International Economic Law

Text, Cases and Materials

Reconciling all fields of international economic law (IEL) and creating bridges between disciplines in a conceptual as well as practical manner, this book stands out as the first modern, comprehensive international economic law textbook.

Containing a technically solid yet critically rich body of knowledge that spans disciplines from trade law to investment, from trade finance to fisheries subsidies, from development to the digital economy and other new-age topics, the book offers the widest possible coverage of issues in current international economic law.

Positioning IEL as a truly global practice, the comprehensive coverage includes various treaty texts, landmark cases and new materials, and is supplemented by case studies, real-life examples, exercises and illustrations. The case extracts and legal texts are selectively chosen, with careful editing and serious deliberation to engage modern law students. Mini chapters show examples of interdisciplinary interactions and provide a window into the future disciplines of international economic law.

Leïla Choukroune is Professor of International Law and Director of the University of Portsmouth thematic area in Democratic Citizenship. She is regularly approached as an independent expert on international economic law and business and human rights. Her research focuses on the interactions between international trade and investment law, human rights, development studies, jurisprudence and social theory. She has published numerous scientific articles, book chapters and special issues in English, French, Spanish and Chinese, and has authored more than ten books, including, recently, *Judging the State in International Trade and Investment Law* (2016), *Exploring Indian Modernities* (2018), and *Handbook of International Investment Law and Policy* (in press). She is the Editor of both *International Law and the Global South* series, and *Human Rights, Citizenship and the Law* series. She is also Associate Editor of the *Manchester Journal of International Economic Law*.

James J. Nedumpara is Professor and Head of the Centre for Trade and Investment Law (CTIL), established by the Government of India at the Indian Institute of Foreign Trade. In this capacity, he advises the government on international trade, investment and dispute settlement matters. He is currently on leave from Jindal Global Law School, where he joined as a founding faculty member. James received his PhD from the National Law School of India University, Bangalore, and holds graduate degrees in Law from the University of Cambridge, UK; the NYU School of Law, USA; and the National University of Singapore. He has appeared in various WTO dispute proceedings as part of the Indian delegation, including *India: Agricultural Products* and *India: Export-Related Measures*, and other dispute consultation proceedings. James has published widely in the field of trade remedy law, most recently, *Non-Market Economies in the Global Trading System: The Special Case of China* (2018).

International Economic Law

Text, Cases and Materials

Leïla Choukroune
University of Portsmouth

James J. Nedumpara
Centre for Trade and Investment Law, Indian Institute of Foreign Trade, New Delhi and Jindal Global Law School
(on leave)

CAMBRIDGE
UNIVERSITY PRESS

CAMBRIDGE
UNIVERSITY PRESS

University Printing House, Cambridge CB2 8BS, United Kingdom

One Liberty Plaza, 20th Floor, New York, NY 10006, USA

477 Williamstown Road, Port Melbourne, VIC 3207, Australia

314–321, 3rd Floor, Plot 3, Splendor Forum, Jasola District Centre, New Delhi – 110025, India

103 Penang Road, #05–06/07, Visioncrest Commercial, Singapore 238467

Cambridge University Press is part of the University of Cambridge.

It furthers the University's mission by disseminating knowledge in the pursuit of education, learning, and research at the highest international levels of excellence.

www.cambridge.org
Information on this title: www.cambridge.org/9781108423885
DOI: 10.1017/9781108500241

© Leïla Choukroune and James J. Nedumpara 2022

First published 2022

Printed in the United Kingdom by TJ Books Limited, Padstow Cornwall 2022

A catalogue record for this publication is available from the British Library.

ISBN 978-1-108-42388-5 Hardback
ISBN 978-1-108-43664-9 Paperback

Additional resources for this publication at www.cambridge.org/choukroune

Contents

Preface

While discussing the fate of international economic law (IEL) during a conference in New Delhi in 2016, we both came to the same conclusion: it is time to see IEL presented in a coherent and integrated manner. The need to defragment international law and look at IEL beyond its technicalities is a pressing urgency. Students, academics and practitioners alike are lost in the meandering density of materials and technical norms deprived of general significance and full of hyper-specialism. How can we simplify this body of law without altering its content? How can we make this fascinating field of law easily approachable for students as well as the teaching and practising communities?

Both of us studied IEL when the field was relatively new and materials were few. But in recent times, the domain of IEL has grown at a speed and complexity that most of us, including experts, cannot keep pace with. The quest for coherence and integration hence informs this textbook. Our very aim is to provide the reader with a technically solid, yet also critically rich body of knowledge spanning disciplines from trade law to investment, from finance to fisheries subsidies, from development to the digital economy. This textbook touches upon and is informed by familiar and newer disciplines of international law. Firmly grounded in general international law, our vision is critical and interdisciplinary. It shows the interactions between disciplines as a reflection of the complexity of international relations and economic globalisation. It revolves around the State as the main subject of international law while also integrating other actors and participants. In addition, our vision is genuinely international in that it shows why and how IEL should not be a thing of the West or the dominating power anymore. It integrates the practices and conceptual approaches of the Global South and intends to participate in a renewed vision of international law.

The latest textbooks in our field are mostly specialised in a given subfield (trade, intellectual property, investment, trade remedies, etc.). There are other good textbooks in individual disciplines, but no other textbook covers such a wide canvas without losing an eye for the details. As surprising as it seems, no recently produced international economic law textbook shares our ambitions. Beyond the above general objectives, this textbook provides the reader with a sound, structured, yet original pedagogy. Texts, cases and materials are found as in other classic textbooks, but we have added a very large number of case studies, examples, exercises and illustrations, to make the reading thought-provoking and always engaging, even when addressing the law as it is. We have selected our case extracts and legal texts with careful editing and serious deliberation. Helping students, academics and practitioners to develop a critical mind and a taste for research has also been at the centre of our approach. This textbook is very much informed by our own research and scholarship. It can be read at different levels, from a simple informative perspective to a truly research-oriented one. In the same vein, we have made sure that the case studies and other legal developments speak to practitioners of international law and international economic law. For years we have advised governments, industry and civil society. Our technical approach, as well as the critical distance that we often take to address a particular issue, is based on pragmatism and the lessons we have learnt from our experiences. Working together, we drew insights from each other, and our combined strengths and perspectives have contributed to the rich array of materials presented in this book.

While this textbook can be read at different levels of specialism, it is also a very agile instrument for teaching and learning IEL. Each chapter, including the introduction, which provides the reader with a conceptual vision of IEL, can be used separately. The chapters are indeed precise enough to cover a given aspect of IEL. It is, as such, a great tool for students who do not need to buy additional resources, including treaty texts, for specialised courses. Yet the textbook forms a very coherent piece of work which opens perspectives and invites the reader to go further, as illustrated by our mini chapters in Part IV, each addressing important contemporary and interdisciplinary issues of IEL. An always evolving instrument, this textbook is also designed to stand the test of time in a fast-changing legal environment. It addresses IEL in a long-term perspective, giving the reader the keys to a deep understanding of contemporary realities informed by past experiences.

We hope to contribute to a new international law scholarship, genuinely international, dynamic, agile and open to all other disciplines and ideas.

James J. Nedumpara and Leïla Choukroune

wife and life's companion, Sharmila; my son, Joseph (Joe); and my parents-in-law, K. V. Joseph and Sophy Joseph. While I spent time working on this book and other things, I missed Joe growing taller. I owe a debt to the large Nedumpara family, whose support was the only reason I thought I could undertake this exercise together with an accomplished scholar located miles across India.

Although not a human incarnation, but maybe the incarnation of humanity, we would like to thank this captivating land (India) for all the beauty and inspiration it provides us with at a temporal and more spiritual level. Most of this book has been written in India and the inspiration we found in many of its welcoming settings has been influential in determining our intellectual journey.

We are humbled by all this support and wish to thank you all again.

Notes on the Text

The drafting of this textbook came to a close at the end of 2020. For updated data, please refer to the sources and references related to a given issue. For the sake of brevity, original footnotes and citations are not included in case and treaty extracts, unless absolutely essential.

Table of Cases

Table of Legislation

Table of Treaties, Instruments and Statutes

International and Regional Instruments

European Union Treaties

Regulations

Commission Regulation (EC) No. 2362/98 of 28 October 1998 laying down detailed rules for the implementation of Council Regulation (EEC) No. 404/93 regarding imports of bananas into the Community, [1998] OJ L 293/32, 130

Commission Regulation (EC) No. 535/94 of 9 March 1994 amending Annex I to Council Regulation (EEC) No. 2658/87 on the tariff and statistical nomenclature and on the common customs tariff, [1994] OJ L 68/15, 101

Council Regulation (EC) No. 2271/96 of 22 November 1996 protecting against the effects of the extra-territorial application of legislation adopted by a third country, and actions based thereon or resulting therefrom, [1996] OJ L 309/1, 402

Regulation (EC) No. 1007/2009 of the European Parliament and of the Council of 16 September 2009 on trade in seal products, [2009] OJ L 286/36, 124

Decisions

2003/97/EC: Commission Decision of 31 January 2003 concerning the validity of certain binding tariff information (BTI) issued by the Federal Republic of Germany (notified under document number C(2003) 77), [2003] OJ L 36/40, 86

Bilateral Investment Treaties

National Legislation

Introduction

Table of Contents

i.1 Introduction

> Peace is the natural effect of trade. Two nations who traffic with each other become reciprocally dependent for if one has an interest in buying, the other has an interest in selling and their union is founded on their mutual necessities. But if the spirit of commerce unites nations, it does not in the same manner unite individuals. We see that in countries where the people move only by the spirit of commerce, they make a traffic of all the humane, all the moral virtues, the most trifling things, those which humanity would demand, are there done, or there given, only for money.[1]

In his 1748 treatise, *The Spirit of Laws*, Montesquieu brilliantly captured the existing tension between the benefits and detriments of trade. 'Commercial laws', he further argued, 'improve manners for the same reason that they destroy them'.[2] This pendulum swing between the need to legislate and the possible negative effects of the same legislation is very much perceived in today's international trade, and, indeed, in international economic law (IEL). While the intellectual legacy of the Enlightenment liberals still largely informs the world of trade ideas, it has also been critically addressed by the new conceptual developments formulated in response to historical evolutions in order to trigger global changes.

By addressing the theoretical foundations of international economics, this introduction further elaborates on the concept of international economic law as the law supporting the architecture and functioning of international economic relations. In doing so, it positions

---

[1] Baron de Montesquieu, 'Book XX: Of Laws in Relation to Commerce Considered in its Nature and Distinctions', in *The Spirit of Laws* (New York: Cosimo Classics, 2007), p. 316.

[2] Montesquieu, *Spirit of Laws*, p. 316.

our own approach within the realm of international law and explains this textbook's foundational principles and pedagogical choices.

i.2   The Law of International Economic Relations

How to define international economic law? What does it comprise of and what does it not cover? Is it public or private law? How international and truly diverse is it? Who are its subjects, actors and other recipients? Why has it been fragmented to the benefit of specialised domains like trade or international investment? Why is it important and timely to approach international economic law as a coherent and yet constantly evolving field?

International economic law has long been defined as the law of international economic relations among States. It is rooted in general public international law and addresses primarily those international economic relations in which the State is the main subject and actor. Yet with the development of international economics, decolonisation and globalisation, international economic relations have evolved dramatically towards much more complex realities. States and private actors interact at local, national, international, regional and global levels. These interactions shape and influence international economic law at its foundations, and in terms of its ability to adapt and provide legal tools to tackle contemporary issues. There is no fixed international legal order. Divisions between international public and private law are not so clear. International economic relations are fluid, in constant movement, and impact all spheres of human life. In addition, the institutions which have shaped the architecture of international economic law have been deeply challenged in their legitimacy and ability to deliver an effective as well as just and equitable world governance. The World Bank, the International Monetary Fund (IMF), the World Trade Organization (WTO), and regional structures like the European Union (EU) and the post-Second World War institutionalisation of international economic relations are in need of great reform. While multilateralism is clearly weakening, alternative scenarios are still unclear, with apparently contradictory trajectories in the direction of a renewed bilateralism on the one hand, and multiple mega-regionalist efforts on the other.

In this general context, defining international economic law proves challenging. But some principles are in place. International economic law is the law of international economic relations with the State as the primary, but not the only, subject and actor. It encompasses a vast array of specialised topics, including trade, investment, finance, development and aid. It is, however, coherent if approached as a component of general international law resting upon the same core principles (sovereignty, equality, *pacta sunt servanda*, good faith, peaceful settlement of disputes, etc.) and the same sources as those outlined in Article 38 of the Statute of the International Court of Justice (ICJ). This defragmented vision supports the unity and diversity of international economic law. It explains and justifies the need for a holistic approach in which other fields of international law (such as human rights or labour, the environment or tax, investment or monetary laws) are not artificially removed from international economic agreements or dispute settlement. Lastly, in line with the vision and conceptual underpinning of this textbook, international economic law is no longer – and in any case, should not be – a thing of the West or the new emerging powers. If not yet truly decolonised, it has been transformed already by the practice of the Global South and will evolve towards more diversity, more complexity, and possibly a new form of universalism.

i.2.1   Economic Foundations

The term 'commerce' derives from the Latin *commercium*, itself composed of *cum* (together) and *merx* (merchandise), while 'trade' comes from Middle English (path, course or track). The exchange of merchandise along many different paths has indeed marked the history of humanity since antiquity. Trade routes were designed as early as the third millennium BCE, when the Harappan civilisation of the Indus Valley, the ancestors of today's South Asians, traded with the Sumerians in Mesopotamia, the fertile crescent now roughly corresponding to Iraq and some parts of Syria and Turkey.[3] The Silk Road, an ancient trade trail, whose name was inspired by the commerce of silk by the Chinese Han dynasty (207 BCE–220 CE), connected the East and West through a vast network of trade routes.[4] Much later, Vasco da Gama took over the spice trade from the Arab powers when, in 1498, he discovered the sea route to India around the Cape of Good Hope and reached Calicut (now Kozhikode).[5] With greater trade came greater interests and greed. The Portuguese, Spanish, Dutch, British and French developed world ambitions through trade, often by using the vehicle of private enterprises, as powerful as today's mega-multinational companies. Backed by various European States that had commercial and military objectives, these companies were key instruments in the States' plans for territorial conquest to achieve economic growth and political hegemony. The various East India Companies created by the Dutch (1602–1799), the French (1664–1769) and the British (1600–1874) reigned over commerce with the East. The latter served as the main device for the subjugation and colonisation of India (see Chapter 11).[6] The sinister reality of corporate looting as the tool of colonial policies claiming a civilising mission echoed another tragic history, that of the trade in humans. An estimated 17 million Africans were shipped across the Atlantic by European powers from the sixteenth century, for over 400 years.[7] While human trafficking and slave routes were not new, European powers systematised, legalised and legitimised this trade, notably with the infamous Code Noir (Black Code), designed by Colbert for French colonisation.[8] This

---

[3] On the Harappan civilisation and how to trace history on the basis of new DNA-related techniques, see T. Joseph, *Early Indians: The Story of Our Ancestors and Where We Came From* (New Delhi: Juggernaut Books, 2018), p. 256.

[4] P. Frankopan, *The Silk Roads: A New History of the World* (London: Bloomsbury, 2016), p. 650.

[5] S. Subrahmanyan, *The Career and Legend of Vasco da Gama* (Cambridge University Press, 1998), p. 428. See also W. L. Bernstein, *A Splendid Exchange: How Trade Shaped the World* (London: Atlantic Books, 2009), p. 488.

[6] William Dalrymple, *The Anarchy: The Relentless Rise of the East India Company* (London: Bloomsbury, 2019), p. 576.

[7] See generally, UNESCO, *The Slave Route*, available at www.unesco.org/new/en/social-and-human-sciences/themes/slave-route (accessed 21 December 2020).

[8] The Code Noir, drafted by Jean-Baptist Colbert, was a decree passed by Louis XIV of France in 1685, to define, legalise and justify the condition and existence of slavery and slave trade.

triangular trade proceeded in three steps: ships left Europe for West and Central Africa with goods to be exchanged for slaves destined for America, where agricultural goods produced by the slaves were later brought to Europe.[9]

It was at this very key moment in the expansion of Europe that trade theorisation took shape with the work of Jean-Baptiste Colbert (1619–83) and Adam Smith (1723–90). Europe started to dominate not only trade, but also its conceptualisation and legitimation. This intellectual domination is still very much perceptible today, considering that the concepts forged from the eighteenth-century Enlightenment provide parts of the theoretical foundations of trade, and most trade textbooks offer only a Western-centric perspective.[10] A true non-Western-centric and critical approach to the history of trade and trade law would require a dedicated study beyond the scope and objectives of this textbook, but it is important to bear in mind the above to understand trade theory and its implications over the centuries.[11]

The theoretical foundations of international economic law are indeed greatly inspired by international trade theory. International trade theory finds its roots in Europe and has been exported – if not imposed at the time of colonisation – to other continents. International trade theory blends international economic theory with international legal scholarship and jurisprudence. International trade theory still very much informs today's international economic law framework, while it has also been critically addressed in the context of the socialist revolutions, decolonisation and the recent development of globalisation.

International economic law must first be approached from an economic theory angle or a political economy perspective, in which economics is understood in relation to other disciplines, from political sciences to history or sociology.[12]

i.2.1.1   Mercantilism

From the sixteenth to the seventeenth century, in Europe, mercantilism emerged as a practice and economic theory to promote the State's regulation of the economy and as a tool to expand its power. While the term, which comes from the Latin *mercari* (to conduct commerce), was coined by the marquis de Mirabeau in France, it was later popularised by the Scottish economist Adam Smith in his 1776 magnum opus, *An Inquiry into the Causes and Nature of the Wealth of Nations*.[13] Mercantilism appeared at the time

---

[9] 'A summary of the triangular slave trade', BBC Bitesize, available at www.bbc.co.uk/bitesize/guides/zy7fr82/ revision/1 (accessed 21 December 2020).

[10] For a Western intellectual history of trade, see, for example, Douglas A. Irwin, *Against the Tide: An Intellectual History of Free Trade* (Princeton University Press, 1998), p. 288.

[11] For a critical approach, see the Introduction to this book, and also Bardo Fassbender and Anne Peters (eds.), *The Oxford Handbook of the History of International Law* (Oxford University Press, 2012), p. 1272; B. S. Chimni, *International Law and the World Order: A Critique of Contemporary Approaches* (Cambridge University Press, 2017), p. 628.

[12] J. Ravenhill, *Global Political Economy* (Oxford University Press, 2016), p. 504.

[13] Adam Smith, *The Wealth of Nations*, Books I–III and IV–V (Penguin Classics, 1982 and 1999), p. 524.

of absolutism (Louis XIV in France) and the conquest of the New World, which corresponded with the beginning of a systematised and theorised colonisation. In this context, 'The Prince', whose power was based on the amount of gold he possessed and the taxes he collected, was to further his reign through industrialisation and commerce. In other words, the dominant thought was that wealth consisted of bullion, and for countries not possessing gold or silver, having a favourable balance of trade was the only way to secure wealth. Commerce was therefore aimed at the taking of other markets and territories to allow the State to have access to precious goods and materials, but not so much to trade freely and on an equal basis. Mercantilists were protectionists.[14] They supported the industrialisation of their own nations, but not that of their colonies or competitors. A mix of defensive (protectionism) and offensive (industrialisation and exportation) policies had to be designed by the State to support its expansion.[15] Mercantilism put economic theory at the heart of the public space. It took various forms, with Antonio Serra in Italy and his work on currency and balance of payments, Jean-Baptiste Colbert in France and his 'Colbertism', supporting a proactive State leading industrialisation and commerce, as well as 'commercialism' in England with Thomas Mun (1571–1641), an economist affiliated with the East India Company, and the German 'cameralism' advocating the centralised management of the economy.

The major assault on mercantilism did not come from political rulers, but from Adam Smith, who laid bare its inherent absurdities. It is partly in response to the mercantilists, and Colbert's theory, that Adam Smith formulated his concepts of the wealth of nations. Smith, now seen as the founder of the British school of classical economics, emphasised the importance of specialisation (division of labour) and viewed international trade as a way to specialise in what one is best at. In *The Wealth of Nations*, Smith advanced a simple yet profound idea: countries can benefit by specialising in those industries at which they excel, and trading in or exchanging those goods with other countries that specialise in other industries. Smith noted, 'if a foreign country can supply us with a commodity cheaper than what we can make, better buy it of them with some part of the produce of our own industry'. To use a simple example, if England was able to produce cloth more efficiently than Portugal, and Portugal was more efficient than England at producing wine, both countries would be better-off if they engaged in bilateral trade. Smith's concept of division of labour and absolute advantage made a strong case for liberal trade and open markets.

Mercantilist theories are revisited today in the context of a contested globalisation, while some would like to favour import substitution based on 'made in' policies and to engage in more protectionist, tariff-based instruments.

---

[14] E. F. Heckscher, *Mercantilism* (London: George Allen and Unwin, 1955).

[15] See Roger Dehem, *Histoire de la pensée économique: des mercantilistes à Keynes* (Paris: Presses de l'Université Laval et Paris, 1993); Lars Magnusson, *Mercantilism: The Shaping of an Economic Language* (London and New York: Routledge, 1994), p. 232.

i.2.1.2   Comparative Advantage

Another classical economist, David Ricardo (1772–1823), further developed the idea of specialisation into the principle of 'comparative advantage'.[16] A truly remarkable and inspirational theory of comparative advantage underpins the economic argument for free trade. According to this theory, a country will specialise in the production of a good in which it has a comparative advantage – that is, where there is labour to produce relatively efficiently, with low opportunity cost.

These principles are detailed in all international trade textbooks. However, a short explanation is in order here. There is specialisation and comparison in trade, but in a rather sophisticated and evolutive fashion.[17] In the example of England and Portugal, which is borrowed from Ricardo's book, assume that Portugal is more efficient than England in making both cloth and wine. It is counterintuitive to suggest that England would still benefit from bilateral trade. It all depends on each country's relative productivity in wine vis-à-vis cloth. The question can be framed as: is it cheaper to produce in England than to import from Portugal? What is the opportunity cost? Is it based only on labour and what labour costs to produce a given good? In assuming that it is, we can define the advantage of country A, where labour is cheap compared to country B, where it is not. When less labour is needed to produce a given good in one country, it has an absolute advantage in producing that good. The Ricardian model assumes international differences in the productivity of labour. It is often referred to as a one factor model. But the issue is that trade cannot be determined on an absolute advantage alone. Absolute advantage and comparative advantage differ. When trade comes into play, the price of a good is not only determined by domestic considerations like the cost of labour, but by supply and demand. The advantage is not absolute, but comparative. Also, countries produce and can hence specialise in a variety of goods. Not to mention that to trade, a country needs to take into consideration transportation and its cost. The reality of trade is naturally much more complex than initially envisaged in Ricardo's 1817 book, *The Principles of Political Economy and Taxation*. States can make multiple policy choices based on domestic resources and other opportunities or constraints. But the Ricardian model, despite its relative simplicity, remains a very useful tool to conceptualise international trade. It shows that productivity differences play an important role in trade and that the trade advantage is comparative rather than absolute.

The essence of comparative advantage is that it is impossible for all countries not to have comparative advantage in something. Producing everything or focusing on self-sufficiency is not a goal to be emulated in itself. As Paul Krugman notes, international trade is about 'mutually beneficial exchange'.[18]

---

[16] D. Ricardo, *The Principles of Political Economy and Taxation* (New York: Dover Publications, 2004), p. 320.

[17] The concept is particularly well explained in Paul R. Krugman, Maurice Obstfeld and Marc J. Melitz, *International Trade: Theory and Policy*, 11th ed., (Boston: Pearson, 2018).

[18] P. R. Krugman, 'What Do Undergraduates Need to Know about Trade', *American Economic Review* (1993), 83(2), p. 24.

i.2.1.3 More Complex Models

As trade has evolved, more complex models have been developed. These trade models introduce multiple factors. In the specific factor model elaborated by Paul Samuelson and Ronald Jones, factors of production other than labour are integrated.[19] Land and capital play a particular role. From a one-factor model (labour) we can move to a three factors conceptualisation, with labour, land and capital. Labour is seen as a mobile factor, which could move from the production of one good to another, while land and capital are specific to the production of a given good. But the complex model, which has received the most attention, was developed by two Swedish economists, Eli Hecksher and Bertil Ohlin, the latter having received the Nobel Prize in Economics in 1977.[20] This model is often referred to as the Heckscher–Ohlin theory or factor proportions theory. It focuses on labour and capital and emphasises the interplay between the proportion in which these factors are available in different countries and used in the same. According to this model, countries tend to trade goods that are intensive in the factor they have in abundance (labour or capital). A country's advantage in production, according to the factor proportions theory, arises solely from the relative factor abundance. Based on these traditional theories, one can rationalise Bangladesh exporting textile products to the United States and the United States exporting microchips and semiconductors to Bangladesh.

There are naturally other elements which could influence trade, from natural resources to economy of scale theories (produce a good in large scale to save on production cost), or the use of technologies providing a trade advantage. In particular, Paul Krugman's 'new trade theory' suggests that significant economies of scale and network effects can determine the patterns of trade.[21] For example, the United States and the European Union, which are both capital-intensive and have similar comparative advantages in several areas of goods or services, trade in the same category of products. Mass production leads to decline in the marginal cost of production and, as a result, in price-competitive goods. The new trade theory affirms that firms compete not only on price but also on considerations such as quality, brandings and perception. The reality and complexity of today's free trade, however, show a mix of all classical theories.

i.2.1.4 The Case for and against Free Trade

According to the World Bank, 'Trade is an engine of growth that creates jobs, reduces poverty and increases economic opportunity. Over one billion people have moved out of

[19] P. Samuelson, 'International Trade and the Equalisation of Factor Prices', *Economic Journal* (1949), 59, pp. 181–96.

[20] B. Ohlin, 'Interregional and International Trade', *Economic Journal* (1933), 44, p. 95. For a commentary on Ohlin's work, see Harry Flam and June Flanders, 'The Young Ohlin on the Theory of "Interregional and International Trade"' (2000), Seminar Papers 684, Stockholm University, Institute for International Economic Studies.

[21] P. R. Krugman received the Nobel Prize in Economics for this seminal work: Paul R. Krugman, 'Scale Economies, Product Differentiation, and the Pattern of Trade', *American Economic Review* (1980), 70(5), pp. 950–9.

poverty because of economic growth underpinned by open trade since 1990.'[22] The case for free trade seems pretty clear for the supporters of globalisation. Yet trade liberalisation is also highly contested today, at a time when protectionism is on the rise. The NAFTA Agreement was scrapped and replaced by a much more diluted version under the moniker USMCA. The Brexit discussions have recently come to a close and opened a new era of cooperation for the UK and Europe. And the quest for alternative and more sustainable, if not yet socially just models, is ongoing.

Arguments for free trade have been made on the basis of the theoretical approaches explained briefly above, as well as pragmatic decisions, often mixing trade liberalisation with offensive and defensive policies. Indeed, there is not a single country totally open to free trade. States use a variety of policy mechanisms to trigger and limit trade at the same time. International economic law is one of these instruments. For its proponents, free trade is seen through a cost–benefit analysis as encouraging productivity and innovation, economies of scale, general economic growth and prosperity. To quote the economist Jagdish Bhagwati, in his book *In Defense of Globalization*, 'free trade means higher growth', and 'higher growth is associated with reduced poverty'.[23] Bhagwati further argues:

only an ignoramus would coach the poor countries to talk of 'unfair trade', for this is the code phrase used by the protectionists in rich countries to cut off imports from the poor countries by alleging that they obtain their competitiveness in ways that amount to unfair competition and unfair trade. Trade experts of all political persuasions have spent decades exposing the cynical use of this phrase and decrying its usage but then in come the know-nothings, who persuade the unsuspecting poor countries to embrace it. When it comes to the two sets of nations, poor and rich, battling it out as to who is the worse unfair trader, do not be surprised when the poor nations find themselves at a disadvantage.[24]

Unfair trade might well refer to the practices of dumping or subsidisation critically addressed by international trade law (see Chapters 5 and 6), but there is more to the question of global fairness and social justice than there might seem.[25] Equity, as noted by Joseph Stiglitz, cannot be left to politics alone, while economists and trade lawyers deal only with efficiency and security.[26] As we will see in Chapter 16, as well as in the following paragraphs, the reality of free trade is much more complex than liberal economists would like it to be. Trade and globalisation have not necessarily benefited all, at least not in the same way. This is where international economic law could have a greater balancing role.

Free traders have not always convinced States and businesses of the validity of their arguments. Alternative schools of thought emerged in response to the classical economists' theories as early as the nineteenth century. Alexander Hamilton (1755–1804) in the United States, John Stuart Mill (1806–1873) in the UK and Friedrich List (1789–1846) in Germany had argued in favour of various forms of protection of the domestic economy to allow infant industries to

---

[22] World Bank, *Trade*, available at www.worldbank.org/en/topic/trade/overview (accessed 5 November 2020).

[23] J. Bhagwati, *In Defense of Globalization* (Oxford University Press, 2007), p. 344.

[24] Bhagwati, *In Defense of Globalization*, p. 6.

[25] J. Stiglitz, *Making Globalization Work: The Next Steps to Global Justice* (London: Penguin, 2007), p. 384.

[26] Stiglitz, *Making Globalisation Work*, p. XIV.

grow. This 'infant industry' theory against free trade, or limiting its development, played a key role throughout the twentieth century, in developing countries in particular, with the concept of import substitution industrialisation (ISI). Indeed, from the Second World War, a number of developing countries reclaimed their independence, using import substitution industrialisation as an engine of economic sovereignty (see Part II and Chapter 16). In this context, the infant industry argument was to support the idea that developing countries have a potential comparative advantage in manufacturing, provided that such industries are initially helped to grow to a significant level to meet international competition. Tariffs and import quotas then need to be used to the benefit of domestic industrialisation. After all, the US or Japan initially protected their economies to grow their national industries. The same is true for China, which gradually liberalised trade from the early 1980s, once Deng Xiaoping had formulated his opening-up theory in 1978. India probably gave the most extreme example of the application of the import-substitution theory in the early 1970s, when its importation of products other than oil was only about 3 per cent.[27] In the context of Latin America, structuralism referred to a form of ISI theory embraced by a number of countries from the 1950s to the 1980s, under the influence of the Argentine economist Raúl Prebisch (1901–86) and with the creation of the United Nations Economic Commission for Latin America and the Caribbean (UNECLAC) (see Chapter 16). This was also related to the dependency theory popularised by Hans Singer and Raúl Prebisch, according to which resources, and natural resources in particular, were exploited in the South to the sole benefit of the North (the coloniser or former coloniser) to maintain the developing world at a stage of underdevelopment. Naturally, the dependency theory shared a number of arguments with earlier Marxist concepts on imperialism. This trade between unequals, described by Karl Marx, fitted the colonial model and its denunciation well.[28] Marxists theories of international law, as we will see below, are regaining a form of popularity at a time of disillusionment with capitalism and discontentment with globalisation.

Import substitution industrialisation, however, was gradually abandoned by most developing countries after the fall of the Soviet Union and under the pressure of World Bank and IMF liberalisation policies (see Chapter 16). The ISI was not short of uncertainties. What industry to invest in? How to reach a stage of competitiveness? What role for the private sector? What policy tools to use – tariffs, quotas, exchange control, domestic content rules? Is the domestic market big enough? These interrogations posed the question of the correct trade policy instruments to apply, an issue still very much debated today when countries need to define their tariffs policy, for example (see Chapter 2). The practice of ISI often revealed the inability of developing countries to effectively implement the theory and, from the early 1990s, revealed a general opening up to the world and free trade.[29] This has

---

[27] A. Panagariya, *India: The Emerging Giant* (Oxford University Press, 2008).

[28] Karl Marx, *Free Trade: An Address Delivered before the Democratic Association of Brussels, Belgium, January 9, 1848* (New York Labour News Co., 1921).

[29] See World Bank, 'Tariff Rate, Applied, Weighted Mean, All Products (%): Low and Middle Income', covering 1988–2017, which shows a sharp decrease in tariffs, in particular for low- and middle-income countries, available at https://data.worldbank.org/indicator/TM.TAX.MRCH.WM.AR.ZS?locations=XO (accessed 5 November 2020).

resulted in an increased share in trade for developing countries, as well as a change in the nature of their commerce, not only in natural resources and agricultural products, but also in manufactured goods. However, the overall picture offered by this apparently simple description can be misleading given that this period also corresponded with the rise of China as a trade superpower. Most of the developing world trade is actually with and by China, which is still considered a developing country and enjoys such status in the WTO (see Chapter 16).

The issue of the inequalities produced by trade liberalisation is at the core of the contestation of globalisation, a phenomenon seen as the product of world capitalism and free trade. The immense echo of the research work of the Paris School of Economics on global inequalities and the resounding success of the book of the French economist Thomas Piketty, *Capital in the Twenty-First Century*, are revealing of contemporary questionings.[30] Since the early 1990s, the anti-globalisation movement has gained world prominence. It has taken multiple shapes and national expressions, resulting in diverse political and economic evolutions, from populism and the rise of extremism, to the contestation of multilateralism and international organisations, (mega)regionalism, renewed bilateralism, trade wars and simply new forms of protectionism. The arguments against globalisation are many and varied, but could be summarised in the words of Joseph Stiglitz, a Nobel laureate in Economics. Stiglitz noted:

1 The benefits of globalisation might well be smaller than advertised and possibly offset by the costs.
2 The disillusionment is proportional to the initial craze for globalisation.
3 Incomes and wealth have not been equally shared, and hence the rise in inequalities.
4 The governance of globalisation is unfair, with the US, for example, having the real power in the IMF to the detriment of other nations, including the now powerful emerging countries.
5 Multinational corporations and international financial institutions are the real decision-makers.
6 The ideology applied to globalisation does not support the interests of all, including sometimes the most powerful.
7 The distribution of powers is affected negatively by globalisation.
8 Globalisation reduces the ability of governments to deal with real issues, in particular international taxation, while a number of super multinational corporations avoid tax.[31]

Stiglitz synthesised brilliantly: 'Globalization is the field on which some of our major societal conflicts – including those over basic values – play out. Among the most important of those conflicts is that over the role of government and markets.'[32] For Dani Rodrik, the paradox of globalisation poses an absolute challenge: 'we cannot simultaneously pursue

---

[30] Thomas Piketty, *Capital in the Twenty-First Century* (Cambridge, MA: Harvard University Press, 2014), p. 696; Thomas Piketty, *Capital and Ideology* (Cambridge, MA: Harvard University Press, 2020), p. 1150.
[31] J. E. Stiglitz, *Globalization and its Discontents Revisited: Anti-Globalization in the Era of Trump* (London: Penguin, 2017), pp. x–xii.
[32] Stiglitz, *Making Globalization Work*, p. xiv.

democracy, national determination, and economic globalisation'.[33] This dramatic tension has been illustrated by the Covid-19 crisis, which has shed some light on the limitations of a certain form of globalisation that is often too reliant on a handful of countries or products to supply medicine and respond to public health priorities. With free trade and globalisation, the question of the State and its regulatory powers is posed with the greatest accuracy and a real sense of urgency.

All these issues are discussed in today's conversations on international economic law, for regulation could help to answer the most pressing problems of our time: whether and to what extent trade and investment agreements should include provisions on labour conditions and wages, the environment, sustainability, or taxation of multinational firms; how can human rights be placed at the core of trade and investment agreements; how to deeply reform the international governance of trade, including international finance for more equitable exchanges.

i.2.2   Law and Legal Theory

As for general international law, legal theory has played a role in the development of international economic law. A number of intellectual currents have marked the field, as well as today's evolutions and reform initiatives. While a detailed study of jurisprudential influences would largely exceed the space of this introduction, we have chosen to highlight a few developments and interrogations to later present contemporary and critical approaches. Beyond its apparent technical aspect, international economic law is not theoretically or politically neutral.

i.2.2.1   Positivism

Positivism remains the most influential approach to international law and today's international economic law. It is the dominant school of thought in jurisprudence. Crystallised in Europe in the seventeenth and eighteenth centuries with the work of Thomas Hobbes (1588–1679), and his *Leviathan*, based on the idea of sovereign powers, positivism was influenced early on by Francis Bacon (1561–1626) and David Hume (1711–76). It was also informed by the codification of Jean-Jacques Rousseau (1712–78) and his *Social Contract*. The term positivism itself was created by the French empirical scientist August Comte (1798–1857). According to Comte, unverified belief systems had to be abandoned in favour of scientific methods based on empiricism and verification. Later, the British empiricist Bertrand Russell (1872–1970) further elaborated the concept of logical positivism. When applied to law and international law, legal positivism aims to identify law *as it is*. But what

---

[33]   D. Rodrik, *The Globalization Paradox: Why Global Markets, States and Democracy Can't Coexist* (Oxford University Press, 2012), p. 368. See also the documentary based on the same by Justin Pemberton, 'Capital in the Twenty-First Century – Official US Trailer' (19 February 2020), available at www.youtube.com/watch?v= TqkjyI1QD2A (accessed 21 December 2020).

law? What is law and what is not law? The property of law is generally attributed by positivists to a product derived from a clear law-making authority. The State is at the centre of the reasoning. The State is the lawmaker. It is seen as the main and often the only actor in the creation of law. Neither morality nor politics is to play a major role in the construction of law. Law is a fact, not a belief. Law is enforced by identified systems and backed by sanctions. The Austrian jurist Hans Kelsen (1881–1973) hence elaborated the theory of a science of law.[34]

In this general context, positivists have questioned the legal nature and authority of international law, where, in contrast to domestic situations, there is not a single sovereign lawmaker, but rather a large variety of actors and influences, not to mention the complex issue of international law enforcement in the absence of a world court competent on all matters of law and to which all subjects and actors of international law could have access. These questions certainly inform today's discussions on international economic law, from the identification of its sources to the settlement of disputes and the enforcement of decisions. In this textbook, law is often presented *as it is*, in its technicality and its apparent objectivity.[35] Yet it is also put into perspective and critically approached. Contemporary positivists would tend to adopt a more open perspective, addressing soft law or moral and political considerations, yet thinking that formal sources are at the very centre of the legal analysis. As alluded to above, positivism remains the main current of jurisprudence and is largely embraced by international lawyers, who see it as an objective tool to tackle legal issues.[36] In this perspective, positivism supports a large adherence to international law from all nations of the world, no matter what their legal culture and history, including a possible colonial legacy. Positivism entails notions of progress, justice and peace and allows international human rights to develop for all. It supports the creation of a range of dedicated international tribunals to enforce the law, thereby furthering the legal character of international law. For all the above reasons, positivism remains extremely influential and is central to international law. But, as we will see below, critical approaches are challenging this relatively simple vision of law, and international economic law in particular, in introducing more complexity.

i.2.2.2 Realism

Another perspective which needs to be acknowledged for its influential interpretation of international law and international economic law is realism. Classical realism developed around the work of the political thinker Hans Morgenthau and his work *Politics Among*

---

[34] C. M. Herrera, 'La théorie du droit international de Hans Kelsen et ses évolutions', in N. Grangé and F. Ramel (eds.), *Le droit international selon Hans Kelsen: Criminalités, responsabilités, normativités* (Lyon: ENS Éditions, 2018), pp. 13–34.

[35] In this regard, we follow an intellectual tradition set up by a number of key figures in the field of twentieth-century international economic law, notably, Dominique Carreau and Patrick Julliard (eds.), *Droit international économique* (Paris: Dalloz, 2007).

[36] Steven R. Ratner and Anne-Marie Slaughter (eds.), *Methods of International Law* (Washington, DC: American Society of International Law, 2004); Jörg Kammerhofer and Jean d'Aspremont, *International Legal Positivism in a Post-Modern World* (Cambridge University Press, 2014).

Nations.[37] Elaborated at the time of the cold war, Morgenthau's scholarship, and the realist approaches, have recently seen a renewed interest. Criticism on globalisation and trade wars can be assessed through this analytical prism, which stresses the overlaps between international law and international relations. For the realists, politics matters first and foremost. It is inherent in human nature and is centrally governed by the idea of power. Power is control and international politics is a struggle for this control. In addition, national interest dominates States' strategies. Hence their engagement in international relations depends mostly on the preservation and growth of their national interest. International law is not disregarded, but should be kept in its place, a relative one. Realists question the relevance and efficiency of international law to prevent war and effectively govern international relations. Scepticism prevails. The validity of international law is interrogated. The American position has often been dominated by this approach to international relations and international law during the cold war era, a tendency that is perceptible today as well when addressing multilateralism.

i.2.2.3   Globalisation: Between Universalism and Fragmentation

In impacting international economic relations, globalisation has naturally made its mark on international law as well. From a jurisprudential perspective, globalisation stresses two apparently opposed tendencies: universalism and fragmentation.

Universalism finds its roots in Christianity, with universal reconciliation referring to the idea that all human beings will eventually be saved, a concept that is also key to other spiritualities – for example, in Buddhism. From a philosophical perspective, it stresses the universal relevance of some ideas and facts regardless of culture, race, religion, nationality or any other distinctive features. It is the opposite of relativism, and of cultural relativism in particular, which insists on judging beliefs and ideas against a given culture. From Christian Europe in the Middle Ages, and later, with the French Revolution and the Declaration of the Rights of Man and the Citizen of 26 August 1789, universalism has shaped international law as much as the principles of equality and sovereignty of States. It often conflicts with the latter in its ambitions to go further and beyond the State. In transcending the nation State, universality enables the application of rights to the entire humanity. It is beyond borders and domestic law. This very idea, already present in the French Declaration, is central to the 1948 Universal Declaration of Human Rights, which opened a process of international codification furthered with the 1966 International Covenant on Civil and Political Rights and the International Covenant on Economic, Social and Cultural Rights, as well as later international and regional human rights instruments.[38]

---

[37]   Hans Morgenthau, *Politics Among Nations* (Boston, MA: McGraw-Hill Education, 2005), p. 752.

[38]   United Nations, Universal Declaration of Human Rights, www.un.org/en/universal-declaration-human-rights/ and Human Rights, www.un.org/en/sections/issues-depth/human-rights/ (both accessed 5 November 2020). See also Dinah Shelton (ed.), *The Oxford Handbook of International Human Rights Law* (Oxford University Press, 2015), p. 1088.

Why is it relevant to international economic law? Because IEL is part of general international law and certainly concerned with human rights (see Mini Chapter 1). In addition, trade also claims a form of universality on the basis of its main principles, the national treatment (NT) and most favoured nation treatment (MFN) that it places at the core of international trade and investment law (see Chapter 13). The architecture of trade exceptions with Article XX of the GATT 1994 is thought to provide for reconciliation between the apparently contradictory objectives of trade liberalisation and rights protection, hence allowing universal adherence to trade and its norms (see Chapter 9). Globalisation, in enhancing trade, has also triggered a form of universalisation. This phenomenon, however, is put under the tension of another product of globalisation: fragmentation.

The fragmentation of international law has been discussed for the past twenty years. Based on the observation that specialised regimes and specialised courts emerged everywhere in the world, fragmentation describes the contemporary technicalisation and strategic division of international law into many subdisciplines eventually read in isolation to meet short-term policy objectives. *Lex specialis* (specialised law) refers to 'self-contained' regimes and regionalism that have been advanced as explanations of the current international law complication. At the same time, and as we will see in the different chapters of this textbook, *jus cogens*, 'systemic integration' and repeated references to Article 31(3)(c) of the Vienna Convention on the Law of Treaties (VCLT)[39] are supposed to provide treaty drafters and judges with solutions in favour of a pluralistic and integrative vision of international law (see Chapter 9). Interpretation would then be the solution to fragmentation.

It has been twenty years since Judge Guillaume, then President of the International Court of Justice, stressed the issue of the 'proliferation' of international law, and fifteen years since the publication of the International Law Commission (ILC) landmark report on fragmentation.[40] The ILC explained but never justified trade law's parallel existence. It actually stressed the irrelevance of the 'self-contained regime' and the idea that trade law was one of these regimes, as general rules of international law do apply to trade law too.

---

[39] Vienna Convention on the Law of Treaties, Vienna, 23 May 1969, in force 27 January 1980, 1155 UNTS 331; (1969) 8 ILM 679; UKTS (1980) 58. See Appellate Body Report, *Peru – Additional Duty on Imports of Certain Agricultural Products*, WT/DS457/AB/R, adopted 31 July 2015, para. 5.104; Appellate Body Report, *United States – Definitive Anti-Dumping and Countervailing Duties on Certain Products from China*, WT/DS379/AB/R, adopted 25 March 2011, paras. 305–316 (noting that while interpreting Art. 1.1(a)(1) of the Agreement on Subsidies and Countervailing Measures (SCM Agreement), the relevant provisions of ILC Articles on State responsibility may be taken into account).

[40] ICJ, *Speech by His Excellency Judge Gilbert Guillaume, President of the International Court of Justice, to the Sixth Committee of the General Assembly of the United Nations*, available at www.icj-cij.org/public/files/press-releases/1/3001.pdf (accessed 21 December 2020); Martti Koskenniemi, ILC (2006), *ILC Analytical Study 2006: ILC Study Group on the Fragmentation of International Law; Fragmentation of International Law: Difficulties Arising from the Diversification and Expansion of International Law; Report of the Study Group of the International Law Commission*, UN Doc A/CN.4/L.682 and Add.1 and Corr. 1. New York: International Law Commission; ILC (2006), *ILC Conclusions 2006: Report of the Study Group, Fragmentation of International Law: Difficulties Arising from the Diversification and Expansion of International Law: Conclusions*, UN Doc. A/CN.4/L.702.

ILC Report on Fragmentation of International Law (2006)

191. The rationale of special regimes is the same as that of *lex specialis*. They take better account of the particularities of the subject-matter to which they relate; they regulate it more effectively than general law and follow closely the preferences of their members. Where the application of the general law concerning reactions to breaches (especially countermeasures) might be inappropriate or counterproductive, a self-contained regime such as, for instance, the system of persona non grata under diplomatic law, may be better suited to deal with such breaches.

    [...]

192. But no regime is self-contained. Even in the case of well-developed regimes, general law has at least two types of function. First, it provides the normative background that comes in to fulfil aspects of its operation not specifically provided by it. In case of dissolution of a State party to a dispute within the WTO dispute settlement system, for instance, general rules of State succession will determine the fate of any claims reciprocally made by and as against the dissolved State. This report has illustrated some of the ways in which this supplementing takes place. Second, the rules of general law also come to operate if the special regime fails to function properly. Such failure might be substantive or procedural, and at least some of the avenues open to regime members in such cases are outlined in the Vienna Convention itself. Also, the rules on State responsibility might be relevant in such situations.

193. Third, the term 'self-contained regime' is a misnomer. No legal regime is isolated from general international law. It is doubtful whether such isolation is even possible: a regime can receive (or fail to receive) legally binding force ('validity') only by reference to (valid and binding) rules or principles outside it. In previous debates within the Commission over 'self-contained regimes', 'regimes' and 'subsystems', there never was any assumption that they would be hermetically isolated from the general law.

No legal regime is artificially separated from general international law. There is no 'clinical isolation' of trade law as stressed by the now ritualistically cited decision of the WTO Appellate Body: 'WTO agreement is not to be read in clinical isolation from public international law'.[41] It might well be that '[t]he general rule of interpretation [as set out in Article 31(1) of the Vienna Convention on the Law of Treaties] has attained the status of a rule of customary or general international law. As such, it forms part of the "customary rules of interpretation of public international law" which the Appellate Body has been

---

[41] See Appellate Body Report, *United States – Standards for Reformulated and Conventional Gasoline*, WT/DS2/AB/R, adopted 20 May 1996, p. 17.

directed, by Article 3(2) of the Dispute Settlement Understanding (DSU),[42] to apply in seeking to clarify the provisions of the General Agreement and the other "covered agreements" of the Marrakesh Agreement Establishing the World Trade Organization (the "WTO Agreement")'.[43]

As we will see in the next chapters, fragmentation does very much exist, particularly because the question is not so much about interpretation as the content of WTO rules and international economic law. When the decoupling of norms is intentionally embedded into the law, there is not much for the adjudicator to interpret in a holistic fashion. The issue is not with interpretation, but with the law itself.

Some have argued that fragmentation was over with the coexistence and coherent integration of international legal regimes.[44] But as we discuss in the following chapters, the parallel existence of specialised norms has not yet been tackled with great success. The theory according to which IEL would be 'multi-sourcing' for equivalent norms is not satisfactory either.[45] The need to see international economic law in a coherent and integrated manner, as proposed throughout this textbook, is even more pressing.

i.2.2.4   Critical Approaches

In questioning the very existence of 'law as a fact' and introducing more complexity in analysing international law, critical approaches (CA) challenge liberal legal theory. CA are particularly relevant to address the issues of the decolonisation of IEL and the quest for sovereign equality. They matter, as well, when looking at the actors of IEL and their impact on law-making and law enforcement.

As discussed above, when addressing different economic theories, liberalism refers to a school of thought that developed from eighteenth-century Enlightenment Europe. The term itself is recent. It gained popularity in the twentieth century to describe individual freedom and its many conceptualisations.

Against the backdrop of Marxism, which had already contested liberal theory on the basis of domination, exploitation of one group by the other, its alienation and class struggle, the critical legal studies (CLS) movement developed an original vision. Born in the United States in the context of the Vietnam War and the fight for civil rights, CLS stressed social inequalities and the political biases of the law.[46] The popular expression 'law is politics' is one of the strong claims made by CLS, which highlights the need for neutrality and

---

[42] Understanding on Rules and Procedures Governing the Settlement of Disputes, 15 April 1994, Marrakesh Agreement Establishing the World Trade Organization, Annex 2, 1869 UNTS 401.

[43] Appellate Body Report, *US – Gasoline*, p. 17.

[44] Mads Andenas and Eirik Bjorge (eds.), *A Farewell to Fragmentation: Reassertion and Convergence in International Law* (Cambridge University Press, 2015), p. 604.

[45] T. Broude and Y. Shany (eds.), *Multi-Sourced Equivalent Norms in International Law* (Oxford: Hart, 2011).

[46] R. M. Unger, *The Critical Legal Studies Movement* (London: Verso Books, 2015); Duncan Kennedy, *The Rise and Fall of Classical Legal Thought* (Washington, DC: Beard Books, 1975); Andrew Altman, *Critical Legal Studies: A Liberal Critique* (Princeton University Press, 1993).

objectivity of law.[47] CLS was influenced by American legal realism (see above) and general critical theory.[48] CLS theorists have marked international legal scholarship, but became less present at the peak of the trade liberalisation era. They now seem to have gained the interest of a new generation of IEL scholars. While acknowledging its dominating character, CLS approaches the law with more complexity than pure Marxist theories. Noted CLS theorists include Roberto M. Unger, Robert W. Gordon, Duncan Kennedy and David Kennedy for international law-related aspects.

In the context of this short presentation, we have chosen to use the term 'critical approaches' as CLS covers a particular school of thought born in the United States and is somehow more limited than CA. It is naturally very reductive to simplify CA to a few traits or currents, but pedagogically helpful, as shown by the paragraphs below.

A first trait of CA lies in its denial of legal neutrality. Indeed law, and IEL in particular, is not politically, economically, morally or culturally neutral. It is the product of a given history, a particular political perspective supporting a certain vision of the economy. In this regard, CA denounces purely positivist approaches to law. It critiques the formalism and the so-called objectivity of the law. It aims at demystifying the celebrated qualities of law.

Going one step further, CA tends to deconstruct the law in a postmodern fashion. Postmodernist theory is characterised by a form of suspicion of reason and stresses the role of ideology and power in the fabric of an idea. It denounces the objectivity of knowledge. In doing so, postmodern scholars pay particular attention to language and how law is expressed. They have been influenced by the French philosopher Jacques Derrida (1930–2004) and, in a different way, by the Swiss linguist Ferdinand de Saussure (1857–1913).

CA also questions the autonomy of the individual and their ability to make free decisions that are not determined by their social, political, cultural or religious environment. In this regard, feminist approaches denounce the intrinsic inequality of the law that supports all forms of discrimination against women. They are often placed in the CA theories. But feminist approaches are not necessarily antiliberal, for a number of liberal thinkers are also in favour of equality and freedom for all. As far as international law is concerned, feminist perspectives have played a role since the early twentieth century, with the development of women's international peace organisations, in particular. A true critique of international law by feminist scholars appeared from the late 1970s, documenting a history of domination in which postcolonial and critical race feminist theory play a significant part. More recently, 'gender' approaches have contributed to a more complex vision of law beyond the male/female binary. These gendered approaches are now found in IEL, with a new current, for example, analysing the impact of trade on gender and vice versa. The work of Hilary Charlesworth and Christine Chinkin is of particular interest.[49]

---

[47] A. Bianchi, *International Law Theories: An Inquiry into Different Ways of Thinking* (Oxford University Press, 2016), p. 136.

[48] S. E. Bronner, *Critical Theory: A Very Short Introduction* (Oxford University Press, 2017).

[49] H. Charlesworth and C. Chinkin, *The Boundaries of International Law: A Feminist Analysis*, Melland Schill Studies in International Law (Manchester University Press, 2000). See also Doris Buss and Ambreena Manji (eds.), *International Law: Modern Feminist Approaches* (Oxford and Portland, OR: Hart, 2005).

Lastly, of great relevance to international economic law is the scholarship of the Third World Approaches to International Law (TWAIL). Born in Harvard Law School around a group of students and scholars in the late 1990s, TWAIL is made of many subdivisions and draws on postcolonial studies.[50] From the early days of the decolonisation era, scholars like Georges Abi-Saab, R. P. Anand, Mohammed Bedjaoui, T. E. Elias and, more recently, M. Sornarajah had already influenced IEL scholarship significantly. They had stressed the North/South divide, historic bias in international law's creation, and contemporary imperialist making and application of international economic law. Along these lines, B. S. Chimni and James Thuo Gathii, the fathers of TWAIL, have produced stimulating scholarship reflecting on the issue of colonial history, identities, differences and their significance for international law.[51] For James Gathii: 'TWAIL is a historically aware methodology – one that challenges the simplistic visions of an innocent third world and a colonising and dominating first world. This methodology proceeds from the assumption that it is not possible to isolate modern forms of domination such as governmentality, from the continuation of older modes of domination (colonial and pre-colonial).'[52]

TWAIL is heterogeneous and evolves in multiple networks, grasping the attention of a wide variety of scholars. While Chimni was one of TWAIL's very first initiators and theoreticians, he is of late proposing what seems to be a more encompassing perspective that is an Integrated Marxist Approach to International Law (IMAIL). In doing so, he offers a theory integrating the different logics he feels are constitutive of the world order: the logics of capital, territory, culture, nature and law.[53]

All the above developments on the economic and legal theoretical underpinnings of international economic law show the importance of conceptual foundations. Being aware of the multiple facets of international law and international economic law makes their study and practice more stimulating and more complete. Being able to critically address the foundations and principles, but also the actors and practices of the field, is a true comparative advantage, as demonstrated below.

i.3   Subjects and Sources

Who are the subjects of international economic law? While the primary subject is the State, is it the only one? What about other players, such as multinational corporations

[50] G. Huggan (ed.), *The Oxford Handbook of Post-Colonial Studies* (Oxford University Press, 2013).

[51] See generally, *Trade, Law and Development: Third World Approaches to International Law* (special issue, 2011), 3(1), and, in particular, J. T. Gathii, 'TWAIL: A Brief History of its Origins, its Decentralised Network, and a Tentative Bibliography', pp. 26–48.

[52] Gathii, 'TWAIL', p. 26.

[53] Chimni, *International Law and the World Order*, p. 447; see also C. Miéville, *Between Equal Rights: A Marxist Theory of International Law* (Chicago: Haymarket Books, 2005); A. Anghie, *Imperialism, Sovereignty and the Making of International Law* (Cambridge University Press, 2012).

or civil society organisations? Is there a distinction between subjects, actors and participants? Here, again, international economic law rules and practices derive from general international law.[54]

i.3.1   Subjects, Actors or Participants

Contrary to national law, in which a large number of legal subjects coexist (notably, individuals, citizens, foreigners residing in the country), international law is much more selective. The State is the primary subject of international law. There are a few other subjects, but with limited legal capacity. These are insurgents, *sui generis* entities, international organisations, national liberation movements and individuals. Before we address the particularities of the later subjects of international law, one needs to understand what makes the State the main subject of international law, and indeed IEL.

The State is a political construct, and sovereignty and independence have been stressed as the crucial constitutive criteria of statehood throughout the entire history of international relations. It was sovereignty, however, that was mostly referred to. This has been true in particular since the 1648 Peace Treaties of Westphalia that ended the Thirty Years War, which devasted parts of today's Germany and killed about 30 per cent of its population. At the core, this 'Westphalian system' was the principle of sovereignty of each State over its territory and the exclusion of interference in other countries' domestic affairs.[55] The two concepts of sovereignty and independence, however, have been more clearly associated in international legal discourse since Max Huber's arbitral decision in the *Island of Palmas Case*.[56] Huber notes:

Sovereignty in the relations between States signifies independence. Independence in regard to a portion of the globe is the right to exercise therein, to the exclusion of any other State, the functions of a State. The development of the national organisation of States during the last few centuries and, as a corollary, the development of international law, have established this principle of the exclusive competence of the State in regard to its own territory in such a way as to make it the point of departure in settling most questions that concern international relations.[57]

---

[54] International economic law requires a preliminary knowledge of general international law. On the State and how international law is made, it is highly recommended to refer to general international law textbooks, for example, Antonio Cassese, *International Law* (Oxford University Press, 2005); Malcom N. Shaw, *International Law* (Cambridge University Press, 2017); Patrick Daillier, Matthias Forteau and Alain Pellet (eds.), *Droit International Public* (Paris: LGDJ, 2009).

[55] Olaf Asbach and Peter Schröder (eds.), *The Ashgate Research Companion to the Thirty Years War* (Farnham: Ashgate, 2014.)

[56] *The Island of Palmas Case (Netherlands, USA)*, *Reports of International Arbitral Awards*, 4 April 1928, Vol. II, pp. 829–871.

[57] *Island of Palmas Case*, p. 838.

While all States are sovereign, they are also *equal*. Sovereign equality between States enjoys a more recent conceptualisation and owes a lot to the two world wars and the postcolonial world order.[58] The Charter of the United Nations, in its Chapter I (Purposes and Principles), Article 2(1), states: 'The Organisation is based on the principle of the sovereign equality of all its Members'. The 1970 Declaration on Principles of International Law, Friendly Relations and Co-operation Among States in Accordance with the Charter of the United Nations brought additional clarification on the concept of sovereign equality and what it covers.[59]

Declaration on Principles of International Law (1970)

All States enjoy sovereign equality. They have equal rights and duties and are equal members of the international community, notwithstanding differences of an economic, social, political or other nature.

In particular, sovereign equality includes the following elements:

(a) States are judicially equal;
(b) Each State enjoys the rights inherent in full sovereignty;
(c) Each State has the duty to respect the personality of other States;
(d) The territorial integrity and political independence of the State are inviolable;
(e) Each State has the right freely to choose and develop its political, social, economic and cultural systems;
(f) Each State has the duty to comply fully and in good faith with its international obligations and to live in peace with other States.

Formulated in a decolonisation context, these elements are of particular interest to IEL students, scholars and practitioners, as they echo the idea of an 'economic sovereignty' and the concepts of the New International Economic Order. In the quest for independence, one of the colonies' prerequisites was control over economic resources, goods and services. This led to the formulation of the principle of permanent sovereignty over natural resources (PSNR), as expressed in the 1962 United Nations General Assembly Resolution, a landmark moment for international economic law (see Chapter 16).

---

[58] U. K. Preuss, 'Equality of States: Its Meaning in a Constitutionalised Global Order', *Chicago Journal of International Law* (2008), 9, pp. 17–49.

[59] UN General Assembly, Declaration on Principles of International Law concerning Friendly Relations and Co-operation Among States in accordance with the Charter of the United Nations, 24 October 1970, A/RES/2625 (XXV).

General Assembly Resolution 1803 (XVII): Permanent Sovereignty over Natural Resources (14 December 1962)

The General Assembly,

[...]

Declares that:

1. The right of peoples and nations to permanent sovereignty over their natural wealth and resources must be exercised in the interest of their national development and of the well-being of the people of the State concerned.

2. The exploration, development and disposition of such resources, as well as the import of the foreign capital required for these purposes, should be in conformity with the rules and conditions which the peoples and nations freely consider to be necessary or desirable with regard to the authorization, restriction or prohibition of such activities.

3. In cases where authorization is granted, the capital imported and the earnings on that capital shall be governed by the terms thereof, by the national legislation in force, and by international law. The profits derived must be shared in the proportions freely agreed upon, in each case, between the investors and the recipient State, due care being taken to ensure that there is no impairment, for any reason, of that State's sovereignty over its natural wealth and resources.

4. Nationalization, expropriation or requisitioning shall be based on grounds or reasons of public utility, security or the national interest which are recognized as overriding purely individual or private interests, both domestic and foreign. In such cases the owner shall be paid appropriate compensation, in accordance with the rules in force in the State taking such measures in the exercise of its sovereignty and in accordance with international law. In any case where the question of compensation gives rise to a controversy, the national jurisdiction of the State taking such measures shall be exhausted. However, upon agreement by sovereign States and other parties concerned, settlement of the dispute should be made through arbitration or international adjudication.

5. The free and beneficial exercise of the sovereignty of peoples and nations over their natural resources must be furthered by the mutual respect of States based on their sovereign equality.

6. International co-operation for the economic development of developing countries, whether in the form of public or private capital investments, exchange of goods and services, technical assistance, or exchange of scientific information, shall be such as to further their independent national development and shall be based upon respect for their sovereignty over their natural wealth and resources.

7. Violation of the rights of peoples and nations to sovereignty over their natural wealth and resources is contrary to the spirit and principles of the Charter of the United

> *(cont.)*
>
> Nations and hinders the development of international co-operation and the mainten-
> ance of peace.
>
> 8. Foreign investment agreements freely entered into by or between sovereign States shall
> be observed in good faith; States and international organizations shall strictly and
> conscientiously respect the sovereignty of peoples and nations over their natural wealth
> and resources in accordance with the Charter and the principles set forth in the
> present resolution.

Along the same lines, a number of key additional international texts were later adopted,
supporting the idea of economic sovereignty:

- The UN General Assembly Resolution 3281 of 1974, the Charter of Economic Rights and
  Duties of States (CERDS).[60]
- The 1986 UN General Assembly Resolution on the right to development as a human right,
  which implies the freedom of people and nations to freely choose their method of develop-
  ment, a text which paved the way to the Millennium Development Goals of 2000.[61]
- The United Nations Conference on the Human Environment 1972 Stockholm
  Declaration, which called for the conservation of natural resources, particularly flora
  and fauna, and the need to manage and preserve the Earth's renewable resources.[62]
- The 1982 UN World Charter for Nature and the UN Convention on the Law of the Sea.
- The 1985 Brundtland Commission report and conceptualisation of 'sustainable develop-
  ment', calling on nations to develop within a framework that includes limiting the
  degradation of the environment.
- The 1992 Rio Conference, providing guidelines for sustainable development.[63]
- The UN Convention on Biological Diversity, which reinforced the idea of sovereignty
  over natural resources, but with some attention for natural resources, biological diversity
  to use these resources in a responsible, sustainable manner.[64]

All these international reference texts stress the possibility of equality through diversity.
Irrespective of their size or power, States have the same rights and duties. There is equality
before the law in the sense of equality of legal personality and capacity. As an example, the
WTO's decision-making process, based on positive consensus, is a recognition of this formal

---

[60] UN General Assembly, Charter of Economic Rights and Duties of States, 12 December 1974, A/RES/29/3281.

[61] UN General Assembly, Declaration on the Right to Development, 4 December 1986, A/RES/41/128; United
Nations Development Program, Millennium Development Goals, available at www.undp.org/content/undp/en/
home/sdgoverview/mdg_goals.html (accessed 5 November 2020).

[62] UN General Assembly, United Nations Conference on the Human Environment, 15 December 1972, A/RES/2994.

[63] United Nations Conference on Environment and Development (UNCED), Earth Summit, available at https://
sustainabledevelopment.un.org/milestones/unced (accessed 5 November 2020).

[64] UN Environment, Convention on Biological Diversity, available at www.cbd.int (accessed 5 November 2020).

equality. To give a trade-related example, all States, if members of the WTO, can have recourse to the dispute settlement system. Naturally, this equality is often more formal than effective when confronted with the reality of power balance in international relations.[65] Some weaker States might not have the financial resources or political margin to bring a WTO case (see Chapter 10).

While sovereignty has fostered the idea that there is no higher power than the nation State, economic interdependence and the reality of globalisation require a new approach to the traditional concept of sovereignty.[66] In recent times, several trade disputes have touched upon the rights of certain States to retain control of various types of natural resources, especially resources that could give them unique economic advantages, such as rare earths and raw materials.[67] The unavailability of such resources has disrupted supply chains in several countries and can impede international trade. To what extent can a country exercise sovereignty over such resources that are vital for orderly international trade? The various disciplines in trade and investment law, such as prohibition on quantitative restrictions, export controls and performance requirements, have redefined the concept of sovereignty in the field of IEL.

Interestingly, when it comes to additional criteria to define statehood, the rules relating to the creation of States are relatively vague. They have not changed much, despite the decolonisation process or the end of the Soviet Bloc, and rely on customary international law (see the sources of IEL below). In this regard, Article 1 of the 1933 Montevideo Convention on Rights and Duties of States had formulated the now widely accepted criteria of statehood in international law. These criteria are a permanent population, a defined territory, a government and the capacity to enter into relations with other States.

Other criteria have been put forward by international law scholars. For example, James Crawford, in a landmark publication on the creation of States in international law, has noted: 'no violation of self-determination or unlawful use of force should be allowed for a State to be created'.[68] But we know from international relations history that these conditions are often difficult to meet. Lastly and very importantly, a large scholarship is dedicated to the question of recognition. While the act of recognition has no legal effect on the international personality of the new State and does not confer rights or obligations, it has a real political significance. Other States welcome the birth of a new member of the international community and de facto support its existence as an international subject. However, as pointed out by Antonio Cassese, there is a political element of inequality, if not domination, in the recognition process: 'the theory is an outmoded survival from the nineteenth century

---

[65] While the WTO legal system has seen lopsided participation of developed countries, several developing countries and small economies continue to play an active role.

[66] J. H. Jackson, 'Sovereignty – Modern: A New Approach to an Outdated Concept', *American Journal of International Law* (2003), 97, pp. 782–80. See also J. H. Jackson, *Sovereignty, the WTO, and Changing Fundamentals of International Law* (Cambridge University Press, 2006), p. 89.

[67] M. Chi, 'Resource Sovereignty in WTO Dispute Settlement: Implications of *China – Raw Materials*, and *China – Rare Earths*', *Manchester Journal of International Economic Law* (2015), 12(1), pp. 2–15.

[68] J. Crawford, *The Creation of States in International Law* (Oxford University Press, 2007).

when [...] European States claimed the right to admit other States to, or exclude from, the "family of nations"'.[69] State practice indeed shows great evolutions and discrepancies on the conditions for the granting of recognition. A more important criterion seems to be that of effectiveness, as pointed out by James Crawford.[70] The State possesses an effective authority that is an effective government.

Being a sovereign State and so a subject of international law grants rights and obligations. These matter greatly and are reflected in IEL practice. The fundamental rights of States can be summarised to three core ideas: independence, equality and peaceful coexistence.[71] However, sovereignty is not absolute and needs to be understood, at the international level, in relation to other States' rights and obligations. The State, first and foremost, is forbidden to interfere in other States' internal affairs or in their territories. This includes the possible submission by the State to the jurisdiction of its courts or foreign States for acts performed as sovereigns – complex questions involving the 'sovereign immunity of States'. In an international economic law context, this issue is of particular interest when dealing with State-owned enterprises (SOEs).[72] What is their ability to bring an investment claim against another State and/or be litigated against? (See Chapters 10 and 14.)

In addition to States, a number of other entities are accepted as international legal subjects, and we explore these below.

i.3.1.1   International Organisations

They are the instruments of a State's international policies. They are endowed with international legal personality. But unlike States, and as explained in a landmark Advisory Opinion of the ICJ in *Legality of the Threat or Use of Nuclear Weapons*, they have much more limited competence and range of action. The ICJ stressed the following:

the Court need hardly point out that international organizations are subjects of international law which do not, unlike States, possess a general competence. International organizations are governed by the 'principle of speciality', that is to say, they are invested by the States which create them with powers, the limits of which are a function of the common interests whose promotion those States entrust to them.[73]

International organisations only exist on the basis of a State's will. They were first designed in the late nineteenth century to deal with technical matters, such as the 1875 Universal Postal Union or the 1883 Union for the Protection of Industrial Property. Naturally, with the First and Second World Wars, political international organisations of great significance were also created: the League of Nations, the International Labour Organization (ILO) and the United Nations. But not all international organisations possess

---

[69] Cassese, *International Law*, p. 74.   [70] Crawford, *Creation of States*, ch. 2.   [71] Shaw, *International Law*, ch. 5.
[72] J. Chaisse and J. Gorski (eds.), *Regulation of State-Controlled Enterprises: An Interdisciplinary and Comparative Examination* (Singapore: Springer, in press).
[73] *Legality of the Threat or Use of Nuclear Weapons, Advisory Opinion, ICJ Reports 1996*, p. 226.

international legal personality. To be considered as an international subject, they need to demonstrate the possibility to exercise their functions and enjoy a form of autonomy from their member States. They can then possess rights and are subjected to certain obligations. These are, principally, the right to enter into international agreements with non-member States on matters within their competences, the right to immunity from jurisdiction of State courts for the acts and activities they perform, the right to protection for their agents in their official capacity as international civil servants, the right to bring an international claim for reparation for damages caused by a member State or third State. These organisations are generally structured on the same basis with a general assembly of member States, a permanent secretariat made of international civil servants and a governing body. They play a great role in international economic law from the WTO, the World Bank or the IMF.

i.3.1.2 *Sui Generis* Entities

Here is a quite interesting and rare category of subjects of international law. *Sui generis* entities, for historical reasons, have acquired the status of subjects while, unlike a State, they do not necessarily have a territory and enjoy only a limited international personality. The Holy See, the seat of the Catholic Church, for example, can enter into international agreements and enjoys immunity from foreign jurisdiction. The Sovereign Order of Malta established in the twelfth century, at the time of the Crusades, and now a charitable organisation, and the International Committee of the Red Cross (ICRC), though initially born as a private entity, all enjoy the status of subjects of international law.

i.3.1.3 Insurgents

Another peculiar category is that of insurgents. It is not very clearly defined. It covers rebellious parties who dissent against a given State. When the insurgents come to acquire effective control over part of the State territory, they may be recognised as belligerents. Their recognition as international legal persons depends greatly on other States. As demonstrated by Antonio Cassese, they are transient – that is, their status is transitory.[74] They are endowed with very limited capacities before they become real sovereigns.

i.3.1.4 National Liberation Movements

A relatively close category to insurgents is that of national liberation movements that could have acquired control over some parts of the territory in which they are fighting (FLN in colonised Algeria, for example). But often, and contrary to insurgents, these movements prepare their operation from the outside and are hosted in another country. Their existence and legitimisation are based on the principle of self-determination (UN Charter, Chapter 1,

---

[74] A. Cassese, 'The Status of Rebels under the 1977 Geneva Protocol in Non-International Armed Conflicts', *International and Comparative Law Quarterly* (1981), 30(2), pp. 416–39.

Article 1 and International Covenant on Civil and Political Rights, and International Covenant of Economic, Social and Cultural Rights, Article 1). Their fight against colonisation or political oppression, as well as their aspiration to become a State, justify their international status.

i.3.1.5 Individuals

Lastly, and certainly important today, individuals pose a new challenge to international law. For many, individuals are not yet subjects of international law, but rather participants in the international community. They were for a long time under the complete control of the State and benefited from its international commitment. In IEL, treaties of friendship, commerce and navigation (FCN treaties) benefited individuals, but such treaties were not made by and for them. Diplomatic protection exercised by the State for the benefit of its citizens derives from the same idea. It was the main basis for the inclusion of individuals in international economic law (see Chapter 14). The situation, however, has evolved with a much greater integration of individuals in international relations over the course of the twentieth and early twenty-first century. From human rights violations to the role of multinational companies in globalisation, their presence is immense. When it comes to disputes, the investor–State dispute settlement system bears testimony to the participation and powers given to individuals. Thus, States have given individuals certain rights that also come with a number of obligations. These obligations derive from customary international law and deal mostly with the need to refrain from violations of international humanitarian law and human rights (such as aggression and international crimes). In terms of rights, individuals may hold a few based on certain treaty provisions. For example, the right granted by the ILO (Article 24 of its Constitution) to associations of workers and employers to submit complaints against a State on the basis of an alleged violation of an ILO Convention it ratified.[75] We can also think about the European Convention on Human Rights, which guarantees the right of any person, non-governmental organisation or group of individuals claiming to be the victim of a violation of their rights under the Convention or its Protocols to introduce an application before the court. In international economic law, the debate very much revolves around two main actors – SOEs and private entities – which notably play a role as investors.[76]

Naturally, other actors are present without being considered as subjects endowed with a legal personality. One can think about civil society organisations and non-governmental organisations (NGOs) or think tanks, which are now welcomed to submit Amicus briefs to a WTO panel or an arbitration tribunal (see Chapters 10 and 14). These civil society organisations are also actors in the WTO-related debates when, for example, they lobby with their governments or engage with the WTO processes on a particular trade topic.

---

[75] Constitution of the International Labour Organization, Art. 24, 1 April 1919.

[76] A. Kjeldgaard-Pedersen, *The International Legal Personality of the Individual* (Oxford University Press, 2018), ch. 8.

i.3.2   Sources

The sources and principles of IEL are also derived from general international law. In this regard, the past fifty years have been key to the codification of IEL.

The sources of IEL, as for general international law, are found in Article 38 of the Statute of the International Court of Justice (ICJ).

ICJ, Article 38

1. The Court, whose function is to decide in accordance with international law such disputes as are submitted to it, shall apply:
   a. international conventions, whether general or particular, establishing rules expressly recognized by the contesting States;
   b. international custom, as evidence of a general practice accepted as law;
   c. the general principles of law recognized by civilized nations;
   d. subject to the provisions of Article 59, judicial decisions and the teachings of the most highly qualified publicists of the various nations, as subsidiary means for the determination of rules of law.
2. This provision shall not prejudice the power of the Court to decide a case ex aequo et bono, if the parties agree thereto.

---

i.3.2.1   International Custom

International custom or customary international law (CIL) has always been approached as a complex and rather controversial source of international law. CIL lacks a 'centralized law maker, a centralized executive, and a centralized authoritarian decision maker'.[77] While apparently easy to identify as a generally accepted usage, custom is more difficult to define. Since the Permanent Court of International Justice (PCIJ) with the *Lotus Case*, international custom is seen as a form of implicit understanding between world nations. According to the Permanent Court: 'The rules of law binding upon States therefore emanate from their own free will as expressed in conventions or by usages generally accepted as expressing principles of law and established in order to regulate the relations between these coexisting independent communities or with a view to the achievement of common aims. Restrictions upon the independence of States cannot therefore be presumed.'[78]

But what are these 'usages generally accepted as expressing principles of law'? Where do we find them? Are they universal, regional or local? International custom has naturally been

---

[77] J. L. Goldsmith and E. A. Posner, 'A Theory of Customary International Law', John M. Olin Law and Economics Working Paper 63 (1998), University of Chicago Law School.
[78] See *S.S. Lotus (France* v. *Turkey), 1927 PCIJ, Series A, No. 10.*

critically addressed by non-European powers, which felt excluded as they were originally not involved in the creation of modern international law.[79]

Article 38 of the Statute of the ICJ does not provide much clarification when it defines international custom as 'evidence of a general practice accepted as law'. Two elements define custom: a general practice and the acceptance by States that this practice is law (*opinio juris*). A third related element has been put forward with the idea of an *opinio necessitatis*, or the fact that international custom is required by social or political forces. An example often given to explain the later element is the use of custom to manage State relations in matters of the sea and, notably, the exploitation of the continental shelf.[80]

The ICJ admitted the possibility of the existence of more local customary rules in the *Asylum* case, in which Colombia relied on a local custom against Peru when granting asylum. However, it is up to the State to prove the existence of such a custom. In the *Asylum* case the, ICJ noted the following.

Asylum (Colombia *v.* Peru), ICJ Reports 1950

The Party which relies on a custom of this kind must prove that this custom is established in such a manner that it has become binding on the other Party. The Colombian Government must prove that the rule invoked by it is in accordance with a constant and uniform usage practised by the States in question, and that this usage is the expression of a right appertaining to the State granting asylum and a duty incumbent on the territorial State. This follows from Article 38 of the Statute of the Court, which refers to international custom 'as evidence of a general practice accepted as law'.[81]

The ICJ also admitted a degree of flexibility in State practice as expressed in its judgment on the *Nicaragua* case: 'In order to deduce the existence of customary rules, the Court deems sufficient that the conduct of states should, in general, be consistent with such rules, and that instances of state conduct inconsistent with a given rule should generally have been treated as breaches of that rule, not as indications of the recognition of a new rule'.[82]

The role of custom is relatively limited today, given that countries have chosen, since the end of the Second World War and the decolonisation process, to resort to a vast effort of codification better encompassing countries' differences in approach and visions of international law.

---

[79] For an international investment law-related perspective, see M. Sornarajah, 'Resistance to Dominance in International Investment Law', in Julien Chaisse, Leïla Choukroune and Sufian Jusoh (eds.), *Handbook of International Investment Law and Policy* (Singapore: Springer, 2021).

[80] *North Sea Continental Shelf Cases (Federal Republic of Germany v. Denmark; Federal Republic of Germany v. Netherlands), ICJ Reports 1969*, p. 3.

[81] *Asylum (Colombia v. Peru), ICJ Reports 1950*, p. 276.

[82] *Case Concerning Military and Paramilitary Activities in and against Nicaragua (Nicaragua v. United States of America), Merits, Judgment, ICJ Reports 1986*, p. 98, para. 186.

i.3.2.2 International Treaties

Treaties are by far the main source of contemporary international law and, consequently, also of IEL. Treaties are also called agreements, conventions, covenants, statutes or acts. No matter what their names and forms are, they are all the product of the will of two (bilateral) or more (multilateral) legal subjects (States mostly, and international organisations sometimes). They are binding for the parties and do not create obligations for third parties. They are often the product of a codification exercise.

Codification has largely occupied international lawyers throughout the second half of the twentieth century. With the emergence of a significant number of new countries, but also more complex international relations, including booming international exchanges, the need for treaty drafting became evident. From the law of the sea to the law of treaties itself, the United Nations and its General Assembly have played a key role in the codification effort, often led by the International Law Commission.[83] The ILC was created by the UN General Assembly in 1947, under Article 13(1)(a) of the Charter of the United Nations, to 'initiate studies and make recommendations for the purpose of [...] encouraging the progressive development of international law and its codification'. However, other major processes of codification were run more directly by the States, as in the case of the General Agreement on Tariffs and Trade (GATT) rounds of negotiation and, later, the creation of the World Trade Organization.

As far as codification is concerned, the 1969 Vienna Convention on the Law of Treaties (VCLT) soon became the reference instrument.[84] The VCLT is routinely invoked in international trade and investment disputes.

Box i.1 Treaty interpretation and the VCLT

Adopted on 23 May 1969 and entered into force on 27 January 1980, the Vienna Convention on the Law of Treaties (VCLT) established a set of comprehensive rules on the negotiation, drafting, reservations, amendment, interpretation and termination of international treaties. It is probably the best example of codification of customary international law. It was drafted by the UN International Law Commission, which started its work as early as 1949. The VCLT has more than a hundred States parties.

Some countries, such as the United States, have not ratified the VCLT, but recognise some of its provisions as customary international law. The VCLT is indeed the authoritative guide on international treaties and is referred to religiously in WTO disputes decisions in matters of interpretation. National courts have also referred to the VCLT, and its role for codification has been acknowledged.[85] The reference to the

---

[83] International Law Commission, available at legal.un.org/ilc/ (accessed 21 December 2020).

[84] O. Corten and P. Klein, *The Vienna Convention on the Law of Treaties: A Commentary* (Oxford University Press, 2011), p. 2071. See also B. J. Codon, 'Lost in Translation: Plurilingual Interpretation of WTO Law', *Journal of International Dispute Settlement* (2010), 1, pp. 191–216.

[85] *Ram Jethmalani* v. *Union of India* (2011) 8 SCC 1.

Box i.1 (cont.)

customary rules of international law on the interpretation of treaties in Article 3.2 of the DSU of the WTO Agreements is considered to be a reference to Articles 31–33 of the VCLT.[86] The International Court of Justice and other international courts and tribunals have also recognised the rules of treaty interpretation under the VCLT, namely Articles 31–33, as customary international law.[87]

The VCLT applies to treaties between States. Section 3 and Articles 31–33 relating to the interpretation of treaties are of particular interest from an IEL perspective. Before the VCLT, treaties were mostly interpreted on the basis of logical reasoning and the legal culture of a given domestic system. Article 31 embodies the textual principle, although it stresses elements such as good faith, the context of the treaty, its object and purpose, subsequent agreements, subsequent practice, relevant rules of international law and any special meaning of the terms of a treaty. According to Article 31(2), the 'context' is limited to the text of the treaty, its preamble and its annexes, alongside other international agreements and instruments related to the treaty. In terms of Article 31(3), a treaty interpreter is required to take into account '[a]ny subsequent agreement between the parties regarding the interpretation of the treaty or the application of its provisions' and '[a]ny relevant rules of international law applicable in the relations between the parties'. 'Supplementary means' of interpretation are then listed in its Article 32 and include 'preparatory work' that took place with a view to drafting the treaty. Article 32 can be availed to confirm an interpretation arrived at by the tools provided in Article 31, or if an application of the Article leaves the meaning ambiguous or obscure or leads to a result that is manifestly absurd or unreasonable. Lastly, Article 33 clarifies the issue of language in a liberal and universal attempt: 'when a treaty has been authenticated in two or more languages, the text is equally authoritative in each language', unless the treaty provides otherwise. Plurilingual interpretation is indeed a difficult task and has been addressed in a number of WTO cases; while English, along with French and Spanish, are WTO official languages, there are discrepancies in different textual versions of the same agreement. For example, the text of the DSU, Article 7.2 is different in the English and French versions compared to the Spanish version, in which the word 'relevant' has been omitted when referring to the provisions to be looked at. Similar discrepancies exist in the English, French and Spanish texts of the important Article XX(b) (General Exceptions) of the GATT 1994. This is to say that the codification of interpretation

---

[86] Appellate Body Report, *US – Gasoline*, p. 17.

[87] *Land, Island and Maritime Frontier Dispute (El Salvador* v. *Honduras), ICJ Reports 1992*, p. 351, para. 380; *Territorial Dispute (Libya* v. *Chad), ICJ Reports 1994*, p. 6, para. 41; *Golder* v. *United Kingdom*, ECHR (1975), Series A, No. 18.

Box i.1 (cont.)

provided by the Vienna Convention on the Law of Treaties is of major importance today for a number of IEL-related matters.

While it may be helpful to organise the analysis in the nature of text, context, object and purpose in turn, treaty interpretation is a holistic exercise that should not be mechanically subdivided into rigid parts.[88]

In addition, the rules also detail the relationship between successive treaties relating to the same subject matter, in Article 30. This rule helps in solving conflicts between treaties on the same subject matter, by laying out rules and principles, which may apply to solve these conflicts.

i.3.2.3   Judicial Decisions and Scholarship

Another important source of international law stems from international judicial decisions. These are, in the words of Article 38 of the Statute of the ICJ, to be utilised as 'subsidiary means' for the determination of rules of law, just as the 'teachings of the most highly qualified publicists of the various nations'. As per Article 59 of the Statute of the ICJ, the decisions of the Court have no binding effect except as between the parties and in respect of the case under consideration. The doctrine of precedent developed in common law does not exist in international law. However, as proven by the practice of international law, international courts' decisions can be of major importance. They serve as a starting point in the court's reasoning and provide elements of comparison. In IEL, too, there is nothing comparable to *stare decisis* or a rule of precedent (see Chapters 10 and 14). But in trade law, WTO decisions in particular are of great significance and follow a certain logical pattern from which one could see a form of consistency, if not precedence as such. Investment law is much less influenced by arbitral cases, for investment decisions have been rather inconsistent, if not contradictory, but here again, cases are of importance in the making and evolution of the field.

The 'teachings of the most highly qualified publicists of the various nations' are not without impact on the creation of international law. Treaty drafters or judges do refer to international law scholarship, either directly in quoting a given reference in a judgment, or indirectly in using various sources to inform their reasoning.

i.3.2.4   International Law and Domestic Law: The Case of the WTO

The relationship between international law and domestic law is governed by States' constitutional order. From a positivist approach, the role of the State is central in the making of

---

[88] Appellate Body Report, *China – Measures Affecting Trading Rights and Distribution Services for Certain Publications and Audiovisual Entertainment Products*, WT/DS363/AB/R, adopted 19 January 2010, para. 348.

international law and its application. The issue of international law before municipal courts is rather complex and goes far beyond the idea that the State needs to act in conformity with its international obligations. Trade law offers an interesting illustration of this complexity. The WTO Agreement mandates all members to ensure conformity of their laws, regulations and administrative procedures with the substantive obligations contained in the Agreement. A failure to do so would engage the State's international responsibility. But it is up to each member of the WTO to implement the Agreement. It may or may not be given direct effect in a given domestic legal order. In the European Union, international agreements concluded by the EU become an integral part of the EU's legal order. EU law, then, needs to be interpreted in light of the WTO Agreement when relevant. However, as the direct effect of WTO law is not specified in the Agreement itself, the European Court of Justice had to determine whether that effect should be attributed to the WTO Agreement or not. In US law, some treaties are held to be self-executing, hence providing them with a direct effect. It is not the case of WTO law. This is equally true for decisions of the WTO dispute settlement panels and the Appellate Body. Both jurisdictions require the implementation of WTO law in their legal orders to translate their internationally binding obligations domestically.

i.3.2.5   General Principles of International Law

The general principles of international law are also recognised as a subsidiary source of international law. The wording of Article 38 of the Statute of the ICJ remains problematic for many, as it refers to the idea of the 'civilised nations' acknowledging these principles. A similar provision was already present in the Statute of the Permanent Court of International Justice. Naturally, the expression 'civilised nations' could be interpreted as referring to those who acknowledge the authority of international law in the conduct of their international affairs, but it also referred to Western powers still dominating international relations at that time. Without universal consensus, these general principles of international law could be difficult to describe, but a few are relatively easy to identify: good faith, *res judicata* or the idea according to which no claim against a settled matter could be made, or estoppel that is not taking a position contrary to a well-established principle.

i.3.2.6   Other Sources and Hierarchy

Sources other than those listed in Article 38 of the Statute of the ICJ play a role today. They are not primary sources, but could be considered subsidiary sources. In particular, the body of soft law that has developed in international relations, around issues of trade, investment and human rights, presents a real interest. This 'soft law', as opposed to the 'hard law' of treaties, is made of standards, commitments, guidelines and other declarations. In an IEL context, we could think, for example, about the UN Guiding Principles on Business and Human Rights.[89]

---

[89] Guiding Principles on Business and Human Rights, United Nations Human Rights, Office of the High Commissioner, UN. Doc. HR/PUB/11/04.

But is there a hierarchy of sources of international law? Is this comparable to what exists in domestic law? The question revolves around the idea of *jus cogens*, or the existence of peremptory norms of international law. These have been defined by the VCLT in its Article 53.

> ### VCLT, Article 53: **Treaties Conflicting with a Peremptory Norm of General International Law ('Jus Cogens')**
>
> A treaty is void if, at the time of its conclusion, it conflicts with a peremptory norm of general international law. For the purposes of the present Convention, a peremptory norm of general international law is a norm accepted and recognized by the international community of States as a whole as a norm from which no derogation is permitted and which can be modified only by a subsequent norm of general international law having the same character.

However, a norm 'accepted and recognized by the international community of States as a whole as a norm from which no derogation is permitted', is not necessarily easy to identify or agree upon. The ban on torture, the ban on slavery or the principle of non-interference in other States' domestic affairs are often put forward as *jus cogens* norms of universal acceptance. The reliance on *jus cogens*, however, remained limited in international law. One could imagine, perhaps, that IEL is not concerned with *jus cogens* norms. However, egregious human rights violations in the context of an international investment or the trade supply chain have showed that *jus cogens* is very much an IEL topic too (see Mini Chapter 1).[90]

i.4 Conclusion

According to Georges Scelle, founder of the sociological objectivist theory of international law, 'every internationalist is attached to a philosophical-legal school which dominates his teaching'.[91] Without adhering to a particular school of thought, we have chosen to critically address international economic law to better unveil its complexity. IEL is not theoretically or politically neutral. While presenting the law 'as it is', in a rather positivist manner, throughout the different chapters of this textbook, we have also systematically put the technical components of IEL into perspective. This critical distance is very much needed to truly comprehend a field at the crossroads between disciplines, yet firmly anchored in general international law. To achieve this objective, we have chosen to refer to a variety of sources and visions. One of our central aims is to participate in a genuine international and

---

[90] Thomas Cottier, 'Improving Compliance: Jus Cogens and International Economic Law', *Netherlands Yearbook of International Law* (2016), 46, pp. 329–56.

[91] The original French text reads: 'Tout internationaliste se rattache à une école philosophico-juridique qui domine son enseignement'. See George Scelle, *Précis de droit des gens: principes et systématique* (Paris: Dalloz, 2008).

comparative approach to IEL, one that is not only focused on the developed world, but which takes into consideration the practice and possible theoretical perspectives of the Global South. In doing so, we have used different pedagogical tools to stimulate the readers' learning and the development of his/her own critical thinking. Another common denominator of this textbook is that it places human beings at the centre of the reflection around international economic law and stresses its role as a true regulator of a globalisation, which could evolve in a fairer and more just manner. Based on years of teaching, research and practice on a large number of IEL topics, this textbook reflects our own teaching, practice and scholarship. We attempt to answer some of the questions that we have encountered in our classroom teaching and in our professional lives as practitioners of IEL. It is very much informed by research and practice, and by all our interactions with students, peers, policy-makers and colleagues all over the world. We hope it will contribute to a better understanding of international relations and their implications for all actors in the field.

FURTHER READING

Abi-Saab, G., Keith, K., Marceau, G. and Marquet, C., *Evolutionary Interpretation and International Law* (Oxford: Hart, 2019).

Benvenisti, E., *The Law of Global Governance* (The Hague: Brill, 2014).

Bianchi, A., *International Law Theories: An Enquiry into Different Ways of Thinking* (Oxford University Press, 2016).

Evenett, S. J., *Cloth for Wine? The Relevance of Ricardo's Comparative Advantage in the Twenty-First Century* (London: CEPR Press, 2017).

Lacharrière, G. L., *L'influence de l'inégalité de développement des Etats sur le droit international* (The Hague: Brill, 1973).

Nicholson, P. and Gillespie, J., *Law and Development and the Global Discourses of Legal Transfers* (Cambridge University Press, 2012).

Scelle, G., *Précis de droit des gens: principes et systématique* (Paris: Dalloz, 2008).

Part I

International Trade Law

1 International Trade Law: Basic Principles

Table of Contents

Highlights

- Non-discrimination is a key principle found in almost all branches of international economic law. It includes principles such as most favoured nation treatment and national treatment.
- Most favoured national treatment under the GATT is the obligation to extend any 'advantage', 'favour', 'privilege' or 'immunity' granted by a WTO member to any product originating in or destined for any other country 'immediately and unconditionally' to the 'like product' originating in or destined for any other members.
- National treatment seeks to ensure that WTO members do not treat imported products less favourably than domestic products once the products enter into internal commerce. The purpose of national treatment is to ensure that no indirect advantage is given to domestic production.
- Less favourable treatment under Article III:4 is overwhelmingly established on the basis of the disparate impact test, unbridled by the significance of regulatory concerns. The Appellate Body rulings in *US – Clove Cigarettes* and *EC – Seal Products* confirm this trend.
- The WTO provides a separate regime (TRIMs Agreement) for trade-related investment measures that are captured in Articles III and XI of the GATT. The TRIMs Agreement includes an Annex of prohibited TRIMs.
- The Enabling Clause that is considered an exception to Article I of the GATT is an integral element in enabling WTO members to provide preferential, non-reciprocal and more advantageous treatment to products originating from developing and least-developed countries.

1.1   Non-Discrimination

Non-discrimination is a key principle of international economic law and is found in almost all branches of this rapidly evolving field. It is an established norm under the General Agreement on Tariffs and Trade (GATT), General Agreement on Trade in Services (GATS), Trade-Related Intellectual Property Rights (TRIPS), and in the field of international investment law.

The non-discrimination principle incorporates most favoured nation (MFN) treatment and national treatment (NT). The two questions that arise under the non-discrimination principle are as follows: is the measure discriminatory between member countries? Does the importing country discriminate between imported and domestic products by using domestic taxation or regulation? The non-discrimination principle is key to preserving the balance of rights and obligations undertaken by countries under the WTO or other trade agreements.

1.1.1   Most Favoured Nation Principle

Article I:1 of the GATT sets out the MFN treatment – a fundamental non-discrimination obligation under the GATT 1994. This principle is broadly considered a 'cornerstone' principle of the multilateral trading system.[1] In the words of the International Court of Justice, 'it is the very intention of the clause to establish and to maintain at all times fundamental equality without discrimination among all of the countries concerned'.[2] MFN treatment seeks to reduce tensions in international relations, specifically in the context of trade relations and the possibility of disputes. The unconditional nature of the MFN principle seeks to render the conclusion of individual agreements superfluous and creates a tendency to foster multilateralism.[3]

The term 'most favoured' is a misnomer because it does not entail any special treatment, but rather an equality of treatment that a Member grants to every other WTO member with respect to import and export of products.

The MFN principle has a long history, although the term appears to have been used first only in the seventeenth century.[4] The peace treaty signed between Great Britain and Sweden on 11 April 1654 contained an MFN clause.[5] MFN clauses were also routinely seen in the friendship, commerce and navigation (FCN) treaties and bilateral treaties concerning diplomatic and consular relations. Although MFN treatment finds a place in a number of

---

[1] Appellate Body Report, *Canada – Certain Measures Affecting the Automotive Industry*, WT/DS139/AB/R, WT/DS142/AB/R, adopted 19 June 2000, para. 69.

[2] *Rights of Nationals of the United States of America in Morocco (France* v. *United States of America), Judgment of 27 August 1952, ICJ Reports 1952*, p. 176.

[3] Meinhard Hilf and Robin Geiß, 'Most-Favoured-Nation Clause', in Rüdiger Wolfrum (ed.), *Max Planck Encyclopedia of Public International Law*, Vol. VII (Oxford University Press, 2012), pp. 384–7.

[4] OECD, *Most-Favoured-Nation Treatment in International Investment Law*, OECD Working Papers on International Investment 2004/02 (Paris: OECD Publishing, 2004).

[5] Hilf and Geiß, 'Most-Favoured-Nation Clause', para. 6.

economic treaties, it cannot be said that MFN treatment is a rule of customary international law.[6] In other words, MFN can be assumed only in situations where a treaty explicitly provides for it. States have the general freedom to enter into preferential treaties and to determine the contours and content of such treaties.

The growth of regional and bilateral trade agreements, to an extent, has affected the functioning of the MFN principle. At the end of 2019, 303 regional trade agreements had been notified to the WTO.[7] For example, the European Union is one of the largest customs unions, whereas the Trans-Pacific Partnership (TPP), and its renamed version, the Comprehensive and Progressive Agreement for Trans-Pacific Partnership (CPTPP), is an example of a large free trade agreement, more popularly known as a 'mega-regional'. These regional trade agreements could be an exception to the MFN clause (see Chapter 2). Despite this trend, an overwhelming volume of merchandise trade is carried out on the basis of the unconditional MFN route.[8]

GATT, Article 1:1: General Most-Favoured-Nation Treatment

With respect to customs duties and charges of any kind imposed on or in connection with importation or exportation or imposed on the international transfer of payments for imports and exports ... and with respect to all matters referred to in paragraphs 2 and 4 of Article III, any advantage, favour, privilege or immunity granted by any contracting party to any product originating in or destined for any other country shall be accorded immediately and unconditionally to the like product originating in or destined for the territories of all other contracting parties.

The obligation under Article I:1 of the GATT is to extend any 'advantage', 'favour', 'privilege' or 'immunity' granted by a WTO member to any product originating in or destined for any other country, 'immediately and unconditionally', to the 'like product' originating in or destined for any other members. The MFN obligation has the objective of preserving the equality of competitive opportunities.[9] The MFN principle has also become a convenient shorthand to incorporate, by way of reference, advantages previously granted in other treaties.[10]

---

[6] G. Schwarzenberger, 'The Most-Favoured-Nation Standard in British State Practice', *British Yearbook of International Law* (1945), 22, p. 103.

[7] World Trade Organization, Regional Trade Agreements Database, RTA Tracker, available at http://rtais.wto.org/UI/PublicMaintainRTAHome.aspx (accessed 5 November 2020).

[8] World Trade Organization, *The WTO and Preferential Trade Agreements: From Co-Existence to Coherence*, World Trade Report 2011 (Geneva: WTO Publications, 2011).

[9] Appellate Body Reports, *European Communities – Measures Prohibiting the Importation and Marketing of Seal Products*, WT/DS400/AB/R, WT/DS401/AB/R, adopted 18 June 2014, para. 5.88.

[10] J. H. Jackson, *The World Trading System: Law and Policy of International Economic Relations*, 2nd ed. (Cambridge, MA: MIT Press, 1997).

The importance of MFN treatment is self-evident and cannot be overemphasised. For decades, China negotiated permanent normal trading relations (PNTR) with the United States on an annual basis. The PNTR status was negotiated under the provisions of the Jackson–Vanik waiver,[11] a provision related to the freedom of emigration, from the 1980s.[12] Receiving periodic extensions of the PNTR was not easy, as the US Congress had often attempted to terminate the status for alleged failure to comply with statutory conditions, including concerns in the area of human rights.[13] On the other hand, the MFN treatment guaranteed under Article I:1 of the GATT is permanent and unconditional. In other words, when China joined the WTO in 2001, China qualified for the non-discriminatory tariff and other concessions that the United States had extended to its other trading partners.

Article I:1 of the GATT is considerably broad and includes not only 'customs duties and charges of any kind', but also internal taxes and internal regulations within the meaning of paragraphs 2 and 4 of Article III. The following discussion focuses on the meaning of the MFN clause under Article I:1 of the GATT through GATT and WTO jurisprudence.

BELGIAN FAMILY ALLOWANCES

Belgian Family Allowances is a remarkable case under the GATT; it is, perhaps, the shortest ever, but it was the first case where a GATT panel ruled that a GATT violation had occurred.[14]

The subject matter of the dispute was a 1939 Belgian law which imposed *ad valorem* duty of 7.5 per cent on goods purchased by local government bodies for their use. The tax was not imposed on all imports, but only on purchases made by local bodies. Under Belgian law, products imported from a particular country could be exempt from the import duty if that country had a family allowances regime corresponding to that of Belgium. On this basis, exemptions were given to France, Italy, Luxembourg, the Netherlands and the United Kingdom. Later, in 1950, Sweden was also given the exemption, but not Denmark or Norway.

The facts of this case point out that the 7.5 per cent tax was collected not at the time of importation, but rather when the purchase price was paid by the public body. Even the GATT panel was inclined to call the measure an 'internal tax' under Article III:2 of the GATT,[15] but the application of the internal tax based on the origin also made it a presumptive violation under Article I:1 of the GATT.

---

[11] Jackson–Vanik Amendment, Section 402, 19 USC 2432.

[12] H.Con.Res.204, *A concurrent resolution approving the extension of nondiscriminatory treatment to the products of the People's Republic of China*, 96th Congress (1979–80).

[13] V. N. Pregelj, *Most-Favored-Nation Status of the People's Republic of China* (Washington, DC: Congressional Research Service, Library of Congress, 2001).

[14] R. E. Hudec, *The GATT Legal System and World Diplomacy*, 2nd ed. (Salem: Butterworth, 1990).

[15] GATT Panel Report, *Belgian Family Allowances*, G/32, adopted 7 November 1952, BISD 1S/59.

Belgian Family Allowances *(GATT Panel)*

3. ... If the General Agreement were definitely in force in accordance with Article XXVI, it is clear that that exemption would have to be given unconditionally to all other contracting parties (including Denmark and Norway). The consistency or otherwise of a system of family allowances in force in the territory of a given contracting party with the requirements of Belgian law would be irrelevant in this respect, and the Belgian legislation would have to be amended in so far as it introduced a discrimination between countries having a given system of family allowances and those which had a different system or no system at all, and made the granting of the exemption dependent on certain conditions.

In *Belgian Family Allowances*, the tax exemption was available only to countries meeting certain qualifications. This was an origin-based discrimination and was not related to the intrinsic characteristics of the product or the production methods. The ruling of the panel forbade discrimination based on which policies the exporting countries had pursued.[16]

SPAIN – UNROASTED COFFEE

Spain – Unroasted Coffee is one of the earlier cases in the field of non-discrimination. Spain introduced different tariff rates on different categories of unroasted, non-caffeinated coffee beans. Spain's customs classification differentiated between five different categories of products (see Table 1.1).

Brazil's complaint was that there were higher rates of duty on 'unwashed arabica', which constituted almost the entirety of Spain's imports of coffee from Brazil.[17] Brazil argued that

Table 1.1 Spain's tariff treatment for unroasted non-decaffeinated coffee (Royal Decree 1764/79)

Product Description	Duty rate
Colombian mild	Free
Other mild	Free
Unwashed arabica	7% ad valorem
Robusta	7% ad valorem
Other	7% ad valorem

[16] S. Charnovitz, 'Belgian Family Allowances and the Challenge of Origin-Based Discrimination', *World Trade Review* (2005), 4(1), p. 12.

[17] GATT Panel Report, *Spain – Tariff Treatment of Unroasted Coffee*, L/5135, adopted 11 June 1981, BISD 28S/102, para. 2.11.

coffee was a single product, and that for the purposes of Article I:1 of the GATT must be considered a 'like product'.[18] According to Brazil, 'mild' and 'unwashed arabica' originated from the same species of plant, and often from the same variety of tree.[19] Brazil also argued that the classification 'unwashed arabica' or 'mild' would depend exclusively on the treatment given to the berries.[20] In other words, the differences, if any, between groups of coffee were essentially of an organoleptic nature, which includes aroma and taste.[21]

Brazil also argued that the classification system used by Spain had been introduced by the International Coffee Organization (ICO) in 1965/66, when the ICO decided to create groupings of coffee-producing countries as part of a system for the limited adjustment export quotas for 'mild arabicas', 'unwashed arabicas' and 'robustas'. Mild arabicas, including the 'Colombian mild', are produced through the wet method, whereas 'unwashed arabica' coffee is produced through the dry method.

Spain admitted that both 'mild' and 'unwashed arabica' belong to the group of arabica.[22] Spain also argued, however, that differences in quality existed between these categories as a result of climatic and growing conditions as well as methods of cultivation. According to Spain, the aroma and taste, which are essential in determining the trade and consumption, were completely different in 'washed' and 'unwashed' arabica coffees.[23] In addition, according to Spain, for historical reasons, consumer preference for the various types of coffee was established in the Spanish market, whereas, in contrast, the use of blends was more generalised in other markets. The core of Spain's argument was that various types of unroasted coffee (in this case, 'mild' and 'unwashed Arabica') were not the same products.

The GATT Panel found that the Spanish tariff treatment discriminated against unroasted coffee originating in Brazil. The Panel stated that the treatment of the entire group of unroasted coffee was discriminatory.

Spain – Unroasted Coffee *(GATT Panel)*

4.4. The Panel found that there was no obligation under the GATT to follow any particular system of classifying goods, and that a contracting party had the right to introduce in its customs tariff new positions or sub-positions as appropriate. The Panel considered, however, that, whatever the classification adopted, Article I:1 required that the same tariff treatment be applied to 'like products'.

[...]

---

[18] GATT Panel Report, *Spain – Unroasted Coffee*, para. 3.9.
[19] GATT Panel Report, *Spain – Unroasted Coffee*, para. 3.9.
[20] GATT Panel Report, *Spain – Unroasted Coffee*, para. 3.9.
[21] GATT Panel Report, *Spain – Unroasted Coffee*, para. 3.10.
[22] GATT Panel Report, *Spain – Unroasted Coffee*, para. 3.7.
[23] GATT Panel Report, *Spain – Unroasted Coffee*, para. 3.7.

(cont.)

4.6. The Panel examined all arguments that had been advanced during the proceedings for the justification of a different tariff treatment for various groups and types of unroasted coffee. It noted that these arguments mainly related to organoleptic differences resulting from geographical factors, cultivation methods, the processing of beans, and the genetic factor. The Panel did not consider that such differences were sufficient reason to allow for a different treatment. It pointed out that it was not unusual in the case of agricultural products that the taste and aroma of the end-product would differ because of one or several of the above-mentioned factors.

4.7. The Panel furthermore found relevant to its examination of the matter that unroasted coffee mainly, if not exclusively, sold in the form of blends, combining various types of coffee, and that coffee in its end-use, was universally regarded as a well-defined and single product for drinking.

[…]

4.10. The Panel further noted that Brazil exported to Spain mainly 'unwashed Arabica' and Robusta coffee which were both presently charged with higher duties than that applied to 'mild' coffee. Since these were considered to be 'like products', the Panel concluded that the tariff regimes as presently applied by Spain was discriminatory vis-à-vis unroasted coffee originating in Brazil.

It is noteworthy that the Panel considered that the tariff treatment of the entire group of unroasted coffee was discriminatory based on the measure's asymmetric impact on Brazil's coffee exports. Some commentators argue that the GATT Panel did not pay enough regard to the role of consumer preferences and that this case would have yielded a different outcome if decided today.[24]

An equally important issue was whether an importing country had the freedom to introduce new tariff classifications or positions to offer different duty treatment. While the Panel in the *Spain – Unroasted Coffee* case acknowledged this right, it upheld the principle that notwithstanding the tariff classification, the same treatment needs to be given to various types of the good that are generally accepted to be one product.[25] However, a slightly different position was taken by another GATT panel in *Japan – SPF (Canada)*, which recognised the right of a GATT contracting party to use tariff classification as a legitimate means of trade policy.

---

[24] J. H. B. Pauwelyn, A. T. Guzman and J. A. Hillman, *International Trade Law*, 3rd ed. (New York: Wolters Kluwer, 2016).

[25] W. J. Davey, 'Un-Conditional Most Favoured Nation Treatment', in T. Cottier and K. N. Scheffer (eds.), *Elgar Encyclopedia of International Economic Law* (Cheltenham: Edward Elgar, 2017), p. 170.

JAPAN – SPF (CANADA)

In *Japan – SPF (Canada)*, Canada complained that Japan had developed a tariff classification system in such a manner that a significant part of the Canadian exports of spruce, pine and fir (SPF) dimension lumber was subjected to a higher tariff (8 per cent), whereas comparable dimension lumber (mainly exported by the United States) attracted a zero rate of duty. In other words, according to Canada, Canadian SPF products were placed in a less favoured category. The GATT Panel noted in this case that the tariff structure and classification system left wide discretion to the contracting parties to structure the system.[26]

Japan – SPF (Canada) *(GATT Panel)*

5.10. Tariff differentiation being basically a legitimate means of trade policy, a contracting party which claims to be prejudiced by such practice bears the burden of establishing that such tariff arrangement has been diverted from its normal purpose so as to become a means of discrimination in international trade. Such complaints have to be examined in considering simultaneously the internal protection interest involved in a given tariff specification, as well as its actual or potential influence on the pattern of imports from different extraneous sources …

In other words, the Panel noted that the GATT left 'wide discretion to the contracting parties in relation to the structure of the national tariffs and the classification of goods in the framework of that structure'.[27]

1.1.1.1   The Meaning of 'Advantage'

The following section will examine the meaning of 'advantage' under Article I:1 of the GATT. *US – Footwear (Brazil)* is one of the pioneering cases in this field. There is a certain amount of confusion even among experienced trade practitioners or scholars about the remit of MFN treatment. Article I:1 is not just limited to customs duties. The following case is helpful in understanding the scope of MFN with respect to non-customs duty-related matters.

US – FOOTWEAR (BRAZIL)

Brazil was a major exporter of non-rubber footwear to the United States. In 1974, the United States imposed a countervailing duty (CVD) on non-rubber footwear from Brazil, following a request from the US domestic industry. The countervailing duties were imposed based on Section 303 of the US Tariff Act, more commonly known as the Smoot–Hawley

---

[26] GATT Panel Report, *Canada/Japan: Tariff on Imports of Spruce, Pine, Fir (SPF) Dimension Lumber*, L/6470, adopted 19 July 1989, BISD 36S/167, paras. 5.7–5.10.

[27] GATT Panel Report, *Japan – SPF Dimension Lumber*, para. 5.8.

Tariff Act of 1930. In 1974, the United States passed the Trade Act, Section 331, which provides for an affirmative determination of injury in CVD investigations. It is pertinent to note that the injury determination in CVD investigations was not part of the 1930 Tariff Act, which was grandfathered by the GATT 1947.[28] Furthermore, the 1930 Act covered countervailing duties on imports of dutiable products. At the same time, the 1974 Act provided for injury determination in the case of duty-free products. The 1974 Act applied to duty-free imports from all countries that are GATT contracting parties, but not signatories to the Tokyo Subsidies Code.

Detailed disciplines on subsidy and injury were put together for the first time during the Tokyo Round of trade negotiations. These outcomes of the negotiations were incorporated in the Tokyo Round Subsidies Code (1979). The United States implemented the Tokyo Round commitments in the Trade Agreement Act of 1979, which came into force on 1 January 1980. This legislation provided for an injury test, prior to the imposition of CVD on both duty-free and dutiable products imported from Tokyo Subsidies Code signatories.[29] Section 104 of the Trade Agreement Act provided for a transitional procedure under which a party subject to CVD under the 1930 Act could request an injury review within a three-year period from 1980.

Brazilian footwear was subject to CVD under the 1930 Act during 1974. Brazil requested an injury review and the United States International Trade Commission (USITC) notified the Department of Commerce of the request on 28 October 1981. The USITC conducted a review that resulted in a negative injury determination on 24 May 1983. The US Department of Commerce implemented the revocation (backdated) only with effect from 28 October 1981, which was the date of the request.

On the other hand, certain duty-free products that were subject to CVD measures from India, Mexico and Trinidad and Tobago had their duties revoked effectively from the date of assuming obligations under the 1974 Act. This duty was revoked from the date when the obligation for an injury test arose (which would be the date these countries' products became duty-free).

US – Footwear (Brazil) (GATT Panel)

6.8. ... The Panel considered that the *rules and formalities* applicable to countervailing duties, including those applicable to the revocation of countervailing duty orders, are rules and formalities imposed in connection with importation, within the meaning of Article I:1.

---

[28] It would have been in violation of Art. VI:6(a), but as pre-GATT legislation, it was covered by the 'existing legislation' clause of the Protocol of Provisional Application (PPA) of the General Agreement.

[29] GATT Panel Report, *United States – Denial of Most-Favoured-Nation Treatment as to Non-Rubber Footwear from Brazil*, DS18/R, adopted 19 June 1992, BISD 39S/128, para. 2.11.

(cont.)

6.9. The Panel proceeded to consider whether the United States, through the operation of Section 331 of the Trade Act of 1974, accords an *advantage* to countries subject to pre-existing countervailing duty orders on products designated as duty-free under the US Generalised System of Preferences programme. In the view of the Panel, the automatic backdating of the effect of revocation of a pre-existing countervailing duty order, without the necessity of the country subject to the order making a request for an injury review, is properly considered to be an advantage within the meaning of Article I:1. It was equally clear from the record that this advantage is not accorded, under Section 104(b) of the Trade Agreements Act of 1979, to contracting parties signatories to the Subsidies Agreement. When such a signatory contracting party seeks revocation of a pre-existing countervailing duty order on a dutiable product originating in its territory, it is required to request the United States authorities for an injury review, following which the United States authorities conduct a review investigation and revoke the countervailing duty order, presuming there is a negative injury determination, but with the revocation effective as of the date of the request for the review.

6.10. The Panel recalled that the United States had argued that countries subject to the automatic backdating procedure under Section 331 could conceivably make the opposite argument from that of Brazil: that they were treated less favourably than those Subsidies Agreement signatories availing themselves of the three-year period for requesting an injury review under Section 104(b). The Panel however considered that Article I:1 does not permit balancing more favourable treatment under some procedures against a less favourable treatment under others. ... In the view of the Panel, such an interpretation of the most-favoured-nation obligation of Article I:1 would defeat the very purpose underlying the unconditionality of that obligation.

CANADA – AUTOS

In this case, the European Communities and Japan challenged certain Canadian measures which provided duty-free exemption for the importation of automobiles, buses and other specified commercial vehicles. The conditions under which the import duty exemptions were decided were based on the terms set out in the Motor Vehicle Tariff Order 1998 (MVTO 1998), the special remission orders (SROs) and the Letters of Undertaking.

Under the MVTO 1998, an importer was required to meet three conditions in order to avail themselves of the import duty restriction. These conditions were broadly classified under (1) production during the designated base year, (2) ratio requirements, and (3) the amount of Canadian value added (CVA) requirement.[30] The companies that met the

---

[30] Panel Report, *Canada – Autos*, para. 10.182.

requirements of MVTO 1998 were eligible to import motor vehicles duty-free. In addition, through the SROs, Canada also designated certain other companies as eligible to import motor vehicles duty-free. More specifically, the SROs permit remission of duties on imports of motor vehicles where the conditions specific to production-to-sale ratio and CVA requirements are met. Furthermore, in accordance with its commitments under the Canada–United States Free Trade Agreement (CUSFTA), Canada had not designated any additional manufacturers to receive the duty-free treatment.

The historical context of the measure offers some useful insights. The import duty exemption indeed stemmed from the bilateral agreement negotiated between Canada and the United States to resolve their long-standing dispute in the trade in automotive products.[31] The Canada–US Auto Pact signed in 1965 provided the backbone for building Canada's auto industry. The import duty exemption served as encouragement to the US automobile industry to expand its operations in Canada.

On the face of it, Canada's measures appeared origin-neutral, and were not intrinsic to any country. One of the issues was whether Article I:1 of the GATT also covers de facto discrimination. According to Japan, the complainant in this case, the measure constituted an 'advantage' in as much as the import duty exemption was available only for imports of motor vehicles originating in some countries, but not for imports of motor vehicles from all WTO members. On the other hand, Canada argued that its measure only imposed conditions on the car manufacturing companies themselves, and did not prescribe any limitation on the origin of the products that they can import. According to Canada, this was not prohibited by Article I:1, as it was dependent on the sourcing decisions of private companies.[32]

The Appellate Body addressed this issue as follows:

Canada – Autos *(Appellate Body)*

70. In examining the measure at issue, we note that the import duty exemption is afforded by Canada to imports of some, but not all, motor vehicles. We observe, first of all, that the Canadian Customs Tariff provides that a motor vehicle normally enters Canada at an MFN tariff rate of 6.1 percent. This is also the bound *ad valorem* rate in Canada's WTO Schedule of Concessions. The MVTO 1998 and the SROs modify this rate by providing the import duty exemption for motor vehicles imported by certain manufacturers meeting certain ratio requirements and CVA requirements. The MVTO 1998 accords the import duty exemption in the form of a 'reduced rate of customs duty', established in the amended Canadian Customs Tariff as 'free'. The SROs accord the import duty exemption in the form of a full duty 'remission'.

[. . .]

---

[31] Panel Report, *Canada – Autos*, para. 10.48.   [32] Appellate Body Report, *Canada – Autos*, para. 66.

(cont.)

72. ... [I]n practice, a motor vehicle imported into Canada is granted an 'advantage' of the import duty exemption only if it originates in one of a small number of countries in which an exporter of motor vehicles is affiliated with a manufacturer/importer in Canada that has been designated as eligible to import motor vehicles duty free under MVTO 1998 or under an SRO.

73. Since 1989, no manufacturer not already benefitting from the import duty exemption on motor vehicles has been able to qualify under the MVTO 1998 or under an SRO. The list of manufacturers eligible for the import duty exemption was closed by Canada in 1989 in fulfilment of Canada's obligations under CUSFTA.

74. Thus, in sum, while the Canadian Customs Tariff normally allows a motor vehicle to enter Canada at the MFN duty rate of 6.1 percent, the same motor vehicle has the 'advantage' of entering Canada duty free when imported by a designated manufacturer under the MVTO 1998 or under the SROs.

The concept of 'advantage' under GATT Article I:1 has been interpreted in several other cases. *Colombia – Ports*[33] and *EC – Seal Products*[34] are two prominent cases. *Colombia – Ports* examined various measures purportedly taken by Colombia under domestic anti-smuggling policies, which also included certain restrictions on ports of entry and their implications on Panama, a neighbouring country. Around twenty-six ports of entry were normally available for Panama's exports into Colombia, eleven of which had been authorised to import textiles and footwear. However, the Colombian Resolutions limited the entry of the named products to Bogotá airport and Barranquilla seaport. The consequence for non-compliance included seizure and forfeiture of the goods. In the case of textiles, additional special legalisation requirements had to be met. Panama succeeded in a claim of Article I:1. The Panel also reiterated that Article I:1 protected potential future trade and the conditions governing competition between suppliers of different origin, irrespective of trade volumes.[35]

The meaning of the term 'unconditionally' in Article I:1 is examined in the context of *EC – Tariff Preferences* discussed in the section below.

1.1.1.2   Exception to the MFN Principle: The Enabling Clause

In 1971, the GATT contracting parties adopted a waiver decision for authorising developed countries to offer tariff preferences to goods originating in developing countries aimed at their economic development.[36] Under this arrangement, the obligations under Article I of

---

[33] Panel Report, *Colombia – Indicative Prices and Restrictions on Ports of Entry*, WT/DS366/R, Corr.1, adopted 20 May 2009, para. 7.325.

[34] *European Communities – Measures Prohibiting the Importation and Marketing of Seal Products*, WT/DS 401/AB/R, adopted 16 June 2014.

[35] Panel Report, *Colombia – Ports of Entry*, para. 7.325.

[36] GATT contracting parties, *Generalized System of Preferences*, Decision of 25 June 1971, BISD 18S/24.

the GATT were waived for a period of ten years. Subsequently, in 1979, this decision was formalised through the adoption of the so-called Enabling Clause.[37] The Generalised System of Preferences (GSP) is implemented under the Enabling Clause.

EC – Tariff Preferences

The Appellate Body, in an appeal from a panel ruling in *EC – Tariff Preferences* examined the legal nature of the Enabling Clause. In this case, India, the complainant, had challenged the conditions under which the European Communities had provided certain tariff preferences to certain developing countries while implementing a scheme of generalised tariff preferences. The EC Regulation provided tariff preferences based on grounds such as protection of labour rights and the environment and special arrangements for least-developed countries, in addition to the preferences under the Drug Arrangements whereby twelve predetermined countries, namely, Bolivia, Colombia, Costa Rica, Ecuador, El Salvador, Guatemala, Honduras, Nicaragua, Pakistan, Panama, Peru and Venezuela, were accorded tariff preferences.

India alleged that the EC tariff preferences under the Drug Arrangements are inconsistent with Article I:1 of the GATT. According to India, Article I:1 imposes an obligation on WTO members to treat 'like products … equally irrespective of their origin'.[38] India argued that the Enabling Clause is an exception to Article I:1 of the GATT. India relied on the ordinary meaning of 'exception', which according to Black's Law Dictionary is 'something that is excluded from a rule's operation'.[39] According to India, the Enabling Clause was an affirmative defence and the European Communities bore the burden of proof.[40]

The EC, on the other hand, defended the tariff preferences under the Enabling Clause. Paragraph 1 of the Enabling Clause provides as follows:

The Enabling Clause: Key Elements

1. Notwithstanding the provisions of Article I of the General Agreement, contracting parties may accord differential and more favourable treatment to developing countries, without according such treatment to other contracting parties. [Notes omitted]

   [. . .]

Note 3: As described in the Decision of the contracting parties of 25 June 1971, relating to the establishment of 'generalized, non-reciprocal and non-discriminatory preferences beneficial to the developing countries'.

---

[37] GATT, Decision of the contracting parties of 28 November 1979 on 'Differential and More Favourable Treatment, Reciprocity and Fuller Participation of Developing Countries', BISD 26S/203.

[38] Appellate Body Report, *European Communities – Regime for the Importation, Sale and Distribution of Bananas*, WT/DS27/AB/R, adopted 25 September 1997, para. 190.

[39] Panel Report, *European Communities – Conditions for the Granting of Tariff Preferences to Developing Countries*, WT/DS246/R, adopted 20 April 2004, as modified by Appellate Body Report, WT/DS246/AB/R, para. 7.25 (quoting para. 62 of India's Second Written Submission).

[40] Panel Report, *EC – Tariff Preferences*, para. 7.21 (quoting para. 43 of India's First Written Submission).

The Appellate Body turned to the text of the 1979 Enabling Clause, which had become part of GATT 1994.

EC – Tariff Preferences *(Appellate Body)*

90. ... The ordinary meaning of the term 'notwithstanding' is, as the Panel noted, '[i]n spite of, without regard to or prevention by'. By using the word 'notwithstanding', paragraph 1 of the Enabling Clause permits Members to provide 'differential and more favourable treatment' to developing countries 'in spite of' the MFN obligation of Article I:1. Such treatment would otherwise be inconsistent with Article I:1 because that treatment is not extended to all Members of the WTO 'immediately and unconditionally'. Paragraph 1 thus excepts Members from complying with the obligation contained in Article 1:1 for the purpose of providing differential and more favourable treatment to developing countries, provided that such treatment is in accordance with the conditions set out in the Enabling Clause. As such, the Enabling Clause operates as an 'exception' to Article I:1.

In essence, the arguments of the EC are captured in the Appellate Body Report.

EC – Tariff Preferences *(Appellate Body)*

93. According to the European Communities, the Enabling Clause, as the 'most concrete, comprehensive and important application of the principle of Special and Differential Treatment', serves to achieve one of the fundamental objectives of the WTO Agreement. In the view of the European Communities, provisions that are exceptions permit Members to adopt measures to pursue objectives that are 'not ... among the WTO Agreement's own objectives'; the Enabling Clause does not fall under the category of exceptions. Pointing to the alleged difference between the role of measures falling under the Enabling Clause and that of measures exception provisions such as Article XX, the European Communities contends that the WTO Agreement does not 'merely tolerate' measures under the Enabling Clause, but rather 'encourages' developed country Members to adopt such measures. According to the European Communities, to require the preference-granting countries to invoke the Enabling Clause in order to invoke to justify or defend their GSP schemes cannot be reconciled with the intention of WTO Members to encourage these schemes.

    [...]

146. In light of the above, we do not agree with European Communities' assertion that the Panel's interpretation of the word 'non-discriminatory' in footnote 3 of the

> **(cont.)**
>
> Enabling Clause is erroneous because the phrase 'generalized, non-reciprocal and non-discriminatory' in footnote 3 merely refers to the description of the GSP in the 1971 Waiver Decision and, of itself, does not impose any legal obligation on preference granting countries. Nor do we agree with the United States that the Panel erred in 'assum[ing]' that the term 'non-discriminatory' in footnote 3 imposes obligations on preference granting countries, and that, instead, footnote 3 'is simply a cross reference to where the Generalized System of Preferences is described'.

In *EC – Tariff Preferences*, the Appellate Body held that the term 'non-discriminatory' in footnote 3 of the Enabling Clause requires that identical tariff treatment be 'available' to all 'similarly-situated' GSP beneficiaries. In this regard, the Appellate Body clarified that 'similarly-situated' GSP beneficiaries means all GSP beneficiaries that have similar 'development, financial and trade needs' to which the GSP measure is intended to respond. However, this interpretation leaves the possibility of permitting a GSP regime where tariff preferences are provided only to a set of developing countries without providing similar benefits to another set of developing countries, so long as the favoured group has distinct development needs.

Concerning the term 'unconditionally' under Article I:1, the Panel noted that it has a broader meaning than simply that of not requiring compensation for trade concessions. The Panel interpreted the term in its ordinary meaning as that 'not limited by or subject to any conditions'.[41]

Concerning the burden of proof, the recent WTO dispute of *Brazil – Taxation*[42] had the opportunity to reiterate the findings in *EC – Tariff Preferences*.

Brazil – Taxation *(Appellate Body)*

5.365 A complaining party is therefore required to raise the Enabling Clause and identify the relevant provisions thereof in its panel request when a measure according differential and more favourable treatment is: (i) plainly taken pursuant to the Enabling Clause, or when it is clear from the face of the measure itself that it has been adopted pursuant to the Enabling Clause; and/or (ii) notified pursuant to paragraph 4(a) of the Enabling Clause. However, the complaining party 'is merely to identify those provisions of the Enabling Clause with which

---

[41] Panel Report, *EC – Tariff Preferences*, para. 7.59.

[42] Appellate Body Reports, *Brazil – Certain Measures Concerning Taxation and Charges*, WT/DS472/AB/R, Add.1, WT/DS497/AB/R, Add.1, adopted 11 January 2019, paras. 5.361–5.366.

(cont.)

the [measure] is allegedly inconsistent, without bearing the burden of establishing the facts necessary to support such inconsistency'. Thus, while it is for the complaining party to identify the relevant provision(s) of the Enabling Clause in its panel request, the burden to 'prove' that the measure 'satisf[ies] the conditions set out in the Enabling Clause' still 'remains on the responding party' relying on 'the Enabling Clause as a defence'.

1.1.2 National Treatment

Article III of the GATT embodies another key principle of non-discrimination. The national treatment principle is the bedrock of the international trading system established by the WTO. In essence, Article III states that a WTO member shall not treat imported products less favourably than domestic products once the products have entered internal commerce. In *Italian Discrimination Against Imported Agricultural Machinery*, one of the earlier cases under GATT 1947, the Panel noted that the purpose of Article III is to ensure that 'no indirect protection' is given to domestic products.[43] This principle was reiterated by the Appellate Body in *Japan – Alcoholic Beverages II*, where it emphasised that the broad and fundamental purpose of Article III is to avoid protectionism in the application of internal taxes and regulatory measures.[44] Article III requires WTO members to provide equality of competitive opportunities in the marketplace. In other words, 'Article III protects expectations not of any particular trade volume, but rather of the equal competitive relationship between domestic and imported products'.[45] At the same time, Article III also allows a member to pursue bona fide domestic measures, including fiscal and domestic regulatory functions. In the exercise of their sovereignty, WTO members are free to pursue various domestic goals and values; however, the exercise of sovereignty needs to be constrained by what the members have negotiated and agreed with other nations internationally.

The language of non-discrimination under Article III is different from the most favoured nation treatment obligation under Article I of the GATT. While Article I states that a product from a WTO member shall be offered any favourable treatment or advantage offered to a like product from any other country, Article III introduces the 'less favourable' treatment standard, which implies that an imported product from a WTO member shall not

---

[43] GATT Panel Report, *Italian Discrimination Against Imported Agricultural Machinery*, L/833, 23 October 1958, BISD 7S/60, para. 11.

[44] Appellate Body Report, *Japan – Taxes on Alcoholic Beverages*, WT/DS8/AB/R, WT/DS10/AB/R, WT/DS11/AB/R, adopted 1 November 1996, p. 16.

[45] Appellate Body Report, *Japan – Alcoholic Beverages II*, p. 16; GATT Panel Report, *United States – Taxes on Petroleum and Certain Imported Substances*, L/6175, adopted 17 June 1987, BISD 34S/136 (hereafter, *US – Superfund*), para. 5.1.9.

be treated less favourably than the like or directly competitive domestic product. To restate the difference, MFN treatment ensures a WTO member the best possible treatment, and NT guarantees protection from any disadvantageous treatment in comparison with like domestic products.

GATT 1994, Article III: National Treatment on Internal Taxation and Regulation

1. The contracting parties recognize that internal taxes and other internal charges, and laws, regulations and requirements affecting the internal sale, offering for sale, purchase, transportation, distribution or use of products, and internal quantitative regulations requiring the mixture, processing or use of products in specified amounts or proportions, should not be applied to imported or domestic products so as to afford protection to domestic production.*
2. The products of the territory of any contracting party imported into the territory of any other contracting party shall not be subject, directly or indirectly, to internal taxes or other internal charges of any kind in excess of those applied, directly or indirectly, to like domestic products. Moreover, no contracting party shall otherwise apply internal taxes or other internal charges to imported or domestic products in a manner contrary to the principles set forth in paragraph 1.*

    [...]

Annex I: Notes and Supplementary Provisions

Ad Article III

Paragraph 2

A tax conforming to the requirements for the first sentence of paragraph 2 would be considered to be inconsistent with the provisions of the second sentence only in cases where competition was involved between, on the one hand, a directly competitive or substitutable product which was not similarly taxed.

It is important to remember that Article III of the GATT does not generally deal with border measures. However, Interpretative Note to Article III, or Ad Article III, clarifies that internal taxes or other charge, law, regulation or requirement which applies to an imported product and to the like products and is collected or enforced against the imported product at the border, could be subject to the provisions of Article III.

1.1.2.1 Taxes

Historically, taxes have been used by governments to discourage the consumption or use of certain products. Taxes on alcohol and tobacco products have a long history and have been the subject matter of several GATT/WTO disputes. Internal taxes have been used for the distribution of economic resources and for pursuing public policy goals. The common complaint is that the internal or consumption taxes have been applied in a manner such that they discriminate against imported products. The most important question is how tribunals can design a test for Article III:2 that does not encroach upon the fiscal sovereignty of a WTO member.

1.1.2.2 Aim-and-Effects Test

As the foregoing analysis in some of the GATT/WTO cases has indicated, most complainants in trade disputes seek to establish a national treatment violation by highlighting a different treatment of one imported product as against a like domestic product. This can also apply to the MFN examination, as was seen in the case of *Spain – Unroasted Coffee*.

Governments often distinguish between products for non-trade related concerns or meeting certain regulatory objectives. A GATT Panel in *US – Malt Beverages* noted that 'it is imperative that determinations made in the context of Article III … not necessarily infringe upon the regulatory authority and the domestic policy options of contracting parties'.[46] The jurisprudence under GATT 1947 developed a subjective standard under the so-called 'aim-and-effect' test. If the measure is designed to protect or promote a particular concern, for example, enforcing fuel emission norms, then the concerned products are compared for the national treatment analysis based on their fuel efficiency. Based on this approach, the GATT Panel in *US – Malt Beverages* ruled that low and high alcohol content beers are not 'like' for the purposes of GATT Article III:4.[47] In the Panel's view, the measures restricting sale, distribution and labelling were aimed at encouraging the consumption of low alcohol content beer in the place of high alcohol content beer.[48] Similarly, in *US – Taxes on Automobiles*, also known as the 'gas guzzler' case, the issue was whether differential taxation based on fuel efficiency was compatible with Article III. The GATT panel concluded that notions of likeness and direct competition cannot be separated from the objectives of the regulatory scheme.[49] Despite the physical similarities, the various classifications of automobiles were not treated as 'like products' based on the gasoline consumption norms. In other words, addressing externalities in the production and consumption of a product was an integral component in the national treatment analysis, especially in the 'likeness' inquiry.

---

[46] GATT Panel Report, *United States – Measures Affecting Alcoholic and Malt Beverages*, DS23/R, adopted 19 June 1992, BISD 39S/206, para. 5.72.

[47] GATT Panel Report, *US – Malt Beverages*, para. 5.75.

[48] GATT Panel Report, *US – Malt Beverages*, paras. 5.71–5.72.

[49] GATT Panel Report, *United States – Taxes on Automobiles*, DS31/R, 11 October 1994. The Panel Report in this case was not adopted by the GATT Panel.

The major distinction between the aim-and-effects test and the traditional likeness analysis is that the former consigns the metaphysics of 'likeness' to a lesser role.[50] Rather, the aim-and-effects test looks in particular at the trade effects of the measure and the regulatory purpose or, more importantly, the *bona fides* of the measure. By necessary implication, if a measure is not intended to provide protection to domestic production, regulatory distinction between the products should be treated as 'legitimate'.

To meet the aim-and-effects test, the trade or competitive effects should be clear enough or inherent enough to be called 'protective'.[51] From the perspective of 'effects', the question is whether the tax affords protection to domestic production or not. Concerning the 'aim', a number of considerations can be weighed. For example, *ex ante* knowledge of the protective operation of the measure, its structural incentives, the arbitrary and irrational nature of categories, and the legislative statement or preparatory work can all constitute the elements of an aim-and-effects test.

The origins of the aim-and-effects test could be traced to Article III:1, which contains the language 'so as to afford protection' to domestic production. However, in the first sentence of Article III:2, which deals with national treatment obligations among 'like products', there is no textual reference to the policy statement in Article III:1. *Japan – Alcoholic Beverages II* provided a ground-breaking examination and, ultimately, a rejection of the aim-and-effects test. In short, this case examined, among other important issues, whether the language 'so as to afford protection' has a purposive connotation or meaning.

1.1.2.3 Aim-and-Effects Test and Likeness of Products

JAPAN – ALCOHOLIC BEVERAGES II (WTO)

Japan's domestic tax regime for alcoholic beverages was challenged in the mid-1980s in the GATT. In fact, the Japanese tax regime on liquor dates back to 1940, when alcoholic beverages were classified into broad categories and differential tax rates were imposed.[52] The taxes were imposed not only on the basis of the degree of alcohol, but also on the basis of the tax-bearing ability of the consumers. Japan replaced the tax regime with new differential taxes on various categories of alcohol.

Under the Japanese Liquor Tax Law, duties on imported spirits such as brandy, cognac, genever, gin, rum, vodka, whiskey and others were significantly in excess of the duty on domestically produced shochu, a distilled white spirit. For example, as provided in Figure 1.1, the tax on shochu was between one-fourth and one-seventh of the tax on imported brandy and whiskey. According to other major alcohol exporters, such as the

---

[50] R. E. Hudec, 'GATT/WTO Constraints on National Regulation: Requiem for an "Aim and Effects" Test', *International Lawyer* (1998), 32(3), p. 619.

[51] A. Matoo and A. Subramanian, 'Regulatory Autonomy and Multilateral Discipline: The Dilemma and a Possible Solution', *Journal of International Economic Law* (1998), 1(2), pp. 303–22.

[52] GATT Panel Report, *Japan – Customs Duties, Taxes and Labelling Practices on Imported Wines and Alcoholic Beverages*, L/6216, adopted 10 November 1987, BISD 34S/83, para. 2.1.

Figure 1.1 *Japan – Alcoholic Beverages II*
In *Japan – Alcoholic Beverages II*, the United States and the European Communities complained that imported products such as vodka, gin, genever and rum (white and brown spirits) were discriminately taxed vis-à-vis Japanese shochu.

SHOCHU

¥155.70
per litre

VODKA

¥377.23
per litre

BRANDY

¥982.30
per litre

European Communities, Canada and the United States, the imported products were predominantly subjected to higher specific tax rates.

The complainants argued that the liquors they had exported were either 'like' or 'directly competitive or substitutable' products with shochu, the Japanese alcohol in question. The complainants also referred to the 1987 GATT Panel Report, where it was stated that 'Japanese shochu (Group A) and vodka could be considered as like products in terms of Article III:2 because they were both white/clear spirits, made of similar raw materials, and their end-uses were virtually identical'.[53] In essence, the complainants had based their claims on Article III:2, first sentence and second sentence, respectively.

The United States, one of the complainants, agreed with the outcome in the Panel proceeding. However, the United States appealed the Panel's approach for determining a violation of Article III:2 and offered the aim-and-effects test as an alternative. The United States argued that the specific obligations of Article III:2 must be read in the light of Article III:1, which formed the context of Article III:2. In short, the case boiled down to the type of interpretation to be given to the general terms of Article III:1 under the interpretative principles embodied in Articles 31–33 of the VCLT.

Japan – Alcoholic Beverages II *(Appellate Body)*

G. Article III:1. The terms of Article III must be given their ordinary meaning – in their context and in the light of the overall object and purpose of the *WTO Agreement*. Thus, the words actually used in the Article provide the basis for an interpretation that must give meaning and effect to all its terms. The proper interpretation of the Article is, first of all, a textual interpretation. Consequently, the Panel is correct in seeing a distinction between Article III:1 which 'contains general principles', and Article III:2, which 'provides for specific

---

[53] Panel Report, *Japan – Taxes on Alcoholic Beverages*, WT/DS8/R, WT/DS10/R, WT/DS11/R, adopted 1 November 1996, as modified by Appellate Body Report WT/DS8/AB/R, WT/DS10/AB/R, WT/DS11/AB/R, para. 5.7.

> **(cont.)**
>
> obligations regarding internal taxes and internal charges'. Article III:1 articulates the general principle that internal measures should not be applied so as to afford protection to domestic production. This general principle informs the rest of Article III. The purpose of Article III:1 is to establish the general principle as a guide to understanding and interpreting the specific obligations contained in Article III:2 and in the other paragraphs of Article III, while respecting, and not diminishing in any way, the meaning of words actually used in the text of those other paragraphs. In short, Article III:1 constitutes part of the context of Article III:2, in the same way that it constitutes part of the context of each of the other paragraphs in Article III. Any other reading of Article III would have the effect of rendering the words of Article III:1 meaningless, thereby violating the fundamental principle of effectiveness in treaty interpretation. Consistent with the principle of effectiveness, and with the textual differences in the two sentences, we believe that Article III:1 informs the first sentence and the second sentence of Article III:2 in different ways.

In essence, the Appellate Body noted that the first sentence of Article III:2 is, in effect, an expression of the general principle set forth in Article III:1.[54]

US – Clove Cigarettes, albeit not being a discriminatory taxation case, provides useful insights on the continuing significance of the aims-and-effect test in WTO law.

US – Clove Cigarettes

In *US – Clove Cigarettes*,[55] the role of regulatory purpose in the Article III:4 analysis came up for consideration. The United States imposed restrictions on certain categories of flavoured cigarettes under the Family Smoking Prevention and Tobacco Control Act of 2009. According to the United States, this was intended to prohibit the manufacture and sale of cigarettes with certain 'characterising flavours' that appeal to youth. Indonesia, the complainant in this case, argued that while banning clove cigarettes and permitting like menthol cigarettes in the market, the United States had accorded less favourable treatment to the imported clove cigarettes.[56] In other words, the Appellate Body reiterated that 'likeness' is about the 'nature and extent of competitive relationship between and among the products'.[57] The Appellate Body conclusively rejected the regulatory purpose and intent in the following words:

---

[54] Appellate Body Report, *Japan – Alcoholic Beverages II*, p. 18.

[55] Panel Report, *United States – Measures Affecting the Production and Sale of Clove Cigarettes*, WT/DS406/R, adopted 24 April 2012, as modified by Appellate Body Report WT/DS165/AB/R.

[56] Panel Report, *US – Clove Cigarettes*, para. 7.293.

[57] Appellate Body Report, *United States – Measures Affecting the Production and Sale of Clove Cigarettes*, WT/DS406/AB/R, adopted 24 April 2012, para. 120.

US – Clove Cigarettes *(Appellate Body)*

113. We further observe that measures often pursue a multiplicity of objectives, which are not always easily discernible from the text or even from the design, architecture, and structure of the measure. Determining likeness on the basis of the regulatory objectives of the measure, rather than on the product's competitive relationship, would require identification of all relevant objectives of a measure, as well as an assessment of which objectives amongst others are relevant or should prevail in determining whether the products are like. It seems to us that it would not always be possible for a complainant or a panel to identify all the objectives of a measure and/ or be in a position to determine which among multiple objectives are relevant to the determination of whether two products are like or not.

[...]

117. Nevertheless, in concluding that the determination of likeness should not be based on the regulatory purpose of the technical regulation, we are not suggesting that the regulatory concerns underlying technical regulations may not play a role in the determination of whether or not products are like. In this respect, we recall that, in *EC – Asbestos*, the Appellate Body found that regulatory concerns and considerations play a role in applying certain of the 'likeness' criteria (that is, physical characteristics and consumer preferences) and, thus, in the determination of likeness under Article III:4 of the GATT 1994.

In short, the Appellate Body noted that the concept of 'like products' (albeit within the meaning of a technical regulation) does not lend itself to distinctions based on the regulatory objectives of a measure. However, regulatory concerns that can be considered as relevant to the assessment of the traditional *Border Tax Adjustments* criteria can be taken into consideration in the like product analysis.[58] (See the discussion on *Japan – Alcoholic Beverages II* and *EC – Asbestos* in this chapter.) The Appellate Body's approach in *US – Clove Cigarettes* also affirms the competition-based approach to likeness based on the interaction between the products in the marketplace.[59] This was consistent with its approach taken since *Japan – Alcoholic Beverages II*.[60]

---

[58] Appellate Body Report, *US – Clove Cigarettes*, paras. 116–121. See also T. Voon, 'The WTO Outlaws Discrimination in US Flavored Cigarettes Ban', *ASIL Insights* (2012), 16(15).

[59] F. Pierola, 'The Treatment of "Likeness" and a New Rejection of the "Aims and Effects" Test in *US – Clove Cigarettes*', *Global Trade and Customs Journal* (2012), 7(7/8), pp. 347–8.

[60] Appellate Body Reports, *United States – Certain Country of Origin Labelling (COOL) Requirements*, WT/DS384/ AB/R, WT/DS386/AB/R, adopted 23 July 2012; Panel Reports, *European Communities – Measures Prohibiting the Importation and Marketing of Seal Products*, WT/DS400/R, Add.1, WT/DS401/R, Add.1, adopted 18 June 2014, as modified by Appellate Body Reports WT/DS400/AB/R, WT/DS401/AB/R, para. 7.258.

1.1.2.4 Like Product in Article III:2, First Sentence

Japan – Alcoholic Beverages II will long be considered as a pioneering case in understanding the meaning of 'likeness' between products. The meaning of 'like products' is crucial to determining the scope of WTO obligations, especially in relation to domestic taxes. Concerning Article III:2, first sentence, the AB noted that a determination of WTO consistency requires only two elements:[61] (1) whether the imported and domestic products are 'like'; and (2) whether the taxes imposed on imported products are 'in excess of' those applied to the like domestic product.

The Appellate Body affirmed the Panel's finding that shochu and the imported vodka are 'like'.[62] The Appellate Body stressed that the analysis of 'likeness' should be undertaken on a case-by-case basis. While the text of the GATT was silent on the width and breadth of this concept – that is, how broad or narrow the concept should be – the Appellate Body referred to a little-known GATT *Report by the Working Party on Border Tax Adjustments* of 1970. This report had specified the following criteria for determination of likeness, namely: the product's end-uses in a given market; consumers' tastes and habits, which range from country to country; the product's properties, nature and quality (in other words, the products' physical similarity).[63] In line with previous GATT practice, the Appellate Body included the tariff classification as an additional element.[64] The Appellate Body, however, caveated that the tariff classification had to be sufficiently detailed if it were to serve as a useful sign of product similarity.[65] In addition, the Appellate Body introduced the famous metaphor of 'accordion' in the likeness inquiry.

> ### Japan – Alcoholic Beverages II *(Appellate Body)*
>
> **Page 21, second para.** No one approach to exercising judgement will be appropriate for all cases. The criteria in *Border Tax Adjustments* should be examined, but there can be no precise and absolute definition of what is 'like'. The concept of 'likeness' is a relative one that evokes the image of an accordion. The accordion of 'likeness' stretches and squeezes in different places as different provisions of the WTO Agreement are applied. The width of the accordion in any one of those places must be determined by the particular provision in which the term 'like' is encountered as well as by the context and the circumstances that prevail in any given case to which that provision may apply. . . . We believe that, in Article III:2, first sentence of the GATT 1994, the accordion of 'likeness' is meant to be narrowly squeezed.

---

[61] Appellate Body Report, *Japan – Alcoholic Beverages II*, pp. 18–19.

[62] Appellate Body Report, *Japan – Alcoholic Beverages II*, p. 23.

[63] GATT, Working Party Report, *Border Tax Adjustments*, L/3464, adopted 20 November 1970, BISD 18S/97, para. 18.

[64] GATT Panel Report, *Japan – Alcoholic Beverages I*, the 1987 case, had also provided a reference to using tariff classification as an additional element.

[65] Appellate Body Report, *Japan – Alcoholic Beverages II*, p. 21; see also Appellate Body Reports, *Philippines – Taxes on Distilled Spirits*, WT/DS396/AB/R, WT/DS403/AB/R, adopted 20 January 2012, para. 163.

1.1.2.5   Article III:2, First Sentence and Meaning of 'in Excess of'

The Appellate Body provided important clarification on the meaning of 'in excess of'. According to the Appellate Body, even the smallest amount of 'excess' is too much.[66] The Appellate Body also noted that the prohibition of discriminatory taxes under the first sentence of Article III:2 is not conditional on a 'trade effect test' or qualified by any *de minimis* standard.[67]

1.1.2.6   Directly Competitive and Substitutable Products under Article III:2, Second Sentence

Article III:2, second sentence, does not deal with 'like products'; rather, it deals with 'directly competitive and substitutable products' (DCS). While the concept of 'like products' comprises perfect substitutes, the category of DCS could also include imperfect substitutes. It is also clear that the width of Article III:2, second sentence, is significantly broader than the first sentence.

The Appellate Body noted that unlike the first sentence of Article III:2, the second sentence specifically invokes the introductory paragraph of Article III:1. It states that the directly competitive and substitutable imported product and the like domestic product should not be dissimilarly taxed *'so as to afford protection to domestic production'*.

> ## Japan – Alcoholic Beverages II *(Appellate Body)*
>
> **Page 29, second para.** Although it is true that the aim of the measure may not be easily ascertained, nevertheless its protective application can most often be discerned from the design, the architecture, and the revealing structure of the measure. The very magnitude of the dissimilar taxation in a particular case may be evidence of such a protective application, as the Panel rightly concluded in this case. Most often, there will be other factors to be considered as well.

In other words, even if two products are substitutes and are otherwise in competition, the Appellate Body's ruling requires a panel to examine whether the dissimilar taxation has been imposed 'so as to afford protection'. It is useful to remember that the Appellate Body has rejected the aim-and-effects test. However, a WTO panel may have to look at the protective application of the measure. A WTO panel, as suggested by the Appellate Body, may have to look at the 'structure, the architecture and the revealing nature' of the measure. This is not a rehabilitation of the old aim-and-effects test, but an objective inquiry of the nature of application of the measure.

---

[66] Appellate Body Report, *Japan – Alcoholic Beverages II*, p. 23, para. 2.
[67] GATT Panel Report, *US – Superfund*, para. 5.1.9.

KOREA – ALCOHOLIC BEVERAGES

Korea – Alcoholic Beverages bears close similarity to *Japan – Alcoholic Beverages II*. In this case, imported distilled beverages, including whiskey, vodka and gin, were taxed pursuant to the Korean Liquor Tax Law, in excess of the tax on the domestic product, namely soju (see Table 1.2).

Table 1.2 Tax rates on alcohol in *Korea – Alcoholic Beverages*

Alcohol	Ad valorem tax rate (%)
Diluted soju	35
Distilled soju	50
Liqueur	50
Other liquors (brandy, whiskey, gin, rum, tequila, vodka and mixed distilled drinks)	80–100

This is, perhaps, the first dispute under the GATT/WTO where the Panel recognised the merits of a quantitative determination of product likeness. The Panel noted that a high degree of substitution, as indicated by elasticity of substitution or cross-price elasticity, was probative of a directly competitive and substitutable relationship. The Panel found that the soju and the imported alcoholic products were directly competitive and substitutable products, and that the tax differential in this case exceeded the *de minimis* levels.

The Appellate Body noted that the actual consumer demand for imported products may be influenced by other measures, such as previous protectionist tax regimes and import prohibitions. The issue of latent consumer demand is particularly relevant for items like food and beverages because consumers tend to purchase those brands with which they are already familiar.[68] The Appellate Body thus upheld the Panel's decision to include a 'strong potentially direct competitive relationship' within the ambit of 'directly competitive or substitutable'. In completing its analysis, the Panel was correct in assessing evidence for consumer behaviour from the Japanese market, because it had characteristics similar to the market at issue.[69]

Korea – Alcoholic Beverages *(Appellate Body)*

118. The first sentence of Article III:2 also forms part of the context of the term. 'Like' products are a subset of directly competitive or substitutable products: all like products are, by definition, directly competitive or substitutable products, whereas

---

[68] Appellate Body Report, *Korea – Taxes on Alcoholic Beverages*, WT/DS75/AB/R, WT/DS84/AB/R, adopted 17 February 1999, para. 123.

[69] Appellate Body Report, *Korea – Alcoholic Beverages*, para. 124.

> **(cont.)**
>
> not all 'directly competitive or substitutable' products are 'like'. The notion of like products must be construed narrowly but the category of directly competitive or substitutable products is broader. While perfectly substitutable products fall within Article III:2, first sentence, imperfectly substitutable products can be assessed under Article III:2, second sentence.

The categories of 'like products' and 'directly competitive and substitutable products' are not often amenable to a clear definition. Products that are perfect substitutes may be considered like; on the other hand, imperfect substitutes may be treated as directly competitive and substitutable. Importantly, such an analysis has to be done on a case-by-case basis.

In relation to Article II:2, second sentence, the Appellate Body equally relied on the fact that 'the tax operates in such a way that the lower tax brackets cover almost exclusively domestic production, whereas the higher tax brackets embrace almost exclusively imported products'.[70] In other words, in *Korea – Alcoholic Beverages*, the Appellate Body reiterated its finding in *Japan – Alcoholic Beverages II* that the existence of protection is not based on the subjective intent of the members, but on the 'objective design, revealing structure and architecture'.[71]

Philippines – Distilled Spirits, discussed below, addresses certain issues of an internal tax regime where the taxes are determined on the basis of the raw materials used.

PHILIPPINES – DISTILLED SPIRITS

This was a complaint brought by the European Union and the United States against a certain Philippines excise tax on distilled spirits. In the Philippines, distilled spirits are mainly produced from sugar cane molasses, which may involve stripping ethyl alcohol from its natural congeners. Thereafter, natural or artificial flavours are added to make sure that the alcohol is replicated as closely as possible with distilled spirit made from traditional materials.

According to Philippine law, if the distilled spirits were manufactured from certain designated materials, such as coconut, cassava, buri palm, nipa, juice, syrup or sugar of the cane, and if such designated materials were produced commercially in the country where they were processed into distilled spirits, such products were subjected to flat tax rate of 14.68 Philippines pesos (PHP) per proof. For example, for 1 litre of distilled spirit made from coconut having 10 per cent alcohol content, the tax will be calculated in accordance with the following formula:

$$\text{Tax Rate}(14.68 \text{ PHP}) \times \text{Proof}(\% \text{of alcohol} \times 2) \times \text{Bottle Volume} = \text{Tax}$$

Based on this formula, the tax for a litre of spirit will be:

$$14.68 \times [(10/100) \times 2] \times 1 = \text{PHP } 2.94.$$

---

[70] Appellate Body Report, *Korea – Alcoholic Beverages*, para. 150.
[71] Appellate Body Report, *Korea – Alcoholic Beverages*, paras. 70–71.

If the distilled spirits do not meet the above description, they will not qualify for the flat tax rates. In that scenario, the distilled spirits will be subject to a different tax rate based on the net retail price (NRP). The volume for net retail price is 750 ml, which is the standard unit for sale in the Philippines. If the NRP of a 750 ml bottle of spirit is less than PHP 250.00, then the tax rate of PHP 158.72 ppl would apply; if the NRP is between PHP 250.00 and PHP 675.00, then the tax rate of PHP 317.44 ppl would apply; and if the NRP is more than PHP 675.00, then PHP 634.90 ppl would apply (see Figure 1.2 for the tax rates). Further calculation is done as per the above formula.

The Philippines excise tax on distilled spirits did not formally differentiate between domestic products and imported products. But according to the evidence placed before the Panel, all of the distilled spirits in the Philippines were made from designated materials, usually sugar molasses, and benefited from the flat tax rate; at the same time, the vast majority of the imported distilled spirits were not made from designated materials and faced one of the higher tax rates.[72] Apparently, there was no de jure discrimination, but the

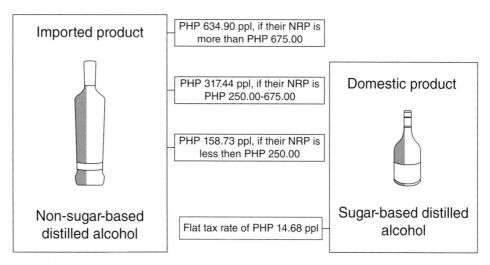

Figure 1.2 *Philippines – Distilled Spirits* (PHP = Philippine pesos, ppl = per proof litre, NRP = net retail price)
The Philippines imposed differential rates of excise duty on distilled spirits based on the raw materials used for making alcoholic beverages. The designated raw materials included saps of nipa, coconut, cassava, buri-palm or cane juice, syrup or sugar.

---

[72] Panel Report, *Philippines – Distilled Spirits*, para. 2.17.

complainants argued that the measure was de facto discriminatory with respect to imported products.[73] For example, the most sold domestic gin in the Philippines was Ginebra San Miguel, which attracted an excise tax of PHP 14.68 ppl, whereas the most sold imported gin, Bombay Sapphire, attracted a duty of PHP 370.44 ppl (see Figure 1.2). As the Panel noted, in most cases, the imported distilled spirits were subject to an excise duty ten to forty times the taxes applied on a directly competitive or substitutable domestic product.

The complainants argued that non-sugar-based (non-designated) imported distilled spirits were 'like' and/or 'directly competitive' to sugar-based (designated) domestic spirits in their respective types or categories. The Philippines argued that the distilled spirits made from designated materials are different from distilled spirits made from non-designated materials, since they differ in their chemical composition, especially in regard to 'congeners'.[74] Congeners are chemical compounds that provide flavour and aroma to the products. Although the distilled spirits were meant for the same use (namely, 'thirst-quenching, socialization, and pleasant intoxication'), the drinks each served a different, non-interchangeable audience.[75] On the criterion of consumer perception, the Panel noted that nothing on the label of the products indicated the raw materials, thereby negating the role of raw materials in consumer preference.

The complainants had also argued that the Philippines' measures violated Article III:2, second sentence. In addition to examining the four criteria under the *Report on Border Tax Adjustments*, the Panel also looked at factors including distribution channels and internal regulations – for example, the regulations relating to drunk-driving and the sale and distribution of alcohol.[76] The Philippines argued that distilled spirits made from designated raw materials are sold in local *sari-sari* stores (small local stores) and belonged to a different channel of distribution. The Panel, however, noted that all distilled spirits share some common distribution channels.

The Appellate Body upheld most of the Panel's findings in the appeal. The key paragraphs are extracted below.

Philippines – Distilled Spirits *(Appellate Body)*

125. We consider that, in spite of differences in the raw materials used to make the products, if these differences do not affect the final products, these products can still be found to be 'like' within the meaning of Article III:2 of the GATT. Article III:2, first sentence, refers to 'like products', not to their raw material base. If differences in raw materials leave fundamentally unchanged the competitive relationship among the

---

[73] Panel Report, *Philippines – Distilled Spirits*, para. 7.182.
[74] Panel Report, *Philippines – Distilled Spirits*, para. 7.40.
[75] Panel Report, *Philippines – Distilled Spirits*, para. 7.128.
[76] Panel Report, *Philippines – Distilled Spirits*, para. 7.135.

> *(cont.)*
>
> products, the existence of these differences would not necessarily negate a finding of 'likeness' under Article III:2.
>
> [...]
>
> 148. We observe that both the analysis of 'likeness' under Article III:2, first sentence, of the GATT 1994, and the analysis of direct competitiveness and substitutability under Article III:2, second sentence, require consideration of the competitive relationship between imported and domestic products. However, 'likeness' is a narrower category than 'directly competitive and substitutable'. Thus, the degree of competition and substitutability that is required under Article III:2, first sentence, must be higher than that under Article III:2, second sentence. On this point, we recall that, in *Canada – Periodicals*, the Appellate Body considered that a relationship of 'imperfect substitutability' would still be consistent with the notion of 'directly competitive or substitutable products', under the second sentence of Article III:2 of the GATT 1994, and that '[a] case of perfect substitutability would fall within Article III:2, first sentence'. In *Korea – Alcoholic Beverages*, the Appellate Body observed that '"like products" are a subset of directly competitive or substitutable products', so that 'perfectly substitutable products fall within Article III:2, first sentence', while 'imperfectly substitutable products can be assessed under Article III:2, second sentence'.

According to the Appellate Body, the mere fact that imported and domestic distilled spirits are manufactured from different raw materials is not a good enough reason to treat the products as not 'like'. The Philippines had argued that the difference in chemical composition, such as taste, flavour and aroma, are reasons to differentiate the products. As the GATT panel in *Spanish Unroasted Coffee* noted, the difference in organoleptic properties alone will not make the products fundamentally different. On the other hand, if the difference in raw materials, as we will further elaborate in *EC – Asbestos* later in this chapter, has a non-protectionist regulatory objective which, inter alia, affects consumer preferences, it can be considered a reasonable basis to treat the products as 'unlike'.[77] However, this view is undoubtedly not free from contestation.

In an older case, namely, *Chile – Alcoholic Beverages*, the Appellate Body noted that 'it is irrelevant that protectionism was not the intended objective if the particular tax measure is nevertheless, to echo Article III, applied to "imported or domestic products so as to afford protection to domestic production"'.[78]

---

[77] See also N. Damien and J. P. Trachtman, '*Philippines – Taxes on Distilled Spirits*: Like Products and Market Definition', *World Trade Review* (2013), 12(2), pp. 297–326.

[78] Appellate Body Report, *Chile – Taxes on Alcoholic Beverages*, WT/DS87/AB/R, WT/DS110/AB/R, adopted 12 January 2000, para. 29.

In short, it can be opined that the pendulum has swung from the extremes of the aim-and-effects test developed in the *US – Malt Beverages* case to the current 'protective application' test. If the objective of Article III is to curb lurking protectionism, one has to pierce the veil masking most of the governmental policies, at least in a subtle way. The protective application has significance in that context.

1.1.2.7   Internal Regulation

1.1.2.7.1 Law, Regulation or Requirement   Regulatory differences between imported and domestic products could affect conditions of competition. If the regulations place disproportionate costs on foreign producers or products, it could tilt the level playing field. At the same time, the right to regulate is a foundational principle that informs the balance of rights and obligations within the WTO system.[79]

> ## GATT, Article III:4
>
> The products of the territory of any contracting party imported into the territory of any other contracting party shall be accorded treatment no less favourable than that accorded to like products of national origin in respect of all laws, regulations and requirements affecting their internal sale, offering for sale, purchase, transportation, distribution or use.

To establish an inconsistency with Article III:4, the three following elements should be met: (1) the measure at issue is a 'law, regulation, or requirement affecting the internal sale, offering for sale, purchase, transportation, distribution, or use' of the products at issue; (2) the imported and domestic products at issue are 'like' products; (3) the treatment accorded to imported products is 'less favourable' than that accorded to like domestic products. This three-stage examination is well recognised in WTO jurisprudence.

The term 'laws, regulations and requirements' encompasses a variety of governmental measures, from mandatory rules which apply across the board to government action that merely creates incentives or disincentives for otherwise voluntary action by private persons.[80]

US – Gasoline, the first ever WTO dispute, had addressed one such issue. The challenge was against the US Clean Air Act of 1990, which specified certain 'baselines' for the year 1990 for the sale of reformulated gasoline. The US domestic refiners had three possible means of establishing their 1990 baseline, whereas the foreign refiners had only one method to establish

---

[79] M. A. Crowley and R. Howse, '*Tuna – Dolphin II*: A Legal and Economic Analysis of the Appellate Body Report', *World Trade Review* (2014), 13(2), p. 321.

[80] Panel Reports, *Brazil – Certain Measures Concerning Taxation and Charges*, WT/DS472/R, Add.1, Corr.1, WT/DS497/R, Add.1, Corr.1, adopted 11 January 2019, as modified by Appellate Body Reports WT/DS472/AB/R, WT/DS497/AT/R.

their baseline, failing which a statutory baseline was specified.[81] In other words, the baselines were based on the nature of the entity. The complaint was that the regulatory process under the Clean Air Act tilted the level playing field in favour of the domestic refiners and therefore constituted a violation of Article III:4 of the GATT. *US – Gasoline* provided a flavour of the type of national treatment claims which were to come to WTO dispute settlement.

1.1.2.8   Like Product in Article III:4

Japan – Alcoholic Beverages II clarified the scope of 'like product' under Article III:2 of the GATT, first sentence. However, the meaning of 'like product' under Article III:4 was rather unclear. Governments often distinguish between products for regulatory purposes. The important question was whether the WTO panels should follow the same test for 'likeness' analysis under Article III:4 of the GATT, as was identified for Article III:2 in *Japan – Alcoholic Beverages II.*

*EC – A*sbestos

EC – Asbestos – a watershed case in the WTO – revolved around the legal consistency of a French Decree that imposed a ban on the import and use of asbestos containing chrysotile fibres, widely considered as a carcinogenic substance. Before the partial ban was introduced, Canada (the Quebec province in particular) had exported a significant quantity of chrysotile fibre to France.

The Panel considered whether cement-based products containing asbestos fibres are 'like' cement-based products containing PCG (PVA, cellulose and glass) fibres. The Panel had noted, inter alia: 'taking into account the properties criterion, chrysotile fibres are like PVA, cellulose and glass fibres'.[82] The Appellate Body discussed the approach of the Panel, which concluded that the PCG fibres and the chrysotile asbestos fibres are 'like products'.

EC – Asbestos *(Appellate Body)*

105. ... [W]e think it helpful to summarize the way in which the Panel assessed the 'likeness' of chrysotile asbestos fibres, on the one hand, and the PCG fibres – PVA, cellulose and glass fibres – on the other. It will be recalled that the Panel adopted the approach in the *Border Tax Adjustments* report, using the four general criteria mentioned above. After reviewing the first criterion, 'properties, nature and quality of products', the Panel 'conclude[d] that ... chrysotile fibres *are like* PVA, cellulose and glass fibres'. In reaching this 'conclusion', the Panel found that it was not decisive that that the products 'do not have the same structure or chemical composition', nor that asbestos is 'unique'. Instead, the Panel focused on 'market access'

---

[81] Appellate Body Report, *US – Gasoline*, pp. 5–6.
[82] Panel Report, *European Communities – Measures Affecting Asbestos and Asbestos-Containing Products*, WT/DS135/R, Add.1, adopted 5 April 2001, as modified by Appellate Body Report WT/DS135/AB/R, para. 8.126.

(cont.)

and whether the products have the same 'applications' and can 'replace' each other for some industrial uses. The Panel also declined to '[i]ntroduce a criterion on the risk of the product'.

106. Under the second criterion, 'end-use', the Panel stated that it had already found, under the first criterion, that the products have 'certain identical or at least similar end-uses' and that it did not, therefore, consider it necessary to elaborate further on this criterion. The Panel declined to 'take a position' on 'consumers' tastes and habits', the third criterion, [b]ecause this criterion would not provide clear results. The Panel observed that consumers' tastes and habits are 'very varied'. Finally, the Panel did not regard as 'decisive' the different 'tariff classification' of the products.

The Appellate Body articulated its view on the Panel's approach in examining the four criteria under the 1970 *Report by the Working Party on Border Tax Adjustments*, as follows:

EC – Asbestos *(Appellate Body)*

109. ... It is our view that, having adopted an approach based on the four criteria set forth in *Border Tax Adjustments*, the Panel should have examined the evidence relating to each of those four criteria and, then, weighed *all* of that evidence, along with any other relevant evidence, in making the overall determination of whether the products at issue could be characterized as 'like'. Yet, the Panel expressed a 'conclusion' that the products were 'like' after examining only the first of the four criteria. The Panel then repeated that conclusion under the second criterion – without further analysis – before dismissing altogether the relevance of the third criterion and also before rejecting the different tariff classifications under the fourth criterion. In our view, it was inappropriate for the Panel to express a 'conclusion' after examining only one of the four criteria.

   [...]

111. We believe that physical properties deserve a separate examination that should not be confused with the examination of end-uses. Although not decisive, the extent to which products share common physical properties may be a useful indicator of 'likeness'. Furthermore, the physical properties of a product may also influence how the product can be used, consumer attitudes about the product, and tariff classification. It is, therefore, important for a panel to examine fully the physical character of a product. We are also concerned that it will be difficult for a panel to draw the appropriate conclusions from the evidence examined under each criterion if a panel's approach does not clearly address each criterion separately, but rather entwines different, and distinct, elements of the analysis along the way.

> **(cont.)**
>
> [. . .]
> 113. . . . Moreover, as we have said, in examining the 'likeness' of products, panels must evaluate *all* relevant evidence. We are very much of the view that evidence relating to the health risks associated with a product may be pertinent in an examination of 'likeness' under Article III:4 of the GATT 1994. We do not, however, consider that the evidence relating to health risks associated with chrysotile asbestos fibres need be examined under a *separate* criterion, because we believe that this evidence can be evaluated under the existing criteria of physical properties, and of consumer's tastes and habits.

The Appellate Body noted that the 'physical properties deserve a separate examination and should not be confused with the examination of end-uses'.[83] In this case, the physical properties of chrysotile fibres and the PCG fibres were distinctly different. The Appellate Body noted that it would be difficult for a Panel to reach a conclusion on each criterion unless the Panel approaches the relevant criterion separately. In the opinion of the Appellate Body, the Panel 'entwined' different and distinct elements of the likeness criteria.

1.1.2.9 Less Favourable Treatment

Article III:4 of the GATT provides that the treatment accorded to imported products shall not be less favourable. In certain cases, application of different formal legal requirements for imported products and domestic products could amount to a less favourable treatment to the imported products. A different treatment of imported and domestic products purely based on the origin of the product may give an inference that there is a less favourable treatment. But such a finding is not dispositive. In certain cases, different treatment of imports could also confer such products certain advantages.[84] Similarly, application of formally identical treatment on both imported and domestic products could also result in discrimination in certain cases.

KOREA – VARIOUS MEASURES ON BEEF

Korea had implemented a dual retail system for beef products. In 1999, Korea introduced the *Management Guidelines for Imported Beef*. Outlets selling domestic beef could not have sold imported beef. Small retailers that were a 'Specialised Imported Beef Store' could sell any beef other than domestic beef and were also required to display a separate 'Special Import Beef Store' sign to clearly distinguish them from domestic sellers of beef.

---

[83] Appellate Body Report, *European Communities – Measures Affecting Asbestos and Asbestos-Containing Products*, WT/DS135/AB/R, adopted 5 April 2001, para. 111.

[84] GATT Panel Report, *United States – Section 337 of the Tariff Act of 1930*, L/6439, adopted 7 November 1989, BISD 36S/345, para. 5.11.

Furthermore, large-scale distributors, including department stores and supermarkets, were required to set apart a separate sales area for imported beef.

The Panel in *Korea – Various Measures on Beef* observed that 'treatment no less favourable' under Article III:4 requires that a member accord to imported products 'effective equality of opportunities' with like domestic products in respect of the application of laws, regulations and requirements.[85] The question, however, was whether a formal difference in treatment between the imported and the domestic product could qualify as 'treatment no less favourable'. The Panel stated as follows:

Korea – Various Measures on Beef *(Panel)*

627. Any regulatory distinction that is based exclusively on criteria relating to the nationality or the origin of the products is incompatible with Article III and this conclusion can be reached even in the absence of any imports (as hypothetical imports can be used to reach this conclusion) confirming that there is no need to demonstrate the actual and specific trade effects of a measure for it to be found in violation of Article III.

The trade effects were hardly an issue. Since the days of *Brazilian Internal Taxes*, a dispute decided in 1949, the provisions of Article III are considered to be applicable whether or not the trade is 'substantial, small or inconsistent'.[86] The Appellate Body, however, clarified that all regulatory distinctions that are based on the nationality of products need not be inconsistent with Article III:4.

Korea – Various Measures on Beef *(Appellate Body)*

135. The Panel stated that 'any regulatory distinction that is based exclusively on criteria relating to the nationality or origin' of products is incompatible with Article III:4. We observe, however, that Article III:4 requires only that a measure accords treatment to imported products that is 'no less favourable' than that accorded to like domestic products. A measure that provides treatment to imported products that is different from that accorded to like domestic products is not necessarily inconsistent with Article III:4, as long as the treatment provided by the measure is 'no less favourable'. According 'treatment no less favourable' means, as we have previously said, according conditions of competition no less favourable to the imported product than to the like domestic product.

---

[85] Panel Report, *Korea – Measures Affecting Imports of Fresh, Chilled and Frozen Beef*, WT/DS161/R, WT/DS169/R, adopted 10 January 2001, as modified by Appellate Body Report WT/DS161/AB/R, WT/DS169/AB/R, para. 450.

[86] Working Party Report, *Brazilian Internal Taxes*, GATT/CP.3/42 (First Report), adopted 30 June 1949, BISD II/ 181.

In other words, a formal difference in treatment between imported and like domestic products is neither necessary nor sufficient to establish 'treatment no less favourable'. The Panel drew reference to the *US – Section 337* dispute. In that dispute, the GATT Panel was examining the issue whether the United States patent enforcement measures, which were formally different for imported and for domestic products, violated Article III:4. According to the GATT Panel, as recalled by the Appellate Body in *Korea – Various Measures on Beef*, 'the mere fact that imported products are subject under Section 337 to legal provisions that are different from those applying to products of national origin is in itself not conclusive in establishing inconsistency with Article III:4'. In other words, Article III:4 of the GATT does not necessarily require identical treatment.

As explained earlier, the objective of Article III and Article III:4 in particular is to ensure equality of competitive opportunities between the imported and the like domestic product. Traditionally, the WTO panels examine whether the measure has a detrimental impact on the conditions of competition. The test of 'detrimental impact' came into prominence in the *US – Section 337* case.[87] It has been applied consistently in examining discrimination since then.[88]

An equally interesting issue is the notion of balancing more favourable treatment of some imported products against less favourable treatment of other imported products. In *EC – Asbestos*, the Panel considered whether there were *any* imported products that were banned, and *any* 'like' domestic products that were permitted. The *Asbestos* Panel examined on the basis of the diagonal approach whether a distinction in law triggers a de jure examination[89] (see Table 1.3). Traditionally, such distinctions, seen in origin-neutral measures, were not the subject matter of a de jure discrimination, but, at best a de facto discrimination.

Table 1.3 Application of a diagonal test. See also *EC – Asbestos (AB)*, DSC, WorldTradelaw.net.

Type of products	Regulatory regime	Imports	Domestic
Polyvinyl, cellulose and glass	Allowed	Not considered	Allowed
Chrysotile fibre	Prohibited	Prohibited	Not considered

[87] GATT Panel Report, *US – Section 337*. However, the concept of detrimental impact was suggested in a few GATT cases involving Art. I:1 of the GATT; see GATT Panel Report, *United States – Measures Affecting the Importation, Internal Sale and Use of Tobacco*, DS44/R, adopted 4 October 1994, BISD 41S/131; GATT Panel Report, *EEC – Import Regime for Bananas*, DS38/R, 11 February 1994, unadopted; GATT Panel Report, *US – Footwear (Brazil)*.

[88] For example, Appellate Body Report, *Korea – Measures Affecting Imports of Fresh, Chilled and Frozen Beef*, WT/DS161/AB/R, WT/DS169/AB/R, adopted 10 January 2001, para. 137; Appellate Body Report, *Thailand – Customs and Fiscal Measures on Cigarettes from the Philippines*, WT/DS371/AB/R, adopted 15 July 2011, para. 134; Appellate Body Reports, *EC – Seal Products*, para. 5.101.

[89] Panel Report, *EC – Asbestos*, paras. 8.155–8.156.

The diagonal test used by the *Asbestos* Panel can also result in unwarranted outcomes. There will always be *some* imported products that fall into the disfavoured category and *some* domestic products that fall into the favoured category. While the diagonal test is controversial, the more appropriate test will be to examine whether the measure affects the imports *as a group* more than it affects the domestic product as a group. For example, in *EC – Seal Products*, the Panel noted that while *most* of the seal products from Canada and Norway could not qualify for the exception, most products from Sweden would qualify, and therefore could be placed on the market.[90] It held the mere fact that *some* imported products from Canada and Norway could be placed on the market did not negate the fact that there was less favourable treatment. In other words, the more rational test will be to assess how the imported and domestic products are spread or distributed in different regulatory categories. This will ensure that a panel will not be able to cherry-pick and compare products that are distributed in different regulatory categories.

The Appellate Body's approach in *Korea – Various Measures on Beef* provides some practical application of the detrimental impact test.

Korea – Various Measures on Beef *(Appellate Body)*

137. ... Whether or not imported products are treated 'less favourably' than like domestic products should be assessed instead by examining whether a measure modifies the conditions of competition in the relevant market to the detriment of imported products.

  [...]

145. When beef was first imported into Korea in 1988, the new product simply entered into the pre-existing distribution system that had been handling domestic beef. The beef retail system was a unitary one, and the conditions of competition affecting the sale of beef were the same for both the domestic and the imported product. In 1990, Korea promulgated its dual retail system for beef. Accordingly, the existing small retailers had to choose between, on the one hand, continuing to sell domestic beef and renouncing the sale of imported beef or, on the other hand, ceasing to sell domestic beef in order to be allowed to sell the imported product. Apparently, the vast majority of the small meat retailers chose the first option. The result was the virtual exclusion of imported beef from the retail distribution channels through which domestic beef (and, until then, imported beef, too) was distributed to Korean households and other consumers throughout the country. Accordingly, a new and separate retail system had to be established and gradually built from the ground up for bringing the imported product to the same households and other consumers if the imported product was to compete at all with the domestic product.

---

[90] Panel Reports, *EC – Seal Products*, paras. 7.143, 7.144.

> *(cont.)*
>
> Put in slightly different terms, the putting into legal effect of the dual retail system for beef meant, in direct practical effect, so far as imported beef was concerned, the sudden cutting off of access to the normal, that is, the previously existing distribution outlets through which the domestic product continued to flow to consumers in the urban centres and countryside that make up the Korean national territory. The central consequence of the dual retail system can only be reasonably construed, in our view, as the imposition of a drastic reduction of commercial opportunity to reach, and hence to generate sales to, the same consumers served by the traditional retail channels for domestic beef. In 1998, when this case began, eight years after the dual retail system was first prescribed, the consequent reduction of commercial opportunity was reflected in the much smaller number of specialised imported beef shops (approximately 5,000 shops) as compared with the number of retailers (approximately 45,000 shops) selling domestic beef.

Korea – Various Measures on Beef explains how detrimental impact on account of different treatment between imported and like domestic product could be indicative of less favourable treatment. An adjudicator may be required to examine the reasons for the detrimental impact. This view was reiterated by the Appellate Body in *Dominican Republic – Cigarettes.*[91]

Box 1.1 Detrimental impact: *Dominican Republic – Cigarettes* and its significance

Dominican Republic imposed a selective consumption tax on certain products, among them, cigarettes. The measure required both domestic producers and importers of cigarettes to post a bond amount of RD$ 5 million. The bond amount apparently served to secure as a guarantee of tax liabilities for compliance with internal tax obligations as well as the selective consumption tax. The bond requirement was imposed equally on domestic producers and importers, although the timing of settling of the Selective Consumption Tax was different. According to Honduras, the complainants in this case, the per unit cost of the bond requirement for imported products was significantly higher on Honduras products.

In this dispute, the Appellate Body found that the detrimental impact on the competitive opportunities for the like imported product was not attributable to the specific measure at issue. In this case, the detrimental effect due to the measure (the

---

[91] Appellate Body Report, *Dominican Republic – Measures Affecting the Importation and Internal Sale of Cigarettes*, WT/DS302/AB/R, adopted 19 May 2005.

Box 1.1 (cont.)

high per-unit cost of the bond requirement for imported cigarettes) was not due to the foreign origin of the cigarettes (which would have been discriminatory), but because these cigarettes occupied lower market share, which is an external factor.

The Appellate Body found that the existence of a detrimental effect on a given imported product resulting from a measure does not necessarily imply that this measure accords less favourable treatment to imports if the detrimental effect could be explained by factors unrelated to the foreign origin of the product.

To Go Further

United States Trade Representative, *Report on the Appellate Body of the World Trade Organization* (February 2020), pp. 90–3.

The reasoning of the Appellate Body in *Dominican Republic – Cigarettes* was subject to critical review in subsequent cases. *Thailand – Cigarettes (Philippines)* examined in detail the detrimental impact test elaborated in *Dominican Republic – Cigarettes*. This case dealt with a value added tax (VAT) and other fiscal measures, as well as their administration. According to the Philippines, resellers of imported cigarettes had to pay VAT, while resellers of domestic cigarettes, such as Thailand Tobacco Monopoly, which had a market share of 78 per cent, were exempt. The Appellate Body made a notable ruling in this case that for a measure to be found to modify the conditions of competition in the marketplace to the detriment of imported products, there must be a 'genuine relationship' between the measure and the detrimental impact.[92] The Appellate Body further held that the analysis of whether a measure has a detrimental impact on imports 'need not be based on empirical evidence as to the actual effects of the measure at issue in the internal market of the Member concerned'.[93] However, the complainant cannot establish a claim of less favourable treatment merely on 'simple assertion', but is required to identify and elaborate the implications of the measure on 'conditions of competition'.[94]

In a later WTO dispute, namely, *US – Tuna II (Mexico)*, the Panel reasoned that denying a 'dolphin-safe' label to tuna caught by setting on dolphins does not necessarily imply that less favourable treatment is given to Mexican tuna products.[95] The Panel concluded that any adverse impact felt by Mexican tuna products in the US market was the 'result of factors or

---

[92] Appellate Body Report, *Thailand – Cigarettes*, para. 134.

[93] Appellate Body Report, *Thailand – Cigarettes*, para. 29.

[94] Appellate Body Report, *Thailand – Cigarettes*, para. 130.

[95] Panel Report, *United States – Measures Concerning the Importation, Marketing and Sale of Tuna and Tuna Products*, WT/DS381/R, adopted 13 June 2012, as modified by Appellate Body Report WT/DS381/AB/R, para. 7.305.

circumstances unrelated to the foreign origin of the product, including the choices made by Mexico's own fishing fleet and canners'.[96]

1.1.2.10 Summary of Interpretation of Article III:4

The interpretation of the 'less favourable treatment' has waxed and waned in WTO jurisprudence. In more recent cases, such as *US – Clove Cigarettes* and *EC – Seal Products*, the approach is to find a less favourable treatment upon finding a detrimental impact.[97] The regulatory rationale, although considered a crucial balancing factor, is not given much importance.[98]

The reasoning of the Appellate Body in *EC – Asbestos* continues to have appeal, although the 'less favourable treatment' element of Article III:4 was not appealed by the parties.[99] Trade regulations can promote societal objectives, including health, environment and other public goods or values, by drawing certain distinctions between products.[100] Disparate impact or protective effect should not be wholly dispositive in a finding of 'less favourable treatment'; at the same time, and more importantly, the Appellate Body is not endorsing a regulatory purpose test in *Asbestos*.[101] *EC – Asbestos* is not an authority for the proposition that there is a need to examine the 'design, architecture and the structure' of the challenged measure in an Article III:4 analysis.[102] This view was confirmed by the Appellate Body in *EC – Seal Products*, where it noted that the interpretative direction of Article III:1 influences the various paragraphs of Article III in different ways.[103] In short, the protective application test designed in *Japan – Alcoholic Beverages II* may have a limited role in finding 'less favourable treatment' under Article III:4. On the whole, *EC – Asbestos* strikes a fine balance between preserving regulatory freedom and the need to maintain equality of competitive opportunities between imported and domestic products that compete in the marketplace.

To summarise, an examination under Article III:4 takes into account the *configuration* of competition between imported and domestic products at any given point in time in order to evaluate whether the challenged measure modifies the competitive relationship between imported products and the like domestic products. The analysis does not take into account the actual trade effects – a concept which has been explicitly rejected; on the other hand, the

---

[96] Panel Report, *US – Tuna II (Mexico)*, para. 7.378.

[97] Appellate Body Report, *US – Clove Cigarettes*, para. 372; Appellate Body Reports, *EC – Seal Products*, para. 5.101.

[98] J. Flett, 'WTO Space for National Regulation: Requiem for a Diagonal Vector Test', *Journal of International Economic Law* (2013), 16(1), pp. 64, 73.

[99] Appellate Body Report, *EC – Asbestos*, para. 100.   [100] Appellate Body Report, *EC – Asbestos*, para. 100.

[101] R. Hudec, one of the pioneers in international trade law, remarked that the Appellate Body decision in *EC – Asbestos* had brought back the aim-and-effects test. See A. Porges and J. P. Trachtman, 'R. Hudec and Domestic Regulation: The Resurrection of Aim and Effects', *Journal of World Trade* (2003), 37(4), pp. 783–99.

[102] Such a view, however, was raised in the Panel Report, *European Communities – Regime for the Importation, Sale and Distribution of Bananas, Complaint by Ecuador*, WT/DS27/R/ECU, adopted 25 September 1997, as modified by Appellate Body Report WT/DS27/AB/R, para. 7.181.

[103] Appellate Body Reports, *EC – Seal Products*, para. 5.114.

analysis takes into account the overall competitive relationship between the imported products and like domestic products. The potential imports are of paramount importance in this analysis.[104] Furthermore, the 'less favourable treatment' test is increasingly considered to be an objective examination stripped of a measure's legislative intent.

1.1.2.11   Government Procurement Exception

GATT Article III:8(a) permits governments to purchase domestic products for their own use in preference to imported products, making government procurement an exception to the national treatment principle. This exception was invoked notably in the *Canada – Renewable Energy / Canada – Feed-In Tariff Program* dispute.

CANADA – RENEWABLE ENERGY / CANADA – FEED-IN TARIFF PROGRAM

The Canadian province of Ontario was predominantly dependent on hydroelectric power generation in the first half of the twentieth century.[105] Over a period of time, the Hydroelectric Power Commission of Ontario added coal and nuclear power to the mix. Around 2009, Ontario implemented a feed-in-tariff (FIT) programme. The FIT was one of the latest in a series of programmes initiated by the Ontario Ministry of Energy and Infrastructure, under the Green Energy and Green Economy Act of 2009, to increase the supply of renewable electricity in the Ontario electricity system, in order to diversify the supply mix and replace coal-fired electricity generation plans.[106]

Under the FIT programme, generators of electricity produced from renewable energy sources (for example, wind power and solar PV technologies) were paid a guaranteed price per kilowatt hour (kWh) of electricity delivered, under twenty- or forty-year contracts.[107] Under the FIT programme, electricity generation facilities using renewable sources had to comply with minimum required local content, which was a minimum of 50 per cent for large wind installations and 60 per cent for solar PV technologies.

The European Union and Japan, the complainants in this matter, argued that the FIT programme and its related contracts imposed domestic content requirements on wind and solar PV electricity generators that affected the 'internal sale, purchase, or use' of renewable energy equipment and components, causing less favourable treatment to products of foreign origin.[108] In addition, the complainants argued that the domestic contents requirements fell under paragraph 1(a) of the Illustrative List, thereby violating Article 2.1 of the TRIMs Agreement.[109]

---

[104] L. Ehring, 'De Facto Discrimination in WTO Law: National and Most-Favored-Nation Treatment – or Equal Treatment?', *Journal of World Trade* (2002), 36(5), pp. 921–77.

[105] Panel Reports, *Canada – Certain Measures Affecting the Renewable Energy Generation Sector / Canada – Measures Relating to the Feed-In Tariff Program*, WT/DS412/R, Add.1, WT/DS426/R, Add.1, adopted 24 May 2013, as modified by Appellate Body Reports, WT/DS412/AB/R, WT/DS426/AB/R, para. 7.21.

[106] Panel Reports, *Canada – Renewable Energy / Canada – Feed-In Tariff Program*, para. 7.65.

[107] Panel Reports, *Canada – Renewable Energy / Canada – Feed-In Tariff Program*, para. 7.68.

[108] Panel Reports, *Canada – Renewable Energy / Canada – Feed-In Tariff Program*, paras. 3.1, 3.4.

[109] Panel Reports, *Canada – Renewable Energy / Canada – Feed-In Tariff Program*, para. 3.5.

In defence, Canada argued that the FIT and the micro-FIT programmes are not subject to the disciplines of Article III, as the challenged measures governed the procurement of renewable electricity with the governmental purpose of securing an electricity supply for Ontario consumers.[110] Canada argued that the procured electricity was not subject to commercial resale.[111]

Canada – Renewable Energy / Canada – Feed-In Tariff Program (Appellate Body)

5.60. ... The word agency is 'used' in connection with the word 'governmental' and, accordingly, Article III:8(a) refers to entities acting for or on behalf of government. The Appellate Body has held that the meaning of 'government' is derived, in part, from the functions that it performs and, in part, from the authority under which it performs those functions.

[...]

5.75. [...] the product that is subject to the Minimum Required Domestic Content Levels of the FIT Programme and Contracts challenged by the complainants as discriminatory under Article III:4 of the GATT 1994 and the TRIMs Agreement is certain renewable energy generation equipment. The product purchased by the Government of Ontario under the FIT Programme and Contracts, however, is electricity and not generation equipment. The generation equipment is purchased by the generators themselves. Accordingly, the product being purchased by a government agency for purposes of Article III:8(a) – namely, electricity – is not the same as the product that is treated less favourably as a result of the Minimum Required Domestic Content Levels of the FIT Programme and the Contracts.

The Appellate Body noted that Article III:8(a) of the GATT provides a derogation from the national treatment obligation of Article III:4 of the GATT. According to the Appellate Body, Article III:8(a) is limited to products purchased for the use of the government, consumed by the government or provided by the government to recipients in discharge of its public functions.

In this case, the local content requirements created discrimination between imported (EU or Japanese) renewable energy parts and components and the corresponding Canadian products. The government procurement exception under Article III:8(a) of the GATT was

---

[110] Panel Reports, *Canada – Renewable Energy / Canada – Feed-In Tariff Program*, para. 7.86.
[111] Panel Reports, *Canada – Renewable Energy / Canada – Feed-In Tariff Program*, para. 7.86.

meant to justify the discrimination stemming from the local content requirement (LCR), especially in relation to entirely different categories of products.

A similar issue arose in *India – Solar Cells*. The case related to certain LCRs contained in India's Jawaharlal Nehru National Solar Mission, introduced in 2012. The LCRs were introduced, apparently, to address the lack of manufacturing capability in the upstream products.

The WTO Panel and the Appellate Body unambiguously held that the LCRs enshrined in this measure violated the core national treatment obligations under Article III:4 of the GATT and Article 2.1 of the TRIMs Agreement. India had claimed that the LCRs were exempt from the obligations under Article III:4 of the GATT by virtue of Article III:8(a), an argument that the Panel rejected.[112]

1.1.2.11.1 Subsidy to Domestic Producers

Subsidies are recognised to be an effective policy tool for achieving a number of policy goals and members have certain latitude in supporting certain sectors. Subsidies given to the agriculture sectors are governed separately by the Agreement on Agriculture.

It appears that the GATT makes some distinction in payments made to consumers and producers.[113] Payments made to consumers for purchasing local products will indeed come under Article III:4, while payments made to domestic producers, without something more, cannot attract Article III:4.[114] Subsidies to domestic producers can stimulate production and, in certain situations, lead to adverse effects, which will be governed by Article XXIII:1(b) of the GATT or the Agreement on Subsidies and Countervailing Measures (SCM Agreement). While it is the prerogative of the member to provide subsidies only to domestic producers, such subsidies can have an impact on the conditions of competition on imported like products that might not have received such subsidies. Article III:8(b) of the GATT carves out an exemption from Article III of the GATT for payment of subsidies exclusively to domestic producers.

Brazil – Taxation

In *Brazil – Taxation*,[115] the issue was whether Article III:8(b) of the GATT served as an exception to the non-discrimination obligations imposed by, inter alia, Articles III:2 and III:4 of the GATT for subsidies paid exclusively to domestic producers. Brazil provided tax incentives that conformed to the Brazilian productive process, which resulted in a violation of Article III:2 of the GATT. The WTO Panel, and later the Appellate Body, ruled on whether the exception provided for in Article III:8(b) of the GATT was available for subsidies that introduced discrimination between domestic and imported products.

The Panel and the Appellate Body held that subsidies that are paid through the proceeds of discriminatory taxation would fall outside the scope of the exception in Article III:8(b)

---

[112] Panel Report, *India – Certain Measures Relating to Solar Cells and Solar Modules*, WT/DS456/R, Add.1, adopted 14 October 2016, as modified by Appellate Body Report WT/DS456/AB/R, para. 7.135.

[113] GATT Panel Report, *Italy – Agricultural Machinery*, p. 60.

[114] Appellate Body Report, *United States – Conditional Tax Incentives for Large Civil Aircraft*, WT/DS487/AB/R, Add.1, adopted 22 September 2017, para. 5.16.

[115] Appellate Body Reports, *Brazil – Taxation*.

by virtue of the first example and would therefore continue to be subject to the national treatment obligation.[116] When the internal taxes are higher on imported products than on like domestic products, or otherwise accord less favourable treatment to imported products and are thus inconsistent with Article III, the payment of subsidies derived from the proceeds of such GATT-inconsistent taxes would not be justified under Article III:8(b).[117]

1.1.2.12   Relationship between Article III:4 of the GATT and the TRIMs Agreement

The GATT rules only extended to a very narrow range of investment measures. During the Uruguay Round, it was reaffirmed that investment measures 'inconsistent with the provisions of Article III or XI of the GATT' are also prohibited.[118] An illustrative list of such measures was provided that included local content, sourcing and some trade balancing requirements. Furthermore, developing and least developed countries were provided five and seven years, respectively, for the elimination of TRIMs that were not consistent with Articles III or XI of the GATT.

In particular, paragraph 1(a) of the Illustrative List, which is referenced in Article 2.2 of the TRIMs Agreement, provides as follows:

> ## *TRIMs (Illustrative List)*
>
> TRIMs that are inconsistent with the obligation of national treatment provided for in paragraph 4 of Article III of GATT 1994 include those which are mandatory or enforceable under domestic law or under administrative rulings, or compliance with which is necessary to obtain an advantage, and which require:
>
> (a) the purchase or use by an enterprise of products of domestic origin or from any domestic source, whether specified in terms of particular products, in terms of volume or value of products, or in terms of a proportion of volume or value of its local production.

Canada – Renewable Energy / Canada- Feed-In Tariff Program and *India – Solar Cells* exemplify how certain industrial policy measures can sometimes undermine ostensibly sound environmental policies. Both these measures sought to create additional production in renewable energy and, overall, a shift away from fossil fuel-based energy policies to biothermal and solar energy production. While these policies resulted in a violation of Article III:4 of the GATT, they also fell foul of the TRIMs Agreement.

---

[116] Panel Reports, *Brazil – Taxation*, para. 7.87; Appellate Body Reports, *Brazil – Taxation*, para. 5.120.

[117] Appellate Body Reports, *Brazil – Taxation*, para. 5.89.

[118] M. Trebilcock, R. Howse and A. Eliason, *The Regulation of International Trade*, 4th ed. (London: Routledge, 2013), p. 584.

1.2   Conclusion

The concepts of MFN and NT constitute the pillars of non-discrimination. The multilateral trading system sustains and retains its perennial appeal on the strength of these basic legal obligations. Even in preferential trade agreements, these principles are incorporated, at least in the relationship between the parties to such groupings or arrangements.

While MFN and NT remain the basic principles of the overarching 'non-discrimination' obligation, members often draw distinctions between products – often for legitimate, and sometimes for non-legitimate purposes. A differential taxation or a differential regulatory treatment for such purposes can often face scrutiny at the dispute settlement stage. It is well-accepted in GATT/WTO law that if a differential treatment modifies the conditions of competition between products which are otherwise 'like', it may result in the violation of the non-discrimination obligation. In that context, certain GATT panels had examined the 'regulatory purpose' as an implicit part of the aim-and-effects test. This test was rejected in the famous *Japan – Alcoholic Beverages II*, but has found a subtle application in the form of the 'protective application' test. Panels often examine the 'structure, the design and the revealing architecture' of the measure to discern discrimination. This is widely considered an objective test. The regulatory purpose can be considered in an objective manner either under the 'like product' analysis or the 'less favourable treatment'.

The 'like product' examination has to be conducted on a case-by-case basis. An objective, economic analysis may be applied either individually or in combination for such examination. The Appellate Body in *EC – Asbestos* has also held that risks such as carcinogenicity, toxicity or such other considerations that inevitably influence the definition of physical properties of the product can be considered in the like product analysis.

For the purposes of Article III:4, a formal difference in treatment between imported and like domestic products is neither necessary, nor sufficient to establish a violation of Article III. Formal distinctions based on an origin basis need not be inconsistent with Article III of the GATT, if such distinctions can be explained by some rationale. The *Dominican Republic – Cigarettes* case is an authority for this proposition. The WTO panels often employ the detrimental impact test in assessing 'less favourable treatment'.

1.3   Summary

- The non-discrimination provision is a key pillar of the rule-based multilateral trading system.
- The MFN and NT provisions under Articles I and III of the GATT deal with both de jure and de facto discrimination.
- The concept of 'likeness' is a key touchstone in the non-discrimination analysis. For the determination of 'likeness', the WTO panels generally refer to the 1970 Working Party on Border Tax Adjustment.

- The concept of likeness is often compared to the metaphor of an accordion. The concept of 'likeness' expands and squeezes depending on the context. For example, the meaning of 'like product' under Article III:2 is narrower than 'like product' under Article III:4.
- The NT treatment obligation under Article III:4 of the GATT does not require the identical treatment of the imported and the like domestic products, but equality of competitive conditions between the two.
- The key exceptions to the MFN principle include the exception under Article XXIV (Customs Unions and Free Trade Areas) and the Generalised System of Preferences implemented under the 1979 Enabling Clause.

1.4   Review Questions

1. The Minnesota solar photovoltaic (PV) rebate grants incentives and rebates for the use of solar PV modules made in Minnesota. Products that are manufactured outside Minnesota do not receive the incentives. If you assume that the PV rebate scheme is a violation of Article III:4 of the GATT, is there any need, in your view, to provide a detailed like product analysis, using the *Border Tax Adjustments* criteria in a WTO challenge?

2. The Appellate Body in *US – Clove Cigarettes* suggested that the 'regulatory concerns underlying a measure such as health risks associated with a product' are relevant in determining whether products are 'like' only to the extent that these concerns affect the traditional concerns, such as 'physical characteristics or consumer preferences'. Has the Appellate Body indirectly used an aim-and-effects test in this finding?

3. In *EC – Asbestos*, paragraph 100, the Appellate Body notes that 'a Member may draw distinctions between products which have been found out to be "like", without, for this reason, alone, according to the group of "like" imported products "less favourable treatment" than that accorded to the group of "like" domestic products'. Does this view mean that the detrimental impact test is not dispositive for the purposes of Article III:4? Can regulatory intent be used to differentiate products that are otherwise competitive for the purpose of Article III:4?

4. In *US – Clove Cigarettes*, the group of like imported products that originated from Indonesia included not only clove cigarettes, but also non-clove cigarettes, such as cinnamon- and cocoa-flavoured cigarettes. Likewise, the group of like domestic products, or American products, included not only menthol cigarettes, but also other categories of flavoured cigarettes. However, the share of non-clove cigarettes imported from Indonesia into the United States and the share of non-menthol-flavoured cigarettes domestically manufactured in the United States was very low. The complainants in this case followed a comparison between imported clove cigarettes and domestic menthol cigarettes. Does the complainant's analysis follow a de jure analysis or a de facto analysis of Article III:4? Do you find any concern in following the 'detrimental impact' analysis?

1.5   Exercise

The Republic of Vega Land, a WTO member, has been adopting a number of policies to achieve a sustainable energy policy. Vega Land has identified that biodiesel, which is produced from renewable energy sources such as plant oils, animal fats and animal feedstock, can be used in motor vehicles. Biodiesel is biodegradable, non-toxic and free from sulphur and other aromatics. However, after the approval of biodiesel as a permitted motor fuel, most of the gas stations/fuel outlets started selling biodiesels in blended forms. The blended products are designated as BX, X being a number (for example, B10 means 10 per cent biodiesel is blended with 90 per cent petroleum diesel). The domestic retail sales tax on the products in Vega Land was designated in 2015 as shown in Table 1.4.

Table 1.4 Tax structure of the Republic of Vega Land on biodiesel

Product	Harmonised System	Sales tax (%)
Biodiesel	3824.90.4020	10
Blended diesel or mixtures thereof	3824.90.4030	15
Petroleum diesel	2710.19.4010	50

The Trade Policy Division in Vega Land would like to be assured that this tax structure is consistent with their WTO obligations. Prepare a short memo on the above tax structure and its WTO consistency.

FURTHER READING

Davey, W. J., *Non-Discrimination in the World Trade Organization: The Rules and Exceptions* (The Hague: Academy of International Law, 2012).

Ehring, L., '*De Facto* Discrimination in World Trade Law: National and Most-Favoured-Treatment – or Equal Treatment?', *Journal of World Trade* (2002), 36(5), pp. 921–77.

Horn, H. and Weiler, J. H., 'EC – Asbestos: European Communities – Measures Affecting Asbestos and Asbestos-Containing Products', in H. Horn and P. C. Mavroidis (eds.), *The WTO Case Law of 2001: The American Law Institute Reporters' Studies* (Cambridge University Press, 2003), pp. 14–40.

Hudec, R., 'GATT/WTO Constraints on National Regulation: Requiem for an "Aims and Effects" Test', *International Lawyer* (1998), 32(3), pp. 619–49.

Verhoosel, G., *National Treatment and WTO Dispute Settlement: Adjudicating the Boundaries of Regulatory Autonomy* (London: Bloomsbury, 2002).

2 Tariffs, Quotas and Preferential Trade Agreements

Table of Contents

Highlights

- Tariffs are taxes imposed on imported commodities. They may be imposed for a variety of reasons, including revenue for the importing country, coercion or to protect infant industries.
- Tariff binding seeks to preserve the value of tariff concessions negotiated by a member with its trading partners during the Uruguay Round of negotiations and is a basic object of the GATT 1994.
- The specific commitments are listed in Schedules of Concessions, which reflect specific tariff concessions and other commitments that members have given in the context of trade negotiations.
- Quantitative restrictions (QRs) refer to non-tariff, border measures that are capable of impeding trade, directly or indirectly, actually or potentially. QRs are not permitted either under the GATT or under the Agreement on Agriculture except under certain specific circumstances.
- A WTO member may maintain QRs to avert a balance-of-payment crisis or under certain limited exceptions under Article XI or the safeguard provisions under Article XIX.

- WTO members are permitted to form customs unions as well as free trade agreements, as long as the conditions to enter into economic integration agreements are met. Such arrangements constitute an exception to the MFN principle under the GATT.
- Preferential trade agreements (PTAs) in goods are permissible under the GATT once the PTA is comprehensive and includes 'substantially all trade', and as long as the liberalisation does not result in higher or more restrictive duties or other barriers to trade for members who are not parties to such an agreement.
- In implementing PTAs, rules of origin determine the nationality of a product. This is important since tariffs under PTAs are applied based on the originating status of a good, and not on an MFN basis.

2.1   Introduction

Import tariffs are not a new phenomenon, although their effects are poorly understood.[1] In economic terms, a tariff is a tax imposed on 'commodities imported from foreign countries'.[2] Tariffs are generally either *ad valorem* in nature, where the tax is imposed on the value of the goods, or specific, where the tax is an amount based on the quantity of the concerned good.

There are essentially three reasons why tariffs are imposed.[3] First, import tariffs can be an important source of revenue for an importing country. The developing world is more dependent on tariffs as a form of revenue than the developed world. Second, tariffs can also be imposed as a coercive instrument. Sometimes, tariffs are imposed for a political reason, especially to coerce or induce a nation to adopt certain policies or to comply with certain international obligations. Third, tariffs serve as a protective instrument. Import tariffs have routinely been imposed to protect the domestic industry, particularly against import price fluctuations.[4] Tariffs were widely considered a necessary complement to infant industry protection.[5]

Imposition of a tariff on an imported product may lead to varied outcomes. When a tariff is imposed on an imported product, the cost is often passed on to domestic consumers, unless they shift to an equally competitive domestic product. On the other hand, if the domestic product is less efficient, the tariff will encourage the production of a less efficient domestic product, which will lead to welfare losses.[6]

The modern tale of tariff protection begins with the imposition of French duties in 1664 and 1667, which affected Dutch and English imports of textiles and sugar in particular.

---

[1] Smith, *Wealth of Nations*, pp. 358, 701.   [2] D. A. Wells, *A Primer of Tariff Reform* (Palala Press, 2015), p. 5.

[3] A. Chatzky, 'The Truth about Tariffs' (Council on Foreign Relations, updated 2019), available at www.cfr.org/backgrounder/truth-about-tariffs (accessed 21 December 2020).

[4] F. Langdana and P. T. Murphy, *International Trade and Global Macropolicy* (New York: Springer, 2014).

[5] D. A. Irwin, 'Did Late Nineteenth-Century US Tariffs Promote Infant Industries? Evidence from the Tinplate Industry', *Journal of Economic History* (2000), 60(2), pp. 335–60.

[6] Irwin, 'Late Nineteenth-Century US Tariffs', pp. 355–8.

These duties ultimately resulted in the Franco-Dutch War in 1668.[7] In the United States, Alexander Hamilton's Report on Manufactures in 1791 led to Congress imposing customs duties on a number of imported goods, as a form of infant industry protection against European industries.[8] Similarly, the tariffs on corn introduced by the United Kingdom in 1815 proved to be quite controversial, due to their impact on wheat prices, and opponents of these tariffs formed the Anti-Corn Law League to promote free trade.[9] In the twentieth century, the notorious Smoot–Hawley tariffs in the United States are widely considered to have contributed to the Great Depression of the 1930s.[10] The Smoot–Hawley tariffs resulted in an increase in the already high tariff rates, which caused retaliatory responses from other countries and ultimately worsened the economic crisis in the 1930s.[11]

The Great Depression and the unforgettable experiences of the Second World War led to discussions to establish a multilateral framework to reduce tariffs and other barriers to trade. Although efforts in the 1940s to establish the International Trade Organization failed, trading nations established the General Agreement on Tariffs and Trade (GATT) in 1947, initially through an ad hoc mechanism. One of the key objectives of the GATT 1947 was to reduce tariffs and other barriers to trade across the board. Over the course of more than four decades, the GATT contracting parties met for eight rounds of negotiations for trade liberalisation, the last of which was the Uruguay Round.[12]

The Uruguay Round of negotiations and the resultant WTO can both be credited with a major role in promoting free trade, with tariff reduction in particular being a significant success.[13] Tariff protection against industrial products is at a historically low level in almost all countries and applied tariffs have also dropped to their lowest levels in recent history.[14] There have been instances of slight aberration in this trend, such as the increase in the average tariffs in the United States post-2019.[15]

Another hinderance to free trade is import licensing, which refers to the administrative procedures to be complied with prior to importation of goods. The Tokyo Round Import

---

[7] Smith, *Wealth of Nations*, p. 358.

[8] A. Hamilton, 'Report on Manufactures', submitted to US Congress on 5 December 1791; see also D. A. Irwin, 'The Aftermath of Hamilton's "Report on Manufactures"', *Journal of Economic History* (2004), 64(3), pp. 800–21.

[9] H. D. Jordan, 'The Political Methods of the Anti-Corn Law League', *Political Science Quarterly* (1927), 42(1), pp. 58–76.

[10] R. Pomfret, *International Trade: An Introduction to Theory and Policy* (Cambridge, MA and Oxford: Basil Blackwell, 1991), p. 164.

[11] C. P. Bown, *Self-Enforcing Trade: Developing Countries and WTO Dispute Settlement* (Washington, DC: Brookings Institution Press, 2009), p. 11.

[12] Bown, *Self-Enforcing Trade*, p. 12.

[13] A. Aggarwal, 'Impact of Tariff Reduction on Exports: A Quantitative Assessment of Indian Exports to the US', ICRIER Working Paper 120 (New Delhi: Indian Council for Research on International Economic Relations, 2004), p. 1.

[14] J. N. Bhagwati, P. Krishna and A. Panagariya, 'The World Trade System Today', in J. N. Bhagwati, P. Krishna and A. Panagariya (eds.), *The World Trade System: Trends and Challenges* (Cambridge, MA: MIT Press, 2016), p. 4.

[15] K. Rapoza, 'Average Tariff for China to Hit 17.5%. Was Around 5% Pre-Trump', *Forbes*, 7 August 2019.

Licensing Code was concluded in 1980, with the aim of preventing such import licensing procedures from serving as unnecessary restrictions to trade. These procedures were subsequently revised in the Uruguay Round Agreement on Import Licensing Procedures.

Quantitative restriction (QR) in the nature of import or export quotas is another protectionist tool. QRs can be in the form of government-imposed restriction on quantity, or sometimes a specification of value, which by its nature, limits the quantity of imports. QRs are typically administered with import licences. Import quotas may be sold or directly allocated to individuals or firms, domestic or foreign.[16] These measures are regulated largely by Articles XI and XIII of the GATT. The difference between tariffs and quotas is that the government receives revenue from tariffs whereas private parties receive quota rents in the latter. Both tariffs and quotas can lead to welfare losses. Import quotas provide absolute protection to the domestic industry and create monopoly power more effectively than tariffs.[17]

2.2   Tariff Bindings

The 'basic object and purpose' of the GATT 1994, as reflected in Article II, is to 'preserve the value of tariff concessions negotiated by a member with its trading partners, and bind the tariffs in that member's Schedule'.[18] Generally, in the context of trade in goods, tariffs are bound under Article II of the GATT. In the case of agricultural products, the commitments and concessions also relate to tariff rate quotas and domestic support, as well as export subsidies. Once a tariff concession is agreed and bound in a member's schedule, the member is committed not to introduce measures that would upset the balance of concessions among members. The bound commitments are included in the Schedules of Concessions, which are integral parts of the WTO treaty. The Schedules of Concessions are attached either to the Marrakesh Protocol to the GATT 1994 or to protocols of accessions for members who acceded after the establishment of the WTO.

GATT 1994, Article II: Schedules of Concessions

1. (a) Each contracting party shall accord to the commerce of the other contracting parties treatment no less favourable than that provided for in the appropriate Part of the appropriate Schedule annexed to this Agreement.

   (b) The products described in Part I of the Schedule relating to any contracting party, which are the products of territories of other contracting parties, shall, on their

---

[16] A. V. Deardorff, *Terms of Trade: Glossary of International Economics* (Hackensack: World Scientific, 2006), p. 226.

[17] Krugman et al., *International Trade*, p. 252.

[18] Appellate Body Report, *Argentina – Measures Affecting Imports of Footwear, Textiles, Apparel and Other Items*, WT/DS56/AB/R, Corr.1, adopted 22 April 1998, para. 47.

(cont.)

importation into the territory to which the Schedule relates, and subject to the terms, conditions or qualifications set forth in that Schedule, be exempt from ordinary customs duties in excess of those set forth and provided therein. Such products shall also be exempt from all other duties or charges of any kind imposed on or in connection with the importation in excess of those imposed on the date of this Agreement or those directly and mandatorily required to be imposed thereafter by legislation in force in the importing territory on that date.

[...]

2. Nothing in this Article shall prevent any contracting party from imposing at any time on the importation of any product:

(a) a charge equivalent to an internal tax imposed consistently with the provisions of paragraph 2 of Article III in respect of the like domestic product or in respect of an article from which the imported product has been manufactured or produced in whole or in part;

[...]

Ad note Article II

Paragraph 2(a)

The cross-reference, in paragraph 2(a) of Article II, to paragraph 2 of Article III shall only apply after Article III has been modified by the entry into force of the amendment provided for in the Protocol Modifying Part II and Article XXVI of the General Agreement on Tariffs and Trade, dated September 14, 1948.

Paragraph 2(b)

See the note relating to paragraph 1 of Article I.

WTO members are obliged not to exceed their applied tariffs on goods beyond their bound levels. WTO panels and the Appellate Body have examined members' obligations under Article II of the GATT in several disputes. *Argentina – Textiles and Apparel* is one such dispute.

ARGENTINA – TEXTILES AND APPAREL

Argentina maintained minimum specific import duties (referred to as DIEM) on textiles, apparel and footwear, which had a bound rate of 35 per cent.[19] Under the DIEM, Argentina calculated an average import price of each Harmonized System tariff line of textiles,

---

[19] Panel Report, *Argentina – Measures Affecting Imports of Footwear, Textiles, Apparel and Other Items*, WT/DS56/R, adopted 22 April 1998, as modified by Appellate Body Report WT/DS56/AB/R, para. 2.2.

apparels and footwear, on which it applied its bound rate of 35 per cent.[20] The resultant duty was applied to all products under that Harmonized System tariff line as a specific minimum duty. During importation, either the determined specific minimum duty or the *ad valorem* rate, whichever was higher, was applied.[21] The United States challenged this measure before a WTO panel, and it was subsequently appealed to the Appellate Body, which noted:

Argentina – Textiles and Apparel (US) *(Appellate Body)*

45. ... Article II:1 ... Paragraph (b) prohibits a specific kind of practice that will always be inconsistent with paragraph (a): that is, the application of ordinary customs duties in excess of those provided for in the Schedule.

    [...]

47. ... Article II:1(a) is part of the context of Article II:1(b); it requires that a Member must accord to the commerce of the other Members 'treatment no less favourable than that provided for' in its Schedule. It is evident to us that the application of customs duties in excess of those provided for in a Member's Schedule, inconsistent with the first sentence of Article II:1(b), constitutes 'less favourable' treatment under the provisions of Article II:1(a).

    [...]

55. We conclude that the application of a type of duty different from the type provided for in a Member's Schedule is inconsistent with Article II:1(b), first sentence, of the GATT 1994 to the extent that it results in ordinary customs duties being levied in excess of those provided for in that Member's Schedule. In this case, we find that Argentina has acted inconsistently with its obligations under Article II:1(b), first sentence, of the GATT 1994, because the DIEM regime, by its structure and design, results, with respect to a certain range of import prices in any relevant tariff category to which it applies, in the levying of customs duties in excess of the bound rate of 35 per cent *ad valorem* in Argentina's Schedule.

The Appellate Body in *Argentina – Textiles and Apparel* held that the text of Article II:1(b), first sentence, does not address whether applying a type of duty different from the type provided for in a member's schedule is, in itself, inconsistent with the schedule. The application of a type of duty different from the type provided for in a member's schedule is inconsistent with Article II:1(b), first sentence of the GATT, to the extent that it can result in customs duties being levied in excess of those provided for in that member's schedule.[22]

---

[20] Panel Report, *Argentina – Textiles and Apparel*, para. 2.6.

[21] Panel Report, *Argentina – Textiles and Apparel*, para. 2.6.

[22] Appellate Body Report, *Argentina – Textiles and Apparel*, para. 55.

2.3   WTO and Border Tax Adjustment

The GATT 1947 and, later, the WTO Agreements (especially the SCM Agreement) have provided some distinction in the treatment of direct and indirect taxes.[23] The underlying rationale of the distinction, significantly flawed as it might be,[24] is that indirect taxes are entirely passed forward in product prices, whereas direct taxes are entirely absorbed in lower factor incomes. In addition, it is well-recognised in GATT jurisprudence that fiscal measures may adopt the destination principle.[25] The destination principle requires that all internal charges imposed on an exported product should be relieved or rebated in the exporting country, whereas all imported products sold to consumers should be levied with some or all of the tax levied in the importing country, in respect of like domestic products.[26] This principle is also specifically mentioned in Footnote 1 of the SCM Agreement and Article XVI of the GATT. (See our discussion in Chapter 6.)

In the 1970 GATT *Report on Border Tax Adjustments*, the Working Party stated that only the taxes directly levied on products, such as credit invoice VAT, excise and sales tax, and other consumption taxes are eligible for border adjustment.[27] In *US – Superfund*, the GATT contracting parties added that the tax adjustment rules of the GATT distinguish between taxes on products and taxes not directly levied on products, but they do not distinguish between taxes with different policy purposes.[28] Neither does the *Report on Border Tax Adjustments* provide a list of products that are eligible or not eligible for border tax adjustment.

Discerning whether a duty is a 'customs duty' or an 'internal charge' is not easy. The Appellate Body in *China – Auto Parts* spelt out the distinction between an 'ordinary customs duty', within the scope of Article II:1(b), first sentence, and an 'internal charge' within the meaning of Article III:2.

China – Auto Parts

This was China's first case at the WTO and has symbolic and interpretative relevance. As the *Economist* magazine noted, this case drew attention to China's increasingly fractious trade relationships and governmental intervention in certain key industries.[29]

The measures at issue were the Policy on Development of the Automotive Industry (Policy Order 8), Decree 125 and Announcement 4 (collectively referred to as 'China's Auto policies').[30]

---

[23] 'Border-Adjusted Taxes and the Rules of the World Trade Organization: The Distinction between Direct and Indirect Taxes (Part I)', CRS Reports and Analysis (Washington, DC: Federation of American Scientists, 22 March 2017).

[24] G. C. Hufbauer and Z. Lu, 'Border Tax Adjustments: Assessing Risks and Rewards', Peterson Institute for International Economics Policy Brief (January 2017), p. 5.

[25] GATT, *Border Tax Adjustments*, para. 4.

[26] GATT, *Border Tax Adjustments*, para. 4; see also GATT Panel Report, *US – Superfund*, para. 5.2.4.

[27] GATT, *Border Tax Adjustments*, para. 14.   [28] GATT Panel Report, *US – Superfund*, para. 5.2.4.

[29] 'Inevitable Collision', *The Economist*, 23 February 2003, pp. 82–3.

[30] Panel Reports, *China – Measures Affecting Imports of Automobile Parts*, WT/DS339/R, Add.1, Add.2, WT/DS340/R, Add.1, Add.2, WT/DS342/R, Add.1, Add.2, adopted 12 January 2009, upheld (WT/DS339/R) and as modified (WT/DS340/R, WT/DS342/R) by Appellate Body Reports WT/DS340/AB/R, WT/DS342/AB/R, para. 7.1.

China had a fast-developing automobile market, and US companies such as Delphi Corp and Visteon Corp had a sizeable market share in China. In the meantime, domestic companies such as Weichai Power Co. Ltd and Chanchun FAW – Sihuan Automobile Co. Ltd came along.[31]

Under the measures at issue, China imposed a charge on imported auto parts equivalent to tariff rates applicable to motor vehicles, if the parts were characterised as complete motor vehicles under the measure. The charges imposed under the disputed measures were 25 per cent if the auto parts were characterised as a complete vehicle, and 10 per cent if they were not.[32] The determination of whether an imported part was a complete vehicle or not was based on whether it was used in the assembly of a certain vehicle model. China had bound its MFN duty at 25 per cent for complete motor vehicles and 10 per cent for auto parts.[33] Manifestly, China's automobile policy was 'to discourage foreign car makers from importing vehicles in large parts to circumvent the higher tariff'.[34]

The imposition of the charge was only upon assembly in China, regardless of whether all the parts were imported together, at the same time or within the same shipment.[35] If the imported parts used in a particular vehicle met or exceeded the relevant threshold, then all of the imported parts used to assemble that model of vehicle were characterised as complete vehicles. In other words, China rolled all the imported parts together and assumed that the imported parts imparted the essential character of a completed vehicle.[36] Various combinations of assemblies also met the characterisation of a complete vehicle. For example, a vehicle body including cabin assembly and engine assembly, or five or more assemblies other than vehicle body (including cabin) and engine assemblies could fit the description of a complete vehicle for tax purposes. Accordingly, imported parts used for complete vehicles had a 25 per cent duty levied. Such duties also applied to completely knocked down and semi-knocked down kits. On the other hand, if the imported vehicle parts were not characterised as a complete vehicle, such parts were subject to a duty of 10 per cent.

The complainants argued that these measures were adopted to favour domestic auto parts over imported ones, whereas China argued that the measures were only to ensure that correct tariffs were paid on imports. China stated that its measures were customs duties consistent with Article II of the GATT. According to the complainants, it could not constitute an ordinary customs duty, since it was only triggered on the actual use of the parts in the assembly of vehicles after importation, and it is not imposed solely on the status/ condition of the goods at the time of importation.[37]

---

[31] D. Pruzin, 'Citing Carmaker's Woes, US, EU Urge China to Implement Quickly WTO Auto Parts Ruling', *International Trade Reporter* (Washington, DC: Bureau of National Affairs, 2009), 26, p. 77.

[32] Panel Reports, *China – Auto Parts*, para. 7.24.   [33] Panel Reports, *China – Auto Parts*, para. 7.24.

[34] R. Bhala and D. A. Gantz, 'WTO Case Review 2009', *Arizona Journal of International and Comparative Law* (2010), 27(1), p. 108.

[35] Panel Reports, *China – Auto Parts*, para. 7.31.

[36] Panel Reports, *China – Auto Parts*, para. 7.120 (referring to China's first written submission).

[37] Panel Reports, *China – Auto Parts*, para. 7.119.

China – Auto Parts *(Appellate Body)*

114. ... The measures set out ... the criteria that determine when imported parts used in a particular vehicle model must be deemed to have the 'essential character' of complete vehicles and are thus subject to the 25 per cent charge. These criteria are expressed in terms of particular combinations or configurations of imported auto parts or the value of imported parts used in the production of a particular vehicle model. The use in the production of a vehicle model of specified combinations of 'major parts' or 'assemblies' that are imported requires characterization of *all* parts imported for use in that vehicle model as complete vehicles. Various combinations of assemblies will meet the criteria, for example: a vehicle body (including cabin) assembly and an engine assembly; or five or more assemblies other than the vehicle body (including cabin) and engine assemblies. The use, in a specific vehicle model, of imported parts with a total price that accounts for at least 60 per cent of the total price of the complete vehicle also requires characterization of *all* imported parts for use in that vehicle model as complete vehicles. Imports of CKD [completely knocked down] and SKD [semi-knocked down] kits are also characterized as complete vehicles.

    [...]

120. By the tenth working day of the month following issuance of the Verification Report, the automobile manufacturer must make a declaration of duty payable, and submit additional documentation, to the district customs office, in respect of all relevant complete vehicles assembled from when production of the vehicle model began through to the end of the month in which the Verification Report was issued. The district customs office then proceeds to classify the auto parts as complete vehicles and to collect the 'duty' and import VAT for all imported auto parts used in assembling those complete vehicles. It is this 'duty' that constitutes the 'charge' under the measures ...

121. When the imported parts used in the production of a specific vehicle model meet the criteria under the measures at issue, then the 25 per cent charge and the requirements under the measures apply in respect of *all* imported parts assembled into the relevant vehicle model. It is immaterial whether the auto parts that are 'characterized as complete vehicles' were imported in multiple shipments – that is at various times, in various shipments, from various suppliers and/or from various countries – or in a single shipment. It is also immaterial whether the automobile manufacturer imported the parts itself or obtained the imported parts in the domestic market through a third party supplier such as an auto part manufacturer or other auto part supplier.

    [...]

> **(cont.)**
>
> 153. ... a key criterion for a charge to constitute an ordinary customs duty under Article II:1(b) is that it accrue at the moment of importation.
>
>   [...]
>
> 162. ... [I]n examining the scope of application of Article III:2, in relation to Article II:1(b), first sentence, the time at which a charge is collected or paid is not decisive. In the case of Article III:2, this is explicitly stated in the GATT 1994 itself, where the Ad Note to Article III specifies that when an internal charge is 'collected or enforced in the case of the imported product at the time or point of importation', such a charge 'is nevertheless to be regarded' as an internal charge. What is important, however, is that the *obligation* to pay a charge must accrue due to an internal event, such as the distribution, sale, use or transportation of the imported product.

The Appellate Body affirmed the finding of the Panel that China's measure is an 'internal charge' and not an ordinary customs duty. Again, in *China – Publications and Audiovisual Products (US)*, the Appellate Body had an opportunity to dwell on the distinctions between a border tax and an internal charge. According to the Appellate Body, the key determinant is that the case of an 'internal charge' arises because of an internal event, for instance, the product was used internally or resold internally.[38]

In *India – Additional Import Duties* (discussed below), the Panel and the Appellate Body had occasion to examine whether a measure falls under Article II:2(a) or the Ad Note to Article III.[39]

INDIA – ADDITIONAL IMPORT DUTIES

In India, for historical reasons, the power to impose taxes on liquor remained with the provincial units. Excise duty on liquor traditionally forms one of the most important sources of revenue for the provincial states.

India placed imported liquor under QR until 2001. After the QRs were eliminated, the central government rationalised the different excise duties and imposed an additional duty in lieu of state excise duties. The additional duty was a charge calculated on the basis of average rates of state excise duties.

---

[38] Appellate Body Report, *China – Publications and Audiovisual Products*, para. 163.

[39] Appellate Body Reports, *China – Measures Affecting Imports of Automobile Parts*, WT/DS339/AB/R, WT/DS340/AB/R, WT/DS342/AB/R, adopted 12 January 2009, fn. 233. See also J. Dasgupta, '*India – Additional Import Duties*: Tax Reforms via WTO', in A. Das and J. Nedumpara (eds.), *WTO Dispute Settlement at Twenty: Insiders' Reflections on India's Participation* (Singapore: Springer, 2016), p. 188.

India had undertaken tariff bindings on the basic customs duty on these products at the rate of 150 per cent.[40] The Indian Customs also levied an additional duty in the range of 20–150 per cent based on the cost, insurance, freight (CIF) price per case.[41] Over and above this, Customs also levied such additional duties at 4 per cent.[42] The duty structure is provided in Table 2.1.

Table 2.1 Duties imposed on alcoholic beverages by India

Goods	Price bands of goods	Basic custom duty	Additional duty	Such additional duty
Beers and wines	CIF price not exceeding US$25 per case	100% *ad valorem*	75% ad valorem	4%
	CIF price US$25–40 per case		50% *ad valorem* or US$37 per case, whichever is higher	
	CIF price greater than US$40 per case		20% *ad valorem* or US$40 per case, whichever is higher	
Distilled spirits	CIF price not exceeding US$10 per case	150% *ad valorem*	150% *ad valorem*	4%
	CIF price US$10–20 per case		100% *ad valorem* or US$40 per case, whichever is higher	
	CIF price US$20–40 per case		50% *ad valorem* or US$53.2 per case, whichever is higher	
	CIF price exceeding US$40 per case		25% *ad valorem* or US$53.2 per case, whichever is higher	

The United States complained that both the additional duties, when imposed in conjunction with the basic customs duty on alcoholic products such as beer, wine and distilled spirits, resulted in less favourable treatment than what India had scheduled in its tariff bindings. In other words, these measures amounted to a violation of India's commitments under Article II:1(a) and (b) of the GATT. The United States also argued that these measures qualified as an 'ordinary customs duty' or 'other duties and charges'.[43]

India, in defence, argued that these measures can be classified as import border tax adjustments within the meaning of Article II:2 of the GATT. In particular, Article II:2(a) states that 'nothing in Article II prevents a contracting party from imposing a charge equivalent to an internal tax consistently with paragraph of Article III in respect of a like domestic product' at the time of importation.[44] In other words, India was arguing that the additional duties were imposed at the border only in lieu of internal taxes.[45] India argued

---

[40] Panel Report, *India – Additional and Extra-Additional Duties on Imports from the United States*, WT/DS360/R, adopted 17 November 2008, as reversed by Appellate Body Report WT/DS360/AB/R, para. 4.18.

[41] Panel Report, *India – Additional Import Duties*, para. 7.15.

[42] Panel Report, *India – Additional Import Duties*, para. 7.17.

[43] Panel Report, *India – Additional Import Duties*, paras. 7.26, 7.27.

[44] Panel Report, *India – Additional Import Duties*, para. 7.30.

[45] Panel Report, *India – Additional Import Duties*, para. 7.121.

that the similar domestic charges in the form of excise duties, value added taxes as well as sales taxes were already in place on like domestic products.[46]

In the interrelationship between Article II:1(b) and II:2(a), there is a potential issue regarding whether Article II:2(a) is an exception to a violation of Article II:1(b). If that be the case, who should bear the burden in establishing consistency or non-consistency with II:2(a)? The Appellate Body noted as follows:

> ### India – Additional Import Duties *(Appellate Body)*
>
> 190. Not every challenge under Article II:1(b) will require a showing with respect to Article II:2(a). In the circumstances of this dispute, however, where the potential for application of Article II:2(a) is clear from the face of the challenged measures, and in the light of our conclusions above concerning the need to read Articles II:1(b) and II:2(a) together as closely interrelated provisions, we consider that, in order to establish a prima facie case of a violation of Article II:1(b), the United States was also required to present arguments and evidence that the Additional Duty and the Extra-Additional Duty are not justified under Article II:2(a).

In addition, the Appellate Body made the following key observations:

> ### India – Additional Import Duties *(Appellate Body)*
>
> 192. ... [D]ue to the characteristics of the measures at issue or the arguments presented by the responding party, there is a reasonable basis to understand that the challenged measure may not result in a violation of Article II:1(b) because it satisfies the requirements of Article II:2(a), then the complaining party bears some burden in establishing that the conditions of Article II:2(a) are not met.

In other words, if there is a reasonable presumption that the measure is a border tax adjustment, then the complainant is also required to adduce evidence as to why the measure need not get the benefit of Article II:2(a).

If the additional duty is not an ordinary customs duty or a border adjustment duty, then the question is whether it is levied on imported products at an amount or rate no higher than the rate/amount levied on domestically produced like products to be consistent with GATT Article III:2. The Appellate Body ruled that India's additional duties were not justified as they resulted in import charges in excess of the excise duty imposed on like domestic products. This was because India employed the process of averaging of excise rates in

---

[46] Panel Report, *India – Additional Import Duties*, para. 7.30.

various states to calculate additional duty to be imposed on the imports, and in some states, the additional duty exceeded the excise duty applicable on like domestic products.[47]

In conclusion, Table 2.2 summarises the GATT provisions on various categories of import or border taxes, as well as the conditions necessary to meet the requirements on border tax adjustments.

Table 2.2 GATT provisions: tariffs and border tax adjustments

Charge/tax	Principle	Legal provisions
Ordinary customs duties	Permitted, but must not exceed level of tariff binding	Art. II:1(b)
Other duties and charges	Prohibited on bound items except if validly recorded in the schedule	Art. II:1(b) and Understanding
Internal charges collected at the point of importation	Permitted, provided that the charge is consistent with Art. III:2	Note to Art. III of the GATT
Charges on importation equivalent to internal taxes	Permitted, provided that the charge is consistent with Art. III:2	Art. II:2(a) of the GATT

Source: Frieder Roessler, 'India – Additional and Extra-Additional Duties on Imports from the United States: Comment', World Trade Review (2010), 9, p. 269.

2.4   Tariff Classification

The Schedules of Concessions of a WTO member form an integral part of the WTO Agreement. Such schedules are present both under the GATT and the GATS. However, members quibble over which products are bound and which products are unbound; whether commitments are indeed given on a product line, or whether there are limitations to certain concessions, and so on.[48] This is especially true in technological products where product descriptions could be vague or based on generic terms or technologies. Assume that a WTO member had undertaken commitments on mobile phones in 1996. It is not clear whether the category of mobile phone (in the technology jargon, 'telephone for cellular networks') could include a 'smart phone'. At the same time, it is possible to argue that a 'smart phone' is a computing device which has a communication function and therefore could come under computer products (under the technological category 'automated data processing machines').

---

[47] Appellate Body Report, *India – Additional and Extra-Additional Duties on Imports from the United States*, WT/DS360/AB/R, adopted 17 November 2008, paras. 213–214.

[48] Panel Report, *European Communities and its Member States – Tariff Treatment of Certain Information Technology Products*, WT/DS375/R, WT/DS376/R, WT/DS377/R, adopted 21 September 2010. See also Appellate Body Report, *United States – Measures Affecting the Cross-Border Supply of Gambling and Betting Services*, WT/DS285/AB/R, adopted 20 April 2005, para. 166.

Tariff classification issues are exacerbated when members are required to transpose product codes and descriptions from older versions of Harmonized System (HS) nomenclature into newer versions of the HS system. The World Customs Organization undertakes these changes periodically, usually every four to six years, and WTO members update these schedules.[49] There is a real need to preserve the original tariff commitments and the product commitment unchanged – a task which can be onerous.

In *EC – Computer Equipment*, the Appellate Body noted that the terminology of the schedules should be interpreted as if one were interpreting the GATT itself or any other treaty in the WTO single undertaking.[50] In this connection, an important issue is the interpretative value of the various transpositions and amendments made to the Harmonized System at the World Customs Organization.

In Chapter 1 of this book we examined the importance of the interpretative rules under Articles 31–33 of the VCLT. International tribunals have unambiguously recognised the rules of treaty interpretation under the VCLT, namely, Articles 31–33, as customary international law.[51] While it may be helpful to organise the analysis in the nature of text, context, object and purpose, in that order, it is important to bear in mind that treaty interpretation is a holistic exercise that should not be mechanically subdivided into rigid parts.[52]

One way to learn the nuances of such a complicated exercise is to examine a good case. *EC – Chicken Cuts*[53] is a primer in treaty interpretation in WTO law.

EC – Chicken Cuts

Brazil and Thailand, the complainants, challenged the change in EC classification practice and the consequent tariff treatment for *frozen boneless salted chicken cuts*. Before 2002, frozen boneless chicken cuts with a salt content of 1.2–3.0 per cent was classified under subheading 0210.90.20 and was subject to an *ad valorem* tariff of 15.4 per cent (see Table 2.3). Later, by 2003, the said products were classified under subheading 0207.41.10 and were subject to a tariff of €102.4/100kg/net.[54] According to the complainants, this measure amounted to a treatment less favourable than that

[49] D. Yu, 'The Harmonized System: Amendments and their Impact on WTO Members' Schedules', Staff Working Paper ERSD-2008-02 (WTO Economic Research and Statistics Division, 2008).

[50] Appellate Body Report, *European Communities – Customs Classification of Certain Computer Equipment*, WT/DS62/AB/R, WT/DS67/AB/R, WT/DS68/AB/R, adopted 22 June 1998, para. 84.

[51] *Land, Island and Maritime Frontier Dispute (El Salvador* v. *Honduras)*, ICJ Reports 1992, p. 351, para. 380; *Territorial Dispute (Libya* v. *Chad)*, ICJ Reports 1994, p. 6, para. 41; *Golder* v. *United Kingdom*, ECHR (1975), Series A, No. 18.

[52] Appellate Body Report, *China – Publications and Audiovisual Products*, para. 348.

[53] Appellate Body Report, *European Communities – Customs Classification of Frozen Boneless Chicken Cuts*, WT/DS269/AB/R, WT/DS286/AB/R, Corr.1, adopted 27 September 2005.

[54] Panel Reports, *European Communities – Customs Classification of Frozen Boneless Chicken Cuts*, WT/DS269/R (*Brazil*), WT/DS286/R (*Thailand*), adopted 27 September 2005, as modified by Appellate Body Report WT/DS269/AB/R, WT/DS286/AB/R, para. 7.3.

provided for in the European Communities Schedule LXXX in violation of Article II:1(a) and/or Article II:1(b) of the GATT 1994.[55] This dispute appears to be a dispute on tariff classification, while some would argue that this dispute is truly a matter of treaty interpretation.[56]

Table 2.3 Tariff classification and duty

Tariff classification	Description	Duty
0207	Meat and edible offal, of the poultry of heading no. 0105, fresh, chilled or frozen:	1024 ECU/T [€102.4/ 100kg/net]
02.07	– Of fowls of the species *Gallus domesticus*:	
	— Cuts:	
0207.41.10	—— Boneless	
02. 10	Meat and edible meat offal, in brine, dried, smoked; edible flours and meals of meat or meat offal:	15.4%
0210.90	– Other, including edible flours and meals of meat or meat offal:	
	— Meat:	
0210.90.20	—— Other	

The WTO Panel framed the issue as to whether chicken cuts in question were 'salted' within the meaning of tariff heading 02.10, without separately examining whether they also fell within the meaning of tariff heading 02.07. The respondent argued that 'salted' necessarily has a connotation of 'long-term preservation'.[57]

The Panel examined whether the measures at issue (EC Regulation 1223/2002 and EC Decision 2003/97/EC) resulted in the imposition of duties and conditions on the products at issue in excess of those provided for in the EC Schedule. The Panel examined the ordinary meaning of the term 'salted' in heading 02.10 of the EC Schedule.[58] In this analysis, the Panel examined exclusively the dictionary meaning of the term 'salted', which stated 'to season, to add salt, to flavour with salt, to treat, to cure or to preserve'.[59] The Panel also examined the relevant terms in the concession, namely, 'in brine', 'dried' and 'smoked' as context under Article 31(2) of the VCLT. The Panel concluded that 'there is nothing in the range of meanings comprising the ordinary meaning of term "salted" that indicates that chicken to which salt has been added is not covered by the concession contained in heading 02.10 of the EC Schedule'.[60]

---

[55] Panel Reports, *EC – Chicken Cuts*, paras. 2.1, 7.60.

[56] H. Horn and R. Howse, '*European Communities – Customs Classification of Frozen Boneless Chicken Cuts*', *World Trade Review* (2008), 7(1), p. 10.

[57] Panel Reports, *EC – Chicken Cuts*, para. 7.86.   [58] Panel Reports, *EC – Chicken Cuts*, para. 7.108.

[59] Panel Reports, *EC – Chicken Cuts*, para. 7.116.   [60] Panel Reports, *EC – Chicken Cuts*, paras. 7.116, 7.151.

EC – Chicken Cuts *(Appellate Body)*

176. ... [W]e would agree with the European Communities that there is no reference in the *Vienna Convention* to 'factual context' as a separate analytical step under Article 31. Nevertheless, we do not believe that the Panel was incorrect to consider elements such as the 'products covered by the concession contained in heading 02.10', 'flavour, texture, [and] other physical properties' of the products falling under heading 02.10, and 'preservation' when interpreting the term 'salted' as it appears in heading 02.10. The Panel's consideration of these elements under 'ordinary meanings' of the term 'salted' complemented its analysis of the dictionary definitions of that term. In any event, even if we were to agree with the European Communities that these elements are not considered under the 'ordinary meaning', they certainly could be considered as 'context'. Interpretation pursuant to customary rules codified in Article 31 of the Vienna Convention is ultimately a holistic exercise that should not be mechanically divided into rigid components.

The Panel noted that, 'in essence, the ordinary meaning of the term "salted" indicates that the character of the product has been altered through the addition of salt'.[61] The Appellate Body divided the inquiry into two parts: (i) does the term 'salted' in heading 02.10, when considered in its context, indicate that meat to which salt has been added is to be considered 'salted', even if such salting is not sufficient to place the meat in a state of 'preservation'? (ii) Must the salting be such as to place the meat in a state of 'preservation'?[62]

In essence, the Appellate Body examined whether the customary rules of treaty interpretation suggest that 'salting' under heading 02.10 of the EC schedule contemplates exclusively the notion of 'preservation'. In other words, reading an element of preservation could narrow the ordinary meaning of heading 02.10.[63]

The Appellate Body examined the immediate context of heading 02.10 to understand whether 'salting' under this heading contemplates exclusively the notion of 'preservation'.

EC – Chicken Cuts *(Appellate Body)*

212. At the same time, we are not convinced that the terms 'dried, in brine and smoked' refer *exclusively* to the concept of 'preservation'. We note that the dictionary meaning of the term 'to dry' is, in relevant part, 'to remove the moisture from by wiping, evaporation, draining; preserve (food etc.) by the removal of its natural moisture'; in turn, the dictionary meaning of the term 'to smoke' is to 'dry or cure

---

[61] Panel Reports, *EC – Chicken Cuts*, para. 7.150.   [62] Appellate Body Report, *EC – Chicken Cuts*, para. 208.
[63] Appellate Body Report, *EC – Chicken Cuts*, para. 187.

> **(cont.)**
> (meat, fish, etc.) by exposure to smoke'. The ordinary meanings of these terms suggest that the relevant processes can be applied to meat in various ways and degrees of intensity, thereby producing different effects on the meat, effects that may or may not place the meat in a state of 'preservation' . . .
> 213. We, therefore, do not agree with the European Communities that the terms of heading 02.10 of the EC Schedule other than 'salted', considered alone or together, suggest that the term 'salted' must be read as referring exclusively to products that have a level of salt content sufficient to ensure 'preservation' by salting.

The Appellate Body later turned to the structure of chapter 2 of the EC Schedule and the Harmonized System and the notes thereto to support a reading of heading 02.10 as referring exclusively to the process of 'preservation' (see Table 2.4). The relevant notes to the chapters concerned are reproduced below.

Table 2.4 Chapter notes

Chapter note to chapter 16	Explanatory note to chapter 2	Explanatory note to heading 02.10
This chapter does not cover meat, meat offal, fish, crustaceans, molluscs, or other aquatic invertebrates, prepared or preserved by the processes specified in chapter 2 or 3 or heading 05.04	This chapter covers meat and meat offal in the following states only, whether or not they have been previously scalded or similarly treated but not cooked	This heading applies to all kinds of meat and edible meat offal which have been prepared as described in the heading, other than pig fat, free of lean meat and poultry fat, not rendered or otherwise extracted (heading 02.09)

The EC argued that heading 02.10 does not make any reference to refrigeration. In other words, according to the EU, refrigeration is of 'little or no importance' for heading 02.10. The EC, therefore, argued that heading 02.10 covers only meat products that have been 'preserved' by the processes mentioned in that heading. While the Appellate Body agreed with the EC regarding this proposition, it also noted that refrigeration 'will not influence whether a product falls under heading 02.10'.[64] Furthermore, according to the Appellate Body, the chapter note to chapter 16 and the explanatory note to heading 02.10 confirmed that chapter 2 covered both preserved and prepared products.

---

[64] Appellate Body Report, *EC – Chicken Cuts*, para. 218.

EC – Chicken Cuts *(Appellate Body)*

229. As a result, we conclude that the Harmonized System and the relevant Chapter and Explanatory Notes thereto do not support the view that heading 02.10 is characterized exclusively by the concept of preservation. Furthermore, the term 'salted' in heading 02.10, when considered in its context, suggests that meat to which salt has been added, so that its character has been altered, will be 'salted' within the meaning of heading 02.10, even if such salting does not place the meat in a state of 'preservation'. Heading 02.10 of the Harmonized System, read in its context, suggests that it is neither limited to, nor excludes, meat that is 'prepared' by salting or that has been preserved by 'salting'. Specifically, for resolving this dispute, heading 02.10 does not contain a *requirement* that salting must, itself, ensure 'preservation'.

The Panel, and then the Appellate Body, turned to the subsequent practice of WTO members, as this could shed light on the understanding of parties to a treaty.[65] The Panel analysed the classification practice related to salted chicken cuts with a salt content of 1.2–3 per cent, while the Appellate Body extended this to all meat that falls within heading 02.10 of the EC Schedule. In this regard, the Appellate Body noted that the Schedules of Concessions of members other than the European Communities include tariff bindings under headings 02.07 and 02.10 and could be useful in establishing subsequent practice.[66] The Appellate Body also concluded that the mere fact that there was lack of protest from one member does not mean that there was equal agreement with that practice. According to the Appellate Body, it would be difficult to establish a 'concordant, common and discernible pattern' based on the acts or pronouncements of one or very few parties to a multilateral treaty.[67] Therefore, it concluded that no subsequent practice could be established regarding the tariff classification.[68] The Appellate Body also examined the supplementary means of interpretation (i.e. the negotiating history and the circumstances of its conclusion) under Article 32 of the VCLT.

EC – Chicken Cuts *(Appellate Body)*

305. In our view, it is possible that documents published, events occurring, or practice followed subsequent to the conclusion of the treaty may give an indication of what were, and what were not, the 'common intention of the parties' at the time of the

---

[65] Appellate Body Report, *EC – Chicken Cuts*, para. 255.
[66] Appellate Body Report, *EC – Chicken Cuts*, para. 262.
[67] Appellate Body Report, *EC – Chicken Cuts*, para. 259.
[68] Appellate Body Report, *EC – Chicken Cuts*, para. 272.

(cont.)

conclusion. The relevance of such documents, events or practice would have to be determined on a case-by-case basis ...

[...]

344. ... the term 'salted' in heading 02.10 of the Harmonized System does not contain a requirement that salting must, by itself, ensure long-term preservation; but, at the same time, it does not exclude the notion of 'preservation'. Therefore, we are of the view that, if a specific criterion of long-term preservation – such as the one advocated by the European Communities, namely, that salting, by itself, must ensure long-term preservation and that therefore it must be 'much higher than 3%' – is to form a part of the tariff commitment of the European Communities under its Schedule relating to heading 02.10, then there must be clear evidence that such a criterion was agreed upon by the parties for the European Communities' WTO Schedule. We see no such evidence on record; nor do we see it stated explicitly in the European Communities' customs legislation in force at the time of conclusion of the WTO Agreement, namely, EC Regulation 535/94; nor do we find it clearly enshrined in the ECJ's case-law prior to the enactment of EC Regulation 535/94. Rather, we find that the products at issue in this dispute were invariably classified by the customs authorities under heading 02.10 between 1996 and 2002, when the European Communities adopted EC Regulation 1223/2002, introducing the phrase 'provided ... salting ensures long-term preservation'.

2.5   Quantitative Restrictions

Quantitative restrictions (QRs) refer to non-tariff measures. According to WTO notification procedures, QRs include licensing requirements (both automatic and non-automatic licensing); global and bilateral quotas; minimum prices triggering quantitative restrictions; imports affected through State trading enterprises and voluntary export restraints.

GATT, Article XI: General Elimination of Quantitative Restrictions

1. No prohibitions or restrictions other than duties, taxes or other charges, whether made effective through quotas, import or export licences or other measures, shall be instituted or maintained by any contracting party on the importation of any product of the territory of any other contracting party or on the exportation or sale for export of any product destined for the territory of any other Member.

Article XI:1 spells out the types of border measures that can be instituted by a WTO member. A ban on the trade or exportation of a commodity will be a 'prohibition' within the meaning of Article XI of the GATT. The WTO Appellate Body noted in *China – Raw Materials* that the title of Article XI 'suggests that Article XI of the GATT 1994 covers those prohibitions and restrictions that have a limiting effect on the quantity or amount of a product being imported or exported'.[69] In other words, measures, which are capable of impeding trade, directly or indirectly, actually or potentially, could come within the broad category of QRs. Importantly, QRs are border measures that affect imports and are prohibited. However, in certain cases concerning domestic regulations, which may regulate or incidentally prohibit trade, measures may apply to both domestic and imported products. In such cases, by virtue of *Ad Note* to Article III, the measures are examined under Article III of the GATT, which deals with national treatment. Cases such as *US – Tuna (I), US – Shrimp*[70] and *EC – Asbestos*[71] spurred a debate on whether the challenged measures should have been examined as an import restriction under Article XI of the GATT or as an internal regulation under Article III:4 of the GATT.[72] While the respondents admitted that the measures were import prohibitions under Article XI of the GATT in the first two cases, in *EC – Asbestos* the challenged measure was examined under Article III of the GATT.

An important exception to QRs includes measures taken to safeguard an external financial position. Economies that could experience a balance-of-payments (BoP) crisis, arising mainly due to efforts to expand their internal market or from the instability in their terms of trade, can take advantage of this exception.

INDIA – QUANTITATIVE RESTRICTIONS

This dispute related to QRs maintained by India on 2,714 tariff lines at the 8-digit level based on balance-of-payments grounds.[73] India had been consulting regularly under Article XVIII:B of the GATT with the Committee on Balance-of-Payments Restrictions since 1957.[74]

During the consultations held in January 1997, the IMF informed the BoP Committee that India's current monetary reserves were adequate and were not threatened by a serious decline.[75] India advised of its plan to phase out QRs in nine years in a BoP Committee meeting held on 19 May 1997;[76] in another meeting, on 10–11 June 1997, India offered to revise the phase-out plan to seven years.[77] However, no consensus could be achieved in these

---

[69] Appellate Body Reports, *China – Measures Related to the Exportation of Various Raw Materials*, WT/DS394/AB/R, WT/DS395/AB/R, WT/DS398/AB/R, adopted 22 February 2012, para. 320.

[70] Appellate Body Report, *United States – Import Prohibition of Certain Shrimp and Shrimp Products*, WT/DS58/AB/R, adopted 6 November 1998.

[71] Appellate Body Report, *EC – Asbestos*.   [72] Trebilcock et al., *Regulation of International Trade*, p. 671.

[73] Panel Report, *India – Quantitative Restrictions on Imports of Agricultural, Textile and Industrial Products*, WT/DS90/R, adopted 22 September 1999, para. 2.1.

[74] Panel Report, *India – Quantitative Restrictions*, para. 2.2.

[75] Panel Report, *India – Quantitative Restrictions*, para. 2.4.

[76] Panel Report, *India – Quantitative Restrictions*, para. 2.5.

[77] Panel Report, *India – Quantitative Restrictions*, para. 2.6.

BoP Committee meetings. On 16 July 1997, the United States requested consultations with India.[78] The United States alleged that India's measures were inconsistent with Article XI:1, Article XVIII:11, Article 4.2 of the Agreement on Agriculture (AoA), and Article 3 of the Agreement on Import Licensing Procedures.

GATT, Article XVIII: Governmental Assistance to Economic Development

Section B

9. In order to safeguard its external financial position and to ensure a level of reserves adequate for the implementation of its programme of economic development, a contracting party coming within the scope of paragraph 4(a) of this Article may, subject to the provisions of paragraphs 10 to 12, control the general level of its imports by restricting the quantity or value of merchandise permitted to be imported; Provided that the import restrictions instituted, maintained or intensified shall not exceed those necessary:
   (a) to forestall the threat of, or to stop, a serious decline in its monetary reserves ...
      [...]
11. In carrying out its domestic policies, the contracting party concerned shall pay due regard to the need for restoring equilibrium in its balance of payments on a sound and lasting basis and to the desirability of assuring an economic employment of productive resources. It shall progressively relax any restrictions applied under this Section as conditions improve, maintaining them only to the extent necessary under the terms of paragraph 9 of this Article and shall eliminate them when conditions no longer justify such maintenance; Provided that no contracting party shall be required to withdraw or modify restrictions on the ground that a change in its development policy would render unnecessary the restrictions which it is applying under this Section.*

Ad Note Article XVIII:11

The second sentence in paragraph 11 shall not be interpreted to mean that a contracting party is required to relax or remove restrictions if such relaxation or removal would thereupon produce conditions justifying the intensification or institution, respectively, of restrictions under paragraph 9 of Article XVIII.

India could maintain restrictions for BoP purposes, as long as specific conditions mentioned in Article XVIII:9 and Article XVIII:11 were respected.[79]

The issue to be decided under Article XVIII:9 was whether India was facing a serious decline or threat thereof in its reserves (Article XVIII:9(a)) or had inadequate reserves

---

[78] Panel Report, *India – Quantitative Restrictions*, para. 1.1.
[79] Panel Report, *India – Quantitative Restrictions*, para. 5.156.

(Article XVIII:9(b)). To determine this issue, the Panel had to consider the adequacy of India's reserves. The Panel opined that large decline need not necessarily be a serious one if the reserves are more than adequate.[80] Moreover, the IMF had reported an adequate level of reserves and the Reserve Bank of India also stated that India's reserves were 'well above the conventional thumb rule of reserve adequacy'.[81] The Panel ruled that India was not facing a serious decline or a threat of a serious decline in monetary reserves and did not face the situation of inadequate reserves.[82] According to the Panel, India's measures exceeded those necessary under the terms of Article XVIII:9(a) or (b) and, therefore, India would appear to be in violation of the requirements of Article XVIII:11 unless the measures could be justified under the Ad Note to Article XVIII:11.[83]

The next issue to be decided was whether India was entitled under the Ad Note Article XVIII:11 to maintain measures for BoP purposes. India argued that it should not be required to remove its quantitative restrictions immediately, because it would create the conditions for their reinstatement.[84] The Panel opined that the Ad Note could cover situations where the conditions of Article XVIII:9 are no longer met but are threatened.[85] As the situation improves, there should be gradual relaxation.[86] But this notion of 'gradual relaxation' should be read in the context of Article XVIII:9, implying that as conditions improve, measures must be relaxed in proportion to the improvements in monetary reserves.[87] The logical conclusion is that the measures will be eliminated when conditions no longer justify the continuation of measures.[88]

The Panel stated that measures under Ad Note to Article XVIII:11 could be maintained if the relaxation or removal of the measures 'would thereupon produce' conditions justifying the intensification or institution, respectively, of restrictions under paragraph 9 of Article XVIII.[89] The Panel examined the terms of paragraph 11 as follows:

India – Quantitative Restrictions *(Panel)*

5.196. ... Dictionary definitions of the term 'thereupon' are 'upon that or it', 'on that being done or said', '(directly) after that', 'in consequence of that', 'immediately' or 'at

---

[80] Panel Report, *India – Quantitative Restrictions*, para. 5.173.

[81] Panel Report, *India – Quantitative Restrictions*, paras. 5.174, 5.12 (the IMF was consulted under Art. 13 of the DSU, as it had expertise in BoP issues, and therefore was a relevant source under Art. 13.2).

[82] Panel Report, *India – Quantitative Restrictions,* paras. 5.169–5.173.

[83] Panel Report, *India – Quantitative Restrictions*, para. 5.184.

[84] Panel Report, *India – Quantitative Restrictions*, para. 5.185.

[85] Panel Report, *India – Quantitative Restrictions*, para. 5.189.

[86] Panel Report, *India – Quantitative Restrictions*, para. 5.190.

[87] Panel Report, *India – Quantitative Restrictions*, para. 5.190.

[88] Panel Report, *India – Quantitative Restrictions*, para. 5.190.

[89] The meaning 'immediately' is stated as the most appropriate meaning for 'thereupon'. Panel Report, *India – Quantitative Restrictions*, paras. 5.196–5.197.

(cont.)

once'. While several variations of meaning can be identified in those definitions, we are of the view that the most appropriate meaning should be 'immediately'. In particular, we note that this interpretation is consistent with, and arguably compelled by the Spanish and French versions of the Agreement ('inmediatamente' and 'immédiatement', respectively). The context of the term tends to confirm this choice. If 'thereupon' had been intended to mean only 'in consequence of that', the word would not have been necessary. The causality between the removal of the measures and the occurrence of the 'conditions' is clear without that word.

[. . .]

5.198. . . . Our interpretation of the term 'thereupon' as a notion of time is also consistent with the structure of the sentence which deals with the moment when measures may have to be removed. We do not mean that the term 'thereupon' should necessarily mean within the days or weeks following the relaxation or removal of the measures; this would be unrealistic, even though instances of very rapid deterioration of balance-of-payments conditions could occur. We consider that the purpose of this word is to ensure that measures are not maintained because of some distant possibility that a balance-of-payments difficulty may occur, which would be possible if India's interpretation was accepted.

Based on the information available to it, the Panel concluded that a removal of the measures at issue would not *immediately* produce conditions justifying the reimposition of import restrictions for balance-of-payments reasons and, therefore, the measures were not justified under Ad Note Article XVIII:11.[90] India appealed to the Appellate Body on whether the Panel correctly interpreted the Ad Note Article XVIII:11 of the GATT 1994 and, in particular, the word 'thereupon'.[91] The Appellate Body agreed with the Panel in the following manner:

India – Quantitative Restrictions *(Appellate Body)*

114. We agree with the Panel that the Ad Note, and, in particular, the words 'would thereupon produce', require a causal link of a certain directness between the removal of the balance-of-payments restrictions and the recurrence of one of the three conditions referred to in Article XVIII:9. As pointed out by the Panel, the Ad Note demands more than a mere possibility of recurrence of one of these three

---

[90] Panel Report, *India – Quantitative Restrictions*, para. 5.125; C. Thomas, 'Balance-of-Payments Crises in the Developing World: Balancing Trade, Finance and Development in the New Economic Order', *American University International Law Review* (2000), 15, pp. 1273–5.

[91] Appellate Body Report, *India – Quantitative Restrictions*, paras. 29–30.

> **(cont.)**
>
> conditions and allows for the maintenance of balance-of-payments restrictions on the basis only of clearly identified circumstances. In order to meet the requirements of the Ad Note, the probability of occurrence of one of the conditions would have to be clear.
>
> 115. We also agree with the Panel that the Ad Note and, in particular, the word 'thereupon', expresses a notion of temporal sequence between the removal of the balance-of-payments restrictions and the recurrence of one of the conditions of Article XVIII:9. We share the Panel's view that the purpose of the word 'thereupon' is to ensure that measures are not maintained because of some distant possibility that a balance-of-payments difficulty may occur

In sum, the Appellate Body affirmed the Panel's finding on the meaning of 'thereupon' to the adverb 'immediately',[92] although the Appellate Body added that the Panel should have used the words 'soon after' to express the temporal sequence required by the word.[93] The Appellate Body upheld the Panel's interpretation of the Ad Note.[94]

2.5.1   Interaction between GATT Article XI:1 and Article 4.2 of the Agreement on Agriculture

QRs are not tolerated within either the GATT or the AoA. However, the GATT does include certain exceptions – for instance, export prohibitions or restrictions temporarily applied to prevent critical shortages of feedstuff or import restrictions necessary for the removal of temporary surplus of the like domestic product. *Indonesia – Import Licensing Regimes*, a dispute brought by New Zealand and the United States, touched upon the interaction between Article XI:1 of the GATT and Article 4.2 of the AoA.[95] This matter is examined in Chapter 3.

2.6   Preferential Trade Agreements

Article XXIV of the GATT permits WTO members to form two special types of agreements, namely free trade agreements (FTAs) and customs unions (CUs). Similarly, Article V of the

---

[92] Appellate Body Report, *India – Quantitative Restrictions*, para. 117.

[93] Appellate Body Report, *India – Quantitative Restrictions*, para. 119.

[94] Appellate Body Report, *India – Quantitative Restrictions*, para. 120.

[95] Panel Report, *Indonesia – Importation of Horticultural Products, Animals and Animal Products*, WT/DS477/R, WT/DS478/R, Add.1, Corr.1, adopted 22 November 2017, as modified by Appellate Body Report WT/DS477/AB/R, WT/DS478/AB/R, paras. 3.1, 3.3.

GATS lays down the conditions under which economic integration agreements (EIAs) are considered to serve the objectives of liberalisation of trade in services among WTO members. Collectively, they are referred to as preferential trade agreements (PTAs) and serve as an exception to the non-discrimination rule of MFN in GATT and GATS.

According to the Vinerian theory, PTAs allow some domestic production to be replaced by imports from efficient firms located in countries that are preferential partners – that is, trade creation resulting in certain welfare gains.[96] At the same time, PTAs may reduce imports from more efficient non-party countries, resulting in trade diversion and loss of welfare.[97] In other words, trade creation can lead to welfare gains, whereas trade diversion can result in welfare losses. However, governments are not often influenced by welfare considerations alone in signing PTAs. A number of recent free trade agreements focus on regional economic integration that may have geopolitical considerations as well.

The concept of customs unions or free trade agreements, to an extent, is antithetical to the concept of MFN-based trade. However, the drafters of the GATT 1947 considered that voluntary agreements could advance closer integration between economies through freedom of trade.[98] In other words, even at the drafting stage of the GATT, it was considered that an MFN-based system could coexist with regionalism.

> ## GATT, Article XXIV:8: Territorial Application – Frontier Traffic – Customs Unions and Free-Trade Areas
>
> (a) A customs union shall be understood to mean the substitution of a single customs territory for two or more customs territories, so that
>   (i) duties and other restrictive regulations of commerce (except, where necessary, those permitted under Articles XI, XII, XIII, XIV, XV and XX) are eliminated with respect to substantially all the trade between the constituent territories of the union or at least with respect to substantially all the trade in products originating in such territories, and,
>   (ii) ... substantially the same duties and other regulations of commerce are applied by each of the members of the union to the trade of territories not included in the union.
> (b) A free-trade area shall be understood to mean a group of two or more customs territories in which the duties and other restrictive regulations of commerce (except, where necessary, those permitted under Articles XI, XII, XIII, XIV, XV and XX) are eliminated on substantially all the trade between the constituent territories in products originating in such territories.

---

[96] J. Viner, *The Customs Union Issue* (Oxford University Press, 2014).

[97] J. Cheong and K. Wong, 'Economic Integration, Trade Diversion and Welfare Change', unpublished paper (University of Washington, 2007), p. 1.

[98] GATT, Art. XXIV:4.

Free trade agreements and customs unions have not often been the subject matter of dispute settlement in the WTO. Nevertheless, some disputes have examined the relationship between Article XXIV of the GATT and other WTO-covered agreements. *Turkey – Textiles*, a dispute brought by India against Turkey, is one of the landmark disputes that examine this.

TURKEY – TEXTILES

The European Communities–Turkey Customs Union (1995) was the culmination of a long and protracted negotiation that commenced with the 'Ankara Agreement' of 1963.[99] The entry into force of the final phase of the customs union also entailed that the partner countries had to enforce common and harmonised rules for imports of goods from third countries. The European Communities had imposed QRs on certain textile items from countries including India, whereas Turkey did not have such restrictions. However, Turkey agreed to adopt the relevant EC regulations and, in particular, Regulation 3030 of 1993 and to enter into bilateral agreements with supplier countries. Turkey proposed a draft memorandum of understanding with India, which India rejected.[100] Turkey went ahead and imposed QRs on nineteen categories of textiles and clothing.

On 21 March 1996, India requested consultations with Turkey concerning Turkey's imposition of QRs. India claimed that those measures were inconsistent with Articles XI and XIII of the GATT 1994, as well as with Article 2 of the Agreement on Textiles and Clothing. Earlier, India had requested to be joined in the consultations between Hong Kong and Turkey on the same subject matter.

Can Turkey maintain such QRs consistently with its WTO obligations? Turkey's defence was Article XXIV of the GATT. The Panel, and later the Appellate Body that dealt with these issues in some depth, provide valuable clarifications. To an extent, the following paragraphs can be summarised as a rule book for WTO members that seek to negotiate and enter into regional trade agreements.

Turkey – Textiles *(Appellate Body)*

44. To determine the meaning and significance of the chapeau of paragraph 5, we must look at the text of the chapeau, and its context, which, for our purposes here, we consider to be paragraph 4 of Article XXIV.

45. First, in examining the text of the chapeau to establish its ordinary meaning, we note that the chapeau states that the provisions of GATT 1994 'shall not prevent' the formation of a customs union. ... Thus, the chapeau makes it clear that Article XXIV may, under certain conditions, justify the adoption of a measure which is inconsistent

[99] This is formally known as the Agreement establishing an Association between the European Economic Community and Turkey, signed 1963.

[100] S. Rajagopal, 'Recollections and Reflections of a Stakeholder in WTO Disputes', in Das and Nedumpara, *WTO Dispute Settlement at Twenty*, pp. 107–33, at p. 112.

(cont.)

with certain other GATT provisions, and may be invoked as a possible 'defence' to a finding of inconsistency.

46. Second in examining the text of the chapeau, we observe also that it states that the provisions of the GATT shall not prevent *'the formation of a customs union'*. This wording indicates that Article XXIV can justify the adoption of a measure which is inconsistent with certain other GATT provisions only if the measure is introduced upon the formation of a customs union, and only to the extent that the formation of the customs union would be prevented if the introduction of the measures were not allowed.

    [...]

48. Sub-paragraph 8(a)(i) of Article XXIV establishes the standard for the internal trade between constituent members in order to satisfy the definition of a 'customs union'. It requires the constituent members of a customs union to eliminate 'duties and other restrictive regulations of commerce' with respect to 'substantially all the trade' between them. Neither the GATT Contracting Parties nor the WTO Members have ever reached an agreement on the interpretation of the term 'substantially' in this provision. It is clear, though, that 'substantially all the trade' is not the same as all the trade, and also that 'substantially all the trade' is something considerably more than merely some of the trade. We note also that the terms of sub-paragraph 8(a)(i) provide that members of a customs union may maintain, where necessary, in their internal trade, certain restrictive regulations of commerce that are otherwise permitted under Articles XI through XV and under Article XX of the GATT 1994. Thus, we agree with the Panel that the terms of sub-paragraph 8(a)(i) offer 'some flexibility' to the constituent members of a customs union when liberalising their internal trade in accordance with this sub-paragraph. Yet we caution that the degree of 'flexibility' that sub-paragraph 8(a)(i) allows is limited by the requirement that 'duties and other restrictive regulations of commerce' be 'eliminated with respect to substantially all' internal trade.

49. Sub-paragraph 8(a)(ii) establishes the standard for the trade of constituent members *with third countries* in order to satisfy the definition of a 'customs union'. It requires the constituent members of a customs union to apply 'substantially the same' duties and other regulations of commerce to external trade with third countries. The constituent members of a customs union are thus required to apply a common external trade regime, relating to both duties and other regulations of commerce. However, sub-paragraph 8(a)(ii) does not require each constituent member of a customs union to apply the same duties and other regulations of commerce with respect to trade with third countries. Instead, it requires that *substantially the same* duties and other regulations of commerce shall be applied.

The Appellate Body noted in this case that the Panel referred to the chapeau of paragraph 5 of Article XXIV only in a passing and perfunctory way. According to the Appellate Body, the following language of the chapeau, viz. 'the provisions of this Agreement *shall not prevent*, as between the territories of the contracting parties, *the formation of a customs union ...; Provided* that' (emphasis original), indicates that the chapeau should have been central to the Panel's analysis.

Furthermore, the WTO panel assumed that the agreement between Turkey and the European Union was a 'customs union' within the meaning of Article XXIV of the GATT.[101] No GATT/WTO panel had hitherto examined the issue of whether a dispute settlement panel had the jurisdiction to assess the overall compatibility of a customs union with the requirements of Article XXIV. At best, such matters had been submitted to the examination of the Committee on Regional Trade. This specific issue was not appealed and the Appellate Body preferred to exercise judicial economy. However, the Appellate Body gave enough indications based on its earlier ruling in *India – Quantitative Restrictions* that the issue of examining the compatibility of customs unions or free trade agreements with Article XXIV was not beyond the jurisdiction of the panel.

The meaning of the term 'substantially all trade' was yet another critical issue in this matter. Turkey argued that had it not introduced the QRs on textile and clothing products from India that were at issue, the European Communities would have 'exclud[ed] these products from free trade within the Turkey/EC customs union'. According to Turkey, such an action might have been warranted to avoid trade diversion. Turkey further noted that its exports of these products accounted for 40 per cent of the total exports to the European Communities. Turkey expressed strong doubts about whether the requirement of Article XXIV:8(a)(i) that duties and other restrictive regulations of commerce be eliminated with respect to 'substantially all trade' between Turkey and the European Communities could be met if 40 per cent of Turkey's total exports to the EC were excluded. According to Turkey, it would be prevented from forming a customs union with the European Communities but for the QRs.

Turkey – Textiles *(Appellate Body)*

58. ... First, the party claiming the benefit of this defence must demonstrate that the measure at issue is introduced upon the formation of a customs union that fully meets the requirements of sub-paragraphs 8(a) and 5(a) of Article XXIV. And, second, that party must demonstrate that the formation of that customs union would be prevented if it were not allowed to introduce the measure at issue. Again, both these conditions must be met to have the benefit of the defence under Article XXIV.

---

[101] Appellate Body Report, *Turkey – Restrictions on Imports of Textiles and Clothing Products*, WT/DS34/AB/R, adopted 19 November 1999, para. 59.

2.6.1   Preferential Trade Agreements and Fragmentation of Law

Preferential trade agreements can also interact in multiple ways with the WTO legal system. Fragmentation of international trade rules is often a major concern raised by policymakers and the international trade law community.[102] One of the recent WTO cases to touch upon this matter is the *Peru – Additional Duty* dispute.

PERU – ADDITIONAL DUTY

Peru introduced a price range system (PRS) (*sistema de franja de precios*) for four categories of agricultural products (milk, maize, rice and sugar). According to the PRS, Peru's tariffs on these products could vary every fortnight as a function of historical world prices. The PRS system was apparently in conflict with the WTO Agreement on Agriculture, especially Article 4.2. Peru's price band was similar to a variable import levy and a minimum import price, which are prohibited under Article 4.2. However, Peru and Guatemala had agreed in a bilateral FTA that 'Peru may maintain its Price Range System'.[103] The FTA further provided that 'in the event of any inconsistency' between other agreements (such as the WTO Agreement) and FTA rules, the FTA rules 'shall prevail'.

In short, the question was whether Peru can rely upon the provisions of the Guatemala–Peru FTA to interpret the obligations under Article 4.2 of the AoA. In this regard, Peru relied upon Paragraph 9 of Annex 2.3 to the FTA and the International Law Commission's Article 20 (consent precluding the wrongfulness of an act) and Article 50 (which pertains to the loss of the right to invoke responsibility). Article 41 of the Vienna Convention provides that two parties may modify a multilateral treaty between themselves, under certain conditions, reflecting the *lex posterior* rule.

> ### *Peru – Additional Duty (Appellate Body)*
>
> 5.91. Peru contends that the Panel should have interpreted the term 'shall not maintain' in Article 4.2 of the Agreement on Agriculture in the light of the provisions of the FTA between Peru and Guatemala as allowing Peru to maintain the PRS. More specifically, Peru argues that paragraph 9 of Annex 2.3 to the FTA, providing that 'Peru may maintain its Price Range System' with regard to the imports of certain products, is relevant to the interpretation of Article 4.2 of the Agreement on Agriculture and Article II:1(b) of the GATT in accordance with Article 31(3)(a) and (c) of the Vienna Convention. Peru also contends that, according to ILC Article 20, Guatemala's approval and ratification of the FTA amounts to 'consent' precluding the wrongfulness of Peru's maintenance of the PRS, and that 'Guatemala's ratification of the FTA amounts to a waiver in the sense of Article 45(a) of the ILC Articles'.

---

[102] G. Shaffer and L. A. Winters, 'FTA Law in WTO Dispute Settlement: *Peru – Additional Duty* and the Fragmentation of Trade Law', *World Trade Law* (2017), 16(2), pp. 303–26, at p. 304.

[103] Guatemala–Peru Free Trade Agreement, signed on 6 December 2011, paragraph 9, Annex 2.3.

(cont.)

[. . .]

5.94. While context is a necessary element of an interpretative analysis under Article 31 of the Vienna Convention, its role and importance in an interpretative exercise depends on the clarity of plain textual meaning of the treaty terms. If the meaning of the treaty terms is difficult to discern, determining the ordinary meaning under Article 31 may require more reliance on the context and the object and purpose of the treaty and other elements considered 'together with the context' and the tools mentioned in Article 32. However, we do not see how, in an interpretative exercise under Article 31, elements considered 'together with context' can be used to reach the conclusion that the textual terms 'shall not maintain' in Article 4.2 of the Agreement on Agriculture should be read as 'may maintain' based on a particular provision found in the FTA. We do not consider that Article 31 can be used to develop interpretations based on asserted subsequent agreements or asserted 'relevant rules of international law applicable in the relations between the parties' under Article 31(3)(a) and (c) that appear to subvert the common intention of the treaty parties as reflected in the text of Article 4.2 and Article II:1(b).

5.95. Moreover, Peru clarified at the oral hearing that it is advocating an interpretation of Article 4.2 of the Agreement on Agriculture and Article II:1(b) of the GATT as permitting the PRS exclusively in the relations between Peru and Guatemala, who are parties to the FTA. Article 31(1) of the Vienna Convention states that '[a] treaty shall be interpreted' such that the object of the interpretative exercise is the treaty as a whole, not the treaty as it may apply between some of the parties. We thus understand that, with multilateral treaties such as the WTO covered agreements, the 'general rule of interpretation' in Article 31 of the Vienna Convention is aimed at establishing the ordinary meaning of the treaty reflecting the common intention of the parties to the treaty, and not just the intentions of some of the parties. While an interpretation of the treaty may in practice apply to the parties to the dispute, it must serve to establish the common intention of the parties to the treaty being interpreted.

The Appellate Body, based on the above analysis, did not consider that the textual terms 'shall not maintain' could be considered as 'may maintain' based on Paragraph 9 of Annex 2.3 to the FTA or the ILC articles. According to the Appellate Body, in order to be 'relevant' rules within the meaning of Article 31(3)(c) of the Vienna Convention, the rules of international law, including the FTA provision, should be 'agreements bearing specifically upon the interpretation of a treaty'.[104]

---

[104] Appellate Body Report, *Peru – Additional Duty*, para. 5.101.

2.6.2 Rules of Origin

Rules of origin are important criteria to determine the nationality of a product. They are especially important in implementing PTAs. If tariffs are applied on an MFN basis, the country of origin of the product is not of particular concern. However, the originating status of the good is a matter of significance in the context of PTAs. Under most PTAs, tariff concessions or other benefits are given only to parties to the agreement. Restrictive definitions were often used by countries to limit the grant of preferences only to partner countries or to attract investments. However, the determination of the origin of goods has become increasingly complex with the advent of globalisation.

The rise of transnational corporations and the fragmentation of production processes have resulted in a phenomenon known as 'global value chains'. In a world where several components of a good flow from different countries and territories, it is often difficult to identify the precise origin of the good concerned, necessitating the rules of origin. Traditionally, countries looked at two broadly recognised concepts: (a) did the product undergo substantial transformation in the exporting country? and (b) was there significant value addition? However, the concepts of 'substantial transformation' and 'significant value addition' are not entirely clear. In the ordinary sense, substantial transformation entails a product acquiring distinctive or unique features. In most cases, the concept is facts-relative and agreement-specific. What may amount to substantial transformation may vary from agreement to agreement. Therefore, unique preferential origin rules have come up in recent trade agreements. Some of the criteria include specified changes in tariff classification, undergoing specific manufacturing or processing operations, minimum operations, specified value-added requirements and so on. In addition, certain agreements provide product-specific rules of origin, for instance, the special rules of origin for textiles and apparels under the Trans-Pacific Partnership (TPP).[105]

Domestic sensitivities and trade protectionist concerns may also play an active role in the negotiations on rules of origin under most trade agreements.[106] For example, a regional trade partner may grant tariff benefits on pasta, but it can insist that the wheat flour required to make pasta is sourced internally and not from import sources. If this requirement is too cumbersome for the partner country, the other partner may insist on value addition criteria. For example, the parties can agree that for conferring originating status, the cost, insurance and freight value of the imported materials does not exceed X per cent of the total cost of the materials used in the production of the goods. Parties also sometimes exclude certain operations, such as packing, bottling, assembly, simple mixing, preservation and labelling from conferring origin. Therefore, it is not uncommon to find product-specific rules of origin in most regional trade agreements.

---

[105] The TPP has provided for the 'fiber-forward' and the 'yarn-forward' rule. See NAFTA, Chapter 5 Provisions for Specific Sectors, Textile and Apparel Products (US Customs and Border Protection, 2014), available at www.cbp.gov/trade/nafta/guide-customs-procedures/provisions-specific-sectors/textiles (accessed 21 December 2020).

[106] D. C. Lazaro and E. M. Medalla, 'Rules of Origin: Evolving Best Practices for RTAs/FTAs', Discussion Paper Series 2006-01 (Philippine Institute for Development Studies, January 2006), p. 3.

PTAs also provide for cumulation of rules of origin. Materials originating from, or working or processing in a PTA partner can count towards meeting the country of origin. Materials, inputs or parts imported from the identified countries will be treated as being of domestic origin for the purposes of preferential access.

Cumulation is of three specific types: bilateral cumulation; diagonal cumulation and full cumulation. In the case of *bilateral cumulation*, products imported from a bilateral partner and produced in accordance with the applicable rules of origin could qualify as an originating product of the other PTA partner. Under *diagonal cumulation*, originating materials from regional partners (for example, the Association of South East Asian Nations) to be further processed within a signatory to the regional grouping will be treated as originating from the exporting partner, provided the value addition requirement in the country of export is sufficiently met.[107] Finally, in respect of *full cumulation*, any manufacturing or processing activities undertaken within a regional grouping can be considered as qualifying content, irrespective of whether the concerned activity was good enough to confer originating status.

Few GATT or WTO negotiators or the countries paid attention to the discriminatory rules of origin issues. Although rules of origin issues can be and have been used as non-tariff barriers by some countries, only a few disputes have arisen in this area under the GATT or WTO. The preferential treatment under PTAs depends on the origin of the product, which is mostly based on the share of the content in the final product. The arbitrariness in deciding the share specification is coupled with the arbitrariness practised in the computation of this share.[108] Further, the increasing proliferation of PTAs is leading to varying rules of origin on different products depending on the source of origin. This phenomenon has been termed 'the spaghetti bowl phenomenon'.[109] However, in a world of criss-crossing rules of origin, harmonising such rules will soon be a pressing need.

Box 2.1 'Fiber-forward' and 'yarn-forward' rule

The 'yarn-forward' rule is a widely popular and well-established principle of establishing rule of origin. In the context of the TPP, the yarn used to form the fabric (which may later be used to produce wearing apparel or other textile articles) must originate in a CPTPP party. Thus, a wool shirt made in Mexico from fabric woven in Mexico of wool yarn imported from China would not be considered originating for special concession in Canada. In this case, the yarn does not originate within a CPTPP party.

---

[107] P. Bombarda and E. Gamberoni, 'Firm Heterogeneity, Rules of Origin, and Rules of Cumulation', *International Economic Review* (2013), 54, p. 307.

[108] J. Bhagwati, D. Greenway and A. Panagariya, 'Trading Preferentially: Theory and Policy', *Economic Journal* (1998), 108, p. 1138.

[109] J. Bhagwati, 'US Trade Policy: The Infatuation with FTAs', Discussion Paper Series 726 (Department of Economics, Columbia University, April 1995), p. 4.

> **Box 2.1 (cont.)**
>
> On the other hand, if the Chinese wool fibre is imported into Mexico and spun into wool yarn in Mexico, which is then used to produce the wool fabric and then a shirt, that shirt would be considered originating within a CPTPP party.
>
> **To Go Further**
>
> United States–Korea Free Trade Agreement, Annex A4 (revised 2014), available at ustr.gov/trade-agreements (accessed 21 December 2020).

2.7   Conclusion

Tariffs have traditionally been collected for a variety of purposes. While generating revenue is a key consideration, tariffs are also used for protecting domestic industries and for pursuing a unilateral political or economic agenda. Tariff negotiations at the GATT/WTO and in other preferential trade agreements have yielded substantial tariff reductions over the last several decades. Most of these tariff reductions are now the subject of tariff commitments under multilateral or preferential trade agreements. The tariff bindings reflected in the Schedules of Concessions are an integral part of the WTO Treaty (as well as that of other trade agreements) and are to be interpreted as an operative part of the treaty using the rules of the Vienna Convention.

No less significant is the elimination of quotas on most items, barring a few agricultural tariff lines at the WTO. Discretionary import licensing measures are also in decline. WTO members seldom rely on QRs, even on balance-of-payments grounds. At the same time, the WTO has not achieved much success in the harmonisation of rules of origin, which, contrary to expectations, have become more complex as well as more difficult to administer. Country- and product-specific rules of origin are often seen in preferential trade agreements.

2.8   Summary

- Import tariffs are the most common and traditional form of restriction on international trade.
- Each WTO member maintains a schedule of tariff concessions which are also known as bound commitments. These commitments can be suspended only in situations where an importing member applies emergency actions or takes recourse to general exceptions or security exceptions. In addition, an importing member is also permitted to take anti-dumping or countervailing duty measures in conformity with Article VI of the GATT 1994 and the respective covered agreements.

- WTO members use the Harmonized Commodity and Coding System developed by the World Customs Organization for tariff classification.
- Import tariffs are also called border taxes since they are applied at the border. Some of the internal taxes are also collected at the border; however, the border tax adjustment should be applied consistently with the non-discrimination principle under Article III:2.
- There is a general prohibition of quantitative restrictions. Restrictions should be transparent and should be in the nature of duties, taxes or other charges.
- Quantitative restrictions, whenever applied, shall be applied in a non-discriminatory manner.
- Preferential trade agreements are considered an exception to the MFN principle under Article I:1 of the GATT. However, members are required to meet the requirements of Article XXIV by eliminating duties and other restrictive regulations of commerce between the constituent territories of the customs union or the free trade area.
- A WTO member seeking to justify a GATT-inconsistent measure should establish two cumulative conditions in order to avail the defence under Article XXIV: (i) the measure at issue is introduced upon the formation of a customs union or FTA, and (ii) the customs union or FTA would be prevented if the member were not allowed to introduce the concerned measure.

2.9   Review Questions

1 What is the proper characterisation of a variable import duty under the GATT? Can it be considered as an 'ordinary customs duty' or 'other duties and charges'?

2 Are export duties covered under the discipline of the GATT?

3 Does the GATT permit border tax adjustments? What principles need to be followed in implementing a regime for border taxes?

4 Who bears the burden of proof in WTO complaints which may possibly involve a border tax adjustment defence? (See *China – Autos (US)* and *India – Additional Duties.*)

5 Explain the importance of rules of origin. Why do they gain a special significance in the context of PTAs? Explain the variance found between such rules.

6 What is the meaning of 'substantially all trade' in relation to free trade agreements? Can partial-scope trade agreements be justified under Article XXIV?

2.10   Exercise

The Republic of Lohapur is a WTO member and its economy is heavily dependent on steel, coal and cement production. In the early 2000s, Lohapur's industrial pollution levels rose drastically. As a result, the government introduced a national carbon reduction programme to disincentivise carbon-intensive industrial processes under the Clean Energy Act 2017. The Act authorises the Environment Protection Board (EPB) to recommend the imposition of a tax on carbon dioxide from industrial production. Steel, in particular, is a big contributor to global carbon emissions.

The tax on carbon emissions for steel was proposed to be collected on the basis of carbon emissions as calculated and certified by the (EPB). In the case of imports, carbon dioxide emissions are considered difficult to ascertain. Lohapur provided an opportunity to foreign exporters to demonstrate the exact amount of carbon emissions in steel production. Given the multiple production lines in the steel industry, this information was seldom provided. Hence, the average carbon dioxide emissions per tonne of steel produced in Lohapur is taken as the standard emission rate for imported steel. It was found that the average carbon dioxide emission is 1.7 tonnes of carbon dioxide per tonne of steel in Lohapur (the international benchmarks are around 1 tonne/per tonne of steel). It is widely reported that the coking coal extracted from the mining sites of Lohapur has a higher content of coal, sulphur and other impurities. Lohapur's EPB decided to impose the carbon tax at the rate of US$17 per tonne of steel on imported steel, the same tax the EPB had recommended for carbon content in domestic steel. The carbon tax is collected, along with other applicable custom duties, at the point of custom clearance. Lohapur's bound rate of duty (specific duty) on steel is US$20 per tonne, whereas the MFN basic customs duty is US$10 per tonne of steel.

This border tax is applied in addition to the ordinary customs duty on steel.

The kingdom of Ahanastan, a WTO member, exports 50 per cent of its domestic steel production to Lohapur. According to industry sources, the steel from Ahanastan has carbon emissions ranging from 1 to 1.5 tonnes of carbon dioxide per tonne of steel. Due to increased costs from the carbon border tax, steel manufacturers from Ahanastan have witnessed a sharp decline in their exports. The Kingdom of Ahanastan has filed a WTO dispute against the Republic of Lohapur, claiming a violation of Article II:1(a) and (b), Article II:2(a) and Article III:2 of the GATT. Ahanastan argues that Lohapur has violated its commitments on steel by imposing the carbon tax at the border in addition to its ordinary customs duty.

As a lawyer representing the Republic of Lohapur, how would you defend its measures? On the flipside, what would be your arguments if you were representing Ahanastan? You may also focus on issues such as the burden of proof of the relevant parties.

FURTHER READING

Bhala, R. and Gantz, D. A., 'WTO Case Review 2009', *Arizona Journal of International and Comparative Law* (2010), 27(1), pp. 85–190.

Dasgupta, J., '*India – Additional Import Duties*: Tax Reforms via WTO', in A. Das and J. J. Nedumpara (eds.), *WTO Dispute Settlement at Twenty: Insiders' Reflections on India's Participation* (Singapore: Springer, 2016), pp. 179–93.

Hoda, A., *Tariff Negotiations and Renegotiations under the GATT and the WTO*, 2nd ed. (Cambridge University Press, 2019).

Metcalf, G. and Weisbach, D. A., 'The Design of a Carbon Tax', University of Chicago Public Law and Legal Theory Working Paper 254 (2009).

Shaffer, G. and Winters, A., 'FTA Law in WTO Dispute Settlement: *Peru – Additional Duty* and the Fragmentation of Trade Law', *World Trade Review* (2017), 16(2), pp. 303–26.

3 Trade in Agriculture

Table of Contents

Highlights

- Agriculture is a sensitive sector and has been one of the most contentious areas of international trade. Agriculture remained as an outlier to other disciplines of the GATT for several decades.
- The 'three pillars' of the Agreement on Agriculture (AoA) are market access, domestic support and export competition.
- As part of the market access commitments, members were required to convert all their non-tariff measures into tariff equivalents. In addition, the tariffs were subject to a reduction commitment over a period of time.
- Members are permitted to impose a special safeguard duty on selected products, subject to meeting the volume or price triggers specified in Article 5 of the AoA.

- Under export competition, members were permitted to reserve the right to provide export subsidies. However, these were also subject to reduction commitments. The export subsidy disciplines in the AoA are different from the provisions of the SCM Agreement.
- Establishing disciplines on domestic support measures is one of the major contributions of the Uruguay Round. Based on the effects of the subsidies on trade distortion, domestic support is classified into amber box, blue box and green box under the AoA.
- Green box subsidies have no or minimal trade-distorting effects.
- The concept of domestic support is captured by the Aggregate Measurement of Support (AMS). The AMS was subject to reduction commitments. Measures subject to AMS calculation are termed amber box subsidies.
- Direct payments associated with production-limiting programmes (blue box) are excluded from AMS calculation.
- *De minimis* provision for AMS permits exclusion of product-specific and non-product-specific support not exceeding 10 per cent of respective current output value, for developing countries.

3.1   Introduction

Agriculture has been one of the principal areas of contention in the multilateral trading system. Agriculture is often referred to as the 'multifunctional' sector. Multifunctionality refers to the overall importance of agriculture, primarily the non-trade benefits of agriculture for a community.[1] A country may wish to treat its agriculture sector differently for various reasons, including, for example, the maintenance of food security, increasing price stability and the preservation of the environment. While a 'fair and market-oriented agricultural trading system' is an important goal, agricultural reform can also have adverse impact on vulnerable populations in several countries in Asia, Africa and Latin America. The quest for providing a balance between various trade and non-trade concerns lies at the heart of agriculture negotiations.

The Uruguay Round Agreement on Agriculture (AoA) introduces itself as part of a 'reform process'.[2] An important objective of the AoA is to provide for substantial progressive reductions in agricultural support, in an equitable way, having regard to non-trade concerns, including food security and the need to protect the environment.[3] The AoA also adopted a calibrated approach to regulating domestic support through disciplines based on the nature and extent of market distortion.

---

[1] F. Smith, '"Multifunctionality" and "Non-Trade Concerns" in the Agriculture Negotiations', *Journal of International Economic Law* (2000), 3(4), p. 707; Organisation for Economic Co-operation and Development, *Multifunctionality: Towards an Analytical Framework* (Paris: OECD, 2001), p. 76.

[2] Agreement on Agriculture, 15 April 1994, Marrakesh Agreement Establishing the World Trade Organization, Annex 1A, 1867 UNTS 410, Preamble, para. 1.

[3] AoA, Preamble, paras. 3, 6.

This chapter discusses the existing disciplines under the AoA, with particular emphasis on the 'three pillars', namely, market access, domestic support, and export competition. It also discusses some of the subsequent developments, including the decisions adopted in various WTO Ministerial Conferences.

3.2   Negotiating History

Agriculture trade was affected by discriminatory trade policies for decades. Tariff quotas, tariff peaks and tariff escalations were rampant in agriculture trade even after the formation of the GATT 1947. In fact, agriculture was effectively excluded from GATT disciplines until the Uruguay Round (1986–94). The GATT contracting parties were permitted to use export subsidies and import restrictions, with the result that the agriculture trade was replete with trade barriers and other distortions on a scale that was uncommon to the merchandise trade. Efforts to undertake agriculture reforms started with the 1982 GATT Ministerial Meeting.[4]

In 1982, long before the launch of the Uruguay Round, the OECD Ministerial Council adopted a declaration indicating that 'agriculture trade should be more fully integrated into and within the open and multilateral trading system' and agreeing that multilateral negotiations should address 'adjustment in domestic policies'.[5] The 1986 Punta del Este Declaration, which launched the Uruguay Round, stated that 'there is an urgent need to bring more discipline and predictability to world agricultural trade'.[6] The Ministerial Declaration also called for the need to correct and prevent 'restrictions and distortions including those related to structural surpluses'.[7] The Cairns Group – a group of developed and developing countries with export interests in agricultural products – pushed hard for ambitious agriculture reforms. These initiatives led to the 1987 Ministerial Declaration. The scope of reforms was to include measures meant to prevent increases in excess supplies by reducing guaranteed prices and other types of production incentives.[8]

Political considerations and transitional issues delayed any breakthrough in negotiations between the US and the EU – the two principal parties – over the proper approach to trade liberalisation.[9] The 1991 'Dunkel Draft' represented an attempt at a compromise aimed at breaking the impasse between the US and the EU.

The US and the EU reached a bilateral agreement in November 1992, known as the Blair House Agreement.[10] These commitments included reducing domestic support by 20 per cent

---

[4] World Trade Organization, Ministerial Declaration of 29 November 1983, GATT Doc. L/5424, para. 7(v).

[5] D. J. Blair, *Trade Negotiations in the OECD: Structures, Institutions and States* (London and New York: Kegan Paul, 1993), pp. 120–1.

[6] World Trade Organization, Ministerial Declaration on the Uruguay Round of Punta del Este, Uruguay, 20 September 1986, p. 6, available at www.wto.org/gatt_docs/English/SULPDF/91240152.pdf (accessed 21 December 2020).

[7] Punta del Este Declaration, p. 6.   [8] Punta del Este Declaration, p. 6.

[9] Trebilcock et al., *Regulation of International Trade*, p. 448.

[10] Trebilcock et al., *Regulation of International Trade*, p. 450, fn. 93.

in terms of the Aggregate Measurement of Support (AMS) (a concept that will be explained later in this chapter), with 1986–88 as a base period, and reducing export subsidies with the base period as defined in the Dunkel Draft. Furthermore, income support to farmers was to be exempted from domestic support reduction commitments, if given on only a limited part of total production of each farm.[11]

The AoA, in terms of its general structure and basic principles, reflects the Dunkel Draft. The AoA requires binding commitments in the following areas: market access, domestic support and export competition, with negotiations aimed at progressive liberalisation. With respect to specific commitments, the Agreement is largely based upon the Blair House Agreement, as modified by the 7 December 1993 meeting between US Trade Representative Micky Kantor and EU Trade Commissioner Leon Brittan.

3.3   Relationship with Other Agreements

The relationship between the AoA and other multilateral trade agreements is given in Article 21.1 of the AoA. In particular, certain disciplines of the AoA have significant overlap with the GATT and the SCM Agreement.

> ### *AoA, Article 21.1*
>
> The provisions of GATT 1994 and of other Multilateral Trade Agreements in Annex 1A to the WTO Agreement shall apply subject to the provisions of this Agreement.

This relationship was examined in greater details in *EC – Bananas III*, discussed below.

EC – BANANAS III

This case was a WTO complaint brought by Ecuador, Guatemala, Honduras, Mexico and the United States against the European Communities' (EC) banana regime. The EC had operated a complex regime, including the use of tariff rate quotas (TRQ) on banana imports from third countries.

The complainants challenged the country-specific allocation of tariff quota shares to the African, Caribbean and Pacific (ACP) and the Banana Framework Agreement (BFA) countries as inconsistent with the tariff quota allocation rules of Article XIII of the GATT 1994. While quotas are generally prohibited under Article XI of the GATT, TRQs are permitted under Article XIII, subject to the condition that the distribution of tariff quotas reflects 'as closely as possible the shares various Members must be expected to obtain' in the

---

[11] 'United States Department of Agriculture Statement on US–EC Accord on Oil Seeds and the Uruguay Round', *International Trade Reporter* (Washington, DC: Bureau of National Affairs, 1992), 9, p. 2028; T. P. Stewart, *The GATT Uruguay Round: A Negotiating History (1986–1992)*, 4 vols. (Deventer: Kluwer Law and Taxation Publishers, 1993), p. 7.

absence of restrictions.[12] One of the goals of the AoA is to convert the quota restrictions into tariff measures. On the interaction between the GATT and the AoA, the *EC – Bananas III* Panel made the following observations:[13]

EC – Bananas *III (Panel)*

7.122. ... It is clear from Article 21.1 that the provisions of the Agreement on Agriculture prevail over GATT and the other Annex 1A agreements. But there must be a provision of the Agreement on Agriculture that is relevant in order for this priority provision to apply. It is not the case that Article 21.1 of the Agreement on Agriculture means that no GATT/WTO rules apply to trade in agricultural products unless they are explicitly incorporated into the Agreement on Agriculture. We note that one of the purposes of the Agreement on Agriculture is to bring agriculture under regular GATT/WTO disciplines.

The AoA has a relationship with several WTO-covered agreements. Since 'subsidies' constitute a key pillar of the AoA, it has significant interactions with the SCM Agreement. To an extent, the AoA has been carved out from the SCM Agreement, especially in relation to subsidies.[14] This mutual interaction can lead to certain complexities, especially since both the AoA and the SCM Agreement provide different disciplines for subsidies, especially export subsides. But they still interact, as our subsequent discussions on *US – Upland Cotton* will demonstrate.

SCM Agreement, Article 3: Prohibition

3.1 Except as provided in the Agreement on Agriculture, the following subsidies, within the meaning of Article 1, shall be prohibited:
   (a) subsidies contingent, in law or in fact, whether solely or as one of several other conditions, upon export performance, including those illustrated in Annex I;
   (b) subsidies contingent, whether solely or as one of several other conditions, upon the use of domestic over imported goods.
3.2 A Member shall neither grant nor maintain subsidies referred to in paragraph 1.

---

[12] Appellate Body Reports, *European Communities – Regime for the Importation, Sale and Distribution of Bananas – Second Recourse to Article 21.5 of the DSU by Ecuador*, WT/DS27/AB/RW2/ECU, Corr.1, adopted 11 December 2008, *European Communities – Regime for the Importation, Sale and Distribution of Bananas – Recourse to Article 21.5 of the DSU by the United States*, WT/DS27/AB/RW/USA, Corr.1, adopted 22 December 2008, para. 338.

[13] Panel Report, *EC – Bananas III*, para. 7.122.

[14] R. Lawrence and N. Stankard, Should Export Subsidies Be Treated Differently? (mimeo, 2005, on file with authors).

The AoA also includes provisions on domestic support and export subsidies. It is instructive to refer to Article 10.1 of the AoA.

AoA, Article 10: Prevention of Circumvention of Export Subsidy Commitments

10.1. Export subsidies not listed in paragraph 1 of Article 9 shall not be applied in a manner which results in, or which threatens to lead to, circumvention of export subsidy commitments; nor shall non-commercial transactions be used to circumvent such commitments.

US – UPLAND COTTON

The relationship between the two was addressed in *US – Upland Cotton*. In this case, Brazil challenged the US cotton support programme on the ground that the US cotton subsidies were depressing international cotton prices and were unfairly affecting or influencing the value and quantity of Brazil's exports. The nature of support provided by the US included marketing loan payments, direct payments, counter-cyclical programmes, crop insurance and export guarantee. The Appellate Body interpreted Article 21.1 of the AoA to mean that the provisions of the GATT 1994 and of other multilateral trade agreements in Annex 1A apply, 'except to the extent that the Agreement on Agriculture contains specific provisions dealing specifically with the same matter'.[15] The analysis started with the AoA, followed by the SCM Agreement and, finally, the GATT.

The WTO Panel in this case noted that it had to decide initially whether the US programmes were consistent with the export subsidy provisions of the AoA and, if necessary, to conduct an analysis under the relevant provisions of the SCM Agreement and the GATT 1994. The Appellate Body reviewed this approach in the appeal as follows:

US – Upland Cotton *(Appellate Body)*

532. ... where, for example, the domestic support provisions of the Agreement on Agriculture would prevail in the event that an explicit carve-out or exemption from the disciplines in Article 3.1(b) of the SCM Agreement existed in the text of the Agreement on Agriculture. Another situation would be where it would be impossible for a Member to comply with its domestic support obligations under the Agreement on Agriculture and the Article 3.1(b) prohibition simultaneously. Another situation might be where there is an explicit authorization in the text of the Agreement on Agriculture that would authorize a measure that, in the absence of such an express authorization, would be prohibited by Article 3.1(b) of the SCM Agreement.

---

[15] Appellate Body Report, *United States – Subsidies on Upland Cotton*, WT/DS267/AB/R, adopted 21 March 2005, para. 532.

The AoA also has an important overlap with GATT Article XI. Article XI prohibits quantitative restrictions on trade, subject to certain exceptions. Some of these exceptions are pertinent for agricultural products. With respect to agricultural products, Article XI:2(c)(i)–(iii) of the GATT permits limited use of otherwise outlawed measures. Some of these measures seek to protect farmers or the processing industry from exigencies such as critical shortage of foodstuffs, temporary surplus of perishable commodities or other vagaries of weather and nature.[16] This issue discussed later in this chapter, in the context of *Indonesia – Import Licensing Regimes*.

Safeguard measures are also permissible under the AoA. The following section deals specifically with special safeguard measures. Agricultural products are also subject to the traditional safeguard actions under the GATT (Article XIX). The WTO dispute in *Korea – Dairy*[17] is an example of a safeguard measure taken on an agricultural product addressed exclusively under Article XIX of the GATT and the Agreement on Safeguards.[18] In other words, safeguard actions, other than special safeguards under Article 5 of the AoA, shall be governed by Article XIX of the GATT and the Agreement on Safeguards.

In conclusion, an examination of the WTO compatibility of agricultural support measures must not end with an analysis of the provisions of the AoA. The measure may have to meet the standards under other multilateral agreements unless the latter is specifically pre-empted or excluded by AoA provisions.[19]

3.4   Market Access

In order to understand the disciplines of the AoA on market access, it is important to know the product coverage of the Agreement. Article 2, read with Annex 1 to the AoA, indicates the product coverage of the Agreement arranged by the customs classification or the Harmonized System (HS) Code.[20] The product coverage relates to Chapters 1–24, other than fish and fish products, under the Harmonized System, and thirteen other categories. These additional thirteen categories are mentioned under Annex 1 of the AoA. The Panel in *Canada – Dairy* had to determine whether butter, cheese and milk fell within the ambit of the AoA. The Panel observed that the agricultural products set

---

[16] Panel Report, *Indonesia – Import Licensing Regimes*.

[17] Panel Report, *Korea – Definitive Safeguard Measure on Imports of Certain Dairy Products*, WT/DS98/R, Corr.1, adopted 12 January 2000, as modified by Appellate Body Report WT/DS98/AB/R.

[18] Korea could not invoke the SSG provisions of Art. 5 of the AoA in this case. Therefore, to the extent that its domestic industry was being seriously injured by increased imports, Korea had to impose a safeguard measure consistent with the Agreement on Safeguards. Panel Report, *Korea – Dairy*, para. 4.54.

[19] M. Matsushita et al., *The World Trade Organization: Law, Practice, and Policy*, 3rd ed. (Oxford University Press, 2015), p. 261.

[20] Current Situation of Schedules of WTO Members, Revision, G/MA/W/23/Rev.9.

out in Annex 1 included the products at issue (under HS, Chapter 4) and would thus be covered under the AoA.[21]

Members may regulate market access for agricultural products under the AoA through multiple ways. This may be achieved through imposition of tariffs, by providing for TRQs or special safeguard duty (SSG). Part III and Annex 5 of the AoA are the main provisions governing market access.

3.4.1 Tariffs

Non-tariff measures in agriculture include import licensing measures, voluntary export restraints or other requirements to export or import through State trading enterprises, to name a few. Tariffication refers to the process by which non-tariff import barriers are converted into their tariff equivalents.[22] The integration of the agricultural sector into the rules-based multilateral trading system was achieved through the tariffication of agricultural import barriers. This key obligation of tariffication and market access is provided in Article 4.2 of the AoA. It forbids the use of 'any measures of the kind which have been required to be converted into ordinary custom duties'.[23] The exceptions to this principle are those measures that are justified under the special safeguard provisions of Article 5 and the special treatment provisions of Annex 5 to the AoA. Footnote 1 to Article 4.2 of the AoA contains a further exception to tariffication – that is, measures maintained under balance-of-payment provisions[24] or other general, non-agriculture-specific provisions of the GATT 1994 or of other multilateral agreements in Annex 1A to the WTO Agreement.

For the purpose of completing a draft schedule of concessions and commitments, the GATT Secretariat had issued a provisional document entitled 'Modalities for the Establishment of Specific Binding Commitments under the Reform Programme'.[25] Annex 3 provided for the calculation of tariff equivalents and related provisions. Paragraph 2 of Annex 3 provided that the calculation of tariff equivalents shall be made

---

[21] Panel Report, *Canada – Measures Affecting the Importation of Milk and the Exportation of Dairy Products*, WT/DS103/R, WT/DS113/R, adopted 27 October 1999, as modified by the Appellate Body Report WT/DS103/AB/R, WT/DS113/AB/R, para. 7.18.

[22] The WTO argues that there is 'a solid economic rationale' for the choice of tariffs over non-tariff barriers. The fact that non-tariff barriers result in 'quota rents' particularly encourages domestic petitioners to engage in lobbying activities for putting in place such barriers. See World Trade Organization, *Annual Report 1998* (Geneva: WTO Publications, 1998), p. 39.

[23] Fn. 1 to Art. 4.2 gives a non-exhaustive list of the type of measures that have to be converted into ordinary customs duties. They include quantitative import restrictions, variable import levies, minimum import prices, discretionary import licensing, non-tariff measures maintained through State-trading enterprises, voluntary export restraints and similar border measures other than ordinary customs duties, whether or not the measures are maintained under country-specific derogations from the provisions of the GATT 1947.

[24] Panel Report, *India – Quantitative Restrictions*, para. 5.241.

[25] Note by the Chairman of the Market Access Group, 'Modalities for the Establishment of Specific Binding Commitments under the Reform Programme', MTN.GNG/MA/W/24, 20 December 1993.

using the actual difference between internal and external prices in a transparent manner, using data, data sources, and so on. Thus, members had the incentive to opt for periods for which the highest internal prices coincided with the lowest external prices. This was fully reflected in the selection of the years 1986–88 to serve as the base period for market access commitments.[26] The base period for tariffication is considered to be a 'generous' choice, since world market prices for a number of important agricultural products during 1986–88 were notably low compared to longer-run averages and world market prices.[27] The rationale behind tariffication was to convert the non-tariff barriers into tariffs that provided an equivalent level of protection. However, several members over-estimated the levels of protection offered by non-tariff barriers in order to obtain a higher operative level of base customs duty. Such an approach is captured by the phrase 'dirty tariffication'.

During the Uruguay Round, developed country members agreed to reduce tariffs over a six-year period by an average of 36 per cent, with a minimum reduction of 15 per cent for each product. Developing countries agreed to reduce tariffs over a ten-year period by an average of 24 per cent, with a minimum reduction of 10 per cent for each product. Least developed countries were not required to make tariff reduction commitments.

3.4.1.1   Quotas and Other Border Measures in the AoA

The text of Article XI:1 of the GATT provides a general prohibition on quantitative restrictions. In other words, border restrictions have to take a more transparent form and should be in the nature of duties, taxes or other charges.[28]

Agricultural products are also often subject to price band or price range systems, which are designed to insulate agricultural products from the vagaries of international price movements. Such systems generally operate on the basis of a floor price and a reference price.[29] In *Chile – Price Band System*, Chile determined the actual tariff applied on certain agricultural products by using a price band based on the fluctuating world prices of the concerned agriculture commodities.[30] Argentina, the complainant in this dispute, contended that the Chilean measure was a 'variable import levy', a 'minimum import price' or a 'similar border measure other than ordinary customs duties'. In other words, the price band mechanism impeded the transmission of international price movements to the domestic market. The Appellate Body also indicated that Article 4 'is appropriately viewed as the legal vehicle for requiring the conversion

---

[26] M. G. Desta, *The Law of International Trade in Agricultural Products* (London: Kluwer Law International, 2002), p. 73.

[27] S. Tangermann, 'Implementation of the Uruguay Round Agreement on Agriculture by Major Developed Countries', UNCTAD/ITD/16, 3 October 1995, p. 5.

[28] GATT Panel Report, *Japan – Trade in Semi-Conductors*, L/6309, adopted 4 May 1988, BISD 35S/116.

[29] E.g. Appellate Body Report, *Peru – Additional Duty*.

[30] Panel Report, *Chile – Price Band System and Safeguard Measures Relating to Certain Agricultural Products*, WT/DS207/R, adopted 23 October 2002, as modified by Appellate Body Report WT/DS207/AB/R.

into ordinary customs duties of certain market access barriers affecting imports of agricultural products'.[31]

The overlap between the provisions of Article XI:1 of the GATT 1994 and Article 4.2 of the AoA raises certain interpretative issues. As the Panel in *Korea – Various Measures on Beef* noted, 'a violation of Article XI of GATT and its Ad Note relating to state-trading operations would necessarily constitute a violation of Article 4.2 of the Agreement on Agriculture and its footnote which refers to non-tariff measures maintained through state-trading enterprises'.[32] This relationship was examined in *Indonesia – Import Licensing Regimes* (more popularly referred to as *Indonesia – Horticulture*).

INDONESIA – IMPORT LICENSING REGIMES

The co-complainants, New Zealand and the United States, challenged a total of eighteen measures concerning Indonesia's import licensing regime, which imposed, among others, restrictions such as limited application windows for import licences, 80 per cent realisation requirement, storage ownership and capacity requirement and use, sale and distribution requirements. The measures affected fruits, vegetables, flowers, dried fruits, vegetables, juices and animal products including beef and poultry. These measures were challenged under Article XI:1 of the GATT 1994 and Article 4.2 of the AoA.

Indonesia relied upon Article XI:2(c)(ii) of the GATT 1994 to exclude measure 4 (Harvest period requirement), measure 7 (Reference prices for chillies and shallots) and measure 16 (Beef reference price) from the scope of Article XI:1.[33] In Indonesia's view, these measures were necessary to remove a temporary surplus of horticultural products, animals and animal products in its domestic market, as provided in Article XI:2(c)(ii).

Indonesia – Import Licensing Regimes *(Panel)*

7.60. ... Article XI:2(c) by its terms concerns agricultural products and therefore does not qualify under the exclusion for general, non-agriculture-specific provisions. Therefore, Indonesia cannot rely upon Article XI:2(c)(ii) of the GATT 1994. This is confirmed by Article 21 of the Agreement on Agriculture, which provides that '[t]he provisions of GATT 1994', including Article XI:2(c)(ii) of the GATT 1994, *'shall apply subject to the provisions of this Agreement'*. Accordingly, we conclude that Indonesia cannot rely upon Article XI:2(c)(ii) of the GATT 1994 to exclude Measures 4, 7 and 16 from the scope of Article XI:1 of the GATT 1994 because, with respect to agricultural measures, Article XI:2(c) has been rendered inoperative by Article 4.2 of the Agreement on Agriculture. (Emphasis supplied)

---

[31] Appellate Body Report, *Chile – Price Band System and Safeguard Measures Relating to Certain Agricultural Products*, WT/DS207/AB/R, adopted 23 October 2002.

[32] Panel Report, *Korea – Various Measures on Beef*, para. 732.

[33] Panel Report, *Indonesia – Import Licensing Regimes*, para. 7.60.

In essence, the conflict between Article XI:2(c) of the GATT and Article 4.2 of the AoA was ruled in favour of the AoA. The systemic question is whether Article XI:2(c) is the only provision that has been rendered inoperative in relation to the AoA. In any case, this dispute has far-reaching implications for WTO members that maintain temporary quantitative restrictions.[34]

3.4.2 Tariff Rate Quotas

As discussed earlier, quantitative restrictions are prohibited under the GATT. However, several quantitative restrictions were replaced with tariffs having a similar effect during the Uruguay Round. Several countries, even now, maintain TRQs on agricultural products such as cereals, fruits, meat, cotton and sugar. Under the AoA, forty-three members have reserved the right to impose a total of 1,425 TRQs.[35]

A TRQ is the quota of imports that is allowed to enter a country at below the normal tariff rates. Products imported within the quota are charged a lower tariff, while imports above the quota incur a higher tariff.[36] To give an illustration, in relation to the banana regime, the EC maintained the tariff quota of 2.2 million tonnes in its Schedule. In 1995, the EC autonomously expanded this quota by 353,000 upon the enlargement of the EC. In this exercise, the EC's banana regime differentiated between ACP countries and Latin American bananas. A detailed explanation of the EC banana regime is provided in Box 3.1.

Box 3.1 TRQs and the European Union banana regime

The *EC – Bananas* dispute is perhaps one of the most controversial, complex and convoluted disputes in WTO history. From the founding of the EEC until 1993, the EC member States maintained independent banana import regimes. Each of the twelve countries within the EC had its own import regime for bananas. Bananas were not eligible for free circulation within the Community. Some countries (Irish Republic, Denmark, Luxembourg, Belgium, Netherlands) imposed a 20 per cent duty on bananas, whereas others (France, Greece, Italy, Portugal, Spain, UK) imposed a duty alongside a quota. Germany provided a free market system and did not impose tariffs. The objective of the EC banana regime was to provide preferential access to the bananas exported by ACP countries, which were the former colonies of the European Communities.

---

[34] J. J. Nedumpara and P. Bhardwaj, 'Trade Disputes and the Agriculture Policies in the Developing World: Time to Claw Back the Development Space under the WTO', *Global Trade and Customs Journal* (2019), 14(7–8), pp. 343–51.

[35] World Trade Organization, Agriculture Negotiations briefing document, 'The Issues, and Where We Are Now' (updated 1 December 2004), available at www.wto.org/English/tratop_e/agric_e/negs_bkgrnd00_contents_e.htm (accessed 21 December 2020).

[36] United Nations, 'Dispute Settlement: World Trade Organization, 3.15 Agriculture', available at https://unctad.org/en/Docs/edmmisc232add32_en.pdf (accessed 21 December 2020).

Box 3.1 (cont.)

The Lomé IV Convention, signed in 1989, allowed imports of bananas from ACP countries, duty-free.[37] Under Protocol 5 of this convention, the EEC had committed to maintain the traditional advantage of ACP banana suppliers in their market.

On 1 July 1993, the EEC introduced a common organisation of the market in bananas (COMB)[38] replacing the various banana import systems of the member States. Title IV of this regulation discussed banana trading arrangements with third countries. It distinguished four categories of suppliers: traditional imports from ACP countries; non-traditional imports from ACP countries; imports from non-ACP countries; and EEC bananas.

Traditional ACP suppliers were allowed to supply bananas up to a maximum quantity fixed for each of these countries – this collectively amounted to 857,700 tonnes. Imports of non-traditional ACP bananas and bananas from third countries were subject to a tariff quota of 2 million tonnes[39] (increased in 1994 to 2.1 million tonnes and to 2.2 million tonnes in 1995). ACP bananas (from Côte d'Ivoire, Cameroon, Somalia, Cape Verde, St Lucia, Jamaica, Belize, St Vincent and the Grenadines, Dominica, Surinam and Grenada) entered at zero duty within this quota, while third-country bananas were subject to a tariff of 100 ECUs per tonne. For imports above this quota, a duty of 750 ECUs per tonne was prescribed for ACP countries and 850 ECUs per tonne for third countries (see Figure 3.1).

Although the share of bananas from ACP countries was small (less than 10.0 per cent), the operators who marketed Community or ACP bananas received a 30.0 per cent share, while the traders of non-ACP or dollar bananas received 66.5 per cent of the TRQ. This necessitated traders of dollar bananas to purchase market share from the traders of ACP or Community bananas. The remaining 3.5 per cent was for new EC operators.

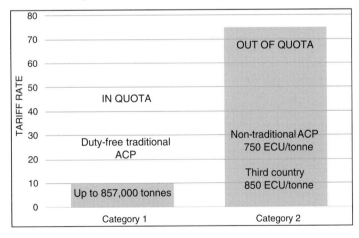

Figure 3.1 EC banana regime import quotas

---

[37] Lomé IV Convention, Art. 168(1).   [38] Council Regulation (EEC) 404/93.

[39] Council Regulation (EEC) 404/93, Art. 18.

Box 3.1 (cont.)

Five Latin American countries (Colombia, Costa Rica, Guatemala, Nicaragua and Venezuela – countries exporting dollar bananas) filed a complaint against the EC in 1993, widely known as *EC – Bananas II*. The GATT Panel ruled against the EC, but the Panel ruling was not adopted. As of 1995, the Banana Framework Agreement (BFA) allocated substantial shares of the 2,200,000 tonne tariff quota (established by EC Regulation 404/1993) to the suppliers of Colombia and Costa Rica. This had been notified to the GATT.[40]

Ecuador and the United States challenged the BFA again under the newly established WTO dispute settlement system (*EC – Bananas III*). The Appellate Body overruled the Panel's interpretation and held that the Lomé Waiver does not cover inconsistencies with Article XIII. The GATT waiver provided a limited waiver from GATT Article 1, only to the extent necessary to allow the European Communities to provide preferential treatment for products originating from the ACP, as required by the Lomé IV Convention.

The EC modified the banana regime introduced in 1998 by Regulation 1637/98, in combination with EC Regulation 2362/98. Under this revised regime, there were no country-specific allocations to twelve traditional ACP countries. According to the US, the EC was required to adopt a single TRQ covering all suppliers, and the allocation of quota among the supplying countries should be based on the principles of Article XIII of the GATT. The EC also removed the system of licensing allocations based on the type of operators, namely A, B, C categories. At the compliance stage, the Appellate Body ruled in *EC – Bananas III (Article 21.5 – Ecuador)* that allocating the TRQs exclusively to a group of ACP countries, without reserving shares to non-ACP suppliers, could not be considered an allocation that closely reflects members' market shares.[41] Accordingly, it was held that the exclusion of non-ACP suppliers from the tariff quota was inconsistent with the requirements of Article XIII of the GATT.

The EC later stated that it would introduce a tariff-only regime for bananas no later than 1 January 2006. Later, the Doha Ministerial Conference in 2001 adopted two short-term waivers for the EC's banana import regime, namely, Article I and Article XIII waivers. Importantly, the EC's interim banana regime (2001–05) was not disputed by any WTO member.

To Go Further

Schropp, S. A. B. and Palmeter, D., 'Commentary on the Appellate Body Report in *EC – Bananas III* (Article 21.5): Waiver-Thin, or Lock, Stock, and Metric Ton?', *World Trade Review* (2010), 9(1), pp. 7–57.

---

[40] 'General Agreement on Tariffs and Trade: Dispute Settlement Panel Report on the European Economic Community – Import Regime for Bananas', *International Legal Materials* (1995), 34(1), pp. 177–234.

[41] Appellate Body Report, *EC – Bananas III (Article 21.5 – Ecuador)*, para. 340.

The administration of TRQs is governed, in part, by Article XIII of the GATT. Article XIII regulates the non-discriminatory administration of quantitative restrictions, including, where applicable, the allocation of shares among WTO members. This provision can be used to ensure that exporters from a particular country have access to a portion of the TRQ that broadly resembles their share in world trade in the product at issue.[42] The Agreement on Import Licensing Procedures also governs the TRQ administration procedures.[43]

The administration of TRQs is also contentious, especially in countries which have State control[44] over imports and exports. In agricultural products, the extent of under-fill (i.e. use of lower duty rates within quotas) in TRQs, has also been a specific concern. The 2013 Bali Ministerial Conference on tariff rate quotas clarifies the procedure for administering quotas.[45] If the quotas are persistently under-filled, for example, where the fill rates remain less than 65 per cent for two consecutive years, the importing members are required to take certain specific action, including the modification of the administration of the tariff quota.

3.5   Special Safeguard Provision

In 1955, the United States obtained a 'waiver' under the GATT 1947 for certain agricultural measures that restricted imports of certain types of agricultural goods. In response to removing these import restrictions, the United States and other members succeeded in incorporating a 'special safeguard' provision (SSG) in the AoA. The purpose of the SSG was to retain certain restrictions on imports that were previously covered by the waiver (or similar provisions by other countries).[46]

The purpose of Article 5 of the AoA is to allow members to temporarily deviate from their obligations under Article II of the GATT (bound tariff rates) in cases where trigger levels of quantities and/or prices are met. The purpose of the SSG is to prevent a large surge in the volume of imports, or to avoid depressing effects on domestic prices pursuant to a fall in import prices. The reference price for calculating the price trigger is the average unit value of the cost, insurance, freight (CIF) price during the 1986–88 base period, expressed in domestic currency. It may also be an 'appropriate' price in terms of the quality of the product and its stage of processing. Members are not required to conduct an investigation or to demonstrate that the domestic industry is injured in order to impose the SSG.

---

[42] A. E. Appleton and P. F. J. Macrory, 'Non-Tariff Barriers: The Agreements on Sanitary and Phytosanitary Measures and Technical Barriers to Trade', in A. E. Appleton and P. F. J. Macrory (eds.), *Business Guide to Trade and Investment* (Paris: International Chamber of Commerce, 2017), p. 181.

[43] World Trade Organization, Ministerial Conference, Ninth Session, Bali, 3–6 December 2013, 'Understanding on Tariff Rate Quota Administration Provisions of Agricultural Products, as Defined in Article 2 of the Agreement on Agriculture', Ministerial Decision of 7 December 2013, WT/MIN(13)/39, WT/L/914.

[44] State control is mostly exercised through State trading enterprises.

[45] WTO, 'Understanding on Tariff Rate Quota Administration Provisions of Agricultural Products'.

[46] Jackson, *World Trading System*, pp. 314–15.

The option to invoke the special safeguard is only available to those countries that have specifically reserved a right to do so by selecting the products that they consider sensitive and designating them with the SSG symbol in their Schedules. According to the WTO, a total of thirty-nine members have reserved the right to use an SSG, on a combined 6,027 agricultural products.[47] An illustration of a member reserving a right to impose a special safeguard measure is provided below.

Table 3.1 EC's WTO Schedule: illustration of SSG

Tariff item number	Description of products	Final bound rate of duty	Special safeguard
0207	Meat and edible offal, of the poultry of heading No. 0105, fresh, chilled or frozen:		
(...)			
	-Poultry cuts and offal other than livers, frozen:		
0207.41	–Of fowls of the species Gallus domesticus:		
	—Cuts:		
0207.41.10	——Boneless	1024 ECU/T	SSG

Source: EC's WTO Schedule.

In *EC – Poultry*, Brazil's claim was that the EC had not followed the procedures set out in Article 5.1 in the imposition of the special safeguard on imports of frozen poultry. Brazil argued that the import price referred to therein should be 'c.i.f. price plus ordinary customs duty', whereas the EC argued that Article 5.1(b) referred to the CIF price itself.[48] The Appellate Body interpreted the phrase 'price at which that product may enter the customs territory' to mean the price at which the product may enter the customs territory, not the price at which the product may enter the domestic market of the importing member. Accordingly, they held that price in Article 5.1(b) does not include custom duties and internal charges.[49]

3.5.1   Special Safeguard Mechanism

The 2015 Nairobi Decision on a Special Safeguard Mechanism for Developing Country Members reaffirmed the goal to negotiate a right for developing countries to a special

[47] WTO, 'The Issues, and Where We Are Now', p. 39.

[48] Art. 5.1(b): 'the price at which imports of that product may enter the customs territory of the Member granting the concession, as determined on the basis of the c.i.f. import price of the shipment concerned expressed in terms of its domestic currency, falls below a trigger price equal to the average 1986 to 1988 reference price for the product concerned'.

[49] Appellate Body Report, *European Communities – Measures Affecting the Importation of Certain Poultry Products*, WT/DS69/AB/R, adopted 23 July 1998, para. 145.

safeguard mechanism, as agreed in the Hong Kong Ministerial Declaration, and directed members to undertake the relevant negotiations in the Committee on Agriculture.

3.6   Domestic Support

Production subsidies are defined in popular literature as 'Domestic or production subsidies ... granted for the benefit of products regardless of whether those products are exported or not'.[50] Domestic subsidies are the most perplexing, because they subsume a variety and range of government interventions, many of which may be justifiable as exercises of sovereign activity.[51]

WTO members have agreed to reduce the level of domestic support pursuant to Article 6 of the AoA. The commitment of members on the reduction of domestic agricultural support measures are set out in Part IV of their GATT Schedule of Concessions.

Box 3.2 Aggregate measurement of support (AMS)

AMS refers to support for a single agricultural product (that is, in one specific subsector). Total AMS refers to the support provided to all agricultural products (i.e. all farming sectors taken together), and Current Total AMS refers to the Total AMS in any given year. The term 'commitment level' refers to the promise made by a WTO member regarding the Current Total AMS in a given year. That AMS is not to exceed the commitment level. Each WTO member sets forth these promises – that is, enlists the annual commitment levels – in its Schedule of Concessions.

Equivalent Measurement of Support (EMS)

EMS is the annual level of support, expressed in monetary terms, provided to producers of basic agricultural products through the application of one or more measures, the calculation of which, based on AMS methodology, is impracticable.

The AMS commitment for developed countries under the AoA is to reduce the aggregate trade distorting support by 20 per cent over a period of six years, where the base period of measurement is derived from the 1986–88 average. A member is considered to be in compliance with its domestic support reduction commitments in any year in which its domestic support in favour of agricultural producers expressed in Current Total AMS does not exceed the corresponding Annual or Final Bound Commitment Levels specified in Part IV of its Schedule.[52]

---

[50] Jackson, *World Trading System*, p. 280.   [51] Jackson, *World Trading System*, p. 280.   [52] AoA, Art. 6.3.

Members who have undertaken reduction commitments in their Schedules are not allowed to provide domestic support measures in excess of their commitment levels.[53] These domestic support measures pertain to the 'amber box' measures and do not include measures that are exempt from the calculation of AMS. All other members who have not undertaken any reduction commitments in their Schedules are not allowed to provide support to agricultural producers in excess of the relevant *de minimis* levels set out in paragraph 4 of Article 6.[54]

3.6.1   Classification of Domestic Support Measures

Given the variety of WTO members' domestic support subsidies, the AoA classifies domestic support measures based on their presumed trade-distorting nature into three categories: amber box, green box and blue box.

3.6.1.1   Green Box

Green box subsidies are considered to be subsidies with no or minimal trade-distorting effects. Green box subsides are not subject to limits on the amount of support that can be provided.

Annex 2 to the AoA provides a detailed but non-exhaustive list of measures for which governments may claim exemption from including in their calculation of AMS. The fundamental requirement is that any support claimed under Annex 2 should have no, or at most minimal, trade-distorting effects on production. All measures for which exemption is claimed need to meet the general and policy-specific criteria. The general criteria are stated under paragraph 1 to Annex 2. According to the general criteria, all green box measures shall be provided through a publicly funded government programme not involving transfers from consumers. Besides, such support shall not have the effect of providing price support to producers. The policy-specific criteria and conditions depend on the nature of the particular policy under consideration in Annex 2. These include, among others, public stockholding for food security purposes, domestic food aid, decoupled income support, payments under environmental programmes and payments under regional assistance programmes.

Paragraph 3 of Annex 2 lists the eligibility criteria of a public stockholding for food security programmes. Food purchase and sales by the government are required to be made at current market prices. In the case of food security programmes involving the procurement of foodstuffs at an administered price, the difference between the acquisition price and the external reference price is to be accounted for in the AMS.[55] Most developing countries are unable to avail themselves of the green box for food security purposes as they implement public stockholding programmes using administered prices. These administered prices are usually higher than market prices.

---

[53] AoA, Art. 3.2.   [54] AoA, Art. 7.2(b).   [55] AoA, Annex 2, para. 3, fn. 5.

Direct payments to producers that are not linked to production decisions are considered to be decoupled income support. Although a farmer receives a payment from the government, this payment does not influence the type or volume of agricultural production. In addition, no production shall be required in order to receive such payments. For example, the provision of basic income support to a small farmer not linked to production would be considered as decoupled income support.

In practice, green box programmes such as decoupled programmes are seen to distort trade by affecting the risk behaviour of the producers.[56]

3.6.1.2   Blue Box

Blue box support consists of direct payment to farmers subject to the following conditions: (1) it must embody limitations on production, and (2) payments must be based on (a) fixed area or yield, (b) no more than 85 per cent of a base level of production, or (c) a fixed number of livestock. Article 6.5 of the AoA permits domestic support subsidies that conform to the above requirements to be exempt from reduction commitments. The exemption from reduction commitments for payment under blue box is required to be reflected separately in the Supporting Table to the Domestic Support notification made to the WTO.[57]

The addition of the blue box was a result of the Blair House Accord and is rooted in the *EEC – Oilseeds I* dispute between the US and the EEC.[58] As a result of the inclusion of Article 6.5, neither the United States deficiency payments (as authorised under the 1990 Farm Bill) nor the compensation payments under the European Union's Common Agricultural Policy had to be included in AMS calculations.[59]

3.6.1.3   Amber Box

Amber box support is presumed to be production- and trade-distorting and is subject to the Uruguay Round reduction commitments. These subsidies are to be included in the calculation of AMS.

Article 1 of the AoA sets out the definitions of AMS. AMS relates to a monetary value of the support granted to producers of basic agricultural products. AMS may be product- or non-product-specific. Total AMS is the sum of all the separate product-specific AMS, as well as any non-product-specific AMS measures that exceed the prescribed de minimis levels provided under Article 6.4 of the AoA. Domestic support that is provided under programmes that qualify under Annex 2 to the Agreement are excluded from the scope of the definition.

---

[56] S. Sharma, *The WTO and Food Security: Implications for Developing Countries* (Singapore: Springer Nature, 2017).

[57] AoA, Art. 6.5(b).

[58] GATT Panel Report, *European Economic Community – Payments and Subsidies Paid to Processors and Producers of Oilseeds and Related Animal-Feed Proteins*, L/6627, adopted 25 January 1990, BISD 37S/86.

[59] T. Josling, *Agricultural Trade Policy: Completing the Reform* (Washington, DC: Peterson Institute for International Economics, 1998), p. 32.

Annex 3 to the Agreement details the calculation of AMS. In the case of product-specific support, the AMS is calculated for each basic agricultural product receiving market price support and any kind of non-exempt payments.[60] In the case of non-product specific support, all support given across all agricultural products is to be converted into its monetary equivalent and totalled into one figure. Finally, the Total AMS, which is the sum total of all domestic support provided in favour of agricultural producers, is to be determined.

Article 6, paragraph 4 of the AoA provides an exemption from inclusion in Total AMS of product-specific domestic support of less than 5 per cent of the total value of production of a basic agricultural product during a relevant year, or 10 per cent for a developing country.

Article 7, paragraph 2 of the AoA states that '[w]here no Total AMS commitment exists in Part IV of a Member's Schedule, the Member shall not provide support to agricultural producers in excess of the relevant *de minimis* level set out in paragraph 4 of Article 6'. For instance, India does not have a Total AMS commitment in Part IV of the Schedule.

A schematic representation of support measures that are exempt from inclusion in the calculation of AMS is provided in Figure 3.2.

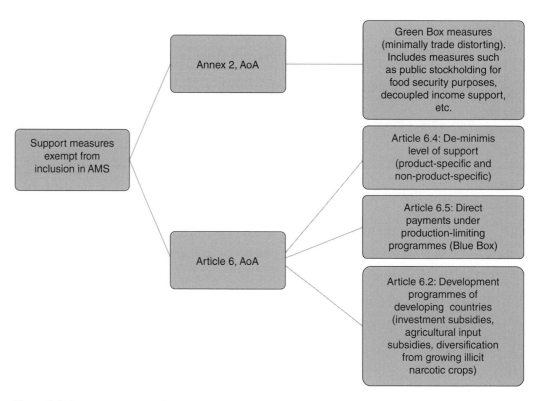

Figure 3.2 Support measures that are exempt from inclusion in the calculation of AMS

---

[60] AoA, Annex 3, para. 1.

3.6.2 Market Price Support

The concept of market price support is not defined in the AoA. It is one of the three listed categories of support mentioned in the amber box, the other two being non-exempt direct payments and other non-exempt subsidies. There is a view that quantification of market price support need not be based on the expenditure of the government or budgetary outlays.[61] According to this view, market price support gauges the effect of a government policy measure on agricultural producers of a basic product which need not be based on the budgetary cost of the measure. For example, a government administrative action that is regulatory in character could function as a market price support. On the other hand, the reference to the terms in paragraph 2 of Annex 3 that 'subsidies ... shall include both budgetary outlays and revenue forgone by the government or their agents' gives an indication that the amber box category could entail a certain cost to the government. Some illustrations of market price support include minimum support price and minimum procurement price.

Market price support is to be calculated in the following manner:

AoA, Annex 3, para. 8

[M]arket price support shall be calculated using the gap between a fixed external reference price and the applied administered price multiplied by the quantity of production eligible to receive the applied administered price.

The first element of market price support is the determination of applied administered price (AAP). Although the term is undefined in the AoA, the WTO Panel in *China – Agricultural Producers* provides some useful clarity. Based on the dictionary meaning of the terms, the Panel noted that 'AAP is the price set by the government at which specified entities will purchase certain basic agricultural products'.[62]

The fixed external reference price is based on the years 1986–88. The formula for the calculation of market price support is:

[Fixed External Reference Price – Applied Administered Price]
× Quantity of production eligible to receive the applied administered price.

The 1986–88 fixed external reference price is outdated and bears little resemblance to current market conditions.[63] Another significant issue is the interpretation of the term 'eligible production'.

---

[61] Panel Report, *Korea – Various Measures on Beef*, para. 827.

[62] Panel Report, *China – Domestic Support for Agricultural Producers*, WT/DS511/R, Add.1, adopted 26 April 2019, para. 7.177.

[63] T. Josling, 'Rethinking the Rules for Agricultural Subsidies: E15 Initiative', E15 Initiative (Geneva: International Centre for Trade and Sustainable Development and World Economic Forum, 2015), available at www.e15initiative.org/ (accessed 21 December 2020).

Korea – Various Measures on Beef

In *Korea – Various Measures on Beef*, one of the arguments of the complainants, the United States and Australia, was that Korea calculated its domestic support for the beef industry incorrectly for the years 1997 and 1998, as Korea did not include Current AMS for beef in its Current Total AMS. In other words, according to the complainants, had Korea's domestic support for beef, which had allegedly exceeded its *de minimis* level, been taken into account, Korea would have breached its domestic support commitments.[64] The Panel made certain significant observations on the concept of market price support.[65]

Korea – Various Measures on Beef *(Panel Report)*

827. ... There may, of course, be circumstances where eligible production may be less than total marketable production as, for example, where the minimum price support is only available to producers in certain disadvantaged regions. Another possible example would be where there is a legislatively predetermined, non-discretionary, limitation on the quantity of marketable production that a governmental intervention agency could take off the market at the administered price in any year. In the latter case, the particular design and operation of the price support mechanism would have to be taken into account in determining eligible production, since even governmental purchases at a level below the legislatively predetermined quantity limit could, depending on market conditions, suffice to maintain market prices at above the minimum levels for all marketable production. Hence, with these qualifications, eligible production for the purposes of calculating the market price support component of current support should comprise *the total marketable production of all producers which is eligible to benefit from the market price support*, even though the proportion of production which is actually purchased by a governmental agency may be relatively small or even nil. (Emphasis added)

The Appellate Body in *Korea – Various Measures on Beef* considered the meaning of the phrase 'quantity of production eligible to receive the applied administered price' and reached a similar understanding to that of the Panel.[66] The Appellate Body found that Korea erred in calculating the market price support by using the amount of production actually purchased instead of production declared eligible to receive the applied administered price, according to the provisions of paragraph 8 of Annex 3. The Appellate Body made the following observations:

---

[64] For a detailed discussion, see J. J. Nedumpara and S. Janardhan, 'Developing Countries and Domestic Support Measures in Agriculture: Walking a Tightrope', *Journal of World Trade* (2020), 54(1), pp. 81–102.

[65] Panel Report, *Korea – Various Measures on Beef*, para. 827.

[66] Appellate Body Report, *Korea – Various Measures on Beef*, para. 120.

Korea – Various Measures on Beef *(Appellate Body)*

120. We share the Panel's view that the words 'production eligible to receive the applied administered price' in paragraph 8 of Annex 3 have a different meaning in ordinary usage from 'production actually purchased'. The ordinary meaning of 'eligible' is 'fit or entitled to be chosen'. Thus, 'production eligible' refers to production that is 'fit or entitled' to be purchased rather than production that was actually purchased. In establishing its program for future market price support, a government is able to define and to limit 'eligible' production. Production actually purchased may often be less than eligible production.

The meaning of the term 'eligible production' has significant implications for a WTO member's AMS commitments. While most developing countries argue that this concept can only relate to the amount actually purchased,[67] others argue that it should include the value of total production, unless otherwise limited.[68]

In early 2019, the WTO panel in *China – Domestic Support for Agricultural Producers* revisited the terms 'eligible production'. The United States, the complainant, had contended that certain Chinese support for wheat, corn and rice exceeded China's commitments under the AoA in the years 2012–15. The WTO panel in this case inquired, 'the pertinent question is whether the [agricultural product] that was produced would be able to benefit from the [applied administered price] if the seller so desired'.[69]

3.6.3 Due Restraint or Peace Clause

Article 13 of the AoA, known in WTO parlance as the 'Peace Clause', limited the possibility to challenge subsidies in agricultural products under the dispute settlement mechanism until the end of the implementation period (2003). The Peace Clause was essentially a compromise negotiated between the United States and the European Communities on some of their differences concerning agriculture.[70] There are no limitations at present regarding the applicability of trade remedy provisions, after the expiry of Article 13 of the AoA. Brazil's challenge against the United States against certain US Cotton subsidies (in *US – Upland Cotton*) has confirmed the expiry of the Peace Clause.

US – Upland Cotton

Brazil challenged the United States' domestic support to upland cotton in *US – Upland Cotton*. The United States was the third largest producer of cotton and the world's leading

---

[67] China's Second Written Submission, para. 365, cited in Panel Report, *China – Agricultural Producers*, para. 7.280.

[68] Panel Report, *China – Agricultural Producers*, Integrated executive summary of the arguments of Australia, WT/DS511/R/Add.1.

[69] Panel Report, *China – Agricultural Producers*, para. 7.314.

[70] Matsushita et al., *World Trade Organization*, p. 287.

exporter. Some of the programmes challenged in this dispute included marketing loan payments, direct payments, counter-cyclical payments, crop insurance, export credit guarantees and 'Step 2' payments. These domestic support measures were price-contingent and were determined by market prices falling below certain price triggers. Decoupled income support was provided under the direct payments programme. Payments under this programme were, for the most part, pegged to fixed, historical production levels. While they were not contingent upon the production of cotton, they were only given under the circumstances of a recipient refraining from planting fruit, vegetables or wild rice, or by not producing at all.[71]

Brazil contended that the two categories of payments – production flexibility contracts (PFCs) under the 1996 Farm Bill and direct payments (DP) under the 2002 Farm Bill – do not satisfy the requirements of decoupled income support, a green box measure under paragraph 6 of Annex 2 of the AoA.

The provision under consideration was a green box measure in paragraph 6 of Annex 2, which stated that '[t]he amount of such payments in any given year shall not be related to, or based on, the type of volume of production (including livestock units) undertaken by the producer in any year after the base year'.

US – Upland Cotton *(Panel)*

7.371. The object and purpose of Annex 2 is to set out the terms on which certain domestic support measures can be exempt from reduction commitments. The first sentence of paragraph 1 provides that 'domestic support measures for which exemption from the reduction commitment is claimed shall meet the fundamental requirement that they have no or at most minimal trade-distorting effects or effects on production'. Brazil submits that the chapeau of paragraph 1 of Annex 2 forms part of the context for interpreting paragraph 6(b). The United States submits that the purpose of the criteria in Annex 2 is to determine compliance with that fundamental requirement. Therefore, on either view, that fundamental requirement should be taken into account in interpreting the criterion in paragraph 6(b).

7.386. ... the Panel notes that the planting flexibility limitations provide a monetary incentive for payment recipients not to produce the prohibited crops. USDA data presented by Brazil shows that the planting flexibility limitations in this dispute cover a wide range of types of production which represent approximately 22 per cent of farm income from crops in the seventeen states of the United States producing upland cotton, peaking at over 70 per cent in California, a major upland cotton producing state. The United States has not suggested that these farms are

---

[71] Federal Agriculture Improvement and Reform (FAIR) Act 1996, Section 118, subsection (b)(1).

> *(cont.)*
>
> covered by the special eligibility criterion which would permit them to plant fruits and vegetables without penalty. These limitations therefore significantly constrain production choices available to PFC and DP payment recipients and effectively eliminate a significant proportion of them. Whilst these programmes permit recipients to produce nothing, this alone does not remove the significant constraint that the planting flexibility limitations have in certain regions on the choices of those PFC and DP payment recipients who do produce something, which the evidence shows is the overwhelming majority.

The Panel concluded that planting flexibility limitations in the direct payment programme do not fully conform with paragraph 6(b) of Annex 2 to the AoA. The Panel also analysed Article 13 of the AoA, which provides that domestic support that conforms with Article 6 is exempt from the subsidies provisions of the GATT and the actionable subsidies under the SCM Agreement, provided that such measures do not grant support to a specific commodity in excess of that decided during the 1992 marketing year. The Panel concluded that Brazil had discharged its burden that the US domestic support measures did not fall under Article 13 and thus are vulnerable to challenge under the SCM Agreement.[72]

The WTO decision is significant since it represents a victory to developing countries in challenging agricultural protection in developed countries.[73]

3.6.4 Implementation and Surveillance of the Disciplines under the AoA

The main vehicle for monitoring and surveillance in agricultural trade is the notification to the Committee on Agriculture (CoA)[74] of the levels of domestic support, along with parallel notifications on export subsidies, tariff-rate quotas and new measures. The obligation of WTO members to submit notifications is contained in Article 18 (Review of the Implementation of the Commitments) of the AoA.[75] Members are required to 'promptly' notify all modifications of existing measures or the introduction of new domestic support measures.[76] The CoA adopted detailed notification requirements and formats in order to facilitate the review process to be undertaken at each formal meeting. These are contained in documents G/AG/2 and G/AG/2/Add.1. The main task of the CoA is to review the

---

[72] Panel Report, *United States – Subsidies on Upland Cotton*, WT/DS267/R, Add.1–Add.3, Corr.1, adopted 21 March 2005, as modified by Appellate Body Report WT/DS267/AB/R, paras. 7.598, 7.608.

[73] K. H. Cross, 'King Cotton, Developing Countries and the "Peace Clause": The WTO's US Cotton Subsidies Decision', *Journal of International Economic Law* (2009), 9, p. 153.

[74] AoA, Art. 17.

[75] The terms of reference are contained in the Decision by the General Council on 31 January 1995 (WT/L/43).

[76] AoA, Art. 18.3.

member's implementation of their commitments. This notification mechanism is a useful tool for facilitating transparency in the agricultural trading system.

Any member may bring to the attention of the CoA any measure that it considers ought to have been notified by another member, termed 'counter-notification'.[77]

3.6.5   Bali Ministerial Decision on Public Stockholding for Food Security Purposes

The Ministerial Decision on Public Stockholding for Food Security Purposes exempts food purchases at State-determined prices for the purposes of food security from developing countries' maximum trade-distorting support. Developing countries can avail themselves of the benefit in relation to support provided for traditional staple food crops, in pursuance of public stockholding programmes for food security purposes existing as of the date of the Decision, where these are consistent with the criteria of paragraph 3, footnote 5 and footnotes 5 and 6 of Annex 2 to the AoA, when the developing member complies with the terms of the Decision.[78]

In order to take advantage of the decision, the concerned member must notify that it is exceeding or is at the risk of exceeding its domestic support obligations under the AoA.[79] The developing member is also required to ensure that its stockholding programme does not distort trade or adversely affect the food security of other countries.[80]

In November 2014, the WTO General Council accepted an arrangement by the United States and India to extend the Peace Clause indefinitely, provided that the conditions set out in paragraphs 3 to 6 of the Bali Decision are met, and to continue their endeavours to reach a more permanent solution.[81] Achieving a permanent solution may require certain changes to the AoA or the WTO DSU.

3.7   Export Subsidies

Prior to the onset of the Uruguay negotiations, the Leutwiler Report suggested that the goal of reform should be 'the total elimination of … export subsidies, as they produce many of the major distortions in world agricultural markets'.[82] Agriculture export subsidies held the key to the success or failure of the negotiations in this regard.

---

[77] AoA, Art. 18.6; WTO Committee on Agriculture, 'Organisation of Work and Working Procedures of the Committee on Agriculture', G/AG/1, adopted 28 March 1995, para. 11.

[78] Ministerial Decision of 7 December 2013 on Public Stockholding for Food Security Purposes, WT/MIN(13)/38-WT/L/913 (11 December 2013) (Bali Decision), para. 2.

[79] The Bali Decision refers to the AMS limits, which could either be total bound AMS or the *de minimis* product level support, as the case may be.

[80] Bali Decision, para. 4.

[81] General Council, Decision of 27 November 2014, WT/L/939, concerning the Decision on Public Stockholding for Food Security Purposes (contained in WT/GC/W688).

[82] GATT, *Trade Policies for a Better Future: The 'Leutwiler Report', the GATT and the Uruguay Round* (Dordrecht: Martinus Nijhoff, 1987), p. 44.

The term 'export subsidies' is defined under Article 1(e) of the AoA as referring to subsidies contingent upon export performance, including export subsidies listed in Article 9 of the Agreement. Article 9.1 provides only an illustrative list of the types of practices that fall within the scope of agricultural export subsidies. However, the AoA does not define the key term 'subsidy'.

With respect to export subsidies on agricultural products, (a) agricultural products that are specified in Section II of Part IV of a member's GATT Schedule of Concessions are subject to reduction commitments, and (b) agricultural products that are not specified in the Schedule are not to be provided by members. Export subsidy commitments in a member's Schedule must be expressed in terms of both budgetary outlay and quantity commitment levels (during the base period 1986–90).[83]

Box 3.3 Export subsidies: vilified and condemned

Subsidies can serve a multitude of policy goals. However, there is a general consensus among economists and policymakers that subsidies can subvert negotiated market access commitments. However, some subsidies can lead to positive externalities and in making available valuable public goods. Subsidies also have a major role in addressing poverty and food security concerns, especially in net food-importing countries. Sometimes, a bumper production during a year may result in marketable surplus for which certain governments may not have storage or stockholding facilities.

The GATT 1954–55 Review session introduced certain amendments to Article XVI of the GATT. Specific rules on subsidies were created. Subsidising the export of 'primary products' was permissible, whereas all other export subsidies (especially for non-primary products) were prohibited. The GATT 1960 Working Party also drew an illustrative list of subsidies. While export subsidies on industrial goods attracted a rigorous regime, subsidies to domestic producers remained non-actionable, with the possible exception of countervailing duties.

In short, the special treatment given for export subsidies for agricultural products under the GATT has been carried forward to the WTO. The export subsidy disciplines under the AoA were not as rigorous as the disciplines under the SCM Agreement. However, this distinction has been almost done away with by virtue of the Nairobi Ministerial Decision on Export Competition in 2015, where the ministers have agreed to phase out their export subsidies over time. Around sixteen WTO members (counting the European Union as one) have already committed to eliminate their scheduled export subsidy commitments at the time of the Nairobi Decision, and most of the developed countries are on the path to removing their export subsidies. The Nairobi Decision states that developing members shall continue to benefit from the provisions of Article 9.4 in terms of providing export subsidies for reducing the cost of

---

[83] AoA, Arts. 3, 9.2.

Box 3.3 (cont.)

marketing and other types of international and internal transport and freight for a period of five years – that is, up to 2020. Least developed countries and net food-importing developing members shall continue to enjoy this benefit until 2030.

The Nairobi Decision has also introduced obligations in relation to export credits, export credit guarantees and insurance programmes. The Nairobi Decision has established the maximum repayment term for any new support as eighteen months for developed members, whereas developing members are given a four-year phase-in period. However, after 2019, the maximum repayment term even for developing members is only eighteen months. It is important to bear in mind that with respect to export credit guarantees, export credits and insurance programmes, under Article 10.2 of the AoA, members have undertaken to work towards the development of internationally agreed disciplines.

The types of export subsidies encompassed in Article 9.1 include:

- direct subsides, contingent on export performance, by government or their agencies to producers of an agricultural product;
- sales, or disposal for export, of agricultural product stocks at prices lower than domestic market prices;
- payments, including those financed by levies, on the export of agricultural products financed by government action;
- subsidies to reduce the costs of marketing exports of agricultural products;
- internal transport and freight charges on export terms on terms more favourable than for domestic shipments; and
- subsidies on agricultural products contingent on their incorporation in export products.

Article 10.1 of the AoA is a residual provision which does not allow members to grant export subsidies that are not listed in Article 9.1 in a manner that results in or threatens to lead to circumvention of export subsidy commitments. Non-listed export subsidies on scheduled agricultural products may be used by members subject to the anti-circumvention provisions.

Canada – Dairy

In *Canada – Dairy*, New Zealand and the United States challenged certain elements of Canada's Special Milk Classes Scheme as export subsidies, which are not authorised by the AoA. The Canadian government had established a fairly old and very comprehensive supply management system for industrial milk. Three major entities were involved in the implementation and management of the Canadian regulatory regime (see Figure 3.3).

The Canadian Dairy Commission established the national target prices for industrial milk and set the support price for milk and skimmed milk powder; the Canadian Milk Supply Management Committee oversaw the implementation of the milk pooling scheme, which formed the basis of the Special Milk Classes Scheme. During the period in question, the Committee established the production quota for industrial milk, based on the production and demand forecasts made by the Commission. The provincial marketing boards purchased the milk from producers and sold it to processors for the making of dairy products.

The Special Milk Classes Scheme established five different classes, four of which dealt with the domestic market, with the fifth category concerned with exports, comprising five classes that dealt with 'Special Milk'.

Figure 3.3 Operation of Canada's Special Milk Classes Scheme

Under the Special Milk Classes 5(d) and 5(e), milk was used in products exported to traditional export markets such as the US and the UK and for the removal of surplus milk from the domestic market. The prices of milk negotiated for these activities were substantially lower than prices of milk meant for domestic use and therefore constituted export subsidies.[84]

The WTO Panel found that Canada had provided agricultural export subsidies, as described in Articles 9.1(a) and 9.1(c) of the AoA.[85] The Appellate Body examined the concept of 'payments' further, and observed as follows:

Canada – Dairy *(Appellate Body)*

107. We have found that the word 'payments', in the term 'payments-in-kind' in Article 9.1(a), denotes a transfer of economic resources. We believe that the same holds true for the word 'payments' in Article 9.1(c). The question which we now address is whether, under Article 9.1(c), the economic resources that are transferred by way of a 'payment' must be in the form of money, or whether the resources transferred may take other forms. As the Panel observed, the dictionary meaning of the word 'payment' is not limited to payments made in monetary form. In support of this, the Panel cited the Oxford English Dictionary, which defines 'payment' as 'the

---

[84] Appellate Body Report, *Canada – Measures Affecting the Importation of Milk and Exportation of Dairy Products*, WT/DS103/AB/R, WT/DS113/AB/R, Corr.1, adopted 27 October 1999, paras. 14–15.

[85] Panel Report, *Canada – Dairy*, paras. 7.116, 7.113, 8.1.

> **(cont.)**
>
> remuneration of a person with money *or its equivalent*' (emphasis added). Similarly, the Shorter Oxford English Dictionary describes a 'payment' as a 'sum of money (*or other thing*) paid' (emphasis added). Thus, according to these meanings, a 'payment' could be made in a form, other than money, that confers value, such as by way of goods or services. A 'payment' which does not take the form of money is commonly referred to as a 'payment in kind'.
>
> 113. In our view, the provision of milk at discounted prices to processors for export under Special Classes 5(d) and 5(e) constitutes 'payments', in a form other than money, within the meaning of Article 9.1(c). If goods or services are supplied to an enterprise, or a group of enterprises, at reduced rates (that is, at below market rates), 'payments' are, in effect, made to the recipient of the portion of the price that is not charged. Instead of receiving a monetary payment equal to the revenue foregone, the recipient is paid in the form of goods or services. But, as far as the recipient is concerned, the economic value of the transfer is precisely the same.

Canada eliminated Special Milk Class 5(e) and restricted exports of dairy products under Special Milk Class 5(d) following the Appellate Body ruling. However, Canada added a new category of milk for export process termed 'commercial export milk' (CEM). Under the CEM, producers could sell any quantity of milk to Canadian processors for export processing.[86] The Appellate Body suggested that the notion of 'proper value'[87] necessitates an objective benchmark and that this benchmark may change depending on the facts and circumstances of a disputed measure, including the regulatory framework surrounding the measure.[88] The Appellate Body, however, could not complete its analysis on whether there was 'payment' under the CEM, since the panel did not make any factual findings pertaining to the cost of production.[89] Finally, in a second challenge under Article 21.5 of the DSU, with additional evidence, the Panel and Appellate Body found Canada to have acted inconsistently with its commitments under the AoA.[90]

---

[86] Appellate Body Report, *Canada – Measures Affecting the Importation of Milk and the Exportation of Dairy Products – Recourse to Article 21.5 of the DSU by New Zealand and the United States*, WT/DS103/AB/RW, WT/DS113/AB/RW, adopted 18 December 2001, para. 4.

[87] Appellate Body Report, *Canada – Dairy (Article 21.5 – New Zealand and US)*, para. 73. The Appellate Body indicated that when the price charged by a producer of milk is less than the milk's proper value to the producer, there are 'payments' under Art. 9.1(c).

[88] Appellate Body Report, *Canada – Dairy (Article 21.5 – New Zealand and US)*, paras. 74–76.

[89] Appellate Body Report, *Canada – Dairy (Article 21.5 – New Zealand and US)*, para. 102.

[90] Panel Report, *Canada – Measures Affecting the Importation of Milk and the Exportation of Dairy Products – Second Recourse to Article 21.5 of the DSU by New Zealand and the United States*, WT/DS103/AB/RW2, WT/DS113/AB/RW2, adopted 17 January 2003, as modified by Appellate Body Report WT/DS103/AB/RW2, WT/DS113/AB/RW2.

*EC – E*XPORT *S*UBSIDIES ON *S*UGAR

European Communities – Export Subsidies on Sugar involves certain significant findings on the export subsidy disciplines under the AoA. The EC had maintained a certain quota system for sugar. Two categories, namely A sugar and B sugar, were eligible for domestic support and export refunds. The third category, C sugar, represented any sugar that was in excess of the production quotas under A sugar and B sugar and had to be exported.

Thailand, the complainant in this case, argued that C sugar was provided with export subsidies under Article 9.1(c) in violation of Articles 3.3 and 8 of the AoA. In addition to other issues, the panel examined whether 'payment in the form of cross-subsidization resulting from the profits made on sales of A and B sugar [was] used to cover the fixed costs of production/export of C sugar'.[91] In this regard, the Panel observed as follows:

EC – Export Subsidies on Sugar *(Panel)*

7.310.   The Panel finds that there is clear evidence that the relatively high EC administered domestic market (above-intervention) prices for A and B quota sugar allow the sugar producers to recover fixed costs and to sell exported C sugar over average variable costs but below the average total cost of production. Sugar is sugar whether or not produced under an EC created designation of A, B or C sugar. A, B or C sugar are part of the same line of production and thus to the extent that the fixed costs of A, B and C are largely paid for by the profits made on sales of A and B sugar, the EC sugar regime provides the advantage which allows EC sugar producers to produce and export C sugar at below total cost of production. For the Panel this cross-subsidization constitutes a payment in the form of a transfer of financial resources.

The Panel and, later, the Appellate Body found that the elements of Article 9.1(c) – that is, whether or not there were 'payments' and whether these payments were 'on the export' and 'financed by virtue of governmental action' – were met in this case. According to the Appellate Body, payment under the AoA does not require a particular form.[92]

Article 8 of the AoA implies that members are not precluded from providing export subsidies. However, they need to do it in conformity with the rules of the Agreement and their respective Schedules of Commitments. Reference needs to be made to Article 3.3 in this regard, which addresses the use of export subsidies on agricultural products that are specified in the Schedule and those that are not. In essence, the provision of listed export

---

[91] Panel Report, *European Communities – Export Subsidies on Sugar, Complaint by Thailand*, WT/DS266/R, adopted 19 May 2005, as modified by Appellate Body Report WT/DS265/AB/R, WT/DS266/AB/R, WT/DS283/AB/R, para. 7.252.

[92] Panel Report, *EC – Export Subsidies on Sugar (Thailand)*, paras. 7.334–7.335.

subsidies on specified agricultural products is allowed, but within the limits set by the Schedules, and the provision of listed export subsidies on non-specified agricultural products is prohibited.[93]

The WTO consistency of an export subsidy for agricultural products has to be examined under the AoA, in the first place. Agricultural export subsidies are also subject to the actionable subsidy disciplines under the SCM Agreement, where a member will be required to prove the adverse effects.[94]

The Panel in *US – FSC* stated, 'Article 1 of the SCM Agreement, which defines the term "subsidy" for the purposes of the SCM Agreement, represents highly relevant context for the interpretation of the word "subsidy" within the meaning of the Agreement on Agriculture, as it is the only article in the WTO Agreement that provides a definition of that term'.[95]

The Nairobi Ministerial Conference in 2015 marked a significant decision on export subsidies. Under the Ministerial Decision on Export Competition, developed countries agreed to immediately eliminate their remaining scheduled export subsidy entitlements. Developing countries were required to eliminate their export subsidy entitlements by the end of 2018, subject to certain exceptions. However, it was agreed that the benefit of the provisions of Article 9.4 of the AoA, especially subsidies related to marketing, handling, upgrading and international transport, would be available to developing country members until the end of 2023.[96]

3.8   Conclusion

The AoA under the Uruguay Round is an incomplete agreement. Mandated negotiations on the AoA started in the year 2000 itself. However, members have not achieved positive and successful outcomes on a number of areas, including: market access, domestic support and export competition. Although the AoA succeeded in tariffing quota restrictions and other non-tariff barriers, the market access restrictions remain high. 'Box-shifting' is also fairly common in several countries, with members apparently shifting trade-distorting support to blue and green boxes. The AoA needs reconsideration in determining the AMS, especially in relation to identifying the 'eligible quantity of production'. The Panel and Appellate Body ruling in *Korea – Various Measures on Beef* and the recent Panel ruling in *China – Agricultural Producers* raise certain valid concerns.

One of the major achievements after the conclusion of the Uruguay Round was the sectoral initiative on cotton, as well as the Bali Ministerial Declaration on Public

---

[93] Desta, *Law of International Trade in Agricultural Products*, p. 232.   [94] Panel Report, *US – Upland Cotton.*

[95] Panel Report, *United States – Tax Treatment for 'Foreign Sales Corporations'*, WT/DS108/R, adopted 20 March 2000, as modified by Appellate Body Report WT/DS108/AB/R, para. 7.150.

[96] WTO, Ministerial Conference, Tenth Session, Nairobi, 15–18 December 2015, 'Export Competition', Ministerial Decision, WT/MIN(15)/45, WT/L/980, dated 21 December 2015, paras. 6, 7, 8; AoA, Art. 9.4 does not require a developing country member to undertake commitments in respect of the export subsidies listed in subparagraphs (d) and (e) of Art. 9.1, during the implementation period.

Stockholding for Food Security Programmes. A permanent peace clause in this regard will provide considerable comfort to WTO members that have a substantial number of income-poor and resource-poor farmers and consumers.

3.9   Summary

- The AoA has contributed to radically reforming the agricultural policies of several WTO members.
- The AOA has played a key role in the removal of non-tariff barriers, but tariffs remain very high in agricultural products.
- The tariff rate quotas that are rampant in the agricultural trade remain non-transparent and, in many cases, not fully utilised.
- Undue reliance on price supports is a continuing concern in agriculture. Several members have increased support for direct payments that are decoupled from production. Subsidies of this nature, although not tied to output and prices, encourage farmers to remain in farming and have trade-distorting potential.
- The calculation of domestic support captured in the phrase 'aggregate measurement of support' has been one of the controversial elements of the AoA. The benchmark for comparison, namely, the fixed external reference, is based on outdated historic data and bears no resemblance to current market realities. Reforms in this area are urgent.
- The provisions of the AoA create difficulties for members, especially developing and least developed countries, to engage in public stockholding programmes for food security purposes. A lasting and durable solution is required in this area.

3.10   Review Questions

1 What is the exact relationship between the AoA and the SCM Agreement? Can a WTO member challenge a domestic support measure provided by a member that is in accordance with the provisions of the AoA under the SCM Agreement?
2 Can market price support exist under the AoA even if the government does not provide any budgetary support?
3 In determining the 'quantity of eligible production' for domestic support determination, should a WTO member take into account all production eligible for the applied administered price, whether or not actually procured by a member's government? What was the finding of the WTO Panel and the Appellate Body in *Korea – Various Measures on Beef* in this regard?
4 Are import and export quotas permitted under the AoA? What is the relationship between Article XI and footnote 1 to Article 4.2 of the AoA?

5 Article XI:2(c) of the GATT permits certain exceptions for agriculture and fisheries products. Can a WTO member maintain non-tariff restrictions on agricultural products and seek the benefit of Article XI:2(c)? Do you agree with the finding of the Appellate Body in *Indonesia – Import Licensing Regimes*?

6 Is the 'Peace Clause' under the Bali Ministerial Decision applicable for domestic support measures for all agricultural products?

3.11 Exercises

Exercise 1

Minerva is a developing member of the WTO. In order to support its farmers who grow corn, the government fixes the price (fixed reference price) at which it would procure the corn from the farmers. The procurement by the government is triggered only in case the price of corn in the market falls below the fixed reference price. This programme is applicable in three out of six provinces of Minerva.

Corn farmers also enjoy other benefits from the government. These include certain agricultural input subsidies, such as fertiliser subsidies, which are available to the low-income and resource-poor category of corn farmers.

In Minerva's notification on domestic support to the Committee on Agriculture, Minerva calculates its domestic support to the corn farmers based on the quantity of production that was procured by the government. Minerva has also notified of the agricultural input subsidies under Article 6.2 of the Agreement on Agriculture.

Based on this, Saratoga, another WTO member, decides to challenge Minerva's method of calculation of AMS in its domestic support notification.

1 How should Minerva calculate the domestic support to its corn farmers? Has Minerva calculated the AMS correctly in considering the quantity of production that was actually procured by the government as the 'quantity of eligible production'?

2 Is Minerva's notification on agricultural input subsidies compliant with Article 6 of the Agreement on Agriculture?

Exercise 2

The National Edible Oils Association has requested the government of Xanadu, a WTO member, to encourage the production of palm oil and curb the importation of products such as canola oil, sunflower oil and other vegetable oils. Xanadu has significant domestic and export sales of palm oil. The Association represented to the Bureau of Trade in Xanadu that farmers are giving up palm oil production in view of the non-remunerative prices. The Association has suggested the following measures for consideration.

1 Fixing the minimum selling price at US$150 per MT.

2 Creating a price stabilisation fund by allocating 5 per cent of the import duties on palm oil to the fund.

3 Creating a cess with a view to compensating oil palm growers in the event that international prices fall below a certain average price mark of the last five years.

Examine the compatibility of these measures with the WTO Agreements, especially the AoA.

FURTHER READING

Desta, M. G., *The Law of International Trade in Agricultural Products* (London: Kluwer Law International, 2002).

McMahon, J., *The WTO Agreement on Agriculture: A Commentary*, Oxford Commentaries on the GATT/WTO Agreements (Oxford University Press, 2007).

Matsushita, M., Schoenbaum, T. J., Mavroidis, P. C. and Hahn, M., *The World Trade Organization: Law, Practice, and Policy*, 3rd ed. (Oxford University Press, 2015).

Smith, F., *Agriculture and the WTO: Towards a New Theory of International Agricultural Trade Regulation*, Elgar International Economic Law (Cheltenham: Edward Elgar, 2009).

Trebilcock, M., Howse, R. and Eliason, A., *The Regulation of International Trade*, 4th ed. (London: Routledge, 2013).

4   Technical Barriers to Trade and Sanitary and Phytosanitary Measures

Table of Contents

Highlights

- The Agreement on Technical Barriers to Trade (TBT) and the Agreement on Sanitary and Phytosanitary Measures (SPS) seek to discipline behind-the-border regulatory measures.

- The TBT and SPS Agreements aim to discipline unnecessary barriers to trade through harmonisation, equivalence and conformity assessment procedures.
- Both the agreements include provisions for addressing disguised restrictions on trade while safeguarding the interests of WTO members for pursuing legitimate regulatory objectives.
- While the TBT Agreement focuses on non-discriminatory aspects, the SPS Agreement highlights the role of science and the need for conducting risk assessments.
- Both the TBT and the SPS Agreements put emphasis on exploring measures that are least trade-restrictive. The SPS Agreement includes a special provision on regionalisation to ensure that SPS measures do not disrupt trade from areas or parts of a country that are disease-, pest- or risk-free.
- Participation in international standards-making activities is one of the recommended ways of achieving coherence and uniformity in domestic standards.
- Both the agreements place emphasis on timely notification and information exchange.

4.1   TBT Agreement

The Agreement on Technical Barriers to Trade (TBT)[1] was finalised and signed at the end of the Uruguay Round of GATT negotiations in 1994. Even at the launch of the Tokyo Round, it was fairly clear that the provisions of the GATT 1947 were inadequate to deal with non-tariff barriers to trade.[2] Various types of non-tariff measures, which have been couched in the nature of health or consumer protection policies, can also serve as protectionist instruments.[3] Testing, inspection, labelling and certification procedures can impede trade in a manner that tariffs cannot. The delays and costs involved in complying with administrative procedures can severely inhibit trade. In that context, the GATT 1947 did not specifically provide disciplines in regulating the use of non-tariff barriers such as mandatory product regulations, product standards, certification requirements, labelling and other formalities that can have a restrictive impact on trade.

In December 1969, the Committee on Trade in Industrial Products established Working Group 3 to deal specifically with the issue of technical regulations and to propose ways to address concerns related to non-tariff barriers.[4] Working Group 3 and its successor groups eventually formulated the Standards Code of 1979, which became the precursor to the TBT Agreement. The Standards Code dealt with mandatory and voluntary technical specifications encompassing both industrial and agricultural goods. Although the Standards Code

---

[1] Agreement on Technical Barriers to Trade, 1868 UNTS 120 (1994).
[2] Trebilcock et al., *Regulation of International Trade*, p. 292.   [3] Jackson, *World Trading System*, p. 222.
[4] WTO, Note by the Secretariat, 'Negotiating History of the Coverage of the Agreement on Technical Barriers to Trade with Regard to Labelling Requirements, Voluntary Standards, and Process and Production Methods Unrelated to Product Characteristics', G/TBT/W/11 (29 August 1995), para. 4.

was a direct result of the Tokyo Round, it was not signed by all contracting parties to the GATT 1947. It was a plurilateral agreement. The Standards Code established the principle that technical regulations should not be used as barriers to trade. The TBT Agreement which evolved from the Standards Code became an integral part of the 'single undertaking' of the Uruguay Round Agreements.

4.1.1 Scope of the Agreement

The TBT is a specialised legal regime that applies solely to a limited class of measures. For these measures, the TBT Agreement imposes obligations on members that seem to be different from, and additional to, the obligations imposed on members under the GATT 1994.[5]

The TBT Agreement applies to:

- *Technical regulations*: measures that lay down product characteristics or their related processes and production methods, with which compliance is mandatory.
- *Standards*: measures approved by a recognised body that provide, for common and repeated use, rules, guidelines or characteristics for products or related processes and production methods, with which compliance is voluntary.
- *Conformity assessment procedures*: procedures used, directly or indirectly, to determine the fulfilment of relevant requirements contained in technical regulations or standards.

The TBT Agreement applies to final products and/or to related processes and production methods. Technical regulations and standards include terminology, symbols, packaging, marking or labelling requirements, among others. However, two areas of trade in goods are excluded from the TBT Agreement: sanitary and phytosanitary measures, and government procurement specifications.[6] Technical measures relating to services are dealt with under Article VI:4 of the GATS, and do not come under the TBT Agreement.

The SPS Agreement covers regulations with very specific objectives, such as to prevent risks arising from food, and animal or plant-carried diseases and pests. If a measure qualifies according to the definition set out in Annex A(1) of the SPS Agreement, then the SPS Agreement applies to the exclusion of the TBT Agreement. It has been considered that the relationship between the agreements is one of 'mutual exclusivity'.[7] Some have also considered that the SPS Agreement has been carved out from TBT and is intended to deal with a 'limited set of measures'.[8] The Panel in *EC – Hormones* referred to Article 1.5 of the TBT

---

[5] Appellate Body Report, *EC – Asbestos*, para. 80.

[6] Government procurement specifications are addressed in the Government Procurement Agreement and are not subject to the provisions of the TBT Agreement: TBT Agreement, Art. 1.4.

[7] P. V. D. Bossche and W. Zdouc, *The Law and Policy of the World Trade Organization: Text, Cases and Materials* (Cambridge University Press, 2013), p. 943.

[8] D. A. Motaal, 'The Multilateral Scientific Consensus and the World Trade Organization', *Journal of World Trade* (2004), 38, p. 856.

Agreement and stated: '[s]ince the measures in dispute are sanitary measures, we find that the TBT Agreement is not applicable to this dispute'.[9]

The SPS Agreement covers all measures intended to protect human or animal health from food-borne risks, human health from animal- or plant-carried diseases, and animals and plants from pests or diseases; and to prevent other damage from pests. On the other hand, the TBT Agreement covers all technical regulations, standards and conformity assessment procedures, regardless of their objectives, except when these are sanitary or phytosanitary measures, as defined by Annex A of the SPS Agreement.

4.1.2 Technical Regulation

As stated above, the TBT Agreement applies only to a limited class of measures, prominent among which are technical regulations. In Annex 1.1 of the TBT Agreement, a technical regulation is defined as:

> ### *Technical Regulations – Definition*
>
> ### Annex 1:1
>
> Document that lays down product characteristics or their related processes and production methods, including the applicable administrative provisions, with which compliance is mandatory. It may also include or deal exclusively with terminology, symbols, packaging, marking or labelling requirements as they apply to a product, process or production method.

For example, a regulation that a product should be 'pesticide-free' is a technical regulation. The hallmark of a technical regulation is that it stipulates that in order to be marketed or sold, a product must or must not contain certain product characteristics.

The determination of whether a measure constitutes a technical regulation 'must be made in light of the characteristics of the measure at issue and the circumstances of the case'.[10] In some recent cases, namely, *EC – Asbestos, EC – Sardines, US – COOL* and *EC – Seal Products*, the Appellate Body established a three-tier test for determining whether a measure is a 'technical regulation' under the TBT Agreement.

---

[9] Panel Report, *European Communities – Measures Concerning Meat and Meat Products (Hormones), Complaint by Canada*, WT/DS48/R/CAN, adopted 13 February 1998, as modified by Appellate Body Report WT/DS26/AB/R, WT/DS48/AB/R, para. 8.32; Panel Report, *European Communities – Measures Concerning Meat and Meat Products (Hormones), Complaint by the United States*, WT/DS26/R/USA, adopted 13 February 1998, as modified by Appellate Body Report WT/DS26/AB/R, WT/DS48/AB/R, para. 8.29.

[10] Appellate Body Report, *United States – Measures Concerning the Importation, Marketing and Sale of Tuna and Tuna Products*, WT/DS381/AB/R, adopted 13 June 2012, para. 188.

- First, the document must apply to an identifiable product or group of products.
- Second, the document must lay down one or more characteristics of the product. These product characteristics may be intrinsic or they may be related to the product. They may be prescribed or imposed in either a positive or a negative form.
- Third, compliance with the product characteristics must be (directly or indirectly) mandatory.

The heart of the definition of a technical regulation is that the 'document' must 'lay down' – that is, set forth, stipulate or provide – 'product characteristics'.[11] The term 'product characteristics' in Annex 1.1 of the TBT Agreement should be interpreted in accordance with its ordinary meaning.

EC – Asbestos

On 24 December 1996, the French Government adopted Decree No. 96-1133 (Decree), which entered into force on 1 January 1997. Article 1 of the Decree provides for a ban on asbestos, stating in relevant part:

I. **For the purpose of protecting workers,** ... the manufacture, processing, sale, import, placing on the domestic market and transfer under any title whatsoever of all varieties of asbestos fibres shall be prohibited, regardless of whether these substances have been incorporated into materials, products or devices.
II. **For the purpose of protecting consumers,** ... the manufacture, import, domestic marketing, exportation, possession for sale, offer, sale and transfer under any title whatsoever of all varieties of asbestos fibres or any product containing asbestos fibres shall be prohibited.

Article 2 provides certain limited exceptions to the ban for chrysotile asbestos (also called white asbestos) fibres:

2.1. On an exceptional and temporary basis, the bans instituted under Article 1 shall not apply to certain existing materials, products or devices containing chrysotile fibre when, to perform an equivalent function, no substitute for that fibre is available which:
On the one hand, in the present state of scientific knowledge, poses a lesser occupational health risk than chrysotile fibre to workers handling those materials, products or devices;
On the other, provides all technical guarantees of safety corresponding to the ultimate purpose of the use thereof.

Canada argued that the Decree is a technical regulation within the meaning of Article 2.1 of the TBT Agreement and violated Articles 2.2, 2.4 and 2.8. The WTO Panel held that the TBT Agreement does not apply to the part of the Decree concerning the ban on imports of asbestos and asbestos-containing products within the meaning of Annex 1:1.[12] The Panel, however, held that the TBT Agreement applies to the part of the Decree relating to the exceptions to the ban.[13] Since Canada did not make specific claims concerning the exceptions to the general ban, the case was ultimately decided under Article III:4 of the GATT.

---

[11] Appellate Body Report, *EC – Asbestos*, para. 65.   [12] Panel Report, *EC – Asbestos*, para. 8.72.
[13] Panel Report, *EC – Asbestos*, para. 8.72.

(See Chapter 1 for a detailed analysis of Article III:4.) However, the Panel's finding was overturned on appeal. The Appellate Body observed:

EC – Asbestos *(Appellate Body)*

64. In our view, the proper legal character of the measure at issue cannot be determined unless the measure is examined as a whole. Article 1 of the Decree contains broad, general prohibitions on asbestos and products containing asbestos. However, the scope and generality of those prohibitions can only be understood in light of the exceptions to it which, albeit for a limited period, permit, *inter alia*, the use of certain products containing asbestos and, principally, products containing chrysotile asbestos fibres. The measure is, therefore, not a *total* prohibition on asbestos fibres, because it also includes provisions that *permit*, for a limited duration, the use of asbestos in certain situations. Thus, to characterise the measure simply as a general prohibition, and to examine it as such, overlooks the complexities of the measure, which include both prohibitive and permissive elements. In addition, we observe that the exceptions in the measure would have no autonomous legal significance in the absence of the prohibitions. We, therefore, conclude that the measure at issue is to be examined as an integrated whole, taking into account, as appropriate, the prohibitive and the permissive elements that are part of it.

    [...]

68. The definition of a 'technical regulation' in Annex 1.1 of the TBT *Agreement* also states that '*compliance*' with the 'product characteristics' laid down in the 'document' must be '*mandatory*'. A 'technical regulation' must, in other words, regulate the 'characteristics' of products in a binding or compulsory fashion. It follows that, with respect to products, a 'technical regulation' has the effect of *prescribing* or imposing one or more 'characteristics' – 'features', 'qualities', 'attributes', or other 'distinguishing mark'.

69. 'Product characteristics' may, in our view, be prescribed or imposed with respect to products in either a positive or a negative form. That is, the document may provide, positively, that products *must possess* certain 'characteristics', or the document may require, negatively, that products must *not possess* certain 'characteristics'. In both cases, the legal result is the same: the document 'lays down' certain binding 'characteristics' for products, in one case affirmatively, and in the other by negative implication.

70. A 'technical regulation' must, of course, be applicable to an identifiable product, or group of products. Otherwise, enforcement of the regulation will, in practical terms, be impossible. ... Clearly, compliance with this obligation requires identification of the product coverage of a technical regulation. However, in contrast to what the

> **(cont.)**
>
> Panel suggested, this does not mean that a 'technical regulation' must apply to '*given*' products which are actually *named, identified* or *specified* in the regulation.[14] Although the *TBT Agreement* clearly applies to 'products' generally, nothing in the text of that Agreement suggests that those products need be named or otherwise *expressly* identified in a 'technical regulation'. Moreover, there may be perfectly sound administrative reasons for formulating a 'technical regulation' in a way that does *not* expressly identify products by name, but simply makes them identifiable – for instance, through the 'characteristic' that is the subject of regulation.

In *EC – Asbestos*, the Appellate Body found that a general ban on asbestos containing asbestos fibres, together with the exceptions, provide for 'product characteristics'. The Appellate Body, however, noted that a prohibition of asbestos in its natural state is not a technical regulation.[15] The French Decree was a regulation on *products that contain asbestos*. Accordingly, on a broad generalisation, if the market placing of a product is dependent upon the absence or presence of certain product characteristics, there is a strong possibility of treating such a measure as a technical regulation.

The characterisation of a measure as a technical regulation has significant implications in a WTO dispute. *EC – Seal Products*, yet another landmark dispute, addresses some of these issues.

EC – Seal Products

EC – Seal Products relates to a certain legislative scheme adopted by the EU to regulate the importation and marketing of seal products. The EU considered that the methods typically used to kill and extract seal skins amounted to significant pain and suffering.[16] In essence, the EU measures were rooted in non-instrumental values such as public moral or animal welfare considerations.[17] The EU seal regime laid down that seal products (pure seal products and seal-containing products) were permitted only in three situations: (1) the seal products result from traditional seal hunts, namely by the Inuit community ('IC hunts'); (2) the seal products derived from marine resource management hunts ('MRM hunts'); and (3) imports by travellers for non-commercial purposes ('travellers' exceptions').

Canada was a major exporter in seal products. In 2008, the year before the European ban, Canada exported approximately CAD$2.5 million in seal products to the EU.[18] The ban on

---

[14] Panel Reports, *EC – Seal Products*, para. 8.57. [15] Appellate Body Report, *EC – Asbestos*, para. 71.

[16] Regulation (EC) 1007/2009 of the European Parliament and of the Council of 16 September 2009 on Trade in Seal Products, 2009 Official Journal (L286), p. 36.

[17] R. Howse and J. Langille, 'Permitting Pluralism: The Seals Product Dispute and Why the WTO Should Accept Trade Restrictions Justified by Noninstrumental Moral Values', *Yale Journal of International Law* (2012), 37, p. 368.

[18] Howse and Langille, 'Permitting Pluralism', p. 370.

commercially hunted seal products had an immediate trade impact on Canada. Norway also filed a separate dispute.[19]

The nature and structure of the EC seal regime was remarkably similar to the measure in *EC – Asbestos*. The measure in *EC – Asbestos* imposed bans on the importation of not only asbestos fibres, but also products that contained asbestos fibres. Both the measures had prohibitive and permissive aspects.

The Panel in *EC – Seal Products* highlighted the fact that 'the prohibition on seal-containing products under the EU seal regime lays down a product characteristic in the negative form by requiring that all products . . . not contain seal', and concluded that the EC seal regime falls into the ambit of the TBT Agreement.[20] Nevertheless, the Appellate Body afterwards reversed the Panel finding that the EC seal regime was a technical regulation. According to the Appellate Body, a Panel must carefully examine the design and operation of the measure while seeking to identify its 'integral and essential' aspects. These features of the measure are to be accorded the most weight for the purpose of characterising the measure. The conclusion as to the legal characterisation of the measure must be made in respect of the measure as a whole.[21]

EC – Seal Products *(Appellate Body)*

5.58. . . . [W]hen the prohibitive aspects of the EU Seal Regime are considered in the light of the IC and MRM exceptions, it becomes apparent that the measure is not concerned with banning the placing on the EU market of seal products as such. Instead, it establishes the conditions for placing seal products on the EU market based on criteria relating to the identity of the hunter or the type or purpose of the hunt from which the product is derived. We view this as the main feature of the measure. That being so, we do not consider that the measure as a whole lays down product characteristics.

There were certain apparent distinctions between *EC – Asbestos* and *EC – Seal Products*. In *EC – Asbestos*, the asbestos-containing products were regulated in view of their carcinogenic properties, whereas the regulation in *EC – Seal Products* was not purely on account of whether the product contained seal as an input or not. There was a complete exception for IC hunts. Stated differently, 'the identity of the hunter, the type of hunt, or the purpose of the hunt', are per se not product characteristics. According to the Appellate Body, the exceptions under *EC – Seal Products* did not lay down product characteristics.[22]

---

[19] Request for Consultations, *European Communities – Measures Prohibiting the Importation and Marketing of Seal Products*, WT/DS401/1, 10 November 2009.

[20] Panel Reports, *EC – Seal Products*, para. 7.106.   [21] Panel Reports, *EC – Seal Products*, para. 7.125.

[22] Appellate Body Reports, *EC – Seal Products*, para. 5.45.

The EC seal regime indeed involved a process and production method (PPM), based on the identity of the hunter or the nature of the hunt.

4.1.2.1 Process and Production Method

The TBT Agreement allows WTO members to make regulatory interventions in the market, under certain conditions, to ensure quality and standards of a product. The regulations can apply on product characteristics or their *related* processes and production methods. It is, however, widely debated within the scholarly community whether technical regulations can apply to measures that specify the non-physical aspects of a product.[23] In *EC – Sardines*, the Appellate Body emphasised that product characteristics include not only 'features and qualities intrinsic to the product', but also those that are related to it, such as means of identification.[24] In *EC –Seal Products*, the Appellate Body noted that the definition of a technical regulation also provides that a regulation may prescribe 'product characteristics or their related processes and production methods'.[25] However, most of these decisions point to the fact that the processes and production methods prescribed by the measure have a sufficient nexus to the characteristics of a product.[26] Otherwise, it is impossible to argue that these attributes are 'related to' those characteristics.

The applicability of the TBT Agreement on non-product-related processes or production methods (npr-PPM) is still debated. The last sentence of Annex 1.1 stipulates that a technical regulation may also include or deal exclusively with terminology, symbols, packaging, marking or labelling requirements as they apply to a product, process or production method. Interestingly, the last sentence does not include the word 'related' before process or production method. The rationale for this omission seems to be that packaging, labelling, marking, and so on, are all visible forms of the product itself and could be an intrinsic part of the product characteristics.[27]

The Appellate Body in *US – Tuna II (Mexico)* held that labelling schemes depicting how tuna are harvested fall within the Annex 1.1 definition of 'technical regulation'.[28] Although the first sentence of Annex 1.1 refers to the terms 'their related' processes and production methods, these terms are conspicuous by their absence in the second sentence. While there is

---

[23] Bossche and Zdouc, *Law and Policy of the World Trade Organization*, p. 887; M. Du, 'What Is a "Technical Regulation" in the TBT Agreement?', *European Journal of Risk Regulation* (2015), 6, p. 396; Robert Howse, 'WTO Seals: What Is it Really that Makes the AB Think that TBT Doesn't Apply?', *International Economic Law and Policy Blog* (25 May 2014), available at http://worldtradelaw.typepad.com/ielpblog/2014/05/wto-sealswhat-is-it-really-that-makes-the-ab-think-that-tbt-doesnt-apply.html (accessed 5 November 2020).

[24] Appellate Body Report, *European Communities – Trade Description of Sardines*, WT/DS231/AB/R, adopted 23 October 2002, para. 189.

[25] Appellate Body Reports, *EC – Seal Products*, para. 5.12.

[26] Appellate Body Reports, *EC – Seal Products*, para. 5.12.

[27] Appellate Body Reports, *Australia – Certain Measures concerning Trademarks, Geographical Indications and other Plain Packaging Requirements applicable to Tobacco Products and Packaging*, WT/DS441/AB/R, Add.1, adopted 29 June 2020, para. 6.4.

[28] Appellate Body Report, *US – Tuna II (Mexico)*, para. 199.

a view that these two sentences should be read together,[29] there are also contrasting views as to whether npr-PPMs may be applicable to labelling requirements.[30]

4.1.3 Standards

Standards are different from technical regulations. They are voluntary in nature. Annex 1.2 to the TBT Agreement defines a 'standard' as follows:

TBT Agreement, Annex 1.2

Standard

Document approved by a recognized body, that provides, for common and repeated use, rules, guidelines or characteristics for products or related processes and production methods, with which compliance is not mandatory. It may also include or deal exclusively with terminology, symbols, packaging, marking or labelling requirements as they apply to a product, process or production method.

Explanatory note

The terms as defined in ISO/IEC Guide 2 cover products, processes and services. This Agreement deals only with technical regulations, standards and conformity assessment procedures related to products or processes and production methods. Standards as defined by ISO/IEC Guide 2 may be mandatory or voluntary. For the purpose of this Agreement standards are defined as voluntary and technical regulations as mandatory documents. Standards prepared by the international standardization community are based on consensus. This Agreement covers also documents that are not based on consensus.

The term 'recognized body' is defined neither in the TBT Agreement nor in the ISO/IEC Guide 2. However, Annex 1 (paragraphs 4–8) refers to the different types of bodies whose documents are either covered by, or referred to, in the TBT Agreement. These include: international body or system; regional body or system; central government body; local government body; and non-governmental body.

The obligations related to standards in the TBT Agreement are found in two provisions:

- Preparation, Adoption and Application of Standards (Article 4)
- Code of Good Practice for the Preparation, Adoption and Application of Standards (Annex 3)

---

[29] Bossche and Zdouc, *Law and Policy of the World Trade Organization*, p. 887.

[30] A. E. Appleton, 'The *US – Shrimp* Appeal: Twenty Years On', in Das and Nedumpara, *WTO Dispute Settlement at Twenty*, p. 631.

Article 4 of the TBT Agreement establishes the Code of Good Practice for the Preparation, Adoption and Application of Standards. Its text is contained in Annex 3 (Code of Good Practice). Annex 3(B) stipulates that the Code is open to acceptance by any standardising body within the territory of a member of the WTO, whether a central government body, a local government body, a non-governmental body, any governmental or non-governmental regional standardising body to which a member (or body within its territory) is a party to.[31]

US – Tuna II (Mexico)

In *US – Tuna II (Mexico)*, the Panel and the Appellate Body considered the meaning of the term 'international standard'. The issue was whether tuna labelling schemes prepared by the Agreement on the International Dolphin Conservation Program (AIDCP) was an 'international standard' or not. According to US law, tuna caught by 'setting on dolphin' in the Eastern Tropical Pacific Ocean was not eligible for the dolphin-safe label. Mexico argued that the US labelling scheme for 'dolphin-safe' tuna had not used the AIDCP requirements 'as a basis'. The Panel and, later, the Appellate Body examined the meaning of the term 'international standard'.

US – Tuna II (Mexico) *(Panel)*

7.663. The term 'international standard' is not defined in Annex 1 of the TBT Agreement, but is defined in the ISO/IEC Guide 2. In accordance with the terms of Annex 1, in the absence of a specific definition of this term in Annex 1, the term 'international standard' should be understood to have the same meaning in the TBT Agreement as in the ISO/IEC Guide 2, which defines it as a 'standard that is adopted by an international standardizing/standards organization and made available to the public'.

The Panel found that the AIDCP was a standardising body.[32]

US – Tuna II (Mexico) *(Appellate Body)*

353. ... The term 'international standard' is defined in the ISO/IEC Guide 2:1991 as a 'standard' that is adopted by an international standardizing/standards organization and made available to the public. This definition suggests that it is primarily the characteristics of the entity approving a standard that lends the standard its 'international' character. By contrast, the subject matter of a standard would not appear to be material to the determination of whether the standard is 'international'.

[...]

---

[31] TBT Agreement, Annex 3(B).   [32] Panel Report, *US – Tuna II (Mexico)*, paras. 7.686–7.687.

(cont.)

355. With respect to the type of entity approving an 'international standard', the ISO/IEC Guide 2:1991 refers to an 'organization', whereas Annex 1.2 of the TBT Agreement stipulates that a 'standard' is to be approved by a 'body'. According to the ISO/IEC Guide 2:1991, a 'body' is a 'legal or administrative entity that has specific tasks and composition', whereas an 'organization' is a 'body that is based on the membership of other bodies or individuals and has an established constitution and its own administration'. The answer to the question of whether an 'international' standard has to be approved by a 'body' or an 'organization' thus determines whether the entity can be a 'legal or administrative entity that has specific tasks and composition', or whether the entity must also be 'based on the membership of other bodies or individuals' and must have 'an established constitution and its own administration'.

The United States argued in this case that 'neither the AIDCP nor the parties constitute a body'. Furthermore, only a limited number of countries participated in the adoption of the AIDCP resolution. The Appellate Body while addressing this issue noted that Annex 1.2 of the TBT Agreement referred to a 'body' and not to an 'organization'. According to the Appellate Body, the definitions in Annex 1 to the TBT Agreement prevailed over the definitions in the ISO:IEC Guide 1:1991. The Appellate Body held that in order to constitute an 'international standard' for the purposes of the TBT Agreement, a standard has to be adopted by an 'international standardizing body'.

US – Tuna II (Mexico) *(Appellate Body)*

359. We consider, therefore, that a required element of the definition of an 'international' standard for the purposes of the TBT Agreement is the approval of the standard by an 'international standardizing body', that is, a body that has recognized activities in standardization and whose membership is open to the relevant bodies of at least all members.

To summarise, an 'international standard' is thus composed of three elements: a standard, adopted by an international standardising/standards body, and made available to the public. The Appellate Body in *US – Tuna II (Mexico)* noted that a 'standardizing body' is defined as a 'body that has recognized activities in standardization', whereas a 'standards body' is a 'standardizing body recognized at national, regional or international level, that has as a principal function, by virtue of its statutes, the preparation, approval or adoption of standards that are made available to the public'.[33]

---

[33] Appellate Body Report, *US – Tuna II (Mexico)*, para. 357.

4.1.4 International Standards and Harmonisation

The TBT Agreement embodies the concept of harmonisation. The principle of harmonisation was first introduced during the Tokyo Round.[34] Harmonisation means the uniform application of technical regulations and standards across different countries and organisations.[35] The TBT Agreement furthers the concept of harmonisation for technical regulations, conformity assessment procedures and international standards.

1 Technical Regulation – Articles 2.4–2.6
2 Standards – Annex 3(F)–(G) of the Code of Good Practice
3 Conformity Assessment Procedures – Articles 5.4 and 5.5

According to Article 2.4 of the TBT Agreement, members are required to use international standards as a basis for their technical regulations, except where such international standards would be ineffective or inappropriate for the fulfilment of legitimate objectives.

The determination of relevant international standards came up in *EC – Sardines*, which is discussed below.

EC – Sardines

The case dealt with an EC regulation, which had set out a number of prescriptions for the sale of 'preserved sardines', including the requirement that they contain only one named species of sardine, namely, *sardina pilchardus*. The standard at issue was Codex Stan 94 – Standard for Canned Sardines and Sardine-Type Products. Peru contended that the EC Regulations were not 'based' on the international standards as provided under Article 2.4 of the TBT Agreement. The EC, however, contested that Codex Stan 94 was not a 'relevant international standard'. According to the EC, Codex Stan 94 was accepted by only eighteen countries, of which only four had accepted it fully. Again, the EC contended that none of the member States of the EU, or even Peru, had accepted Codex Stan 94.[36]

In order to examine the notion of 'relevant international standard' under Article 2.4, the Appellate Body considered the relationship between the definitions under Annex 1 of the TBT Agreement and the ISO/IEC Guide.

EC – Sardines *(Appellate Body)*

224. ... The definition of a standard in Annex 1 to the TBT Agreement departs from that provided in the ISO/IEC Guide precisely in respect of whether consensus is expressly required.

---

[34] *Proposed GATT Code of Conduct for Preventing Technical Barriers to Trade*, GATT Doc. Spec (71) 143, 30 December 1971 (Revised Draft 1979); Agreement on Technical Barriers to Trade, BISD 26S/8, 12 April 1979 (Tokyo Rounds Standards Code).

[35] Revised Draft 1979; H. Z. Schroder, *Harmonization, Equivalence and Mutual Recognition of Standards in WTO Law* (Alphen aan den Rijn: Kluwer Law International, 2011), p. 46.

[36] Panel Report, *EC – Sardines*, para. 4.33.

4.1.4.1 Meaning of 'Consensus' in International Standard Setting

Consensus is defined in ISO/IEC Guide 2 as 'general agreement, characterised by the absence of sustained opposition to substantial issues by any important part of the concerned interests and by a process that involves seeking to take into account the views of all parties concerned and to reconcile any conflicting arguments'.[37]

The Appellate Body in *EC – Sardines* upheld the Panel's conclusion that even if not adopted by consensus, an international standard can constitute a 'relevant international standard'.[38] The Appellate Body agreed with the following interpretation by the Panel of the last two sentences of the Explanatory note to the definition of the term 'standard', as contained in Annex 1, paragraph 2:

EC – Sardines *(Appellate Body)*

222. The first sentence reiterates the norm of the international standardization community that standards are prepared based on consensus. The following sentence, however, acknowledges that consensus may not always be achieved and that international standards that were not adopted by consensus are within the scope of the TBT Agreement. This provision therefore confirms that even if not adopted by consensus, an international standard can constitute a relevant international standard.

An important issue is whether a standard that is not adopted by 'unanimity' could still be considered as a 'relevant international standard'. Although *EC – Sardines* has by and large clarified this position, there remain certain apparent contradictions in the language of Annex 1.2. In particular, the penultimate line of the Explanatory note to Annex 1.2 clearly indicates that '[s]tandards prepared by the international standardization community are based on consensus'. At the same time, the last line of the Explanatory note states that '[t]his Agreement also covers documents that are not based on consensus'. In any case, the Appellate Body's statement in *EC – Sardines*, that the 'omission of a consensus requirement in the definition of a "standard" in Annex 1.2 was a deliberate choice on the part of the drafters of the TBT Agreement', may remain somewhat questionable.[39]

4.1.4.2 'Ineffective or Inappropriate Means' for the Fulfilment of 'Legitimate Objectives'

In *EC – Sardines*, the Appellate Body held that the interpretation of the second part of Article 2.4 raises two questions: first, the meaning of the term 'ineffective or inappropriate means'; and second, the meaning of the term 'legitimate objectives'.

---

[37] *ISO/IEC Guide 2: 1991: General Terms and their Definitions Concerning Standardization and Related Activities*, 6th ed. (1991).

[38] Appellate Body Report, *EC – Sardines*, paras. 222–227.   [39] Appellate Body Report, *EC – Sardines*, para. 225.

The term 'ineffective or inappropriate means' refers to two aspects – the *effectiveness* of the measure and the *appropriateness* of the measure. The Appellate Body clarified the meaning of the two concepts as follows:

EC – Sardines *(Appellate Body)*

285. Thus, in the context of Article 2.4, an ineffective means is a means which does not have the function of accomplishing the legitimate objective pursued, whereas an inappropriate means is a means which is not especially suitable for the fulfilment of the legitimate objective pursued. An inappropriate means will not necessarily be an ineffective means and vice versa. That is, whereas it may not be especially suitable for the fulfilment of the legitimate objective, an inappropriate means may nevertheless be effective in fulfilling that objective, despite its 'unsuitability'. Conversely, when a relevant international standard is found to be an effective means, it does not automatically follow that it is also an appropriate means. The question of effectiveness bears upon the results of the means employed, whereas the question of appropriateness relates more to the nature of the means employed.

On the other hand, 'legitimate objectives' referred to in Article 2.4 must be interpreted in the context of Article 2.2 of the TBT Agreement, which provides an illustrative and open list of objectives, considered 'legitimate'. The Appellate Body in *US – COOL* noted that in identifying the objective pursued by a member, a panel should take into account the member's articulation of its objectives. The Appellate Body, however, clarified that a panel is not bound by a member's characterisation of such objectives.[40]

4.1.5 Substantive Obligations in the TBT Agreement

4.1.5.1 Non-Discrimination Obligation

Article 2.1 of the TBT Agreement establishes the key obligations – that is, the requirement that WTO members accord products originating from the territories of other WTO members a treatment 'no less favourable than that accorded to like products of national origin and to like products originating in any other country'. It is a combination of both the MFN and the NT requirements. In *US – COOL*, the Appellate Body noted that the MFN treatment obligation prohibits discrimination through technical regulations among like products imported from different countries, while the national treatment obligation prohibits discrimination between domestic and imported like products.[41]

The examination of a claim under Article 2.1 of the TBT is very similar to the examination under the GATT. Given the wording of Article III:4 of the GATT 1994 and Article 2.1

---

[40] Appellate Body Reports, *US – COOL*, para. 371.   [41] Appellate Body Reports, *US – COOL*, para. 267.

of the TBT Agreement, the same measure can be challenged at the same time under both agreements. Nonetheless, there are important differences between the two provisions, which are eloquently brought out in *US – Clove Cigarettes*.

US – CLOVE CIGARETTES

In 2009, the US Congress passed the Family Smoking Prevention and Tobacco Control Act,[42] which introduced an amendment in Section 907 of the Federal Food, Drug, and Cosmetic Act. This amendment prohibited the production and sale of cigarettes with 'characterising flavours', including fruit, chocolate, cinnamon and clove, among others.[43]

The purported objective of the US legislation was to 'protect the public health, including by reducing the number of children and adolescents who smoke cigarettes', by introducing a ban on the manufacture and sale of cigarettes with certain 'characterising flavour' that appeal to the youth. However, the US legislation exempted menthol cigarettes, a flavoured category of cigarettes, from the ban, while not according the same treatment to a number of other flavoured cigarettes, such as clove, cinnamon, cocoa. Indonesia largely exported clove cigarettes, although its share in the US market was extremely low, somewhere between 0.13 and 0.6 per cent during the period 2000–2009.[44] On the other hand, menthol cigarettes were largely produced by domestic tobacco manufacturers and represented a quarter of the US cigarette market.

Indonesia brought a complaint against the United States that the US measure had violated the national treatment obligation under Article 2.1 and the obligation to explore less trade-restrictive alternatives under Article 2.2.

US – Clove Cigarettes *(Appellate Body)*

91. While this recital [the second recital to the TBT Agreement] may be read as suggesting that the TBT Agreement is a 'development' or 'step forward' from the disciplines of GATT 1994, in our view, it also suggests that two agreements overlap in scope and have similar objectives. If this were not true, the TBT Agreement could not serve to 'further the objectives' of the GATT 1994. The second recital indicates that the TBT Agreement expands on pre-existing GATT disciplines and emphasizes that the two agreements should be interpreted in a coherent and consistent manner.

While examining the consistency of a measure under Article 2.1, a panel must examine (1) whether the measure is a technical regulation; (2) whether the imported and domestic products are 'like'; and (3) whether the imported products are treated less favourably than

---

[42] Family Smoking Prevention and Tobacco Control Act, Public Law No. 111-31, 123 Stat. 1776.
[43] Family Smoking Prevention and Tobacco Control Act, Sections 101(b), 907(a)(1)(A).
[44] Executive Summary of the Second Written Submission of the United States to the Panel in *US – Clove Cigarettes*, available at the website of the Office of the US Trade Representative, available at https://ustr.gov/node/1457 (accessed 21 December 2020), para. 21.

like domestic products. The measure was unarguably a technical regulation, whereas the United States contested the Panel's finding that clove and menthol cigarettes are like products.

While the Appellate Body did not object to the Panel's reliance on the likeness criteria developed in the jurisprudence under Article III of the GATT 1994, it disagreed with the particular weight the Panel attached to the health objective of the technical regulation at issue in its assessment of the products' physical characteristics and consumers' tastes and habits. The Appellate Body noted:

US – Clove Cigarettes *(Appellate Body)*

111. We agree that the very concept of 'treatment no less favourable' which is expressed in the same words in Article III:4 of the GATT 1994 and in Article 2.1 of the TBT Agreement, informs the determination of likeness, suggesting that likeness is about the 'nature and extent of the competitive relationship between and among products'. Indeed, the concept of 'treatment no less favourable' links the products to the market place, because only in the market place can it be determined how the measure treats like imported and domestic products . . .

112. In the light of the above, we disagree with the Panel that the text and context of the TBT Agreement support an interpretation of the concept of 'likeness' in Article 2.1 of the TBT Agreement that focuses on the legitimate objectives and purposes of the technical regulation, rather than on the competitive relationship between and among the products.

116. More importantly, however, we do not consider that the concept of 'like products' in Article 2.1 of the TBT Agreement lends itself to distinctions between products that are based on the regulatory objectives of a measure. As we see it, the concept of 'like products' serves to define the scope of products that should be compared to establish whether less favourable treatment is being accorded to imported products. If products that are in a sufficiently strong competitive relationship to be considered like are excluded from the group of like products on the basis of a measure's regulatory purposes, such products would not be compared in order to ascertain whether less favourable treatment has been accorded to imported products. This would inevitably distort the less favourable treatment comparison, as it would refer to a 'marketplace' that would include some like products, but not others.

The Appellate Body further elaborated on why likeness is a determination about competitiveness. The Appellate Body differed from the Panel and adopted an approach that accorded limited weight to policy objectives or regulatory concerns underlying the measure. The Appellate Body noted: '[t]he regulatory concerns underlying a measure, such as the health risks associated with a given product, may be relevant to an analysis of the 'likeness' criteria under Article III:4 of the GATT 1994, as well as under Article 2.1 of the TBT Agreement, to the extent they have an impact on the competitive relationship between and among the products concerned'.[45] *US – Clove Cigarettes* also provided analytical clarity on the interpretation of several likeness criteria, especially on 'end-use' and 'consumer tastes and habits', which form part of the *Border Tax Adjustments* criteria. On the end-use criterion, the Appellate Body found:

US – Clove Cigarettes *(Appellate Body)*

129. An analysis of end-use should be comprehensive and specific enough to provide meaningful guidance as to whether the products in question are like products. It is not disputed that both clove and menthol cigarettes are 'to be smoked'. Nevertheless, 'to be smoked' does not exhaustively describe the functions of cigarettes. As a consequence, to find, as the Panel did, that the end-use of both clove and menthol cigarettes is 'to be smoked' does not, in our view, provide sufficient guidance as to whether such products are like products within the meaning of Article 2.1 of the TBT Agreement.

132. In the light of the above, we disagree with the Panel that the end-use of cigarettes is simply 'to be smoked' and agree with the United States that there are more specific end-uses of cigarettes such as 'satisfying an addiction to nicotine' and 'creating a pleasurable experience associated with the taste of the cigarette and the aroma of the smoke'.

Notwithstanding the above observation, the Appellate Body did not overturn the Panel finding that clove and menthol cigarettes are like products.

In terms of consumer tastes and preferences, the Appellate Body agreed with the United States that the Panel should not have limited its analysis only to young smokers.

US – Clove Cigarettes *(Appellate Body)*

144. The Panel's consideration of consumer tastes and habits was too limited. At the same time, the mere fact that clove cigarettes are smoked disproportionately by youth, while menthol cigarettes are smoked more evenly by young and adult smokers does not necessarily affect the degree of substitutability between clove and menthol cigarettes.

---

[45] Appellate Body Report, *US – Clove Cigarettes*, para. 119.

In conclusion, the Appellate Body found that since both clove and menthol cigarettes are used by young smokers, there was still enough substitutability between the products to find likeness under Article 2.1 of the TBT Agreement.

4.1.5.2 'Treatment no Less Favourable'

As discussed above, a regulatory measure can have implications on the national treatment obligation. A regulatory measure that imposes a prohibition or onerous requirements on essentially imported products while providing a carve-out or a relaxed regime for domestic products could result in a treatment less favourable to the imported product.

The TBT Agreement has no analogous provision to Article XX of the GATT, which provides a list of general exceptions. However, the sixth recital to the preamble of the TBT Agreement provides that countries may take measures necessary for the protection of animal or human life, so long as the measures do not constitute arbitrary or unjustifiable discrimination or a disguised restriction on international trade. The preamble forms an important context in treaty interpretation in customary international law.

Based on previous GATT jurisprudence[46] under Article III:4 of the GATT, and drawing inspiration from the sixth recital, the Appellate Body explained:

US – Clove Cigarettes *(Appellate Body)*

182. [W]here the technical regulation at issue does not *de jure* discriminate against imports, the existence of a detrimental impact on competitive opportunities for the group of imported vis-à-vis the group of domestic like products is not dispositive of less favourable treatment under Article 2.1. Instead, a panel must further analyse whether the detrimental impact on imports stems exclusively from a legitimate regulatory distinction rather than reflecting discrimination against the group of imported products. In making this determination, a panel must carefully scrutinize the particular circumstances of the case, that is, the design, architecture, revealing structure, operation, and application of the technical regulation at issue, and, in particular, whether that technical regulation is even-handed, in order to determine whether it discriminates against the group of imported products.

In subsequent cases, this analytical approach crystallised into the following two-step assessment of whether the technical regulation at issue accords de facto less favourable treatment under Article 2.1: (1) whether the technical regulation modifies the conditions of competition to the detriment of imported products vis-à-vis like products of domestic origin and/or like products originating in any other country; and (2) whether such detrimental

---

[46] Appellate Body Report, *Japan – Alcoholic Beverages II*, p. 29, second paragraph; Appellate Body Report, *US – Gasoline*, p. 20. The Appellate Body obviously did not refer to these cases in reaching this finding.

impact 'stems exclusively from a legitimate regulatory distinction'.[47] The concept of legitimate regulatory distinction[48] requires that the measures are designed and applied in an even-handed manner and not as a means of arbitrary or unjustifiable discrimination.[49]

US – COOL

The matter at issue was US country-of-origin labelling for beef and pork, which was introduced pursuant to the 2002 Farm Bill as amended in 2008. Under this law, most retail food stores were required to inform consumers about the country of origin of a number of agricultural products, including beef and pork. The original measure in *US – COOL* required that muscle cuts of meat from imported and domestic livestock should be sold at retail stores with one of the labels shown in Figure 4.1. The retailer of a covered commodity was required to inform consumers at the final point of sale about the country of origin of the covered commodity. In addition, any person engaged in the business of supplying a covered commodity to the retailer was required to provide information indicating the country of origin of the commodity.[50]

A key issue under Article 2.1 of the TBT Agreement was whether the COOL measure had altered conditions of competition in the market to the detriment of livestock imported from Mexico and Canada. For retailers to ensure that appropriate labels are fixed, meat producers segregated the livestock according to their origin. This would enable them to keep records regarding livestock origin. Furthermore, the COOL measure required details of exactly where each production step took place – that is, the place where the livestock was born, raised and slaughtered. Since the imported livestock constituted a small percentage of the overall US market, the least expensive way of complying with the COOL measure was to avoid segregation by relying exclusively on US livestock.[51] Although the measure did not explicitly require meat producers to adopt the policy of segregation, the measure created incentives for private actors to make choices in ways that would benefit domestic products to the detriment of like imported products, resulting in less favourable treatment in breach of TBT Article 2.1.[52]

---

[47] Appellate Body Report, *US – Tuna II (Mexico)*, para. 215; Appellate Body Reports, *US – COOL*, para. 271; Appellate Body Report, *United States – Measures Concerning the Importation, Marketing and Sale of Tuna and Tuna Products – Recourse to Article 21.5 of the DSU by Mexico*, WT/DS381/AB/RW, Add.1, adopted 3 December 2015, para. 7.26. See also Panel Report, *United States – Measures Concerning the Importation, Marketing and Sale of Tuna and Tuna Products – Recourse to Article 21.5 of the DSU by Mexico*, WT/DS381/RW, Add.1, Corr.1, adopted 3 December 2015, as modified by Appellate Body Report WT/DS381/AB/RW, para. 7.73; Panel Reports, *United States – Certain Country of Origin (COOL) Requirements – Recourse to Article 21.5 of the DSU by Canada and Mexico*, WT/DS384/RW, Add.1, WT/DS386/RW, Add.1, adopted 29 May 2015, as modified by Appellate Reports WT/DS384/AB/RW, WT/DS386/AB/RW, paras. 7.60–7.62.

[48] The concept of using 'legitimate regulatory and policy concerns' in evaluating treatment concerns finds expression in the US gas guzzler tax dispute. See GATT Panel Report, *US – Taxes on Automobiles* (not adopted).

[49] Appellate Body Reports, *US – COOL*, para. 270.

[50] The original COOL measures included the COOL statute passed by the US Congress and its implementing regulation passed by the US Department of Agriculture's Agriculture Market Service (2009 Final Rule).

[51] Panel Reports, *US – COOL*, para. 7.349.

[52] Appellate Body Reports, *US – COOL*, paras. 288, 349; see also Appellate Body Report, *Korea – Various Measures on Beef*, para. 145.

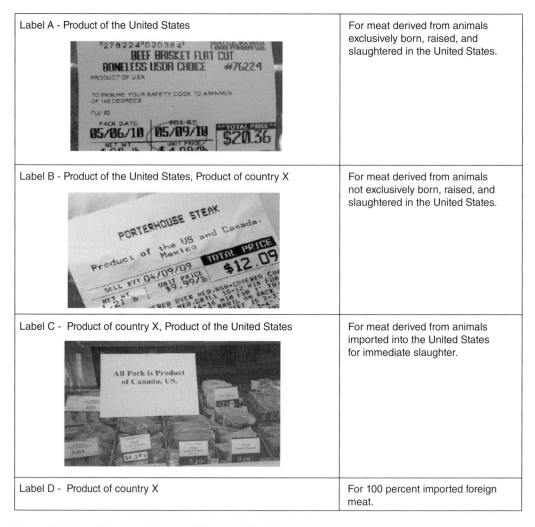

Label A - Product of the United States	For meat derived from animals exclusively born, raised, and slaughtered in the United States.
Label B - Product of the United States, Product of country X	For meat derived from animals not exclusively born, raised, and slaughtered in the United States.
Label C - Product of country X, Product of the United States	For meat derived from animals imported into the United States for immediate slaughter.
Label D - Product of country X	For 100 percent imported foreign meat.

Figure 4.1 *United States – Country of Origin of Labelling*
Canada and Mexico argued that the COOL measure had an adverse impact on their trade.

US – COOL *(Appellate Body)*

288. ... The relevant question is whether it is the governmental measure at issue that affects the conditions under which like goods, domestic and imported, compete in the market. While a measure may not legally require certain treatment of imports, it may nevertheless create incentives for market participants to behave in certain ways, and thereby have the 'practical effect' of treating imported products less favourably.

> **(cont.)**
>
> Thus, the findings in *Korea – Various Measures on Beef* are consistent with, and support the proposition that, whenever the operation of a measure in the market creates incentives for private actors systematically to make choices in ways that benefit domestic products to the detriment of like imported products, then such a measure may be found to treat imported products less favourably.

The Appellate Body also noted that a detrimental impact on the imported goods in itself is not dispositive of a violation of Article 2.1. In other words, the Appellate Body applied the additional test of whether the regulatory distinction stemmed exclusively from a legitimate regulatory distinction that it enunciated in *US – Clove Cigarettes*.

US – COOL *(Appellate Body)*

293. ... The Panel seems to have considered its finding that the COOL measure alters the conditions of competition to the detriment of imported livestock to be dispositive, and to lead, without more, to a finding of violation of the national treatment obligation in Article 2.1 ... The Panel should have continued its examination and determined whether the circumstances of this case indicate that the detrimental impact stems exclusively from a legitimate regulatory distinction, or whether the COOL measure lacks even-handedness. As noted above, where a regulatory distinction is not designed and applied in an even-handed manner – for example, because it is designed or applied in a manner that constitutes a means of arbitrary or unjustifiable discrimination – that distinction cannot be considered legitimate and, thus, the detrimental impact will reflect discrimination prohibited under Article 2.1.

The Appellate Body then noted that since the recordkeeping and verification requirements imposed a disproportionate burden on upstream producers and processors compared to origin information conveyed to consumers, the measure discriminated against imported livestock.[53] Importantly, the origin-related information required to be tracked and verified by upstream producers and processors was not necessarily reflected in the labels. In other words, there was a 'disconnect' between the information that was sought and the information ultimately conveyed to consumers.[54] This regulatory distinction drawn by the COOL measure was therefore not legitimate within the meaning of Article 2.1.[55]

To sum up the larger question of the meaning of 'treatment no less favourable', the Appellate Body clarified in *EC – Seal Products* that the mere similarity of obligations in

---

[53] Appellate Body Reports, *US – COOL*, para. 347.   [54] Appellate Body Reports, *US – COOL*, para. 347.
[55] Appellate Body Reports, *US – COOL*, para. 349.

GATT Article III:4 and TBT Article 2.1 does not mean that the two provisions must be given identical meanings.[56] In addition, the use of the sixth recital in TBT Article 2.1 analysis, which is reflected in the 'legitimate regulatory distinction' test, adds certain elements of the Article XX chapeau analysis into Article 2.1. Yet TBT Article 2.1 and Article XX are quite different.[57]

The Appellate Body has certainly provided a creative and imaginative interpretation of Article 2.1 and has introduced some flexibility for members adopting different regulatory treatment that could detrimentally impact imported products. However, a practical problem with this approach is that a WTO panel could reach diverse and possibly contradictory outcomes while interpreting Article III:4 in combination with Article XX of the GATT, as opposed to interpreting Article 2.1 of the TBT independently, concerning the same measure entailing almost the same type of obligations. In fact, one of the criticisms has been that the Appellate Body's approach leads to different interpretations of similarly worded provisions.[58]

4.1.6   Obligation to Explore Less Trade-Restrictive Measures

Article 2.2 requires that regulations be no more 'trade-restrictive than necessary'. This provision encapsulates the object and purpose of the TBT Agreement by proscribing obstacles to trade, but only those considered unnecessary to attain legitimate objectives.

> ### TBT Agreement, Article 2.2
>
> Members shall ensure that technical regulations are not prepared, adopted or applied with a view to or with the effect of creating unnecessary obstacles to international trade. For this purpose, technical regulations shall not be more trade-restrictive than necessary to fulfil a legitimate objective, taking account of the risks non-fulfilment would create. Such legitimate objectives are, inter alia: national security requirements; the prevention of deceptive practices; protection of human health or safety, animal or plant life or health, or the environment. In assessing such risks, relevant elements of consideration are, inter alia: available scientific and technical information, related processing technology or intended end-uses of products.

The first step in examining the legitimacy of the objective is the identification of the objective of the measure at issue. The objective of any measure can be determined by considering the text of the statute, legislative history and other evidence regarding the structure and operation of the measure.[59] Moreover, the respondent member's

---

[56] Appellate Body Reports, *EC – Seal Products*, para. 5.123.

[57] Appellate Body Reports, *EC – Seal Products*, paras. 5.311–5.313.

[58] United States Trade Representative, 'Report on the Appellate Body of the World Trade Organization', February 2020, p. 93.

[59] Appellate Body Report, *US – Tuna II (Mexico)*, para. 314.

characterisation of the objective can be taken into account, although the Panel is not bound by it. A legitimate objective 'refers to an aim or target that is lawful, justifiable, or proper'.[60]

The definition of 'necessary' that appears in Article 2.2 of the TBT Agreement is derived from GATT cases interpreting Article XX, which set forth the 'least trade-restrictive' test. In determining whether or not a measure is 'more trade-restrictive than necessary to fulfil a legitimate objective', the degree of contribution made by the measure to the legitimate objective at issue must be considered. According to the Appellate Body, the precise inquiry in this respect is to what degree the challenged technical regulation, as written and applied, is capable of contributing and/or actually contributes to the achievement of the legitimate objective pursued by the member.[61]

The Panel in *US – Tuna II (Mexico)* considered that the 'risks of non-fulfilment' language in Article 2.2 required consideration of the 'likelihood and the gravity of potential risks'. In assessing such risks, the relevant elements of consideration are, *inter alia*: available scientific and technical information, related processing technology or intended end-uses of products.[62]

In *US – Tuna II (Mexico)*, the Appellate Body found that an analysis of whether a technical regulation is 'not more trade-restrictive than necessary taking account of the risks non-fulfilment would create' involves a 'relational analysis' and a 'comparative analysis'. According to the Appellate Body, the use of the comparative 'more … than' in the second sentence of Article 2.2 suggests that the existence of an 'unnecessary obstacle to international trade' in the first sentence of Article 2.2 can be established on the basis of a comparative analysis.[63] Stated in plain terms, while technical regulations can have 'some trade restrictiveness', it shall not have a limiting effect on trade more than what is needed to achieve a certain degree of contribution towards the achievement of a legitimate objective.[64]

It is fair to state that some of these 'conceptual tools' can indeed look more complicated than what the plain language of Article 2.2 states. It is reasonably instructive to examine the concluding observations of the Appellate Body in *US – Tuna II (Mexico)*.

US – Tuna II (Mexico) *(Appellate Body)*

322. In sum, we consider that an assessment of whether a technical regulation is 'more trade-restrictive than necessary' within the meaning of Article 2.2 of the TBT Agreement involves an evaluation of a number of factors. A panel should begin by considering factors that include: (i) the degree of contribution made by the measure to the legitimate objective at issue; (ii) the trade-restrictiveness of the measure; and (iii) the nature of the risks at issue and the gravity of consequences that would arise from non-fulfilment of the objective(s) pursued by the Member through the

---

[60] Appellate Body Reports, *US – COOL*, para. 370.   [61] Appellate Body Reports, *US – COOL*, para. 373.
[62] Appellate Body Report, *US – Tuna II (Mexico)*, para. 321.
[63] Appellate Body Reports, *US – COOL*, para. 376.   [64] Appellate Body Reports, *US – COOL*, para. 375.

> *(cont.)*
>
> measure. In most cases, a comparison of the challenged measure and possible alternative measures should be undertaken. In particular, it may be relevant for the purpose of this comparison to consider whether the proposed alternative is less trade-restrictive, whether it would make an equivalent contribution to the relevant legitimate objective, taking account of the risks non-fulfilment would create, and whether it is reasonably available.

In *US – COOL*, the Appellate Body has outlined how the burden of proof in Article 2.2 of the TBT can be met.[65] First, the complainant may identify a possible alternative measure that is less trade-restrictive, makes an equivalent contribution to the relevant objective, and is reasonably available. The respondent may rebut the claim by presenting evidence and arguments that the alternative measure claimed by the complainant is not (1) reasonably available, (2) is not less trade restrictive, or (3) does not make an equivalent contribution to the achievement of the relevant legitimate objective.

More recently, in *Australia – Tobacco Plain Packaging*, the Appellate Body affirmed the use of comparative and relational analysis. The Appellate Body further reaffirmed that such an analysis is not required when the measure is not trade-restrictive at all or when the trade restriction makes no contribution to the achievement of the relevant legitimate objective.[66]

4.1.7   Conformity Assessment Procedures

Conformity assessment procedures (CAPs) are mechanisms to demonstrate that requirements relating to a product, process, system or body are fulfilled.[67] In other words, CAPs provide confidence to regulators, consumers, producers, users and, importantly, the marketplace that certain requirements have been satisfied. CAPs also serve to avoid unnecessary obstacles to international trade, as specified in Article 5.1.2 of the TBT Agreement, which is similar to Article 2.2.[68]

---

[65] Appellate Body Reports, *US – COOL*, para. 379.

[66] Appellate Body Report, *Australia – Certain Measures concerning Trademarks, Geographical Indications and other Plain Packaging Requirements applicable to Tobacco Products and Packaging (Honduras)*, WT/DS435/AB/R, Add.1, adopted 29 June 2020, para. 6.4.

[67] ISO/IEC 17000:2004: 'Conformity assessment – Vocabulary and general principles'.

[68] TBT Agreement, Art. 5.1.2 states that conformity assessment procedures are not prepared, adopted or applied with a view to or with the effect of creating unnecessary obstacles to international trade. This means, inter alia, that conformity assessment procedures shall not be more strict or be applied more strictly than is necessary to give the importing member adequate confidence that products conform to applicable technical regulations or standards, taking account of the risks that non-conformity would create.

A CAP is defined in TBT Annex 1, paragraph 3 as: 'Any procedure used, directly or indirectly, to determine that relevant requirements in technical regulations or standards are fulfilled'.

Out of fifteen Articles in the TBT Agreement, five deal with CAP. Articles 5 and 6 contain the primary disciplines with respect to central government bodies. Articles 7–9 stipulate the application of these basic principles to: local government bodies; non-governmental bodies; and international and regional systems.

The Explanatory note to Annex 1.3 presents a non-exhaustive list of CAPs, which includes: procedures for sampling, testing and inspection; evaluation, verification and assurance of conformity; and registration, accreditation and approval, as well as their combinations.[69]

Under the TBT Agreement, members are required to grant no less favourable access to CAPs for suppliers of like products, domestic and foreign,[70] and to make CAPs no stricter than what is necessary to ensure conformity of products with technical regulations and standards.[71] The TBT Agreement contains no relevant definitions of the types of procedures used for conformity assessment. Testing, inspection and certification procedures, for example, are defined in the document ISO/IEC Guide 2:1991.

EC – TRADEMARKS AND GEOGRAPHICAL INDICATIONS (AUSTRALIA)

The Panel in *EC – Trademarks and Geographical Indications (Australia)* differentiated between conformity assessment procedures and technical regulations and standards.[72] Noting the definition of 'conformity assessment procedures' in Annex 1.3, the Panel observed:

EC – Trademarks and Geographical Indications (Australia) *(Panel)*

7.512. This definition shows that 'conformity assessment procedures' assess conformity with 'technical regulations' and 'standards'. This suggests that they are not only distinct from one other, but mutually exclusive. Whilst a single measure can combine both a technical regulation and a procedure to assess conformity with that technical regulation, it would be an odd result if a conformity assessment procedure could fall within the definition of a technical regulation as well.

---

[69] TBT Agreement, Explanatory note to Annex 1.3.   [70] TBT Agreement, Art. 5.1.1.
[71] TBT Agreement, Art. 5.1.2.
[72] Panel Report, *European Communities – Protection of Trademarks and Geographical Indications for Agricultural Products and Foodstuffs, Complaint by Australia*, WT/DS290/R, adopted 20 April 2005.

4.1.8   Transparency Obligations

All technical regulations, standards and conformity assessment procedures adopted by members must be published in the interests of perusal by other Members.[73] Articles 2.9 and 2.10 together provide that should members seek to formulate technical regulations that do not conform to any existing international standards, they must notify other members of the WTO by detailed notifications, through the WTO Secretariat. This is to ensure that other members are given adequate time to react to such changes and take appropriate actions.

The obligations under Articles 2.9 and 2.10 are triggered when the measure is foreseen to have a significant effect on trade of other members. It also provides that notifications must be made in the early stages of development of the measures, to allow for amendments to be proposed and incorporated therein.

4.1.9   TBT Committee

Article 13.1 of the TBT Agreement sets up the TBT Committee. It allows members to consult on any matter related to operation of the TBT Agreement and the furtherance of its objectives. The Committee is to be composed of representatives from all members and must meet at least once a year. In addition to WTO members and observer governments, the TBT Committee also includes seventeen intergovernmental organisations as observers.[74] Article 13.2 empowers the Committee to set up working parties or other bodies to carry out appropriate responsibilities under the Agreement. Under Article 13.3 it is also tasked with ensuring that unnecessary duplication of work under the TBT Agreement is reduced.

TBT Committee discussions allow for an alternate route to be taken for dispute resolution, rather than reference to the Dispute Settlement Body (DSB). Such discussions are more informal and could result in mutually acceptable resolutions. Given the presence of all members and observers in the Committee, it is sometimes more strategically advisable to bring up issues before the TBT Committee as opposed to the dispute settlement panels. Furthermore, in light of the Appellate Body's ruling in *US – Tuna II (Mexico)*, the decisions of the TBT Committee have legal force and are considered 'subsequent agreements' within the meaning of Article 31(3)(a) of the VCLT.[75]

4.1.10 Conclusion

The TBT Agreement seeks to ensure that technical regulations, standards, rules and conformity assessment procedures do not pose any unnecessary obstacles to trade. The Agreement aims to facilitate international trade in a non-discriminatory manner. The

---

[73] TBT Agreement, Art. 2.11, Annex 3.L, M, N and O contain similar provisions for standards. Arts. 5.6, 5.7, 5.8 and 5.9 have similar provisions for conformity assessment procedures.

[74] *International Intergovernmental Organizations: Observer Status in the Committee on Technical Barriers to Trade – Note by the Secretariat*, WTO Doc. G/TBT/GEN/2, 4 March 2004.

[75] Appellate Body Report, *US – Tuna II (Mexico)*, para. 372.

TBT Agreement builds on the non-discriminatory requirements under the GATT, namely MFN treatment and national treatment. Moreover, the TBT Agreement aims to create a predictable trading environment by introducing specific provisions on transparency and conformity assessment procedures.

4.2   Sanitary and Phytosanitary Measures Agreement

4.2.1   Introduction

The Agreement on Sanitary and Phytosanitary Measures is a covered agreement in the WTO. Much like the TBT Agreement, the SPS Agreement was formulated after the provisions of the GATT 1947 were perceived as inadequate to prevent trade distortions arising from increasingly complex trade regulations.[76] In the Tokyo Round, the Standards Code was formulated with the specific goal of removing non-tariff barriers to trade. The Standards Code applied to 'all products, including industrial and agricultural products'.[77] However, in the decade following the Tokyo Round (1974–79), a consensus emerged that the Standards Code had failed to stem disruptions, especially of trade in agricultural products.[78]

At the beginning of the Uruguay Round, the Punta del Este Declaration specifically mentioned the goal of 'minimising the adverse effects that sanitary and phytosanitary regulations and barriers can have on trade in agriculture',[79] recognising that this area in particular was susceptible to governmental regulation and potential abuse.[80] In the Uruguay Round, specific work was done to address issues identified in the working of the GATT 1947. The decision on SPS measures was arrived at after a long, winding process of negotiations. It started with discussions on a general level, later on expanding to more specialised areas negotiated within a working group assigned to the task, the details of which are elaborated below.

While measures concerning national food safety, animal and plant health were somewhat covered by Article XX(b) of the GATT 1947, the provisions were not adequate to establish a holistic framework to regulate the intersection of the interests of domestic health and the interests of liberal trade. The negotiations also focused on clarifications to Article XX(b) of the GATT 1947 to include SPS measures. Eventually, negotiations ended with the conclusion that the existing legal framework was ineffective in regulating the trade effects of SPS measures, and all efforts to amend the Standards Code were dropped.[81]

---

[76] Trebilcock et al., *Regulation of International Trade*, p. 292.   [77] Tokyo Round Standards Code, Art. 1.

[78] *Sanitary and Phytosanitary Regulation Affecting Trade in Agriculture – Background Note by the Secretariat*, GATT Doc. MTN.GNG/NG5/W/41, 2 February 1988, pp. 2–4; D. Roberts, 'Preliminary Assessment of the Effects of the WTO Agreement on Sanitary and Phytosanitary Trade Regulations', *Journal of International Economic Law* (1998), 1, p. 380.

[79] Punta del Este Declaration, p. 6.

[80] Markus Wagner, 'Interpreting the SPS Agreement: Navigating Risk, Scientific Evidence and Regulatory Autonomy' (19 December 2016), available at https://ssrn.com/abstract=2887361 (accessed 21 December 2020).

[81] *Summary of the Main Points Raised during the Meetings of the Working Group on Sanitary and Phytosanitary Regulations and Barriers*, GATT Doc. No. MTN.GNG/NG5/WGSP/W/2, 14 November 1988.

The SPS issues were also discussed under the general aegis of the Agriculture Committee. Agricultural products were most prone to barriers based on health and safety measures. However, in view of the high political stakes involved in the negotiations on farm subsidies and the technical nature of SPS matters, a different forum for the SPS Agreement was suggested.[82] The Agriculture Committee set up a working group tasked with introducing a new agreement to resolve the issue.[83]

The main task before the working group was to devise ways to differentiate genuine national health and regulatory measures from measures that were designed as disguised barriers to trade. Negotiators realised that international standards were the most cost-effective way of preventing protectionist interventions.[84] The level of potential threat from the trade of a product, and the health and safety standards it is supposed to conform to would be regulated based on a uniform international standard. Adherence to such standards was expected to provide a presumption of consistency or legitimacy.

In the early stages of the negotiations, the need for scientific justification of SPS measures was not deemed necessary.[85] Instead, focus was on a country's ability to determine its own perception of risk. However, such a rule – based solely on a country's self-perception – would hardly represent progress from the existing international regulations on trade. It was quietly acknowledged that regulation of SPS measures cannot be accomplished through international standards alone. Where scientific evidence is available in certain areas, members could rely on such materials. However, risks to human, animal or plant life or health arise from multiple sources, from unknown pathogens and in numerous pathways. Epidemiological conclusions often require detailed study and structured approaches. In reality, choosing an objective risk prevention or mitigation strategy cannot often be based on existing scientific knowledge and materials. At the same time, various SPS measures were not genuinely concerned about existing risks or concerns, but were aimed at protecting the domestic sectors. In other words, there was a need to strike a fine balance by negotiating a new agreement.

The working group developed norms to distinguish genuine health and safety concerns from illicit or bad faith considerations. By 1991, all key issues had been resolved and the parties started working on a legal draft of the negotiation results. Ultimately, the SPS Agreement was negotiated and signed as a part of the 'single undertaking' of the Uruguay Round, making it a part of the WTO regime.

4.2.2 Scope of the SPS Agreement

SPS measures are taken to protect human, animal and plant life or health risks arising from diseases, pests or contaminants. The word 'sanitary' relates to human and animal health,

---

[82] B. Rigod, 'The Purpose of the WTO Agreement on the Application of Sanitary and Phytosanitary Measures (SPS)', *European Journal of International Law* (2013), 24, p. 508.

[83] *Communication from the US on a Health and Sanitary Working Group*, GATT Doc. No. MTN.GNG/ NG5/77, 13 September 1988.

[84] Rigod, 'The Purpose of the WTO Agreement', p. 508.   [85] Rigod, 'The Purpose of the WTO Agreement', p. 507.

while 'phytosanitary' concerns plant protection. Generally, the SPS measures include quarantine treatments; labelling and packaging requirements directly relating to food safety; testing, inspection, certification and approval procedures; and permissible limits of toxins, additives, contaminants and pesticide residue in foods, beverages and feedstuff.[86] Additives and artificial substances are very much part and parcel of modern food and present significant health risks.[87] Importantly, the risk profile of various substances also evolve over time.

With the coming into force of the Agreement, the development and application of SPS measures has to be in accordance with the provisions of the Agreement. Annex A of the SPS Agreement defines SPS measures as follows:

SPS Agreement, Annex A

1. Sanitary or phytosanitary measure – Any measure applied:
   (a) to protect animal or plant life or health within the territory of the Member from risks arising from the entry establishment or spread of pests, diseases, disease-carrying organisms or disease-causing organisms;
   (b) to protect human or animal life or health within the territory of the Member from risks arising from additives, contaminants, toxins or disease-causing organisms in foods, beverages or feedstuffs;
   (c) to protect human life or health within the territory or the Member from risks arising from diseases carried by animals, plants or products thereof, or from the entry, establishment or spread of pests; or
   (d) to prevent or limit other damage within the territory of the Member from the entry, establishment or spread of pests.

This list is exhaustive, designed to limit the application of the SPS Agreement to a specific category of measures, broadly speaking those that aim to protect human, animal or plant life or health, or the territory of a member, from specified risks in food/feed or risks from pests or diseases.[88] For a specific measure to be viewed as an SPS measure, the decisive factor is a subjective one, namely, what counts as the objective or purpose of the regulation.[89] The Appellate Body in *Australia – Apples* noted that the central element in defining an SPS

---

[86] Appleton and Macrory, 'Non-Tariff Barriers', p. 91.

[87] N. Michail, 'EFSA Sets Safe Intake Level for MSG and Glutamate Additives, Urging New Maximum Levels', *Food Navigator* (11 July 2017), available at www.foodnavigator.com/Article/2017/07/12/EFSA-sets-safe-intake-level-for-MSG-and-glutamate-additives-urging-new-maximum-levels (accessed 21 December 2020).

[88] D. Prevost, 'Opening Pandora's Box: The Panel's Findings in the *EC – Biotech Products* Dispute', *Legal Issues of Economic Integration* (2007), 34(1), pp. 67–101.

[89] J. Pauwelyn, 'WTO Agreement on Sanitary and Phytosanitary (SPS) Measures as Applied in the First Three SPS Disputes *EC – Hormones, Australia – Salmon* and *Japan – Varietals*', *Journal of International Economic Law* (1999), 2, p. 641.

measure is the purpose or intention of the measure in question – in other words, its text, structure, design and application.[90]

EC – Approval and Marketing of Biotech Products

The *EC – Approval and Marketing of Biotech Products* dispute had at stake not only the US$ billion agricultural gene technology industry, but also 'the viability of organic farming practices, future food security in developing countries, agricultural sustainability, global biodiversity, long-term human health, and national regulatory autonomy regarding health and environmental concerns'.[91] The dispute involved a complaint by the United States, Canada and Argentina against the EC in relation to genetically modified organisms (GMOs). Around the time of the dispute, an international debate had developed regarding the consumption and production of GMO food products.[92] The United States was pushing for the acceptance of GMO-based products, and the EC, backed by consumer groups and other activists, had tried to restrict their use through various regulations.[93]

This dispute concerned two distinct issues: (1) the operation and application by the EC for approval of biotech products; and (2) certain measures adopted and maintained by specific EC member States prohibiting or restricting the marketing of biotech products. Out of these two issues, three measures were challenged:

First, the de facto moratorium on new approvals of biotech products by the European Communities;

Second, the European Communities measures affecting the approval of biotech products; and

Third, the ban imposed by the six EU member States.

A key threshold issue was whether the measures were within the scope of the SPS Agreement.

EC – Approval and Marketing of Biotech Products *(Appellate Body)*

7.149. Annex A(1) indicates that for the purposes of determining whether a particular measure constitutes an 'SPS measure' regard must be had to such elements as the purpose of the measure, its legal form and its nature. The purpose element is addressed in Annex A(1)(a) through (d) ('any measure applied to'). The form

[90] Appellate Body Report, *Australia – Measures Affecting the Importation of Apples from New Zealand*, WT/DS367/AB/R, adopted 17 December 2010, para. 172.
[91] J. Peel, R. Nelson and L. Godden, 'GMO Trade Wars: The Submissions in the *EC – GMO* Dispute in the WTO', *Melbourne Journal of International Law* (2005), 6, p. 141.
[92] S. Lester and D. Bodansky, '*European Communities – Measures Affecting the Approval and Marketing of Biotech Products*, WT/DS291/R, WT/DS292/R, and WT/DS293/R', *American Journal of International Law* (2007), 101, pp. 453–9.
[93] Lester and Bodansky, '*Biotech Products*'.

> ***(cont.)***
> element is referred to in the second paragraph of Annex A(1) ('laws, decrees, regulations'). Finally, the nature of measures qualifying as SPS measures is also addressed in the second paragraph of Annex A(1) ('requirements and procedures, including, inter alia, end product criteria; processes and production methods; testing, inspection, certification and approval procedures; [etc.]').

4.2.3   Substantive Obligations in the SPS Agreement

4.2.3.1   Basic Rights and Obligations

Article 2 of the SPS Agreement lays down the basic principles of the SPS Agreement. Article 2.1 preserves the right of WTO members to take SPS measures necessary for the protection of human, animal or plant life or health. However, such a right is subject to compliance with all of the obligations set out in the SPS Agreement.[94] The sovereign right to take SPS measures can be exercised only to the extent necessary to protect human, animal or plant life and health, and shall not be maintained without sufficient scientific evidence.[95] The Appellate Body has made clear that the provision has to be read in conjunction with Article 5.1 (risk assessment), as it is a 'specific application of the basic obligations contained in Article 2.2'.[96] The basic obligations set out in Article 2 are generally fulfilled 'through the "particular routes" or "specific obligations" set out in Article 5'.[97]

The Appellate Body in *EC – Hormones* held that the requirements of a risk assessment under Article 5.1, as well as 'sufficient scientific evidence' under Article 2.2, are essential for the maintenance of the delicate and carefully negotiated balance in the SPS Agreement between the shared but competing interests of promoting international trade and protecting the life and health of human beings.[98] Not every evidence can be 'scientific evidence', but only evidence gathered through scientific methods.[99] In *Japan – Apples*, Japan relied upon 'indirect' evidence of a risk of disease transmission through US apple imports. Indirect evidence might include scientific studies or experiences that suggest a link between trade in a product and the occurrence of disease, without establishing causation. Neven and Weiler

---

[94] Appellate Body Report, *India – Measures Concerning the Importation of Certain Agricultural Products*, WT/DS430/AB/R, adopted 19 June 2015, para. 5.21.

[95] SPS Agreement, Art. 2.2.

[96] Appellate Body Report, *European Communities – Measures Concerning Meat and Meat Products (Hormones)*, WT/DS26/AB/R, WT/DS48/AB/R, adopted 13 February 1998, para. 180.

[97] Appellate Body Report, *India – Quantitative Restrictions*, para. 5.25.

[98] Appellate Body Report, *EC – Hormones*, para. 171.

[99] Panel Report, *Japan – Measures Affecting the Importation of Apples*, WT/DS245/R, adopted 10 December 2003, paras. 8.92–8.93, 8.98.

argue that scientific evidence should be based on the quantification of probability of an occurrence to the extent possible; but, in reality, experts are invited to assess the 'risk' which involves a combined evaluation of 'both the scientific probability of an occurrence and a political determination of acceptable danger'.[100]

Article 2, however, requires that the scientific evidence should be 'sufficient' in nature. In other words, Article 2.2 requires a rational or objective relationship between the SPS measure and the scientific evidence, a relationship that is to be determined on a case-by-case basis.[101]

Article 2.3 further states that SPS measures should not discriminate arbitrarily or unjustifiably and should not be applied in a manner that constitutes a disguised restriction on international trade. The non-discrimination requirement in Article 2.3 of the SPS Agreement differs significantly from the non-discrimination principle in the GATT and TBT Agreement. The non-discrimination in Article 2.3 recognises that 'it is the similarity of the risks, rather than the similarity of the products, that matters'.[102] Accordingly, even if the products are different, but the risks posed by them are similar, they should be treated in a similar manner.

4.2.3.2 Harmonisation

The SPS Agreement seeks to promote the harmonisation of national SPS measures.[103] Article 3 of the SPS Agreement deals with the relationship between domestic SPS regulations and international standards.[104] Under Article 3 of the SPS Agreement, members have three options with respect to international standards. They may choose to: (1) base the SPS measures on relevant international standards (Article 3.1); (2) conform the SPS measures to international standards (Article 3.2); or (3) impose SPS measures that would result, in effect, in a higher standard of protection than that aimed to be achieved by the relevant international standards (Article 3.3).

Article 3.2 provides that the SPS measure, which conforms to international standards, guidelines or recommendations, shall be deemed necessary to protect human, animal or plant life or health, and shall be presumed to be consistent with the relevant provisions of this Agreement and of the GATT 1994. In *US/Canada – Continued Suspension*, the Appellate Body noted:[105]

---

[100] D. J. Neven and J. H. H. Weiler, '*Japan – Measures Affecting the Importation of Apples* (AB – 2003–4): One Bad Apple? (DS245/AB/R): A Comment', *World Trade Review* (2006), 5, pp. 280–310.

[101] Appellate Body Report, *Japan – Measures Affecting Agricultural Products*, WT/DS76/AB/R, adopted 19 March 1999, para. 84.

[102] Bossche and Zdouc, *Law and Policy of the World Trade Organization*, p. 951.   [103] SPS Agreement, Annex A(2).

[104] Trebilcock et al., *Regulation of International Trade*, p. 293.

[105] Appellate Body Report, *Canada – Continued Suspension of Obligations in the EC – Hormones Dispute*, WT/DS321/AB/R, adopted 14 November 2008, para. 694; Appellate Body Report, *United States – Continued Suspension of Obligations in the EC – Hormones Dispute*, WT/DS320/R, Add.1–Add.7, adopted 14 November 2008, as modified by Appellate Body Report WT/DS320/AB/R, para. 694.

> ## US/Canada – Continued Suspension *(Appellate Body)*
>
> 694. ... This presumption, however, does not apply where a Member has not adopted a measure that conforms with an international standard. Article 3.2 is inapplicable where a Member chooses a level of protection that is higher than would be achieved by a measure based on an international standard. The presumption in Article 3.2 cannot be interpreted to imply that there is sufficient scientific evidence to perform a risk assessment where a Member chooses a higher level of protection.

Moreover, under Article 3.3, WTO members may introduce or maintain an SPS measure, which results in a higher level of protection, in two cases: if there is a scientific justification; or as a consequence of the level of protection a member determines to be appropriate, in accordance with the relevant provisions of Article 5. In other words, there is scientific justification for an SPS measure within the meaning of Article 3.3, if there is a rational relationship between the SPS measure and the available scientific information.[106]

4.2.3.3   International Standard-Setting Bodies

According to Article 3.4 of the SPS Agreement, there is an express recognition of three standardisation bodies (popularly known as the 'three sisters') relevant for SPS-related purposes: (1) the Codex Alimentarius Commission (Codex) for food safety; (2) the International Office of Epizootics (OIE) for animal health and zoonoses, and (3) the International Plant Protection Convention Secretariat (IPPC) for plant health. These standards are laid out in codes or manuals. For example, the OIE standards on animal health are contained in the *Terrestrial Code.*

The SPS Agreement recognises the role of these international organisations in the development and periodic review of standards guidelines and recommendations, with a view to harmonising SPS measures. Articles 3.5 and 12.4 of the SPS Agreement require the Committee to develop a procedure to monitor the process of international harmonisation and the use of international standards, guidelines or recommendations.

EC – Hormones

The *EC – Hormones* dispute arose from the prohibition on the entry of US beef treated with growth hormones in the EU market. The EC, through a series of Council Directives, prohibited the placing on the market and importation of meat and meat products that had been treated with any of six specific hormones for growth purposes.

Canada and the United States argued that by banning the importation of meat and meat products from cattle to which any of the six hormones had been administered for the purposes of promoting growth, the EC measures violated Articles 2, 3 and 5 of the SPS

---

[106] Appellate Body Report, *EC – Hormones*, para. 175, fn. 12.

Figure 4.2 International standard-setting bodies: the 'three sisters'

The SPS Agreement encourages members to use international standards. The Codex, OIE and IPCC also collaborate on cross-cutting issues, such as certification, testing, inspection and risk analysis. Photo credits left to right: miakievy / DigitalVision Vectors / Getty Images; t-lorien / E + / Getty Images; PeopleImages / E + / Getty Images.

Agreement. The Panel found that the EC measures were in violation of Articles 3.1, 5.1 and 5.5 of the SPS Agreement. The EC first appealed the Panel's interpretation of 'based on' in Article 3.1 of the SPS Agreement.

EC – Hormones *(Appellate Body)*

163. In the first place, the ordinary meaning of 'based on' is quite different from the plain or natural import of 'conform to'. A thing is commonly said to be 'based on' another thing when the former 'stands' or is 'founded' or 'built' upon or 'is supported by' the latter … The reference of 'conform to' is to 'correspondence in form or manner', to 'compliance with' or 'acquiescence', to 'follow[ing] in form or nature'. A measure that 'conforms to' and incorporates a Codex standard is, of course, 'based on' that standard. A measure, however, based on the same standard might not conform to that standard, as where only some, not all, of the elements of the standard are incorporated into the measure.

164. In the second place, 'based on' and 'conform to' are used in different articles, as well as in differing paragraphs of the same article. Thus, Article 2.2 uses 'based on', while

> **(cont.)**
>
> Article 2.4 employs 'conform to'. Article 3.1 requires the Members to 'base' their SPS measures on international standards; however, Article 3.2 speaks of measures which 'conform to' international standards. Article 3.3 once again refers to measures 'based on' international standards. The implication arises that the choice and use of different words in different places in the SPS Agreement are deliberate, and that the different words are designed to convey different meanings.

The Appellate Body essentially held that the ordinary meaning of 'based on' is different from 'conform to'. 'Based on' requires simply that a thing should be 'supported' by another thing. It is less strict than the 'conform to' standard. Additionally, the object and purpose of Article 3 envisages harmonisation of standards as a future goal, not as a present obligation, as implied by the Panel's reliance on the term 'conform to'.[107]

The EC also appealed the Panel's interpretation of the relationship between SPS Agreement Articles 3.1, 3.2 and 3.3. The Panel had introduced a 'general rule – exception' relationship of the various articles of the SPS Agreement.[108] The Appellate Body overturned the Panel's interpretation and noted that the three provisions apply together, each addressing a separate situation. According to the Appellate Body, the three paragraphs provide three distinct approaches for WTO members for implementing their SPS measures.

> ## EC – Hormones *(Appellate Body)*
>
> 170. Under Article 3.2 of the SPS Agreement, a Member may decide to promulgate an SPS measure that conforms to an international standard. Such a measure would embody the international standard completely and, for practical purposes, converts it into a municipal standard. Such a measure enjoys the benefit of a presumption (albeit a rebuttable one) that it is consistent with the relevant provisions of the SPS Agreement and of the GATT 1994.
>
> 171. Under Article 3.1 of the SPS Agreement, a Member may choose to establish an SPS measure that is based on the existing relevant international standard, guideline or recommendation. Such a measure may adopt some, not necessarily all, of the elements of the international standard. The Member imposing this measure does not benefit from the presumption of consistency set up in Article 3.2.
>
> 172. Under Article 3.3 of the SPS Agreement, a Member may decide to set for itself a level of protection different from that implicit in the international standard, and to

---

[107] Appellate Body Report, *EC – Hormones*, para. 165.   [108] Appellate Body Report, *EC – Hormones*, para. 169.

(cont.)

implement or embody that level of protection in a measure not 'based on' the international standard. The Member's appropriate level of protection may be higher than that implied in the international standard. The right of a Member to determine its own appropriate level of sanitary protection is an important right.

4.2.4   Risk Assessment

Article 5 of the SPS Agreement deals with the assessment of risk and determination of appropriate level of protection. It requires that the SPS measures be based on a risk assessment carried out by taking into account the available scientific evidence.[109] As noted by the Panel in *EC – Approval and Marketing of Biotech Products*, two issues may be addressed to determine whether there is a violation of Article 5.1. First, whether there is a 'risk assessment' within the meaning of SPS Agreement and, second, whether the SPS measure is 'based on' this risk assessment.[110]

Risk assessment, in a generic sense, focuses on the identification or evaluation of the likelihood of entry or pest or disease, including the magnitude of biological and economic consequences, according to the SPS measures to be applied.

In *EC – Hormones*, the Appellate Body noted that Article 5.1 does not insist that a member that adopts a sanitary measure shall have to carry out its own risk assessment. It only requires that the SPS measures be 'based on an assessment, as appropriate for the circumstances'. The SPS measure might well find its objective justification in a risk assessment carried out by another member or an international organisation.[111]

SPS Agreement

Article 5: Assessment of Risk

1. Members shall ensure that their sanitary or phytosanitary measures are based on an assessment, as appropriate to the circumstances, of the risks to human, animal or plant life or health, taking into account risk assessment techniques developed by the relevant international organizations.

---

[109] SPS Agreement, Arts. 5.1, 5.2.

[110] Panel Reports, *European Communities – Measures Affecting the Approval and Marketing of Biotech Products*, WT/DS291/R, Add.1–Add.9, Corr.1, WT/DS292/R, Add.1–Add.9, Corr.1, WT/DS293/R, Add.1–Add.9, Corr.1, adopted 21 November 2006, para. 7.3030.

[111] Appellate Body Report, *EC – Hormones*, para. 190.

Annex A: Definitions *(cont.)*

4. **Risk assessment** – The evaluation of the likelihood of entry, establishment or spread of a pest or disease within the territory of an importing Member according to the sanitary or phytosanitary measures which might be applied, and of the associated potential biological and economic consequences; or the evaluation of the potential for adverse effects on human or animal health arising from the presence of additives, contaminants, toxins or disease-causing organisms in food, beverages or feedstuffs.

4.2.4.1 Types of Risk Assessment

The risks assessed in risk assessment must be 'ascertainable' risks, and not the 'uncertainty that theoretically always remains since science can never provide absolute certainty that a given substance will not ever have adverse health effects'.[112] WTO members might maintain SPS measures in respect of *de minimis* risks – risks not supported by available scientific evidence but which, given the limitations of the scientific method, cannot be ruled out by science.[113]

There are mainly two kinds of risk assessments arising under Annex A(4) of the SPS Agreement. This was acknowledged in *Australia – Salmon*. These include risks arising from pests or diseases or food-borne risks.

Australia – Salmon *(Appellate Body)*

121. On the basis of this definition, we consider that, in this case, a risk assessment within the meaning of Article 5.1 must: (1) identify the diseases whose entry, establishment or spread a Member wants to prevent within its territory, as well as the potential biological and economic consequences associated with the entry, establishment or spread of these diseases; (2) evaluate the likelihood of entry, establishment or spread of these diseases, as well as the associated potential biological and economic consequences; and (3) evaluate the likelihood of entry, establishment or spread of these diseases according to the SPS measures which might be applied.

---

[112] J. Peel, 'Risk Regulation Under the WTO SPS Agreement: Science as an International Normative Yardstick?', Jean Monnet Working Paper 02/04 (2004).

[113] Peel, 'Risk Regulation'.

Articles 5.2 and 5.3 of the SPS Agreement provide certain factors that Members must take into account while undertaking a risk assessment, but do not specify the methodologies to be used. These include: (1) available scientific evidence; (2) relevant processes and production methods; (3) relevant inspection, sampling and testing methods; (4) prevalence of specific diseases or pests; (5) existence of pest- or disease-free areas; (6) relevant ecological and environmental conditions; and (7) quarantine and other treatment.

According to the Appellate Body of *EC – Hormones*, Article 5.2 shows that a risk assessed under Article 5.1 'is not only risk ascertainable in a science laboratory operating under strictly controlled conditions, but also risk in human societies as they actually exist, in other words, *the actual potential for adverse effects on human health in the real world where people live and work and die*' (emphasis added).[114] These memorable words signify that risk assessment is not just the assessment that is carried out in simulated conditions or laboratories, but also a consideration of the real-world concerns that people may have.

Article 5.3 mandates that certain economic factors should also be taken into account while assessing risks to animal or plant life or health. These factors include the potential damage in terms of loss of production or sales in the event of the entry, establishment or spread of a pest or disease; the costs of control or eradication in the territory of the importing member; the relative cost-effectiveness of alternative approaches to limiting risks and so on.

In *Australia – Salmon*, the Panel noted that Articles 5.2 and 5.3 only qualify the way in which a risk assessment has to be carried out, not the substantive obligation to base a sanitary measure on a risk assessment.[115] Regarding the scope of a member's obligation under Article 5.3, the Panel in *Russia – Pigs (EU)* found this provision to refer to two different situations.[116]

Russia – Pigs (EU) *(Panel)*

7.759. The first situation is when a Member is 'assessing the risk to animal or plant life or health'. The second is when a Member is 'determining the measure to be applied for achieving the appropriate level of sanitary or phytosanitary protection'. Pursuant to Article 5.3, in both these situations Members 'shall take into account' as relevant economic factors, those listed at the end of this provision. We observe that there is no indication in the text that the factors listed are only by way of example, rather this is presented as a complete list.

---

[114] Appellate Body Report, *EC – Hormones*, para. 187.

[115] Panel Report, *Australia – Measures Affecting Importation of Salmon*, WT/DS18/AB/R, Corr.1, adopted 6 November 1998, as modified by Appellate Body Report WT/DS18/AB/R, para. 8.57.

[116] Panel Report, *Russian Federation – Measures on the Importation of Live Pigs, Pork and Other Pig Products from the European Union*, WT/DS475/R, Add.1, adopted 21 March 2017, as modified by Appellate Body Report WT/DS475/AB/R, para. 7.759.

In situations where a risk assessment sets out a divergent opinion and this opinion comes from qualified and respected sources, it can be reasonably said that an SPS measure which reflects the divergent opinion is 'based on' the risk assessment in question inasmuch as the divergent opinion is expressed in that risk assessment.[117]

4.2.5 Consistency

Article 5.5 of the SPS Agreement contains the consistency requirement, which means that members must avoid unjustifiable differences in the level of health protection if such differences result in discrimination or a disguised restriction on international trade.

In *EC – Hormones*, the Appellate Body found that three elements must be demonstrated to establish an inconsistency with Article 5.5 and that these elements are cumulative in nature:

- The member imposing the measure complained of has adopted its own appropriate levels of sanitary protection against risks to human life or health in several different situations.
- Those levels of protection exhibit arbitrary or unjustifiable differences ('distinctions' in the language of Article 5.5) in their treatment of different situations.
- The arbitrary or unjustifiable differences result in discrimination or a disguised restriction of international trade.[118]

In *Australia – Apples*, in view of the special circumstances of the case, the Panel departed from a strict application of the 'three elements' test. The Panel found that New Zealand had not demonstrated the first or second elements of the three-pronged Article 5.5 test. Given that the elements of the test are cumulative, the Panel did not proceed to the third element and dismissed New Zealand's claim under Article 5.5.[119]

The issue of consistency in the application of SPS measures was comprehensively examined in *Australia – Apples*.

AUSTRALIA – SALMON

The dispute concerned an import restriction that Australia had imposed on fresh, chilled and frozen salmon (specifically adult, wild, ocean-caught Pacific salmon) from Canada and the United States. Australia identified twenty-four 'disease agents' that were present in Canadian and US salmon. Australia considered this a threat to the health of the Australian salmon population. To deal with this threat, Australia promulgated Quarantine Proclamation 86A, which provided for the prohibition of imports of salmon if such products had not been treated so as to prevent the spread of disease prior to

---

[117] Panel Reports, *EC – Approval and Marketing of Biotech Products*, para. 7.3060; see also Appellate Body Report, *EC – Hormones*, paras. 193–194.

[118] Appellate Body Report, *EC – Hormones*, para. 214.

[119] Panel Report, *Australia – Measures Affecting the Importation of Apples from New Zealand*, WT/DS367/R, adopted 17 December 2010, as modified by Appellate Body Report WT/DS367/AB/R, para. 7.985.

importation. Pursuant to the Proclamation, Australia permitted the importation of only those salmon that had been 'heat-treated', which eliminated the risk of disease.

Canada and the United States claimed that the import prohibition on salmon that had not been heat-treated was inconsistent with SPS Agreement Articles 2, 3 and 5. The Panel found that the measure at issue was inconsistent with Articles 5.1 and 5.2, because it was not 'based on' a risk assessment. In addition, the measure was inconsistent with Article 5.5, because it adopted arbitrary or unjustifiable distinctions in levels of protection in different but comparable situations that resulted in discrimination or a disguised restriction on international trade and Article 5.6, since it is more trade-restrictive than required.

With respect to Article 5.5, the Panel identified the import prohibition on fresh, chilled or frozen salmon for human consumption – that is, the measure at issue – and contrasted it with the admission of imports of (1) uncooked Pacific herring, cod, haddock, Japanese eel and plaice for human consumption; (2) uncooked Pacific herring, Atlantic and Pacific cod, haddock, European and Japanese eel and Dover sole for human consumption; (3) herring in whole, frozen form used as bait ('herring used as bait'); and (4) live ornamental finfish. The Panel determined that the above constituted 'different' situations that can be compared under Article 5.5 of the SPS Agreement.

What 'different situations' can be 'comparable'? The situations are comparable if the situations involve either a risk of entry, establishment or spread of the same or a similar disease, *or* a risk of the same or similar 'associated potential biological and economic consequences'.[120] According to Australia, *both* of these elements are required in order for two situations to be comparable. The Appellate Body disagreed and upheld the Panel's finding that situations can be compared under Article 5.5 if these situations involve *either* a risk of entry, establishment or spread of the same or a similar disease, *or* a risk of the same or similar 'associated potential biological and economic consequences'. The Appellate Body observed that it was sufficient for the comparison situation to have one disease in common, rather than all diseases.

Australia – Salmon *(Appellate Body)*

146. Situations which involve a risk of entry, establishment or spread of the same or a similar disease have some common elements sufficient to render them comparable under Article 5.5. Likewise, situations with a risk of the same or similar associated potential biological and economic consequences also have some common elements sufficient to render them comparable under Article 5.5. We, therefore, consider that for 'different' situations to be comparable under Article 5.5, there is no need for both the disease and the biological and economic consequences to be the same or similar. We recognize that, as pointed out by Australia, the risk which needs to be

---

[120] Panel Report, *Australia – Salmon*, para. 8.117.

> **(cont.)**
> examined in a risk assessment, pursuant to Article 5.1 and the first definition of risk assessment of paragraph 4 of Annex A, is the risk of both the entry, establishment or spread of a disease and the associated potential biological and economic consequences. However, we fail to see how this can be of relevance to the question of comparability of different situations under Article 5.5 which is the issue addressed by the Panel.

With respect to the second element, the Panel held that the different levels of protection provided to imports of salmon as compared to imports of herring used as bait and imports of finfish were 'arbitrary or unjustifiable'. The Panel had found that these two comparison situations present at least as high, if not higher, of a risk as do imports of salmon, yet they are treated much more leniently.

Australia argued on appeal that the Panel erred by limiting its examination to disease agents 'positively detected' in ocean-caught Pacific salmon. The Appellate Body rejected this argument, stating that the Panel explicitly took into account other disease agents. Furthermore, it considered that taking into account all disease agents would have been impractical.

> ### Australia – Salmon *(Appellate Body)*
>
> 158. Australia determined explicitly that its appropriate level of protection with respect to ocean-caught Pacific salmon is 'a high or "very conservative" level of sanitary protection aimed at reducing risk to "very low levels", "while not based on a zero-risk approach".' The level of protection reflected in Australia's treatment of herring used as bait and live ornamental finfish is definitely lower. We note the Panel's factual finding that herring used as bait and live ornamental finfish can be presumed to represent at least as high a risk – if not a higher risk – than the risk associated with ocean-caught Pacific salmon.

Regarding the third element under Article 5.5, the Panel had found that the distinctions in levels of protection result in a 'disguised restriction on international trade'. In support of this conclusion, the Panel set out three 'warning signals' that the measure resulted in a 'disguised restriction on international trade'. The warning signals are, broadly:

- the 'arbitrary character' of the differences in the levels of protection;
- the 'rather substantial difference' in the different levels of protection; and
- the fact that the measure at issue is not 'based on' a risk assessment under Article 5.1.

The Appellate Body reviewed each of the warning signals and upheld the Panel's finding. The Appellate Body upheld the Panel's finding that Australia acted inconsistently with Article 5.5 and, by implication, Article 2.3.[121]

4.2.6   Appropriate Level of Protection

The SPS Agreement allows WTO members to determine the appropriate level of protection they want to achieve for the protection of human, animal or plant life or health. The concept of the appropriate level of protection appears at various places throughout the SPS Agreement. They may depart from relevant international standards where such standards would not secure the level of SPS protection determined to be appropriate by the member in question.[122] Similarly, members need only accept 'third country' SPS measures as equivalent to their own, where these third country SPS measures are demonstrated to achieve the importing member's appropriate level of SPS protection.[123]

The concept of an 'appropriate level of sanitary or phytosanitary protection' is defined in Annex A(5) of the SPS Agreement as: 'The level of protection deemed appropriate by the Member establishing a sanitary or phytosanitary measure to protect human, animal or plant life or health within its territory'. A note to this definition provides that '[m]any Members otherwise refer to this concept as the "acceptable level of risk"'. Appropriate level of protection (ALOP) and acceptable level of risk seem to be two sides of the same coin. When members make a determination about the level of protection to be secured, they also – explicitly or implicitly – make a corresponding determination about the level of risk they are willing to tolerate.

In *Australia – Salmon*, the Appellate Body observed:

Australia – Salmon *(Appellate Body)*

206. ... the *SPS Agreement* contains an implicit obligation to determine the appropriate level of protection. We do not believe that there is an obligation to determine the appropriate level of protection in quantitative terms. This does not mean, however, that an importing Member is free to determine its level of protection with such vagueness or equivocation that the application of the relevant provisions of the *SPS Agreement*, such as Article 5.6, becomes impossible. It would obviously be wrong to interpret the *SPS Agreement* in a way that would render nugatory entire articles or paragraphs of articles of this Agreement and allow Members to escape from their obligations under this Agreement.

---

[121] Appellate Body Report, *Australia – Measures Affecting Importation of Salmon*, WT/DS18/AB/R, adopted 6 November 1998, paras. 177–178.
[122] SPS Agreement, Art. 3.3.   [123] SPS Agreement, Art. 4.1.

(cont.)

207. … where a Member does not determine its appropriate level of protection, or does so with insufficient precision, the appropriate level of protection may be established by panels on the basis of the level of protection reflected in the SPS measure actually applied. Otherwise, a Member's failure to comply with the implicit obligation to determine its appropriate level of protection – with sufficient precision – would allow it to escape from its obligations under this Agreement and, in particular its obligations under Articles 5.5 and 5.6.

KOREA – RADIONUCLIDES

Korea – Radionuclides is based on measures imposed by Korea in relation to food imports from Japan subsequent to its Fukushima Daiichi Nuclear Power Plant disaster. Korea had placed bans on certain marine products affected by the nuclear accident. Among other issues, the Appellate Body provided important guidance in the determination of ALOP under the SPS Agreement.[124]

Korea – Radionuclides *(Appellate Body)*

5.21. … under Article 5.6, a complainant must establish that an alternative measure: (i) is reasonably available taking into account technical and economic feasibility; (ii) achieves the Member's ALOP; and (iii) is significantly less restrictive to trade than the contested SPS measure. These cumulative elements entail an assessment of a proposed alternative measure that serves as a conceptual tool to be used for the analysis under Article 5.6.

5.24. In examining a claim under Article 5.6 of the SPS Agreement, a panel is charged with, *inter alia*, identifying the level of protection of the Member whose SPS measure is challenged and the level of protection of the proposed alternative measure. A panel would typically be expected to accord weight to the respondent's articulation of its ALOP, particularly where that appropriate level of protection was specified in advance of the adoption of the SPS measure, where the ALOP is specified with sufficient precision, and where it has been consistently expressed by the responding Member. A panel, however, is not required to defer completely to a respondent's characterization of its own ALOP, particularly where the respondent has not expressed its ALOP with sufficient precision. Rather, a panel must ascertain the respondent's ALOP on the basis of the totality of the arguments and

---

[124] Appellate Body Report, *Korea – Import Bans, and Testing and Certification Requirements for Radionuclides*, WT/DS495/AB/R, Add.1, adopted 26 April 2019, paras. 5.21, 5.24, 5.31.

> *(cont.)*
>
> evidence on the record, which may include the level of protection reflected in the SPS measure actually applied.

Before the Panel, Korea contended that its ALOP consisted of: (i) radioactive levels in food consumed by Korean consumers that exist in the ordinary environment (i.e. in the absence of radiation from a major nuclear accident); (ii) at levels of radioactive contamination in food that are 'as low as reasonably achievable' (ALARA); (iii) below the quantitative dose exposure of 1 mSv/year. While the Panel accepted Korea's ALOP, it found that the alternative measure proposed by Japan of allowing the import of fish products with less than 100 Bq/kg of caesium was a less restrictive measure that was capable of satisfying Korea's ALOP. This measure in the Panel's view would result in Korean consumers being exposed to less than 1 mSv/year dose limit even in a scenario where 100 percent of the food products were of Japanese origin. According to the Appellate Body, the Panel overlooked the multi-faceted objective of Korea's measures and had failed to consider whether each of the elements referred to above represented a distinct component of Korea's ALOP, and how they interacted as parts of Korea's overall ALOP. While the Appellate Body noted that ALOPs cannot be overly vague in respect of how they should be implemented, the Panel had erred in reducing Korea's ALOP to a sole quantitative aspect (i.e. 'below 1 mSv/year' or 'significantly lower than 1mSv/year') when determining whether Korea's SPS measures were more restrictive than necessary.

4.2.6.1 'No More Trade-Restrictive than Required'

Article 5.6 obliges members to adopt measures no more trade-restrictive than required to achieve the chosen level of SPS protection, considering technical and economic feasibility. The Panel in *US – Poultry (China)* held that a finding, under Article 5.5, that a member is applying different ALOPs does not take away the right of the importing member to determine its ALOP, particularly for the purpose of the analysis under Article 5.6.[125]

In the context of Article 5.6, the complainant has to demonstrate that another measure that is less trade-restrictive and still achieves the appropriate level of protection is reasonably available, taking into account the technical and economic feasibility. In *Australia – Salmon*, the Appellate Body differentiated 'appropriate level of protection' established by a member from the 'SPS measure'. The first is an objective; the second is an instrument chosen to attain or implement that objective.[126]

---

[125] Panel Report, *United States – Certain Measures Affecting Imports of Poultry from China*, WT/DS392/R, adopted 25 October 2010, para. 7.333.

[126] Appellate Body Report, *Australia – Salmon*, paras. 200–204.

4.2.7   Provisional Measures

Article 5.7 of the SPS Agreement permits the taking of provisional measures when there is insufficient scientific evidence to permit the assessment of health risks. These measures, however, should be based on available information, and assessed and reviewed reasonably.

EC – Hormones was the first SPS dispute under the WTO that examined the scope of provisional measures under the SPS Agreement. The EC did not claim that its import ban was a provisional measure. It invoked the 'precautionary principle' more generally. The Appellate Body agreed with the Panel that the 'precautionary principle' (other than that expressed in SPS Article 5.7 on provisional measures) does not override the obligation to base SPS measures on a risk assessment.[127] On the status of the 'precautionary principle' in international law, the Appellate Body noted as follows:

> ## EC – Hormones *(Appellate Body)*
>
> 123. The status of the precautionary principle in international law continues to be the subject of debate among academics, law practitioners, regulators and judges. The precautionary principle is regarded by some as having crystallized into a general principle of customary international environmental law. Whether it has been widely accepted by members as a principle of general or customary international law appears less than clear.

In *Japan – Agricultural Products II*, the Appellate Body noted that Article 5.7 operates as a qualified exemption from the obligation under Article 2.2 not to maintain SPS measures without sufficient scientific evidence. In other words, Article 5.7 can apply only to 'situations where deficiencies in the body of scientific evidence do not allow a WTO Member to arrive at a sufficiently objective conclusion in relation to risk'.[128]

In *Japan – Agricultural Products II*, the Appellate Body also outlined the conditions that must be cumulatively met for the invocation of the measure.

- The provisional measure must be adopted on the basis of available pertinent information.
- The member adopting the measure must seek to obtain the additional information necessary for a more objective assessment of risk.
- The SPS measure must be reviewed accordingly within a reasonable period of time.[129]

Whenever one of the above requirements is not met, the measure will be considered as inconsistent with the SPS Agreement.[130] In *Japan – Apples*, the Appellate Body noted that

---

[127] Appellate Body Report, *EC – Hormones*, paras. 120–125.
[128] Appellate Body Report, *Canada – Continued Suspension*, para. 677.
[129] Appellate Body Report, *Japan – Agricultural Products II*, para. 89.
[130] J. Pauwelyn, 'First Three SPS Disputes', p. 650.

the relevant scientific evidence will be 'insufficient' within the meaning of Article 5.7 if the body of available scientific evidence does not allow, in quantitative or qualitative terms, the performance of an adequate assessment of risks as required under Article 5.1 and as defined in Annex A to the SPS Agreement.[131]

4.2.8 Regionalisation

The SPS Agreement mitigates the potential effects of trade barriers as a result of SPS measures by limiting such measures geographically. Article 6.1 mandates that when implementing measures, members must take at least the following elements into account: 'the level of prevalence of specific diseases or pests, the existence of eradication or control programmes, and appropriate criteria or guidelines which may be developed by the relevant international organizations'.

Article 6.1 is an overarching obligation concerning the adaptation of SPS measures to regional conditions followed by two specific obligations provided in Articles 6.2 and 6.3.[132] Article 6.2 recognises the concepts of pest- or disease-free areas and areas of low pest or disease prevalence guided by factors such as geography, ecosystems, epidemiological surveillance, and the effectiveness of sanitary or phytosanitary controls. On the other hand, Article 6.3 requires exporting members to provide evidence to the importing Member to objectively demonstrate that its areas are, and are likely to remain, pest- or disease-free or areas of low pest or disease prevalence.[133]

In interpreting Article 6, the Appellate Body noted in *India – Agricultural Products* that the relevant areas subject of the adaptation obligation can 'vary, and may entail a territory that can be smaller than, the same size as, or bigger than, a country'.

India – Agricultural Products *(Appellate Body)*

5.154. ... [T]he general 'adaptation' obligation in Article 6.1 may well encompass both a requirement to adapt appropriately at the time the SPS measure is adopted, as well as a requirement to adapt appropriately if and when relevant SPS characteristics in relevant areas in the territory of the importing or exporting Member change or are shown to warrant an adaptation of a specific SPS measure.

---

[131] Appellate Body Report, *Japan – Measures Affecting the Importation of Apples*, WT/DS245/AB/R, adopted 10 December 2003, para. 179.

[132] J. J. Nedumpara, A. Chandra and G. S. Deepak, '*India – Agricultural Products*: Defending India's First SPS Dispute', in Das and Nedumpara, *WTO Dispute Settlement at Twenty*, p. 228.

[133] Panel Report, *United States – Measures Affecting the Importation of Animals, Meat and Other Animal Products from Argentina*, WT/DS447/R, Add.1, adopted 31 August 2015, para. 7.649.

The Appellate Body noted in *India – Agricultural Products* that Article 6 does not indicate the specific manner in which a member could 'ensure' the adaptation of the SPS within the meaning of Article 6.1 or 'recognise' the concepts listed in Article 6.2. However, if a member's domestic regime forecloses the possibility of recognition of the concepts of pest- or disease-free areas and areas of low pest or disease prevalence, such a situation will not satisfy the requirements of Article 6.2. The WTO Panel in this case had found that by imposing a prohibition on the import of poultry products, India had contradicted the requirement to recognise the concept of pest- or disease-free areas and areas of low pest or disease prevalence.[134]

More recently, the EU had challenged Russia's failure to comply with the regionalisation requirements in *Russia – Pigs (EU)*.[135] Russia had imposed import restrictions on live pigs, pork and certain pig products from the EU following the outbreak of African swine fever.

A key aspect of this dispute is the role of panels in making findings on certain aspects of the SPS Agreement. Exporting members that claim under Article 6.3 that regions within their territories are 'pest- or disease-free areas or areas of low pest or disease prevalence' are required to provide 'necessary evidence' to the importing member. The Appellate Body noted that the panel's role, in such situations, is confined to evaluating whether the nature, quality and quantity of evidence provided by the exporting member is sufficient for the importing member to make a determination regarding the pest- or disease free status of the area. The Appellate Body noted that a panel is not required to 'determine for itself, based on the evidence provided by the exporting Member, whether the relevant areas are, and are likely to remain, pest- or disease free or of low pest or disease prevalence'.[136]

4.2.9 Equivalence

Equivalence refers to a situation where the sanitary measures proposed by the exporting member could be considered as an alternative if they serve the importing member's level of sanitary or phytosanitary protection. This principle is reflected in Article 4 of the SPS Agreement. In order to facilitate the evaluation of equivalence, reasonable access to the importer for inspection should be granted by the exporting party. This involves inspection, testing and other relevant procedures.[137]

The WTO Panel in *US – Poultry (China)* reviewed and examined the SPS Committee Decision on Equivalence and the text of Article 4.

---

[134] Panel Report, *India – Measures Concerning the Importation of Certain Agricultural Products*, WT/DS430/R, Add.1, adopted 19 June 2015, as modified by Appellate Body Report WT/DS430/AB/R, para. 7.702.

[135] Appellate Body Report, *Russian Federation – Measures on the Importation of Live Pigs, Pork and Other Pig Products from the European Union*, WT/DS 475/AB/R, adopted 21 March 2017.

[136] Appellate Body Report, *Russia – Pigs (EU)*, para. 5.66.

[137] FAO, *Guidelines for the Design, Operation, Assessment and Accreditation of Food Import and Export Inspection and Certification Systems* (CAC/GL 26-1997).

US – Poultry (China) *(Panel)*

7.136. [T]he Panel sees nothing in Article 4 or the Decision which suggests that Article 4 is the only provision in the SPS Agreement which regulates the operation of equivalence regimes, including their 'procedural requirements' or that it should be applied in isolation from other relevant provisions of the SPS Agreement. In fact, the Decision states that the importing Member should explain its SPS measures by identifying the risk and provide a copy of the risk assessment or technical standard on which the measure is based. Further, it requires the importing Member to analyse the science-based and technical information provided by the exporting Member with respect to that Member's own SPS measure(s) to examine if the measure achieves the importing Member's ALOP.

4.2.10 Transparency Obligations in the SPS Agreement

Under Article 7 of the SPS Agreement, each member of the WTO has an obligation to notify any change in their SPS measures, and to provide information on their measures according to Annex B to the SPS Agreement. In this regard, pursuant to Annex B, paragraph 10, of the SPS Agreement, countries are required to identify a single central government authority to be responsible for the notification requirements of the SPS Agreement ('notification authority'). In addition, countries are also required to establish an enquiry point that will be responsible for answering questions from other countries about SPS measures and related issues ('enquiry point').

Article 5.8 of the SPS Agreement also contains an important obligation for the promotion of transparency. It obliges members to provide information, upon request, regarding the reasons for their SPS measures where such measures are not 'based on' international standards or no relevant international standards exist. In sum, the transparency obligations set forth in the SPS Agreement can be grouped into three sets of obligations, namely: (1) SPS notifications and the establishment of a notification authority; (2) publication (of all regulations); (3) establishment and functioning of SPS enquiry points.

4.2.11 SPS Committee

Article 12.1 of the SPS Agreement sets up the SPS Committee. It has the mandate to carry out functions necessary for the implementation of the SPS Agreement and furtherance of its objectives. The Committee is to be composed of representatives from all WTO members. Governments, which have an observer status in WTO bodies (such as the Council for Trade in Goods), are also eligible to be observers in the SPS Committee. International intergovernmental organisations, such as Codex, OIE, IPPC, WHO, UNCTAD and the International

Standards Organization (ISO), have been granted observer status. It meets three times a year and takes decisions by consensus. The SPS Committee also holds occasional joint meetings with the TBT Committee on notification and transparency procedures. Informal or special meetings may be scheduled as needed. Article 12.2 empowers the Committee to encourage and facilitate ad hoc consultations or negotiations among members on specific sanitary and phytosanitary issues.

4.2.12 Conclusion

The SPS Agreement is one of the important outcomes of the Uruguay Round and has introduced key disciplines for regulating domestic regulations aimed at human, animal, plant health and safety. In simple terms, the SPS Agreement has brought science into the heart of international trade regulations. The Agreement also highlights the importance of conducting risk assessments while formulating SPS measures. In addition to developing disciplines on sanitary and phytosanitary regulations, the Agreement aims at harmonisation through international standards, conformity assessment procedures and equivalence. The SPS Agreement also recognises the concept of regionalisation, which permits imports from parts or regions of a country not affected by the concerned disease. Overall, the Agreement seeks to reduce unnecessary barriers to international trade.

4.3   Summary

- The TBT Agreement covers technical regulations, standards and conformity assessment procedures.
- Technical regulations apply to identifiable products and set out product characteristics or their related process and production methods. Technical regulations are mandatory, whereas standards are not mandatory.
- Conformity assessment procedures establish whether a product satisfies the requirements of a technical regulation or standard.
- The TBT Agreement requires that technical regulations, standards and conformity assessment procedures do not discriminate, do not create unnecessary obstacles to international trade and are 'based on' international standards when they exist.
- The 'necessity test' under the TBT Agreement involves a comparative and relational analysis. Instead of applying the traditional 'least trade restrictive' test, the panels examine the degree of contribution a TBT measure makes in furtherance of a legitimate objective, as well as the risk of non-fulfilment of the objective. This view was affirmed by the Appellate Body in *US – Clove Cigarettes, US – Tuna (II), US – COOL* and *Australia – Tobacco Plain Packaging (Honduras)*.
- WTO members have the right to apply SPS measures to protect human, animal, plant life or health within their territory, as long as they satisfy the conditions set forth in the SPS Agreement.

- The SPS Agreement stipulates that SPS measures are based on scientific principles and are not maintained without sufficient scientific evidence. If the SPS measures 'conform' to international standards, there is a presumption that such measures are necessary to protect human, animal or plant life or health.
- While members adopt SPS measures, they shall ensure that such measures are based on a risk assessment as appropriate to the circumstances by taking into account the risk assessment techniques developed by relevant international organisations.
- While implementing SPS measures, members generally should not impose countrywide prohibitions. Article 6 requires members to adapt SPS measures to regional characteristics and recognise the concepts of pest- or disease-free areas or areas of low pest or disease prevalence.

4.4   Review Questions

1 How does the 'necessity test' under Article 2.2 of the TBT Agreement differ from the traditional necessity test under Article XX of the GATT?
2 Is 'consensus' required for establishing an international standard under the TBT Agreement? (See *EC – Sardines*.)
3 Who can set international standards under the TBT Agreement. (See *US – Tuna II (Mexico)*.)
4 Does the TBT Agreement incorporate non-product-related PPMs? (See *US – Tuna II (Mexico)*.)
5 What are the reasons based on which the Appellate Body overturned the Panel's characterisation of the EC seal regime as a 'technical regulation'?
6 Explain the difference between 'basing' and 'conforming to' under the harmonisation requirement of the SPS Agreement. Under what circumstances can a member deviate from the international standard? (See *EC – Hormones*.)
7 Can a WTO member meet the requirements of basing an SPS measure on 'scientific principle(s)' without a risk assessment under Article 5 of the SPS Agreement?
8 What is the meaning of ALOP? (See Appellate Body Reports in *Australia – Salmon* and *Korea – Radionuclides*.)

4.5   Exercises

Exercise 1

The Office of Foreign Trade, Republic of Minerva, a WTO member, issued a trade notice in 2017. Under the notice, items or products of reptiles, mink, fox (whole, with or without head, tail or paws) are prohibited either for domestic sale or imports. However, the trade notice exempts limited sale of products from chinchillas, especially for the production of famed chinchilla garments manufactured by the Inchan community, an indigenous group within Minerva. Although the world population is declining, the chinchilla population in Minerva has seen an increase, mainly attributable to conservation policies adopted by Minerva's Wildlife Department. Minerva's chinchilla population is mainly seen around the Andes mountain range, which is home to the Inchan community.

Minerva's neighbours include Unandoga along the Andes mountains on the eastern side, and Ithaca and Machu on the western side. Among these countries, Unandoga has a sizeable population of chinchillas, whereas Ithaca and Machu have no known habitats of chinchillas. However, other categories of wild animals like fox and mink are seen in Ithaca and Machu. The trade notice contains the following schedule.

HS code	Item description	Existing policy	New trade policy
41133000	Of reptiles	Free	Prohibited (based on CITES)
43011000	Of mink, whole, with or without head, paws or tail	Free	Prohibited (based on CITES)
43016000	Of fox, whole, with or without head, tail or paws	Free	Prohibited (based on CITES)
43018000	Other fur skins, whole, with or without head, tail or paws	Free	Prohibited (based on CITES) Fur skins made of chinchillas seen in the Andes mountain ranges permitted, subject to appropriate certification

After the publication of the trade policy, Machu and Ithaca lost the entire market for fur skins (both countries exported fur skins from mink) that are used in customised winter clothing. Machu and Ithaca consider a trade action under the WTO, initially raising the matter before the TBT Committee.

Examine the legal issues.

Exercise 2

The Republic of Zion, a WTO member, recently witnessed a mystery illness that killed more than a hundred children in the northern part of its territory. It was reported that the children had consumed lychee imported from its neighbour, Manchin, another WTO member. Researchers and scientists in Zion commented that the disease was caused by the Ackee fruit, which contained hypoglycin, a toxin that prevents the body from making glucose. It was reported, however, that the Ackee fruit, which is also grown in Zion, has been consumed by generations of people without any adverse effects. In order to protect human health against food-borne diseases, the Ministry of Health in Zion decides to restrict the entry of Ackee fruit to its territory.

What requirements in the SPS Agreement should the regulatory body in Zion abide by before adopting any SPS measure? Prepare a checklist of items that the regulatory agency in Zion will have verify to ensure that its measures are consistent with the SPS Agreement.

FURTHER READING

Durán, G. M., 'NTBs and the WTO Agreement on Technical Barriers to Trade: The Case of PPM-Based Measures Following *US – Tuna II* and *EC – Seal Products*', in C. Hermann, M. Krajewski and J. P. Terhechte (eds.), *European Yearbook of International Economic Law* (Berlin: Springer, 2015), pp. 87–136.

Lester, S. and Stemberg, W., 'The GATT Origins of TBT Agreement Articles 2.1 and 2.2', *Journal of International Economic Law* (2014), 17, pp. 215–32.

Mavroidis, P. C., Bermann, G. A. and Wu, M., *The Law of the World Trade Organization (WTO): Documents, Cases and Analysis* (St Paul: West, 2010).

Neven, D. J. and Weiler, J. H. H., '*Japan – Measures Affecting the Importation of Apples* (AB – 2003–4): One Bad Apple? (DS245/AB/R): A Comment', *World Trade Review* (2006), 5, pp. 280–310.

Wagner, M., 'Law Talk v. Science Talk: The Languages of Law and Science in WTO Proceedings', *Fordham International Law Journal* (2011), 35, pp. 151–200.

5 Anti-Dumping

Table of Contents

Highlights

- Dumping is essentially price discrimination in international markets. Anti-dumping is a specific action against dumping, which may result in imposition of higher duties, price undertaking or provisional measures in the form of cash security or bond. Anti-dumping is widely recognised and applied as one of the key components of trade remedy instruments; the other two include countervailing duty measures and safeguard actions.

- Certain domestic anti-dumping laws implemented in the early part of the twentieth century also addressed predatory pricing in addition to international price discrimination; predatory pricing is no longer addressed in anti-dumping law, although certain home market below costs sales are disregarded from anti-dumping determinations.
- The Anti-Dumping (AD) Agreement seeks to protect the domestic industry in the importing country against injurious dumping; the extent of anti-dumping protection is limited to the price differences between an exporter's home market and exports sales to the country applying the anti-dumping remedy. In addition to dumping, injury and causation are also required to be established.
- The AD Agreement provides detailed substantive rules for the conduct and implementation of anti-dumping proceedings and reviews.
- The extent of anti-dumping duty cannot in any case exceed the margin of dumping. Certain countries implement the 'lesser duty rule', where the duties are sufficient to offset the injury.
- One of the controversial topics in anti-dumping is the practice of 'zeroing'. As a practice, zeroing is prohibited in most forms of anti-dumping proceedings, including original proceedings, periodic/interim reviews and expiry reviews.
- Anti-dumping provisions are also negotiated as part of free trade agreements.

5.1   Introduction

Anti-dumping laws are one of the most common and frequently used instruments of trade contingent protection. At a fundamental level, the purpose of antidumping measures is to offset the injury to the domestic industry in the importing country attributable to dumped imports. In international trade, dumping essentially refers to a pricing behaviour of an exporter. The first internationally accepted definition of the term 'dumping' was provided under Article VI of the GATT 1947.[1] According to this definition, 'dumping' is a sale of products abroad at a price lower than the 'normal value' or, roughly speaking, the home market price. It consequently formed the basis for drafting the Anti-Dumping Agreement during the Uruguay Round of trade negotiations. The AD Agreement is formally known as the Agreement on Implementation of Article VI of the General Agreement on Tariffs and Trade 1994. The object of the AD Agreement is to recognise the right of members to counteract injurious dumping, while at the same time imposing substantive conditions and rules on the conduct of the investigations and the imposition of anti-dumping measures.[2]

The AD Agreement aims to expand and clarify the application of Article VI of the GATT 1994.[3] It allows WTO members, when taking action against dumping, to depart from key

---

[1] M. J. Trebilcock, *Understanding Trade Law* (Cheltenham: Edward Elgar, 2013), p. 65.

[2] Appellate Body Report, *European Union – Anti-Dumping Measures on Biodiesel from Argentina*, WT/DS473/AB/R, Add.1, adopted 26 October 2016.

[3] Appellate Body Report, *EU – Biodiesel (Argentina)*.

GATT principles, including the MFN principle.[4] The AD Agreement allows WTO members to impose anti-dumping duties in excess of the tariffs as negotiated among members as part of their Schedule of Concessions.[5]

There is a widely held criticism that the AD Agreement is not based on any economic rationale, but on political or other considerations.[6] Certain scholars perceive that anti-dumping is a threat to trade liberalisation.[7] However, there has been a general understanding among the negotiating parties, even before the establishment of the WTO, that each importing member should have the right to impose anti-dumping duties on goods that are dumped in its market and to protect its domestic industry.[8]

5.2   Rationale for Anti-Dumping

The current text of the AD Agreement contains detailed rules for national anti-dumping investigation procedures and stipulates methods for defining the phrases used in Article VI, such as 'dumping', 'normal value', 'export price' and 'injury'.[9] Article 1 of the AD Agreement clarifies that the national anti-dumping measures shall be adopted only pursuant to investigations initiated and conducted in accordance with the provisions of the AD Agreement.[10]

There are three broad theories that support the application of anti-dumping duties. These are not economic theories per se. These three theories consider anti-dumping measures as a:

- response to international price discrimination
- mechanism of special protection
- strategic tool.

Response to international price discrimination. Anti-dumping laws were always characterised as a response to international price discrimination.[11] There could be several reasons for international price discrimination, but one overwhelming reason is that price competition is generally intense in international markets, whereas an exporter may enjoy

---

[4] MFN treatment under the GATT 1994, Art. I, and the obligation to not impose duties in excess of bound duties under the GATT 1994, Art. II.

[5] GATT 1947, Art. II:2(a).

[6] P. C. Mavroidis, P. A. Messerlin and J. M. Wauters, *The Law and Economics of Contingent Protection in the WTO* (Cheltenham: Edward Elgar, 2008), pp. 7–25.

[7] J. M. Finger, *Antidumping: How it Works and Who Gets Hurt* (Ann Arbor: University of Michigan Press, 1993).

[8] J. H. Jackson, J. V. Louis and M. Matsushita, 'Implementing the Tokyo Round: Legal Aspects of Changing International Economic Rules', *Michigan Law Review* (1981), 81(2), p. 273.

[9] Jackson et al., 'Implementing the Tokyo Round', p. 273.

[10] Jackson et al., 'Implementing the Tokyo Round', p. 273.

[11] J. J. Nedumpara, 'Rules on Anti-Dumping Measures, in Cottier and Schefer, *Elgar Encyclopedia of International Economic Law*, p. 86.

tariff or other forms of protection at home.[12] Anti-dumping mechanisms could level the playing field in that sense.

Mechanism of special protection. The second argument provides that anti-dumping measures facilitate trade liberalisation by allowing countries to increase tariffs in order to protect domestic industries that are injured by imports.[13] This has been referred to as the safety valve theory. According to this argument, anti-dumping measures act as a safeguard mechanism.[14] Although the safeguard mechanism under the WTO is a better mechanism to achieve this goal, the legal hurdle for imposing safeguard duties is higher. In practice, however, anti-dumping has swayed from its original purpose of serving as a 'safety valve' and is often used as an excuse for special interests to shield themselves from competition.[15]

Strategic tool. The third argument provides that anti-dumping duties are a strategic or protectionist policy in the hands of WTO members. It is also known as the retaliation theory. Michael Finger notes that countries using anti-dumping protection form a 'club' and tend to apply anti-dumping duties against one another rather than against the 'non-club'.[16] In their findings, in a way, Prusa and Skeath reject the notion that the rise in anti-dumping activity can be solely explained by an increase in unfair trade.[17] According to Prusa, during the 1980s and 1990s, two-thirds of the anti-dumping actions involved countries that were anti-dumping users.[18] Anti-dumping actions are also used by countries to advance their government's industrial policy or for improving the competitive position of firms in an oligopolistic industry.[19]

GATT, Article VI

1. ... a product is to be considered as being introduced into the commerce of an importing country at less than its normal value, if the price of the product exported from one country to another
   (a) is less than the comparable price, in the ordinary course of trade, for the like product when destined for consumption in the exporting country, or,

---

[12] M. J. Trebilock, *Understanding Trade Law* (Cheltenham: Edward Elgar, 2011), pp. 60–75.

[13] Jackson et al., 'Implementing the Tokyo Round', p. 273.

[14] K. W. Bagwell, G. A. Bermann and P. C. Mavroidis, 'Introduction', in Bagwell, Bermann and Mavroidis, *Law and Economics of Contingent Protection in International Trade* (Cambridge University Press, 2009), pp. 1–7, at 3; Jackson et al., 'Implementing the Tokyo Round', p. 273.

[15] N. Mankiw and P. Swagel, 'Anti-Dumping: The Third Rail of Trade Policy', *Foreign Affairs* (2005), 84(4), pp. 107–19, at 107.

[16] Finger, *Antidumping*, p. 7.

[17] T. J. Prusa and S. Skeath, 'The Economic and Strategic Motives for Antidumping Filings', NBER Working Paper 8424, available at www.nber.org/papers/w8424 (accessed 21 December 2020).

[18] Thomas J. Prusa, 'On the Spread and Impact of Anti-Dumping', *Canadian Journal of Economics/Revue canadienne d'économique* (2001), 34(3), pp. 591–611.

[19] M. Moore and M. Wu, 'Antidumping and Strategic Industrial Policy: Tit-for-Tat Trade Remedies and the *China – X-Ray Equipment* Dispute', *World Trade Review* (2015), 14(2), pp. 239–86.

> ## *(cont.)*
> (b) in the absence of such domestic price, is less than either
>   (i) the highest comparable price for the like product for export to any third country in the ordinary course of trade, or
>   (ii) the cost of production of the product in the country of origin plus a reasonable addition for selling cost and profit.

Article VI of the GATT does not provide much guidance in ensuring that this instrument is not used in a protectionist manner. However, significant regulations and clarifications in this respect were included in the Kennedy and, later, in the Tokyo anti-dumping code. The AD Agreement builds on the general provisions contained in Article VI of the GATT 1994 and was a significant improvement over the Tokyo code, which was the previous attempt by a group of select GATT contracting parties to provide detailed disciplines on the conditions under which members are authorised to act against dumped imports.[20]

It should be noted that both Article VI of the GATT 1994 and the provisions of the AD Agreement elaborate the permissible responses against 'dumping'. Furthermore, Article 18 of the AD Agreement provides that any specific action against dumping should be in accordance with the provisions of Article VI of the GATT 1994 and the AD Agreement. The combined scope of the GATT Article VI and the AD Agreement was the subject matter of a dispute in the early days of the WTO.

US – 1916 ACT

The *United States – Anti-Dumping Act of 1916*[21] examined this relationship between Article VI:1 of the GATT and the AD Agreement. The United States enacted the Anti-Dumping Act of 1916 as part of the Revenue Act of 1916. This was the first legislation passed by the United States to address the problem of international price discrimination that could be predatory. The 1916 Act provided for civil actions and criminal proceedings against importers who 'commonly and systematically' have sold or imported into the United States goods with the intent of 'destroying competition or eliminating a competitor'. The 1916 Act remained on the statute books for more than eight decades, but was rarely applied.

In the appeal, the Appellate Body clarified that Article VI:1 GATT 1994 must be read together with the provisions of the AD Agreement.[22] The Appellate Body referred to the text of Article 1 of the AD Agreement and noted that anti-dumping measures taken under the AD Agreement must also adhere to Article VI of the GATT 1994.[23]

---

[20] Moore and Wu, 'Antidumping and Strategic Industrial Policy'.
[21] Appellate Body Report, *United States – Anti-Dumping Act of 1916*, WT/DS136/AB/R, WT/DS162/AB/R, adopted 26 September 2000.
[22] Appellate Body Report, *US – 1916 Act*, para. 118.   [23] Appellate Body Report, *US – 1916 Act*, para. 120.

US – 1916 Act *(Appellate Body)*

132. The requirement of intent to destroy, injure, or prevent the establishment of an American industry, or to restrain or monopolize any part of trade, does not affect the applicability of Article VI of the GATT to the 1916 Act. As already noted, action may be taken under the 1916 Act only when the constituent elements of dumping are present. The fact that an importer can only be found to have violated the 1916 Act when the sales of the dumped product in the United States were carried out with a certain intent does not mean that the actions under the 1916 Act are not 'specific action against dumping'. Proof of requisite intent under the 1916 Act only constitutes an additional requirement for the imposition of the civil and criminal penalties set out in that Act. Even if the 1916 Act allowed the imposition of penalties *only* if the intent proven were an intent to monopolize or an intent to restrain trade (i.e., an 'antitrust'-type intent), this would not transform the 1916 Act into a statute which does not provide for 'specific action against dumping', and, thus would not remove the 1916 Act from the scope of application of Article VI.

    [...]

137. ... Article VI of the GATT and the Anti-Dumping Agreement apply to 'specific action against dumping'. Article VI, and, in particular, Article VI:2, read in conjunction with the Anti-Dumping Agreement, limit the permissible responses to dumping to definitive anti-dumping duties, provisional measures and price undertakings. Therefore, the 1916 Act is inconsistent with Article VI:2 and the Anti-Dumping Agreement to the extent it provides for 'specific action against dumping' in the form of civil and criminal proceedings and penalties.

The Appellate Body, therefore, agreed with the WTO Panel that the 1916 Act, by providing for the imposition or for the recovery of treble damages, violated Article VI:2 of the GATT 1994, since it provided for a 'specific action against dumping', which was not authorised by Article VI of the GATT or the AD Agreement.

US – OFFSET ACT (BYRD AMENDMENT)

A similar issue arose in *United States – Continued Dumping and Subsidy Offset Act of 2000*. The Byrd Amendment (named after the former West Virginia Senator Robert Byrd, who inserted the amendment in the annual Agricultural Appropriations Bill) was introduced in 2000 to address the continued dumping or subsidising of products imported into the United States, after an anti-dumping or countervailing duty (CVD) order was imposed. The Byrd Amendment explicitly provided that duties collected pursuant to anti-dumping/CVD orders would be paid entirely to the US companies that supported the anti-dumping/CVD petition. In order to collect the disbursements under the Byrd Amendment, a domestic producer was required to establish its eligibility on the grounds that: (1) the domestic producer was a petitioner or interested party in support of a petition that resulted in an anti-dumping investigation; and that (2) the domestic producer remained in operation at the time of the claim for disbursement.[24] It is important to recall that anti-dumping/CVD petitions can only be filed by companies or producers who account for a major proportion of the production of the product under investigation and should also have claimed 'material injury' (see Section 5.4 of this chapter) on account of the dumped/subsidised imports.

Similar to the grounds in *US – 1916 Act*, the complainants in *US – Offset Act (Byrd Amendment)*[25] argued that US law violated key elements of the AD and SCM Agreements, in as much as it permitted 'specific action' against dumping and subsidisation that are not expressly authorised by the GATT 1994, the AD Agreement or the SCM Agreement, respectively. Specifically, the Byrd Amendment provided financial incentives for the domestic industry in the United States to file and support anti-dumping or CVD cases. As identified by the Appellate Body, the offset payments under the Continued Dumping and Subsidy Offset Act (CDSOA) were inextricably linked to a determination of dumping and subsidisation. The Appellate Body provided detailed analysis of the scope of the AD Agreement in this dispute.

US – Offset Act (Byrd Amendment) *(Appellate Body)*

256. All these elements lead us to conclude that the CDSOA has an adverse bearing on the foreign producers/exporters in that the imports into the United States of the dumped or subsidized products (besides being subject to anti-dumping or counter-vailing duties) result in the financing of United States competitors – producers of like products – through the transfer to the latter of the duties collected on those exports. Thus, foreign producers/exporters have an incentive not to engage in the practice of exporting dumped or subsidized products or to terminate such practices. Because the CDSOA has an adverse bearing on, and more specifically, is designed and structured so that it dissuades the practice of dumping or the practice of sub-sidization, and because it creates an incentive to terminate such practices, the CDSOA is undoubtedly an action 'against' dumping or a subsidy, within the meaning of Article 18.1 of the *Anti-Dumping Agreement* and of Article 32.1 of the *SCM Agreement*.

The Appellate Body found that the CDSOA had an adverse bearing on the foreign producers/exporters (in addition to being subject to anti-dumping or countervailing duties) in as much as their imports of the product into the United States could result in the financing

---

[24] Continued Dumping and Subsidy Offset Act of 2000, 19 USC §1675 c(b)(4).

[25] Appellate Body Report, *United States – Continued Dumping and Subsidy Offset Act of 2000*, WT/DS217/AB/R, WT/DS234/AB/R, adopted 27 January 2003, p. 375.

of US competitors – producers of like products – through the transfer to the latter of the duties collected on those exports.

5.3   Determination of Dumping

One of the key issues in an anti-dumping investigation is whether a product is being dumped and, if so, the determination of the dumping margin. Article 2 of the AD Agreement provides detailed rules on the determination of dumping. First of all, an investigating authority (IA) will have to determine the 'normal value' and the 'export price'.

5.3.1   Normal Value

Article 2.2 of the AD Agreement provides that normal value is the price of a 'like product' in the home market of the exporting country during the 'ordinary course of trade'. Determining home market sales or domestic sales transactions is the standard way to determine normal value for the purposes of calculating dumping margins. There is a four-pronged inquiry in the determination of normal value under Article VI of the GATT and the AD Agreement.

- Sale must be in the *ordinary course of trade*;
- Sale must be of the *like product*;
- Products must be destined for *consumption in the exporting country*;
- Price must be *comparable*.

5.3.1.1   Sales in the Ordinary Course of Trade (OCT Test)

Article 2.1 of the AD Agreement authorises the investigating agencies to exclude sales not made in the 'ordinary course of trade' (OCT) from the calculation of normal value. The purpose of the OCT test is to ensure that normal value is, indeed, the 'normal' price of the like product, in the home market of the exporter.[26] Article 2.2.1 of the AD Agreement does not define the concept 'in the ordinary course of trade', but it provides examples of certain sales that are not in the OCT. Article 2.1 provides that 'sales made below per unit (fixed and variable) cost of production plus selling, general and administrative expenses (S,G&A) may, under certain circumstances, be considered as not in the ordinary course of trade' (see Figure 5.1). It needs to be further inquired if such sales were made within an extended period of time,[27] in substantial quantities,[28] and at prices that do not allow for the recovery

---

[26] Appellate Body Report, *United States – Anti-Dumping Measures on Certain Hot-Rolled Steel Products from Japan*, WT/DS184/AB/R, adopted 23 August 2001, para. 140.

[27] Normally one year, but in no case less than six months.

[28] If the weighted average selling price of the transactions under consideration is below the weighted average per unit costs, or if the volume of sales at a loss represents at least 20 per cent of the volume of transactions.

of all costs. For example, sales that are below cost at the time of sale can still fall within the OCT if the losses on such sales can be recovered within the period of investigation. In this case, the term 'cost' refers to the cost of making and selling the product. Article 2.2.1 of the AD Agreement states that prices that are below total cost at the time of sale, but above the weighted average total cost during the period of investigation, can be considered to provide for cost recovery within a reasonable period of time. Although the term 'reasonable period of time' is not specified, it is often considered as the period of investigation, by implication.[29] This assumption is supported by virtue of footnote 4 to Article 2 of the AD Agreement, which states that 'the extended period of time should normally be one year but shall in no case be less than six months'.

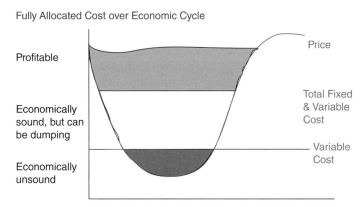

Figure 5.1 Rationale of below-cost sales

An assessment as to whether sales in the domestic market of the exporting member are made in the OCT can be a complex task. There are many situations where the transactions are not in the OCT. Such circumstances include: (1) sales below cost; (2) sales to affiliated parties; and (3) aberrationally high-priced sales/abnormally low-priced sales.

To determine whether the below-cost sales are made in substantial quantities, the AD Agreement also provides for the 80:20 test, popularly known as the Pareto test. Sales below total cost are made in substantial quantities when sales below cost represent 20 per cent or more, in volume, of all domestic sales in the country of export or export sales to a third country. When home market sales or sales to third countries do not satisfy the 80:20 test, such sales can be treated as not being in the OCT and may be disregarded for determining normal value. Sales not made in the OCT may be ignored in determining normal value.[30] The normal value would then be determined on the basis of the remaining sales.

---

[29] Panel Report, *European Communities – Anti-Dumping Measures on Farmed Salmon from Norway*, WT/DS337/R, Corr.1, adopted 15 January 2008, para. 7.277.

[30] See explanation as provided in fn. 28.

Box 5.1 OCT and below-cost test

Determining whether sales are made in the ordinary course of trade:

- Calculate the cost of manufacturing.
- Calculate the general expenses.
- Calculate the total cost (add the cost of manufacture and general expenses).
- Calculate the domestic price.
- Compare net domestic prices to total cost (adjusted).
- Verify whether sales made below cost are made (1) within an extended period of time; (2) in substantial quantities of time; and (3) whether cost recovery is possible within a reasonable period of time.

US – Hot-Rolled Steel

US – Hot-Rolled Steel provides significant clarity on issues such as determination of normal value, related party sales, and injury and causation. The case was brought by Japan regarding the preliminary and final determinations of the United States Department of Commerce (USDOC) and United States International Trade Commission on the anti-dumping investigation of certain hot-rolled steel products.

US – Hot-Rolled Steel *(Appellate Body)*

140. Article 2.1 requires investigating authorities to exclude sales 'not made in the ordinary course of trade', from the calculation of normal value, precisely to ensure that normal value is, indeed, the 'normal price' of the like product, in the home market of the exporter. Where a sales transaction is concluded on terms and conditions that are incompatible with 'normal' commercial practice for sales of the like product, in the market in question, at the relevant time, the transaction is not an appropriate basis for calculating 'normal value'.

141. We can envisage many reasons for which transactions might not be 'in the ordinary course of trade'. For instance, where parties to a transaction have common ownership, although they are legally distinct persons, usual commercial principles might not be respected between them. Instead of a sale between these parties being a transfer of goods between two enterprises, which are economically *interdependent*, transacted at market prices, the sale effectively involves a transfer of goods within a *single* economic enterprise. In that situation, there is reason to suppose that the sales price might be fixed according to criteria which are not those of the marketplace. The sales transaction *might* be used as a vehicle for transferring resources within the single economic enterprise. Thus, the sales price may be *lower* than the 'ordinary

> **(cont.)**
>
> course' price, if the purpose is to shift resources to the buyer, who then receives goods worth more than the actual sales price. Or, conversely, the sales price may be *higher* than the 'ordinary course' price, if the purpose is to shift resources to the seller, who receives higher revenues for the sale than would be the case in the marketplace. There are many reasons relating to corporate law and strategy, and to fiscal law, which may lead to resources being allocated, in these ways, within a single economic enterprise.

The Appellate Body in *US – Hot-Rolled Steel* confirmed that the AD Agreement does not define the term 'in the ordinary course of trade'. The issue in this case was whether the USDOC could exclude some of the sales of hot-rolled steel within the Japanese market from the calculation of the normal value. The USDOC had used a methodology which excluded from the dumping calculation home market sales by an exporter to a related or affiliated party, unless the price was at least 99.5 per cent of the average price charged to unaffiliated or independent third-party customers. However, the US methodology failed to take into consideration high-priced transactions between affiliates. It is axiomatic that sale price between affiliates could be higher or lower than the ordinary sales price.

The Appellate Body noted that the USDOC's conduct of the OCT test in this case was asymmetric and that the investigating authorities should exercise discretion in an *even-handed manner*, which is fair to all parties.[31]

> ## US – Hot-Rolled Steel *(Appellate Body)*
>
> 148. ... In particular, the discretion must be exercised in an *even-handed* way that is fair to all parties affected in an anti-dumping investigation. If a Member elects to adopt general rules to prevent distortion of normal value through sales between affiliates, those rules must reflect, even-handedly, the fact that both high- and low-priced sales between affiliates might not be 'in the ordinary course of trade'.
>
>   [...]
>
> 150. We observe that, under the 99.5 per cent test, a great range of low-priced sales to affiliates can be excluded from the calculation of normal value because they are deemed not to be 'in the ordinary course of trade'. The effect of the test is to minimize, to an extreme degree, possible downward distortion of normal value that might result from sales to affiliates.

---

[31] Appellate Body Report, *US – Hot-Rolled Steel*, para. 148.

As opposed to the 99.5 per cent test for low-priced transactions, there was no similar rule for OCT determination for high-priced transactions between affiliates in the methodology applied by the USDOC. As far as high-priced transactions were concerned, the USDOC excluded those sales from the calculation of normal value only if those prices were 'aberrationally' or 'artificially high'. According to the Appellate Body, there was a lack of *even-handedness* in the tests applied by the US. The Appellate Body observed that the combined application of these two rules operated systematically to raise or skew the normal value, through the automatic exclusion of all high-priced sales.[32]

5.3.1.2 Alternative Methods to Calculate Normal Value

The preferred method is to assess domestic sales transaction of the product in the exporting country's domestic market. In the event the normal value cannot be determined on the basis of domestic market sales, two other alternatives have been provided in the AD Agreement – third-country market price and constructed normal value. The alternative methods are employed in the following circumstances:

- when there are no sales of the *like product* in the *ordinary course of trade* in the exporting country, or
- when the particular market situation does not permit a proper comparison, and the
- low volume of sales in the domestic market of the exporting country does not permit a proper comparison.

The foregoing discussion has already examined the meaning of sales within the *ordinary course of trade*. The other two scenarios are explained in detail below.

Particular Market Situation   Particular market situation is broadly understood as a situation when the market of the exporting country operates, either directly or indirectly, in a distorted manner on account of factors such as undue government intervention, taxes, regulations and industrial policies, such that the determination of normal value could be questionable.[33] However, the negotiating history of the WTO contributes little to explaining the term and what situations are included in it.[34] A GATT Panel (*EEC – Cotton Yarn*)[35] found that hyperinflation combined with a fixed exchange rate did not necessarily constitute a particular market situation.[36] What needs to be demonstrated is whether or not the sales concerned would permit a proper comparison. In *EEC – Cotton Yarn*, the Panel considered that the complainant had failed to demonstrate that prices used as the basis of normal value

---

[32] Appellate Body Report, *US – Hot-Rolled Steel*, para. 154.

[33] W. Zhou and A. Percival, 'Debunking the Myth of "Particular Market Situation" in WTO Anti-Dumping Law', *Journal of International Economic Law* (2016), 19(4), p. 868.

[34] Zhou and Percival, 'Debunking the Myth of "Particular Market Situation"', p. 868.

[35] GATT Panel Report, *European Economic Community – Imposition of Anti-Dumping Duties on Imports of Cotton Yarn from Brazil*, ADP/137, adopted 30 October 1995, BISD 42S/17.

[36] GATT Panel Report, *EEC – Cotton Yarn*, p. 17.

were themselves so affected by the combination of high domestic inflation and a fixed exchange rate that those sales did not permit a proper comparison.[37] On the whole, while the meaning of particular market situation is unclear in WTO law, it could be argued that State intervention and price distortion, especially in the market for inputs and raw materials, could amount to particular market situation in appropriate circumstances.[38] Recently, the WTO Panel in *Australia – Anti-Dumping Measures on Paper* had the opportunity to examine the meaning of particular market situation.[39] The Panel adopted the approach that particular market situation did not have to be defined in a manner to include all possible situations that would prevent a proper comparison between domestic and export prices.[40] According to the Panel, particular market situation 'does not lend itself to a definition that foresees all the varied situations that an investigating authority may encounter that would fail to permit a "proper comparison"'.[41]

Insufficient or Low Volume of Sales   Sufficiency of sales in the home market is a key determinant in the OCT analysis.[42] The volume expressed in relative terms is determinative of the number of sales made in the domestic market compared with the number of export sales. Footnote 2 of the AD Agreement states that sales shall normally be considered sufficient in volume if they represent at least 5 per cent of the sales of the product to the importing/investigating country. It is clear that the 5 per cent benchmark is not an absolute criterion. Assuming that evidence of sales at a lower ratio are still of sufficient magnitude to provide for a proper comparison, a lower volume of sales should be acceptable for the purposes of the normal value determination.[43] Furthermore, it is not very clear whether the sufficiency of domestic sales relates to all domestic sales by an investigated exporter, or only to those sales by the exporter that are made in the OCT. In any case, the purpose of the sufficient volume test is to determine whether the domestic market is sufficiently significant to enable domestic sales to serve as a legitimate measure of normal value.

Third-Country Price Method   Article 2.2 of the AD Agreement provides that the calculation of normal value on the basis of export price to a third market should be 'appropriate', and that the export price to that county should be 'representative'. However, there is no other guidance under the AD Agreement as to the method of calculation while using the data from a third country. Some WTO members generally test the volume of exports to a given third country against the volume of exports to the importing member.

[37] GATT Panel Report, *EEC – Cotton Yarn*, p. 17.

[38] J. J. Nedumpara and A. Subramanian, 'China's Long March to Market Economy Status: An Analysis of China's WTO Protocol of Accession and Member Practices', in J. J. Nedumpara and W. Zhou (eds.), *Non-Market Economies in the Global Trading System: The Special Case of China* (Singapore: Springer, 2018), pp. 13–63, at 50–1.

[39] Panel Report, *Australia – Anti-Dumping Measures on A4 Copy Paper*, WT/DS529/R, Add.1, adopted 28 January 2020.

[40] Panel Report, *Australia – Anti-Dumping Measures on Paper*.

[41] Panel Report, *Australia – Anti-Dumping Measures on Paper*, para. 7.21.   [42] AD Agreement, fn. 2.

[43] AD Agreement, fn. 2.

Box 5.2 Normal value determination involving non-market economy/use of surrogate country

The non-market economy (NME) is not a properly defined concept and refers to States that were previously State-controlled economies. The ex-communist countries were treated as NMEs during the GATT days, especially between 1955 and 1995. However, once the NMEs had joined the GATT/WTO, the market economy treatment was almost certainly guaranteed. Exception to this rule could be China and Vietnam. NME treatment continues to be a controversial topic in the WTO.[44]

The NME methodology is especially important in the case of anti-dumping. A number of GATT/WTO members do not accept prices or costs in non-market economies as an appropriate basis for the calculation of normal value on the ground that such prices and costs are controlled by the government and therefore are not subject to market forces.[45] There is no definition of NME in the GATT/WTO, other than a rather incomplete description provided in the Interpretative Ad Note to Article VI of the GATT, which refers to 'a country which has a complete or substantially complete monopoly of its trade and where all domestic prices are fixed by the state'.

While using NME methodology, an investigating agency will resort to prices or costs in a third country as the basis for normal value, which is commonly referred to as the 'surrogate country' methodology. A number of investigating agencies collect production costs from firms or enterprises situated in market economy surrogate countries. The choice of the surrogate country is often an arbitrary selection.

Notwithstanding the NME methodology, several countries provide individual market economy treatment if the exporters prove that they operate under market economy conditions. The definition of what constitutes a market economy is, by and large, similar in most jurisdictions employing anti-dumping measures, and the focus is on criteria such as the absence of State interference and of market distortions carried over from former economic systems, currency convertibility, absence of bankruptcy laws, and the freedom to hire employees and negotiate wages.[46]

To Go Further

Nedumpara, J. J. and Zhou, W. (eds.), *Non-Market Economies in the Global Trading System: The Special Case of China* (Singapore: Springer, 2018).

Shadikhodjaev, S., 'Non-Market Economies, Significant Market Distortions and the 2017 EU Anti-Dumping Amendment', *Journal of International Economic Law* (2018), 21, pp. 885–905.

---

[44] Request for Consultations by China, *European Union – Measures Related to Price Comparison Methodologies*, WTO Doc. WT/DS516/1, 12 December 2016.

[45] Appellate Body Report, *US – Anti-Dumping and Countervailing Duties (China)*, para. 17.68.

[46] World Trade Organization, Communication from United States, Draft General Council Decision, *The Importance of Market-Oriented Conditions to the World Trading System*, WT/GC/W/796, 20 February 2020.

5.3.1.3 Constructed Normal Value

The purpose of the constructed normal value is to establish an 'approximate proxy for the price of the like product in the ordinary course of trade in the domestic market of the exporting country when the normal value cannot be determined on the basis of the domestic sale'.[47] Article 2.2 of the AD Agreement collapses the three elements of constructed normal value as follows:

- cost of production;
- reasonable amount for S,G&A;
- reasonable amount for profits.

On the basis of the above three elements, the investigating agency (IA) can calculate the constructed normal value. The additional details for the constructed normal value are provided in Articles 2.2.1.1 and 2.2.2 of the AD Agreement.

Calculation of Cost of Production   Article 2.2.1.1 sets out three types of obligations relating to an IA's cost calculations for constructing the normal value. Article 2.2.1.1 of the AD Agreement, first sentence, requires the IA to normally base its calculation on actual cost data of the examined producer or exporter, provided that:

- such records are in accordance with the generally accepted accounting principles (GAAP) of the exporting country, and
- they reasonably reflect the costs associated with the production and sale of the product under consideration.

Article 2.2.1.1 imposes certain positive obligations on the IAs. The first sentence requires that costs shall normally be calculated on the basis of records kept by the exporter or producer under investigation, provided that such records are in accordance with the generally accepted accounting principles of the exporting country and reasonably reflect the costs associated with the production and sale of the product under consideration. In other words, the records of the exporter or producer being investigated are the preferred source. The second sentence of Article 2.2.1.1 of the AD Agreement requires the investigating agency to consider all available evidence on the proper allocation of costs, including that which is made available by the exporter or producer in the context of an anti-dumping investigation, provided that such allocations have historically been utilised by the exporter or producer. The final sentence then provides for the appropriate adjustment of costs for non-recurring items of cost that benefit future and/or current production or for circumstances in which costs during the period of investigation are affected by start-up operations.

---

[47] Panel Report, *Thailand – Anti-Dumping Duties on Angles, Shapes and Sections of Iron or Non-Alloy Steel and H-Beams from Poland*, WT/DS122/R, adopted 5 April 2001, as modified by Appellate Body Report WT/DS122/AB/R, para. 7.112.

The IAs will also examine whether the allocations have been utilised historically by the exporter or producer, in particular in relation to establishing appropriate amortisation and depreciation periods, and allowances for capital expenditures and other development costs.[48] The third rule in Article 2.2.2.1 provides that costs shall be adjusted appropriately for non-recurring components that benefit future and/or current production. An adjustment is also foreseen for circumstances in which the costs during the period of investigation have been affected by start-up operations. Cases such as *China – Broiler Products*[49] and *EU – Biodiesel (Argentina)* (discussed below) provide that determining the appropriate cost allocation methodology necessarily includes the consideration of the methodologies used in the exporter's books and records.

Box 5.3 Cost allocation in anti-dumping duty investigations: a case study of broiler chicken

The normal value for a product cannot be determined unless the costs of production are properly allocated to the product under investigation. Exporters and producers that have multiple production lines or product profiles are often called on to allocate costs at an intricate level for the concerned product in an anti-dumping investigation. The cost allocation in anti-dumping can be more nuanced and detailed than the cost allocation in normal accounting.

The United States is a leading exporter of poultry products and China is one of the major importers. Interestingly, an important category of broiler products exported by the United States to China is chicken feet, otherwise known as chicken paws, which are hardly consumed in the United States or are regarded as a waste or, at best, used in animal feed products. In China, by contrast, they are a delicacy or a popular snack and command higher prices.

Since the anti-dumping investigation by China at the WTO involved broiler chicken products and not the whole chicken, it was important to allocate the costs. While the cost of rearing a live broiler chicken may include the cost of feed and other overhead costs, it is important to allocate the costs properly for both edible and non-edible products that emerge from the production process. For example, non-edible products, such as feathers, blood, viscera or offal, can emerge as by-products, which in turn can be used for animal feed. Among these, chicken paws indeed have a market outside the United States.

Chicken products have common costs up to the point of split-off from the whole chicken. The various broiler products after the split-off include breast, legs, quarters

---

[48] Appellate Body Report, *EU – Biodiesel (Argentina)*, para. 6.15.

[49] Panel Report, *China – Anti-Dumping and Countervailing Duty Measures on Broiler Products from the United States*, WT/DS427/R, Add.1, adopted 25 September 2013, para. 7.195.

Box 5.3 (cont.)

and chicken feet. Companies or firms producing joint or co-products that have a single production cost up to a certain point allocate that cost across the various resulting products. For example, if a single chicken worth $10 was divided up and the breast was sold for $5, the thighs for $3, wings for $1 and paws for $1, then 50 per cent of the pre-split-off production cost would be allocated to the breast, 30 per cent to the thighs and 10 per cent each to the wings and paws. Generally, for low-value by-products, no split-off costs are assigned.

Some US producers that were affected by the Chinese anti-dumping investigation, namely Pilgrim's Pride, Tyson and Keystone, had their own company-specific cost allocation methodologies. For instance, Tyson historically used a 'relative sales value' allocation methodology ('value based allocation'). The other allocation methodology is the 'weight-based allocation', according to which the split-up costs would be allocated according to the weight of the product concerned.

According to the Ministry of Commerce, the Chinese investigating agency, in the cost allocation methodologies of the three US producers, paws were given very little attention in the cost calculation. According to MOFCOM, broiler products such as paws, which accounted for most of the US exports to China, were allocated a relatively small portion or none of the total costs, which led to distortion of the constructed normal value. MOFCOM, therefore, ignored the cost allocation methodology of the investigated firms. According to the US exporters, their own cost allocation methodology should have been the basis for determination of constructed normal value. It is important to recall that the normal value was constructed because US domestic sales of the products were not in the ordinary course of trade.

Article 2.2.1.1 of the AD Agreement states that costs shall normally be calculated on the basis of records kept by the exporter or producer under investigation, if those books and records are consistent with the GAAP of the exporting country, and reasonably reflect the costs associated with the production and sale of the product under consideration.

According to the Panel in *China – Broiler Products*, use of the term 'normally' in Article 2.2.1.1 has some relevance. If the exporter's data are ignored, an investigating agency is bound to explain why it departed from the norm and declined to use the US producer's books and records. In other words, there is a presumption that the books and records of the investigated companies shall be used in order to calculate the cost of production to determine the normal value. The Panel, accordingly, found that China acted inconsistently with the first sentence of 2.2.1.1 when MOFCOM declined to use Tyson's and Keystone's books and records. MOFCOM devised and applied its own allocation methodology, as opposed to the alternate methodology suggested by the investigated companies.

Box 5.3 (cont.)

To address this question, the Panel examined the analytical framework established by the Appellate Body in *US – Softwood Lumber V* and certain other disputes, such as *EC – Salmon (Norway)* and *China – GOES*. Borrowing the reasoning of the Appellate Body ruling in *US – Softwood Lumber V*, the Panel observed that in cases where there is 'compelling evidence' available to the agency that more than one allocation methodology may potentially be appropriate to ensure that there is a proper allocation of costs, the investigating agency may be required to 'reflect on' and 'weigh the merits of' evidence that relates to such alternative allocation methodologies. In the assessment of the Panel, such an approach was necessary to meet the requirement to 'consider all available evidence'.

In more recent times, certain investigating agencies tend to ignore the cost of production as reflected in the exporter's accounting records, on the ground that the costs do not reflect the 'actual costs'. In other words, cost distortions induced by government intervention or the absence of competitive markets in the exporting country in the input market is often considered a ground to disregard the costs reflected in the books of accounts. The facts relating to *EU – Biodiesel*, a case that deliberated this matter in great detail, is discussed below. In *Ukraine – Ammonium Nitrate*, Ukraine argued that natural gas, which was an input for the production of the fertiliser, was artificially priced low (much lower than the export price to other countries) in view of the government control in Russia.

WTO panels, and the Appellate Body in particular, have clarified that the second condition in Article 2.2.1.1 is not concerned with the issue of whether the costs in themselves are 'reasonable'. In other words, according to the Appellate Body, there is nothing in the second condition that would allow an investigating authority to disregard domestic input costs on the ground that such costs are lower than international prices. According to this view, once the records correspond to or accurately record the costs, including the allocation for depreciation or amortization and their consistency with accounting standards, there is no additional standard of 'reasonableness'. Having noted this, it should be stated that the exact meaning of the second condition of Article 2.2.1.1 is far from clear. This is more than evident from the reasoning of the Appellate Body in *Ukraine – Ammonium Nitrate*.[50]

To Go Further

Prusa, T. J. and Vermulst, E., '*China – Anti-Dumping and Countervailing Duty Measures on Broiler Products from the United States*: How the Chickens Came Home to Roost', *World Trade Review* (2015), 14(2), pp. 287–335.

---

[50] Appellate Body Report, *Ukraine – Anti-Dumping Measures on Ammonium Nitrate*, WT/DS493/AB/R, Add.1, adopted 30 September 2019, paras. 6.68–6.108, at paras. 6.88 and 6.89.

The construction of cost of production was, yet again, a matter of dispute in *EU – Biodiesel (Argentina)*, discussed below.

EU – Biodiesel (Argentina)

EU – Biodiesel (Argentina) related to the imposition of anti-dumping duties on biodiesel exports from Argentina and Indonesia. In the investigation, the EU authorities determined that the domestic sale of biodiesel in Argentina was not made in the ordinary course of trade in view of State intervention in the domestic market. The major input for the production of biodiesel was soybeans. It was found that the Argentinian government had imposed a differential export tax on soybeans and soybean oil. EU authorities noted that the domestic price of soybeans was 'artificially' lower than the international price, in view of the distortion caused by export taxes. EU authorities therefore noted that the records of the Argentinian exporters did not 'reasonably reflect' the raw material cost on the product. Accordingly, EU authorities replaced the domestic Argentinian raw material cost with average reference prices of the raw materials published by the Argentine Ministry of Agriculture. One of the key issues in this dispute was the use of actual input costs by domestic producers.

EU – Biodiesel (Argentina) *(Appellate Body)*

6.73. ... In circumstances where the obligation in the first sentence of Article 2.2.1.1 to calculate cost on the basis of the records kept by the exporter or producer under investigation does not apply, or where relevant information from the exporter or producer is not available, an investigating authority may have recourse to alternative bases to calculate some or all such costs. Yet, Article 2.2 does not specify precisely to what evidence an authority may resort. This suggests that, in such circumstances, the authority is not prohibited from relying on information other than that contained in the records kept by the exporter or producer, including in-country and out-of-country prices. This, however, does not mean that an investigating authority may simply substitute the costs from outside the country of origin for the 'cost of production in the country of origin'. Indeed, Article 2.2 of the Anti-Dumping Agreement and Article VI:1(b)(ii) of the GATT make clear that the determination is of the 'cost of production [...] in the country of origin'. Thus, whatever the information that it uses, an investigating authority has to ensure that such information is used to arrive at the 'cost of production in the country of origin'.

Since the EU authorities used a surrogate price of soybeans that did not represent its cost of production in Argentina when constructing the normal value of biodiesel, the Appellate Body ruled that the EU had acted inconsistently with Article 2.2 of the AD Agreement. In an important finding, the Appellate Body noted that the EU authority's determination that the domestic price of soybeans in Argentina was artificially lower than international prices, in view of the Argentine export tax system, was, in itself, not a sufficient ground for concluding that Argentine exporters' accounting records did not 'reasonably reflect the costs' of soybeans that were used as inputs in producing biodiesel.[51]

S,G&A and Profits in Constructed Normal Value   According to Article 2.2.2 of the AD Agreement, the S,G&A are to be calculated on the basis of actual sales and production data obtained in the OCT of the product under investigation. However, when the data are not available, paragraphs (i), (ii) and (iii) of Article 2.2.2 of the AD Agreement provide alternative methods for calculating S,G&A. The three options are as follows:

- the *actual amounts incurred and realized* by the *exporter* or *producer* in question in respect of production and sales in the domestic market . . . of the *same general category of products*;
- the weighted average of the *actual amounts incurred and realized by other exporters or producers* . . . in respect of production and sales of the *like product* . . .;
- any reasonable method . . . (Emphasis added)

Article 2.2.2 paragraph (i) provides that the amounts can be based on the actual amounts incurred and realised by the investigated exporter for the same general category of products (which may include the like product). How broad the general category of products can be is not defined in the AD Agreement. The Panel in *Thailand – H-Beams* found that the text of Article 2.2.2 of the AD Agreement does not provide precise guidance as to the required breadth or narrowness of the product category.[52] It did note, however, that the narrower the category, the fewer products other than the like product will be included in the category, and this would seem to be fully consistent with the goal of obtaining results as close as possible to the price of the like product in the OCT in the domestic market of the exporting country.[53]

EC – Bed Linen

In the underlying investigation in *EC – Bed Linen*,[54] a landmark dispute involving India and the European Communities, the respondent relied on the constructed normal value under Article 2.2.2 of the AD Agreement for certain exporters of cotton-type bed linen products from India. One of the issues involved in this dispute was the determination of constructed normal value of Indian exporters who did not have representative domestic sales in the OCT of the product under investigation – that is, bed linen.

The Indian exporters who were selected by the European Commission in the sample included Anglo-French Textiles, Madhu, Omkar, Prakash and Bombay Dyeing. Since the sampled exporters did not have domestic sales in the OCT for the like product, the European Commission constructed the normal value for all investigated Indian producers. Among these companies, only Bombay Dyeing had some representative sales of the product in the Indian domestic market. Since the other Indian companies did not

---

[51] Appellate Body Report, *EU – Biodiesel (Argentina)*, para. 6.56.
[52] Panel Report, *Thailand – H-Beams*, para. 7.111.   [53] Panel Report, *Thailand – H-Beams*, para. 7.113.
[54] Panel Report, *European Communities – Anti-Dumping Duties on Imports of Cotton-Type Bed Linen from India*, WT/DS141/R, adopted 12 March 2001, as modified by Appellate Body Report WT/141/AB/R.

have profitable sales of the like product, the European Commission used the S,G&A of a very few other product types. The European Commission selected an amount of 29.4 per cent for the S,G&A and profits for Bombay Dyeing, the only Indian producer that had a few sales of the product types in the OCT. Importantly, the profit margin of Bombay Dyeing on the like product was higher than the profit margin of other Indian exporter, except one.[55]

To restate, in the underlying anti-dumping investigation, the European Commission determined the S,G&A and profits based on the data of one 'other producer' (Bombay Dyeing) without calculating the weighted average of the actual amounts incurred and realised by other exporters or producers. India contended that the relevant part of Article 2.2.2(ii) provides that the amounts for S,G&A and profits shall be based on: 'the actual amounts *incurred and realized by* other *producers or exporters*' (emphasis added).

According to India, the reference under Article 2.2.2 to the terms 'other exporters and producers' and 'weighted average' meant that the production and sales amounts are required to be averaged among more than one firm and thus could not be based on one firm's data. The Panel rejected India's claim, saying that a mere implication that plural words in the provision envisaged situations consisting of more than one exporter should not be a basis to reject the EC methodology.[56] According to the Panel, the existence of data of more than one exporter or producer is not a necessary prerequisite for the application of the weighted average approach in calculating the S,G&A.

However, the Appellate Body overruled the Panel's reasoning as this was not a correct interpretation of Article 2.2.2(ii) of the AD Agreement:

EC – Bed Linen *(Appellate Body)*

80. Here, we note especially that Article 2.2.2(ii) refers to 'the weighted average of the actual amounts incurred and realized by other exporters or producers'. In referring to 'the actual amounts incurred and realized', this provision does not make any exceptions or qualifications. In our view, the ordinary meaning of the phrase 'actual amounts incurred and realized' includes the SG&A actually incurred, and the profits or losses actually realized by other exporters or producers in respect of production and sales of the like product in the domestic market of the country of origin. There is no basis in Article 2.2.2(ii) for excluding some amounts that were actually incurred or realized from the 'actual amounts incurred or realized'. It follows that, in the calculation of the 'weighted average', all of 'the actual amounts incurred and realized' by other exporters or producers must be included, regardless of whether those amounts

---

[55] F. Graasfma and S. Rajagopal, 'An Overview of WT/DS 141: *EC – Anti-Dumping Duties on Imports of Cotton-Type Bed Linen from India*', in Das and Nedumpara, *WTO Dispute Settlement at Twenty*, pp. 135–59, at 143, 145.

[56] Panel Report, *EC – Bed Linen*, para. 7.65.

> **(cont.)**
>
> are incurred and realized on production and sales made in the ordinary course of trade or not. Thus, in our view, a Member is not allowed to exclude those sales that are not made in the ordinary course of trade from the calculation of the 'weighted average' under Article 2.2.2(ii).

In addition, the European Commission refused to accept the information on S,G&A for Indian companies that did not have profitable sales. India argued that in contrast to the chapeau of Article 2.2.2, the second paragraph of Article 2.2.2 did not contain the terms 'ordinary course of trade'. The Appellate Body noted:

> ## EC – Bed Linen *(Appellate Body)*
>
> 82. In contrast to Article 2.2.2(ii), the first sentence of the chapeau of Article 2.2.2 refers to 'actual data pertaining to production and sales *in the ordinary course of trade*' (emphasis added). Thus, the drafters of the *Anti-Dumping Agreement* have made clear that sales *not* in *the ordinary course of trade* are to be *excluded* when calculating amounts for S,G&A and profits using the method set out in the chapeau of Article 2.2.2.
> 83. The exclusion in the chapeau leads us to believe that, where there is no such explicit exclusion elsewhere in the same Article of the *Anti-Dumping Agreement*, no exclusion should be implied. And there is no such explicit exclusion in Article 2.2.2(ii). Article 2.2.2(ii) provides for an *alternative* calculation method that can be employed precisely when the method contemplated by the chapeau cannot be used. Article 2.2.2(ii) contains its own specific requirements. On their face, these requirements do not call for the exclusion of sales not made in the ordinary course of trade. Reading into the text of Article 2.2.2(ii) a requirement provided for in *the chapeau* of Article 2.2.2 is not justified either by the text or by the context of Article 2.2.2(ii).

The Appellate Body clarified that all of the 'actual amounts incurred and realized' by other exporters or producers must be included, regardless of whether the amounts are incurred and realised on production and sales in the ordinary course of trade or not.[57]

Similarly, in *EC – Tube or Pipe Fittings*,[58] a dispute involving Brazil and the European Communities, the question arose whether data relating to sales that had been discarded by

---

[57] Appellate Body Report, *European Communities – Anti-Dumping Duties on Imports of Cotton-Type Bed Linen from India*, WT/DS141/AB/R, adopted 12 March 2001, para. 80.

[58] Appellate Body Report, *European Communities – Anti-Dumping Duties on Malleable Cast Iron Tube or Pipe Fittings from Brazil*, WT/DS219/AB/R, adopted 18 August 2003.

the European Commission under Article 2.2 of the AD Agreement could still be used for the purposes of constructing S,G&A and profits in the context of Article 2.2.2 of the AD Agreement. It may be worth noting that the term OCT is not expressly mentioned in paragraphs (i), (ii) and (iii) of Article 2.2.2. The Appellate Body expressly stated that the investigating agency can make use of the actual data for the calculation of S,G&A when constructing the normal value.[59]

Concerning the meaning of 'reasonable' in the context of Article 2.2.2(iii) of the AD Agreement, the Panel in *EC – Salmon (Norway)* noted that the actual domestic profit data and actual S,G&A data should not be excluded because of the low volume of domestic sales or the low level of profitability of the sales to which they pertain.[60]

The determination of what could be S,G&A itself is not free from ambiguities. The Panel in *US – Softwood Lumber V* noted that Article 2.2.2 of the AD Agreement does not provide guidance on the cost items that should be considered to be general or administrative costs.[61] The Panel noted that the ordinary meaning of general costs includes costs affecting all or nearly all products manufactured by a company, while administrative costs were defined as costs concerning or relating to the management of the company's affairs.[62]

5.3.2 Export Price

Export price is the price at which the exporter sells the product in an importing country market. It is ordinarily based on the transaction price.[63] The AD Agreement provides no specific guidelines on the determination of export price.

Ex-factory export prices are arrived at after making numerous adjustments. According to Article 2.4 of the AD Agreement, adjustments are provided for differences in taxes, quantities, level of trade (wholesale or retail sales) physical characteristics and other factors that affect price comparability. The adjustments could include, for example, discounts and rebates, packaging costs, costs relating to transport, maintenance, insurance, loading and unloading and handling costs, and other allied costs. When there is no export price or when it appears to the IA that it is significantly different from the average price charged to the related importers in comparison with other importers, or that it is unreliable because of association or a compensatory arrangement between the exporter and the importer or a third party, the export price has to be constructed. The export price is constructed on the basis of the price at which the imported products are first resold to an independent buyer, or on such reasonable basis as the authorities may determine.[64]

---

[59] Appellate Body Report, *EC – Tube or Pipe Fittings*, para. 101.
[60] Panel Report, *EC – Salmon (Norway)*, paras. 7.309, 7.318.
[61] Panel Report, *United States – Final Dumping Determination on Softwood Lumber from Canada*, WT/DS264/R, adopted 31 August 2004, as modified by Appellate Body Report WT/DS264/AB/R, para. 7.263.
[62] Panel Report, *US – Softwood Lumber V*, para. 7.263.
[63] Bossche and Zdouc, *Law and Policy of the World Trade Organization*, p. 520.   [64] AD Agreement, Art. 2.3.

The Panel in *US – Stainless Steel (Korea)*[65] provided the following function of constructed export price:

> ## US – Stainless Steel (Korea) *(Panel)*
>
> 6.99. … rather, an export price is constructed, and the appropriate allowances made, because it appears to the investigating authorities that the export price is unreliable because of association or a compensatory arrangement between the exporter and the importer or third party. By working backwards from the price at which the imported products are first resold to an independent buyer, it is possible to remove the unreliability. Thus, we agree with the US that the purpose of these allowances is to construct a reliable export price to use in lieu of the actual export price or … to arrive at the price that would have been paid by the related importer had the sale been made on a commercial basis.

The Panel further held that, as the constructed export price should be a reliable export price, costs incurred between importation and resale can only be deducted if they were foreseen.[66] Only such foreseen costs can be considered to be reflected in the price.[67]

5.3.3 Fair Price Comparison

Article 2.4 lays down as key principle that a fair comparison shall be made between export price and the normal value. It also provides that the comparison *shall be made at the same level of trade, normally at the ex-factory level, and in respect of sales made as nearly as possible at the same time.* Although the AD Agreement does not prohibit the use of FOB (free-on-board) or CIF (cost, insurance, freight) prices, it appears that the normal way to perform a fair comparison at the same level of trade is by comparing prices at the ex-factory level.

Article 2.4 further provides that due allowances for any differences affecting price comparability must be made in accordance with the AD Agreement. The purpose of the above provision is to neutralise differences in a transaction that an exporter could be expected to have reflected in his pricing.[68] Article 2.4 of the AD Agreement provides a mere indicative list, and requires that due allowance shall be made for any explicitly listed differences that

---

[65] Panel Report, *United States – Anti-Dumping Measures on Stainless Steel Plate in Coils and Stainless Steel Sheet and Strip from Korea*, WT/DS179/R, adopted 1 February 2001.

[66] Panel Report, *US – Stainless Steel (Korea)*, paras. 6.100–6.101.

[67] Panel Report, *US – Stainless Steel (Korea)*, paras. 6.100–6.101.

[68] Panel Report, *United States – Final Anti-Dumping Measures on Stainless Steel from Mexico*, WT/DS344/R, adopted 20 May 2008, as modified by Appellate Body Report WT/DS344/AB/R; Panel Report, *Egypt – Definitive Anti-Dumping Measures on Steel Rebar from Turkey*, WT/DS211/R, adopted 1 October 2002, para. 7.333.

are also demonstrated to affect price comparability.[69] For example, in *EC – Tube or Pipe Fittings*, the Panel accepted that due allowance could be made for packing expenses, an item not explicitly mentioned in Article 2.4 of the AD Agreement.[70] In other words, Article 2.4 of the AD Agreement does not require that an adjustment be made automatically in all cases where differences are found to exist.

The burden of proof on various parties in ensuring fair comparison under Article 2.4 of the AD Agreement is a matter of debate. In *EC – Tube or Pipe Fittings*, the parties differed in their views of the nature of evidence that should be submitted in support of a claim for such an adjustment, and whether it is the IA or the exporter that bears the burden of identifying and substantiating the claimed adjustment.[71] According to the WTO Panel, the investigating agency retains the discretion for accepting or disregarding certain claims for due allowances.[72] However, in situations where normal value or export price is constructed or based on information from third sources (for example, NMEs), the IA must inform the parties of the type of information that is needed for a fair comparison.[73]

5.3.3.1 Comparison between Normal Value and Export Price

The AD Agreement includes three methods that could, theoretically, be used by an IA when comparing the normal value and export price for establishing a dumping margin.

AD Agreement, Article 2.4.2

Methods of Comparison

Subject to the provisions governing fair comparison in paragraph 4, the existence of margins of dumping during the investigation phase shall normally be established on the basis of a comparison of a weighted average normal value with a weighted average of prices of comparable export transactions or by a comparison of normal value and export price on a transaction-to-transaction basis. A normal value established on a weighted average basis may be compared to prices of individual export transactions if the authorities find a pattern of export prices which differ significantly among different purchasers, regions or time periods, and if an explanation is provided as to why such differences cannot be taken into account appropriately by the use of weighted average to weighted average or transaction-to-transaction comparison.

---

[69] Panel Report, *US – Softwood Lumber V*, para. 7.207.

[70] Panel Report, *European Communities – Anti-Dumping Duties on Malleable Cast Iron Tube or Pipe Fittings from Brazil*, WT/DS219/R, adopted 18 August 2003, as modified by Appellate Body Report WT/DS219/AB/R, para. 7.184.

[71] Panel Report, *EC – Tube or Pipe Fittings*, para. 7.158.   [72] Panel Report, *EC – Tube or Pipe Fittings*, para. 7.158.

[73] Appellate Body Report, *European Communities – Definitive Anti-Dumping Measures on Certain Iron or Steel Fasteners from China – Recourse to Article 21.5 of the DSU by China*, WT/DS397/AB/RW, Add.1, adopted 12 February 2016, para. 5.172.

As clearly spelt out in Article 2.4.2, the three standard methods to calculate the dumping margin by the IA are:

- Weighted average to weighted average (WA-WA)
- Transaction to transaction (T-T)
- Weighted average to transaction (WA-T).

The choice of methodology for calculating the margin will have an important impact on whether dumping is found to exist or not. In practice, the WA-WA methodology is often the preferred one. The Appellate Body in *EC – Tube or Pipe Fittings* made it clear that two methods (WA-WA, T-T) are offered as alternatives, and WTO members are free to choose one or other of them.[74] The Appellate Body rejected all arguments indicating any preference, arguing that nothing in the AD Agreement privileges one methodology over the other.[75]

The T-T methodology does not involve an evaluation of all sales either. There could be a discrepancy in the number of sales in the home and export markets. As a result, in such cases, in practice, an investigating agency will look for the domestic sale as close in time as possible to each of the export transactions. In other words, it will compare the two transactions that are contemporaneous.

A third exceptional methodology is provided for in Article 2.4.2 of the AD Agreement, which allows, in specific circumstances, a comparison between weighted average normal value and prices of specific export transactions. The use of the third methodology has been controversial, especially in the case of targeted dumping, and has been the subject matter of a few recent cases at the WTO.

5.3.3.2   Concept of Zeroing

'Zeroing' has been one of the controversial elements of dumping margin calculation. Zeroing is a methodology whereby an IA treats as 'zero' the negative dumping margins, while calculating the overall dumping margin. Such a practice often inflates the margin of dumping as it disregards the negative dumping margin and sets to 'zero' the negative margins. Several WTO cases have treated this practice as a violation of Article 2.4.2 of the AD Agreement. The impact of zeroing is that it eliminates 'negative dumping margins' from the overall dumping margin calculation. In such cases, dumping will look more serious than it actually is.

The negative dumping occurs because the export price is actually higher than the normal value. If the negative dumping can be used to offset the positive amount, no dumping will be found to exist. However, it has been the practice of some WTO members not to allow such offset and to attribute a zero value to negatively dumped transactions. This is known as the practice of zeroing.

---

[74] Appellate Body Report, *EC – Tube or Pipe Fittings*.
[75] Appellate Body Report, *EC – Tube or Pipe Fittings*, para. 76.

Table 5.1 Example of zeroing

Home market sale	Quantity	Domestic sales value	Weighted average unit normal value	Export price	Quantity	Export value	Weighted average unit export price
100	10	1000		95	10	950	
120	10	1200		135	10	1350	
115	10	1150		110	10	1100	
105	10	1050		105	10	1050	
95	10	950		90	10	900	
Total	50	5350	107	535	50	5350	107
Dumping margin without zeroing				0			
Dumping margin with zeroing				3.75%			

Source: Author's own.

Investigating authorities tend to divide the product under investigation into several subgroups or product categories or models for comparison purposes. Zeroing was common when such models or subgroups were compared. The Appellate Body in *US – Softwood Lumber V* stated that zeroing occurs mainly at the stage of aggregation of the results of the subgroups in order to establish an overall margin of dumping for the product under investigation as a whole.[76] In other words, according to the Appellate Body, the terms 'margins of dumping' and '*all* export transactions' should encompass the results of all model-specific comparisons (emphasis added).[77]

5.3.3.3 Zeroing and Targeted Dumping

Targeted dumping is dumping that is targeted at certain purchasers, periods of time or geographical locations. This practice stems from the exceptional methodology (i.e. W-T) outlined in Article 2.4.2 of the AD Agreement. For example, Boxing Day (26 December) sales or festival sales could be one such example. It is deemed to be present upon the identification of 'a pattern of export prices which differ significantly among different purchasers, regions or time periods', in terms of what is popularly known as the pattern clause in the second sentence of Article 2.4.2 of the AD Agreement.

If the pattern clause is satisfied, the latter part of the second sentence of Article 2.4.2 becomes relevant. This requirement is known as the explanation clause, which needs an

---

[76] Appellate Body Report, *United States – Final Dumping Determination on Softwood Lumber from Canada*, WT/DS264/AB/R, adopted 31 August 2004, para. 64.

[77] Appellate Body Report, *United States – Measures Relating to Zeroing and Sunset Reviews*, WT/DS322/AB/R, adopted 23 January 2007, para. 124.

explanation as to why the W-W and W-T comparisons are inadequate to address the dumping pattern.

The identification of these two clauses is a necessary and sufficient condition for a departure from the preferred price methodology of either a W-W or T-T comparison. The purpose of a W-T comparison is to 'unmask' or reveal the price differences present in a targeted dumping scenario. The rationale for the targeted dumping methodology is that significant price differences that are concentrated in a targeted dumping situation may remain suppressed or lost in a W-W or T-T comparison. In *US – Washing Machines*,[78] a case involving a challenge of the methodologies applied by the United States, the Appellate Body noted that the exceptional W-T comparison methodology under the second sentence of Article 2.4.2 requires a comparison of the weighted average normal value and the entire universe of export transactions that fall within the pattern, irrespective of whether the export price of the individual pattern transactions is above or below the normal value. The Appellate Body clarified that W-T comparison methodology should be applied only to pattern transactions. Thus, zeroing the negative intermediate comparisons within the pattern is inconsistent with Article 2.4.2. The United States violated the law by applying the W-T methodology to transactions other than those constituting the pattern in the *US – Washing Machines* investigation.

However, recently, in *US – Differential Pricing Methodology*,[79] a WTO Panel held that the US Department of Commerce, in an investigation on softwood lumber from Canada, aggregated the export price variations in different categories to find a single pattern, acting inconsistently with Article 2.4.2 of the AD Agreement. Regarding the inclusion of significantly different export prices in a pattern, the Panel held that targeted dumping is masked when significantly lower prices to certain purchasers, or certain regions, or in certain time periods, are masked by significantly higher export prices to certain other purchasers, or to certain other regions, or in certain other time periods.[80] According to the Panel, to successfully unmask targeted dumping reflected in the pattern transactions, an investigating authority should be permitted to adopt a methodology that deals with such significantly higher-priced export sales, which may be masking the significantly lower-priced export sales, as well as those lower-priced sales that may be masked.[81] Accordingly, on the question of zeroing in targeted dumping under the second sentence of Article 2.4.2 of the AD Agreement, the Panel disagreed with the Appellate Body in *US – Washing Machines* and held that non-pattern sales must not be excluded and W-W methodology may be used for such comparisons. In other words, all sales must be take into account in order to 'properly

[78] Appellate Body Report, *United States – Anti-Dumping and Countervailing Measures on Large Residential Washers from Korea*, WT/DS464/AB/R, Add.1, adopted 26 September 2016.

[79] Panel Report, *United States – Anti-Dumping Measures Applying Differential Pricing Methodology to Softwood Lumber from Canada*, WT/DS534/R, Add.1, circulated on 9 April 2019.

[80] Panel Report, *United States – Differential Pricing Methodology*, para. 7.57.

[81] Panel Report, *United States – Differential Pricing Methodology*, para. 7.58.

assess the pricing behaviour of a foreign producer or exporter and accurately measure the magnitude of dumping'.[82]

5.3.4 Like Product in Anti-Dumping Investigations

The determination of what constitutes a like product is important for determining dumping, as well as material injury or threat of material injury in anti-dumping investigations. It is also critical in determining the identification and the standing of the domestic industry to file an anti-dumping petition.

Article 2.6 of the AD Agreement defines *like product* to mean a product identical to or having characteristics closely resembling the product at issue. However, the IAs have wide latitude and discretion in choosing the 'product under investigation' and the competing domestic industry like product. The Panel in *EC – Salmon (Norway)* rejected Norway's argument that in defining 'like product', Article 2.6 of the AD Agreement required an assessment of 'likeness' in respect of the product under investigation 'as a whole', which required a comparison of all product categories considered as potentially 'like'.[83]

EC – Salmon (Norway) *(Panel)*

7.51. Where a broad basket of goods under consideration and a broad basket of domestic goods have been found by an investigating authority to be 'like', this does not mean that each of the goods included in the basket of domestic goods is 'like' each of the goods included within the scope of the product under consideration.

The Panel in *EC – Fasteners (China)* held that Articles 2.1 and 2.6 of the AD Agreement do not require the IAs to define the product under consideration to include only products which are like.[84] The Panel stated that the mere fact that a dumping determination is ultimately made with respect to a product provides no clarity about the scope of that product. Although the product under investigation and the like product are well-defined at the beginning of an investigation, it is possible that the precise nature of the product evolves during the course of the investigation. In other words, there is no requirement that the product under investigation should comprise a homogeneous category of products, which are like each other. Similarly, in *EC – Salmon*, the WTO Panel noted that the mere fact that a dumping determination is ultimately with respect to a product, provides no

---

[82] Panel Report, *United States – Differential Pricing Methodology*, para. 7.90.
[83] Panel Report, *EC – Salmon (Norway)*, para. 7.51.
[84] Panel Report, *European Communities – Definitive Anti-Dumping Measures on Certain Iron or Steel Fasteners from China*, WT/DS397/R, Corr.1, adopted 28 July 2011, as modified by Appellate Body Report WT/DS397/AB/R, para. 7.263.

guidance in the determination of the scope of the product under investigation or its internal consistency.[85]

5.4   Determination of Injury

5.4.1   Investigation of Injury

Dumping alone is not sufficient for invoking anti-dumping relief. The domestic industry should have suffered certain 'injury' as a result of dumping. In the context of the AD Agreement, the term 'injury' includes the following:

- *Material injury*: injury to the domestic industry;
- *Threat of material injury*: threat of injury to the domestic industry and not merely an allegation or a conjecture;
- *Material retardation of the establishment of a domestic industry*: a situation where an industry was about to be established, but its establishment was materially retarded because of the dumped imports.

The AD Agreement provides further details and guidance relating to the determination of material injury and threat of material injury, but provides no further guidance on the consideration of material retardation of the establishment of a domestic industry. The Appellate Body and various WTO Panels have shown that Article 3.1 of the AD Agreement provides more detailed obligations with respect to determination of injury.[86] Article 3.1 provides that the investigating authorities must ensure that a determination of injury is made on the basis of positive evidence and an objective examination of the volume and effect of dumped imports. 'Positive evidence' relates to the quality of the evidence that authorities may rely upon in making a determination. On the other hand, an objective examination requires that the examination process must conform to the basic principles of good faith and fundamental fairness.[87]

In anti-dumping investigations, injury is often assessed through the volume and price effects of dumping. Article 3.1 of the AD Agreement provides that the injury shall be based on positive evidence and involve an objective examination of the: (i) volume of dumped imports and the effect of such imports on prices in the domestic market for the like product; (ii) consequent impact of these imports on domestic producers of the like domestic product.

Article 3.2 of the AD Agreement provides that an investigating agency shall *consider* whether there has been a significant increase in dumped imports, either in absolute terms or relative to production or consumption in the importing member with regard to the volume

---

[85] Panel Report, *EC – Salmon*, para. 7.48.

[86] Panel Report, *Mexico – Anti-Dumping Investigation of High Fructose Corn Syrup (HFCS) from the United States*, WT/DS132/R, Corr.1, adopted 24 February 2000, para. 7.119.

[87] Appellate Body Report, *US – Hot-Rolled Steel*, para. 196.

of the dumped imports. It further provides that as regards the effects of the dumped imports on prices of the like domestic product, the IA shall consider:

- whether there has been significant price undercutting by the dumped imports as compared with the price of a like product of the importing member; or
- whether the effect of such imports is otherwise to depress prices to a significant degree or prevent price increases (price suppression), which otherwise would have occurred to a significant degree.

The AD Agreement does not subject the injury analysis to a prior finding of dumping. In practice, both the dumping and the injury investigations proceed simultaneously. In certain jurisdictions, such as the European Union, India and Australia, the injury and dumping investigations are conducted by the same agency; however, in jurisdictions such as Canada and the United States, different agencies are tasked with these responsibilities. In order to establish injury, most investigating agencies examine the volume of dumped imports, their price effects, and the injury parameters relating to the domestic industry. The various indicators of injury are specifically reflected in Article 3.4 of the AD Agreement. Article 3.5 of the AD Agreement deals with causation.

5.4.1.1 Injury to Domestic Industry

The injury referred to in Article 3 of the AD Agreement should be an injury caused to the 'domestic industry' by reason of dumping. Article 4.1 of the AD Agreement provides the definition of domestic industry 'as the domestic producers as a whole of the like products or ... those of them whose collective output of the products constitutes a major proportion of the total domestic production of those products'.

It should be noted that if a domestic producer is related to an exporter or exporters of the product under investigation, then the IAs have the discretion to exclude such producer from the definition of domestic industry. The rationale is that a producer who is economically related to the exporter does not require protection by AD duties.[88] Domestic producers will be considered as 'related' to the exporters if: a domestic producer directly or indirectly controls an exporter, or vice versa; or both are directly or indirectly controlled by a third party. There is an exhaustive definition of related parties in footnote 11 under Article 4 of the AD Agreement.

In *US – Hot-Rolled Steel*, the Appellate Body dealt with an issue whether or not production of hot-rolled steel by the domestic industry for in-house or captive consumption can be excluded from the scope of domestic industry. The Appellate Body ruled that an injury determination should be based on the entirety of the domestic industry and not simply on one part of the domestic industry.[89]

---

[88] Matsushita et al., *World Trade Organization*, p. 426.
[89] Appellate Body Report, *US – Hot-Rolled Steel*, para. 190.

The Appellate Body in *EC – Fasteners (China)* had occasion to examine the definition of domestic industry.

EC – Fasteners (China) *(Appellate Body)*

412. ... 'A major proportion', therefore, should be understood as a proportion defined by reference to the total production of domestic producers as a whole. 'A major proportion' of such total production will standardly serve as a substantial reflection of the total domestic production.

[...]

413. ... As footnote 9 to Article 3 of the Anti-Dumping Agreement indicates, the domestic industry forms the basis on which an investigating authority makes the determination of whether the dumped imports cause or threaten to cause material injury to the domestic producers ... Thus, 'a major proportion of the total domestic production' should be determined so as to ensure that the domestic industry defined on this basis is capable of providing ample data that ensure an accurate injury analysis.

414. ... to ensure the accuracy of an injury determination, an investigating authority must not act so as to give rise to a material risk of distortion in defining the domestic industry, for example, by excluding a whole category of producers of the like product.

5.4.1.2   Injury Examination

Articles 3.1 and 3.2 of the AD Agreement both mention that the volume and price effect analysis are relevant only for like products. Prices are comparable only when the products are like.[90] Before beginning with the price and volume effects under Article 3.1, the IA needs to ascertain price comparability of the products at issue.[91] This is especially important if the IA is developing subcategories or models for injury assessment.

The following discussion focuses on the examination of price effects of the dumped imports.

Price Suppression   As set out by the Appellate Body in *US – Upland Cotton*,[92] price suppression refers to a situation where the price or value of the domestic like product are prevented from rising (i.e. they do not increase when they otherwise would have) or an

---

[90] Panel Report, *China – Definitive Anti-Dumping Duties on X-Ray Security Inspection Equipment from the European Union*, WT/DS425/R, Add.1, adopted 24 April 2013, para. 7.41.

[91] Panel Report, *China – X-Ray Equipment*, para. 7.41.

[92] Appellate Body Report, *US – Upland Cotton*, para. 350.

increase is less than it otherwise would have been.[93] The Appellate Body in *China – GOES*[94] held:

> ## China – GOES *(Appellate Body)*
>
> 141. ... With regard to price suppression, Articles 3.2 and 15.2 require the investigating authority to consider 'whether the effect of' subject imports is '[to] prevent price increases, *which otherwise would have occurred*, to a significant degree'. By the terms of these provisions, price suppression cannot be properly examined without a consideration of whether, in the absence of subject imports, prices 'otherwise would have' increased.

In respect of price comparability, the Appellate Body noted in *China – GOES* that Article 3.2 of the AD Agreement involves a comparison of prices of dumped imports with the prices of the like domestic product.[95] In the *China – X-Ray Equipment* case,[96] the EU argued that China compared the prices of an entire range of products covered by the investigation, without taking into account the considerable differences among the products, particularly between 'high-energy' and 'low-energy' scanners.

> ## China – X-Ray Equipment *(Panel)*
>
> 7.50. ... If two products being analysed in an undercutting analysis are not comparable, for example in the sense that they do not compete with each other, it is difficult to conceive how the outcome of such an analysis could be relevant to the causation question. Further, if two products are compared at different levels of trade, without adjustment, the outcome of this comparison would not lead to an objective, unbiased analysis under Article 3.5 regarding the injury arising due to the difference in the prices of the products.

Price Depression   Price depression refers to the situation where prices of the domestic like products are pressed down or reduced.[97] The Appellate Body in *China – GOES* stated:

---

[93] J. J. Nedumpara, *Injury and Causation in Trade Remedy Law* (Singapore: Springer, 2016), pp. 83–91.

[94] Appellate Body Report, *China – Countervailing and Anti-Dumping Duties on Grain Oriented Flat-Rolled Electrical Steel from the United States*, WT/DS414/AB/R, adopted 16 November 2012, paras. 141, 144, 145.

[95] Appellate Body Report, *China – GOES*, para. 129.   [96] Panel Report, *China – X-Ray Equipment*.

[97] Panel Report, *US – Upland Cotton*, para. 7.1277.

China – GOES *(Appellate Body)*

141. Price depression refers to a situation in which prices are pushed down, or reduced, *by something*. An examination of price depression, by definition, calls for more than a simple observation of a price *decline*, and also encompasses an analysis of *what is* pushing down the prices.

According to the Appellate Body, an examination of price depression calls for 'more than a simple observation of a price decline, and also encompasses an analysis of what is pushing down the prices'.[98] In other words, the concepts of price suppression and price depression implicate an examination of what brings about or leads to such price phenomena. In this regard, the Appellate Body held:

China – GOES *(Appellate Body)*

159. . . . 'merely showing the existence of significant price depression does not suffice for the purposes of Article 3.2 of the Anti-Dumping Agreement and Article 15.2 of the SCM Agreement'. We recall our interpretation, set out above, that Articles 3.2 and 15.2 contemplate an inquiry into the relationship between two variables, whereby an authority must consider whether a first variable – that is, subject imports – has explanatory force for the occurrence of depression or suppression of a second variable – that is, domestic prices. Thus, as the Panel rightly found, it is not sufficient for an authority to confine its consideration to what is happening to domestic prices alone for purposes of the inquiry stipulated in Articles 3.2 and 15.2.

The difference between price suppression and price depression was explained by the Panel Body in *US – Upland Cotton*.[99] The Appellate Body held that unlike price suppression, price depression is a directly observable phenomenon.[100] While falling prices can be observed, price suppression concerns whether the prices are less than what they would have been but for the dumped imports. According to the Appellate Body, the identification of price suppression presupposes a comparison of observable facts (prices) with a counterfactual situation (what prices would have been), where one has to determine if, in the absence of some controlling phenomenon, prices would have increased or would have increased more than they actually did. On the other hand, price depression exists in a situation where prices are pressed down or reduced and are easily observable.[101]

---

[98] Panel Report, *US – Upland Cotton*, para. 141.   [99] Panel Report, *US – Upland Cotton*, para. 7.1277, fn. 1388.

[100] Appellate Body Report, *United States – Subsidies on Upland Cotton – Recourse to Article 21.5 of the DSU by Brazil*, WT/DS267/AB/RW, adopted 20 June 2008, para. 351.

[101] Appellate Body Report, *US – Upland Cotton (Recourse to Article 21.5)*, para. 424.

Injury and Cumulation

> ### *AD Agreement, Article 3.3*
>
> Where imports of a product from more than one country are simultaneously subject to anti-dumping investigations, the investigating authorities may cumulatively assess the effects of such imports only if they determine that (a) the margin of dumping established in relation to the imports from each country is more than *de minimis* as defined in paragraph 8 of Article 5 and the volume of imports from each country is not negligible and (b) a cumulative assessment of the effects of the imports is appropriate in light of the conditions of competition between the imported products and the conditions of competition between the imported products and the like domestic product.

Cumulation is a useful tool for injury analysis when imports take place from multiple sources. If imports are found to compete with each other and the domestic like product, then the IA may cumulate the volume and effect of such imports for injury assessment. The Panel in *EC – Bed Linen* observed that when a producer is found not to be dumping the product, the imports attributable to such a producer/exporter should be excluded from the volume of dumped imports and not considered for injury analysis.[102]

5.4.1.3 Determination of Injury

The injury examination requires an evaluation of the impact of dumping on domestic producers of a majority of like products. Article 3.4 of the AD Agreement provides that an examination of the impact of the dumped imports on the domestic industry concerned shall evaluate all relevant economic factors and indices having a bearing on the state of industry and an actual or potential decline in: sales, profits, output, market share, productivity, return on investments, capacity utilisation, factors affecting domestic prices, magnitude of the margin of dumping, actual and potential negative effects on cash flow, inventories, employment, wages, growth, ability to raise capital or investments.

The Appellate Body in *EC – Tube or Pipe Fittings* stated that Article 3.4 of the AD Agreement does not impose any obligation as to the manner in which the mentioned factors should be examined. It may be sufficient under Article 3.4 to implicitly examine the factors.[103] Article 3.4 of the AD Agreement requires an IA to carry out a reasoned analysis and a thorough evaluation of the state of the domestic industry.

The list of factors included in Article 3.4 of the AD Agreement seems to combine both indicators of the state of the domestic industry and factors that may be relevant in resolving the causation question. Certain parameters, such as market share, profitability and factors affecting domestic prices, could be indicative of injury and causation. Finally, an IA must

---

[102] Panel Report, *EC – Bed Linen*, para. 6.138.   [103] Appellate Body Report, *EC – Tube or Pipe Fittings*, para. 161.

examine all relevant economic factors and not only those mentioned in Article 3.4 of the AD Agreement.

The Panel in *US – Hot-Rolled Steel* stated that it is necessary for the IA to evaluate data and not merely mention it in its analysis.

US – Hot-Rolled Steel *(Panel)*

7.232. ... An evaluation of a factor implies putting of data in context and assessing such data both in their internal evolution and vis-à-vis other factors examined. Only on the basis of the evaluation of data in the determination would a reviewing Panel be able to assess whether the conclusions drawn from the examination are those of an unbiased and objective authority.

The Panel in *EC – Tube or Pipe Fittings*, after recalling previous Panel and Appellate Body decisions, held that the indicators listed under Article 3.4 contain a mandatory, rather than an illustrative list of factors that must be addressed in every investigation.[104] The domestic industry is not required to show injury in respect of all fifteen injury parameters. After evaluating each of these parameters, an IA is required to provide an overall assessment of the domestic industry, including the weight attached to the injury parameters.

5.4.1.4   Threat of Injury

The term 'injury' in the AD Agreement refers to both material injury and threat of material injury to a domestic industry. Article 3.7 of the AD Agreement sets forth the requirements that an IA has to comply with in the case of a threat of injury examination: (1) a determination of threat of injury must be based on facts and not merely on allegations, conjecture or a remote possibility; (2) the expected injury must be imminent and clearly foreseen.

In a threat of injury scenario, the IA should determine whether (1) dumped imports have been increasing at a significant rate that indicates the likelihood of substantially increased importation; (2) there is sufficiently freely disposable or an imminent substantial increase in the capacity of the exporter, indicating a likelihood of substantially increased dumped exports; (3) the prices of the dumped imports are such that they have a significant price-depressing or price-suppressing effect on domestic prices and would therefore likely increase demand for further imports; and (4) the State of the investors of the subject product inventories.

---

[104] Panel Report, *EC – Tube or Pipe Fittings*, para. 7.304.

The list of factors mentioned in Article 3.7 is not an exhaustive list, but only an indicative one.[105] The Appellate Body in *Mexico – Corn Syrup*[106] made an important observation in the establishment of threat of injury.

Mexico – Corn Syrup (Article 21.5 – US) *(Appellate Body)*

85. ... In determining the existence of the *threat* of material injury, the investigating authorities will necessarily have to make assumptions relating to 'the occurrence of future events' since such future events 'can never be definitively proven by facts'. Notwithstanding this intrinsic uncertainty, a 'proper establishment' of facts in a determination of threat of material injury must be based on events that, although they have not yet occurred, must be 'clearly foreseen and imminent', in accordance with Article 3.7 of the Anti-Dumping Agreement.

Therefore, the IA is permitted to have recourse to Article 3.7 to justify imposition of anti-dumping duties when the injury is imminent and not a mere conjecture or allegation.

5.4.2 Determination of Causation

Article 3.5 of the AD Agreement requires the IA to demonstrate that dumped imports, through the effects of dumping, as set forth in Articles 3.2 and 3.4 of the AD Agreement, are causing injury within the meaning of the AD Agreement.[107] Accordingly, Article 3.5 provides that the volume and price effects of the imports need to be assessed to establish a causal link between the imports and the injury to the domestic industry.[108]

An IA's determination of the causal relationship between the imports of the product at issue and injury must be reasoned and adequate.[109] In making the determination, the IA is required to demonstrate a relationship of cause and effect, such that the products at issue are shown to have caused the injury to the domestic industry.[110] There could be factors other than dumped imports that might have caused injury to the domestic industry. As the Panel in *China – Autos (US)* noted, the role of any other factor that might have caused simultaneous injury should be identified and separated – a concept known as non-attribution.[111]

[105] Panel Report, *United States – Investigation of the International Trade Commission in Softwood Lumber from Canada*, WT/DS277/R, adopted 26 April 2004, para. 7.68.
[106] Appellate Body Report, *Mexico – Anti-Dumping Investigation of High Fructose Corn Syrup (HFCS) from the United States – Recourse to Article 21.5 of the DSU by the United States*, WT/DS132/AB/RW, adopted 21 November 2001.
[107] Panel Report, *China – X-Ray Equipment*, para. 7.251.
[108] See, generally, Nedumpara, *Injury and Causation in Trade Remedy Law*.
[109] Panel Report, *China – Anti-Dumping and Countervailing Duties on Certain Automobiles from the United States*, WT/DS440/R, Add.1, adopted 18 June 2014, para. 7.322.
[110] Panel Report, *China – Autos (US)*, para. 7.323.   [111] Panel Report, *China – Autos (US)*, para. 7.323.

5.4.3   Non-Attribution

Article 3.5 of the AD Agreement imposes a dual obligation on an IA, which must ensure that injury is attributed to dumped imports and that injury attributable to other factors is not attributed to dumping.

The second obligation is commonly known as the non-attribution requirement. Such a requirement is also present in the case of CVD, as well as safeguard investigations. It merely means that when assessing factors causing the injury, the IA needs to consider whether factors other than those caused by the dumped products are also causing injury at the same time. The injury caused by factors other than dumping (other known factors) should not be wrongly attributed to the dumped goods. An illustrative list of other factors is provided in Article 3.5 of the AD Agreement and includes: (1) volume and prices of imports not sold at dumped prices; (2) contraction in demand or changes in the patterns of consumption; (3) trade-restrictive practices of and competition between foreign and domestic producers; (4) development in technology; and (5) export performance and productivity of the domestic industry.

The list of other factors mentioned above is indicative.[112] Any factor raised by an interested party can be an 'other factor' that needs to be assessed as to its impact on the domestic industry during the investigating period.[113] According to the WTO Panel in *China – Autos*, whether a causal factor was 'known' to an IA would depend on an evaluation of the extent to which that factor was 'clearly raised' by the interested parties during an investigation.[114] The Panel, however, underlined that an IA is 'under no obligation to seek out and identify all possible other factors causing injury to the domestic industry in a given investigation.[115]

Concerning the methodology for carrying out the non-attribution test, the Appellate Body in *US – Hot-Rolled Steel* noted:

US – Hot-Rolled Steel *(Appellate Body)*

244. We emphasize that the particular methods and approaches by which WTO Members choose to carry out the process of separating and distinguishing the injurious effects of dumped imports from the injurious effects of the other known causal factors are not prescribed by the Anti-Dumping Agreement. What the Agreement requires is simply that the obligations in Article 3.5 be respected when a determination of injury is made.

There is no requirement to determine the impact of the other factors individually or collectively, as it depends upon the subjective facts of each case.[116]

---

[112] Panel Report, *EC – Tube or Pipe Fittings*, para. 7.359.
[113] Panel Report, *EC – Tube or Pipe Fittings*, para. 7.359.   [114] Panel Report, *China – Autos*, para. 7.323.
[115] Panel Report, *China – Autos*, para. 7.323.
[116] Appellate Body Report, *EC – Tube or Pipe Fittings*, paras. 191–192.

5.5   Administration of Anti-Dumping Proceedings

Dumping or dumping margin is determined by the national investigating authorities of the respective WTO member States.

Anti-dumping investigations are initiated based on the application of the domestic industry. Article 5.3 of the AD Agreement provides the obligation of the importing member authorities to examine, before initiation of the investigation, the accuracy and adequacy of the evidence in the application. Before initiation, the importing member authorities must notify the government of the exporting member. The AD Agreement does not contain rules on the form of such notification.

5.5.1   Industry Standing and Interested Parties

Article 5.4 of the AD Agreement provides that the IA shall examine the basis of the degree of support for or against the initiation of investigation, and whether the application expressed by the domestic producers of the like product has been made by or on behalf of the domestic industry. A failure to properly determine standing before initiation is a fatal error that cannot be rectified retroactively. An application is said to be made by or on behalf of the domestic industry if it is supported by domestic producers whose collective output constitutes more than 50 per cent of the total production of the like product produced by that part of the domestic industry expressing either support for or opposition to the application. There can be no standing if the collective output of the domestic producers in support of the application is less than 25 per cent of the total output. This is called the 50-25 test.

The parties most directly affected by an AD investigation are the domestic producers, foreign producers and exporters, and their importers/end-users. However, the government of the exporting country and representative trade associations also qualify as interested parties. Article 6.11 provides that other domestic or foreign parties may also be included as interested parties by the importing member. Although interested parties are provided with an opportunity to participate in the anti-dumping proceedings, few countries provide a public interest examination.

5.5.2   Due Process Rights

Articles 6 and 12 of the AD Agreement contain various due process rights of interested parties. In *Thailand – H-Beams*, the Appellate Body had occasion to elaborate the scope of due process rights.[117] The Appellate Body held that Article 6 of the AD Agreement

---

[117] Appellate Body Report, *Thailand – Anti-Dumping Duties on Angles, Shapes and Sections of Iron or Non-Alloy Steel and H-Beams from Poland*, WT/DS122/AB/R, adopted 5 April 2001.

establishes a framework of procedural and due process obligations that requires investigating authorities to disclose certain evidence to interested parties. Further, Articles 6.9 and 12 set out procedural obligations in respect of the final determination.

5.5.2.1   Public Notices and Reasoned Determinations

Article 12 of the AD Agreement lays down detailed rules concerning public notice by an investigating agency of initiation of an investigation, preliminary and final determinations, and price undertakings. Upon initiation of an investigation, the respective exporting countries, as well as interested parties, shall be notified, and a public notice shall be made. The notification requirements also apply to preliminary and final determinations and price undertakings.

5.5.2.2   Confidentiality and Disclosure of Essential Facts

Anti-dumping investigations involve confidential business proprietary information of various parties, especially in relation to costing and pricing and various managerial decisions. However, in the interests of due process, the interested parties need access to the confidential information. Article 6.5 of the AD Agreement states that information that is by its nature confidential or is provided on a confidential basis shall, 'upon good cause shown', be treated as confidential by the authorities and 'shall not be disclosed without specific permission of the party submitting it'.

At the same time, the authorities shall require interested parties providing confidential information to provide meaningful non-confidential summaries of the same. Parties generally prepare both confidential and non-confidential versions of the submission. Most parties redact the confidential information in their non-confidential submissions. In most WTO members, only the IA will have access to the confidential file, whereas in certain jurisdictions, such as the US, the authorised attorneys can access the confidential file.[118]

5.5.2.3   Best Information Available or Facts Available

It is a fact that not all parties cooperate, or cooperate fully, in anti-dumping investigations. As the WTO Panel in *Egypt – Steel Rebar* noted, IAs face a dilemma in basing their finding on normal value or export prices and any other matters, where the data or information might not have been submitted by the parties or is not available.[119] In other cases, the submitted information may not be reliable.

Article 6.8 and Annex II to the AD Agreement recognise the right of the importing member to base findings on the facts available where an interested party refuses access to,

---

[118] In the US, the parties access the file under the Administrative Protection Order.

[119] Panel Report, *Egypt – Definitive Anti-Dumping Measures on Steel Rebar from Turkey*, WT/DS211/R, adopted 1 October 2002, para. 7.146.

or otherwise does not provide necessary information within a reasonable period or significantly impedes the investigation. In such cases, preliminary and final determinations, affirmative or negative, may be made on the basis of the facts available.

5.5.3 Anti-Dumping Measures

There are three types of remedies: provisional measures, price undertakings and definitive or final measures.

Provisional measures should preferably take the form of a security (cash deposit or bond equal to the amount of anti-dumping duty provisionally estimated), may not be applied sooner than 60 days from the date of initiation, and may not last longer than four months or, on the decision of the importing member authorities, upon request by exporters representing a significant percentage of the trade involved, a maximum of six months.

5.5.4 Price Undertakings

If the injurious effect of the dumping can be eliminated by maintaining appropriate price levels, anti-dumping duties can be suspended. Price undertaking is one such mechanism. Use of the word 'may' indicates that authorities have complete discretion in this regard and, indeed, some authorities are reluctant as a matter of policy to accept price undertakings. Price undertakings are often the preferred solution by exporters and are often indexed to the costs of the inputs used.

5.5.5 Duration of Anti-Dumping Measures

The validity of an anti-dumping duty is for a period of five years, counted from the date of imposition of the duty. The duration of duties can be extended for a further period of five years based on an expiry review (or sunset review). However, where a reasonable period of time has elapsed after the imposition of the anti-dumping duty, the IA assessing the need for continuing the imposition of the duty may undertake a review, either on its own initiative or at the request of any interested party and on the substantiation of such a request.

5.5.6 Anti-Dumping and Developing Countries

The AD Agreement contains special provisions regarding developing countries. According to Article 15 of the AD Agreement, when imposition of anti-dumping duties would affect the essential interests of developing country members, possibilities of constructive remedies must be considered. However, definite obligations of the developed countries towards the developing countries seem to be ambiguous. In *EC – Bed Linen*, a WTO Panel noted:

> ### EC – Bed Linen *(Panel)*
>
> 6.238. ... Pure passivity is not sufficient, in our view, to satisfy the obligation to explore possibilities of constructive remedies, particularly where the possibility of an undertaking has already been broached by the developing country concerned. Thus, we consider that the failure of the European Communities to respond in some fashion other than bare rejection particularly once the desire to offer undertaking had been communicated to it constituted a failure to 'explore possibilities of constructive remedies' ...

5.5.7   Special Standard of Review in the Anti-Dumping Agreement

Article 17.6 of the AD Agreement provides a special standard of review for panels examining AD actions. This review is independent of the general standard of review provided in Article 11 of the DSU. Article 17.6(i) is designed to provide certain deference to the evaluation of the facts by the investigating authorities. Article 17.6(ii) requires the panels to uphold the interpretations (which are otherwise permissible) of the Agreement by national authorities in cases where such provisions permit more than one interpretation.

5.5.8   Judicial Review

Domestic anti-dumping measures can be reviewed before national courts and tribunals. Article 13 of the AD Agreement provides that members shall maintain independent judicial, arbitral or administrative tribunals or procedures for the purpose or prompt review of administrative decisions regarding final determinations and review of determinations. This opportunity permits the interested parties to raise their legal disputes before the national forums. However, availability of this measure does not prevent a party from approaching WTO dispute panels.

5.6   Conclusion

Anti-dumping actions have become the main line of defence for several trading nations in the aftermath of the substantial decline in tariffs on non-agricultural products. The applied tariffs on the bulk of commodities in most of the jurisdictions have fallen to single digits. The anti-dumping actions are generally clustered around intermediary goods and inputs. On some of these products, anti-dumping measures have remained for decades.

On a positive note, the AD Agreement has been singularly responsible for curbing the protectionist instincts of several key users of this instrument. WTO Panels and the Appellate Body have reviewed and ruled against several inconsistent member practices in this field.

This rigorous review has also resulted in an improvement in the way anti-dumping investigations are conducted.

While anti-dumping measures are targeted at unfair pricing, they have also been used to target certain types of government intervention. Most of the anti-dumping actions against China seek to address the role of the State in the allocation of resources. While distortions in costs and prices in determining normal value and export price could be central to anti-dumping, it is unclear whether the AD Agreement is the correct instrument to deal with such issues. Some of these emerging issues will be explored in greater detail in the next chapter, on subsidies.

5.7   Summary

- Anti-dumping is a response to international price discrimination in goods, particularly when such price discrimination is injurious to the domestic industry. Dumping, injury and causation are the three important requirements in order to successfully initiate an anti-dumping investigation.
- The normal value should be the price of the product in the exporting country in the ordinary course of trade. Since dumping involves comparison with an export price, it is important to identify a comparison price, which is ideally a price at the ex-factory level. The AD Agreement provides clear guidance on the principles to be used for fair comparison in arriving at a conclusion of dumping.
- Having found dumping, determination of material injury is the next challenge. The economic and non-economic parameters of the domestic industry have to be identified to assess injury. An equally important task is the determination of causation between dumping and injury.
- An anti-dumping determination hinges on defining the scope of the product under investigation and the like domestic product. Furthermore, in order to determine the price and volume effects of the imports, accurate and reliable data on imports and various domestic industry factors need to be selected.
- Anti-dumping measures last for a period of five years, unless they are extended, terminated, modified or revised. In addition to duties, the AD Agreement provides for price undertaking in lieu of duty.
- Anti-dumping inquiries are rigorous and time-consuming. They are also very data-intensive, involving sales and cost data of the domestic industry and the exporters. Most of this information is collected from the interested parties through questionnaire responses.

5.8   Review Questions

1 Explain the significance of the 'ordinary course of trade' (OCT) test in the context of the various provisions of the Anti-Dumping Agreement. Is the OCT related to below-cost sales? (See Appellate Body Report, *US – Hot-Rolled Steel*.)

2 Can an anti-dumping agency ignore the domestic costs and prices of an exporting firm in an anti-dumping investigation? Is the situation different if the exporting country is a State capitalist economy where the State has strong control over resources and industrial policies? (See Panel and Appellate Body Reports, *EC – Fasteners (China)* and *EU – Biodiesel (Argentina)*.)

3 The use of zeroing is considered an egregious method of calculation in dumping margin determination. Provide a summary of the various categories of zeroing observed in dumping margin calculations among various WTO members. (See Panel and Appellate Body Reports, *EC – Bed Linen* and *US – Washing Machines*.)

4 What are the differences between 'price depression' and 'price suppression' in injury analysis? (See Appellate Body Report, *US – Upland Cotton* and *China – GOES*.)

5 Explain the concept of 'like product' in anti-dumping law. (See Panel Report, *EC – Salmon (Norway)*.)

5.9   Exercise

You are an intern at the trade law practice of a large law firm in Zion, the capital of Khemed. The partner has assigned you a trade remedy matter where the firm is representing Company Z – a major manufacturer and exporter of e-cigarettes (HS Code 85437099) in a third country – Springfield. Company X and Company Y (major manufacturers of e-cigarettes in Khemed) have filed an anti-dumping investigation against imports of e-cigarettes originating in Springfield. Companies X and Y account for 35 per cent of the total production of e-cigarettes (Company X – 20 per cent and Company Y – 15 per cent) in Khemed and are supported by other Khemedian manufacturers of e-cigarettes (who collectively account for 52 per cent of the total production of e-cigarettes in Khemed). Companies X and Y's application contains information relating to dumping, injury and causal link. The application contains information on the volume of the dumped imports for two calendar years, but not for the previous years. The application lists Company Z (your client) as one of the exporters of the dumped products. Company Z and Company Y have a common shareholder owning a 26 per cent share and majority voting rights (based in a third country – Hogsmeade), which specialises in health- and technology-related products. Company A, the other major manufacturer in Khemed, which has a share of 25 per cent of the production, is not in favour of the anti-dumping action. There are also rumours that the market for e-cigarettes in Khemed was affected by imports of cheap regular cigarettes (HS Code 24022090) from neigbouring countries.

The application filed with the Khemedian anti-dumping authorities contains certain information on the imports of e-cigarettes from Springfield, which indicate that the product is being imported at significantly lower prices. The Khemedian anti-dumping authorities took into account the injury data submitted by Companies X and Y, which indicate that the profits, market share, employment, wages and so on in Khemed have declined over the period of investigation (2014–19). The Khemedian authorities determined that the dumped imports from Springfield have caused injury to the domestic Khemedian producers. Based on these findings, provisional duties were recommended.

Your client, Company Z, has requested your advice on whether the imposition of provisional duties can be challenged before a local court, or even the WTO DSB, and on what grounds. You may also examine the legal grounds, including the adequacy and accuracy of the evidence for initiating the investigation.

FURTHER READING

Bhala, R., 'Rethinking Anti-Dumping Law', *George Washington Journal of International Law and Economics* (1995), 29, pp. 1–144.

Finger, J. M., *Antidumping: How it Works and Who Gets Hurt* (Ann Arbor: University of Michigan Press, 1993).

Mankiw, G. N. and Swagel, P., 'Anti-Dumping: The Third Rail of Trade Policy', *Foreign Affairs* (2005), 84(4), pp. 107–19.

Mavroidis, P. C., Bermann, P. G. and Wu, M., *The Law of the World Trade Organization (WTO): Documents, Cases and Analysis* (St Paul: West, 2010), ch. 17.

Nedumpara, J. J., 'Anti-Dumping Proceedings and "Zeroing" Practices: Have We Entered the Endgame?', *Global Trade and Customs Journal* (2012), 7(1), pp. 14–26.

Pauwelyn, J. H. B., Guzman, A. T. and Hillman, J. A., 'Dumping and Anti-Dumping Duties', in Pauwelyn, Guzman and Hillman, *International Trade Law*, 3rd ed. (New York: Wolters Kluwer, 2016), ch. 15.

6 Subsidies, Countervailing Measures and Safeguards

Table of Contents

Highlights

- Multilateral disciplines on subsidies are aimed at eliminating or reducing trade-distorting subsidies.
- Not all government support or financial contribution can amount to a subsidy. The SCM Agreement requires certain fundamental elements to be met to constitute an actionable subsidy. These elements are financial contribution and benefit. In addition, for a subsidy to be actionable, it should be 'specific'.
- The SCM Agreement addresses subsidies provided by a government or any public body within the territory of a member.

- Not all subsidies in the economic sense are captured by the SCM Agreement. Subsidies to domestic producers are permissible, but actionable if they cause 'adverse effects'. In addition, such subsidies should be given in conformity with Article III:8(b) of the GATT 1994 to remain compliant with the GATT.
- The SCM Agreement deals with three categories of subsidies, namely, prohibited subsidies, actionable subsidies and non-actionable subsidies. The category of non-actionable subsidies expired in 1999.
- Export subsidies and import substitution subsidies are specific and are prohibited. These subsidies can be challenged directly before the WTO DSB.
- There are certain limited exceptions to export subsidies under Part VII of the SCM Agreement. Members that are included in Annex VII of the SCM Agreement can provide certain export subsidies.
- CVD measures can be imposed by importing countries, based on a proper investigation and subject to finding subsidy, injury and causal link.
- Safeguard measures are available to WTO members to restrict imports from other members, provided that the surge in imports causes or threatens to cause serious injury to the domestic industry. Safeguard measures are temporary and are meant to facilitate structural adjustment within the industry.

6.1   Subsidies and Countervailing Measures

6.1.1   Introduction

There are few topics in the field of international trade law and economics that are as contentious and complicated as subsidies. During the early years of the GATT, emphasis was placed on reduction of tariffs, although non-tariff barriers started receiving attention from the mid-1960s.[1] Under Articles XVI and VI of the GATT 1947, the contracting parties were authorised to take domestic actions against injurious effects of subsidies in the form of countervailing duties.

As time elapsed, concerns over subsidies as an alternative form of protection began to grow. Several countries started providing subsidies for industrial activities, such as aircraft, automobiles, shipbuilding and fisheries, to name a few. Subsidies assumed various forms, such as grants and cash transfer, low-interest loans, tax incentives or the provision of goods. Agricultural subsidies also continued to distort the field of international trade, a topic that is exhaustive in itself and the subject matter of Chapter 3 in this book. In addition, export promotion and import substitution subsidies became rampant. Export credits were also used as a tool to gain advantage in trade.

Countries decided to act by making the subsidies discipline more compact during the Tokyo Round through the Subsidies Code. However, it was the Agreement on Subsidies and

---

[1] A. F. Lowenfeld, *International Economic Law* (Oxford University Press, 2008), p. 217.

Countervailing Measures (SCM Agreement), concluded at the historic Uruguay Round, that established the primary rules concerning the regulation of subsidies and the use of countervailing measures.[2]

6.1.2 How Do Subsidies Affect International Trade?

Subsidies are an inherent attribute of governmental functioning. Subsidies are critical tools for governments to achieve a variety of public policy goals. It may be used for supporting the livelihood of small farmers, delivering essential public services or in unexpected contingencies, such as certain financial, industrial or health crises. Subsidies need not distort trade in all situations; however, in most situations, subsidies may distort international trade, disrupt production processes and affect business performance.[3]

Subsidies can generally be categorised into those that have a negative externality (for example, export subsidies or pernicious forms of subsidies, such as subsidies for illegal, unreported and unregulated (IUU) fishing[4]), and those that have a positive externality (education, environment protection, health, etc.).[5] In principle, public goods are non-excludable and are available to all.[6] As Trebilcock and Howse point out, investing in basic infrastructure or education alters a country's comparative advantage and thus affects domestic resource allocation.[7] However, the fact that a subsidy will de facto almost always benefit some industries over others implies that this trade distortion rationale is not watertight.[8] The provision of non-specific goods or services with public goods characteristics is considered non-trade-distorting, not so much because it might not affect trade in all situations, but because it would do so in a corrective rather than in a distortive manner.[9] This is at least the overwhelming economic creed.

A subsidy can have similar trade effects as an import tariff. A government that subsidises an industry simply reduces the cost of the subsidy recipient. This in turn allows the subsidised industry to lower its prices and become more competitive vis-à-vis imports. Thus, a subsidy may represent a government-induced obstacle to international trade in the same way as an import tariff.[10] Subsidies in such cases can affect market access

---

[2] Lowenfeld, *International Economic Law*, p. 238.

[3] P. R. Krugman and M. Obstfeld, *International Economics: Theory and Policy* (Boston: Pearson/Addison Wesley, 2009).

[4] G. Shaffer, R. Wolfe and V. Le, 'Can Informal Law Discipline Subsidies?', *Journal of International Economic Law* (2015, updated 2018), 18(4), pp. 711–41.

[5] D. Coppens, *WTO Disciplines on Subsidies and Countervailing Measures: Balancing Policy Space and Legal Constraints* (Cambridge University Press, 2014).

[6] P. Samuelson, 'The Pure Theory of Public Expenditure', *Review of Economics and Statistics* (1954), 36(4), pp. 387–9.

[7] Trebilcock and Howse, *Regulation of International Trade*, p. 391.

[8] Mavroidis et al., *Law and Economics of Contingent Protection*, pp. 350–1.

[9] Coppens, *WTO Disciplines on Subsidies and Countervailing Measures*, p. 481.

[10] W. Muller, *WTO Agreement on Subsidies and Countervailing Measures: A Commentary* (Cambridge University Press, 2017), p. 5; Jackson, *World Trading System*, pp. 280–1.

commitments. This was the underlying logic for introducing some subsidy disciplines into the GATT 1947, notably Articles VI and XVI.[11]

The theory of comparative advantage represents an adaptation to international trade of the basic notion that the value of domestic output will be maximised if resources are allocated through private market transaction. The objection to subsidies within this framework is that they distort the resource-allocating function of the market and thereby reduce the benefits derived from specialisation reflecting comparative advantage coupled with trade.[12] It can also lead to countries engaging in competitive subsidisation programmes, which could ultimately result in waste of scarce public resources.

6.1.3 Historical Perspective

Legal provisions dealing with subsidies were incorporated in the GATT 1947 (enshrined in Articles VI and XVI of the GATT 1947). These provisions were general and remarkably vague. Article XVI of the GATT 1947 did not define the term 'subsidy'.[13] Further, there was no clarity regarding the types of adverse effects that could be caused by subsidies. Also, the text of the GATT 1947 did not provide clarity on the remedies or response actions a contracting party could take in response to subsidies.[14] In fact, Article VI of the GATT 1947 contained only three paragraphs regarding the use of countervailing measures (as discussed in Section 6.1.4).

The issue of disciplining subsidies came into focus during the Tokyo Round of GATT negotiations (1973–79). Negotiations during this round resulted in the Code on Subsidies and Countervailing Duties, also known as the Tokyo Subsidies Code.[15] Only a few countries participated in the Tokyo Code. Subsequently, the Uruguay Round negotiations (1986–94) successfully negotiated the SCM Agreement, which was applicable to all members of the WTO. It must also be noted that no changes were made to the provisions of the original GATT that dealt with subsidies – Articles VI and XVI of the GATT 1994.

6.1.4 Article VI of the GATT 1994

Article VI of the GATT 1994 permits members to impose duties (and other measures) on goods originating in other member State(s) and receiving subsidies.[16] Article VI of the

---

[11] Bagwell et al., *Law and Economics of Contingent Protection in International Trade*, p. 170.

[12] W. F. Schwartz and E. W. Harper Jr, 'The Regulation of Subsidies Affecting International Trade', *Michigan Law Review* (1972), 70(5), p. 840.

[13] B. M. Hoekman, *Trade Laws and Institutions: Good Practices and the World Trade Organization* (Washington, DC: World Bank Publications, 1995), p. 19.

[14] A. E. Appleton and M. G. Plummer, *The World Trade Organization: Legal, Economic and Political Analysis* (Dordrecht: Springer, 2007), p. 688.

[15] Agreement on Interpretation and Application of Articles VI, XVI and XXIII of the General Agreement on Tariffs and Trade, 5 April 1979, GATT Doc. MTN/NTM/W/236.

[16] Agreement on Interpretation and Application of Articles VI, XVI and XXIII, Art. VI.

GATT specifically imposes certain important conditions on the imposition of countervailing duties.[17] The purpose of CVD is not to impose a penalty, but to offset the distortion that has been caused by the subsidy.[18] The concept of CVD actions is not often supported by economists, who argue that subsidised imports represent an improvement in the terms of trade for the importing country and could provide national welfare gain.[19]

Paragraph 3 of Article VI stipulates that imposition of CVDs shall not be in excess of the estimated subsidy.[20] The Appellate Body reiterated this view in *US – Countervailing Measures on Certain EC Products*, a dispute initiated by the US against certain EU subsidies.[21] The subsidies were allegedly provided to certain EC companies that were previously State-owned entities. The Appellate Body emphatically stated, quoting Article VI:3, '[n]o countervailing duty shall be levied on any product of the territory of any contracting party ... in excess of an amount equal to the estimated bounty or subsidy determined to be granted'.[22]

In short, Article VI of the GATT 1994 still remains relevant and will have to be read together with the SCM Agreement. Article VI(3) of the GATT and the SCM Agreement identify the permissible responses when subsidies are found to exist. Furthermore, CVDs can only be levied when it is demonstrated that the effect of subsidisation is causing 'material injury' to an established domestic industry, according to paragraph 6 of Article VI of the GATT 1994.

6.1.4.1 Relationship between Article VI of the GATT and the SCM Agreement

The relationship between Article VI of the GATT and the SCM Agreement is not expressly mentioned in the concerned agreements. However, certain WTO Panel and Appellate Body decisions have touched upon this relationship. In *Brazil – Desiccated Coconut*, the Philippines had challenged CVDs imposed by Brazil on the Philippines' exports of desiccated coconut.[23] The question was whether Article VI of the GATT 1994 created rules that were separate and distinct from those of the SCM Agreement.

In approaching this issue, the *Desiccated Coconut* Panel made it clear that the SCM Agreement did not supersede Article VI of the GATT 1994. The Panel noted that Article VI of the GATT 1994 and the SCM Agreement have force, effect and purpose within the WTO Agreement. In a subsequent dispute, namely *US – Carbon Steel*, the Appellate Body noted

---

[17] Agreement on Interpretation and Application of Articles VI, XVI and XXIII, Arts. VI(3) and VI(6).

[18] Bossche and Zdouc, *Law and Policy of the World Trade Organization*, p. 858; GATT 1994, Art. VI:3.

[19] A. O. Sykes, 'The Questionable Case for Subsidies Regulation: A Comparative Perspective', *Journal of Legal Analysis* (2010), 2(2), pp. 473–523.

[20] GATT 1994, Art. VI:3.

[21] Appellate Body Report, *United States – Countervailing Measures Concerning Certain Products from the European Communities*, WT/DS212/AB/R, adopted 8 January 2003.

[22] Appellate Body Report, *US – Countervailing Measures on Certain EC Products*, para. 139.

[23] Panel Report, *Brazil – Measures Affecting Desiccated Coconut*, WT/DS22/R, adopted 20 March 1997, upheld by Appellate Body Report WT/DS22/AT/R.

that the object and purpose of the SCM Agreement is to improve the GATT disciplines on subsidies and the use of CVDs.[24]

6.1.5   The Concept of 'Subsidy'

The standard economic definition of 'subsidy' under the SCM Agreement involves the notion of a monetary contribution by a government or a public body to firms, business enterprises or producers. Under the SCM Agreement, a subsidy is deemed to exist if two conditions are met: (1) a 'financial contribution' is made by the 'government or any public body', or any form of 'income or price support' exists; and (2) a 'benefit' is conferred.[25] For a subsidy to be actionable, it must be 'specific' to an enterprise, industry or group of enterprises or industries. In other words, a financial contribution in itself will not constitute a subsidy. The financial contribution must confer a benefit to a recipient and must be specific. The details of these elements are explained in the following paragraphs.

SCM Agreement, Article 1: Definition of a Subsidy

1.1. For the purpose of this Agreement, a subsidy shall be deemed to exist if:
  (a)(1) there is a financial contribution by a government or any public body within the territory of a Member (referred to in this Agreement as 'government'), i.e. where:
   (i) a government practice involves a direct transfer of funds (e.g. grants, loans and equity infusion), potential direct transfer of funds or liabilities (e.g. loan guarantees);
   (ii) government revenue that is otherwise due is foregone or not collected (e.g. fiscal incentives such as tax credits);
   (iii) a government provides goods or services other than general infrastructure, or purchases goods;
   (iv) a government makes payments to a funding mechanism, or entrusts or directs a private body to carry out one or more of the type of functions illustrated in (i) to (iii) above which would normally be vested in the government and the practice, in no real sense, differs from practices normally followed by governments;
   or

---

[24] Appellate Body Report, *United States – Countervailing Duties on Certain Corrosion-Resistant Carbon Steel Flat Products from Germany*, WT/DS213/AB/R, Corr.1, adopted 19 December 2002, para. 73.

[25] SCM Agreement, Art. 1.1.

> **(cont.)**
>
> (a)(2) there is any form of income or price support in the sense of Article XVI of
>   GATT 1994;
>   and
> (b)   a benefit is thereby conferred.
> 1.2. A subsidy as defined in paragraph 1 shall be subject to the provisions of Part II or shall
>   be subject to the provisions of Part III or V only if such a subsidy is specific in
>   accordance with the provisions of Article 2.

Subsidies often do not require a monetary payment. Certain tax exemptions, debt forgiveness, deferrals or even tax credits, which selectively draw up the beneficiaries, can result in a subsidy. A financial contribution will also exist if a government makes payments to a funding mechanism, or 'entrusts' or 'directs' a private body to carry out one or more of the type of functions described above rather than directly doing so itself (see Figure 6.1). Article 1.1(a)(1) of the SCM Agreement provides a closed list of the types of financial contribution.[26]

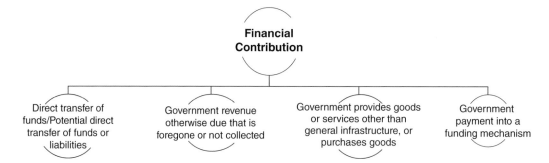

Figure 6.1 Types of financial contribution

The categories of financial contributions shown in Figure 6.1 make it appear that the SCM Agreement is self-contained and exhaustive with respect to the categories of industrial subsidies. One of the reasons for providing an exhaustive list of government actions that could come within the ambit of 'financial contribution' is to limit the kind of government actions that could fall within the scope of the SCM Agreement.[27] The closed nature of this list theoretically provides certain latitude to WTO members in structuring their assistance programmes.

---

[26] SCM Agreement, Art. 1. See also Panel Report, *United States – Measures Affecting Trade in Large Civil Aircraft (Second Complaint)*, WT/DS353/R, adopted 23 March 2012, as modified by Appellate Body Report WT/DS353/AB/R, para. 7.164.

[27] Panel Report, *United States – Measures Treating Exports Restraints as Subsidies*, WT/DS194/R, Corr.2, adopted 23 August 2001, para. 8.69.

CANADA – RENEWABLE ENERGY / CANADA – FEED-IN TARIFF PROGRAM

Canada – Renewable Energy / Canada – Feed-In Tariff Program examined the overlapping nature of the various subparagraphs of Article 1.1 and, in particular, whether they are exclusive.

In this case, the EU claimed that Canada's measures relating to domestic content requirements in the feed-in tariff (FIT) programme established by the Ontario Power Authority (OPA) was inconsistent with the SCM Agreement. In that case, the OPA, a public body, entered into FIT and micro-FIT contracts with suppliers and paid for the price of the electricity delivered into the Ontario electricity grid. Another entity, namely Hydro One, transmits the electricity.

A transaction may apparently fit one or more descriptions of a financial contribution under Article 1.1(a)(1). This is especially true when government transactions are multifaceted and complex in their nature. The WTO Panel and, later, the Appellate Body had the opportunity in this case to adjudicate how a measure should be characterised and examined when it can meet one or several of the legal requirements. The Panel noted that the coverage of some of the subparagraphs was exclusive. More specifically, the Panel noted that 'government purchase of goods' could not also be characterised as 'direct transfer [of] funds',[28] a finding that was rejected by the Appellate Body.

> ## Canada – Renewable Energy / Canada – Feed-In Tariff Program
> ### *(Appellate Body)*
>
> 5.120. When determining the proper legal characterization of a measure under Article 1.1(a)(1) of the SCM Agreement, a panel must assess whether the measure may fall within any of the types of financial contributions set out in that provision. . . . Having done so, the transaction may naturally fit into one of the types of financial contributions listed in Article 1.1(a)(1). However, transactions may be complex and multifaceted. This may mean that different aspects of the same transaction may fall under different types of financial contribution. It may also be the case that the characterization exercise does not permit the identification of a single category of financial contribution and, in that situation, as described in the *US – Large Civil Aircraft (2nd complaint)* Appellate Body report, a transaction may fall under more than one type of financial contribution. We note, however, that the fact that a transaction may fall under more than one type of financial contribution does not mean that the types of financial contributions set out in Article 1.1(a)(1) are the same or that the distinct legal concepts set out in this provision would become redundant, as the Panel suggests.

---

[28] Panel Reports, *Canada – Renewable Energy / Canada – Feed-In Tariff Program*, para. 7.246.

A detailed analysis of the various types of financial contribution is provided below.

6.1.5.1   Direct Transfer of Funds

There are two terms that require discussion: direct transfer of funds and potential transfer of funds.

Direct transfer of funds includes a financial contribution involving direct transfer of funds from government or a public body to a private body or entity. In this case, the transfer of funds is made directly through 'grants, loans and equity infusion'. As the text of Article 1.1 (a)(1)(i) suggests, these terms are illustrative. Examples of direct transfer of funds include debt forgiveness, extension of a loan maturity, interest rate deductions, debt-to-equity swaps, joint ventures and so on.[29] Again, the term 'funds' includes not only money, but also financial resources and other financial claims generally.[30]

US – LARGE CIVIL AIRCRAFT (2ND COMPLAINT)

US – Large Aircraft (Second Complaint) is one of the key cases in understanding the concept of financial contribution, especially direct transfer of funds. While the term 'grant' has a gratuitous element, the term 'loans and equity infusion' may entail certain reciprocal obligations.[31]

In *US – Large Civil Aircraft (2nd complaint)*, the EC had claimed that ten categories of measures implemented by the United States (including tax and non-tax benefits from the state of Washington, property and sales tax breaks from the state of Kansas, for example) amounted to subsidies to Boeing – a US multinational company that designs and manufactures large civil aircraft. The Panel and, later, the Appellate Body confirmed that two of the measures relating to payments and access to facilities, equipment and employees constituted financial contributions within the meaning of Article 1.1(a)(1) of the SCM Agreement. In this regard, the Appellate Body interpreted the term 'direct transfer of funds' as follows:[32]

US – Large Civil Aircraft (2nd Complaint) *(Appellate Body)*

617. It is clear from the examples in subparagraph (i) that a direct transfer of funds will normally involve financing by the government to the recipient. In some instances, as in the case of grants, the conveyance of funds will not involve a reciprocal obligation on the part of the recipient. In other cases, such as loans and equity infusions, the recipient assumes obligations to the government in exchange of funds provided. Thus the provision of funding may amount to a donation or may involve reciprocal rights and obligations.

---

[29] Appellate Body Report, *United States – Measures Affecting Trade in Large Civil Aircraft (Second Complaint)*, WT/DS353/AB/R, adopted 23 March 2012, para. 616; see also Appellate Body Report, *Japan – Countervailing Duties on Dynamic Random Access Memories from Korea*, WT/DS336/AB/R, Corr.1, adopted 17 December 2007, para. 251.

[30] Appellate Body Report, *Japan – DRAMS (Korea)*, para. 250.

[31] Appellate Body Report, *US – Large Civil Aircraft (2nd Complaint)*, para. 617.

[32] Appellate Body Report, *US – Large Civil Aircraft (2nd Complaint)*, para. 617.

6.1.5.2 Potential Transfer of Funds

The word 'potential' constitutes a financial contribution when the government promises to transfer money under certain conditions. The SCM Agreement itself has given the example of 'loan guarantees' as a form of potential transfer of funds. A financial contribution exists, regardless of whether these funds have to be paid in the end and whether the potential transfer effectively materialises.[33] Determination of this type of transfer is more difficult to identify when compared to those under the category of direct transfer of funds.

US – Large Civil Aircraft (2nd Complaint) discussed whether the alleged measure was a 'potential direct transfer of funds'. The Panel established that 'mere possibility that a government may transfer funds' upon the fulfilment of any predefined condition is not enough to satisfy the definition of a financial contribution. According to the Panel, a potential transfer of funds indicates a 'possibility', due to the uncertainty of whether the 'triggering event' would occur or not.[34] For example, payments contingent on a debt default, insured risk, and so on, could fall in this category.

6.1.5.3 Revenue Foregone that Is Otherwise Due

A financial contribution also exists when a government does not collect or foregoes revenue that is otherwise due. This kind of financial contribution is more complicated in nature. A fiscal incentive, such as a tax credit, could come within the ambit of this category. In *Canada – Autos*,[35] an import duty exemption was granted to certain imported cars, specifically from the United States as opposed to European countries and Japan. This was found to be revenue 'otherwise due', as the exemption implied that the normal MFN import duty of 6 per cent would not have to be paid to the Canadian Government.

US – FSC is one of the early WTO cases that examined the question of revenue foregone. Several WTO members challenged the tax exemptions given to offshore foreign sales corporations established by US firms. The FSCs were generally subsidiaries of US corporations selling goods in foreign markets.[36] In a highly instructive finding, the Appellate Body noted that there must be 'some defined, normative benchmark against which the comparison can be made between the revenue actually raised and the revenue that would have been raised "otherwise"'.[37] This is a tricky inquiry, since sovereign governments have the power to tax or not to tax virtually all income or activities. The mere fact that certain revenue is not due from a fiscal perspective is not determinative of the existence of revenue forgone.

---

[33] Panel Report, *European Communities – Countervailing Measures on Dynamic Random Access Memory Chips from Korea*, WT/DS299/R, adopted 3 August 2005, para. 7.87.

[34] Panel Report, *US – Large Civil Aircraft (2nd Complaint)*, para. 7.164.

[35] Appellate Body Report, *Canada – Autos*, para. 91.

[36] Appellate Body Report, *United States – Tax Treatment for 'Foreign Sales Corporations'*, WT/DS108/AB/R, adopted 20 March 2000.

[37] Appellate Body Report, *US – FSC*, para. 90.

One of the methods of conducting this inquiry is identifying a 'general rule of taxation' and its 'exceptions'. In *US – FSC*[38] and *US – FSC (Article 21.5 – EC)*[39] the Appellate Body observed that the general rule of taxation and its exceptions should represent two fiscal situations that can legitimately be compared. This approach is embodied in the 'but for' test. While applying this test, the challenged measure could be considered the 'exception', while the general rule of taxation could be the 'normative benchmark'. While the Appellate Body had expressed reservations in the universal applicability of this test, it serves as a useful frame of analysis.

US – Large Civil Aircraft (2nd Complaint) exemplifies how this analytical framework can be put to use. A WTO Panel must: (1) identify the tax treatment that applies to the income of the alleged subsidy recipients; (2) identify a benchmark for comparison; and (3) compare the challenged tax treatment and the reasons for it with the benchmark tax treatment. In other words, a comparison has to be made between the revenue 'actually raised' and the revenue that would 'otherwise' have been raised. In many ways, this inquiry should be on the nature of the relationship between the contested tax measure and the overall tax regime. It is not wholly inapposite to characterise this inquiry in the form of a rhetorical expression – whether the glass is half-full or half-empty.

Brazil – Taxation[40] examined the meaning of 'revenue foregone that is otherwise due' in great detail.

Brazil – Taxation

Brazil had suspended IPI tax for certain exporting companies under the programme for predominantly exporting companies (PEC) and the special regime for purchase of capital goods for exporting companies (RECAP). A similar tax suspension was made in respect of the ICT programmes (i.e. the Informatics, PADIS, PATVD and Digital Inclusion Programmes). IPI tax is a Brazilian federal non-cumulative indirect tax applicable to all domestic and foreign manufactured goods. It is a non-cumulative value-added tax in the sense that when a taxpayer remits an IPI tax on a given transaction, the taxpayer is entitled to deduct the IPI tax paid in the earlier stages of the supply chain. Under the PEC programme, a legal person registered as a PEC is entitled to the suspension of IPI tax on its purchase of raw materials, intermediate goods and packaging materials.[41] The IPI tax is implemented through the use of a credit system. Furthermore, in order to be eligible for the IPI tax suspension, the entities will have to be accredited with concerned government agencies.

According to Brazil, the IPI tax was an administrative tax mechanism to prevent credit accumulation, especially for companies that would not be able to generate enough tax debits to offset the tax credits generated. The WTO Panel in this case, while determining 'revenue forgone', compared the sectors receiving the IPI tax suspension with companies with

---

[38] Appellate Body Report, *US – FSC*, paras. 90–91.

[39] Appellate Body Report, *United States – Tax Treatment for 'Foreign Sales Corporations' – Recourse to Article 21.5 of the DSU by the European Communities*, WT/DS108/AB/RW, adopted 29 January 2002, paras. 89–90.

[40] Appellate Body Reports, *Brazil – Taxation*.   [41] Panel Reports, *Brazil – Taxation*, para. 7.1134.

structurally accumulating credits. The Panel noted that other credit-accumulating companies (i.e. other than ICT companies) cannot qualify for the IPI tax suspension.[42] In the Panel's view, the challenged tax treatments were 'suspensions' of economy-wide tax treatments that apply to all transactions by all businesses.[43] In the Panel's view, the IPI tax suspension did not directly link to the problem of credit accumulation.[44]

Brazil challenged the decision and the Appellate Body addressed the choice of this benchmark comparator during the appeal.

Brazil – Taxation (Appellate Body)

5.163. The determination of a benchmark comparison entails, instead, identifying the 'tax treatment of comparable income of comparably situated tax payers'. This exercise 'involves an examination of the structure of the domestic tax regime and its organizing principles' and requires the panel 'to develop an understanding of the tax structure and the principle that best explains the Member's tax regime'. Such an examination must be conducted on the basis of the 'rules of taxation that each Member, by its own choice, establishes for itself'. In its identification of a benchmark, a panel must be aware of the limitations inherent in identifying and comparing a general rule of taxation and an exception from that rule since such an approach 'could result in a finding that a government revenue otherwise due has been foregone anytime the tax applicable to a recipient is lowered.

According to the Appellate Body, in determining a benchmark for comparison, the panels must be 'cognizant of the limitations inherent in seeking to identify a general rule of taxation and an exception from that rule'. In the Appellate Body's view, it is not sufficient, after identifying the general rule of taxation, to conduct an analysis of whether a higher tax liability would have arisen but for the challenged measure.[45] Stated differently, after identifying the existence of a general rule–exception relationship, 'a panel is expected to examine the structure of the tax measure and its organizing principles'.[46] The Appellate Body accordingly ruled that instead of identifying the general rule of taxation for structurally credit-accumulating companies (generally, producers of low-taxed products), the Panel should have determined the tax treatment of comparably situated taxpayers.[47] The Appellate Body noted that there were other companies covering a broad number of entities in addition to the PECs that were entitled to the tax suspension.[48] According to the Appellate Body, the Panel should have

---

[42] Panel Reports, *Brazil – Taxation*, para. 7.486.   [43] Panel Reports, *Brazil – Taxation*, para. 7.1164.

[44] Panel Reports, *Brazil – Taxation*, para. 7.1167.   [45] Appellate Body Reports, *Brazil – Taxation*, para. 5.167.

[46] Appellate Body Reports, *Brazil – Taxation*, para. 5.167; Appellate Body Report, *US – Large Civil Aircraft (2nd Complaint)*, para. 815.

[47] Appellate Body Reports, *Brazil – Taxation*, para. 5.168.

[48] Appellate Body Reports, *Brazil – Taxation*, para. 5.170.

examined in detail the treatment of these companies. Based on this view, the Appellate Body reversed the Panel's analysis under Article 1.1(a)(1)(ii).[49]

6.1.5.4 Revenue Foregone and Defence under Footnote 1 of the SCM Agreement

A footnote to Article 1.1(a)(1)(ii) of the SCM Agreement implements the 'destination principle' in taxation. According to footnote 1, exemption of duties or taxes borne by like domestic products when destined for domestic consumption or remission of such duty not in excess of those that have accrued, shall not be deemed to be a subsidy if it is in accordance with Article XVI of the GATT and Annexes I–III of the SCM Agreement.[50] In other words, a WTO member can exempt, remit, rebate or refund taxes that were levied on the inputs consumed in the production of exported products. The Appellate Body in *EU – PET (Pakistan)* observed that the paragraphs (g), (h) and (i) of Annex I all refer to exemptions or remission 'in excess', thus mirroring the language of footnote 1 of the Agreement.[51] This is termed the 'excess remission principle'.[52]

The principle embodied in footnote 1 is capable of application in advance authorisation and duty drawback schemes, whereby import duties borne on raw materials and inputs can be refunded or rebated if such raw materials are incorporated in the finished products. However, such flexibility was not extended to capital goods that were not 'consumed' within the meaning of the SCM Agreement.[53]

6.1.5.5 Government Provision of Goods and Services and Purchase of Goods Other than General Infrastructure

Where government provides goods or services, it has the effect of lowering the cost of production. By the same logic, where government purchases goods, it has the potential to artificially increase revenues to the seller.[54] In *Canada – Renewable Energy / Canada – Feed-In Tariff Program*, the Panel found that a government 'purchase [of] goods' within

---

[49] Appellate Body Reports, *Brazil – Taxation*, para. 5.172.

[50] Appellate Body Report, *European Union – Countervailing Measures on Certain Polyethylene Terephthalate from Pakistan*, WT/DS486/AB/R, Add.1, adopted 28 May 2018, para. 5.97.

[51] Appellate Body Report, *EU – PET (Pakistan)*, para. 5.134.

[52] Appellate Body Report, *EU – PET (Pakistan)*, para. 5.134:

> In sum, a harmonious reading of Article 1.1(a)(1)(ii), footnote 1, and Annexes I(i), II, and III to the SCM Agreement and the *Ad* Note to Article XVI of the GATT 1994 confirms that duty drawback schemes can constitute an export subsidy that can be countervailed only if they result in a remission or drawback of import charges 'in excess' of those actually levied on the imported inputs that are consumed in the production of the exported product.

[53] Panel Report, *India – Export Related Measures*, WT/DS541/R, Add.1, circulated to WTO members 31 October 2019 [appealed by India 19 November 2019 – the Division suspended its work on 10 December 2019].

[54] Appellate Body Report, *United States – Final Countervailing Duty Determination with Respect to Certain Softwood Lumber from Canada*, WT/DS257/AB/R, adopted 17 February 2004, para. 53.

the meaning of Article 1.1(a)(1)(iii) takes place when a government or public body obtains possession (including in the form of entitlement) by making a payment, either monetary or otherwise. The product in question was electricity, an intangible good that cannot be stored and must be consumed almost at the same time it is produced. The Panel found that given the specific characteristics of electricity, the purchase of electricity could be considered as involving the transfer of entitlement to electricity, rather than the taking of physical possession over electricity.[55]

On appeal, the Appellate Body upheld the finding of the Panel that the FIT programme and micro-FIT contracts are government purchases of goods.[56]

6.1.5.6 Payment to Funding Mechanisms/Entrustments or Direction of a Private Body

In this type of financial contribution, the government involves a private entity to perform one of the three earlier mentioned kinds of financial contribution. According to the wordings of the text, the government may make payments to a 'funding mechanism' or can 'entrust or direct' a private body to do so.

The criteria for 'entrustment or direction' was interpreted by the WTO Panel in *US – Export Restraints*.[57] The Panel stated that the words 'entrust' and 'direct' contain a notion of delegation (in the case of entrustment) or command (in the case of direction).[58]

The above interpretation was discussed in *US – Countervailing Duty Investigation on DRAMS*. In this case, the US measures imposing CVD on certain Dynamic Random Access Memory Semiconductors (DRAMS) and memory modules containing DRAMS imported from Korea were challenged. The concerned Korean companies were Hynix and Samsung. Korea alleged that the United States had incorrectly imposed CVD since it considered private creditors that were not 100 per cent owned by the Korean Government as private bodies 'entrusted' or 'directed' by the Government of South Korea.

The Appellate Body disagreed with the view held in *US – Export Restraints*, since the interpretation by the Panel in that case effectively replaced the terms 'entrusts' and 'directs' with two other terms, 'delegation' and 'command', whose scope the Panel did not define. According to the Appellate Body, 'there must be a demonstrable link between the government and the conduct of the private body'.[59] The Appellate Body further observed that policy pronouncements or actions that are a by-product of government regulation are insufficient for qualifying certain actions as 'entrustment' or 'direction'.[60]

---

[55] Panel Reports, *Canada – Renewable Energy / Canada – Feed-In Tariff Program*, para. 7.229.

[56] Appellate Body Reports, *Canada – Certain Measures Affecting the Renewable Energy Generation Sector / Canada – Measures Relating to the Feed-In Tariff Program*, WT/DS412/AB/R, WT/DS426/AB/R, adopted 24 May 2013, para. 5.128.

[57] Panel Report, *US – Export Restraints*, para. 8.29.   [58] Panel Report, *US – Export Restraints*, para. 8.29.

[59] Appellate Body Report, *United States – Countervailing Duty Investigation on Dynamic Random Access Memory Semiconductors (DRAMS) from Korea*, WT/DS296/AB/R, adopted 20 July 2005, para. 112.

[60] Appellate Body Report, *US – Countervailing Duty Investigation on DRAMS*, paras. 112–115.

In other words, 'entrustment' occurs when the government gives a responsibility to a private body, whereas 'direction' refers to a situation where the government exercises authority over the private body.[61] The government uses a private body, as a proxy or agent, to effectuate a government function or objective. The Appellate Body further noted that in most cases, entrustment or direction of a private body could involve some form of threat or inducement.[62] Panels may look at the extent of government ownership of the entities in question, the nature of government action,[63] commercial feasibility and so on.

CHINA – GOES

In *China – GOES*, the US challenged Chinese measures imposing anti-dumping and countervailing duties on grain oriented flat-rolled electrical steel (GOES) from the United States. China asserted that evidence indicating one of the measures – that is, voluntary restraint agreements – established under the Steel Import Stabilization Act of 1984 resulted in 'pecuniary benefits' to the US steel industry. China pointed out a transfer of wealth from steel purchasers to the US steel industry, in effect constituting transfer of funds in the form of higher prices. China argued that this was a financial contribution under Article 1.1(a)(1)(iv). However, the Panel disagreed.[64]

> ## China – GOES *(Panel)*
>
> 7.91. … when the action of a private party is a mere side-effect resulting from a government measure, this does not come within the meaning of entrustment or direction under Article 1.1(a)(1)(iv). … [T]he increased revenue that the steel industry received after the VRAs came into existence cannot be characterised as evidence of a financial contribution.

6.1.5.7 Income or Price Support

Article 1.1(a)(2) of the SCM Agreement also treats any form of 'income or price support' as a subsidy if it confers a benefit. It is also mentioned in Article XIV of the GATT. The term 'support' is often used in the context of agriculture, especially with respect to government support programmes for farm products.[65] In the ordinary meaning, 'support' denotes 'the action of contributing to the success or maintaining the value of something'.[66] In the context of subsidies, the term 'support' within Article 1.1(a)(2) refers to the action of

---

[61] Appellate Body Report, *US – Countervailing Duty Investigation on DRAMS*, para. 116.

[62] Appellate Body Report, *US – Countervailing Duty Investigation on DRAMS*, para. 116.

[63] Panel Report, *EC – Countervailing Measures on DRAM Chips*, para. 7.53.

[64] Panel Report, *China – Countervailing and Anti-Dumping Duties on Grain Oriented Flat-Rolled Electrical Steel from the United States*, WT/DS414/R, Add.1, adopted 16 November 2012, upheld by Appellate Body Report WT/DS414/AB/R, para. 7.91.

[65] AoA, Art. 6 and Annexes II, III, IV.   [66] Oxford English Dictionary Online.

the government that directly or indirectly increases an activity. The Appellate Body in *US – Softwood Lumber IV* noted that the range of government measures capable of providing subsidies is broadened by the concept of 'income or price support'.[67]

In practice, Article 1.1(a)(2) is hardly applied in determining a financial contribution. The Panel in *Canada – Renewable Energy / Canada – Feed-In Tariff Program* exercised judicial economy on a claim based on this article, which was later affirmed by the Appellate Body.[68]

6.1.6   Who Should Provide a Subsidy? The Relevance of 'Public Body'

For a financial contribution to be deemed a subsidy for the purposes of the SCM Agreement, the financial contribution must be made by the government or a public body. The definition of public body has attracted significant debate in recent times, especially in light of the alleged subsidies provided by Chinese State-owned enterprises (SOEs).[69] (See Chapter 12 for additional discussion.) In a narrow sense, SOEs may not be equated with government. However, the larger question is whether SOEs, State-owned banks and similar entities should be considered an 'extension of the State'.[70] At least from the point of State-induced distortion, several WTO members have raised concerns about the financial support provided by governments through their SOEs. In the United States, in particular, the policy articulation in the Kitchen Shelving and Decision Memorandum,[71] which was subsequently challenged in *US – Countervailing Measures (China)*, stated that majority government-owned enterprises are 'public bodies', although this presumption is rebuttable.[72] This presumption raises a number of questions. For instance, if a commercial bank provides certain preferential loans to certain targeted industries, it need not fall within the disciplines of the SCM Agreement. However, what if the loan is provided by a State-owned commercial bank? Although SOEs are entities run on a commercial basis and are responsible for their own profits and losses, there is a view that they are 'government actors'.[73] The other point of view is that SOEs or like entities are 'private bodies' – in such a case, any financial contribution made by such entities will not qualify as a subsidy unless there is entrustment of direction.

There are two ways of approaching this issue. The first is a type of 'structural test', where an entity is considered to be a public body if it is controlled by the government; the second approach is more 'functional', where the inquiry is whether such entities perform a

---

[67] Appellate Body Report, *US – Softwood Lumber IV*, para. 52.

[68] Appellate Body Reports, *Canada – Renewable Energy / Canada – Feed-In Tariff Program*, para. 5.139.

[69] Ru Ding, 'Public Body or Not: Chinese State-Owned Enterprises,' *Journal of World Trade* (2014), 48(1), pp. 167–89.

[70] Mark Wu, 'The "China, Inc." Challenge to Global Trade Governance', *Harvard Journal of International Law* (2016), 57(2), pp. 261–323, at 301–5.

[71] Certain Kitchen Appliance Shelving and Racks from the People's Republic of China Investigation, Final Affirmative Countervailing Duty Determination, 74 Federal Register 37012 (27 July 2009).

[72] Panel Report, *United States – Countervailing Duty Measures on Certain Products from China*, WT/DS437/R, Add.1, adopted 17 January 2015, as modified by Appellate Body Report WT/DS437/AB/R, para. 7.66.

[73] Report of the Working Party on the Accession of China in document WT/ACC/CHN/49, 1 October 2001, para. 172.

government function. This issue has come up in several WTO disputes, especially in challenges of CVD determinations.

KOREA – COMMERCIAL VESSELS

In *Korea – Commercial Vessels*, the key issue was whether the Export–Import Bank of Korea (KEXIM) was a public body. KEXIM was created and operated on the basis of a public statute, giving the government control over its decision-making. According to the Panel, an entity constitutes a 'public body' if it is controlled by the government (or other public bodies). In the Panel's view, if an entity is controlled by the government (or other public bodies), then any action by that entity is attributable to the government.[74]

> ## Korea – Commercial Vessels *(Panel)*
>
> 7.50. In our view, an entity will constitute a 'public body' if it is controlled by the government (or other public bodies). If an entity is controlled by the government (or other public bodies), then any action by that entity is attributable to the government, and should therefore fall within the scope of Article 1.1(a)(1) of the SCM Agreement.

Importantly, the Panel in this case noted that the determination of whether an entity is a public body or not 'should not depend on an examination of whether the entity acts pursuant to commercial principles'.[75]

US – ANTI-DUMPING AND COUNTERVAILING DUTIES (CHINA)

The control test was contested in *US – Anti-Dumping and Countervailing Duties (China)*.[76] The USDOC had imposed CVD on several products imported from China (for example, circular welded carbon quality steel pipe, light-walled rectangular pipe and tube laminated woven sacks, certain new pneumatic off-the-road tyres). The Panel upheld the finding of the USDOC that certain SOEs and State-owned commercial Banks (SOCBs) in China were 'public bodies' for the purposes of the SCM Agreement. According to the Panel, SOEs and SOCBs were 'controlled by the government'.

The Panel findings were challenged before the Appellate Body. The Appellate Body noted that the term 'public body' in Article 1.1(a)(1) covers only an entity that 'possesses, exercises or is vested with "governmental authority"'[77] – a finding that has raised several concerns.

---

[74] Panel Report, *Korea – Measures Affecting Trade in Commercial Vessels*, WT/DS273/R, adopted 11 April 2005, para. 7.50.

[75] Panel Report, *Korea – Commercial Vessels*, para. 7.44.

[76] Appellate Body Report, *US – Anti-Dumping and Countervailing Duties (China)*, para. 318.

[77] Appellate Body Report, *US – Anti-Dumping and Countervailing Duties (China)*, para. 317.

US – Anti-Dumping and Countervailing Duties (China) *(Appellate Body)*

317. ... just as no two governments are exactly alike, the precise contours and characteristics of a public body are bound to differ from entity to entity, State to State, and case to case. Panels or investigating authorities confronted with the question of whether conduct falling within the scope of Article 1.1(a)(1) [of the SCM Agreement] is that of a public body will be in a position to answer that question only by conducting a proper evaluation of the core features of the entity concerned, and its relationship with government in the narrow sense.

6.1.6.1   Whether Government Ownership Is Relevant for Government Control

One of the key questions in this case was whether government ownership was relevant for exercising governmental control. The USDOC has held in several domestic CVD proceedings that majority government ownership is sufficient in itself to treat an entity as a 'public body'. The Appellate Body explained the nature of governmental authority as follows:

US – Anti-Dumping and Countervailing Duties (China) *(Appellate Body)*

318. ... There are many different ways in which government in the narrow sense could provide entities with authority. Accordingly, different types of evidence may be relevant to showing that such authority has been bestowed on a particular entity. Evidence that an entity is, in fact, exercising governmental functions may serve as evidence that it possesses or has been vested with governmental authority, particularly where such evidence points to a sustained and systematic practice. It follows, in our view, that evidence that a government exercises meaningful control over an entity and its conduct may serve, in certain circumstances, as evidence that the relevant entity possesses governmental authority and exercises such authority in the performance of governmental functions. We stress, however, that apart from an express delegation of authority in a legal instrument, the existence of mere formal links between an entity and government in the narrow sense is unlikely to suffice to establish the necessary possession of governmental authority. Thus, for example, the mere fact that a government is the majority shareholder of an entity does not demonstrate that the government exercises meaningful control over the conduct of that entity, much less that the government has bestowed it with governmental authority. In some instances, however, where the evidence shows that the formal indicia of government control are manifold, and there is also evidence that such control has been exercised in a meaningful way, then such evidence may permit an inference that the entity concerned is exercising governmental authority.

Importantly, the Appellate Body reversed the Panel finding on the issue of government control. The Appellate Body drew a distinction between entities merely owned or controlled by a government and entities that exercise some degree of 'governmental authority'. The key issue according to the Appellate Body was whether these SOEs and SOCBs exercise governmental functions on behalf of the Chinese Government. According to the Appellate Body, evidence that a government exercises meaningful control over an entity and its conduct may serve, in certain circumstances, to show that the relevant authority possesses government authority. The Appellate Body concluded that the Panel's analysis lacked proper legal basis as even if a government is the majority shareholder of an entity, that fact alone did not demonstrate whether the government exercised *meaningful control over the conduct of that entity or not.*[78]

US –Anti-Dumping and Countervailing Duties (China) remains one of the landmark decisions in trade remedy jurisprudence. The attributes of a 'public body' were soon strongly contested in *US – Carbon Steel (India)*, as well as in a series of other cases, such as *US – Countervailing Measures (China)*. The *Carbon Steel* case involved the imposition of CVDs by the US on imports of certain hot-rolled carbon steel flat products from India. India argued before the Panel that the USDOC improperly focused on the Government of India's (GOI's) 98 per cent shareholding in the National Mineral Development Corporation (NMDC), a public sector undertaking. The Panel rejected India's claim and India appealed. The Appellate Body explained that although the Panel had reviewed 'some aspects of control by the GOI', it had failed to 'address the question of whether there was evidence that the NMDC was performing governmental functions on behalf of the GOI. Consequently, the Appellate Body reversed the Panel's finding in which it rejected India's claim.

US – Carbon Steel (India)

The Panel held in this case that the GOI had 'meaningful control' over NMDC. In relation to 'control', the Appellate Body noted that 'a government's exercise of "meaningful control" over an entity and its conduct, including control such that the government can use the entity's resources as its own may certainly be relevant'.[79] Importantly, the Appellate Body held that 'an entity constitutes a public body if it performs governmental function and has the power and authority to perform that function'.[80]

US – Carbon Steel (India) *(Appellate Body)*

4.54. In sum, the USDOC did not evaluate the relationship between NMDC and the GOI within the Indian legal order, and the extent to which the GOI in fact 'exercised'

---

[78] Appellate Body Report, *US – Anti-Dumping and Countervailing Duties (China)*, para. 4.43.

[79] Appellate Body Report, *United States – Countervailing Measures on Certain Hot-Rolled Carbon Steel Flat Products from India*, WT/DS436/AB/R, adopted 19 December 2014, paras. 4.54–4.55.

[80] Appellate Body Report, *US – Carbon Steel (India)*, para. 4.20.

(cont.)

meaningful control over NMDC and over its conduct in order to conclude properly that the NMDC is a public body within the meaning of Article 1.1(a)(1) of the SCM Agreement. Instead, the USDOC examined evidence which, in our view, would be seen more appropriately as evidence of 'formal indicia' of control such as the GOI's ownership interest in the NMDC and the GOI's power to appoint or nominate directors. These factors are certainly relevant but do not provide a sufficient basis for a determination that an entity is a public body that possesses, exercises, or is vested with governmental authority. Moreover, the USDOC did not refer in its determinations to evidence contained on the USDOC's administrative record that was referred to by the United States in the panel proceedings as well as on appeal. Nor did the USDOC discuss in its determinations evidence on record regarding NMDC's status as *Miniratna* or *Navratna* company that could have been relevant to the question of whether the USDOC's determinations contain a sufficient and adequate evaluation of the relationship between the GOI and the NMDC, and, in particular, the degree of control exercised by the GOI over the conduct of the NMDC and the degree of autonomy enjoyed by the NMDC.

4.55. For all these reasons, we conclude that the USDOC did not provide a reasoned and adequate explanation of the basis for its finding that the NMDC is a public body within the meaning of Article 1.1(a)(1) of the SCM Agreement, as interpreted by the Appellate Body.

In sum, the critical consideration in the public body inquiry is whether the concerned enterprise has the authority to perform government functions. In other words, the public body inquiry under the SCM Agreement does not hinge on the conduct of the investigated entity or firm, but rather on the core characteristics of the entity itself and its relationship with government, in light of the legal and economic environment in which the entity operates.[81]

6.1.7 Determination of Benefit

The existence of the financial contribution or income/price support is not sufficient for the existence of a subsidy. There must also be a benefit that has been conferred. Article 1 of the SCM Agreement identifies the practices that constitute a 'financial contribution', but it does not define the term 'benefit' or set out criteria for measurement of whether a benefit is conferred.

The SCM Agreement does not precisely state who should receive a benefit either. However, it could be broadly stated that the 'benefit' must be received by a legal person, but not necessarily the producer.

---

[81] Appellate Body Report, *US – Anti-Dumping and Countervailing Duties (China)*, paras. 291, 317, 318, 319.

CANADA – AIRCRAFT

The Panel Report in *Canada – Aircraft* provides guidance on the term 'benefit'. In fact, the finding of the Panel on the concept of 'benefit' has almost attained 'treaty status' and is quoted invariably in all WTO cases relating to this subject. In this dispute, Brazil alleged that Canada had granted certain subsidies with the intention of supporting the export of civilian aircraft, namely regional aircraft manufactured and exported by Bombardier. Brazil primarily contended that these measures were inconsistent with Article 3 of the SCM Agreement. In its opinion, the Panel noted that the ordinary meaning of 'benefit' does not involve a 'net cost' to the government. The Panel stated that the ordinary meaning of 'benefit' encompasses some form of 'advantage',[82] a finding that was later affirmed by the Appellate Body.

Canada – Aircraft *(Appellate Body)*

157. We also believe that the word 'benefit' as used in Article 1.1(b), implies some kind of comparison. This must be so, for there can be no 'benefit' to the recipient unless the 'financial contribution' makes the recipient 'better off' than it would otherwise have been, absent that contribution. In our view, the marketplace provides an appropriate basis for comparison in determining whether a 'benefit' has been 'conferred', because the trade-distorting potential of a 'financial contribution' can be identified by determining whether the recipient has received a 'financial contribution' on terms more favourable than those available to the recipient in the market.

In sum, the Panel in *Canada – Aircraft* found that a 'financial contribution' conferred a 'benefit' and constituted a subsidy under Article 1 of the SCM Agreement when it was provided on terms that were more advantageous than those otherwise available to the recipient on the market. In appeal, the Appellate Body concurred with the Panel finding on the 'benefit' concept.

While conducting the benefit analysis, the panel in *EC – Countervailing Measures on DRAM Chips* agreed with the Appellate Body in *Canada – Aircraft* that the proper standard is whether the recipient is 'better off' than it would have been absent the contribution.[83] As a corollary, it found that the appropriate basis for determining the existence of a benefit is the marketplace. This view has also been upheld in *Canada – Renewable Energy / Canada – Feed-In Tariff Program*, where the Appellate Body noted that a financial contribution conferred a benefit within the meaning of Article 1.1(b), 'when it conferred an advantage on its recipient, and that such an advantage was to be determined by comparing the position of the recipient in the market place with or without the financial contribution'.[84]

---

[82] Panel Report, *Canada – Measures Affecting the Export of Civilian Aircraft*, WT/DS70/R, adopted 20 August 1999, upheld by Appellate Body Report WT/DS70/AB/R, para. 9.112.

[83] Panel Report, *EC – Countervailing Measures on DRAM Chips*, para. 7.176.

[84] Appellate Body Reports, *Canada – Renewable Energy / Canada – Feed-In Tariff Program*, para. 5.159.

6.1.7.1   Calculating the Benefit

An understanding of the meaning of the term 'benefit' is also crucial in determining the quantum of subsidy. It is therefore necessary to read Article 1.1(b) of the SCM Agreement along with Article 14. As noted earlier, Article 14 of the SCM Agreement provides that the term 'benefit' refers to 'benefit to recipient'. It appears that the definition of benefit in Article 1.1(b) has been influenced by the context of Article 14. According to the Appellate Body in *US – Countervailing Measures (China)*, the determination of whether the remuneration paid for a government-provided good is less than adequate entails the selection of a benchmark or comparator similar to the benefit analysis under Article 1.1(b) of the SCM Agreement.[85]

Article 14 of the SCM Agreement is concerned with the calculation of the subsidy in countervailing investigations specified by Part V of this Agreement. In addition to Article 14, Annex IV of the SCM Agreement also deals with the calculation of the total ad valorem subsidisation (paragraph 1(a) of Article 6). The approach under Annex IV of the SCM Agreement is based on the notion of *cost-to-government* approach, while the former is based on *benefit-to-recipient*.[86]

Although existence of a benefit is a necessary part of identifying a subsidy, cost to government may still be used while calculating the amount of the subsidy.[87] In any case, neither of the two provisions is amply clear.[88] Article 14 of the SCM Agreement establishes that any method of calculating benefit shall conform to certain guidelines.

SCM Agreement, Article 14: Calculation of the Amount of a Subsidy in Terms of the Benefit to the Recipient

[...]

(a) government provision of equity capital shall not be considered as conferring a benefit, unless the investment decision can be regarded as inconsistent with the usual investment practice (including for the provision of risk capital) of private investors in the territory of that Member;

(b) a loan by a government shall not be considered as conferring a benefit, unless there is a difference between the amount that the firm receiving the loan pays on the government loan and the amount the firm would pay on a comparable commercial loan which the firm could actually obtain on the market. In this case the benefit shall be the difference between these two amounts;

(c) a loan guarantee by a government shall not be considered as conferring a benefit, unless there is a difference between the amount that the firm receiving the guarantee

---

[85] Appellate Body Report, *US – Countervailing Measures (China)*, para. 4.44.
[86] Mavroidis et al., *Law and Economics of Contingent Protection*, p. 384.
[87] Mavroidis et al., *Law and Economics of Contingent Protection*, p. 384.
[88] Mavroidis et al., *Law and Economics of Contingent Protection*, p. 384.

> *(cont.)*
>
> pays on a loan guaranteed by the government and the amount that the firm would pay on a comparable commercial loan absent the government guarantee. In this case the benefit shall be the difference between these two amounts adjusted for any differences in fees;
>
> (d) the provision of goods or services or purchase of goods by a government shall not be considered as conferring a benefit unless the provision is made for less than adequate remuneration, or the purchase is made for more than adequate remuneration. The adequacy of remuneration shall be determined in relation to prevailing market conditions for the good or service in question in the country of provision or purchase (including price, quality, availability, marketability, transportation and other conditions of purchase or sale).

The Appellate Body in *Japan – DRAMs (Korea)* made the following observations regarding the requirements of the chapeau of Article 14:[89]

Japan – DRAMs (Korea) *(Appellate Body)*

190. The chapeau of Article 14 sets out three requirements. The first is that 'any method used' by an investigating authority to calculate the amount of a subsidy in terms of benefit to the recipient shall be provided for in the national legislation or implementing regulations of the Member concerned. The second requirement is that the 'application' of that method in each particular case shall be transparent and adequately explained. The third requirement is that 'any such method' shall be consistent with the guidelines contained in paragraphs (a)–(d) of Article 14.

Notwithstanding the reference to the 'benefit to the recipient' language in Article 14, one could argue that other approaches, such as cost of production test, could also be relevant in the determination of subsidy where the domestic market price is distorted by government intervention, or the incumbent is a government monopoly, or where there is no marketplace. The existence of a fully competitive market, in which prices are determined by demand and supply, free from governmental interference, is an essential consideration.[90] In *US – Softwood Lumber IV*,[91] both the Panel and the Appellate

---

[89] Appellate Body Report, *Japan – DRAMs (Korea)*, para. 190.

[90] Julian Qin, 'Market Benchmarks and Government Monopoly: The Case of Land and Natural Resources under Global Subsidies Regulation', *University of Pennsylvania Journal of International Law* (2019), 40(3), p. 575.

[91] Panel Report, *United States – Investigation of the International Trade Commission in Softwood Lumber from Canada*, WT/DS257/R, adopted 26 April 2004, para. 7.68.

Body examined the USDOC's calculation of the benefit conferred on the lumber produ-cers. Emphasis was laid on identifying the prevailing market conditions. While the Panel in the *Softwood Lumber IV* dispute noted that the prevailing market conditions would be the stumpage fee of trees in private land in Canada, the Appellate Body held otherwise. According to the Appellate Body, the Canadian market was too distorted to be used as a benchmark. The Appellate Body noted: '[t]he determination of whether private prices are distorted because of the government's predominant role in the market, as a provider of certain goods, must be made on a case-by-case basis, according to the particular facts underlying each countervailing duty investigation'. The Appellate Body in this case endorsed the use of out-of-country benchmarks.[92] As the Appellate Body stated in *US – Carbon Steel (India)*, the purpose of the inquiry is to determine whether the 'proposed benchmark prices are market determined such that they can be used to assess whether [the] remuneration is less than adequate'.[93]

CANADA – RENEWABLE ENERGY / CANADA – FEED-IN TARIFF PROGRAM
In *Canada – Renewable Energy / Canada – Feed-In Tariff Program*, the Appellate Body had occasion to dwell on government interventions that create markets that did not exist earlier. This is a novel, yet not entirely unusual situation. For instance, governments may intervene to reduce excessive reliance on fossil fuel energy resources and to promote sustainable forms of energy.

Canada – Renewable Energy / Canada – Feed-In Tariff Program (Appellate Body)

5.188. Nevertheless, a distinction needs to be drawn between, on the one hand, govern-ment interventions that create markets that would otherwise not exist and, on the other hand, other types of government interventions in support of certain players in markets that already exist, or to create market distortions therein. Where a government creates a market, it cannot be said that the government intervention distorts the market, as there would not be a market if the government had not created it. While the creation of markets by a government does not in and of itself give rise to subsidies within the meaning of the SCM Agreement, government interventions in the existing market may amount to subsidies when they take the form of financial contribution, or income or price support, and confer a benefit to specific enterprises or industries.

Although a financial contribution was found in the context of Canada's FIT pro-grammes, the Appellate Body noted that it had insufficient factual evidence on record to

---

[92] Panel Report, *US – Softwood Lumber IV*, para. 102.
[93] Appellate Body Report, *US – Carbon Steel (India)*, para. 4.152.

establish whether the programme conferred benefit on the producers of wind or solar PV generated electricity.[94]

6.1.7.2 Pass-Through and Privatisation Issues

The application of the benefit-to-the-recipient had presented particular problems in the case of State-owned enterprises, which had been subsequently privatised. When a non-recurring subsidy was paid to an SOE, one particular issue was whether the benefit would remain with the firm, or with the firm's owners or its productive assets. Most of these subsidies were one-time payments for building new capacity or updating equipment. The USDOC, in several cases especially involving steel products, has held that even after change of ownership of an SOE pursuant to sale at arm's length and at fair market value, it could continue to impose CVD on the premise that pre-privatisation subsidies have not been fully exhausted. In other words, the crux of the argument is whether the benefit to the productive operations of the original contribution continues to exist even after the privatisation or even if the value of the subsidies has been extinguished with privatisation.[95]

The issue was addressed in *US – Lead and Bismuth II*, wherein the Appellate Body held that privatisation for arm's length and at fair market value will necessarily extinguish the remaining benefit of any non-recurring subsidy paid to a former SOE. The Appellate Body somewhat softened this stand in *US – Countervailing Measures on Certain EC Products.*

US – Countervailing Measures on Certain EC Products *(Appellate Body)*

94. ... Privatization at arm's-length and for fair market value must lead to the conclusion that the privatized producer paid for what he got and thus did not get any benefit or advantage from the prior financial contribution bestowed upon the state-owned producer. While Members may maintain a rebuttable presumption that the benefit from financial contributions (or subsidization) continues to accrue to the privatized producer, privatization at arm's length and for fair market value is sufficient to rebut such a presumption.

6.1.8 Specificity

In principle, a government can uniformly support all activities of the economy. In an economic sense, if the government were to support all goods supplied and all services

---

[94] Appellate Body Reports, *Canada – Renewable Energy / Feed-In Tariff Program*, para. 5.129. See also R. Pal, 'Has the Appellate Body Decision in *Canada – Renewable Energy/ Canada – Feed-in Tariff Program* Opened the Door for Production Subsidies?', *Journal of International Economic Law* (2014), 17(1), pp. 126–9, at p. 125.

[95] T. J. Prusa, 'The Use of Economics in Appellate Body Decisions', EUI Working Paper RSCAS 2013/12 (European University Institute, Robert Schuman Centre for Advanced Studies, Global Governance Programme 38), available at https://cadmus.eui.eu/bitstream/handle/1814/26074/RSCAS_2013_12.pdf?sequence (accessed 21 December 2020).

provided uniformly across the economy, the relative prices would not change and exchange rates would adjust to keep the trade flows nearly the same.[96] The foreign producers or markets will not be distorted in such cases. However, governments do not have unlimited budgets and State support is often managed by special interests, in several economies. The specificity test excludes or insulates legitimate government activities from the purview of subsidies regulation.

The question is whether the granting authority limits subsidy to certain enterprises or groups of enterprises, industry or certain regions. There are four types of 'specificity':

1 *Enterprise specificity* – a government targets a particular enterprise or enterprises for subsidisation (Article 2.1);
2 *Industry specificity* – a government targets a particular enterprise or enterprises belonging to the same industry for subsidisation (Article 2.1);
3 *Regional specificity* – a government targets producers in specified parts of its territory for subsidisation (Article 2.2);
4 *Prohibited subsidies* – that is, export subsidies and domestic content subsidies are deemed to be specific (Article 2.3).

US – Softwood Lumber provides very good guidance on the concept of 'specificity'. At the heart of the dispute is the claim that the Canadian lumber industry was being unfairly subsidised by federal and provincial governments, as most timber in Canada is owned by the provincial governments. The charges for logging on Canada's government-owned lands (known also as the 'stumpage fee') were set administratively, rather than through the competitive marketplace. Competitive marketplace pricing was the practice in the United States, Canada's neighbour. The US claimed that this act by Canada constituted an unfair subsidy. The Canadian government and lumber industry contended before the US authorities and in the GATT that Canadian timber was sold to such a wide range of industries that the lack of specificity made it ineligible to be considered a subsidy under the US law. From 1982, there have been six major iterations of the dispute.

Once the existence of a financial contribution, along with the conferment of benefit, has been established, a subsidy is deemed to exist. However, only 'specific' subsidies are subject to regulation under the SCM Agreement. Therefore, a discussion on the concept of specificity is central to classifying a government support as a 'subsidy'.

For a subsidy to be actionable, it must be specific to 'certain enterprises'.[97] This means that the subsidy in question must be specific to an enterprise, industry or group of enterprises or industries within the jurisdiction of the authority that is granting the subsidy. The Appellate Body in *US – Anti-Dumping and Countervailing Duties (China)* observed that

---

[96] Alan O. Sykes, 'The Limited Economic Case for Subsidies Regulation', E15 Initiative (Geneva: International Centre for Trade and Sustainable Development and World Economic Forum, 2015), available at www.e15initiative .org/ (accessed 21 December 2020).
[97] SCM Agreement, Art. 2.

the definition of the terms 'certain enterprises' suggests that relevant enterprises must be 'known and particularized', but not necessarily 'explicitly identified'.

In determining whether a subsidy is specific to 'certain enterprises', the inquiry has to focus on the principles set out in paragraphs (a)–(c) of Article 2.1. The specificity analysis normally begins by examining the evidence under the above subparagraphs. Under subparagraph (a), the inquiry is whether the granting authority, or the legislation pursuant to which the granting authority operates, explicitly limits the subsidy to certain enterprises.[98] Subparagraph (b) provides that specificity 'shall not exist' if the granting authority or the legislation pursuant to which the granting authority operates, establishes objective criteria or conditions governing the eligibility for, and amount of subsidy, provided that the eligibility is automatic, that such criteria or conditions are strictly adhered to, and that they are clearly spelled out in law, regulation or other official document so as to be capable of verification. These are the elements of a de jure specificity analysis. The de jure specificity analysis will normally proceed on this sequential basis.[99]

It is important to note that Article 2 does not provide a clear definition of the terms 'enterprise or industry or group of enterprises or industries' or what constitutes 'certain enterprises'. In *US – Anti-Dumping and Countervailing Duties (China)*, the Appellate Body noted that it 'involves "a certain amount of indeterminacy at the edges"', which subjects it to wider interpretations.[100]

The SCM Agreement covers not only de jure specificity, but also de facto only to 'certain enterprises'.[101] The elements of de facto specificity are provided in Article 2.1(c). The key differences between de jure and de facto specificity are mentioned in the table below.

Table 6.1 Differences between de jure and de facto specificity

De jure specificity	De facto specificity

• Where a subsidy is explicitly limited sectorally or regionally, either by the granting authority, or by legislation, it is de jure specific.
• Where the authority or legislation establishes an objective criteria or condition governing the eligibility for, and amount of, a subsidy, the specificity will not exist.
	• It is quite possible that a subsidy on its face is non-specific, but could be administered in a specific manner, for example:
	  ◦ the subsidy programme is used by a limited number of certain enterprises;
	  ◦ predominantly by certain enterprises;
	  ◦ the granting of disproportionately large amounts of subsidy to certain enterprises.
	• The extent of diversification of economic activities within the jurisdiction, as well as of the length of time during which the subsidy programme has been in operation, should be taken into account.

---

[98] Appellate Body Report, *US – Anti-Dumping and Countervailing Duties (China)*, para. 367.

[99] Appellate Body Report, *US – Large Civil Aircraft (2nd Complaint)*, para. 873.

[100] *US – Anti-Dumping and Countervailing Duties (China)*, para. 373.   [101] SCM Agreement, Art. 2.1(b).

In considering the above factors, one should take into account the diversification of economic activities within the relevant jurisdiction, as well as the length of time that a subsidy programme has been in operation.

Article 2.2 of the SCM Agreement specifies the scope of 'regional specificity' to 'a designated geographic area'. The Panel in *US – Anti-Dumping and Countervailing Duties (China)* interpreted the term a 'designated geographic region' to 'encompass any identified tract of land within the jurisdiction of a granting authority'.[102]

Under Article 2.3 of the SCM Agreement, all export subsidies and import substitution subsidies within the meaning of Article 3 of the SCM Agreement are automatically deemed to be specific.

6.1.9 Treatment of Subsidies under the SCM Agreement

Articles 3–9 of the SCM Agreement establish a three-tier framework for the categorisation of subsidies and subsidy remedies.[103] Export and import substitution subsidies are prohibited. Other categories of subsidies are actionable only if they cause adverse effects outside the territory of the country and in certain exceptional situations within the country providing such subsidies.

6.1.9.1 Prohibited Subsidies

Article 3 of the SCM Agreement lists subsidies that are prohibited under all circumstances.[104] These include export subsidies and import substitution subsidies. Export subsidies are subsidies that are contingent, in law or in fact, whether solely or as one of several other conditions, on export performance. The term 'contingent' was interpreted in *Canada – Aircraft* to mean 'conditional' or 'dependent for its existence on something else'. Therefore, Article 3.1(a) allows for both de jure and de facto contingency. In order for subsidy to qualify as de jure export contingent, 'it must be derived from the words actually used in the measure itself'. The criteria for de facto contingency has been explained in footnote 4 to the SCM Agreement, which identifies three elements: 'granting of a subsidy'; 'tied to'; and 'anticipated'.[105] As the Appellate Body noted in *Canada – Aircraft*, de jure contingency is established on the basis of the 'very words of the measure', whereas a de facto contingency is 'inferred from the total configuration of facts and circumstances surrounding the granting of the subsidy'.[106] A WTO Panel considering complaints of de facto contingency may, in addition to the terms of the measure, examine the design,

---

[102] Panel Report, *United States – Definitive Anti-Dumping and Countervailing Duties on Certain Products from China*, WT/DS379/R, adopted 25 March 2011, as modified by Appellate Body Report WT/DS379/AB/R, para. 9.144.

[103] SCM Agreement, Art. 9.   [104] SCM Agreement, Art. 3.

[105] Appellate Body Report, *Canada – Aircraft*, paras. 169–172.

[106] Appellate Body Report, *Canada – Aircraft*, para. 167.

structure, modalities of operation and other relevant factual circumstances.[107] An Illustrative List of the types of export subsidies that would fall within the scope of Article 3.1(a) is provided for in Annex I of the SCM Agreement. One such prohibited item is certain types of export credits, discussed in Box 6.1.

Box 6.1 Export credits and international trade finance

At the crossroads between trade and finance, export credit payments represent an interesting yet controversial form of financing. It is often said that purchasers shop for the goods and for the most attractive financing terms. The cost of capital in most developing countries remains very high and continues to stifle export growth. Development assistance banks provide several types of assistance, including interest subvention, concessional financing, lines of credit, tied aid and officially supported export credits (seller's credit or buyer's credit), in order to reduce the financing cost.

Export credits extended by the supplier of goods – such as when the importer of goods and services is allowed to defer payment – are known as supplier's credits. Export credits extended by a financial institution or an export credit agency (ECA) in the exporting country are known as buyer's credits. Several governments provide officially supported export credits to industries through ECAs, which are semi-public banks. Export financing is provided in the nature of loans, guarantees or insurance. In certain cases, the official support is provided at rates that are not adequate to meet the cost of funds employed. Certain types of such export finance programmes can be used as a tool to promote certain strategic sectors. Export subsidy cases involving Brazil (relating to Embraer) and Canada (relating to Bombardier) in the field of regional aircraft led to long and prolonged trade disputes at the WTO.

Export subsidies are prohibited under the SCM Agreement, but there is a thin margin for other types of export credits other than those described above. Items (j) and (k) of the Illustrative List of Export Subsidies of the SCM Agreement identify certain categories of export credit guarantee, insurance or export credit programmes as prohibited export subsidies. Item (j) disciplines export credit guarantee or insurance programmes that are provided at premium rates and are inadequate to cover the long-term operating costs and losses of the programmes. 'Premium' is the amount to be paid for the contract of insurance. 'Long-term' is understood to mean a period of sufficient duration so as to ensure an objective examination. Item (j) establishes a cost-to-government standard – that is, government activities in the nature of insurances and guarantees constitute export subsidies only if the premium rates are inadequate to cover the long-term operating costs and losses.

Item (k), on the other hand, disciplines the grant by governments of export credits at rates below which they actually have to pay for funds so employed (or such

---

[107] Appellate Body Report, *US – Tax Incentives*, para. 5.48.

Box 6.1 (cont.)

institutions have to pay had they borrowed in international capital markets to obtain funds of the same maturity and credit terms). The proviso to Item (k) states that if the measure meets all the requirements of an international undertaking on official export credits to which at least twelve original members of the SCM Agreement have subscribed, it shall not be considered to be a prohibited export subsidy. There is only one such undertaking – that is, the OECD Arrangement on Officially Supported Export Credits of 1979. The OECD Arrangement places limitations on the financing terms and conditions (repayment terms, minimum premium rate, minimum interest rates) to be applied when providing officially supported export credits, as well as on the use of tied aid by the participants. The Arrangement contains various transparency provisions among participants to ensure that these limitations are effectively applied.

The export credit payments shall not be considered as prohibited export subsidies if the interest rate provisions of the OECD Arrangement are applied in practice. It does not matter whether or not a WTO member is a party to the OECD Arrangement. In *Canada – Aircraft (Article 21.5 – Brazil)*, the WTO Panel observed that commercial interest reference rates (CIRR) and sectoral minimum interest rate rules in the OECD Arrangement have to be complied with by members who would like to use the safe harbour provisions of the OECD Arrangement. CIRR refers to the fixed interest rates established for various currencies over a period of five years or more. Considering the limitations of the OECD Arrangement, an initiative led by the United States, China, and other OECD and BRICS (Brazil, Russia, India, China, South Africa) economies to establish guidelines for medium- to long-term export credit with tenor of two years and above, formally known as the International Working Group (IWG) on export credits, has been established.

The IWG arrangement seeks to replace the existing OECD Arrangement for export credits and is likely to be its successor.

To Go Further

Badin, M., 'Developmental Responses to the International Trade Legal Game', in D. Trubek, H. Alviar Garcia, D. Coutinho and A. Santos (eds.), *Law and the New Developmental State: The Brazilian Experience in Latin American Context* (Cambridge University Press, 2013), pp. 246–301.

Muller, Wolfgang, *WTO Agreement on Subsidies and Countervailing Measures: A Commentary* (Cambridge University Press, 2017), pp. 601–34.

Import substitution subsidies is the second category of prohibited subsidy. Such subsidies are contingent, whether solely or as one of several other conditions, on the use of domestic rather than imported goods. These often take the form of local content requirements.

To challenge a prohibited subsidy in WTO dispute settlement proceedings, a complaining member need only prove that the subsidy exists; there is no need to demonstrate that the subsidy resulted in adverse trade effects. CVD action under domestic law may also be taken against prohibited subsidies, but an affirmative injury determination to the domestic industry as well as the necessary causal link needs to be made.

6.1.9.2 Actionable Subsidies

Part II of the SCM Agreement deals with actionable subsidies. Such subsidies are not prohibited outright, but an action against the measure may be brought if it causes adverse effects on the interests of other members. For a subsidy to constitute as an actionable subsidy, it must be specific and must cause 'adverse effects'. Article 5 of the SCM Agreement identifies three types of adverse effects: (1) injury to the domestic industry of another WTO member; (2) serious prejudice; (3) nullification and impairment of benefits (accruing under the GATT, and in particular the benefits of concessions bound under Article II of the GATT).

6.1.9.3 Injury

Footnote 45 of the SCM Agreement clarifies the term 'injury' to mean 'material injury to a domestic industry, threat of material injury to a domestic industry or material retardation of the establishment of such an industry. The concept of injury under Article 15 of the SCM Agreement is substantially similar to the concept of injury under the AD Agreement. The concept of injury is discussed in greater detail in Section 6.1.10, dealing with countervailing duty measures.

6.1.9.4 Serious Prejudice

Article 6 of the SCM Agreement addresses 'serious prejudice'. Serious prejudice arises where the effect of a subsidy is demonstrated in various ways, such as import displacement or impediment in either the subsidising country or third-country markets; significant price undercutting, significant price suppression, price depression or lost sales in any market; or an increase in world market share. In other words, serious prejudice addresses the negative effects of the subsidies in the market of the subsidising member, as well as in a third-country market. A member can invoke this provision when certain subsidies disadvantage or adversely affect its export opportunities in world markets.[108] Footnote 13 of the SCM Agreement clarifies that the term 'serious prejudice to the interests of another member' is used in the same sense as in Article XVI:1 of the GATT 1994, and includes the threat of serious prejudice.

---

[108] Sykes, 'The Questionable Case for Subsidies Regulation', p. 9.

Under the SCM Agreement, a determination of serious prejudice must be based on measurable, accurate and verifiable data. Articles 6.4–6.6 of the SCM Agreement provide more detailed guidance on the criteria set out in Article 6.3.

SCM Agreement, Article 6.3

Serious prejudice in the sense of paragraph (c) of Article 5 may arise in any case where one or several of the following apply:

(a) the effect of the subsidy is to displace or impede the imports of a like product of another Member into the market of the subsidizing Member;

(b) the effect of the subsidy is to displace or impede the exports of a like product of another Member from a third country market;

(c) the effect of the subsidy is a significant price undercutting by the subsidized product as compared with the price of a like product of another Member in the same market or significant price suppression, price depression or lost sales in the same market;

(d) the effect of the subsidy is an increase in the world market share of the subsidising Member in a particular subsidized primary product or commodity as compared to the average share it had during the previous period of three years and this increase follows a consistent trend over a period when subsidies have been granted.

If one of the conditions of Article 6.3 is met, then 'serious prejudice' may exist. The SCM Agreement gives no additional guidance as to whether the conditions listed in Article 6.3 are sufficient for serious prejudice to exist. However, according to the Panel in *Korea – Commercial Vessels*, there must be a 'causal relationship' between the subsidy and the significant price suppression or price depression to constitute serious prejudice.[109]

In the case of actionable subsidies, the complainant must establish adverse effects. Therefore, in claims involving serious prejudice, adverse effects are required to be established. In *US – Upland Cotton*, the adverse effects were found to entail price suppression for the concerned product in the world market. The US domestic subsidies on cotton were considered as the cause for the price suppression. Similarly, in the case of *EC – Large Aircraft*, subsidies by EU member countries to Airbus were considered to have adverse effects on Boeing, the US competitor. The adverse effects were noticed in the nature of displacement of imports in the European market, displacement of export from other third-country markets and lost sales.

Where serious prejudice is presumed, the burden is placed on the government that has allegedly provided the subsidy to demonstrate that serious prejudice did not result from

---

[109] Panel Report, *Korea – Commercial Vessels*, paras. 7.604–7.621.

the subsidisation in question. The four categories of subsidies that can cause 'serious prejudice' are:

1 total subsidisation of a product exceeding 5 per cent *ad valorem*, which is calculated in accordance with Annex IV on a cost-to-the-government basis;
2 subsidies to cover operating losses sustained by an industry;
3 subsidies to cover operating losses sustained by an enterprise other than one-time measures that are non-recurrent and cannot be repeated for that enterprise and that are given merely to provide time for the development of long-term solutions and to avoid acute social problems;
4 direct forgiveness of debt.

Korea – Commercial Vessels *(Panel)*

7.578. ... [W]e see serious prejudice as an entirely different concept from injury. Rather than having to do with the condition of a particular domestic industry within the territory of a Member (the subject matter of injury analysis), in our view, serious prejudice has to do in the first instance with negative effects on a Member's trade interests in respect of a product caused by another Member's subsidization. Article 6.3 demonstrates this in providing that the recognized 'adverse effects' of subsidies on these interests include, in the context of serious prejudice, lost import or export volume or market share in respect of a given product (displacement or impedance, more than equitable share), and adverse price effects ..., in variously defined markets.

6.1.9.5   Non-Actionable Subsidies

Article 8.2 of the SCM Agreement sets out the criteria for non-actionable subsidies. These include subsidies for: government assistance for industrial research and pre-competitive development activity; government assistance to disadvantaged regions; and government assistance to adapt existing plant and equipment to new environmental requirements.

The non-actionable subsidies were introduced only for a period of five years and expired on 31 December 1999. In the absence of consensus, the concept of non-actionable subsidies no longer exists. Specific actions against such subsidies are not possible at present.

6.1.10 Countervailing Duty Measures

Part V of the SCM Agreement speaks about countervailing measures, which can be imposed only after conducting investigations in accordance with the SCM Agreement. The three substantive requirements that are required to be met for the imposition of a CVD measure are: subsidy; material injury to the domestic industry; and causation.

SCM Agreement, Article 15: Determination of Injury

15.1. A determination of injury for purposes of Article VI GATT 1994 shall be based on positive evidence and involve an objective examination of both (a) the volume of the subsidized imports and the effect of the subsidized imports on prices in the domestic market for like products and (b) the consequent impact of these imports on the domestic producers of such products.

The evaluation of volume requires an investigating agency to consider whether there has been a significant increase in subsidised imports (whether in absolute or relative terms). The Panel Report in *US – Countervailing Duty Investigation on DRAMS* provides some useful guidance.[110]

US – Countervailing Duty Investigation on DRAMS *(Panel)*

7.233. There are three ways in which an investigating authority may comply with the Article 15.2 requirement to 'consider whether there has been a significant increase in subsidized imports'. First, the investigating authority may consider whether there has been a significant increase in the volume of subsidized imports in absolute terms. Second, the investigating authority may consider whether there has been a significant increase in the volume of subsidized imports relative to domestic production. Third, the investigating authority may consider whether there has been a significant increase in the volume of subsidized imports relative to domestic consumption. Article 15.2 provides that '[n]o one or several of these factors can necessarily give decisive guidance'.

Article 15.4 of the SCM Agreement requires that the examination of the impact of the dumped imports on the domestic industry shall include an evaluation of all relevant economic factors and indices having a bearing on the state of the industry. Similar to the AD Agreement, there are fifteen factors under the SCM Agreement. Article 15.4 states that this list is not exhaustive and that no single or several of these factors can necessarily give decisive guidance.

In *US – Carbon Steel (India)*, where India claimed that the imposition of countervailing duties on certain Indian hot-rolled carbon steel flat products was inconsistent with the SCM Agreement. It was alleged that the measure at issue, in certain situations, led to a

---

[110] Panel Report, *United States – Countervailing Duty Investigation on Dynamic Random Access Memory Semiconductors (DRAMS) from Korea*, WT/DS296/R, adopted 20 July 2005, as modified by Appellate Body Report WT/DS296/AB/R, para. 7.223.

single injury assessment for both subsidised imports and dumped imports when simultaneous AD/CVD proceedings were conducted on the same product from different countries.[111]

US – Carbon Steel (India) *(Panel)*

7.360. ... Articles 15.1, 15.2, 15.4 and 15.5, which set out the different elements required for injury analysis, consistently refer only to 'subsidized imports' ... [T]he express limitation of the imports to be considered under Article 15 suggests to us that, in an injury analysis under that provision, the effects of other 'unfairly traded' imports is not a relevant consideration because such imports are not 'subsidized imports'. Thus, in our view, the use of the term 'subsidized imports' in these provisions limits the scope of the investigating authority's injury assessment only to subsidized imports.

6.1.10.1 Threat of Injury

The SCM Agreement provides for a remedy when there is a threat of injury on account of subsidised imports. Threat of injury must have occurred and cannot be based on conjecture or remote possibility.[112] The Panel in *US – Softwood Lumber VI* held that the authorities do not have to specify one particular event that has occurred, which will cause damage in 'progression' of the given circumstances. It was elaborated by the Appellate Body in *US – Upland Cotton (Article 21.5 – Brazil)* that the threat of injury 'relates to prejudice that does not yet exist, but is imminent such that it will materialize in the near future'.[113]

6.1.10.2 Causal Nexus between Subsidy and Injury

Article 15.5 of the SCM Agreement requires a causal nexus between the subsidy and the material injury. The evaluation of import volumes, prices and their impact on the domestic industry is helpful in assessing whether the domestic industry has suffered material injury. Footnote 47 of the SCM Agreement states that the demonstration of the causal link must be based on an examination of all relevant evidence before the investigating agencies.[114] The agencies must also examine factors other than the subsidised imports injuring the domestic

---

[111] Panel Report, *United States – Countervailing Measures on Certain Hot-Rolled Carbon Steel Flat Products from India*, WT/DS436/R, Add.1, adopted 19 December 2014, as modified by Appellate Body Report WT/DS436/AB/R, para. 7.360.

[112] Panel Report, *US – Softwood Lumber VI*, para. 7.60.

[113] Appellate Body Report, *US – Upland Cotton (Article 21.5 – Brazil)*, para. 244.

[114] For a detailed analysis, see Nedumpara, *Injury and Causation in Trade Remedy Law*.

industry at the same time. The resulting injury caused by these factors must not be attributable to the dumped imports. The concept of non-attribution applies both to the AD Agreement and the Agreement on Safeguards.

6.1.10.3 Imposition of CVDs: How to Calculate the Benefit

The general rules for calculation of the value of subsidy followed among certain WTO members are identified in Table 6.2.

Table 6.2 General rules for calculation of value of subsidy

Allocation period, allocation and appropriate benchmark	The subsidy amount has to be established during the product under investigation during the period of investigation (POI), which is normally the most recent financial year. For recurring subsidies (tax incentives, discounts on utilities, wage subsidies), the year-to-year amount can be attributed to the year of grant, that is, the POI. Some non-recurring subsidies (grants, equity infusion, debt forgiveness) have effects that outlast the year of grant; in that case, subsidies granted before the POI should also be investigated and the portion attributable to the POI should be determined. The allocation largely involves two exercises:
	1 Attribution to the POI of subsidies granted before the POI; and 2 Allocation of the subsidy amount per unit of the like product.
	The subsidy amount should be calculated on a per unit basis. After determining the subsidy amount for the POI, the per unit amount is derived by allocating it over the appropriate denominator. Appropriate denominators for various categories of subsidies are generally considered as follows:
	1 Export subsidies: export volume during the POI; 2 Non-export subsidies: total sales (domestic plus export).
	If the benefit of a subsidy is limited to a particular product or market, the denominator should reflect only sales of that product or in that market.
Allocation to the POI of subsidies granted before the POI	Recurring subsidies are generally identified as those that are available on a year-to-year basis and which are not linked to capital assets. For recurring subsidies whose effects are felt immediately after granting, the whole amount can be attributed in the POI and should normally be increased by the annual commercial interest rate. Non-recurring subsidies are generally tied to capital assets or capital structure of the firm. For non-recurring subsidies, the total amount should be spread over the normal life of the assets and the amount in the POI is to be taken.
Allowed deduction from amount of subsidy	Allowed deductions from the amount of subsidy that are commonly recognised are: 1 Any application fee or cost necessarily incurred to qualify for, or to obtain the subsidy, directly paid to the government in the POI; 2 Export taxes, duties or other charges levied on the export of a product, specifically intended to offset the subsidy.

Sources: Allocation of benefit to a particular time period, 19 Code of Federal Regulations § 351.524 (US); Article 7 of Regulation on Protection against Subsidized Imports from Countries not Members of the EU, Council Regulation 2016/1037, OJ 2016 No. L176 (EU); Annex IV, Part C, Customs Tariff (Identification, Assessment and Collection of Countervailing Duty on Subsidized Articles and for Determination of Injury) Rules, 1995 (India).

Once the IA establishes that a subsidy is countervailable on the product under investigation, the subsidy has to be allocated over an appropriate denominator. In general terms, the *per unit* subsidy is determined by dividing the subsidy by the number of units produced (in the case of domestic subsidies) or exported (in the case of export subsidies).

The benefits or effects of the subsidy may have lingering effects. The SCM Agreement assumes that an important effect of a subsidy is to reduce a firm's costs and the subsidy calculation methodology is adopted to nullify the effects. The objective of the calculation is to arrive at the amount of subsidy per unit of production during the investigation period. The per unit subsidy can be converted into an *ad valorem* rate by expressing the per unit subsidy as a percentage of the average CIF (duty unpaid) unit import price. In this way, it can be established whether the subsidy amount is *de minimis* (where subsidy is less than 1 per cent *ad valorem*).

6.1.11 Double Remedies

It should be noted that the AD and CVD measures are trade remedies that address two distinct trade practices and have different purposes and effects.[115]

US – ANTI-DUMPING AND COUNTERVAILING DUTIES (CHINA)

In *US – Anti-Dumping and Countervailing Duties (China)*, China challenged the US practice of concurrent application of AD duties and CVDs on the same product when the investigating agencies have calculated the normal value by using the surrogate country (NME) methodology.

GATT, Article VI:5

No product . . . shall be subject to both anti-dumping and countervailing duties to compensate for the same situation of dumping or export subsidization

GATT, Article VI:3

No countervailing duty shall be levied on any product of the territory of any contracting party imported into the territory of another contracting party in excess of an amount equal to the estimated bounty or subsidy determined to have been granted, directly, or indirectly . . .

The Appellate Body in *US – Anti-Dumping and Countervailing Duties (China)* considered the provision 'in excess of an amount equal to the estimated bounty or subsidy' in Article VI:3 of the GATT and contrasted it with the obligations under Articles 19.3 and 19.4 of the SCM Agreement.

SCM Agreement, Article 19.3

When a countervailing duty is imposed in respect of any product, such countervailing duty shall be levied, in the appropriate amount in each case, on a non-discriminatory basis on imports of such product . . .

---

[115] Appellate Body Report, *US – Anti-Dumping Countervailing Duties (China)*, para. 239.

(cont.)

SCM Agreement, Article 19.4

No countervailing duty shall be levied on any imported product in excess of the amount of the subsidy found to exist, calculated in terms of subsidization per unit of the subsidized and exported product.

Given Article VI of the GATT is the founding provision for both the AD and SCM Agreements; it aids and informs the conjoint application of AD and CVD measures. The Appellate Body in *US – Anti-Dumping and Countervailing Duties (China)* held as erroneous the Panel's holding that 'the imposition of anti-dumping duties calculated under an NME methodology has no impact on whether the amount of the concurrent countervailing duty is "appropriate" or not', and that Article 19.3 does not address the double remedy issue. The Appellate Body noted that the Panel failed to give meaning to all the terms of Article 19.3 of the SCM Agreement and stated:

US – Anti-Dumping and Countervailing Duties (China) *(Appellate Body)*

582. ... the appropriateness of the amount of the countervailing duties cannot be determined without having regard to anti-dumping duties imposed on the same product to offset the same subsidization. The amount of a countervailing duty cannot be 'appropriate' in situations where that duty represents the full amount of the subsidy and where the anti-dumping duties, calculated at least to some extent on the basis of the same subsidization, are imposed concurrently to remove the same injury to the domestic industry. Dumping margins calculated based on an NME methodology are, for the reasons explained above, likely to include some component that is attributable to subsidization.

The Appellate Body also held that an investigating agency has an affirmative obligation to establish whether or to what degree the concurrent application of CVD and AD would offset the same subsidisation twice.[116] The Appellate Body distinguished between the legal and factual issue of double remedies and reasoned that double remedies do not necessarily exist in every case of concurrent application of duties where the NME methodology is used.[117] The offsetting of the same subsidisation twice depends on whether and to what extent domestic subsidies have affected the export price of a product, and on whether the IA has taken the necessary steps to adjust its methodology to take this fact into account.[118]

---

[116] Appellate Body, *US – Anti-Dumping and Countervailing Duties (China)*, para. 604.
[117] Appellate Body, *US – Anti-Dumping and Countervailing Duties (China)*, para. 599.
[118] Appellate Body, *US – Anti-Dumping and Countervailing Duties (China)*, para. 599.

In conclusion, regulation of subsidies has been a major achievement of the WTO. Disputes relating to subsidies and countervailing duty investigations form a key area of dispute settlement. In addition, discussions are under way at the national and international level to ensure accurate reporting of various subsidies, given at different tiers of government. While the WTO jurisprudence on subsidies is comprehensive and detailed, there is a greater need to focus on and develop economically sound tools for addressing trade-distorting subsidies.

6.2   Emergency Actions and Safeguard Measures

Safeguard measures are defined as 'emergency' actions with respect to increased imports of particular products, where such imports have caused or threatened to cause serious injury to the importing member's domestic industry.[119] A WTO member may apply a temporary 'safeguard' measure in cases where increase in imports of the product is causing, or is threatening to cause, serious injury to the industry. Safeguards could be in the form of additional duty, or any other measures on the import of a product. Notably, safeguard measures were permitted under the GATT 1947 regime under Article XIX and are broader than other trade remedies and apply on a non-discriminatory basis. Other trade remedy measures are often targeted at 'unfair trade' against select countries, narrower product categories and, more often than not, are limited to the imposition of *ad valorem* duties.

The WTO Agreement on Safeguards establishes procedural and substantive rules, including time limits, on the use of safeguards and, importantly, prohibits 'grey area' measures, such as voluntary export restraints and voluntary restraint arrangements.[120]

6.2.1   Historical Background

Under the GATT 1947, safeguards were regulated only by Article XIX. The provisions of Article XIX were reinforced with the conclusion of the Agreement on Safeguards as part of the Uruguay Round of trade negotiations.

GATT, Article XIX:1(a)

If, as a result of unforeseen developments and of the effect of the obligations incurred by a contracting party under this Agreement, including tariff concessions, any product is being imported into the territory of that contracting party in such increased quantities and under such conditions as to cause or threaten serious injury to domestic producers in that territory of like or directly competitive products, the contracting party shall be free, in respect of such product, and to the extent and for such time as may be necessary to prevent or remedy such injury, to suspend the obligation in whole or in part or to withdraw or modify the concession.

---

[119] Agreement on Safeguards, Art. 2.   [120] Agreement on Safeguards, Art. 11.

Article XIX of the GATT provides for the suspension of obligations. The Agreement on Safeguards was negotiated especially in the backdrop of several GATT contracting parties using grey area measures. These included bilateral voluntary export restraints, voluntary export arrangements and orderly marketing agreements. These measures were not imposed pursuant to Article XIX and thus were not subject to multilateral discipline through the GATT. The Agreement on Safeguards clearly prohibits such measures. Grey area measures are primarily bilateral or plurilateral measures that are trade-restrictive. The Agreement on Safeguards required the phase-out of all grey area measures that were in effect when the Agreement entered into force. Members were given a period within which they had to notify all such measures that they maintained, as well as timetables for phasing them out.

The Agreement on Safeguards sets forth the rules for the application of safeguard measures pursuant to Article XIX of GATT 1994.

US – LINE PIPE

Safeguard measures are often conceived as 'safety valves' in international trade. In *US – Line Pipe*, the Appellate Body noted the importance of safeguard measures as follows.[121]

US – Line Pipe *(Appellate Body)*

82. ... Agreement on Safeguards both reiterates, and further elaborates on, much of what long prevailed under the GATT 1947. Nevertheless, part of the raison d'être of Article XIX of the GATT 1994 and the Agreement on Safeguards is, unquestionably, that of giving a WTO Member the possibility, as trade is liberalized, of resorting to an effective remedy in an extraordinary emergency situation that, in the judgement of that Member, makes it necessary to protect a domestic industry temporarily.

The guiding principles of the Agreement with respect to safeguard measures are:

1 Such measures must be temporary.
2 They may be imposed only when imports are found to cause or threaten serious injury to a competing domestic industry (that produces 'like' or ' 'directly competitive' product).
3 They be applied on a non-selective (MFN) basis.
4 They will be progressively liberalised while in effect.
5 The member imposing them must pay compensation to the members whose trade is affected, subject to certain limitations in Article 8.3. Additionally, the member imposing the measure has to establish 'unforeseen developments' – developments that could not have been anticipated at the time the relevant WTO tariff concession was offered.

---

[121] Appellate Body Report, *United States – Definitive Safeguard Measures on Imports of Circular Welded Carbon Quality Line Pipe from Korea*, WT/DS202/AB/R, adopted 8 March 2002, para. 82.

The characterisation of a member's measure as a safeguard measure was recently discussed in *Indonesia – Iron or Steel Products*.[122]

INDONESIA – IRON OR STEEL PRODUCTS

In 2014, Indonesia imposed a specific duty on galvalume, a type of flat-rolled iron or steel, after an investigation under Indonesian domestic safeguard legislation. This duty was notified to the WTO Committee on Safeguards and was applied on imports from all sources, although most developing countries were exempted. The complaining parties, namely Vietnam and Chinese Taipei, argued that this duty violated the Agreement on Safeguards and, as an arguendo, even if it was not a safeguard measure, it was inconsistent with Article I of the GATT. Indonesia agreed that the measure was a safeguard measure and consistent with the Agreement. Interestingly, on challenge, the Panel noted that Indonesia had no binding tariff obligation under GATT with respect to galvalume and therefore the measure did not constitute a safeguard measure. The Appellate Body upheld this ruling of the Panel. The Appellate Body identified two features that are necessary constituents to ensure the applicability of the WTO safeguard regime on a measure. First, that measure must suspend, in whole or in part, a GATT obligation or withdraw or modify a GATT concession.[123] Second, the suspension, withdrawal or modification in question must be designed to prevent or remedy serious injury to the member's domestic industry caused or threatened by increased imports of the subject product.[124] A Panel must make an assessment of the design, structure and expected operation as a whole of a measure to properly characterise it as a safeguard measure.[125] The Appellate Body further noted that in carrying out an analysis of whether a measure constitutes a safeguard measure, it is important to distinguish between the features that determine whether a measure can be properly characterised as a safeguard measure from the conditions that must be met in order for the measure to be consistent with the Agreement on Safeguards and the GATT 1994.[126]

6.2.2 Conditions for the Application of Safeguard Measures

Article 2 sets forth the conditions under which safeguard measures may be applied. These conditions are: increased imports; serious injury or threat thereof; and the existence of the causal link between increased imports of the products concerned and serious injury or threat thereof.

---

[122] Appellate Body Report, *Indonesia – Safeguard on Certain Iron or Steel Products*, WT/DS490/AB/R, WT/DS496/AB/R, Add.1, adopted 27 August 2018.

[123] Appellate Body Report, *Indonesia – Iron or Steel Products*, para. 5.60.

[124] Appellate Body Report, *Indonesia – Iron or Steel Products*, para. 5.60.

[125] Appellate Body Reports, *China – Auto Parts*, para. 171. The characterisation of a measure as a safeguard measure is before the WTO Panel in the challenge against US measures under Section 232, where the United States has invoked the national security defence under Art. XXI of the GATT 1994.

[126] Appellate Body Report, *Indonesia – Iron or Steel Products*, para. 5.57.

6.2.2.1 Increased Imports

Article 2.1 of the Agreement on Safeguards specifies two scenarios where there can be an increase in imports: an absolute increase or a relative increase. In *US – Steel Safeguards*, the Appellate Body, when determining whether safeguard measures imposed by the US on a wide range of steel products are consistent with Article XIX of the GATT and the Agreement on Safeguards, stated as follows:[127]

US – Steel Safeguards *(Appellate Body)*

354. ... A determination of whether there is an increase in imports cannot, therefore, be made merely by comparing the end points of the period of investigation. Indeed, in cases where an examination does not demonstrate, for instance, a clear and uninterrupted upward trend in import volumes, a simple end-point-to-end-point analysis could easily be manipulated to lead to different results, depending on the choice of end points. A comparison could support either a finding of an increase or a decrease in import volumes simply by choosing different starting and ending points.

ARGENTINA – FOOTWEAR (EC)

Argentina – Footwear (EC) is a landmark decision in the field of safeguards.[128] The Appellate Body developed in this case certain parameters while interpreting the requirement of 'increased imports'. These parameters were later reaffirmed in *US – Steel Safeguards*.[129]

Argentina – Footwear (EC) *(Appellate Body)*

131. ... the determination of whether the requirement of imports 'in such increased quantities' is met is not a merely mathematical or technical determination. In other words, it is not enough for an investigation to show simply that imports of the product this year were more than last year – or five years ago. Again, and it bears repeating, not just any increased quantities of imports will suffice. There must be

---

[127] Appellate Body Report, *United States – Definitive Safeguard Measures on Imports of Certain Steel Products*, WT/DS248/AB/R, WT/DS249/AB/R, WT/DS251/AB/R, WT/DS252/AB/R, WT/DS253/AB/R, WT/DS254/AB/R, WT/DS258/AB/R, WT/DS259/AB/R, adopted 10 December 2003, para. 354.

[128] Appellate Body Report, *Argentina – Safeguard Measures on Imports of Footwear*, WT/DS121/AB/R, adopted 12 January 2000.

[129] Appellate Body Report, *US – Steel Safeguards*, para. 354.

> **(cont.)**
>
> 'such increased quantities' as to cause or threaten to cause serious injury to the domestic industry in order to fulfil this requirement for applying a safeguard measure. And this language in both Article 2.1 of the Agreement on Safeguards and Article XIX:1(a) of the GATT 1994, we believe, requires that the increase in imports must have been recent enough, sudden enough, sharp enough, and significant enough, both quantitatively and qualitatively, to cause or threaten to cause 'serious injury'.

6.2.2.2   Serious Injury or Threat Thereof

Establishing 'serious injury or threat thereof' is essential to introducing a safeguard measure. Article 4.1(a) of the Agreement on Safeguards defines serious injury as 'a significant overall impairment in the position of the domestic industry'. The Appellate Body in *US – Lamb* observed that 'serious' connotes a much higher standard of injury than the word 'material'. In other words, the injury standard for the application of a safeguard measure should be higher than the injury standard for anti-dumping or countervailing measures.[130]

In determining whether serious injury is present, investigating authorities are to evaluate all relevant factors having a bearing on the condition of the industry. Factors that must be analysed include:

- absolute and relative rate and amount of increase in imports;
- market share taken by the increased imports;
- changes in level of sales, production, productivity, capacity, utilisation, profits and losses;
- employment of the domestic industry.

When examining whether increased imports have caused serious injury or threat, the authorities must evaluate all relevant factors listed above. This analysis, however, is extremely fact-intensive and case-specific.

6.2.2.3   Causal Link between Increased Imports and Serious Injury

In a Safeguard investigation, causation plays a central role.[131] With respect to this requirement, in *US – Lamb*, the Appellate Body determined that 'a panel must review whether the

---

[130] Appellate Body Report, *United States – Safeguard Measures on Imports of Fresh, Chilled or Frozen Lamb Meat from New Zealand and Australia*, WT/DS177/AB/R, WT/DS178/AB/R, adopted 16 May 2001, para. 124.

[131] Appellate Body Report, *United States – Definitive Safeguard Measures on Imports of Wheat Gluten from the European Communities*, WT/DS166/AB/R, 19 January 2001, para. 91.

authorities have provided a *reasoned and adequate explanation* of how the facts support their determination'.[132] Developing the link of causation essentially involves an attribution element and a non-attribution element. Whereas the former requires establishing a genuine cause–effect relationship between increased imports and serious injury or threat thereof, the latter requires identification of injury due to factors other than increased imports and non-attribution of the injury to these factors. The purpose is to segregate the injury caused by other factors and not to attribute this cause to increased imports.

6.2.3   Nature of Safeguard Measures

The Agreement on Safeguards specifies requirements with respect to the manner in which safeguard measures can be implemented, which are as follows:

Table 6.3 Difference between definitive safeguard and provisional safeguard

	Definitive safeguard Article 7	Provisional safeguard Article 6
Maximum duration	4 years unless extended under the Agreement on Safeguards	200 days
Type of measure	The Agreement on Safeguards provides no guidance on the form of safeguard measures. It can be an increase in the tariff above the bound rate, quantitative restrictions, TRQs, etc.	Only increase in tariffs
Criteria for imposing safeguard	Prevention or remedy of serious injury	Critical circumstances, where delay would cause damage that would be difficult to repair

Safeguard measures shall not be imposed for more than four years, with an outer timeline of eight and ten years (including provisional measures and extensions) in the case of developed and developing members. Progressive liberalisation of the measure is also required if the measure extends over one year.

A WTO member proposing a safeguard measure shall endeavour to maintain a substantially equivalent level of concession and other obligations between it and the affected exporting member. Exporting members are also free to suspend concessions if members are unable to reach an agreement on the compensation based on consultation. However, the right of suspension shall not be used in the first three years of the application of the safeguard measure, provided that the safeguard measure is taken as a result of the increase in imports and the measure otherwise conforms with the Agreement on Safeguards.[133]

---

[132] Appellate Body Report, *US – Lamb*, para. 103; Appellate Body Report, *US –Steel Safeguards*, para. 474.
[133] Agreement on Safeguards, Art. 8.

6.3   Conclusion

This chapter examined the use of two complex instruments in the field of trade remedies. The discipline of subsidies is perhaps the most controversial topic in international trade regulation at present. The provision of subsidies is also intrinsically linked to the role of the State and the use of State resources.

Most subsidies can distort resource allocation and international trade, while certain types of subsidies can address market failure and externality problems. The SCM Agreement primarily addresses two closely related topics: multilateral disciplines regulating the provision of industrial subsidies, and the use of countervailing measures to offset injury caused by subsidised imports. Agriculture subsidies are mainly addressed in the Agreement on Agriculture. More recently, the WTO has launched targeted negotiations in addressing harmful fisheries subsidies. In recent times, there is also an effort to discipline areas such as currency misalignment, unlimited State guarantees and debt forgiveness.

The Agreement on Safeguards, on the other hand, disciplines the use of safeguard measures that are addressed in response to an increase in imports causing or threatening to cause a serious injury or serious impairment to the domestic industry. Safeguard measures are implemented in cases where a sudden increase in imports of the product is causing, or is threatening to cause, serious injury to the industry. As in the case of AD and CVD measures, a proper investigation has to be conducted to identify whether there is an increase in imports causing injury to the domestic industry. Safeguard measures are meant for the suspension of GATT obligations in certain emergent situations and are not to be maintained for indefinite periods of time.

6.4   Summary

- Most subsidies can distort resource allocation and international trade, while certain types of subsidies can address market failures and externality problems.
- The SCM Agreement addresses three categories of subsidies: prohibited subsidies; actionable subsidies; and non-actionable subsidies. Notably, the category of non-actionable subsidies expired in 1999.
- The SCM Agreement has established the constituent elements of subsidy, such as 'financial contribution' and 'benefit'. In addition, subsidies need to be 'specific'. Export subsidies and import substitution subsidies are deemed to be 'specific'.
- WTO members can initiate specific actions against subsidies on imported goods when such goods cause serious injury to the domestic industry.
- Under-reporting of subsidies is one of the major difficulties in identifying and disciplining subsidies.
- Safeguard actions are emergency actions and could be used only when there is a sudden surge in imports on products that are subject to tariff commitments. In addition, the increase in imports should be on account of 'unforeseen developments'.

6.5   Review Questions

1 What are the various steps in identifying a subsidy under the SCM Agreement? Why were FIT contributions provided in *Canada – Renewable Energy / Canada – Feed-In Tariff Program* not considered a subsidy?

2 Article 1.1(a)(1) contains the phrase 'by a government or public body within the territory of the Member'. Do the terms 'government' and 'public body' have distinct meanings? (See *US – Anti-Dumping and Countervailing Duties (China)*.) Does a subsidy provided by a member to a corporation located in a third country come under the coverage of the SCM Agreement?

3 Can a government-sponsored study to examine the problems faced by an industry and requesting corrective actions be considered 'a provision of service other than general infrastructure', and therefore a 'financial contribution'? (See Panel Report, *China – GOES*.)

4 Why was the concept of specificity introduced in the SCM Agreement? (See *US – Carbon Steel (India)*.)

5 What is the meaning of 'serious prejudice'? Is it the same as 'injury'? (See Panel Report, *Korea – Commercial Vessels, US – Upland Cotton*.)

6 What are the essential features and characteristics of emergency safeguard measures? (See *Indonesia – Iron or Steel Products*.)

7 Why are grey area measures prohibited under the Agreement on Safeguards?

6.6   Exercise

Manchow is an emerging economy and a member of the WTO. Kachina is a developed WTO member.

The consumer electronic goods industry is a burgeoning sector in Manchow. In order to boost this sector, Manchow enacted an administrative order, the Framework for Rapid Improvement in Electronic Goods, 2018. Pursuant to this, the Technology Goods Promotion Corporation (TGPC), which was partially owned (49 per cent) and controlled by the Government of Manchow, was empowered to grant loans to enterprises involved in the manufacture of consumer electronic goods. The secretary general of TGPC was a senior government official. However, the majority of the board members were private individuals. These loans were granted at an interest rate of 7 per cent per annum, whereas similarly placed commercial loans were available at 10 per cent. Furthermore, the loan programme was made available based on criteria such as the turnover of the enterprise and the number of persons employed.

The consumer electronic goods industry in Kachina was not performing well for a host of reasons, such as lack of automation and the high cost of inputs. The imports from Manchow seemed to have aggravated the situation. Under pressure from the domestic industry, the

CVD agency of Kachina held a preliminary discussion. It found that the imported consumer electronic goods from Manchow had increased by 30 per cent over the past year and that domestic prices in Kachina had reduced. The market share of the domestic industry had been steadily decreasing over the past few years (2015–19) and many of the smaller manufacturers were going out of business.

Manchow has not undertaken any commitments on consumer electronic goods at the WTO.

Based on this, Kachina explored the possibilities of taking a CVD action against the imports from Manchow.

1 Would the measures of Manchow be considered a 'subsidy' under the SCM Agreement?
2 Assuming that Manchow's measure constitutes a 'subsidy', do you think that Kachina has sufficient grounds to take a CVD action?
3 Do you think that safeguards is a viable remedy for Kachina?

FURTHER READING

Horlick, G. and Clarke, P. A., 'Rethinking Subsidy Disciplines for the Future: Policy Options for Reform', *Journal of International Economic Law* (2017), 20(3), pp. 673–703.

Jackson, J. H., *The World Trading System: Law and Policy of International Economic Relations*, 2nd ed. (Cambridge, MA: MIT Press, 1997).

Mavroidis, P. C., Bermann, G. A. and Wu, M., *The Law of the World Trade Organization (WTO): Documents, Cases and Analysis* (St Paul: West, 2010).

Sykes, A. O., 'The Questionable Case for Subsidies Regulation: A Comparative Perspective', *Journal of Legal Analysis* (2010), 2(2), pp. 473–523.

Van der Bossche, P. and Zdouc, W., *The Law and Policy of the World Trade Organization: Text, Cases and Materials* (Cambridge University Press, 2017).

7 Trade-Related Aspects of Intellectual Property Rights

Table of Contents

Highlights

- TRIPS is the first major international treaty on trade providing standard protection for patents. The purpose was to provide 'effective and adequate' protection of intellectual property rights as part of a multilateral trade agreement. The TRIPS embodies the key principles of MFN and national treatment.
- TRIPS provides a minimum level of substantive protection for copyright, trademarks, geographical indications, industrial designs, patents and layout designs (topographies) of integrated circuits; TRIPS also provides protection against unfair competition, protection of undisclosed information and so on.
- TRIPS specifically incorporates the Paris Convention (1967) for the Protection of Industrial Property and the Berne Convention (1971) for the Protection of Literary and Artistic Works.

- TRIPS provides the intellectual property holder with the exclusive right to authorise or control his or her work.
- TRIPS provides a twenty-year period for patent protection, and a copyright protection of the life of the author plus fifty years.
- The WTO General Council, while giving effect to the Doha Declaration of 2001, decided that a WTO member could issue compulsory licences for the export of medicines to LDCs that may lack manufacturing capacity in order to ensure access to patented medicines. An amendment to the TRIPS Agreement in this regard entered into force in January 2017.
- 'TRIPS plus' provisions – provisions that provide additional IP protection – are increasingly seen in some of the new preferential trade agreements and mega-regional trade agreements.

7.1   Introduction

Intellectual property (IP) protection is the protection granted to inventions, literary and artistic works, symbols, names and images created by the mind. Internationally, this protection is provided by countries through treaties such as the Paris Convention for the Protection of Industrial Property of 1883 (Paris Convention)[1] and the Berne Convention for the Protection of Literary and Artistic Works of 1886 (Berne Convention).[2] The Paris Convention and the Berne Convention were some of the very first multilateral agreements in the field of intellectual property rights law, and provided the foundation for the protection of IP rights.[3] The TRIPS Agreement, under the WTO, was designed to provide a comprehensive system of protection of intellectual property rights, including copyrights, trademarks, geographical indications, industrial designs and layout designs of integrated circuits. The agreement also enlists the rights conferred, permissible exceptions to rights and the minimum duration of protection for all WTO members. It further sets out minimum standards of protection to be provided by each member and the procedures and remedies available for rights holders to effectively enforce their rights. The minimum standards of protection in the TRIPS Agreement provide only the minimum protection, whereas WTO members are free to provide more extensive protection of IP rights if they wish to do so.[4]

This chapter will mainly focus on the general provisions and basic principles of the TRIPS Agreement. The enforcement aspects of IP rights are not specifically addressed in this chapter.

---

[1] Paris Convention for the Protection of Industrial Property, 20 March 1883.

[2] Berne Convention for the Protection of Literary and Artistic Works, 9 September 1886, as revised at Paris on 24 July 1971 and amended in 1979.

[3] T. Cottier, 'Working Together Towards TRIPS', in J. Watal and A. Taubman (eds.), *The Making of the TRIPS Agreement: Personal Insights from the Uruguay Round Negotiations* (Geneva: World Trade Organization, 2015), pp. 79–94, at 79, 88.

[4] A. D. Mitchell and T. Voon, 'The Nature of the TRIPS Agreement', in D. Bethlehem et al., *The Oxford Handbook of International Trade Law* (Oxford University Press, 2009), p. 187.

7.2   TRIPS and its Negotiating History

Before the TRIPS Agreement came into force, the Paris Convention and the Berne Convention were the key multilateral agreements that provided certain intellectual property protection.[5] Both these conventions came to be administered by the World Intellectual Property Organization (WIPO), established by the WIPO Convention in 1967, which is a specialised agency of the United Nations whose mandate is to promote the protection of IP universally.[6]

Under the Paris Convention, signatories were required to provide national treatment and to implement minimum levels of intellectual property protection for industrial properties such as patents, trademarks, industrial designs, trade names, appellations of origin and utility models. Right of priority, which confers on an inventor a certain period of priority after filing for patents and trademarks, is a unique feature of the Paris Convention. The Berne Convention was drafted for the protection of literary and artistic works. The major point of difference between the two conventions is that the Paris Convention covers industrial property whereas the Berne Convention covers copyright.

The 1970s saw a rise in piracy and counterfeiting of intellectual property, especially in literary and artistic works, which provided the impetus for seeking protection for IP rights.[7] To address this problem, developed countries led a movement to revise the existing treaties for effective internal and border enforcement.[8] A plurilateral code on trade in counterfeit goods was one of the US proposals. However, the IP standards administered by the WIPO did not oblige the signatories to institute domestic monitoring and enforcement mechanisms for protection of IP rights. Unlike the developed countries, developing countries were aiming to introduce revisions seeking greater transfer of technology for their scientific and economic development. Developing countries also sought revisions that allowed them to retain the use of compulsory licensing, especially in the field of pharmaceuticals and to reduce the compensation payable to authors of protected works.[9] These contrasting and divergent positions impeded the successful renegotiations of the Paris Convention.[10]

In the interim, the United States pursued unilateral approaches to improve IP protection in foreign markets.[11] The United States Generalised System of Preferences, introduced pursuant to the Trade Act of 1974, placed these interests before the commencement of the Uruguay Round. In addition, the Trade and Tariff Act of 1984 explicitly provided for

---

[5] Stewart, *The GATT Uruguay Round*, p. 2245.

[6] Convention Establishing the World Intellectual Property Organization, 828 UNTS 3 EIF, 26 April 1970; see also A. Bogsch, *Brief History of the First Twenty-Five Years of the World Intellectual Property Organisation* (Geneva: World Intellectual Property Organization, 1992).

[7] Lowenfeld, *International Economic Law*, p. 105.

[8] A. Otten, 'The TRIPS Negotiations: An Overview', in Watal and Taubman, *The Making of the TRIPS Agreement*, p. 61.

[9] P. D. S. Tarrago, 'Negotiating for Brazil', in Watal and Taubman, *The Making of the TRIPS Agreement*, pp. 246–8.

[10] Stewart, *GATT Uruguay Round*, p. 2255.   [11] Stewart, *GATT Uruguay Round*, p. 2256.

IP protection by recourse to Section 301 of the 1974 Trade Act.[12] This controversial section allowed the US President to seek the elimination of 'unjustified and unreasonable' trade practices to improve IP rights protection in foreign markets.[13] Once the Uruguay Rounds had begun, the United States strengthened its stand for the protection of intellectual property by enacting the Special 301[14] provision under the Omnibus Trade and Competitiveness Act of 1988.[15] The Special 301 provision gives the United States the power to initiate actions against countries that have the most 'onerous or egregious acts, policies or practices' that 'deny adequate and effective intellectual property rights' to US products, and declare such countries 'Priority Foreign Countries'. In addition, the Special 301 provision also authorises the US Trade Representative to place countries on the Priority Watch List and the Watch List, based on levels of intellectual property protection and enforcement. The determination is subject to an assessment of whether the proposed action is detrimental to US economic interests or not.[16] A combination of the GSP programme, Section 301 and Special 301 provided the United States with strong leverage to seek enhanced standards of IP protection from its trading partners. As A. V. Ganesan, India's chief negotiator during the Uruguay Round, notes, '[r]etaliatory action against Indian garment and other exports to the United States was looming large over India like a Damocles' sword', and it was necessary to 'avoid trade friction'.[17] This was true for other countries, such as Brazil and Thailand, which improved their domestic laws and commitment for the protection of IP rights.[18] Although improvement in IP protection through domestic laws was a possibility, effective international protection could only be achieved through multilateral negotiations and the Uruguay Round turned out to be a viable forum. In addition, several developing countries felt that they could extract reciprocal concessions in areas such as textiles and clothing and agriculture, which had escaped the rigorous GATT disciplines for decades. This is the how intellectual property rights entered the agenda of multilateral trade negotiations.

There are other factors that also contributed to the inclusion of IP protection as part of trade agreements.[19] In addition, it is evident and amply borne out by anecdotal reports that some technology-driven industries had actively pursued their business interests in these

---

[12] Title III of the Trade Act of 1974 (Sections 301–310, 19 USC Sections 2411–2420), titled 'Relief from Unfair Trade Practices', often collectively referred to as 'Section 301'. See N. D. Palmeter, 'The Trade and Tariff Act of 1984: From the Customs Treatment of Manhole Covers to the Return of Goods from Outer Space', *Syracuse Journal of International Law and Commerce* (2004), 11(3), p. 487.

[13] Panel Report, *United States – Tariff Measures on Certain Goods from China*, WT/DS543, circulated 15 September 2020.

[14] The basis of the Special Report issued by the US Trade Representative can be traced to Section 182 of the Trade Act of 1974 (19 USC 2242), as amended by the Omnibus Trade and Competitiveness Act of 1988 and the Uruguay Round Agreements Act of 1994.

[15] A. V. Ganesan, 'Negotiating for India', in Watal and Taubman, *The Making of the TRIPS Agreement*, pp. 212–38, at 219.

[16] Stewart, *GATT Uruguay Round*, p. 2257.   [17] Ganesan, '*Negotiating for India*', p. 219.

[18] Stewart, *GATT Uruguay Round*, p. 2259.   [19] Stewart, *GATT Uruguay Round*, p. 2259.

negotiations.[20] In 1979, during the Tokyo Round, the International Anti-Counterfeiting Coalition (IACC) was formed in order to discourage the importation of counterfeit products.[21] These disparate yet compelling initiatives outside the GATT steered the negotiations within the GATT towards a movement for the inclusion of intellectual property rights as part of the Uruguay Round negotiations.

During the GATT Ministerial Meeting of 1982, the United States formalised its position regarding the inclusion of counterfeit products. This effort was opposed by the developing countries, particularly Brazil and India.[22] Brazil and India argued that the GATT's jurisdiction was limited to tangible goods and, therefore, IP conflicts could not be addressed within the GATT.[23] Both these countries also argued that intellectual property should be left to the exclusive domain of the WIPO.[24]

Despite the opposition of several developing countries, the Punta del Este Declaration of 1986 provided a mandate to clarify the GATT provisions and to elaborate new rules on the trade-related aspects of intellectual property rights, including trade in counterfeit goods.[25] Many developing as well as developed countries opposed the inclusion of intellectual property rights such as patents and copyrights.[26] During the early phase of the negotiations, several draft text proposals were submitted to the GATT Council, including the Swiss-Colombian compromise proposal and the Brazil–Argentina proposal.[27] By the end of 1989, the TRIPS negotiations produced numerous proposals by countries participating in the negotiations.[28]

Early views on the TRIPS negotiations pointed to a tussle between the global North and South and the developed against the developing world. However, as negotiations progressed, countries aligned on the basis of specific issues. Even the Quad countries had disagreements amongst themselves. The US and Japan had divergent views with respect to rental rights. Geographical indication was an area where the European Communities had

---

[20] Stewart, *GATT Uruguay Round*, p. 2260.

[21] F. Sterlacci and J. Arbuckle, *Historical Dictionary of the Fashion Industry*, 2nd ed. (Lanham: Rowman and Littlefield, 2017), p. 235; Stewart, *GATT Uruguay Round*, p. 2261.

[22] C. S. Harrison, *The Politics of the International Pricing of Prescription Drugs* (Westport: Praeger, 2004), p. 163; Stewart, *GATT Uruguay Round*, p. 2261.

[23] Stewart, *GATT Uruguay Round*, p. 2261. For a discussion of this issue, see, generally, D. Gervais, *The TRIPS Agreement: Drafting History and Analysis* (London: Sweet and Maxwell, 1998).

[24] Stewart, *GATT Uruguay Round*, p. 2261; see also A. Dearndorff, 'What Might Globalization's Critics Believe?', Research Seminar in International Economics Discussion Paper 492 (2002), pp. 653–4.

[25] GATT Contracting Parties, Thirty-Eighth Session: Ministerial Declaration, adopted 29 November 1982, GATT document L/5424.

[26] Otten, 'TRIPS Negotiations', p. 72.

[27] J. Croome, *Reshaping the World Trading System: A History of the Uruguay Round*, 2nd ed. (The Hague: Kluwer International, 1999), pp. 28–9.

[28] C. A. P. Braga, 'Trade-Related Intellectual Property Issues: The Uruguay Round Agreement and its Economic Implications', in W. Martin and L. A. Winters (eds.), *The Uruguay Round and the Developing Economies* (Washington, DC: World Bank, 1995), p. 382; Stewart, *GATT Uruguay Round*, p. 2264.

differences with the United States.[29] At the same time, Japan and the EC were pitted against the US on patent laws.[30]

The draft final act released by GATT Director General Arthur Dunkel on 20 December 1991 clearly exceeded the initial negotiating mandate articulated in Uruguay in 1986.

7.3   Framework of the TRIPS Agreement

The Preamble to the TRIPS Agreement requires WTO members to provide adequate standards and principles (i.e. minimum standards) concerning the availability, scope and use of intellectual property rights (IPRs), as well as mechanisms for parties to obtain these rights. Importantly, the Preamble also reinforces the long-held belief that IPR are 'private rights', meaning that rights holders (such as individuals or companies), rather than governments (unless, of course, the government is the rights holder), are responsible for enforcing their own IPRs (i.e. bringing actions in national court systems for injunctions, damages and so on).

Article 7 of the TRIPS Agreement states that the protection and enforcement of IPRs should contribute to the 'promotion of technological innovation and to the transfer and dissemination of technology'. Article 7 also encapsulates the need to implement the IP provisions 'to the mutual advantage of producers and users of technological knowledge and in a manner conducive to social and economic welfare'.

The TRIPS Agreement, as stated before, only sets minimum standards of IP protection. The Agreement is divided into seven parts: Parts I and II provide the substantive rules that WTO members must implement and apply domestically. Part III relates to the enforcement obligations. Part IV includes provisions for acquiring and maintaining the IPRs. Part V addresses dispute settlement rules for the TRIPS Agreement. Part VI provides for transitional agreements; while Part VII deals with various institutional and other matters.

The TRIPS Agreement also incorporates most of the substantive obligations of the Paris Convention and the Berne Convention, and certain provisions of the Treaty on Intellectual Property in Respect of Integrated Circuits and the Rome Convention.[31]

In addition, the TRIPS Agreement provides certain limited exceptions for patents, which are embodied in Article 30. Article 31 is another significant provision, which deals with compulsory licensing. Compulsory licences are a contentious issue between the developing and the developed world, even today. Other exceptions include those on copyright in Article 13, which confines limitations or exceptions to exclusive rights to certain special cases that do not conflict with a normal exploitation of the work and do not unreasonably prejudice

---

[29] Otten notes, 'GIs were not a North–South negotiation but essentially one between the "old world" and the "new world"' (Otten, 'TRIPS Negotiations', p. 72).

[30] Stewart, *GATT Uruguay Round*, p. 2313.

[31] Section 2.1 of the TRIPS Agreement incorporates, by reference, the Paris Convention, while Art. 9.1 incorporates the Berne Convention.

the legitimate interests of the rights holder. Article 17 allows limited exception to rights conferred by trademark, such as fair use of descriptive terms.

7.4 Principles of Non-Discrimination

Two of the most important principles of the TRIPS Agreement are the national treatment and most favoured nation treatment obligations. Importantly, the signing of the TRIPS Agreement helped to integrate trade law principles into IP law.

7.4.1 National Treatment Obligation under TRIPS

The NT obligation requires each WTO member to give nationals from other member countries treatment that is no less favourable than that which it gives to its own nationals with respect to the protection of intellectual property. For example, if the European Union provides a simple regime for an EU national to register and protect geographical indications, and a more difficult or onerous regime for a non-EU national, it could violate the national treatment obligation. In *EC – Trademarks and Geographical Indications*,[32] the EU prescribed different regimes for the registration of geographical indication by EU and non-EU nationals. A WTO Panel held that the 'extra hurdle' faced by non-EU applicants, which required their domestic authorities to review and send their applications to the European Commission, while not insisting on similar requirements for applications within the EU, resulted in a violation of national treatment.

The most pertinent exception to NT is included in Article 7(8) of the Berne Convention, which states that the term of protection for copyright shall be equal to the right given in the country of origin. For example, Indian authors can get only life plus sixty years in the United States, while US citizens can get life plus seventy years in India. This is explained by the fact that the term of copyright protection last for the life of the author plus seventy years in the United States, while it lasts only for life of the author plus sixty years in India.

7.4.2 Most Favoured Nation Treatment Obligation under TRIPS

The TRIPS Agreement has incorporated the MFN principle, which is a fundamental principle under the GATT and WTO regime. In the context of TRIPS, the MFN principle requires that any benefit of IP protection extended to any WTO member or other countries shall also be extended to all WTO members. However, under the TRIPS Agreement, the MFN provision applies subject to four types of exceptions, which are listed in Article 4.

In the *Havana Club* case (discussed below), the WTO Appellate Body found that Section 211 of the Omnibus Appropriation Act of 1998 violated the MFN provision of the TRIPS

---

[32] Panel Reports, *European Communities – Protection of Trademarks and Geographical Indications for Agricultural Products and Foodstuffs*, WT/DS290/R *(Australia)* / WT/DS174/R *(US)*, adopted 20 April 2005.

Agreement. Such a violation arose by virtue of the definition of 'designated national' under US law, whereby a Cuban national was treated differently from a non-Cuban national for the purposes of trademarks.

US – Section 211 Appropriations Act

The dispute between the United States and the European Communities presents an interesting set of facts. It was essentially a dispute between Havana Club International, S.A. (HCI) and Bacardi-Martini USA Inc., over the rights of the trademark 'Havana Club' (also known as the *Havana Club* case).

Prior to the Cuban Revolution in 1959, Havana Club was one of the largest companies selling rum, in Cuba and internationally. Until 1960, the Cuban corporation José Arechabala, SA (JASA) held the original Havana Club trademark and also manufactured the product. In 1960, Fidel Castro's regime confiscated most large private holdings in Cuba for State purposes, including JASA. No compensation was paid to the Arechabala family, who later fled to Spain.[33] Following the Cuban Missile Crisis in 1962, the United States government imposed sanctions on the Cuban government in 1963.[34] From 1972 to 1993, a Cuban State foreign trade enterprise established by the Cuban Ministry of Foreign Commerce, was the exclusive exporter of Havana Club rum. The Arechabala family could not restart the business and allowed the US trademark of 'Havana Club' to expire. In the meantime, the Havana Club mark was registered in the United States in 1976 by a Cuban State-owned enterprise called *Empresa Cubana Exportadora de Alimentos y Productos Varios* ('Cubaexport'). Cubaexport continued to market Havana Club rum internationally from 1972 until 1993. In 1993, Cubaexport decided to seek a foreign partner for its Havana Club rum business. Cubaexport reached an agreement with Pernod Ricard, SA, a French company and an international distributor of liquor.

Following this agreement, the reorganisation of the companies took place to form two companies: Havana Club Holding (HC Holding), a Luxembourg corporation, and Havana Club International (HCI), a Cuban corporation. These companies had a 50-50 equity split between Havana Rum & Liquors and Pernod Ricard. According to Cubaexport, all the assets associated with the Havana Club trademark were transferred to Havana Rum and Liquors, which then transferred them to HC Holding. HC Holding then granted HCI an exclusive licence to sell Havana Club rum and to use the Havana Club trademark.

Prior to Pernod Ricard entering into its agreement with Cubaexport, the Arechabala family was in talks with multiple parties to discuss purchasing their waiver of any claims to the Havana Club name. After a series of negotiations, the Arechabalas finally entered into a formal sale purchase agreement with Bacardi & Co. in April 1995. Pursuant to this

---

[33] E. Taylor, 'The Havana Club Saga: Threatening More than Just "Cuba Coke"', *Northwestern Journal of International Law and Business* (2004), 24(2), pp. 513–32, at 513–15.

[34] The US Government passed the Cuban Asset Control Regulations. See D. R. Dinan, 'An Analysis of the United States–Cuba "Havana Club" Rum Case before the World Trade Organization', *Fordham International Law Journal* (2002), 26, p. 337.

agreement, Bacardi & Co. purchased the Havana Club trademark, the related goodwill and any rum business assets that still existed, from the Arechabala family.

On 5 October 1995, the companies HC Holding and HCI applied to the Office of Foreign Asset Control (OFAC), an agency of the US government, for a specific licence authorising the assignment of the Havana Club trademark. In 1997, the OFAC revoked the licence retroactive to the date of application, stating that fresh facts and circumstances that were not included in the application for a licence on 5 October 1995, had been brought to its notice.

Legislative actions took place in the United States. The United States enacted the Omnibus Appropriation Act 1998, Section 211 of which intended to prevent the registration and enforcement in the US of trademarks requisitioned by Cuba. This section dealt with 'trademarks, trade names, and commercial names which were similar or substantially similar to trademarks, trade names and commercial names used in connection with businesses or assets sequestered by the Cuban Government on or after July 1, 1959'. This legislative measure effectively stopped Pernod Ricard from being able to enforce its rights in the trademark 'Havana Club'.

In 1995, Bacardi-Martini, a company headquartered in Bermuda, began to distribute rum in the United States bearing the trademark Havana Club. The dispute was first taken up in the District Courts. In December 1996, HC Holding and HCI filed their lawsuit for trademark infringement against Bacardi, alleging violation of Sections 32 and 43(a) of the Lanham Act.[35] Bacardi responded by alleging that the licence received by HC Holding and HCI from OFAC authorising the US trademarks was obtained by fraud.

The District Court concluded that HCI lacked standing to assert its claims under the Lanham Act because it was barred from selling its rum in the United States by virtue of the Cuban embargo, and therefore could not suffer commercial injury because of Bacardi's action. The Court also found that any injury HCI might suffer once the embargo was lifted was too remote to grant HCI standing.[36]

In short, HC Holding was unable to protect its trademark 'Havana Club' in the United States. In June 2000, the EC, representing the interests of Pernod Ricard, requested the establishment of a WTO Panel under Article 6 of the DSU and Article 64.1 of the TRIPS Agreement.[37] The EC alleged that Section 211 of the Omnibus Appropriations Act[38] was in

---

[35] US District Court for the Southern District of New York, 974 F. Supp. 302 (SDNY 1997), 12 August 1997.

[36] *Havana Club Holding, SA* v. *Galleon, SA*, 62 F.Supp.2d 1085, 1089 (SDNY 1999), para. 1099.

[37] Panel Report, *United States – Section 211 Omnibus Appropriations Act of 1998*, WT/DS176/R, adopted 1 February 2002, as modified by Appellate Body Report WT/DS176/AB/R, para. 1.1.

[38] The Omnibus Appropriations Act Section 211(a)(1) reads:

> Notwithstanding any other provision of law, no transaction or payment shall be authorized or approved pursuant to Section 515.527 of title 31, Code of Federal Regulations, as in effect on September 9, 1998, with respect to a mark, trade name, or commercial name that is the same as or substantially similar to a mark, trade name, or commercial name that was used in connection with a business or assets that were confiscated unless the original owner of the mark, trade name, or commercial name, or the bona fide successor-in-interest has expressly consented.

violation of the TRIPS Agreement. Specifically, the EC challenged the provisions of the Omnibus Appropriations Act that prohibited the US courts from enforcing trademarks, tradenames or commercial names that were used in connection with a business or assets that were confiscated, unless the original owner or its successor-in-interest had consented. More specifically, according to the EC, Section 211(a)(2) of the Act violated Article 42 of the TRIPS Agreement, which enables trademark holders to enforce their marks by means of fair and equitable procedures. The EC also considered Sections 211(a)(2) and (b) to be at variance with US obligations under Articles 2.1, 3 and 4 of the TRIPS Agreement, together with Article 2(1) of the Paris Convention.

The EC claimed that Section 211 violated the MFN and NT obligations of the TRIPS Agreement by favouring US or third-country successors-in-interest to trademarks by exempting them from the additional requirements that are otherwise imposed on Cuban successors-in-interest. Cuban nationals were required to undergo a hearing under Section 211(a)(2) before they were granted access to US courts regarding the enforcement of their trademark rights. The Panel found that Sections 211(a)(2) and (b) did not violate the MFN provision as enshrined in Article 4 of the TRIPS Agreement.[39] The Appellate Body, on the other hand, ruled to the contrary and overturned the Panel's decision.

> ### US – Section 211 Appropriations Act *(Appellate Body)*
>
> 307. Pointing to this particular situation, the European Communities argues that, on the face of the statute, the original owner who is a Cuban national is subject to Sections 211(a)(2) and (b), and the original owner who is a non-Cuban foreign national is not. This alone, as the European Communities sees it, is sufficient for us to find that Sections 211(a)(2) and (b) violate the most-favoured-nation obligation of the United States.
> 308. We agree with the European Communities that the situation it describes on appeal is within the scope of the statute on its face. As we explained earlier, the term 'designated national' as defined in Section 515.305 of 31 CFR and Section 211(d)(1) includes non-Cuban foreign nationals only when they are successors-in-interest to Cuba or a Cuban national. Non-Cuban foreign nationals who are original owners are not covered by the definition of 'designated national' and are thereby not subject to Sections 211(a)(2) and (b).

The Appellate Body arrived at a similar reasoning with respect to the NT claim. On the EC's claim on Article 42, the Panel and, later, the Appellate Body ruled in favour of the United States.

---

[39] Panel Report, *US – Section 211 Appropriations Act*, para. 9.1(h), (n).

US – Section 211 Appropriations Act *(Appellate Body)*

215. The first sentence of Article 42 requires Members to make certain civil judicial procedures 'available' to right holders. Making something available means making it 'obtainable', putting it 'within one's reach' and 'at one's disposal' in a way that has sufficient force or efficacy. We agree with the Panel that the ordinary meaning of the term 'make available' suggests that 'right holders' are entitled under Article 42 to have access to civil judicial procedures that are effective in bringing about the enforcement of their rights covered by the Agreement.

    [. . .]

227. With this in mind, we turn to the alleged inconsistency of Section 211(a)(2) with Article 42. Section 211(a)(2) does not prohibit courts from giving right holders access to fair and equitable civil judicial procedures and the opportunity to substantiate their claims and to present all relevant evidence. Rather, Section 211(a)(2) only requires the United States courts not recognize, enforce or otherwise validate any assertion of rights by designated nationals or successors-in-interest who have been determined, after applying United States Federal Rules of Civil Procedure and Federal Rules of Evidence, not to own the trademarks referred to in Section 211(a)(2). As we have said, Section 211(a)(2) deals with the substance of ownership. Therefore, we do not believe that Section 211(a)(2) denies the *procedural* rights that are guaranteed by Article 42.

7.5   Substantial Provisions of TRIPS

7.5.1   Copyrights

Copyright is a legal concept that appears to have its roots in the advent of the printing press in the fifteenth century. It is a form of IPR that grants the creator of the original work the legal right to seek protection against any unauthorised use. Copyright relates to literary and artistic creations such as books, music, paintings and sculptures, films and technology-based works (such as computer programs and electronic databases).

Broadly speaking, copyright laws exist for three basic reasons:[40]

1 to confer economic rights or moral rights on authors for their creative works;
2 to encourage the availability and dissemination of creative works;
3 in this process, to facilitate the access to and use of creative works by the general public.

---

[40] J. H. Bruwelheide, *The Copyright Primer for Librarians and Educators*, 2nd ed. (Chicago: American Library Association, 1995).

It is pertinent to note that while US laws focus on economic rights, EU laws focus on moral rights.

The substantive provisions for the protection of copyright and related rights are contained in Section 1 of Part II – that is, Articles 9–14 of the TRIPS Agreement. Article 9 stipulates the principle that WTO members have to comply with the substantive provisions of the Berne Convention. The Berne Convention provides that members must ensure that copyright owners have certain economic rights. The Berne Convention also prescribes certain other rights in relation to communication of copyright, such as moral rights.

Article 9.2 of the TRIPS Agreement states that copyright protection extends to expressions and not to the ideas, procedures and methods of operation or mathematical concepts as such. It is pertinent to note that the TRIPS Agreement excludes recognition of moral rights by excluding certain rights conferred under Article 6*bis* of the Berne Convention.

Article 12 of the Agreement provides minimum standards for the term of protection of copyrighted works. The term of protection for literary works is the life of the author plus fifty years. Article 10.1 reiterates the basic principle of copyright that computer programs, whether in source or object code, shall be protected as literary works under the Berne Convention (1971).

United States – Section 110(5) Copyright Act

This was the first TRIPS copyright case and the first dispute to interpret the three-step test, as embodied by Article 13 of the TRIPS Agreement. At issue in this dispute was the Fairness in Music Licensing Act (FMLA), an amendment to Section 110(5) of the Copyright Act. The amendment was enacted by the US Congress in October 1998.[41]

As a general principle under the US Copyright Act, the owner of a music copyright has the 'exclusive right' to publicly perform the copyrighted work through digital or audio transmission.[42] Traditionally, restaurants or public food outlets also play music through radio or television sets for the benefit of customers. In fact, the music contributes to the ambience of the dining experience. However, in the case of small fast-food restaurants or hotels, as clarified by the US Supreme Court in the landmark *Twentieth Century Music Corp* v. *Aiken*, there was no 'performance'.[43] The Supreme Court decision, popularly known as the Aiken exception, later gave to the 'home-style exception', under which anybody was allowed to run or display in his or her premises, on a single receiving apparatus typically used in private homes, copyrighted performances of non-dramatic compositions such as plays, operas or musicals from radio or television transmissions without the consent of the copyright holder.[44] The homestyle exception was expected to serve small eating, drinking and retail establishments that merely turned on their standard

---

[41] Fairness in Music Licensing Act of 27 October 1998, Pub. L. No. 105-298, 112 Stat. 2830, 105th Cong., 2nd Session (1998).

[42] United States Copyright Act of 1976, 19 October 1976, Pub. L. 94-553, 90 Stat. 2541 (as amended).

[43] *Twentieth Century Music Corp* v. *Aiken*, 422 US 151 (1975).

[44] Panel Report, *United States – Section 110(5) of the US Copyright Act*, WT/DS160/R, adopted 27 July 2000, para. 2.7.

radio or television equipment for their customers' enjoyment, but was not meant to include the use of commercial or sound systems or apparatus that could convert standard home sound or stereo systems into commercial sound systems. The purpose was to permit broadcasting of dramatic works by a non-commercial radio or television system. Similarly, the 'business exemption' applied to food service establishments with limited size and area, to communicate radio or television transmissions of 'nondramatic music' without the consent of the copyright holder. Particular spatial restrictions and other conditions applied to the business exemption.

Several European associations of music right holders, such as the Irish Music Rights Organisation, took up the matter with the EU Commission.[45] The EC filed a WTO complaint on the ground that the amended law resulted in royalty losses to the European companies. The EC contested the amended subparagraphs (A) and (B) of Section 110(5) of the Copyright Act. The subparagraphs refer, in particular, to the 'homestyle' exemption defined in subparagraph (A)7, and the 'business' exemption defined in subparagraph (B) of Section 110(5). Both subparagraphs grant exceptions to the provisions of Section 106 of the Copyright Act. According to the EC, Section 110(5) of the US Copyright Act permitted, under certain conditions, the playing of radio and television music in public places (bars, shops, restaurants and so on) without the payment of a royalty fee.

The EC claimed that, as a result of these exceptions, the EC's rights under Article 9.1 of the TRIPS Agreement were impaired and nullified. Article 9.1 of the TRIPS Agreement requires all members to comply with Articles 1–21 of the Berne Convention of 1971. According to the EC, Article 11*bis*(1)(iii) and Article 11(1)(ii) of the Berne Convention (1971) provide protection, which was altered by the amended Copyright Act of 1976. Article 11*bis*(1)(iii) provides the authors of literary and artistic works with the exclusive right to authorise 'the public communication by loudspeaker or any analogous instrument transmitting, by signs, sounds or images, the broadcast of the work', while Article 11(1)(ii) grants to authors of dramatic and musical works the exclusive right to authorise 'any communication to the public of the performance of these works'.

The United States, on the other hand, argued that the provisions on the home-style exemption and the business exemption were justified under Article 13 of the TRIPS Agreement.

> ### TRIPS Agreement, Article 13: Limitations and Exceptions
> Members shall confine limitations or exceptions to exclusive rights to certain special cases which do not conflict with a normal exploitation of the work and do not unreasonably prejudice the legitimate interests of the right holder.

---

[45] L. A. McCluggage, 'Section 110(5) and the Fairness in Music Licensing Act: Will the WTO Decide the United States Must Pay to Play?', *IDEA: The Journal of Law and Technology* (2000), 40, p. 1.

The Panel applied Article 13 of the TRIPS Agreement, taking Article 11*bis*(2) of the Berne Convention as a guide.

United States – Section 110(5) Copyright Act *(Panel)*

4.10. While not in the foreground of the TRIPS negotiations, the history of Berne suggests that the specific balance of interests involved in relation to the public performance of broadcast works appears to be between the right of the author to remuneration, and the need for broadcasting media to develop and contribute to social and economic well-being. What factors should be considered in maintaining this balance? Clearly, it was not intended to give the author the right to prohibit the public communication of the broadcast of the work, as this would be an unreasonable constraint on the use of broadcast material. Some de minimis or public interest exceptions to the right were also entertained in relation to some jurisdictions at least – use within the family or domestic circle, in religious or educational contexts. The author, also, did not have an unlimited right to obtain remuneration – in effect, the author was not given monopoly bargaining power, and it was acknowledged that an independent authority may establish the level of remuneration that would be equitable.

4.11. Hence the balance struck was for an undiminished right of equitable remuneration in relation to use of works that did not fall within the 'minor exception' or de minimis category. When, at the Rome Conference, Article 11*bis* was introduced in its initial form, the Sub-Committee on Broadcasting reported that the Article was intended 'to bring the author's rights into harmony with the general public interests of the State, the only ones to which specific interests are subordinate', while it 'emphatically confirms the author's right'.

The Panel then laid down the three-step test for the limitations and exceptions under Article 13 of the TRIPS Agreement.[46] The limitations or exceptions are confined to certain special cases, which do not conflict with a normal exploitation of the work, and which do not unreasonably prejudice the legitimate interests of the right holder. The three-step test had its roots in changes to the Berne Convention, inserted through the 1967 Stockholm Conference for the Revision of the Berne Convention.[47]

---

[46] A. Kur, 'Of Oceans, Islands, and Inland Water: How Much Room for Exceptions and Limitations Under the Three-Step Test?', *Richmond Journal of Global Law and Business* (2009), 8, pp. 287–350, at 287, 315.

[47] C. Geiger, D. Gervais and M. Senftleben, 'The Three-Step Test Revisited: How to Use the Test's Flexibility in National Copyright Law', PIJIP Research Paper 2013-04 (2013); see also J. Oliver, 'Copyright in the WTO: The Panel Decision on the Three-Step Test', *Columbia Journal of Law and Arts* (2002), 25, p. 119.

The Panel found that one of the two exemptions provided by Section 110(5) of the Copyright Act was inconsistent with US obligations.

US – Section 110(5) Copyright Act *(Panel)*

6.247. We recall our conclusion that in the application of the three conditions of Article 13 to an exemption in national law, both actual and potential effects of that exception are relevant. As regards the third condition in particular, we note that if only actual losses were taken into account, it might be possible to justify the introduction of a new exception to an exclusive right irrespective of its scope in situations where the right in question was newly introduced, right holders did not previously have effective or affordable means of enforcing that right, or that right was not exercised because the right holders had not yet built the necessary collective management structure required for such exercise. While under such circumstances the introduction of a new exception might not cause immediate additional loss of income to the right holder, he or she could never build up expectations to earn income from the exercise of the right in question. We believe that such an interpretation, if it became the norm, could undermine the scope and binding effect of the minimum standards of intellectual property rights protection embodied in the TRIPS Agreement.

In regard to the home-style exemption, the WTO Panel found that this met the requirements of Article 13 and, therefore, was consistent with Berne Convention Article 11*bis*(1)(iii) and 11(1)(ii), as incorporated into the TRIPS Agreement, Article 9.1:(1) the exemption was confined to 'certain special cases', as it was well-defined and limited in its scope and reach (only 13–18 per cent of establishments covered); (2) the exemption did not conflict with a normal exploitation of the work, as there was little or no direct licensing by individual rights holders for 'dramatic' musical works (i.e. limited for opera, operetta or similar dramatic work); and (3) the exemption did not cause unreasonable prejudice to the legitimate interests of the rights holders in light of its narrow scope. In other words, the beneficiaries or potential beneficiaries of the home-style exemption were limited.

In relation to the business exemption, the WTO Panel found that this did not meet the requirements of Article 13. The Panel relied on the statistical data provided by the US and the EC. According to the Panel, the business exemption resulted in significant royalty losses for copyright holders. The Panel used the three-step reasoning for rejecting the business exemption: (1) the exemption did not qualify as a 'certain special case' under Article 13, as its scope in respect of potential users covered 'restaurants' (70 per cent of eating and drinking establishments and 45 per cent of retail establishments), which is one of the main types of establishments intended to be covered by Article 11*bis*(1)(iii); (2) the exemption interfered with a 'normal exploitation of the work', as it deprived the rights holders of musical works of compensation, as appropriate, for the use of their work from broadcasts of radio and television; and (3) the 1998 amendment exempts 70 per cent of eating and drinking establishments and 45 per cent of all retail establishments from paying such fees. In other words, the business exemption was available to too many[48] and caused prejudice to the legitimate interests of the rights holders.[49] The Panel, however, recognised the difficulty in quantifying the economic value of the prejudice.[50]

In conclusion, subparagraphs (A) and (B) of Section 110(5) of the Copyright Act were deemed to be clearly defined, but their scope and extent were different. While the home-style exemption was narrow in scope and reach, the business exemption was broad and hence was considered impermissible. The WTO Panel has made it clear that the three conditions under Article 13 of the TRIPS Agreement are distinct requirements that apply on a cumulative basis. In other words, a failure to comply with any one of the three conditions could result in a rejection of the exemptions.

In addition, from the perspective of the TRIPS Agreement, the Panel noted that the three-step test in Article 13 applies to Article 11(1)(ii) and 11 *bis*(1)(iii) of the Berne Convention, and also in respect of any national law that is predicated on the 'minor exception' doctrine, as incorporated into the TRIPS Agreement.[51]

The application of Article 13 is of particular importance to several WTO members. In several countries, there are 'permissible free use' provisions. For example, WTO members provide limited exceptions for educational purposes. This may include using photocopies or extracts of published materials, audio recordings or videos of copyrighted materials for educational purposes. Although there is a broad understanding that the extent of copying should not prejudice the legitimate rights of the copyright holder, the extent of 'prejudice' itself is not clearly defined.[52]

Box 7.1 Delhi University photocopying case

What is the extent of 'fair use' for educational purposes? In *University of Oxford* v. *Rameshwari Photocopy Services*,[53] several leading publishers, led by Oxford University Press, sought an injunction against a private photocopier service provider, which operated from the premises of the Delhi School of Economics (part of Delhi University), from photocopying, reproducing and distributing certain portions of published works. The respondent in this case used to take photocopies from books published by the petitioners for the purpose of compiling prescribed readings and course materials. This was a cheaper option for the students and universities were also

---

[48] Panel Report, *US – Section 110(5) Copyright Act*, para. 6.206.
[49] Panel Report, *US – Section 110(5) Copyright Act*, para. 6.249.
[50] Panel Report, *US – Section 110(5) Copyright Act*, para. 6.251.
[51] Panel Report, *US – Section 110(5) Copyright Act*, paras. 6.53–6.55.
[52] Panel Report, *US – Section 110(5) Copyright Act*, para. 6.260.
[53] *University of Oxford* v. *Rameshwari Photocopy Services*, 235 (2016) Delhi Law Times 409.

Box 7.1 (cont.)

relieved of the burden of stocking sufficient numbers of books for individual student use. The publishers, on the other hand, felt that it was an infringement of copyright under Section 14 of the Indian Copyright Act, 1957. Section 52(1)(a) of the Copyright Act 1957 provided a type of 'fair use exception', which allowed fair dealing with 'literary, dramatic, musical and artistic' copyrighted work for certain specific purposes. Interestingly, there was no such term as 'fair use' under Indian copyright law, although it contained the term 'fair deal'. The Delhi High Court ruled in favour of the respondent on the ground that the fair use provision exempts reproduction of any work from copyright infringement used for educational purposes and the respondent did not make any additional profit. The Delhi High Court, while noting that national copyright laws must fulfil the three-step test provided in the Berne Convention, left it to the Indian government to determine whether a given copyright exception is justified under the three-step test.

The matter is still contentious. While copyrights are important for fostering creativity, socio-economic conditions in certain countries may demand some flexibility. The Delhi photocopying case only illustrates the vague nature of the obligations under domestic law and even under the TRIPS Agreement.

To Go Further

S. Sivakumar and L. P. Lukose, 'On the Right to Photocopy', *The Hindu*, 26 September 2016.

7.5.2 Trademark

Trademark is another form of IP and it grants the right to exclusively use a sign or combination of signs that are capable of distinguishing the good or services of one undertaking from those of another.[54] This might include a symbol, word, term or logo. Trademarks play a key role in international trade and protect the owners from risks arising from counterfeiting, which are fairly common in several markets. In other words, trademarks enable an owner to preserve its established goodwill in the concerned jurisdictions.

The TRIPS Agreement is the first multilateral agreement to define a trademark. Trademark was available only for goods under the Paris Convention. This was extended to cover both goods and services under the TRIPS Agreement.

The substantive provisions for the protection of trademarks and related rights are contained in Section 2 of Part II – that is, Articles 15–21 of the TRIPS Agreement. Articles 15.1 and 16.1 enlist the criteria capable of constituting a trademark. Article 15.2 reinforces the

---

[54] TRIPS Agreement, Art. 15.

Paris Convention (1967) and prohibits any derogation from the provisions of this convention. Article 16.2 provides that exclusive rights must provide for well-known marks – an issue that came up in the *Australia – Tobacco Plain Packaging* case, discussed later in this chapter. Article 18 provides for a term of protection from the initial registration, and each renewal of registration for a term of no less than seven years.

US – Section 211 Appropriations Act ('Havana Club')

The Havana Club case examined some interesting claims in relation to trademarks and tradenames. The WTO Panel found that trade names and commercial names were not categories of IP rights protected by the TRIPS Agreement.

US – Section 211 Appropriations Act *(Panel)*

8.65. In respect of the EC's argument that signs constituting trademarks used in connection with confiscated assets that meet the criteria set out in Article 15.1 can come within the purview of Section 211(a)(1) and therefore be denied registration as trademarks, we note that Section 211(a)(1) does not deny trademark registration to those signs that constitute trademarks as such; it denies trademark registration to those who are not deemed to be the proper owner under US law. Thus, the effect of Section 211(a)(1) is that the original owner, the successor-in-interest or a person who has the original owner's or the successor-in-interest's consent can register the signs constituting trademarks that were used in connection with confiscated assets which meet the requirements of Article 15.1 because they are considered the proper owner under Section 211(a)(1). It is also for this reason that we do not share the EC's view that Articles 16 to 21 of the TRIPS Agreement would be reduced to inutility; the original owner, the successor-in-interest or a person who has the original owner's or the successor-in-interest's consent would obtain rights and benefits stemming from these provisions. Therefore, Section 211 (a)(1) is not inconsistent with Article 15.1 on the basis that Section 211(a)(1) denies trademark registration to those signs constituting trademarks that were used in connection with confiscated assets which meet the requirements of Article 15.1.

Importantly, the Appellate Body reversed the decision of the Panel and held that if the negotiators had intended to exclude trade names, there would not have been any reason to incorporate Article 8 of the Paris Convention (relating to trade names) into the TRIPS Agreement.[55]

---

[55] Appellate Body Report, *United States – Section 211 Omnibus Appropriations Act of 1998*, WT/DS176/AB/R, adopted 1 February 2002, para. 338.

One of the more recent cases on trademarks is the high-profile *Australia – Tobacco Plain Packaging* case,[56] discussed below.

AUSTRALIA – TOBACCO PLAIN PACKAGING

The challenged measures were Australia's Plain Packaging Act 2011 and Tobacco Plain Packaging Regulations 2011 (TPP Measures). (See also Chapter 14.) The measures sought to discourage the use of tobacco products and required that tobacco products be sold logo-free, in 'plain, drab, dark brown packets'.[57] Plain packaging of tobacco products was an optional measure provided under the guidelines of the 1996 WHO Framework Convention on Tobacco Control.

These measures standardised the visual appearance of tobacco products by banning the use of logos, symbols, colours and promotional text, and requiring all tobacco products to be in a standard size, colour and so on.[58] Several WTO members, namely Ukraine (later dropping out), Honduras, the Dominican Republic, Cuba and Indonesia, challenged the measures as inconsistent with Articles 15.4, 16.3 and 20 of the TRIPS Agreement and Article 6*quinquies* of the Paris Convention (1967), as incorporated into the TRIPS Agreement by Article 2.1 thereof.

7.5.2.1 Article 6 *quinquies* of the Paris Convention (1967)

The Panel ruled that complainants had not demonstrated that the TPP measures are inconsistent with Article 6*quinquies* of the Paris Convention (1967), as incorporated into the TRIPS Agreement by Article 2.1 thereof. According to the complainants, Australia does not accept for filing and protection an 'as is' basis for every trademark duly registered in the country of origin.

---

[56] Panel Report, *Australia – Certain Measures concerning Trademarks, Geographical Indications and other Plain Packaging Requirements applicable to Tobacco Products and Packaging*, WT/DS435/R, Add.1 and Suppl.1, adopted 27 August 2018 (*Australia – Tobacco Plain Packaging (Cuba)*); Appellate Body Report, *Australia – Certain Measures concerning Trademarks, Geographical Indications and other Plain Packaging Requirements applicable to Tobacco Products and Packaging*, WT/DS441/AB/R, Add.1, adopted 29 June 2020 (*Australia – Tobacco Plain Packaging (Dominican Republic)*); Appellate Body Report, *Australia – Certain Measures concerning Trademarks, Geographical Indications and other Plain Packaging Requirements applicable to Tobacco Products and Packaging*, WT/DS435/AB/R, Add.1, adopted 29 June 2020 (*Australia – Tobacco Plain Packaging (Honduras)*); Panel Report, *Australia – Certain Measures concerning Trademarks, Geographical Indications and other Plain Packaging Requirements applicable to Tobacco Products and Packaging*, WT/DS467/R, Add.1 and Suppl.1, adopted 27 August 2018 (*Australia – Tobacco Plain Packaging (Indonesia)*).

[57] Panel Report, *Australia – Tobacco Plain Packaging*, para. 2.11.

[58] Panel Report, *Australia – Tobacco Plain Packaging*, paras. 2.20–2.31.

Figure 7.1 Tobacco plain packaging.
Regulations on the packaging and presentation of
tobacco products are becoming increasingly
common, especially for creating public
health awareness.
Photo: Australian Government / Getty Images
News / Getty Images AsiaPac / Getty Images.

7.5.2.2   Articles 16.1 and 16.3.3 of TRIPS

Article 16.1 of the TRIPS Agreement provides that

the owner of a registered trademark shall have the exclusive right to prevent all third parties not having
the owner's consent from using in the course of trade identical or similar signs for goods or services
which are identical or similar to those in respect of which the trademark is registered where such use
would result in a likelihood of confusion.

The complainants argued that the prohibition on the use of certain tobacco-related products
diminishes the distinctiveness of these trademarks. The Panel clarified the role of distinctiveness in the context of Article 16.1 as follows:

Australia – Tobacco Plain Packaging (Cuba) *(Panel)*

7.2010.   ... A registered trademark is likely to be distinctive in the relevant jurisdiction, as
distinctiveness is a condition for registration under Article 15.1. The decision to
register a trademark is generally based on a finding under domestic law that it
was (or has become) distinctive in that jurisdiction at the time of that determination. As the text of Article 16.1 refers only to 'owners of the registered trademark', rights under that provision become available upon registration. It is thus
clear that Article 16.1 does not relate to the acquisition of distinctiveness through
use as a prerequisite for registration. As concerns registered trademarks, Article
16.1 itself does not mention distinctiveness, but identifies 'likelihood of confusion' as one of the infringement criteria. As under Article 15, a Member's
obligation under Article 16.1 is to provide a right for the trademark owner to

(cont.)

prevent situations that fulfil the infringement criteria. Article 16.1 does not make Members responsible for the conditions in which those infringement criteria, such as a 'likelihood of confusion', can be fulfilled, let alone obligated to refrain from regulatory conduct that might impair a trademark owner's ability to maintain the distinctiveness of a sign in order to satisfy the 'likelihood of confusion' criteria.

Indonesia and Cuba argued that the TPP measures violate Article 16.3 of the TRIPS Agreement, since the challenged measures prevent existing well-known tobacco trademarks from maintaining their trademark status and also prevent other registered marks from acquiring well-known trademark status through use. It is pertinent to note that Article 16.3 of the TRIPS Agreement incorporates Article 6*bis* of the Paris Convention, *mutatis mutandis*.

*Paris Convention, Article 6*bis

(1) The countries of the Union undertake, ex officio if their legislation so permits, or at the request of an interested party, to refuse or to cancel the registration, and to prohibit the use, of a trademark which constitutes a reproduction, an imitation, or a translation, liable to create confusion, of a mark considered by the competent authority of the country of registration or use to be well known in that country as being already the mark of a person entitled to the benefits of this Convention and used for identical or similar goods. These provisions shall also apply when the essential part of the mark constitutes a reproduction of any such well-known mark or an imitation liable to create confusion therewith.

The Panel examined the claims under Article 16.3 as follows:

Australia – Tobacco Plain Packaging *(Panel)*

7.2116. We recall our assessment ... that Article 16.3, together with Article 6*bis* of the Paris Convention (1967), formulates an obligation for Members to refuse or cancel a registration and to prohibit the use of a trademark conflicting with a registered well-known trademark that is used on non-similar goods and services under certain factual conditions. We also recall that Members' compliance with this obligation is independent of the actual occurrence of these factual conditions in the market. In light of this understanding, and in line with our assessment under Article 16.1 above, we disagree that a reduction in the factual occurrence

> **(cont.)**
>
> in the marketplace of the situations that would trigger well-known trademark protection constitutes a reduction in the availability of such protection mandated by Article 16.3 of the TRIPS Agreement and Article 6*bis* of the Paris Convention (1967). In other words, while Article 16.3 and Article 6*bis* oblige Members to protect currently well-known trademarks in the manner specified in these provisions, they do not require Members to provide such protection for trademarks that do not, or do no longer, fulfil these criteria – and not doing so is therefore not a violation of Article 16.3.

The Panel agreed with Australia that Article 16.3 does not establish a positive right to use a well-known trademark, but on the contrary, only obligates a member to provide a possibility for refusing or cancelling the registration, and of prohibiting the use of a trademark, where it conflicts with a well-known trademark or a trademark that is used on non-similar goods.[59]

7.5.2.3   Article 20 of TRIPS

A trademark owner has a legitimate interest in preserving the distinctiveness or the capacity to distinguish the relevant goods or services.[60] In relation to the plain packaging requirements, Honduras and Indonesia argued that the prohibition on the use of stylised word marks, composite marks and other figurative marks 'unjustifiably' encumbers the use of trademarks in the course of trade protected under Article 20 of the TRIPS Agreement.

> ### *TRIPS Agreement, Article 20: Other Requirements*
>
> The use of a trademark in the course of trade shall not be unjustifiably encumbered by special requirements, such as use with another trademark, use in a special form or use in a manner detrimental to its capability to distinguish the goods or services of one undertaking from those of other undertakings. This will not preclude a requirement prescribing the use of the trademark identifying the undertaking producing the goods or services along with, but without linking it to, the trademark distinguishing the specific goods or services in question of that undertaking.

---

[59] Panel Report, *Australia – Tobacco Plain Packaging*, paras. 7.2093–7.2099. See also E.-U. Petersmann, 'How to Reconcile Human Rights, Trade Law, Intellectual Property, Investment and Health Law? WTO Dispute Settlement Panel Upholds Australia's Plain Packaging Regulations of Tobacco Products', EUI Law 2018/19, European University Institute Research Repository.

[60] Panel Report, *EC – Trademarks and Geographical Indications (Australia)*, para. 7.664.

The complainants, namely Honduras, the Dominican Republic, Cuba and Indonesia, claimed that the TPP measures violated Article 20 of the TRIPS Agreement, since they imposed 'special requirements', which encumbered the use of trademarks in the course of trade; in addition, according to the complainants, the use was encumbered 'unjustifiably'.[61]

Under Article 20 of the TRIPS Agreement, a member cannot create a special requirement that reduces the distinguishing capability of a mark of one undertaking from another undertaking. First, the Panel stated that 'special requirement' means the trademark be used in a particular way or a prohibition on the use of the trademark altogether.[62] The Panel noted that 'encumbrance' means complete prohibition or the usage of the trademark in a certain way.[63] For example, if a measure prohibits the use of a trademark, it hinders or encumbers the trademark 'to the greatest possible extent'.[64] The meaning of 'use in course of trade' under Article 20 is not only limited to use on packaging of the product; it also includes a wider range of commercial, advertising and promotion activities.[65] The Panel held that TPP measures constitute a special requirement that encumbers the use of a trademark in the course of trade within Article 20.[66] Second, with respect to the adverb 'unjustifiably', the Panel noted that unjustifiable needs should be determined by taking into account the nature and extent of encumbrance, reasons for 'special requirements' including societal concern it seeks to safeguard, and whether those reasons sufficiently support the encumbrance.[67] This is akin to a 'weighing and balancing' test very commonly used in the context of the necessity test under the GATT Article XX or Article 2.2 of the TBT Agreement. The Panel held that the TPP measures are not unjustifiable as the reason supporting the encumbrance on the usage of trademark – that is, global health concerns that involve a high level of preventable morbidity and mortality are a legitimate causes of policy intervention.[68]

Australia – Tobacco Plain Packaging (Panel)

7.2604. Overall, we are not persuaded that the complainants have demonstrated that Australia has acted beyond the bounds of the latitude available to it under Article 20 to choose an appropriate policy intervention to address its public health concerns in relation to tobacco products, in imposing certain special requirements under the TPP measures that encumber the use of trademarks in the course of

---

[61] Panel Report, *Australia – Tobacco Plain Packaging*, para. 7.2132.
[62] Panel Report, *Australia – Tobacco Plain Packaging*, para. 7.2231.
[63] Panel Report, *Australia – Tobacco Plain Packaging*, paras. 7.2236–7.2239, 7.2244–7.2245.
[64] Panel Report, *Australia – Tobacco Plain Packaging*, para. 7.2236.
[65] Panel Report, *Australia – Tobacco Plain Packaging*, paras. 7.2285–7.2286.
[66] Panel Report, *Australia – Tobacco Plain Packaging*, para. 7.2292.
[67] Panel Report, *Australia – Tobacco Plain Packaging*, para. 7.2430.
[68] Panel Report, *Australia – Tobacco Plain Packaging*, paras. 7.2556–7.2574, 7.2592, 7.2604.

> *(cont.)*
>
> trade. While recognising that trademarks have substantial economic value and that the special requirements are far-reaching in terms of the trademark owners' possibilities to extract economic value from the use of figurative or stylised features of trademarks, we note that the TPP measures, including their trademark restrictions, are an integral part of Australia's comprehensive tobacco control policies, and designed to complement the pre-existing measures. As noted above, the fact that the special requirements, as part of the overall TPP measures and in combination with other tobacco-control measures maintained by Australia, are capable of contributing, and do in fact contribute, to Australia's objective of improving public health by reducing the use of, and exposure to, tobacco products, suggests that the reasons for which these special requirements are applied provide sufficient support for the application of the resulting encumbrances on the use of trademarks. We further note that Australia, while having been the first country to implement tobacco plain packaging, has pursued its relevant domestic public health objective in line with the emerging multilateral public health policies in the area of tobacco control as reflected in the FCTC and the work under its auspices, including the Article 11 and Article 13 FCTC Guidelines.

The WTO Panel accordingly rejected the Article 20 claim, arguably the strongest claim of the complainants. Overall, the Panel noted that Article 20 of the TRIPS Agreement reflects the balance between the existence of the legitimate interests of trademark owners in using such rights in the marketplace and the rights of WTO members to adopt and implement measures that seek to protect certain societal interests.[69]

7.5.3   Geographical Indications

A geographical indication (GI) or appellation of origin is a type of intellectual property that is a sign used on a product that has a specific geographical origin, process, quality or reputation that is intrinsic to its origin. Certain geographic locations may be associated with a unique product quality, aroma, taste or other characteristics. For example, champagne is associated with sparkling wine produced in the Champagne area of France. The same may apply to Darjeeling tea.

Within the TRIPS Agreement, Articles 22, 23 and 24 provide the legal framework for GI protection. The substantive provisions for the protection of patent rights are contained in Section 3 and 4 of Part II – that is, Articles 22–26 of the TRIPS Agreement.

---

[69] Panel Report, *Australia – Tobacco Plain Packaging*, para. 7.229.

Two distinct levels of protection are offered to products under the Agreement:

- GI protection for geographical indications related to all products under Article 22.2;
- GI protection for wines and spirits under Article 23.2.

Article 23 covers additional protection for both wines and spirits. Article 23.1 requires members to provide the legal means to prevent the use of the name where true geographical origin is indicated but it is not a product that is originally made in that region. Article 23.2 outlines the action that can be taken, such as refusal of registration or invalidation. The enhanced protections under Article 23 and certain exceptions under Article 24 are applicable to all wine and spirits, and not other GIs. Furthermore, under Article 23, a member can refuse or invalidate the registration of any wine or spirit trademark consisting of a false or inaccurate geographic indication. According to Article 24.5, the protection for GIs does not prejudice the registration or right to use of the trademarks that are identical or similar to a GI, when those trademarks were acquired in good faith, and before the provisions of the TRIPS Agreement came into force.

Article 23.4 states that further negotiations shall take place in the Council for TRIPS in order to facilitate the establishment of a multilateral system of notification and registration of geographical indications for wines eligible for protection in those members participating in the system. Specifically, the two issues that were debated under the Doha mandate are: creating a multilateral register for wines and spirits; and extending the higher level of protection beyond wines and spirits. Many developing members consider that the emphasis on GI in the TRIPS Agreement, especially for alcoholic beverages, is both culturally discriminatory and an impediment for collection of higher economic rent on other categories of products that are of importance to them.[70] Although these discussions have taken place over several years, no major progress has yet been made.

7.5.4 Patents

Patents are a type of intellectual property that confers on its owner the exclusive rights to products or services. Prior to the TRIPS Agreement, many countries provided only process – but not product – patents. The TRIPS Agreement provided substantive standards for patent protection for both processes and products, without limitations to the fields of technology. The Agreement specifies that the invention shall be new, involve an inventive step and is capable of industrial application.[71]

The substantive provisions for the protection of patent rights are contained in Section 5 of Part II – that is, Articles 27–34 of the TRIPS Agreement.

Article 28.1 enforces exclusive rights on the owner to the subject matter of their patent by preventing third parties from making, using, offering for sale, selling or importing products that

[70] S. Frankel and D. K. Gervais, *Advanced Introduction to International Intellectual Property* (Cheltenham: Edward Elgar, 2016), pp. 103–4.
[71] TRIPS Agreement, Art. 27.1.

are granted patents without the consent of the owner of the patent. Similarly, Article 28.2 confers exclusive rights on the owner to the subject matter of their patent by preventing third parties from using, offering for sale, selling or importing for these purposes at least the product obtained directly by that process. Patents are granted for a minimum of twenty years from the date of filing.[72]

The Agreement provides for a three-pronged exception under Article 30. The provision allows members to provide a limited exception to the exclusive rights conferred by a patent. This clause is qualified by three criteria:

1 The exceptions do not unreasonably conflict with a normal exploitation of the patent.
2 The exceptions do not unreasonably prejudice the legitimate interests of the patent owner.
3 The exceptions take into account the legitimate interest of the third parties.

The role of exceptions in relation to patents was examined in *Canada – Pharmaceutical Patents*.

Canada – Pharmaceutical Patents

Canada – Patent Protection of Pharmaceutical Products involved a complaint brought by the European Communities against Canada. The complaint targeted certain provisions under Canada's Patent Act, especially the 'regulatory review provision' (Sec. 55.2(1)) and the 'stockpiling provision' (Sec. 55.2(2)). The regulatory review provision allowed a third party to use the patent for purposes reasonably related to the development and submission of information required for the marketing approval of the new drug. Such information could expedite the release of a competing generic drug upon the expiration of the product. The stockpiling provision allowed third parties to make, construct or use the patented invention, during the applicable period, for the manufacture and storage of articles intended for sale after the date on which the patent expired.

Box 7.2 Regulatory review exceptions or 'Bolar exceptions'

The regulatory review exception is also known as the Bolar exception, after a well known case, *Roche Products* v. *Bolar Pharmaceuticals* (1984),[73] decided in the United States. The Federal Court held that 'Bolar's intended experimental use is solely for business reasons and not for amusement, to satisfy idle curiosity, or for strictly philosophical inquiry'.[74] This exception allows some pharmaceutical companies to use patents for purposes reasonably related to the development and submission of information required under the law.

Some products, like pharmaceutical products, cannot be marketed without obtaining marketing approval from the appropriate regulatory authority. A generic drug's commercial success depends on how quickly it is placed on the market after a

---

[72] TRIPS Agreement, Art. 33.   [73] *Roche Products* v. *Bolar Pharmaceuticals*, 733 F.2d 858 (1984).
[74] *Roche Products* v. *Bolar Pharmaceuticals*.

Box 7.2 (cont.)

patent expires, and the approval process can take time. In order to avoid this de facto extension of a patent term and encourage competition in the market as soon as the patent term expires, the regulatory review exception is permitted by several WTO members.

The European Communities, the complainant, contended that the provisions of the TRIPS Agreement entitled third parties to use patented inventions without the consent of the patent holder before the expiry of the patent term and, therefore, Canada was in violation of Articles 28.1 and 33.[75] It is pertinent to note that under Article 33 of the TRIPS Agreement, a patent must last no less than twenty years from the date of filing the application.

TRIPS Agreement, Article 30: Exceptions to Rights Conferred

Members may provide limited exceptions to the exclusive rights conferred by a patent, provided that such exceptions do not unreasonably conflict with a normal exploitation of the patent and do not unreasonably prejudice the legitimate interests of the patent owner, taking account of the legitimate interests of third parties.

Canada contended that these provisions relating to patents were subject to exceptions provided in Article 30 of the TRIPS Agreement. Interpreting the first prong of the Article 30 exception, the Panel held:

Canada – Pharmaceutical Patents (Panel)

7.30. ... the narrower definition is the more appropriate when the word 'limited' is used as part of the phrase 'limited exception'. The word 'exception' by itself connotes a limited derogation, one that does not undercut the body of rules from which it is made. When a treaty uses the term 'limited exception', the word 'limited' must be given a meaning separate from the limitation implicit in the word 'exception' itself. The term 'limited exception' must therefore be read to connote a narrow exception – one which makes only a small diminution of the rights in question.

The WTO Panel considered the exploitation to be 'normal' when it is 'essential to the achievement of the goals of patent policy'. Interestingly, the wording of Article 30 relating to

---

[75] Panel Report, *Canada – Patent Protection of Pharmaceutical Products*, WT/DS114/R, adopted 7 April 2000.

patents is different from the corresponding provision dealing with copyrights under Article 13 of the TRIPS Agreement.

The Panel could not agree with the EC's claim that the mere existence of the patent owner's rights to exclude was a sufficient reason, by itself, for treating all gains derived from such rights as flowing from 'normal exploitation' of the patent.[76] In the Panel's view, the EC's arguments contained no evidence or analysis addressed to the various meanings of 'normal', in the sense of demonstrating that most patent owners often extract the value of their patents in the additional period of market exclusivity that has been barred by Section 55.2(1) of the Canadian law, nor an argument that the prohibited manner of exploitation was 'normal' as being essential to the achievement of the goals of the patent policy.[77]

Canada – Pharmaceutical Patents *(Panel)*

7.45. In the Panel's view, however, Canada's regulatory review exception is a 'limited exception' within the meaning of TRIPS Article 30. It is 'limited' because of the narrow scope of its curtailment of Article 28.1 rights. As long as the exception is confined to conduct needed to comply with the requirements of the regulatory approval process, the extent of the acts unauthorized by the right holder that are permitted by it will be small and narrowly bounded. Even though regulatory approval processes may require substantial amounts of test production to demonstrate reliable manufacturing, the patent owner's rights themselves are not impaired any further by the size of such production runs, as long as they are solely for regulatory purposes and no commercial use is made of resulting final products.

   [...]

7.57. The Panel considered that Canada was on firmer ground, however, in arguing that the additional period of de facto market exclusivity created by using patent rights to preclude submissions for regulatory authorization should not be considered 'normal'. The additional period of market exclusivity in this situation is not a natural or normal consequence of enforcing patent rights. It is an unintended consequence of the conjunction of the patent laws with product regulatory laws, where the combination of patent rights with the time demands of the regulatory process gives a greater than normal period of market exclusivity to the enforcement of certain patent rights. It is likewise a form of exploitation that most patent owners do not in fact employ. For the vast majority of patented products, there is no marketing regulation of the kind covered by Section 55.2(1), and thus there is no possibility

---

[76] Panel Report, *Canada – Pharmaceutical Patents*, para. 7.58.
[77] Panel Report, *Canada – Pharmaceutical Patents*, paras. 7.57, 7.58.

(cont.)

to extend patent exclusivity by delaying the marketing approval process for competitors.

[. . .]

7.59. In sum, the Panel found that the regulatory review exception of Section 55.2(1) does not conflict with a normal exploitation of patents, within the meaning of the second condition of Article 30 of the TRIPS Agreement. The fact that no conflict has been found makes it unnecessary to consider the question of whether, if a conflict were found, the conflict would be 'unreasonable'. Accordingly, it is also unnecessary to determine whether or not the final phrase of Article 30, the calling for consideration of the legitimate interests of third parties, does or does not apply to the determination of 'unreasonable conflict' under the second condition of Article 30.

With respect to the stockpiling exception, the Panel noted that allowing unlimited production of the patent product during the term of the patent went too far and was not consistent with the Agreement.

Canada – Pharmaceutical Patents *(Panel)*

7.34. In the Panel's view, the question of whether the stockpiling exception is a 'limited' exception turns on the extent to which the patent owner's rights to exclude 'making' and 'using' the patented product have been curtailed. The right to exclude 'making' and 'using' provides protection, additional to that provided by the right to exclude sale, during the entire term of the patent by cutting off the supply of competing goods at the source and by preventing use of such products however obtained. With no limitations at all upon the quantity of production, the stockpiling exception removes that protection entirely during the last six months of the patent term, without regard to what other, subsequent, consequences it might have. By this effect alone, the stockpiling exception can be said to abrogate such rights entirely during the time it is in effect.

7.5.4.1   Term of Patent Protection

In a different case, namely *Canada – Patent Term*,[78] again involving Canada, the issue was whether Section 45 of Canada's Patent Act was inconsistent with Article 33 of the TRIPS

---

[78] Appellate Body Report, *Canada – Term of Patent Protection*, WT/DS170/AB/R, adopted 12 October 2000.

Agreement. Canada argued that since patents regularly took four to five years to issue, the grant of seventeen years of protection from the date of grant provided the same 'substantive' or 'effective' protection for the patentee as provided under Article 13.[79] The Appellate Body noted in this case that the concept of 'effective' protection did not exist in Article 33 of the TRIPS Agreement.

7.6   TRIPS Agreement and Public Health

The Doha Declaration on the TRIPS Agreement and Public Health (2001) was a major development in the field of trade and IPR.[80] There were widespread concerns that patent rules might restrict and impede access to affordable medicines, especially in developing countries that had to combat several public health emergencies, such as HIV, tuberculosis and malaria.

The Doha Declaration reaffirms that 'the TRIPS Agreement does not and should not prevent Members from taking measures to protect public health'. The Doha Declaration refers to several aspects of TRIPS, including the right to grant compulsory licences and the freedom to determine the grounds upon which licences are granted. In addition, members have the right to determine what constitutes a national emergency and circumstances of extreme urgency, and the freedom to establish the regime of exhaustion of intellectual property rights.

The Doha Declaration has also clarified the doctrine of exhaustion of rights under the TRIPS Agreement. According to the principle of exhaustion, once a patented product has been sold anywhere with the authorisation of the patent holder, the latter cannot legally prevent the subsequent sale or importation anywhere in the world.[81] Parallel importing is a concept used for importing a legally produced good from a low-priced distributor instead of buying directly from a manufacturer. The Declaration has also clarified that members are free to establish their own regime for exhaustion of IP rights, subject to the mandatory non-discriminatory clauses, such as national treatment and MFN treatment. This decision will enable countries that do not have the manufacturing facility for pharmaceuticals to import medicines from countries such as Brazil, India and Thailand, for example, under a compulsory licence, to meet their needs. The Doha Declaration is a major clarification in the context of the debate on TRIPS and access to medicines.[82]

The Doha Declaration on Public Health is a landmark decision and seeks to overcome the various difficulties that countries face in ensuring access to affordable medicines and public

---

[79] Appellate Body Report, *Canada – Patent Term*, para. 20.

[80] WTO, 'Doha Ministerial Declaration on the TRIPS Agreement and Public Health', WT/MIN(01)/DEC/2, 14 November 2001.

[81] Matsushita et al., *World Trade Organization*, pp. 654–5.

[82] J. Watal, 'Exhaustion of Rights and Parallel Importation in Intellectual Property', in Cottier and Schefer, *Elgar Encyclopedia of International Economic Law*, pp. 375–7.

health in general, without limitation to certain diseases. The WTO Panel in *Australia – Tobacco Plain Packaging* noted that the Doha Declaration on TRIPS and Public Health is a 'subsequent agreement' to the TRIPS Agreement within the meaning of Article 31(3)(a) of the Vienna Convention on the Law of Treaties.[83]

7.7   Intellectual Property Rights in New Trade Agreements

After the TRIPS Agreement entered into force in 1995, several treaties on the protection of IP rights have been concluded. The WIPO Copyright Treaty entered into force in 1996; the WIPO Performance and Phonogram Treaty also entered into force the same year; the Singapore Treaty on the Law of Trademarks was concluded in 2006 and entered into force in 2009; in the meantime, several members (around seventy-four) have acceded to the International Union for the Protection of New Varieties of Plants (UPOV). Some of these treaties have substantive IP components.

In addition to the above developments, some of the recent preferential trade agreements have set higher standards of IPR protection. These provisions are commonly referred to as 'TRIPS-plus' provisions. Generally speaking, TRIPS-plus provisions include broadening of protectable subject matter, longer periods of IP protection, special protection for biologicals, weakening of flexibilities such as tougher conditions for use of compulsory licensing, and dilution of special and differential treatment provisions.[84]

The TPP (and the renamed CPTPP) also allows evergreening as well as adjustment for patent term if the issue of patent takes more than five years from date of filing and the patent examination takes more than three years.[85] Unlike other international trade or IPR agreements, CPTPP makes express provision for the protection of encrypted program-carrying satellite and cable signals.[86] It also makes provision for internet safe harbour and strong liability for internet service providers.[87]

The recently concluded United States–Mexico–Canada Agreement (USMCA) introduces certain innovations in the field of intellectual property. A Committee on IPR under the USMCA aims to strengthen the broader enforcement of IPRs, sharing of trade secret information, fairness in patent litigation, implementation of multilateral agreements and so on.[88] It establishes a provision for pre-established damages in cases of civil proceedings concerning IPR infringement.[89] The USMCA also specifically includes a provision on adjustment in the term of the patent if there is a delay in the issuance of the patent.[90]

---

[83] Panel Report, *Australia – Tobacco Plain Packaging*, paras. 7.2407–7.2411.

[84] B. Mercurio, 'The Impact of Preferential Trade Agreements on Intellectual Property Right Protection', in Cottier and Schefer, *Elgar Encyclopedia of International Economic Law*, pp. 524–6.

[85] TPP, Art. 18.46.4. See, generally, C. Raina, 'IPR and New Rule-Making', in A. Das and S. Singh (eds.), *Trans-Pacific Partnership: A Framework for Future Trade Rules* (New Delhi: Sage, 2018), pp. 112–53.

[86] TPP, Art. 18.79.   [87] TPP, Art. 8.82.   [88] USMCA, Art. 20.B.3.2.   [89] USMCA, Art. 20.J.4.6.

[90] USMCA, Art. 20.F.9.

The EU–Canada Comprehensive Economic and Trade Agreement (CETA) is another treaty with broad IPR features. CETA confers the right to performers to either authorise or prohibit the broadcast of their work by wireless means, and makes a provision for their appropriate remuneration.[91] CETA also creates a provision for limitation of intermediary liability for copyright infringement via communication network services.[92] CETA mandates the parties to provide protection for undisclosed data relating to new and innovative pharmaceutical products and plant varieties.[93]

Intellectual property is also considered a protected investment under the investment provisions/chapters of free trade agreements. Some of the high-profile investment disputes, such as the *Australia –Tobacco Plain Packaging* challenge[94] and the Eli Lilly case,[95] involved claims on the protection of IPRs as protected investments. (See Chapter 13 for a detailed review.)

7.8   Conclusion

The linkage between trade and IP has been contested and is controversial. While defenders of IP protection insisted that widespread counterfeiting, piracy and infringement of IP rights could constitute barriers to trade, there were equally strong, compelling arguments to suggest that IP issues should be kept outside the domain of trade agreements. Although this debate is still valid, all major trade agreements, especially preferential trade agreements concluded after the creation of the WTO, have incorporated specific chapters on IP. While resistance to the inclusion of IP in trade agreements has become weaker, the nature and degrees of IP protection in trade agreements remains contentious. More specifically, the impact of patents on public health policies is a topic of continuing relevance for a large number of developing countries that may not have the domestic capability to innovate and produce newer versions of medicines.

Based on a reasonable assessment of the experience of the last twenty-five years, the TRIPS Agreement has served the interests of the international trading community by protecting innovation and creativity. The TRIPS Agreement introduced a certain harmonisation in IP standards across the globe. The Agreement also provided certain policy flexibility – for example, the definition of 'patentable subject matter' in Article 27 and some permitted exceptions. While several developing members have experienced adjustment difficulties, the strong global and local civil society movements have ensured that the Agreement is applied and enforced in a fair and equitable manner. The Doha Declaration on TRIPS and Public Health and the subsequent amendment to the TRIPS Agreement in 2017 are illustrations of how the Agreement has adapted to new realities.

As this chapter has highlighted, the TRIPS Agreement is still a work in progress, as several areas, including use of genetic resources, protection of traditional knowledge,

---

[91] CETA, Art. 20.8.   [92] CETA, Art. 20.11.   [93] CETA, Arts. 20.30, 20.39.
[94] *Philip Morris Asia Ltd* v. *Australia*, PCA case no. 2012-12.
[95] *Eli Lilly and Company* v. *Canada*, ICSID case no. UNCT/14/2.

development of disciplines on geographical indication on products other than wine and spirits, the continuation of the moratorium on non-violation, nullification and impairment complaints, are still under discussion. In addition, with the developments in technology, newer fields and challenges have emerged, including internet and digital economy, data protection and privacy and forced technology transfer. While some of these issues are addressed in preferential trade agreements, the need for multilateral engagements on some of the newer areas is worth considering.

7.9   Summary

- The TRIPS Agreement introduced enforceable and binding rules on IP protection under the aegis of the WTO. The possibility of suspension of concessions or retaliation in other sectors (for example, goods) ensured that the agreement has teeth and enforceability.
- By incorporating the provisions of the Paris Convention on Industrial Property and the Berne Convention on Copyrights, the TRIPS Agreement built on the progress achieved in several IP-related treaties.
- The TRIPS Agreement provided meaningful flexibilities, including extended timelines and transition periods for introducing IP rights. However, some of the TRIPS flexibilities are disappearing from the recent preferential trade agreements with IP chapters.
- Regulatory data protection and forced technology transfer requirements are some of the new and emerging controversial areas of IP protection.
- The extension of the moratorium on non-violation complaints is another long-standing issue under the TRIPS Agreement.
- Outside the TRIPS Agreement, negotiations on IPRs continue at the WIPO or agencies or forums such as UPOV or the Anti-Counterfeiting Trade Agreement.

7.10   Review Questions

1 What is the minimum period of patent protection provided under the TRIPS Agreement? Can a member extend this period unilaterally?

2 What is the principle laid down under the Bolar exception? (See Panel Report, *Canada – Pharmaceutical Patents*.)

3 How useful are the non-discrimination provisions under the TRIPS Agreement?

4 What is the scope of GI protection under the TRIPS Agreement? Which are the two distinct categories of GI protection in the TRIPS Agreement?

5 The Doha Declaration on the TRIPS Agreement and Public Health was a historic moment. Explain.

6 What flexibilities are available under the TRIPS Agreement for meeting public health emergencies?

7.11 Exercise

1. Minerva, a WTO member, has introduced a copyright law which has a section entitled 'Fair and Reasonable Use'. The section reads: 'Reproduction by photocopier or other similar means of parts of published works or of small works, as well as the recording of parts of films and other audiovisual works on audio or video media by educational institutions and their use for educational purposes shall not amount to copyright infringement.' It was later discovered that several photocopying centres in Minerva used to take copies of the published books and then distribute these in bulk to universities. However, the photocopying centres only charged for the cost of services and did not make any profit. Examine the legality of the measure under Article 13 of the TRIPS Agreement.

2. Fezland is a developed country with a large population and a fast-growing economy. The health care system in Fezland had been at the centre of much criticism. The activists complained that many citizens did not have proper health insurance and were unable to pay their medical bills or access expensive medicines. They demanded that the government guarantee to every Fezian citizen the right to health care. After protests broke out in support of this demand, the government decided to introduce a law guaranteeing the right to health care and amended some of the existing laws.

   An amendment was made to the Foreign Investment Act by virtue of the Foreign Investment (Amendment) Act. Amended Article 1(a) required that all foreign investors, who were preparing to invest or had already invested in Fezian pharmaceutical companies, must share patented technology and technical know-how with Fezian companies in certain situations. This had to be done through a technology transfer agreement. Moreover, under Article 1(b), all Fezian pharmaceutical companies could be asked to share patented technology or allow access to confidential data in case of a health emergency. A health emergency was defined in terms of the spread of an epidemic or an acute shortage of medicines in the domestic market, as defined under the National Epidemics Act.

   Bologia is a small but developed country that is also known as a 'start-up nation'. In the last two decades, Bologian companies have emerged as some of the largest investors in health care sectors across the globe. Bologian companies have invested heavily in the health care sector in Fezland.

   After the Foreign Investment (Amendment) Act was implemented in 2019, several Bologian companies were asked to provide access to patented technology and technical know-how through technology transfer agreements with the Fezian investee company. In the case of non-compliance, fines amounting to 5 per cent of annual net profits could be imposed for each proven incident of non-compliance. The affected Bologian companies approached the Bologian government to help them. Both Fezland and Bologia are members of the WTO. Bologia alleges that the Foreign Investment (Amendment) Act is inconsistent with Articles 3, 27, 28 and 39 of the TRIPS Agreement. Fezland defended the Foreign Investment (Amendment) Act, saying that the measure was necessary in order to guarantee access to medicines and universal health care for Fezian citizens. According to Fezland, the measure was necessary to bring foreign investors onto an equal footing with Fezian companies in terms of the government's access to patented technology and technical know-how in the pharmaceutical sector, especially in the light of COVID-19.

Draft a legal memo evaluating whether the Foreign Investment (Amendment) Act is consistent with the provisions of the TRIPS Agreement.

FURTHER READING

Correa, C., *Trade-Related Aspects of Intellectual Property Rights: A Commentary on the TRIPS Agreement* (Oxford University Press, 2007).

Frankel, S. and Gervais, D. K., *Advanced Introduction to International Intellectual Property* (Cheltenham: Edward Elgar, 2016).

Gervais, D., *The TRIPS Agreement: Drafting History and Analysis* (London: Sweet and Maxwell, 1998).

Matsushita, M., Schoenbaum, T. J., Mavroidis, P. C. and Hahn, M., *The World Trade Organization: Law, Practice, and Policy* (Oxford University Press, 2015).

Watal, J. and Taubman, A. (eds.), *The Making of the TRIPS Agreement: Personal Insights from the Uruguay Round Negotiations* (Geneva: World Trade Organization, 2015).

8 Trade in Services

Table of Contents

Highlights

- The services sector is an integral part of the global economy and has been growing dynamically since the 1990s. Statistics reveal that value added from services accounts for approximately one-third of the total manufacturing exports of developed economies.
- The General Agreement on Trade in Services (GATS) was a key achievement of the Uruguay Round. The GATS is a work in progress and negotiations continue to take place under the auspices of the Council for Trade in Services, as well as the specialised working groups formed under the mandate of the GATS.
- Four modes of supply are recognised under the GATS, namely cross-border supply, consumption abroad, commercial presence and movement of natural persons.
- The GATS includes a framework of general disciplines (such as transparency, domestic regulations) that apply to all forms of services trade and member-specific commitments listed in the schedules, which apply to specific obligations.

- General disciplines are divided into unconditional and conditional obligations, the latter being applicable only in sectors where individual members have undertaken specific commitments.
- A member's Services Schedule comprises sector-specific commitments on market access (Article XVI), national treatment (Article XVII) in each mode of supply, and the additional commitments (Article XVIII) that a member may undertake voluntarily.
- The GATS follows a 'positive list' approach and is perceived to be generally flexible. However, this inherent flexibility has also contributed to insubstantial trade commitments.
- The true benefits of GATS are yet to be fully realised. Disciplines on domestic regulations are considered to contribute to the liberalisation process.

8.1   Introduction

Services represent the fastest-growing sector of the global economy. A study by the International Monetary Fund has estimated that services constitute one-quarter of world trade.[1] In the period 1980–2015, the share of services in GDP increased in all income level groups, ranging from 61 to 76 per cent in developed economies and 42 to 55 per cent in the case of developing economies.[2]

Services form the backbone for the production of goods and services. Telecommunications, banking, insurance, construction, logistics and transportation are not only consumed in their own right, but are strategically important inputs across all sectors, including both goods and services. In the same vein, business services, such as professional services, architectural services, engineering services, real estate services, rental and leasing services, also play an important role.

The General Agreement on Trade in Services is the first multilateral trade agreement to cover trade in services. It entered into force on 1 January 1995. As outlined in its Preamble, the GATS envisages the expansion of trade in services, based on the principles of transparency, progressive liberalisation and inclusive growth. Although the GATS appears to have broad scope, it includes only a few substantive general obligations. Furthermore, it provides exemptions from these obligations based on various grounds. In fact, the GATS disciplines apply only to the sectors wherein members have undertaken commitments. Importantly, the GATS permits members to determine the extent of their commitments and obligations, based on their level of development and domestic sensitivities.

The GATS architecture includes a three-tiered structure: (1) a framework agreement that outlines the general disciplines and key substantive obligations; (2) eight annexes; and

---

[1] P. Loungani, S. Mishra, C. Papageorgiou and K. Wang, 'World Trade in Services: Evidence from a New Dataset', IMF Working Paper 17/77 (2017).

[2] UNCTAD, 'The Role of the Services Economy and Trade in Structural Transformation and Inclusive Development', Note by the UNCTAD Secretariat, Trade and Development Commission, TD/B/C.I/MEM.4/14, 6 June 2017, p. 2.

(3) schedules of specific commitments in which each member enumerates the sectors and the extent to which the commitments apply. In addition to the text, the annexes and the schedules of specific commitments form an integral part of the GATS.

Has the GATS been an underperformer? The flexibility permitted within the GATS has played its part in the GATS failing to achieve any significant liberalisation in trade in services that was envisaged at the establishment of the WTO. There is a wide gap between the existing level of openness in the services sector among most members and the commitments they have undertaken under the GATS. Some progress was made in terms of initial offers and revised offers in the early stages of the Doha Round, but members were unable to convert the progress into binding commitments. At the same time, rapid expansion of global value chains, increasing advancement in the classification of services, and technological advancements in several sectors of the services economy pose a continuing challenge to the relevance of GATS obligations.

8.2   General Agreement on Trade in Services

8.2.1   Brief Overview of the GATS

8.2.1.1   Negotiating History

In the 1980s, trade in services witnessed huge growth, despite the lack of a multilateral framework. This was spurred by advancements in technology, information and communications technology, transport and entertainment services. The advancements in technology, especially the invention of the Internet, also made the cross-border delivery of services technically feasible. At the same time, certain protectionist barriers emerged, including regulatory and administrative barriers. These barriers centred around local employment, infant industry protection, privacy concerns and regulatory freedom.

The United States pushed for the inclusion of a comprehensive framework for trade in services within the multilateral trading system.[3] During the Uruguay Round, developing countries were apprehensive of opening up the services sector and thereby compromising their regulatory space.[4] Very few market access offers were tabled during the Uruguay Round and the concessions exchanged were far short of the desired level. Interestingly, the unique architecture of the GATS admitted considerable flexibility. In addition, a number of disciplines, such as domestic regulations, emergency safeguard measures and subsidies were reserved for future negotiation. In short, the GATS remained an incomplete agreement, perhaps more than any other WTO Agreement.

---

[3] J. A. Mancheti and P. C. Mavroidis, 'The Genesis of the GATS (General Agreement on Trade in Services)', *European Journal of International Law* (2011), 22(3), pp. 689–721, at p. 692 (noting that US financial interests systematically argued in favour of a new round); see also J. E. Spero, 'Tear Down Barriers to Export of Services', *New York Times* (30 July 1991).

[4] Mancheti and Mavroidis, 'The Genesis of the GATS', p. 690.

Article XIX of the GATS embodies the idea of progressive liberalisation. The WTO members are committed to entering into subsequent rounds of trade-liberalising negotiations. The first round of these negotiations began in 2000. These were later integrated into the Doha Development Agenda, which commenced in 2001. These negotiations have faltered, owing to divergences among different groupings with conflicting interests. Despite this slow and unsatisfactory progress, many argue that 'it is possible to make improvements in the GATS, and to make it a more effective instrument of liberalization, without fundamental structural changes'.[5]

8.2.1.2 Structure of the GATS

The GATS includes the text of the Agreement (a Preamble, twenty-nine Articles categorised into six parts, and eight annexes,[6] along with an Understanding on Financial Services); and a schedule of specific commitments for each WTO member. The GATS is comprised of the following parts:

- Preamble: Basic Objectives and Principles of the GATS
- Part I: Scope and Definition
- Part II: General Obligations and Disciplines (conditional and unconditional)
- Part III: Specific Commitments
- Part IV: Progressive Liberalization
- Part V: Institutional Provisions
- Part VI: Final Provisions.

A unique feature of the GATS is that it provides members with the flexibility to determine the extent to which they would like to liberalise. The main body of the GATS outlines members' obligations concerning their use of measures (measures which may be in the form of laws, rules, regulations, procedures, decisions or administrative actions) affecting trade in services. These obligations essentially fall into two main groups: unconditional obligations that must be adhered to by all members in all the sectors covered by the GATS; and conditional obligations, the scope of which is confined only to those sectors and modes for which a member has undertaken specific commitments.

The unconditional obligations under the GATS are with respect to MFN treatment (Article II), transparency provisions (Article III), availability of legal remedies (Article VI:2), compliance of monopolies and exclusive service providers with the MFN obligation (Article VIII:1), business practices (Article IX) and subsidies that are deemed to affect trade

---

[5] A. Mattoo, 'Shaping Future GATS Rules for Trade in Services', Policy Research Working Paper 2596 (Washington, DC: World Bank, 2001), p. 5.

[6] Annex on Article II Exemptions; Annex on Movement of Natural Persons; Annex on Air Transport Services; Annex on Financial Services; Second Annex on Financial Services; Annex on Negotiations on Maritime Transport Services; Annex on Telecommunications; Annex on Negotiations on Basic Telecommunications.

(Article XV:2). Members must comply with these obligations automatically, irrespective of their schedules of commitments.

The GATS includes twelve broad categories of sectors, based on the 'Services Sectoral Classification List' (W/120) – a comprehensive list of services compiled by the GATT in July 1991.[7] The sectors include: Business and professional services; Communications services; Construction services; Distribution services; Education services; Environment services; Financial services; Health and social services; Tourism services; Recreation and cultural services; Transport services; and Other services. These sectors are further divided into approximately 160 subsectors.

8.2.1.3   Scope and Applicability

Article I of the GATS states that it applies to 'measures by Members affecting trade in services'. Measures by members would include measures taken by central, regional or local governments and authorities, and non-governmental bodies in the exercise of power delegated by central, regional, local governments or authorities.[8] It is understood that such measures not only include direct measures aimed at influencing the trade in services, but may also include any indirect or de facto restrictions affecting trade in services. The ambit of the above provision is further clarified by an illustrative list of measures contained in Article XXVIII of the GATS. Article XXVIII, clause (c) provides an inclusive list of measures that may affect trade in services.

GATS, Article XXVIII

(c) 'measures by Members affecting trade in services' include measures in respect of
   (i) purchase, payment or use of a service;
   (ii) the access to and use of, in connection with the supply of a service, services which are required by those Members to be offered to the public generally;
   (iii) the presence, including commercial presence, of persons of a Member for the supply of a service in the territory of another.

The term 'measure' itself has been defined in Article XXVIII(a) of the GATS as 'measure means any measure by a Member, whether in the form of a law, regulation, rule, procedure, decision, administrative action, or any other form'.

Affecting   The requirement for a measure to 'affect' trade in services has been identified as crucial by the WTO Appellate Body in *EC – Bananas III*.[9] The Appellate Body held that

---

[7] Group of Negotiations on Services, Uruguay Round, 'Services Sectoral Classification List: Note by the Secretariat', MTN.GNS/W/120, 10 July 1991.
[8] GATS, Art. I:3.   [9] Appellate Body Report, *EC – Bananas III*, para. 220.

the term 'affecting' has a broad scope of application, and is wider in scope than similar terms, such as 'regulating' or 'governing'.[10] The Appellate Body made the following observation in this regard:

EC – Bananas III *(Appellate Body)*

220. ... In our view, the use of the term 'affecting' reflects the intent of the drafters to give a broad reach to the GATS. The ordinary meaning of the word 'affecting' implies a measure that has 'an effect on', which indicates a broad scope of application. This interpretation is further reinforced by the conclusions of the previous panels that the term 'affecting' in the context of Article III of the GATT is wider in scope than such terms as 'regulating' or 'governing'.

In *Canada – Autos*, the Appellate Body held that the proper analysis of whether the measure is 'affecting trade in services' under Article I:1 would have required the Panel to examine all the relevant facts, including who supplies services (in this case, it was wholesale trade services of motor vehicles through a commercial presence in Canada), and how such services are supplied.[11] A somewhat debatable issue is whether the term 'affecting trade in services' applies purely in respect of the provision of services or whether it also applies to meeting various essential steps, especially obtaining government approvals, permits, authorisations and so on, which may be necessary for all or part of the process of delivering the service in question. A WTO Panel has held that measures related to the 'constitution' or 'acquisition' of a legal person within the territory of a member for the purpose of supplying a service could come within the meaning of measures 'affecting trade in services'.[12]

Trade in Services The phrase 'trade in services' is one of the crucial elements of the GATS. In the case of services, trade takes place through multiple means. A major category of international trade is cross-border supply of services, which can take place when a service is rendered by telephone, internet or other digital or other physical[13] means. In certain cases, individuals themselves travel in order to consume services in a foreign country. International tourists or students travelling to enrol in foreign universities fall within this category. Services conducted via commercial presence – that is, by establishing branches or offices – is demonstrably the most important category of trade

---

[10] Appellate Body Report, *EC – Bananas III*, para. 220.

[11] Appellate Body Report, *Canada – Autos*, paras. 163–165.

[12] Panel Report, *Argentina – Measures Relating to Trade in Goods and Services*, WT/DS453/R, Add.1, adopted 9 May 2016, as modified by Appellate Body Report WT/DS453/AB/R, para. 7.88.

[13] For example, cross-border educational or legal services performed via post or courier could fall within this category.

in services and falls broadly within the domain of investment. In other words, GATS is one of the multilateral agreements governing certain aspects of investment. In an interconnected world, a potentially significant form of delivery is cross-border movement of service providers themselves. These four modes of service delivery are captured in Article 1:2 of the GATS.

Box 8.1 Meaning of trade in services

The supply of a service

(a) from the territory of one member into the territory of any other member;
(b) in the territory of one member to the service consumer of any other member;
(c) by a service supplier of one member, through commercial presence in the territory of any other member;
(d) by a service supplier of one member, through presence of natural persons of a member in the territory of any other member.

The phrase 'supply of service' includes the production, distribution, marketing, sale and delivery of a service. This effectively includes all the steps of value addition that a service undergoes from the producer to the consumer. The underlying basis for the different means of supply of services, listed in Article I:2(a)–(d) of the GATS is the location of the service supplier and the consumer at the time of the transaction. Some examples of the four modes of supply of services are provided in Table 8.1.

Table 8.1 Modes of supply

Supplier presence	Other criteria	Mode	Examples
Service supplier *not present* within the territory of the member	Service delivered *within* the territory of the member, from the territory of another member	Mode 1 Cross-border trade	*Cross-border online education services*
	Service delivered *outside* the territory of the member, in the territory of another member, to a service consumer of the member	Mode 2 Consumption abroad	*A student moving abroad to enrol in a course*
Service supplier *present* within the territory of the member	Service delivered within the territory of the member, through the commercial presence of the supplier	Mode 3 Commercial presence	*A university setting up an offshore campus*
	Service delivered within the territory of the member, with supplier present as a *natural person*	Mode 4 Movement of natural persons	*A professor travelling to an overseas university to deliver visiting lectures*

Trade disputes are relatively few in the GATS. Nonetheless, some disputes have arisen. *Canada – Periodicals*[14] was one of the initial cases. This case defined the scope of the GATS.

CANADA – PERIODICALS

The applicability of the GATS was one of the many issues in this case. The case mainly related to a GATT claim on the importation of certain split-run periodicals into Canada. Split-run periodicals are local editions of a foreign magazine with local advertisements. For decades, Canada had imposed an import ban on foreign split-run magazines.[15] *Time* magazine and *Reader's Digest* were the only two magazines permitted to have split-run editions in Canada. However, with the innovations in technology, the contents of the periodicals were transmitted through satellites and then printed in Canada. To respond to this, Canada imposed a tax equal to 80 per cent of the value of all the advertisements contained in certain periodicals under the amended provisions of the Canadian Excise Tariff Act.[16] An obvious target of this measure was the advertisement revenue of *Sport's Illustrated*, published by *Time Warner*.[17]

The issue was whether the excise tax was imposed on a good or service, and therefore whether the GATT or the GATS should apply. Since Canada had not undertaken any commitments in respect of 'advertising services' in its GATS Schedule, Canada argued that it was not bound to provide national treatment to members for advertising services in its market.[18] Canada went a step further and argued that since Part V.I of the Excise Act was a measure on advertising services, the measure fell under the GATS and not the GATT.[19]

The Panel and later the Appellate Body rejected Canada's argument that the GATT and the GATS are mutually exclusive. The Appellate Body held that the actual target of the tax was periodicals themselves and not services.[20] Agreeing with the Panel, the Appellate Body noted at page 19: 'The entry into force of the GATS, as Annex 1B of the WTO Agreement, does not diminish the scope of application of the GATT 1994.'

The ordinary meaning of the texts of the GATT 1994 and the GATS, as well as Article II:2 of the WTO Agreement, taken together, indicate that the obligations under the GATT 1994 and the GATS can coexist and that one does not override the other. The case, incidentally, gave a landmark ruling on the meaning of the national treatment principle under Article III:2 of the GATT.

Canada – Periodicals paved the way for an expansive interpretation of the scope of the GATS, encompassing all 'measures affecting trade in services'. A similar issue arose in *EC – Bananas III.*[21]

---

[14] Appellate Body Report, *Canada – Certain Measures Concerning Periodicals*, WT/DS31/AB/R, adopted 30 July 1997.

[15] R. Eberschlag, 'Culture Class: Canadian Periodical Policies and the World Trade Organization', *Manitoba Law Journal* (1998), 26(1), pp. 65–95, at p. 66.

[16] Panel Report, *Canada – Certain Measures Concerning Periodicals*, WT/DS31/R, Corr.1, adopted 30 July 1997, as modified by Appellate Body Report WB/DS31/AB/R, para. 2.6.

[17] Eberschlag, 'Culture Class', p. 70.   [18] Appellate Body Report, *Canada – Periodicals*, p. 4, last para.

[19] Appellate Body Report, *Canada – Periodicals*, p. 4.

[20] Appellate Body Report, *Canada – Periodicals*, pp. 18–19.   [21] Panel Report, *EC – Bananas III.*

EC – Bananas III

The measure at issue was related to the legal regime within the European Communities for the importation, distribution and sale of bananas. According to the complainants (United States, Mexico, Honduras, Ecuador and Guatemala), the banana regime favoured the EC distributors and those of the traditional ACP countries.[22] The EC regime was challenged under both the GATT and the GATS. The complainants argued that the EC regime granted less favourable treatment to their suppliers of wholesale trade services of bananas compared to the EC and ACP suppliers, and thereby violated Articles II (MFN) and XVII (NT) of the GATS. However, the EC argued that the measure at issue did not fall within the scope of the GATS and therefore should be examined solely under the GATT.

In addressing this claim, the Panel first focused on whether the EC regime met the threshold requirement of falling within the ambit of the GATS. Thus, the Panel concluded that the EC regime fell within the scope of the GATS. This finding was upheld by the Appellate Body. The Appellate Body followed the observation made in *Canada – Periodicals*, reiterating that the GATT and the GATS are not mutually exclusive.

EC – Bananas III *(Panel)*

7.285. [N]o measures are excluded *a priori* from the scope of the GATS as defined by its provisions. The scope of the GATS encompasses any measure of a Member to the extent it affects the supply of a service regardless of whether such measure directly governs the supply of a service or whether it regulates other matters but nevertheless affects trade in services.

8.2.2   Non-Discrimination Obligations

8.2.2.1   Most Favoured Nation Treatment

The above discussion underlined the broad scope of application of the GATS. Part II of the GATS contains key substantive obligations that are unconditionally applicable to all the measures taken by members affecting trade in services. These include, among others, the MFN treatment (Article II), transparency (Article III), domestic regulation (Article VI) and recognition (Article VII).

The MFN obligation is applicable to all services and service suppliers (including all modes of supply of services), except where members have incorporated exemptions in accordance with the terms and conditions of the Annex on Article II exemptions.

---

[22] Panel Report, *EC – Bananas III*, para. 4.1.

GATS, Article II: Most-Favoured-Nation Treatment

1. With respect to any measure covered by this Agreement, each Member shall accord immediately and unconditionally to services and service suppliers of any other Member treatment no less favourable than it accords to like services and service suppliers of any other country.

The essential elements of the MFN principle, their interpretation and evolution in the GATS jurisprudence are discussed below.

EC – BANANAS III

EC – Bananas III is also a fairly well-cited case in relation to the MFN treatment under the GATS. (The facts have already been discussed in the previous section, as well as in Chapter 3.) One of the allegations was that the European Community market was by and large closed to US and Latin American banana distribution companies. According to the complainants, the bananas distributed in the key markets such as France, Spain and the UK were almost exclusively sourced and distributed by companies having EC or ACP interests.[23] The Panel found that the EC had undertaken commitments for wholesale trade services for both Mode 1 (cross-border supply) and Mode 3 (commercial presence) and that the EC banana regime indeed had an effect on these commitments specified in EC's services schedule. Since the discrimination was de facto, the Panel had to conduct a quantitative analysis of the EC, ACP and third-country service suppliers within the formally origin-neutral categories, to establish who received the differential treatment under the regime.

The Panel found that all the complainants' origin suppliers were classified in Category A, and suppliers of EC or ACP origin were classified in Category B, mainly for their past marketing of bananas under the EC regime. This categorisation resulted in Category A service suppliers not having the same opportunity to obtain access to import licences as Category B service suppliers. Consequently, the Panel concluded that service suppliers of the complainants were subject to less favourable conditions of competition in their ability to compete vis-à-vis service suppliers of EC or ACP origin. Accordingly, the measure was inconsistent with the GATS Articles II and XVII. The Appellate Body upheld the Panel's finding.

EC – Bananas III also examined the MFN obligation under the GATS Article II:1. The question was whether the MFN obligation under the GATS extends to de facto claims, since the measures at issue did not prima facie discriminate, but were considered discriminatory in fact. The Panel cleared up this ambiguity by stating that Article II of the GATS does apply to both de facto discrimination and de jure discrimination. On the EC's appeal on this matter, the Appellate Body upheld the Panel's finding.

---

[23] Panel Report, *EC – Bananas III*, para. 4.603.

EC – Bananas III *(Appellate Body)*

233. The GATS negotiators chose to use different language in Article II and Article XVII of the GATS in expressing the obligation to provide 'treatment no less favourable'. The question naturally arises: if the GATS negotiators intended that 'treatment no less favourable' should have exactly the same meaning in Articles II and XVII of the GATS, why did they not repeat paragraphs 2 and 3 of Article XVII in Article II? The question here is the meaning of 'treatment no less favourable' with respect to the MFN obligation in Article II of the GATS. There is more than one way of writing a de facto non-discrimination provision. Article XVII of the GATS is merely one of the many provisions in the WTO Agreement that require the obligation of providing 'treatment no less favourable'. The possibility that the two Articles may not have exactly the same meaning does not imply that the intention of the drafters of the GATS was that a de jure, or formal, standard should apply in Article II of the GATS. If that were the intention, why does Article II not say as much? The obligation imposed by Article II is unqualified. The ordinary meaning of this provision does not exclude de facto discrimination.

The nature and contours of the MFN obligation were also the subject matter of a dispute in *Canada – Autos*,[24] discussed below.

CANADA – AUTOS

In *Canada – Autos*, Japan and the EC challenged the duty-free treatment accorded by Canada to imports of motor vehicles by certain manufacturers from the US. This duty-free treatment arose out of an agreement concerning automotive products between Canada and the US (the Auto Pact). The complainants argued that the import duty exemption granted to only some manufacturers/wholesalers of motor vehicles was inconsistent with Canada's obligations under Article II of the GATS.

The Panel noted that like the measures at issue in *EC – Bananas III*, this case also involved an import duty exemption granted only to manufacturer beneficiaries, which affected conditions of competition in the supply of distribution services.[25] Therefore, in this case, the service at issue was the wholesale trade service of automobiles through commercial presence (Mode 3).

Interestingly, this case also involved the issue of de facto discrimination under both the GATT and the GATS. The complainants claimed that although the criteria for eligibility for the import duty exemption were not explicitly based on nationality, the import duty exemption constituted de facto discrimination under Article II of the GATS. As a matter of fact,

---

[24] Panel Report, *Canada – Certain Measures Affecting the Automotive Industry*, WT/DS139/R, WT/DS142/R, adopted 19 June 2000, as modified by Appellate Body Report WT/DS139/AB/R, WT/DS142/AB/R.

[25] Panel Report, *Canada – Autos*, para. 10.239.

almost all the services suppliers that benefited from the exemption were from the United States. However, Canada argued that this was not the case because two European companies and a Japanese-American joint venture company also benefited from the import duty exemption. In order to figure out the nationality of these companies, the Panel relied on the definition of a 'juridical person of another Member' under Article XXVIII(m) of the GATS. Accordingly, the Panel found that the measure at issue allowed only three US service suppliers and one Swedish service supplier to qualify for the import duty exemption.[26] Therefore, the Panel held that the Canadian measure constituted de facto discrimination and was inconsistent with Article II.

On this, Canada appealed that the Panel had failed to examine whether the measure is one 'affecting trade in services', as required under Article I:1 of the GATS. The Appellate Body was critical of the Panel's assumption that the import duty exemption enjoyed by certain manufacturers in Canada also affected wholesale trade services of motor vehicles.[27] It noted that the Panel did not examine any evidence relating to the provision of wholesale trade services of motor vehicles within the Canadian market and, hence, did not make any factual findings on the structure of Canada's market for motor vehicles.[28] Therefore, the Appellate Body reversed the Panel's conclusion that the import duty exemption is inconsistent with Article II:1 of the GATS, as well as the Panel's findings leading to that conclusion.[29]

The disputes *Canada – Autos* and *EC – Bananas III* can be considered very similar, where the services at issue were distribution services, and the respondents in both these cases also argued that the measures at issue were not actually about distribution services for goods, but about the goods themselves, and therefore the GATS should not apply. However, unlike *EC – Bananas III*, in *Canada – Autos*, the Appellate Body found the Panel's analysis to be inadequate and noted that the threshold requirement of the measure at issue falling within the scope of the GATS could not be based on a mere assumption. It requires detailed examination of relevant facts, including who supplies the service at issue and evidence of how the service is supplied, in order to determine whether a particular measure actually 'affects trade in services' within the meaning of Article I:1.[30]

As specified above, Article II:2 of the GATS enables a member to maintain measures inconsistent with MFN treatment as long as such measures are listed in and meet the conditions of the Annex on Article II Exemptions. The Annex on Article II Exemptions allowed members to seek exemptions not exceeding a period of ten years.[31] As stipulated under the Annex on Article II Exemptions attached to the GATS, MFN exemptions should terminate at the date provided for the exemption and should not exceed ten years. It is understood that such exemption may be redundant going forward, although most of the members who have scheduled such exemptions have not automatically terminated them. Additionally, another exception to the MFN obligations enshrined under Article V of the

---

[26] Panel Report, *Canada – Autos*, para. 10.261.   [27] Appellate Body Report, *Canada – Autos*, paras. 164, 165.
[28] Appellate Body Report, *Canada – Autos*, para. 163.   [29] Appellate Body Report, *Canada – Autos*, para. 171.
[30] Appellate Body Report, *Canada – Autos*, paras. 151–167.   [31] Annex on Article II Exemptions, para. 6.

GATS, which is similar to the GATT (Article XXIV), is the opportunity to enter into free trade agreements between members.

8.2.3 National Treatment

Article XVII of the GATS, which embodies the national treatment principles, provides as follows:

GATS, Article XVII: National Treatment

1. In the sectors inscribed in its Schedule, and subject to any conditions and qualifications set out therein, each Member shall accord to services and service suppliers of any other Member, in respect of all measures affecting the supply of services, treatment no less favourable than it accords to its own like services and service suppliers.[10]
2. A Member may meet the requirement of paragraph 1 by according to services and service suppliers of any other Member, either formally identical treatment or formally different treatment to that it accords to its own like services and service suppliers.
3. Formally identical or formally different treatment shall be considered to be less favourable if it modifies the conditions of competition in favour of services or service suppliers of the Member compared to like services or service suppliers of any other Member.

[Original footnote 10] Specific commitments assumed under this Article shall not be construed to require any Member to compensate for any inherent competitive disadvantages which result from the foreign character of the relevant services or service suppliers.

National treatment obligations under the GATS originate primarily from the specific commitments that members undertake in their schedules with respect to specific sectors and modes of delivery of service. For the sectors committed, a Member cannot formulate and apply laws, regulations and policies that discriminate foreign services and service suppliers from domestic ones. In other words, a measure that discriminates explicitly on the basis of the origin of the service or service supplier would constitute a formal de jure violation of national treatment. It is a well-established principle in GATT law that, if the origin of the product is the 'sole criterion' for distinction of the goods, a detailed examination of likeness based on the traditional *Border Tax Adjustments* criteria is not required.[32]

---

[32] Panel Report, *India – Measures Affecting the Automotive Sector*, WT/DS146/R, WT/DS175/R, Corr.1, adopted 5 April 2002, para. 10.74; Panel Report, *Turkey – Measures Affecting the Importation of Rice*, WT/DS3334/R, adopted 22 October 2007, para. 7.21; Panel Report, *Canada – Measures Relating to Exports of Wheat and Treatment of Imported Grain*, WT/DS276/R, adopted 27 September 2004, upheld by Appellate Body Report WT/DS276/AB/R, para. 6.164.

The same principle also applies to the GATS.[33] (See discussion on *Argentina – Financial Services* below.)

Unlike in the GATT, in the GATS, members have flexibility to undertake only qualified national treatment obligations. In other words, members are entitled to include qualifications or conditions in the national treatment obligations to limit the scope of application to particular sectors or modes of supply. Thus, while both MFN and national treatment are non-discrimination obligations, MFN is a general obligation and national treatment (Article XVII) is a specific obligation.

Importantly, according to Article XVII:2, a member may provide 'either formally identical or formally different treatment' to foreign services and service suppliers vis-à-vis the domestic services and service suppliers. Article XVII:3 further clarifies that a treatment will be considered no less favourable if 'it modifies the conditions of competition' in favour of services or service suppliers of a member compared to like services or service suppliers of any other member. Articles XVII:2 and XVII:3 thus include a de facto national treatment obligation.

Box 8.2 Limitation of national treatment (example)

Under telecommunication services, for the issuance of a licence, a mandatory requirement of a minimum period of residence can be considered a limitation. Such a limitation could be protected by including it within the schedule of commitments.

The meaning of the national treatment obligation was further elaborated by the Appellate Body in *China – Electronic Payment Services*.[34]

CHINA – ELECTRONIC PAYMENT SERVICES

In this case, the US challenged several Chinese requirements relating to electronic payment services under the GATS. Electronic payment services include payment and money transmission services, such as credit, charge and debit cards, traveller's cheques and bankers draft's. In this case, the United States had challenged a host of Chinese measures that established requirements for electronic payment services. The measures at issue, among others, mandated the use of China Union Pay (CUP) and/or established CUP as the sole supplier of all electronic payment services for all domestic transactions denominated and paid in renminbi (RMB). In addition, China had imposed a requirement for all the point-of-sale (POS) equipment to have interoperability with the CUP payment network/system. It also mandated the use of the CUP logo for all automated teller machines (ATMs), merchant card-processing equipment and POS terminals. The United States argued that the net effect

---

[33] See also Appellate Body Report, *Argentina – Measures Relating to Trade in Goods and Services*, WT/DS453/AB/R, Add.1, adopted 9 May 2016, para. 6.36.

[34] Panel Report, *China – Certain Measures Affecting Electronic Payment Services*, WT/DS413/R, Add.1, adopted 31 August 2012.

of these measures led to an economy-wide monopoly of CUP. This dispute arose in light of the unique position that CUP had built for itself in the Chinese electronic payment system market, which led to it being the third largest electronic payment services network globally, along with Visa and Mastercard, while overtaking American Express.[35]

The Panel in *China – Electronic Payments* laid out the following requirements in order to demonstrate a violation of Article XVII of the GATS.

China – Electronic Payments *(Panel)*

7.641. ... Accordingly, in order to sustain its claim that China's measures are in breach of Article XVII, the United States as the complaining party needs to establish all of the following three elements:

(i) China has made a commitment on national treatment in the relevant sector and mode of supply, regard being had to any conditions and qualifications, or limitations, set out in its Schedule;

(ii) China's measures are 'measures affecting the supply of services' in the relevant sector and mode of supply; and

(iii) China's measures accord to services or service suppliers of any other Member treatment less favourable than that China accords to its own like services and service suppliers.

On Article XVII claims, the Panel first made an assessment of whether the services supplied by CUP and the US electronic payment services companies, namely Mastercard and Visa, were 'like'. This claim required an analysis of whether the services in question were essentially the same in competitive terms.[36] The Panel examined all the relevant evidence, including the memorandum and articles of association, annual reports and prospectus of CUP and other electronic payment services suppliers. Although the evidence provided by the US was not extensive, it was sufficient to raise a presumption that the electronic payment services provided by CUP and the US suppliers were essentially the same in competitive terms.[37] The Panel came to the conclusion that China's requirements modified the conditions of competition in favour of CUP and were inconsistent with Article XVII of the GATS.

8.2.3.1   The 'Likeness' Test

'Likeness' is a key element of Article XVII. The GATS, like the GATT 1994, does not specifically incorporate the definition of 'likeness' to determine whether the services in

---

[35] P. Delimatsis, 'The WTO Outlaws the Privileges of the Chinese Payment Services Giant', *American Society of International Law Insights* (2012), 16(31).

[36] Panel Report, *China – Electronic Payment Services*, para. 7.702.

[37] Panel Report, *China – Electronic Payment Services*, para. 7.704.

question are alike. The GATS jurisprudence has also remained fairly underdeveloped in this area.

The 'likeness' determination under the GATS was tested in *EC – Bananas III*. According to the complainants, the various measures under the EC banana regime had an impact on the wholesale trade services that they could supply through commercial presence. Such an impact, the complainants argued, was inconsistent with the unqualified national treatment commitment in the EC's schedule, covering the supply of 'wholesale trade services' in relation to Mode 3, commercial presence. To explain, the supply of wholesale trade services covered activities associated with reselling bananas, as described in the headnote to Section 6 of the Central Product Classification, which included 'maintaining inventories, physically assembling, sorting, grading in large lots, breaking bulk, redistribution in smaller lots, refrigeration and delivery services'.[38]

EC – Bananas III *(Panel)*

7.322. The nature and the characteristics of wholesale transactions as such, as well as each of the different subordinated services mentioned in the headnote to section 6 of the CPC, are 'like' when supplied in connection with wholesale services, irrespective of whether these services are supplied with respect to bananas of EC and traditional ACP origin, on the one hand, or with respect to bananas of third country or non-traditional ACP origin, on the other. Indeed, it seems that each of the different services activities taken individually is virtually the same and can only be distinguished by referring to the origin of the bananas in respect of which the service activity is being performed. Similarly, ... to the extent that entities provide these like services, they are like service suppliers.

To summarise, according to the Panel in *EC – Bananas III*, wholesale transactions, as well as each of the different subordinate categories of services mentioned in the headnote to section 6 of the CPC, are 'like' when supplied in connection with wholesale services.

The recent Panel and Appellate Body rulings in *Argentina – Financial Services*[39] addressed the circumstances in which 'likeness' can be presumed.

ARGENTINA – FINANCIAL SERVICES
Argentina – Financial Services has provided some important clarifications on the general jurisprudence on 'likeness', as well as the specific issue of 'presumption of likeness' within the GATS. The case involved eight measures implemented by Argentina addressing financial, taxation, foreign exchange and registration measures, which allegedly affected services and services suppliers from jurisdictions (for example, Panama) that do not exchange

---

[38] Panel Report, *EC – Bananas III*, para. 7.294.   [39] Panel Report, *Argentina – Financial Services*.

information with Argentina for purposes of tax transparency, or prevention of money laundering and terrorist financing. Argentina labelled such jurisdictions as 'non-cooperative', whereas 'cooperative' jurisdictions were those that had an agreement with Argentina for the effective exchange of information or that enabled potential negotiation of such agreements. Panama contended that differential treatment accorded under the measure at issue to services and service suppliers violated the non-discrimination provisions under the GATS. With respect to three of the eight measures, the Panel found that Argentina did not accord non-discriminatory treatment to the 'like' services and services suppliers of non-cooperative countries and, hence, violated the MFN obligation under the GATS.

Argentina appealed the Panel's findings that the services and services suppliers at issue were 'like' under the GATS Articles II and XVII. The Panel, for instance, had taken into account the regulatory aspects or concerns that could potentially justify the application of the inconsistent measure in the 'likeness' determination.

Argentina – Financial Services *(Panel)*

7.514. [A] central issue in this dispute is whether the exchange of tax information between Argentina and other non-cooperative jurisdictions constitutes a regulatory aspect that modifies the conditions of competition on the Argentine market in such a way that it converts different and, in principle, less favourable treatment into 'treatment no less favourable'.

According to the Panel, such concerns could affect the 'conditions of competition'.[40] However, the Appellate Body overturned the Panel's finding and found that the regulatory aspects or objectives need not be influencing the 'likeness' determination.

Argentina – Financial Services *(Appellate Body)*

6.136. In our view, although the Panel used the words 'modify the conditions of competition' ..., the Panel's consideration of the relevant regulatory aspects does not actually speak to the question of whether the measures at issue modify the conditions of competition to the detriment of services and service suppliers of non-cooperative countries. Indeed, ... the Panel had already concluded that the measures at issue modify the conditions of competition in such a manner. In the Panel's analysis of the 'regulatory aspects', we do not find any assessment of the implications of these measures for the competitive

---

[40] Appellate Body Report, *Argentina – Financial Services*, paras. 7.493, 7.494.

> ***(cont.)***
>
> opportunities of the services and service suppliers of non-cooperative countries vis-à-vis those of cooperative countries. Rather, in analysing the relevant 'regulatory aspects', the Panel appears to have been looking at something akin to the second step of the analysis regarding 'treatment no less favourable' under Article 2.1 of the TBT Agreement, as developed in the relevant jurisprudence. Although the Panel did not use such words to describe its analysis, statements made by the Panel indicate that the Panel was effectively looking at whether the detrimental impact on like services and service suppliers, which it had already established, 'stems exclusively from a legitimate regulatory distinction', even though such an analytical step is not foreseen under the GATS non-discrimination clauses.

According to the Appellate Body, examination of the regulatory aspects was an additional step of inquiry that was not envisaged by the GATS. In the view of the Appellate Body, where a measure is inconsistent with non-discriminatory provisions, regulatory aspects or concerns that could potentially justify such a measure are more appropriately addressed in the context of the relevant exceptions.

The Appellate Body reversed the Panel's finding that the services and services suppliers of cooperative countries were 'like' the services and services suppliers of non-cooperative countries because it failed to make a finding that the difference in treatment was based 'exclusively' on origin (the 'presumption of likeness' approach). In the absence of a finding that the measures at issue provide for a distinction based exclusively on origin, and by failing to conduct an analysis of 'likeness' on the basis of the arguments and evidence presented by Panama, the Appellate Body noted that the Panel had erred. But the Appellate Body did not determine for itself whether the services at issue were 'like'.

The Appellate Body, however, noted that the determination of 'likeness' could be a more complex task in the context of the GATS when compared to its counterpart, the GATT 1994, especially considering the role that domestic regulation may play in shaping, for example, the characteristics of services and services suppliers and consumer preferences.[41]

In addition, the Panel committed a legal error by making a prima facie case for Panama in the absence of evidence and legal argument. The Appellate Body reversed the Panel's conclusion on both Articles II and XVII of the GATS.[42]

---

[41] Appellate Body Report, *Argentina – Financial Services*, para. 6.39.
[42] Appellate Body Report, *Argentina – Financial Services*, paras. 6.71, 6.80.

8.3   Market Access

Article XVI of the GATS incorporates the provision on market access.

> ### GATS, Article XVI: Market Access
>
> 1. With respect to market access through the modes of supply identified in Article I, each Member shall accord services and service suppliers of any other Member treatment no less favourable than that provided for under the terms, limitations and conditions agreed and specified in its Schedule.

Market access commitments under the GATS also fall within the category of specific commitments. Thus, their application is limited with respect to the service sectors that are inscribed in a member's schedule. For sectors not listed, a member would not be subject to any of the market access obligations.

8.3.1   Scope of Market Access in the GATS

Considering the fact that services have a much broader coverage than goods and are traded across four different modes of supply, market access in the GATS has certain inherent complexities. Under Mode 1 (cross-border supply), the service is delivered across the border, similar to goods. Under Modes 2 and 4, the consumer or the provider of the service will have to cross the border. Mode 3 is similar to investment, in as much as the capital crosses the border. Therefore, a member has to make commitments in a given sector with respect to each of the four modes of supply of services.

8.3.1.1   Conditions Prohibited

In addition to the general provision on market access enshrined in Article XVII:1, Article XVII:2 prohibits certain conditions that restrict market access. These measures cannot be applied unless they have been inscribed in the specific conditions or qualifications of a member's schedule of commitments. These measures have been listed in Table 8.2.

Specifically, rules, regulations or laws in the form of restrictions, such as those allowing only a specified number of branches within the territory of a member, are prohibited unless they are inscribed in the member's schedule.

Some of the GATS disputes have addressed the issue of market access violations. In 2003, Antigua and Barbuda brought a dispute against the US concerning certain violations of

Table 8.2 Market access limitations (prohibited unless scheduled in the GATS)

GATS Article	Market access limitations	Illustrative examples
XVI(a)	Limitations on the number of service suppliers, whether in the form of numerical quotas, monopolies, exclusive service suppliers or the requirements of an economic needs test	Limitation on the opening of foreign bank branches to 10
XVI(b)	Limitations on the total value of service transactions or assets in the form of numerical quotas or the requirement of an economic needs test	Investment by a foreign company in another company not to exceed 30 per cent of the invested company's capital
XVI(c)	Limitations on the total number of service operations or the total quantity of service output expressed in terms of designated numerical units in the form of quotas or the requirement of an economic needs test	Restrictions on the broadcasting time available for foreign films
XVI(d)	Limitations on the total number of natural persons that may be employed in a particular service sector or that a service supplier may employ and who are necessary for, and directly related to, the supply of a specific service in the form of numerical quotas or the requirement of an economic needs test	Board of directors cannot include more than 30 per cent non-citizens
XVI(e)	Measures that restrict or require specific types of legal entity or joint venture through which a service supplier may supply a service	Only institutions incorporated with threshold capital base eligible to seek authorisation for services supply
XVI(f)	Limitations on the participation of foreign capital in terms of maximum percentage limit on foreign shareholding or the total value of individual or aggregate foreign investment	A company registered for a given service sector must not exceed 25 per cent total equity

market access for cross-border recreational services under the GATS. The *US – Gambling*[43] dispute is discussed below.

US – GAMBLING

US – Gambling is one of the landmark decisions dealing with the scope of market access and is also the first WTO dispute to deal with the Internet and e-commerce.[44] Antigua and Barbuda, a tiny island nation, challenged several US federal and state laws, including the Wire Act, the Travel Act and the Illegal Gambling Business Act (IGBA), which prohibited the provision of cross-border gambling and betting services to US consumers from online gambling services situated outside the United States. Antigua and Barbuda brought its complaint to the WTO, after Jay Cohen, a US citizen and operator of an Antigua and Barbuda-based internet sports book service, World Sports Exchange, was jailed in the US

---

[43] Panel Report, *United States – Measures Affecting the Cross-Border Supply of Gambling and Betting Services*, WT/DS285/R, adopted 20 April 2005, as modified by Appellate Body Report WT/DS285/AB/R.

[44] D. A. Irwin and J. H. Weiler, 'Measures Affecting the Cross-Border Supply of Gambling and Betting Services (DS 285)', *World Trade Review* (2005), 7(1), pp. 71–113, at p. 73.

for the remote supply of gambling services, in violation of the 1961 US Wire Communications Act.[45] This dispute involved a number of substantive GATS provisions: Articles XVI (Market Access), XVII (National Treatment) and XIV (General Exceptions). The discussion on the exceptions (invoked by the US under Article XIV to justify its measure) is included in Chapter 9.

Antigua and Barbuda argued that the United States had made full market access commitments on cross-border supply (Mode 1) of gambling and betting services. In other words, the United States had inscribed 'none' in the market access column under the heading of 'Other Recreational Services (except sporting)'. The precise US commitment on gambling was ambiguous, since the US schedule did not provide any reference to 'gambling'. Antigua and Barbuda contended that the measures at issue constituted limitations within Article XVI:2(a) and (c) of the GATS, thereby violating US commitments. The United States argued that none of the measures at issue specified any numerical units, and it was not in the form of quotas.

The Panel held that the US measures prohibiting the use of one, several or all means of delivery included in Mode 1 constituted a 'zero quota', which acted as a limitation for the service suppliers for those means of delivery and was inconsistent with Article XVI:2(a) and (c). Hence, the US measures provided less favourable treatment than that provided for in its schedule, contrary to the terms of Article XVI of the GATS.

The United States appealed the Panel ruling. In its view, the complainant had not identified the precise source of 'prohibition' on the cross-border supply of gambling and betting services. According to the United States, the Panel had ignored the meaning of *form* and *numerical quotas*, and had erroneously included measures that had the *effect* of limiting the number of service suppliers within the scope of Article XVI:2(a) of the GATS. Responding to the US argument, the Appellate Body observed:

US – Gambling *(Appellate Body)*

227. The words 'in the form of' in sub-paragraph (a) relate to all four of the limitations identified in that provision. It follows, in our view, that the four types of limitations, themselves, impart meaning to 'in the form of'. Looking at these four types of limitations in Article XVI:2(a), we begin with 'numerical quotas'. These words are not defined in the GATS. According to the dictionary definitions provided by the United States, the meaning of the word 'numerical' includes 'characteristic of a number or numbers'. The word 'quota' means, inter alia, 'the maximum number or quantity belonging, due, given, or permitted to an individual or group'; and 'numerical limitations on imports or exports'. Thus, a 'numerical quota' within

---

[45] J. Pauwelyn, 'Rien ne Va Plus? Distinguishing Domestic Regulation from Market Access in GATT and GATS', *World Trade Review* (2005), 4(2), pp. 131–70.

> **(cont.)**
>
> Article XVI:2(a) appears to mean a quantitative limit on the number of service suppliers. The fact that the word 'numerical' encompasses things, which 'have the characteristics of a number', suggests that limitations 'in the form of a numerical quota' would encompass limitations which, even if not in themselves a number, have the characteristics of a number.

In a finding of the Panel, which was upheld by the Appellate Body, it was found that US federal laws, by prohibiting the cross-border supply of gambling and betting services where specific commitments had been undertaken, amounted to a 'zero quota'. The measures, accordingly, fell within the scope of, and were prohibited by Article XVI:2(a) and (c). In this case, the individual measures in themselves need not give rise to a violation, but the cumulative effect of the measures is to bring about a violation of the GATS commitment.[46] In other words, Article XVI captures not only quantitative restrictions, but also measures that take a different form but have an equivalent effect.[47] The Appellate Body upheld the Panel's decision concerning US federal laws, but reversed similar findings of the Panel relating to the state laws, as Antigua and Barbuda failed to establish a prima facie case in respect of such laws.[48]

China – Publications and Audiovisual Products

This dispute involved a series of Chinese measures regulating the importation and distribution of certain audiovisual products and services, such as reading materials, audiovisual home entertainment, sound recordings and films for theatrical release.[49] The United States alleged that these measures violated GATS Articles XVI and XVII. Specifically, the United States claimed that the Chinese rules governing the electronic distribution of sound recordings prohibited foreign-invested enterprises from engaging in that service sector and accordingly violated China's commitments[50] on 'Sound recording distribution services'.

According to China, the scope of the commitment covered only the distribution of sound recording in physical form, such as compact discs, but not by electronic means. While relying on the principle of *dubio mitius*, China argued that it cannot be assumed that a sovereign State intends to impose upon itself the more onerous, rather than the less

---

[46] Irwin and Weiler, 'Cross-Border Supply of Betting and Gambling Services', p. 82.

[47] E. H. Leroux, 'Twenty Years of GATS Case Law: Does it Taste Like a Good Wine?', in P. Sauvé and M. Roy (eds.), *Research Handbook on Trade in Services* (Cheltenham: Edward Elgar, 2016), pp. 191–215.

[48] U. Turksen and R. Holder, 'Contemporary Problems with the GATS and Internet Gambling', *Journal of World Trade* (2015), 49(3), pp. 457–93.

[49] Panel Report, *China – Measures Affecting Trading Rights and Distribution Services for Certain Publications and Audiovisual Entertainment Products*, WT/DS363/R, Corr.1, adopted 19 January 2010, as modified by Appellate Body Report WT/DS363/AB/R.

[50] The People's Republic of China, 'Schedule of Specific Commitments', GATS/SC/135, 14 February 2002.

burdensome obligations.[51] China claimed that electronic distribution constituted a new service, which did not exist at the time of negotiation. Therefore, China's GATS commitment could not be interpreted to include it.

The Panel rejected China's argument based on its assessment of China's Schedule of Commitments in accordance with Articles 31 (General Rule of Interpretation) and 32 (Supplementary Means of Interpretation) of the VCLT. In light of the object and purpose, the Panel held that China's commitment on sound recording distribution services included the supply of such services 'electronically', and did not limit the commitments to only those supplied through a physical, tangible medium.[52] The Panel finally held that the Chinese measures were inconsistent with respect to Articles XVI and XVII of the GATS.

China appealed the Panel's findings, arguing, inter alia, that the Panel erred in interpreting China's GATS schedule. The Appellate Body upheld the Panel's findings. While relying on the finding in *US – Gambling*, the Appellate Body referred to the 1993 Scheduling Guidelines, the W/120 Classification List and the 1991 UN Provisional Central Product Classification for evaluating the scope of 'Sound recording distribution services' under China's schedule.

Importantly, the Appellate Body noted that a product can simultaneously have a goods and a services component and that a measure could be subject to both the GATT and the GATS to the extent that it affects 'goods' or 'services'. This approach indicates a cumulative interpretation of the GATT and the GATS.[53]

Box 8.3 Technological neutrality

When the GATS was drafted, the commercial use of the Internet was gradually taking root and could not be fully assessed by the negotiators. However, a few years later, WTO members examined whether the existing modes of supply under the GATS covered electronic deliveries or not. In the discussion regarding the Work Programme on Electronic Commerce, which began in 1998, a general view among members was that the GATS was *technologically neutral*, as it does not contain any provisions distinguishing between the different technological means of supplying a service.[54] However, some delegations were of the view that these issues were complex and needed further examination.[55]

---

[51] Panel Report, *China – Publications and Audiovisual Products*, para. 7.1165. This principle was discussed in Appellate Body Report, *EC – Hormones*, fn. 154.

[52] Panel Report, *China – Publications and Audiovisual Products*, para. 7.1171.

[53] J. Pauwelyn, 'Squaring Free Trade in Culture with Chinese Censorship: The WTO Appellate Body Report on China – Audiovisuals', *Melbourne Journal of International Law* (2006), 11(2), pp. 119–40, at 127.

[54] Work Programme on Electronic Commerce, Progress Report to the General Council, adopted by the Council for Trade in Services on 19 July 1999, S/L/74 (27 July 1999).

[55] Work Programme on E-Commerce, para. 4.

Box 8.3 (cont.)

While relying on the Work Programme on E-Commerce, the Panel in *US – Gambling* held that the GATS includes within its scope the supply of services through any means of delivery, including the Internet. Further, in *China – Publications and Audiovisual Products*, the Appellate Body confirmed this view. However, this still remains contentious.[56]

Another issue in the GATS with the advancement in technology is the integration of Mode 5 of service supply under the schedule of commitments. Under Mode 5, the service supplied forms an integral part of the goods being traded internationally. Since such services are bundled with goods, the framework on trade in goods is made applicable on them therefore limiting their liberalisation. However, as the aforesaid modes of services delivery are a pure creation of the GATS, creating a new mode would require fresh negotiations or renegotiations, which seems unlikely.

CHINA – ELECTRONIC PAYMENT SERVICES

In this case, the US challenged China's measures relating to electronic payment services for payment card transactions for violating Articles XVI:1, XVI:2(a) and XVII of the GATS. The US argued that China imposed limitations, despite having made market access (MA) and NT commitments in Modes 1 and 3 in subsector 7(d) on Banking and other financial services,[57] which covered the supply of electronic payment services. The Panel found that China had undertaken MA and NT commitments in Mode 3, but not in Mode 1.[58]

One of the main issues was on the scope of Article XVI:2(a). The US claimed that six legal requirements (as listed by the US) established and maintained CUP as both a 'monopoly' supplier and an 'exclusive service supplier' for all RMB bank card transactions in respect of Article XVI:2(a). China argued that the scope of Article XVI:2(a) extended only to 'quantitative' or 'quantitative-type measures'.[59] The Panel relied on *US – Gambling* and held that even a measure that is not a 'quota' can fall within the scope of Article XVI:2(a), if it is quantitative in its thrust and limits the supply of a service in the same way as a quota does. The Panel then proceeded to evaluate the measures individually, examining their consistency with Article XVI:2(a).

The Panel noted that CUP enjoyed exclusivity as the sole electronic payment services supplier only in certain relevant transactions, and for those transactions CUP acted as a monopoly.[60] Accordingly, it found that certain Chinese measures at issue imposed a

---

[56] S. Smith, 'GATS and Technology Neutrality', South Centre Workshop on E-Commerce and Domestic Regulation (Geneva, 2017); J. Kelsey, *Serving Whose Interests? The Political Economy of Trade in Services Agreements* (Abingdon and New York: Routledge-Cavendish, 2008).

[57] 'Services Sectoral Classification List'.

[58] Panel Report, *China – Electronic Payment Services*, paras. 7.573, 7.633–7.634.

[59] Panel Report, *China – Electronic Payment Services*, para. 7.584.

[60] Panel Report, *China – Electronic Payment Services*, para. 7.623.

limitation on the number of service suppliers in the form of a monopoly within the meaning of Article XVI:2(a) of the GATS for the supply of electronic payment services for RMB bank card transactions. The Panel hence concluded that this limitation on service suppliers imposed by China did not meet the qualification requirements specified in China's Mode 3 MA entry in its schedule and was therefore inconsistent with Article XVI:2(a) of the GATS.

Box 8.4 Overlapping GATS obligations and scheduling concerns

It is important to draw a line between measures that constitute de facto MA limitations within Article XVI of the GATS and those that fall outside its scope. This can be tricky, since there are scenarios where it may overlap with other GATS obligations. For example, certain regulatory measures may have the same effect as a quota or other limitation, as spelled out in Article XVI:2, but may fall broadly within the category of qualitative as opposed to quantitative. Such measures would be beyond the scope of Article XVI and might fall under Article XVII on national treatment or under Article VI on domestic regulation.[61]

Interestingly, in case of overlap between MA and NT, Article XX:2 of the GATS states that '[m]easures inconsistent with both Articles XVI and XVII shall be inscribed in the column relating to Article XVI'. This language suggests that Article XX:2 contemplates overlap between measures prohibited by both Articles XVI and XVII, namely, those quantitative restrictions enumerated in Article XVI:2(a)–(d) which are also discriminatory against foreign services or suppliers and any restrictions covered by XVI:2(e)–(f), which are inherently discriminatory.

In *China – Electronic Payment Services*, China had undertaken full NT commitments (i.e. inscribed 'None') and no commitments under MA (i.e. inscribed 'Unbound') under Mode 1 in Banking and other financial services. Therefore, an interpretative issue arose as to whether measures inconsistent with both Articles XVI and XVII should be evaluated based on the existence of a NT commitment, or on the absence of an MA commitment. The Panel noted that unlike Article XVII, the scope of MA is limited to six defined categories of measures and does not extend to 'all measures affecting the supply of services'. Importantly, the Panel held that Article XX:2 of the GATS establishes a *scheduling* primacy that the obligations in Article XVI:2 can extend to measures that are also within the scope of Article XVII.[62] In other words, the Panel found that China's MA entry concerning subsector (d) and Mode 1 allowed it to maintain measures in that subsector and mode that are inconsistent with both Articles XVI and XVII.

---

[61] Leroux, 'Twenty Years of GATS Case Law'.
[62] Panel Report, *China – Electronic Payment Services*, para. 7.664.

Box 8.4 (cont.)

To Go Further

R. Block, 'Market Access and National Treatment in *China – Electronics Payment Services*: An
Illustration of the Structural and Interpretative Problems in GATS', *Chicago Journal of
International Law* (2014), 14(2), p. 652.

8.4 Other Provisions and Concerns under the GATS

This chapter has focused largely on the relatively substantive provisions of the GATS that
have been challenged under the WTO dispute settlement system. The other provisions,
although in the form of soft obligations, are significant, nevertheless. These provisions serve
multiple functions and aim at: streamlining the supply of services through expedited application procedures, establishment of enquiry points and so on (Articles III:4, IV:2 and VI);
and developing future disciplines on domestic regulation (Article VI), emergency safeguards
(Article X), government procurement (Article XIII) and so on. However, these provisions
have lost their significance as the multilateral negotiations have gone astray. Overall, the
GATS is still considered an incomplete contract, having been drafted in a somewhat
ambiguous manner with built-in agendas, which are yet to be finalised.[63]

The GATS has not achieved its liberalising objectives for a number of reasons. The
flexibilities allow parties to undertake obligations that are way below the existing openness
in their services sector. In addition, unlike the GATT, quantitative restrictions are possible if
adequately scheduled. Furthermore, like the HS classification for goods, a proper classification methodology is yet to emerge for services in GATS. To top it all, a number of
obligations are soft obligations or best endeavour clauses.

Some of the key provisions of the GATS are explored below.

8.4.1 Article V: Economic Integration Agreements

Article V of the GATS allows economic integration or regional agreements. Article V is an
exception to the MFN obligation embodied under Article II. This exception is on the same
lines as Article XXIV:4 of the GATT 1994. The essential requirements within Article V are
twofold: (1) the agreements must have substantial sectoral coverage (understood in terms of
factors such as volume of trade affected, number of sectors covered and so on); and (2) such

---

[63] H. Horn, G. Maggi and R. W. Staiger, 'Trade Agreements as Endogenously Incomplete Contracts', NBER
Working Paper 12745 (National Bureau of Economic Research, 2006); Delimatsis, 'WTO Outlaws Privileges of
Chinese Payment Services Giant', p. 6.

agreements provide for the elimination of substantially all discrimination between the parties (in a national treatment sense).

Considering the increasing proliferation of free trade agreements, Article V of the GATS is critical. While Article V is in the nature of an exception to the fundamental MFN obligation, the requirements of 'substantial sectoral coverage' and 'elimination of substantially all discrimination' ensure that the services liberalisation has to be a deep economic integration.

8.4.2 Article VI: Domestic Regulation

The Preamble to the GATS recognises members' right to 'regulate, and to introduce new regulations on the supply of services within their territories in order to meet national policy objectives'. Article VI strikes a balance in this regard by stipulating a number of general disciplines protecting the legitimate right of members to regulate for public policy reasons, while ensuring that such measures (such as qualification and licensing requirements, technical standards) do not constitute unnecessary trade barriers. Article VI of the GATS requires members to comply with the fundamental principles of transparency and due process. The provision contains both conditional and unconditional obligations.

Article VI:4 provides the Council for Trade in Services with the mandate to develop necessary disciplines aimed at ensuring that measures relating to qualification requirements and procedures, technical standards and licensing requirements do not constitute 'unnecessary barriers to trade in services'. The GATS Council in 1998 adopted the first and only set of disciplines under Article VI:4, applicable to domestic regulation in the accountancy sector.[64] However, these disciplines did not take immediate legal effect.

A Working Party on Domestic Regulation (WPDR) was established in 1999 for the purpose of the negotiations, replacing the Working Party in Professional Services.[65] The WPDR was entrusted with developing horizontal disciplines that shall be applicable to all service sectors under the GATS. However, there has been little or no development in the negotiations on domestic regulation. In the Eleventh WTO Ministerial Conference, held in Buenos Aires in December 2017, proposals on domestic regulations were on the agenda. To date, no outcome has been achieved by the WPDR on developing domestic regulation disciplines. On the other hand, a Joint Ministerial Statement by fifty-eight WTO members was presented in 2017 in Buenos Aires to strengthen the Disciplines on Domestic Regulation, pursuant to the mandate under Article VI:4 of the GATS.[66] Since then, around

---

[64] Disciplines on Domestic Regulation in the Accountancy Sector, Decision of the GATS Council of 14 December 1998, S/L/64.

[65] Decision on Domestic Regulation, adopted by the Council for Trade in Services on 26 April 1999, S/L/70 (28 April 1999).

[66] 'Communication from Albania; Argentina; Australia; Canada; Chile; China; Colombia; Costa Rica; The European Union; Hong Kong; China; Iceland; Israel; Japan; The Republic of Kazakhstan; The Republic of Korea; Liechtenstein; The Former Yugoslav Republic of Macedonia; Mexico; The Republic of Moldova; Montenegro; New Zealand; Norway; Peru; The Russian Federation; Switzerland; The Separate Customs Territory of Taiwan, Penghu, Kinmen and Matsu; Turkey; Ukraine; and Uruguay: Disciplines on Domestic Regulation', Ministerial Conference, Eleventh Session, Buenos Aires, WT/MIN(17)/7/Rev.2, WT/GC/190/Rev.2, 13 December 2017.

sixty-three members who are part of the Joint Initiative have met regularly at the WTO[67] and have formulated their draft indicative schedules.[68]

8.4.3 Article VII: Recognition

Recognition, in simple terms, is acceptance of the standards, qualifications and so on of foreign service suppliers. As a matter of fact, countries have absolute discretion in accepting or rejecting the applications of foreign service suppliers for not meeting the required or even desired criteria. Naturally, this also has a risk of members using such measures for protectionist purposes. In practice, a better level of services liberalisation requires certain cohesiveness in the regulatory regimes of the various members (in addition to disciplines governing the autonomous regimes of members).

Article VII of the GATS, in furtherance of the above-mentioned objective, encourages members to enter into mutual recognition agreements or arrangements with other members for the purpose of recognising the education or experience achieved, or the standards, licences or certification granted in particular member States. Importantly, Article VII is non-binding, so long as it does not result in a disguised restriction on trade.

8.4.4 Payments and Transfers

Article XI:1 of the GATS states that 'a Member shall not apply restrictions on international transfers and payments for current transactions relating to its specific commitments. The purpose of Article XI is to preserve the value of specific commitments undertaken by members under GATS. However, a carve-out has been provided in Article XII of the GATS whereby members may maintain restrictions on international transfers and payments to safeguard their balance-of-payments on account of serious external financial difficulties or threat thereof. In addition, the GATS Annex on Financial Services permits members to implement measures to ensure the stability of financial systems.

Payments and transfers is one area where members will be guided by the Articles of Agreement of the International Monetary Fund, and the provisions of the GATS provided certain deference to the IMF. Payment and transfers directly affecting current transactions fall within the jurisdiction of the IMF. Article VIII, Section 2(a) of the Articles of Agreement of the IMF provides that 'no [IMF member] shall, without the approval of

---

[67] The membership of the Joint Initiative on Services Domestic Regulation was sixty-three in December 2020, with Thailand the last to participate; see WTO, 'Thailand Joins Negotiations on Services Domestic Regulation, available at www.wto.org/english/news_e/news20_e/jssdr_11nov20_e.htm (accessed 21 December 2020).

[68] 'Progress on the JSIs: Communication by the Co-ordinators of the JSIs', available at www.wto.org/english/news_e/news20_e/jsec_18dec20_e.pdf; see also WTO, 'Coordinators of Joint Initiatives Cite Substantial Progress in Discussions', available at www.wto.org/english/news_e/news20_e/jsec_18dec20_e.htm (both accessed 21 December 2020).

the Fund, impose restrictions on the making of payments and restrictions for current international transactions'. However, the IMF approves such measures only in the case of a serious balance of payments crisis.

8.4.5   Article XIX: Negotiation of Specific Commitments

Article XIX is unique as it obligates members to negotiate a progressively higher level of liberalisation. Such a mandate for future negotiation does not feature in other agreements, including the GATT and the TRIPS. Article XIX:2 introduces certain flexibility to developing countries by giving due consideration to the level of development and national policy objectives of members.

Article XI:3 attempts to streamline the negotiations by mandating the development of negotiating guidelines and procedures. The Council for Trade in Services, as required by Article XIX:3 of the GATS, approved the Guidelines and Procedures for the Negotiations on Trade in Services in a Special Session.[69] Article XIX:4 provides members with the flexibility of conducting bilateral, plurilateral or multilateral negotiations for increasing the overall level of specific commitments.

The services negotiations began on 1 January 2000, in accordance with Article XIX:1 of the GATS. Later, the services negotiations were integrated into the Doha Round. Unfortunately, there has been little to no progress on this front.

8.5   Specific Obligations and Scheduling

As against some of the general obligations discussed above, the GATS provides members with the flexibility (both in terms of extent and the type of sectors/subsectors covered) to undertake commitments on the obligations in Part III of the GATS, namely market access (Article XVI), national treatment (Article XVII) and additional commitments (Article XVIII).

Article XX of the GATS requires each member to submit a schedule of commitment, but does not prescribe the sector scope or the extent of liberalisation. Members have the option of limiting their commitments in the sectors they list. Article XX specifies the core elements that must be covered in a member's schedule and provides that the schedules form 'an integral part' of the GATS.[70] Article XX:1 of the GATS reads as follows:

---

[69] 'Guidelines and Procedures for the Negotiations on Trade in Services', adopted by the Special Session of the Council for Trade in Services on 28 March 2001, S/L/93.

[70] GATS, Art. XX:3.

GATS, Article XX:1: Schedule of Specific Commitments

1. Each Member shall set out in a schedule the specific commitments it undertakes under Part III of this Agreement. With respect to sectors where such commitments are undertaken, each Schedule shall specify:
   (a) terms, limitations and conditions on market access;
   (b) conditions and qualifications on national treatment;
   (c) undertakings relating to additional commitments;
   (d) where appropriate the timeframe for implementation of such commitments; and
   (e) the date of entry into force of such commitments.

It is important to note that these commitments specify the minimum level of market access and national treatment granted in a specific sector and may not necessarily reflect the actual conditions.

Interestingly, Article XX does not indicate the method of scheduling commitments. While Article XXVIII (e) defines the term 'sector', it does not explain how the service sectors are to be scheduled. In fact, details regarding the scheduling of commitments in services is contained in the Scheduling Guidelines of 1993 (revised in 2001)[71] and the 'Services Sectoral Classification List'.[72] The latter consists of twelve core service sectors that are subdivided into a total of around 160 subsectors and is based on the more refined United Nations Provisional Central Product Classification (UN CPC Provisional).[73] As members were allowed flexibility in specifying the extent of their commitments, to ensure consistency in language and terminology, these documents were significant.[74] The GATS also includes other internationally recognised ad hoc classifications, like the Annex on Financial Services, Annex on Air Transport, the Telecom Model Schedule and the Maritime Model Schedule.[75]

With time, the GATS has increasingly been faced with a challenge regarding the classification and scheduling of services. The Classification List has failed to keep up with the advancements in classification made at the UN CPC level. Its subsequent revisions were never taken up and adopted in the GATS, although members are not prevented from

---

[71] Group of Negotiations on Services, Uruguay Round, 'Scheduling of Initial Commitments in Trade in Services: Explanatory Note, Addendum', MTN.GNS/W/164,/Add.1, 30 November 1993; WTO, Trade in Services, 'Guidelines for the Scheduling of Specific Commitments under the GATS', adopted by the Council for Trade in Services on 23 March 2001, S/L/92.

[72] 'Services Sectoral Classification List'.

[73] Department of International Economic and Social Affairs, Statistical Office of the United Nations, 'Provisional Central Product Classification', Statistical Papers Series M, No. 77 (New York: United Nations, 1991).

[74] Panel Report, *US – Gambling*.

[75] 'Guidelines for the Scheduling of Specific Commitments under the GATS', para. 23.

using further revisions of UN CPC Provisional.[76] This lack of adaptability of the Classification Lists becomes problematic in the identification of newer sectors, given the evolving nature of services.[77]

The Schedule of Specific Commitments is also relatively complex when compared to tariff schedules. While a tariff schedule lists tariff rates per product, a services schedule contains at least eight entries in each sector – that is, a commitment each on market access and national treatment across the four modes of supply, in each service sector.

Accordingly, each GATS Schedule has four columns that specify the following: (1) Description of committed sector or subsector; (2) Market access limitations under Article XVI; (3) National treatment limitations under Article XVII; and (4) Additional commitments under Article XVIII. The sample schedule of XYZ country in Table 8.3 illustrates this.

Table 8.3 Sample schedule of commitments for country XYZ

Modes of supply: (1) Cross-border supply; (2) Consumption supply; (3) Commercial presence; (4) Presence of natural persons

Sector or subsector	Limitations on market access	Limitations on national treatment	Additional commitments
I. Horizontal commitments			
All sectors included in this schedule	(4) Unbound, other than for: (a) temporary presence, as intra-corporate transferees, of essential senior executives and specialists; and (b) presence for up to 120 days of representatives of a service provider to negotiate sales of services	(3) Authorisation is required for acquisition of land by foreigners	
II. Sector-specific commitments			
Tourism and travel-related services A. Hotels and other lodging services (CPC 641 – 643)	(1) None (2) None (3) None, except that establishment of commercial presence would only be through incorporation of company in XYZ (4) Unbound, except as indicated in horizontal section	(1) None (2) None (3) None (4) Unbound	

[76] For example, the United Nations updated the Central Product Classification and released CPC Version 2.1 on 11 August 2015. However, GATS Schedules continue to refer to the 1991 'Provisional Central Product Classification', which makes it difficult to identify the scope of commitments in light of technological developments in the services sector today.

[77] Delimatsis, 'WTO Outlaws Privileges of Chinese Payment Services Giant', p. 6.

In a GATS schedule, the terms 'none' and 'unbound' are significant:

- **None** (full commitment): Inscribing 'none' implies that the member undertakes not to limit market access or national treatment in a given sector and mode of supply through any inconsistent measure.[78] The term 'none' means full commitment.[79]
- **Unbound**' (no commitment): Inscribing 'unbound' implies that the member retains absolute flexibility to introduce or maintain any measures inconsistent with market access and/or national treatment obligations for the given sector and modes.[80] In *China – Electronic Payment Services*, the Panel noted that the term 'unbound' would indicate an absence of constraint or obligation.[81]

It is pertinent to note that the Council for Trade in Services has adopted guidelines for scheduling specific commitments under GATS.[82] When 'none' or 'unbound' is not specified next to a particular sector and mode of supply, it implies that the member is providing some degree of commitment while specifying limitations.[83] Further, members are also entitled to list conditions and limitations that apply across all scheduled sectors. These are referred to as horizontal commitments.[84] Importantly, the sector-specific commitments in each mode of supply are subject to the horizontal commitments for that mode. The commitments for 'tourism and travel-related services' in the sample schedule for country XYZ are illustrated below:

- **Mode 1**: Full commitments for both market access and national treatment.
- **Mode 2**: Full commitments for both market access and national treatment.
- **Mode 3**: Limited commitment for market access, since establishment of commercial presence is allowed only through incorporation of company in XYZ. Full sector-specific commitment for national treatment, but subject to horizontal limitation specifying requirement for authorisation for acquisition of land by foreigners.
- **Mode 4**: Limited commitments for market access only to the extent specified in the horizontal commitments. No commitments for national treatment.

US – GAMBLING

This case has been discussed in the section on market access. It may be pertinent here to note that the WTO Panel interpreted the meaning and scope of 'betting and gambling services' as inscribed in the GATS schedule of commitments of the United States.[85] The relevant extract of the United States GATS schedule is reproduced in Table 8.4.

---

[78] 'Guidelines for the Scheduling of Specific Commitments under the GATS', para. 42.
[79] Appellate Body Report, *US – Gambling*, para, 215.
[80] 'Guidelines for the Scheduling of Specific Commitments under the GATS', para. 46.
[81] Panel Report, *China – Electronic Payment Services*, para. 7.652.
[82] 'Guidelines for the Scheduling of Specific Commitments under the GATS'.
[83] 'Guidelines for the Scheduling of Specific Commitments under the GATS', para. 44.
[84] 'Guidelines for the Scheduling of Specific Commitments under the GATS', para. 36.
[85] The United States of America, 'Schedule of Specific Commitments', GATS/SC/90, 15 April 1994, p. 72.

Table 8.4 US GATS schedule on recreational, cultural and sporting services

Sector or subsector	Limitations on market access	Limitations on national treatment
10. Recreational, cultural and sporting services		
A. Entertainment services (including theatre, live bands and circus services)	1) None 2) None 3) None 4) Unbound, except as indicated in the horizontal section	1) None 2) None 3) None 4) None
B. News agency services	[...]	[...]
C. Libraries, archives, museums and other cultural services	[...]	[...]
D. Other recreational services (except sporting)	1) None 2) None 3) The number of concessions available for commercial operations in federal, state and local facilities is limited 4) Unbound, except as indicated in the horizontal section.	1) None 2) None 3) None 4) None

For interpreting the United States' GATS Schedule, the Panel relied on the customary rules of treaty interpretation, embodied in Articles 31 and 32 of the VCLT,[86] an approach previously employed by panels for interpreting members' GATT schedules. The Panel found the context for the GATS schedules to be contained in the document W/120 and the 1993 Scheduling Guidelines.[87] The Panel concluded that subsector 10.D of the US schedule included specific commitments on gambling and betting services. The Panel based its evaluation on W/120, which refers to UN CPC Provisional 964 and includes CPC subclass 96492, entitled 'Gambling and betting services'.[88] The US appealed the finding.

In its appeal, the United States alleged that the Panel erred in treating the documents W/120 and the 1993 Scheduling Guidelines[89] as relevant context within the meaning of Article 31(2) of the VCLT. Principally, the United States argued that these documents were drafted by the GATT Secretariat, not by the parties themselves, and therefore did not form the relevant context for interpreting the US schedule. Importantly, this argument was upheld by the Appellate Body. Nonetheless, the Appellate Body held that W/120 and the 1993 Scheduling Guidelines constituted 'supplementary means of interpretation' under Article 32 of the VCLT.[90]

The US further argued that gambling and betting services were excluded from the scope of 'other recreational services', since it had included the phrase 'except sporting'.[91] The Appellate Body noted that the UN CPC Provisional classification that corresponds to 'Sporting services'

---

[86] Appellate Body Report, *US – Gambling*, para. 159.   [87] Panel Report, *US – Gambling*, para. 6.82.

[88] Panel Report, *US – Gambling*, para. 6.93.

[89] Group of Negotiations on Services, Uruguay Round, 'Scheduling of Initial Commitments in Trade in Services: Explanatory Note', MTN.GNS/W/164, 3 September 1993, para. 19.

[90] Appellate Body Report, *US – Gambling*, para. 196.   [91] Appellate Body Report, *US – Gambling*, para. 158.

(CPC 9641) does not include gambling and betting services, which instead fall under the Class 'Other recreational services' (CPC 9649).[92] Accordingly, the Appellate Body rejected the US appeal on this issue and upheld the Panel's conclusions, albeit for different reasons.[93]

This dispute clarified that the interpretation of a GATS Schedule requires a holistic approach where the panels must have recourse to a range of interpretative elements, including context, object, purpose of the treaty and its preparatory work.

A major difficulty in using the old service classification system is that such system often fails to capture the various types of services that are being delivered today or will be delivered tomorrow. The issue of development and lack of adaptability could be addressed through the principle of *technological neutrality*. Notably, the Panel in this dispute concluded that Mode 1 includes all means of delivery and noted that 'this is especially so in sectors and sub-sectors where cross-border supply is effected essentially . . . through the internet'.[94]

Box 8.5 Scheduling methodology

There are two ways to schedule sector-specific commitments in a member's schedule of commitments in a trade agreement. First is the GATS-like 'positive' style of scheduling, in which members inscribe the sectors that are covered and/or restricted (to whatever extent). Second is the 'negative' style of scheduling that is largely witnessed in the newer FTAs, which, in an ideal form would list only the sectors that are restricted or not open and the corresponding measures (non-conforming measures).[95] The proponents of the negative listing methodology of scheduling state that such style allows for the coverage of new service sectors that were not conceptualised at the time the agreement was negotiated. However, in practice, members often carve out unrecognised or technologically unfeasible services from their commitments through their horizontal commitments.

8.6 Conclusion

Although the GATS has been in existence for more than two decades, jurisprudence on GATS is scarce and is evolving only gradually. Out of the 598 WTO disputes that have been initiated since 1995, only 30 involve violations of the GATS provisions.[96] Out of these, only

---

[92] Appellate Body Report, *US – Gambling*, paras. 198–201.   [93] Appellate Body Report, *US – Gambling*, para. 213.

[94] Panel Report, *US – Gambling*, para. 6.287.

[95] For greater certainty, 'non-conforming measures' could be understood as measures that are exempt from the substantive obligations of the trade in services chapter.

[96] WTO, Chronological list of disputes cases, available at www.wto.org/english/tratop_e/dispu_e/dispu_status_e.htm (accessed 21 December 2020).

eight disputes have resulted in Panel and/or Appellate Body Reports that have been adopted by the DSB. On substantive issues, GATS jurisprudence has contributed to resolving certain fundamental issues regarding the interpretation and application of the GATS, in areas such as Article XVI (Market Access), Article XVII (National Treatment) and Article II (MFN).[97]

The novelty of service-related issues, especially the application of the positive listing rule, has resulted in reluctance of members to make any substantial progress in negotiations after the entry into force of the GATS.[98] In addition, the commitments undertaken under the GATS are significantly below the liberalisation that most members have autonomously pursued. Further, given the overlap between commercial presence under the GATS and investment protection under bilateral investment treaties, most members pursue liberalisation goals outside the context of the GATS and in different fora. While GATS has substantial liberalising potential in regard to services, the progress achieved in certain areas, such as Mode 4 (movement of natural persons), is disappointing. In addition to the extremely low level of commitments in Mode 4, the benefits originally envisaged under this mode are denied to labour-resourceful countries on the ground that the GATS does not apply to measures affecting movement of natural persons seeking access to the employment market of a member. Notably, other disciplines, such as subsidies and emergency safeguard measures, are yet to be developed in the GATS. These asymmetries have to be addressed if the GATS is to achieve its true potential.

8.7   Summary

- The GATS consists of a framework of general rules and disciplines (including annexes addressing individual sectors and modes) and commitments on market access and national treatment listed in each member's schedule of commitments.
- The obligations fall into two main groups: unconditional obligations, which apply across the board, and 'conditional obligations', which apply only to those sectors and modes for which a member has undertaken commitments.
- The scope of GATS extends to all measures affecting trade in services, with the exception of services supplied in the exercise of governmental authority, and measures affecting air traffic rights and services directly related.
- Each member is required to submit a schedule of specific commitments specifying the limitations on market access (Article XVI), conditions on national treatment (Article XVII) and any additional obligations (Article XVIII) in each subsector and mode of supply.
- Article XVI:2 of the GATS provides an exhaustive list of six categories of restrictions that must not be maintained, unless specifically scheduled as an MA limitation.

---

[97] Leroux, 'Twenty Years of GATS Case Law', pp. 203–7.
[98] Delimatsis, 'WTO Outlaws Privileges of Chinese Payment Services Giant', p. 14.

- Article XVII of the GATS mandates WTO members not to discriminate between 'like' domestic and foreign services and service suppliers. It extends to formally identical and formally different treatment – that is, it includes both de jure and de facto discrimination.
- In the event of a claim under Article II or XVII, a 'likeness' analysis must be conducted as a threshold issue. A presumption of 'likeness' arises if the sole criterion of distinction is the place of origin of the service.
- During the Uruguay Round, members relied upon the 1993 Scheduling Guidelines, the W/120 and the 1991 UN CPC Provisional for scheduling. These documents have been used as supplementary means of interpretation under the customary rules of interpretation.
- The GATS has several negotiating mandates, including Article X (Emergency Safeguard Measures), Article XIII (Government Procurement), Article XV (Subsidies), Article VI (Domestic Regulation) and Article XIX (Negotiations of Specific Commitments). Among these topics, disciplines on domestic regulation have received increased attention in recent times.

8.8   Review Questions

1 What is the scope of the GATS? (Refer to *EC – Bananas III.*)

2 In *EC – Bananas III*, the measure at issue was challenged both under the GATT and the GATS. What is the threshold requirement for challenging a measure under the GATS? What is the relationship between the GATT and the GATS? (Refer to *Canada – Periodicals*).

3 In *EC – Bananas III*, the measure at issue was challenged as prima facie origin-neutral. However, the Panel and later the Appellate Body held that the EC was inconsistent with Articles XVII and II of the GATS. How did the Panel come to the conclusion that there was a violation of Articles XVII and II? Is the same standard applicable for both Articles XVII and II, even though there is a difference in language in the provisions?

4 In *Canada – Autos*, why did the Appellate Body reverse the decision of the Panel that there was a violation of Article II of the GATS, although the dispute was similar to the *EC – Bananas III* case?

5 What are the supplementary materials available to interpret a member's GATS schedule of commitments? (Refer to *US – Gambling* and *China – Publications and Audiovisual Products.*)

6 What types of measures are to be scheduled under Article XVI:2(a)–(f)? Please provide examples for each subparagraph. (Refer to Scheduling Guidelines (S/L/92).)

7 In the light of *US – Gambling*, what constitutes a limitation in the form of a numerical quota under Article XVI:2 of the GATS?

8 In *China – Publications and Audiovisual Products*, China had undertaken commitments under Mode 1 for sound recording services. What do we mean by 'technological neutrality' of the GATS? Provide examples.

9 In light of *China – Electronic Payment Services*, is it reasonable to conclude that there is an overlap between Articles XVI and XVII of the GATS?

10 What comprises the threshold test of 'likeness' in any claim under Articles XVII and II of the GATS? What does the 'presumption of likeness' mean? (Refer to *Argentina – Financial Services* and *China – Electronic Payment Services*.)

11 What is the test to determine 'treatment no less favourable' under Article XVII? (Refer to *China – Publications and Audiovisual Products*, *China – Electronic Payment Services* and *Argentina – Financial Services*.)

8.9   Exercises

Exercise 1

Boshland and Kolabia are members of the WTO. Boshland is a developed country and the world leader in providing entertainment services; it has several popular bands and DJs that are constant chart toppers. Kolabia is a rapidly growing developing country.

Bhut Entertainment Services Team Ltd (BEST), an entertainment services and event management company based in Bhut, the cultural hub of Boshland, was incorporated in 2010. BEST organises all sorts of events (such as concerts, award shows, weddings and theatre) and has quickly become a very successful enterprise around the globe. BEST is renowned for organising elaborate international music festivals and bringing the music of the Bosh bands and DJs to many countries.

BEST has a wholly owned subsidiary in Kolobo, Kolabia, called BEST-K, which provides entertainment services across the territories of Kolabia. BEST-K was incorporated in 2015 and received the approval from the Entertainment Ministry. BEST-K has organised several events in Kolabia, including its national film industry's function, KOL Awards, and the wedding of the Kolabian President's daughter.

In December 2019, BEST is planning to organise its flagship music festival, BESTIES, in Kolobo, capital of Kolabia. BESTIES festivals will be taking place simultaneously in four other countries around the world. BESTIES will not only include performances by famous musicians, but will also broadcast live performances from all the other BESTIES at each venue.

Meanwhile, the Kolabian government implemented the following different measures:

1 Enhancement of Culture Act, which requires that at least two Kolabian folk musicians be engaged in the event of any musical programme or festival.

2 Entertainment Act Amendment, which prohibits the supply of cross-border entertainment services.

3 Entertainment Act Rules that specify that ownership and control of a company approved by Entertainment Ministry must remain at all times in the hands of resident Kolabian citizens or companies, which are owned and controlled by resident Kolabian citizens.

In view of these new legal changes, BEST is unable to organise BESTIES in Kolabia. Aggrieved, BEST has approached the Boshland Trade Ministry to help them deal with the measures implemented by the Kolabian government.

You work at the Boshland Trade Ministry and have been asked to assess whether Boshland can challenge these measures implemented by Kolabia under the GATS. Accordingly, you have been requested to draft a legal brief evaluating whether any of the Kolabian measures are inconsistent with Articles XVI and XVII of the GATS.

Kolabia's Schedule of Commitments is provided below.

Kolabia: GATS schedule of specific commitments (original schedule, 1995)

Sector or subsector	Limitations on market access	Limitations on national treatment
All sectors included in the schedule		4) Unbound
Sector-specific commitments		
A. Entertainment services (including theatre and live bands) (CPC 9619*)	1) None 2) None 3) None, except commercial presence is only through incorporation of a company and with the approval of the Entertainment Ministry 4) Unbound, except as indicated in the horizontal commitments	1) Unbound 2) None 3) None 4) None

* Kolabia has no additional commitments in the above schedule.

Exercise 2

Boshland and Kolabia are members of the WTO. Boshland is a developed country and the world leader in providing education services. Boshland has several internationally acclaimed and highly accredited universities and educational institutions. Kolabia is a developing country with one of the fastest-growing economies. The major population demographic in Kolabia is between the ages of eighteen and thirty-five years.

Every year, a large number of students from Kolabia are admitted to the universities of Boshland to pursue studies at undergraduate and graduate level. However, students from Kolabia prefer the educational institutions of Arkina. Arkina is also a WTO member and a developing country with a high growth rate. Arkina is also becoming a leader in providing education services. In Arkina, Kolabian students form 45 per cent of the overall foreign student demographic.

In December 2019, to facilitate higher education for its citizens, Kolabia implemented a programme that subsidised the education fee for Kolabian students who travel to Boshland to pursue higher education. The programme stipulates that if a Kolabian student gets accepted into an educational institution ranking within the top twenty of Boshland (as published on the website of the Ministry of Human Resources of Boshland), half of the academic tuition will be borne by the Government of Kolabia. The implementation of such programme led to a decline in the number of students travelling from Kolabia to Arkina to pursue education. Also, news reports from

Arkina suggest that the education industry in Arkina is in decline, due to the non-availability of students from Kolabia.

Draft a legal brief, evaluating whether any of the Kolabian measures are inconsistent with Articles II, XVI and XVII of the GATS. You may need to refer to other chapters and include any possible defences that Kolabia might invoke.

Kolabia's relevant GATS schedule of commitments is provided below.

Kolabia: GATS schedule of specific commitments (original schedule, 1995)

Sector or subsector	Limitations on market access	Limitations on national treatment
All sectors included in the schedule		4) Unbound
Sector-specific commitments		
A. Other higher education services (CPC 92390*)	1) Unbound 2) None 3) None, except that the number of persons who can pursue medical degrees will be limited depending on the total supply of doctors 4) Unbound, except as indicated in the horizontal commitments	1) None 2) None 3) None 4) Unbound

* Kolabia has no additional commitments in the above schedule.

FURTHER READING

Cossy, M., 'Determining "likeness" under the GATS: Squaring the circle?', WTO Staff Working Paper ERSD-2006-08 (Geneva: World Trade Organization, Economic Research and Statistics Division, September 2006).

Delimatsis, P., 'Trade in Services and Regulatory Flexibility – Twenty Years of GATS, Twenty Years of Critique', TILEC Discussion Paper No. 2015-016 (Tilburg Law and Economics Center, 2015).

Marchetti, J. A. and Mavroidis, P. C., 'The Genesis of the GATS', *European Journal of International Law* (2011), 22(3), pp. 689–721.

Munin, N., *Legal Guide to GATS* (Alphen aan den Rijn: Wolters Kluwer, 2010).

Pauwelyn, J., 'Rien Ne Va Plus? Distinguishing Domestic Regulation from Market Access in GATT and GATS', *World Trade Review* (2005), 4(2), pp. 131–70.

Sauvé, P. and Roy, M., *Research Handbook on Trade in Services* (Cheltenham: Edward Elgar, 2016).

Turksen, U. and Holder, R., 'Contemporary Problems with the GATS and Internet Gambling', *Journal of World Trade* (2015), 49(3), pp. 453–93.

9 Trade Exceptions

Table of Contents

Highlights

- Trade exceptions protect the State's normative autonomy in allowing derogations from its trade obligations under certain precise conditions.
- Trade exceptions are generally categorised in four groups: general exceptions, security exceptions, economic emergency exceptions and regional trade exceptions.
- General exceptions (GATT 1994, Article XX and GATS Article XIV) are the most widely referred to and, as such, the main topic of this chapter.
- The consistency of general exceptions and security exceptions within the WTO regime has been largely discussed and interpreted by the WTO DSB.
- Other areas of international economic law, such as international investment law, also draw upon the GATT Article XX type of exceptions.

9.1   Introduction

In a trade context, exceptions are conceived as a way to protect certain fundamental policy objectives of the State. These exceptions preserve the State's autonomy to regulate for public policy purposes by offering a margin to adjust domestic policies to various societal goals, for instance, health, environment, labour or public morals. The State's independence to legislate is protected. The State may derogate from its international trade obligations when trade liberalisation, market access or the principles of non-discrimination or other obligations directly conflict with various sovereign choices and rights. As a matter of fact, WTO members are allowed to enact trade-restrictive legislation and other measures deviating from their GATT 1994 and GATS obligations in a general or specific manner. However, these legislative and restrictive measures have to be adopted only under specific conditions. These 'conditions', expressed in a number of criteria, vary according to the importance of the measure and the societal interests that it promotes. The general exceptions in the GATT/GATS have been subjected to intense scrutiny by the WTO dispute settlements panels.

Among the trade exceptions, general exceptions are the most widely referred to, most frequently invoked exception in trade disputes. Nevertheless, it is important to note that trade exceptions are generally categorised in four groups: general exceptions (GATT 1994 Article XX and GATS Article XIV), security exceptions (GATT 1994 Article XXI and GATS Article XVI*bis*), economic emergency exceptions (balance-of-payment measures and safeguard measures) and regional trade agreement exceptions. We have discussed this second group of exceptions briefly in other parts of this book (Chapters 2 and 6).

9.2   General Exceptions

9.2.1   Main Features

Article XX of the GATT 1994 permits a WTO member to maintain certain measures, which would otherwise be inconsistent with WTO obligations. In particular, Article XX of the GATT 1994 seeks to exempt governmental measures taken, for example, to protect public morals; protect human, animal or plant life or health; discourage products of prison labour; prevent deceptive practices or conserve natural resources.

The Article XX subparagraphs reflect broad public policy goals, which are either constituent or part of the measure being challenged as inconsistent with specific WTO rules. The scope of Article XX of the GATT 1994 is also considered to be sufficiently broad. Importantly, Article XX chapeau contains the words 'nothing in this agreement', indicating it could be available with respect to any obligations under the GATT 1994.

Interestingly, in 1948, the Commercial Policy chapter of the Havana Charter for an International Trade Organization had already included an exception clause quite similar to the general exceptions we now find under the GATT 1994.[1] Article 45 of the Havana Charter (General Exceptions to Chapter IV – Commercial Policy) also included a preamble, conceived to prevent the abuse of such exceptions. The preambular part of the GATT 1994 Article XX, or the introductory paragraph, is known as the chapeau (literally meaning 'hat'). The chapeau has a particular importance in the application of the general exceptions. In addition to this chapeau, specific exceptions are provided in a list under paragraphs (a)–(j).

GATT 1994, Article XX: General Exceptions

Subject to the requirement that such measures are not applied in a manner which would constitute a means of arbitrary or unjustifiable discrimination between countries where the same conditions prevail, or a disguised restriction on international trade, nothing in this Agreement shall be construed to prevent the adoption or enforcement by any contracting party of measures:

(a) necessary to protect public morals;

(b) necessary to protect human, animal or plant life or health;

(c) relating to the importations or exportations of gold or silver;

(d) necessary to secure compliance with laws or regulations which are not inconsistent with the provisions of this Agreement, including those relating to customs enforcement, the enforcement of monopolies operated under paragraph 4 of Article II and Article XVII, the protection of patents, trade marks and copyrights, and the prevention of deceptive practices;

(e) relating to the products of prison labour;

(f) imposed for the protection of national treasures of artistic, historic or archaeological value;

(g) relating to the conservation of exhaustible natural resources if such measures are made effective in conjunction with restrictions on domestic production or consumption;

(h) undertaken in pursuance of obligations under any intergovernmental commodity agreement which conforms to criteria submitted to the contracting parties and not disapproved by them or which is itself so submitted and not so disapproved;

(i) involving restrictions on exports of domestic materials necessary to ensure essential quantities of such materials to a domestic processing industry during periods when the domestic price of such materials is held below the world price as part of a governmental stabilization plan; Provided that such restrictions shall not operate to increase the

---

[1] See Chapter 12 for a contextualisation of the Havana Charter's objectives, and later failure to create an international trade organisation.

> ### *(cont.)*
>
> exports of or the protection afforded to such domestic industry, and shall not depart from the provisions of this Agreement relating to non-discrimination;
>
> (j) essential to the acquisition or distribution of products in general or local short supply; Provided that any such measures shall be consistent with the principle that all contracting parties are entitled to an equitable share of the international supply of such products, and that any such measures, which are inconsistent with the other provisions of the Agreement shall be discontinued as soon as the conditions giving rise to them have ceased to exist. The contracting parties shall review the need for this sub-paragraph not later than 30 June 1960.

As the Appellate Body noted in *US – Shrimp*,[2] Article XX of the GATT 1994 recognises the need to maintain a balance between the right of a given member to invoke exceptions and the substantive rights of other members under this agreement. The domestic policies embodied in exceptions (a)–(j) also reflect certain fundamental societal interests. Typically, some of the measures that called for justification under the general exceptions under the GATT/WTO included the protection of animal welfare under public moral considerations,[3] reduction of risks to human health posed by certain type of hazardous products, such as asbestos[4] or waste tyres,[5] or policies aimed at the conservation of exhaustible natural resources, such as tuna,[6] herring,[7] salmon,[8] dolphins,[9] turtles,[10] clean air,[11] certain types of metals[12] or rare earths.[13]

To qualify as an exception, a measure has to satisfy one of the exceptions listed in paragraphs (a)–(j), as well as the requirements of the chapeau. In *US – Gasoline*, the Appellate Body had the opportunity to lay down the interpretative scheme and application of Article XX.

---

[2] Appellate Body Report, *US – Shrimp*, para. 156.

[3] Appellate Body Reports, *EC – Seal Products*; Panel Reports, *Brazil – Taxation*.

[4] Appellate Body Report, *EC – Asbestos*.

[5] Appellate Body Report, *Brazil – Measures Affecting Imports of Retreaded Tyres*, WT/DS332/AB/R, adopted 17 December 2007.

[6] GATT Panel Report, *United States – Prohibition of Imports of Tuna and Tuna Products from Canada*, L/5198, adopted 22 February 1982, BISD 29S/91.

[7] GATT Panel Report, *Canada – Measures Affecting Exports of Unprocessed Herring and Salmon*, L/6268, adopted 22 March 1988, BISD 35S/98.

[8] GATT Panel Report, *Canada – Herring and Salmon*.   [9] Appellate Body Report, *US – Tuna II (Mexico)*.

[10] Appellate Body Report, *US – Shrimp*.   [11] Appellate Body Report, *US – Gasoline*.

[12] Appellate Body Reports, *China – Raw Materials*.

[13] Appellate Body Reports, *China – Measures Related to the Exportation of Rare Earths, Tungsten, and Molybdenum*, WT/DS431/AB/R, WT/DS432/AB/R, WT/DS433/AB/R, adopted 29 August 2014.

US – Gasoline *(Appellate Body)*

Page 22. In order that the justifying protection of Article XX may be extended to it, the measure at issue must not only come under one or another of the particular exceptions – paragraphs (a) to (j) – listed under Article XX; it must also satisfy requirements imposed by the opening clauses of Article XX. The analysis is, in other words, two-tiered: first, provisional justification by reason of the characterization of the measure under Article XX(g); second, further appraisal of the same measure under the introductory clauses of Article XX.

In *US – Gasoline*, the Appellate Body also noted that while evaluating the consistency of a particular measure under the subparagraphs of Article XX, divergent standards could be taken into consideration, despite the fact that the chapeau represents in itself a unitary standard.

US – Gasoline *(Appellate Body)*

Pages 17–18. In enumerating the various categories of governmental acts, laws or regulations which WTO Members may carry out or promulgate in pursuit of differing legitimate state policies or interests outside the realm of trade liberalization, Article XX uses different terms in respect of different categories:

'necessary' – in paragraphs (a), (b) and (d); 'essential' – in paragraph (j); 'relating to' – in paragraphs (c), (e) and (g); 'for the protection of' – in paragraph (f); 'in pursuance of' in paragraph (h); and 'involving' – in paragraph (i).

It does not seem reasonable to suppose that the WTO Members intended to require, in respect of each and every category, the same kind of degree of connection between the measure under appraisal and the state interest or policy sought to be promoted or realized.

In *US – Shrimp*, the Appellate Body noted that following the above sequence of steps reflects no inadvertence or random choice, but rather the fundamental structure and logic of Article XX.[14] An examination of the GATT/WTO cases in the last three decades indicates that some of the commonly used exceptions under the GATT include Article XX(b), (d) and (g). A few cases have also arisen under Article XX(a), relating to the public moral exception. *EC – Seal Products* and *Brazil – Taxation* fall under this category. *India – Solar Cells*[15] involved an analysis of exceptions under XX(j). Generally, in the context of the GATT 1994 Article XX, divergent standards such as 'necessary', 'relating to' or 'essential' have gathered a specific meaning and gloss, which is addressed in the following section. For the

---

[14] Appellate Body Report, *US – Shrimp*, para. 119.
[15] Appellate Body Report, *India – Certain Measures Relating to Solar Cells and Solar Modules*, WT/DS456/AB/R, Add.1, adopted 14 October 2016.

sake of brevity, we are limiting our analysis only to the 'necessity', 'relating to' and 'essential' tests in the context of GATT Article XX.

9.2.2   First-Tier Examination: the 'Necessity' Test

9.2.2.1   Necessity and the GATT 1994, Article XX

Necessity is a defence to responsibility under international law.[16] However, in the context of international trade law, the concept of necessity has evolved rather independently, although the colour and import of the necessity test varies even within the iterated exceptions of Article XX of the GATT.

THAILAND – CIGARETTES

In *Thailand – Cigarettes*[17](a prominent case under the GATT 1947), the Panel noted that the principal health objectives highlighted by Thailand to justify the import restrictions on cigarettes were to protect the public from harmful components and to reduce the consumption of cigarettes. The Panel noted that smoking constituted a serious risk to human health. Consequently, the measures designed to reduce the consumption of cigarettes fell within the scope of Article XX(b).The second question addressed by the Panel was whether the Thailand ban on importation of cigarettes was unavoidable and 'necessary' within the meaning of Article XX of the GATT.

The Panel referred to an earlier decision of the GATT in *US – Section 337 Tariff Act*:[18]

> ## Thailand – Cigarettes *(GATT Panel)*
>
> 5.26. It was clear to the Panel that a contracting party cannot justify a measure inconsistent with another GATT provision as 'necessary' in terms of Article XX(d) if an alternative measure which it could reasonably be expected to employ and which is not inconsistent with other GATT provisions is available to it. By the same token, in cases where a measure consistent with other GATT provisions is not reasonably available, a contracting party is bound to use, among the measures reasonably available to it, that which entails the least degree of inconsistency with other GATT provisions.

---

[16] International Law Commission, Articles on Responsibility of States for Internationally Wrongful Acts, adopted by the ILC at its fifty-third session, in 2001, published in *Yearbook of the International Law Commission*, 2001, Vol. II, Part Two.

[17] GATT Panel Report, *Thailand – Restrictions on Importation of and Internal Taxes on Cigarettes*, DS10/R, adopted 7 November 1990, BISD 37S/200.

[18] GATT Panel Report, *United States Section 337 of the Tariff Act of 1930*, L/6439, adopted 7 November 1989, BISD 36S/345, para. 5.26.

The *Thailand – Cigarettes* Panel examined other reasonable opportunities available to Thailand to achieve these health objectives consistently with the General Agreement. In particular, the Panel examined whether Thailand's concerns about the quantity of cigarettes consumed could be met by other measures, reasonably available to it.[19] The Panel noted that Thailand had already implemented some non-discriminatory controls, including information programmes, both direct and indirect bans on advertising, warnings on cigarettes packs and bans on smoking in public places.[20] The Panel also noted that the GATT contracting parties could use governmental monopolies, such as the Thai Tobacco Monopoly, to restrict the supply of cigarettes, on the importation and domestic sale of cigarettes.[21] The Panel found, therefore, that Thailand's practice of permitting the sale of domestic cigarettes, while not permitting the importation of foreign cigarettes, was an inconsistency with the General Agreement not 'necessary' within the meaning of Article XX(b). For these reasons, the Panel did not accept the argument that Thailand had no option but to prohibit cigarette imports.[22]

The 'necessity' test developed in *Thailand – Cigarettes* attained a certain jurisprudential status in GATT law. The concept of necessity examined in this case has been used not only in the context of Article XX(a), (b) and (d) of the GATT, but also in relation to GATS Article XIV and possibly the TRIPS Agreement. The Appellate Body examined this concept for the first time in *Korea – Various Measures on Beef*,[23] the findings of which are often cited in subsequent WTO Panel and Appellate Body Reports.

Korea – Various Measures on Beef

In *Korea – Various Measures on Beef*, the United States challenged Korea's dual retail system for beef, which provided for separate retail shops or separate display of imported and domestic beef and labelling in department stores. The measure was held to be inconsistent with Article III:4 of the GATT. Korea relied upon the Article XX(d) exception, which allows WTO members to adopt or enforce measures 'necessary to secure compliance' with GATT-consistent 'laws or regulations'. In particular, Korea used this defence to justify the inconsistencies stemming from the enforcement of the Korean Unfair Competition Act, which was a GATT-consistent law or regulation. The Appellate Body looked at dictionaries as a starting point to define the meaning of the term 'necessary'.

Korea – Various Measures on Beef *(Appellate Body)*

160. The word 'necessary' normally denotes something 'that cannot be dispensed with or done without, requisite, essential, needful. ...

161. We believe that, as used in the context of Article XX(d), the reach of the word 'necessary is not limited to that which is 'indispensable' or 'of absolute necessity' or

---

[19] GATT Panel Report, *Thailand – Cigarettes*, para. 78.   [20] GATT Panel Report, *Thailand – Cigarettes*, para. 78.
[21] GATT Panel Report, *Thailand – Cigarettes*, para. 79.   [22] GATT Panel Report, *Thailand – Cigarettes*, para. 79.
[23] Appellate Body Report, *Korea – Various Measures on Beef*.

(cont.)

'inevitable'. Measures which are indispensable or of absolute necessity or inevitable to secure compliance certainly fulfil the requirements of Article XX(d). But other measures, too, may fall within the ambit of this exception. As used in Article XX(d), the term 'necessary' refers, in our view, to a range of degrees of necessity. At one end of this continuum lies 'necessary' understood as 'indispensable'; at the other end, is 'necessary' taken to mean as 'making a contribution to'. We consider that a 'necessary' measure is, in this continuum, located significantly closer to the pole of 'indispensable' than to the opposite pole of simply 'making a contribution to'.

162. ... It seems to us that a treaty interpreter assessing a measure claimed to be necessary to secure compliance of a WTO-consistent law or regulation may, in appropriate cases, take into account the relative importance of the common interests or values that the law or regulation to be enforced is intended to protect. The more vital or important those common interests or values are, the easier it would be to accept as 'necessary' a measure designed as enforcement instrument.

163. There are other aspects of the enforcement measure to be considered in evaluating that measure as 'necessary'. One is the extent to which the measure contributes to the realization of the end pursued, the securing of compliance with the law or regulation at issue. The greater the contribution, the more easily a measure might be considered to be 'necessary'. Another aspect is the extent to which the compliance measure produces restrictive effects on international commerce, that is, in respect of a measure inconsistent with Article III:4, restrictive effects *on imported goods*. A measure with a relatively slight impact upon imported products might more easily be considered as 'necessary' than a measure with intense or broader restrictive effects.

164. In sum, determination of whether a measure, which is not 'indispensable', may nevertheless be 'necessary' within the contemplation of Article XX(d), involves in every case a process of weighing and balancing a series of factors which prominently include the contribution made by the compliance measure to the enforcement of the law or regulation at issue, the importance of the common interests or values protected by that law or regulation, and the accompanying impact of the law or regulation on imports or exports.

Importantly, the Appellate Body decision in *Korea – Various Measures on Beef* introduced the 'weighing and balancing' test, which remains a major analytical contribution in the application of the necessity test. Until this dispute, the existence of a less trade-restrictive alternative measure made it exceedingly difficult for a respondent member to meet the necessity test. However, the new approach entails a more nuanced and complex weighing and balancing of the trade restrictiveness of the measure against the importance of fulfilling vital societal values or non-trade values.[24] The necessity test under Article XX(a), (b) and (d) also calls for the need for a similar treatment.

The following discussion focuses on the application of the necessity test under the GATS.

9.2.2.2 Necessity Test under the GATS Article XIV

In *US – Gambling*,[25] Antigua and Barbuda challenged the United States' ban on internet gambling on the ground that the United States had committed, in its GATS schedule, to open its market for cross-border trade in gambling and betting services. In this case, the WTO Panel and the Appellate Body examined the scope of Article XIV(a) of the GATS, which is similar to Article XX(a) of the GATT 1994. The Panel and, later, the Appellate Body found that three United States federal laws (the Wire Act, the Travel Act and the Illegal Gambling Business Act) and some state laws (for example, in Louisiana, Massachusetts, South Dakota and Utah) within the United States prohibit one, several or all means of delivery included in Mode 1 (cross-border delivery of service) of the GATS. Antigua and Barbuda alleged that these measures are inconsistent with the United States' specific market access commitments for gambling and betting services under cross-border delivery of services (Mode 1) of the GATS. In addition, it was found that the United States discriminated against the services and service suppliers of Antigua and Barbuda. The United States, in response to Antigua and Barbuda's claims, relied upon the defence under Article XIV of the GATS. This was the first time a WTO Panel and Appellate Body had occasion to interpret the necessity test under the GATS.

In this dispute, the United States defended the ban by arguing that the measure was necessary to protect public morals and to maintain public order.

US – Gambling *(Appellate Body)*

310. Rather, it is for a responding party to make a prima facie case that its measure is 'necessary' by putting forward evidence and arguments that enable a panel to assess the challenged measure in the light of the relevant factors to be 'weighed and balanced' in a given case. The responding party may, in so doing, point out why alternative measures would not achieve the same objectives as the challenged measure, but it is under no obligation to do so in order to establish, in the first instance, that its measure is 'necessary'. If the panel concludes that the respondent has made a prima facie case that the challenged measure is 'necessary' – that is, 'significantly closer to the pole of "indispensable" than to the opposite pole of simply "making a contribution to"' – then a panel should find that challenged measure 'necessary' within the terms of Article XIV(a) of the GATS.

---

[24] A. Lang, *World Trade Law after Neoliberalism: Reimagining the Global Economic Order* (Oxford University Press, 2011), pp. 320–1.

[25] Appellate Body Report, *US – Gambling*.

The United States had argued that the challenged measures were aimed at addressing concerns such as money laundering, organised crime, underage gambling, pathological gambling and fraud. The Panel earlier had noted that the mechanisms available to the United States to control these societal issues could not be considered as reasonably available alternatives.[26] Under the 'weighing and balancing' test, the respondent does not have to positively exclude all possible alternative measures, but it needs only to show that the measures proposed by the complainant are not 'reasonably available'.[27] An alternative measure may be found not to be reasonably available where it is 'merely theoretical in nature, for instance, where the responding member is not capable of taking it, or where the measure imposes an undue burden on that member, such as prohibitive costs or substantial technical difficulties'.[28] Furthermore, in order to qualify as a 'genuine alternative', the proposed measure must be not only less trade-restrictive than the original measure at issue, but should also 'preserve for the responding member its right to achieve its desired level of protection with respect to the objective pursued'.[29]

9.2.2.3   *Brazil – Retreaded Tyres* and the Necessity Test: A Turning Point?

The necessity test formulated by the Appellate Body in *Korea – Various Measures on Beef*[30] was applied to several other WTO cases, such as *EC – Asbestos*,[31] *Dominican Republic – Import and Sale of Cigarettes*[32] and *Mexico – Taxes on Soft Drinks*.[33] However, *Brazil – Retreaded Tyres* expanded the contours of the necessity test in Article XX of the GATT in an unparalleled way. This case relates to an import ban on used and retreaded tyres. The European Communities, the complainant, did not contest the ban on used tyres, while Brazil conceded that the import ban on retreaded tyres is a violation of Article XI:1 of the GATT. Brazil, however, sought to justify the measures under Article XX(b). According to Brazil, the measure was taken with a view to reducing the exposure of human, animal, plant life and health to risk emanating from the accumulation of waste tyres. According to Brazil, around 40 million tyres become waste in Brazil and the import ban was necessary for the reduction of waste tyres.[34]

---

[26] Panel Report, *US – Gambling*, para. 6.521.   [27] Appellate Body Report, *US – Gambling*, para. 307.

[28] Appellate Body Report, *US – Gambling*, para. 308.

[29] Appellate Body Reports, *EC – Seal Products*, para. 5.261 (quoting Appellate Body Report, *US – Gambling*, para. 308).

[30] Appellate Body Report, *Korea – Various Measures on Beef*, paras. 171 and 172.

[31] Appellate Body Report, *EC – Asbestos*, para. 171.

[32] Appellate Body Report, *Dominican Republic – Measures Affecting the Importation and Internal Sale of Cigarettes*, WT/DS461/AB/R, adopted 19 May 2005, paras. 65, 68, 71.

[33] Appellate Body Report, *Mexico – Tax Measures on Soft Drinks and Other Beverages*, WT/DS308/AB/R, adopted 24 March 2006, para. 74.

[34] Panel Report, *Brazil – Measures Affecting Imports of Retreaded Tyres*, WT/DS332/R, adopted 17 December 2007, as modified by Appellate Body Report WT/DS332/AB/R, para. 4.20.

In terms of trade restrictiveness, no measure could be as trade-restrictive as an import ban. The Panel noted that the objective of the import ban was the reduction of the 'exposure to the risks to human, animal or plant life or health arising from the accumulation of waste tyres',[35] and further added that 'few interests are more "vital" and "important" than protecting human beings from health risks, and that protecting the environment is no less important'.[36] The Appellate Body revisited various aspects of Article XX(b).

Brazil – Retreaded Tyres *(Appellate Body)*

150. As the Panel recognized, an import ban is 'by design as trade-restrictive as can be'. We agree with the Panel that there may be circumstances where such a measure can nevertheless be necessary, within the meaning of Article XX(b). We also recall that, in *Korea – Various Measures on Beef*, the Appellate Body indicated that 'the word "necessary" is not limited to that which is "indispensable"'. Having said that, when a measure produces restrictive effects on international trade as severe as those resulting from an import ban, it appears to us that it would be difficult for a panel to find that measure necessary unless it is satisfied that the measure is apt to make a material contribution to the achievement of its objective. Thus, we disagree with Brazil's suggestion that, because it aims to reduce risk exposure to the maximum extent possible, an import ban that brings a marginal or insignificant contribution can nevertheless be considered necessary.

The Appellate Body agreed with the Panel that a key focus of inquiry is whether the import ban was 'apt to make a contribution' to the objective. The Appellate Body also noted that the degree of contribution could be gauged through quantitative or qualitative reasoning.

According to the Appellate Body, the CONAMA (Brazilian regulation) scheme provided additional support for and was consistent with the design of Brazil's overall strategy for reducing the number of waste tyres. In other words, the import ban and the import ban on used tyres were mutually reinforcing pillars of Brazil's overall strategy in ensuring that the demand for retreaded tyres in Brazil must be met by domestic retreaders, and that these retreaders, in principle, could use only domestic used tyres as raw material. The Appellate Body evaluated the additional requirements of the necessity test, such as the application of the 'least trade-restrictive test'. The order of analysis followed by the Appellate Body is of useful guidance in seeking provisional justification for GATT-inconsistent measures under Article XX of the GATT.

---

[35] Panel Report, *Brazil – Retreaded Tyres*, para. 7.100.   [36] Panel Report, *Brazil – Retreaded Tyres*, para. 7.108.

Brazil – Retreaded Tyres (Appellate Body)

156. In order to determine whether a measure is 'necessary' within the meaning of Article XX(b) of the GATT 1994, a panel must assess all the relevant factors, particularly the extent of the contribution to the achievement of a measure's objective and its trade restrictiveness, in the light of the importance of the interests or values at stake. If this analysis yields a preliminary conclusion that the measure is necessary, this result must be confirmed by comparing the measure with its possible alternatives, which may be less trade restrictive while providing an equivalent contribution to the achievement of the objective pursued. It rests upon the complaining Member to identify possible alternatives to the measure at issue that the responding Member could have taken. As the Appellate Body indicated in *US – Gambling*, while the responding Member must show that a measure is necessary, it does not have to 'show, in the first instance, that there are *no* reasonably available alternatives to achieve its objectives'. We recall that, in order to qualify as an alternative, a measure proposed by the complaining Member must be not only less trade restrictive than the measure at issue, but should also 'preserve for the responding Member its right to achieve its desired level of protection with respect to the objective pursued'. If the complaining Member has put forward a possible alternative measure, the responding Member may seek to show that the proposed measure does not allow it to achieve the level of protection it has chosen and, therefore, is not a genuine alternative. The responding Member may also seek to demonstrate that the proposed alternative is not, in fact, 'reasonably available'.

The Appellate Body in *Brazil – Retreaded Tyres* applied a necessity test, which was considerably deferential to the interests of the respondent member. The Appellate Body also took into consideration 'the capacity of a country to implement remedial measures that would be particularly costly, or would require advanced technologies'[37] in the assessment of reasonably available alternatives. The Appellate Body stated that a panel enjoys certain latitude in setting out its approach to determine the nature of material contribution, and such an approach may be performed in qualitative or quantitative terms.[38]

The Appellate Body's analysis in this case was a reaffirmation of its approach in *EC – Asbestos*, where it held that where issues of human life and health are concerned, the challenged measure is entitled to a 'margin of appreciation'.[39] Based on this approach, greater discretion is available to members in choosing the type of measures that may be appropriate to meet the stated objective.

---

[37] Panel Report, *Brazil – Retreaded Tyres*, para. 171.   [38] Panel Report, *Brazil – Retreaded Tyres*, para. 145.

[39] Appellate Body Report, *EC – Asbestos*, para. 161.

9.2.3   The 'Relating to' Test

In the 1980s, Canada maintained certain regulations prohibiting the exportation or sale for export of certain unprocessed herring and salmon, which constituted the largest share of the West Coast fishery of Canada.[40] In *Canada – Herring and Salmon*,[41] this measure was challenged before a GATT Panel. According to Canada, this requirement was an essential component of resource conservation, as it mandated that the fish should have landed in Canada before being transported for on-shore processing.[42] Canada argued that the expression 'relating to' could not be read to mean 'essential' or 'necessary to', terms used elsewhere in Article XX and the GATT 1947.[43] In an often-cited GATT Panel Report, the Panel notes that measures 'relate to' the conservation objective when they are 'primarily aimed at' that objective.[44] According to the Panel, although the trade measure did not have to be necessary or essential to conservation of exhaustible natural resources, it had to be 'primarily aimed' at conservation to satisfy the requirements of Article XX(g).

In *US – Gasoline*, the Appellate Body clarified that the phrase '"primarily aimed at" itself is not a treaty language and was not designed as a litmus test for inclusion or exclusion from Article XX(g)'.[45] However, if a measure is designed as a conservation goal, despite the difficulties in predicting its possible effects or outcomes, it could meet the 'relating to' requirement.[46] In fact, the interpretation of Article XX(g) has meandered through differing judicial approaches. During the pre-WTO days indeed, the GATT Panel decisions in US – *Tuna (Mexico)*[47] and *US – Tuna (EEC)*[48] had provided narrow interpretations of this exception.

Box 9.1 Tuna-dolphin cases under the GATT/WTO

In 1972, the United States Congress enacted the Marine Mammal Protection Act (MMPA), which prohibited the 'taking' (harassment, hunting, killing or any such acts) of marine mammals. In the 1980s, the United States amended the MMPA to introduce two requirements: (1) the government of the harvesting country should have a programme regulating the taking of marine mammals, comparable to that of the United States; and (2) the average rate of incidental taking of marine mammals by vessels of the harvesting nation should be comparable to the average rate of such taking by US vessels. This measure amounted to an import ban unless the exporting country – that

---

[40] The Canadian Regulations mandated: 'No person shall export from Canada any sockeye or pink salmon unless it is canned, salted, smoked, dried, pickled or frozen and has been inspected in accordance with the Fish Inspection Act'.

[41] GATT Panel Report, *Canada – Herring and Salmon*.

[42] GATT Panel Report, *Canada – Herring and Salmon*, para. 3.35.

[43] GATT Panel Report, *Canada – Herring and Salmon*, para. 3.26.

[44] GATT Panel Report, *Canada – Herring and Salmon*, para. 4.6.   [45] Appellate Body Report, *US – Gasoline*, p. 18.

[46] Appellate Body Report, *US – Gasoline*.

[47] GATT Panel Report, *United States – Restrictions on Imports of Tuna*, DS21/R, 3 September 1991, unadopted, BISD 39S/155.

[48] GATT Panel Report, *United States – Restrictions on Imports of Tuna*, DS29/R, 16 June 1994, unadopted.

Box 9.1 (cont.)

is, a country exporting a commercially traded product such as tuna – demonstrated to the concerned US authorities that it had met the dolphin protections standards established by the United States.

The stated objective of the US measure was to protect marine mammals such as dolphin, which has a close association with yellow fin tuna, especially in the Eastern Tropical Pacific ocean. Schools of tuna often used to swim beneath dolphin and this was used by trawlers to catch tuna. More importantly, the purse-seine technology, which was widely applied in tuna fishing, was estimated to incidentally trap and kill dolphins. In addition, some fishing vessels used the method of setting on dolphin to catch tuna.

Mexico was a major exporter of tuna to the United States. Initially, its exports of tuna to the United States were banned. Mexico complained in 1991, under the GATT dispute settlement in *US – Tuna (Mexico)*. The embargo was also applied to 'inter-mediary' countries handling the tuna en route from Mexico to the United States. This often happened when the industries in the export countries were engaged in the tuna processing or canning industries. In this dispute, the 'intermediary' countries that faced the embargo included Costa Rica, Italy, Japan and Spain, and, earlier, France, the Netherlands Antilles and the United Kingdom. Others, including Canada, Colombia, the Republic of Korea and members of the Association of Southeast Asian Nations, were also named as 'intermediaries'. In 1994, some of these intermediary countries filed a dispute, *US – Tuna (EEC)*. Both the *Tuna* cases remained unadopted by the GATT Council.

Subsequently, the United States introduced the Dolphin Protection Consumer Information Act and sought to regulate tuna fishing methods that are harmful to dolphin through labelling schemes. The US implementation measures were also subsequently challenged at the WTO, which resulted in multiple rulings. But the later *Tuna* cases were generally considered within the backdrop of the TBT Agreement and form part of the trilogy of TBT cases discussed by the WTO Panels and the Appellate Body (see Chapter 4 for further discussion).

To Go Further

M. A. Crawley and R. Howse, '*US – Tuna/Dolphin II*: A Legal and Economic Analysis of the Appellate Body Report', *World Trade Review* (2014), 13(2), pp. 321–55.

In *US – Tuna (Mexico)*, Mexico challenged a US measure imposing import bans on tuna under the MMPA. The GATT Panel noted that the measure was in breach of Article XI, and the United States took recourse to Article XX exceptions. Specifically in relation to Article XX(g), the GATT Panel held that this exception could apply to measures that affected only the production and consumption in the country enacting the measure.[49] The Panel further noted that the United States could not impose restrictions on a product merely because it was harvested or originated in a country with different environment regulations. In other words, an interpretation providing an extraterritorial application to the provisions of Article XX(g) could jeopardise the rights of other contracting parties of the GATT.

The scope and extent of application of Article XX(g) was far from settled. In *US – Tuna (EEC)* – which involved challenges by the EEC against the primary and secondary embargos for dolphin conservation in non-territorial waters – the Panel found the embargo to be a violation of Article XI. The EEC and the Netherlands contended that the natural resources seeking conservation had to be within the territorial jurisdiction of the country enforcing the measure.[50] The Panel, however, noted that the text of Article XX does not spell out any limitation on the location of the natural resource to be conserved.[51] This was a significant development with respect to the scope of the Article XX(g) exception.

In order for a measure to fall within the ambit of subparagraph (g) of Article XX, it must 'relate to the conservation of exhaustible natural resources'. According to the dictionary definition, the term 'relate to' is defined as 'having some connection with, being connected to'.

Later, in *US – Shrimp*, the Appellate Body revisited the 'relating to' test. The United States had introduced an import prohibition against shrimp harvested with commercial fishing technology that adversely affected sea turtles. Even if shrimpers' home countries did not have a regulatory programme comparable to the regime in the United States, so long as they used turtle excluder devices, they were eligible to export shrimp to the United States. However, the Court of International Trade in the United States directed the State Department 'to prohibit not later than May 1, 1996, the importation of shrimp or products of shrimp' from countries where their harvest might have an adverse impact on sea turtles – a decision that further reduced the flexibilities in the programme. In other words, the US measure prohibited shrimp from certain countries, which did not have a turtle conservation programme that was comparable to that of the United States. The United States invoked Article XX(g) of the GATT to justify its measures.

US – Shrimp

In *US – Shrimp*, the Appellate Body indeed acknowledged that subparagraph (g) referred to measures 'primarily aimed at conservation'. However, the Appellate Body described this relationship as 'a close and genuine relationship of ends and means' that requires an examination of the connection between the general structures and design of a measure and the policy goal it purports to serve.[52]

---

[49] GATT Panel Report, *US – Tuna (Mexico)*, para. 5.30.   [50] GATT Panel Report, *US – Tuna (EEC)*, para. 3.15.

[51] GATT Panel Report, *US – Tuna (EEC)*, para. 5.15.

[52] Jayati Srivastava and Rajeev Ahuja, 'Mainstreaming Environment through Jurisprudence: Implications of the Shrimp-Turtle Decision in the WTO for India and other Developing Countries', ICRIER Working Paper 78 (New Delhi: Indian Council for Research on International Economic Relations, 2002).

> ## US – Shrimp *(Appellate Body)*
>
> 141. ... Section 609, *cum* implementing guidelines, is not disproportionately wide in its scope and reach in relation to the policy objective of protection and conservation of sea turtle species. The means are, in principle, reasonably related to the ends. The means and ends relationship between Section 609 and the legitimate policy of conserving an exhaustible and, in fact, endangered species is observably a close and real one, a relationship that is every bit as substantial and as that which we found in *United States – Gasoline*.

Regarding the location of the natural resources in question, the Appellate Body noted:

> ## US – Shrimp *(Appellate Body)*
>
> 121. ... It is not necessary to assume that requiring from exporting countries compliance with, or adoption of, certain policies (although covered in principle by one or another of the exceptions) prescribed by the importing country, renders a measure a priori incapable of justification under Article XX. Such an interpretation renders most, if not all, of the specific exceptions of Article XX inutile, a result abhorrent to the principles of interpretation we are bound to apply.

CHINA – RARE EARTHS

China – Rare Earths[53] is one of the more recent cases that has examined the application of Article XX(g) of the GATT. China maintained export duties and export restrictions on rare earths as well as on tungsten and molybdenum. Heavy rare earth metals have wide application for the manufacture of technology products. China was the world's dominant producer, with a share of almost 97 per cent. A WTO Panel found that China violated its GATT commitments and other obligations under China's Accession Protocol by restricting its rare earth exports to other countries while making these products available to domestic manufacturers.[54] China, on the other hand, argued that these measures[55] were justified on health and environment grounds, under Article XX(b) and (g) of the GATT.

---

[53] Panel Reports, *China – Measures Related to the Exportation of Rare Earths, Tungsten, and Molybdenum*, WT/DS431/R, Add.1, WT/DS432/R, Add.1, WT/DS433/R, Add.1, adopted 29 August 2014, upheld by Appellate Body Reports WT/DS431/AB/R, WT/DS432/AB/R, WT/DS433/AB/R.

[54] China had undertaken certain additional obligations in its Protocol of Accession. Art. 11.3 of China's Protocol of Accession states: 'China shall eliminate all taxes and charges applied to exports unless specifically provided for in Annex 6 of this Protocol or applied in conformity with the provisions of Article VIII of the GATT 1994'.

[55] The Panel and the Appellate Body noted that China cannot rely on Art. XX(g) of the GATT for its export duties which are regulated by Article 11.3 of the Protocol, whereas China's export restrictions were subject to the defences under Art. XX of the GATT 1994. See E. W. Bond and J. Trachtman, 'China – Rare Earths: Export Restrictions and the Limits of Textual Interpretation', *World Trade Review* (2016), 15(2), pp. 189–209.

China – Rare Earths *(Panel)*

7.379. ... The Panel recalls, however, that according to the Appellate Body, the test for whether a challenged measure 'relates to' conservation turns on an examination of its 'general design and structure', and in particular on whether the measure is 'disproportionately wide in its scope and reach in relation to the policy objective of protection and conservation' or whether, conversely, it is 'reasonably related' to the conservation objective, such that its relationship with conservation is 'close and real' and 'substantial'. As the Panel explained in its discussion of the legal test, the test in Article XX(g) focuses on the written measure, on the design and architecture of the challenged export quota, and its operation, while under the chapeau of Article XX, the Panel will review the manner in which the quota system is applied. ... The Panel is thus not required to examine whether a challenged measure has in fact improved the level of conservation of exhaustible natural resources. There is therefore no need for the Panel to decide, in quantitative or qualitative terms, precisely what level of contribution a challenged measure has made to the conservation objective. Instead, the Panel looks at the nature of the challenged measures to determine whether, as a matter of design and architecture, they assist, support or further the goal of conservation.

China challenged the ruling of the Panel. In particular, China challenged the requirement of 'even-handedness' which, in China's view, imposed a burden of resource conservation between foreign and domestic consumers and producers. The Appellate Body made the following observations on the interpretation of 'relating to':

China – Rare Earths *(Appellate Body)*

5.107. In our view, two issues arise from China's claim of error: (i) whether the Panel made the findings attributed to it by China, i.e. that the assessment of whether a measure 'relates to' conservation must be limited to an examination of the design and structure of the measure at issue; and (ii) whether it was proper for the Panel to place an analytical emphasis on the design and structure of the measures at issue.

The Appellate Body noted that an assessment under Article XX(g) of the GATT does not require an examination of the actual effects of the challenged measure, although a panel is not precluded from conducting such an exercise.[56] The Appellate Body further noted that

---

[56] Appellate Body Reports, *China – Rare Earths*, para. 5.137.

the predictable effects of a measure that are discernible from the design and structure of the measure could still be relevant. While the Panel considered that evidence relating to the actual operation and impact of the measure at issue was primarily relevant to the analysis under the chapeau of Article XX, it did not consider itself precluded from considering such evidence in the context of the analysis under subparagraph (g). The Appellate Body found that the Panel did not err in focusing on the design and structure of the measures at issue in its analysis under subparagraph (g). The Appellate Body also noted that due regard must be paid to the words used by the WTO members themselves to express their intent and purpose.[57] In conclusion, the Appellate Body noted that in the 'absence of a nexus' between China's measure and the conservation objective, it would be difficult to attribute any positive evidence on conservation to the challenged measure.[58]

9.2.4   The Role of Effective Domestic Restrictions

China – Raw Materials

In *China – Raw Materials*,[59] the Appellate Body examined in detail the application of Article XX(g), especially the meaning of the terms 'made effective in conjunction with'. The case related to certain export restraints, such as export duties, export quotas, export licensing requirements, export quota administration and allocation, and minimum export price requirements on industrial raw materials. Paragraph 11.3 of China's Protocol of Accession, which mandated China to eliminate all taxes and charges applied to exports, was in contention in this dispute. Annex 6 of the Protocol had listed only eighty-four tariff lines on which China had reserved its right to impose export duties. China breached these obligations by imposing export duties on raw materials such as coke, magnesium, various types of metal scraps and some forms of fluorspar. China used to revise its export taxes evidently in response to price fluctuations and market conditions.

According to China, the challenged measures sought to implement a wide-ranging mineral conservation policy, bearing in mind China's special social and economic development needs. China initially sought to defend the measures under Article XI:2(a) of the GATT, which protected measures 'temporarily applied' to 'prevent or relieve critical shortages of essential products'. China failed to establish that resource depletion could not amount to a critical shortage within the meaning of Article XI:2.

China contended that the sovereign right on natural resources[60] that is protected by Article XX(g) has to be exercised in light of the concept of sustainable right enshrined in the WTO Preamble (see Introduction). It is important to recall that Article XX(g) requires that a WTO member, while imposing trade restrictions for the conservation of natural resources, must also adopt measures imposed at restricting domestic consumption or

---

[57] Appellate Body Reports, *China – Rare Earths*, para. 5.113.
[58] Appellate Body Reports, *China – Rare Earths*, para. 5.113.
[59] Appellate Body Reports, *China – Raw Materials*, paras. 359–361.
[60] Resolution 1803 (XVIII), Permanent Sovereignty Over Natural Resources, 14 December 1962.

production. In *US – Gasoline*, the Appellate Body noted this was a requirement of even-handedness.[61] The Appellate Body in *China – Raw Materials* elaborated on this concept.

China – Raw Materials (Appellate Body)

359. As noted above, the Panel in the present case appears to have considered that, in order to prove that a measure is 'made effective in conjunction with' restrictions on domestic production or consumption in the sense of Article XX(g), it must be established, first, that the measure is applied jointly with restrictions on domestic production or consumption, and, second, that the purpose of the challenged measure is to make 'effective restrictions on domestic production or consumption'. In particular, the Panel's use of the words 'not only ... but, in addition', as well as the reference at the end of the sentence to the GATT Panel Report in *Canada – Herring and Salmon*, indicate that the Panel did in fact consider that two separate conditions have to be met for a measure to be considered 'made effective in conjunction with' in the sense of Article XX(g).

360. As explained above, we see nothing in the text of Article XX(g) to suggest that, in addition to being 'made effective in conjunction with restrictions on domestic production or consumption', a trade restriction must be aimed at ensuring the effectiveness of domestic restrictions, as the Panel found. Instead, we have found above that Article XX(g) permits trade measures relating to the conservation of exhaustible natural resources if such trade measures work together with restrictions on domestic production or consumption, which operate so as to conserve an exhaustible natural resource.

361. Based on the foregoing, we find that the Panel erred in interpreting the phrase 'made effective in conjunction with' in Article XX(g) of the GATT 1994 to require a separate showing that the purpose of the challenged measure must be to make effective restrictions on domestic production or consumption. Accordingly, we reverse this interpretation by the Panel in paragraph 7.397 of the Panel Reports.

This formulation of the Appellate Body in *China – Raw Materials* was emphasised by the Appellate Body in *China – Rare Earths*. To summarise, there is no requirement under Article XX(g) of the GATT that the purpose of the challenged measure must be to make effective restrictions on domestic production or consumption. In the Appellate Body's view, the term 'even-handedness' was a synonym or shorthand reference for the requirement that the conservation restrictions be imposed not only on international trade, but also on domestic production and consumption.[62] In other words, 'even-handedness' is not a separate requirement, but only ensures that the GATT-inconsistent measure and the domestic restriction

---

[61] Appellate Body Report, *US – Gasoline*, pp. 20–1.   [62] Appellate Body Reports, *China – Rare Earths*, para. 5.124.

must work together in order to meet the conditions laid down in the second clause of Article XX(g).[63] In this case, while Chinese export taxes and quotas could reduce domestic output and global consumption, the measures were poised to increase Chinese consumption. This factor might have weighed with the Panel and the Appellate Body in concluding that the measures do not 'relate to' conservation.

9.2.5   The Criterion of 'Essential'

Article XX(j) allows WTO members to take measures that are essential to the 'acquisition or distribution of products in general or local short supply', provided that they are 'discontinued as soon as the conditions giving rise to them have ceased to exist'. Although this provision was part of the original GATT 1947, it was seldom put to use.

India – Solar Cells was the first GATT/WTO case to address this claim. India invoked the exception of Article XX(j) to justify the domestic content requirements under India's solar mission programme, which was found to be inconsistent with the requirements of Article III:4 of the GATT. India argued that 'solar cells and modules are "products in general or local short supply" in India on account of its lack of domestic manufacturing capacity'.[64] India contended that 'the risk of [solar power developers] being unable to access these products makes the "products in general or local short supply" in India'. The Appellate Body held:

> ### India – Solar Cells *(Appellate Body)*
>
> 5.62. ... The Appellate Body has explained in this regard that, in a continuum ranging from 'indispensable' to 'making a contribution to', a 'necessary' measure is 'located significantly closer to the pole of "indispensable" than to the opposite pole of simply "making a contribution to"'. The word 'essential', in turn, is defined as '[a]bsolutely indispensable or necessary'. The plain meaning of the term thus suggests that this word is located at least as close to the 'indispensable' end of the continuum as the word 'necessary'.
>
> 5.63. Having said this, we recall that a 'necessity' analysis under Article XX(d) involves a process of 'weighing and balancing' a series of factors. We consider that the same process of weighing and balancing is relevant in assessing whether a measure is 'essential' within the meaning of Article XX(j). In particular, we consider it relevant to assess the extent to which the measure sought to be justified contributes to: 'the acquisition or distribution of products in general or local short supply'; the relative

---

[63] Appellate Body Reports, *China – Rare Earths*, para. 5.127.

[64] Panel Report, *India – Certain Measures Relating to Solar Cells and Solar Modules*, WT/DS456/R, Add.1, adopted 14 October 2016, as modified by Appellate Body Report WT/DS456/AB/R, para. 7.190.

> *(cont.)*
> importance of the societal interests or values that the measure is intended to protect; and the trade-restrictiveness of the challenged measure. In most cases, a comparison between the challenged measure and reasonably available alternative measures should then be undertaken.

In other words, the terms 'essential' and 'necessary' are almost synonymous in their application. To that extent, the examination of 'essential' could also involve an inquiry whether the respondent member could have chosen a less trade-restrictive measure that could have fulfilled the stated objectives.[65]

9.2.6 'Products in General or Local Short Supply'

INDIA – SOLAR CELLS

The Panel interpreted the term 'products in general or local short supply' to refer to 'a situation in which the quantity of available supply of a product does not meet demand in the relevant geographical area or market'.[66] It observed that 'the words "products in general or local short supply" do not refer to "products of national origin in general or local short supply"'.[67] The Panel considered that 'the effect of adopting India's interpretation of Article XX(j) would be tantamount to interpreting the words "products in general or local short supply", in the first part of Article XX(j), as though they meant "products in general or local short production"'.[68] The Panel rejected such an interpretation. The Panel thus concluded that the term 'products in general or local short supply' did not refer to 'products in respect of which there merely is a lack of domestic manufacturing capacity'.[69] According to the Panel, it was not India's case that the 'quantity of solar cells and modules available from all sources, i.e. both international and domestic, is inadequate to meet the demand' of Indian solar power developers. It also ruled that 'the terms "products in general or local short supply" do not cover products at risk of becoming in short supply'. According to the Panel, although it could envisage a situation of including 'products *at risk of* being in short supply' (emphasis added), at least for argument's sake, it could include only products which face 'imminent risks of such shortage'.[70] Based on this reasoning, the Panel ruled that 'solar cells and modules were not "products in general or local short supply" in India'.

The Appellate Body later affirmed the ruling of the Panel on the meaning of the terms 'local short supply'.

---

[65] Panel Report, *India – Solar Cells*, para. 7.349.
[66] Panel Report, *India – Solar Cells*, para. 7.225.
[67] Panel Report, *India – Solar Cells*, para. 7.223.
[68] Panel Report, *India – Solar Cells*, para. 7.224.
[69] Panel Report, *India – Solar Cells*, para. 7.235.
[70] Panel Report, *India – Solar Cells*, para. 7.255.

> ## India – Solar Cells *(Appellate Body)*
>
> 5.66. We note that 'supply' is defined as the 'amount of any commodity actually produced and available for purchase', and that, in its ordinary meaning, the word 'supply' is the 'correlative' of the word 'demand'. An assessment of whether there is a 'deficiency' or 'amount lacking' in the 'quantity' of a product that is available would therefore appear to involve a comparison between 'supply' and 'demand' . . .

According to the Appellate Body, 'Article XX(j) does not limit the scope of potential sources of supply to "domestic" products manufactured in a particular country that may be "available" for purchase in a given market'.[71] Therefore, if India can meet its demand by importing the product in question, the defence under Article XX(j) is bound to be unavailable.

9.2.7 Second Tier of Analysis under Article XX: Interpretation of the Chapeau

In *US – Gasoline*, the Appellate Body pointed out that the chapeau of Article XX, 'by its express terms addresses, not so much as the questioned measure or its specific contents as such, but rather the manner in which the measure is applied'.[72]

The Appellate Body further noted that it is 'important to underscore that the purpose and object of the introductory clauses of Article XX is generally the prevention of "abuse of the exceptions of [Article XX]"'.[73] In other words, the chapeau functions as a second tier of examination and is horizontally applicable across measures. This view was reiterated by the Appellate Body in *US – Shrimp*.

> ## US – Shrimp *(Appellate Body)*
>
> 116. The general design of a measure, as distinguished from its application, is, however, to be examined in the course of determining whether that measure falls within one or another of the paragraphs of Article XX following the chapeau. The Panel failed to scrutinize the *immediate* context of the chapeau: i.e., paragraphs (a) to (j) of Article XX. Moreover, the Panel did not look into the object and purpose of the whole of the GATT 1994 and the WTO Agreement . . . Thus, the Panel arrived at the very broad formulation that measures which 'undermine the

---

[71] Appellate Body Report, *India – Solar Cells*, para. 5.68.   [72] Appellate Body Report, *US – Gasoline*, p. 22.
[73] Appellate Body Report, *US – Gasoline*, p. 22.

> *(cont.)*
>
> multilateral trading system' must be regarded as 'not within the scope of measures permitted under the chapeau of Article XX'. Maintaining, rather than undermining, the multilateral trading system is necessarily a fundamental and pervasive premise underlying the WTO Agreement; but it is not right or an obligation, nor is it an interpretative rule which can be employed in the appraisal of a given measure under the chapeau of Article XX.

In most GATT/WTO cases, the defence under Article XX is used by the respondent to justify a violation of non-discrimination, either of the MFN or of national treatment under the GATT. However, in addition to satisfying one of the elements of subparagraphs (a)–(j) of the GATT, the measure has to meet the requirements of a non-discrimination provision, albeit of a different type. This non-discrimination requirement is embodied in the language 'arbitrary or unjustifiable discrimination where the same conditions prevail' of the introductory part (or chapeau) of Article XX.

In *US – Shrimp*, the Appellate Body provided the following general guidelines for the interpretation of the non-discrimination provision of the chapeau:

US – Shrimp *(Appellate Body)*

150. We commence the second tier of our analysis with an examination of the ordinary meaning of the words of the chapeau. The precise language of the chapeau requires that a measure not be applied in a manner which would constitute a means of 'arbitrary or unjustifiable discrimination between countries where the same conditions prevail' or a 'disguised restriction on international trade'. There are three standards contained in the chapeau: first, arbitrary discrimination between countries where the same conditions prevail; second, unjustifiable discrimination between countries where the same conditions prevail; and third, a disguised restriction on international trade. In order for a measure to be applied in a manner which would constitute 'arbitrary or unjustifiable discrimination between countries where the same conditions prevail', three elements must exist. First, the application of the measure must result in discrimination. As we stated in *United States – Gasoline*, the nature and quality of this discrimination is different from the discrimination in the treatment of products which was already found to be inconsistent with one of the substantive obligations of the GATT 1994, such as Articles I, III or XI. Second, the discrimination must be arbitrary or unjustifiable in character. We will examine this element of arbitrariness or unjustifiability in detail below.

> **(cont.)**
>
> Third, this discrimination must occur between countries where the same conditions prevail. In *United States – Gasoline*, we accepted the assumption of the participants in that appeal that such discrimination could occur not only between different exporting Members, but also between exporting Members and the importing Member concerned. Thus, the standards embodied in the language of the chapeau are not only different from the requirements of Article XX(g); they are also different from the standard used in determining that Section 609 is violative of the substantive rules of Article XI:1 of the GATT 1994.

In the above decision, the Appellate Body provided important insights on the role of the chapeau. While the subparagraphs discuss the right of a WTO member to pursue certain legitimate objectives, the chapeau deals mainly with the 'abuse' of those rights. According to the Appellate Body, the chapeau also marks a 'line of equilibrium'. This line of equilibrium is supposed to balance the conflicting rights of the members. The Appellate Body stressed the importance of a fine balance as follows:

> ## US – Shrimp *(Appellate Body)*
>
> 159. The task of interpreting and applying the chapeau is, hence, essentially the delicate one of locating and marking out a line of equilibrium between the rights of a Member to invoke an exception under Article XX and the rights of other Members under varying substantive provisions (e.g. Article XI) of the GATT 1994, so that neither of the competing rights will cancel out the other . . .

In the subsequent paragraphs of its decision, the Appellate Body examined the application of the measure at issue. The Appellate Body noted a finding by the Panel that the United States did not propose the negotiation of an agreement to any of the complaining countries until after the conclusion of the Inter-American Convention for the Protection and Conservation of Sea Turtles, in September 1996 – that is, well after the deadline for the imposition of the import ban of 1 May 1996. The Panel had concluded that in spite of the possibility offered by the United States legislation, the United States did not enter into negotiations before it imposed the import ban.

9.2.8   Arbitrary or Unjustifiable Discrimination

In *US – Shrimp*, the Appellate Body also elaborated on the standards for applying the 'arbitrary or unjustifiable' discrimination enquiry between countries where the same conditions prevail.

US – Shrimp *(Appellate Body)*

177. We next consider whether Section 609 has been applied in a manner constituting 'arbitrary discrimination between countries where the same conditions prevail'. We have already observed that Section 609, in its application, imposes a single, rigid and unbending requirement that countries applying for certification under Section 609(b)(2)(A) and (B) adopt a comprehensive regulatory program that is essentially the same as the United States' program, without inquiring into the appropriateness of that program for the conditions prevailing in the exporting countries. Furthermore, there is little or no flexibility in how officials make the determination for certification pursuant to these provisions. In our view, this rigidity and inflexibility also constitute 'arbitrary discrimination' within the meaning of the chapeau.

In short, the complainants were able to establish that the shrimp caught abroad using harvesting methods identical to those employed in the United States did not receive the same treatment, which did result in the breach of the chapeau. The Appellate Body also concluded that the operation of the measure could not 'reconcile with the declared objective of protecting and conserving sea turtles'.[74]

BRAZIL – RETREADED TYRES

Brazil – Retreaded Tyres provides a clear exposition of the meaning of 'arbitrary or unjustifiable discrimination' under Article XX of the GATT. Brazil's import ban resulted in discriminatory treatment between MERCOSUR and non-MERCOSUR countries in relation to retreaded tyres.[75] A MERCOSUR tribunal had earlier held that the import ban was incompatible with the terms of the MERCOSUR Agreement. The Appellate Body held:

Brazil – Retreaded Tyres *(Appellate Body)*

228. In this case, the discrimination between MERCOSUR countries and other WTO Members in the application of the Import Ban was introduced as a consequence of a ruling by a MERCOSUR tribunal. The tribunal found against Brazil because the restriction on imports of remoulded tyres was inconsistent with the prohibition of new trade restrictions under MERCOSUR law. In our view, the ruling issued by the MERCOSUR arbitral tribunal is not an acceptable rationale for the discrimination, because it bears no relationship to the legitimate objective pursued by the Import Ban that falls within the purview of Article XX(b), and even goes against this

---

[74] Appellate Body Report, *US – Shrimp*, para. 165.
[75] Appellate Body Report, *Brazil – Retreaded Tyres*, para. 227.

> **(cont.)**
>
> objective, to however small a degree. Accordingly, we are of the view that the MERCOSUR exemption has resulted in the Import Ban being applied in a manner that constitutes arbitrary or unjustifiable discrimination.
>
> 232. Like the Panel, we believe that Brazil's decision to act in order to comply with the MERCOSUR ruling cannot be viewed as 'capricious' or 'random'. Acts implementing a decision of a judicial or quasi-judicial body – such as the MERCOSUR arbitral tribunal – can hardly be characterized as a decision that is 'capricious' or 'random'. However, discrimination can result from a rational decision or behaviour, and still be 'arbitrary or unjustifiable'; because it is explained by a rationale that bears no relationship to the objective of a measure provisionally justified under one of the paragraphs of Article XX, or goes against that objective.

The Appellate Body also held in this case that arbitrary or unjustifiable discrimination would result if the 'reasons given for this discrimination bear no rational connection to the objective falling within the purview of a paragraph of Article XX, or would go against that objective'.[76] The Appellate Body also noted that the analysis on arbitrary or unjustifiable discrimination 'should focus on the cause of the discrimination, or the rationale put forward to explain its existence'.[77]

However, the interpretation of Article XX of the GATT 1994 has seen several ebbs and flows in the recent past, especially in *EC – Seal Products*,[78] where the Appellate Body made subtle modifications to the interpretation of the chapeau of Article XX.

EC – SEAL PRODUCTS

EC – Seal Products related to a challenge on the EU seal regime. The EU imposed a ban on seals and seal products based on concerns related to seal welfare. However, the ban provided exceptions for seals hunted by the Inuit community (IC exception), and for seal products hunted for the purpose of marine resource management and sold on a non-profit basis (MRM exception). The import ban was motivated by public concerns arising from the cruel manner in which seals are hunted and killed, whereas the IC exception was made to protect the traditional lifestyle and livelihood of indigenous peoples, especially the Inuit community; the MRM exception, on the other hand, took into consideration the need for sustainable management of marine resources.

The EU seal regime was an origin-neutral measure and did not, *ex facie*, discriminate against the products based on origin. However, under the IC exception, most seal products from Norway and Canada were unable to enter the EU market. On the other hand, the bulk of seal products from Greenland came from the Inuit community, who were able to make use of the exception. Similarly, seal products from Norway and Canada were unable to

---

[76] Appellate Body Report, *Brazil – Retreaded Tyres*, para. 227.

[77] Appellate Body Report, *Brazil – Retreaded Tyres*, para. 226.

[78] Appellate Body Reports, *EC – Seal Products*, paras. 5.296–5.306.

make use of the MRM exception, whereas seal products from certain EU countries, such as Sweden and Finland, were able to qualify under the exception.

The Panel concluded that the IC exception under the EU seal regime violated Article I:1 of the GATT 1994 because an advantage granted by the EU to seal products originating in Greenland (specifically, its Inuit population) was not accorded immediately and unconditionally to like products originating in Norway.[79] In relation to the MRM exception, the WTO Panel found that it violated Article III:4 of the GATT 1994, since it accorded seal products from Canada treatment less favourable than that accorded to like domestic seal products. The Panel also found that the IC exception and the MRM exception were not justified under Article XX(a) of the GATT 1994 ('necessary to protect public morals') because they failed to meet the requirements under the chapeau of Article XX. Additionally, the Panel found that the EU failed to make a prima facie case that the EU seal regime is justified under Article XX(b) of the GATT 1994.

The Panel, as well as the Appellate Body, had no difficulty in concluding that the EU seal regime was necessary to protect public morals under Article XX(a).[80] However, the Appellate Body made the following findings with respect to the chapeau:

EC – Products (Appellate Body)

5.306. One of the most important factors in the assessment of arbitrary or unjustifiable discrimination is the question of whether the discrimination can be reconciled with, or is rationally related to, the policy objective with respect to which the measure has been provisionally justified under one of the subparagraphs of Article XX. In *Brazil – Retreaded Tyres*, the Appellate Body considered this factor particularly relevant in assessing the merits of the explanations provided by the respondent as to the cause of the discrimination. As the Appellate Body stated, it had 'difficulty understanding how discrimination might be viewed as complying with the chapeau of Article XX when the alleged rationale for discriminating does not relate to the pursuit of or would go against the objective that was provisionally found to justify a measure under a paragraph of Article XX'. In *US – Shrimp*, the Appellate Body considered this factor as one element in a 'cumulative' assessment of 'unjustifiable discrimination'.

[. . .]

5.339. For these reasons, we find that the European Union has not demonstrated that the EU Seal Regime, in particular with respect to the IC exception, is designed and applied in a manner that meets the requirements of the chapeau of Article XX of the GATT 1994. It follows that the European Union has not justified the EU Seal Regime under Article XX(a) of the GATT 1994.

---

[79] Panel Reports, *EC – Seal Products*, para. 8.3(a).
[80] Panel Reports, *EC – Seal Products*, para. 7.639; Appellate Body Reports, *EC – Seal Products*, paras. 5.290 and 5.339.

EC – Seal Products is a unique and ground-breaking case in the interpretation of Article XX. The EU seal regime was provisionally justified under Article XX of the GATT, as it sought to protect public moral concerns about animal welfare. However, satisfying the chapeau was more difficult. In essence, this difficulty arose from the exceptions, namely the IC exception and the MRM exception. In other words, this case dealt with the issue of reconciling multiple non-trade values.[81] While protecting animal welfare was an important non-trade value, it conflicted with the objectives of the IC and the MRM exceptions, which had pro-trade effects, albeit for different reasons. The Appellate Body obviously considered the need for accommodating such multiple values. The Appellate Body was equally concerned with the fact that the EU did not seek to ameliorate animal welfare conditions, especially in relation to indigenous hunts in seals – a concern which formed the bedrock of this measure.

Second, the Appellate Body ruling in *EC – Seal Products* appears to have somewhat modified the finding of the Appellate Body in *Brazil – Retreaded Tyres* that the chapeau must bear a rational connection with, and must not go against, the objectives falling under the subparagraphs of Article XX.[82] In *Brazil – Retreaded Tyres*, the Appellate Body noted that it would be difficult to find any discrimination consistent with the chapeau, where such discrimination 'does not relate to the pursuit of or would go against the objective' that was provisionally justified. In *EC – Seal Products*, however, the Appellate Body noted that the relationship between the discrimination and policy objectives in subparagraphs (a)–(j) need not be the sole test while evaluating the chapeau. To this extent, it diluted the strong relationship mandated between the discriminatory aspects of the measure and policy objective enumerated in the subparagraphs of Article XX.[83] Furthermore, this approach obviously helps in accommodating various other non-trade values in the Article XX calculus.

9.2.9 Disguised Restriction

It is a well-accepted principle that a WTO member, while adopting measures for the fulfilment of a legitimate objective, shall not give occasion for disguised restriction on international trade. In *US – Gasoline*, the Appellate Body provided guidance for understanding these terms.

US – Gasoline *(Appellate Body)*

Page 25. It is clear to us that 'disguised restriction' includes disguised *discrimination* in international trade. It is equally clear that *concealed* or *unannounced* restriction or discrimination in international trade does *not* exhaust the meaning of 'disguised restriction'.

---

[81] J. Y. Qin, 'Accommodating Divergent Policy Objectives under WTO Law: Reflections on *EC – Seal Products*', *American Journal of International Law Unbound* (2015), 108, pp. 308–14.

[82] Appellate Body Report, *Brazil – Retreaded Tyres*, para. 227.

[83] Appellate Body Reports, *EC – Seal Products*, para. 5.321.

> **(cont.)**
>
> We consider that 'disguised restriction', whatever else it covers, may properly be read as embracing restrictions amounting to arbitrary or unjustifiable discrimination in international trade taken under the guise of a measure formally within the terms of an exception listed in Article XX. Put in a somewhat different manner, the kinds of considerations pertinent in deciding whether the application of a particular measure amounts to 'arbitrary or unjustifiable discrimination', may also be taken into account in determining the presence of a 'disguised restriction' on international trade. The fundamental theme is to be found in the purpose and object of avoiding abuse or illegitimate use of the exceptions to substantive rules available in Article XX.

The purpose of Article XX exceptions is to permit trade-restrictive or discriminatory measures if they are intended to pursuing a legitimate objective. By the same logic, measures that are implemented for protective or improper purposes could constitute disguised restrictions. This consideration is a key component of the chapeau.[84]

9.2.10 Conclusion

General exceptions are intended to provide a balance between the rights of States to regulate and their trade obligations incurred under the GATT. These exceptions serve two main purposes: to enhance regulatory flexibility on the one hand, and to provide for legal certainty in an adjudicatory context on the other.

There has been a trend in recent times to defer to the regulatory autonomy of the State, especially in relation to protecting vital societal interests, such as the right to health, public morals or environment. This is a stark departure from the days of the *US – Tuna (Mexico)* and *US – Tuna (EEC)* cases, where the focus was on preserving negotiated market access commitments. The creation of the two-tier analysis in Article XX seeks to ensure that the regulatory State can pursue certain legitimate societal interests and non-trade values, provided such measures are implemented in a non-discriminatory and non-protectionist manner.

The application of the two-tier analysis, however, is not without problems. Some of the measures, which have been accorded provisional justification, could stumble at the second tier of analysis – that is, while assessing the conformity of the measure with the chapeau. This could especially be true in situations where the challenged measure has provided some exceptions to certain targeted categories. The MERCOSUR exceptions in *Brazil – Retreaded Tyres* and the IC exceptions in *EC – Seal Products* possibly provide illustrations. While the chapeau may not be the appropriate place to evaluate the functional capability of

---

[84] L. Bartels, 'The Chapeau of the General Exceptions in the WTO GATT and GATS', *American Journal of International Law* (2015), 109, p. 125.

the measure to meet the declared public policy objectives, a clearly lopsided application of various State policies could still be reined in by the chapeau.

Of late, a large number of preferential trade agreements and international investment agreements are also finding inspiration from the GATT Article XX and GATS Article XIV general exceptions. These provisions include a number of common elements: an exhaustive list of permissible policy objectives (protection of human health, public morals and conservation of natural resources); and a general prohibition of the arbitrary or unjustifiable discrimination in the application of the designed exceptions.[85] The inclusion of the chapeau in such treaties is yet another noteworthy fact.

9.3   Other Exceptions

9.3.1   Security Exceptions

WTO law also provides for security exceptions in the GATT Article XXI and GATS Article XIV*bis*. As a matter of fact, these security exceptions have very rarely been invoked in GATT/WTO practice, although this practice is fast changing. The security exceptions can be invoked when States feel that their security interests are threatened,[86] or in relation to protecting strategic domestic industries (military, energy, health, food, etc.). For example, in 1975, Sweden invoked the GATT Article XXI security exceptions on certain footwear imports, presumably on the ground that footwear was an essential domestic industry that had to be preserved to maintain certain minimum production capacity. Sweden later withdrew the measure.[87]

As illustrated in Article XXI of the GATT 1994, security exceptions directly relate to general international law and the UN Charter's objective of maintenance of international peace and security. An interesting balance has to be kept here: while the sovereign State 'must be the judge of last resort on questions relating to its own security', the international system's equilibrium should be maintained by appropriate procedures justifying the essential character of necessary trade-restrictive measures (GATT 1994, Article XXI, paragraphs (a) and (b)).[88] Ultimately, States have to abide by their other international obligations and the

---

[85] See Chapter 13 for an analysis of the GATT, Art. XX-type of investment exceptions.

[86] P. C. Mavroidis, G. A. Bermann and M. Wu, *The Law of the World Trade Organization (WTO): Documents, Cases and Analysis* (St Paul: West, 2010), pp. 684–746. GATT 1994, Art. XXI was indeed only invoked in the following cases: *Summary Record of the Twenty-Second Meeting* (*US – Export Restrictions (Czechoslovakia)*), GATT CP.3/SR22, 8 June 1949, BISD II/28; GATT Panel Report, *United States – Imports of Sugar from Nicaragua*, L/5607, adopted 13 March 1984, BISD 31S/67; GATT Panel Report, *United States – Trade Measures Affecting Nicaragua*, L/6053, 13 October 1986, unadopted; *United States – The Cuban Liberty and Democratic Solidarity Act*, WT/DS38/6, 24 April 1998 (Lapse of the Authority for Establishment of the Panel); Communication from the European Communities, *Trade Measures Taken by the European Community against the Socialist Federal Republic of Yugoslavia*, GATT, L/6948, 2 December 1991.

[87] Alan O. Sykes, 'Editorial Comment: Economic "Necessity" in International Law', *American Journal of International Law* (2015), 109(2), pp. 296–323.

[88] Contracting Parties Decision, *Article XXI – United States Exports Restrictions*, 8 June 1949, BISD II/28.

UN Charter, which itself provides for the possible 'complete or partial interruption of economic relations' in its Article 41.[89]

GATT, Article XXI

Nothing in this Agreement shall be construed

(a) to require any contracting party to furnish any information the disclosure of which it considers contrary to its essential security interests; or

(b) to prevent any contracting party from taking any action which it considers necessary for the protection of its essential security interests (i) relating to fissionable materials or the materials from which they are derived; (ii) relating to the traffic in arms, ammunition and implements of war and to such traffic in other goods and materials as is carried on directly or indirectly for the purpose of supplying a military establishment; (iii) taken in time of war or other emergency in international relations; or

(c) To prevent any contracting party from taking any action in pursuance of its obligations under the United Nations Charter for the maintenance of international peace and security.

Trade sanctions are a good example of these interactions between general international law and international trade law. Although extremely controversial as they directly impact civilians in their daily lives, trade sanctions indeed remain a key instrument of State foreign policy. This is evident from the first case related to security exceptions that was brought to the WTO, namely, *United States – The Cuban Liberty and Democratic Solidarity Liberty Act of 1996*, popularly known as *US – Helms Burton*.

Box 9.2 The US, Cuba and the EU
Trade Sanctions and Extraterritoriality

The Cuban Liberty and Democratic Solidarity (Libertad) Act of 1996 (Helms–Burton Act, named after the two US Senators who sponsored the text) was a United States federal law that strengthened and continued the United States embargo against Cuba. The law was passed by the 104th United States Congress on 6 March 1996 and enacted into law by the 42nd President of the United States, Bill Clinton, on 12 March 1996.

---

[89] 'The Security Council may decide what measures not involving the use of armed force are to be employed to give effect to its decisions, and it may call upon the Members of the United Nations to apply such measures. These may include complete or partial interruption of economic relations and of rail, sea, air, postal, telegraphic, radio, and other means of communication, and the severance of diplomatic relations' (United Nations, Charter of the United Nations, 24 October 1945, 1 UNTS XVI).

Box 9.2 (cont.)

The Helms–Burton Act was considered to contain a number of provisions that imposed sanctions on products of Cuban origin or products from other countries that have a certain percentage of Cuban value addition. Under the Act, 'trafficking' (ownership) by third-country companies of Cuban properties once owned by Americans was opened up to lawsuits in the US, and required the exclusion from the US of owners or shareholders of companies 'trafficking' in property formerly owned or claimed by American nationals. It also alleged that this measure sought to restrain the freedom of third countries in transiting through US ports.

As explained at the time by Professor John Jackson, the law had frozen 'the 35-year-old US embargo against trade with and investment in Cuba, which applies not only to US firms but also to overseas firms owned or controlled by "US persons"'.[90]

The extraterritorial character of the text immediately revealed itself to be problematic and was condemned by the Council of Europe, the EU, Canada, Brazil, Argentina and Mexico, since the US was threatening to punish lawful activity – trade, investment and tourism carried out by residents of third countries with another independent country, Cuba. It was also denounced by civil society and humanitarian NGOs, as creating more hardship for a Cuban population directly suffering from the trade embargo.

The European Union introduced a Council Regulation declaring the extraterritorial provisions of the Helms–Burton Act to be unenforceable within the EU, and permitting recovery of any damages imposed under it.[91] In addition, the EC eventually challenged this measure before the WTO. The EC claimed that the US restrictions on goods of Cuban origin, as well as the possible refusal of visas and the exclusion of non-US nationals from US territory, were inconsistent with its obligations under the GATT Articles I, III, V, XI and XIII, and the GATS Articles I, III, VI, XVI and XVII. The WTO consultations were inconclusive and a Panel was established to adjudicate the matter on 20 November 1996. Subsequent to the establishment of the Panel and the refusal of the US to participate in the procedure, the EC made a request for the suspension of the Panel in its submission on 21 April 1997. Although the WTO was not notified of a mutually agreed solution, the EC has not resurrected the original Panel.

The GATS also provides for security exceptions in its Article XIV*bis*, whose language is quite similar to Article XXI of the GATT 1994. Similarly, Article 73 of the TRIPS provides for security exceptions. Article XXI of the GATT 1994 and Article 73(b)(iii) of the TRIPS

---

[90] J. H. Jackson, 'Helms–Burton, the US, and the WTO', *American Society of International Law Insights* (1997), 2(1), available at www.asil.org/insights/volume/2/issue/1/helms-burton-us-and-wto (accessed 21 December 2020).

[91] Council Regulation (EC) No. 2271/96, 22 November 1996.

were the subject matter of two recent WTO disputes, *viz.*, *Russia – Traffic in Transit* and *Saudi Arabia – Protection of IPRs*, discussed below.

RUSSIA – TRAFFIC IN TRANSIT

Russia imposed transit restrictions of varying degrees by preventing traffic coming from Ukraine and/or going to Kazakhstan or the Kyrgyz Republic through Russian territory. Ukraine claimed violations of several provisions of the GATT and, in particular, Article V:2, which guarantees freedom of transit of goods.[92] Russia, in its defence, invoked Article XXI(b)(iii) of the GATT 1994, arguing that the Panel lacked the jurisdiction to evaluate measures in respect of which Article XXI is invoked.[93] Russia's jurisdiction argument was based on its interpretation of Article XXI(b)(iii) as being totally 'self-judging'.[94] Russia argued that the Panel's only role was to recognise that Russia had invoked Article XXI.

The Panel, at the beginning, decided to address the jurisdictional issues before going into the merits of the case.[95] In a normal case, a panel would not have considered the applicability of the exception without examining the legality of the substantive claims.[96] Russia had argued that 'the explicit wording of Article XXI confer[red] sole discretion on the Member invoking this Article to determine the necessity, form, design and structure of the measures taken pursuant to Article XXI'.[97]

In the Panel's view, international adjudicative tribunals have an inherent jurisdiction to determine all matters arising in relation to the exercise of their own substantive jurisdiction under the principle of *Kompetenz-Kompetenz*.[98] The Panel then interpreted the meaning of Article XXI(b)(iii).

The introductory chapeau of Article XXI(b) contains the adjectival clause 'which it considers'. The question was whether this clause qualifies only the terms 'necessary' or 'essential security interests', which are part of the chapeau, or if it qualifies the determination of the circumstances in the subparagraphs of Article XXI(b).[99] The Panel first tested the last and the most extensive hypothesis.

The three subparagraphs of Article XXI(b) operate as limiting qualifying clauses on the exercise of the discretion of members.[100] They are substantially different and establish alternative, rather than cumulative, requirements.[101] The phrases 'relating to', 'taken in time of', 'war'

---

[92] Ukraine also alleged violation of paragraph 2 of Part I of the Protocol of Accession of Russia, which incorporates commitments in paragraph 1161 of the Working Party Report on the Accession of Russia and commitments in paragraphs 1426, 1427 and 1428 of Russia's Working Party Report, Panel Report, *Russia – Measures Concerning Traffic in Transit*, WT/DS512/R, adopted 26 April, 2019, para. 3.1.

[93] Panel Report, *Russia – Traffic in Transit*, para. 3.2.   [94] Panel Report, *Russia – Traffic in Transit*, para. 7.26.

[95] Panel Report, *Russia – Traffic in Transit*, paras. 7.24–7.25.

[96] Tania Voon, 'Russia – Measures Concerning Traffic in Transit', *American Journal of International Law* (2020), 114(1), pp. 96–103.

[97] Panel Report, *Russia – Traffic in Transit*, para. 7.28.

[98] Panel Report, *Russia – Traffic in Transit*, para. 7.53 and fn. 145.

[99] Panel Report, *Russia – Traffic in Transit*, para. 7.63.   [100] Panel Report, *Russia – Traffic in Transit*, para. 7.65.

[101] Panel Report, *Russia – Traffic in Transit*, para. 7.68.

and 'emergency in international relations' are amenable to objective determination. The Panel examined the text and context of Article XXI, including its negotiating history, and concluded that the circumstances in subparagraph (ii) are an 'objective fact, subject to objective determination'.[102] The Panel thus concluded that the clause 'which it considers' did not extend to determination of the subparagraphs of Article XXI(b).[103]

The Panel next determined whether the measures at issue fall within the scope of Article XXI(b)(iii). It opined that a war or other emergency in international relations involves a fundamental change of circumstances.[104] An 'emergency in international relations', in particular, refers generally to a situation of armed conflict, or of latent armed conflict, or of heightened tension or crisis, or of general instability engulfing or surrounding a State. It also gives rise to particular types of interests – that is, defence or military interests, or maintenance of law and public order interests.[105] The situation cannot be one of mere political or economic differences between members. Based on the evidence, that the situation between Ukraine and Russia was recognised by the UN General Assembly as involving armed conflict and a number of countries had imposed sanctions against Russia, the Panel concluded that measures were taken in time of an emergency in international relations.[106]

Finally, the issue was whether the chapeau of Article XXI(b) was satisfied. The Panel was of the view that 'essential security interests' generally mean 'those interests relating to the quintessential functions of the State, namely, the protection of its territory and its population from external threats, and the maintenance of law and public order internally'.[107] However, the determination of essential security interests and the necessity of the measures have to be determined by the member itself.[108] This discretion is subject to the good faith obligation of articulating or defining essential security interests and of proving their connection with the measures at issue.[109] In conclusion, the Panel determined that Russia met the requirements for invoking Article XXI(b)(iii) of the GATT 1994.[110]

9.3.2 Security Exceptions in other WTO Cases

The United States, by Presidential Proclamation, imposed 25 per cent and 10 per cent *ad valorem* import duties on steel and aluminium imports against a number of WTO countries.[111]

---

[102] Panel Report, *Russia – Traffic in Transit*, para. 7.77.   [103] Panel Report, *Russia – Traffic in Transit*, para. 7.101.
[104] Panel Report, *Russia – Traffic in Transit*, para. 108.   [105] Panel Report, *Russia – Traffic in Transit*, para. 7.76.
[106] Panel Report, *Russia – Traffic in Transit*, para. 7.125.
[107] Panel Report, *Russia – Traffic in Transit*, para. 7.130.
[108] Panel Report, *Russia – Traffic in Transit*, paras. 7.131, 7.146.
[109] Panel Report, *Russia – Traffic in Transit*, paras. 7.130–7.132, 7.134, 7.138.
[110] Panel Report, *Russia – Traffic in Transit*, para. 7.149.
[111] Adjusting Imports of Steel into the United States, including the Annex: To Modify Chapter 99 of the Harmonized Tariff Schedule of the United States (Presidential Proclamation 9705, issued 8 March 2018), 83 FR 11625–11630, 15 March 2018; Adjusting Imports of Aluminum into the United States, including the Annex: To Modify Chapter 99 of the Harmonized Tariff Schedule of the United States (Presidential Proclamation 9704, issued 8 March 2018), 83 FR 11619–11624, 15 March 2018.

The measure resulted in a series of WTO disputes.[112] The United States has relied on national security concerns while defending its measures in a DSB meeting and subsequent Panel proceedings.[113] It reasoned that 'the tariffs imposed under Section 232 of the US Trade Expansion Act were necessary for the protection of its essential security interests given the key role steel and aluminum plays in US national defense'.[114]

In *United Arab Emirates – Goods, Services and IP Rights*, Qatar claimed that the United Arab Emirates (UAE) had violated its rights under the WTO's GATT, GATS and the TRIPS Agreement.[115] Saudi Arabia had also severed diplomatic and consular relations with Qatar and imposed comprehensive measures putting an end to all economic and trade relations between the two countries. In the dispute against Saudi Arabia, the respondent has relied on essential security exceptions.[116] In June 2017, Saudi Arabia imposed a scheme of diplomatic, political and economic measures against Qatar. In addition to severing diplomatic and consular relations with Qatar, Saudi Arabia had closed all its ports for Qatari use, prevented Qatari nationals from crossing into Saudi territory, and expelled Qatari residents and visitors in Saudi territories.[117] Such measures impacted the ability of Qatari nationals to protect intellectual property rights in Saudi Arabia.[118]

The worsening of the political relationship also had its impact on commercial businesses. In particular, the measures affected beIN Media Group LLC (beIN), a global sports and entertainment company headquartered in Qatar.[119] It had obtained the exclusive rights to broadcast and to authorise others to broadcast, prime sporting competitions in the MENA region, including in Saudi Arabia.[120] Following Saudi Arabia's severance of relations with Qatar, beIN's website in Saudi Arabia was blocked by the Saudi government and a circular

---

[112] DS544: *United States – Certain Measures on Steel and Aluminium Products* (China); DS548: *United States – Certain Measures on Steel and Aluminium Products* (EU); DS552: *United States – Certain Measures on Steel and Aluminium Products* (Norway); DS554: *United States – Certain Measures on Steel and Aluminium Products* (Russia); DS564: *United States – Certain Measures on Steel and Aluminium Products* (Turkey); DS547: *United States – Certain Measures on Steel and Aluminium Products* (India); DS556: *United States – Certain Measures on Steel and Aluminium Products* (Switzerland).

[113] Summary of the DSB meeting: Panels established to review US steel and aluminium tariffs, countermeasures on US imports, 21 November 2018, available at www.wto.org/english/news_e/news18_e/dsb_19nov18_e.htm (accessed 21 December 2020).

[114] Summary of DSB Meeting.

[115] Request for Consultations by Qatar, *United Arab Emirates – Measures Relating to Trade in Goods and Services, and Trade-Related Aspects of Intellectual Property Rights*, WT/DS526/1, 4 August 2017, para. 2.

[116] Request for the Establishment of a Panel by Qatar, *Saudi Arabia – Measures Concerning the Protection of Intellectual Property Rights*, WT/DS567/3, 9 November 2018; see also Minutes of Meeting, WT/DSB/M/422, held on 4 December 2018, para. 5.3.

[117] Panel Report, *Saudi Arabia – Measures Concerning the Protection of Intellectual Property Rights*, WT/DS567/R, 16 June 2020, para. 2.29.

[118] Panel Report, *Saudi Arabia – Protection of IPR*, para. 2.18.

[119] Panel Report, *Saudi Arabia – Protection of IPR*, para. 2.30.

[120] Panel Report, *Saudi Arabia – Protection of IPR*, para. 2.32.

was issued, stating that beIN was not licensed to distribute media content and did not have the right to operate in Saudi Arabia.[121]

Since Saudi Arabia had invoked the security exception in Article 73(b)(iii) of the TRIPS Agreement, the Panel had to decide whether the measures constituted actions 'which it considers necessary for the protection of its essential security interests' and 'are taken in time of war or other emergency in international relations'.[122] The Panel followed the various steps enunciated in *Russia – Transit* while addressing this matter.

The Panel found that an 'emergency in international relations' existed in this case and that the measures were taken in time of an 'emergency in international relations'.[123] The Panel also analysed whether Saudi Arabi had sufficiently articulated its relevant 'essential security interests' in terms of protecting itself from the stated 'dangers of terrorism and extremism', and eventually concluded that Saudi Arabia's articulation of its relevant 'essential security interests' was sufficient.[124] Finally, the Panel examined whether the relevant actions were so remote from, or unrelated to, the 'emergency in international relations' as to make it *implausible.*

In relation to the last test (the test of 'implausibility'), the Panel first analysed the measures that prevented beIN from obtaining Saudi legal counsel to enforce its IP rights through civil enforcement procedures before Saudi courts and tribunals ('anti-sympathy measures').[125] Given that Saudi Arabia had imposed a travel ban on all Qatari nationals and expelled all Qatari nationals in Saudi Arabia as part of the comprehensive measures, the Panel held that it was not implausible that Saudi Arabia might take measures to prevent Qatari nationals from having access to courts, tribunals and other institutions in Saudi Arabia.[126] There were also claims that beoutQ[127] had begun the unauthorised distribution and streaming of media content that is created by or licensed to beIN. It was alleged that Saudi Arabia has not provided for criminal procedures and penalties to be applied to beoutQ, despite having significant evidence in this regard.[128] The Panel, however, found no rational or logical connection between the comprehensive measures aimed at ending interaction with Qatar and Qatari nationals, and the non-application of Saudi criminal procedures and penalties to beoutQ.[129]

The Panel concluded that the requirements for invoking the security exception under Article 73(b)(iii) are met in relation to one category of measures, namely the anti-sympathy measures that involved inconsistency with Articles 42 and 41.1 of the TRIPS Agreement, whereas the Panel found that the security exception failed to apply to the category of

---

[121] Panel Report, *Saudi Arabia – Protection of IPR*, para. 2.37.
[122] Panel Report, *Saudi Arabia – Protection of IPR*, para. 7.229.
[123] Panel Report, *Saudi Arabia – Protection of IPR*, paras. 7.269–7.270.
[124] Panel Report, *Saudi Arabia – Protection of IPR*, paras. 7.280–7.282.
[125] Panel Report, *Saudi Arabia – Protection of IPR*, para. 7.285.
[126] Panel Report, *Saudi Arabia – Protection of IPR*, para. 7.286.
[127] The name 'beoutQ' – that is, 'be out Qatar' – is a play on the name beIN Sports.
[128] Panel Report, *Saudi Arabia – Protection of IPR*, para. 8.1.
[129] Panel Report, *Saudi Arabia – Protection of IPR*, para. 7.292.

measures under Saudi Arabia's non-application of criminal procedures and penalties to beoutQ falling under Article 61 of the TRIPS Agreement.[130]

9.4   Economic Emergency and Regional Trade Agreements Exceptions

Can exception become the norm? This is indeed what has happened as far as economic emergency exceptions and regional trade agreements exceptions are concerned. While originally considered under the exception category, one can easily argue that the very wide recourse to these trade measures has de facto modified their categorisation. For this reason, economic emergency measures, as well as regional trade agreements, are covered at greater length in Chapter 2. However, for the sake of understanding, we now briefly address some of their main features.

Economic emergency exceptions allow WTO members to adopt two types of 'emergency' measures (for example, safeguards and balance-of-payment solutions) to react to an unexpected trade situation threatening a member's economy. Safeguards are covered by the GATT 1994 Article XIX and the WTO Agreement on Safeguards, and may be adopted in case a surge in a particular import 'causes or threatens to cause serious injury to the domestic industry that produces like or directly competitive products'.[131] On the other hand, balance-of-payment measures under the GATT 1994 Articles XII and XVIII:B and the GATS Article XII:1 allow members to adopt specific measures to protect their financial situation.

Economic emergency exceptions are particularly relevant today, in times of health emergencies, and the Covid-19 crisis in particular. While there is no general international law definition of economic emergency, State constitutions often provide for a series of emergency-related measures. For example, Article 360 (Part XVIII Emergency Provisions) of the Indian Constitution includes 'Provisions as to Financial Emergency'. These provisions are to be read in conjunction with available trade-related economic emergency measures. In this regard, balance-of-payment measures are likely to play a greater role in countries' responses to the Covid-19 crisis, an economic and health emergency indeed.[132] If a country is grappling with a major balance-of-payments difficulty, it may not be able to expand imports. Instead, the country may be tempted to impose measures to restrict imports and discourage capital outflows in order to improve the balance-of-payments situation.

Regional trade agreements are often presented as exceptions allowing WTO members to adopt otherwise inconsistent measures when forming regional trade groupings. The recent proliferation of regional trade agreements and other mega trade deals has largely complicated an already complex situation so much that the differentiation between regional trade

---

[130] Panel Report, *Saudi Arabia – Protection of IPR*, para. 7.294.   [131] Agreement on Safeguards, Art. 2.

[132] Martin Wolf, 'The Virus Is an Economic Emergency Too', *Financial Times* (17 March 2020), available at www.ft .com/content/348e05e4-6778-11ea-800d-da70cff6e4d3 (accessed 21 December 2020). See IMF, Policy Responses to Covid-19, for an account of economic emergency measures taken by States in response to the Covid-19 crisis: www .imf.org/en/Topics/imf-and-covid19/Policy-Responses-to-COVID-19 (accessed 21 December 2020).

agreements themselves and the measures considered as regional trade exceptions has become problematic. For these reasons, regional trade exceptions under the GATT and the GATS are addressed in Chapters 2 and 8.

9.5   Summary

- Four types of trade exceptions are generally identified: general exceptions, security exceptions, economic emergency exceptions and regional trade exceptions.
- These general exception provisions are intended to strike a balance between the State's right to regulate and its trade obligations. In particular, the below tests and criteria have been developed for the GATT Article XX:
  - ○ a first-tier examination based on the 'necessity' test;
  - ○ a first-tier examination based on the 'relating to' test;
  - ○ whether the measure was made effective 'in conjunction with' (other measures);
  - ○ whether the measure was 'essential to the acquisition or distribution of products in general or local short supply';
  - ○ a second-tier examination based on the interpretation of the chapeau of the GATT 1994 Article XX and whether the measure was an arbitrary or unjustifiable discrimination or a disguised restriction to trade.
- Security exceptions have rarely been used in the past, but their use has risen since 2017. Security exceptions are not purely self-judging, in the sense that a WTO member cannot insist on a panel not to exercise its jurisdiction in a matter that involves a national security defence. In other words, a member does not have unfettered discretion in invoking security exceptions, thereby precluding the scrutiny of the challenged measure by a panel.
- Economic emergency exceptions and regional trade exceptions have somehow become the norm. While originally considered under the category exceptions, recourse to these measures has become so widespread as to impact on their categorisation. For this reason, economic emergency measures as well as regional trade agreements are covered at greater length in Chapters 2 and 8.
- There is a general requirement of 'even-handedness' in applying trade exceptions. Measures taken to protect States' regulatory autonomy need to be neutral and even-handed in their approach – that is, they should not result in discriminatory and/or arbitrary application of laws and regulations among members.

9.6   Review Questions

1 In *China – Raw Materials*, the respondents first relied on the exceptions under Article XI:2 (c)(i) of the GATT 1994. Can a WTO member rely on the Article XX exceptions in addition to other specific exceptions listed under the GATT?

2 In *China – Rare Earths*, China sought to justify its export duties that violated Paragraph 11.3 of China's Accession Protocol to the WTO, by asserting that these duties were justifiable as measures 'necessary to protect human, animal, or plant life or health' under Article XX(b) of the GATT 1994. Can the GATT Article XX be used to defend violations of other instruments under the WTO umbrella? Are general exceptions available for derogations from the provisions of the Protocol of Accession of WTO members? (Refer to *China – Publications and Audiovisual Products*, *China – Raw Materials* and *China – Rare Earths*. Search for the China Accession Protocol (WT/L/432) and see what is specific in it in relation to trade restrictions.)

3 Is it possible to use an Article XX general exception to defend a violation of specific provisions of agreements covered by Annex IA? (Refer to Panel Report, *US – Poultry (China)*.)

4 In *US – Gasoline*, the measure at issue was the different 'baseline' standards applicable to US and Venezuelan gasoline producers. The nature of examination of discrimination under the Article XX chapeau is different to the standard by which a violation of the substantive rule – for example, a violation of NT under Article III:4 – has been determined to have occurred. Consider what standards should be employed by a Panel or Appellate Body when appraising a measure under the Article XX chapeau, when it has already been found that the measure has violated the substantive non-discrimination provisions of the GATT. (Examine how the Appellate Body approached this issue in *EC – Seal Products*.)

5 In light of the *EC – Seal Products* case, is it reasonable to conclude that the non-discrimination requirement mentioned in the Article XX chapeau is similar to the substantive non-discrimination requirement under various substantive obligations of the GATT?

6 Are the meanings of 'necessary' under Article XX(b) and 'essential' in Article XX(j) nearly the same? Should these terms have the same content, meaning and application in the context of the WTO disputes? (Refer to *India – Solar Cells*.)

7 Do the subparagraphs of Article XX contain any inherent territorial limitation? Can a regulating State adopt a measure to protect natural resources outside its jurisdiction? What are the findings of the *US – Tuna (Mexico)* and *US – Tuna (EEC)* GATT Panels in this regard? How did the Appellate Body respond to this proposition in *US – Shrimp*?

8 Is Article XXI of the GATT 'self-judging'? Or is it justiciable?

9.7   Exercise

Trade relations are very tense between the Mare Nostrum Union (MNU), a regional trade union of developed countries, and its developing countries partners of the CAP region.

While the MNU has recently declared that it would not put 'undue pressure' on developing countries to conclude their controversial economic partnership deals (EPDs), the MNU's commercial policy is very badly perceived by most of its developing and least-developed trading partners of the CAP. Numerous violent demonstrations have taken place in Grecka, the administrative capital of the MNU. International NGOs and trade unions are particularly active in denouncing the negative consequences that a new trade deal could imply for the developing world, and for the CAP region in particular. But the MNU insists on the need to 'rethink trade cooperation for a better and more sustainable development'.

On 13 March 2011, Indoustani, Saint Luciou, Pakoustan and Ivory Land, four developing countries, requested consultations with the MNU at the WTO concerning the ban on importation of scallops and scallops products from their countries, imposed by the MNU under Section IX of its Regional Harmonized Trade Code. MNU's measures were introduced under the *Conservation of Fisheries and Prevention of Harmful Harvesting Act.* Violations of Articles I, III, XI and XIII of the GATT 1994, as well as nullification and impairment of trade benefits, are alleged by the complainants.

Your firm, Freuden Und Recht Partners, is well-known for its expertise in agricultural disputes. Indeed, it was in charge of Thailand's interests during the 'shrimp war'. You have been requested to advise the complainants and to write a legal brief supporting their position. To do so, please reply clearly (in a structured and logical way) to the two following questions:

1 Your team of lawyers is firmly convinced that the best way to advance the complainants' position is to use Article XI of the GATT 1994 in a clever manner. How would you put forward your arguments in relation to the other articles mentioned above? (Please refer to other chapters of this book and think about possible recourse to Article XI:2 as an alternative or complementary measure to Article XX.)

2 In an interview given to the French daily *Le Monde* and reproduced on the Financial Times website, the MNU Trade Secretary, Mrs La Mer, argued that most of the MNU importation control policies (and Section IX of their Trade Code) fall under Article XX(g) of the GATT 1994. She added: 'The techniques used by Indoustani, Saint Luciou, Pakoustan and Ivory Land fishermen to collect baby scallops are not in line with the imperative to protect the environment as they impair scallops' reproduction and harmonious development.' You are not convinced by this argument and think one needs to find a 'line of equilibrium'. Accordingly, you should prepare a counterargument based on your understanding of Article XX of the GATT 1994.

FURTHER READING

Baroncini, E., 'An Impossible Relationship? Article XX GATT and China's Accession Protocol in the China – Raw Materials Case', *Biores* (2012), 6(1), pp. 18–22.

Bartels, L., 'The Chapeau of the General Exceptions in the WTO GATT and GATS Agreement', *American Journal of International Law* (2015), 109, pp. 95–125.

Howse, R., 'The Appellate Body Rulings in the Shrimp/Turtle Case: A New Legal Baseline for the Trade and Environment Debate', *Columbia Journal of Environmental Law* (2002), 27(2), pp. 489–519.

Mavroidis, P. C., Bermann, G. A. and Wu, M., *The Law of the World Trade Organization (WTO): Documents, Cases and Analysis* (St Paul: West, 2010), chs. 20, 21, 22.

Pauwelyn, J. H. B., Guzman, A. T. and Hillman, J. A., *International Trade Law* (New York: Wolters Kluwer: 2016), chs. 13 and 14.

Quin, J. Y., 'Accommodating Divergent Policy Objectives under WTO Law: Reflections on EC – Seal Products', *AJIL Unbound* (2014), 108, pp. 308–14.

Reagan, D. H., 'The Meaning of "Necessary" in GATT Article XX and GATS Article XIV: The Myth of Cost–Benefit Balancing', *World Trade Review* (2007), 6, pp. 347–60.

10 WTO Dispute Settlement

Table of Contents

Highlights

- The dispute settlement mechanism of the WTO is rooted in Articles XXII and XXIII of the GATT 1947.
- The WTO Dispute Settlement Understanding (DSU) improved on the dispute settlement mechanism under the GATT 1947. It governs the rules and procedures for all disputes arising under the covered agreements of the Final Act of the Uruguay Round.
- The DSU's key success was in establishing an enforceable, compulsory and automatic dispute resolution mechanism at the WTO.
- The DSU provides strict timelines for the dispute settlement mechanism and consists of four key steps:
  1 **Consultations**: Initial non-judicial diplomatic method through which members can resolve a dispute.
  2 **Panel stage**: It begins the adjudicative process and includes written submissions, arguments and evidence before the panellists.
  3 **Appellate stage**: Appeals lie from the Panel to the Appellate Body.
  4 **Implementation**: After the Panel and Appellate Body Reports are adopted by the DSB, the losing member is required to implement the DSB ruling.
- Since its establishment, the WTO dispute settlement system has received almost 600 dispute consultation requests, making it one of the most active international law tribunals.
- The WTO DSU is facing a major crisis, with the Appellate Body becoming dysfunctional in December 2019. The restoration of the two-tier appeal mechanism envisaged under the DSU will be the biggest challenge for the members.

10.1 Introduction

Dispute settlement under the WTO is a legacy of the GATT 1947. Since the GATT was only a provisional agreement, it did not provide for an elaborate dispute settlement mechanism. Dispute settlement under the GATT 1947 relied mainly on Articles XXII and XXIII, which provided only a skeletal framework. Initially, in the event of a complaint, the parties discussed the matter with a view to finding an acceptable solution. If no solutions were found, the GATT membership as a whole investigated the matter and made rulings or recommendations. The GATT dispute settlement system, however, evolved significantly over several decades and provided the basis for a much improved Understanding on Rules and Procedures Governing the Settlement of Disputes (DSU), as specified in Annex 2 of the WTO Agreement.

The WTO dispute settlement mechanism has been prolific. As of December 2020, 598 disputes had been initiated at the WTO. Of these, at least half (256 disputes) have resulted in Panel Reports. In comparison with other international tribunals, this is a significant achievement.

As the number of disputes being filed under the WTO dispute settlement system keeps increasing, some of the controversies relating to the role and functioning of the Appellate

Body has unexpectedly exposed the dispute settlement system to a troubling and tumultuous future. In other words, this is also a period for undertaking certain reforms or addressing procedural weaknesses within the DSU. This chapter, among other topics, discusses some of the key reform proposals to the DSU.

10.2 Developments from the GATT to the WTO

10.2.1 History of the DSU

The GATT 1947 came into force as an interim arrangement. The United States Congress did not adopt the Havana Charter, which left the much-envisioned International Trade Organization stillborn. With this setback, countries fell back on the GATT 1947, which became the default framework for the multilateral trading system.

As the GATT 1947 was a provisional agreement, its drafters did not envisage the requirement for comprehensive provisions on dispute settlement. Articles XXII and XXIII of the GATT 1947, which pertain to the settlement of disputes, do not even mention the terms 'working parties', 'dispute settlement' or 'panel'. However, these two provisions evolved to provide over a hundred Panel Reports, authored by 'working parties' of experts prior to the establishment of the WTO, successfully contributing to a body of jurisprudence that remains relevant even today. In the words of John Jackson, the GATT 1947 was far more successful than what might have been fairly predicted in the late 1940s.[1]

The GATT signatories were called contracting parties. Article XXII, entitled 'Consultations', allows contracting parties to consult with one another and find a solution with respect to 'any matter affecting the operation of this Agreement'. On the other hand, Article XXIII, entitled 'Nullification and Impairment', provided for the contracting parties to make written representations or proposals to seek resolution of their concerns if any benefits accruing under the GATT 1947 were nullified or impaired. The GATT Article XXIII:1 also provides that a contracting party shall give sympathetic consideration to such representations or proposals. Article XXIII:2 provides for retaliatory measures through suspension of concessions if the 'circumstances are serious enough to justify such actions'.

Article XXIII:2 of the GATT 1947 outlines certain basic concepts regarding dispute settlement. Initially, the disputes were decided by rulings of the Chairman of the GATT Council, later by working parties composed of representatives from all interested contracting parties, and eventually by panels of independent experts (three or five in number) drawn from countries unrelated to the dispute.[2] However, the recommendations of the Panels were adopted by way of *positive consensus*, which meant that all contracting parties, including the parties to the dispute, have to agree for their adoption. Since the consensus of the respondent

---

[1] J. H. Jackson, 'Dispute Settlement and the WTO: Emerging Problems', *Journal of International Economic Law* (1998), 1(3), pp. 329–51.

[2] C. VanGrasstek, *The History and Future of the World Trade Organization* (Geneva: World Trade Organization, 2013), p. 51.

to the dispute was also required, it effectively provided a veto power to the respondent party to block any stage of the dispute settlement process. Nonetheless, the informal and more or less diplomatic nature of the proceedings ensured that the dispute resolution process was characterised by flexibility and generally devoid of hostility.[3]

The contracting parties of the GATT made efforts to legalise and codify the dispute settlement practices in the form of decisions that laid down procedural aspects of dispute settlement.[4] Furthermore, in order to enhance the legal aspects of the dispute settlement system, a GATT Office of Legal Affairs was established within the GATT Secretariat in 1983.[5]

The GATT 1947 was envisaged to be an interim solution, and its dispute settlement mechanism was by and large ad hoc. Gradually, the dispute settlement mechanism under the GATT 1947 transformed from a mediation or diplomatic discussion between the contracting parties to a more rules-oriented approach, involving a much larger membership. The power-oriented GATT 1947 system had its own nimbleness and the flexibility to deal with certain special sensitivities of the contracting parties. Even John Jackson, who passionately argued for a rule-based system, understood the importance of institutional space for political and/or diplomatic adjustment for rule-based outcomes.[6] Some of the obvious shortcomings of the GATT dispute settlement system are set out in Box 10.1.

Box 10.1 Shortcomings of the GATT 1947 dispute settlement system

- Positive consensus was essential for the adoption of GATT Panel Reports.
- No strict timelines or effective and transparent procedures for dispute settlement.
- Lack of clarity in the language of Articles XXII and XXIII of the GATT 1947.
- No appellate mechanism.
- No institutional framework for dispute settlement.

During the initial part of the Uruguay Round negotiations, the negotiating parties attempted to remedy some of these shortcomings and adopted the Decision of 12 April 1989 on Improvements to the GATT Dispute Settlement Rules and Procedures, but failed to agree upon a number of critical issues. Finally, at the end of the Uruguay Round, a rules-based dispute settlement procedure with strict timelines was implemented through the DSU.

---

[3] Y. Xu and P. Weller, *The Governance of World Trade: International Civil Servants and GATT/WTO* (Cheltenham: Edward Elgar, 2004), p. 199.

[4] Decision of 5 April 1966 on Procedures under Art. XXIII, BISD 14S/18; Understanding on Notification, Consultation, Dispute Settlement and Surveillance, adopted 28 November 1979, BISD 26S/10; Decision on Dispute Settlement, contained in the Ministerial Declaration of 29 November 1982, BISD 29S/13; Decision on Dispute Settlement of 30 November 1984, BISD 31S/9.

[5] For a history of the evolution of legal institutions, such as the legal secretariat for GATT Panel Reports, see, generally, G. Marceau, *A History of Law and Lawyers in the GATT/WTO* (Cambridge University Press, 2015).

[6] J. H. Jackson, *Restructuring the GATT System* (New York: Council on Foreign Relations, 1990). See also R. L. Howse, 'The House that Jackson Built: Restructuring the GATT System', *Michigan Journal of International Law* (1997), 20(2), 107–19.

10.2.1.1   Dispute Settlement Systems of the GATT 1947 and the WTO DSU

The DSU came into force on 1 January 1995. As one of the key results of the Uruguay Round, the DSU introduced a comprehensive dispute settlement process under the WTO, which included a two-tier dispute settlement system, including specific timelines for the resolution and implementation of the disputes. Article 3.1 of the DSU specifies that it adheres to and elaborates on Articles XXII and XXIII of the GATT 1947. The key differences between the GATT 1947 dispute settlement mechanism and the DSU are discussed in Table 10.1.

Table 10.1 Differences between the GATT 1947 and the DSU

GATT 1947	DSU
A single contracting party can veto adopting of a Panel Report, due to positive consensus, which requires all contracting parties to agree to the adoption of a Panel Report, known as 'positive consensus'	No single member has the power to block/delay the adoption of a Panel Report, which is adopted unless there is a consensus among the Membership not to do so – known as negative/reverse consensus
No detailed timelines specified for the completion of the dispute	Prompt timelines specified where members are required to adopt Panel Reports within 12.5 months, or 15.5 months if there is an appeal to the Appellate Body, followed by a reasonable period for implementation
No institutional body created to oversee dispute settlement	The Marrakesh Treaty has an established Dispute Settlement Body (DSB) and a well-staffed secretariat to oversee and assist in dispute settlement, respectively
No compulsory jurisdiction	Provides compulsory jurisdiction over disputes arising under the covered agreements
No procedure for appeal	Establishment of the Appellate Body to preside over appeals
Third parties could not participate in a dispute	DSU allows for third parties that have 'substantial interest' in a matter to participate in a dispute
No interim review of arguments	DSU allows Panels to issue an interim Panel Report prior to the issuance of the final report
No provision to seek information from non-contracting parties	DSU Article 13 allows Panel to seek information and technical advice from any individual or body

10.2.2 WTO Dispute Settlement Understanding

10.2.2.1   Structure and Scope of the DSU

The DSU consists of twenty-seven Articles. The DSU also includes four Appendices, namely: (1) list of WTO Agreements governed by the DSU; (2) special or additional rules and procedures contained in the covered agreements that prevail in the event of conflict with the DSU; (3) working procedures for the Panel; and (4) rules for panels to seek information from expert review groups.

The DSU is designed to provide a unified system of dispute resolution of all Uruguay Round Agreements, with some minor exceptions. Article 1.1 states that the DSU applies to all the Agreements specified in Appendix 1 and refers to these as 'covered agreements'. The covered agreements include the WTO Agreement, the Agreements in Annexes 1 and 2, and any plurilateral trade agreement in Annex 4 where its committee of signatories has taken a decision to apply the DSU.[7] But some covered agreements have special rules and procedures that are specified in Appendix 2 of the DSU. Article 1.2 of the DSU specifies the principle of *lex specialis* and, in the event of a conflict between the DSU and the special rules and procedures identified in Appendix 2 of the DSU, the special rules in Appendix 2 shall prevail. (See Introduction.)

10.2.2.2 Purpose of the DSU

The DSU does not contain a Preamble, which usually specifies the purpose of the Agreement. However, Article 3.2 of the DSU specifies the central element of the WTO dispute settlement system:

DSU, Article 3.2

The dispute settlement system of the WTO is a central element in providing security and predictability to the multilateral trading system. The Members recognize that it serves to preserve the rights and obligations of Members under the covered agreements, and to clarify the existing provisions of those agreements in accordance with customary rules of interpretation of public international law. Recommendations and rulings of the DSB cannot add to or diminish the rights and obligations provided in the covered agreements.

Furthermore, Article 3.7 of the DSU prescribes that the dispute settlement mechanism is aimed at securing a positive solution that is mutually acceptable to the parties to the dispute. In the absence of a mutually agreed solution, the first objective is to secure the withdrawal of the measure, if such measure is found to be inconsistent with the provisions of the covered agreement.

Therefore, unlike Article XXII of the GATT 1947, the DSU's main aim is to seek a positive solution that is mutually acceptable to the parties to the dispute. Furthermore, Articles 3.3 and 3.4 state that the dispute settlement system 'is essential to the effective functioning of the WTO' and is aimed at achieving 'a satisfactory settlement' of disputes.

---

[7] Appellate Body Report, *Brazil – Measures Affecting Desiccated Coconut*, WT/DS22/AB/R, adopted 20 March 1997, p. 13.

10.2.2.3   DSU and Compulsory Jurisdiction

Article 23.1 of the DSU confers compulsory jurisdiction to the WTO's DSB in relation to recourse to remedies concerning violations of obligation or other nullification or impairment of benefits under the covered agreement.

> ## DSU, Article 23.1
>
> When Members seek the redress of a violation of obligations or other nullification or impairment of benefits under the covered agreements or an impediment to the attainment of any objective of the covered agreements, they shall have recourse to, and abide by, the rules and procedures of this Understanding.

This provision ensures the exclusivity of jurisdiction of the DSU over WTO Agreements. Therefore, the complaining member is required to bring any dispute arising under the covered agreements to the WTO dispute settlement system. A WTO Panel has interpreted Article 23.1 to impose an obligation on members to have recourse to the DSU 'to the exclusion of any other system, in particular a system of unilateral enforcements of WTO rights and obligations'.[8] The prohibition in Article 23.1 would also bar tribunals formed under free trade agreements to interpret provisions of the covered agreements.

The respondent member also has to submit to the jurisdiction of the WTO dispute settlement system, since DSU Article 6.1 requires that a Panel be established on the request of the complaining party. The establishment of a Panel can be blocked only if there is a consensus not to establish a Panel.

Finally, panels and the Appellate Body do not have the power to issue advisory opinions. In other words, the WTO dispute settlement system is actively discouraged from providing rulings outside the context of a specific dispute.[9]

10.2.2.4   Decision-Making under the DSU

A major shortcoming of the GATT 1947 dispute settlement system was that essential steps, such as the establishment and adoption of Panel Reports, were based on positive consensus. There were also other ways in which a contracting party could avoid the dispute settlement procedures – for example, by blocking the appointment of panellists. In many ways, the blocking of the Panel Report was considered to be the most serious defect of the GATT dispute settlement system. This was modified in the DSU. Article 2.4 of the DSU provides that the DSB will take decisions by way of consensus.[10]

---

[8] Panel Report, *United States – Sections 301–310 of the Trade Act of 1974*, WT/DS152/R, adopted 27 January 2000, para. 7.43.
[9] DSU, Arts. 3.2, 19.2.   [10] DSU, fn. 1.

Accordingly, the DSU has ensured that all Appellate Body (and Panel) Reports are adopted automatically and accepted unconditionally by the parties to the dispute, unless the DSB decides by consensus not to adopt such a report within thirty days following its circulation to members.[11]

10.3 Stages in WTO Dispute Settlement

10.3.1 Overview

The DSU specifies a strict time line for the WTO dispute settlement system, as shown in Figure 10.1.

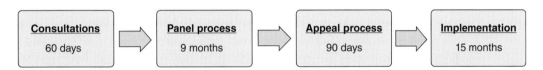

Figure 10.1 Timeline of WTO dispute settlement

10.3.2 Consultations

Bilateral consultation between members is the first stage of the WTO dispute settlement process. Consultation is a non-judicial diplomatic method through which members can resolve a dispute. This was the practice even under the GATT. As a GATT Panel pointed out, it was a fundamental tenet of the dispute settlement process that only matters on which the parties to a dispute had consulted, and on which consultations had not proven successful were subject to a Panel process.[12]

During consultations, members exchange information about the measure being challenged, respond to the specific questions of the parties (especially by the complainant member) and, in some cases, reach a mutually agreed solution, as specified in Article 3.7 of the DSU. The consultation stage is critical and is considered mandatory. If a member fails to respond to or to enter into consultations within the stipulated time period, in accordance with Article 4.3 of the DSU, the member that requested the consultations can proceed directly to request the establishment of a Panel. Nonetheless, the parties have the option to explore a mutually agreed solution at any stage of the dispute settlement process.[13] Lastly, the request for consultation must state the reasons for the dispute in writing and be notified to the DSB and the relevant Councils and Committees of the WTO.[14]

---

[11] DSU, Art. 17.14.   [12] GATT Panel Report, *US – Malt Beverages*, para. 3.1.   [13] DSU, Art. 3.6.
[14] DSU, Art. 4.4.

10.3.3 Panel Stage

If consultations are not successful, the complainant may request the establishment of a Panel, any time after sixty days from the date of the request for consultations. While the upper limit for a Panel or Appellate Body to provide its report is one year and three months respectively, disputes tend to take longer, due to the overwhelming number of cases, constraints at the WTO Secretariat and delays in translation.[15]

The complainant can request the establishment of a Panel at any time after the sixty-day period by submitting a formal request in writing. Article 6.2 of the DSU specifies that a panel request shall: (1) indicate whether consultations were held; (2) identify the specific measure; and (3) provide a brief summary of the legal basis of the complaint sufficient to present the problem clearly.

The party requesting a panel must clearly identify the measure and provide a brief summary of the challenged measure(s) with the legal provisions in question. The form and substance of the panel request is critical, since it cannot subsequently be amended and forms the basis of the Panel's terms of reference. Furthermore, panel requests are required to be clear and precise in providing the information specified in Article 6.2 to inform the parties of the legal basis of the complaint and defend the case properly. Accurately identifying the basis of a legal complaint is considered part of the due process requirement.[16] In one of the earlier cases involving Mexico's challenge of Guatemala's anti-dumping investigation of an industrial product, Mexico's failure to specifically identify the 'final antidumping measure' resulted in a contention that the Panel lacked the jurisdiction to examine the claim.[17] It is interesting to note that most of Mexico's claims related to procedural aspects of the investigation.[18] In essence, there is limited room for correcting a drafting or pleading error with respect to panel requests.

The panel request must be 'sufficient to present the problem clearly'. In other words, the claims, as opposed to the arguments, must be clearly specified in the panel request.[19]

10.3.3.1   Preliminary Ruling

The DSU does not specify any provision with regard to preliminary rulings. However, parties to the dispute sometimes seek a preliminary ruling from the Panel on certain issues. These issues often arise under Article 6.2 of the DSU. A preliminary ruling usually consists of issues that are procedural in nature or that relate to the jurisdiction of the Panel or the Appellate Body.

---

[15] For a statistical analysis of caseload at the Panel and the Appellate Body stage, as of 30 April 2018, see J. Pauwelyn and W. Zhang, 'Busier than Ever? A Data-Driven Assessment and Forecast of WTO Caseload', CTEI Working Paper 2018-02 (Graduate Institute of Geneva, Centre for Trade and Economic Integration, 2018).

[16] Appellate Body Report, *European Communities – Conditions for the Granting of Tariff Preferences to Developing Countries*, WT/DS246/AB/R, adopted 20 April 2004, para. 113.

[17] Panel Report, *Guatemala – Anti-Dumping Investigation Regarding Portland Cement from Mexico*, WT/DS60/R, adopted 25 November 1998, as reversed by Appellate Body Report WT/DS60/AB/R, paras. 4.3–4.8.

[18] Appellate Body Report, *Guatemala – Anti-Dumping Investigation Regarding Portland Cement from Mexico*, WT/DS60/AB/R, adopted 25 November 1998, para. 89.

[19] Appellate Body Report, *EC – Bananas III*, para. 143.

Past practice has indicated that disputing parties have requested preliminary rulings in respect of a wide range of issues,[20] including: (1) the adequacy of consultations; (2) admissibility of claims with respect to new or expired measures; (3) issues related to panel composition; (4) alleged conflicts of interest; (5) enhanced third-party rights; (6) admissibility of evidence; (7) procedures for business confidential information and other confidentiality issues; (8) participation of private counsel; (9) the Panel's working procedures; (10) *amicus curiae* briefs; (11) open hearings; and (12) consultations with scientific experts.

It is relevant to note that panels and the Appellate Body have chosen to defer the preliminary rulings and include them only in the final report. However, in certain cases, panels have circulated the preliminary rulings prior to the final report.[21]

10.3.3.2 Terms of Reference

Article 7 of the DSU governs the rules regarding the terms of reference of panels. The terms of reference of a panel lays down the scope of the dispute, which consists of the 'measure at issue' and the claims that are legal issues to be determined by the panel. Panels have standard terms of reference, unless the parties to the dispute agree otherwise within twenty days from the establishment of the panel.[22]

The document referred to in these standard terms of reference is usually the request for the establishment of a panel, and the panel's terms of reference only includes within its scope those claims that have been identified in the panel request. There is also a provision that allows for non-standard terms of reference.[23] However, it has been noted that, to date, there has been only one dispute where the parties agreed to special terms of reference.[24]

10.3.3.3 Identification of Measure

What can be considered a 'measure' for the purposes of a dispute settlement proceeding? The Appellate Body has observed that, in principle, any act or omission by a WTO member could be considered a measure.[25] Actions by private parties cannot be challenged under the WTO dispute settlement system. However, actions by private parties that can be attributed to the government can be challenged at the WTO. In *Japan – Film*, the Panel held that it could not rule out the possibility that private conduct 'may be deemed to be governmental if there is sufficient governmental involvement with it'.[26]

---

[20] *WTO Analytical Index: Guide to WTO Law and Practice*, Annex 2: Dispute Settlement Understanding, Article 6: Establishment of Panels (Jurisprudence), 18 June 2018, para. 1.4.6.

[21] *WTO Analytical Index*, Annex 2, Art. 6 (Jurisprudence), para. 1.4.6.3.   [22] DSU, Art. 7.1.   [23] DSU, Art. 7.1.

[24] WTO Secretariat, *A Handbook on the WTO Dispute Settlement System* (Cambridge University Press, 2017), p. 64.

[25] Appellate Body Report, *United States – Sunset Review of Anti-Dumping Duties on Corrosion-Resistant Carbon Steel Flat Products from Japan*, WT/DS244/AB/R, adopted 9 January 2004, para. 81.

[26] Panel Report, *Japan – Measures Affecting Consumer Photographic Film and Paper*, WT/DS44/R, adopted 22 April 1998, para. 10.56.

The DSU allows both de jure and de facto measures to be challenged. De jure measures can be accurately identified by the name, number, date and place of promulgation of a law, rule, regulation and so on. De facto governmental measures might entail patterns of conduct by the government, which may be comparatively difficult to identify precisely. Interestingly, even when measures have expired after the commencement of the dispute, the Appellate Body has held that the Panel must make findings if the complainant continues to request a final determination and if there is a possibility that similar measures may be reimposed.[27] Unlike the duty of the Panel to provide findings on an expired measure, the situation regarding recommendations under Article 19.1 relating to expired measures is a lot more complex. Over the years, this issue has been decided in an ad hoc, inconsistent and contradictory manner.[28]

10.3.3.4   Legal Basis of the Dispute

The legal basis of the complaint comprises the claims raised in the dispute. However, substantive arguments of the complainant are not required to be disclosed in the terms of reference. The panel request must succeed in demonstrating that the measure is the source of the alleged violation of the provisions of the covered agreement.

Members can claim that measures at issue are 'as such' or 'as applied' inconsistent with WTO Agreements. Members can claim that a measure is 'as such' inconsistent if it has general and prospective application, and that a claim is 'as applied' inconsistent if it challenges one or more specific instances of the application of such a measure. An example of an 'as such' claim is provided below.

US – Carbon Steel (India)

India claimed that the countervailing duty investigation, related measures as well as the United States Tariff Act 1930 were inconsistent with the GATT 1994 and the SCM Agreement.[29] India challenged the relevant legislation 'as such' and the specific determinations leading to the imposition of countervailing duties as an 'as applied' measure. The differences between an 'as such' and 'as applied' claim are discussed in Table 10.2.

Table 10.2 Differences between 'as such' and 'as applied' claims

As such	As applied
Challenges the measure itself or the language of the measure	Challenges the application of the measure in one or more scenarios
Challenges measures that mandate WTO-inconsistent action	Challenges measures that give discretion to apply the law in a WTO-inconsistent manner
Example: US Tariff Act 1930	**Example:** *Imposition of CVD on certain Indian products under US Tariff Act 1930*

---

[27] Appellate Body Report, *EU – PET (Pakistan)*, para. 7.13.

[28] P. Bhardwaj, 'Towards a Coherent Theory of Panel Recommendations for Expired Measures', *Journal of International Economic Law* (2019), 22(3), pp. 483–502.

[29] Panel Report, *US – Carbon Steel (India)*.

10.3.3.5 Composition of a Panel and Panel Procedure

Article 8 of the DSU specifies the rules for the composition of a panel and the qualifications of panellists. The selection of the panellists is made from an indicative list maintained by the Secretariat, and new persons are periodically proposed by members to be included in the list, on approval by the DSB.[30]

The Secretariat proposes certain panellists to the parties, which the parties cannot reject without providing compelling reasons for the rejection.[31] Reasons for rejection usually entail apprehensions regarding the objectivity of the panellists or their expertise in the subject matter of the dispute. When the parties are unable to reach an agreement, the director general, in consultation with the chairman of the DSB and the relevant council/committee, shall determine the composition, after consulting with the parties to the dispute.

In certain cases, more than one WTO member requests the establishment of a panel regarding the same matter. It is also a routine practice for different WTO members to challenge the same measure.[32] In this regard, Article 9.1 of the DSU provides for the establishment of a single panel to examine similar complaints, taking into account the rights of all members concerned, whenever feasible.

After the composition of the panel, the panellists are required to fix a timetable for the panel process.[33] All panels are required to follow the working procedures specified in Appendix 3 of the DSU, unless otherwise agreed.[34] However, according to Article 12.1, panels have the discretion to depart from Appendix 3. In practice, panels generally follow the working procedures of Appendix 3 to the DSU, with additional rules for specific disputes.

The panel process comprises of oral hearings (usually two) on the basis of written submissions.[35] The entire panel proceedings are confidential and are conducted in closed sessions.

If there are no preliminary issues, the parties start by exchanging their written submissions. The first written submission is filed by the complainants, then the respondents, followed by third-party written submissions. After the first round of submissions, each party also presents its rebuttal submissions. The panel is allowed to ask questions at any time during the course of the proceedings. The general burden of proof lies on the complainant to establish prima facie the violation of specific provisions of the covered agreement, after which the burden shifts to the respondent to refute the claimed violation.[36] In *US – Wool Shirts and Blouses*, the

---

[30] DSU, Art. 8.4.   [31] DSU, Art. 8.6.

[32] For recent examples of multiple complaints against the same measure, refer to the requests for consultations by India, European Union, Canada, Mexico, Norway, Russia and Switzerland relating to complaints filed against the United States with respect to the steel tariffs enforced under Section 232 of the Trade Expansion Act 1962. Other illustrations include *China – Raw Materials*; *China – Rare Earths*; *Canada – Renewable Energy / Canada – Feed-In Tariff Program*.

[33] DSU, Art. 12.3.   [34] DSU, Art. 12.1.

[35] Recently, in the *India – Export Related Measures* dispute, the Panel provided only one substantive hearing. See Panel Report, *India – Export Related Measures*, Addendum, Annex D-1: Communication dated 22 January 2019 from the Panel to the parties concerning the issues of a single substantive meeting and partially open meeting, pp. 84–91.

[36] Appellate Body Report, *EC – Hormones*, para. 98.

Appellate Body stated that the general principle applicable to the allocation of the burden of proof requires the complainant to prima facie prove its claim.[37]

10.3.3.6   Mandate of the Panel

According to Article 11 of the DSU, it is the function of the panel to make an objective assessment of the matter before it, including an objective assessment of the facts of the case and applicability and conformity with the relevant agreements. The panel may also make findings that will assist the DSB in making recommendations/rulings.

10.3.3.7   Standard of Review

The term 'standard of review' refers to the role of a court or tribunal in reviewing decisions taken by domestic authority – for example, the legislative or executive branches of the government.[38] Administrators or regulators take decisions based on certain facts or considerations, and provided that their decisions rest firmly on those factual premises or considerations, it may not be appropriate for courts or judges to second-guess their decisions. In other words, standard of review represents the intensity of scrutiny by courts or tribunals and is always a topic of political contention. WTO panels have the unenviable task of reviewing decisions taken by national authorities – for instance, health regulatory measures or the conduct of trade remedy investigations. The standard of review under Article 11 of the DSU applies to all disputes unless a more specific rule exists under another covered agreement.[39] *EC – Hormones*, a landmark dispute, examines the issue of 'objective assessment' under Article 11 of the DSU.

EC – HORMONES

In this case, the United States and Canada challenged a series of EC directives that prohibited the use of six hormones in livestock farming for growth purposes. The United States argued that the EC directives banning the importation of meat and meat products from cattle to which any of the six hormones had been administered were inconsistent with Articles 2, 3 and 5 of the SPS Agreement and Article 2 of the TBT Agreement.

The Panel found that the measure was inconsistent with Articles 3.1, 5.1 and 5.5 of the SPS Agreement. The EC appealed the Panel Report on the ground that the Panel had failed to apply the appropriate standard of review in assessing certain scientific evidentiary material submitted by the respondent.

---

[37] Appellate Body Report, *United States – Measure Affecting Imports of Woven Wool Shirts and Blouses from India*, WT/DS33/AB/R, Corr.1, adopted 23 May 1977, pp. 12–17.

[38] J. Bohanes and N. Lockhart, 'Standard of Review in WTO Law', in D. Bethlehem, D. McRae, R. Neufeld and I. Van Damme (eds.), *The Oxford Handbook of International Trade Law* (Oxford University Press, 2009), pp. 378–435, at 379.

[39] Agreement on Implementation of Article VI of the GATT 1994, Art. 17.6. There is a special standard of review in relation to anti-dumping investigations; see J. Durling, 'Deference, But Only When Due: WTO Review of Anti-Dumping Measures', *Journal of International Economic Law* (2003), 6(1), pp. 125–53.

The Appellate Body classified standard of review into two categories. First, *de novo* review, which is when the panel gathers its own facts and makes an independent assessment without deferring to a member's (implicit or explicit) assessment; second, the deferential standard, which would require the panel to rely on the member's assessment.

Although the Appellate Body was aware of the limited scope of appeal under Article 17.6 of the DSU (discussed in detail in the next section), it asked a legal question: When does a panel fail to discharge its duty under Article 11 of the DSU to make an objective assessment of the facts before it? In this regard, the Appellate Body made the following observation:[40]

EC – Hormones *(Appellate Body)*

133. ... Clearly, not every error in the appreciation of the evidence (although it may give rise to a question of law) may be characterized as a failure to make an objective assessment of the facts. In the present appeal, the European Communities repeatedly claims that the Panel disregarded or distorted or misrepresented the evidence submitted by the EC and even the opinions expressed by the Panel's own expert advisors. The duty to make an objective assessment of the facts is, among other things, an obligation to consider the evidence presented to a panel and to make factual findings on the basis of that evidence. The deliberate disregard of, or refusal to consider, the evidence submitted to a panel is incompatible with a panel's duty to make an objective assessment of the facts. The wilful distortion or misrepresentation of the evidence put before a panel is similarly inconsistent with an objective assessment of the facts. 'Disregard' and 'distortion' and 'misrepresentation' of the evidence, in their ordinary signification in judicial and quasi-judicial processes, imply not simply an error of judgment in the appreciation of evidence but rather an egregious error that calls into question the good faith of a panel. A claim that a panel disregarded or distorted the evidence submitted to it is, in effect, a claim that the panel, to a greater or lesser degree, denied the party submitting the evidence fundamental fairness, or what in many jurisdictions is known as due process of law or natural justice.

Accordingly, the Appellate Body undertook an examination of the EC's claim that the Panel did not consider or had misquoted the statements of some of the expert scientific opinions provided. The Appellate Body observed that these statements did not contradict the Panel's conclusion and that the errors pointed out by EC did not rise to the level of 'deliberate disregard' or 'wilful distortion' of the evidence. Therefore, the Appellate Body found that the Panel did comply with Article 11 of the DSU. Over the years, the Appellate

---

[40] Appellate Body Report, *EC – Hormones*, para. 133.

Body has departed from the high threshold prescribed in *EC – Hormones*. For instance, in *Korea – Various Measures on Beef*, the Appellate Body reversed the Panel's fact-finding because it had misinterpreted the information contained in Korea's schedules showing values for domestic support commitments.[41] In *US – Wheat Gluten*, the Appellate Body noted that a finding of inconsistency with respect to Article 11 could be established if the Panel 'exceeded the bounds of its discretion, as the trier of facts, in its appreciation of the evidence'.[42]

Article 11 claims constitute the bulk of claims under appeal. For instance, in *EC and Certain Member States – Large Civil Aircraft*, the Appellate Body held that '[a]s an initial trier of facts, a panel must provide a "reasoned and adequate" explanation for its findings and coherent reasoning'. It has to base its findings on sufficient evidentiary basis on the record, may not apply a double standard of proof, and a panel's treatment of the evidence must not lack 'even-handedness'.[43]

10.3.3.8   Rights of Third Party

Article 10 of the DSU governs the rules regarding third parties. A third party is any member that is neither the complainant nor the respondent. Article 10.2 specifies that any member that has a 'substantial interest' in a matter before the panel shall be provided the opportunity to be heard and make submissions before the panel. Although this is not set out in the DSU, a practice has evolved whereby third parties notify their interest within ten days of the establishment of a panel.

The term 'substantial interest' is subjective. Any member that considers that it has a substantial interest and notifies its interest to the DSB has the opportunity to be heard. Third parties also have the right to receive the submissions of the parties to the dispute.[44] It is also relevant to note that under Article 4.11 of the DSU regarding consultations, a member wishing to participate must have 'a substantial trade interest', as compared to Article 10.2 of the DSU, which only requires 'a substantial interest' in the matter. Accordingly, third parties with substantial interest can be granted the right to be heard. Furthermore, a member cannot participate in an appeal if it was not a third party during the panel proceedings.

While third-party rights are largely participatory in nature, panels have the discretion to grant enhanced rights to third parties that allow them to participate in a greater way than as prescribed under the DSU. In practice, panels have been cautious, and enhanced third-party rights have only been granted in a few disputes on a case-by-case basis.[45] The

---

[41] Appellate Body Report, *Korea – Various Measures on Beef*, paras. 97–105.

[42] Appellate Body Report, *US – Wheat Gluten*, para. 151.

[43] Appellate Body Report, *European Communities and Certain Member States – Measures Affecting Trade in Large Civil Aircraft*, WT/DS316/AB/R, adopted 1 June 2011, para. 881.

[44] DSU, Art. 10.3.

[45] See, for example, Panel Report, *European Communities – Regime for the Importation, Sale and Distribution of Bananas, Complaint by the United States*, WT/DS27/R/USA, adopted 25 September 1997, as modified by Appellate Body Report WT/DS27/AB/R, paras. 7.4–7.8.

enhanced third-party rights include the right to attend the entirety of substantive meetings, receive copies of written submissions and rebuttal submissions, including responses to questions, the right to respond to questions and so on.[46] A variety of considerations are taken into account while granting enhanced third-party rights, which include the relationship of parties, the relevance of the measure to third parties, and the economic and/or social effect on third parties.[47]

10.3.3.9   Adoption of Panel Reports

The recommendations and rulings made by a panel in a WTO dispute become binding only if the Panel Report is adopted by the DSB. Article 16 of the DSU governs the adoption of Panel Reports. In view of the negative consensus principle, Panel Reports are usually adopted automatically by the DSB.

10.3.4   Appeal Mechanism

An appeal mechanism where parties to a panel proceeding can appeal certain aspects of the legal findings of a panel is one of the distinctive features of the WTO dispute settlement system – a feature that has been at the heart of an unresolved crisis at the WTO as of the time of writing this book. The relevant provisions with regard to the appellate process are as follows:

- DSU, Article 16.4;
- DSU, Article 1;
- DSU, Articles 1, 3, 18, 19 (which prescribe general rules);
- Working Procedures for Appellate Review.[48]

10.3.4.1   Structure/Composition of the Appellate Body

Article 17.1 of the DSU establishes the Appellate Body, which is a permanent body, unlike the panels. It comprises seven persons, who are not called judges, but 'members'. The procedure for appointment of the members is laid out in the Working Procedures. Article 17.2 of the DSU specifies that these members are appointed for a four-year period and can be reappointed once.

Article 17.3 of the DSU specifies that an Appellate Body member must be a person of recognised authority who is unaffiliated with any government and has 'demonstrated expertise' in law, international trade and the subject matter of the covered agreements.

---

[46] *WTO Analytical Index*, Annex 2, Article 10: Third Parties (Jurisprudence), para. 1.6.4; Panel Report, *European Union – Measures Affecting Tariff Concessions on Certain Poultry Meat Products*, WT/DS492/R, Add.1, adopted 19 April 2017, para. 7.33; Panel Report, *US – Large Civil Aircraft (2nd Complaint)*, para. 7.16.

[47] *WTO Analytical Index*, Annex 2, Article 10 (Jurisprudence), para. 1.6.4.

[48] Working Procedures for Appellate Review, WT/AB/WP/6, 16 August 2010. The Working Procedures were originally adopted in 1996 and have been amended six times since then.

Members of the Appellate Body are also subject to the rules of conduct that are followed by panellists.

The Appellate Body members elect a chair each year who is responsible for the overall direction of the Appellate Body.[49] Further, the Appellate Body has its own secretariat for legal and administrative support. This is separate from the WTO Secretariat.

10.3.4.2   Procedure for Appeal

Almost 70 per cent of all Panel Reports are appealed each year.[50] At least this was the trend until December 2019. An appeal may be filed by either the complainant or the respondent.[51] Third parties do not have a right to appeal, but those members that have a substantial interest in the matter at the panel stage can make written submissions and have the opportunity to be heard at the appellate stage.[52]

The Working Procedures requires that both the notice of appeal and the appeal submissions be filed on the same day. Further, after one party initiates the appeal, the other party also has the right to appeal and raise any alleged errors by the panel.[53] After the notice of appeal is filed, the parties are informed of the Appellate Body Division (comprising three members) that will hear the appeal. The Appellate Body Secretariat also prepares and intimates a working schedule for the appeal.

Article 17.5 of the DSU specifies that the appeal procedure shall be completed within sixty days and in no circumstances shall exceed ninety days. However, due to the overwhelming number of cases appealed and non-appointment of members to the Appellate Body, this timeline has generally not been complied with.[54]

10.3.4.3   Issues of Law versus Issues of Facts

Article 17.6 of the DSU limits the scope of an appeal to issues of law and legal interpretations: 'An appeal shall be limited to issues of law covered in the panel report and legal interpretations developed by the panel'. In other words, issues that relate to pure findings of fact by the panel cannot be appealed. Any material, submissions and/or pleadings that constitute new factual evidence fall outside the scope of Article 17.6 of the DSU.

A key aspect that comes into question is whether the issues being raised in appeal are issues of law; issues of fact; or mixed issues of law and fact. There are no definitions of these terms, although the Appellate Body is required to evaluate these matters on a case-by-case basis. In *EC – Hormones*, discussed in the previous section, the Appellate Body made some critical observations as to what such issues are comprised of.[55]

---

[49] Working Procedures, Rule 5(1).

[50] World Trade Organization, *Appellate Body Annual Report for 2017*, WT/AB/28, 22 June 2018, Annex 7, p. 87.

[51] DSU, Art. 17.4.   [52] DSU, Art. 17.4.   [53] Working Procedures, Rule 23(1).

[54] *WTO Analytical Index*, Annex 2, Article 17: Appellate Review (Jurisprudence), para. 1.4.1.

[55] Appellate Body Report, *EC – Hormones*, para. 132.

EC – Hormones *(Appellate Body)*

132. Under Article 17.6 of the DSU, appellate review is limited to appeals on questions of law covered in a panel report and legal interpretations developed by the panel. Findings of fact, as distinguished from legal interpretations or legal conclusions, by a panel are, in principle, not subject to review by the Appellate Body. The determination of whether or not a certain event did occur in time and space is typically a question of fact; for example, the question of whether or not Codex has adopted an international standard, guideline or recommendation on MGA is a factual question. Determination of the credibility and weight properly to be ascribed to (that is, the appreciation of) a given piece of evidence is part and parcel of the fact-finding process and is, in principle, left to the discretion of a panel as the trier of facts. The consistency or inconsistency of a given fact or set of facts with the requirements of a given treaty provision is, however, a legal characterization issue. It is a legal question. Whether or not a panel has made an objective assessment of the facts before it, as required by Article 11 of the DSU, is also a legal question which, if properly raised on appeal, would fall within the scope of appellate review.

It cannot be overemphasised that 'it is often difficult to clearly distinguish between issues that are purely legal, purely factual, or are mixed issues of law and fact'.[56] To better understand the distinction, examples of issues of law, fact, and mixed issues of law and fact are given in Table 10.3.

Table 10.3 Examples of issues of law, fact and mixed issues

Fact	Law	Mixed
What was the share of imports from a member during a calendar year in a safeguard proceeding?	What constitutes a 'financial contribution' under Article 1 of the SCM Agreement?	Did the competent authority exercise its discretion in an 'even-handed manner'?
What are the economic effects of subsidised imports on prices in the domestic market?	What are the elements of the 'likeness' test under Article XVII of the GATS?	Are clove and menthol cigarettes 'like' products within the meaning of Article III:2 of the GATT?
What are the potential health risks in smoking clove as opposed to menthol cigarettes?	Can remedies be only 'prospective' in nature under the DSU?	Has an investigating agency established 'unforeseen developments' under the Agreement on Safeguards?
Is avian flu exotic to a particular location?	What is the meaning of 'seek information' under Article 13 of the DSU?	Has the respondent member conducted a risk assessment before taking an SPS measure?

---

[56] Appellate Body Report, *EC and Certain Member States – Large Civil Aircraft*, para. 1313.

The following decision in *EC and Certain Member States – Large Civil Aircraft* is instructive for understanding the difference between claims relating to assessment of facts and application of law.

E C A N D C E R T A I N M E M B E R S T A T E S – L A R G E C I V I L A I R C R A F T

This dispute arose out of a long-term dispute between the US and the EU regarding subsidies being provided to the aircraft industry, specifically with regard to the funding provided to the respective aircraft companies in each country, namely Boeing and Airbus. Before the Panel, the US claimed that each of the challenged EC measures is a specific subsidy within the meaning of Articles 1 and 2 of the SCM Agreement, and that the use of these subsidies caused 'adverse effects' to US interests under Articles 5(a) and (c) and 6.3 of the SCM Agreement. The Panel found that various subsidies (not all) for a number of Airbus models had 'adverse effects' in the form of 'serious prejudice' under Article 6.3 of the SCM Agreement. On appeal, the EC challenged a number of the Panel's findings and certain aspects of its reasoning.

For each aspect of the Panel's assessment that the EC raised, it made parallel claims under the SCM Agreement, alleging an error of application of law, and under Article 11 of the DSU, alleging a failure by the Panel to make an objective assessment of the facts. In this regard, the Appellate Body observed as follows:

EC and Certain Member States – Large Civil Aircraft *(Appellate Body)*

872. The Appellate Body has noted that 'an appellant is free to determine how to characterize its claims on appeal'. Furthermore, we recognize that it is often difficult to distinguish clearly between issues that are purely legal or purely factual, or are mixed issues of law and fact. We also recognize that a failure to make a claim under Article 11 of the DSU on an issue that the Appellate Body determines to concern a factual assessment may have serious consequences for the appellant. An appellant may thus feel safer putting forward both a claim that the Panel erred in the application of a legal provision and a claim that the Panel failed to make an objective assessment of the facts under Article 11 of the DSU. In most cases, however, an issue will either be one of application of the law to the facts or an issue of the objective assessment of facts, and not both.

Accordingly, the Appellate Body analysed each of the EC's parallel claims, to see if these alleged errors of the Panel were issues of application of the law to the facts or an issue of the objective assessment of facts. The Appellate Body noted that not every error in the appreciation of a particular piece of evidence will suffice to prove that the Panel failed in its duty to comply with Article 11. The Appellate Body carried out a review of the Panel's assessment of specific facts in order to evaluate whether the Panel fulfilled its duties under DSU Article 11. In some instances, the Appellate Body found that the Panel had erred in its objective assessment, while in others it concluded that it fell within the Panel's bounds of discretion as initial trier of facts. For example, on the determination of 'serious prejudice' under Articles 5(c) and 6.3(c) of the SCM Agreement, the EC claimed that the Panel's assessment relating to causation of lost sales of the A380 (a particular type of large civil aircraft) was erroneous and that it violated Article 11 of the DSU. In this regard, the Appellate Body examined the Panel's assessment of factual evidence and rejected the EC's claim that the Panel failed to conduct an objective assessment of the counterfactual submitted by the EC.

10.3.4.4   Mandate of the Appellate Body

Article 17.13 of the DSU specifies that the Appellate Body may *uphold, modify or reverse* the legal findings and conclusions of a panel, its mandate being as follows:

- *Uphold:* Appellate Body agrees with the panel reasoning and conclusion.
- *Modify:* Appellate Body agrees with the panel conclusion, but not the reasoning.
- *Reverse:* Appellate Body disagrees with the panel conclusion.

The Appellate Body's analysis of whether a statement by the panel amounts to a legal finding or conclusion is evaluated on a case-by-case basis, while taking into account the context in which the statement was made. Further, in cases where the Appellate Body has modified or reversed a finding by the panel, and a related statement or observation made by the panel has no bearing or effect on the conclusion, the Appellate Body has sometimes declared such observations/statements as 'moot and of no legal effect'.

10.3.4.5   Completion of Analysis

In many cases, the Appellate Body has gone beyond the mandate of Article 17.13 of the DSU and has explicitly or implicitly completed the panel's legal analysis. This usually arises in two types of scenarios: (1) where the Appellate Body has reversed or modified the panel's legal interpretation; or (2) to make a finding on a claim that the panel has failed to address.

The second scenario arises because panels often decline to rule on whether the measure at issue violates a provision of the covered agreements if it has already found that the measure violates another provision under WTO Agreements. This is known as *judicial economy*, which is when the panel chooses to rule only on those claims that are necessary to resolve the dispute, to the exclusion of other claims.[57] In other words, even when a panel has validly exercised jurisdiction, it does not follow that it has to rule on the substantive merits of each of the claims raised before it.[58] In a scenario where an appellate tribunal has to rule on an issue that requires factual or legal

---

[57] The power of the Appellate Body to exercise judicial economy is somewhat unclear in view of Art. 17.12 of the DSU. See A. Alvarez-Jiménez, 'The WTO Appellate Body's Exercise of Judicial Economy', *Journal of International Economic Law* (2009), 12(2), pp. 393–415.

[58] Appellate Body Report, *European Communities and Certain Member States – Measures Affecting Trade in Large Aircraft – Recourse to Article 21.5 of the DSU by the United States*, WT/DS316/AB/RW, Add.1, adopted 28 May 2018, para. 5.23.

determinations to be made by the court of first instance, dispute is usually remanded back to the court of first instance. However, since the DSU does not grant remand authority to the Appellate Body, one may argue that it is necessary for the Appellate Body to undertake the task of completing the panel's analysis and to determine a 'positive solution' to a dispute.

The Appellate Body can complete the analysis only in those cases where the panel has made sufficient factual findings in its report or recorded undisputed facts to enable the Appellate Body to carry out the legal analysis.[59] Without sufficient factual findings or undisputed facts, the Appellate Body will have to decline completing the analysis, since it does not have any fact-finding authority.[60] Further, the Appellate Body has also declined to complete the analysis if it concerns an entirely new issue that had not been raised at the panel stage.[61] For example, in *EC and Certain Member States – Large Civil Aircraft*, although the Appellate Body reversed the Panel's finding in relation to the 'benefit' analysis, it ruled that it could not complete the analysis with regard to determining 'benefit' under Articles 1.1(b) and 14(a) of the SCM Agreement. This was because the Panel did not make affirmative findings regarding the investment costs and the expected returns associated with the underlying transaction, which are necessary for a benefit determination.[62]

10.3.4.6   Adoption of Appellate Body Reports

The Appellate Body Report is circulated to the WTO members and, along with the Panel Report as modified by the Appellate Body Report, is to be adopted by the DSB within thirty days after circulation.[63]

In practice, the Appellate Body has taken significantly more than the sixty to ninety days specified in the DSU to complete its review for most cases. One recent estimate by the United States indicates that the average time taken by the Appellate Body, in the period from 2014 to mid-2018, was 163 days.[64]

10.3.5 Implementation of DSB Ruling

An important hallmark of the WTO dispute settlement mechanism is the prompt implementation and compliance with the recommendation and rulings of the DSB. Accordingly, if the Appellate Body Report and Panel Report conclude that the respondent violated provisions of the covered agreements, then the respondent member is to secure the withdrawal of the measures concerned. Article 21 of the DSU, which governs implementation, has the following parts: surveillance of implementation; disagreement on the implementation; and remedies, including suspension of concessions.

---

[59] Appellate Body Report, *Australia –Salmon*, para. 118.

[60] Appellate Body Report, *Korea – Definitive Safeguard Measure on Imports of Certain Dairy Products*, WT/DS98/AB/R, adopted 12 January 2000, para. 92.

[61] Appellate Body Report, *EC – Asbestos*, para. 82.

[62] Appellate Body Report, *EC and Certain Member States – Large Civil Aircraft*, para. 1023.   [63] DSU, Art. 17.14.

[64] Statements by the United States at the Meeting of the WTO Dispute Settlement Body, Geneva, 22 June 2018.

To aid understanding, the step-by-step procedure for compliance is provided in Box 10.2.

Box 10.2 Implementation by respondent

Within thirty days following the adoption of the Appellate Body and Panel Reports, the member concerned needs to inform the DSB of its intention with regard to implementation of the Appellate Body and Panel Reports. The concerned member will have to provide a reasonable period of time by when it can implement the DSB rulings.

↓

Reasonable period of time (RPT)

DSU Article 21.3

↙	↓	↘
1 Period of time as proposed by the concerned member, provided that such period is approved by the DSB	2 Period of time mutually agreed by the parties to the dispute within 45 days after the date of adoption	3 Period of time determined through binding arbitration within 90 days of adoption of the Appellate Body Report; arbitrator to decide on the RPT, which should not exceed 15 months from the date of adoption

Compliance Panel	**Compensation and the suspension of concessions**
DSU Article 21.5	*DSU Article 22.2*
If the parties disagree on whether the concerned member has implemented the recommendations and rulings, *either of them* can request a compliance panel. The DSB, in such a scenario, shall refer this matter to the original panel, which is supposed to decide in an expedited fashion (within 90 days) whether the implementing measure fully complies with the recommendations and rulings adopted by the DSB.	If the member concerned fails to bring the measures into compliance within the RPT, then parties shall, no later than the expiry of the RPT, enter into negotiations, with a view to developing mutually acceptable compensation. If no satisfactory compensation has been agreed within 20 days after the date of expiry of the RPT, *any party* may request authorisation from the DSB to suspend the application of concessions to the respondent or other obligations under the covered agreements.

Sequencing problem

There is lack of clarity from the DSU as to which of the two procedures above (i.e. the compliance proceeding or the suspension of obligations) should follow after the expiry of the RPT.

10.3.5.1 Determination of Reasonable Period of Time

Article 21.3 of the DSU allows the member concerned to implement the recommendations and ruling within a 'reasonable period of time' when immediate compliance is impracticable. There are three ways of determining the RPT: (1) member proposes and the DSB approves;

(2) a period of time is mutually agreed by the parties to the dispute; or (3) a period of time is determined through binding arbitration.[65]

In practice, the parties to the dispute often mutually agree for an RPT, which ranges from four to fifteen months, depending upon the legislative, regulatory or other requirements the respondent member may need to follow.[66] This agreement has to be reached between the parties within forty-five days from the date of the adoption of the Panel and/or Appellate Body report. When the parties fail to agree on an RPT, they may choose to determine the RPT through binding arbitration under Article 21.3(c) of the DSU.

The DSU does not indicate who can serve as an arbitrator, other than specifying that it can be both an individual and a group of individuals. Usually, arbitrations are conducted by sitting or former Appellate Body members. The parties are to decide on an arbitrator by mutual agreement, but if they fail to do so within ten days after referring the matter to arbitration, the director general of the WTO will appoint an arbitrator within ten days, after consulting the parties.[67]

In the arbitration proceedings, under Article 21.3(c), the burden of proof lies on the party seeking to prove that there are 'particular circumstances' justifying a shorter or longer time and a variety of factors are taken into consideration. Generally speaking, the RPT is that period of time that is the 'shortest possible within the legal system of the Member to implement the relevant recommendations and rulings of the DSB'.[68] A study reviewing all thirty-four awards issued under Article 21.3(c) until the year 2017, concluded that the *EC – Bananas III (Article 21.3(c))* dispute was the only one where the RPT exceeded the fifteen-month guideline.[69]

10.3.5.2 Compliance Panel

Before the expiry of the RPT, the respondent member must withdraw or amend the inconsistent measure to comply with the rulings of the DSB. However, if there is a disagreement over whether the implementation measure leads to compliance with the covered agreements, the parties have recourse to dispute settlement procedures under Article 21.5 of the DSU. The panel that examines the measure taken to comply can be referred to as the compliance panel, for convenience.

Article 21.5 of the DSU also states that the compliance panel should circulate its report within ninety days, but this timeline seems unrealistic. Although the DSU does not specify whether the possibility to hold consultations between the parties and the appeal of the Panel

---

[65] DSU, Art. 21.3.

[66] *WTO Analytical Index*, Annex 2, Article 21: Surveillance of Implementation of Recommendations and Rulings (Practice), para. 1.2.1.

[67] DSU, Art. 21, fn. 12.

[68] Award of the Arbitrator, *Chile – Price Band System and Safeguard Measures Relating to Certain Agricultural Products – Arbitration under Article 21.3(c) of the DSU*, WT/DS207/13, 17 March 2003, para. 34.

[69] P. C. Mavroidis, N. Meagher, T. J. Prusa and T. Yanguas, 'Ask for the Moon, Settle for the Stars: What Is a Reasonable Period to Comply with WTO Awards?', *World Trade Review* (2017), 16(2), pp. 395–425.

Report fall within the scope of the Article 21.5 panel, the term 'recourse to dispute settlement procedures' under DSU Article 21.5 is understood to refer to Articles 4–20 of the DSU.[70] In other words, the assessment of the compliance measure is also subject to consultations and an appeal.

10.3.5.3 Mandate of the Panel under Article 21.5

The DSU does not specify the scope of the inquiry by the compliance panel under Article 21.5 of the DSU.

CANADA – AIRCRAFT (ARTICLE 21.5 – BRAZIL)

The panel's mandate under DSU Article 21.5 was examined in *Canada – Aircraft (Article 21.5 – Brazil)*,[71] where the Appellate Body made the following observations:

> ## Canada – Aircraft (Article 21.5 – Brazil) *(Appellate Body)*
>
> 41. [I]n carrying out its review under Article 21.5 of the DSU, a panel is *not* confined to examining the 'measures taken to comply' from the perspective of the claims, arguments and factual circumstances that related to the measure that was the subject of the original proceedings. Although these may have some relevance in proceedings under Article 21.5 of the DSU, Article 21.5 proceedings involve, in principle, not the original measure, but rather a new and different measure which was not before the original panel. In addition, the relevant facts bearing upon the 'measure taken to comply' may be different from the relevant facts relating to the measure at issue in the original proceedings. It is natural, therefore, that the claims, arguments and factual circumstances which are pertinent to the 'measure taken to comply' will not, necessarily, be the same as those which were pertinent in the original dispute.

In other words, the compliance panel is required to examine the 'measure taken to comply' holistically and not only in light of the recommendations and rulings of the DSB.

The measure taken to comply is any measure implemented by the respondent taken in the direction of, or for the purpose of achieving, compliance.[72] It is for the panel to decide whether certain measures have been 'taken to comply' with a DSB ruling. This assessment may entail a review of other measures that have a *close relationship* to the declared 'measure

---

[70] Bossche and Zdouc, *Law and Policy of the World Trade Organization*, p. 293.

[71] Appellate Body Report, *Canada – Measures Affecting the Export of Civilian Aircraft – Recourse by Brazil to Article 21.5 of the DSU*, WT/DS70/AB/RW, adopted 4 August 2000, para. 41.

[72] Appellate Body Report, *United States – Final Countervailing Duty Determination with Respect to Certain Softwood Lumber from Canada – Recourse by Canada to Article 21.5 of the DSU*, WT/DS257/AB/RW, adopted 20 December 2005, para. 66.

taken to comply' and to the DSB rulings. The panel's examination of the 'close nexus' requires the examination of *'timing, nature, and effects of the various measures'*.[73]

Table 10.4 illustrates the differences between a regular panel and a compliance panel proceeding.

Table 10.4 Differences between an original panel and a compliance panel

Original panel	Compliance panel
• Scope of the original panel extends to the matter before it as put forth by the complainants in its panel request and the legal basis of the complaint • Longer time frame of up to 6–9 months • Composition of the panel is determined by the parties to the dispute, as provided under Article 8 of the DSU • Panel proceedings can be initiated only by the complainant	• Scope of the compliance panel is limited to the measure taken to comply and its inconsistency with the DSB ruling, as well as the covered agreements • Shorter time frame of 90 days prescribed in the DSU, which is not followed in practice • Composition of a compliance panel is, in principle, already determined – Article 21.5 specifies that it must be the original panel, wherever possible • The complainant or the respondent can initiate compliance panel proceedings

Source: based on Appellate Body Report, *US – Softwood Lumber IV (Article 21.5 – Canada)*, paras. 71–72.

It is important to note that scope of the panel under DSU Article 21.5 does not allow a claim to be reasserted after the original panel or the Appellate Body has made a finding of WTO inconsistency.[74]

US – Tuna II (Mexico)

This case involves Mexico challenging a variety of measures implemented by the United States that established conditions for the use of a 'dolphin-safe' label on tuna products.[75] Mexico alleged that these US measures were discriminatory and inconsistent with provisions of the GATT 1994 and the TBT Agreement. The DSB ruled that the US dolphin-safe labelling provisions were inconsistent with Article 2.1 of the TBT Agreement.

During the RPT, the United States implemented a legal instrument known as the '2013 Final Rule'[76] and some additional regulations. Mexico collectively referred to the US measures as the 'Amended Tuna Measure'. Mexico alleged that the United States failed to comply with the DSB rulings because the Amended Tuna Measure remained inconsistent with the TBT Agreement and the GATT.

---

[73] Appellate Body Report, *United States – Laws, Regulations and Methodology for Calculating Dumping Margins ('Zeroing') – Recourse to Article 21.5 of the DSU by the European Communities*, WT/DS294/AB/RW, Corr.1, adopted 11 June 2009, para. 207.

[74] Appellate Body Report, *European Communities – Anti-Dumping Duties on Imports of Cotton-Type Bed Linen from India – Recourse to Article 21.5 of the DSU by India*, WT/DS141/AB/RW, adopted 24 April 2003, para. 98.

[75] Appellate Body Report, *US – Tuna II (Mexico)*.

[76] US Department of Commerce, NOAA, Enhanced Document Requirements to Support Use of the Dolphin Safe Label on Tuna Products, US Fed. Reg. Vol. 78, No. 131 (9 July 2013), pp. 40997–41004.

The parties disagreed as to the identity of the measure taken to comply. Mexico argued that the measure taken to comply is the Amended Tuna Measure as a whole. On the other hand, the US argued that it is only the 2013 Final Rule, which was adopted with the goal of complying with the DSB ruling.

The Panel agreed with the United States that the 2013 Final Rule was the measure it had taken to comply with the DSB ruling. However, in the Article 21.5 proceedings, the Panel's task was not only to determine whether the 2013 Final Rule was in itself WTO-consistent, but rather, to assess whether the 2013 Final Rule succeeded in bringing the tuna measure as a whole (a measure that had already been found to be inconsistent by the Appellate Body) into conformity with the covered agreements. Therefore, the Panel's finding that the 'measure taken to comply' is the 2013 Final Rule in no way precluded the Panel from considering the elements of the 2013 Final Rule itself, or from examining how the 2013 Final Rule interacted with the other elements that constituted the Amended Tuna Measure. In other words, the Panel found that the scope of the compliance panel extended to claims raised against both the 2013 Final Rule and the amended tuna measure.

10.3.6 Compensation and Suspension of Concessions

The provisions relating to compensation and suspension of concession gain salience in situations of non-implementation.

Article 21.6 of the DSU provides the DSB with a mechanism for monitoring the respondent to ensure whether it is compliant with the rulings and recommendations of the DSB within the RPT. However, if the respondent still fails to bring its measure into conformity, then it can seek recourse under DSU Article 22, which deals with compensation and suspension of concessions.

Article 22 provides temporary measures that can be resorted to by the complainant, in the event of the impossibility of or delay in implementing the DSB ruling by the respondent. It is important to note that the remedy of compensation and suspension of concessions under Article 22 does not constitute punitive measures, but is provisional, voluntary and negotiated.

10.3.6.1 Compensation

Article 3.7 of the DSU specifies that compensation should be resorted to only if the immediate withdrawal of the measure is impracticable. Under the WTO, there is no compensation for past economic harm attributable to the legal violation.[77] It is supposed to be only a temporary measure, pending the withdrawal of the measure that is inconsistent with a covered agreement. The term compensation in this context does not mean monetary

---

[77] R. E. Hudec, 'Broadening the Scope of Remedies in WTO Dispute Settlement', in F. Weiss (ed.), *Improving WTO Dispute Settlement Procedures: Issues and Lessons from the Practice of Other International Courts and Tribunals* (London: Cameron May, 2000).

payment, but rather the offering of additional market access, like a tariff reduction on products of export interest to the complainant to be given on an MFN basis.

If the respondent fails to comply at the end of the RPT, then the complainant can request negotiations with the respondent in order to decide on mutually acceptable compensation.[78] In the event that the parties involved agree on compensation, the agreed compensation must be in conformity with the covered agreements.

10.3.6.2 Suspension of Concessions

As a last resort, the DSU provides the complaining member with the possibility of suspending the application of concessions or other obligations under the covered agreements on a discriminatory basis against the respondent, subject to authorisation by the DSB of such measures.[79] In common parlance, it is called 'retaliation'.

If the negotiations fail to decide satisfactory compensation within twenty days after the expiry of the RPT,[80] the complainant seeks permission to impose trade sanctions, which are inconsistent with the covered agreements, in response to the respondent's failure to comply with the DSB. The DSB authorises through reverse consensus and, accordingly, authorisation to retaliate is quasi-automatic.

The exact content of the request for suspension of concessions is not defined in the DSU. However, the DSU does prescribe the level and form of permissible suspension, as specified in Articles 22.3 and 22.4 of the DSU. According to Article 22.4, the level of concession must be equivalent to the nullification or impairment resulting from non-compliance.[81] The DSB cannot authorise any suspension of concession or other obligations if a covered agreement prohibits such suspensions.[82]

Article 22.3(a) requires that the complainant first seek to suspend concessions or obligations in the same sector as that in which the violation or other nullification or impairment was found.[83] This is based on the notion that suspension of concessions should correspond with the underlying obligation violated by the respondent. The term 'sector' is defined in Article 22.3(f) to mean all goods, a principal services sector and the different categories of intellectual property in accordance with the GATT 1994, the GATS and the TRIPS respectively. For example, a WTO-inconsistent tariff on steel (a good) can be countered with a tariff increase on steel (a good) or any other good, and a response to a violation in the area of patents should also relate to patents.

Article 22.3(b), however, specifies that if the complainant considers it impracticable or ineffective to remain within the same sector, the sanctions can be imposed in a different sector, but under the same agreement. This option is only relevant with regard to violations

---

[78] DSU, Art. 22.2.   [79] DSU, Art. 3.7.   [80] DSU, Art. 3.7.

[81] See, generally, W. Zdouc, 'Cross-Retaliation and Suspension under the GATS and TRIPS Agreements', in Chad P. Bown and Joost Pauwelyn (eds.), *The Law, Economics and Politics of Retaliation in WTO Dispute Settlement* (Cambridge University Press, 2010), pp. 515–35.

[82] DSU, Art. 22.5.   [83] DSU, Art. 22.3(a).

under the GATS and the TRIPS, because a violation with regard to patents could be countered with countermeasures on copyrights, and a violation in financial services could be countered with a measure in the area of educational services.

Further, Article 22.3(c) allows the complainant to apply countermeasures under another agreement, if it is impracticable or ineffective to retaliate within the same agreement and the circumstances are serious enough. This process of suspending concessions in other sectors or under another agreement is often referred to as cross-retaliation. In the famous case of *EC – Bananas III*, Ecuador, a complainant, sought retaliation against the EC in the field of the TRIPS, although the dispute involved issues under the GATT and the GATS.[84] Authorisations for cross-retaliation were also granted in *US – Gambling* and *US – Upland Cotton*. Cross-retaliation is effective in situations where the complainant member may not have meaningful trade in sectors involved in the dispute or could hurt its own economic interests through suspension of concessions. However, in practice, members do not wish to exercise this right and generally attempt to seek diplomatic solutions. In all the above cases, the parties settled the matter through mutual agreements or trade cooperation.[85]

10.3.6.3   Arbitration under DSU Article 22.6

Article 22.6 of the DSU provides the respondent with recourse to arbitration in the event it objects to the level or form of the suspension of concession proposed by the complainant. This arbitration can be carried out by the original panel or by an arbitrator and must be completed within sixty days after the expiry of the RPT.

Under Article 22.6 of the DSU, the arbitrator's mandate comprises:

- identifying the level of suspension of concessions or other obligations: the arbitrator determines whether the proposed level is equivalent to the level of nullification or impairment as per Article 22.4 of the DSU;
- the form of suspensions of concessions/choice of agreement and sectors: the arbitrator determines whether the principles and procedures of Article 22.3 of the DSU have been followed.

In structuring the suspension of concessions, arbitrators have observed that it is better to be as precise as possible in the request for suspension of concessions.[86]

---

[84] DSB, Minutes of Meetings held on 18 May 2000, WT/DSB/M/80, 26 June 2000, paras. 48–58.

[85] R. Schnepf, 'Status of the WTO Brazil – US Cotton Case', CRS Report R43336 (Washington, DC: Congressional Research Service, 12 December 2013), available at https://fas.org/sgp/crs/row/R43336.pdf (accessed 21 December 2020).

[86] Decision by the Arbitrator, *European Communities – Measures Concerning Meat and Meat Products (Hormones), Original Complaint by the United States – Recourse to Arbitration by the European Communities under Article 22.6 of the DSU*, WT/DS26/ARB, 12 July 1999, fn. 16; Decision by the Arbitrator, *European Communities – Regime for the Importation, Sale and Distribution of Bananas – Recourse to Arbitration by the European Communities under Article 22.6 of the DSU*, WT/DS27/ARB/ECU, 24 March 2000, fn. 12.

UNITED STATES – TUNA II (MEXICO)

In *US – Tuna II (Mexico)*, the United States was required to comply with the Panel and Appellate Body Reports of the Article 21.5 compliance proceedings. Subsequently, Mexico requested authorisation from the DSB to suspend concessions or other obligations and the United States objected to the proposed level of suspension, which led the matter to be referred to arbitration under DSU Article 22.6.

One of the preliminary issues was whether the determination of the consistency of the form and level of suspension should be on the basis of the original measure that was taken to comply (2013 Tuna Measure) or the modified compliance measure adopted after compliance proceedings (2016 Tuna Measure).

The United States argued that the relevant measure was the one that existed at the time of the arbitration rather than the one that existed at the time of the expiry of the RPT. The Arbitrator stated as follows:[87]

US – Tuna II (Mexico) (Article 22.6 – US) *(Decision by the Arbitrator)*

3.19. Given that Article 22.6 of the DSU explicitly refers to 'the situation' described in Article 22.2, that latter provision clearly provides relevant context for the interpretation of Article 22.6. To recall, the text of Article 22.2 provides in relevant part that in a situation where a Member fails to bring a measure previously found to be inconsistent with the covered agreements into compliance therewith, and where no satisfactory compensation is agreed within 20 days of the expiry of the applicable RPT, the complaining Member may request authorization from the DSB to suspend concessions or other obligations. The 'situation' referred to in Article 22.6 thus occurs where (a) a Member has failed to bring a measure into compliance with the covered agreements before the expiry of the applicable RPT; and (b) the parties have failed to agree on satisfactory compensation.

3.20. Read together, Articles 22.2 and 22.6 of the DSU thus establish that a complaining Member may seek authorization to suspend concessions in situations where the responding Member has failed, within the RPT, to bring into conformity a measure that has previously been found to be inconsistent with the covered agreements. It is therefore the continued WTO-inconsistency of the original or a compliance measure (where a compliance measure was taken within the RPT) at the time the RPT expires that forms the basis for any request for authorization to suspend concessions. In turn, a request for authorization to suspend concessions typically triggers a request for arbitration under Article 22.6.

---

[87] Decision by the Arbitrator, *United States – Measures Concerning the Importation, Marketing and Sale of Tuna and Tuna Products – Recourse to Article 22.6 of the DSU by the United States*, WT/DS381/ARB, 25 April 2017, para. 3.19.

The Arbitrator found that the relevant measure was the 2013 Tuna Measure, not the 2016 Tuna Measure. The Arbitrator concluded that, in accordance with Article 22.4 of the DSU, Mexico could request authorisation from the DSB to suspend concessions up to a level not exceeding US$163.23 million annually.

Under Article 22.6, the arbitrator's report is not susceptible for appeal and also does not require adoption. It is also important to note that the concessions or other obligations will not be suspended while the panel/arbitrator decides on the level or form of suspension of concession. The DSB grants authorisation for the suspension of obligations in accordance with the decision of the arbitrator, unless the request is rejected by negative consensus.[88]

10.3.7 Sequencing

A controversial issue in the DSU is the conflict in time frame between Articles 21.5 and 22.6 of the DSU. Under Article 22.6, the DSB has to grant authorisation to the requesting party to suspend concessions within thirty days of the expiry of the RPT, unless the DSB, by consensus, rejects the request for authorisation. However, the complainant can request to suspend concessions only if the respondent has failed to implement a measure to comply with the covered agreements.

The recourse under DSU Article 21.5 requires the compliance panel to evaluate whether the measure taken to comply is consistent with the DSB ruling and with the covered agreements. Therefore, it is impossible to obtain authorisation for retaliation within thirty days of expiry of the RPT in cases where the complainant challenges the respondent's measure taken to comply. In certain cases in the face of a retaliation, the respondent itself has taken recourse to Article 21.5.[89] This issue has come up in many older disputes, such as *EC – Bananas III*, and even in recent disputes such as *India – Solar Cells*[90] and *India – Quantitative Restrictions*. The controversy relating to *EC – Bananas III* is discussed below.

EC – Bananas III

This was a dispute brought by the United States, Mexico, Ecuador, Honduras and Guatemala against the EC bananas regime.[91] The EC lost the dispute and had to comply with the DSB recommendations and rulings. The implementing measures were under review in a compliance panel under Article 21.5 of the DSU and, in the meantime, the complainants also filed for suspension of concessions under Article 22.2.

There were two retaliation requests, one from the United States and the other from Ecuador. The United States insisted on its right to retaliation, whereas the EC argued that the compliance panel under DSU Article 21.5 be established first to assess whether the EC measures taken to comply were consistent with its obligations under the covered agreements. In April 1999, the DSB authorised the United States to suspend concessions to the EC in

---

[88] DSU, Art. 22.7.

[89] *United States – Measures Concerning the Importation, Marketing and Sale of Tuna and Tuna Products – Recourse to Article 21.5 of the DSU by the United States (Request for the Establishment of a Panel)*, WT/DS381/32, 12 April 2016.

[90] Appellate Body Report, *India – Solar Cells*.   [91] Appellate Body Report, *EC – Bananas III*.

view of its failure to comply with the DSB rulings, and in May 2000 the DSB authorised Ecuador to suspend concessions. However, the lack of clarity in the sequencing in timeline between DSU Articles 21.5 and 22.2 generated a major controversy. Finally, in April 2001, the United States and the EC reached a provisional settlement in this dispute.[92] Under the terms of this agreement, the US sanctions were suspended on 1 July 2001, and were to be removed once the EU modified its banana import regime. Eventually, the parties notified the DSB of a mutually agreed solution pursuant to DSU Article 3.6 on 8 November 2012.

It has been observed that parties have largely agreed on an ad hoc basis on the procedures to resolve the sequencing issue – that is, whether the evaluation relating to the consistency of the measure taken to comply with the covered agreements should be completed prior to seeking authorisation for retaliation.[93] These are called sequencing agreements.[94] Over the years, the procedure and practice developed appear to suggest that the compliance panel proceedings should come first and complainants can resort to suspension of concessions only once the Article 21.5 proceedings are over.

10.4   Alternative Remedies under the DSU

It is important to note that the DSU provides for alternative means of resolving disputes other than through adjudicating by a panel and the Appellate Body and the imposition of retaliatory measures.

10.4.1 Mutually Agreed Solutions

Article 3.6 of the DSU pertaining to mutually agreed solutions states:

> ### DSU, Article 3.6
>
> Mutually agreed solutions to matters formally raised under the consultation and dispute settlement provisions of the covered agreements shall be notified to the DSB and the relevant Councils and Committees, where any Member may raise any point relating thereto.

Mutually agreed solutions are a common route utilised by WTO members to resolve disputes amicably and parties can enter into a mutually acceptable solution at any stage of the dispute settlement proceedings. Article 3.5 specifies that all mutually agreed solutions

---

[92] Understanding between the European Communities and the United States, WT/DS27/59, G/C/W/270, WT/DS27/ 58, Enclosure 1, 11 April 2000; WTO, Notification of Mutually Agreed Solution of 8 November 2012, WT/DS364/ 3, G/L/822/Add.1, 12 November 2012.

[93] Bossche and Zdouc, *Law and Policy of the World Trade Organization*, p. 297, fn. 809.

[94] The first such sequencing agreement was signed between Australia and Canada in the aftermath of *Australia – Salmon*, an SPS dispute. See Panel Report, *Australia – Measures Affecting Importation of Salmon – Recourse to Article 21.5 of the DSU by Canada*, WT/DS18/RW, adopted 20 March 2000, para. 1.3.

must be consistent with the WTO Agreements. Mutually agreed solutions must be notified to the DSB and the relevant Councils and Committees. In the *EC – Bananas III* dispute, the issue of establishing compliance panel proceedings, after a mutually agreed solution was entered into, was discussed. In this regard, the Appellate Body found that entering into a mutually agreed solution did not necessarily imply that the parties had waived their right to have recourse to compliance panel proceedings. The Appellate Body further noted that there must be a clear indication in the agreement between the parties of a relinquishment of the right to have recourse to Article 21.5.

10.4.2 Good Offices, Conciliation or Mediation

Article 5 of the DSU provides members with recourse to settle disputes through good offices, conciliation and mediation. At any stage of the dispute settlement process, parties to the dispute can opt to settle a dispute amicably through good offices, conciliation and mediation.[95] Good offices mostly comprise offering logistical support to help the disputing parties negotiate.[96] In conciliation, a third person participates in order to ease discussions and negotiations. The mediator not only participates, but may also propose a solution to the parties,[97] although the parties are not required to accept the suggested solution.

10.4.3 Arbitration under Article 25

Article 25 of the DSU provides members with an alternative dispute resolution mechanism, through expeditious arbitration, to resolve disputes arising out of covered agreements. It is an arbitration that is binding on the parties,[98] and the parties to the dispute decide the scope and procedure of the arbitration process.[99]

Procedures set out in DSU Articles 4–20 are not applicable to arbitration under DSU Article 25.[100] However, Articles 21 and 22 of the DSU are applicable *mutatis mutandis*.[101] In other words, the arbitration award cannot be appealed, but is subject to the provisions dealing with surveillance and implementation of DSB rulings and recommendations under Article 21 and the suspension of concessions under Article 22 of the DSU, respectively. Unlike Panel and Appellate Body Reports, arbitration awards under Article 25 need not be adopted by the DSB and only need to be notified to the DSB and the Council or Committee of the relevant agreement.[102]

Arbitration under DSU Article 25 has only been used once.[103] Interestingly, it has been observed that in light of the present crisis at the Appellate Body, where members are failing

---

[95] DSU, Art. 5.3.
[96] R. R. Babu, *Remedies under the WTO Legal System* (Leiden: Martinus Nijhoff Publishers, 2012), p. 47.
[97] Babu, *Remedies under the WTO Legal System*, p. 47.   [98] DSU, Art. 25.3.   [99] DSU, Art. 25.1.
[100] Babu, *Remedies under the WTO Legal System*, p. 49.   [101] DSU, Art. 25.4.   [102] DSU, Art. 25.4.
[103] Award of the Arbitrator, *United States – Section 110(5) of the US Copyright Act – Recourse to Arbitration under Article 25 of the DSU*, WT/DS160/ARB25/1, 9 November 2001.

to appoint members, Article 25 can provide a unique solution for preserving the two-tier dispute settlement mechanism, unless a lasting solution is found.[104] The multiparty interim arbitration agreement mooted by the European Union and fifteen other countries is based on Article 25 of the DSU.

10.5   Other Issues

10.5.1 Good Faith

The principle of good faith is part of customary international law.[105] (See our discussion in Chapter 1.) The DSU specifically mentions the principle of good faith in Articles 3.10 and 4.3 of the DSU. Article 3.10 states as follows:

> ### DSU, Article 3.10
>
> It is understood that requests for conciliation and the use of the dispute settlement procedures should not be intended or considered as contentious acts and that, if a dispute arises, all Members will engage in these procedures in *good faith* in an effort to resolve the dispute. . . .

Article 3.10 of the DSU is a general good faith obligation with regard to the WTO dispute settlement mechanism as a whole, whereas Article 4.3 of the DSU is limited to applying the principle of good faith in relation to consultations. It is generally considered that due process, a feature of good faith, is an inherent principle in the WTO dispute settlement system.[106]

PERU – AGRICULTURAL PRODUCTS

This dispute concerns an additional duty imposed by Peru on imports of certain agricultural products. Guatemala claimed that this additional duty was inconsistent with certain provisions of the GATT 1994, the (AoA) and Customs Valuation Agreement (CVA).

Peru, as a preliminary issue, asserted that Guatemala did not act in good faith under Articles 3.7 and 3.10 of the DSU in light of the Peru–Guatemala Free Trade Agreement (PGFTA). Peru alleged that Guatemala waived its right to challenge the measure at issue under the WTO dispute settlement mechanism due to Annex 2.3 of the PGFTA.

In this regard, the Panel found that a WTO panel cannot question a member's exercise of its judgement as to whether initiation of a procedure would be fruitful under DSU Article

---

[104] S. Andersen, T. Friedbacher, C. Lau, N. Lockhart, J. Y. Remy and I. Sandford, 'Using Arbitration under Article 25 of the DSU to Ensure the Availability of Appeal', CTEI Working Paper 2017-17 (Graduate Institute of Geneva, Centre for Trade and Economic Integration, 2017), p. 9.

[105] G. Schwarzenberger and E. D Brown, *A Manual of International Law* (Milton: Professional Books, 1976), p. 7.

[106] Appellate Body Report, *Chile – Price Band System*, para. 176.

3.7. Therefore, the Panel ultimately did not examine whether the PGFTA contained a waiver to the WTO dispute settlement mechanism and rejected Peru's claim that Guatemala did not act in good faith under DSU Articles 3.7 and 3.10.

On appeal, Peru challenged the Panel's findings under DSU Articles 3.7 and 3.10, arguing that the Panel failed to correctly interpret the provision of the DSU. Peru contended that the Panel incorrectly limited its analysis to a situation in which Guatemala expressly waived its right, whereas rights under WTO law may be waived either expressly or by necessary implication, provided that the language in the PGFTA reveals clearly that the parties intended to relinquish their rights. In this regard, the Appellate Body decided to examine whether the parties to the dispute clearly stipulated a relinquishment of their right to have recourse to WTO dispute settlement by means of a mutually acceptable solution consistent with the covered agreements in the PGFTA.

The Appellate Body, however, found that Annex 2.3 of the PGFTA does not constitute a solution mutually acceptable to both parties within the meaning of the DSU Article 3.7. Accordingly, the Appellate Body found that, irrespective of the status of the PGFTA, parties to the PGFTA have the right to bring claims under covered agreements to the WTO dispute settlement system. Importantly, the Appellate Body found that Guatemala had not waived its right to have recourse to these dispute settlement proceedings. Therefore, the Appellate Body upheld the Panel's finding that there was 'no evidence that this dispute was initiated in a manner contrary to good faith'.[107]

10.5.2 *Amicus Curiae* Briefs

The WTO has jurisdiction to entertain State-to-State or intergovernmental dispute settlement. Individuals, firms, international organisations and NGOs cannot bring claims before WTO panels. Although the DSU does not contain any provisions specifically regarding *amicus curiae* briefs, Article 13 of the DSU empowers the panels to seek information. Panels may also consult international bodies and scientific or technical experts in areas such as SPS and BoP matters. In a broader sense, *amicus curiae* briefs involve citizen participation in the judicial process. In several domestic jurisdictions, legal or natural persons submit written submissions with a view to influencing the decision-making process.

The Appellate Body observed in *US – Shrimp* that Articles 11, 12 and 13 of the DSU provide panels and the Appellate Body with ample discretionary authority to accept and consider or reject information and advice submitted to it, whether requested by them or not.[108] In a subsequent dispute, the Appellate Body found that DSU Article 17.9 accorded the Appellate Body with the authority to have its own

---

[107] Appellate Body Report, *Peru – Agricultural Products*, para. 6.1.c.
[108] Appellate Body Report, *US – Shrimp*, paras. 104–106. See also Marceau, *A History of Law and Lawyers*, p. 50, fn. 182.

working procedures and, accordingly, to accept and consider any information that is pertinent to the appeal.[109] Many WTO members heavily criticised the Appellate Body's position in *EC – Asbestos* to develop working procedures for accepting *amicus* submissions.[110] However, in *EC – Asbestos*, the submissions by non-State actors were denied in the end.[111]

10.5.3 Business Confidential Information, Confidentiality and Transparency

10.5.3.1 Confidentiality

WTO dispute settlement proceedings are largely confidential in nature at every stage, through consultations, panel proceedings and at the appellate stage. Article 4.6 DSU specifies that consultations shall be confidential; however, the information acquired during consultations can be used by the parties to the dispute.[112]

At the request of the parties to a dispute, additional protection may be accorded to business confidential information. In cases such as *Canada – Aircraft* and *Brazil – Aircraft*, the Panel and the Appellate Body adopted special procedures governing business confidential information that went beyond the protection afforded by Article 18.2 of the DSU.[113]

10.5.3.2 Transparency

Historically, dispute settlement proceedings were confidential under the GATT 1947, as there was no comprehensive dispute settlement mechanism and hearings were primarily diplomatic in nature. Even under the DSU, panel and Appellate Body hearings are usually held behind closed doors. Members such as the EU and Canada have made proposals to allow panel and Appellate Body hearings to be open to the public (if the parties to the dispute agree).[114] In 2005, the EU, Canada and the United States submitted a joint request for the first panel hearings to be open to public observation for the parallel disputes *US –*

---

[109] Appellate Body Report, *United States – Imposition of Countervailing Duties on Certain Hot-Rolled Lead and Bismuth Carbon Steel Products Originating in the United Kingdom*, WT/DS138/AB/R, adopted 7 June 2000, para. 39.

[110] *Decision by the Appellate Body Concerning Amicus Curiae Briefs, Statement by Uruguay at the General Council on 22 November 2000*, WT/GC/38, 4 December 2000.

[111] Panel Report, *European Communities – Measures Affecting Asbestos and Asbestos-Containing Products*, WT/DS135/R, Add.1, adopted 5 April 2001, as modified by Appellate Body Report WT/DS135/AB/R, para. 8.12.

[112] Panel Report, *Korea – Taxes on Alcoholic Beverages*, WT/DS75/R, WT/DS84/R, adopted 17 February 1999, para. 10.23.

[113] Appellate Body Report, *Brazil – Export Financing Programme for Aircraft*, WT/DS46/AB/R, adopted 20 August 1999, para. 9; Appellate Body Report, *Canada – Measures Affecting the Export of Civilian Aircraft* WT/DS70/AB/R, adopted 20 August 1999, para. 6.

[114] Communication from the European Communities, TN/DS/W/1, 13 March 2003, para. 6; and Communication from Canada, TN/DS/W/41, 24 January 2003, para. 5.

Continued Suspension[115] and *Canada – Continued Suspension*,[116] after which, a few panel and Appellate Body hearings have been made open to the public at the request of the parties.

10.5.4 Special Treatment for Developing Countries

The designation of a country as a 'developing country' is self-declaratory under the WTO (see Chapter 16). Whether there should be differentiation between developing countries[117] or enhanced special and differential treatment (S&DT) for least-developed countries[118] is a matter of immense controversy.[119]

The DSU has certain special provisions that provide S&DT to developing countries, such as Article 3.12 and 4.10.[120] At the panel stage, Article 8.10 specifies that at least one panellist must be from a developing country when the case is between a developed country and one or more developing countries. A panel is also required to provide 'sufficient time' for the developing country member to prepare and present its arguments.[121] Panels are also required to explicitly indicate the form in which S&DT has been raised by such members in the course of the dispute settlement procedures.[122]

DSU Article 21.2 specifies that particular attention should be paid to matters affecting the interests of developing countries in the context of compliance. The DSB is required to take appropriate actions in the event that a dispute is raised by a developing country, and take into account not only the trade coverage of measures complained of, but also its impact on the economy of the developing country.[123]

Developing countries suffer from capacity constraints in dispute settlement – 'constraints of legal knowledge, financial endowment, and political power'. Shaffer referred to them as constraints of 'law, money and politics'.[124] The Advisory Centre on WTO Law, an intergovernmental organisation, offers both legal advice and representation to developing

---

[115] Panel Report, *United States – Continued Suspension of Obligations in the EC – Hormones Dispute*, WT/DS320/R, Add.1–Add.7, adopted 14 November 2008, as modified by the Appellate Body Report WT/DS320/AB/R, para. 7.40.

[116] Panel Report, *Canada – Continued Suspension of Obligations in the EC – Hormones Dispute*, WT/DS321/R, Add.1–Add.7, adopted 14 November 2008, as modified by Appellate Body Report WT/DS321/AB/R, para. 7.38.

[117] A. Keck and P. Low, 'Special and Differential Treatment in the WTO: Why, When and How?', Staff Working Paper ERSD-2004-03 (Geneva: World Trade Organization, Economic Research and Statistics Division, 2004), p. 25.

[118] Dispute Settlement Understanding Proposals: Legal Text, *Communication from India on behalf of Cuba, Dominican Republic, Egypt, Honduras, Jamaica and Malaysia*, TN/DS/W/47, 11 February 2003; Special Session of the Dispute Settlement Body, *Text for LDC Proposal on Dispute Settlement Understanding Negotiations: Communication from Haiti*, TN/DS/W/37, 22 January 2003.

[119] Communication from the United States, 'An Undifferentiated WTO: Self-Declared Development Status Risks Institutional Irrelevance', WT/GC/W/757, 16 January 2019 (arguing how self-declaration and its first-order consequence can lead to institutional irrelevance of the WTO). In response, China, India, South Africa and Venezuela submitted a proposal: WT/GC/W/765, 28 February and 1 March 2019.

[120] DSU, Art. 4.10.   [121] DSU, Art. 12.10.   [122] DSU, Art. 12.11.   [123] DSU, Arts. 21.7, 21.8.

[124] G. Shaffer, 'The Challenges of WTO Law: Strategies for Developing Country Adaptation', *World Trade Review* (2006), 5(2), pp. 177–98.

countries in relation to WTO dispute settlement. These services are available to developing country members of the Advisory Centre (thirty-six as of 31 May 2020) and to LDCs that are members of the WTO.

10.5.5 Nullification and Impairment

Article 3.8 of the DSU specifies that there is presumption of nullification or impairment when the complainant demonstrates the existence of the 'violation'. It is doubtful whether this presumption is actually rebuttable.[125] In *EC – Bananas III*, the Appellate Body noted the EC's attempt to rebut the presumption under the GATT 1994 on the basis that the US has never exported a single banana to the EC and, therefore, could not possibly suffer any trade damage. The Appellate Body observed that the US is a producer of bananas and that its potential export interest cannot be excluded. Further, the internal market of the US for bananas could be affected by the EC bananas regime through its effects on world supplies and world prices of bananas. Accordingly, the Appellate Body held that the EC did not rebut the presumption of nullification and impairment.[126]

In the case of situation or non-violation complaints, however, the fact of nullification or impairment or impediment to the attainment of an objective will have to be proved by positive evidence, which would include data showing adverse trade effects.

10.5.6 Non-Violation Claims

The DSU allows members to resort to dispute settlement even when the provisions of a covered agreement have been violated. These are typically called 'violation complaints'. Members can also bring non-violation claims[127] and 'situation' claims,[128] where a member's actions lead to the nullification and impairment of benefits, even if no specific violation of the covered agreement is alleged. During the GATT era, eight non-violation complaints were brought to dispute settlement; however, only five such complaints were successful.[129]

Article 26.1 of the DSU specifies the procedure for filing non-violation complaints, as specified under Article XXIII:1(b) of the GATT 1994. Article 26.2 deals with situation

[125] Bossche and Zdouc, *Law and Policy of the World Trade Organization*, p. 174.
[126] Appellate Body Report, *EC – Bananas III*, para. 251.   [127] GATT, Art. XXIII:1(b); GATS, Art. XXIII:3.
[128] GATT, Art. XXIII:1(c).
[129] Working Party Report, *The Australian Subsidy on Ammonium Sulphate*, GATT/CP.4/39, adopted 3 April 1950, BISD II/188; GATT Panel Report, *Treatment by Germany of Imports of Sardines*, G/26, adopted 31 October 1952, BISD 1S/53; GATT Panel Report, *European Economic Community – Production Aids Granted on Canned Peaches, Canned Pears, Canned Fruit Cocktail and Dried Grapes*, L/5778, 20 February 1985, unadopted; GATT Panel Report, *European Community – Tariff Treatment on Imports of Citrus Products from Certain Countries in the Mediterranean Region*, L/5776, 7 February 1985, unadopted; GATT Panel Report, *EEC – Oilseeds I*; GATT Panel Report, *Uruguayan Recourse to Article XXIII*, L/1923, adopted 16 November 1962, BISD 11S/95; GATT Panel Report, *Japan – Semi-Conductors*; GATT Panel Report, *United States – Restrictions on the Importation of Sugar and Sugar-Containing Products Applied under the 1955 Waiver and under the Headnote to the Schedule of Tariff Concessions*, L/6631, adopted 7 November 1990, BISD 37S/228.

complaints under Article XXIII:1(c) of the GATT 1994. In the case of a non-violation or a situation complaint, the complainant must establish that there is nullification or impairment of a benefit, or that the achievement of an objective is impeded.

Based on the text of Article XXIII:1(b) of the GATT, the Panel in *Japan – Film*, the first WTO panel to interpret and apply this provision, put forward a three-pronged legal standard to demonstrate a valid non-violation complaint. Accordingly, a panel may examine whether there is a commitment/benefit granted, whether there is a governmental action; and whether the action negatively affects the reasonable expectations created by benefit/commitment. The burden of proof in a non-violation case lies on the complainant to submit a 'detailed justification' supporting its case.[130]

10.6 Crisis in the Appellate Body

10.6.1 Stalemate Relating to Appointments to the Appellate Body

A recent crisis that has been plaguing the WTO dispute settlement mechanism is the failure of WTO members to arrive at a consensus to appoint and reappoint Appellate Body members. The United States has always been a vocal critic of the Appellate Body, and this criticism has often been articulated in the statements made by the United States in meetings of the DSB. The United States has previously blocked the appointment of US nationals to the Appellate Body, in 2011 and 2013, namely Jennifer Hillman and James Gathii.[131] In 2016, the United States took the unprecedented step of blocking the reappointment of an Appellate Body member of foreign nationality, specifically, South Korean judge Seung Wha Chang.[132] From 2018, the US has been raising concerns, which it refers to as 'systemic concern[s] about the disregard for the proper role of the Appellate Body'.[133] These issues are not directly related to the substantive legal ruling in the disputes, but rather the manner in which the Appellate Body reached those conclusions. Each of the issues is listed below, along with appropriate references to the statements of the United States for further reading:

- The Appellate Body's disregard for the strict ninety-day timeline prescribed by Article 17.5 of the DSU for the issuance of the Appellate Body Report.[134]
- The Appellate Body authorising members whose terms have expired to serve on pending disputes.[135]

---

[130] Panel Report, *Japan – Film*, paras. 10.41, 10.32.

[131] G. Shaffer, M. Elsig and M. Pollack, 'US Threats to the WTO Appellate Body', University of California Irvine School of Law Research Paper 2017-63 (13 December 2017), available at https://papers.ssrn.com/sol3/papers.cfm?abstract_id=3087524 (accessed 21 December 2020).

[132] Statement by the United States at the Meeting of the WTO Dispute Settlement Body, Geneva, 23 May 2016, p. 9.

[133] Statement by the United States at the Meeting of the WTO Dispute Settlement Body, Geneva, 23 May 2016.

[134] Statement by the United States at the Meeting of the WTO Dispute Settlement Body, Geneva, 22 June 2018.

[135] Statement by the United States at the Meeting of the WTO Dispute Settlement Body, 28 February 2018.

- Legal rulings by the Appellate Body on issues not necessary to resolve the dispute or the issue of 'advisory opinions'.[136]
- Review of facts by the Appellate Body and review of a member's domestic law even after the panel's evaluation.[137]
- Jurisprudence of the Appellate Body that effectively leads to a system of precedent in the WTO DSU system.[138]
- Judicial overreach by the Appellate Body on the grounds that it was adding to the text of the covered agreements rather than interpreting the agreements.[139]

The United States has stated that until all of its concerns have been addressed, it will not support the appointment of members to the Appellate Body. Despite the efforts of several members to resolve this crisis, the United States has not fleshed out its own concrete reform proposal.[140] In the meantime, the Appellate Body's strength was reduced to one on 10 December 2019. Hong Zhao, the remaining AB Member, completed her term on 30 November 2020. Respondents could still formally appeal findings of the Panel Report, a possibility recognised as 'appealing into the void'.[141] In a forward-looking move, the European Union and fifteen other Members have proposed a multi-party interim arbitration agreement as an ad hoc mechanism to preserve the two-tier nature of the WTO DSB and to prevent the possibility of members appealing into the void. This arrangement is envisaged under the arbitration mechanism under Article 25 of the DSU.

As outlined in the Multi-Party Interim Appeal Arbitration Arrangement, participating members will have to complete two separate formalities: endorse the political communication to the DSB; and enter into appeal arbitration agreements for specific disputes. This interim mechanism, based on the EU proposal, is envisaged for all future disputes between the parties and pending disputes, except in situations where the interim report has already been issued. The Multi-Party Interim Arbitration Arrangement is proposed to be based on the substantive and procedural aspects of the appellate review mechanism under Article 17 of the DSU. As Zhou and Wagner note, a failure to act decisively could make tomorrow's WTO look like yesterday's GATT.[142]

---

[136] Statement by the United States at the Meeting of the WTO Dispute Settlement Body, Geneva, 22 November 2017.

[137] Statements by the United States at the Meeting of the WTO Dispute Settlement Body, Geneva, 27 August 2018.

[138] Statements by the United States at the Meeting of the WTO Dispute Settlement Body, Geneva, 18 December 2018.

[139] Statements by the United States at the Meeting of the WTO Dispute Settlement Body, Geneva, 29 October 2018.

[140] Statements made by the United States at the Meeting of the WTO General Council, Geneva, 12 December 2018.

[141] J. Pauwelyn, 'WTO Dispute Settlement Post-2019: What to Expect?', *Journal of International Economic Law* (2019), 22(3), pp. 297–321.

[142] M. Wagner and W. Zhou, 'WTO Dispute Settlement System: Just Another Victim on the Road to Tomorrow's GATT?', *ILA Reporter*, available at http://ilareporter.org.au/2019/07/the-wto-dispute-settlement-system-just-another-victim-on-the-road-to-tomorrows-gatt-markus-wagner-and-weihuan-zhou (accessed 21 December 2020).

10.7 Conclusion

There is no doubt that the WTO dispute settlement system has been the most successful international adjudicatory body, purely in view of the sheer number of cases filed (almost 600) and the number of reports produced. The WTO's dispute settlement system was widely considered efficient and an exemplar in the field of international dispute settlement. But a few cracks have emerged in recent times, especially the failure to nominate judges to the Appellate Body. Reforms relating to sequencing, compensation, degree of deference, remand authority, timelines, staffing of panellists, *amicus curiae* briefs and transparency are some of the areas where reforms are required.

The above discussion has only provided an overview of the WTO dispute settlement system and the DSU. The Appellate Body crisis, precipitated by the non-filling of vacancies, is bound to make the entire WTO system lose its efficacy unless viable interim solutions are found. It is also time to ponder over whether the WTO panels and, in particular, the Appellate Body have become so textually driven that they have lost some of their adjudicative dexterity and pragmatism. These are the areas where the DSB organs may have to do some soul searching. There may be some valid criticisms of the functioning of the Appellate Body, especially in relation to judicial gap filling and advisory opinions; however, these are not good enough reasons to destroy the so-called 'jewel in the crown' of the WTO.

10.8 Summary

- WTO DSU introduced a rule-oriented, legalised and judicialised dispute settlement procedure in the place of the power-oriented GATT. This inherent strength of the system is apparently its greatest challenge at present.
- The negative consensus rule ensured stability and predictability in the adoption of Panel and Appellate Body reports. However, the application of the consensus rule for decisions such as appointment of Appellate Body members has brought the system to the point of collapse. Further, the strict timelines proved inadequate for addressing complex trade disputes. To its credit, the DSB has been able to secure prompt compliance with the vast majority of DSB rulings and recommendations. The number of cases where suspension of concessions were authorised and carried out remains low, which is a testimony to the effectiveness of the system.
- Although the panels and the Appellate Body have received wide recognition for their work in integrating international trade dispute resolution in the wider setting of public international law, some members believe that the WTO panels and the Appellate Body are not performing the tasks assigned to them in the first place. While disagreements may be genuine, returning to the pre-WTO days is not what the majority of members want or what the interconnected world needs.
- Disagreements remain on aspects such as the interpretation of municipal law (whether it can be a question of law subject to appellate review), the role of precedents, the scope of

Article 11 review and advisory opinions. Some of these aspects also indirectly refer to the role, status and prestige of the panels and the Appellate Body in the galaxy of 'international law tribunals'.

10.9 Review Questions

1 What is the difference in the dispute settlement mechanism between the GATT 1947 and the DSU?

2 When does a WTO dispute start? What is the difference between the format for a consultation request and a panel request? What is the level of specificity and accuracy required in a panel request? Is it sufficient to list the provisions of the covered agreements that the complainant has allegedly breached? (See Panel Report, *Korea – Dairy*.)

3 What are the third-party rights available to the WTO DSU? What is the meaning of the concept of 'enhanced third-party rights'? Why do countries increasingly participate as third parties?

4 What is the meaning of the term 'standard of review'? Why is this concept important in dispute settlement? What is the appropriate standard of review in WTO cases? Is it 'de novo' review or 'total deference'?

5 Based on your reading of the WTO cases, give examples of findings of fact and findings of law, illustrating the difference between both types of findings.

6 What is the mandate of the Appellate Body? Can the Appellate Body review questions of facts? When and under what circumstances can the Appellate Body 'complete the legal analysis'? How should the interpretation 'municipal law' be treated in an appeal proceeding?

7 What are the procedures for deciding a 'reasonable period of time'? What considerations apply in deciding the RPT in a given dispute? Can developing countries, as a matter of right, seek additional RPT? (See *Peru – Agricultural Products*, where Peru highlighted various domestic constraints, including the relevance of climate phenomenon El Niño.)

8 How did 'sequencing' become a controversial issue? Can this issue be addressed without making formal amendments to the DSU? How do members address this issue in the post-*EC – Bananas III* scenario?

9 When can a member retaliate? Is it possible to receive monetary payments in WTO law? What is the procedure for retaliation?

10 What reforms are urgently needed to re-establish the efficacy of the WTO DSU?

10.10 Exercise

In the Panel Report issued in the matter of *Lakkidi – Measures Affecting Importation of Pork Products*, the Panel analysed the WTO consistency of a set of food safety standards that subjected pork products originating from Ibutu, another WTO member, to rigorous testing, as they were perceived to contain harmful nutrients. Lakkidi argued that these measures were implemented in conformity with the SPS Agreement and the GATT.

During the Panel processes, the Panel sought scientific details from the OIE, as well as the WHO. Safety Food Warriors, a private non-governmental organisation, submitted an unsolicited brief to the Panel. Safety Food Warriors' submission provided detailed evidence on the unethical veterinary practices in Ibutu and how these could affect the quality and safety of swine products. The documents were accepted by the Secretariat, but later rejected. Lakkidi argued during the Panel process that Safety Food Warriors' brief should be accepted and deemed part of the submission of Lakkidi.

The WTO Panel ruled against Lakkidi. This finding has now been appealed to the Appellate Body. Due to extensive arguments and logistical constraints at the Secretariat, the Appellate Body could not complete the proceedings within ninety days of the filing of the appeal. In fact, almost five months have passed since the appeal was filed.

Did the Panel violate its duty under Article 11, DSU by disregarding the submissions made by Safety Food Warriors from its analysis? Can Lakkidi rely on a report that was not officially part of its submission? Further, can the Appellate Body extend the ninety-day timeline in Article 17?

FURTHER READING

Babu, R., *Remedies under the WTO Legal System*, Nijhoff International Trade Law Series, Vol. 11 (Leiden: Martinus Nijhoff, 2012).

Consultative Board to the Director-General, Supachai Panitchpakdi, *The Future of the WTO: Addressing Institutional Challenges in the New Millennium* (Geneva: World Trade Organization, 2004).

Qian, M. A., 'Reasonable Period of Time in the WTO Dispute Settlement System', *Journal of International Economic Law* (2012), 15(1), pp. 257–85.

Staiger, R. W. and Sykes, A. O., 'Non-Violations', *Journal of International Economic Law* (2013), 16 (4), pp. 741–75.

VanGrasstek, C., *The History and Future of the World Trade Organization* (Geneva: World Trade Organization, 2013).

Voon, T. and Yanovich, A., 'The Facts Aside: The Limitation of WTO Appeals to Issues of Law', *Journal of World Trade* (2006), 40(2), pp. 239–58.

Part II

International Investment Law

11 International Investment Law in the Making

Table of Contents

Highlights

- With around 3,000 international investment agreements (IIAs), including 2,340 bilateral investment treaties (BITs) in force and 319 treaties with investment provisions (TIPs) in force too, the production of economic norms for global and regional integration has reached unprecedented levels.
- While a rather old discipline, when viewed from a historical perspective, contemporary international investment law (IIL) remains very much in the making.
- IIL is characterised by the extremely vast diversity of its sources and rather inconsistent decisions emanating from various international adjudicating bodies.
- IIL has only recently captured the attention of the larger community of international law scholars, while triggering great interest in civil society and student audiences alike.
- This interest also corresponds to the significant increase of foreign direct investment (FDI) in the past two decades.
- The vast majority of developed and developing countries are now directly concerned with IIL.

- The history of IIL reveals a pendulum swing between liberalisation, promotion and protection of FDI on the one hand, and protection of the State's interests on the other.
- Beyond the binary of pro-/anti-FDI doctrines, conceptual approaches could be categorised in three different groups: the liberal perspective, the dependency theory and the regulatory one.
- There are at least four categories of international investment actors: States; foreign investors, in the form of private or public entities; international organisations; and civil society.
- Today's dynamic IIL scholarship supports the need for this discipline to be addressed beyond its technicalities – that is, in an international economic law (IEL) and general international law perspective.

11.1   Introduction

With around 3,300 IIAs and almost 600 FTAs, the production of economic norms for global and regional integration has reached an unprecedented stage.[1] As part of the response to the limited evolution of multilateral trade negotiations conducted by the WTO, myriad mega-regional trade and investment deals are currently negotiated or reshaped to meet the expectations of a now trade-conscious and therefore more demanding global civil society. From the Transatlantic Trade and Investment Partnership's (TTIP) various negotiation projects to the concluded Trans-Pacific Partnership (TPP), the African Continental Free Trade Area (AfCFTA) and the Regional Comprehensive Economic Partnership (RCEP), the magnitude of these proposed new deals has simply been immense.[2] This bewildering array of new legal instruments covers an incredibly vast legal and political landscape at the crossroads between trade, investment and essential societal concerns, such as human rights, labour, health and environmental protection. In response to the fragmentation of international law, and in a quest for renewed coherence, the latest investment treaty initiatives often propose to further 'regulatory cooperation' (i.e. sharing information and good practices) into a more ambitious 'regulatory convergence', aiming at the production of quite similar norms.[3] Whether these deals, even when concluded, are going to be implemented

---

[1] For regular updates, see UNCTAD's *World Investment Report*, generally published in June, available at https://unctad.org/en/pages/PublicationWebflyer.aspx?publicationid=2460 (accessed 21 December 2020).

[2] For an update on recent negotiations and concluded agreements, see WTO Regional Trade Agreement Database, available at www.wto.org/english/tratop_e/region_e/region_e.htm (accessed 21 December 2020). As of 17 January 2020, 303 RTAs were in force. A large number include an investment chapter.

[3] On fragmentation, see Report of the Study Group of the International Law Commission, 'Fragmentation of International Law: Difficulties Arising from the Diversification and Expansion of International Law', UN Doc. A/CN.4/L.682, 13 April 2006. See also Margaret Young (ed.), *Regime Interaction in International Law: Facing Fragmentation* (Cambridge University Press, 2012); Ole Kristian Fauchald and Andreas Nollkaemper (eds.), *The Practice of International and National Courts and the (De-)Fragmentation of International Law* (Oxford: Hart, 2014). On the methodological challenge in international economic law, see Ernst-Ulrich Petersmann, 'Methodological

remains to be seen, as the political pressure surrounding trade and investment regulation is today at a rare high.

In this general context, contemporary IIL, while a rather old discipline when viewed from an historical perspective, remains very much in the making. Indeed, as we will see below, IIL and dispute settlement have been constantly evolving from a conceptual framework to a variety of other approaches, which may apparently refer to the same standards but differ greatly in putting forward different policy objectives and economic development paths. In recent years, profound changes have occurred, hence modifying the landscape designed by the proponents of the 1990s investment liberalisation. Countries like Ecuador, Bolivia or Venezuela have denounced the International Centre for Settlement of Investment Disputes (ICSID) Convention and some of their BITs, as exemplified by Ecuador's decision, in March 2013, to terminate its BIT with the US, a few months after a record US$2.3 billion arbitration award in the *Occidental Petroleum Corporation* v. *Ecuador* case was rendered.[4] Other, usually less vocal, critics of IIL have also joined a growing club of dissenters. In September 2012, South Africa informed the Belgo-Luxembourg Economic Union of its wish not to renew their existing BIT, which was to expire in March 2013. Similarly, in 2015, Indonesia started to terminate all its BITs, beginning with the BIT it had adopted with its former colonial ruler, the Netherlands, and is currently rethinking a new investment treaty model.[5] In the same vein, India suspended all its BITs negotiations in 2013 and adopted a largely debated new investment treaty model in 2015.[6] On this basis, it has entered into a new series of negotiations and signed new BITS with Belarus, Kyrgyzstan and Brazil.[7] The changes did not come as a complete surprise, as all these countries had been facing an increasing number of controversial FDI cases, with extraordinarily high claims against the State. For some, this was totally new and was perceived as unacceptable, and as challenging the State's sovereignty. Interestingly, a shift from the traditional liberal approach to foreign investment protection has taken place in capital-exporting countries too. In 2011, for example, the Australian government decided no longer to include provisions on investor–State dispute settlement in its bilateral and regional trade agreements, although it later agreed to investment arbitration in the 2015 TPP, and its revised version the CPTPP. Other developed countries, including the US, Canada and EU members, have also faced civil society's reaction to unpopular trade deals, as illustrated by the EU–Canada

---

Pluralism and its Critics in International Economic Law Research', *Journal of International Economic Law* (2013), 15(4), pp. 921–70; Ernst-Ulrich Petersmann, 'Methodology Problems in International Economic Law and Adjudication', EUI Law working paper 2016/12 (European University Institute, 2016).

[4] *Occidental Petroleum Corporation* v. *Ecuador*, ICSID Case No. ARB/06/11, main materials available at www.italaw .com/cases/767 (accessed 21 December 2020).

[5] Wenny Setiawati, 'Investment Court System for Indonesia: A Better Outcome for Investment Disputes?', in Chaisse et al., *Handbook of International Investment Law and Policy* (Singapore: Springer, in press).

[6] Prabhash Ranjan, *India and Bilateral Investment Treaties* (Oxford University Press, 2019); Leïla Choukroune and Rahul Donde (eds.), *Adjudicating Global Business in and with India: International Commercial and Investment Disputes Settlement* (London: Routledge, in press).

[7] See UNCTAD Investment Policy Hub for updates, available at https://investmentpolicy.unctad.org/international-investment-agreements/countries/96/india (accessed 21 December 2020).

Comprehensive Economic and Trade Agreement (CETA), eventually signed on 30 October 2016 after a phase of 'legal scrubbing' of the previously adopted text. CETA entered into force provisionally on 21 September 2017, meaning most of the agreement now applies. However, the second treaty text has not yet been ratified by all EU national parliaments and this task has revealed itself to be more complicated than initially anticipated by the trade negotiators. Changes will occur again in accordance with the developments of the global economy and the necessity for countries to readjust their investment law and policy to the needs of a specific situation. It is important to bear in mind that IIL is fast evolving and shaped by politico-economic decisions.

At the centre of today's global controversy, the investor–State dispute settlement (ISDS) system plays a particular role. The number of ISDS disputes has literally exploded in recent years, with an overall number of known treaty-based arbitration cases reaching a total of 1,023, with 674 concluded cases by May 2020.[8] The nature of these investor–State disputes has also evolved, with investors not hesitating to challenge the regulatory activity of host countries, along with their national policies for health, the environment, energy production and security. Developed countries are also targeted and represented 45 per cent of the total disputes in 2015.[9] In addition, intra-EU disputes accounted for about one-quarter of the investment arbitrations initiated in 2016, down from one-third in the three preceding years, but still at a significant level for countries new to ISDS and generally used to *bringing* disputes rather than *responding* to them – a drastic change that also explains a number of political reactions against ISDS, including from the European Union (see Chapter 14). Lastly, the vast majority of investment arbitrations are brought under BITs, most of them dating back to the 1980s and 1990s, and offering generous protection to FDIs. As developing as well as developed countries are sued by powerful businesses, their autonomy to regulate investment liberalisation comes increasingly under pressure. This unbalance has been acknowledged by the EU itself, an original supporter of the ISDS system.[10] Recent awards have indeed reached astronomical levels with a 2014 decision, for example, amounting to US$50 billion in the three closely related *Yukos* cases[11] – the highest known award at that time in investment arbitration. Concerns with the current investor–State dispute settlement system relate, in particular, to a number of clearly identified issues: a democratic deficit, coupled with a deficit of legitimacy in relation to the questionable professionalism, independence and impartiality of arbitrators, and the lack of transparency in the proceedings and the publication of decisions; a deficit of

---

[8] UNCTAD Investment Policy Hub, available at https://investmentpolicy.unctad.org/investment-dispute-settlement (accessed 21 December 2020); UNCTAD, *World Investment Report 2020: International Production beyond the Pandemic* (New York and Geneva: United Nations, 2020).

[9] UNCTAD, *World Investment Report 2020*.

[10] See the EU ISDS reform proposals since 2015, and its multilateral investment court project, available at https://ec.europa.eu/trade/policy/accessing-markets/investment/ (accessed 21 December 2020).

[11] *Hulley Enterprises Limited (Cyprus)* v. *Russian Federation*, UNCITRAL, PCA Case No. AA226, Final Award, 18 July 2014; *Yukos Universal Limited (Isle of Man)* v. *Russian Federation*, UNCITRAL, PCA Case No. AA227, Final Award, 18 July 2014; *Veteran Petroleum Limited (Cyprus)* v. *Russian Federation*, UNCITRAL, PCA Case No. AA228, Final Award, 18 July 2014.

coherence and consistency in the arbitral awards; third-party financing; the cost of arbitration; and, finally the absence of an appeal mechanism. Therefore, international organisations, such as the United Nations Conference on Trade and Development (UNCTAD), but also the pro-investment liberalisation Organisation for Economic Co-operation and Development (OECD), are now publishing a series of roadmap papers for ISDS reform. In July 2016, the G20 countries even adopted the Guiding Principles for Global Investment Policymaking, drawing on UNCTAD's *Investment Policy Framework for Sustainable Development* (see Chapter 14).[12] UNCTAD, as well as the United Nations Commission on International Trade Law (UNCITRAL), in coordination with the ICSID of the World Bank, are very much at the centre of international discussions on investment treaty making and dispute settlement reform (see Chapter 14).[13]

Lastly, it would be a mistake to consider that investment-related disputes are settled only by arbitral tribunals on the basis of investment contracts and BITs. There are indeed many other judicial and non-judicial fora in which these are addressed today, from alternative dispute resolution (ADR) mechanisms to domestic courts. This ever-changing landscape, resulting from the complication of international economic transactions and their globalisation, is illustrated by a number of recent and less recent cases one would usually study in a business and human rights context.

Bhopal in India, *Total* in Burma, *Nike* in China, *Shell* in Nigeria, *Talisman* in Sudan, *Wal-Mart* in the US, *Texaco-Chevron* in Ecuador or *Philip Morris* in Australia, and many other multinational companies have been named and shamed for their responsibility in dramatic violations of international human rights law, including environmental and social disasters.[14] How can these non-State actors be held responsible for such violations? These pressing questions are but a few of the issues addressed in this and the following three chapters, aimed at developing a well-informed and critical approach to one of the most important and truly fascinating fields of contemporary international law: international investment.

This first chapter will pose the basis of our analysis in addressing *why* and *how* IIL is still in the making. In doing so, it will present FDI's contemporary features, IIL's historical background and the main theoretical discussions surrounding it.

---

[12] http://investmentpolicyhub.unctad.org/News/Hub/Archive/508/ (accessed 21 December 2020).

[13] See the work of UNCITRAL, available at https://uncitral.un.org/en/working_groups/3/investor-state, as well as the ICSID reflections on ISDS reform, available at https://icsid.worldbank.org/en/Pages/resources/ICSID-Publications.aspx (both accessed 21 December 2020).

[14] For a general overview of all these cases, which have national and international ramifications, with a series of domestic and international litigation, see the Business and Human Rights Resource Centre database, available at www.business-humanrights.org (accessed 21 December 2020). Some of these cases will be addressed more directly in Chapter 14, in relation to precise ISDS. In this regard, the UNCTAD investment dispute settlement navigator provides very good access to cases. See, for example, the *Philip Morris* case, available at https://investmentpolicy.unctad.org/investment-dispute-settlement/cases/421/philip-morris-v-australia (accessed 21 December 2020).

11.2 FDI Today

11.2.1 Mapping Exercise

11.2.1.1   FDI Global and Regional Trends

FDIs are now of prime importance for most developed and developing economies. Whether FDI *inflows* (FDI coming into a given territory) or *outflows* (FDI going out from a given territory), it represents one of the most salient features of globalisation, while participating (or not) in economic development. The nature of FDIs, and the economic theories supporting their growth, or preventing the same, have long been conflicting, if not controversial. Before engaging further in these more conceptual issues, let us first carry out a simple mapping exercise to introduce recent global FDI trends.[15] According to the UNCTAD *World Investment Report 2019*, global FDI flows continued to fall in 2018, by 13 per cent, to US$1.3 trillion. FDI flows to developed economies reached the lowest point since 2004, declining by 27 per cent.[16] However, flows to developing countries remained stable, rising by 2 per cent. As a result, the share of developing countries in global FDI increased to 54 per cent, a record high, which produces a number of policy implications of importance for the development of international investment law. More active developing economies could have a greater say in treaty making and dispute settlement reforms. Developing Asia is particularly well-placed as the largest recipient of FDI in the developing world. Despite a decline of 6 per cent, flows to developing Asia continued to account for one-third of global FDI in

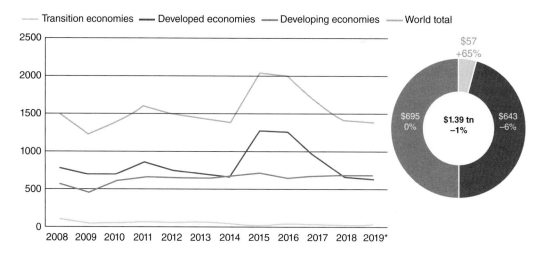

Figure 11.1 FDI inflows, 2008–19. Source: UNCTAD.

---

[15] It is always recommended to start your IIL journey with a simple mapping exercise based on the recently published statistics by UNCTAD, the World Bank, the OECD and other regional organisations.

[16] UNCTAD, *World Investment Report 2019: Special Economic Zones* (New York and Geneva: United Nations, 2019). For updates, see the UNCTAD *World Investment Reports*.

Group of economies/region	2017	2018	2019	Projections 2020
World	1 700	1 495	1 540	920 to 1 080
Developed economies	950	761	800	480 to 600
Europe	570	364	429	240 to 300
North America	304	297	297	190 to 240
Developing economies	701	699	685	380 to 480
Africa	42	51	45	25 to 35
Asia	502	499	474	260 to 330
Latin America and Caribbean	156	149	164	70 to 100
Transition economies	50	35	55	30 to 40
Memorandum: annual growth rate (per cent)				
World	−14	−12	3	(−40 to −30)
Developed economies	−25	−20	5	(−40 to −25)
Europe	−16	−36	18	(−45 to −30)
North America	−40	−2	0	(−35 to −20)
Developing economies	7	0	−2	(−45 to −30)
Africa	−10	22	−10	(−40 to −25)
Asia	7	−1	−5	(−45 to −30)
Latin America and the Caribbean	14	−5	10	(−55 to −40)
Transition economies	−25	−31	59	(−45 to −30)

Figure 11.2 FDI inflows and projections by group of economies and region, 2017–19, and forecast 2020. Source: UNCTAD, FDI/MNE database.

2019. Looking ahead, UNCTAD expected FDI flows to rise marginally in 2020, but with the Covid-19 pandemic crisis, trends are fast-changing and a decline is now evident.

If analysed from a grouping or regional perspective, it is interesting to see that the G20 still represents one-third of the world FDI inflows and remains the largest recipient and source of global FDI, despite the emergence of other dynamic groupings that shape the South–South FDI landscape.

11.2.2 FDI Actors

From a historical and legal perspective, FDI actors were considered as private individuals to whom the law on the State's responsibility for injuries caused to aliens could apply. The complication and development of global economic transactions deeply challenged this initial approach on the basis of a simple observation: there is much more to FDI actors than private individuals. As a matter of fact, one can distinguish four categories of actors (at the very least): the State; investors in the form of private or public entities; international

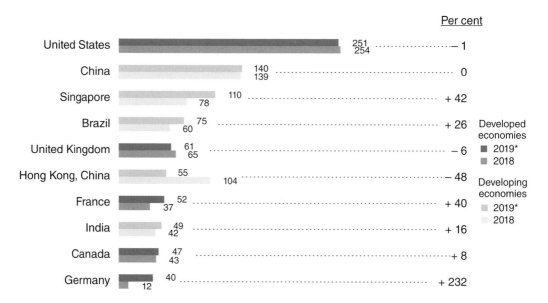

Figure 11.3 FDI inflows: top ten host economies, 2018 and 2019. Source UNCTAD.

organisations and other international institutions, such as arbitral bodies; NGOs and civil society organisations, including professional bodies. In summary, there are State and non-State actors, the latter now taking an extraordinary variety of shapes.

To be more precise, the State very much remains at the centre of FDI reception and exportation. It is referred to as the 'host State' when it welcomes FDI, and the 'home State' when investors originate from it. It regulates FDI at the domestic and international level, according to certain policy priorities and its sovereign right to protect its population and strategic economic sectors, but also the foreign investors towards whom it has certain duties. This balance between rights and duties reveals itself to be essential in the conceptual framing of IIL.

Corporations then obviously account for the vast majority of foreign direct investors. Their internationalisation, although relatively recent, has been a powerful catalyst of globalisation and FDI growth. Two periods have been of particular importance for their expansion: 1993–97 and 2003–10, as analysed by the UNCTAD Transnationality Index reflected in the UNCTAD yearly world investment report.[17] These internationalised actors are referred to as multinational enterprises or transnational companies. There are, of course, numerous definitions encompassing a complex reality, but let us assume that to qualify as an MNE, a company should operate in a number of countries under a common system of decision-making and a harmonised strategy. A parent company is generally identifiable,

[17] See http://unctad.org/en/Pages/DIAE/World%20Investment%20Report/Annex-Tables.aspx (accessed 21 December 2020).

as well as subsidiaries or local entities.[18] The companies are often linked by shared ownership (equity-based, large or small) and/or a contract in which one party retains some control over the other(s). Of course, the task of identifying these entities is not as easy as it seems, as they deliberately use all the tools and other loopholes existing in national and international law to maximise their business activities. MNEs indeed entertain a complex relation with the law, and international law in particular.[19] The State remains their agent for access to international law's protection – for example, through BITs. They are not subject to international law as such, but, as some have argued, 'participants' in the international legal order, an ambiguous status that has posed numerous problems (as we will see in Chapter 14) in the many business and human rights cases settled on the basis of the Alien Tort Claim Act (ATCA).[20] At the same time, corporations have full legal personality, which allows them to enter into legal relationships. However, this legal personality is separated from the legal personality of their owner (or shareholders) and managers through a fictional device: 'the corporate veil', which may be difficult to lift when, for example, the manager of a given company is directly implicated in some unlawful activities. Because of their importance and the impact they produce on economies and societies, the activities of MNEs have been scrutinised, and a number of attempts to frame their conduct have been made, starting with the *OECD Guidelines for Multinational Enterprises*. Interestingly, these guidelines, first adopted in 1976 and later revised in 1979, 1982, 1984, 1991, 2000 and 2011, do not provide a definition of MNEs.[21] Yet they propose recommendations for the conduct of responsible businesses abroad. Later on, a number of other international organisations took a keen interest in framing the conduct of MNEs. This renewed attention naturally corresponded with the expectations of a civil society searching for accountability in response to certain unlawful MNEs' activities, including human rights violations. The International Labour Organization's MNE Declaration is also relevant in that it provides guidance to enterprises on social policy and inclusive, responsible and sustainable workplace practices, and is the only global instrument elaborated and adopted (forty years ago, amended in 2000 and 2006, and revised in 2017) by governments, employers and workers around the world.[22] Lastly, the Human Rights Council's 'Guiding Principles on Business and Human Rights' of 2011 is of particular importance and will be addressed in Chapter 14.[23]

---

[18] UNCTAD, *World Investment Report 2011: Non-Equity Modes of International Production and Development* (New York: United Nations, 2011).

[19] Peter T. Muchlinski, *Multinational Enterprises and the Law* (Oxford University Press, 2007).

[20] For a conservative approach, see J. E. Alvarez, 'Are Corporations "Subjects" of International Law?', NYU School of Law, Public Law Research Paper 10-77 (2010), available at http://ssrn.com/abstract=1703465 (accessed 21 December 2020).

[21] *OECD Guidelines for Multinational Enterprises* (Paris: OECD Publishing, 2011), available at www.oecd.org/daf/inv/mne/ (accessed 21 December 2020).

[22] ILO, Tripartite Declaration of Principles Concerning Multinational Enterprises and Social Policy, available at www.ilo.org/empent/Publications/WCMS_094386/lang–en/index.htm (accessed 21 December 2020).

[23] Report of the Special Representative of the Secretary-General, 'Guiding Principles on Business and Human Rights: Implementing the United Nations "Protect, Respect and Remedy" Framework', Human Rights Council, A/HRC/17/31, 21 March 2011, available at www.ohchr.org/Documents/Issues/Business/A-HRC-17-31_AEV.pdf (accessed 21 December 2020).

Yet these companies, MNEs or not, are not necessarily private entities. Many of today's investors are actually owned, partially or fully, by the State and referred to as State-owned enterprises (SOEs) or State-controlled entities (SCEs), a category that could include sovereign wealth funds (SWFs).

Box 11.1 The return of State capitalism?

How can an entity be qualified as State-controlled or State-owned? Here again, there is no single rule in international law. A government can, for instance, own a certain number of shares in a given company without necessarily claiming any control. There is no threshold of shares to own to qualify the entity as an SCE. After all, the WTO itself searched for a definition of 'public bodies' in a number of China-related cases, including *US – Anti-Dumping and Countervailing Duties (China)*. However, it often happens that government-owned or State-run enterprises are the result of corporatisation that is a form of administrative process in which the structure of the entity is reorganised as a semi-autonomous body and sometimes even listed on stock exchanges.

In addition, and yet differently, SWFs are key FDI players as well. Although they have existed for more than a century with the first American attempts, SWFs have gained phenomenal importance from the year 2000, with the rise of China as a global investor, of course, but also countries like Norway, which possesses the biggest fund, or the United Arab Emirates, Kuwait, Saudi Arabia and Qatar. There is no consensus on their definition. However, SWFs are generally created by governments to manage their excess liquidity at a positive time for their economies (no or little debt) and plan the future in diversifying their sources of revenue. They can virtually invest in anything. In 2009, the International Forum of SWFs was created to share good practices and now comprises thirty-two members and about 70 per cent of all assets managed by the SWFs. The Forum also endorses the Santiago Principles drafted by the International Working Group of SWFs and welcomed by the IMF's International Monetary Financial Committee in 2008, promoting good governance, accountability and transparency (see Part IV, for additional discussion of these Principles).

According to the *World Investment Report 2017*, about 1,500 State-owned MNEs (1.5 per cent of all MNEs) own more than 86,000 foreign affiliates, or close to 10 per cent of all foreign affiliates.[24] They announced greenfield investments accounting for 11 per cent of the global total in 2016, up from 8 per cent in 2010. China is the largest home economy of these companies. Interestingly, with the emergence of the BRICS, the return of State capitalism also seems perceptible. Russian, Chinese or Brazilian investors are often state-owned. This is not exactly a new idea – see, for example, the eighteenth century East India Company (Box 11.2 below) or the presence of many active SOEs in European countries

---

[24] UNCTAD, *World Investment Report 2017: Investment and the Digital Economy* (New York and Geneva: United Nations, 2017).

Box 11.1 (cont.)

like France or rising powers like the 1950s South Korea – but the dynamism of these 'emerging' companies at a time of liberalisation and globalisation is interesting to observe, as it is also sometimes problematic in investment disputes when the claimant is de facto the State against another State in a different form (see Chapter 14).

To Go Further

'The Rise of State Capitalism', *The Economist* (21 January 2012), available at www.economist .com/node/21543160 (accessed 21 December 2020).

Bondy,C., Chaisse, J., Chen, H., Górski, J., Sejko, D. and Weeramantry, R. (eds.), *State-Controlled Entities Regulation, Transnational Dispute Management* (special issue, 2020), 6, available at www.transnational-dispute-management.com/news.asp?key=1719 (accessed 21 December 2020).

Chaisse, J. and Górski, J. (eds.), *The Regulation of State-Controlled Enterprises: An Interdisciplinary and Comparative Examination* (Singapore: Springer, in press).

Chaisse, J. and Sejko, D., '*Investor–State Arbitration Distorted: When the Claimant Is a State*', in L. Choukroune (ed.), *Judging the State in International Trade and Investment Law: Sovereignty Modern, the Law and the Economics* (London: Springer, 2016), pp. 77–103.

Choukroune, L., 'China and the WTO Dispute Settlement System: The Global Trade Lawyer and the State Capitalist', *China Perspectives and Perspectives Chinoises* (2012), 1, pp. 49–57.

International Working Group of Sovereign Wealth Funds, *Generally Accepted Principles and Practices: 'Santiago Principles'* (October 2008), available at www.ifswf.org/santiago-principles-landing/santiago-principles (accessed 21 December 2020).

Wang, J. 'State Capitalism and Sovereign Wealth Funds: Finding a "Soft" Location in International Economic Law' in in C. L. Lim (ed.), *Alternative Visions of the International Law on Foreign Investment: Essays in Honour of Muthucumaraswamy Sornarajah* (Cambridge University Press, 2016), pp. 405–27.

Lastly, other non-State actors are also playing an important role, if not in the making, for the very least in the regulation, settlement of disputes and debate surrounding FDI. These are international organisations (IOs) and other NGOs and professional bodies. As far as IOs are concerned, the World Bank, the IMF, UNCTAD, UNCITRAL and the OECD, for example, have been closely associated with a number of FDI-related initiatives, if not directly involved in these, as in the case of the creation, in 1965, of the ICSID, established under the World Bank for the resolution of disputes between investors and States. Other regional IOs, like the Association of South East Asian Nations (ASEAN), are also playing an important part in the FDI debate.[25]

NGOs have long been absent from this discussion, but are now particularly keen to engage with issues that directly touch upon rights (health, labour, the environment) and

---

[25] See, for example, their FDI statistics, available at http://asean.org/?static_post=foreign-direct-investment-statistics (accessed 21 December 2020).

development. Some have designed a genuine expertise in the field of FDI and (as we will see in Chapter 14) also appeared as *amicus* in a number of investment cases, hence pushing ISDS reform towards more transparency and inclusiveness of civil society (see Chapter 10). Lastly, professional organisations, be it national bar associations, chambers of commerce or private companies associations are also keen to engage in the global FDI debate and adhere to a number of guidelines framing the activities of MNEs.[26]

11.2.3 The Nature and Specificity of FDI

From this general panorama, one can now better gauge the reality of global FDIs, as well as their nature. What are FDIs and how are they approached by economics and law? The definition of FDI has been a controversial issue in international economics and at the centre of conflicting theories. The OECD benchmark definition of FDI, completed in 2008 and revised in 2015, tried to systematise an international standard providing the basis for economic analysis and international comparisons.[27] How can we indeed identify and measure FDI? In reviewing the concept of investment, the OECD argues:

> ### OECD Benchmark Definition of Foreign Direct Investment:
> ### *1.4. An Overview of Foreign Direct Investment Concepts*
>
> 11. Direct investment is a category of cross-border investment made by a resident in one economy (the *direct investor*) with the objective of establishing a lasting interest in an enterprise (the *direct investment enterprise*) that is resident in an economy other than that of the direct investor. The motivation of the direct investor is a strategic long-term relationship with the direct investment enterprise to ensure a significant degree of influence by the direct investor in the management of the direct investment enterprise. The 'lasting interest' is evidenced when the direct investor owns at least 10 per cent of the voting power of the direct investment enterprise. Direct investment may also allow the direct investor to gain access to the economy of the direct investment enterprise which it might otherwise be unable to do. The objectives of direct investment are different from those of portfolio investment whereby investors do not generally expect to influence the management of the enterprise.[28]

---

[26] See, for example, the International Chamber of Commerce initiatives on business and human rights, available at https://iccwbo.org/media-wall/news-speeches/icc-at-the-forefront-on-business-and-human-rights/ (accessed 21 December 2020).

[27] *OECD Benchmark Definition of Foreign Direct Investment*, 4th ed. (Paris: OECD Publishing, 2008), available at www.oecd.org/investment/fdibenchmarkdefinition.htm (accessed 21 December 2020); 'The OECD's Revised Benchmark Definition of Foreign Direct Investment: Better Data for Better Policy', available at http://oecdinsights .org/2015/10/19/the-oecds-revised-benchmark-definition-of-foreign-direct-investment-better-data-for-better-policy/ (accessed 21 December 2020).

[28] *OECD Benchmark Definition of Foreign Direct Investment*, p. 17.

A number of criteria are hence determined: the foreign character of the operation, its long-term duration, the access facilitation to another economy, the difference with portfolio investment.

The IMF's *Balance of Payments and International Investment Position Manual* (BPM6) also approaches the issue of investment in its Chapters 6 (Functional Categories) and 7 (International Investment Position).[29] As such, they identify five 'functional categories', which build on the classification of financial assets and liabilities:

(a) direct investment,
(b) portfolio investment,
(c) financial derivatives (other than reserves) and employee stock options,
(d) other investment, and
(e) reserve assets.

IMF, BPM6, Chapter 6: Functional Categories, I. Definition of direct investment

6.8. *Direct investment is a category of cross-border investment associated with a resident in one economy having control or a significant degree of influence on the management of an enterprise that is resident in another economy.* As well as the equity that gives rise to control or influence, direct investment also includes investment associated with that relationship, including investment in indirectly influenced or controlled enterprises (paragraph 6.12), investment in fellow enterprises (see paragraph 6.17), debt (except selected debt set out in paragraph 6.28), and reverse investment (see paragraph 6.40). The Framework for Direct Investment Relationships (FDIR) provides criteria for determining whether cross-border ownership results in a direct investment relationship based on control and influence. The definition of direct investment is the same as in the fourth edition of the *OECD Benchmark Definition of Foreign Direct Investment*, which provides additional details on the FDIR and the collection of direct investment data. Appendix 6a, Topical Summary – Direct Investment, provides references to paragraphs in which different aspects of direct investment are discussed in this *Manual*.

Here again, a number of important criteria are put forward: the idea of control, the concept of risk, which is central to FDI, the distinction with portfolio investment (see Chapter 12). Yet what about sustainable development (economic, social and environmental development in a holistic approach) and the benefit the host economy could gain from an

---

[29] IMF, *Balance of Payments and International Investment Position Manual*, 6th ed. (Washington, DC: International Monetary Fund, 2010), available at www.imf.org/external/pubs/ft/bop/2007/bopman6.htm (accessed 21 December 2020).

FDI? If not initially a sustainable development, the very idea of economic development has been at the centre of FDI controversies since the early days of their existence.[30] Investing in another country can only benefit the investor, which literally takes foreign resources in kind and/or repatriates its profits without any participation in the local economy and its development. Parts of the colonial model had been based on the exploitation of alien resources, and proponents of the New International Economic Order (NIEO) denounced the status quo of the former imperial economic powers on the basis of this very fact. Lastly, the current opposition to FDI in developed or developing countries is based on the same principles: the need to protect domestic resources and the economy while sharing (or not) certain economic projects through opening up to foreign investors certain selected sectors, if not the economy as a whole. As such, a profound concern remains about the capacity of international law to effectively protect States' interests and their economic development to the benefit of their population. As argued by Howard Mann:

the only significant expansion of the substantive content of investment treaties in their 50-plus years of existence has been to extend investor rights from the protection of existing foreign investments to the rights to establish investments in a foreign State, and then to maximize the profits from these investments – even when at the expense of social and economic development rights in the host states. The broad result is that investment treaties are becoming more supportive of the rights of existing capital owners to extend and expand their capital base, while precluding governments from adopting policies and tools aimed at broadening the base of economic development and intergenerational equity. ... Professor Sornarajah is right that, now more than ever, international investment treaties have become the international economic law support to the law of greed over the law of need.[31]

In the past few years, these issues have actually been acknowledged by the international community, including civil society organisations, which have managed to influence governments in the developing and developed world alike. The new generations of BITs and IIAs show a more balanced picture, with some forms of agile use of international economic law flexibilities and protections (see Chapter 12).

Box 11.2 The East India Company: an early controversial MNE

Founded on 31 December 1600, the East India Company (EIC), also known as the Honourable East India Company (HEIC) and, informally, the John Company, was an English and later British joint stock company, formed to trade with the 'East Indies', the Indian Subcontinent and China. Owned by rich merchants and aristocrats, the company became a very powerful instrument of the monarchy and eventually took control of the declining Indian Mughal Empire in the early nineteenth century. By

---

[30] Howard Mann, 'The New Frontier: Economic Rights of Foreign Investors versus Government Policy Space for Economic Development', in C. L. Lim (ed.), *Alternative Visions of the International Law on Foreign Investment: Essays in Honour of Muthucumaraswamy Sornarajah* (Cambridge University Press, 2016), pp. 289–323.

[31] Mann, 'The New Frontier', p. 323.

Box 11.2 (cont.)

1803, indeed, the company had an army of about 260,000 men – twice the size of the British army at that time. It effectively ruled large parts of India for about a century (1750–1850), until, with the Government of India Act of 1858, the British Crown formed the British Raj under its control. The company was later involved in the illegal opium trade via its Indian merchant of Calcutta, where opium was sold, provided that it was later sent to China, where its trade was banned. This soon resulted in the First Opium War (1839–42), after which the island of Hong Kong was ceded to Britain under the Treaty of Nanking (29 August 1842).

The EIC was, in its own way, a model of internationalised corporation trading and investing abroad for its shareholders' own benefit. In doing so, it had gained large control of territories on which it de facto participated in the governance of local affairs and people. Its extraterritorial features, its complex set of laws allowing for some independence yet a close relation with the British Crown, and its interference in domestic affairs have been denounced on a similar basis as the activities of certain powerful contemporary MNEs in the developing world.

As explained by William Dalrymple in his outstanding historical research monograph, *The Anarchy*: 'We still talk about the British conquering India, but that phrase disguises a more sinister reality. It was not the British government that began seizing great chunks of India in the mid-eighteenth century, but a dangerously unregulated private company headquartered in one small office, five windows wide, in London, and managed in India by a violent, utterly ruthless and intermittently mentally unstable corporate predator – Clive. India's transition to colonialism took place under a for-profit corporation, which existed entirely for the purpose of enriching its investors'.[32]

To Go Further

Dalrymple, W., *The Anarchy: The Relentless Rise of the East India Company* (London: Bloomsbury, 2019).

Dalrymple, W., 'The East India Company: The Original Corporate Raiders', *The Guardian* (4 March 2015), available at www.theguardian.com/world/2015/mar/04/east-india-company-original-corporate-raiders; www.thehindu.com/books/books-authors/goats-kings-and-anarchy-william-dalrymple-on-his-new-book/article20507760.ece?homepage=true (accessed 21 December 2020).

Ghosh, A., *Sea of Poppies / River of Smoke / Flood of Fire* (Ibis Trilogy: three fascinating novels set against the background of the opium trade and wars) (London: John Murray, 2009, 2012, 2016).

Robins, N., *The Corporation that Has Changed the World: How the East India Company Shaped the Modern Multinational* (London: Pluto Press, 2012).

---

[32] Dalrymple, *The Anarchy*, p. xxv.

11.2.3.1 Conflicting Economic Theories

There have been many conflicting economic theories on the nature and benefit of FDI. Beyond the binary of pro-/anti-FDI doctrines, these approaches could probably be categorised in three different groups: the liberal perspective, the dependency theory and the regulatory one. They all very much matter today and are found in the policies of a variety of States all over the world.

Box 11.3 UNCTAD *World Investment Report 2015* on FDI governance reform

There is a pressing need for systematic reform of the global IIA regime. As is evident from the heated public debate and parliamentary hearing processes in many countries and regions, a shared view is emerging on the need for reform of the IIA regime to ensure that it works for all stakeholders. The question is not about *whether* or not to reform, but about the *what*, *how* and *extent* of such reform.

[...]

IIA reform can build on lessons learned from 60 years of IIA rule making: (i) IIAs 'bite' and may have unforeseen risks, and safeguards need to be put in place; (ii) IIAs have limitations as an investment promotion tool, but also underused potential; and (iii) IIAs have wider implications for policy and systemic coherence, as well as capacity-building.

IIA reform should address five main challenges. IIA reform should aim at (i) *safeguarding the right to regulate in the public interest* so as to ensure that IIAs' limits on the sovereignty of States do not unduly constrain public policymaking; (ii) *reforming investment dispute settlement* to address the legitimacy crisis of the current system; (iii) *promoting and facilitating investment* by effectively expanding this dimension in IIAs; (iv) *ensuring responsible investment* to maximise the positive impact of foreign investment and minimise its potential negative effects; and (v) *enhancing the systemic consistency of the IIA regime* so as to overcome the gaps, overlaps and inconsistencies of the current system and establish coherence in investment relationships.

UNCTAD presents policy options for meeting these challenges. ... Some of these reform options can be combined and tailored to meet several reform objectives:

– *Safeguarding the right to regulate: Options include clarifying or circumscribing provisions such as most-favoured-nation (MFN) treatment, fair and equitable treatment (FET), and indirect expropriation, as well as including exceptions, e.g. for public policies or national security.*
– *Reforming investment dispute settlement: Options include (i) reforming the existing mechanism of ad hoc arbitration for ISDS while keeping its basic structure and (ii) replacing existing ISDS arbitration systems. The former can be done by fixing the*

Box 11.3 (cont.)

existing mechanism (e.g. improving the arbitral process, limiting investors' access, using filters, introducing local litigation requirements) and by adding new elements (e.g. building in effective alternative dispute resolution or introducing an appeals facility). Should countries wish to replace the current ISDS system, they can do so by creating a standing international investment court, or by relying on State–State and/or domestic dispute resolution.

- *Promoting and facilitating investment: Options include adding inward and outward investment promotion provisions (i.e. host- and home-country measures), and joint and regional investment promotion provisions, including an ombudsperson for investment facilitation.*
- *Ensuring responsible investment: Options include adding not lowering of standards clauses and establishing provisions on investor responsibilities, such as clauses on compliance with domestic laws and on corporate social responsibility.*
- *Enhancing systemic consistency of the IIA regime: Options include improving the coherence of the IIA regime, consolidating and streamlining the IIA network, managing the interaction between IIAs and other bodies of international law, and linking IIA reform to the domestic policy agenda.*

To Go Further

UNCTAD, *World Investment Report 2015: Reforming International Investment Governance* (New York and Geneva: United Nations, 2015), p. xii. Recent *World Investment Reports* argue along the same lines and have proposed different roadmaps for reform.

As far as the classical liberal theory is concerned, opening up to foreign capital is considered beneficial to the host economy in that it brings new technology, employment, research, upgrading of all working resources and eventually generates profit, growth and development. From the eighteenth century onwards, this approach largely relied on classical economics and was recently revamped by the 'Washington Consensus', named after the 1980s and 1990s liberalisation policies promoted by the World Bank and the IMF (see Chapter 15), partly as a response to the development failure of post-colonial socialist initiatives much less keen on economic opening up.[33] This resulted in the drafting of very liberal – that is, investor-friendly BITs – in the 1990s. These were often inspired by the US treaty model and the later adoption of the North American Free Trade Agreement (NAFTA), which exemplified a number of investor-protective provisions and is still (strangely) very much copied today, despite a great deal of criticism. By an entirely

---

[33] John Williamson, 'What Washington Means by Policy Reform', in J. Williamson (ed.), *Latin American Adjustment: How Much Has Happened?* (Washington, DC: Institute for International Economics, 1990), pp. 224–44.

understandable swing of the pendulum, FDI approaches may indeed develop at opposite sides of the economic spectrum.

The dependency theory offers a completely different approach to the liberal one. Largely deriving from the work of the Argentine economist Raúl Prebisch and its conclusion on Latin America, the dependency theory argues that FDI, while beneficial for MNEs, is detrimental to the host States, in that they deplete their resources without bringing the expected growth and development (see Chapter 16).[34] In a word, Prebisch re-examined Ricardo's classical comparative advantage theory to conclude that trade and FDI were not necessarily a blessing, and often rather a curse, for developing countries relying mostly on their natural resources manna. Import substitution, as well as a critical distance towards FDI and the West, and MNEs in particular, was preferred to liberalisation. Between 1964 and 1969, Raúl Prebisch served as the founding Secretary General of UNCTAD and certainly had an impact on its pro-developed agenda. Many of the dependency theory conclusions could be applied to certain contemporary situations. FDI can still very much bring exploitation and subjugation, as in the colonial period (see Mini Chapter 1 and the business and human rights cases discussed in Chapter 10). Liberalisation as such does not suffice to generate development if the flows of foreign capital are not guided and regulated by a sensible and forward-looking State.

In this regard, what we could call the regulatory approach, tries to strike a balance between investment liberalisation and the expected protection of investor on the one hand, and the right – and duty – of the State to regulate for public purposes, on the other hand. It is a more balanced position, which has learned from past mistakes either in the form of complete trust in the beneficial character of liberalisation or a great hostility towards MNEs. It is embraced by most of the current regulatory initiatives, supported by IOs and NGOs, which may differ on the precise approach to adopt, some key concepts and standards of treatment, the drafting of certain provisions and indeed the degree of liberalisation to offer.

These three approaches are directly reflected in the investment treaties standards of treatment and other treaty provisions (explored further in the rest of Part II).

11.2.3.2 Admission

Another key concern is that of the admission of FDI. In this regard, State policies are fundamental for all parties to the investment treaty. There are, of course, several conceptions of and practical approaches to these notions. The European and American perspectives have generally differed. Let us take, for example, a BIT provision from the 2000 treaty between France and Mexico:

---

[34] Raúl Prebisch, *The Economic Development of Latin America and its Principal Problems* (New York: United Nations, 1950).

France and Mexico 2000 BIT, Article 3: Promotion and Admission of Investment

Each Contracting Party shall admit in its territory and in its maritime area investments made by investors of the other Contracting Party in accordance with its legislation, and promote them under the provisions of this Agreement.

The contracting parties' legislations serve as the reference for admission. There is no particular encouragement to amend these laws in a more investment-friendly direction. Yet the parties may revise the same after the entry into force of the treaty. As such, the BIT may be said to be less protective than other models and the American one in particular. The US BITs indeed tend to create a link between admission and the national treatment standard, as illustrated by the US 2012 Model BIT:

US 2012 Model BIT, Article 3

1. Each Party shall accord to investors of the other Party treatment no less favourable than that it accords, in like circumstances, to its own investors with respect to the establishment, acquisition, expansion, management, conduct, operation, and sale or other disposition of investments in its territory.

Some exceptions to these NT provisions may also be planned and listed accordingly in the treaty, with regard to certain sectors of the economy or governance mechanism. The most commonly used technique in reference to this 'right of admission' is hence to link it to the NT and the MFN Treatment. Of course, it may happen that while a BIT had provided for a 'right of admission' similar to what could be found in the American model, some national rules are seen as inconsistent with the treaty. If not amended by the State, an investor might invoke this issue before an investment tribunal.

11.2.3.3   Performance Requirements

A last related issue is that of performance requirements. These are obligations imposed by the host State on the investor in terms of local content, transfers of technology, employment of local labour, formation of joint venture, level of domestic shares in a given company, level of exportation, research and development and so on. Performance requirements have been prohibited in the American treaties, but have been largely used by other countries such as China or India in the early stages of their opening-up policy.[35] These measures can indeed be

---

[35] International Institute for Sustainable Development, *Performance Requirements in Investment Treaties* (Winnipeg: IISD, 2014), available at www.iisd.org/sites/default/files/publications/best-practices-performance-requirements-investment-treaties-en.pdf (accessed 21 December 2020).

considered an effective tool for economic development, balancing the treaty rights granted to the protection of foreign investors. In addition, the WTO TRIMs Agreement forbids certain performance requirements and states: 'Without prejudice to other rights and obligations under GATT 1994, no Member shall apply any TRIM that is inconsistent with the provisions of Article III or Article XI of GATT 1994'. This implies the prohibition of certain performance requirements listed in the Annex to the Agreement, such as local content or the restriction of exports, and in direct relation to NT and MFN Treatment. As often occurs in a WTO context, developing and least developed countries have been eligible to certain exemptions to this general rule and could use performance requirements under certain conditions for a certain period of time.[36]

The issue of performance requirements remains contentious today, as these serve a particular gradual approach to investment liberalisation, but may be prohibited by the more liberal players in search for new markets in which to invest.

11.3   Brief History of International Investment Law

The history of IIL is revealing of the pendulum swing between protection and opening up that we referred to above. Some would go back to Antiquity and argue that foreign investments have always existed everywhere in the world and have been regulated by States for a long time.[37] After all, Phoenicians, Egyptians and Greeks had invested abroad in a manner one could consider a form of colonisation of the whole Mediterranean region, and the Chinese had done the same in their Asian sphere of influence.

11.3.1 Commerce and Investment

11.3.1.1   Treaties of Friendship and Navigation

But as far as international law is concerned, one generally refers to the 'Treaties of Friendship and Navigation' established between Western powers from the eighteenth century to trace the existence of the early modern manifestations of IIL. The first of these instruments was probably the Treaty of Amity and Commerce between the United States and France, signed on 6 February 1778 at the Hotel de Crillon, Paris.[38] Its Article 2 was already paving the way towards the adoption of the future MFN principle:

---

[36] A list of prohibited TRIMs, such as local content requirements, is part of the TRIMs Agreement. See also Holger Hestermeyer, 'The Legality of Local Content Measures under WTO Law', *Journal of World Trade* (2014), 48(3), pp. 553–9.

[37] Kenneth J. Vandevelde, 'A Brief History of International Investment Agreements', *UC Davis Journal of International Law and Policy* (2005), 12(1), pp. 157–94.

[38] Treaty text available at https://avalon.law.yale.edu/18th_century/fr1788-1.asp (accessed 21 December 2020).

Treaty of Amity and Commerce between the United States and France, 6 February 1778, Article 2

The most Christian King, and the United States engage mutually not to grant any particular Favour to other Nations in respect of Commerce and Navigation, which shall not immediately become common to the other Party, who shall enjoy the same Favour freely, if the Concession was freer made, or on allowing the same Compensation, if the Concession was Conditional.

Many treaties of this type were later signed between the US and European countries. Interestingly, the terminology of 'friendship, commerce and navigation' was still found in the immediate aftermath of decolonisation, for example, with the 1953 Treaty of Friendship, Commerce and Navigation between the Government of India and the Sultanate of Muscat and Oman.[39] Its Articles VII and VIII directly addressed international investment issues:

Treaty of Friendship, Commerce and Navigation between the Government of India and the Sultanate of Muscat and Oman, 1953

Article VII

The nationals of each High Contracting Party shall receive treatment not less favourable than that accorded to the nationals of any other foreign country in regard to the acquisition, possession or disposal of all kinds of movable and immovable property, in conformity with such laws and rules as are in force or may be established in the territories of the other.

Article VIII

The nationals of each High Contracting Party residing in the territories of the other shall receive protection and security for their persons and property and shall enjoy in this respect rights and privileges not less favourable than those accorded to the nationals of any other foreign country, in conformity with the laws and regulations as are in force or may be established in the territories of the other.

However, a global history of IIL is yet to be produced, as many of these treaties of friendship, commerce and navigation were, in fact, also used as the basis for the establishment of colonial domination, as illustrated by the infamous unequal treaties (see Box 11.4).

---

[39] See the treaty text, available at http://mea.gov.in/bilateral-documents.htm?dtl/7627/Treaty+of+Friendship+Commerce+and+Navigation (accessed 21 December 2020).

Box 11.4 China's unequal treaties: trade, war and domination

The unequal treaties refer to a series of agreements signed between Western powers and the Qing dynasty in China and the late Tokugawa dynasty in Japan. In China, notably, they concluded the military defeat of the Middle Kingdom in the Opium Wars. The first treaty referred to as 'unequal' was the Convention of Chuenpi, signed in 1841. Later, China and Great Britain signed the infamous Treaty of Nanjing in 1842. This treaty forced China to open up to foreign trade. The unequal treaties included MFN provision. The concept of extraterritoriality was also introduced in relation to the special protection afforded to foreign nationals, who could be put on trial by their own authorities, for instance, in dedicated courts established by the UK and the US. From the 1920s, with the rise of anticolonial claims, these treaties were systematically referred to as unequal, and were put forward in the nationalist fight as a symbol of colonial domination. They are still very much present in the collective Chinese memory today and are often invoked to justify national policies perceived as protectionist.

To Go Further

Bickers, R. A. and Jackson, I. (eds), *Treaty Ports in Modern China: Law, Land and Power* (Abingdon: Routledge, 2016).

Escarra, J., 'Droits et intérêts étrangers en Chine', *Revue d'économie politique* (1927), 41(4), pp. 1017–53.

11.3.2 The Colonial Period

During the colonial period, the responsibility of host States to foreign investors had never been easy to conceptualise, nor had it always been universally accepted.[40] While late nineteenth-century Western practices tend to show that aliens were entitled to equality of treatment with nationals of the host State, the protection of their property, already proclaimed as an unalienable right by the French 1789 Declaration of the Rights of Man and the Citizen, remained ambiguous. Prior to the 1917 Russian Revolution and the abolition of private property without compensation, the Calvo doctrine (often confused with the Calvo clause that one could find in a number of Latin American constitutions and other international investment agreements) gave an excellent account of the competing approaches to States' responsibility in international law (see Chapter 12). The work of Carlos Calvo, the famous Argentine jurist, is systematically referred to in IIL publications to explain the

---

[40] As clearly exemplified by the United Nations International Law Commission's work on State responsibility, which started as early as 1949 and was concluded in 2001 by the adoption of a set of Draft Articles on the Responsibility of States for Internationally Wrongful Acts.

reluctance of States, and Latin American States in particular, to grant more favourable treatment than the treatment they accorded to their nationals: 'the Calvo doctrine is based on the view that foreigners must assert their rights before domestic courts and that they have no right of diplomatic protection by their home state or access to international tribunals'.[41]

But what was Carlos Calvo writing in his 1868 *Derecho Internacional Teórico y Práctico de Europa y América* and his further elaborated 1896 French edition, *Le droit international théorique et pratique*? Not that much about private property and international investment, as suggested by its many critics, but rather about State equality, sovereignty and independence in the context of the solvency crisis and the many attempts by Western States to resort to the use of force to collect debt, as exemplified by the US 'gunboat diplomacy' performed in 1980s Venezuela. For Calvo, who supports his reasoning by quoting the landmark work of the eighteenth-century scholar, Emer de Vattel, *Droit des gens*, a State cannot be responsible for the prejudices caused to foreigners, as such a principle would create 'an absurd and fateful privilege in favour of the most powerful States and against the weak'.[42] Out of this rather simple 'Calvo doctrine', a number of Latin American countries developed a 'Calvo clause', introduced in their constitutions or in some of the contracts they concluded with aliens. These legal instruments argued more specifically in favour of a strict approach to NT as the best possible treatment accorded to foreigners, who shall then refrain from resorting to any dispute settlement mechanism other than those available at the domestic level, while leaving aside the possibility of calling for diplomatic protection from their home State.[43] The 1917 post-revolution Mexican Constitution exemplifies this approach in framing private property within the boundaries of public interest. So much so, in fact, that the equally famous Hull formula (named after Cordell Hull, the longest-serving US Secretary of State and winner of the 1945 Nobel Peace Prize for his role in the creation of the United Nations), had to firmly express the American view (and most probably the generally held Western view of that time) of the rights and obligations of host States to foreign investors, and their home States in general, and of the protection of private property in particular (see Chapter 13 for concrete IIA illustrations). On 18 March 1938, Mexican President Lazaro Cardenas signed an order of expropriation of nearly all the foreign oil companies operating in Mexico, and later created Petróleos Mexicanos (PEMEX), a State-owned enterprise then holding a monopoly on oil. The US government responded by supporting its companies' effort to gain compensation for the expropriation. Cordell Hull, then Secretary of State, started a dialogue with his Mexican counterpart, Foreign Minister Eduardo Hay. In his

---

[41] Rudolf Dolzer and Christoph Schreuer, *Principles of International Investment Law* (Oxford University Press, 2009), p. 12.

[42] C. Calvo, *Derecho Internacional Teórico y Práctico de Europa y América* (Paris: D'Amyot, 1868). The original quotation is: 'crear un privilegio absurdo y funestísimo a favor de los Estados mas poderosos y en contra de los débiles', p. 388. See also C. Calvo, *Le droit international théorique et pratique: précedé d'un exposé historique des progrès de la science du droit des gens* (Paris: A. Rousseau, 1896).

[43] M. Garcia-Mora, 'The Calvo Clause in Latin American Constitutions and International Law', *Marquette Law Review* (1950), 33(4), pp. 205–19.

correspondence with the Mexican authorities, Hull expressed what has since been referred to as the Hull formula.[44]

US Secretary of State to the Mexican Ambassador (Castillo Najera), Washington, 22 August 1938

[...]

The fundamental issues raised by this communication from the Mexican Government are therefore, first, whether or not universally recognized principles of the law of nations require, in the exercise of the admitted right of all sovereign nations to expropriate private property, that such expropriation be accompanied by provision on the part of such government for adequate, effective, and prompt payment for the properties seized; second, whether any government may nullify principles of international law through contradictory municipal legislation of its own; or, third, whether such Government is relieved of its obligations under universally recognized principles of international law merely because its financial or economic situation makes compliance therewith difficult.

The Government of the United States merely adverts to a self-evident fact when it notes that the applicable precedents and recognised authorities on international law support its declaration that, under every rule of law and equity, no government is entitled to expropriate private property, for whatever purpose, without provision for prompt, adequate and effective payment therefore ...

That 'no government is entitled to expropriate private property, for whatever purpose, without provision for prompt, adequate and effective payment' remained a central argument in international investment law and dispute settlement. The terms 'prompt', 'adequate' and 'effective' have been discussed since Hull formulated them. They have often been challenged by developing countries in a postcolonial environment (see below), and again today in the context of a surge of ISDS. The notion of adequacy has been debated particularly for its vagueness. However, much of the opposition between the 'Calvo' and 'Hull' approaches can also be seen as rhetorical when examining investment treaties provisions. It is indeed interesting to observe how treaties have integrated either one or the other approach and often blended these two visions to achieve their politico-economic objectives.

As far as the NT standard was concerned, nothing had been codified and the unwritten rules of customary international law prevailed. One had to wait for the drafting of the never adopted Havana Charter to find some NT-related provisions, as shown by its Article 12:

---

[44] See also Eduardo Hay to Josephus Daniels, 3 August 1938; and US Secretary of State to the Mexican Ambassador in Washington, DC, 22 August 1938, both in *Foreign Relations of the United States: Diplomatic Papers 1938, Volume V: The American Republics* (Washington, DC: Government Printing Office, 1938).

> ### *Havana Charter for an International Trade Organization, Article 12: International Investment for Economic Development and Reconstruction*
>
> 1. The Members recognize that:
>   (a) international investment, both public and private, can be of great value in promoting economic development and reconstruction, and consequent social progress; ...
> 2. Members therefore undertake: ...
>   (i) to provide reasonable opportunities for investments acceptable to them and adequate security for existing and future investments, and
>   (ii) to give due regard to the desirability of avoiding discrimination as between foreign investments.

While 'due regard' to the 'desirability of avoiding discrimination' was suggested, no real codification effort had been supported, and the Calvo and Hull doctrines remained largely disconnected from States' practices. The waves of expropriations following the socialist revolutions in Eastern Europe and in the developing world, as well as the decolonisation era, forced international investment players to rethink the customary legal basis on which IIL rested.

11.3.3 The Postcolonial Period

11.3.3.1 The NIEO

A fascinating first attempt to reconceptualise IIL took place within the United Nations General Assembly. From the 1962 Resolution 1803 on Permanent Sovereignty over Natural Resources[45] to the 1974 Declaration on the Establishment of a New International Economic Order[46] and the 1986 Declaration on the Right to Development,[47] developing States started to elaborate a special approach to international investment, which today deserves to be reconsidered, as it already showed some of the challenges resulting from foreign investment promotion. While the 1803 Resolution eventually proved quite consensual in affirming a number of fundamental principles – such as the payment of compensation, in accordance with international law, in the event of alien property being taken for public interest, as well as the possibility of resorting to international dispute settlement mechanisms after exhaustion of local remedies – this apparent international agreement did not last for long. The adoption, in

---

[45] General Assembly Resolution 1803 (XVII), 14 December 1962. Procedural history and related documents available at www.ohchr.org/documents/professionalinterest/resources.pdf (accessed 21 December 2020).

[46] General Assembly Resolution 3201 (S-VI), Declaration on the Establishment of a New International Economic Order, 1 May 1974.

[47] General Assembly Resolution 41/128, Declaration on the Right to Development, 4 December 1986.

December 1973, of General Assembly Resolution 3171 and, even more importantly, of the 1974 Charter of Economic Rights and Duties of States designed to support the NIEO, removed all ambiguities. The approach was clearly not sympathetic towards a liberal model promoting States' opening-up policies. After years of what they had perceived as 'exploitation' by 'transnational corporations', the General Assembly's dominant group of 'non-aligned' countries called for a new international economic order supported by the following principles:

General Assembly Resolution 29/3281, Charter of Economic Rights and Duties of States

Article 1

Every State has the sovereign and inalienable right to choose its economic system as well as its political, social and cultural systems in accordance with the will of its people, without outside interference, coercion or threat in any form whatsoever.

Article 2

1. Every State has and shall freely exercise full permanent sovereignty, including possession, use and disposal, over all its wealth, natural resources and economic activities.

From these two fundamental principles derived other equally challenging ideas, questioning some of the officially accepted concepts of an international legal regime that the newly independent States did not recognise as their creation.[48] Although the text of the Charter remains of a general and non-binding nature and cannot be compared to precise treaty provisions, it is clear that 'No State shall be compelled to grant preferential treatment to foreign investment',[49] and 'where the question of compensation gives rise to a controversy, it shall be settled under the domestic law of the nationalizing State and by its tribunals, unless it is freely and mutually agreed by all States concerned that other peaceful means be sought on the basis of the sovereign equality of States and in accordance with the principle of free choice of means'.[50] In this context, national treatment was considered the best available standard of treatment, not one necessarily favouring protectionism, but rather a cautious approach to an economic liberalisation that did not always prove beneficial to the developing world.

Interestingly, a rather different, if not opposed, perspective to investment liberalisation was also adopted, at the same key period, with the drafting of the 1965 Convention on the Settlement of Investment Disputes between States and Nationals of Other States. As history

---

[48] F. Garcia Amador, 'The Proposed New International Economic Order: A New Approach to the Law Governing Nationalization and Compensation', *Lawyer of the Americas* (1980), 12(1), pp. 1–58.

[49] General Assembly Resolution 29/3281, Art. 2(a).   [50] General Assembly Resolution 29/3281, Art. 2(c).

has shown, this liberal approach favouring investors' protection won out over the 1970s NIEO. However, as far as national treatment was concerned, this transformation was not as evident. Indeed, major emerging economic players, such as China[51] or India,[52] did not initially grant this standard to foreign investors in order to protect certain strategic economic sectors. This heterodox strategy eventually revealed itself as positive, as it gave space for regulatory autonomy and gradual economic liberalisation, hence supporting the development of national champions now 'going global' in claiming, in turn, the national treatment standard of protection.[53]

General Assembly Resolution 1803 (XVII), Permanent Sovereignty over Natural Resources (14 December 1962)

The General Assembly,

Recalling its resolutions 523 (VI) of 12 January 1952 and 626 (VII) of 21 December 1952,

Bearing in mind its resolution 1314 (XIII) of 12 December 1958, by which it established the Commission on Permanent Sovereignty over Natural Resources and instructed it to conduct a full survey of the status of permanent sovereignty over natural wealth and resources as a basic constituent of the right to self-determination, with recommendations, where necessary, for its strengthening, and decided further that, in the conduct of the full survey of the status of the permanent sovereignty of peoples and nations over their natural wealth and resources, due regard should be paid to the rights and duties of States under international law and to the importance of encouraging international co-operation in the economic development of developing countries,

Bearing in mind its resolution 1515 (XV) of 15 December 1960, in which it recommended that the sovereign right of every State to dispose of its wealth and its natural resources should be respected,

Considering that any measure in this respect must be based on the recognition of the inalienable right of all States freely to dispose of their natural wealth and resources in accordance with their national interests, and on respect for the economic independence of States,

---

[51] N. Gallagher and W. Shan, *Chinese Investment Treaties: Policies and Practice* (Oxford University Press, 2009). One generally distinguishes three phases in China's investment policy: the early opening-up phase (1979–91) during which the first BITs were concluded; the consolidation phase (1992–2000), with greater liberalisation and some acceptance, from the mid-1990s, of the NT standard, and the phase corresponding to the post-WTO accession (2001–10). To this we should add another phase, which started in the mid-2000s and covers China's 'going global' policy of promotion of Chinese FDI in the developing world, but also, to some extent, in industrialised countries.

[52] P. Ranjan, 'International Investment Agreements and Regulatory Discretion: Case Study of India', *Journal of World Investment and Trade* (2008), 9(2), pp. 209–43.

[53] M. Sornarajah, 'India, China and Foreign Investment', in M. Sornarajah and J. Wang (eds.), *China, India and the International Economic Order* (Cambridge University Press, 2010), pp. 132–66.

(cont.)

Considering that nothing in paragraph 4 below in any way prejudices the position of any Member State on any aspect of the question of the rights and obligations of successor States and Governments in respect of property acquired before the accession to complete sovereignty of countries formerly under colonial rule,

Noting that the subject of succession of States and Governments is being examined as a matter of priority by the International Law Commission,

Considering that it is desirable to promote international co-operation for the economic development of developing countries, and that economic and financial agreements between the developed and the developing countries must be based on the principles of equality and of the right of peoples and nations to self-determination,

Considering that the provision of economic and technical assistance, loans and increased foreign investment must not be subject to conditions which conflict with the interests of the recipient State,

Considering the benefits to be derived from exchanges of technical and scientific information likely to promote the development and use of such resources and wealth, and the important part which the United Nations and other international organizations are called upon to play in that connection,

Attaching particular importance to the question of promoting the economic development of developing countries and securing their economic independence,

Noting that the creation and strengthening of the inalienable sovereignty of States over their natural wealth and resources reinforces their economic independence,

Desiring that there should be further consideration by the United Nations of the subject of permanent sovereignty over natural resources in the spirit of international co-operation in the field of economic development, particularly that of the developing countries,

I

Declares that:

1. The right of peoples and nations to permanent sovereignty over their natural wealth and resources must be exercised in the interest of their national development and of the well-being of the people of the State concerned.
2. The exploration, development and disposition of such resources, as well as the import of the foreign capital required for these purposes, should be in conformity with the rules and conditions which the peoples and nations freely consider to be necessary or desirable with regard to the authorization, restriction or prohibition of such activities.
3. In cases where authorization is granted, the capital imported and the earnings on that capital shall be governed by the terms thereof, by the national legislation in force, and by international law. The profits derived must be shared in the proportions freely

(cont.)

agreed upon, in each case, between the investors and the recipient State, due care being taken to ensure that there is no impairment, for any reason, of that State's sovereignty over its natural wealth and resources.

4. Nationalization, expropriation or requisitioning shall be based on grounds or reasons of public utility, security or the national interest, which are recognized as overriding purely individual or private interests, both domestic and foreign. In such cases the owner shall be paid appropriate compensation, in accordance with the rules in force in the State taking such measures in the exercise of its sovereignty and in accordance with international law. In any case where the question of compensation gives rise to a controversy, the national jurisdiction of the State taking such measures shall be exhausted. However, upon agreement by sovereign States and other parties concerned, settlement of the dispute should be made through arbitration or international adjudication.

5. The free and beneficial exercise of the sovereignty of peoples and nations over their natural resources must be furthered by the mutual respect of States based on their sovereign equality.

6. International co-operation for the economic development of developing countries, whether in the form of public or private capital investments, exchange of goods and services, technical assistance, or exchange of scientific information, shall be such as to further their independent national development and shall be based upon respect for their sovereignty over their natural wealth and resources.

7. Violation of the rights of peoples and nations to sovereignty over their natural wealth and resources is contrary to the spirit and principles of the Charter of the United Nations and hinders the development of international co-operation and the maintenance of peace.

8. Foreign investment agreements freely entered into by or between sovereign States shall be observed in good faith; States and international organizations shall strictly and conscientiously respect the sovereignty of peoples and nations over their natural wealth and resources in accordance with the Charter and the principles set forth in the present resolution.

11.3.4 The Liberal Approach

The liberal approach was crystallised, in the 1990s, in a variety of international instruments that soon became the apparent normative references of international investment law. The introductory remarks of the World Bank's 1992 *Guidelines on the Treatment of Foreign Direct Investment* set the tone in praising the positive role of FDI for the world economy, and developing countries in particular. It was rapidly followed by a surge in BITs and, very importantly, the negotiation of a vast number of investment treaties by major Asian States (China, India and South East Asian nations). Among these international investment initiatives, two instruments are particularly revealing of the 1990s spirit and a number of key standards of treatment: the NAFTA and the Energy Charter Treaty. These treaties and other legal texts will be discussed in great detail in the following chapters, but it is interesting to stop and think for a while about the causes of this liberal landslide, which unleashed a wave of legislative reactions and, a few years later, a second wave of disputes, now critically examined by the challenged States, the international community and civil society. The current disenchantment with ISDS stems from the very liberal architecture established progressively from the 1960s and the creation of the ICSID under the auspices of the World Bank, but also from the very protective nature of a number of core 1990s treaties, which have shaped the burgeoning investment world of the late century. But what is liberalism in investment law? A political and economic project to start with, as well as an endeavour to approach the world from the prism of the American victory over Nazism and the Soviet Union on the basis of certain liberties, including the fundamental idea of the right to property as a human right. It might well, then, be essential to differentiate liberalism from neoliberalism, as the two concepts vary in their formulation and objective. In this regard, Kenneth J. Vandevelde's analysis[54] is particularly interesting in that it clearly links and distinguishes, at the same time, political and economic liberalism:

Liberalism began in the mid-seventeenth century as a political doctrine. John Locke theorized that all persons were born in a state of nature with equal liberty. ... To protect their liberties, individuals consented to the creation of a State with power to protect each against the other through legislation for the common good. The danger existed, however, that a state created to protect liberty would become too strong and would itself become an oppressor. One preventative was constitutionalism, the idea that the state itself is subject to fundamental law.

Political liberalism, then, encompassed at least three principles of relevance here. The first principle is that the State exists to protect individual liberty. The second is that the State possesses the power to regulate for the common good. The third is that the State regulatory power is limited by the rule of law. ... the liberty principle, the regulatory principle, and the legality principle, respectively. ... the regulatory principle exists in tension with the liberty principle. That is State regulatory power threatens, but is also limited by, the liberty of the individual. The tension is mediated by the legality principle, under which law establishes boundaries between the regulatory principle and the liberty principle, putting it in tension with each of these two principles.[55]

Everything is said here about the tension between rights and liberties and regulation. These forces are very much found at work in an international investment context. And, as

---

[54] Kenneth J. Vandevelde, 'The Liberal Vision of the International Law on Foreign Investment', in Lim, *Alternative Visions of the International Law on Foreign Investment*, pp. 43–67.

[55] Vandevelde, 'The Liberal Vision', p. 48.

argued by Kenneth J. Vandevelde again, on the basis of economic liberal thinking first theorised in Adam Smith's *The Wealth of Nations*, the State also has a responsibility to protect property and contract rights, while giving a central role to the market:

Applied to investment policy, economic liberalism includes three principles. The first is the principle that the market rather than the State should allocate capital, the principle of investment neutrality. The second (...) that the State should protect property and contract rights, the principle of investment security. The third is that the State should ensure the proper functioning of the market and should act where the market is inadequate, the principle of market facilitation. Like the three principles of political liberalism, these three principles of economic liberalism exist in tension which each other. For example, a State seeking to ensure that a market is competitive may exercise the principle of market facilitation to prohibit a merger of two enterprises, thereby intruding upon the principle of investment neutrality.[56]

11.3.5 Resistance and Changes: Looking Ahead

In changing times, a form of resistance to the current international investment regime has materialised. From anti-globalisation activists to more mainstream NGOs, but also States, including developed States, a larger number of actors are voicing their concerns with a system they find unbalanced and unfair, as too protective of private interests. Often, the very proponents of the 1970s and 1990s liberalisations and former firm supporters of the ICSID are now denouncing their own creations and formulating new plans to reshape, if not yet IIL itself, at least international investment dispute settlement. The apparent rebellion of the European Union against the ISDS system is hence revealing of a new trend. Developed countries can be targeted by investment disputes, as illustrated in the controversial *Vattenfall AB and others* v. *Federal Republic of Germany*, in which a Swedish company formulated a EUR4.7 billion claim against the German State for violation of its Energy Charter Treaty obligations following its decision to stop nuclear energy production.[57] As a matter of direct consequence of the German humiliation, in May 2015, in the context of the then ongoing trade negotiations with the US, the European Commission published the concept paper, 'Investment in TTIP and beyond – the path for reform', which called for a 'profound reform of the traditional approach to investment protection and the associated ISDS system', and, accordingly, aimed at 'moving from current ad hoc arbitration towards an Investment Court'. Since that time, a number of proposals have been put forward by the EU, which

---

[56] Vandevelde, 'The Liberal Vision', p. 48.

[57] *Vattenfall AB and others* v. *Federal Republic of Germany*, ICSID Case No. ARB/12/12, available at www.italaw .com/cases/1654 (accessed 21 December 2020). While the ICSID decision is still pending, the German Federal Constitutional Court ruled, in November 2020, that Germany must completely rework its system of financial compensation for energy firms hit by the nuclear power phase-out; see 'Vattenfall Wins Case against German Nuclear Phaseout', Deutsche Welle, available at www.dw.com/en/vattenfall-wins-case-against-german-nuclear-phaseout/a-55572736 (accessed 21 December 2020).

is lobbying hard for the creation of an investment court (as illustrated in Chapter 14). But the EU is not the only international organisation to develop a keen interest in these issues. As a matter of fact, in 2013, UNCITRAL adopted the Rules on Transparency in Treaty-Based Investor–State Arbitration, applicable to cases initiated under UNCITRAL Arbitration Rules and based on investment treaties concluded since 1 April 2014.[58] The UN Convention on Transparency in Treaty-Based Investor–State Arbitration, also developed by UNCITRAL, provides an opt-in mechanism for States that wish to extend the application of such Transparency Rules to cases under treaties concluded before 1 April 2014. The Transparency Convention entered into force on 18 October 2017.[59] Lastly, in July 2017, UNCITRAL entrusted its Working Group III with a broad mandate to work on the possible reform of ISDS. A number of proposals have been put forward in this context.[60] The future of IIL and dispute settlement remains challenging and rather unpredictable, as investment law is today, more than ever, a fast-changing discipline.

11.4 Conclusion

International investment law is still very much in the making and at the centre of divergent economic and political perspectives. It is a fast-changing field of international law, influenced by the politico-economic decisions of States and foreign investors alike. Opening up to FDI is a political decision as much as investing abroad is a highly strategic decision. In recent times, the complication of the FDI scene with its many new actors, complex deals and unprecedented disputes had called for a serious evaluation of past regulatory initiatives. The same is true for the international settlement of investment disputes. The lessons learnt through these questionings have improved understanding and possibly helped to reform contemporary IIL, while it continues to search for a global codification effort.

11.5 Summary

- International investment law, while a rather old discipline, if viewed from a historical perspective, remains very much in the making.
- Today, FDIs are of prime importance for most developed and developing economies.

---

[58] See www.iisd.org/project/transparency-and-uncitral-arbitration-rules (accessed 21 December 2020).

[59] See https://uncitral.un.org/en/texts/arbitration/conventions/transparency (accessed 21 December 2020).

[60] See UNCITRAL's work on ISDS reform: United Nations Convention on Transparency in Treaty-Based Investor–State Arbitration (New York, 2014) (the 'Mauritius Convention on Transparency'), available at https://uncitral.un.org/en/working_groups/3/investor-state (accessed 21 December 2020).

- Whether FDI inflows or outflows, they represent one of the most salient features of globalisation while participating (or not) in economic development.
- The nature of FDIs and the economic theories supporting their growth (or preventing the same) have long been conflicting, if not controversial, issues.
- One can, at the very least, distinguish four categories of actors: the State; investors in the form of private or public entities; international organisations and institutions; NGOs and civil society organisations, including professional bodies.
- In brief, there are State and non-State actors, the latter now taking an extraordinary variety of shapes.
- The definition of FDI has been a complicated issue in international economics and is at the centre of conflicting theories.
- Beyond the binary of pro-/anti-FDI doctrines, these approaches could probably be categorised in three different groups: the liberal perspective, the dependency theory and the regulatory one.
- As far as international law is concerned, one generally refers to the treaties of friendship, commerce and navigation established between Western powers from the eighteenth century to trace the existence of the early modern manifestations of IIL.
- The colonial period, decolonisation and the neoliberal era have differently shaped the global approach to IIL.
- Today, IIL and dispute settlement are once again under global scrutiny, often challenged and constantly evolving to adjust to the politico-economic strategies of States and investors alike.

11.6 Review Questions

1 How could you describe today's FDI scene at the global, regional and national levels?
2 What are the selected countries and sectors of particular interest?
3 Which region of the world is receiving the largest amount of FDI?
4 Which countries are leading in terms of inflows and outflows?
5 Is there a form of stability in FDI flows (in and out) or constant evolution?
6 Has the Covid-19 pandemic had an impact on FDI, and if so, how?
7 Who are the actors of international investment law?
8 What is the status of MNEs under international law and why does it matter?
9 Are there historical precedents of MNEs?
10 Were the treaties of friendship, commerce and navigation unequal treaties?
11 What was Calvo's approach?
12 What was Hull's approach?
13 What principle did the NIEO put forward?
14 Is the NIEO still relevant today?

15 What were the underpinnings of the liberal approach to FDI?

16 Is the regulatory approach different from the liberal one and how does it materialise?

11.7   Exercises

Exercise 1: Your Country's FDI – A Mapping Exercise

- What about your own country's FDI inflows and outflows? How can you describe today's FDI situation in relation to your own country?
- Has FDI been regulated, and if so, how? Who are the actors of this FDI regulation? (Refer to Chapter 12 to better understand this question and frame your answers.)
- Is your country a party to BITs and IIAs? Which one? Can you identify policy changes or generations of BITs/IIAs? How do the IIAs to which your country has been a party differ?

Please search the UNCTAD databases, including the Investment Policy Hub, and look at the latest *World Investment Report* to map your country's FDI situation and gather important information on the regulation of FDI: https://investmentpolicy.unctad.org.

Exercise 2: In Search of a 2023 Multilateral Investment Treaty

Phase 1: Preparatory Work

This is a personal (preparation) and collective (negotiation) exercise to be conducted in a two-step approach on the basis of this chapter and the following chapters in Part II.

1 To familiarise yourself with the current BITs/IIAs in force, browse the UNCTAD resources: https://investmentpolicy.unctad.org/international-investment-agreements.

2 Now try to identify competing views and other controversies fuelling the making of investment treaties. To do so, please approach these questions from a historical perspective and on the basis of a large variety of countries and initiatives.

3 What is in the treaty? From your research, try to identify your priorities. What should be in your ideal multilateral investment treaty? Pay attention to each and every single detail, from the preamble of the treaty to the precise wording of given provisions and the mechanisms in place for the settlement of investment disputes. Be rigorous, yet creative. Getting inspiration from existing IIAs does not mean that you have to reproduce them.

Phase 2: Negotiation Work

A group of twenty-five countries have agreed to enter into a multilateral investment treaty negotiation. Developed and developing countries are equally represented. They are hosts and homes of FDIs. They show a variety of political approaches to the regulation of FDI and are all parties to a vast network of existing BITs and IIAs. They have taken part in ISDS as claimants (via some of their enterprises investing abroad) and respondents. Their civil societies are particularly interested in seeing how the State will address FDI opportunities and challenges.

Each country comes to the negotiation table with a first treaty draft. You are representing one of these twenty-five countries and have prepared a multilateral treaty draft suited to your strategic vision and politico-economic priorities.

In the course of the negotiations, some alliances are shaping up. Groups and subgroups are forming around issues of common interest. These negotiation partnerships inform the redrafting of your original treaty text.

After a few months of discussions, you are able to lead a group and present a new treaty draft.

Your new draft has been made public. You have received a large number of comments by national and international civil society organisations, from NGOs to multinational enterprises and lobby groups. These are to be taken into consideration for your redrafting and discussed with your negotiating partners.

A major economic crisis is now impacting the global economy. A number of countries revise their FDI policies and threaten to withdraw from the multilateral treaty discussions.

At the same time, a new group of countries is willing to join the negotiations. Alliances have changed. You have to adjust to the reality of the new composition of the negotiation group. Major actors have left the negotiation table, while a few newcomers have joined it.

Eventually, your draft is going to be discussed as the main draft model for the conclusion of a multilateral treaty on FDI.

You lead the final negotiation discussions and try to accommodate different perspectives to reach an acceptable consensus. For each and every one of the negotiation steps described above, please amend your draft according to the changing circumstances.

For the purposes of this exercise, you may use the following link as the draft text which has been made public for comments: https://www.international.gc.ca/trade-commerce/trade-agreements-accords-commerciaux/agr-acc/tpp-ptp/text-texte/09.aspx?lang=eng.

FURTHER READING

Brabazon, H., *Neoliberal Legality: Understanding the Role of Law in the Neoliberal Project* (Abingdon and New York: Routledge, 2017).

Chaisse, J. and Sejko, D., '*Investor–State Arbitration Distorted: When the Claimant Is a State*', in L. Choukroune (ed.), *Judging the State in International Trade and Investment Law: Sovereignty Modern, the Law and the Economics* (Singapore: Springer, 2016), pp. 77–103.

Chaisse, J., Choukroune, L. and Jusoh, S. (eds.), *Handbook of International Investment Law and Policy* (Singapore: Springer, 2021).

Sornarajah, M., *Resistance and Change in the International Law on Foreign Investment* (Cambridge University Press, 2015).

Vandevelde, K. J., 'A Brief History of International Investment Agreements', *UC Davis Journal of International Law and Policy* (2005), 12(1), pp. 157–94.

'The Liberal Vision of the International Law on Foreign Investment', in C. L. Lim (ed.), *Alternative Visions of the International Law on Foreign Investment: Essays in Honour of Muthucumaraswamy Sornarajah* (Cambridge University Press, 2016), pp. 43–67.

Wang, J., 'State Capitalism and Sovereign Wealth Funds: Finding a "Soft" Location in International Economic Law', in C. L. Lim (ed.), *Alternative Visions of the International Law on Foreign Investment: Essays in Honour of Muthucumaraswamy Sornarajah* (Cambridge University Press, 2016), pp. 405–27.

12 International Investment Law: Foundations and Sources

Table of Contents

Highlights

- Law helps to attract, protect and promote foreign investment. It provides a certain degree of stability and predictability for the investor as well as the State.
- Law also serves as a tool to resolve international investment disputes.
- But is international investment law the only way to regulate FDI?
- There are, in fact, three laws of international investment: national, contractual and international.
- These three laws are naturally interrelated, but our approach is international law-centric.
- IIL is grounded in general public international law and the theory of State responsibility.
- Therefore, the sources of IIL are found in Article 38 of the Statute of the International Court of Justice (ICJ).
- There is an immense variety of national investment regimes. They are all related to a particular politico-economic vision of FDI based on the risks and benefits that FDI can bring.
- This profusion of national norms creates a form of uncertainty for international investors.
- State–investor contracts have been secured to further protect FDI and mitigate the uncertainties of the different national regimes.
- Investment contracts are the product of a negotiation between the State and the investor.

- These contracts are under scrutiny as they often reflect imbalances of power in favour of the investor.
- Controversial provisions are found in investment contracts, such as 'stabilisation' or 'umbrella' clauses.
- Guidelines for fairer and more sustainable contracts are now developed.
- In the past thirty years or so, in parallel with the large increase of FDI and the globalisation of the economy, IIL has evolved quickly.
- While customary international law remains a controversial source of IIL, IIAs, including BITs, have massively expanded since the end of the decolonisation period, and particularly since the 1980s and a new era for trade liberalisation.
- These IIAs provide a vast network of binding obligations for States, with direct impact on non-State actors and investors.
- IIL can be analysed as a 'regime', a *lex specialis* (specialised law) prevailing over more general rules (*lex specialis derogate legi generali*). Yet it is an integral part of general international law.
- The lack of a universal treaty, as well as the very nature of these agreements between States, limits the ability of this legal international regime to truly respond to today's challenges.
- Long debated, a universal investment agreement still seems a faraway objective.
- However, a number of regional or sectoral initiatives provide for some harmonisation of IIL.

12.1 Introduction

Why do we need law for foreign investment? Are there no successful international investments without law? Brazil has failed to ratify almost all the BITs it has signed.[1] The Brazil–Angola BIT is now the only treaty in force since 2017.[2] Yet Brazil has attracted a great deal of FDI and its companies have invested dynamically abroad.[3] Could it be that the widely held virtues of legal transparency, certainty and stability are in fact a complete myth? The question of the need for and importance of international law in regulating international relations has been widely debated, but never fully answered.[4] A clear tension

---

[1] For updates on Brazil's international investment regime, see the UNCTAD dedicated pages, available at https://investmentpolicy.unctad.org/country-navigator/30/brazil (accessed 21 December 2020). It is interesting to note a form of new dynamism, with Brazil signing a number of new BITs, as in January 2020 with India.

[2] See the Brazil–Angola BIT, available at https://investmentpolicy.unctad.org/international-investment-agreements/treaties/bilateral-investment-treaties/3666/angola---brazil-bit-2015- (accessed 21 December 2020).

[3] See the evolution of Brazil FDI net inflows, as reported by the World Bank, available at https://data.worldbank.org/indicator/BX.KLT.DINV.CD.WD?locations=BR; and the outflows, available at https://data.worldbank.org/indicator/BM.KLT.DINV.WD.GD.ZS?locations=BR (both accessed 21 December 2020).

[4] See, generally, Fassbender and Peters, *Oxford Handbook of the History of International Law*; and specifically, Arnulf Becker Lorca, 'Eurocentrism in the History of International Law', in Fassbender and Peters, *Oxford Handbook of the History of International Law*, pp. 1034–57; Chimni, *International Law and the World Order*; Michael Byers (ed.), *The Role of Law in International Politics: Essays in International Relations and International Law* (Oxford University Press, 2001).

remains between the idealistic aspirations of an international society based on the rule of law and the pragmatic reality of power relations with competing States' interests. Not to mention that the bases on which the international legal system has been created are not necessarily as universal as they claim to be. The 'civilised' Western world has long excluded the 'uncivilised' colonies in a law-making process, the consequences of which are still perceptible today, including in IIL and dispute settlement (see Introduction and Chapter 11).[5]

As observed by J. E. Alvarez, IIL can then meet three objectives: 'obligation, precision and delegation'.[6] However, 'these rules are not necessarily coherent or consistent'. They are becoming 'more precise over time, not only as a result of ever more detailed provisions in treaty and national law, but also thanks to the ever more elaborate interpretations of relevant law rendered by international arbitrators sitting in investor–State disputes'.

International investment law can be analysed as a 'regime', a *lex specialis* prevailing over more general rules (*lex specialis derogate legi generali*) (see Introduction). In the absence of a universal treaty or an international organisation dedicated to its administration, this regime is still in the making and lacks the precision, coherence and authority expected in international law.[7] The international investment regime broadly comprises IIAs of different forms, from BITs to FTAs, including an investment chapter such as the now historic NAFTA, to a number of 'softer' international agreements, like the *OECD Guidelines for Multinational Enterprises*. This 'regime' produces some effect vis-à-vis its parties (the States) and is adjudicated by a number of arbitral tribunals and other courts (see Chapter 14). Yet again, the absence of uniformity and the hyperdiversity of the regime, with about 3,300 IIAs, as well as its impact on non-States parties (the individual, either a juridical or natural person), largely complicates the equation.[8] Lastly, it would be misleading to approach IIL in isolation, ignoring its direct relations with domestic and contractual law. As such, international investment law is no exception to the fragmentation of international law (see Introduction). It is a specialised regime, but here again, a regime, which is not strictly separated from other international legal regimes (human rights, the environment, tax, corruption and so on). It interacts directly with all of them as well as with domestic and contractual law, while it is firmly grounded in general public international law and the theory of State responsibility.

After clarifying the three laws of international investment, this chapter goes on to address the sources of IIL and highlights the great variety of its formats.

---

[5] Sornarajah, 'Resistance to Dominance in International Investment Law'.

[6] José E. Álvarez, *The Public International Law Regime Governing International Investment* (The Hague: Hague Academy of International Law, 2011), pp. 24–5.

[7] On the various legal regimes of international economic law and the largely debated issue of the fragmentation of international law, see Introduction.

[8] For a recent account of the number of IIAs, see UNCTAD, available at http://investmentpolicyhub.unctad.org/IIA (accessed 21 December 2020).

12.2   The Three Laws of FDI

There are three laws of international investment: national, contractual and international.[9] *National law* is fundamentally political and so constantly evolving. It addresses the authorisation (entry and exit) and treatment of foreign investments once they have entered the territory of a sovereign State. *Contractual law* creates legally binding obligations for the parties (the foreign investor and a given State), based on a joint negotiation. It is of a particular and precise nature. Lastly, *international law* is the product of the agreements entered into by States. These three laws are naturally interrelated, but our approach is international law-centric and so grounded in general public international law and the theory of State responsibility.

12.2.1 National Law

As we are rightly reminded by M. Sornarajah: 'in the bustle of the controversy that attends this area of the law, it is easy to forget the role of domestic law'. However, 'foreign investment is an inherently internal process as it takes place within territory of the host State and therefore falls under the sovereign powers of the State'.[10] Yet not all countries have a domestic investment law regime. To take an example in the region of ASEAN, Singapore, the most vibrant economy in attracting FDI, has not put in place a very detailed domestic investment law.[11] There is indeed no automaticity in attracting more FDI on the basis of existing national or domestic law. The World Bank itself concluded, in an authoritative study on foreign investment regulation, that while good regulation and efficient processes matter for FDI, 'many other variables such as market size, political stability, infrastructure quality, or level of economic development are likely to better explain the relationship'.[12] When they do have a domestic investment regime, States differ in their way of approaching it. They naturally choose different political options to attract, promote and protect investment, but also limit and restrict the same and possibly litigate disputes. In different countries, different laws serve different purposes. They may encourage foreign investment on the one hand, and control FDI on the other. After all, it is about striking a balance between opening up to the world and protecting the economy, as well as the rights

---

[9] See, in particular, Jeswald W. Salacuse, *The Three Laws of International Investment: National, Contractual and International Frameworks for Foreign Capital* (Oxford University Press, 2013).

[10] M. Sornarajah, *The International Law of Foreign Investment*, 4th ed. (Cambridge University Press, 2017), p. 108.

[11] Jonathan Bonnitcha, *Investment Laws of ASEAN Countries: A Comparative Review* (Winnipeg: International Institute for Sustainable Development, 2017), available at www.iisd.org/library/investment-laws-asean-countries-comparative-review (accessed 21 December 2020). See also the latest figures from the UNCTAD *World Investment Report*.

[12] International Finance Corporation/Multilateral Investment Guarantee Agency/World Bank, *Investing Across Borders 2010: Indicators of Foreign Direct Investment Regulation in Eighty-Seven Economies* (Washington, DC: World Bank, 2010), available at https://openknowledge.worldbank.org/handle/10986/27883 (accessed 21 December 2020). See also the most recent editions of the World Bank's Global Investment Competitiveness Survey, available at www.investorsurvey.net (accessed 21 December 2020).

granted to foreigners and those of nationals. In this regard, the data collected by the World Bank can be quite surprising, if not counterintuitive. For example, it takes sixteen procedures and forty-six days to establish a foreign-owned limited liability company (LLC) in Mumbai, but eighteen procedures and sixty-five days in China (Shanghai), even though the People's Republic is generally reputed for being more investment-friendly than India. However, the arbitration of commercial disputes will be much easier in China (no matter the recent character of its laws and its authoritarian socialist regime) than in India (despite a democratic law-making process and the long presence of commercial courts).[13]

Box 12.1 Top five findings of the World Bank Global Investment Competitiveness Survey 2017/2018

What do foreign investors value when they decide to invest abroad? Through 754 interviews with executives of multinational corporations with investments in the developing world, the World Bank Global Investment Competitiveness Survey 2017/2018 concluded that investors identified the following criteria:

1 Cost-competitive destinations and potential linkages between trade and investment policies such as tax holidays.
2 Policies that help them expand their business rather than policies just to attract FDI.
3 Investment protection guarantees, with 90 per cent of all investors rating various types of legal protection as important (ability to transfer currency, legal protections against expropriation, against breach of contract, and against non-transparent or arbitrary government conduct, for example).
4 Capacity and skills of local suppliers.
5 Stable macroeconomic and regulatory framework.

To Go Further

World Bank, *Global Investment Competitiveness Report 2017/2018: Foreign Investor Perspectives and Policy Implications* (Washington, DC: World Bank, 2018), available at www.worldbank.org/en/topic/competitiveness/publication/global-investment-competitiveness-report (accessed 21 December 2020).

---

[13] World Bank, Investing Across Borders database, available at http://iab.worldbank.org/data/exploreeconomies/india#arbitrating-commercial-disputes for India, and at http://iab.worldbank.org/data/exploreeconomies/china#arbitrating-commercial-disputes for China. On average, it takes around thirty-three weeks to enforce an arbitration award rendered in India, as against twenty-six in China, from filing an application to a writ of execution attaching assets (assuming there is no appeal), and forty-three weeks for a foreign award (thirty-one in China). On commercial and investment arbitration in India, see Leïla Choukroune and Rahul Donde (eds.), *International Commercial and Investment Disputes Settlement in and with India, Transnational Dispute Management* (special issue, 2018), 15(2), available at www.transnational-dispute-management.com/journal-browse-issues-toc.asp?key=77 (accessed 21 December 2020); Choukroune and Donde, *Adjudicating Global Business in and with India.*

While there may be national investment laws, these will have to be understood in conjunction with other regulations influencing investments, such as tax, land or labour laws. Therefore, the national legal framework of investment 'consists of legislations, regulations, administrative acts and judicial decisions of countries and their subdivisions having jurisdiction over the investment or the investor'.[14] As a result, there is an immense diversity of national approaches and regimes. A variety of institutions are generally designated internally to manage the domestic regime, while a number of issues are quite typically raised:

- What are the permitted foreign investments and investors and how should these be defined (sectoral restrictions on the basis of negative lists, restriction of ownership in privatised companies, regulation of equity joint ventures between foreign and local enterprises, screening laws)?[15]
- Is there a difference between FDI and domestic investment law?
- What are the incentives (tax holidays or special trade zones, for example) and guarantees (strength of the legal system and the rule of law, including legal stability) offered to foreign investments and investors?[16]
- What are the rights offered to foreign investments/investors? Are these rights specific and/ or different from those offered to domestic investments/investors?
- What type of control does the State want to establish over foreign investments/investors?
- How will the State approve and administer FDI?
- Are portfolio investments considered investment and how will they be managed?
- Are there conflicts of law between domestic law and international law?
- What law will prevail if a conflict occurs in relation to a particular investment standard or notion?
- How will disputes be settled? Is there a dedicated institution for the settlement of FDI disputes?[17]

To illustrate the above, the ASEAN region provides a set of interesting and sometimes contradicting examples for a number of countries that are also party to the ASEAN Comprehensive Investment Agreement, a treaty aiming at harmonisation of all existing

---

[14] Salacuse, *Three Laws of International Investment*, p. 35.

[15] On the control of inward investment and its encouragement, see Peter T. Muchlinshki, *Multinational Enterprises and the Law* (Oxford University Press, 2010), pp. 177–261; and Salacuse, *Three Laws of International Investment*, pp. 89–131.

[16] World Bank, *Global Investment Competitiveness Report 2017/2018: Foreign Investor Perspectives and Policy Implications* (Washington, DC: World Bank, 2018), and, specifically, its chapter 3: Maria R. Andersen, Benjamin R. Kett and Erik von Uexkull, 'Corporate Tax Incentives and FDI in Developing Countries', pp. 73–99, available at http://pubdocs.worldbank.org/en/964321508856694021/GICR-03.pdf (accessed 21 December 2020). The World Bank concludes that tax incentives are generally not cost-effective for developing countries and should be used only strategically.

[17] For a detailed account and a crystal-clear approach, see Salacuse, *Three Laws of International Investment*, pp. 89–136.

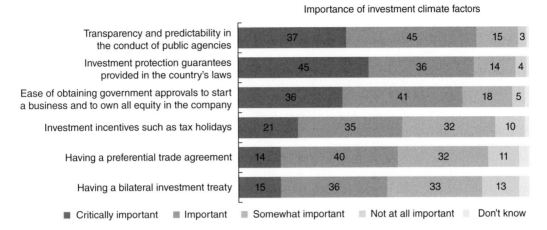

Figure 12.1 Why national law matters. Source: The World Bank, Global Investment Competitiveness Report, 2017–18, p. 9.

regimes.[18] There is only a minimal investment national framework in Singapore, as in Brunei. Yet both countries have an investment agency and do restrict FDI in certain strategic sectors of the economy, such as oil, gas, fisheries and land acquisition for Brunei, and telecommunication, media and land ownership for Singapore. In Laos, national investment law deals with the establishment of investment, new incentives and the operation of special economic zones (SEZ), but does not grant foreign investor national treatment. In Myanmar, on the other hand, investment law guarantees fair and equitable treatment, and offers significant protection for the investment/investor. In Vietnam, investment law encourages the domestic settlement of investment disputes unless an international agreement to which the country is a party requires otherwise.[19] These national policies are fluid and are regularly amended to adjust to new politico-economic challenges. As far as dispute settlement is concerned, the ASEAN Comprehensive Investment Agreement provides for ISDS as well as original ADR mechanisms.[20] The countries of the region are party to the ASEAN–Australia–New Zealand Free Trade Agreement, which came into force in 2010 and also provides for ISDS.

Let us conclude with another quite surprising example of regulatory diversity: while Latin America often appears reluctant to opening up to the world, the World Bank has showed that Chile, Colombia and Peru were among the world's most open economies covered by its

---

[18] This agreement took effect on 29 March 2012 and aims to attract ASEAN as a single investment destination; available at http://asean.org/?static_post=asean-comprehensive-investment-agreement (accessed 21 December 2020). For a comparative analysis of national and international investment regimes in Asia, see Luke Nottage and Vivienne Bath, 'International Investment Agreements and Investor–State Arbitration in Asia', in Chaisse et al., *Handbook of International Investment Law and Policy* (Singapore: Springer, in press).

[19] Bonnitcha, *Investment Laws of ASEAN Countries*; Nottage and Bath, 'International Investment Agreements'.

[20] Julien Chaisse and Sufian Jusoh, *The ASEAN Comprehensive Investment Agreement: The Regionalization of Laws and Policy on Foreign Investment* (Cheltenham: Edward Elgar, 2016).

2013 study on FDI regulations indicators, with almost no restriction on foreign ownership in the thirty-two sectors. Mexico, on the other hand, was the most restricted economy of the region at that time. Naturally, these regimes keep changing with new governments.[21]

The great variety of national investment laws certainly raises questions for the investor, with or without the overarching framework of international law. For this reason, among a few other solutions developed, State–investor contracts have been secured (in national law to start with, and on the basis of licences or permits, for example) to further protect and enhance FDI. Yet they naturally raise a number of issues in relation to the imbalance of power, which often direct their negotiation, the highly demanding clauses they comprise, and the quite general absence of publication, if not secrecy, surrounding their conclusion.

12.2.2 Contractual Law

The investment contract operates within the realm of the three laws of investment, national, contractual per se and international. It is a legal instrument resting upon a precise body of law and interacting with others. While private investment contracts almost all contain a 'choice of law' clause, reflecting the principle of 'parties' autonomy', a concept now largely, if not yet universally, recognised by the courts, investment contracts between the State and a private entity are based on national law and considered 'State contracts'. These very specific contracts aim at different objectives to those of commercial contracts: they support the State in performing certain tasks and thus rely on a different set of national rules. They can be subject to legitimate changes by a government eager to protect its regulatory independence. Because of the risk they entail for the investor, some have argued in favour of the internationalisation of State contracts – that is, their governance by international law.[22] A number of landmark cases that came out of the 1970s postcolonial order have illustrated this tendency in the context of what were referred to as economic development agreements. As explained by Jean Ho, the idea of internationalisation of State contracts is not new and dates back to the post-soviet revolution era, with the emergence of nationalisation policies:

---

[21] World Bank, Regulating Foreign Direct Investment in Latin America, Indicators of Investment Regulations and Options for Investment Climate Reform, October 2013, available at http://iab.worldbank.org/~/media/FPDKM/IAB/Documents/Regulating-FDI-in-Latin-America.pdf. See also World Bank, 'How Developing Countries Can Get the Most Out of Direct Investment', and *Global Investment Competitiveness Report 2017/2018*, available at www.worldbank.org/en/topic/competitiveness/publication/global-investment-competitiveness-report (accessed 21 December 2020).

[22] Salacuse, *Three Laws of International Investment*, p. 165; and A. F. M. Maniruzzaman, 'State Contracts in Contemporary International Law: Monist versus Dualist Controversies', *European Journal of International Law* (2001), 12, pp. 309–28, who rightly observes: 'in the context of the theory of internationalization, the perennial question remains whether or to what extent public international law has any role to play in the situation where the proper law of the contract is some municipal law, and the contract has its being in that law as the proper law of the contract' (p. 310).

the idea of internationalisation likely surfaced in the 1930 arbitral award in *Lena Goldfields* v. *USSR*, and gained more defined contours in the 1950s to the 1970s in the innovative proposal to prevent Iran from interfering with concessionary rights of the Anglo-Iranian Oil Company, as well as a string of arbitral awards on termination of concessions in the Middle East. The proposal called for the inclusion of a non-interference clause in the concession, and its incorporation by reference into a treaty concluded between Iran and the United Kingdom, thereby elevating every breach of contract into a breach of treaty.[23]

UNCTAD formulated a definition of State contract in its 2004 report:[24]

UNCTAD, State Contracts, *Introduction*

A 'State contract' can be defined as a contract made between the State, or an entity of the State, which, for present purposes, may be defined as any organization created by statute within a State that is given control over an economic activity, and a foreign national or a legal person of foreign nationality. State contracts can cover a wide range of issues, including loan agreements, purchase contracts for supplies or services, contracts of employment, or large infrastructure projects, such as the construction of highways, ports or dams. One of the commonest forms of State contracts is the natural resource exploitation contract, sometimes referred to as a 'concession agreement', though this is not a strict term of art (Brownlie, 2003, p. 522). Such agreements feature prominently in the natural resource sectors of developing countries. Historically, these sectors have provided the most important source of income for the domestic economy and have often been State controlled, so that foreign entrants into the sector had to make contracts with the State entity in control.

The UNCTAD definition stresses the discretionary character of the conclusion of these State contracts, often in sensitive and strategic sectors, such as the exploitation of natural resources, as in the case below.

Aminoil v. Kuwait

The seminal *Aminoil* v. *Kuwait* was a case set against the backdrop of a concession agreement granted in 1948, at the time of the British presence, and subject to a stabilisation clause preventing the State from unilaterally altering or annulling the terms of the agreement (see below for more on stabilisation clauses). To settle the dispute and address the question of compensation arising after the nationalisation of the company by the State, the arbitral tribunal largely referred to international law as an integral part of Kuwaiti law, and so a well-'blended' source of interpretation.[25] However, this monist (as opposed to dualist) interpretation, giving great importance, if not supremacy, to international law has

---

[23] Jean Ho, *State Responsibility for Breaches of Investment Contracts* (Cambridge University Press, 2018), p. 238.

[24] UNCTAD, *State Contracts* (New York and Geneva: United Nations, 2004), p. 3, available at https://unctad.org/en/Docs/iteiit200411_en.pdf (accessed 21 December 2020).

[25] *Government of the State of Kuwait* v. *American Independent Oil Company*, Ad Hoc Arbitral Tribunal, 1982.

not been accepted by all scholars and arbitrators, who have also put forward the accepted autonomy of the parties to the contract to choose the applicable law above the State's sovereign independence.[26]

12.2.2.1 Negotiation

In this context, it is important to bear in mind that State contracts are the product of negotiation between the parties, the State and the investor. This negotiation is highly strategic and may reveal itself as extremely complex and sensitive, for the given parties do not always share the same cultural and political backgrounds, nor the same strategic interests and objectives as concerns the investment. Negotiating with the 'sovereign' is a genre in itself in diplomatic and international relations. Negotiation tips and other intercultural approaches are common in contract law literature and are often taught in law or business schools to future investors or counsels.[27] But in the recent past, and against the backdrop of multiple controversies arising from land grabbing and other highly debated infrastructure contracts, a number of agencies, including the United Nations, have crafted guidelines and principles for the negotiation of investment contracts by developing and least developed countries, which resources are much-coveted by other more powerful or emerging economies challenged by demographic and natural commodity scarcity (China, India, Brazil and the Gulf countries). The UN's *Principles for Responsible Contracts: Integrating the Management of Human Rights Risks into State–Investor Contract Negotiations – Guidance for Negotiators*, is probably the most advanced of these voluntary schemes, since it adopts a human rights-based approach while addressing general contractual issues. It identifies negotiation challenges and proposes ten principles for integrating human rights as a risk (and opportunity) in the negotiation of contracts:[28]

OHCHR, Principles for Responsible Contracts

Ten Principles for Integrating the Management of Human Rights Risks into Contract Negotiations

1 Preparation and Planning

Principle 1: The Parties should be adequately prepared and have the capacity to properly address the human rights implications of projects during negotiations.

---

[26] F. A. Mann, 'The Aminoil Arbitration', *British Yearbook of International Law* (1984), 54(1), pp. 213–21.

[27] Salacuse, *Three Laws of International Investment*, p. 197.

[28] Office of the High Commissioner for Human Rights, *Principles for Responsible Contracts: Integrating the Management of Human Rights Risks into State–Investor Contract Negotiations – Guidance for Negotiators* (Geneva: United Nations, 2015), available at www.ohchr.org/Documents/Publications/Principles_ResponsibleContracts_HR_PUB_15_1_EN.pdf (accessed 21 December 2020).

(cont.)

[…]

2 Managing Potential Adverse Human Rights Impact

Principle 2: Responsibility for preventing and mitigating human rights risks associated with the project and its activities should be clarified and agreed before the contract is finalized.

[…]

3 Project Operating Standards

Principle 3: The laws, regulations and standards governing the execution of the project should facilitate the prevention, mitigation and remedy of any negative human rights impact throughout the life cycle of the project.

[…]

4 Stabilization Clauses

Principle 4: Contractual stabilization clauses, if used, should be carefully drafted so that any protections for investors against future changes in law do not interfere with the State's bona fide efforts to implement laws, regulations or policies, in a non-discriminatory manner, in order to meet its human rights obligations.

[…]

5 'Additional Goods or Service Provision'

Principle 5: If the contract envisages that investors will provide additional services beyond the scope of the project, this should be carried out in a manner compatible with the State's human rights obligations and the investor's human rights responsibilities.

[…]

6 Physical Security for the Project

Principle 6: Physical security for the project's facilities, installations or personnel should be provided in a manner consistent with human rights principles and standards.

[…]

7 Community Engagement

Principle 7: The project should have an effective community engagement plan through its life cycle, starting at the earliest stages of the project.

[…]

(cont.)

8 Project Monitoring and Compliance

Principle 8: The State should be able to monitor the project's compliance with relevant standards to protect human rights, while providing the necessary assurances to business investors against arbitrary interference in the project.

[...]

9 Grievance Mechanisms for Harm to Third Parties

Principle 9: Individuals and communities that are affected by the project activities, but not party to the contract, should have access to an effective non-judicial grievance mechanism.

[...]

10 Transparency/Disclosure of Contract Terms

Principle 10: The contract's terms should be disclosed, and the scope and duration of exceptions to such disclosure should be based on compelling justifications.

The above UN holistic human rights-based approach is particularly interesting, as it integrates all legal regimes and reconciles the different branches of international law. Olivier de Schutter performed a quite similar exercise at the time he was UN Special Rapporteur on the right to food. He proposed 'A Set of Core Principles and Measures to Address the Human Rights Challenge' in relation to large-scale land acquisitions and leases, at the centre of which are the concepts of transparency of the negotiations and the rights of local communities, including indigenous people. These rights are fostered by the systematic practice of 'impact assessment' studies in particular.[29] All these guidelines have now largely influenced the field of investment contract negotiations and are often referred to by negotiators, both States and investors. Indeed, today we find similar approaches in the latest generations of BITs, with the idea 'impact assessment' or 'due diligence' gaining momentum (see further below and Chapter 13).

Box 12.2 Fairer and more sustainable rights-based contracts

What is in the contract? How can investment contracts be made more sustainable and fairer in a way that is based on rights for all? This interrogation has gained popularity among a vast series of IIL actors: NGOs advising the 'victims' of land grabbing and

---

[29] Olivier De Schutter (Special Rapporteur on the right to food), 'Large-Scale Land Acquisitions and Leases: A Set of Core Principles and Measures to Address the Human Rights Challenge' (11 June 2009), available at www.oecd.org/site/swacmali2010/44031283.pdf (accessed 21 December 2020).

Box 12.2 (cont.)

other controversial deals related to FDI in the sensitive sectors of mining, oil or even infrastructure, but also international organisations, governments and investors themselves, as they, too, wish to see their rights fully respected and better framed.

In doing so, a number of tools have been identified in line with the work of the UN (Global Compact and *Guiding Principles on Business and Human Rights*) or the OECD (*Guidelines for Multinational Enterprises*). Among these, a consensus seems to be widely established in favour of the following ideas: a well-prepared and informed negotiation, feasibility study and impact assessment; respect of economic, but also social (labour, health, safety, education) and environmental obligations; careful consideration of stabilisation clauses, with regard to fiscal sovereignty and respect for human rights; periodic reviews and possibility of renegotiation, dispute settlement and grievances mechanisms; transparency, including publication of the contract, monitoring and termination of the contract. In a number of instances, some model contracts have also been prepared (for example, the IISD model contract for farmland and water). Some are more daring than others, but a few approach the matter specifically from a rights-based viewpoint, hence also participating in the defragmentation of international law. A vast literature has developed to inform this new approach.

To Go Further

BBC Africa Debate, 'Is "Land Grabbing" Good for Africa?' (podcast, 24 February 2012), available at www.bbc.co.uk/programmes/p00p5qrb (accessed 21 December 2020).

BBC News, 'Analysis: Land Grab or Development Opportunity?' (22 February 2012), available at www.bbc.co.uk/news/world-africa-17099348 (accessed 21 December 2020).

Brauch, M. D., *Contracts for Sustainable Infrastructure: Ensuring the Social and Environmental Co-Benefits of Infrastructure Investment Projects* (Winnipeg: International Institute for Sustainable Development, 2017), available at www.iisd.org/library/contracts-sustainable-infrastructure-ensuring-economic-social-and-environmental-co-benefits (accessed 21 December 2020).

Cotula, L., *Investment Contracts and Sustainable Development: How to Make Contracts for Fairer and More Sustainable Natural Resource Investments* (London: International Institute for Environment and Development, 2010), available at http://pubs.iied.org/pdfs/17507IIED .pdf (accessed 21 December 2020).

International Bar Association, Model Mining Development Agreement Project (MMDA 1.0) (2011), available at www.mmdaproject.org (accessed 21 December 2020).

International Senior Lawyers Project/Columbia Center on Sustainable Investment, 'Guide to Land Contracts: Agricultural Projects' (2016), available at http://ccsi.columbia.edu/files/ 2016/03/Ag-Guide-2016.pdf (accessed 21 December 2020).

Mann, H., *IISD Handbook on Mining Contract Negotiations for Developing Countries, Volume I: Preparing for Success* (Winnipeg: International Institute for Sustainable Development, 2015), available at www.iisd.org/library/iisd-handbook-mining-contract-negotiations-developing-countries-volume-1-preparing-success (accessed 21 December 2020).

> ### Box 12.2 (cont.)
>
> Office of the High Commissioner for Human Rights, *Guiding Principles on Business and Human Rights: Implementing the United Nations 'Protect, Respect and Remedy' Framework* (New York and Geneva: United Nations, 2011), available at www.ohchr.org/Documents/ Publications/GuidingPrinciplesBusinessHR_EN.pdf (accessed 21 December 2020).
> *Principles for Responsible Contracts: Integrating the Management of Human Rights Risks into State–Investor Contract Negotiations – Guidance for Negotiators* (Geneva: United Nations, 2015), available at www.ohchr.org/Documents/Publications/Principles_ResponsibleContracts_HR_ PUB_15_1_EN.pdf (accessed 21 December 2020).
> Organisation for Economic Co-operation and Development, *OECD Guidelines for Multinational Enterprises* (Paris: OECD Publishing, 2011), available at www.oecd.org/daf/ inv/mne/ (accessed 21 December 2020).
> Smaller, C., *The IISD Guide to Negotiating Investment Contracts for Farmland and Water* (Winnipeg: International Institute for Sustainable Development, 2014), available at www .iisd.org/sites/default/files/publications/iisd-guide-negotiating-investment-contracts-farmland-water_1.pdf (accessed 21 December 2020).

12.2.2.2   Types of Contracts

As for national law specific rules, the variety of contractual forms is potentially immense. They largely depend on the objectives the State and the investor want to meet and will serve as a legal framework to achieve these goals. They have also evolved over time, with the diversification of FDI and its actors, the end of the colonial period, countries' political preferences in favour of statist models or models that are more open, as well as the recent liberalisation and regulation efforts they have engaged in (see Chapter 11). One could indeed identify a few generations of contracts – for example, with the oil concession contracts of the colonial era; the production and profit-sharing agreements of the post-decolonisation period; and, later, the private-public partnerships of the 1990s, taking the form of build-own-operate (BOO), according all the benefits (and risks) to the investor, or build-operate-transfer (BOT), which allowed the host country to take over the project after some time elapsed. The nature of these contracts, as well as the law applicable to them, is naturally of great importance for the determination of the existence of an investment and/or an investor, a question that arises quite systematically in the context of a dispute (see Chapter 13). The most commonly found investment contracts can nevertheless be categorised in a few groups.[30]

Wholly Owned FDIs   The foreign investor (either a physical or a legal person) acquires, controls and operates assets abroad for the purpose of making profit. This form of

---

[30] See, generally, Peter T. Muchlinshki, *Multinational Enterprises and the Law* (Oxford University Press, 2010), pp. 45–79; Salacuse, *Three Laws of International Investment*, pp. 204–44; Sornarajah, *International Law of Foreign Investment*, pp. 142–5.

investment can be performed through an existing branch of a company or a subsidiary. Of course, domestic law plays a great role in the determination of the applicable rules. For example, taxation will be key in choosing a given form of company.

International Joint Ventures   In this case, one refers to the decision made by the foreign investor to operate alone or with the support of other foreign business partners. This form of partnership for FDI has gained immense popularity since the 1970s. International joint ventures cover both basic and complex realities. In simple terms, it is an association between at least two investors. Yet such associations can take a variety of forms, according to different domestic laws. However, we tend to distinguish between two generally accepted manifestations: an equity joint venture and a contractual one. International joint venture contracts are particularly complex. They require a clear agreement between the different parties with different legal backgrounds and business objectives.

Box 12.3 *Force majeure*

Does the Covid-19 pandemic constitute a *force majeure* under national and/or international law? This interrogation has been at the centre of law firms' preoccupations since the beginning of the crisis. It is likely that governments will face claims of *force majeure* from multinational companies in relation to the measures they have taken and that have had a direct impact on their operations. A number of States indeed have de facto forbidden economic activity, while, as in case of India, taking restrictive FDI measures. At the same time, States are making the same *force majeure* claim to support their own response measures. This defence strategy arises in contract disputes or ISDS initiated on the basis of an international investment treaty.

Force majeure, as the French expression clearly alludes to (a major force), is used to acknowledge the dramatic consequences of a given event beyond one's control. However, *force majeure* will only be relevant to an international contract if the contract actually contains a specific *force majeure* clause and the precise wording of a definition. One needs to assess the impact of the *force majeure* event – in this case, a global pandemic. The burden of proof will rely on the party trying to demonstrate the *force majeure*. Interestingly, here, the State could be the respondent, but also a party trying to show that Covid-19 was indeed a *force majeure*. The next steps could vary on the basis of the contract (or the international investment treaty) and its possible definitions of *force majeure* in the general context of exceptions (see Chapter 13). The party arguing *force majeure* could be allowed to terminate the contract.

To Go Further

Mann, H., 'Force Majeure and Covid-19: Legal Risks of a Double-Edged Sword' (Ottawa: International Institute for Sustainable Development, May 2020), available at www.iisd.org/library/force-majeure-covid (accessed 21 December 2020).

Public-Private Partnerships   Another interesting and rather popular form of international investment contract is the public-private partnership (PPP). PPPs typically occur in the context of complex infrastructure deals, which were not necessarily permitted by the sovereign State in the immediate decolonisation period, since they impact on strategic aspects of the domestic economy and could interfere with precise policy choices for the population and the lives of sometimes vulnerable indigenous communities.[31] They are generally made on a BOO, BOT or BOOT (build-own-operate-transfer) model. While ownership is controlled by the State, the concession granted to a private foreign investor can be agreed upon for a long period and based on very advantageous terms. International organisations such as the World Bank have been supportive of this model for the developing world, and have put in place a number of guidelines and principles to facilitate its negotiation and implementation.[32] According to the World Bank, PPPs have been signed in 134 countries and contribute about 15–20 per cent of total infrastructure investment. While funding and efficiency are secured, the ability of PPPs to deliver essential services to local populations remains unclear, if not controversial.

International Loans   A last form of investment contract can be described as international loans. They are naturally quite popular in the developing world. In this case, the lender will be an international entity and the borrower located in another country. They provide the borrower with funds for a certain period and are based on either fixed or floating interest rates. They can also be secured (some form of property interest is guaranteed to the lender in the event the borrower fails to repay the loan) or unsecured (the borrower is seen as creditworthy). In these cases, export-import (EXIM) banks are playing a key role. Over the past decade, a number of emerging countries' EXIM banks made a vigorous entry into the loan market, proposing preferential and somehow different conditions to borrowers (less stringent conditionality with regard to governance and regulation in particular). Brazil, India and, mostly, China have become central actors in this financial market for aid (see Chapters 15 and 16). As an example, for the period 2000–2015, China's EXIM bank loaned US$6.9 billion to Angola – that is, 11 per cent of its total financing to Africa.[33] Interestingly, the same Chinese EXIM bank is also lending to Brazilian

---

[31] Josua Loots, 'Public-Private Partnerships for Infrastructure Development in Africa: The Need for Human Rights-Focused Regulation', *Perspectives Africa: Putting People Back into Infrastructure* (2017) 2, pp. 6–10, available at www.boell.de/en/2017/06/14/public-private-partnerships-infrastructure-development-africa-need-human-rights-focused (accessed 21 December 2020). See also World Bank Group, *World Bank Group Support to Public-Private Partnerships* (March 2017), available at https://ieg.worldbankgroup.org/evaluations/world-bank-group-support-ppp (accessed 21 December 2020); and, generally, World Bank policy on the same, available at www.worldbank.org/en/topic/publicprivatepartnerships (accessed 21 December 2020).

[32] See, in particular, for infrastructure-related public-private partnerships, the World Bank dedicated website at www.worldbank.org/en/topic/publicprivatepartnerships (accessed 21 December 2020).

[33] Macau Hub, 'Angola Receives US$6.9 Billion from the Export–Import Bank of China in 2000–2015 Period' (2 May 2017), available at https://macauhub.com.mo/feature/angola-recebeu-69-mil-milhoes-de-dolares-banco-de-exportacoes-e-importacoes-da-china-ate-2015/ (accessed 21 December 2020).

companies (the mining and petroleum giants, Vale and Petrobras) to invest in China and export advanced technologies.[34]

Box 12.4 China's investment regime in and out

According to UNCTAD, in 2016, China received US$133.7 billion (108.1 billion for Hong Kong) and exported US$183.1 billion (62.5 billion for Hong Kong). With the Covid-19 pandemic, China has become the first recipient of FDI in the world, hence surpassing the US. This makes the People's Republic, by far, the top home and host economy for FDI in Asia.

China's domestic investment regime has changed over the years to become more open and welcoming to the FDI it needs to sustain the growth on which its socio-political stability rests. At, the same time, it encourages its companies to invest abroad to source commodities and expand its influence in the developed and the developing world, through strategic deals and massive investments in infrastructure or loans.

Chinese domestic law on FDI is constantly evolving to meet the needs of its new investment strategies. As a matter of fact, in 2016, the Ministry of Commerce introduced a series of new record filings for its administration of foreign invested enterprises. It later refined this regime, in 2017, in the direction of a 'negative list' system. Two regulations are of particular importance, the Catalogue of Industries for Guiding Foreign Investment and a separate list for China Free Trade Zones. In terms of contracts or types of enterprises recorded in the second list, one finds, notably: wholly foreign-owned enterprises, Sino-foreign equity joint venture companies, Sino-foreign invested joint stock limited companies, foreign-invested joint stock limited companies, foreign-invested venture capital companies, and foreign investment projects from Hong Kong, Macao or Taiwan.

On the other hand, the Chinese outward FDI regime has pragmatically encouraged investors. In 2016, China became the second largest investor abroad after the US. Despite the real buzz and legitimate concern about Chinese investments in Africa, China invests essentially in Asia, followed by Europe, Latin America, Africa and Oceania. Since the 2006 Beijing summit and the publication of the first comprehensive Chinese *White Paper on China's African Policy, January 2006*, China's presence in Africa is indeed scrutinised by many observers, from policymakers to businesses and academics. While this 'strategic partnership' is not always welcomed or viewed as the 'win-win cooperation' advertised by Hu Jintao in his 2006 Beijing address, some analysts deliberately take the opposite side, with a view to deconstructing myths and discourses and showing 'the real story' from proven facts. With sixty-five countries and 4.4 billion people in Asia, Europe and Africa, China's Belt and Road Initiative is now at the centre of this renewed effort to reach out to the world on the basis of a

---

[34] China.org, 'China Exim Bank, Brazilian Companies Make Loan Deals' (21 May 2015), available at www.china.org .cn/business/2015-05/21/content_35629475.htm (accessed 21 December 2020).

Box 12.4 (cont.)

carefully planned strategy, mixing clear support of Chinese State-owned companies, the allocation of preferential loans via China's EXIM bank, the strategic acquisition of resources and know-how, and the vast dissemination of a discourse on the pacific and friendly character of a win-win deal for development scientifically broadcast by Chinese media well-versed in using and transforming the propaganda apparatus.

To Go Further

Ahmad, M., Chaisse, J., Cheng, T., Chi, M. and Górski, J., 'One Belt One Road Initiative ("OBOR"): Editorial', *Transnational Dispute Management* (special issue, 2017), 3, available at www.transnational-dispute-management.com/article.asp?key=2469 (accessed 21 December 2020).

Brautigam, D., *The Dragon's Gift: The Real Story of China in Africa* (Oxford University Press, 2009).

Chaisse, J. (ed.), *China's International Investment Strategy* (Oxford University Press, 2019).

Choukroune, L., Book reviews, 'Robert I. Rotberg (ed.), China into Africa: Trade, Aid and Influence / Deborah Brautigam, The Dragon's Gift: The Real Story of China in Africa / David H. Shinn and Joshua Eisenman, China and Africa: A Century of Engagement', *China Perspectives* (2013), 2, pp. 82–4.

Export-Import Bank of China: http://english.eximbank.gov.cn/en/ (accessed 21 December 2020).

Cotula, L., *Land Deals in Africa: What Is in the Contracts?* (London: International Institute for Environment and Development, 2011), available at http://pubs.iied.org/pdfs/12568IIED.pdf (accessed 21 December 2020).

Cotula, L., Weng, X., Ma, Q., Ren, P., *China–Africa Investment Treaties: Do They Work?* (London: International Institute for Environment and Development, 2016), available at http://pubs.iied.org/pdfs/17588IIED.pdf (accessed 21 December 2020).

Ministry of Commerce, People's Republic of China: http://english.mofcom.gov.cn

Shinn, D. H. and Eisenman, J., *China and Africa: A Century of Engagement* (University of Pennsylvania Press, 2012).

12.2.2.3   Stabilisation and Umbrella Clauses

Among the many debated features of international investment contracts are the controversial stabilisation and umbrella clauses.

Stabilisation Clauses   As the name suggests, stabilisation clauses aim at stabilising the terms and conditions of a given investment contract to provide the investment and investor with some stability.[35] While this perspective is understandable from the

---

[35] An interesting and quite comprehensive study on the impact of stabilisation clauses and human rights was released by the International Finance Corporation of the World Bank and John Ruggie, then United Nations

viewpoint of the investor, which may want to limit the risk of its investment in a complex, unstable political or economic context, it is more questionable from the standpoint of a State that is keen to maintain its regulatory autonomy (on the notion of risk as a component of an investment, see Chapter 13). Concretely speaking, the host State will commit not to modify its regulatory framework without the consent of the other parties. Any contravention to the terms of the clause would then result in the payment of compensation. These clauses are very common in large energy or resources projects performed in the developing world and have generated a real public outcry, notably since the Argentine crises and the many arbitral cases following a number of regulatory measures taken by Argentina and perceived by investors as contractual – and treaty – breaches (see Chapter 14). The stabilisation clauses' power is immense, as they can 'freeze' the law to the benefit of the investor, or even exclude the application of certain parts of domestic law if these are perceived as inconsistent with the terms of the contract. Virtually all fields of domestic law are concerned: labour, tax, environment and property.[36] A few categories of clauses emerge in a large variety of contracts:

- Freezing clauses: freezing the law at one point in time.
- Economic stabilisation/equilibrium clauses: providing compensation to the investor in case of economic changes induced by legislative action affecting the investor's business operation.
- Hybrid clauses: representing a mix of the two previous categories.

The following abstract from the 1998 Republic of Equatorial Guinea model clauses provides an example of the typical wording of these clauses at the peak of the liberalisation era.[37]

Special Representative of the Secretary General on Business and Human Rights, 'Stabilization Clauses and Human Rights' (27 May 2009), available at www.ifc.org/wps/wcm/connect/0883d81a-e00a-4551-b2b9-46641e5a9bba/Stabilization%2BPaper.pdf?MOD=AJPERES&CACHEID=ROOTWORKSPACE-0883d81a-e00a-4551-b2b9-46641e5a9bba-jqeww2e (accessed 21 December 2020). It stressed, in particular, the disparities between OECD and non-OECD contracts and the long-term impacts of stabilisation clauses on human rights, including sustainability.

[36] T. Walde and G. Ndi, 'Stabilizing International Investment Commitments: International Law versus Contract Interpretation', *Texas International Law Journal* (1996), 31, pp. 215–42; A. F. M. Maniruzzaman, 'The Pursuit of Stability in International Energy Investment Contracts: A Critical Appraisal of the Emerging Trends', *Journal of World Energy Law and Business* (2008), 1(2), p. 122; Katja Ghene and Romulo Brillo, 'Stabilization Clauses in International Investment Law: Beyond Balancing and Fair and Equitable Treatment', research paper (Institute of Economic Law, Transnational Economic Law Research Centre, Martin Luther University Halle-Wittenberg, March 2017), available at http://telc.jura.uni-halle.de/sites/default/files/BeitraegeTWR/Heft%20143.pdf (accessed 21 December 2020).

[37] See the 1998 Model (Art. 20.3) cited by P. Cameron in *International Energy Investment Law: The Pursuit of Stability* (Oxford University Press, 2010); see also the Model Petroleum Production Sharing Contract Republic of Equatorial Guinea 2006, available at www.ogel.org/legal-and-regulatory-detail.asp?key=11934 (accessed 21 December 2020).

1998 Republic of Equatorial Guinea Stabilisation Clause Model Article

Should the income of the state or the Contractor be materially altered as a result of new laws, orders or regulations then, in such an event, the Parties shall agree to make the necessary adjustments to the relevant provisions of this Contract, observing the principle that the affected Party shall be restored to substantially the same economic condition as it would have been in had such change in laws or regulations not occurred. The cost of such restoration to the other Party may not exceed the benefit received by such other Party as a result of such change.

These clauses are particularly popular in the oil and gas industry and often rely on some forms of fiscal stabilisation.[38] Their effectiveness, however, is now contested. Despite the popularity of these stabilisation clauses, 'their practical value to oil and gas companies is questionable, particularly when the fairness of fiscal regimes is so often called into question'.[39]

AMINOIL V. KUWAIT

Here again, the 1982 *Aminoil* case provides an interesting interpretation of the contractual obligations of the parties (the government of Kuwait and the American company Aminoil) and the applicability of stabilisation clauses. The stabilisation clause can be found in Article 17 of the 1948 Concession Agreement (a contract) agreed upon at the time of colonisation. The Tribunal explained its impact on the possibility of nationalisation.[40]

Aminoil *v.* Kuwait

88. These clauses combined, but especially Article 17, constituted what are sometimes called the 'stabilisation' clauses of the contract. A straightforward and direct reading of them can lead to the conclusion that they prohibit any nationalisation. Such is the view maintained by the Company. The Government of Kuwait on the other hand, in a series of arguments the merits of which the Tribunal must now consider, maintained that, on the contrary, these clauses did not prevent a nationalisation.

---

[38] Mario Mansour and Carole Nakhle, 'Fiscal Stabilization in Oil and Gas Contracts: Evidence and Implications', OIES Paper SP37 (Oxford Institute for Energy Studies, January 2016), available at www.oxfordenergy.org/publications/fiscal-stabilization-in-oil-and-gas-contracts-evidence-and-implications/ (accessed 21 December 2020); Nima Mersadi Tabari, *Lex Petrolea and International Investment Law: Law and Practice in the Persian Gulf* (Abingdon and New York: Routledge, 2017); Jola Gjuzi, *Stabilization Clauses in International Investment Law: A Sustainable Development Approach* (Cham, Switzerland: Springer, 2018).

[39] Gjuzi, *Stabilization Clauses in International Investment Law*, p. 18.

[40] *American Independent Oil Company* v. *Government of the State of Kuwait (Aminoil* v. *Kuwait)*, Final Award, 24 March 1982, Section V, Question A, available at https://jusmundi.com/en/document/decision/en-the-american-independent-oil-company-v-the-government-of-the-state-of-kuwait-final-award-wednesday-24th-march-1982#decision_5370 (accessed 21 December 2020).

Article 17 of the 1948 Concession Agreement was indeed particularly generous to the investor in its formulation:

1948 Kuwaiti Concession Agreement, Article 17

The Shaikh shall not by general or special legislation or by administrative measures or by any other act whatever annul this Agreement except as provided in Article 11. No alteration shall be made in the terms of this Agreement by either the Shaikh or the Company except in the event of the Shaikh and the Company jointly agreeing that it is desirable in the interest of both parties to make certain alterations, deletions or additions to this Agreement.

A number of issues were raised on the basis of this article, the 'most radical' one, in the words of the Tribunal, consisted of affirming that the stabilisation clauses were only embodying general principles of contract law and the legal regime of the contract was the same as any other contract and added nothing to the understanding of the issues at stake. This argument was rejected by the Tribunal, as well as another argument putting forward the colonial character of the provision imposed at the time of the British Protectorate. The latter issue is still very much debated today, as these clauses often express an imbalance of power when the negotiation takes place and can be interpreted as a form of neocolonisation or foreign domination by powerful multinational companies. Then came the argument of the possibility to nationalise, which, according to the investor, was precluded by the contract's stabilisation clauses. The Tribunal, however, took another perspective, insisting on the necessity of such a drastic possibility being limited in time.[41]

Aminoil v. Kuwait

94. The case of nationalisation is certainly not expressly provided against by the stabilisation clauses of the Concession. But it is contended by Aminoil that notwithstanding this *lacuna*, the stabilisation clauses of the Concession (Articles 17 and revised 11) are cast in such absolute and all-embracing terms as to suffice in themselves – unconditionally and in all circumstances – for prohibiting nationalisation. That is a possible interpretation on the purely formal plane; but, for the following reasons, it is not the one adopted by the Tribunal.

95. No doubt contractual limitations on the State's right to nationalise are juridically possible, but what that would involve would be a particularly serious undertaking which would have to be expressly stipulated for, and be within the regulations governing the conclusion of State contracts; and it is to be expected that it should cover only a relatively limited

---

[41] *Aminoil* v. *Kuwait*, Final Award, 24 March 1982, Section V, Question A.

> *(cont.)*
>
> period. In the present case however, the existence of such a stipulation would have to be presumed as being covered by the general language of the stabilisation clauses, and over the whole period of an especially long concession since it extended to 60 years. A limitation on the sovereign rights of the State is all the less to be presumed where the concessionaire is in any event in possession of important guarantees regarding its essential interests in the shape of a legal right to eventual compensation.
>
> 96. Such is the case here, – for if the Tribunal thus holds that it cannot interpret Articles 17 and 7(g) – revised 11 – as absolutely forbidding nationalisation, it is nevertheless the fact that these provisions are far from having lost all their value and efficacity on that account since, by impliedly requiring that nationalisation shall not have any confiscatory character, they reinforce the necessity for a proper indemnification as a condition of it.

Umbrella Clauses   In conjunction with this endeavour to stabilise the contract, umbrella clauses found in international investment treaties provide for additional security to the investor. They have been part of investment treaties since the existence of the first BIT, concluded between Germany and Pakistan in 1959.[42] They take the form of catch-all statements to protect the commitments made at the time of the signing of the agreement. A number of arbitral cases have provided diametrically opposed conclusions on the relevance of these clauses one finds in about 40 per cent of the treaties.

SGS v. *Pakistan* and *SGS* v. *Philippines*

Two cases are of particular importance in this regard: *SGS* v. *Pakistan* and *SGS* v. *Philippines*.[43] They both originate in a breach of contract. In *SGS* v. *Pakistan*, the company argued that the umbrella clause present in Article 11 of the BIT between Pakistan and Switzerland had the effect of 'elevating a simple breach of contract claim to a treaty claim under international law'.[44] The whole debate is indeed positioned on this very argument: a contractual breach becomes a treaty claim under international law through the intervention of an umbrella clause. In the Pakistani case, the tribunal decided in favour of the State, in that it argued that the legal consequences attributed to the umbrella clause were 'far-reaching in scope, and so automatic and unqualified and sweeping in their operation, so

---

[42] Germany–Pakistan BIT of 1959, available at https://investmentpolicy.unctad.org/international-investment-agreements/treaties/bilateral-investment-treaties/1732/germany—pakistan-bit-1959- (accessed 21 December 2020).

[43] *SGS Société Générale de Surveillance S.A.* v. *Islamic Republic of Pakistan*, ICSID Case No. ARB/01/13, available at www.italaw.com/cases/1009; *SGS Société Générale de Surveillance S.A.* v. *Republic of the Philippines*, ICSID Case No. ARB/02/6, available at www.italaw.com/cases/documents/1019 (both accessed 21 December 2020).

[44] *SGS Société Générale de Surveillance S.A.* v. *Islamic Republic of Pakistan*, ICSID Case No. ARB/01/13, Decision of the Tribunal on the Objection to Jurisdiction, para. 98.

burdensome in their potential impact upon a Contracting Party'.[45] However, in the second case, *SGS* v. *Philippines*, the Tribunal concluded just the opposite, in considering that a breach of the contract was a breach of the BIT.[46]

SGS *v.* Philippines

117. Whether collateral guarantees, warranties or letters of comfort given by a host State to induce the entry of foreign investments are binding or not, i.e. whether they constitute genuine obligations or mere advertisements, will be a matter for determination under the applicable law, normally the law of the host State. But if commitments made by the State towards specific investments do involve binding obligations or commitments under the applicable law, it seems entirely consistent with the object and purpose of the BIT to hold that they are incorporated and brought within the framework of the BIT by Article X(2) [the umbrella clause].

This naturally raises the question of the competence of international arbitral tribunals to adjudicate contractual claims, an issue that has been intensely debated and not yet answered (see Chapter 14).[47]

In recent times, however, treaty-making practice has seen a clear decline in umbrella clauses. A number of countries, such as Canada, or regional groupings, like ASEAN, have decided to exclude umbrella clauses from their contemporary treaty negotiation practice. But the practice has not yet disappeared, as acknowledged, for example, by the EU–Singapore FTA, which lists a number of negative requirements to understand and implement the umbrella clause.[48]

EU–Singapore FTA

Where a Party, itself or through any entity mentioned in paragraph 5 of Article 9.1 (Definitions), had given a specific and clearly spelt out commitment in a contractual written obligation towards a covered investor of the other Party with respect to the covered

---

[45] *SGS Société Générale de Surveillance S.A.* v. *Islamic Republic of Pakistan*, ICSID Case No. ARB/01/13, Decision of the Tribunal on the Objection to Jurisdiction, para. 167.

[46] *SSG Société Générale de Surveillance S.A.* v. *Republic of the Philippines*, ICSID Case No. ARB/02/6, para. 117.

[47] Olga Boltenko, 'The Umbrella Revolution: State Contracts and Umbrella Clauses in Contemporary Investment Law', in Chaisse et al., *Handbook of International Investment Law and Policy* (Singapore: Springer, in press). For a synthetic account of umbrella clauses jurisprudence and recent discussions, see Andrés Rigo Sureda, 'The Umbrella Clause', in M. Kinnear et al. (eds.), *Building International Investment Law: The First Fifty Years of ICSID* (Alphen aan den Rijn: Wolters Kluwer, 2016), pp. 375–87.

[48] See the EU–Singapore FTA, ch. 9, Art. 9.4, available at https://ec.europa.eu/trade/policy/in-focus/eu-singapore-agreement/index_en.htm (accessed 21 December 2020).

> ***(cont.)***
>
> investor's investment or towards such covered investment. That Party shall not frustrate or undermine the said commitment through the exercise of its governmental authority either:
>
> (a) Deliberately; or
> (b) In a way which substantially alters the balance of rights and obligations in the contractual written obligations unless the Party provides reasonable compensation to restore the covered investor or investment to a position which it would have been in had the frustration or undermining not occurred.

An interesting way to interpret these umbrella clauses and limit their reach had been put forward by M. Sornarajah, in his Expert Opinion in the case *El Paso* v. *Argentina*.[49]

> ### El Paso *v.* Argentina, *M. Sornarajah Expert Opinion*
>
> 12. Being domestic contracts, contracts of foreign investment create obligations only in domestic law. It is without doubt that, through the use of appropriate language, the rights so created can be lifted up and subjected to an international regime of protection. But, the extent of those rights must depend on domestic law ... they can be protected only to the extent that they exist in domestic law.

Replacing State contracts in a national law context is indeed a good way to limit their internationalisation and the potentially problematic consequences of the same for the State.

Stabilisation and umbrella clauses, analysed as attempts to internationalise the State contract, provide a perfect transition to the third law of FDI: international law.

12.2.3 International Law

12.2.3.1 State Responsibility

The issue of State responsibility for breaches of its international obligations is absolutely fundamental in general public international law. As rightly formulated by James Crawford, the law of international responsibility is 'surpassed by none and paralleled only by the law of treaties'.[50] This principle arises from the doctrine of State sovereignty and equality. It also finds

---

[49] Legal Opinion of M. Sornarajah in *El Paso* v. *Argentina*, ICSID Case No. ARB/03/15, 5 March 2007, para. 12.

[50] James Crawford, *The International Law Commission's Articles on State Responsibility* (Cambridge University Press, 2002); P.-M. Dupuy (ed.), *Obligations multilatérales, droit impératif et responsabilité internationale des états* (Paris: Pedone, 2003); James Crawford, Alain Pellet and Simon Olleson, *The Law of International Responsibility* (Oxford University Press, 2010); René Provost and Robert McCorquodale (eds.), *State Responsibility in International Law* (London: Routledge, 2002).

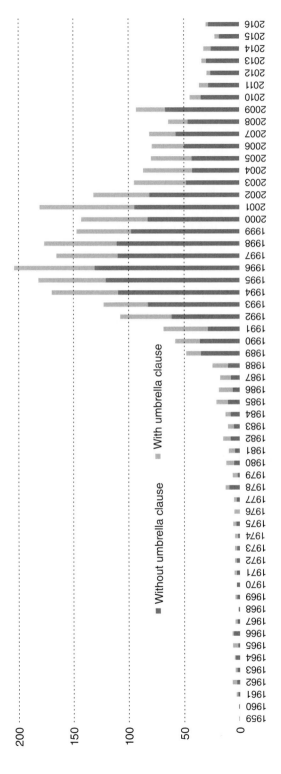

Figure 12.2 Evolution of BITs with umbrella clause signed between 1959 and 2016. Source: UNCTAD Investment Policy Hub, available at https://investmentpolicyhub.unctad.org/Pages/mapping-of-iia-clauses

its roots in the very conflicting nature of international society. In simple terms, it provides for the reparation of an unlawful act of one State against another. A breach of a substantial rule of international law has to be proven – so much so that questions of hierarchy of rules of conflict arise naturally. General treaty law and interpretation hence play a central role (see Introduction).

CHORZÓW FACTORY

Since the *Chorzów Factory* case, an investment dispute adjudicated by the PCIJ (see Chapters 13 and 14), we know that the essential characteristics of State responsibility lie in the following elements:

- the existence of an international legal obligation in force between two States;
- an act of violation of this legal obligation imputable to one of these two States;
- a loss or damage resulting from this breach of international law;
- a duty to repair the loss or damage caused by each breach of an international obligation.

According to the Court:[51]

Chorzów Factory

125. The essential principle contained in the actual notion of an illegal act is that reparation must, so far as possible, wipe out all the consequences of the illegal act and re-establish the situation which would, in all probability, have existed if that act had not been committed. Restitution in kind, or, if this is not possible, payment of a sum corresponding to the value which a restitution in kind would bear; the award, if need be, of damages for loss sustained which would not be covered by restitution in kind or payment in place of it – such are the principles which should serve to determine the amount of compensation due for an act contrary to international law.

However, who can be identified as a State, and how? The seminal issues of fault, attribution or even invocation of State responsibility have long been debated and have been partly clarified by the International Law Commission in its Articles on Responsibility of States for Internationally Wrongful Acts adopted on 20 August 2001. They will be addressed more directly in Chapter 14, as investment case law has indeed shed some light on the matter, while complicating it too. As a matter of fact, in the landmark *Barcelona Traction* case (Box 12.6 below), the ICJ referred to the obligations towards the international community as a whole and not only vis-à-vis a given State.[52] However, one easily understands the

---

[51] *Factory at Chorzów (Germany v. Poland), 1928, PCIJ, Series A, No. 17.*

[52] Two other cases settled by the ICJ and directly related to IIL deserve particular attention: ELSI and Diallo. They will be addressed in greater detail in Chapter 14. See *Elettronica Sicula S.p.A. (ELSI) (United States of America v. Italy)*, Judgment of 20 July 1989, available at www.icj-cij.org/en/case/76; *Ahmadou Sadio Diallo (Republic of Guinea v. Democratic Republic of the Congo)*, Judgment of 30 November 2010, available at www.icj-cij.org/en/case/103 (both accessed 21 December 2020).

consequences that State responsibility theory can produce in IIL. The treaties to which the home and host States are parties have to be honoured according to the general principle of *pacta sunt servanda*. A breach of these treaties (a BIT, for example) can result in the invocation of State responsibility and, as explained above, the need for the respondent to repair its wrongful act (these issues will be covered at length in Chapter 14). As alluded to above, the concept of international responsibility, although still widely debated, if not controversial, has been somehow clarified by the ILC's Articles on Responsibility of States for Internationally Wrongful Acts, 2001.[53] However interesting, timely and vastly commented on by eminent scholars, the work of the Commission remained limited:

ILC, Articles on Responsibility of States for Internationally Wrongful Acts, 2001

General Commentary

(1) These articles seek to formulate, by way of codification and progressive development, the basic rules of international law concerning the responsibility of States for their internationally wrongful acts. The emphasis is on the secondary rules of State responsibility: that is to say, the general conditions under international law for the State to be considered responsible for wrongful actions or omissions, and the legal consequences which flow therefrom. The articles do not attempt to define the content of the international obligations, the breach of which gives rise to responsibility. This is the function of the primary rules, whose codification would involve restating most of substantive customary and conventional international law.

Box 12.5 The *Maria Luz* incident: State responsibility and civilisation

There are many ways to narrate and read the 'incident' that brought Japan and Peru into opposition, after a 370-tonne barque, the *Maria Luz*, which had set out from Macao, was stopped on its way to Peru by a severe storm, unexpectedly ending its journey, in June 1872, in the port of Yokohama. It was not long before one of the 231 listed 'Chinese passengers' threw himself overboard and managed to swim his way to the closest ship in the harbour, a British vessel, named the *Iron Duke*. After a series of questions and investigations, which took the unfortunate Chinese man from the British consulate to the Japanese government, his adventure ended back on the *Maria Luz*, where he was returned after assurances from its captain, Ricardo Hereira, that he would

---

[53] Available at http://legal.un.org/ilc/texts/instruments/english/commentaries/9_6_2001.pdf (accessed 21 December 2020).

Box 12.5 (cont.)

not be ill-treated. Sufficient time had elapsed, however, to gather evidence that the boat was not transporting Chinese passengers, but rather performing 'coolie trade', for these forced labourers were bound to take part in various business exploitations in Peru. Once a second individual escaped the ship, a few days later, the British consul, R. G. Watson, decided to inspect the *Maria Luz* and lodge a detailed complaint to the Japanese minister of foreign affairs, Soejima Taneomi. At the time, Meiji Japan (1868–1912) was embarking on an impressive reform through modernisation of its political and legal system, and the British consul played the card of 'civilisation against barbaric practices'. Modern law – that is, a reaction to an oppressive feudal regime incarnated by a despotic sovereign in the direction of secularism, abstraction, generalisation and professionalisation – had to prevail over the past. But Meiji Japan was also infamously subjected to the 'unequal treaties' (see Box 11.4), imposing extraterritorial obligations to civilise oriental laws and disputes to the benefit of Western powers. Who was the civilised and who the civiliser? In the mid-eighteenth century, indeed, most European colonisers were still struggling with the universal ban on slavery. While the Indian Emperor Ashoka had abolished the slave trade in the third century BCE, and the Qin dynasty (221–206 BCE) had done the same in China, European nation States were literally battling to impose a ban since, in 1315, Louis X of France published a first decree abolishing slavery and proclaiming that 'France signifies freedom', so that any slave entering French territory could be freed. In the mid-nineteenth century, most colonial powers, however, entertained some forms of slavery in their overseas possessions, despite domestic legislation such as the British Slavery Abolition Act of 1833.

Luckily for the Chinese coolies, there was no 'unequal treaty' with Peru, so the British were happy to encourage a judicial solution and the trial of the captain of the *Maria Luz*. In the course of the investigation and procedure, Chinese coolies were invited to testify and expose how they had been kidnapped and made to sign 'labour' contracts of which they could not understand the substance. A second trial was later organised for Hereira to prove, with the assistance of a British lawyer well-versed in Japanese classical studies, a Mr Dickens, that the Chinese coolies were legally obliged to embark to Peru to perform their contractual obligations. The irregularity of the labour contracts, but also the abject nature of the trade, led the Japanese judge to found in favour of the coolies in denouncing slavery in these terms:

> . . . a state . . . which is so repugnant to all sense of natural justice that it has ever been held that it can exist or be recognized only by force of express laws, and which there is no obligation on the part of a sovereign state either in the law or comity of nations to in any manner assist or countenance.

To the great displeasure of a large majority of Western powers supporting Peru, the international responsibility of Japan was hence protected. How could it have violated the law of nations in reaction to such a 'repugnant' situation? Naturally, Peru was of

Box 12.5 (cont.)

another opinion and claimed payment of damages subsequent to the second trial. Japan only agreed to submit the case to the arbitrage of Alexander II of Russia, the very tsar who had emancipated the serfs a decade before. In 1875, Alexander II upheld the Japanese judgment in favour of the liberation of the Chinese coolies, who were all taken back to China except for a thirteen-year-old girl, bought by the *Maria Luz* captain for his own convenience, a rather sad ending for a case that later also influenced Japanese legislation on the sale of people, and prostitutes in particular.

To Go Further

Basset Moore, J. (ed.), *History and Digest of the International Arbitrations to which the United States has been a Party*, 6 vols. (Washington, DC: Government Printing Office, 1898), vol. 5, pp. 5035–6 (for the text of Alexander II's decision), available in Spanish at https://babel .hathitrust.org/cgi/pt?id=uc1.$c184892;view=1up;seq=7 (accessed 21 December 2020).

Botsman, D. V., 'Freedom without Slavery? "Coolies", Prostitutes, and Outcastes in Meiji Japan's "Emancipation Moment"', *American Historical Review* (2011), 116(5), pp. 1323–47, available at https://academic.oup.com/ahr/article/116/5/1323/10956 (accessed 21 December 2020).

Burns, S. L. and Brooks, B. J., *Gender and Law in the Japanese Imperium* (University of Hawaii Press, 2014).

12.2.3.2 Diplomatic Protection

In the context of State responsibility, another key notion has played a fundamental role in international investment law and dispute settlement – that of diplomatic protection. It rests upon the idea of nationality, a link between an individual and the State able to offer 'protection' – that is, a series of benefits and obligations in domestic and international law (on the issue of nationality, see Chapter 13). The International Law Commission adopted the Draft Articles on Diplomatic Protection in 2006.[54] According to the Commission, diplomatic protection could be defined according to the following terms:

Draft Articles on Diplomatic Protection, 2006

Article 1: Definition and Scope

For the purposes of the present draft articles, diplomatic protection consists of the invocation by a State, through diplomatic action or other means of peaceful settlement,

---

[54] Draft Articles on Diplomatic Protection, available at http://legal.un.org/ilc/texts/instruments/english/draft_articles/ 9_8_2006.pdf (accessed 21 December 2020).

(cont.)

of the responsibility of another State for an injury caused by an internationally wrongful act of that State to a natural or legal person that is a national of the former State with a view to the implementation of such responsibility.[...]

Article 3: Protection by the State of Nationality

1. The State entitled to exercise diplomatic protection is the State of nationality.
2. Notwithstanding paragraph 1, diplomatic protection may be exercised by a State in respect of a person that is not its national in accordance with draft article 8.

The problem is naturally more complicated for juridical persons, and the question of corporations is often posed in IIL. Here, the ILC argues:

Draft Articles on Diplomatic Protection, 2006

Article 9: State of Nationality of a Corporation

For the purposes of the diplomatic protection of a corporation, the State of nationality means the State under whose law the corporation was incorporated. However, when the corporation is controlled by nationals of another State or States and has no substantial business activities in the State of incorporation, and the seat of management and the financial control of the corporation are both located in another State, that State shall be regarded as the State of nationality.

If a State is under a duty to protect its nationals, taking up the claims of its subjects ('prendre fait et cause') against other States is not so easy, either technically or diplomatically. The issue of nationality has first to be resolved. Then come a number of problematic considerations in terms of the political and economic impact that such a decision may have in the conduct of the sovereign's international relations, as is demonstrated in the *Mavrommatis Palestine Concession* case.[55]

Mavrommatis Palestine Concession

By taking up the case of one of its subjects and by resorting to diplomatic action or international judicial proceedings on his behalf, a State is in reality asserting its own rights, its right to ensure, in the person of its subjects, respect for the rules of international law.

---

[55] PCIJ, *Mavrommatis Palestine Concessions Case*, Judgment, 30 August 1924, available at www.icj-cij.org/public/ files/permanent-court-of-international-justice/serie_A/A_02/06_Mavrommatis_en_Palestine_Arret.pdf (accessed 21 December 2020).

It is easy, then, to understand why States have been rather reluctant to exercise diplomatic protection in the context of investment disputes and the consequent birth of a hybrid ISDS, better suited to the needs of a very peculiar situation, that of a dispute between a State and a private party, but on the basis of a treaty between two States (see Chapter 14).

Box 12.6 *Barcelona Traction*

The *Barcelona Traction, Light and Power Company (Belgium* v. *Spain)* is probably still the most famous case in IIL.[56] Its realm and repercussions have been immense and still influence conceptual approaches, interpretation and contemporary case law. From admissibility, capacity of applicant government and claims brought on behalf of shareholders in foreign limited liability companies, to the nature of corporate entities and, of course, diplomatic protection, the issues at stake were of crucial importance and largely debated until now. At the time, an alternative hybrid ISDS method was not yet in existence, the ICJ appeared to be the only, albeit problematic, recourse to peacefully solving investment disputes. In this regard, the *Barcelona Traction* case, which was adjudicated by an impressive bench of remarkable international lawyers (notably, Judges Gerald Fitzmaurice, Tanaka and Jessup), remains a landmark decision, highlighting the inherent limitations of the system.

In 1958, Belgium filed an application with the ICJ against Spain, seeking reparation for the damages allegedly caused to the *Barcelona Traction, Light and Power Company* by organs of the Spanish State, in contradiction to international law. The case was later removed (April 1961) from the list of the Court, Belgium having given a notice of discontinuance, in the hope of an out-of-court settlement. The case was reintroduced in June 1962, however, in response to which Spain raised four preliminary objections. The third and fourth objections (joined by the Court to the merits of the case) were of particular interest: the Belgian government lacks any *jus standi* to make a claim or intervene on behalf of Belgian interests in a Canadian company; even if there is *jus standi*, the claim remains inadmissible as local remedies were not exhausted. The ICJ rendered its judgment on 5 February 1970.

Interestingly, the *Barcelona Traction Company* had been incorporated as a holding company in 1911, in Canada, where it had its head office. However, for the purpose of creating and operating an electric power and distribution system in Catalonia (Spain),

---

[56] *Barcelona Traction, Light and Power Company, Limited (Belgium* v. *Spain)*, Judgment of 5 February 1970, *ICJ Reports 1970*, and the Separate Opinions (including of Judge Jessup), available at www.icj-cij.org/en/case/50/judgments (accessed 21 December 2020).

Box 12.6 (cont.)

it formed a number of operating, finance and concession holding companies, some incorporated in Spain, others in Canada. To complicate an already rather complex situation, the shareholders of the company soon became Belgian in majority and the bonds it issued were mostly in sterling. The Spanish Civil War had a considerable impact on its operations and the servicing of the bonds. The company was later declared bankrupt, to the great displeasure of the foreign shareholders, whose countries tried to intervene diplomatically to convince the Spanish government to find a suitable solution.

By way of conclusion to highly complex discussions involving international and comparative law, as well as company law, the ICJ rejected the Belgian claim by fifteen votes to one, twelve votes of the majority being based on the idea that Belgium had no standing to exercise diplomatic protection of the shareholders in a Canadian company in respect of measures taken against this company in Spain. In doing so, it refuted the theory of diplomatic protection of shareholders, since this would open too large a door to many competing claims on the part of various States: 'The danger would be inasmuch as the shares of companies whose activity is international are widely scattered and frequently change hands' (para. 96). The Court therefore agreed that the Company's national State (Canada) was better able to act and that Belgium had no *jus standi* 'by considerations of equity'. The Separate Opinions of the different judges present, although coming to the same conclusion, are absolutely fascinating, for they show the intensity and depth of the discussions and the many different routes by which a similar conclusion can be reached. Justice Jessup, for instance, argued: 'in adjudicating upon the *Barcelona Traction* case, the Court must apply rules from one of the most controversial branches of international law. The subject of the responsibility of States for injuries to aliens (otherwise referred to as the diplomatic protection of nationals), evokes in many current writing recollections of political abuses in past eras' (in reference to gunboat diplomacy). At a time of decolonisation and progressive shaping of a New International Economic Order competing with the rise of new multinational corporations, the question was even more legitimate. But it is striking to see how accurate this remark remains today.

To Go Further

Charpentier, J., 'L'arrêt de la Cour Internationale de Justice dans l'affaire de la Barcelona Traction, Light and Power Company, Limited (nouvelle requête) (Belgique c. Espagne): Exceptions préliminaires, arrêt du 24 juillet 1964', *Annuaire Français de Droit International* (1964), 10, pp. 327–52.

Lillich, R. B., 'Two Perspectives on the Barcelona Traction Case', *American Journal of International Law* (1971), 65(3), pp. 522–32.

12.3 The International Law of Foreign Investment

Firmly resting upon general public international law principles, international investment law naturally finds its sources in Article 38 of the Statute of the International Court of Justice. While customary international law remains controversial, IIAs have massively expanded from the end of the decolonisation period. They provide a vast network of binding obligations for States with a direct impact on non-State actors and investors in particular. However, the lack of a universal instrument, as well as the very nature of these agreements between States, limit the ability of this legal international regime to truly respond to today's challenges.

12.3.1 Sources of International Investment Law

According to Article 38 of the Statute of the ICJ, the sources of international law (see Introduction), and so international investment law, are as follows:

- international conventions
- customary international law
- general principle of law
- secondary sources, such as judicial decisions and scholarly works.

The relationship of IIL to customary international law has been particularly scrutinised. Is there a hierarchy between the sources of law? If so, which source prevails over the others? The reference to custom is indeed quite systematic in IIAs, which can create a number of ambiguities. The formation and identification of rules of customary international law in IIL requires first a definition of 'custom', which is said to exist on the basis of two constitutive elements: a 'general practice' that is accepted by law and the belief that this practice is required by law (*opinio juris sive necessitatis*).[57] Of course, these two elements have been widely debated, if not contested, by the doctrine, and a vast number of investor–State arbitration tribunals have engaged in this discussion (see Chapter 14).[58] In any case, the principles regarding the formation of customary rules investment arbitration are not fundamentally different from those applicable in general international law, a conclusion that, once more, supports the strong inscription of international investment as a discipline of public international law.

---

[57] International Law Commission, 'Identification of Customary International Law', Topic 1.13 in *Analytical Guide to the Work of the International Law Commission*, available at http://legal.un.org/ilc/guide/1_13.shtml (accessed 21 December 2020).

[58] For a precise account of the formation and identification of custom in IIL, see Patrick Dumberry, *The Formation and Identification of Rules of Customary International Law in International Investment Law* (Cambridge University Press, 2016).

Box 12.7 *Jus cogens*

Is there a hierarchy of sources of law in international (investment) law as in the domestic legal order? In the absence of a Constitution, and with the proliferation of international regulations, as well as courts and tribunals, the answer is far from simple. While it is generally acknowledged that judicial decisions and writings, as well a general principle of law, have a subordinate function, as stated in Article 38 of the Statute of the ICJ, the prioritisation between treaty and custom is less evident and even more complex for *jus cogens*. It is agreed that *lex specialis derogat legi generali*: specialised law prevails over a general rule. So much so that IIL could prevail over general international law. In addition, *lex posterior derogat legi priori*: a later law repeals an earlier one. But what about *jus cogens*? Some of these obligations are *erga omnes*, such as the prohibition of genocide, slavery and torture. The same obligations are also put forward to illustrate the idea of *jus cogens* as a 'peremptory norm of general international law' (VCLT, Article 53). Therefore, one has to identify, in a two-step fashion, the existence of a rule of general international law and then its peremptory nature. Yet the issue of universality arises. What is generally accepted by all globally? And what is generally accepted by all globally in the context of *lex specialis* and IIL in particular? When could an investment treaty contradicting *jus cogens* be considered void *ab initio*? Contemporary international law does not offer a clear set of rules able to clarify these interrogations, and neither does international investment case law. What if peremptory norms – in a counterintuitive way – could also be limiting or de facto serve as an excuse to justify the impossibility for the State to take certain decisions on the basis of an 'essential interest' and indeed a 'necessity'? This argument has been elaborated in investment law in the context of the Argentine economic crisis of the 1990s and the decisions taken by the State on the ground of what it later argued as 'necessity'. Such a highly complex debate would first and foremost require the definition of peremptory norms, a task investment law arbitrators do not dare to perform. *Jus cogens* has been regularly invoked in investment disputes by investors (*Methanex* v. *USA*; *Biloune* v. *Ghana*; *Roussalis* v. *Romania*, for example) and by the State (*Aminoil*; *Texaco*; and several Argentine cases), but never directly addressed or clarified. The ICJ itself remained rather ambiguous, despite a number of landmark decisions addressing the issue of definition, including the infamous *Barcelona Traction* case (ban of acts of aggression, genocide, slavery and racial discrimination), which directly related to IIL. One would tend to believe, however, that the dilemma of States between necessity and peremptory norms could only occur with rather controversial norms, for which *jus cogens* nature has not been clearly established, as in the case of the protection of the environment, the still debated economic sovereignty over natural resources or, possibly, State security. Eventually, the very nature of *jus cogens*, as a sort of legacy of *jus naturalis* and at the cutting edge

Box 12.7 (cont.)

of the protection of individual rights, including against the State, remains highly controversial, if not contested.

To Go Further

Biloune and Marine Drive Complex Ltd *v.* Ghana Investments Centre and the Government of Ghana, UNCITRAL, Award on Jurisdiction and Liability, 27 October 1989.

Government of Kuwait *v.* American Independent Oil Co (Kuwait *v.* Aminoil), Ad Hoc Arbitral Tribunal, 24 March 1982.

Methanex v. *USA*, UNCITRAL (NAFTA), Final Award of the Tribunal on Jurisdiction and Merits, 3 August 2005.

Spyridon Roussalis *v.* Romania, ICSID, Award, Case No. ARB/06/1, 7 December 2011.

Texaco Overseas Petroleum Company and California Asiatic Oil Company *v.* Government of the Libyan Arab Republic, International Arbitral Tribunal, Award on Merits, 19 January 1977.

Vadi, V., 'Jus Cogens in International Investment Law and Arbitration', in M. den Heijer and H. van der Wilt (eds.), *Netherlands Yearbook of International Law 2015: Jus Cogens: Quo Vadis?* (The Hague: Asser Press, 2016), pp. 357–88.

Viñuales, J. E., 'State of Necessity and Peremptory Norms in International Investment Law', *Law and Business Review of the Americas* (2008), 14(1), pp. 79–103, available at https://ssrn .com/abstract=1653467 (accessed 21 December 2020).

From the sources of IIL explored above, one can identify a series of natural international regulatory efforts, in the absence of a true universal treaty and thus codification (see Chapter 11). Beyond the first international efforts that materialised with the never adopted 1948 Havana Charter and the NIEO initiatives, BITs soon appeared as a novel pragmatic instrument.

12.3.2 Bilateral Investment Treaties

The first BIT was adopted in 1959 between Germany and Pakistan.[59] Although simple, it set the tone for generations to come and (at the time of writing) 2,946 signed and 2,362 BITs in force.[60] Its structure has somehow been largely followed and consists of the following elements:

- preamble
- definitions
- scope

---

[59] See https://investmentpolicy.unctad.org/international-investment-agreements/treaties/bilateral-investment-treaties/ 1732/germany---pakistan-bit-1959- (accessed 21 December 2020).

[60] See UNCTAD statistics, available at http://investmentpolicyhub.unctad.org/IIA (accessed 21 December 2020).

- market access and non-discrimination
- standards of protection
- dispute settlement
- final provisions in relation to ratification, withdrawal, revision.

Its preamble, once again very simple, was also straightforward.

Germany–Pakistan BIT, 1959, Preamble

THE FEDERAL REPUBLIC OF GERMANY and PAKISTAN,
DESIRING to intensify economic co-operation between the two States,
INTENDING to create favourable conditions for investments by nationals and companies of either State in the territory of the other State, and
RECOGNIZING that an understanding reached between the two States is likely to promote investment, encourage private industrial and financial enterprise and to increase the prosperity of both the States,
HAVE AGREED AS FOLLOWS . . .

With the complication of international relations, the rise of new actors and the need to balance protection for investors and the State's interest and right to regulate, BITs have naturally evolved, so that we generally identify several generations: the initial, postcolonial one, the liberal 1990s attempts, and the post-liberal models with a form of rebalancing between duties and rights, promotion, protection and national interests.

China provides another good example of generations of BITs. One generally identifies three moments, if not three generations of IIAs. The initial phase started with China's first BIT with Sweden, in 1982, and lasted until the late 1990s.[61] It was largely characterised by a prudent, if not reluctant, approach to normative internationalisation, with national treatment seldom granted and international dispute settlement limited to the determination of the amount of compensation for expropriation. From 1998, with the China–Barbados BIT of July 1998, which offered foreign investors unrestricted access to international arbitration for the first time, China entered into a new phase of BIT drafting, inspired by EU model treaties and framing NT in a less restrictive and somehow personalised manner, depending on whether the country was a developed or developing nation. The last phase, starting from 2007 and the China–Korea BIT, is generally described as a more liberal one, partly inspired by NAFTA in the sense that Chinese treaties granted fair and equitable treatment in de facto accepting certain customary international law features, but also the national treatment and MFN treatment often defined by using the now generalised yet difficult to interpret 'in like

---

[61] Agreement on the Mutual Protection of Investments between the Government of the People's Republic of China and the Government of the Kingdom of Sweden, 29 March 1982.

circumstances' terminology (see Chapters 13 and 14).[62] To these three generations, one could add a fourth, corresponding to today's mega-regional trade and investment negotiations and China's expansion as a global investor. As we will see below, this fourth generation may well be characterised – and this is not China-specific – by a certain distancing from the late 1990s NAFTA model in relation to today's new investment issues. In addition, it integrates the lessons learned from China's accession to and participation in the WTO.[63] Lastly, the recent wave of FTA drafting does not seem to add much to China's general BIT approach – contrary to some theses often put forward, according to which a regional negotiation's aim is to further liberalise trade by introducing greater protection and flexibilities.[64]

To use another recent example, the Preamble of the 2016 Morocco–Nigeria BIT, although short and rather simple, is revealing of the spirit of our time.[65]

Morocco–Nigeria BIT, 2016, Preamble

The Government of the Kingdom of Morocco; and the Government of the Federal Republic of Nigeria hereinafter referred to as the 'Parties'

DESIRING to strengthen the bonds of friendship and cooperation between the State Parties;

RECOGNIZING the important contribution investment can make to the sustainable development of the state parties, including the reduction of poverty, increase of productive capacity, economic growth, the transfer of technology, and the furtherance of human rights and human development;

SEEKING to promote, encourage and increase investment opportunities that enhance sustainable development within the territories of the state parties;

UNDERSTANDING that sustainable development requires the fulfilment of the economic, social and environmental pillars that are embedded within the concept;

REAFFIRMING the right of the State Parties to regulate and to introduce new measures relating to investments in their territories in order to meet objectives and taking into

---

[62] On China's investment treaties evolution, see, for example, the recent research of Kate Hadley, 'Do China's BITs Matter? Assessing the Effect of China's Investment Agreements on Foreign Investment Flows, Investors' Rights, and the Rule of Law', *Georgetown Journal of International Law* (2013), 45, pp. 255–321; Axel Berger, 'Investment Rules in Chinese Preferential Trade and Investment Agreements', Discussion Paper 7/2013 (German Development Institute, 2013).

[63] On the accession to and participation of China in the WTO, including dispute settlement, see Leïla Choukroune (ed.), *China's WTO Decade, China Perspectives* (special issue, 2012), 1, available at www.cefc.com.hk/issue/china-perspectives-2012-1/ (accessed 21 December 2020).

[64] Hadley, 'Do China's BITs Matter?'; Berger, 'Investment Rules in Chinese Preferential Trade and Investment Agreements'.

[65] See the 2016 Morocco–Nigeria BIT, available at http://investmentpolicyhub.unctad.org/Download/TreatyFile/5409 (accessed 21 December 2020).

> ***(cont.)***
>
> account any asymmetries with respect to the measures in place, the particular need of developing countries to exercise this right;
>
> SEEKING an overall balance of the rights and obligations among the State Parties, the investors, and the investments under this Agreement;
>
> Have agreed as follows ...

Economic growth is coupled with the reduction of poverty and, interestingly, the 'furtherance of human rights and human development', as well as sustainable development. In addition, the 'right of the State to regulate' is also highlighted. This South–South agreement hence offers a rather different perspective to the North–South agreements of the 1990s, which were generally very protective of the investor/investment and quite unbalanced in terms of rights and obligations. The evolutive nature of the BITs scene is not a surprise. It reflects the change in nature of international relations, the constantly renewed power balances and related State policies to adjust to their strategies and needs. The better drafting quality of recent BITs is also a reflection of the quite massive aid effort brought to developing countries by various donors and other NGOs, in order to raise their awareness of the need for legal protection and quality legislation.[66] In the 1990s indeed, a large number of BITs had been negotiated on the basis of certain State models, typically from Europe or North America, which were not necessarily tailored to the needs of their developing partners. Why have these developing countries agreed to engage in these unbalanced deals? The reasons are necessarily varied and complex (see Chapter 11), but often relate to the perception that FDI was desperately needed for development, regardless of the concessions granted to the investor.[67]

The universalisation of BITs now adopted between various countries from the Global South itself contrasts with initial efforts to protect investors from the North against the hardship of a risky investment in the developing world.

The use, necessity and effectiveness of these treaties has been widely debated. Do we need BITs to attract FDI when domestic law provides sufficient protection and some incentives? Not necessarily, as the case of Brazil, which has not ratified any BIT for many years, could demonstrate.[68] The impact of BITs on the rule of law is equally debated.

---

[66] See, in particular, the work of UNCTAD and that of the IISD, which probably pioneered investment treaty training and guidelines for the developing world. The 2012 Southern African Development Community Model Bilateral Investment Treaty Template provides a good example of this endeavour, available at www.iisd.org/sites/default/files/meterial/6th_annual_forum_sadc_model_template.pdf (accessed 21 December 2020).

[67] On the need for and efficiency of BITs, see Jonathan Bonnitcha, *Substantive Protection under Investment Treaties: A Legal and Economic Analysis* (Cambridge University Press, 2014).

[68] Bonnitcha, *Substantive Protection under Investment Treaties*, pp. 102–41.

Box 12.8 The Indian new model BIT

As a direct result of the shock produced by the *White Industries* case of 2011, in which India breached its BIT with Australia, New Delhi decided to review its investment treaties, and its Model BIT in particular. A draft Model BIT was unveiled in 2015, and after intense public scrutiny and debate, including some recommendations by the Law Commission of India, was eventually adopted, to replace the 2003 model on which most of the more than seventy Indian BITs were based. The 2015 model is at the intersection of various approaches to investment law (liberal and statist). The new model does not always provide a protective and therefore attractive environment for FDI, while it does not necessarily protect so well the interests of the State and its population either, despite some provisions on corporate social responsibility (CSR), for instance, which look rather timid compared to the daring Section 135 of the 2013 Companies Act (mandatory CSR expenditures for private companies on the basis of their net worth, turnover or profit). The 2015 Model BIT Article 12 (CSR) reads as follows:

Investors and their enterprises operating within the territory of each Party shall endeavour to voluntarily incorporate internationally recognized standards of corporate social responsibility in their practices and internal policies, such as statements of principle that have been endorsed or are supported by the Parties. These principles may address issues such as labour, the environment, human rights, community relations and anti-corruption.

This is an example of treaty negotiation and the need to reach a consensus. The non-binding language of the Model BIT provision provides an interesting correspondence, but also an apparent departure from the legalisation of CSR that is now found in Indian domestic law. From a legalisation perspective, Article 12 of the new Model BIT is rather disappointing, for it does not define any obligation, is imprecise and, of course, cannot be clearly implemented. The only element of relative satisfaction could be found in the reference to human rights, a positive move, which could be read in conjunction with other provisions related to 'non-investment concerns' that one can identify in the model and in recent Indian IIA practice more generally.

CSR is a good example. But among the other debatable provisions of the new Indian model BIT are: the stricter definition of investment, the complete exclusion of taxation, the absence of MFN provisions, and the very curiously drafted dispute settlement provisions, which require the exhaustion of local remedies before one could proceed to international arbitration, a quite challenging task in a country where the number of pending cases is infamous. These provisions have to be taken into consideration by Indian investors going global, as they will provide them with less protection than in the past.

In July 2016, India sent notices to fifty-eight countries announcing its intention to terminate or not renew its BITs, although many of these treaties include a 'sunset provision' (protection for an additional period of time, of ten or fifteen years for

Box 12.8 (cont.)

example). Since the adoption of its new model, India has engaged in a series of new negotiations and has successfully signed a series of new BITs.

To Go Further

Choukroune, L., 'Corporate Social Responsibility and Foreign Direct Investment: The Indian Treaty Approach and Beyond', in L. Choukroune and R. Donde (eds.), *International Commercial and Investment Disputes Settlement, Transnational Dispute Management* (special issue, 2018), 15(2), Addendum.

Law Commission of India, 'Analysis of the 2015 Draft Model Indian Bilateral Investment Treaty', Report 260 (August 2015), available at http://lawcommissionofindia.nic.in/reports/Report260.pdf (accessed 21 December 2020).

Ranjan, P., *India and Bilateral Investment Treaties* (Oxford University Press, 2019).
'ISDS Transparency Provisions in the New Indian Model BIT: A Half Hearted Attempt?', in L. Choukroune and R. Donde (eds.), *International Commercial and Investment Disputes Settlement, Transnational Dispute Management* (special issue, 2018), 15(2).

UNCTAD, Investment Policy Hub, India: IIAs, available at https://investmentpolicy.unctad.org/international-investment-agreements/countries/96/india (accessed 21 December 2020).

12.3.3 International Investment Agreements

Without formulating a universal treaty, a number of IIAs have been developed in the attempt to provide a more holistic approach (trade and investment) and/or specialised perspective (regional, sectoral). According to UNCTAD, today there are about 390 treaties with investment provisions (TIPs), including 319 instruments in force.[69] They have recently been growing quickly compared to the relative decrease of BITs – now a more contested instrument than in the liberalisation era of the 1990s.

Among these IIAs and TIPs, two categories can be identified:

- Regional agreements, comprising an investment chapter, often modelled on the NAFTA, which set the tone for the liberal era, and somehow renewed today by a series of mega deals, such as the CETA or the ASEAN Comprehensive Investment Agreement.
- Sectoral agreements, illustrated by the quite popular Energy Charter Treaty, signed in 1994, on which a large number of investment disputes are based, as the Charter remains the most frequently invoked agreement and is now under some form of scrutiny by a number of its parties, including the EU, which is coming forward with reform proposals.[70]

---

[69] For updates, see https://investmentpolicy.unctad.org/international-investment-agreements (accessed 21 December 2020).

[70] The Energy Charter Treaty is available at https://energycharter.org (accessed 21 December 2020). A vast body of literature has developed on the Energy Charter: for a comprehensive approach, see Kaj Hober, *Energy Charter*

> ### *EU Proposal for Modernising the Energy Charter Treaty*
>
> The EU's proposal to modernise the ECT has three main aims.
>
> Firstly, to bring the ECT's provisions on investment protection in line with those of agreements recently concluded by the EU and its Member States.
>
> Secondly, to ensure the ECT better reflects climate change and clean energy transition goals and facilitates a transition to a low-carbon, more digital and consumer-centric energy system, thus contributing to the objectives of the Paris Agreement and our decarbonisation ambition.
>
> Thirdly, to reform the ECT's investor-to-state dispute settlement mechanism in line with the EU's work in the ongoing multilateral reform process in the United Nations Commission on International Trade Law (UNCITRAL).

To these two categories, one could add that of guidelines and principles for responsible investment, as illustrated by the pioneer text of the OECD – the same organisation that had, in the late 1990s, attempted to supervise the negotiation of a universal instrument, the Multilateral Agreement on Investment, which failed under its own too liberal and Western-centric ambitions.[71]

Are investment treaties passé? One could legitimately ask this question with regard to the global scrutiny, agitation and contestation of international investment law in relation to virulently debated recent investment tribunal decisions. No matter what the future of international investment treaties, their provisions remain and provide the basis on which disputes are and will still be settled for some time, as demonstrated in detail by Chapters 13 and 14, on international investment agreements and dispute settlement.

12.4 Conclusion

Lex specialis, 'self-contained' regimes and regionalism have been advanced as many explanations of the current international law complication, while, at the same time, *jus*

Treaty (Oxford University Press, 2020); for the EU proposal on Energy Charter reform and modernisation, see https://trade.ec.europa.eu/doclib/press/index.cfm?id=2148 (accessed 21 December 2020). In December 2020, Belgium asked the European Court of Justice to give an opinion on 'the compatibility of the intra-European application of the arbitration provisions of the future modernised Energy Charter Treaty with the European Treaties'. Concerns over the compatibility of ISDS with EU law have been raised since the 2018 Achmea decision by the Court of Justice of the EU, which held that ISDS was not compatible with EU law: *Slowakische Republik (Slovak Republic) v. Achmea BV (Achmea)*, available at https://eur-lex.europa.eu/legal-content/EN/TXT/HTML/?uri=CELEX:62016CJ0284; see also M. Happold, 'Belgium Asks European Court of Justice to Opine on Compatibility of Energy Charter Treaty's Investor–State Arbitration Provisions with EU Law', *EJIL:Talk!* (blog, 8 December 2020), available at www.ejiltalk.org/belgium-asks-european-court-of-justice-to-opine-on-compatibility-of-energy-charter-treatys-investor-state-arbitration-provisions-with-eu-law/ (both accessed 21 December 2020).

[71] See the Multilateral Agreement on Investment draft of 1998, available at www.oecd.org/investment/internationalinvestmentagreements/multilateralagreementoninvestment.htm (accessed 21 December 2020).

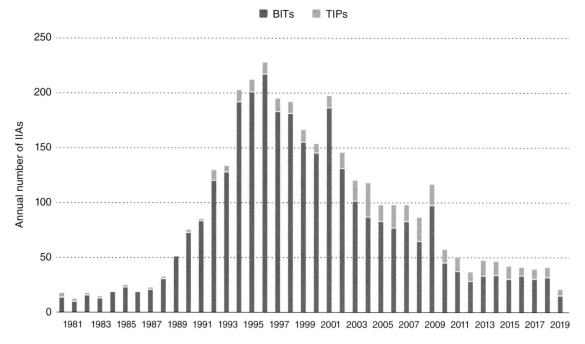

Figure 12.3 Number of IIAs signed, 1980–2019; 2,654 IIAs in force. Source: UNCTAD, IIAs Navigator.

cogens, 'systemic integration' and references to Article 31(3)(c) of the VCLT are supposed to provide drafters and judges with solutions in favour of a pluralistic and integrative vision of international law. But what if the fragmentation of international law was in fact intentional? Could it be that countries are reluctant to negotiate more binding international treaties and prefer to rely on bilateralism, contracts and de facto national law? What strikes astute observers of the evolution of IEL is the inability of States to revive the spirit of a Havana Charter, which provided, as early as 1948, for the creation of an International Trade Organization addressing not only trade liberalisation, but also the link between 'employment and economic activity', and which was already paying special attention to development issues. Kept away by the United States, the International Trade Organization never saw the light of day, and the regulation of international trade liberalisation was done in parallel, almost in isolation, to other advances granted by States.

IIL cannot be read in isolation. It has to be understood as an integral part of the three laws of investment: national, contractual and indeed international. While international law-centric and largely relying on the theory of State responsibility, the approach is also multidisciplinary.

12.5 Summary

- Do we need law for international investments?
- Law encourages or diminishes foreign investment. It provides a certain degree of stability and thus predictability, regulates transactions and serves as a tool to resolve possible investment disputes.
- There are three laws of international investment: national, contractual and international. National law is fundamentally political and so constantly evolving. It addresses the authorisation (entry and exit) and treatment of foreign investments once they have entered the territory of a sovereign State. Contractual law creates legally binding obligations for the parties (the foreign investor and a given State) on the basis of a joint negotiation. It is of a particular and precise nature. Lastly, international law is the product of agreements entered into by States. These three laws are naturally interrelated, but our approach is international law-centric and so grounded in general public international law.
- The sources of IIL are largely found in Article 38 of the Statute of the ICJ. While customary international law remains controversial, IIAs have massively expanded since the end of the decolonisation period. They provide a vast network of binding obligations for States, with a direct impact on non-State actors and investors in particular.
- However, the lack of a universal instrument, as well as the very nature of these agreements between States, limits the ability of this legal international regime to truly respond to today's challenges.

12.6 Review Questions

1 Why is it easy to forget national law when approaching investment law?
2 Why does national law matter? (Think about concrete regulatory examples impacting FDI.)
3 Why do States agree to draft investment contracts?
4 What are the most common types of (State) investment contracts?
5 What principles could be followed for fairer and more sustainable investment contacts?
6 What are the risks and opportunities of stabilisation clauses for the State and the investor?
7 What form do stabilisation clauses generally take?
8 What is an umbrella clause? Has its interpretation been clarified in international investment case law?
9 How is the theory of State responsibility influencing IIL?
10 Why can we say that IIL is a *lex specialis* of general public international law?
11 What is diplomatic protection? What role did it play in the *Barcelona Traction* case?

12 What are the sources of IIL according to Article 38 of the Statute of the ICJ?

13 What is *jus cogens*? Does it play a role in IIL?

14 Are there generations of BITs? If yes, please explain what these are.

15 What are IIAs and what differentiates them from BITs?

16 Why would a universal investment treaty be useful? Why might its negotiation be problematic?

12.7 Exercise

The Hopeland Contract Negotiation and Drafting

Hopeland is a developing country, rich in natural resources, farmland and water. Its magical landscape is home to a number of indigenous communities, whose lifestyles have been preserved from the dangers of environmental degradation and human exploitation, but who also suffer from poverty and great injustice in terms of their basic rights to life, property, language, culture and citizenship. However, these indigenous peoples do not see themselves as poor, as they believe their ancestral land provides them with the necessary means for a happy life.

Gainfame is a large State-owned enterprise (SOE) originating in Gainland, a fast-growing emerging country making major investments abroad to sustain the pace of its tremendous development and the needs of its 1.4 billion population. Gainland EXIM Bank has put in place a generous loan plan for developing and least developed countries, where it seeks to expand its influence.

In late 2019, Hopeland was approached by government officials from Gainland to negotiate a deal with Gainfame for the SOE to invest in the Nordeste farmland, an untouched territory and traditional home of the Rohis, an indigenous community often persecuted for its determination not to abide by the State's rules and its ferociously independent lifestyle. A preferential loan for the much-needed construction of a deep-water port on the developing coastal region of Hopeland was also discussed.

Hopeland and Gainland have ratified a BIT, which comprises a far-reaching umbrella clause on top of generous protection for the foreign investor/investment and some mechanisms for the international settlement of State–investor disputes. Hopeland has recently revised its domestic investment regime and adopted the Hope Invest Framework and Catalogue, which puts in place a modern and welcoming investment climate with equal rights for nationals and foreigners. It comprises a large number of incentives, including tax holidays for investors operating in least developed and indigenous areas.

The Indigenous United Front, an international NGO, has been informed of the land investment negotiations by its Hopeland Nordeste members. It is scandalised by the ambition of the proposed project to grow and harvest crops. It finds its water-intensive character and the likelihood of indigenous people's eviction absolutely contradictory to international law and is ready to support the Rohis in launching a global media campaign. Hopeland government has agreed to listen to their claims and has invited them to the negotiation table. It has reiterated its firm belief in the right to water as a human right recently inscribed in the preamble of the Hopeland Constitution. Yet it is also keen to acquire a loan from Gainland to grow its port capacity. It is hence seeking a balanced land deal.

LJCN is a reputed international law firm. It advises governments and multinational companies alike in the conclusion of sustainable and profitable investment contracts.

As counsel for LJCN, your expert team has been asked to prepare a draft investment contract between Hopeland and Gainfame to massively grow and harvest crops in the Nordeste region. Gainfame is in favour of the adoption of a PPP for the next fifty years. Hopeland is not against this idea, but insists, to satisfy the Rohis and avoid the international naming and shaming campaign planned by the Indigenous United Front, that the negotiations and the contract strictly follow the UN's *Principles for Responsible Contracts: Integrating the Management of Human Rights Risks into State–Investor Contract Negotiations – Guidance for Negotiators.* All principles will have to be implemented, with particular attention on the following:

- preparation and planning, including impact assessment studies
- stabilisation clauses
- community engagement
- grievance mechanisms
- transparency in the conduct of the negotiations and drafting of the contract.

In addition, the negotiations will be informed by the report by the UN's Special Rapporteur on the right to food on 'Large-Scale Land Acquisitions and Leases: A Set of Core Principles and Measures to Address the Human Rights Challenge'. However, time is short and the pressure of the international community perceptible.

You have one month to organise a series of negotiations and come up with a draft contract that is sustainable and beneficial to all parties involved.

FURTHER READING

Álvarez, J. E., *The Public International Law Regime Governing International Investment* (The Hague: Hague Academy of International Law, 2011).

Bonnitcha, J., *Substantive Protection under Investment Treaties: A Legal and Economic Analysis* (Cambridge University Press, 2014).

Chaisse, J., Choukroune, L. and Jusoh, S. (eds.), *Handbook of International Investment Law and Policy* (Singapore: Springer, in press).

Dumberry, P., *The Formation and Identification of Rules of Customary International Law in International Investment Law* (Cambridge University Press, 2016).

Gaillard, E. and Banifatemi, Y., 'The Long March Towards a "Jurisprudence Constante" on the Notion of Investment: Salini v. Morocco, ICSID Case No. ARB/00/4', in M. Kinnear, G. R. Fischer, J. Minguez Almeida, L. F. Torres, M. Uran Bidegain (eds.), *Building International*

Investment Law: The First Fifty Years of ICSID (Alphen aan den Rijn: Wolters Kluwer, 2016), pp. 97–125.

den Heijer, M. and van der Wilt, H. (eds.), *Netherlands Yearbook of International Law 2015: Jus Cogens: Quo Vadis?* (The Hague: Asser Press, 2016).

Hober, K., *Energy Charter Treaty* (Oxford University Press, 2020).

Shelton, D., 'Righting Wrongs: Reparation in the Articles on State Responsibility', *American Journal of International Law* (2002), 96(4), pp. 833–56.

13 International Investment Agreements: Scope, Definitions and Standards

Table of Contents

Highlights

- More than 3,000 IIAs are extremely diverse, but they also share a number of common features.
- Scope, definitions and standards of international investments are typically covered by an IIA.
- The Vienna Convention on the Law of Treaties guides treaty drafting and interpretation.
- The scope of the treaty can be limited temporally and geographically.
- The definitions of investment and investor are key concepts often addressed broadly, but also progressively framed by better treaty drafting.
- In the absence of a unified approach, these definitions have been questioned and further elaborated by a vast body of useful yet often inconsistent case law.
- Standards of treatment and protection are central elements in an IIA.
- National treatment, most favoured nation treatment, fair and equitable treatment, and full protection and security are of particular importance and interpreted at great length by investment tribunals.
- In addition to the above substantive standards, IIAs offer protection against expropriation (direct or indirect), which has also been addressed extensively in a body of case law.

13.1 Introduction

What is the best way to navigate myriad IIAs? While 3,287 agreements (2,897 BITs and 390 TIPs) – of which 2,659 were in force by mid-2020 – are certainly very diverse, they also share a number of common features.[1] Their structure, the definitions and the substantive standards of treatment and protection they encompass reveal many similarities often based on certain popular 'models' adopted at a given period of time. The NAFTA investment Chapter 11, for example, has very much inspired a generation of treaties, which have tried to emulate its rather liberal and investment-friendly traits. At the opposite end of the spectrum, more State-focused treaties are now burgeoning with new sets of provisions. Often better drafted than in the 1990s, they provide greater clarity on controversial issues such as the fair and equitable standard (FET). At a time when the number of international investment agreements terminated exceeds the number of new treaties concluded, regulatory coherence is indeed a must.[2] The structure, scope, definitions and standards of investment covered in international investment treaties have to promote and protect foreign investment, but also create the necessary margin for the State to regulate freely in favour of its own economic and developmental choices. In using the flexibilities offered for treaty drafting in the VCLT, IIAs are anchored in general public international law. Hence, States can benefit from quality international investment, together with greater regulatory protection through a more coherent framework, which is in tune with their national policies and strategies.

In addressing the issues of scope, definitions and standards, this chapter covers a number of essential aspects of contemporary international investment law and paves the way for the next chapter, which addresses the now highly debated ISDS system.

13.2 Scope and Definitions

13.2.1 Scope

13.2.1.1 Framing

Assets, shares, loans and intellectual property, but also taxes and all government entities present over the whole territory of the State parties to the treaty: what is the scope of IIAs? What do they cover beyond the broad definitions of investment and investor? Why is the scope defined, and for what purpose? Are there any limitations or possible exceptions to this scope and, if so, for what reasons?

As discussed below, the issue of definition remains a rather complex and uncertain task, largely interpreted in investment treaties jurisprudence. To narrow down the risk of

---

[1] See the UNCTAD databases for updates, available at https://investmentpolicy.unctad.org/international-investment-agreements (accessed 21 December 2020).

[2] UNCTAD, *World Investment Report 2018: Investment and New Industrial Policies* (New York and Geneva: United Nations, 2018).

interpretation and provide the parties with additional precision and possible 'legal certainty' – as much as this concept does exist – treaty drafters have introduced a number of provisions relating to the *scope of the treaty*, hence framing its application.

In fact, and in addition to the usual definitions of investment and investor, there are generally two dimensions introduced in IIAs: a *geographical* and a *temporal* scope.[3]

The geographical scope depends, first and foremost, on the number of States parties to a given treaty – for example, two countries in the case of a BIT. It will then vary according to the definition of the territory of these States and include all State entities capable of exercising government power. Article 1, para. 22 of the 2012 Canada–China BIT provides an excellent illustration:[4]

Canada–China BIT, 2012, Article 22

22. 'Territory' means:

In respect of Canada:

(a) the land territory, air space, internal waters and territorial sea over which Canada exercises sovereignty;

(b) the exclusive economic zone of Canada, as determined by its domestic law pursuant to Part V of the United Nations Convention on the Law of the Sea (UNCLOS); and

(c) the continental shelf of Canada as determined by its domestic law pursuant to Part VI UNCLOS.

In respect of China:

the territory of China, including land territory, internal waters, territorial sea, territorial air space, and any maritime areas beyond the territorial sea over which, in accordance with international law and its domestic law, China exercises sovereign rights or jurisdiction with respect to the waters, seabed and subsoil and natural resources thereof.

From shell companies practising treaty shopping to delegation of sovereign powers to local governments, the question of territorial scope and so jurisdiction is essential. It has often been addressed by arbitral Tribunals when interpreting an investment treaty.

The second precision brought by the scope of the treaty is *temporal*. It deals with the date of entry into force of the treaty for each party, but also its duration and termination and the related effects of the latter on the parties and their investment and investors. Article XIV of the 1994 US–Argentina BIT provides an example.[5]

---

[3] Jeswald W. Salacuse, *The Law of Investment Treaties* (Oxford University Press, 2015), ch. 7.

[4] Canada–China BIT 2012, available at https://investmentpolicy.unctad.org/international-investment-agreements (accessed 21 December 2020).

[5] US–Argentina BIT, 1994, available at https://investmentpolicy.unctad.org/international-investment-agreements.

US–Argentina BIT, 1994, Article XIV

1. This Treaty shall enter into force thirty days after the date of exchange of instruments of ratification. It shall remain in force for a period of ten years and shall continue in force unless terminated in accordance with paragraph 2 of this Article. It shall apply to investments existing at the time of entry into force as well as to investments made or acquired thereafter.
2. Either Party may, by giving one year's written notice to the other Party, terminate this Treaty at the end of the initial ten year period or at any time thereafter.
3. With respect to investments made or acquired prior to the date of termination of this Treaty and to which this Treaty otherwise applies, the provisions of all of the other Articles of this Treaty shall thereafter continue to be effective for a further period of ten years from such date of termination.
4. The Protocol shall form an integral part of the Treaty.

As clearly highlighted in this article, the treaty enters into force thirty days after ratification, remains in force for a period of ten years and shall continue to be in force after this period unless terminated by either Party by a written notice of one year. If such a termination is decided, the treaty will still apply to the investment 'made or acquired' prior to the date of termination for a further period of ten years from the date of termination. This last provision, described in international investment law as a 'sunset clause', is of particular interest in today's context, where an increasing number of countries are terminating their BITs. As reported by UNCTAD, in 2017, the number of effective treaty terminations (twenty-two) was higher than that of new IIA conclusions (eighteen).[6]

The issue of treaty termination is a fascinating one, often addressed in general public international law, and well-covered by the VCLT in its Part V, Section 3: Termination and Suspension of the Operation of Treaties. Article 54 of the VCLT sets the tone:

VCLT, Part V, Section 3, Article 54: Termination of or withdrawal from a treaty under its provisions or by consent of the parties

The termination of a treaty or the withdrawal of a party may take place:

(a) in conformity with the provisions of the treaty; or
(b) at any time by consent of all the parties after consultation with the other contracting States.

---

[6] 'Overview', in UNCTAD, *World Investment Report 2018*, p. 17.

A treaty can be terminated in conformity with what is planned by this very treaty and at any time if agreed after consultation by the parties.

Article 70 of the VCLT provides precise additions about the consequences of such termination:

> ## VCLT, Part V, Section 3, Article 70: Consequences of the termination of a treaty
>
> 1. Unless the treaty otherwise provides or the parties otherwise agree, the termination of a treaty under its provisions or in accordance with the present Convention:
>   (a) releases the parties from any obligation further to perform the treaty;
>   (b) does not affect any right, obligation or legal situation of the parties created through the execution of the treaty prior to its termination.
> 2. If a State denounces or withdraws from a multilateral treaty, paragraph 1 applies in the relations between that State and each of the other parties to the treaty from the date when such denunciation or withdrawal takes effect.

Paragraph (b) is of particular interest as it clarifies the issue of *retroactivity*. The rights, obligations and legal situations created before the termination of a given treaty shall not be affected by its termination.[7] Therefore, in an IIA context, the investment made prior to the termination of the treaty continues to benefit from its protection, at least for a certain period of time, as often specified in a sunset clause.

What about the investor's right to initiate an arbitration procedure as provided by the IIA? Here, again, the same reasoning applies. The ICSID case *Marco Gavazzi and Stefano Gavazzi v. Romania* has illustrated this very issue.[8] While the BIT between Italy and Romania was terminated on 14 March 2010, a notice of arbitration was formulated on 27 August 2012 and the procedure went on until the conclusion of an award on 18 April 2017.

13.2.1.2 Reservations and Exceptions

Another general public international law question is that of *reservation*, and to a larger extent, *exception* to a treaty. In both cases, the practice preserves and furthers the flexibility of treaty drafters to protect particular interests while achieving certain treaty objectives – in our context, the promotion and protection of foreign investment.

---

[7] See, generally, Olivier Dörr and Kirsten Schmalenbach (eds.), *Vienna Convention on the Law of Treaties: A Commentary* (Berlin: Springer, 2012).

[8] *Marco Gavazzi and Stefano Gavazzi v. Romania*, ICSID Case No. ARB/12/25, Award, 18 April 2017, available at www.italaw.com/sites/default/files/case-documents/italaw9506.pdf (accessed 21 December 2020).

As defined by Article 2(d) of the VCLT, a reservation is a 'unilateral statement, however phrased or named, made by a State, when signing, ratifying, accepting, approving or acceding to a treaty, whereby it purports to exclude or to modify the legal effect of certain provisions of the treaty in their application to that State. A large degree of flexibility prevails here in the *form* and *temporality* of the reservation, as long as the exclusion or modification of the 'legal effect' of certain provisions of a treaty by a given State applies to this very State. Part II, Section 2, Article 19 (Formulation of reservations) of the VCLT, however, limits the exercise to reservations, which are not prohibited or specified by the treaty; and, very importantly, reservations not 'incompatible with the object and purpose of the treaty'. One can easily imagine that this last requirement has given rise to heated scholarly debates and controversial practical situations when drafting human rights-related treaties in particular.[9] Departing from the previous consensus, according to which a reservation could only be made with the consent of all the other States involved in the process, the ICJ, in a 1951 Advisory Opinion on the Genocide Convention – to which some States had made reservation while the treaty did not allow them to – had introduced the concept of compatibility with the 'object and purpose' of a treaty. In doing so, it emphasised the need to preserve the integrity of the text.[10] This view was later accepted by the VCLT. Lastly, VCLT Article 21(a) outlines the effect of treaties reservations, another complex and not yet completely clear issue. It is accepted that a reservation 'modifies for the reserving State in its relations with that other party the provisions of the treaty to which the reservation relates to the extent of the reservation; and modifies those provisions to the same extent for that other party in its relations with the reserving State'.

Of course, the reservation does not modify the provisions of the treaty for the other parties to it. Lastly, if a State has objected to a given reservation, this provision will simply not apply between itself and the reserving State. The question of impermissible reservations and their de facto effect, however, remains largely open and very much debated.

In the context of IIAs, it is interesting to observe a sort of revival of reservations and exceptions, seen and largely encouraged as strategic tools to enhance regulatory flexibility, and so the protection of the State's autonomy to regulate in favour of certain public interests and strategic industrial policies supporting long-term development objectives. Various means are at the disposal of IIA contracting parties to introduce some regulatory flexibility, but two are of particular interest: the GATS-type provision consisting of a *positive list* of sectors open to investment, and the opposite technique, which takes the form of a *negative list* of sectors not open to investment. The negative list seems to be largely preferred by IIA drafters as it provides for certain regulatory clarity. IIA exceptions are also often inspired by the drafting of the GATT Article XX (General Exceptions). These techniques are of

---

[9] See, generally, the work of Professor Alain Pellet, Special Rapporteur on reservations to treaties, available at https://legal.un.org/ilc/guide/1_8.shtml; and International Law Commission, 'Guide to Practice on Reservations to Treaties' (2011), available at http://legal.un.org/ilc/texts/instruments/english/draft_articles/1_8_2011.pdf (accessed 21 December 2020).

[10] *Reservations to the Convention on Genocide, Advisory Opinion, ICJ Reports 1951*, p. 15.

particular interest to developing countries, which have had recourse to them, for example, through the limitation of the NT standard to suit their domestic strategic needs. To take an example, China did not grant NT in its early BITs, in order to protect its own industries. Now that Chinese investors are investing overseas, China is keen to grant NT (and so be granted it in return). However, these techniques are also potentially harmful for investment and development if not well managed administratively.[11]

These reservations/exceptions are often labelled as 'non-conforming measures', while 'carve-out clauses' refer to provisions excluding certain sectors from the scope of the treaty. Contrary to a reservation formulated by a given party to a treaty, a carve-out clause requires the consensual approval of all parties to the treaty, as it is decided that the treaty will not apply to certain sectors of the economy, such as public services, cultural industries, telecommunications or even tobacco.

In the context of the current global surge against ISDS, it is striking to observe that developed countries are now having increasing recourse to exceptions in their recently drafted IIAs. Naturally limiting the scope of the treaty, they also serve as a defence against potential claims.[12] Canada has been one of the proponents of the trend, together with countries like Australia or Japan. In the Canada–China 2012 BIT, for example, a long Article 8 covers exceptions to MFN and NT in particular. Likewise, the recently concluded CETA between the EU and Canada includes some exceptions in its investment chapter:[13]

CETA, Chapter 8, Section E, Article 8.15: Reservations and Exceptions

1. Articles 8.4 through 8.8 do not apply to:
   (a) an existing non-conforming measure that is maintained by a Party at the level of:
      (i) the European Union, as set out in its Schedule to Annex I;
      (ii) a national government, as set out by that Party in its Schedule to Annex I;
      (iii) a provincial, territorial, or regional government, as set out by that Party in its Schedule to Annex I; or
      (iv) a local government;

---

[11] See, generally, UNCTAD, 'Preserving Flexibility in IIAs: The Use of Reservations', UNCTAD Series on International Investment Policies for Development (New York and Geneva: United Nations, 2006), available at http://unctad.org/en/Docs/iteiit20058_en.pdf (accessed 21 December 2020).

[12] Simon Lester and Bryan Mercurio, 'Safeguarding Policy Space in International Investment Agreements', IIEL Issue Brief 12/2017 (Institute of International Economic Law, Georgetown University Law Center, 2017), available at www.law.georgetown.edu/iiel/wp-content/uploads/sites/8/2018/01/Simon-Lester-and-Bryan-Mercurio-General-Exceptions-in-IIAs-IIEL-Issue-Brief-December-2017-Accessible.pdf (accessed 21 December 2020); Caroline Henckels, 'Scope Limitation or Affirmative Defence: The Purpose and Role of Investment Treaty Exception Clauses', in Frederica Paddeu and Lorand Bartels (eds.), *Exceptions and Defences in International Law* (Oxford University Press, 2018), p. 363.

[13] See http://ec.europa.eu/trade/policy/in-focus/ceta/ceta-chapter-by-chapter/ (accessed 21 December 2020).

(cont.)

(b) the continuation or prompt renewal of a non-conforming measure referred to in subparagraph (a); or

(c) an amendment to a non-conforming measure referred to in subparagraph (a) to the extent that the amendment does not decrease the conformity of the measure, as it existed immediately before the amendment, with Articles 8.4 through 8.8.

2. Articles 8.4 through 8.8 do not apply to a measure that a Party adopts or maintains with respect to a sector, subsector or activity, as set out in its Schedule to Annex II.

3. Without prejudice to Articles 8.10 and 8.12, a Party shall not adopt a measure or series of measures after the date of entry into force of this Agreement and covered by its Schedule to Annex II, that require, directly or indirectly an investor of the other Party, by reason of nationality, to sell or otherwise dispose of an investment existing at the time the measure or series of measures become effective.

4. In respect of intellectual property rights, a Party may derogate from Articles 8.5.1(f), 8.6, and 8.7 if permitted by the TRIPS Agreement, including any amendments to the TRIPS Agreement in force for both Parties, and waivers to the TRIPS Agreement adopted pursuant to Article IX of the WTO Agreement.

5. Articles 8.4, 8.6, 8.7 and 8.8 do not apply to:

(a) procurement by a Party of a good or service purchased for governmental purposes and not with a view to commercial resale or with a view to use in the supply of a good or service for commercial sale, whether or not that procurement is 'covered procurement' within the meaning of Article 19.2 (Scope and coverage); or

(b) subsidies, or government support relating to trade in services, provided by a Party.

The overall impression on these recent moves in favour of a sort of rediscovery of treaty flexibility can be confusing. While exceptions to NT are often introduced, it is very rare to find exceptions to the controversial fair and equitable treatment.

Treaties and multilateral treaties, in particular, are necessarily the product of a negotiation. Their outcomes could hence be surprising, despite the good intentions of the parties to improve treaty drafting and adjust their provisions to the needs of a particular situation.

13.2.2 Definitions

The definitions of investment and investor are also very much part of this treaty negotiation and have evolved quite fundamentally from the first ever signed BIT between Germany and Pakistan in 1959, to today's more complex BITs, naturally encompassing even more trade and investment mega-deals.

13.2.2.1 Investment

The Concept of Investment: A Broad Approach   While an investment materialises in a given reality, it is also very much a concept, an idea, which might not be shared or interpreted by all in the same manner. For this very reason, IIAs have defined investment rather broadly and have largely gone beyond the simple protection of basic property rights. Tangible and intangible assets were rapidly covered, but portfolio or purely speculative investments were not accepted at first, as a large number of IIAs initially targeted foreign *direct* investment only.

For India and Australia, 'investment' meant:[14]

India–Australia BIT, 2000

Any kind of asset, including intellectual property rights, invested by an investor of one Contracting Party in the territory of the other Contracting Party in accordance with the laws and investment policies of that Contracting Party, and in particular . . . right to money or to any performance having a financial value, contractual or otherwise.

But for Canada and China in their 2012 BIT, a negative approach was also taken to define investment:

Canada–China BIT, 2012

but investment does not mean:

(k) claims to money that arise solely from
    (i) commercial contracts for the sale of goods or services, or
    (ii) the extension of credit in connection with a commercial transaction, such as trade financing, other than a loan covered by sub-paragraph (d); or
(l) any other claims to money

that do not involve the kinds of interest set out in sub-paragraphs (a) to (j).

The possibilities for framing an investment definition are indeed virtually unlimited.[15]

Whereas the broad character of initial investment definitions had the merit of being encompassing, it also left (too much) room for interpretation. Not to mention that, as surprising as it may seem, the 1966 Convention for the Settlement of Investment Disputes between States and Nationals of Others States on which the work of the ICSID is based,

---

[14] India–Australia BIT 2000, terminated unilaterally on 23 March 2017, available at http://investmentpolicyhub .unctad.org/IIA/mostRecent/treaty/209.

[15] See, generally, UNCTAD, 'Scope and Definition: A Sequel', UNCTAD Series on Issues in International Investment Agreements II (New York and Geneva: United Nations, 2011).

does not define the term investment. Its Article 25 gives some direction in its first paragraph, but no clear definition.

ICSID Convention, Article 25

(1) The jurisdiction of the Centre shall extend to any legal dispute arising directly out of an investment, between a Contracting State (or any constituent subdivision or agency of a Contracting State designated to the Centre by that State) and a national of another Contracting State, which the parties to the dispute consent in writing to submit to the Centre. When the parties have given their consent, no party may withdraw its consent unilaterally.

(2) 'National of another Contracting State' means:

  (a) any natural person who had the nationality of a Contracting State other than the State party to the dispute on the date on which the parties consented to submit such dispute to conciliation or arbitration as well as on the date on which the request was registered pursuant to paragraph (3) of Article 28 or paragraph (3) of Article 36, but does not include any person who on either date also had the nationality of the Contracting State party to the dispute; and

  (b) any juridical person which had the nationality of a Contracting State other than the State party to the dispute on the date on which the parties consented to submit such dispute to conciliation or arbitration and any juridical person which had the nationality of the Contracting State party to the dispute on that date and which, because of foreign control, the parties have agreed should be treated as a national of another Contracting State for the purposes of this Convention.

This consensual approach by default, which at a time of decolonisation and complete reshuffling of the international scene had the merit of accommodating various visions of foreign investment, has also naturally produced a large number of heated discussions and interpretations in investment arbitration. Two methods of interpretation, however, seem to prevail: a liberal and intuitive one largely based on a case-by-case approach, and a more deductive and objective technique resting on the establishment of objective criteria.[16] As we will see below, the adoption of one or the other approach will de facto impact the jurisdiction of the arbitral tribunal and the protection (generous or more restricted) of the investment. As far as the ICSID Convention is concerned, some tribunals have considered that the text of a given IIA only mattered in defining investment, while others decided that the

---

[16] Emmanuel Gaillard, 'Identify or Define? Reflections on the Evolution of the Concept of Investment in ICSID Practice', in Christina Binder, Ursula Kriebaum, August Reinisch and Stephan Wittich (eds.), *International Investment Law for the Twenty-First Century: Essays in Honour of Christoph Schreuer* (Oxford University Press, 2009), pp. 403–16.

provision of Article 25 was also to be taken into consideration in their appreciation of the reality of an investment. This encompassing perspective is often referred to as a 'double keyhole approach'.

Asset- or Enterprise-Based Definition Traditionally, IIAs have used an 'asset-based' definition of investment. As in the 2005 Germany–China BIT, the term investment means: 'every kind of asset invested directly or indirectly by investors of one Contracting Party in the territory of the other Contracting Party'.[17] Then comes a list of accepted forms of investments, including, for example, 'movable and immovable property', 'shares' or 'intellectual property rights'. While a list may give the impression of precision, this type of definition remains broad, as 'every kind of asset' could potentially be considered under an openended approach.

Another option is to use an 'enterprise-based' definition, as in the pioneering US–Canada 1988 FTA, and, later, in the NAFTA, Chapter 11.[18] This approach seems useful in the case of a broader treaty scope (pre-entry and post-entry treatment) for the promotion and protection of investment. In addition, 'an enterprise' has legal personality, which might help to clarify the situation in case a dispute arises.

Assets-based definitions very much dominate the field of IIAs. These definitions have nevertheless been narrowed down using a variety of techniques:

- a 'closed list' of investment (exhaustive approach);
- excluding certain specific assets, such as portfolio investment or loans and debts, as they may not contribute directly to the economy of the host country;
- excluding certain sectors, such as energy and health-related investment or public procurements;
- limiting investments to those made in accordance with the host country law only;
- introducing the idea of a risk related to the investment as criteria to qualify it;
- excluding certain commercial contracts;
- restricting the range of covered intellectual property rights;
- limiting the temporal scope of the investment to a given time (post-establishment, for example).

Objective Criteria or Conceptual Approach? In this relatively confusing context, investment tribunals have tried to delineate the definition of investment and, in particular, to identify objective criteria. In this regard, the *Salini* decision (see Box 13.1) has served as a litmus test and a long-term benchmark, referred to in a vast number of cases. The Tribunal identified four criteria for an investment to be defined as such in international

---

[17] Germany–China BIT 2005, available at www.international.gc.ca/trade-agreements-accords-commerciaux/topics-domaines/disp-diff/nafta.aspx?lang=eng (accessed 21 December 2020).

[18] NAFTA, Chapter 11, Art. 1139: Definitions, available at www.nafta-sec-alena.org/Home/Texts-of-the-Agreement/North-American-Free-Trade-Agreement?mvid=1&secid=539c50ef-51c1-489b-808b-9e20c9872d25#A1139 (accessed 21 December 2020).

investment law: (1) a contribution of money or assets; (2) a certain duration; (3) an element of risk; and (4) a contribution to the economic development of the host State.[19] A problematic question has been whether the four criteria had to be tested systematically all together or if they could exist independently based on different investment circumstances. Here, again, arbitrators have differed very much in their approaches. However, the most controversial element of the objective test is certainly that of the contribution to economic development, for it is rather difficult to prove in the context of financial investment, for example.

PHOENIX ACTION LTD V. CZECH REPUBLIC

Phoenix Action is an Israeli company which purchased two Czech companies, Benet Praha (BP) and Benet Group (BG). The Czech Republic challenged the jurisdiction of the Tribunal on the basis that Phoenix was *ex post* an Israeli entity created by a Czech national in order to establish diversity of nationality. The Czech Republic specifically asked the Tribunal to decide whether a foreign entity could be created for the sole purpose of establishing diversity of nationality.

In the *Phoenix Action Ltd* v. *Czech Republic* case, the Tribunal hence argued:[20]

Phoenix Action Ltd *v.* Czech Republic

85. It is the Tribunal's view that the contribution of an international investment to the *development* of the host State is impossible to ascertain – the more so as there are highly diverging views on what constitutes 'development'. A less ambitious approach should then be adopted, centred on the contribution of an international investment to the *economy* of the host State, which is indeed *inherent in the mere concept of investment as shaped by the elements of contribution/duration/risk*, and should therefore be presumed.

Often, tribunals have used the three first criteria, but not the fourth one on economic development, as in *L.E.S.I.-Dipenta* v. *Algeria*, *Saba Fakes* v. *Turkey*, *RSM* v. *Central African Republic*, *Quiborax* v. *Bolivia* or *Pey Casado* v. *Chile*.[21]

---

[19] This four-criteria definition approach has been followed, notably, in *Jan de Nul N.V. and Dredging International N.V.* v. *Arab Republic of Egypt*, ICSID Case No. ARB/04/13, Award, 6 November 2008, available at www.italaw.com/cases/587; *Saipem S.p.A.* v. *People's Republic of Bangladesh*, ICSID Case No. ARB/05/07, Award, 30 June 2009, available at www.italaw.com/cases/951; *Ioannis Kardassopoulous* v. *Republic of Georgia*, ICSID Case No. ARB/05/18, Award, 30 March 2010, available at www.italaw.com/cases/599; *Bayindir Insaat Turizm Ticaret Ve Sanayi A.S.* v. *Islamic Republic of Pakistan*, ICSID Case No. ARB/03/09, Award, 27 August 2009, available at www.italaw.com/cases/131; and *Millicom International Operations B.V. and Sentel GSM S.A.* v. *Republic of Senegal*, Decision on Jurisdiction of the Arbitral Tribunal, 16 July 2010, available at www.italaw.com/cases/documents/706 (all accessed 21 December 2020).

[20] *Phoenix Action Ltd* v. *Czech Republic*, ICSID Case No. ART/06/5, Award, 15 April 2009, para. 85, available at www.italaw.com/cases/850 (accessed 21 December 2020).

[21] *Consortium Groupement L.E.S.I.-DIPENTA* v. *République algérienne démocratique et populaire*, ICSID Case No. ARB/03/08, Award, 10 January 2005 Award, available at www.italaw.com/cases/323; *Saba Fakes* v. *Republic of*

BIWATER V. TANZANIA

In *Biwater* v. *Tanzania*, the claims arose out of a contractual dispute between the claimant's locally incorporated company and Tanzania's Water and Sewerage Authority. The case is emblematic of the issues surrounding water privatisation, development and the right to regulate. In the *Biwater* v. *Tanzania* decision, the Tribunal argued:[22]

Biwater *v.* Tanzania

312. In the Tribunal's view, there is no basis for a rote, or overly strict, application of the five *Salini* criteria in every case. These criteria are not fixed or mandatory as a matter of law. They do not appear in the ICSID Convention. On the contrary, it is clear from the *travaux préparatoires* of the Convention that several attempts to incorporate a definition of 'investment' were made, but ultimately did not succeed. In the end, the term was left intentionally undefined, with the expectation (inter alia) that a definition could be the subject of agreement as between Contracting States. ...

313. Given that the Convention was not drafted with a strict, objective, definition of 'investment', it is doubtful that arbitral tribunals sitting in individual cases should impose one such definition which would be applicable in all cases and for all purposes.

Interestingly, however, in the *Phoenix* case referred to above, the Tribunal used two additional criteria, *good faith* and *investment's conformity with the law of the host State*.

Turkey, ICSID Case No. ARB/07/20, Award, 14 July 2010, available at www.italaw.com/cases/429; *RSM Production Corporation* v. *Central African Republic*, ICSID Case No. ART/07/2, Award, 11 July 2011, available at www.italaw.com/cases/4880; *Quiborax S.A., Non-Metallic Minervals S.A. and Allan Fosk Kaplún* v. *Plurinational State of Bolivia*, ICSID Case No. ARB/06/2, Award, 16 September 2015, available at www.italaw.com/cases/885; *Victor Pey Casado and President Allende Foundation* v. *Republic of Chile*, ICSID Case No. ARB/98/2, available at www.italaw.com/cases/829, a fascinating series of arbitral episodes leading to the possible annulment of the Award of 13 September 2016 (all accessed 21 December 2020).

[22] *Biwater Gauff (Tanzania) Ltd* v. *United Republic of Tanzania*, ICSID Case No. ARB/05/22, Award, 24 July 2008, available at www.italaw.com/cases/157 (accessed 21 December 2020). See also *Alpha Projektholding GmbH* v. *Ukraine*, ICSID Case No. ARB/07/16, Award, 8 November 2010, para. 312, available at www.italaw.com/cases/71 (accessed 21 December 2020):

> The Tribunal is particularly reluctant to apply a test that seeks to assess an investment's contribution to a country's economic development. Should a tribunal find it necessary to check whether a transaction falls outside any reasonable understanding of 'investment', the criteria of resources, duration, and risk would seem fully to serve that objective. The contribution-to-development criterion, on the other hand, would appear instead to reflect the consequences of the other criteria and brings little independent content to the inquiry. At the same time, the criterion invites a tribunal to engage in a post hoc evaluation of the business, economic, financial and/or policy assessments that prompted the claimant's activities. It would not be appropriate for such a form of second-guessing to drive a tribunal's jurisdictional analysis.

Box 13.1 The *Salini* case: rise and fall of an objective definition test

The Salini Costruttori SPA v. *Kingdom of Morocco* claim arose out of a public procurement agreement for a highway construction and the non-payment of the contract price to the investor, which had been awarded a (investment) contract through a tender. The Moroccan government objected to the jurisdiction of the ICSID, on the basis that the highway project was not an investment. The Arbitral Tribunal hence adopted a 'double-keyhole' approach in analysing the definition of investment in the BIT between Morocco and Italy, but also the scope of the ICSID Convention, which, as we have seen, does not provide for a definition of investment. The Tribunal hence identified four criteria: (1) a contribution of money or assets; (2) a certain duration; (3) an element of risk; and (4) a contribution to the economic development of the host State. One must note that a previous decision, *Fedax N.V.* v. *Republic of Venezuela*, had laid down some of the elements that would later become the four *Salini* criteria.

This 'test' was later referred to quite systematically by a number of arbitrators, apparently keen to find a form of objectivity to support their reasoning. However, more recently, panels have started to question the validity of the test, and its fourth element in particular. While the *Quiborax* v. *Bolivia* case was revealing of this new tendency to question the imperative of development, the Tribunal in *Phillip Morris* v. *Uruguay* seems to have gone one step further: 'whether the so-called *Salini* test relied upon by the Respondent has any relevance in the interpretation of the concept of investment under Article 25(1) of the ICSID Convention is very doubtful', with the panel concluding: 'As shown hereafter, there is no such *"jurisprudence constante"* with respect to acceptance of the *Salini* test'.

That is, indeed, one of the main general issues in international investment arbitration: there is no *jurisprudence constante*, and it may well be that a test can gain popularity, lose it, and then regain importance later.

To Go Further

Fedax N.V. v. *Republic of Venezuela*, ICSID Case No. ARB/96/3, Decision of the Tribunal on Objections to Jurisdiction, 11 July 1997, available at www.italaw.com/cases/432 (accessed 21 December 2020).

Gaillard, E. and Banifatemi, Y., 'The Long March Towards a "Jurisprudence Constante" on the Notion of Investment: *Salini* v. *Morocco*, ICSID Case No. ARB/00/4', in Kinnear et al., *Building International Investment Law*, pp. 97–125.

Grabowski, A. 'The Definition of Investment under the ICSID Convention: A Defense of Salini', *Chicago Journal of International Law* (2014), 15(1), Art. 13, available at http://chicagounbound.uchicago.edu/cjil/vol15/iss1/13 (accessed 21 December 2020).

Joy Mining Machinery Limited v. *Arab Republic of Egypt*, ICSID Case No. ARB/03/11, available at www.italaw.com/cases/590 (accessed 21 December 2020).

Phillip Morris Brands Sàrl, Phillip Morris Products S.A. and Abal Hermanos S.A. v. *Oriental Republic of Uruguay*, ICSID Case No. ARB/10/17, Decision on Jurisdiction, 2 July 2013, para. 204, available at www.italaw.com/cases/460 (accessed 21 December 2020).

Box 13.1 (cont.)

Quiborax S.A., Non-Metallic Minerals S.A. and Allan Fosk Kaplún v. *Plurinational State of Bolivia*, ICSID Case No. ARB/06/2, Decision on Jurisdiction, 27 September 2012, available at www.italaw.com/cases/885 (accessed 21 December 2020).

Salini Costruttori S.p.A. and Italsrade S.p.A. v. *Kingdom of Morocco [I]*, ICSID Case No. ARB/00/4, Decision on Jurisdiction, 23 July 2001, case materials available at www.italaw.com/cases/958 (accessed 21 December 2020).

The Legality of Investment   The last question, which has often been addressed in investment treaty jurisprudence, is that of the legality of the investment. An easy answer can be found in the limitations listed in the treaty itself, in terms of geographical and temporal scope, or simply the laws of the host State.[23]

FRAPORT V. PHILIPPINES

In this regard, the *Fraport* v. *Philippines* cases (I and II – the first case having been annulled) bring some clarification. Centred around the legality of Fraport's investment under Philippines' law, the decision indeed approached the question of legality from various angles: existence of the requirement, origin and meaning, violation of the requirement, and whether, in case of illegality, the respondent State should be estopped from using the argument to object to the jurisdiction of the tribunal. From these two decisions, it seems that this legality argument might be valid only when the treaty contains express requirements and the investment/investor has violated the law of the host State.

13.2.2.2 Investor

Who is an 'investor' in IIL? Is it a juridical or a natural person, or both? As in the case of investment, IIAs comprise a definition of the term investor. For example, the 2001 China–Nigeria BIT provides, in its Article 1:[24]

China–Nigeria BIT, 2001

The term 'investor' includes nationals and companies of both Contracting Parties:

(a) 'Nationals' means, with regards to either Contracting Party, natural persons having the nationality of that Contracting Party;
(b) 'Companies' means, with regards to either Contracting Party, corporations, firms and associations incorporated or constituted under the law in force in the territory of the Contracting Party.

---

[23] Jean Kalicki, Dmitri Evseev and Mallory Silberman, 'Legality of Investment', in Kinnear et al., *Building International Investment Law*, pp. 127–39.

[24] China–Nigeria BIT 2001, available at https://investmentpolicy.unctad.org/international-investment-agreements.

One fundamental issue is easily identifiable here, that of the *nationality* of the individual and/or the company identified as an investor. Here again, Article 25 of the ICSID is not of much help, as it only refers to a 'national' of a contracting State, either a natural person or a juridical person. Seemingly simple, this question of nationality is actually extremely complex and has given rise to a vast number of disputes. Who is entitled to bring a claim? On what basis can arbitration take place if not by the protection by a given State of nationality through an investment treaty? The ICJ landmark *Nottebohm* decision (see Box 13.2) had set strict criteria, going further than the generally accepted idea that national law sets the rules according to which nationality is granted. It must be said that treaties as well as arbitral practice on the nationality of individuals in investment law differ from the principles adopted in general international law about the question of diplomatic protection.

HUSSEIN NUAMAN SOUFRAKI V. UNITED ARAB EMIRATES

For natural persons, the *Hussein Nuaman Soufraki* v. *United Arab Emirates* case has clarified essential aspects of the determination of nationality of an investor:[25]

- The country at issue in a dispute governs the law on nationality.
- It is in the power of the tribunal to determine jurisdiction in relation to the issue of nationality.
- Proof of nationality (passport, ID card) is taken into consideration by the tribunal, which is not bound by this in its reasoning.

That the country at issue governs the rules on nationality and the tribunal has the power to decide questions of nationality have been supported by other decisions, such as *Siag* v. *Egypt* and *Victor Pey Casado* v. *Chile*.[26]

Box 13.2 The *Nottebohm* case: nationality as a condition of the exercise of diplomatic protection and beyond

As IIL finds its roots in the theory of State responsibility, the principle of diplomatic protection has played an important role (see Chapter 12). Diplomatic protection cannot be exercised for all, but only under strict conditions of nationality. Here comes the case of Mr Nottebohm, a landmark decision in public international law. In this case, the ICJ decided that only where a genuine link between the State and its national exists could diplomatic protection be exercised and so claimed as a right. The facts of

---

[25] *Hussein Nuaman Soufraki* v. *United Arab Emirates*, ICSID Case No. ARB/02/7, Award, 7 July 2004, available at www.italaw.com/cases/1041 (accessed 21 December 2020). For a commentary, see Christoph Schreuer, 'Criteria to Determine Investor Nationality (Natural Persons)', in Kinnear et al., *Building International Investment Law*, pp. 153–61.

[26] *Waguih Elie George Siag and Clorinda Vecchi* v. *Arab Republic of Egypt*, ICSID Case No. ARB/05/15, Decision on Jurisdiction, 11 April 2007, available at www.italaw.com/cases/1022 (accessed 21 December 2020); *Pey Casado* v. *Chile*, Award, 8 May 2008.

Box 13.2 (cont.)

this case are critical to understanding the Court's reasoning and the limitations of the same as applied to international investments.

Liechtenstein claimed restitution and compensation from the government of Guatemala, on the ground that it had acted towards Friedrich Nottebohm, a citizen of Liechtenstein, in a manner contrary to international law. Guatemala first objected to the ICJ jurisdiction, an objection that was not accepted by the Court. The ICJ, however, ruled against Lichtenstein in its second judgment of 6 April 1955, for the following reasons: Mr Nottebohm was born in Germany in 1881. He moved and settled in Guatemala in 1905, and resided in this country as a German citizen. In October 1939, just after the beginning of the Second World War, Friedrich Nottebohm applied for naturalisation in Liechtenstein and was indeed granted a new nationality. He then returned to Guatemala in 1940 and resumed his former business activities until he was deported in 1943, as a result of war measures.

The Court first acknowledged that Lichtenstein was entirely free to grant nationality of the basis of its own criteria and national law:

It is for Liechtenstein, as it is for every sovereign State, to settle by its own legislation the rules relating to the acquisition of its nationality, and to confer that nationality by naturalization granted by its own organs in accordance with that legislation. It is not necessary to determine whether international law imposes any limitations on its freedom of decision in this domain. (ICJ Judgment, 6 April 1955, p. 20)

But the ICJ also noted that Guatemala might not be obliged to recognise the exercise of diplomatic protection by Lichtenstein in favour of one of its nationals, Mr Nottebohm. Indeed, the very fact of exercising diplomatic protection brought the issue of nationality beyond the borders of the State and its domestic law.

But the issue which the Court must decide is not one which pertains to the legal system of Liechtenstein. It does not depend on the law or on the decision of Liechtenstein whether that State is entitled to exercise its protection, in the case under consideration. ... It is international law, which determines whether a State is entitled to exercise protection and to seize the Court. (ICJ Judgment, 6 April 1955, p. 20)

The Court emphasised the tenuous nature of the link of Mr Nottebohm with Liechtenstein, a country where he had never really resided, while he had lived for more than thirty years in Guatemala.

Naturalization is not a matter to be taken lightly. To seek and to obtain it is not something that happens frequently in the life of a human being. It involves his breaking of a bond of allegiance and his establishment of a new bond of allegiance. It may have far-reaching consequences and involve profound changes in the destiny of the individual who obtains it. It concerns him personally, and to consider it only from the point of view of its repercussions with regard to his property would be to misunderstand its profound significance. In order to appraise its international effect, it is impossible

Box 13.2 (cont.)

to disregard the circumstances in which it was conferred, the serious character which attaches to it, the real and effective, and not merely the verbal preference of the individual seeking it for the country which grants it to him. (ICJ Judgment, 6 April 1955, p. 24)

These facts clearly establish, on the one hand, the absence of any bond of attachment between Nottebohm and Liechtenstein and, on the other hand, the existence of a longstanding and close connection between him and Guatemala, a link which his naturalization in no way weakened. That naturalization was not based on any real prior connection with Liechtenstein, nor did it in any way alter the manner of life of the person upon whom it was conferred in exceptional circumstances of speed and accommodation. In both respects, it was lacking in the genuineness requisite to an act of such importance, if it is to be entitled to be respected by a State in the position of Guatemala. It was granted without regard to the concept of nationality adopted in international relations. (ICJ Judgment, 6 April 1955, p. 26)

This landmark decision has often been referred to in the case of dual nationality. It has only recently been extended to the question of diplomatic protection and, consequently, has created a number of interrogations. The ILC 2006 Draft Articles on Diplomatic Protection recommended that the perspective taken by the ICJ should be limited to the facts of the *Nottebohm* case alone. In the event of dual nationality, for example, the test of effectiveness is generally adopted as shown in the context of *the* Iran–US Claims Tribunal: 'The dominant and effective' nationality was recognised as a basis for diplomatic protection. As far as corporations are concerned, the *Barcelona Traction* Tribunal acknowledged the right of diplomatic protection of a corporation to the State under the laws of which it is incorporated and registered – a perspective largely confirmed by Article 9 of the ILC Draft Articles. Later, the ICJ in the *Diallo* case noted that:

diplomatic protection of the direct rights of associés of a SPRL or shareholders of a public limited company is not to be regarded as an exception to the general legal regime of diplomatic protection for natural or legal persons as derived from customary international law. (*Diallo* case, Preliminary Objections, *ICJ Reports 2007*, p. 606)

This is to say, the quite daring incursion of the ICJ into international law in the context of the *Nottebohm* case remains exceptional, while the acceptance that domestic law determines the criteria of nationality is generalised.

To Go Further

Ahmadou Sadio Diallo case *(Republic of Guinea* v. *Democratic Republic of the Congo), Preliminary Objections, ICJ Reports 2010*, available at www.icj-cij.org/en/case/103 (accessed 21 December 2020).

de Visscher, P., 'L'affaire Nottebohm', *Revue générale de droit international public* (1956), 2.

Nottebohm case *(Liechtenstein* v. *Guatemala)* materials available at www.icj-cij.org/en/case/18 (accessed 21 December 2020).

For juridical persons, the term 'investor' is defined by sometimes rather different treaty provisions, as in the 2003 China–Germany BIT:[27]

China–Germany BIT, 2003

2. The term 'investor' means
   (a) in respect of the Federal Republic of Germany:
      – Germans within the meaning of the Basic Law for the Federal Republic of Germany,
      – any juridical person as well as any commercial or other company or association with or without legal personality having its seat in the territory of the Federal Republic of Germany, irrespective of whether or not its activities are directed at profit;
   (b) in respect of the People's Republic of China:
      – natural persons who have nationality of the People's Republic of China in accordance with its laws,
      – economic entities, including companies, corporations, associations, partnerships and other organizations, incorporated and constituted under the laws and regulations of and with their seats in the People's Republic of China, irrespective of whether or not for profit and whether their liabilities are limited or not;

While the seat of incorporation of the company matters, the Chinese and German approaches remain different and yet coexist in the same treaty (cf. the importance of national investment law, Chapter 12).

It is generally agreed that the law of the investor home State shall prevail in the event of a dispute, as stated implicitly in Article 25(2)(b) of the ICSID. Arbitration is then closed to the nationals of the State in which the investment is made (host State) unless the parties agree otherwise. The rather elusive drafting of Article 25, here again, left considerable margin for interpretation. In addition to the treaty's terms determining the nationality of a corporation, arbitral tribunals have often had to clarify this extremely important and complex question at a time of globalisation and treaty shopping by companies seeking the best possible protection for their investment and the ideal tax regime, as in the case of shell companies.

It is indeed quite frequent for companies to restructure their investment to achieve investment treaty protection.[28] Nationality planning and corporate restructuring are important topics for investors seeking to expand their business abroad. The issue arises at a number of key moments in the life of an investment. When planning, naturally, but also in the course of the investment's existence, as investors might want to avoid a politically unstable or risky situation and think about bringing a claim against the host State. Therefore, they seek the best

---

[27] China–Germany BIT 2003, available at https://investmentpolicy.unctad.org/international-investment-agreements/treaties/bit/905/china---germany-bit-2003- (accessed 21 December 2020).

[28] Stephen Jagush, Anthony Sinclair and Manthi Wickramasooriya, 'Restructuring Investments to Achieve Investment Treaty Protection', in Kinnear et al., *Building International Investment Law*, pp. 175–90.

possible protection, within the permissible legal limits of the IIA network. There is a legitimate incentive for treaty shopping. This, of course, affects the State greatly, with opinion largely differing on the legitimacy and legality of practices seen as rather cynical if not literally abusive. Some tribunals have clarified the legality of corporate nationality planning in shedding some light on what could constitute an 'abuse of process', and the difference between this abusive practice and a *ratione temporis* objection to the jurisdiction.

LAO HOLDINGS N.V. V. LAO PEOPLE'S DEMOCRATIC REPUBLIC

In *Lao Holdings N.V.* v. *Lao People's Democratic Republic*, the Tribunal has framed the possibility of changing nationality so that it is not considered an 'abuse of process':[29]

> ## Lao Holdings N.V. *v.* Lao People's Democratic Republic
>
> 76. If a company changes its nationality in order to gain ICSID jurisdiction at a moment when things have started to deteriorate so that a dispute is highly probable, it can be considered an abuse of process, but for an objection based on *ratione temporis* to be upheld, the dispute has to have actually arisen before the critical date to conform to the general principle of non-retroactivity in the interpretation and application of international treaties.

To sum up: if a claimant acquires an investment after the date of the disputed State measure, the tribunal will lack jurisdiction *ratione temporis*, as no retroactivity is permitted. However, if a claimant has voluntarily changed nationality while expecting a dispute to arise, this can then be identified as an abuse of process. This abuse naturally remains to be proven and interpreted.

TOKIOS TOKELÉS V. UKRAINE

In this regard, the landmark *Tokios Tokelés* v. *Ukraine* decision, in which the claimant was de facto of the same nationality as the respondent (Ukraine), since the company was controlled by a Ukrainian company, has brought some (temporary) clarification. Ukraine faced an ISDS under the Ukraine–Lithuania BIT. The company Tokios Tokelés was incorporated in Lithuania. The claimant, Tokios Tokelés, had also created a subsidiary in Ukraine, Tokios Spravy, to operate a printing business. Tokios Tokelés claimed that Ukraine had breached its obligations under the Ukraine–Lithuania BIT, in response to its publication of a book favourably portraying a leading Ukrainian opposition leader. Ukraine challenged the standing of Tokios Tokelés, alleging that, although it was incorporated in Lithuania, it was clearly controlled by Ukrainians and should therefore be considered Ukrainian. Ukrainian nationals indeed owned 99 per cent of Tokios Tokelés shares and held two-thirds of the positions on its board of directors.[30]

---

[29] *Lao Holdings N.V.* v. *Lao People's Democratic Republic*, ICSID Case No. ARB(AF)/12/6, Decision on Jurisdiction, 21 February 2014, available at www.italaw.com/cases/2020 (accessed 21 December 2020).

[30] *Tokios Tokelés* v. *Ukraine*, ICSID Case No. ARB/02/18, Decision on Jurisdiction, 29 April 2004, including Dissenting Opinion of Professor Weil, available at www.italaw.com/cases/documents/1101 (accessed 21 December 2020).

Tokios Tokelés *v.* Ukraine

52. In summary, the Claimant is an 'investor' of Lithuania under Article 1(2)(b) of the BIT because it is an 'entity established in the territory of the Republic of Lithuania in conformity with its laws and regulations'. This method of defining corporate nationality is consistent with modern BIT practice and satisfies the objective requirements of Article 25 of the Convention. We find no basis in the BIT or the Convention to set aside the Contracting Parties' agreed definition of corporate nationality with respect to investors of either party in favour of a test based on the nationality of the controlling shareholders. While some tribunals have taken a distinctive approach, we do not believe that arbitrators should read in to BITs limitations not found in the text nor evident from negotiating history sources.

LOEWEN v. *USA*

In addition, in the *Loewen* v. *USA* case, the claims arose out of alleged mistreatment of the investor by the state of Mississippi in the course of commercial litigation between the claimant and one of its competitors in the funeral home and funeral insurance business. The case has shown that nationality should ideally be continuous:[31]

Loewen *v.* USA

225. In international law parlance, there must be continuous national identity from the date of the events giving rise to the claim, which date is known as the *dies a quo*, through the date of the resolution of the claim, which date is known as the dies *ad quem*.

The question was indeed – and very much remains – that of the nationality of the *shareholders* controlling the company, but who are not necessarily of the nationality of the home State and sometimes even hold the nationality of the host State. Here, the tribunal has limited its reasoning to the BIT definition of investor, without considering the effective control by shareholders and their nationality. A number of additional decisions have not always followed *Tokios Tokelés'* conclusions and, beyond the issue of nationality, have sometimes also ventured into another related complex question, that of direct or indirect control of the company by its shareholders, as in *Aguas del Tunari* v. *Bolivia*.[32]

---

[31] *Loewen Group Inc. and Raymond L. Loewen* v. *United States of America*, ICSID Case No. ARB(AF)/98/3, Award, 26 June 2003, para. 225, available at www.italaw.com/cases/632 (accessed 21 December 2020).

[32] *Aguas del Tunari, S.A.* v. *Republic of Bolivia*, ICSID Case No. ARB/02/3, available at www.italaw.com/cases/57 (accessed 21 December 2020).

Aguas del Tunari v. Bolivia

This decision was based on the interpretation of the BIT between the Netherlands and Bolivia, which defined investors as 'legal persons controlled directly or indirectly by nationals of that Contracting Party but constituted in accordance with the law of the other Contracting party'. What, then, was the meaning of 'controlled directly or indirectly'? The Tribunal decided to interpret the phrase in its context and in the light of the object and purpose of the BIT. It concluded that control exists when an 'entity possesses the legal capacity to control the other entity'. In this case, 100 per cent shareholding was accepted as de facto control, no matter the factual reality of the exercise of control on a daily basis. The Dutch claimants were hence not seen as a mere 'shell'.

CMS v. Argentina

In *CMS* v. *Argentina*, another decision on shareholders' standings, the Tribunal found 'no bar in current international law to the concept of allowing claims by shareholders independently from those of the corporation concerned not even if these shareholders are minority or non-controlling shareholders'.[33] This is to say that shareholders' rights protection has largely evolved, together with global economic changes, since the *Barcelona Traction* case and its related developments in terms of diplomatic protection (see Chapter 12). It is now generally accepted that shareholders have standing to claim against a host State's measures affecting a company they hold shares in. However, it would be misleading to believe that shareholders' protection is not an issue anymore, as it still raises numerous questions, from that of standing to the possibility of multiple (frivolous) claims for the same damage.[34]

Seeking jurisprudential uniformity on the interrelated questions of nationality and control remains a very distant dream, as arbitral tribunals continue to agree to disagree.

13.3 Standards of Treatment and Protection

Standards of treatment and protection have also faced the same fate in a large number of epic arbitral interpretations. Some clarifications have been brought by arbitral decisions, which have later had an impact on treaty drafting. So controversial provisions such as the FET, in particular, are today better framed, yet not entirely deprived of ambiguities. At the core of IIAs, these standards of treatment and protection constitute the very essence of IIL

---

[33] *CMS Gas Transmission Company* v. *Republic of Argentina*, ICSID Case No. ARB/01/8, Decision on Jurisdiction, para. 48, available at www.italaw.com/cases/288 (accessed 21 December 2020).

[34] Martin J. Valasek and Patrick Dumberry, 'Developments in the Legal Standing of Shareholders and Holding Corporations in Investor–State Disputes', *ICSID Review: Foreign Investment Law Journal* (2011), 26(1), pp. 34–75.

and will most certainly continue to be challenged and debated. The developments explored below hence address the main substantive provisions covered by international investment treaties. Their violations, the claims against treaty breaches and possible defences to responsibility by the State will be covered in greater detail in Chapter 14 on dispute settlement in relation to precise cases and procedures.

13.3.1 National Treatment

As discussed in our introductory chapters to trade and investment (see Chapters 1 and 11), non-discrimination constitutes the cornerstone of international economic law. The basic principle is simple: foreigners should not be treated less favourably than nationals (national treatment), and one should not differentiate between foreign partners in treating a partner more favourably than the other (MFN). The application of these two core components of non-discrimination has revealed itself to be much more complex than expected and has often been fragmented between the different branches of IEL.[35] However, NT and MFN are fundamental to IIL.

NT, although less debated than the rather obscure minimum standard of treatment or controversial FET, is of prime importance. As highlighted by UNCTAD:[36]

UNCTAD, 'National Treatment'

The national treatment standard is perhaps the single most important standard of treatment enshrined in international investment agreements (IIAs). At the same time, it is perhaps the most difficult standard to achieve, as it touches upon economically (and politically) sensitive issues. In fact, no single country has so far seen itself in a position to grant national treatment without qualifications, especially when it comes to the establishment of an investment.

For a long time, nothing much was codified and the unwritten rules of customary international law initially prevailed to govern NT as an essential component of non-discrimination. Its granting was influenced by late nineteenth-century debates and the Calvo doctrine (see Chapter 12). One had to wait for the drafting of the never adopted Havana Charter to find some NT-related provisions:

---

[35] See, for example, N. DiMascio and J. Pauwelyn, 'Non-Discrimination in Trade and Investment Treaties: Worlds Apart or Two Sides of the Same Coin?', *American Journal of International Law* (2008), 102(1), pp. 48–89.

[36] UNCTAD, 'National Treatment', UNCTAD Series on Issues in International Investment Agreements (New York and Geneva: United Nations, 1999).

> ## Havana Charter, Article 12: International Investment for Economic Development and Reconstruction
>
> 1. The Members recognize that:
>   (a) international investment, both public and private, can be of great value in promoting economic development and reconstruction, and consequent social progress;
>   [. . .]
> 2. Members therefore undertake:
>   [. . .]
>   (i) to provide reasonable opportunities for investments acceptable to them and adequate security for existing and future investments, and
>   (ii) to give due regard to the desirability of avoiding discrimination as between foreign investments.

While 'due regard' to the 'desirability of avoiding discrimination' was suggested, no real codification effort had been supported. The wave of expropriations following the socialist revolutions in Eastern Europe and in the Third World, as well as the decolonisation era, forced international investment players to rethink the customary legal basis on which IIL rested. A fascinating first attempt took place within the United Nations General Assembly in the context of the NIEO (see Chapter 12). However, the NT was not generalised, and countries like China awaited until the early 1900s to introduce it systematically in their BITs.[37] The 1990s marked a turning point, with the adoption of the OECD National Treatment Instrument, NAFTA and the Energy Charter, in particular, observing a concrete evolution in treaty drafting. NT was then quite systematically granted pre- (rarely) or post-establishment.

The OECD National Treatment Instrument addresses the treatment of 'foreign-controlled enterprises after establishment' and consists of two elements: a declaration of principles included into the OECD Declaration on International Investment and Multinational Enterprises and the 1991 OECD Council decision obliging adhering countries (OECD members and a number of other States) to notify their exceptions to NT to the OECD, which establishes follow-up procedures.[38] In this context, NT is defined as follows:[39]

---

[37] Leïla Choukroune, 'Indian and Chinese FDI in Developing Asia: The Standards Battle Beyond Trade', *Indian Journal of International Economic Law* (2015), VII, pp. 89–116.

[38] See the work of the OECD on National Treatment for Foreign-Controlled Enterprises, available at www.oecd.org/daf/inv/investment-policy/nationaltreatmentinstrument.htm (accessed 21 December 2020).

[39] OECD Declaration on International Investment and Multinational Enterprises, adopted by the Governments of OECD member countries on 21 June 1976 and reviewed in 1979, 1984, 1991, 2000 and 2011, available at www.oecd.org/daf/inv/investment-policy/oecddeclarationoninternationalinvestmentandmultinationalenterprises.htm (accessed 21 December 2020).

OECD Declaration on International Investment and Multinational Enterprises

1. That adhering governments should, consistent with their needs to maintain public order, to protect their essential security interests and to fulfil commitments relating to international peace and security, accord to enterprises operating in their territories and owned or controlled directly or indirectly by nationals of another adhering government (hereinafter referred to as 'Foreign-Controlled Enterprises') treatment under their laws, regulations and administrative practices, consistent with international law and no less favourable than that accorded in like situations to domestic enterprises (hereinafter referred to as 'National Treatment');

2. That adhering governments will consider applying 'National Treatment' in respect of countries other than adhering governments;

3. That adhering governments will endeavour to ensure that their territorial subdivisions apply 'National Treatment';

4. That this Declaration does not deal with the right of adhering governments to regulate the entry of foreign investment or the conditions of establishment of foreign enterprises.

This quite demanding approach to national treatment, which directly refers to international law in creating a link between NT and other standards of treatment, finds an echo in the 1994 NAFTA, Chapter 11, defining NT in its famous Article 1102:

NAFTA, Chapter 11, Section A, Article 1102: National Treatment

1. Each Party shall accord to investors of another Party treatment no less favourable than that it accords, in like circumstances, to its own investors with respect to the establishment, acquisition, expansion, management, conduct, operation, and sale or other disposition of investments.

2. Each Party shall accord to investments of investors of another Party treatment no less favourable than that it accords, in like circumstances, to investments of its own investors with respect to the establishment, acquisition, expansion, management, conduct, operation, and sale or other disposition of investments.

3. The treatment accorded by a Party under paragraphs 1 and 2 means, with respect to a state or province, treatment no less favourable than the most favourable treatment accorded, in like circumstances, by that state or province to investors, and to investments of investors, of the Party of which it forms a part.

> *(cont.)*
>
> 4. For greater certainty, no Party may:
>   (a) impose on an investor of another Party a requirement that a minimum level of equity in an enterprise in the territory of the Party be held by its nationals, other than nominal qualifying shares for directors or incorporators of corporations; or
>   (b) require an investor of another Party, by reason of its nationality, to sell or otherwise dispose of an investment in the territory of the Party.

As we will see in our next chapter on dispute settlement, this Article has been extensively interpreted in a rather broad, yet often inconsistent manner, hence providing the basis for NT jurisprudence. Along the same lines, the 1994 Energy Charter Treaty reformulated the NT standard (together with the MFN standard) quite synthetically:

> ## Energy Charter Treaty, 1994, Article 10: Promotion, Protection and Treatment of Investments
>
> 2. Each Contracting Party shall endeavour to accord to Investors of other Contracting Parties, as regards the Making of Investments in its Area, the Treatment described in paragraph (3).
> 3. For the purposes of this Article, 'Treatment' means treatment accorded by a Contracting Party which is no less favourable than that which it accords to its own Investors or to Investors of any other Contracting Party or any third state, whichever is the most favourable.

These three international instruments, designed for wide protection of foreign investment in a post-socialist era promoting trade and investment liberalisation, greatly influenced the drafting of specific IIAs and BITs, in particular.

In the 2000s, treaties diversified to include a variety of approaches to NT. The most striking feature of the recent IIAs, with regard to NT, consists of the introduction of what some have described as 'smart flexibility clauses'.[40] For example, the 2012 US and Canada Model BITs had played very well with States' regulatory autonomy for public purposes, while incorporating some additional flexibility/protection in relation to labour, corporate social responsibility or the environment (see above on exceptions/reservations).[41] Along the

---

[40] A. van Aaken, 'Smart Flexibility Clauses in International Investment Agreements', *Investment Treaty News* (2013), 3(4), pp. 3–5.

[41] 2012 US Model BIT, available at https://ustr.gov/sites/default/files/BIT%20text%20for%20ACIEP%20Meeting.pdf; Canada Model BIT 2012, available at https://investmentpolicy.unctad.org/international-investment-agreements/countries/35/canada (both accessed 21 December 2020).

same lines, the CETA has weaved an interesting canvas of provisions, starting from its Preamble recognising that 'the provisions of this Agreement protect investments and investors with respect to their investments, and are intended to stimulate mutually beneficial business activity, without undermining the right of the Parties to regulate in the public interest within their territories', and followed by Article 8.6 (National treatment), to be read in conjunction with Articles 8.15 (Reservations and exceptions) and 8.16 (Denial of benefits), and Chapter 28 on Exceptions.[42]

CETA, Article 8.6: National treatment

1. Each Party shall accord to an investor of the other Party and to a covered investment, treatment no less favourable than the treatment it accords, in like situations to its own investors and to their investments with respect to the establishment, acquisition, expansion, conduct, operation, management, maintenance, use, enjoyment and sale or disposal of their investments in its territory.
2. The treatment accorded by a Party under paragraph 1 means, with respect to a government in Canada other than at the federal level, treatment no less favourable than the most favourable treatment accorded, in like situations, by that government to investors of Canada in its territory and to investments of such investors.
3. The treatment accorded by a Party under paragraph 1 means, with respect to a government of or in a Member State of the European Union, treatment no less favourable than the most favourable treatment accorded, in like situations, by that government to investors of the EU in its territory and to investments of such investors.

Article 8.15 adds:

CETA, Article 8.15: Reservations and exceptions

5. Articles 8.4, 8.6, 8.7 and 8.8 do not apply to:
   (a) procurement by a Party of a good or service purchased for governmental purposes and not with a view to commercial resale or with a view to use in the supply of a good or service for commercial sale, whether or not that procurement is 'covered procurement' within the meaning of Article 19.2 (Scope and coverage); or
   (b) subsidies, or government support relating to trade in services, provided by a Party.

---

[42] See, generally, the CETA text, available at http://ec.europa.eu/trade/policy/in-focus/ceta/ceta-chapter-by-chapter (accessed 21 December 2020).

And Article 8.16 underlines:

> ## CETA, Article 8.16: Denial of benefits
>
> A Party may deny the benefits of this Chapter to an investor of the other Party that is an enterprise of that Party and to investments of that investor if:
>
> (a) an investor of a third country owns or controls the enterprise; and
> (b) the denying Party adopts or maintains a measure with respect to the third country that:
>   (i) relates to the maintenance of international peace and security; and
>   (ii) prohibits transactions with the enterprise or would be violated or circumvented if the benefits of this Chapter were accorded to the enterprise or to its investments.

As far as arbitration is concerned, only a handful of known cases addressing the NT standard issue are available for analysis, and the vast majority relate to NAFTA. They have not followed a uniform or very coherent approach, but some tools have been crafted to assess NT violation and, in particular, the existence of a differentiation, nationality as a criterion, a 'no less favourable treatment' test and another comparison (like circumstance) test, including WTO case law (see Chapter 10). NT is indeed a *relative standard*, which exists on the basis of a comparison.

13.3.2 Most Favoured Nation Treatment

On the other side of the same non-discrimination coin, the MFN standard has also followed the evolutions of the global economy and adjusted to diverging political decisions. The MFN was more rapidly generalised than the NT and served, specifically, as a way to balance the absence of this standard in the hope that a country party to a web of treaties would grant one of its partners NT, which could then be claimed through MFN. MFN is indeed a rather expansible concept – so much so that a number of countries are now distancing themselves from the standard, like India, which decided not to include the MFN in its latest Model BIT.

In investment law, the MFN is inspired by trade-related practices and provisions, but differs from them. In trade, indeed, the MFN relates to the free circulation of goods and services, and so market access. In investment law, MFN applies to the investors and investments regulated by the host State. The variety of situations is immense and the analogies between trade and investment are thus limited.

As remarkably synthesised by an UNCTAD study, the MFN:[43]

---

[43] UNCTAD, 'Most-Favoured Nation Treatment', UNCTAD Series on Issues in International Investment Agreements II (New York and Geneva: United Nations, 2010), available at http://unctad.org/en/Docs/diaeia20101_ en.pdf (accessed 21 December 2020).

- is a treaty-based standard, which needs to be incorporated in a given IIA;
- is a relative standard in that it implies a comparison with a particular situation;
- can only apply to the same subject matter (principle of *ejusdem generis*, that is, of the same kind) or category;
- requires a basis of comparison (like circumstances, like situations);
- is based on nationality;
- needs the identification of a 'less favourable treatment';
- operates independently from contract law (no obligation for the State to treat other foreign investors in the same way as one is treated in a given contract as MFN is treaty-based);
- is different from trade MFN (like products or services/like circumstances for investors and investments);
- has to be interpreted in the light of the VCLT as a treaty obligation.

MFN was long considered a non-controversial standard and systematically granted at least post-establishment. Its history is naturally long and some examples can be found in treaties of friendship and commerce, such as the 1778 Treaty of Amity and Commerce between the United States and France.

Treaty of Amity and Commerce between the United States and France, 1778

Article 3

The Subjects of the most Christian King shall pay in the Port Havens, Roads, Countries, Lands, Cities or Towns, of the United States or any of them, no other or greater Duties or Imposts of what Nature soever they may be, or by what Name soever called, than those which the Nations most favoured are or shall be obliged to pay; and they shall enjoy all the Rights, Liberties, Privileges, Immunities and Exemptions in Trade, Navigation and Commerce, whether in passing from one Port in the said States to another, or in going to and from the same, from and to any Part of the World, which the said Nations do or shall enjoy.

Article 4

The Subjects, People and Inhabitants of the said United States, and each of them, shall not pay in the Ports, Havens Roads Isles, Cities & Places under the Domination of his most Christian Majesty in Europe, any other or greater Duties or Imposts, of what Nature soever, they may be, or by what Name soever called, that those which the most favoured Nations are or shall be obliged to pay; & they shall enjoy all the Rights, Liberties, Privileges, Immunities & Exemptions, in Trade Navigation and Commerce whether in passing from one Port in the said Dominions in Europe to another, or in going to and from the same, from and to any Part of the World, which the said Nation do or shall enjoy.

The very substance of MFN was already clearly palpable. Two centuries later, in a post-decolonisation era, the ILC acknowledged the importance of MFN treatment in its 1978 Draft Articles on Most Favoured Nation.[44]

ILC, Draft Articles on Most-Favoured-Nation Clauses, 1978, Article 5

Most-favoured-nation treatment is treatment accorded by the granting State to the beneficiary State, or to persons or things in a determined relationship with that State, not less favourable than treatment extended by the granting State to a third State or to persons or things in the same relationship with that third State.

MFN has naturally evolved from the first ever 1959 BIT between Germany and Pakistan to today's more sophisticated IIAs or FTAs with investment provisions. As an example, Article 3 of the 1994 China–Croatia BIT is revealing of a period when China was apparently paying less attention to the drafting of key non-discrimination provisions, mixed with other standards of treatment:[45]

China–Croatia BIT, 1994, Article 3

1. Investments and activities associated with investments of investors of either Contracting Party shall be accorded fair and equitable treatment and shall enjoy protection in the territory of the other Contracting Party.
2. The treatment and protection referred to in Paragraph 1 of this Article shall not be less favourable than that accorded to investments of investors of a third State.
3. The treatment and protection as mentioned in Paragraph 1 and 2 of this Article shall not include any preferential treatment accorded by the other Contracting Party to investment of investors of a third State based on customs union, free trade zone, economic union, agreement relating to avoidance of double taxation or for facilitating frontier trade.

---

[44] International Law Commission, 'Draft Articles on Most-Favoured-Nation Clauses with Commentaries', *Yearbook of the International Law Commission* (1978), II(2), available at http://legal.un.org/ilc/texts/instruments/english/commentaries/1_3_1978.pdf (accessed 21 December 2020).

[45] China–Croatia BIT 1994, available at https://investmentpolicy.unctad.org/international-investment-agreements.

China's most recent BITs offer much greater clarity, as in the 2012 Canada–China BIT:[46]

Canada–China BIT, 2012, Article 5: Most-Favoured-Nation Treatment

1. Each Contracting Party shall accord to investors of the other Contracting Party treatment no less favourable than that it accords, in like circumstances, to investors of a non-Contracting Party with respect to the establishment, acquisition, expansion, management, conduct, operation and sale or other disposition of investments in its territory.

2. Each Contracting Party shall accord to covered investments treatment no less favourable than that it accords, in like circumstances, to investments of investors of a non-Contracting Party with respect to the establishment, acquisition, expansion, management, conduct, operation and sale or other disposition of investments in its territory.

3. For greater certainty, the 'treatment' referred to in paragraphs 1 and 2 of this Article does not encompass the dispute resolution mechanisms, such as those in Part C, in other international investment treaties and other trade agreements.

Contemporary issues are well addressed here with, in particular, a third paragraph limiting the scope of the MFN by the exclusion of dispute settlement provisions. MFN treatment now typically comes with exceptions (economic sectors, regional integration mechanisms, dispute settlement) to avoid 'free-riders' engaging in treaty shopping. The risk of an abusive recourse to the MFN clause is indeed twofold: treaty shopping for better dispute settlement and treaty shopping for better provisions.

Maffezini v. Spain

These scenarios developed after the 2000 landmark *Maffezini* v. *Spain* decision on jurisdiction, which highlighted a possible application of MFN treatment to ISDS provisions.

The dispute at stake dealt with an Argentine national, Mr Maffezini's 70 per cent investment share in a Spanish company, Emilio A. Maffezini S.A. (EAMSA). The other 30 per cent was held by Sociedad para el Desarrollo Industrial de Galicia S.A. (SODIGA). After the conclusion of an environmental impact assessment, EAMSA encountered financial difficulties. The investor sought to use the MFN provision as a tool to access the beneficial dispute resolution clause of another treaty, namely, Spain–Chile BIT. It was one of the first ICSID cases where an individual was partly successful in claiming a violation of a BIT.

Following *Maffezini*, claimants have been seeking to use the MFN treatment to access more favourable substantive protection, as in the 2011 *White Industries* v. *India*, in which the

---

[46] Canada–China BIT 2012, available at https://investmentpolicy.unctad.org/international-investment-agreements.

Tribunal held that a delay by Indian courts violated the State's obligation to provide 'effective means' of asserting a claim, a provision borrowed from the BIT between India and Kuwait through the MFN.[47]

13.3.3 Minimum Standard and Fair and Equitable Treatment

The minimum standard and FET, although different, are interesting to read in conjunction and in a historical perspective. Indeed, FET has often been interpreted in relation to the minimum standard.

The minimum standard was progressively defined together with the expansion of trade and investment in the nineteenth century, a period of colonialism and imperialism. It is crucial to bear in mind this tension between the liberalisation of commerce on the one hand, and the brutal conquest, occupation and subjugation of foreign lands on the other, in order to understand the construction, ambiguities and contemporary controversies surrounding the minimum standard of treatment (see Chapter 16, as well as Introduction).[48] While Europe and the US were investing overseas, a body of texts was progressively emerging to define the international law of State responsibility for violation of international obligations. The main question at that time was that of injuries suffered by aliens (individuals) due to denial of justice or violent actions. In parallel, the US and the UK, in particular, started to consider that the taking of foreign property required systematic compensation on the basis of customary international law.[49] This was seen as a 'standard of justice' by and for all 'civilized countries'. While this treatment was evident to the Western world, it was also ill-defined and not deprived of ambiguities, as acknowledged by Sir Elihu Root, then President of the American Society of International Law and former US Secretary of War and Secretary of State, in his 1910 address to the American Society and the proceedings that followed:

The great accumulation of capital in the money centres of the world, far in excess of the opportunities for home investment, has led to a great increase of international investment extending over the entire surface of the earth, and these investments have naturally been followed by citizens from the investing countries prosecuting and caring for the enterprises in the other countries

   [. . .]

The rule of obligation is perfectly distinct and settled. Each country is bound to give to the nationals of another country in its territory the benefit of the same laws, the same administration, the same protection, and the same redress for injury which it gives to its own citizens, and neither more nor less: provided the protection, which the country gives to its own citizens conforms to the established standard of civilization. There is a standard of justice, very simple, very fundamental,

---

[47] *Emilio Agustín Maffezini* v. *Kingdom of Spain*, ICSID Case No. ARB/97/7, available at www.italaw.com/cases/641; *White Industries Australia Limited* v. *Republic of India*, Final Award, 30 November 2011, available at www.italaw.com/cases/documents/1170 (both accessed 21 December 2020).

[48] Becker Lorca, 'Eurocentrism in the History of International Law'.

[49] Andrew Newcombe and Lluís Paradell, *Law and Practice of Investment Treaties: Standards of Treatment* (Alphen aan den Rijn: Wolters Kluwer, 2009), pp. 11–12.

and of such general acceptance by all civilized countries as to form a part of the international law of the world.[50]

However, not all countries shared this supposedly consensual approach. The Mexican (1910–20) and Russian (1917) revolutions, with their socialist constitutions and drastic reform programmes, including confiscation and redistribution of land, dramatically shook a not so solid conceptual edifice. In the following years, the US and Mexico established a General Claims Commission, which acknowledged the existence of the minimum standard and a number of decisions of the PCIJ, and supported the idea of protecting aliens rights (*Certain German Interests in Polish Upper Silesia*) and private property, which, when taken, required to be compensated (*Factory at Chorzów*).[51] In the late 1920s, the League of Nations started preparing its 1930 Codification Conference with a programme on State responsibility. However, States disagreed on the approach to be taken and a number of host States remained in favour of the Calvo doctrine – that is, equality of treatment between nationals and foreigners, nothing less, but nothing more. The League of Nations 1929 draft Convention on the Treatment of Foreigners and the adopted 1933 Convention on the Rights and Duties of States (Montevideo Convention) also addressed the same issue, without being able to reconcile the differences between the North and the South.[52] National treatment prevailed, as stated in the Montevideo Convention:

Montevideo Convention, Article 9

The jurisdiction of States within the limits of national territories applies to all the inhabitants. Nationals and foreigners are under the same protection of the law and the national authorities and the foreigners may not claim rights other or more extensive than those of the nationals.

The Hull formula was later adopted (see Chapter 12) and integrated in modern investment treaties, with a generalisation in the 1990s. In parallel, the minimum standard of treatment continued to be vehemently debated, including by investment tribunals in relation to the FET (see Chapter 14). That is to say that this apparently resolved issue remains rather controversial and still ambiguous.

---

[50] Elihu Root, 'The Basis of Protection to Citizens Residing Abroad', *Proceedings of the American Society of International Law at its Annual Meeting (1907–1917), Volume 4 (28–30 April 1910)*, pp. 16–27, available at www.jstor.org/stable/25656384?seq=1#page_scan_tab_contents (accessed 21 December 2020).

[51] *Certain German Interests in Polish Upper Silesia (Germany v. Poland), 1926, PCIJ, Series A, No. 7; Factory at Chorzów (Germany v. Poland), 1927, PCIJ, Series A, No. 17.*

[52] League of Nations 1929 draft Convention on the Treatment of Foreigners, available at https://biblio-archive.unog.ch/Dateien/CouncilMSD/C-36-M-21-1929-II_EN.pdf; Montevideo Convention on the Rights and Duties of States, available at www.jus.uio.no/english/services/library/treaties/01/1-02/rights-duties-states.xml (both accessed 21 December 2020).

Box 13.3 *Glamis Gold* v. *USA*

Glamis Gold is undoubtedly one of the most debated cases in recent investment arbitration. The clash of religious beliefs, property rights and environmental concerns, together with a novel approach to the long-lasting controversy surrounding the minimum standard of treatment, have made this decision a landmark in contemporary IIL.

Naturally, the case has to be understood in its context and that of NAFTA in particular. In its Chapter 11 on investment, NAFTA indeed incorporated Article 1105 (Minimum Standard of Treatment), including broadly drafted provisions on 'fair and equitable treatment' and 'full protection and security', which have been extensively interpreted in NAFTA investment case law.

The dispute arose from a claim by Glamis Gold, a Canadian mining company, arguing that the United States had breached its obligations by expropriating its rights to mine gold in southeastern California and had denied the company FET. As a matter of fact, the targeted mining land was situated near the traditional reservation of the Quechan tribe, so had been removed from the list of permitted mining areas. However, Glamis Gold had been offered a permit by the Bush administration, but was later stopped in its operation by the state of California, which promulgated new legislation to protect the area from mining activities. This instability led the company to file a request for arbitration for violation of NAFTA's FET and formulate a compensation claim of US$50 million.

With a view to expanding the transparency of its procedure and engaging with the public, the Tribunal allowed the 'Quechan Indian Nation', as well as the 'Sierra Club' and 'Earthworks', but also the 'National Mining Association', to submit *amicus curiae* briefs. All these submissions quite extensively discussed customary international law, in relation to the protection of indigenous communities' rights and the realm of minimum standard and FET principles. As far as investment protection was concerned, the Tribunal referred to the 1926 *Neer* v. *Mexico* case on the minimum standard of treatment by a State vis-à-vis a foreign investor and concluded:

It appears to this Tribunal that the NAFTA States Parties agree that, at a minimum, the fair and equitable treatment standard is that as articulated in Neer: 'the treatment of an alien, in order to constitute an international delinquency, should amount to an outrage to bad faith, to wilful neglect of duty, or to an insufficiency of governmental action so far short of international standards that every reasonable and impartial man would readily recognize its insufficiency. (2009 Award, para. 612)

Although the Tribunal acknowledged that 'situations may be more varied and complicated today than in the 1920s', it also believed that 'the level of scrutiny is the same', and consequently,

the fundamentals of the Neer standard thus still apply today: to violate the customary international law minimum standard of treatment codified in Article 1105 of the NAFTA, an act

Box 13.3 (cont.)

must be sufficiently egregious and shocking – a gross denial of justice, manifest arbitrariness, blatant unfairness, a complete lack of due process, evident discrimination, or a manifest lack of reasons – so as to fall below accepted international standards and constitute a breach of Article 1105. (2009 Award, para. 616)

This lengthy and well-argued decision of 355 pages also approached the complex issue of 'legitimate expectations'. It concurred with previous decisions, and the *Thunderbird* Tribunal in particular, to conclude that this question related to an examination under NAFTA, Article 1105: 'in such situations where a Contracting Party's conduct creates reasonable and justifiable expectations on the part of an investor (or investment) to act in reliance on said conduct' (2009 Award, para. 621). It thus felt that legitimate expectations, as well as FET generally, were not violated and dismissed Glamis' claims.

While this decision has become a seminal one for the complexity of the issues at stake and the involvement of a variety of stakeholders, it is also quite surprising, as one might have expected the Tribunal to be more protective of the investors' rights in a rather unstable context and against the backdrop of a number of previous investor-friendly decisions.

To Go Further

Dumberry, P., *The Formation and Identification of Rules of Customary International Law in International Investment Law* (Cambridge University Press, 2016), p. 61.

Glamis Gold Ltd v. *United States of America*, case materials, including Award, 8 June 2009, available at www.italaw.com/cases/487 (accessed 21 December 2020).

NAFTA, Chapter 11, available at www.nafta-sec-alena.org/Home/Texts-of-the-Agreement/North-American-Free-Trade-Agreement?mvid=1&secid=539c50ef-51c1-489b-808b-9e20c9872d25#A1139 (accessed 21 December 2020).

Sharpe, J. K., 'The Minimum Standard of Treatment, Glamis Gold and Neer's Enduring Influence', in Kinnear et al., *Building International Investment Law*, pp. 269–81.

The obligation to grant FET to foreign investors/investments is now found in the vast majority of contemporary IIAs in relation to the minimum standard (or not – autonomy of the standard). The first use of the FET provision was by Article I of the 1959 Draft Convention on Investments Abroad, launched by groups of European businessmen and lawyers, under the leadership of Hermann Abs, Chairperson of the Deutsche Bank in Germany, and Lord Shawcross, former Attorney General of the United Kingdom:[53]

---

[53] Draft Convention on Investments Abroad, available at www.international-arbitration-attorney.com/wp-content/uploads/137-volume-5.pdf (accessed 21 December 2020).

Draft Convention on Investments Abroad, 1959, Article I

Each Party shall at all times ensure fair and equitable treatment to the property of the nationals of the other Parties. Such property shall be accorded the most constant protection and security within the territories of the other Parties and the management, use and enjoyment thereof shall not in any way be impaired by unreasonable or discriminatory measures.

This first attempt was soon followed by the OECD Draft Convention on the Protection of Foreign Property and inspired a large number of OECD countries in their BIT negotiations.[54]

The FET generalisation corresponded to the drafting of the ambiguous NAFTA Chapter 11, Article 1105, mixing FET with full protection and security without defining them.[55] The absence of definition and the implicit link to the minimum standard later gave rise to a vast body of disputes, which have partially clarified the meaning of Article 1105.

NAFTA, Article 1105

1. Each Party shall accord to investments of investors of another Party treatment in accordance with international law, including fair and equitable treatment and full protection and security.
2. Without prejudice to paragraph 1 and notwithstanding Article 1108(7)(b), each Party shall accord to investors of another Party, and to investments of investors of another Party, non-discriminatory treatment with respect to measures it adopts or maintains relating to losses suffered by investments in its territory owing to armed conflict or civil strife.
3. Paragraph 2 does not apply to existing measures relating to subsidies or grants that would be inconsistent with Article 1102 but for Article 1108(7)(b).

FET, however, is an autonomous and absolute standard. It can exist on its own, with or without a link to the minimum standard and does not require a comparison, contrary to NT and MFN, which are hence relative. As observed by UNCTAD, a sort of typography of FET treaty provisions can be established.[56] The FET can take the form of:

---

[54] OECD, Draft Convention on the Protection of Foreign Property, available at www.oecd.org/daf/inv/internationalinvestmentagreements/39286571.pdf (accessed 21 December 2020).

[55] See Bonnitcha, *Substantive Protection under Investment Treaties*.

[56] UNCTAD, 'Fair and Equitable Treatment: A Sequel', UNCTAD Series on Issues in International Investment Agreements II (New York and Geneva: United Nations, 2012).

– unqualified obligation;
– obligation linked to international law;
– FET obligation related to the minimum standard of treatment of aliens under customary international law;
– FET obligation with additional substantive content, such as denial of justice.

Its interpretation in the context of NAFTA will be covered at length in Chapter 14. This vast body of cases and related controversies (see Box 13.3) have directly influenced contemporary treaties drafters, who are now proposing better-defined provisions, as in CETA, Article 8.10:

CETA, Article 8.10: Treatment of investors and of covered investments

1. Each Party shall accord in its territory to covered investments of the other Party and to investors with respect to their covered investments fair and equitable treatment and full protection and security in accordance with paragraphs 2 through 7.
2. A Party breaches the obligation of fair and equitable treatment referenced in paragraph 1 if a measure or series of measures constitutes:
   (a) denial of justice in criminal, civil or administrative proceedings;
   (b) fundamental breach of due process, including a fundamental breach of transparency, in judicial and administrative proceedings;
   (c) manifest arbitrariness;
   (d) targeted discrimination on manifestly wrongful grounds, such as gender, race or religious belief;
   (e) abusive treatment of investors, such as coercion, duress and harassment; or
   (f) a breach of any further elements of the fair and equitable treatment obligation adopted by the Parties in accordance with paragraph 3 of this Article.
3. The Parties shall regularly, or upon request of a Party, review the content of the obligation to provide fair and equitable treatment. The Committee on Services and Investment, established under Article 26.2.1(b) (Specialised committees), may develop recommendations in this regard and submit them to the CETA Joint Committee for decision.
4. When applying the above fair and equitable treatment obligation, the Tribunal may take into account whether a Party made a specific representation to an investor to induce a covered investment, that created a legitimate expectation, and upon which the investor relied in deciding to make or maintain the covered investment, but that the Party subsequently frustrated.
5. For greater certainty, 'full protection and security' refers to the Party's obligations relating to the physical security of investors and covered investments.
6. For greater certainty, a breach of another provision of this Agreement, or of a separate international agreement does not establish a breach of this Article.

> *(cont.)*
>
> 7. For greater certainty, the fact that a measure breaches domestic law does not, in and of itself, establish a breach of this Article. In order to ascertain whether the measure breaches this Article, the Tribunal must consider whether a Party has acted inconsistently with the obligations in paragraph 1.

A series of observations needs to be formulated with regard to this Article: the FET and the full protection and security standard coexist in the same article; the FET is defined on the basis of a breach of one or several of the listed components (denial of justice, fundamental breach of due process, manifest arbitrariness, targeted discrimination, abusive treatment of investors, and a breach of any further elements of the fair and equitable treatment obligation adopted by the Parties); and the Parties reserve their right to regularly review the content of the FET. Although both encompassing and flexible, this approach leaves some margin for interpretation among a group of countries (Canada and EU members) whose legal systems differ greatly and might not have exactly the same understanding of what constitutes a 'fundamental breach of due process', for instance.

13.3.4 Full Protection and Security

The above association of FET and full protection and security (FPS) is quite telling with regard to the as yet limited clarifications brought to the comprehension of the FPS standard. It is an essential element of the risk protection construction and should be seen from a risk-avoidance perspective. Apparently obvious, if not innocuous, FPS deserves special attention, as a number of disputes have addressed its possible application at a time of global instability and local turmoil (see Chapter 14).

As far as treaty drafting is concerned, two main possibilities exist. First, FPS is integrated in a general provision also covering FET, as in the Energy Charter Treaty:

> ### Energy Charter Treaty, 1994, Article 10: Promotion, Protection and Treatment of Investments
>
> 1. Each Contracting Party shall, in accordance with the provisions of this Treaty, encourage and create stable, equitable, favourable and transparent conditions for Investors of other Contracting Parties to make Investments in its Area. Such conditions shall include a commitment to accord at all times to Investments of Investors of other Contracting Parties fair and equitable treatment. Such Investments shall also enjoy the most constant protection and security and no Contracting Party shall in any way impair by unreasonable or discriminatory measures their management, maintenance, use, enjoyment or disposal. In no case shall such Investments be accorded treatment less favourable than that required by international law, including treaty obligations.

This relatively vague phrasing de facto leaves a large margin for interpretation of the scope covered in relation to highly ambiguous terms, such as 'most constant' or 'unreasonable'. Some recent treaties, such as the 2012 US Model BIT, have tried to clarify these ambiguities, while still including the FPS standard in a broader article, together with the FET.

US Model BIT, 2012, Article 5: Minimum Standard of Treatment

1. Each Party shall accord to covered investments treatment in accordance with customary international law, including fair and equitable treatment and full protection and security.
2. For greater certainty, paragraph 1 prescribes the customary international law minimum standard of treatment of aliens as the minimum standard of treatment to be afforded to covered investments. The concepts of 'fair and equitable treatment' and 'full protection and security' do not require treatment in addition to or beyond that which is required by that standard, and do not create additional substantive rights. The obligation in paragraph 1 to provide:
   (a) 'fair and equitable treatment' includes the obligation not to deny justice in criminal, civil, or administrative adjudicatory proceedings in accordance with the principle of due process embodied in the principal legal systems of the world; and
   (b) 'full protection and security' requires each Party to provide the level of police protection required under customary international law.

In this context, the FPS would clearly refer to the 'level of police protection' required under 'customary international law' and is associated with the minimum standard, which leaves a rather wide margin for interpretation.

Another option is offered by the use of standalone provisions, as in the Southern African Development Community (SADC) 2012 Model BIT:[57]

SADC Model BIT, 2012, Article 9: Protection and Security

9.1. A State Party shall accord Investments of Investors of the other State Party protection and security no less favourable than that which it accords to investments of its own investors or to investments of investors of any third State.
9.2. Investors of one State Party whose Investments in the territory of the other State Party suffer losses as a result of a breach of paragraph 9.1, in particular owing to war or

---

[57] SADC Model BIT 2012, available at www.iisd.org/itn/wp-content/uploads/2012/10/sadc-model-bit-template-final .pdf (accessed 21 December 2020).

> ***(cont.)***
>
> other armed conflict, revolution, revolt, insurrection or riot in the territory of the Host State shall be accorded by the Host State treatment, as regards restitution, indemnification, compensation or other settlement, no less favourable than that which the Host State accords to investors of any third State.

This last option has the merits of clarifying the scope of the FPS as a separate standard from the FET. International investment jurisprudence indeed reflects two opposite views: one anchoring FPS to the FET standard and customary international law, and the other separating the two issues to insist on the independent existence of a specific standard implying equally specific obligations. Therefore, there are two possible approaches of risks and disasters.[58]

This stresses the State's need for a cautious approach to FPS. While avoidance of the standard is not required, a sound definition is essential, as the FPS standard and its due diligence expectations could eventually become complicated for developing States to meet.[59] As we will see in Chapter 14, investment tribunals have all interpreted FPS as protection against violent activities, either from third parties or from the State itself.

13.3.5 Taking of Foreign Property

At the very core of investment treaty protection, the issue of taking of foreign property remains the most essential, debated and controversial, for it relates to and impacts directly on the right (or duty) of the State to regulate. IIAs were originally drafted to prevent, protect and remedy the taking of aliens' property by the host State, be it expropriation or nationalisation, as these terms are often used in an apparently interchangeable fashion, although they are sometimes clarified in treaty drafting or investment jurisprudence. Expropriation breaches, claims and remedies fall under State responsibility and so question fundamental aspects of general public international law. In addition, the concept of expropriation resonates within the whole treaty's architecture in echoing the definitions of investment and investors, as well as the scope of the agreement. It is a complex and fascinating legal device. It is not an investment standard as such, but is often addressed in the same sections by textbooks and other scholarly articles, for it is central to IIL. It is a substantive principle indeed.

---

[58] Leïla Choukroune, 'Disasters and International Trade and Investment Law: The State's Regulatory Autonomy between Risk Protection and Exception Justification', in S. Breau and K. L. H. Samuel (eds.), *Research Handbook on Disasters and International Law* (Cheltenham: Edward Elgar, 2016), pp. 204–24.

[59] Mahnaz Malik, *The Full Protection and Security Standard Comes of Age: Yet Another Challenge for States in Investment Treaty Arbitration?*, Best Practices series (Winnipeg: International Institute for Sustainable Development, 2011).

The basic principle is simple, in a way: in international law, States have a sovereign right to take property held by nationals and aliens equally. But this taking is associated with a number of conditions, developed progressively through political and scholarly approaches and jurisprudence. The taking must be:

– for a public purpose;
– non-discriminatory;
– in accordance with due process of law;
– accompanied by compensation.[60]

However, from a relatively simple concept based on the sovereign right of the State, the taking of foreign property has evolved, in parallel with international economic realities, into a complex right challenged by numerous restrictions and disputes. So much so that from a positive formulation of a sovereign right (the State 'has the right to expropriation but needs to . . .'), treaty drafting has moved to a negative perspective (the 'state shall not expropriate unless it . . .').

As alluded to above, the first massive wave of expropriations took place at the time of the Mexican and Russian revolutions. In his correspondence with Eduardo Hay, the Mexican Minister for Foreign Affairs, then American Secretary of State Cordell Hull put forth what has become the leading formulation of the full compensation standard (see Chapter 12):[61]

The Government of the United States cannot admit that a foreign government may take the property of American nationals in disregard of the universally recognized rule of compensation under international law or admit that the rule of compensation can be nullified by any country through its own local legislation.

Hull insisted that compensation must be 'prompt, adequate and effective' – a formula later largely accepted and found in most of the post-1990s IIAs.

The second wave of nationalisations and expropriations occurred in the context of decolonisation, at a time when newly independent States benefited from a certain legitimacy and implicit international support to recover their lost resources and properties. Hence the formulation of the NIEO within the UN General Assembly and the adoption of a series of resolutions protecting the permanent economic sovereignty of States (see Chapter 12). In this regard, the provisions on expropriation of the Charter of Economic Rights and Duties of States are illustrative of a particular era:

[60] UNCTAD, 'Expropriation', UNCTAD Series on Issues in International Investment Agreements II (New York and Geneva: United Nations, 2012).
[61] Jeffrey F. Taffet and Dustin Walcher, *The United States and Latin America: A History with Documents* (New York: Routledge, 2017).

Charter of Economic Rights and Duties of States, Article 2

1. Every State has and shall freely exercise full permanent sovereignty, including possession, use and disposal, over all its wealth, natural resources and economic activities.
2. Each State has the right:
   a. To regulate and exercise authority over foreign investment within its national jurisdiction in accordance with its laws and regulations and in conformity with its national objectives and priorities. No State shall be compelled to grant preferential treatment to foreign investment;
   b. To regulate and supervise the activities of transnational corporations within its national jurisdiction and take measures to ensure that such activities comply with its laws, rules and regulations and conform with its economic and social policies. Transnational corporations shall not intervene in the internal affairs of a host State. Every State should, with full regard for its sovereign rights, cooperate with other States in the exercise of the right set forth in this subparagraph;
   c. To nationalize, expropriate or transfer ownership of foreign property, in which case appropriate compensation should be paid by the State adopting such measures, taking into account its relevant laws and regulations and all circumstances that the State considers pertinent. In any case where the question of compensation gives rise to a controversy, it shall be settled under the domestic law of the nationalizing State and by its tribunals, unless it is freely and mutually agreed by all States concerned that other peaceful means be sought on the basis of the sovereign equality of States and in accordance with the principle of free choice of means.

Interestingly and quite rightly so, the right to regulate is put forward as a sort of introduction to another right, that of nationalisation, expropriation and transfer of ownership of foreign property. In the event of such a decision, 'appropriate compensation' (not 'full, prompt and effective' compensation) has to be paid and disputes settled under the domestic law of the nationalising State and its tribunals unless freely and mutually agreed otherwise.

The NIEO consensus did not last long. With the waves of liberalisation of the late 1980s and early 1990s, a diametrically opposed approach was adopted, as illustrated by numerous BITs, and NAFTA as the quintessential example.

NAFTA, Chapter 11, Article 1110: Expropriation and Compensation

1. No Party may directly or indirectly nationalize or expropriate an investment of an investor of another Party in its territory or take a measure tantamount to nationalization or expropriation of such an investment ('expropriation'), except:
   (a) for a public purpose;

(cont.)

(b) on a non-discriminatory basis;

(c) in accordance with due process of law and Article 1105(1); and

(d) on payment of compensation in accordance with paragraphs 2 through 6.

2. Compensation shall be equivalent to the fair market value of the expropriated investment immediately before the expropriation took place ('date of expropriation') and shall not reflect any change in value occurring because the intended expropriation had become known earlier. Valuation criteria shall include going concern value, asset value including declared tax value of tangible property, and other criteria, as appropriate, to determine fair market value.

3. Compensation shall be paid without delay and be fully realizable.

4. If payment is made in a G7 currency, compensation shall include interest at a commercially reasonable rate for that currency from the date of expropriation until the date of actual payment.

5. If a Party elects to pay in a currency other than a G7 currency, the amount paid on the date of payment, if converted into a G7 currency at the market rate of exchange prevailing on that date, shall be no less than if the amount of compensation owed on the date of expropriation had been converted into that G7 currency at the market rate of exchange prevailing on that date, and interest had accrued at a commercially reasonable rate for that G7 currency from the date of expropriation until the date of payment.

6. On payment, compensation shall be freely transferable as provided in Article 1109.

7. This Article does not apply to the issuance of compulsory licences granted in relation to intellectual property rights, or to the revocation, limitation or creation of intellectual property rights, to the extent that such issuance, revocation, limitation or creation is consistent with Chapter Seventeen (Intellectual Property).

8. For purposes of this Article and for greater certainty, a non-discriminatory measure of general application shall not be considered a measure tantamount to an expropriation of a debt security or loan covered by this Chapter solely on the ground that the measure imposes costs on the debtor that cause it to default on the debt.

The perspective is clearly negative. When interpreted broadly, the article could give the impression that there is no right to nationalise or expropriate and almost an interdiction to do so. If the taking does occur, the conditions are rather drastic and everything seems to be aimed at avoiding the occurrence of nationalisation and expropriation – not to mention the formation of a new complication, that of the identification and distinction between 'direct' and 'indirect' expropriation or nationalisation. This rather allusive wording has naturally given rise to a very vast body of disputes, which, to some extent, has clarified the concepts of *legality* and *illegality* of *direct* and *indirect* expropriations assorted with *compensation*.

Direct and *indirect* expropriation claims make for a large part of investment disputes and are addressed at length in specialised reports, monographs and research articles.[62]

As we have seen from the above treaty provisions, the absence of uniformity in treaty drafting, if not the vagueness in the terms employed in specific provisions, has led to a case-by-case approach by arbitrators, often adding to the confusion. Without entering into the detailed intricacies of the cases addressing the issues of direct and indirect expropriation, as one could do in a dedicated investment textbook, let us cover the essential traits of this important discussion.

13.3.5.1 Direct Expropriation

The typical situation of an expropriation was, for a long time, a blatant case of a State's seizure of foreign property. With the development of IIAs, the situation was complicated by the rather vague distinctions between direct and indirect expropriation exemplified in the above NAFTA discussion. Progressively, ISDS cases shed some form of light. From the 1990s, indeed, a number of important decisions have marked the IIL field.

Waste Management v. Mexico

A landmark decision was adopted with the settlement of the *Waste Management* case.[63] The claims arose from a fifteen-year waste management concession held by the claimant's local subsidiary company. The concession was granted by the state of Guerrero and the municipality of Acapulco in Mexico. The *Waste Management* Award approached the distinction between direct and indirect expropriation.

Waste Management *v.* Mexico

143. It may be noted that Article 1110(1) distinguishes between direct or indirect expropriation on the one hand and measures tantamount to an expropriation on the other. An indirect expropriation is still a taking of property. By contrast where a measure tantamount to an expropriation is alleged, there may have been no actual transfer, taking or loss of property by any person or entity, but rather an effect on property which makes formal distinctions of ownership irrelevant. This is of particular significance in the present case, at least as concerns the enterprise of Acaverde as a whole.

---

[62] See UNCTAD ISDS databases on breaches of IIAs (alleged and found) for updated figures, available at https://investmentpolicy.unctad.org/investment-dispute-settlement (accessed 21 December 2020); the landmark report published by UNCTAD, 'Expropriation'; Johanne M. Cox, *Expropriation in Investment Treaty Arbitration* (Oxford University Press, 2019); Campbell McLachlan, QC, Laurence Shore and Matthew Weiniger, *International Investment Arbitration: Substantive Principles* (Oxford University Press, 2010).

[63] *Waste Management Inc.* v. *United Mexican States ('Number 2')*, ICSID Case No. ARB(AF)/00/3, Award, 30 April 2004, available at www.italaw.com/cases/1158 (accessed 21 December 2020).

(cont.)

144. Evidently the phrase 'take a measure tantamount to nationalization or expropriation of such an investment' in Article 1110(1) was intended to add to the meaning of the prohibition, over and above the reference to indirect expropriation. Indeed there is some indication that it was intended to have a broad meaning, otherwise it is difficult to see why Article 1110(8) was necessary. As a matter of international law a 'non-discriminatory measure of general application' in relation to a debt security or loan which imposed costs on the debtor causing it to default would not be considered expropriatory or even potentially so. It is true that paragraph (8) is stated to be 'for greater certainty', but if it was necessary even for certainty's sake to deal with such a case this suggests that the drafters entertained a broad view of what might be 'tantamount to an expropriation'.

While the Tribunal acknowledged the distinction between direct and indirect expropriation, it did not really clarify it.

METALCLAD CORPORATION V. MEXICO

In *Metalclad*, another influential NAFTA-based decision (see Box 14.5), the Tribunal had already interpreted the language of Article 1110[64] to find that:

Metalclad Corporation *v.* Mexico

103. … expropriation under NAFTA includes not only open, deliberate and acknowledged takings of property, such as outright seizure or formal or obligatory transfer of title in favour of the host State, but also covert or incidental interference with the use of property which has the effect of depriving the owner, in whole or in significant part, of the use or reasonably-to-be-expected economic benefit of property even if not necessarily to the obvious benefit of the host State.

The breath of interpretation is such that a vast number of situations could fall under the category of 'incidental interference with the use of property which has the effect of depriving the owner in whole or in significant part, of the use or reasonable-to-be-expected economic benefit of property'. The interpretation is very broad and the Tribunal does not even clarify the benefit.

We understand from this extremely broad interpretation why NAFTA cases have long been controversial. As we will see below, the category of indirect expropriation poses

---

[64] *Metalclad Corporation* v. *United Mexican States*, ICSID Case No. ARB(AF)/97/1, Award, 30 August 2000, available at www.italaw.com/cases/671 (accessed 21 December 2020).

multiple challenges. As far as direct expropriation is concerned, other tribunals have been more straightforward.

T E C M E D v . M E X I C O

In *Tecmed* v. *Mexico*, a case that arose out of Mexico's alleged non-renewal of a licence necessary to operate a landfill of hazardous industrial waste, the Tribunal argued that expropriation meant 'a forcible taking by the Government of tangible or intangible property owned by private persons by means of administrative or legislative action to that effect', but observed that:

> the term also covers a number of situations defined as de facto expropriation, where such actions or laws transfer assets to third parties different from the expropriating State or where such laws or actions deprive persons of their ownership over such assets, without allocating such assets to third parties or to the Government.[65]

Here again, we understand that the issue is not so much with the definition of a simple expropriation ('a forcible taking'), but rather with all that is not clearly said and simply alluded to when using the term 'indirect' expropriation.

13.3.5.2 Indirect Expropriation

Indirect expropriation has occupied international law scholarship and IIL actors alike for decades. Without clarity in treaty drafting, there cannot be much clarity in ISDS cases. This simple observation is important to bear in mind to understand the absence of consistency in ISDS cases. However, a number of cases remain of importance as they have marked the IIL field, sometimes by the reach of the decision adopted or the quality of the legal reasoning.

There are different forms of indirect expropriations. Several terms have been used, often quite liberally, in IIAs: 'creeping' expropriation, 'de facto' expropriation, 'equivalent' to expropriation, 'tantamount' to expropriation. Here again, the *Tecmed* Award provided some explanation:

Tecmed *v.* Mexico

114. Generally, it is understood that the term 'equivalent to expropriation' or 'tantamount to expropriation' included in the Agreement and in other international treaties related to the protection of foreign investors refers to the so-called 'indirect expropriation' or 'creeping expropriation', as well as to the above-mentioned de facto expropriation. Although these forms of expropriation do not have a clear or

---

[65] *Técnicas Medioambientales Tecmed S.A.* v. *United Mexican States*, ICSID Case No. ARB(AF)/00/2, Award, 29 May 2003, para 113, available at www.italaw.com/sites/default/files/case-documents/ita0854.pdf (accessed 21 December 2020).

(cont.)

unequivocal definition, it is generally understood that they materialise through actions or conduct, which do not explicitly express the purpose of depriving one of rights or assets, but actually have that effect. This type of expropriation does not necessarily take place gradually or stealthily – the term 'creeping' refers only to a type of indirect expropriation – and may be carried out through a single action, through a series of actions in a short period of time or through simultaneous actions. Therefore, a difference should be made between creeping expropriation and de facto expropriation, although they are usually included within the broader concept of 'indirect expropriation' and although both expropriation methods may take place by means of a broad number of actions that have to be examined on a case-by-case basis to conclude if one of such expropriation methods has taken place.

From the tribunal reasoning we understand that the 'effects' of the State's action matter. This particular focus on the 'effect' of a State decision has contributed to the development of a given approach known as 'the sole effect doctrine'. In adhering to this vision, tribunals have not regarded the initial intention of the State to concentrate only on the effect of the decision. This approach challenges the State regulatory autonomy for public interest.[66]

A 'creeping' expropriation will not necessarily result from a single action of the State. A creeping expropriation takes place on another temporal plane. It will often be gradual. Measures 'tantamount' to expropriation found in Article 1110 of NAFTA are often explained as something approaching 'equivalent' to, as in the *Pope & Talbot* v. *Canada* and *S.D. Myers* v. *Canada* cases.[67]

S.D. MYERS V. CANADA

In a case arising out of Canada's ban on the export of polychlorinated biphenyl wastes from Canada to the United States, and the alleged economic consequences for the investor resulting from the imposition of such ban, the Tribunal clarified the concept of expropriation and what should be understood as 'tantamount' to expropriation:[68]

---

[66] For an interesting recent example of how a tribunal has focused on the 'sole effect doctrine', as well as the regulatory autonomy of the State (often referred to as 'police power'), see the *Philip Morris Brands Sàrl, Philip Morris Products S.A. and Abal Hermanos S.A.* v. *Oriental Republic of Uruguay*, ICSID Case No. ARB/10/7, Award, 8 July 2016, available at www.italaw.com/cases/460 (accessed 21 December 2020). (See also *Philip Morris* case-related developments in Chapters 4 and 7.) See also Prabhash Ranjan, 'Police Powers, Indirect Expropriation in International Investment Law, and Article 31(3)(c) of the VCLT: A Critique of *Philip Morris* v. *Uruguay*', *Asian Journal of International Law* (2019), 9(1), pp. 98–124.

[67] *Pope & Talbot Inc.* v. *Canada*, UNCITRAL, proceedings and Award available at www.uncitral.org/transparency-registry/registry/data/can/pope_talbot_inc.html; *S.D. Myers Inc.* v. *Government of Canada*, UNCITRAL, proceedings and Award available at www.italaw.com/cases/969 (both accessed 21 December 2020).

[68] *S.D. Myers* v. *Canada*, Partial Award, 13 November, 2000, available at www.italaw.com/sites/default/files/case-documents/ita0747.pdf (accessed 21 December 2020).

S.D. Myers *v.* Canada

280. The term 'expropriation' in Article 1110 must be interpreted in light of the whole body of state practice, treaties and judicial interpretations of that term in international law cases. In general, the term 'expropriation' carries with it the connotation of a 'taking' by a governmental-type authority of a person's 'property' with a view to transferring ownership of that property to another person, usually the authority that exercised its de jure or de facto power to do the 'taking'.

    [...]

285. SDMI relied on the use of the word 'tantamount' in Article 1110(1) to extend the meaning of the expression 'tantamount to expropriation' beyond the customary scope of the term 'expropriation' under international law. The primary meaning of the word 'tantamount' given by the Oxford English Dictionary is 'equivalent'. Both words require a tribunal to look at the substance of what has occurred and not only at form. A tribunal should not be deterred by technical or facial considerations from reaching a conclusion that an expropriation or conduct tantamount to an expropriation has occurred. It must look at the real interests involved and the purpose and effect of the government measure.

Tantamount and equivalent are the same in the Tribunal's perspective. But the last sentence of the paragraph cited is of particular interest, as the Tribunal concludes that it must look 'at the real interests involved and the purpose and effect of the government measure'. Here is a mix between several approaches for a more balanced interpretation: the interests at stake, the objective of the measure taken by the State and the effect of it.

13.3.5.3 Legitimate Expectation

As alluded to above, ISDS decisions are many and not particularly consistent. However, in the course of their examination of the concept of indirect expropriation, tribunals have also addressed the controversial issue of the investor's 'legitimate expectations'. In this regard, the *Methanex* case is of particular interest (see Box 14.5).

METHANEX v. UNITED STATES

In a case arising out of alleged injuries on the investor Methanex, resulting from a California ban on the use or sale in California of the gasoline additive methyl tert-butyl ether, the Tribunal shed some light on the question of legitimate expectations.[69]

---

[69] *Methanex Corporation* v. *United States of America*, UNCITRAL, Final Award, 3 August 2005, Part IV, Chapter D, para. 7, available at www.italaw.com/sites/default/files/case-documents/ita0529.pdf (accessed 21 December 2020).

Methanex *v.* United States

Part IV, 7. In the Tribunal's view, Methanex is correct that an intentionally discriminatory regulation against a foreign investor fulfils a key requirement for establishing expropriation. But as a matter of general international law, a non-discriminatory regulation for a public purpose, which is enacted in accordance with due process and, which affects, inter alios, a foreign investor or investment is not deemed expropriatory and compensable unless specific commitments had been given by the regulating government to the then putative foreign investor contemplating investment that the government would refrain from such regulation.

The question revolves around the possibility for the investor to have expected that the regulatory measures taken by the State could deprive him of his property. The situation becomes complicated when expectations of economic benefit generated by the investment come into play. The issue of legitimate expectation has to be understood in conjunction with the treatment of the investor and FET in particular, as well as the idea of risk.[70]

13.3.5.4   Compensation

The last important issue addressed in the context of expropriation is the determination of compensation on the basis of whether the expropriation is legal or not, and direct or indirect. Here again, a vast body of cases and literature has developed over the years.[71] The issue of compensation is one of the most complex and controversial in ISDS. It has clearly arisen at a theoretical level since the debate between Calvo and Hull, and Hull's proposal for 'prompt, adequate, and effective' compensation. It has been influenced by early international decisions, such as the landmark PCIJ *Factory at Chorzów* (see Box 13.4). Compensation has also been at the centre of the NIEO discussions and is a question of general international law relating to the issue of State responsibility.

Box 13.4 *Factory at Chorzów*

In the aftermath of the First World War and against the backdrop of States succession and the Treaty of Versailles, the fascinating *Factory at Chorzów* case addressed the issue of damages for breaches of a treaty resulting from the taking of foreign property.

---

[70] Emmanuel T. Laryea, 'Legitimate Expectations in Investment Treaty Law: Concept and Scope of Application', in Chaisse et al., *Handbook of International Investment Law and Policy.*

[71] Borzu Sabahi, *Compensation and Restitution in Investor–State Arbitration: Principles and Practice* (Oxford University Press, 2011); R. Rajesh Babu, 'Standard of Compensation for Expropriation of Foreign Investment', in Chaisse et al., *Handbook of International Investment Law and Policy.*

Box 13.4 (cont.)

Despite its many and contradictory interpretations, the case remains an authority in contemporary ISDS discussions and still justifies the theory of full compensation. In the Iran–US Claims Tribunal, for example, it was referred to as 'the most authoritative exposition of the principles applicable' (to compensation).

The *Chorzów* case was filed with the Registry of the PCIJ on 8 February 1927, after a series of domestic decisions and bilateral negotiations, and arose out of the question of the responsibility of the Polish government for the taking of a nitrate factory situated at Chorzów, owned by Oberschlesische Stickstoffwerke and Bayerische Stickstoffwerke, two German companies, and operating on the basis of a contract it had concluded, in 1915, with the German Reich. In May 1922, the Geneva Convention between Germany and Poland settled the issue of Upper Silesia, which was ceded to Poland after the war and was where the factory was located. However, a few months later, the Polish government, on the basis of a 1 July 1922 Polish Court decision declaring null and void the registration of the company and citing the Treaty of Versailles, concluded that the property rights of the lands in question were to be registered in the name of the Polish treasury. The Polish State took control of the factory two days later. Two major questions were naturally posed at the time: the legality of the taking and the reparations for the damages caused by this very taking.

The PCIJ remained rather confused in its reasoning on the legality of the taking and it would be exaggerated to conclude that it deemed the taking of foreign property generally illegal. However, it was quite assertive on the idea of compensation (reparation) for the damages caused by the taking and provided the parties with rather precise injunctions on the amount to be paid and the methods of payment, including a clear timeline. In a famous reasoning often quoted in contemporary decisions, the Court demonstrated that:

It is a principle of international law that the breach of an engagement involves an obligation to make reparation in an adequate form. Reparation, therefore is the indispensable complement of a failure to apply a convention and there is no necessity for this to be stated in the convention itself. (*PCIJ, Series A, No. 9, 26 July 1927*, p. 21)

Reparation was seen here as the 'indispensable complement of a failure to apply a convention' – that is, a breach of State responsibility, and a 'principle of international law'.

In addition, the Court explained that the reparation should, as much as possible, be a 'restitution in kind', or, if this was not possible, the payment of reparation equivalent to this restitution in kind as the reparation needed to 'wipe out' all 'the consequences of the illegal act' and 're-establish the situation'. If need be, damages could also be awarded:

Box 13.4 (cont.)

The essential principle contained in the actual notion of an illegal act – a principle which seems to be established by international practice and in particular by the decisions of arbitral tribunals – is that reparation must, as far as possible, wipe out all the consequences of the illegal act and re-establish the situation which would, in all probability, have existed if that act had not been committed. Restitution in kind, or, if this is not possible, payment of a sum corresponding to the value which a restitution in kind would bear; the award, if need be, of damages for loss sustained which would not be covered by restitution in kind or payment in place of it – such are the principles which should serve to determine the amount of compensation due for an act contrary to international law.

In this regard one can indeed easily understand why and how this PCIJ decision provided food for thought for the approach later known as the Hull formula and a number of arbitral decisions supporting 'prompt, adequate, and full compensation'.

To Go Further

Amco International Finance Corp. v. *Iran* (1987), 15 Iran–US CTR 189.
Factory at Chorzów (Germany v. *Poland), 1927, PCIJ, Series A, No. 9*, 26 July 1927, Jurisdiction, and *1928, PCIJ, Series A, No. 17*, 13 September 1927, Merits, available at www.icj-cij.org/en/pcij-series-a (accessed 21 December 2020).

The obligation to compensate is clearly stated in the ILC's Articles on Responsibility of States for Internationally Wrongful Acts, 2001. Article 31(1) obligates the responsible State to 'make full reparation for the injury caused by the internationally wrongful act'.[72]

In the absence of formal unified guidelines on this issue, tribunals have adopted a large variety of approaches, often on a case-by-case basis, in trying to quantify the right value (*valuation*) of an investment. There are several methods in this regard, from the book value of an investment that is the difference between the investment's assets and liabilities, as shown in its financial records, to the much more complex and debated discounted cash flow, which values the investment on the basis of its future probable profits. This method has been quite popular with tribunals, but has also generated a lot of controversy – for the sum calculated, in taking into account a sometimes rather unpredictable future, can be enormous and extremely challenging for a state to gather. The World Bank has published interesting guidelines on the *Legal Framework for the Treatment of Foreign Investment*, in which the issue of compensation is addressed.[73]

---

[72] Articles on Responsibility of States for Internationally Wrongful Acts with Commentaries, Art. 31.
[73] World Bank, *Legal Framework for the Treatment of Foreign Investment, Volume II: Guidelines* (Washington, DC: World Bank, 1992), available at http://documents.worldbank.org/curated/en/955221468766167766/Guidelines (accessed 21 December 2020).

To close this discussion on takings, it is interesting to take a look at recent efforts. In terms of IIA drafting, more balanced and yet also more precise positions can be found today – for example, CETA, Article 8.12.

CETA, Chapter 8, Section D, Article 8.12: Expropriation

1. A Party shall not nationalise or expropriate a covered investment either directly, or indirectly through measures having an effect equivalent to nationalisation or expropriation ('expropriation'), except:
   (a) for a public purpose;
   (b) under due process of law;
   (c) in a non-discriminatory manner; and
   (d) on payment of prompt, adequate and effective compensation.

   For greater certainty, this paragraph shall be interpreted in accordance with Annex 8-A.

2. The compensation referred to in paragraph 1 shall amount to the fair market value of the investment at the time immediately before the expropriation or the impending expropriation became known, whichever is earlier. Valuation criteria shall include going concern value, asset value including the declared tax value of tangible property, and other criteria, as appropriate, to determine fair market value.

3. The compensation shall also include interest at a normal commercial rate from the date of expropriation until the date of payment and shall, in order to be effective for the investor, be paid and made transferable, without delay, to the country designated by the investor and in the currency of the country of which the investor is a national or in any freely convertible currency accepted by the investor.

4. The affected investor shall have the right, under the law of the expropriating Party, to a prompt review of its claim and of the valuation of its investment, by a judicial or other independent authority of that Party, in accordance with the principles set out in this Article.

5. This Article does not apply to the issuance of compulsory licences granted in relation to intellectual property rights, to the extent that such issuance is consistent with the TRIPS Agreement.

6. For greater certainty, the revocation, limitation or creation of intellectual property rights, to the extent that these measures are consistent with the TRIPS Agreement and Chapter Twenty (Intellectual Property), do not constitute expropriation. Moreover, a determination that these measures are inconsistent with the TRIPS Agreement or Chapter Twenty (Intellectual Property) does not establish an expropriation.

Yet treaty drafters could use a number of other techniques and wording to better frame the issue of taking of foreign property, in order to support their right and de facto duty to regulate in favour of public purposes. We will address the question of the right to regulate, or what has been called the 'regulatory chill effect' (limitation of this right) in Chapter 14, but let us briefly suggest a few of the drafting techniques translating policy options available to the States. Parties to an IIA can:[74]

- clarify the meaning of direct and indirect expropriation in using precise criteria to assess their existence;
- clarify the difference between legitimate 'police power' or the right to regulate and indirect expropriation;
- explain why and how such a legitimate and non-discriminatory regulatory action could justify the taking as well as the absence of compensation;
- list the circumstances and/or criteria according to which such a non-regulatory action could take place;
- use exceptions and other treaty flexibilities in the form of WTO general exceptions list type or any other more specific format (provisions, economic sectors, period of time, geographical scope);
- strictly define and frame compensation, including the exact valuation and time period.

13.4 Conclusion

While IIAs are extremely diverse, they also share a number of common features: their structure, the attention they pay to their scope, and the essential definitions of investments and investors, as well as the incorporation of substantive standards of protection from non-discrimination with the NT and MFN treatment to the more controversial FET and FPS often approached together, with the yet to be fully clarified minimum standard of treatment of aliens in customary international law. In addition, international investment treaties protect foreign investors/investment from the taking of property, while ideally, they also protect the State's margin to use its sovereign right to regulate for public purposes. At the time of writing, numerous discussions are taking place internationally to modernise old treaties and adopt new ones, but also, while more treaties are denounced than signed, it is crucial to bear in mind that IIAs are part of general public international law, and therefore to approach their study with a multidisciplinary mindset.[75]

13.5 Summary

- IIAs are extremely diverse, but they also share a number of common features.
- To narrow down the risk of interpretation and provide the parties with additional precision and possible 'legal certainty' – as much as this concept does exist – treaty drafters

---

[74] UNCTAD, 'Expropriation, 2012'.

[75] See the work of UNCTAD on modernisation of IIAs, available at http://unctad.org/en/PublicationsLibrary/diaepcb2017d3_en.pdf and http://unctad.org/en/PublicationsLibrary/webdiaepcb2014d6_en.pdf (both accessed 21 December 2020).

have introduced a number of provisions relating to the *scope of the treaty*, hence framing its application.

- The practice of reservations and exceptions preserves and furthers the flexibility of treaty drafters to protect particular interests while achieving certain treaty objectives – in our context, the promotion and protection of foreign investment.
- The definitions of investment and investor are also very much part of this treaty negotiation and have quite fundamentally evolved from the first BIT ever signed, between Germany and Pakistan in 1959, to today's more complex BITs and, naturally, even more encompassing trade and investment mega-deals.
- Traditionally, IIAs have used an 'asset-based' definition of investment. Another option is to use an 'enterprise-based' definition.
- IIAs comprise a definition of the term investor (juridical and natural person).
- One fundamental issue is easily identifiable here – that of the *nationality* of the individual and/or the company identified as an investor.
- At the core of IIAs, these standards of treatment and protection constitute the very essence of IIL and will most certainly continue to be challenged and debated.
- Also at the centre of investment treaty protection, the issue of taking of foreign property remains the most essential, debated and controversial, for it relates to and impacts directly on the right (or duty) of the State to regulate.

13.6   Review Questions

1 Can a country limit the geographical scope of an IIA? If so, how?

2 Can a country limit the temporal scope of an IIA? If so, how?

3 Can a country terminate its IIAs at any point in time?

4 South Africa, Ecuador, Indonesia and India have recently terminated some of their BITs. Does this mean that the treaties have stopped applying to the investments and investors covered at the very moment these countries denounced their agreements? If not, what rule will prevail? Please research some of these precise BITs to give country-specific answers (2000 India–Australia BIT; 2003 Belgium-Luxembourg Economic Union–South Africa BIT; 1997 Ecuador–Cuba BIT; 2007 Indonesia–Germany BIT). A useful resource is the UNCTAD Investment Policy Hub, available at http://investmentpolicyhub.unctad.org/IIA (accessed 21 December 2020).

5 How is a reservation defined by the VCLT?

6 What is the difference between an exception and a carve-out clause?

7 What are the exceptions planned in the investment chapter of CETA?

8 How was investment defined in the first ever BIT between Germany and Pakistan? How has this definition evolved compared to the 2009 treaty? Please search BITs texts available at https://investmentpolicy.unctad.org/international-investment-agreements (accessed 21 December 2020).

9 Based on a search of recent and less recent German and American BITs, please identify treaties with assets-based definitions of investments and other examples of enterprise-based definitions.

10 What does the *Nottebohm* case bring to the definition of investor?

11 How is an investor defined in the latest Dutch BITs in force? Can it be ambiguous and support treaty shopping? See https://investmentpolicy.unctad.org/international-invest ment-agreements (accessed 21 December 2020).

12 Why is national treatment central to investment law?

13 What is the difference between MFN treatment in trade and investment law?

14 Are FET and FPS relative or absolute standards? Why?

15 Is the taking of foreign property a sovereign right? Is it conditional or unconditional?

13.7 Exercise

Building on its successful contract negotiation with Hopeland, your international law firm, LJCN, is now at the centre of the first truly multilateral investment treaty negotiation. Its team has been chosen by UNCTAD to coordinate a vast effort between the very diverse groups of stakeholders participating in the negotiation.

Several issues have to be negotiated in parallel, hence you are coordinating three working groups. They all consist of a variety of countries, with often quite opposed, if not conflicting interests and visions of what should be the best possible treaty to protect foreign investments, but also their right to regulate in favour of public interest.

The first working group is in charge of the identification and framing of treaty flexibilities. It has to propose a number of exceptions and carve-out clauses to protect the interest of the States parties. Yet a few parties to the negotiation, and Gainland, in particular, are very much opposed to these techniques.

Your role is to convince all of the benefits they could bring and reach an acceptable consensus.

The second working group has been designated to work on the complex question of the definition of investors and the issue of shareholder control. Multinational companies have been lobbying the Conference for a long time and have convinced a number of States parties to the negotiation of the interest of treaty shopping.

You are to clarify all positions and come up with an acceptable definition for all parties, including capital recipient countries, which fear abuse of process and threaten to introduce stringent denial of benefits provisions.

The third working group will have to find a way to rebalance State and investor rights, if reaffirming the taking of foreign property as a right assorted with certain conditions. NGOs associated with the negotiation are trying to convince parties to revert to the NIEO approach. Some also argue that the right to regulate should be introduced as a duty for the State. In playing with the treaty's preamble, scope, exceptions and provisions on expropriation, you are confident you will be able to accommodate all interests and perspectives.

Each working group needs to consult with partners and come up with a written draft proposal.

FURTHER READING

Chaisse, J., Choukroune, L. and Jusoh, S. (eds.), *Handbook of International Investment Law and Policy* (Singapore: Springer, 2021).

Cox, J. M., *Expropriation in Investment Treaty Arbitration* (Oxford University Press, 2019).

Dörr, O. and Schmalenbach, K. (eds.), *Vienna Convention on the Law of Treaties: A Commentary* (Berlin: Springer, 2012).

Dumberry, P., *The Formation and Identification of Rules of Customary International Law in International Investment Law* (Cambridge University Press, 2016).

Kalicki, J., Evseev, D. and Silberman, M., 'Legality of Investment', in M. Kinnear, G. R. Fischer, J. Minguez Almeida, L. Fernanda Torres, M. Uran Bidegain (eds.), *Building International Investment Law: The First Fifty Years of ICSID* (Alphen aan den Rijn: Wolters Kluwer, 2016), pp. 127–39.

Kinnear, M., Fischer, G. R., Minguez Almeida, J., Torres, L. F., Uran Bidegain, M. (eds.), *Building International Investment Law: The First Fifty Years of ICSID* (Alphen aan den Rijn: Wolters Kluwer, 2016).

Kulick, A., *Reassertion of Control over the Investment Treaty Regime* (Cambridge University Press, 2017).

Paddeu, F. and Bartels, L. (eds.), *Exceptions and Defences in International Law* (Oxford University Press, 2020).

Valasek, M. J. and Dumberry, P., 'Developments in the Legal Standing of Shareholders and Holding Corporations in Investor–State Disputes', *ICSID Review: Foreign Investment Law Journal* (2011), 26(1), pp. 34–75.

14   Settlement of International Investment Disputes

Table of Contents

Highlights

- The settlement of international investment disputes has been under intense scrutiny and at the centre of heated discussions for a number of years.
- ISDS remains quite controversial for it is a unique system at the crossroads between public and private international law.
- However, ISDS needs to be approached from a public international law perspective, as the disputes at stake are largely based on IIAs between States.
- From negotiation to litigation, the State's responsibility is engaged when settling an international investment dispute.
- Contract-based arbitration has also influenced ISDS.

- Treaty-based arbitration can take the form of State-to-State (relatively rare) or investor–State arbitration (around 1,000 known cases), conducted in a variety of fora.
- The ICSID remains the most popular forum and benefits from structured proceedings and clear rules.
- Other fora are nevertheless available to the parties to an international investment dispute.
- While one could try to argue in favour of the existence of some *jurisprudence constante* (consistent case law) based on a number of 'persuasive cases', there is certainly no *stare decisis* in IIL, as investment tribunals are not bound by their previous decisions.
- From transparency and ethics, to access to justice and the right to regulate, a number of controversies and challenges are addressed today by a variety of actors (States, international organisations, civil society and so on).
- ISDS reform proposals have been put forward, including by the European Union, along the lines of the establishment of a permanent investment court; while others support ADR solutions or a return to domestic settlement.

14.1 Introduction

The settlement of international investment disputes has been under intense scrutiny and at the centre of heated discussions for a number of years. With the release of controversial reports and documentaries designed to impact on a large global audience, the rather technical issue of ISDS has gone far beyond the confines of highly specialised law firms and obscure arbitral tribunals.[1] So much so that it has captured the imagination and reform frenzy of a variety of stakeholders, from governments to international organisations and civil society, now ready to fight for their own ISDS reform proposals as the best solution to mitigate disputes and eventually improve social justice. Naming and shaming the powerful abusers of the system, be it mega-multinational companies or global corporate lawyers, has certainly helped to shed some light on a rather opaque practice now willing to improve its ethics and transparency. Interrogating the very basis of a hybrid mechanism at the crossroads between private and public international law, which indeed addresses questions of public interest, and so the livelihood of millions of people lacking quality services and essential public goods from water to energy, has had the great merit of liberating the voices

---

[1] See, for example, Pia Eberhardt and Cecilia Olivet, *Profiting from Injustice* (Brussels/Amsterdam: Corporate Europe Observatory/Transnational Institute, 2012), available at https://corporateeurope.org/international-trade/2012/11/profiting-injustice (accessed 21 December 2020); Pia Eberhardt, *The Zombie ISDS: Rebranded as ICS, Rights for Corporation to Sue States Refuse to Die*, updated version (Corporate Europe Observatory, 2016), available at https://corporateeurope.org/sites/default/files/attachments/the_zombie_isds_0.pdf; 'Company vs. Country' (BBC Radio 4 documentary, March 2015), available at www.bbc.co.uk/programmes/b05ntj7p; 'Multinationale contre Etat: la loi du plus fort' (France 2, 16 November 2017), available at www.youtube.com/watch?v=fLFOeJa8p8w (accessed 21 December 2020).

of the silent and deprived. ISDS controversy has undoubtedly proven to be a powerful instrument to reclaim rights and put a rights-based approach at the centre of IIL and dispute settlement, with treaty drafting as its very starting point (see Chapter 12). But is this perception of injustice a true rendition of the reality of ISDS? Are States the sole victims of an unbalanced mechanism that always favours investors? Is the much-criticised ICSID the worst forum to resolve investment issues? Is an international investment court modelled on the now rather weakly supported World Trade Organization system a true improvement? Are ISDS reforms triggered by the developing world or simply the new incarnation of Western-centric ideals reshaped in the light of their own failure and the recent shock waves hitting quite a number of European countries, which perceive themselves as the new and unexpected victims of ISDS?

The settlement of international investment disputes is a complex task. It engages the State's responsibility and finds its roots in practices of negotiation and contract-based arbitration alike. It involves multiple actors, fora and rules. This chapter will therefore cover international investment dispute settlement starting from negotiation and the role of international courts. It then moves progressively to contemporary ISDS and addresses its functioning and the challenges it faces at a time of much expected reforms. In doing so, the chapter focuses on a number of key disputes often related to the issue of the taking of foreign property and the capacity of States to regulate in favour of the protection of public interest, hence echoing our previous investment chapters presenting IIL making and standards. Lastly, it shows a number of developing world-related cases and examples to better balance global views, expectations and practices.

14.2 From Negotiation to Litigation

14.2.1 Engaging State Responsibility

As demonstrated in Chapter 12, international State responsibility is at the centre of IIL. A breach of treaty results in the invocation of the State's responsibility and the need to repair a wrongful act by this very State. Diplomatic protection has sometimes been considered a solution by investors, but is reluctantly used by States. As we will see below, very few cases have been brought to the ICJ and its predecessor, the PCIJ, on this basis, while State-to-State arbitration remains rare. But prior to any litigation effort, there is one step to follow – that of negotiation.

14.2.1.1   Negotiation

Be it compulsory or not, negotiation remains a central element of international investment dispute settlement. This negotiation can take place between the investor and the host State or, at the diplomatic level, between the home State of the investor and the host State, hence bringing us back to the question of diplomatic protection.

Let us consider the issue of negotiation between the investor and the host State, keeping in mind that both parties could actually break their contractual and/or treaty obligations.

As mentioned above, IIL is centred on State responsibility, but this should not preclude the possibility of breaches by the investor. The situation is not so different from a commercial dispute, but one aspect remains crucial here: the State is involved and needs to be duly represented at the negotiation table. Investor–State disputes negotiation could well preserve both parties from acrimonious and costly procedures, including international arbitration, the results of which might be published and so damage their reputation. This negotiation could take place at the domestic level and is often encouraged by international agreements themselves, as a way to further a long-term relationship in which important financial interests are at stake. The possibility of negotiation touches upon two different aspects: the (re)negotiation of the contract and/or the treaty prior to a dispute, and the negotiation of the settlement of the dispute once it has arisen.

In relation to the first possibility listed above, there is sometimes a duty to (re)negotiate a foreign investment contract or treaty, in the context of changing circumstance, and to prevent the escalation of the problem into a dispute. This duty to negotiate can be recognised in contract law by the introduction of a specific clause (hardship or *force majeure* – see Chapter 12), but also in treaty law on the basis of the flexibility offered by Article 62 of the VCLT.

VCLT, Article 62: Fundamental change of circumstances

1. A fundamental change of circumstances which has occurred with regard to those existing at the time of the conclusion of a treaty, and which was not foreseen by the parties, may not be invoked as a ground for terminating or withdrawing from the treaty unless:
   (a) The existence of those circumstances constituted an essential basis of the consent of the parties to be bound by the treaty; and
   (b) The effect of the change is radically to transform the extent of obligations still to be performed under the treaty.
2. A fundamental change of circumstances may not be invoked as a ground for terminating or withdrawing from a treaty:
   (a) If the treaty establishes a boundary; or
   (b) If the fundamental change is the result of a breach by the party invoking it either of an obligation under the treaty or of any other international obligation owed to any other party to the treaty.
3. If, under the foregoing paragraphs, a party may invoke a fundamental change of circumstances as a ground for terminating or withdrawing from a treaty it may also invoke the change as a ground for suspending the operation of the treaty.

This article is particularly interesting and important in that it provides stability and flexibility at the same time, hence preserving a long-term commitment between the parties.

Box 14.1 *Aminoil*: a case of contract renegotiation and arbitration

What if a contract renegotiation *leads* to a dispute rather than prevent it? The case of *Aminoil* (see Chapter 12) can be viewed from a variety of angles, all related to the much publicised and political arbitration that followed the company's nationalisation. It has become a landmark case for the study of stabilisation clauses and the role of arbitration to settle disputes related to changes of contractual circumstances.

In 1948, a concession contract had been signed between the Ruler of Kuwait and the American Company Aminoil, for the exploitation of petroleum and natural gas. Once Kuwait acceded to independence from the British Empire, the initial contract was amended, in 1961, by a 'Supplemental Agreement'. The 1948 contract contained a stabilisation clause. The 1961 amendments essentially modified the financial clauses to the benefit of the new State and to the detriment of the company, which was required to pay taxes. All this took place in the context of decolonisation and the acknowledgement of the principle of State sovereignty over natural resources, alongside the NIEO debates and resolutions adopted by the United Nations (see Chapters 11 and 12). A new series of contractual renegotiations followed and ended with several agreements between the parties in 1973 and 1977. After the latest wave of renegotiations failed, in 1997, the company was eventually nationalised and its concession terminated. Kuwait was willing to compensate the company for the taking and play by the rules of international arbitration. Interestingly, the majority of the Arbitral Tribunal considered that the language of the stabilisation clause did not prohibit nationalisation, especially as Kuwait had agreed to compensate the company for this taking. In a now famous Separate Opinion, the arbitrator appointed by Aminoil, Sir Fitzmaurice, opposed the majority's view in providing a different interpretation of the effect of a stabilisation clause in the case of renegotiation and changing circumstances. In addition, the Tribunal clarified the question of renegotiation of contracts in stating that it was different from an 'obligation to agree' – so much so that the failure to come to an agreement cannot be seen as a contractual breach.

To Go Further

Peter, W., de Kuyper, J.-Q. and de Cnadolle, B. (eds.), *Arbitration and Renegotiation of International Investment Agreements* (The Hague: Kluwer Law International, 1995).

Weiler, T. (ed.), *International Investment Law and Arbitration: Leading Cases from the ICSID, NAFTA, Bilateral Investment Treaties and Customary International Law* (London: Cameron May, 2011), pp. 347–81.

Once a dispute has arisen, as per our second listed possibility above, a number of treaties impose a duty to negotiate the *settlement of disputes* before resorting to any international forum. Numerous examples are found in BITs, but the recent Chinese Model BIT provides for a clear illustration of a quite firm requirement to negotiate. As a matter of fact, the

Canada–China BIT (2012) lists a number of detailed conditions to meet prior to submitting a dispute to arbitration in its Article 21:[2]

Canada–China BIT (2012), Article 21: Conditions Precedent to the Submission of a Claim to Arbitration

1. Before a disputing investor may submit a claim to arbitration, the disputing parties shall first hold consultations in an attempt to settle a claim amicably. Consultations shall be held within 30 days of the submission of the notice of intent to submit a claim to arbitration, unless the disputing parties otherwise agree. The place of consultation shall be the capital of the disputing Contracting Party, unless the disputing parties otherwise agree.

2. Subject to the Party-specific requirements set out in Annex C.21, a disputing investor may submit a claim to arbitration under Article 20 only if:

   (a) the investor consents to arbitration in accordance with the procedures set out in this Agreement and delivers notice of such consent to the disputing Contracting Party together with the submission of a claim to arbitration;

   (b) at least six months have elapsed since the events giving rise to the claim;

   (c) the investor has delivered to the disputing Contracting Party written notice of its intent to submit a claim to arbitration at least four months prior to submitting the claim;

   (d) the investor has delivered, with its notice of intent to submit a claim to arbitration under sub-paragraph (c), evidence establishing that it is an investor of the other Contracting Party;

   (e) the investor has waived its right to initiate or continue dispute settlement proceedings under any agreement between a third State and the disputing Contracting Party in relation to the measure alleged to be a breach of an obligation under Part B of this Agreement; and

   (f) not more than three years have elapsed from the date on which the investor first acquired, or should have first acquired, knowledge of the alleged breach and knowledge that the investor or a covered investment of the investor has incurred loss or damage thereby.

Naturally, a duty to negotiate is also present for the States parties to the treaty before they submit their dispute to an arbitral tribunal, as in Article 15 (Disputes between the

---

[2] See the 2012 Agreement between the Government of Canada and the Government of the People's Republic of China for the Promotion and Reciprocal Protection of Investments, available at https://investmentpolicy.unctad.org/international-investment-agreements/treaties/bilateral-investment-treaties/778/canada---china-bit-2012- (accessed 21 December 2020).

Contracting Parties) of the Canada–China BIT (2012), which encourages consultations through diplomatic channels and the respect of a six-month latency period.

Lastly, as we will see below regarding developments dedicated to ISDS challenges and pathways to reform, there is today a real interest in ADR as means to resolve investment conflict. The possibility of mediation/conciliation, while already offered by an institution such as the ICSID, is very much coming further to the fore.

14.2.1.2 Domestic Resolution

Another step to follow prior to resorting to international litigation is that of domestic remedies whether these have to be first exhausted or not. We have shown (see Chapter 11) that the work of the Argentine jurist Carlos Calvo has deeply influenced certain approaches to IIL, and the settlement of investment disputes in particular. According to these approaches, international investment disputes should first and foremost be settled domestically. States' international responsibility and diplomatic protection are not to be called on, as they are seen as offering an artificially higher protection to foreigners than that which is offered to nationals. National treatment is the best and sufficient standard of protection. As a consequence, the only tribunals that have the jurisdiction to settle international investment disputes are the domestic tribunals of the host State. A lighter approach to the same reasoning requires, *a minima*, the pursuit and sometimes exhaustion of local remedies (P/ELR) prior to engaging in any international procedure.

Pursuit and Exhaustion of Local Remedies   Popular in the 1970s, at the time of decolonisation and indeed affirmation of the NIEO of which the sovereignty over natural resources was a central pillar, P/ELR (whether administrative and/or judicial) lost its importance in the liberal era starting from the late 1980s. Interestingly, it is resurfacing today in the context of ISDS controversies. Quite recently, Argentina, India, Turkey, the United Arab Emirates, the SADC and the East African Community (EAC) have reintroduced a mandatory requirement to pursue or exhaust local remedies (P/ELR). The EU, as we will see below, is now quite tempted to require the same, although not yet ready to fully distance itself from ISDS.

There are a few distinctions to make to clarify the options available to the parties and the investor-claimant in particular:

- P/ELR is not similar to a negotiation or mediation moment often required in investment agreements and referred to as a 'cooling-off period'.
- P/ELR is to be distinguished from the requirement of exclusivity of a given (domestic) forum. It does not preclude recourse to another international forum.
- P/ELR is different from 'fork in the road' provisions, which makes the choice of a given forum rather final (see below).
- P/ELR can be waived in exceptional circumstances when the option is made available by an agreement or when it would be unreasonable, unfair, futile, absolutely ineffective and

cause major undue delay or denial of justice. But these arguments have to be demonstrated and can lead to major disagreements between the parties and to disputes.

- P/ELR has been considered 'an important principle of customary international law' by the ICJ in the ELSI case opposing Italy and the US in the taking of a foreign investment.[3]
- In addition, Article 26 of the ICSID Convention acknowledges the State's right to require P/ELR as a precondition of consent to treaty arbitration.
- IIAs can be silent or explicitly require P/ELR.
- IIAs can make a distinction between the 'pursuit' and the 'exhaustion' of local remedies. This is often based on a given timeline for the claimant to respect before it resorts to international arbitration.
- Investment jurisprudence has largely interpreted P/ELR. Its conclusions vary, but one could see a general leniency in accepting cases for arbitration unless P/ELR is strictly stipulated in IIAs – hence the need for the State to be attentive at the treaty drafting phase, and the new wave of IIAs, including specific provisions on P/ELR.
- As demonstrated in Chapter 13, standards of treatment and the MFN standard in particular can be tricky, as the claimant can well try to import another IIA where the P/ELR is not specified and apply it to the dispute it claims.[4]

EMILIO AGUSTÍN MAFFEZINI V. KINGDOM OF SPAIN

With regard to the possible avoidance of P/ELR through the importation of MFN provisions, the *Maffezini* case proved a landmark. In a dispute arising out of the discontinuance of the investor's activities due to an internal financial crisis allegedly attributed to Spain, the investor attempted to use the MFN clause to overcome a qualifying condition, such as a waiting period, in the dispute settlement provisions of a BIT. The investor indeed argued that he did not need to pursue local remedies because the MFN clause allowed him to go straight to international arbitration. Precisely, *Maffezini* demonstrated that the MFN clause in the Argentina–Spain BIT allowed him to invoke more favourable provisions in another treaty, the Chile–Spain BIT, as the latter did not include a requirement to seek local remedies prior to recourse to international arbitration. In a quite broad interpretation of the BIT, the Tribunal rejected Spain's objections to jurisdiction, agreeing with the investor's reasoning. In contrast to the Spain–Argentina BIT, the Spain–Chile BIT permitted the investor to submit the dispute to ICSID arbitration without first accessing the Spanish courts.

On the basis of the above observations, States have found a new interest in P/ELR and have recently produced a series of interesting new provisions in this regard, as illustrated by the precise wording of Article 15 of the 2015 Indian Model BIT.[5]

---

[3] ELSI, available at www.icj-cij.org/en/case/76 (accessed 21 December 2020).

[4] See *Emilio Agustín Maffezini* v. *Kingdom of Spain*, Decision on Objections to Jurisdiction, para. 22, available at www .italaw.com/cases/641 (accessed 21 December 2020).

[5] Indian Model BIT (2015), available at https://investmentpolicy.unctad.org/international-investment-agreements/ treaty-files/3560/download (accessed 21 December 2020).

Indian Model BIT (2015), Article 15: Conditions precedent to submission of a claim to arbitration

15.1 In respect of a claim that the Defending Party has breached an obligation under Chapter II, other than an obligation under Article 9 or 10, a disputing investor must first submit its claim before the relevant domestic courts or administrative bodies of the Defending Party for the purpose of pursuing domestic remedies in respect of the same measure or similar factual matters for which a breach of this Treaty is claimed. Such claim before the relevant domestic courts or administrative bodies of the Defending Party must be submitted within one (1) year from the date on which the investor first acquired, or should have first acquired, knowledge of the measure in question and knowledge that the investment, or the investor with respect to its investment, had incurred loss or damage as a result.

For greater certainty, in demonstrating compliance with the obligation to exhaust local remedies, the investor shall not assert that the obligation to exhaust local remedies does not apply or has been met on the basis that the claim under this Treaty is by a different party or in respect of a different cause of action. Provided, however, that the requirement to exhaust local remedies shall not be applicable if the investor or the locally established enterprise can demonstrate that there are no available domestic legal remedies capable of reasonably providing any relief in respect of the same measure or similar factual matters for which a breach of this Treaty is claimed by the investor.

15.2 Where applicable, if, after exhausting all judicial and administrative remedies relating to the measure underlying the claim for at least a period of five years from the date on which the investor first acquired knowledge of the measure in question, no resolution has been reached satisfactory to the investor, the investor may commence a proceeding under this chapter by transmitting a notice of dispute ('notice of dispute') to the Defending Party.

Fork in the Road Distinct from P/ELR, the 'fork in the road' provision basically confines the parties to one specific forum. The investor is limited in its choice of recourses and needs to specify its preferences between the different forms of redress available. The choice is generally simple: domestic procedures (court or administration) versus international arbitration. However, the fork in the road provision is not necessarily so easy to implement. It has to be shown that the dispute litigated before an international tribunal is the 'same dispute' as the dispute addressed by domestic procedures.

CHEVRON-TEXACO V. *ECUADOR*

The *Chevron-Texaco* v. *Ecuador* case has clarified the concept of 'sameness' in a detailed reasoning of which the following elements are of importance:[6]

Chevron-Texaco *v.* Ecuador, *Part IV, (F) Fork in the Road*

4.72 The BIT's fork in the road provision appears in Article VI(3) of the BIT . . .

4.73 The question is whether 'the dispute' submitted to this Tribunal has already been submitted to the national courts of Ecuador or New York so as to trigger the fork in the road provision in Article VI(3). There is no suggestion that the Parties have agreed to any other settlement procedure under Article VI(2)(b) of the BIT.

4.74 In the Tribunal's view, 'the dispute' in this context must mean 'the same dispute': it is not suggested that the submission of a different dispute between the Claimants and the Respondent could trigger the fork in the road provision in relation to the Parties' dispute before this Tribunal. Plainly, what is literally one and the same dispute cannot be before two tribunals simultaneously. 'Sameness' must refer to material identity or sameness determined in the context of a fork in the road provision. The question is therefore: what is required to establish this particular 'sameness'?

4.75 Tribunals in earlier investment cases have applied a 'triple identity' test, requiring that in the dispute before the domestic courts and the dispute before the arbitration tribunal there should be identity of the parties, of the object, and of the cause of action. In the present case, there is no identity of parties, of object or of cause of action between the Lago Agrio litigation or, indeed, in the Aguinda litigation in the New York Courts.

For the Arbitral Tribunal, it seems clear that sameness can be simplified to the very idea that 'one and the same dispute cannot be before two tribunals simultaneously'. In addition, it refers to a 'triple identity test' used by previous tribunals: *identity of the parties, the object* and *the cause of action*. Naturally, this test might be difficult to meet in the context of highly complex multinational operations with a large number of stakeholders. Not to mention, as demonstrated by M. Sornarajah on the basis of a distinction made between contractual and treaty cases in the *Vivendi* case, that the variety of legal grounds on which the dispute arises (contract or IIAs) could give even greater flexibility to the investor to have recourse to different fora for a dispute, where exact 'sameness' is difficult to show.[7]

---

[6] *Chevron Corporation and Texaco Petroleum Corporation* v. *Republic of Ecuador*, UNCITRAL, PCA Case No. 2009-23, Third Interim Award on Jurisdiction and Admissibility, 27 February 2012, available at www.italaw.com/sites/default/files/case-documents/ita0175.pdf (accessed 21 December 2020).

[7] M. Sornarajah, *The International Law on Foreign Investment*, 4th ed. (Cambridge University Press, 2018), p. 323; *Compañía de Aguas del Aconquija S.A. and Vivendi Universal S.A.* v. *Argentine Republic*, ICSID Case No. ARB/97/3, Decision on Annulment, 3 July 2003, available at www.italaw.com/cases/309/ (accessed 21 December 2020).

Box 14.2 *Texaco-Chevron* v. *Ecuador*: the major global investment dispute

In September 2015, following twenty-two years of an epic class action lawsuit filed in New York US Federal Court in 1993, on behalf of the victims of the massive pollution resulting from Texaco-Chevron's operations in the Amazon region, the Supreme Court of Canada ruled unanimously that the plaintiffs could seek to enforce the Ecuadorian landmark decision that found Chevron liable for US$9.5 billion in environmental clean-up costs in the Canadian court of Ontario, on the basis of the assets owned by the company in the country. Why would a Canadian court intervene in a dispute between the Ecuadorian Parties and a private multinational company, which took place in Ecuador and was (partially) litigated in the same country?

In August 2018, the Permanent Court of Arbitration in the Hague held Ecuador liable for 'denial of justice' to Chevron and violation of the company's fundamental procedural rights by allowing its courts to issue the $9.5 billion judgment. The Arbitration Tribunal ruled that no part of the said judgment should be recognised or enforced by any State.

Far beyond a simple international investment dispute, the never-ending episodes of this incredibly complex case make it *the* major global investment dispute calling for law reunification and the creation of a proper unique forum to sue multinational corporations for human rights abuses. As we will see below, the company, in a magisterial demonstration of legal mastery of forum and norms shopping has used, and maybe abused, all possible judicial and non-judicial fora to get rid of a now extremely embarrassing, as well as extremely costly, litigation.

The dispute is complicated and revealing of developing countries' dependency on primary goods, and oil in particular, but also how this dependency eventually transforms into a curse rather than a blessing. Ecuador's history with oil had long been a tumultuous one: while the first petroleum concession was granted in 1879 to MG Mier Co., not much was done before the 1910s, with the intervention of the Anglo-Ecuadorian Oil Fields, a subsidiary of British Petroleum and the Ecuador Oil Fields. Following a rather timid attempt to develop the industry in the 1930s, the real take-off only happened from the late 1960s, with the involvement of Texaco Inc., after a time of intense political instability. From 1920 to 1948, Ecuador was governed by no fewer than thirty-five presidents, including eight dictatorships, twelve transitional regimes and four ad hoc administrative structures designated by Constitutional Assemblies. In search of investment for growth and so a form of stability, Texaco Inc., and its subsidiary Texaco Petroleum Company, as well as Gulf Oil, were invited by Ecuador, in March 1964, to participate in a consortium to explore and produce oil in the Oriente region of the Amazon, in partnership with the government. Soon after 1964, the nationalists and the military regimes claimed State sovereignty over the oil resources. The Ecuadorian government created a State-owned oil company (Corporación Estatal Petrolera Ecuatoriana (CEPE), now Petroecuador)

Box 14.2 (cont.)

and demanded a 25 per cent participating share when the operations began in 1974. While the spectre of nationalisation faded away, the Ecuadorian government was very much willing to acquire majority ownership in the company. Hence, in June 1992, Petroecuador acquired 100 per cent of the trans-Ecuador pipeline and 100 per cent of all remaining consortium facilities. Here lies the ambiguity of the relationship between Texaco-Chevron and the Ecuadorian government: while Chevron claims that the Amazon pollution is the main responsibility of an Ecuadorian government, which has progressively acquired the consortium ownership and managed and monitored the whole operation, the plaintiffs, supported by a variety of NGOs and counsels, adopt a pragmatic approach, showing that Chevron was still de facto controlling the exploration and production, despite appearances.

This unprecedented case is not only unique for its political intricacies and the magnitude of the environmental devastation of the rainforest, but also because of the incredible length and complexity of global legal proceedings, which are now reaching their most concrete phase, for a multinational corporation supported on all continents by an army of lawyers, and which has tried all possible legal recourses, from American tribunals to The Hague Permanent Court of Arbitration in relation to the BIT existing at the time between the United States and Ecuador, while some accusations of corruption and illegal behaviours were raised about the plaintiffs' side. At least seven different fora at the national, foreign and international levels have been/ are being considered by the complainant and respondent to seek justice, including Ecuador, the US, the Permanent Court of Arbitration, Canada, Brazil, Argentina and the International Criminal Court.[8]

---

[8] The different proceedings are important to understand the intricacies of international investment dispute settlement and can be explained simply as follows. First, a case in the US where, in 1993, a group of Ecuadorian citizens of the Oriente region filed a class action lawsuit in US Federal Court against Texaco (*Aguinda* v. *Texaco*), and, in 1994, a group of Peruvian citizens also filed a class action lawsuit against Texaco (*Jota* v. *Texaco*). Both lawsuits were dismissed by the US Federal Court, in 2002, on forum non conveniens grounds (Ecuador was a more appropriate venue for litigating these claims). Texaco agreed that courts in Ecuador and/or Peru would have better jurisdiction over the claims. Then, in Ecuador, in 2003, a class action lawsuit was brought against Texaco (acquired by Chevron in 2001), alleging severe environmental contamination of the land, which has led to increased rates of cancer as well as other serious health problems for the residents of the region. On 14 February 2011, an Ecuadorian judge issued a ruling against Texaco-Chevron, which was ordered to pay US$8.6 billion in damages and clean-up costs, with the damages increasing to US$18 billion if the company did not issue a public apology. For Chevron, the ruling was 'illegitimate' and 'unenforceable', and it filed an appeal. On 3 January 2012, a panel of three judges from the Provincial Court of Justice of Sucumbios upheld the February 2011 ruling against Chevron. Chevron tried many tactics to block the judgment, including an order from the Permanent Court of Arbitration, which asked Ecuador's government to suspend the litigation and block the plaintiffs from enforcing the judgment, and, in September 2014, a claim against Woodsford Litigation Funding, which had financed lawyers working on enforcing the US$9.5 billion Ecuadorian judgment against Chevron, which it says was achieved by fraud and bribery. On their side, in an effort to enforce the judgment, the Ecuadorian plaintiffs filed a lawsuit in Canada, in May 2012, and in Brazil, in June 2012, and in Argentina, in November 2012, targeting Chevron's assets in those countries. On 12 November

Box 14.2 (cont.)

Has there been any comparable case in the history of international (investment) law and the efforts to sue multinational corporations for human rights violations? No. This multifaceted transnational litigation is particularly revealing of the many implications and ambiguities brought by foreign direct investment in complicated socio-political contexts, as it deeply questions the ability of developing States to fully exercise their sovereignty over natural resources when in an unbalanced relationship with super-powerful multinational corporations, themselves directly contributing to the development of these very States. Paradigmatic in many ways, the *Chevron* case embodies the numerous facets of global litigation as an emerging practice of forum and norms shopping, drawing upon a vast array of national and international texts and practices, at the centre of which lies the tension between various legal disciplines, and international human rights and economic law in particular.

To Go Further

Aguinda v. *Texaco, Inc.*, No. 93 Civ 7527, SDNY, 3 November 1993 (*Aguinda* complaint); *Ashanga Jota* v. *Texaco, Inc.*, No. 94 Civ.9266, SDNY, 28 December 1994 (*Ashanga Jota* complaint).

Chevron Corporation and Texaco Petroleum Corporation v. *Ecuador (II)*, PCA Case No. 2009-23, award(s) and procedure available at www.italaw.com/cases/257; while the general context is available at www.business-humanrights.org/en/companies/texaco-part-of-chevron/ (both accessed 21 December 2020).

2013, the Ecuador Supreme Court upheld the August 2012 ruling against Texaco-Chevron for environmental damage, but halved the damages to $9.51 billion. In the Permanent Court of Arbitration, in December 2006, and again in September 2009, Chevron filed an international arbitration claim, alleging that the government of Ecuador had violated the US–Ecuador BIT. In March 2010, the PCA ruled that Ecuador's government had violated the BIT and international law by delaying rulings on the commercial dispute currently pending in Ecuador's courts. But the government of Ecuador and the plaintiffs in the Ecuadorian lawsuit filed a lawsuit in US Federal Court, seeking an injunction, barring Chevron from proceeding further under the BIT. In February 2011, the international arbitration tribunal issued an Interim Measures Order in favour of Chevron, ordering Ecuador to suspend enforcement of the Ecuadorian judgment. In a sort of opposite move, however, in March 2015, the arbitration tribunal held that the settlement between Chevron and Ecuador did not preclude residents from suing over the pollution in the future. But in January 2016, the district court of The Hague ruled in favour of Chevron over Ecuador being bound by the US–Ecuador investment agreement and the interim measures decided by the arbitrations. Again in 2018, it ruled in favour of Chevron. In the US again, following the Ecuadorian judgment, Chevron filed a racketeering lawsuit against the plaintiffs' lawyers and representatives in US Federal Court on 1 February 2011. In October 2012, after many judicial episodes, the US Supreme Court refused to hear Chevron's appeal of the lower court's decision, ruling that a US judge lacked authority to issue the injunction, blocking enforcement of the Ecuadorian judgment. In Canada, as alluded to above, in an effort to enforce the US$9.51 billion Ecuadorian judgment, in September 2015, the Canadian Supreme Court ruled that the plaintiffs were able to sue Chevron and its Canadian subsidiary in Canada. In the International Criminal Court, in October 2014, Ecuadorian rainforest communities filed a communication in respect of Chevron's chief executive's acts to prevent the ordered clean-up of toxic waste in the Amazon.

14.2.1.3   International Tribunals

Once the question of the possible resolution of investment dispute by negotiation or at the domestic level has been addressed, the internationalisation of the case in question comes as the natural next step. The hybrid nature of international investment law, which generally involves the State and a foreign private investor, poses the problem of an adequate international forum. A logical approach is to engage the international responsibility of the State and activate the mechanism of diplomatic protection. As explained previously, States (and investor alike) have been rather reluctant to move in this direction, for it is not well-suited to the conduct and realities of international investments (see Chapter 13).

Only a small number of cases have been brought to the PCIJ and then to the ICJ. This was true before the signature of the first BIT in 1959 between Pakistan and Germany, and the later creation, in 1965, of the ICSID. It has been even more true since these major turning points. However, the below cases remain of particular importance for they have clarified a number of key principles, but have also limited the ambit of the Court. They are often referred to in investment arbitration and ICSID case law in particular. But the opposite is not true. The ICJ, 'mindful of its "prestige"', as Alain Pellet puts it, will not refer to arbitration case law, for it is not consistent. This is a very important point. While one could try to argue in favour of the existence of some *jurisprudence constante* based on a number of 'persuasive cases', there is certainly no *stare decisis* in IIL, as investment tribunals are not bound by their previous decisions.[9]

Permanent Court of International Justice
- *Factory at Chorzów*: damages for breaches of a treaty resulting from the taking of foreign property in the aftermath of the First World War and the succession of States between Poland and Germany (see Box 13.4).
- *Oscar Chinn*: whether the Belgian government had violated its obligations vis à vis a British national operating fluvial transport, Mr Chinn, in implementing a programme benefiting a company with significant ties to the Belgian government to offer discount transportation services in Congo.
- *Serbian Loans*: under what conditions the holders of Serbian bonds were entitled to obtain payment of the nominal amount of their coupons.[10]

International Court of Justice
- *Anglo-Iranian Oil Co. (United Kingdom v. Iran)*: in 1933, an oil concession agreement was concluded between the government of Iran and the Anglo-Iranian Oil Company. In 1951,

---

[9] Alain Pellet, 'The Case Law of the ICJ in Investment Arbitration', *ICSID Review – Foreign Investment Law Journal* (2013), 28(2), pp. 223–40, available at https://doi.org/10.1093/icsidreview/sit022 (accessed 21 December 2020).

[10] *Factory at Chorzów, 1927, PCIJ, Series A, No. 9; Factory at Chorzów, 1928, PCIJ, Series A, No. 17; Oscar Chinn (United Kingdom v. Belgium), Judgment, 1934, PCIJ, Series A/B, No. 63; Payment of Various Serbian Loans Issued in France (France v. Kingdom of the Serbs, Croats, and Slovenes), Judgment, 1929, PCIJ, Series A, No. 20.*

laws were passed in Iran for the nationalisation of the oil industry. The UK took up the company's case and instituted proceedings before the ICJ.

- *Barcelona Traction, Light and Power Company, Limited (Belgium v. Spain)*: admissibility of the claims, capacity of applicant government and claims brought on behalf of shareholders in foreign limited liability companies, nature of corporate entities and, of course, diplomatic protection, were all issues of crucial importance and widely debated up to the present day (see Chapter 12).
- *ELSI*: on 6 February 1987, the United States instituted proceedings against Italy in respect of a dispute arising out of the requisition, by the government of Italy, of the plant and related assets of Raytheon-Elsi S.p.A., an Italian company (previously known as Elettronica Sicula S.p.A. – ELSI), which was stated to have been 100 per cent owned by two US corporations (issues of shareholders' rights and nationality; see Chapter 13).
- *East Timor (Portugal v. Australia)*: treaty between Australia and Indonesia, which created a zone of cooperation in a maritime area between 'the Indonesian Province of East Timor and Northern Australia'. Possible failure by Australia to observe the obligation to respect the duties and powers of Portugal as the Administering Power of East Timor and the right of the people of East Timor to self-determination.
- *Gabčíkovo-Nagymaros Project (Hungary v. Slovakia)*: certain issues arising out of differences that had existed between the Republic of Hungary and the Czech and Slovak Federal Republic regarding the implementation and the termination of the Budapest Treaty of 16 September 1977 on the Construction and Operation of the Gabčíkovo-Nagymaros Barrage System and on the construction and operation of the 'provisional solution'.
- *Ahmadou Sadio Diallo (Republic of Guinea v. Democratic Republic of the Congo)*: dispute concerning 'serious violations of international law' alleged to have been committed upon the person of Mr Ahmadou Sadio Diallo, a Guinean national, imprisoned by the authorities of the Democratic Republic of the Congo, after being resident in that State for thirty-two years, despoiled of his sizeable investments, businesses, movable and immovable property and bank accounts, and then expelled. This expulsion came at a time when Mr Diallo was pursuing recovery of substantial debts owed to his businesses by the Congolese State and by oil companies of which the State was a shareholder.[11]

World Trade Organization Although not an international court as such, the WTO Dispute Settlement Mechanism (see Chapter 10) has received more than forty cases in relation to the TRIMs Agreement.[12] Part of the WTO Multilateral Agreements, the rather short TRIMs agreement deals with trade in goods and prohibits trade-related investment measures, such as performance requirements, that are inconsistent with the GATT

---

[11] *Anglo-Iranian Oil Co. (United Kingdom v. Iran)*, available at www.icj-cij.org/en/case/16; *Barcelona Traction*, available at www.icj-cij.org/en/case/50/judgments; ELSI, available at www.icj-cij.org/en/case/76; *East Timor (Portugal v. Australia)*, available at www.icj-cij.org/en/case/84; *Gabčíkovo-Nagymaros Project (Hungary/Slovakia)*, available at www.icj-cij.org/en/case/92; *Diallo*, available at www.icj-cij.org/en/case/103 (all accessed 21 December 2020).

[12] See www.wto.org/english/tratop_e/dispu_e/dispu_agreements_index_e.htm (accessed 21 December 2020).

1994 basic provisions (Articles III and XI). The TRIMs provides a trade perspective limited to prohibiting trade-related investment measures, which could have a restrictive and distorting effect on trade. Performance requirements (see Chapter 11) are obligations imposed on the investor by the host State (local content, transfers of technology, employment of local labour, formation of joint venture, level and so on). They have been prohibited by US treaties, but have been largely used by developing countries to protect their domestic growth and support their industrial take-off. The TRIMs will typically address this type of measure, perceived as impacting the good conduct of trade. National treatment (see Chapters 2, 12 and 13) is at the centre of the TRIMs' legal approach. Foreigners should not be treated less favourably than nationals in having to abide by certain specific domestic requirements to invest. A few recent illustrations provide good examples of how Article 2 (National Treatment and Quantitative Restrictions) could be invoked. For instance, in the case *India – Certain Measures Relating to Solar Cells and Solar Modules* (see Chapter 9), the US challenged certain Indian domestic content requirements for solar cells and solar modules. In *China – Certain Measures Granting Refunds, Reductions or Exemptions from Taxes and Other Payments*,[13] Mexico considered certain Chinese measures granting refunds, reductions or exemptions from taxes and other payments owed to the government by enterprises in China to be in violation of the TRIMs Article 2, as the Chinese government provided refunds, reductions or exemptions to enterprises operating in China on the condition that they purchase domestic over imported goods and meet certain export performance criteria.

Beyond the TRIMs, investment-related cases could also be brought before the DSB on the basis of the GATS, addressing foreign investment in services as one of the four modes of supply of services (see Chapter 8).

Iran–US Claims Tribunal   An ad hoc court has also made a mark on IIL and arbitration: the Iran–US Claims Tribunal.[14] It was established, on 19 January 1981, by the Islamic Republic of Iran and the United States of America, to resolve certain disputes by nationals of one State party against the other State party, as well as State-to-State disputes. To date, the Tribunal has settled over 3,900 cases. It has produced a major body of work on States' international responsibility. Although forming a *lex specialis*, these decisions constitute an important jurisprudential source in international investment arbitration. Some have so argued in favour of the idea of 'persuasive precedent' (cases with non-binding authority) to qualify certain landmark decisions taken by this Tribunal.[15] A vast number of important questions have been addressed in the many awards rendered from nationality of investment and investor, interim measures of relief to expropriation and standard of compensation.

---

[13] *China – Certain Measures Granting Refunds, Reductions or Exemptions from Taxes and Other Payments*, available at www.wto.org/english/tratop_e/dispu_e/cases_e/ds359_e.htm (accessed 21 December 2020).

[14] See www.iusct.net (accessed 21 December 2020).

[15] Christopher S. Gibson and Christopher R. Drahozal, *The Iran–US Claims Tribunal at Twenty-Five: The Cases Everyone Needs to Know for Investor–State and International Arbitration* (Oxford University Press, 2007).

14.3 Contract-Based Arbitration

The influence of contract law and contract-based arbitration on ISDS has been tremendous. Although private actors, and investors in particular, are not international law subjects, they have managed to engage with the international legal system of nation States in creating and preserving a place of choice. The entirety of IIL and litigation rests upon these ambiguous interactions between private and public actors and private and public international law (see Chapters 11 and 12). After all, as evidenced by M. Sornarajah, 'many of the legal techniques, particularly in the field of foreign investment, were created through the exercise of private powers'.[16] The contractual protection negotiated with the host State implies the respect of contractual obligations for the State (and the investor alike), and the consent of the parties to resort to arbitration in the event of a dispute. With the early concession agreements drafted from US expansion in Latin America and, later, the exploitation of energy resources, and oil in particular, the State's liability for breaches of contractual commitments is based on the ability of the investor to negotiate a number of essential contractual requirements. Be it a choice of law clause or a stabilisation provision (see Chapter 12), all these contractual devices have supported the possibility of settling a dispute by an (ad hoc) international (private) arbitration. The creation and procedure to be followed by these tribunals is well-established in the investor–State contracts and, again, has influenced the hybrid system found in international treaties.

14.4 Treaty-Based Arbitration

Treaty-based investor–State arbitration has appeared progressively with the signing of the first BITs. At the centre of this novel and hybrid dispute resolution technique is the idea of consent to arbitration itself deriving from two key elements: the presence of dispute settlement provisions in the treaty text and the satisfaction of the nationality criteria. Therefore, the definitions of investment and investor (see Chapter 13) are of crucial importance. On this basis, the tribunal's jurisdiction can be challenged and/or accepted. According to UNCTAD statistics, more than 40 per cent of the 1,000 plus known investment cases concluded are decided in favour of the State (around 30 per cent in favour of the investor); the proportion is different when discussing the merits of the case (see figures below).[17] It is easy to imagine that the first step for the State is to challenge jurisdiction. Treaty-based arbitration can take two major forms: State-to-State or investor–State arbitration. While the latter form is under much scrutiny, the first option, although available quite systematically in the treaties signed between States parties, is hardly talked about and sometimes avoided in the study of international investment dispute. It is rare, but State-to-State treaty-based arbitration exists and remains as interesting as it is important.

---

[16] Sornarajah, *International Law on Foreign Investment*, p. 278.

[17] See UNCTAD, ISDS statistics, available at https://investmentpolicyhub.unctad.org/ISDS (accessed 21 December 2020).

14.4.1 State-to-State

From *Italy* v. *Cuba* in 2003, to *Ecuador* v. *USA* in 2011, recent investment cases have triggered a renewed interest in State-to-State arbitration, quickly followed by natural interrogations on the political nature of the process and the possible lack of independence and, hence, protection for the investor.[18] But there is much more to State-to-State arbitration than a diplomatic process. It may also be seen as a way to rebalance a system judged (or maybe misjudged) as too favourable to the investor.

Typically, BITs and IIAs provide for the possibility of State-to-State arbitration. The below provision from the 1993 BIT between Ecuador and the US is quite revealing:[19]

Ecuador–USA BIT (1993), Article VII

1. Any dispute between the Parties concerning the interpretation or application of the Treaty which is not resolved through consultations or other diplomatic channels, shall be submitted, upon the request of either Party, to an arbitral tribunal for binding decision in accordance with the applicable rules of international law. In the absence of an agreement by the Parties to the contrary, the arbitration rules of the United Nations Commission on International Trade Law (UNCITRAL), except to the extent modified by the Parties or by the arbitrators, shall govern.

2. Within two months of receipt of a request, each Party shall appoint an arbitrator. The two arbitrators shall select a third arbitrator as Chairman, who is a national of a third State. The UNCITRAL Rules for appointing members of three member panels shall apply mutatis mutandis to the appointment of the arbitral panel except that the appointing authority referenced in those rules shall be the Secretary General of the Centre.

3. Unless otherwise agreed, all submissions shall be made and all hearings shall be completed within six months of the date of selection of the third arbitrator, and the Tribunal shall render its decisions within two months of the date of the final submissions or the date of the closing of the hearings, whichever is later.

4. Expenses incurred by the Chairman, the other arbitrators, and other costs of the proceedings shall be paid for equally by the Parties. The Tribunal may, however, at its discretion, direct that a higher proportion of the costs be paid by one of the Parties.

---

[18] *Italian Republic* v. *Republic of Cuba*, ad hoc State-to-State arbitration, available at www.italaw.com/cases/580; *Republic of Ecuador* v. *United States of America*, PCA Case No. 2012-5, available at www.italaw.com/cases/1494 (both accessed 21 December 2020). Andrea Roberts, 'State-to-State Investment Treaty Arbitration: A Hybrid Theory of Interdependent Rights and Shared Interpretive Authority', *Harvard International Law Journal* (2014), 55(1), pp. 1–70.

[19] Ecuador–USA BIT (1993), available at https://investmentpolicy.unctad.org/international-investment-agreements/treaty-files/1065/download (accessed 21 December 2020).

A rapid typology of the types of claims a State can bring suggests that these are limited to three options: a *claim for diplomatic protection*, a *claim for treaty interpretation* or application (as suggested by the above BIT article), and a *claim for a declaratory relief* – that is, a declaration that the host State has breached its treaty obligations.[20]

The question remains regarding the multiplicity of arbitrations – that is, claims for the same case but brought on the basis of different procedures and before different fora, with a State-to-State and an investor–State arbitration, for example. In this regard, Article 27 of the ICSID Convention seems to argue in favour of exclusivity:

ICSID Convention, Article 27

1. No Contracting State shall give diplomatic protection, or bring an international claim, in respect of a dispute which one of its nationals and another Contracting State shall have consented to submit or shall have submitted to arbitration under this Convention, unless such other Contracting State shall have failed to abide by and comply with the award rendered in such dispute.
2. Diplomatic protection, for the purposes of paragraph (1), shall not include informal diplomatic exchanges for the sole purpose of facilitating a settlement of the dispute.

While this article clarifies a few issues, the timeline remains vague, as does the possibility of bringing other claims than that of diplomatic protection. It is clear from the *Ecuador v. US* case that the *Chevron-Texaco* dispute (see Box 14.2) has been addressed in an incredibly vast array of fora. Other treaties and BITs do not preclude the possibility of State-to-State arbitration in parallel with investor–State arbitration claims.

On the basis of the recent renewal of interest in this long-planned possibility to settle international investment disputes, it will be interesting to see if the new IIAs will comprise better drafted provisions, allowing for clearer interpretation of the possibilities available to all stakeholders.

14.4.2 Investor–State

Treaty-based investor–State dispute settlement constitutes the very core of international investment disputes. It is generally referred to as ISDS. A relatively recent activity, it came into existence after the signing of the first IIAs, but really burgeoned in the early 2000s on the grounds of the 1990s investor-friendly treaties offering significant protection to the investor and thus equally vast possibilities to challenge the State. ISDS is made possible on the basis of treaties, most of which are BITs, but also TIPs. In this last category, the Energy Charter Treaty and NAFTA dominate. The recent popularity of the Energy Charter Treaty as a

---

[20] Roberts, 'State-to-State Investment Treaty Arbitration'; Nathalie Bernasconi-Osterwalder, *State–State Dispute Settlement in Investment Treaties*, Best Practices series (Winnipeg: International Institute for Sustainable Development, 2014).

basis for the investor to bring a claim against the State has become quite controversial and has been deemed to have altered energy transition and participated in climate change.[21] The Energy Charter, as a consequence, is undergoing a series of reforms. As demonstrated previously (see Chapter 11), it would be misleading to believe that the investor is always favoured by these arbitral decisions. The State actually wins most of the concluded cases, while, on the merits, the investor wins. The depth and importance of the issues at stake for public policies, and indeed population rights, has triggered natural scrutiny and intense debates on the legitimacy and merits of this apparently unbalanced (the investor sues the State) and sometimes biased (see Section 14.7.1) system.

Let us remind ourselves of a few interesting statistics generated by the work performed by UNCTAD on the basis of the more than 1,000 known ISDS cases.

Total:	1,023
Pending:	343
Concluded:	674
Unknown:	6

Figure 14.1 Known treaty-based ISDS cases. Updated as of 31 December 2019.
Source: UNCTAD, available at https://investmentpolicy.unctad.org/investment-dispute-settlement

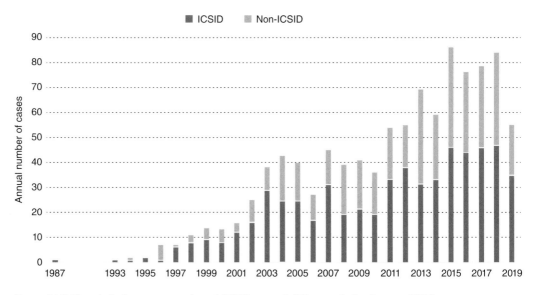

Figure 14.2 Trends in known treaty-based ISDS cases; 1,023 cumulative known ISDS cases.
Source: UNCTAD, ISDS Navigator.

---

[21] Pia Eberhardt, Cecilia Olivet and Lavinia Steinfort, *One Treaty to Rule them All: The Ever-Expanding Energy Charter Treaty and the Power it Gives Corporations to Halt the Energy Transition* (Brussels/Amsterdam: Corporate Europe Observatory/Transnational Institute, 2018), available at www.tni.org/en/energy-charter-dirty-secrets; Energy Charter, available at https://energycharter.org (both accessed 21 December 2020).

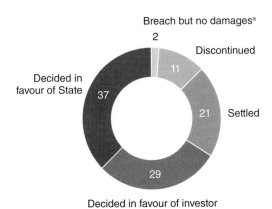

Figure 14.3 Results of concluded cases. Source: UNCTAD, ISDS Navigator. [a] Decided in favour of neither party (liability found but no damages awarded).

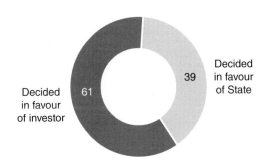

Figure 14.4 Results of concluded cases. Source: UNCTAD, ISDS Navigator.
Note: Excluding cases (i) dismissed by tribunals for lack of jurisdiction, (ii) settled, (iii) discontinued for reasons other than settlement (or for unknown reasons), and (iv) decided in favour of neither party (liability found but no damages awarded).

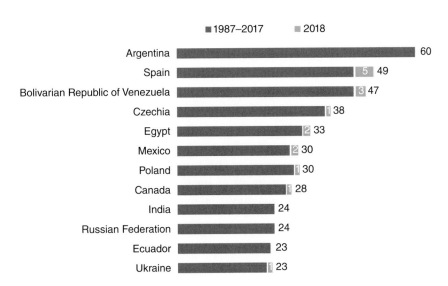

Figure 14.5 Most frequent respondent States, 1987–2018. Source: UNCTAD, ISDS Navigator.

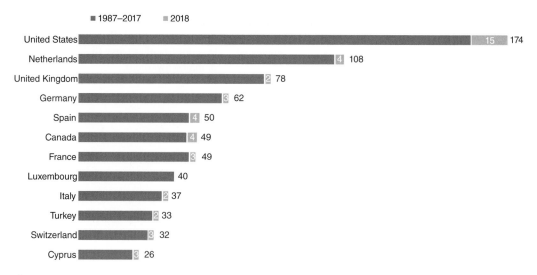

Figure 14.6 Most frequent home State of claimants, 1987–2018. Source: UNCTAD, ISDS Navigator.

14.5 Investor–State Dispute Settlement

14.5.1 The ICSID

At the very core of ISDS is the ICSID. While also in the middle of a number of controversies, it remains the most popular forum to settle investor–State disputes, and is certainly the most transparent, as it now publishes a large amount of information. It is, however, not without major challenges, and other fora are available to the parties for the settlement of their disputes.

14.5.1.1 History and Structure

In the context of decolonisation and the cold war, tensions arose between capital exporting States (mostly the former colonial powers) and the recipients of foreign investments (mostly recently decolonised countries). With its central role in development assistance and promotion of international good governance, the World Bank took the lead in the negotiation of what became a hybrid system for international investment dispute settlement. After a few rounds of negotiations, starting in 1961, the ICSID was established, in 1966, by the 1965 Convention on the Settlement of Investment Disputes between States and Nationals of Other States (ICSID Convention), a multilateral treaty.[22] Its main objective was to

---

[22] ICSID Convention text available at https://icsid.worldbank.org/en/Documents/icsiddocs/ICSID%20Convention%20English.pdf; and its history, available at https://icsid.worldbank.org/resources/publications/the-history-of-the-icsid-convention (both accessed 21 December 2020).

promote greater confidence in investment dispute settlement, at a time (in the developing world) when domestic systems were thought to be unfriendly to international investors and rather inefficient. Its Preamble set the tone:

ICSID Convention, Preamble

The Contracting States

Considering the need for international cooperation for economic development, and the role of private international investment therein;

Bearing in mind the possibility that from time to time disputes may arise in connection with such investment between Contracting States and nationals of other Contracting States;

Recognizing that while such disputes would usually be subject to national legal processes, international methods of settlement may be appropriate in certain cases;

Attaching particular importance to the availability of facilities for international conciliation or arbitration to which Contracting States and nationals of other Contracting States may submit such disputes if they so desire;

Desiring to establish such facilities under the auspices of the International Bank for Reconstruction and Development;

Recognizing that mutual consent by the parties to submit such disputes to conciliation or to arbitration through such facilities constitutes a binding agreement which requires in particular that due consideration be given to any recommendation of conciliators, and that any arbitral award be complied with; and

Declaring that no Contracting State shall by the mere fact of its ratification, acceptance or approval of this Convention and without its consent be deemed to be under any obligation to submit any particular dispute to conciliation or arbitration.

The ICSID procedures are available for investor–State and State-to-State disputes under IIAs. ICSID provides for the settlement of disputes by conciliation, arbitration or fact-finding. The 'negotiation' element, as demonstrated above, is still very much present in the treaty. More than 600 cases have been administered by the ICSID.[23]

---

[23] See the ICSID data for updates, available at https://icsid.worldbank.org/en/Pages/cases/AdvancedSearch.aspx (accessed 21 December 2020). A major effort for transparency has been made in the past few years and a large number of cases are now available online.

Its structure is relatively light and simple, with an Administrative Council and a Secretariat. Each member State has one seat on the Administrative Council, which addresses the organisation of the Institution and not the cases themselves. The Secretariat (around seventy persons), on the other hand, deals with cases. There are 154 contracting States to the Convention and eight signatory States, including, for example, the Russian Federation. A number of important countries, such as India and Brazil, have chosen not to become member States to the ICSID.[24] They are, however, able to resort to ICSID arbitration on the basis of the Centre's Additional Facility Rules. Disputes between a State and a national of another State are indeed eligible for arbitration under this additional facility if there is an investment dispute for which one party is not an ICSID member State or national of a member State, but the other is. The member States take part in the Administrative Council, which meets once a year. They are also entitled to designate up to four individuals to the ICSID panels of conciliators and arbitrators (ICSID Convention, Articles 12–16). The designees may be of any nationality and will serve for a renewable term of six years. These lists of arbitrators and conciliators are available to the parties to a dispute and are mostly used when they are not able to agree on a nominee to an arbitral tribunal.

The constitution of the arbitral tribunal is of particular importance and must be performed as soon as possible after the registration of a request for arbitration (see Figure 14.8). Based on the consent of the parties and quite typical private arbitration practices, the ICSID rules provide the parties with a large margin to determine the number of arbitrators and the method by which to appoint them. They are, for example, not required to select arbitrators from the ICSID lists, but are welcome to do so should they wish.[25] The nationality criteria are also quite flexible. While the majority of arbitrators must be nationals of another State than the parties to the dispute, some flexibility exists if these parties agree. In addition, ICSID arbitrators must satisfy a number of basic ethical considerations, which, unfortunately, have been challenged in recent cases (see Section 14.7.1).[26]

---

[24] James Nedumpara and A. Laddha, 'India Joining the ICSID: Is it a Valid Debate?', in L. Choukroune and R. Donde (eds.), *International Commercial and Investment Disputes Settlement, Transnational Dispute Management* (special issue, 2018), 15(2), available at www.transnational-dispute-management.com/article.asp?key=2539 (accessed 21 December 2020).

[25] ICSID, Selection and Appointment of Tribunal Members, available at https://icsid.worldbank.org/en/Pages/process/Selection-and-Appointment-of-Tribunal-Members-Convention-Arbitration.aspx (accessed 21 December 2020).

[26] UNCTAD provides data on arbitrators on a case-by-case basis, available at https://investmentpolicy.unctad.org/investment-dispute-settlement (accessed 21 December 2020). Professor B. Stern remains the most sought-after arbitrator, with experience of 114 cases at time of writing. See also the updated ICSID caseload statistics, available at https://investmentpolicy.unctad.org/investment-dispute-settlement (accessed 21 December 2020).

The Convention plans for a few types of processes: arbitration, conciliation, additional facilities (arbitration, conciliation and fact-finding), non-ICSID arbitration, mediation and other forms of ADR.

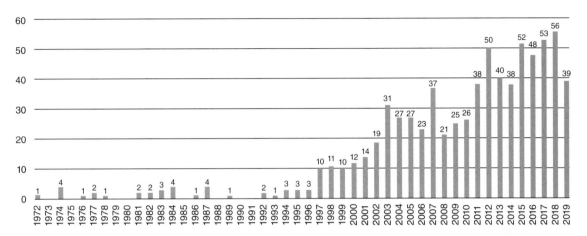

Figure 14.7 Cases registered by ICSID under the ICSID Convention and Additional Facility Rules. Source: ICSID Caseloads Report, 2020–1.

The most popular of these processes is certainly the ICSID arbitration, the steps of which are summarised in Figure 14.8.

14.5.1.2   Dispute Proceedings

Jurisdiction   The issue of jurisdiction of the arbitral tribunal is of major significance. This is about determining the competence of the tribunal to hear the case on the basis of Article 41 of the ICSID Convention and four major elements, including the crucial issue of nationality and Article 25 of the ICSID (see Chapter 13), as well as that of the legal character of the dispute:

• There is a dispute between an ICSID member State and an investor of another contracting party to the Convention.
• There is a dispute between an ICSID member State and another member State (State-to-State arbitration).
• Consent by the parties to submit the dispute to arbitration has been established.
• It is a legal dispute.
• The dispute arises 'out of an investment made in the host contracting State'.

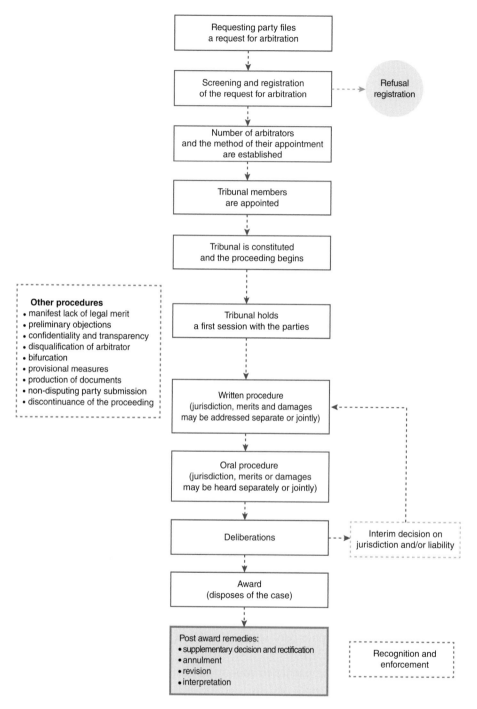

Figure 14.8 Conduct of ICSID arbitration. Source: ICSID, available at https://icsid.worldbank.org/en/
Pages/process/Arbitration.aspx

ICSID Convention, Article 41

1. The Tribunal shall be the judge of its own competence.
2. Any objection by a party to the dispute that that dispute is not within the jurisdiction of the Centre, or for other reasons is not within the competence of the Tribunal, shall be considered by the Tribunal which shall determine whether to deal with it as a preliminary question or to join it to the merits of the dispute.

Applicable Law and Precedent   Once the competence of the arbitral tribunal has been established, the merits of the case are addressed. Here again, the influence of private contractual obligations is quite perceptible. The parties have resorted voluntarily to arbitration, they have given their consent and thus are free to select from a variety of legal regimes. However, this choice is also framed by the IIA on the basis of which the dispute has been brought to the court, as well as Article 42 of the ICSID Convention, which brings additional clarification.

ICSID Convention, Article 42

1. The Tribunal shall decide a dispute in accordance with such rules of law as may be agreed by the parties. In the absence of such agreement, the Tribunal shall apply the law of the Contracting State party to the dispute (including its rules on the conflict of laws) and such rules of international law as may be applicable.
2. The Tribunal may not bring in a finding of *non liquet* on the ground of silence or obscurity of the law.
3. The provisions of paragraphs (1) and (2) shall not prejudice the power of the Tribunal to decide a dispute *ex aequo et bono* if the parties so agree.

International law plays a major part in this approach. But what are the rules of international law, different from the IIA, that can be applied? This remains a vastly debated and contentious issue. IIAs are no more precise on the matter than the ICSID, as illustrated for example, by Article 40 of the 2004 Canada Model BIT:

Canada Model BIT (2004), Article 40: Governing Law

1. A Tribunal established under this Section shall decide the issues in dispute in accordance with this Agreement and applicable rules of international law.
2. An interpretation by the Commission of a provision of this Agreement shall be binding on a Tribunal established under this Section, and any award under this Section shall be consistent with such interpretation.

Another important point remains highly controversial, that of the issue of precedent. As alluded to above, there is no *stare decisis* in ICSID case law, as arbitral tribunals are not bound by previous decisions of other ICSID tribunals. However, there is a form of continuity, if not yet consistency. Tribunals do refer to previous decisions and create a body of law, a *lex specialis* of key relevance and persuasiveness. One may speak of the development of a sort of 'soft precedent' doctrine in light of the greater transparency of ICSID proceedings and the recent publications effort of decisions. Indeed, until recently, very few decisions were available to the public and only a handful of investment arbitration cases were disclosed.[27]

Claims and Counterclaims   What are the causes of actions to bring a claim to the ICSID, or, more precisely, what are the treaty breaches claimed by the investors? UNCTAD provides an interesting overview of the alleged breaches and, later, of the breaches found. Alleged breaches touch mostly on FET and the minimum standard of treaty and, secondly, indirect expropriation. Then come full protection and security, expropriation, umbrella clauses and national treatment. The breaches found follow the same order of importance.[28]

While the investor can claim against the State on the basis of the IIA (and/or contract), the State is able to make *counterclaims*. These have to meet two major conditions: *consent* for counterclaims (these are made possible in a treaty) and *connectedness* to the main claim countered. The most recent IIAs tend to provide for the possibility of counterclaims in an effort to rebalance treaty obligations in favour of the State.

The example often given to illustrate this practice is that of Ecuador, which claimed against the investor Perenco in ICSID proceedings. Perenco had initially claimed against a change in Ecuadorian legislation. But Quito later claimed that the investor had violated Ecuadorian environmental legislation, including not informing the State of several oil spills, and this had led to a massive environmental disaster in the Amazon. Ecuador claimed for US$2.5 billion for cleaning-up damages. The *Perenco* v. *Ecuador* case was settled in September 2019, after eleven years and more than US$89 million in costs, but the saga is not over.[29]

Award, Annulment, Enforcement   Arbitral decisions under the ICSID are to be final. There is no appeal mechanism (ICSID Convention, Article 53). Common in private arbitration, the lack of an appeal mechanism is widely criticised, for in ISDS the State is also involved and so are public policies.

---

[27] Patrick M. Norton, 'The Role of Precedent in the Development of International Investment Law', *ICSID Review – Foreign Investment Law Journal* (2018), 33(1), pp. 280–301.

[28] See UNCTAD at https://investmentpolicyhub.unctad.org/ISDS/FilterByBreaches (accessed 21 December 2020).

[29] *Perenco Ecuador Ltd* v. *Republic of Ecuador and Empresa Estatal Petróleos del Ecuador (Petroecuador)*, ICSID Case No. ARB/08/6, available at www.italaw.com/cases/819 (accessed 21 December 2020). See also, for a contextual note, Daniela Páez-Salgado and Natalia Zuleta, 'Perenco v. Ecuador: An Example of a "Lengthy, Complex, Multi-Faceted, Hard-Fought and Very Expensive" Investment Arbitration?', *Kluwer Arbitration Blog* (14 November 2019), available at http://arbitrationblog.kluwerarbitration.com/2019/11/14/perenco-v-ecuador-an-example-of-a-lengthy-complex-multi-faceted-hard-fought-and-very-expensive-investment-arbitration/?doing_wp_cron=1592919328.6397409439086914062500 (accessed 21 December 2020).

However, a few possibilities are available to the parties in the ICSID Convention and its Articles 50 (Interpretation), 51 (Revision) and 52 (Annulment). Resorted to in a number of recent procedures, Article 52 has been under intense scrutiny as its provisions are limited to annulment and cannot be used as an appeal mechanism by default.

ICSID Convention, Article 52

(1) Either party may request annulment of the award by an application in writing addressed to the Secretary-General on one or more of the following grounds:
  (a) that the Tribunal was not properly constituted;
  (b) that the Tribunal has manifestly exceeded its powers;
  (c) that there was corruption on the part of a member of the Tribunal;
  (d) that there has been a serious departure from a fundamental rule of procedure; or
  (e) that the award has failed to state the reasons on which it is based.

(2) The application shall be made within 120 days after the date on which the award was rendered except that when annulment is requested on the ground of corruption such application shall be made within 120 days after discovery of the corruption and in any event within three years after the date on which the award was rendered.

(3) On receipt of the request the Chairman shall forthwith appoint from the Panel of Arbitrators an *ad hoc* Committee of three persons. None of the members of the Committee shall have been a member of the Tribunal which rendered the award, shall be of the same nationality as any such member, shall be a national of the State party to the dispute or of the State whose national is a party to the dispute, shall have been designated to the Panel of Arbitrators by either of those States, or shall have acted as a conciliator in the same dispute. The Committee shall have the authority to annul the award or any part thereof on any of the grounds set forth in paragraph (1).

(4) The provisions of Articles 41–45, 48, 49, 53 and 54, and of Chapters VI and VII shall apply *mutatis mutandis* to proceedings before the Committee.

(5) The Committee may, if it considers that the circumstances so require, stay enforcement of the award pending its decision. If the applicant requests a stay of enforcement of the award in his application, enforcement shall be stayed provisionally until the Committee rules on such request.

(6) If the award is annulled the dispute shall, at the request of either party, be submitted to a new Tribunal constituted in accordance with Section 2 of this Chapter.

As we have set out above, there are five listed conditions to request the annulment of an award: the Tribunal was not properly constituted; it manifestly exceeded its powers; there was corruption on the part of a member of the Tribunal; there has been serious departure from a fundamental rule of procedure; or the award failed to state the reasons on which it is based. Tribunals have generally been rather strict in their approaches, but a handful of awards have indeed been annulled, in full or in part, starting in 1986 with *Amco Asia Corporation and others* v. *Republic of Indonesia*, and moving to the infamous *Sempra Energy International* v. *Argentine Republic* in 2010 or *Occidental* v. *Ecuador*, only partly annulled.[30]

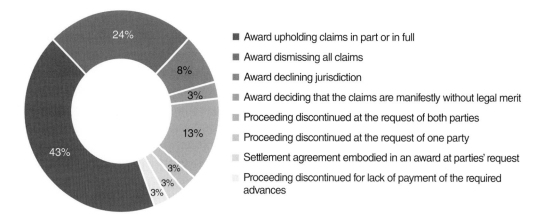

■ Award upholding claims in part or in full
■ Award dismissing all claims
■ Award declining jurisdiction
■ Award deciding that the claims are manifestly without legal merit
▨ Proceeding discontinued at the request of both parties
▨ Proceeding discontinued at the request of one party
▨ Settlement agreement embodied in an award at parties' request
▨ Proceeding discontinued for lack of payment of the required advances

Figure 14.9 Arbitration proceedings under the ICSID Convention and Additional Facility Rules concluded in 2019 – tribunal rulings, settlement and discontinuances. Source: ICSID Caseloads Report, 2020–1.

Box 14.3 *Churchill Mining Plc and Planet Mining Pty Ltd* v. *Indonesia*

Here is a real arbitral saga full of rocambolesque developments involving fraud and forgery, State decentralisation, local powers and no fewer than twenty procedural orders issued by the ICSID arbitral tribunal, as well as an application for annulment by the complainant, the result of which is yet to be seen.

The facts and the procedure were complex. But to simplify, while trying not to alter the essence of the problems, the situation could be summarised as follows: the case was brought under the UK–Indonesia and Australia–Indonesia BITs respectively, and related to expropriation claims arising from a coal project in East Kalimantan (Borneo). Churchill is indeed a British company listed in the Alternative Investment Market of the London Stock Exchange, while Planet is an Australian subsidiary of Churchill. The two original cases brought by Churchill and Planet were joined, for they addressed similar factual issues. At the time of the investment, in 2005, Indonesia's mining law regime was decentralised, with the head of each Bupati (a regency and form of administrative unit) given the power to license and regulate foreign investment for, as in this case, the exploration and mining of coal. Indonesia

---

[30] See the list of annulment procedures and decisions established by the ICSID, available at https://icsid.worldbank.org/en/Pages/process/Decisions-on-Annulment.aspx (accessed 21 December 2020).

Box 14.3 (cont.)

is an extremely diverse and resource-rich country, with its territory spread across about 18,000 islands. It is then understandable that decentralisation could be seen as a good governance mechanism, albeit a challenging one, as we shall see. Three main types of licences could be granted: general survey, exploration and exploitation. These three licences were consecutively granted to the investors. However, without prior notice, the Regent later issued decrees revoking the licences. Following several domestic procedures, the claimants attempted to ascertain the status of their investment and engage with the government of Indonesia. The case eventually went to the Indonesian Supreme Court, without success.

Hence, in May 2012, Churchill filed a request for arbitration with the ICSID, alleging that its investments had been unlawfully expropriated and treated in a manner that violated the FET standard of the BIT (revocation of the licences). In November 2012, Planet filed a similar request for arbitration under the Australia–Indonesia BIT this time. The two arbitrations were later consolidated, while the claimants were asking for over US$1.3 billion in damages for Indonesia's treaty violations. Naturally, this came as a massive shock to Indonesia and public opinion there, which soon started questioning the value of ISDS and BITs.

Indonesia's defence was based on the claim of fraud. The claimants were said to have forged licences. Giving a sort of hint to the claimants about its future decision, a few months prior to it, in September 2016, the Tribunal pointed to the *Minnotte v. Poland* decision, in which three important questions were addressed:

1. the admissibility in international law of claims tainted by fraud or forgery where the alleged perpetrator is a third party;
2. the lack of due care or negligence of the investor to investigate the factual circumstances surrounding the making of an investment; and
3. the deliberate 'closing of eyes' to indications of serious misconduct or crime, or an unreasonable failure to perceive such indications (the *Minnotte* direction).

As a logical consequence, in December 2016, the Tribunal rendered its Award, finding that as the documents on which the case was based were not authentic or authorised, and the perpetrator of the fraud was most likely the claimants' local partner, possibly including the Regent himself, it decided to dismiss the claims. The facts revealed a large 'fraudulent scheme' to obtain mining concessions. The whole project was thus an 'illegal enterprise'. However, this decision is not without raising the question of State responsibility, as pointed out by the claimants, who later requested an annulment.

While deciding in favour of the State after a long and costly procedure involving fraud and forgery, with annulment now pending, this case remains fascinating as it basically addresses all contemporary issues in investment arbitration, from due diligence in complex resources-led investment to decentralisation of powers and possibly

---

Box 14.3 (cont.)

corrupt local authorities, procedural complexities and the question of annulment of arbitral awards. It led Indonesia to terminate its BITs and to question the delegation of certain strategic powers to local government in a country where governance remains a complicated problem.

To Go Further

Churchill Mining Plc and Planet Mining Pty Ltd v. *Indonesia*, ICSID Case Nos. ARB/12/14 and ARB/12/40, including Application for Annulment, 31 March 2017, para. 39, available at www.italaw.com/cases/1479 (accessed 21 December 2020).
David Minnotte & Robert Lewis v. *Republic of Poland*, ICSID Case No. ARB(AF)/10/1, available at www.italaw.com/cases/707 (accessed 21 December 2020).

Final and binding, the ICSID award has to be enforced by the parties. But this remains a quite complicated task due to the sovereign nature of the respondent. The enforcement of an ICSID award is not necessarily easier than that of an ad hoc tribunal. Theoretically, the liable host State can be made to enforce the award in a variety of jurisdictions. The claimant can seek to have the award recognised and enforced in the courts of any ICSID member State as though it were a final judgment of that State's courts (ICSID Convention, Article 54(1)). But this possibility is limited by the wording of the ICSID Convention, Articles 54(3) and 55, dealing with national sovereign immunities rules – that is, the rules of domestic law governing a State's sovereign immunity to the enforcement and execution of the award.[31] In this regard, ICSID is not different from any other arbitration. As explained by M. Sornarajah:

> The difficulties stem from the presence of a sovereign party. The existence of a sovereign defendant immediately raises issues relating to sovereign immunity and act of state. Sovereign immunity has been a bar to the jurisdiction of courts and act of state has been a substantive requirement that courts do not pronounce upon the legality of the act of a foreign sovereign performed within its own territory.[32]

'Sovereign immunity' is a plea against the jurisdiction of a domestic court to touch on another sovereign's interest and, in this case, the enforcement of an international arbitral award. It has nothing to do with the merits of the case, but rather with general international law and the conduct of international relations between equal sovereigns. The same could be said about the 'Act of State doctrine'. It bears the court to pronounce itself on the legality of a sovereign act of a foreign State (in our context, the legality, for example, of a taking later arbitrated internationally). One may easily imagine that a powerful State's court enforcing an award against a weaker State could damage diplomatic relations and the global power

---

[31] Inna Uchkunova and Oleg Temnikov, 'Enforcement of Awards under the ICSID Convention: What Solutions to the Problem of State Immunity?', *ICSID Review – Foreign Investment Law Journal* (2014), 29(1), pp. 187–211.

[32] M. Sornarajah, *The Settlement of Foreign Investment Disputes* (The Hague: Kluwer Law International, 2000), p. 289.

equilibrium. Here again, ISDS and IIL demonstrate and suffer from their hybrid character at the same time. The State, in welcoming FDI, performs an economic role. It is not simply a government act, but also a commercial one. The US, with the 1976 Foreign Sovereign Immunity Act, opened the door to a distinction between government and commercial act, supposedly to make the enforcement or international investment award easier. But domestic courts have remained rather reluctant to depart from the sovereign immunity theory. As a comparison, another interesting avenue for non-ICSID awards could be the activation of the New York Convention on the Enforcement of Foreign Arbitral Awards. ICSID award mechanisms of enforcement are provided and limited by the Convention, but a possibly greater margin of enforcement is offered to non-ICSID awards now becoming relatively popular (see Section 14.6 on the role of the Permanent Court of Arbitration) in the context of the absence of an ICSID appeal mechanism and intensified scrutiny of the institution. Obviously, the New York Convention is made for private parties and not sovereigns, but it could possibly be activated to bypass sovereign immunity. This reasoning was followed by the Energy Charter Treaty drafters, who required that arbitration be held in a new convention party State. However, what brings a State to enforce an award is mostly its international reputation and the additional collateral damage on its FDI attractiveness that an obstructive attitude could generate.

14.6 Other Fora

ISDS is also available in other fora on the basis of the flexibilities provided by international arbitration. UNCTAD has gathered useful information on the most popular institutions, together with applicable arbitration rules. ICSID and ICSID Additional Facilities Rules remain by far the most popular, as does the ICSID as an institution, but the Permanent Court of Arbitration, with around 110 investor–State arbitration cases, followed by the International Chamber of Commerce, to a much lesser extent, and the London Court of International Arbitration deserve special attention.[33] The International Chamber of Commerce is actually the world-leading arbitral institution, but it is mostly focused on commercial arbitration. The Permanent Court of Arbitration has made headlines with its recent Chevron-Texaco decisions (see Box 14.2). Located in The Hague, it was established in 1899 during the first Hague Peace Conference, to facilitate arbitration and other forms of dispute resolution between States. But today it provides the space for international arbitrations involving various combinations of States, State entities, international organisations and private parties.[34] It is acting in more than a hundred investor–State arbitrations, and its popularity seems to have increased with the negative attention generated by the ICSID. It

---

[33] See the work of the International Chamber of Commerce on arbitration and mediation, available at https://iccwbo.org/dispute-resolution-services/ (accessed 21 December 2020).

[34] See the PCA website for updates, available at https://pca-cpa.org/en/cases/ (accessed 21 December 2020).

has made a clear effort of transparency in publishing a significant number of materials related to arbitrated cases.

14.7 ISDS: The Way Forward

14.7.1 Controversies and Challenges

In 2015, the European Commission published the results of a public consultation with the largest number of responses in the history of the European Union – more than 145,000 submissions by civil society on ISDS. Since then, the EU has engaged in major discussions on ISDS reform, leading to the EU-sponsored project of a world investment court. Challenges faced by ISDS have made the headlines for a number of years. So much so that a large variety of stakeholders are interested in its reform, all proposing what they deem to be the best possible alternative to a failed system lacking impartiality and leading to unfair and unethical decisions, jeopardising the State's independence and ability to regulate in the public interest. Let us first address criticism and then move on to present some of the main traits of the proposed reforms.[35]

14.7.1.1 Transparency and Ethics

The very first critique made against ISDS is that of transparency or, more precisely, the lack of thereof. For years, most of the ISDS awards were not available to the public and nothing much was known about proceedings and stakeholders. In this regard, the ICSID has recently made a great effort in opening up its resources to the public. It publishes a large amount of information and, under the influence of the international community, seems to have quite drastically changed its approach to transparency. It has recently published a compendium of State and public comments on proposed amendments to the Centre's procedural rules for resolving international investment disputes.[36]

At the centre of this reformative effort is UNCITRAL. Its Rules on Transparency in Treaty-Based Investor–State Arbitration, amended a number of times, have provided guidelines for the publication of documents and submission of a non-disputing party. The Mauritius Convention on Transparency, known as the United Nations Convention on Transparency in Treaty-Based Investor–State Arbitration, which entered into force in 2017, is considered a landmark.[37] The Convention is an instrument by which the parties express their consent to apply the UNCITRAL rules on Transparency in Treaty-Based Investor–State Arbitration. In addition, UNCITRAL manages a working group on ISDS

---

[35] OECD, *Public Consultation on Investor–State Dispute Settlement*, 16 May – 23 July 2012, available at www.oecd .org/investment/internationalinvestmentagreements/publicconsultationisds.htm (accessed 21 December 2020).

[36] 'Proposals for Amendment of the ICSID Rules', Working Paper 4 (ICSID, February 2020), available at https://icsid .worldbank.org/sites/default/files/WP_4_Vol_1_En.pdf (accessed 21 December 2020).

[37] Convention available at https://uncitral.un.org/en/texts/arbitration/conventions/transparency (accessed 21 December 2020).

reform, the sessions of which are of particular interest in that they are able to gather diverse actors, including the academic community.[38] It has been working, for example, on the establishment of an advisory centre, somehow modelled on the Advisory Centre on WTO Law (see Chapter 10).[39] UNCITRAL, in a joint effort with the ICSID, released a Draft Code of Conduct for Adjudicators on 1 May 2020.[40] It provides applicable principles and provisions on independence and impartiality in the conduct of ISDS and finds inspiration in IIAs and arbitration rules, but also in other international courts, which often have more detailed and stringent requirements on ethics.

Ethical considerations indeed form another large part of ISDS – naming and shaming. From the selection of arbitrators to their role, the general public has recently discovered a world that had long remained opaque and rather endogamous. Arbitrators are lawyers, professors and former judges, who have reached a respectable level of seniority in their field. But private international law specialists dominate the field, which naturally generates concerns for a procedure at the centre of which is the State. The pool of eligible arbitrators long remained limited to what looked as a small, elitist club of maybe fifteen people, as shown by UNCTAD's publicly available statistics.[41] The same arbitrators have repeatedly been appointed in numerous cases and a few nationalities dominate the group, not to mention the lack of diversity, with barely more than 10 per cent of women appointed in ICSID arbitrations (see Figure 14.10).

Questions of independence, impartiality, nationality and disclosure – that is, the potential of revealing information to key stakeholders, from corporations to law firms – are often raised when addressing the issue of ethics.[42] In addition, there is a form of duty to investigate possible conflicts of interest.

---

[38] See UNCITRAL Working Group, available at https://uncitral.un.org/en/working_groups/3/investor-state (accessed 21 December 2020).

[39] Karl P. Sauvant, 'An Advisory Centre on International Investment Law: Key Features', Academic Forum on ISDS Concept Paper 2019/14 (10 September 2019), available at www.jus.uio.no/pluricourts/english/projects/leginvest/academic-forum/papers/papers/sauvant-advisory-center-isds-af-14-2019.pdf (accessed 21 December 2020).

[40] See the UNCITRAL-ICSID Draft Code of Conduct for Adjudicators in Investor–State Dispute Settlement, available at https://uncitral.un.org/en/working_groups/3/investor-state (accessed 21 December 2020).

[41] For a rather critical approach, see the work of Corporate Europe Observatory, for example, 'Lawyers Subverting the Public Interest: Lobby Group EFILA's Stake in Investment Arbitration', Briefing (April 2015).

[42] A number of ICSID cases are of particular interest: *Compañía de Aguas del Aconquija S.A. and Vivendi Universal S.A. v. Argentine Republic*, ICSID Case No. ARB/97/3, Decision on the Challenge to the President of the Committee, 3 October 2001, para. 20, available at www.italaw.com/cases/309; *EDF International S.A., SAUR International S.A. and León Participaciones Argentinas S.A. v. Argentine Republic*, ICSID Case No. ARB/03/23, Challenge Decision Regarding Professor Gabrielle Kaufmann-Kohler, 25 June 2008, paras. 65–68, available at www.italaw.com/cases/372; *ConocoPhillips Petrozuata B.V., ConocoPhillips Hamaca B.V. and ConocoPhillips Gulf of Paria B.V. v. Bolivarian Republic of Venezuela*, ICSID Case No. ARB/07/30, Decision on the Proposal to Disqualify L. Yves Fortier, Q.C., Arbitrator, 27 February 2012, para. 55, available at www.italaw.com/cases/321; *Total S.A. v. Argentine Republic*, ICSID Case No. ARB/04/01, Decision on the Proposal to Disqualify Teresa Cheng, 26 August 2015, available at www.italaw.com/cases/1105; *Blue Bank International & Trust (Barbados) Ltd v. Bolivarian Republic of Venezuela*, ICSID Case No. Arb/12/20, Decision on the Parties' Proposals to Disqualify a Majority of the Tribunal, 12 November 2013, para. 59, available at www.italaw.com/cases/1513 (all accessed 21 December 2020).

Nationality/Nationalities	As of Dec 31, 2019	Nationality/Nationalities	As of Dec 31, 2019
France	261	Korea, Rep.of	13
United States of America	253	Morocco	13
United Kingdom	222	Slovak Republic	13
Canada	145	Switzerland/Brazil	13
Switzerland	137	Bangladesh	12
Spain	122	France/Switzerland	12
Australia	101	Iran, Islamic Rep. of/France	12
Germany	99	Malaysia	12
Mexico	74	Peru	12
Italy	72	Greece	11
Belgium	68	Philippines	11
Argentina	64	Germany/Austria	10
Chile	62	Ireland/Germany	10
Netherlands	52	Nigeria	10
New Zealand	49	Denmark	9
Bulgaria	44	Uruguay	9
Colombia	44	Venezuela	9
Egypt, Arab Rep. of	37	Australia/Ireland	8
Costa Rica	32	Colombia/France	8
Sweden	30	Somalia	8
France/Sweden	28	Ecuador	7
Singapore	25	Senegal	7
United Kingdom/France	25	Thailand	7
Austria	22	Argentina/United States of America	6
Canada/New Zealand	20	India	6
United States of America/Switzerland	19	Switzerland/Ireland	6
Brazil	18	Canada/Lebanon	5
Argentina/Spain	18	Guyana	5
Finland	15	United States of America/France	5
China	14	United States of America/United Kingdom	5
Lebanon/France	14	Algeria	4
Pakistan	14	Bahamas	4
Canada/United Kingdom	13	Barbados	4
Guatemala	13	Cyprus	4

Figure 14.10 State of nationality of arbitrators, conciliators and ad hoc committee members appointed in cases registered under the ICSID Convention and Additional Facilities Rules. Source: ICSID Caseloads Report, 2020–1.

Blue Bank International v. Venezuela

In this regard, the definitions provided by the Tribunal in the *Blue Bank International & Trust (Barbados) Ltd* v. *Bolivarian Republic of Venezuela*, a case that arose out of the alleged indirect expropriation of certain tourism and hospitality facilities by Venezuela, are of particular interest. They also clarify the burdens of proof with regard to Articles 57 and 14(1) of the ICSID Convention.

Blue Bank International & Trust (Barbados) Ltd *v.* Bolivarian Republic of Venezuela

59. Impartiality refers to the absence of bias or predisposition towards a party. Independence is characterized by the absence of external control. Independence and impartiality both *'protect parties against arbitrators being influenced by factors other than those related to the merits of the case'*. Articles 57 and 14(1) of the ICSID Convention do not require proof of actual dependence or bias; rather it is sufficient to establish the appearance of dependence or bias.

A few awards have been annulled by the ICSID itself on the basis of conflicts of interest,[43] but the tribunals remain quite reluctant to engage in this direction.

Recent treaty initiatives have tried to address these concerns in providing for public access, including public hearings, and better framing the role and profiles of arbitrators on the basis of consideration of independence and impartiality. For example, CETA or the Indian Model BIT (2015) contain rather long developments on these issues.

14.7.1.2 *Amicus Curiae* Briefs

Public access to ISDS has been a major issue. Influenced by commercial arbitration, but also by the very fact that major economic interests are at stake in large FDI, parties have long preferred to keep the proceedings and awards strictly confidential. Knowing that public policies are also involved, civil society developed a keen interest in ISDS related to public goods, natural resources and the protection of the environment, in particular.

The first ever arbitration to accept *amicus curiae* briefs – that is, submissions by a non-disputing party, which has a significant presence in the area disputed or an interest in the case – was the *Methanex* case (see Box 14.4). This practice is now quite broadly acknowledged and defined by IIAs, as exemplified by the Canada Model BIT (2012).[44]

---

[43] On the question of ethics and crime in ISDS, see Krista Nadakavukaren Schefer, 'Crime in International Investment Arbitration', in Chaisse et al., *Handbook of International Investment Law and Policy* (Singapore: Springer, in press).

[44] Civil society has also contributed significantly to the issue with a number of publications; for example, for a detailed approach, see 'Third-Party Rights in Investor–State Dispute Settlement: Options for Reform', Submission to UNCITRAL Working Group III on ISDS Reform, contributed by Columbia Center on Sustainable Investment, International Institute for Environment and Development, and International Institute for Sustainable Development (15 July 2019), available at https://uncitral.un.org/sites/uncitral.un.org/files/media-documents/uncitral/en/wgiii_reformoptions_0.pdf (accessed 21 December 2020).

Canada Model BIT (2012), Article 39: Submissions by a Non-Disputing Party

1. Any non-disputing party that is a person of a Party, or has a significant presence in the territory of a Party, that wishes to file a written submission with a Tribunal (the 'applicant') shall apply for leave from the Tribunal to file such a submission, in accordance with Annex C.39. The applicant shall attach the submission to the application.

2. The applicant shall serve the application for leave to file a non-disputing party submission and the submission on all disputing parties and the Tribunal.

3. The Tribunal shall set an appropriate date for the disputing parties to comment on the application for leave to file a non-disputing party submission.

4. In determining whether to grant leave to file a non-disputing party submission, the Tribunal shall consider, among other things, the extent to which:

   (a) the non-disputing party submission would assist the Tribunal in the determination of a factual or legal issue related to the arbitration by bringing a perspective, particular knowledge or insight that is different from that of the disputing parties;

   (b) the non-disputing party submission would address a matter within the scope of the dispute;

   (c) the non-disputing party has a significant interest in the arbitration; and

   (d) there is a public interest in the subject-matter of the arbitration.

5. The Tribunal shall ensure that:

   (a) any non-disputing party submission does not disrupt the proceedings; and

   (b) neither disputing party is unduly burdened or unfairly prejudiced by such submissions.

6. The Tribunal shall decide whether to grant leave to file a non-disputing party submission. If leave to file a non-disputing party submission is granted, the Tribunal shall set an appropriate date for the disputing parties to respond in writing to the non-disputing party submission. By that date, the non-disputing Party may, pursuant to Article 32 (Participation by the Non-Disputing Party), address any issues of interpretation of this Agreement presented in the non-disputing party submission.

7. The Tribunal that grants leave to file a non-disputing party submission is not required to address the submission at any point in the arbitration, nor is the non-disputing party that files the submission entitled to make further submissions in the arbitration.

8. Access to hearings and documents by non-disputing parties that file applications under these procedures shall be governed by the provisions pertaining to public access to hearings and documents under Article 38 (Public Access to Hearings and Documents).

Box 14.4 *Methanex Corp.* v. *US*: opening to the *amicus curiae*

The Canadian Methanex Corporation was marketing and distributing methanol, an ingredient used to manufacture methyl tert-butyl ether (MTBE), a gasoline additive. Although Methanex was a leading producer of methanol for the American market, some 47 per cent of the market was supplied by American companies.

In 1999, Methanex submitted a claim to ICSID arbitration under the UNCITRAL Rules and on the basis of the NAFTA treaty Chapter 11 (Investment). The claim was based on the following situation: environmental groups and experts had raised concerns over the use of MTBE because of its role in the pollution of surface and groundwater. The state of California then banned the use of MTBE. However, according to Methanex, this ban was not made on the basis of environmental considerations, but rather on economic and political objectives, as a rival American company, Archer Daniel Midland (ADM), was producing ethanol, a substitute for MTBE and methanol. ADM was said to have used political donation to influence the decision of the Governor of California to ban MTBE.

As a consequence, Methanex argued that the ban resulted in a discriminatory treatment and a breach of US obligations under NAFTA's Chapter 11. Three claims were put forward: a breach of Article 1102 (National Treatment), a breach of the obligation to accord minimum standard of treatment and, in particular, Article 1105 (Fair and Equitable Treatment), and a breach of Article 1110 relating to the obligation not to take measures tantamount to expropriation without compensation.

The Tribunal rejected all of these arguments, finding in favour of the US and even ordering Methanex to pay full arbitral expenses (approximately US$4 million).

This much-debated case deserves particular attention for a number of reasons:

– It made an important contribution to public access to international arbitration in allowing *amicus curiae* briefs. In August 2000, the Institute for Sustainable Development submitted the first ever recorded *amicus* brief and was then followed by other US-based NGOs.
– As we have seen, it also brought some clarification to the possible application of the national treatment (and minimum treatment) standard for legitimate State regulatory purposes. The same can be said about the interpretation of expropriation.
– However, the *Methanex* decision could not have happened without the very controversial *Metalclad* v. *Mexico*, which preceded *Methanex* by five years and for which a completely different approach had been taken in interpreting expropriation in a very broad context – hence provoking the ire of the international community and the defenders of the environment in particular.

The contrast is striking, the absence of consistency and coherence in arbitral reasoning evident, and so the need to approach these two decisions together and with great care, as they involve considerable political elements, which go far beyond simple treaty

> ### Box 14.4 (cont.)
>
> interpretation and the protection of investment and/or the State's autonomy to regulate in favour of environmental protection.
>
> ### To Go Further
>
> *Methanex* legal materials are available at www.italaw.com/cases/683 (accessed 21 December 2020).

14.7.1.3 Access to Arbitration

Another quite contentious aspect in recent ISDS relates somehow to the idea of access to arbitration, both by those directly concerned by it and others who are not, but who find a pecuniary benefit in the settlement of a given dispute. The latter aspect has been particularly criticised, while some are proposing a novel legal aid solution for (developing) States to better protect their interests.

Third-Party Funding   ISDS third-party funding (TPF) has been vastly denounced in recent years. Present in commercial arbitration, too, the practice consists of a relatively simple equation: a party that is not directly involved in the dispute provides the fund to argue it in exchange of an agreed return.[45] The high cost of ISD and potential high damages of an ISDS have transformed the settlement of international investment disputes into a financially attractive business. TPF, however, tends to strengthen the asymmetry already present in a hybrid system in which the investor is the only one able to sue (the State). TPF is generally not disclosed, which adds to questions surrounding ISDS legitimacy.[46] A number of recently drafted IIAs, such as CETA, Article 8.26, provide for systematic disclosure of TPF. Common law jurisdictions have historically banned TPF under prohibitions against maintenance and champerty. There is a growing trend to ban it and this might translate into new IIAs.

Legal Aid   At the other end of the access-to-justice spectrum is the question of legal aid. This would enable respondents and developing States, in particular, to rebalance the ISDS system in their favour. Scholars draw upon the positive experience of the Advisory Centre on

---

[45] Frank J. Garcia, Hyun Ju Cho, Tara Santosuosso, Randall Scarlett and Rachel Denae Thrasher, 'The Case Against Third-Party Funding in ISDS: Executive Summary', Boston College Law School – PUC University of Chile, Working Group on Trade & Investment Law Reform, Third-Party Funding Task Force (2018), available at https://lawdigitalcommons.bc.edu/cgi/viewcontent.cgi?article=2130&context=lsfp; see also International Council for Commercial Arbitration, *Report of the ICCA–Queen Mary Task Force on Third-Party Funding in International Arbitration* (April 2018), ICCA Reports 4, available at www.arbitration-icca.org/media/10/40280243154551/icca_reports_4_tpf_final_for_print_5_april.pdf (accessed 21 December 2020).

[46] Sai Ramani Garimella, 'Interrogating Third-Party Funding in Investment Arbitration: The Need for Regulation in the UK and India', *Manchester Journal of International Economic Law* (2019), 16(2), p. 213.

World Trade Organization Law to put forward similar proposals for ISDS in the context of the UNCITRAL ISDS reform discussions.[47] But what could legal aid offer without the right treaty or/and contract? As demonstrated in Chapter 13, the legal basis on which the dispute is settled and the very provision of the same matter immensely.

14.7.1.4 Proportionality, Reasonableness and Right to Regulate

On firmer legal ground, a number of issues are also discussed as additional sources of criticism of the ISDS system: proportionality, reasonableness and right to regulate. A vast scholarly literature has been produced in recent years on these aspects of international investment dispute settlement in relation to a series of awards. Eventually, these technical elements relate to the idea that the State should be able to protect its regulatory rights (if not duty) and act in this regard without breaching its international obligations. This approach draws on general international law and human rights in taking into account the political, economic and social context of a given case.

Box 14.5 *Piero Foresti, Laura de Carli and others* v. *Republic of South Africa*: the right to regulate at risk

On 8 November 2006, Piero Foresti, Laura de Carli and others filed an ICSID request for arbitration (under the ICSID Additional Facilities Rules) against the Republic of South Africa. The proceedings were brought pursuant to the Italy–South Africa BIT and the Belgium–Luxembourg–South Africa BIT.

The group of investors who held an interest in granite-quarrying companies in South Africa claimed that South Africa had breached its obligations under the BITs and effectively extinguished their rights without providing compensation. Under the 2002 Mineral and Petroleum Resources Development Act, private ownership of mineral rights was replaced by a system of licences. These licences were granted to investors, provided they met certain requirements, including a number of 'Black Empowerment' objectives, aimed at achieving equality at work for historically marginalised black South Africans.

The investors claimed for expropriation, but also for breaches of national treatment and fair and equitable treatment provisions.

In view of the large public outcry the case raised, the ICSID granted an NGO coalition the opportunity to file a written submission. This NGO coalition included four human rights groups – the Centre for Applied Legal Studies, the Legal Resources Centre, the Centre for International Environmental Law, and the International Centre for the Legal Protection of Human Rights. In addition, for

---

[47] Robert W. Schwieder, 'Legal Aid and Investment Treaty Disputes: Lessons Learned from the Advisory Centre on WTO Law and Investment Experiences', *Journal of World Investment and Trade* (2018), 19(4), pp. 628–66.

Box 14.5 (cont.)

the first time ever, an ICSID tribunal ordered the parties in the arbitration to disclose their key legal filings to a set of public interest organisations, despite the strong objections of the claimants.

However, the case was eventually discontinued in 2010, and the August 2010 Award does not address the merits of the case.

To Go Further

Piero Foresti, Laura de Carli and others v. *Republic of South Africa* legal materials are available at www.italaw.com/cases/683 (accessed 21 December 2020).

14.7.1.5 Damages

The last related criticism deals with damages and, in particular, the amount of damages required by the investor and awarded by the tribunal. How are these calculated? On what basis? Are they proportionate and reasonable? Are we calculating material damages only or is there space for moral damages? Is risk taken into account? Non-pecuniary remedies can also be planned. The latest IIAs pay particular attention to this issue in the drafting of their expropriation-related provisions in particular (see Chapter 13).

14.8 Reform Proposals

14.8.1 The EU and a Multilateral Investment Court

A previously fervent supporter of ISDS, the EU is now firmly opposed to the existing system, if not to ISDS itself. The unexpected victim of international arbitration, with intra-EU cases accounting for one-fifth of the total known ISDS cases in 2017, and the landmark *Vattenfall AB and others* v. *Federal Republic of Germany* (ICSID Case No. ARB/ 12/12) filed under the Energy Charter treaty for EUR4.7 billion by a Swedish company against German changes of regulation in the nuclear energy sector, the EU has changed its perspective. Under significant pressure from civil society, it is championing the establishment of a multilateral investment court (MIC). This court will draw upon the positively perceived experience of the WTO dispute settlement system, but does not seem to really challenge the very basis of ISDS.

According to the EU, this MIC would:

- have a first-instance tribunal;
- have an appeal tribunal;
- have tenured, highly qualified judges, obliged to adhere to the strictest ethical standards and a dedicated secretariat;

- be a permanent body;
- work transparently;
- rule on disputes arising under future and existing investment treaties;
- only apply where an investment treaty already explicitly allows an investor to bring a dispute against a State;
- would not create new possibilities for an investor to bring a dispute against a State;
- prevent disputing parties from choosing which judges ruled on their case;
- provide for effective enforcement of its decisions;
- be open to all interested countries to join.[48]

Box 14.6 *Pope & Talbot, Inc.* v. *Government of Canada*: WTO as a benchmark

In *Pope & Talbot, Inc.*, an American company with a subsidiary in Canada operating a softwood lumber factory there, filed a claim against Canada under the UNCITRAL rules, alleging that Canada's implementation of the May 1996 US–Canada Softwood Lumber Agreement was in breach of the NAFTA treaty Chapter 11 provisions. Precisely, the investor claimed that under the Softwood Lumber Agreement, Canada did not properly allocate a fee on issuance of a permit for exports of softwood lumber to the US above the established base in a given year. For this reason, *Pope & Talbot, Inc.* claimed violations of NAFTA Articles 1102 (National Treatment), 1105 (Minimum Standard of Treatment), 1106 (Performance Requirements) and 1110 (Expropriation).

On 26 June 2006, the Tribunal issued a Partial Award, dismissing the claims under Articles 1106 and 1110. On 10 April 2001, the issued Award on the Merits rejected the Article 1102 claim, but found a breach under Article 1105.

This case is particularly important from an NT standard point of view, as the Tribunal ventured into a quite sophisticated analysis on the semantics of NAFTA Article 1102 and elaborated a quite developed comparison with WTO jurisprudence. In our opinion, this decision is probably the best-argued NAFTA NT award.

To Go Further

Pope & Talbot Inc. v. *Government of Canada* legal materials are available at www.international .gc.ca/trade-agreements-accords-commerciaux/topics-domaines/disp-diff/pope.aspx?lang= eng (accessed 21 December 2020).

What about a true rebalancing of the system? What about the possibility for the State to claim equally? What about regional diversity and representation or even human rights? The

---

[48] See http://trade.ec.europa.eu/doclib/press/index.cfm?id=1608 (accessed 21 December 2020).

EU approach remains silent on numerous aspects. It seems also quite defensive, as illustrated by the recent *Achmea* case, in which the Court of Justice of the European Union ruled that the arbitration provision contained in Article 8 of the 1991 Netherlands–Slovakia BIT had an adverse effect on the autonomy and supremacy of EU law, and is therefore incompatible with it.[49] This case is certainly a resounding decision that has produced a great debate amongst practitioners and academics alike.

14.8.2 Other Initiatives

Other countries are adopting a different approach. For example, Brazil's Cooperation and Investment Facilitation Agreements do not contain ISDS provisions, but a rather innovative system combining investment prevention provisions and State-to-State arbitration inspired by the WTO dispute settlement mechanism. Brazil has always been quite a special player. Although Brazil signed fourteen traditional BITs between 1994 and 1999, they were never approved by the country's National Congress. Brazil did not sign the ICSID Convention. Even so, it continued to receive significant amounts of FDI.[50] The proposed Brazilian model also supports the idea of ADR, with a large role potentially played by dispute prevention and negotiation.

Others, like India, as alluded to above, now seem to favour domestic settlement of investment disputes.

Box 14.7 *Vodafone* v. *India*: the role of domestic courts in ISDS

In what has become a real legal saga, India managed to – momentarily – twist some legal arguments in its favour, hence creating a stimulating debate on the limitations of international arbitration and the role that domestic courts could play in framing international investment disputes.

The first episode began in 2006, when Vodafone BV International (a Dutch company) bought Hutchison Telecommunications International Ltd (a Cayman Island company), which acquired a 67 per cent share in an Indian Company, Hutchison Essar Ltd for the amount of US$ 11 billion. In reaction to this transaction, Indian tax authorities imposed a tax bill of US$ 2.2 billion on Vodafone. But the multinational giant contended that the transaction did not involve assets based in India and so was not taxable in India, a fascinating and recurring argument at the centre of multinational corporations' approaches to investment (see Chapter 13 on the definition of investor).

---

[49] *Slovak Republic* v. *Achmea B.V.*, CJEU, Case C-284/16, available at http://curia.europa.eu/juris/document/document.jsf?text=&docid=199968&pageIndex=0&doclang=EN&mode=req&dir=&occ=first&part=1&cid=404057 (accessed 21 December 2020).

[50] Geraldo Vidigal and Beatriz Stevens, 'Brazil's New Model of Dispute Settlement for Investment: Return to the Past or Alternative for the Future?', *Journal of World Investment and Trade* (2018), 19(3), pp. 474–512.

Box 14.7 (cont.)

In 2010, the Bombay High Court decided in favour of the State. This decision was then challenged by the company in the Indian Supreme Court, which reversed the Bombay ruling, for this was an offshore transaction on which India had no territorial tax jurisdiction. The saga did not stop there. In an unpredictable move, the Indian government amended its tax law and tried to impose its new rules on Vodafone retroactively. This, naturally, did not give the image of a stable and rule-of-law-based country – on the contrary, it is likely to have triggered a series of new tax-related investment disputes. As a logical consequence, Vodafone decided to challenge the Indian government in bringing an arbitration claim under the India–Netherlands BIT. In addition, and while the first case is still pending, Vodafone served a new notice of arbitration, in January 2017, this time under the India–UK BIT, challenging the same tax imposition.

Here comes a new domestic episode. The Indian government decided to play the 'abuse of process' card to counter the second arbitration deemed superfluous. The Delhi High Court took the case and rendered a controversial decision, concluding with an abuse of process as the two companies were de facto owned by the same shareholders. The Delhi High Court then passed an *ex parte* interim order, in August 2017, restraining Vodafone from pursuing the second arbitration. While the issue of abuse of process in arbitration is fascinating and still very much debated, the real question remains of whether an Indian court has any legal ground to issue a sort of anti-arbitration pronouncement. One then has to look into domestic arbitration legislation to see if it can apply to BITs, but also the very BITs for the dispute in question, as the countries (India, the Netherlands and the UK) gave explicit consent to arbitration. A more logical path would have been to push in favour of a joint arbitration of the different disputes. In any case, international tribunals do not seem particularly impressed by domestic courts' anti-arbitration injunctions, as illustrated by the *SGS* v. *Pakistan* case, in which the Supreme Court of Pakistan failed to stop the arbitration from issuing an order. The arbitration process initiated by a Swiss company went on, but was eventually discontinued. One more episode of the Vodafone saga, however, took place in May 2018, at the very same Delhi High Court. In a new, well-argued and lengthy decision addressing the questions of the applicability of the Indian Arbitration and Conciliation Act of 1996 (amended in 2015) to BITs, as well as India's international obligations, the Court reversed its previous judgment and concluded in favour of the consolidation of the two arbitrations (if agreed by the parties) and, in any event, vacated its 2017 order. In September 2020, the Permanent Court of Arbitration ruled against India, arguing that retrospective taxation was a breach of the UK–India BIT. In December, India challenged the decision in Singapore.

To Go Further

SGS Société Générale de Surveillance S.A. v. *Islamic Republic of Pakistan*, ICSID Case No. ARB/01/13, available at www.italaw.com/cases/1009 (accessed 21 December 2020).

Box 14.7 (cont.)

Union of India v. Vodafone Group Plc United Kingdom, 22 August 2017, CS(OS) 383/2017, available at https://indiankanoon.org/doc/150205803/ (accessed 21 December 2020).

Union of India v. Vodafone Group Plc United Kingdom, 7 May 2018, CS(OS) 383/2017 & I.A. No. 9460/2017, available at https://indiankanoon.org/doc/15132051/ (accessed 21 December 2020).

Vodafone International Holdings B.V. v. Union of India, 3 December 2008, Writ Petition No. 2550 of 2007, available at https://indiankanoon.org/doc/1190473/ (accessed 5 November 2020).

Vodafone International Holdings B.V. v. Union of India, Civil Appeal No. 733 of 2012, 20 January 2012, Supreme Court of India, available at https://indiankanoon.org/doc/115852355/ (accessed 21 December 2020).

Vodafone International Holdings B.V. v. India (I), PCA Case No. 2016-35, available at http://investmentpolicyhub.unctad.org/ISDS/Details/581 (accessed 21 December 2020).

Vodafone Group Plc and Vodafone Consolidated Holdings Limited v. India (II), available at http://investmentpolicyhub.unctad.org/ISDS/Details/819 (accessed 21 December 2020).

14.9 Conclusion

There is more than ISDS to the settlement of investment disputes. The international responsibility of States remains at the centre of the process, while at the same time, international contract law and private arbitration have deeply impacted this hybrid exercise. From negotiation to local remedies, diplomatic protection and arbitration, be it contract-based or treaty-based, a number of tools are available to the parties to the dispute. The recent controversies surrounding ISDS, and the work of the ICSID in particular, have brought a rather obscure and technical field of law under a new light. They have also greatly contributed to its reform in the direction of more transparency and responsibility. However, one fundamental element of the system remains intact: that of the possibility for the investor to sue the State, while the opposite is not true. Created in the context of the post-decolonisation era, mostly to protect the interests of Western investors, ISDS benefits and suffers from its hybridity. Now confronted with new challenges, including a fast-growing number of Western or intra-European disputes, ISDS needs to adapt to a global economy in which developing countries are ready to sue their former colonisers. Setting up a world investment court will not address these major issues without rebalancing the system in favour of greater equality between the actors of international investment, the State, the investor, but also civil society and the many regions of the world in their diversity.

14.10 Summary

- There is more than ISDS to international investment dispute settlement.
- The controversies now generated by ISDS proceedings and decisions perceived as non-transparent and unfair hide a much more complex field of international law at the crossroads between private and public interests.

- Negotiation remains a key moment in international investment dispute settlement.
- Domestic procedures (administrative or judicial) are as important.
- Contract law and international commercial arbitration have greatly influenced the field.
- Contract-based or treaty-based, the settlement of investment disputes can happen in a variety of fora.
- International courts have played a significant role.
- The PCIJ or ICJ, although involved in few cases, have taken landmark decisions often referred to in contemporary ISDS.
- The ICSID remains the most important forum for ISDS.
- It is well-structured and evolving in the direction of greater transparency and a more ethical approach.
- There are, however, other fora available to investors.
- The Permanent Court of Arbitration has seen renewed interest.
- Enforcement of ISDS awards remains a complex task.
- ISDS is at the centre of global criticism.
- Lack of transparency, ethics, access to justice, legal quality of the decisions, limitation of the State's right to regulate, costs of the proceedings and amount of damages awarded are mostly put forward to denounce a system perceived as illegitimate and unfair.
- Reform proposals, including the creation of a world investment court, are put forward.
- Others would prefer to opt for alternative dispute settlement or re-engage in domestic avenues for the settlement of international investment disputes.
- Rebalancing the settlement of international investment implies a greater equality between the actors at stake (State, investor, civil society), but also the many regions of the world in integrating their diversity.

14.11 Review Questions

1 Is negotiation a compulsory step in international investment dispute settlement?
2 What can be negotiated?
3 Is the exhaustion of local remedies systematically required by IIAs?
4 On the basis of recent IIA examples, and the Indian Model BIT (2015) in particular, what are the steps to follow before submitting an international investment claim to arbitration?
5 Could P/ELR be waived?
6 Why could it be complex to implement a 'fork in the road' provision?
7 How should domestic court intervention in the *Vodafone* v. *India* case be interpreted?
8 How should State-to-State arbitration be defined? What are its benefits and limits?
9 How has contract-based arbitration influenced ISDS?
10 What is the ICSID?
11 Is a non-ICSID member State able to resort to an ICSID arbitral tribunal?

12 How is the jurisdiction of the Tribunal determined?

13 On what basis is the choice of law made?

14 What are the criteria to annul an ICSID award?

15 Why are ISDS awards delicate to enforce?

16 How transparent is ISDS?

17 Are *amicus* briefs accepted by arbitration tribunals?

18 What are the UNCITRAL rules on transparency?

19 What is the EU proposing in order to reform ISDS?

20 How can stakeholders' interests be rebalanced?

21 What could be the priorities of ISDS reforms?

14.12 Exercise

(For background on the issue, please refer to previous Exercises in Chapters 12 and 13.)

Gainfame, a State-owned enterprise originating in Gainland, is facing a major conflict relating to the investor's operations in the Nordeste region of Hopeland. Indeed, under the pressure of the Indigenous United Front, an international NGO supporting the Rohis indigenous population, Hopeland has decided to modify its investor-friendly tax regime in favour of more social equality and the preservation of natural resources, in particular, water, a precious good that Rohis could be deprived of by the operations of Gainfame. It will now tax all water-intensive foreign investment by 30 per cent and redistribute the benefit of this tax policy to public interest projects, such as the construction of a new dam designed to efficiently redirect water resources and irrigate the whole Nordeste region. Local investors will also be taxed for the same purpose, but at 15 per cent.

Gainfame sees this change of policy as confiscatory. It is breaching Articles 11 (National Treatment), 12 (Fair and Equitable Treatment) and 14 (Takings) of the BIT, and a number of contractual clauses as well. It is also in contradiction to the Hope Invest Framework and Catalogue, which put in place a modern and welcoming investment climate, with equal rights for nationals and foreigners, and included a large number of incentives, including tax holidays for investors operating in least developed and indigenous areas.

Hopeland and Gainland had ratified a BIT, which comprised a far-reaching umbrella clause on top of generous protection for foreign investor/investment, and some mechanisms for the international settlement of State–investor disputes. The BIT makes negotiation a compulsory step at the initial stage of dispute settlement. In its detailed Article 23, the BIT also requires the pursuit and/or exhaustion of local remedies prior to any other means to settle disputes. Hopeland is not a State party to the ICSID, but Gainland is. The two countries had also included a specific grievance mechanism in their contract negotiations to possibly benefit aggrieved local populations. It is, in fact, open to all stakeholders, thanks to its innovative features.

A former employee of LJCN, the reputed international law firm, which had helped the parties at the negotiation stage, you have an impeccable reputation of independence and professionalism. You are approached by Gainfame to advise them on the recourses available and the strategy to follow to get redress for what the company perceives as numerous contractual and treaty breaches by Hopeland. In a written memo, you should develop several scenarios that you feel are the best options for both parties in order to sustain their business relationship while settling the current dispute.

FURTHER READING

Brauch, M. D., *Exhaustion of Local Remedies in International Investment Law*, IISD Best Practices series (Winnipeg: International Institute for Sustainable Development, 2017).

Chaisse, J., Choukroune, L. and Jusoh, S. (eds.), *Handbook of International Investment Law and Policy* (Singapore: Springer, in press).

Gaillard, E., 'Abuse of Process in International Arbitration', *ICSID Review – Foreign Investment Law Journal* (2017), 32(1), pp. 17–37.

Kaufmann-Kohler, G. and Postesta, M. (eds.), *Investor–State Dispute Settlement and National Courts: Current Framework and Reform Options* (Cham, Switzerland: Springer, 2020).

Leal-Arcas, R. (ed.), *Commentary on the Energy Charter Treaty* (Cheltenham: Edward Elgar, 2018).

Linarelli, J., Salomon, M. E. and Sornarajah, M., *The Misery of International Law: Confrontation with Injustices in the Global Economy* (Oxford University Press, 2018).

Roberts, A., 'State-to-State Investment Treaty Arbitration: A Hybrid Theory of Independent Rights and Shared Interpretive Authority', *Harvard International Law Journal* (2014), 55(1), pp. 1–70.

Schwieder, R. W., 'Legal Aid and Investment Treaty Disputes: Lessons Learned from the Advisory Centre on WTO Law and Investment Experiences', *Journal of World and Investment Trade* (2018), 19, pp. 628–66.

Sornarajah, M., *The Settlement of Foreign Investment Disputes* (The Hague: Kluwer Law International, 2000).

Vidigal, G. and Stevens, B., 'Brazil's New Model of Dispute Settlement for Investment: Return to the Past or Alternative for the Future?', *Journal of World and Investment Trade* (2018), 19(3), pp. 475–512.

Weiler, T. (ed.), *International Investment Law and Arbitration: Leading Cases from the ICSID, NAFTA, Bilateral Investment Treaties and Customary International Law* (London: Cameron May, 2011).

Part III

Finance, Development and Aid

15 International Monetary Law and Finance

Table of Contents

Highlights

- International monetary law and finance are at the centre of complex interactions between trade and investment, public and private actors.
- The Bretton Woods System, named after the Conference that took place in the US in July 1944, created the two main institutional pillars for finance and development: the International Monetary Fund and the International Bank for Reconstruction and Development, which soon became the World Bank and is now part of the World Bank Group.
- The Bretton Woods Conference also designed a financial system, aimed at world economic stability and prosperity based on a (neo)Gold Standard.
- All national reserve currencies were valued in relation to the US$, which was convertible to gold at a fixed rate, and so became the dominant reserve currency and the de facto standard.
- The IMF was integrated into the (neo)Gold Standard mechanism in that it was the only authority to enable its members to change the par value of their currencies in case of 'fundamental disequilibrium'.

- This system ended in 1971, with the American decision to terminate the convertibility of the US$ to gold.
- It was replaced by floating exchange rates, but two of its main aspects remained: the IMF as an international organisation governed by and accountable to its 190 member countries (at time of writing), and the US$ as the world reserve currency.
- The IMF's structure consists of the Board of Governors, the Executive Board and a Managing Director.
- The IMF is a quota-based institution. Quotas determine members' voting power, financial access and share in drawing rights allocations.
- The IMF today performs three main functions: surveillance, lending and capacity development.
- The IMF has been at the centre of major financial crisis management in Latin America, Asia and Europe for the past thirty years.
- The 'Washington Consensus', named after the recommendations of the IMF and the World Bank, and the IMF system of 'conditionalities', have been criticised as the very causes of the developing world's economic difficulties, rather than the solutions to them.
- Other international financial organisations and systems exist, as in the eurozone.
- Private activity is also regulated at the crossroads between international public and private law.

15.1 Introduction

In early 2019, the President of the World Bank, Jim Yong Kim, resigned three and a half years before the end of his term. His departure from the organisation echoes a long series of critical voices (among them, the Nobel laureate Joseph Stiglitz) who have repeatedly denounced the flaws of an international financial system resting on the now outdated Bretton Woods institutions – the IMF and the World Bank.[1]

International monetary law and finance occupy a central role in the global economy, which is only partially reflected in international law. Although of prime importance, these topics are not systematically addressed in international economic law courses and manuals, which often prioritise international trade and, to a lesser extent in recent times, IIL. The complexity of international monetary law and finance, which naturally requires a minimal, yet solid background in international economics, has deterred many from engaging further in a field largely conceptualised and taught by economists. The international legal literature covering these topics is itself limited, as only a few scholars seem daring enough to venture into the theoretical underpinnings of a complex field in which law is not always central.[2] Interestingly, the

---

[1] Stiglitz, *Globalization and its Discontents* (London: Penguin, 2002); Stiglitz, *Globalization and its Discontents Revisited*.

[2] A few textbooks dedicate significant sections to these issues. Among these, A. F. Lowenfeld, *International Economic Law* (Oxford University Press, 2008) is certainly the most comprehensive. Its coverage of the financial crisis of the

intertwined nature of money, finance, trade and investment, but also of public and private law, has resurfaced with a series of rather dramatic contemporary events, from the numerous financial crises of the 1990s in Latin America and Asia, to the still perceptible global financial crisis of the late 2000s or the consequences of the Covid-19 pandemic on countries' finances and debt. With the expanding globalisation of the economy (and its domestic questioning), it might well be that international monetary law and finance now elicit the same interest as IIL, a largely underdeveloped discipline only a few decades ago.

In approaching international monetary law against the backdrop of globalisation, but also its interactions with trade, investment and development, this chapter provides a solid introduction to the field. It has to be read in conjunction with Chapter 16 (International Development and Aid), which furthers our discussions on the place of money in economic transformations, and the role played by the institutions and rules created from the Bretton Woods Conference, in the aftermath of the Second World War. After a presentation of the Bretton Woods system itself, starting with the definition of key concepts, this chapter addresses IMF contemporary missions and the challenges it faces. It closes with a brief overview of other existing systems and rules.

15.2 The Bretton Woods System

15.2.1 Standards, Exchange Rates and Balance of Payments

Before engaging further in presenting the specifics of the Bretton Woods system, and the role and functioning of the IMF in particular, let us first briefly explain a few core notions relating to standards, exchange rates and balance of payments.

15.2.1.1   The Gold Standard

The use of gold coins probably dates back to around 700 BCE, when gold became a monetary unit. For centuries, and until very recently, gold and silver were seen as the most precious possessions and remained at the centre of the economy. A State was said to be rich if its reserves in gold and silver were large. Today, countries still keep a substantial amount of gold reserves. In fact, beginning in 2010, central banks around the world became net importers of gold.[3] The US holds the biggest pot of gold, followed by Germany, Italy, France, Russia, China, Switzerland, Japan, the Netherlands and India. Gold has always been viewed as a safe-haven asset, performing well in times of uncertainty. It represents 68.2

1980s and 1990s is particularly remarkable. D. Carreau and P. Juillard, *Droit international économique* (Paris: Dalloz, 2017), throughout its numerous editions, has always provided the reader with important developments in the field. See also R. M. Lastra, *International Financial and Monetary Law* (Oxford University Press, 2015).

[3] 'Top 10 Countries with Largest Gold Reserves', *Forbes* (5 July 2018), available at www.forbes.com/sites/greatspeculations/2018/07/05/top-10-countries-with-largest-gold-reserves/#77524d695334 (accessed 21 December 2020).

per cent of the Dutch foreign reserve, 63.9 per cent of the French, 70.6 per cent of the German reserve and 75.2 per cent of that in the US, the majority of which is held in the infamous Fort Knox.[4] The IMF itself also holds a gold reserve.[5] With skyrocketing global debt and market fluctuations, gold is not yet to lose its attractiveness. It remains an important asset in the reserve holdings of a large number of countries, as well as the IMF.[6]

The Gold Standard is a system in which a country's currency has a given value directly linked to gold. Countries agree to convert paper money into a fixed amount of gold. For example, if the UK sets the price of gold at £300 an ounce, the value of the British pound would then be 1/300th of an ounce of gold. In such a system, gold backs up the value of money. The Gold Standard dates back to the mid-nineteenth century when, in 1821, England became the first country to officially adopt it. For about fifty years, up until the First World War, the Gold Standard was broadly used in relatively stable economic times. Such a situation could be seen as ideal from a commercial angle, as all currencies were related to gold, hence making trade easier. With the eruption of the First World War, governments' finances deteriorated and the Gold Standard started to suffer a loss in confidence, to the benefit of the British pound sterling and the US\$. In 1931, after the 1929 world financial crisis and in the midst of the Great Depression (1929–39), the UK abandoned the Gold Standard, while the US took the lead on the gold market, thus becoming the true, and for a long time the only, financial world leader, with the US\$ and gold.

From an international monetary perspective, gold played a central role at the initial stage of the Bretton Woods system, with a sort of indirect return to the Gold Standard. In the interest of the US, gold was not really the standard on which the system was based. Indeed, all national reserve currencies were valued in relation to the US\$, which was convertible to gold at a fixed rate, and so became the dominant reserve currency and the de facto standard. The IMF was integrated into the (neo-)Gold Standard mechanism in that it was the only authority to enable its members to change the par value of their currencies in case of 'fundamental disequilibrium'. This fixed system, based on the US\$ and gold, had the merit of stability. However, the US saw its gold reserves drop with its global post-war engagement, and its balance of payments soon began to shrink. In 1971, Nixon put an end to the direct convertibility of the US\$ into gold. The connections of the global markets to gold were lost and the US\$ became the central element of financial transactions.

At the IMF level, the 1978 Second Amendment to the Articles of Agreement of the organisation established the right for members to adopt exchange rates arrangements of their choice.[7] This major change represented a complete departure from the par value system, referring to a stated value or face value. However, as alluded to above, gold

---

[4] 'Top 10 Countries with Largest Gold Reserves'.

[5] IMF, 'Gold in the IMF', Factsheet (23 March 2020), available at www.imf.org/en/About/Factsheets/Sheets/2016/08/01/14/42/Gold-in-the-IMF (accessed 21 December 2020).

[6] Peter L. Bernstein, *The Power of Gold: The History of an Obsession* (New York: John Wiley, 2004).

[7] IMF, Articles of Agreement, available at www.imf.org/external/pubs/ft/aa/index.htm; and IMF chronology, available at www.imf.org/external/np/exr/chron/chron.asp (both accessed 21 December 2020).

remained a key element in the IMF functioning, while not a standard, as such. The IMF holds around 90.5 million ounces (2,814.1 tonnes) of gold, valued at about $137.8 billion using end-December 2019 exchange rates.[8] These gold holdings come from four main sources: the 25 per cent initial quota subscription and subsequent quota increases of members paid in gold; the payment of IMF credit interest by members; the acquisition of currencies of other members by members selling gold; and repayment of credit to the IMF.

15.2.1.2 Convertibility and Exchange Rates

From our initial discussion on the role of gold and the Gold Standard, another key aspect of international monetary relations naturally arises, that of convertibility and exchanges rates. *Convertibility* is the quality allowing a given currency to be 'converted' into another one. It is naturally a central element of trade. Freely convertible currencies are exchanged on the foreign exchange market. However, some currencies are not 'freely convertible', as countries may decide that only certain amounts are convertible (see Box 15.1) or that a currency is not convertible at all (North Korean won, Cuban peso). The most convertible currency in the world is the US$. It is the most traded and gives a comparative advantage to the US in its trading relations.

Defined in simple terms, an *exchange rate* is the value of one country's currency against the value of another country's currency. For example, how many Japanese yen does it take to get one US$? The same is true when applied to a currency area, like the eurozone. How many Indian rupees does it take to buy one euro? Exchange rates can be of different types:

- *Free or floating*: the exchange rates rise and fall freely in accordance with the foreign exchange market variations. This system flourished from the 1970s, when the initial Bretton Woods arrangement collapsed with the end of the Gold Standard.
- *Restricted or controlled*: government sets the value of a currency and/or limits its exchange within the country's borders. The Chinese yuan provides a contemporary example (see Box 15.1).
- *Pegged*: a country pegs (attaches) its currency to another country's currency based on a fixed exchange rate. This provides stability to the given currency and a form of comparative advantage in trade. There are today more than sixty countries whose currencies are pegged to the US$ (the world's reserve currency and the leading currency for trade and financial transactions). The currency then falls and rises along with the US$, the value of which changes along floating exchange rates. About twenty countries peg their currencies to the euro. Other currencies (like the Chinese yuan) are pegged to a basket of currencies.
- *Onshore* v. *offshore*: when the exchange rate differs inside and outside a country. Generally, a more favourable rate is offered within the borders of the given country.
- *Spot* v. *forward*: this distinguishes between the on-the-spot value (current) and the forward (prospective) value of a currency.

---

[8] IMF, 'Gold in the IMF'.

Box 15.1 The Chinese currency controversy

For years, the controversy over the Chinese yuan or renminbi (RMB), the currency of the People's Republic of China, has made international headlines. From the US to the EU or Brazil, numerous countries have repeatedly denounced what they have perceived as unfair competition and unfair trade based on cheap goods and unlawful export subsidisation (see Chapters 5 and 6). China is indeed the only major economy to allow capital control, although it is increasingly accepting market forces to determine the RMB's value. The People's Bank of China has the power to intervene in currency markets, buying or selling currencies and so impacting the value of the Chinese yuan, which has been pegged, since 2005, to a basket of different currencies, including the US$, the yen and the euro. In doing so, it can maintain the yuan at a certain value suiting the economic strategy of the State and its legitimate policy objectives. However, an artificially undervalued currency can equal a protectionist policy, creating a barrier to imports on the one hand, and a form of subsidisation of exports on the other. So much so that the balance of payments and trade surplus of the country at stake become a major international issue. On the contrary, if the yuan is above its real value, it enables the Chinese government to buy more in absorbing global resources and, at the same time, lending to developing and emerging markets. The monetary roots of the trade issue are often seen as crystal clear by Chinese competitors and have been alluded to in a series of WTO disputes. From a trade perspective, the issue could potentially be taken to the WTO on the basis of the SCM Agreement. Nevertheless, one would have to prove a violation of the Agreement (unlawful subsidy) by showing that it is a 'financial contribution' conferring a 'benefit' (see Chapter 6). The task thus appears difficult. One could also try to show that market intervention by the People's Bank of China results in prohibited export subsidies on the basis of the SCM Agreement and the Chinese Protocol of Accession to the WTO. Some have also tried to demonstrate that Chinese intervention could be seen as 'currency dumping', something difficult to prove, and rather misleading in terminology, if not reasoning. While the task of challenging Chinese monetary policies might seem simple, it reveals itself to be much more complex. International monetary law and international trade law form two different regimes, often contemplated in isolation and thus difficult to mobilise in a non-fragmented manner. If a currency is manipulated, it may well be that the IMF is the sole competent authority to tackle the problem.

Once again, the incomplete and fragmented nature of a system, put in place at Bretton Woods and voluntarily delinking finance from trade, development and labour, reveals its very limitations and inability to address contemporary issues of global importance.

Box 15.1 (cont.)

To Go Further

Lim, C. L., 'The Law Works itself Pure: The Fragmented Disciplines of Global Trade and Monetary Cooperation, and the Chinese Currency Problem', in C. L. Lim and Bryan Mercurio (eds.), *International Economic Law after the Global Crisis* (Cambridge University Press, 2015), pp. 134–59.

Stiglitz, J. E., 'The US Is at Risk of Losing a Trade War with China', *Project Syndicate* (30 July 2018), available at www.project-syndicate.org/commentary/trump-loses-trade-war-with-china-by-joseph-e-stiglitz-2018-07?barrier=accesspaylog (accessed 21 December 2020).

Yanliang, M., 'China's Quiet Central Banking Revolution', *Project Syndicate* (6 March 2019), available at www.project-syndicate.org/commentary/china-central-bank-communication-exchange-rate-by-miao-yanliang-2019-03 (accessed 21 December 2020).

As we have seen above, in the context of the Bretton Woods system, exchange rates were first fixed on the basis of the (neo-)Gold Standard and then de facto floating from the early 1970s. This situation was legally acknowledged with the Second Amendment of the Articles of Agreement of 1978. This major change was prepared by the IMF from the mid-1970s and adopted during the course of the Kingston Conference in Jamaica (the Jamaica Accords of 8 January 1976). Article IV provides for a rather flexible framework:

IMF, Amended Articles of Agreement, Article IV: Obligations Regarding Exchange Arrangements

Section 1. General obligations of members

Recognizing that the essential purpose of the international monetary system is to provide a framework that facilitates the exchange of goods, services, and capital among countries, and that sustains sound economic growth, and that a principal objective is the continuing development of the orderly underlying conditions that are necessary for financial and economic stability, each member undertakes to collaborate with the Fund and other members to assure orderly exchange arrangements and to promote a stable system of exchange rates. In particular, each member shall:

(i) endeavour to direct its economic and financial policies toward the objective of fostering orderly economic growth with reasonable price stability, with due regard to its circumstances;

(ii) seek to promote stability by fostering orderly underlying economic and financial conditions and a monetary system that does not tend to produce erratic disruptions;

> **(cont.)**
>
> (iii) avoid manipulating exchange rates or the international monetary system in order to prevent effective balance of payments adjustment or to gain an unfair competitive advantage over other members; and
>
> (iv) follow exchange policies compatible with the undertakings under this Section.
>
> ### Section 2. General exchange arrangements
>
> (a) Each member shall notify the Fund, within thirty days after the date of the second amendment of this Agreement, of the exchange arrangements it intends to apply in fulfilment of its obligations under Section 1 of this Article, and shall notify the Fund promptly of any changes in its exchange arrangements.
>
> (b) Under an international monetary system of the kind prevailing on January 1, 1976, exchange arrangements may include (i) the maintenance by a member of a value for its currency in terms of the special drawing right or another denominator, other than gold, selected by the member, or (ii) cooperative arrangements by which members maintain the value of their currencies in relation to the value of the currency or currencies of other members, or (iii) other exchange arrangements of a member's choice.
>
> (c) To accord with the development of the international monetary system, the Fund, by an eighty-five percent majority of the total voting power, may make provision for general exchange arrangements without limiting the right of members to have exchange arrangements of their choice consistent with the purposes of the Fund and the obligations under Section 1 of this Article.

While a stable system of exchange rate is seen as the main tool to support prosperity, the second section, in its paragraph (b), leaves quite a large margin of flexibility to the members of the organisation. The natural result of a negotiation between States, this Article nevertheless provides for some obligations and, in particular, that of collaborating 'with the Fund and other Members to assure orderly exchange arrangements and to promote a stable system of exchange rates'. A system of surveillance and conditionalities was also put in place to mitigate the relative flexibility proposed by the reform.

15.2.1.3   Balance of Payments

Another important concept to address at this stage is that of balance of payments (BoP). The BoP is a statistical statement summarising the transactions between residents and non-residents of a country during a given period (quarter or year) and consists of several

United States, BOP Analytic Presentation (Millions of US Dollars)	
	Q1 2020
Current account (excludes reserves and related items)	−90,338.0
Goods, credit (exports)	3,96,869.0
Goods, debit (imports)	5,73,140.0
Balance on goods	−1,76,271.0
Services, credit (exports)	1,99,473.0
Services, debit (imports)	1,29,937.0
Balance on goods and services	−1,06,735.0
Primary income, credit	2,53,410.0
Primary income, debit	1,99,629.0
Balance on goods, services, and primary income	−52,954.0
Secondary income, credit	34,696.0
Secondary income, debit	72,080.0
Capital account (excludes reserves and related items)	−2,962.0
Capital account, credit	6.0
Capital account, debit	2,968.0
Balance on current and capital account	−93,300.0
Financial account (excludes reserves and related items)	−1,83,938.0
Direct investment, assets	−19,110.0
Equity and investment fund shares	13,413.0
Debt instruments	−32,523.0
Direct investment, liabilities	48,083.0
Equity and investment fund shares	57,813.0
Debt instruments	−9,730.0
Portfolio investment, assets	1,44,705.0
Equity and investment fund shares	3,06,370.0
Debt instruments	−1,61,665.0
Portfolio investment, liabilities	21,313.0
Equity and investment fund shares	2,70,997.0
Debt instruments	−2,49,684.0
Financial derivatives (other than reserves) and employee stock options	−21,830.0
Other investment, assets	6,14,578.0
Other equity	1,298.0
Debt instruments	6,13,280.0
Other investment, liabilities	8,32,885.0
Debt instruments	8,32,885.0
Balance on current, capital, and financial account	90,638.0
Net errors and omissions	−90,878.4
Reserves and related items	−240.4
Reserve assets	−240.4
Net credit and loans from the IMF (excluding reserve position)	0.0
Exceptional financing	0.0
Scale: Millions	

Figure 15.1 Example of the US BoP according to the IMF model. Source: https://data.imf.org/?sk=
7A51304B-6426-40C0-83DD-CA473CA1FD52&sId=1542635306163.

Please note that, for space reasons, we are only showing the first quarter of year 2020 (Q1).

components: the *current account*, measuring international trade (goods and services), net income on investments and direct payments; the *financial account*, describing ownership of the assets (gold, commodities, stocks); and the *capital account*, including any other financial transactions, which do not affect the country's income, production or savings. In recent years indeed, a number of countries have followed the IMF model of BoP presentation, splitting the capital account into two (financial and capital accounts).[9]

The BoP is revealing of a country's financial and economic strength, and informs its government's fiscal and trade policy. Monetary law and trade law meet when discussing BoP, as illustrated by the special provisions of the WTO on BoP and related exceptions (see Chapter 9).[10] In a WTO context, the BoP is governed by the GATT 1994 Articles XII and XVIII:B, the Understanding on the Balance-of-Payments Provisions of the GATT 1994, and Article XII of the GATS. There is, however, more than trade in the BoP, although trade is at its centre. A balanced current account shows the strength of a healthy economy. When a current account is in deficit, a country imports more than it exports (trade deficit), and saves. Trade deficits have multiple causes, but the globalisation of the economy could be identified as one of them. Indeed, multinational companies producing abroad for a given country's market fuel the imports of this country, and hence the trade deficit. The US is the archetypical country facing a massive trade deficit. It can still afford this deficit with the US$ being the global reserve currency and the main instrument of international transaction, as well as its other economic assets. A number of economists do not believe that the US trade deficit hurts the economy, for it can also be the result of a stronger economy in which consumers spend more on imports, and cheap imports from China in particular.[11] In addition, not only trade in goods, but also trade in services has to be taken into consideration in order to gauge the impact of a deficit on the economy. But 2018 showed a new high since 2008.[12] The US monthly trade deficit indeed widened to US$59.8 billion in December 2018, with the goods gap with China jumping to a record high, despite tariffs on US$250 billion worth of Chinese imports and the 'trade wars' going on between the US and its main trading partners.[13]

---

[9] IMF BoP definition and data available at http://datahelp.imf.org/knowledgebase/articles/484330-what-is-the-balance-of-payments-bop; IMF, *Balance of Payments Manual* is also of interest, available at www.imf.org/external/np/sta/bop/bopman.pdf (both accessed 21 December 2020).

[10] Understanding on the Balance-of-Payments Provisions of the General Agreement on Tariffs and Trade 1994, available at www.wto.org/english/docs_e/legal_e/09-bops_e.htm (accessed 21 December 2020).

[11] J. McBride and A. Chatzky, 'The US Trade Deficit: How Much Does it Matter?' (Council on Foreign Relations, 8 March 2019), available at www.cfr.org/backgrounder/us-trade-deficit-how-much-does-it-matter (accessed 21 December 2020).

[12] The IMF provides BoP updated data, for example, the US BoP, available at https://data.imf.org/?sk=7A51304B-6426-40C0-83DD-CA473CA1FD52&sId=1542635306163 (accessed 21 December 2020).

[13] Bureau of Economic Analysis, US Department of Commerce, 'US International Transactions, Second Quarter 2020', available at www.bea.gov/data/intl-trade-investment/international-transactions (accessed 21 December 2020).

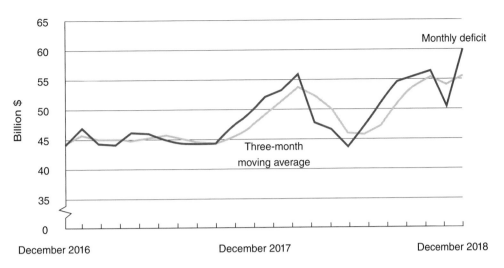

Figure 15.2 US goods and services trade deficit (seasonally adjusted), 6 March 2019. Source: www.bea
.gov/system/files/trade1218-chart-01.png

15.2.2 A Short History

The Bretton Woods system originated in the US on the occasion of the conference formally
known as the United Nations Monetary and Financial Conference held from 1 to 22 July
1944 at the Mount Washington Hotel situated in Bretton Woods, New Hampshire. There
were 730 delegates from all forty-four Allied nations taking part in the Conference. Prepared
as early as the beginning of the Second World War, by John Maynard Keynes of the British
Treasury and Harry Dexter White of the US Treasury, this large conference's objective was
to re-establish a financial order conducive to the growth and development of the Allies, in
the general context of reconstruction and the start of the decolonisation period. Ambitions
were initially high and Keynes, for instance, supported the establishment of an international
clearing union (see Box 15.2). However, the US opposed all initiatives that could eventually
challenge its supremacy.

Box 15.2 John Maynard Keynes

John Maynard Keynes is not guilty of the contemporary failures of a Bretton Woods
system he conceived in a very different light. The British economist and father of what
became the 'Keynesian school of thought', was born in 1883 in Cambridge, England.
He studied at Eton College and King's College, Cambridge. He then started a Civil
Service career in the India Office, but returned rapidly to academia. In 1911, he
became editor of the *Economic Journal* and published his first book in 1913, *Indian*

Box 15.2 (cont.)

Currency and Finance. He then took up an official government position at the UK Treasury during the First World War and continued to advise the government. He was appointed financial representative of the Treasury to the 1919 Versailles Peace Conference, at which he unsuccessfully argued in favour of reparations that were more reasonable for Germany – that is, reparations that would not create a feeling of humiliation and so a desire for revenge, as predicted in his book, *The Economic Consequences of Peace*, published in 1919. In the 1920s, he worked mostly on his academic research, but also as a consultant, arguing in favour of pro-stimulus approaches, encouraging the government to spend on job creation to support the economy as well as an end to the Gold Standard. In the midst of the Great Depression, his work caught the attention of the US President Roosevelt. His major piece of work, *The General Theory of Employment, Interest and Money*, was published in 1936 and sought to demonstrate how cheap money, combined with 'socialisation of investment', could maintain full employment. In supporting State intervention, he was dramatically departing from 'classical' economy – and economists like Friedrich Hayek – and the idea of self-regulation. The Keynesian school of economy was born and remains highly influential today. Elevated to the House of Lords in 1942, as Baron Keynes of Tilton, he was able to make a mark on post-war policies and planned for an International Clearing Union (1941), which was designed to avoid deflationary shocks and the impact of negative BoP. He argued in favour of a radical change of monetary policies, including the creation of a world currency, the 'bancor', which would be exchangeable with national currencies at fixed rates, as well as new institutions, an International Central Bank and a Clearing Union. These were designed to manage international trade, to avoid major deficits or surpluses, hence maintaining a healthy BoP. In an ingenious manner, Keynes invented a system in which creditor countries would be encouraged to spend their surplus money into the economy of the indebted nations. In this framework, every country would benefit from an overdraft facility in its 'bancor' account, equivalent to half the average value of its trade over a five-year period. Disciplines would be put in place on the basis that countries with too large trade deficits would be charged interest and made to reduce the value of their currencies to prevent export of capital. On the other hand, countries with too large a surplus would also be subject to disciplines (interest and increase of their currency's value, as well as possible confiscation of the surplus). This global system, designed to balance power and de facto create a form of equality between nations, was adopted as Britain's official position for the Bretton Woods negotiations, but did not acquire the favour of the most powerful country, the USA. As the biggest creditor of the world, the US was not prepared to abandon the US$ and agree to a stabilisation system that it felt would

Box 15.2 (cont.)

develop to the detriment of the USA. Moreover, it was right: in keeping the US$ and gaining veto power at the IMF, the US maintained its supremacy even when becoming highly indebted, while at the same time, the monetary system created by the IMF resulted in catastrophe for the poorest and most indebted countries.

One of the most influential thinkers of the twentieth century, and certainly Britain's most famous modern (liberal) economist, Keynes has had an impact on generations of decision makers, despite a period of disgrace at the peak of the neoliberal era of the 1980s and 1990s. The return of Keynes' influence materialised in the late 2000s, with a number of responses to the global financial crisis of 2007–08. From James K. Galbraith to Nobel laureates Paul Krugman and Joseph Stiglitz, a large number of contemporary leading economists advocated robust (Keynesian) government intervention to fight the financial crisis and mitigate the negative effects of globalisation in a coordinated fashion. While this might well have been a defeat of the orthodoxy that had prevailed in the past several decades, it did not last long. Austerity policies returned quickly and the Bretton Woods system, once again, has struggled to reform itself in the aftermath of a new crisis, that of the Covid-19 pandemic.

To Go Further

Allen, R. C., *Global Economic History: A Very Short Introduction* (Oxford University Press, 2011).

Keynes, J. M., *The Essential Keynes*, ed. R. Skidelsky (London: Penguin, 2015).

Skidelsky, R., *John Maynard Keynes, 1883–1946: Economist, Philosopher, Statesman* (London: Penguin, 2013).

Stiglitz, J., *Globalization and its Discontents* (London: Penguin, 2002).

Wolff, R. D., *Contending Economic Theories: Neoclassical, Keynesian and Marxian* (Cambridge, MA: MIT Press, 2012).

The monetary system put in place at Bretton Woods was the first example of a fully negotiated order governing independent States. Its main features revolved around exchange rates stability and, as demonstrated above, the (neo-)Gold Standard. Members were to peg their currencies to the US$, which was convertible to gold at a fixed exchange rate. Members were, however, permitted to adjust their currency exchange rate by 1 per cent in case of a 'fundamental disequilibrium', a concept never clearly defined, but envisaged as a fairly rare possibility.

With the 1971 American decision to terminate the convertibility of the US$ to gold, the Bretton Woods system was on the brink of collapse. Yet institutions remained and adapted to a new world order in which the role of the US$ as the world reserve currency became even more evident. A system of subscriptions and quotas had been put in place to provide the IMF with a fund of contributions from members, in gold and their own currencies (25 per cent in gold or a currency convertible to gold (US$), and 75 per cent in their own currency). The quota assigned to the members reflected their relative economic power. Quotas were key in determining the voting powers of IMF members, as well as access to financing. They are still in place today, together with a more complex mechanism of Special Drawing Rights, and are reviewed on a regular basis. Naturally, this system of quota-based voting power rapidly became controversial, as the richest nations, and the US in particular, which held one-third of all IMF quotas and a de facto veto power, exerted a preponderant influence on the organisation.

The initial system worked in supporting the post-war reconstruction efforts, but became increasingly untenable from the 1960s, with American domestic policies supporting full employment, the decolonisation era and the increasing international involvement of the US, and the Vietnam War in particular. Special Drawing Rights were created to counterbalance American difficulties and the flow of dollars out of the US. The December 1971 Smithsonian Agreement (named after the institution where the meeting of a group of ten countries took place) failed to stop the dollar drain. In February 1973, Japan and the European Community countries decided to let their currency float, definitively ending the Bretton Woods system, which had already suffered a major blow in 1971 with the American decision to terminate US$ convertibility. The Jamaica Accords of 1976 formally ended the Bretton Woods system.

Box 15.3 The IMF at major moments

- 1–22 July 1944, formulation of IMF and World Bank Articles of Agreement, Bretton Woods, New Hampshire
- 27 December 1945, Articles of Agreement come into force
- March 1947, IMF begins operations
- 8 May 1947, first drawing by France
- 13–14 August 1952, Germany and Japan become members of the IMF
- 28 July 1969, First Amendment to the Articles of Agreement establishing a facility based on the Special Drawing Rights (SDR)
- 1 January 1970, first allocation of SDR
- 15 August 1971, end of par values and convertibility of the US$
- March 1973, generalisation of floating rates
- 7–8 January 1976, Amendment of Article IV, Jamaica Accords
- 1 April 1978, Second Amendment of Articles of Agreement
- 17 September 1980, unification and simplification of SDR on the basis of a basket of five currencies (US$, pound sterling, French franc, Deutsche mark, Japanese yen)

Box 15.3 (cont.)

- August 1982, Mexican Crisis
- 27 March 1986, establishment of Structural Adjustment Facilities
- 22 February 1987, Louvre Accord to intensify policy cooperation
- November 1992, third amendments to the Articles of Agreement
- September 1997, amendments of Articles of Agreement allowing members to receive an equitable share of cumulative SDR allocations
- December 1997, Asian Crisis
- 20 July 1998, General Arrangement to Borrow is activated for the first time in favour of Russia
- 1 January 1999, creation of the euro
- 2 February 2001, IMF approves increase of Chinese quota after Hong Kong handover
- 2008 Financial Crisis, the IMF enters a phase of reforms
- December 2010, the Board of Governors of the IMF completes the 14th General Review of Quotas
- January 2016, implementation of new governance mechanism more favourable to emerging and developing countries' representation.

15.2.3 The IMF: An International Organisation

The IMF was conceived to build a framework for international economic cooperation and avoid repeating the competitive currency devaluations that contributed to the Great Depression of the 1930s. The IMF's primary mission was to ensure the stability of the international monetary system – the system of exchange rates and international payments that enables countries and their citizens to transact with each other. The IMF is an international organisation governed by and accountable to its 189 member countries.

Box 15.4 The IMF in brief

- Membership: 189 countries
- Headquarters: Washington DC, US
- Objectives:
  - Promote international monetary cooperation
  - Support expansion of international trade
  - Promote exchange stability

Box 15.4 (cont.)

    – Assist the establishment of a multilateral system of payments
    – Make resources available to members facing balance of payments issue
- 2700 staff from 150 countries
- Governance: 24 directors
- Resources: SDR 477 billion or US$661 billion
- Borrowed resources: SDR 500 billion or US$693 billion
- Largest borrowers: Argentina, Ukraine, Greece, Egypt
- Largest precautionary loans: Mexico, Colombia, Morocco

Source: IMF, 'The IMF at a Glance', Factsheet (22 March 2019), available at imf.org/en/About/Factsheets/IMF-at-a-Glance (accessed 21 December 2020).

Article XII of the Articles of Agreement of the IMF established its governing structure, which consists of:[14]

- *Board of Governors* (one governor and one alternate governor from each member country, often chosen from among the top officials from the central bank or finance ministry), which meets once a year at the IMF-World Bank Annual Meeting. It has delegated most of its powers to the Executive Board, but retains the right to approve quota increases, SDR allocations, new member entries, withdrawal of members and amendments of the Articles of Agreement and By-Laws. The Board of Governors also elects Executive Directors. Decisions are made by majority vote unless otherwise specified in the Articles of Agreement. The Board of Governors is advised by two ministerial committees, the International Monetary and Financial Committee and the Development Committee (common to the IMF and the World Bank).
- *Executive Board* of twenty-four members overseeing the day to day work of the organisation. It was reformed in 2016 for the better participation of all members. It makes decisions on the basis of consensus, but sometimes by vote on the basis of quota-determined voting powers.
- *Managing Director*, head of the IMF staff and Chair of the Executive Board, who is assisted by four Deputy Managing Directors. The Managing Director is appointed by the Executive Board for a renewable term of five years.

---

[14] IMF, Articles of Agreement, Article XII, Section 1: Structure of the Fund:

> The Fund shall have a Board of Governors, an Executive Board, a Managing Director, and a staff, and a Council if the Board of Governors decides, by an eighty-five percent majority of the total voting power, that the provisions of Schedule D shall be applied.

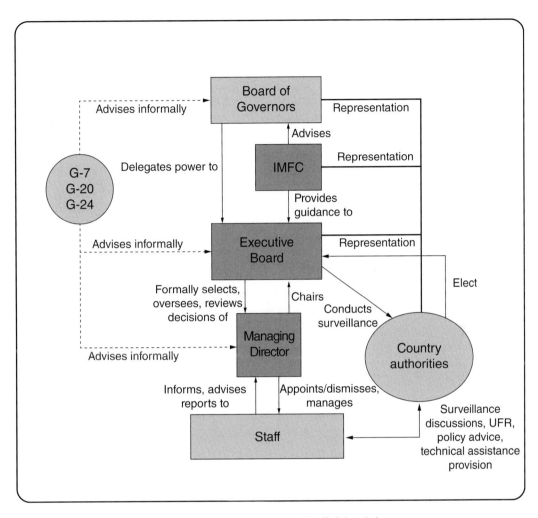

Figure 15.3 Stylised view of IMF governance. Source: IMF official website.

Decision-making at the IMF was designed on the basis of quotas to reflect the relative economic power of members. The governance of the institution has recently been reformed to better balance interests and powers, in the context of the increasing challenges faced by the organisation and a form of legitimacy crisis related to the perceived domination of the Fund by a few of the richest members, and the US in particular. In December 2010, the Board of Governors of the IMF completed the 14th General Review of Quotas, which involved a series of governance measures, which were finally implemented from January 2016. They included a quota increase and realignment of quota and voting shares to emerging and developing countries, plus the protection of the poorest countries' quotas. The 2010 reform also included an amendment to the Articles of Agreement towards the selection of a more representative Executive Board in favour of emerging and developing countries and at the detriment of EU countries, who have accepted a reduction in their participation. In addition, the work of the IMF is based on a Code of Conduct for Staff and another Code of Conduct for Members of the Executive Board.

15.2.4 Resources and Drawing Rights

One of the main objectives of the Fund was to create a pool of resources based on mandatory contributions from its members. These resources could then be drawn by members when in need and in the case of BoP problems in particular. The IMF is a quota-based institution. Quotas determine members' voting power, financial access and share in drawing rights allocations. Quotas were first determined at the Bretton Woods Conference (IMF Articles of Agreement, Schedule A) and were later decided for new members by the Board of Governors based on economic data (GDP, current account transactions in its BoP and official reserves). At the initial stages of the IMF, quotas were to be paid in gold for 25 per cent and in the member's currency for the remaining 75 per cent. Quotas have been reviewed periodically to better reflect members' economic situations and, as explained above, to better balance the representation of all nations, and emerging and developing countries especially. The latest (14th) review was concluded in 2010. The quota increases became effective in 2016. Accordingly, the quota resources doubled to SDR 477 billion (about US$661 billion). In addition, another pool of resources is available: a credit arrangement between the IMF and a group of members and institutions for about SDR 182 billion (US$253 billion). A third line of resource is also available in the form of bilateral borrowing agreements totalling about SDR 317 billion (US$440 billion).

On the basis of these contributions, IMF members were allowed to draw (Drawing Rights) on the resources of the Fund. Keynes' initial idea was that all members would automatically be entitled to draw on the resources of the IMF. But the US, the main creditor country, disagreed and made sure a set of conditions was defined to allow drawing. Hence the idea of 'conditionality' was born and remains one of the most controversial features of the IMF. The Executive Board then agreed on a series of conditions for members to draw IMF resources on the basis of a time period and a percentage of quotas (generally 25 per cent, so the equivalent of the gold share of the quota). Naturally, if additional help was required, expectations (conditions) could become more stringent.

In 1969, the SRD was created as a reserve asset to supplement members' official reserves. In the early 1970s, these drawing rights were thought to provide liquidity in supplementing members' official reserves. The SDR also serves as the unit of account of the IMF and some other international organisations. It is not a currency as such, but a potential claim on the currencies of IMF members. SDR was initially defined on the basis of 0.888671 grams of fine gold (US$ at that time) and redefined as a basket of currencies after the Bretton Woods system came to an end. The SDR basket is reviewed every five years. These currencies amounts remain fixed over the five years, while the weight of the

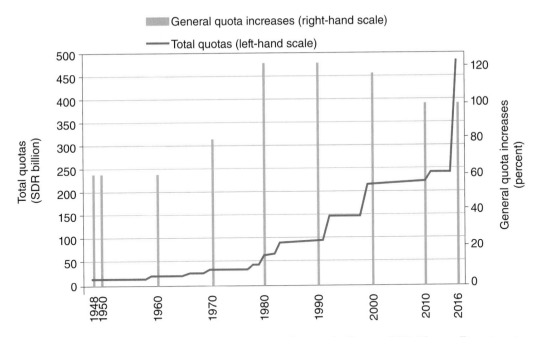

Figure 15.4 Entry into effect of general quota increase, by decade. Source: IMF, Finance Department statistics.

currencies in the basket fluctuate on the basis of exchange rates and is determined daily. Today, the value of the SDR is based on the US$, the euro, the Chinese renminbi, the Japanese yen and the British pound sterling. The decision to include the Chinese renminbi was taken, in November 2015, to reflect the important role of China in the global economy. In addition, SDR provides for the basis of calculation of the interest rate charged to members on their non-concessional borrowings, as well as interest paid to the members who lend and on their holdings. Lastly, members can buy and sell SDRs, and the IMF, if required, can designate members to buy SDRs. The total global allocations are currently about SDR 204 billion (some $283 billion).[15]

15.2.5 The IMF: An Evolving Organisation

The IMF today performs three main functions: surveillance, lending and capacity development.

---

[15] For regular updates on figures, see IMF, 'Special Drawing Right (SDR)', Factsheet (24 March 2020), available at www.imf.org/en/About/Factsheets/Sheets/2016/08/01/14/51/Special-Drawing-Right-SDR (accessed 21 December 2020).

15.2.5.1   Surveillance

The IMF oversees the international monetary system and monitors the economic and financial policies of its 189 member countries. As part of this process, which takes place both at the global level and in individual countries, the IMF highlights possible risks and advises on needed policy adjustments. These policies have often been criticised, and have sometimes proved controversial.

This activity of surveillance, or monitoring, takes the form of country visits and reporting, once the IMF has met with governments and central banks.

> ### *IMF, Articles of Agreement, Article IV: Obligations Regarding Exchange Arrangements*
>
> ### Section 3. Surveillance over exchange arrangements
>
> (a) The Fund shall oversee the international monetary system in order to ensure its effective operation and shall oversee the compliance of each member with its obligations under Section 1 of this Article.
>
> (b) In order to fulfil its functions under (a) above, the Fund shall exercise firm surveillance over the exchange rate policies of members, and shall adopt specific principles for the guidance of all members with respect to those policies. Each member shall provide the Fund with the information necessary for such surveillance, and, when requested by the Fund, shall consult with it on the member's exchange rate policies. The principles adopted by the Fund shall be consistent with cooperative arrangements by which members maintain the value of their currencies in relation to the value of the currency or currencies of other members, as well as with other exchange arrangements of a member's choice consistent with the purposes of the Fund and Section 1 of this Article. These principles shall respect the domestic social and political policies of members, and in applying these principles the Fund shall pay due regard to the circumstances of members.

While monetary policy is scrutinised, all aspects of the country's macroeconomic choices are also addressed, from regulatory and fiscal policies to structural reforms. In doing so, the Fund shall 'respect the domestic social and political policies of members, and in applying these principles the Fund shall pay due regard to the circumstances of members'. While facing major international criticism indeed, the IMF is now more transparent and seems to better take into consideration domestic specificities, for example, in engaging further with civil society and publishing its reports more broadly (World Economic Outlook, Global Financial Stability Report, Fiscal Monitor and so on). IMF surveillance activities are systematically reviewed and discussed with members.

15.2.5.2 Assistance: Lending and Conditionality

The IMF provides loans to member countries experiencing actual or potential BoP problems. This is designed to help them rebuild their international reserves, stabilise their currencies, pay for imports, and restore conditions for strong economic growth.[16] The Fund also addresses structural problems through a system of conditionalities. IMF lending is tailored to the needs of each specific situation and country. Unlike development banks, the IMF does not lend for specific economic development projects, but rather to mitigate the effects of crisis (see Chapter 16).

In 2009, the IMF strengthened its lending capacity, and loan resources available to low-income countries were largely increased, while average limits under the IMF's concessional loan facilities were doubled. Access limits under the IMF's non-concessional lending facilities were reviewed and increased again in 2016. In addition, zero interest rates on concessional loans were extended through end-June 2019, and the interest rate on emergency financing is permanently set at zero. Borrowing indeed takes two forms: *non-concessional and concessional* loans.

Non-concessional lending is based on Article V Section 3(a) of the Articles of Agreement:

> ## IMF, Articles of Agreement, Article V: Operations and Transactions of the Fund
>
> ## Section 3. Conditions governing use of the Fund's general resources
>
> (a) The Fund shall adopt policies on the use of its general resources, including policies on stand-by or similar arrangements, and may adopt special policies for special balance of payments problems, that will assist members to solve their balance of payments problems in a manner consistent with the provisions of this Agreement and that will establish adequate safeguards for the temporary use of the general resources of the Fund.

The Fund is here entitled to help its members facing BoP issues. These non-concessional loans are provided to IMF members through standby arrangements, flexible credit lines, precautionary and liquidity lines, the Extended Fund Facility and the Rapid Financing Instrument for emergency situations.

The IMF *concessional lending* activities began in 1976 through its trust fund (terminated in 1981). The objective was to support developing economies in creating a system departing from the general rules and the idea of non-discrimination, allowing resources to be made available to all members on the same basis. The 1978 Second Amendment of

---

[16] The IMF has set up a Covid-19 emergency response to tackle the issue of debt, available at www.imf.org/en/Topics/imf-and-covid19 (accessed 21 December 2020).

the IMF Articles of Agreement designed special provisions to allow for the surplus from IMF sales of gold to be used for concessional lending. With the 2010 reforms, the IMF Poverty Reduction and Growth Trust (PRGT) provides financial assistance, with the support of three facilities: the Extended Credit Facility (ECF), the Standby Credit Facility (SCF) and the Rapid Credit Facility (RCF). The ECF was created under the PRGT to make the IMF finance support more flexible and better tailored to low-income countries (LICs). It is the IMF's main tool for medium-term support. ECF access is determined on a case-by-case basis and granted with conditionalities.[17] The SCF provides financial assistance to LICs with short-term BoP needs. It can range from twelve to thirty-six months and is based on a country's BoP needs and its economic strength and ability to repay. It is also based on some conditionalities in the form of policies agreed upon.[18] The RCF provides rapid concessional financial assistance with limited conditionality. It is designed for LICs that face urgent BoP needs. Here again, access is determined on a case-by-case basis. In response to the Covid-19 crisis, access to the RCF has temporarily been made easier by the IMF.[19]

Administered accounts were also established to provide financing in the form of debt relief to poor countries. These concessional loans are based on an agreement between the IMF and the country at stake to reform its economy and adopt specific policies. The agreed programme to reform is presented to the Fund's Executive Board in a Letter of Intent and detailed in a Memorandum of understanding between the parties. Most IMF financing is paid out in instalments and linked to demonstrable policy actions on the basis of the defined conditions. These 'conditionalities' form an integral part of IMF lending (as shown in Figure 15.5) and have been at the centre of major controversies.[20] The controversial 'Washington Consensus', referring to the IMF and World Bank austerity policies calling for structural adjustment through market liberalisation and privatisation, has yet to be truly addressed. Scrutiny is high, but the reforms very few.

According to the IMF, conditionalities can take the following concrete forms:

- *Prior actions*: actions taken before the IMF approves financing, for example, fiscal reform or elimination of price control.
- *Quantitative performance criteria*: these are the conditions for monetary and credit aggregates, international reserves, fiscal balances and external borrowing.

---

[17] IMF, 'IMF Extended Credit Facility (ECF)', Factsheet (3 March 2020), available at www.imf.org/en/About/Factsheets/Sheets/2016/08/02/21/04/Extended-Credit-Facility (accessed 21 December 2020).

[18] IMF, 'IMF Standby Credit Facility (SCF)', Factsheet (27 March 2020), available at www.imf.org/en/About/Factsheets/Sheets/2016/08/02/21/10/Standby-Credit-Facility (accessed 21 December 2020).

[19] IMF, 'Enhancing the Emergency Financing Toolkit: Responding to the Covid-19 Pandemic', Policy Papers (9 April 2020), available at www.imf.org/en/Publications/Policy-Papers/Issues/2020/04/09/Enhancing-the-Emergency-Financing-Toolkit-Responding-To-The-COVID-19-Pandemic-49320?sc_mode=1 (accessed 21 December 2020).

[20] David Vines and Christopher L. Gilbert (eds.), *The IMF and its Critics: Reform of the Financial Architecture* (Cambridge University Press, 2004); Joseph E. Stiglitz, *People, Power, and Profits: Progressive Capitalism for an Age of Discontent* (New York: W.W. Norton, 2020).

Purpose	Facility	Financing	Duration	Conditionality
Present, Prospective, or Potential BoP need	SBA	GRA	Up to 3 years, but usually 12–18 months	Ex-post
	SCF	PRGT	1 to 2 years	
Protracted BoP need/ medium-term assistance	EFF	GRA	Up to 4 years	Ex-post, with focus on structural reforms
	ECF	PRGT	3 to 4 years, extendable to 5 years	
Actual and urgent BoP need	RFI	GRA	Outright purchase	No Fund-supported program/ex-post conditionality, but prior actions possible
	RCF	PRGT	Outright disbursement	
Present, Prospective, or Potential BoP need (very strong fundamentals and policies)	FCL	GRA	1 or 2-year	Ex-ante (qualification criteria) and annual reviews for the two year arrangements
Present, Prospective, or Potential BoP need (sound fundamentals and policies)	PLL	GRA	6 month (liquidity window) or 1 or 2-year	Ex-ante (qualification criteria) and ex-post
Non-financial/ signaling instruments	PSI	n/a	1 to 4 year, extendable to 5 years	Ex-post
	PCI	n/a	6 months to 4 years	

Figure 15.5 Examples of IMF conditionalities. Source: IMF official website.

- *Indicative targets*: objectives to be pursued, for example, in terms of primary balance.
- *Structural benchmarks*: these are certainly the most controversial type of reforms as they have an impact on sovereign policies, such as social or fiscal reforms.

All these requirements are systematically monitored and evaluated by the IMF. In its endeavour to reform under the Mandate of former Director Christine Lagarde, the IMF seems to have gone some distance with austerity policies and now better approaches the diversity of local economic conditions, as is illustrated by its capacity development activities.

15.2.5.3 Capacity Development

The IMF provides technical assistance and training to help members, and developing country members in particular, to reform and strengthen their economies, from institutional to human capacity building. Assistance and training courses are offered in a variety of fields, from central banking to monetary and exchange rate policies, tax administration, legal framework or statistics. It is now one of the core activities of the IMF, which echoes that of the World Bank and other regional banks and donors.[21] The topics covered are indeed quite closely related, and so is the rhetoric on the benefits of 'capacity development' work to 'reduce inequalities', tackle 'gender equality' and support 'climate action'.

In the recent past, low-income developing countries benefited from around 40 per cent of the Fund's resources used in capacity development activities. This assistance is delivered in Washington, DC, as well as at the IMF regional centre or with the support of external partners, and is reviewed by the Executive Board periodically, the last review having been completed in 2018.[22]

15.3 The International Monetary System in Crisis

IMF policies have not managed to avoid a long series of financial crises. On the contrary, some have long argued that IMF policies have fuelled these dramatic economic moments for countries at the mercy of the financial markets and austerity policies applied to reform their economy.[23] A combination of factors leads to a financial crisis (financial imbalances,

---

[21] IMF, 'IMF Capacity Development', Factsheet (21 October 2020), www.imf.org/en/About/Factsheets/imf-capacity-development (accessed 21 December 2020).

[22] IMF Capacity Development Strategy and Policies, available at www.imf.org/en/Capacity-Development/strategy-policies (accessed 21 December 2020).

[23] See, for example, Carlos De Resende and Shinji Takagi, 'Assessing the Effectiveness of IMF Programs Following the Global Financial Crisis: How Did it Change Since the Asian Crisis?', ADBI Working Paper Series 838 (Asian Development Bank Institute, April 2018), available at www.adb.org/publications/assessing-effectiveness-imf-programs-following-global-financial-crisis (accessed 21 December 2020); and listen to 'The Amartya Sen Lecture 2014', LSE Podcasts (with Christine Lagarde, Managing Director of the IMF), available at https://soundcloud.com/lsepodcasts/the-amartya-sen-lecture-2014 (accessed 21 December 2020). See also Paul Krugman, *The Return of Depression Economics and the 2008 Crisis* (New York: W. W. Norton, 2009); and Vines and Gilbert, *The IMF and its Critics*.

monetary policies, inadequate supervision, economic dependence and so on). Its remediation depends on a variety of political choices, which should be based on economic sovereignty. As we will see below, in briefly addressing a few major contemporary crises, this regulatory freedom (or lack of thereof), echoing the issues discussed in IIL, has not always been able to manifest itself, hence the controversies surrounding the legitimacy of the IMF and its need for change, a reform discussed for several decades and partially embraced for the past ten years or so.

15.3.1 A Long Series of Regional Crises

15.3.1.1 The Latin American Crisis

The Latin American debt crisis relates to a series of events originating in early 1980s Latin America and often referred to as 'La década perdida' (the lost decade), when these countries could not repay their foreign debt. In the 1960s and 1970s, indeed, Mexico, Brazil and Argentina borrowed massive amounts of money to support ambitious infrastructure programmes and other development-related initiatives. These countries did not only borrow through the international institutional route (World Bank or regional development banks), but also via the private system, on the basis of apparently attractive offers from private banks. Often reliant on natural resources, as in the case of Mexico and its oil, these Latin American countries were in fact very vulnerable. The oil crisis of the late 1970s had a significant impact on the economy.

Unable to repay their debt and the interest, Latin American countries turned to the IMF. The Mexican crisis hence became a textbook case of interactions between poor governance, international intervention and the many side effects of the same.[24] The IMF required structural adjustments to open its lending facilities. These took the form of austerity plans and programmes lowering the total spending of the States. Naturally, these plans had an impact on the well-being of citizens, who, at least in the short-term, sank deeper into poverty. Growth rates fell while unemployment rose. So much so that at the end of the 1980s, a country like Brazil declared that it would never again collaborate with the IMF. This very Latin American crisis generated immense anger and frustration against the international financial system, for it was said to have aggravated economic distress by forcing developing countries to rely even more on the financial markets. From a longer-term perspective, the impact of IMF intervention could be viewed in a more nuanced manner. A country like Mexico indeed repaid its debt and managed to grow quite significantly in the following decades. So did Brazil in the 2000s.

---

[24] For a comparative approach of sovereign debt crises, see Jerome E. Roos, *Why Not Default? The Political Economy of Sovereign Debt* (Princeton University Press, 2019).

15.3.1.2   The South East Asian Crisis

The 1997 South East Asian crisis provides another example of controversial IMF intervention. The crisis began in Thailand with the collapse of the Thai baht, which added to an already difficult situation of debt repayment. In a sort of domino effect, most of the countries of the region found themselves in similar situations. By the end of 1997, South Korea, the largest economy in Asia, with Japan, also found itself in a dramatic debt crisis. Indonesia was seriously affected too, while Hong Kong, Malaysia and the Philippines were significantly hurt. The crisis had repercussions in the whole region, also affecting Singapore, Taiwan and Vietnam, and even Japan, albeit to a much lesser extent.

Countries turned to the IMF, which put in place a very ambitious plan and injected US$40 billion to stabilise currencies in South Korea, Thailand and Indonesia in particular. In going far beyond its traditional adjustment plans, which were essentially targeting macroeconomic policies (BoP, inflation, fiscal deficit and so on), the IMF got involved in very precise structural reforms (regulation, banking, trade policy, private property and FDI, but also social policies including health programmes and how to tackle HIV/AIDS for countries like Thailand and Indonesia). This rather intrusive nature of the Fund's new policies, which also required transparency and publication of the governments' commitments and initiatives, came under global scrutiny. Indonesia managed a major political transition with the end of the Suharto's dictatorship, supported indirectly for the previous thirty years by the same international institutions that later questioned its legitimacy in denouncing corruption. The very same countries, which collapsed in 1997, had been praised a few months before by the IMF for their daring liberal policies. As in Latin America, IMF policies (or the crisis itself) at first seemed to worsen the situation.[25] Austerity measures were applied in a downturn and may well have transformed a recession into a depression.[26] In the longer run, economies recovered and many of them performed extremely well, with Asia being at the forefront of globalization. But the weight of public debt repayment remains very high, while the benefits of growth are not shared by all, thus leading to rising inequalities. Today, in Vietnam, the country's richest man earns more in a day than the poorest person earns in a decade.[27] A similar comparison could be made for most Asian States. In a 2016 report, the IMF itself acknowledged the need for Asia to tackle increasing inequalities:

more recently inequality has risen in many countries in Asia, with growth less beneficial to the poor compared with the past. The report concludes that structural reforms, along with fiscal policy, can help reduce inequality and foster more inclusive growth. Countries will need to address inequality of

---

[25] Elaine Hutson and Colm Kearney, 'The Asian Financial Crisis and the Role of the IMF', *Journal of the Asia Pacific Economy* (1999), 4, pp. 393–412.

[26] B. Thirkell-White, *The IMF and the Politics of Financial Globalization: From the Asian Crisis to a New International Financial Architecture?* (New York: Palgrave Macmillan, 2005); Paul Blustein, *The Chastening: Inside the Crisis that Rocked the Global Financial System and Humbled the IMF* (New York: Public Affairs, 2003).

[27] Deborah Hardoon, 'An Economy for the 99%', Oxfam Briefing Paper (January 2017), available at https://d1tn3vj7xz9fdh.cloudfront.net/s3fs-public/file_attachments/bp-economy-for-99-percent-160117-en.pdf (accessed 21 December 2020).

opportunities, in particular the need to broaden access to education, health, and financial services, as well as tackle labour-market duality and informality. Reforms should avoid costly, across-the-board subsidy schemes while focusing instead on the expansion of social spending through well-targeted interventions and more-progressive tax codes. Recent reforms, such as the elimination of fuel-price controls in most major economies of the region, bode well for the future.[28]

Will the IMF's new policies be conducive to inclusive growth for a more human economy in developing Asia? Time will tell, but one must stress the need for economic independence and sovereign policy choices.

15.3.1.3   The Russian Transition

Another fascinating example of IMF intervention is provided by the Russian transition from a socialist economy towards a more capitalistic one, if not a clear market economy.[29] After the fall of the Berlin Wall and the opening up of the former Eastern bloc, in the early 1990s, Russia joined the IMF in 1992. Reflecting on a series of initial substantial plans put in place by the IMF, Michel Camdessus, Managing Director of the Organisation at the time, noticed with satisfaction, during his April 1998 address:

The Russian economy has passed from the brink of hyperinflation to single-digit inflation; from substantial isolation to substantial integration in global markets; from the demise of central planning to the rise of a dynamic private sector; and from output collapse to a long-awaited renewal of output growth.[30]

However, much remained to be done in terms of regulation and transparency in particular. The Nobel Prize winner, Joseph Stiglitz, was much less impressed by the IMF intervention and the liberal policies applied to Russia, which also seemed to be conducive to corruption (through a massive privatisation plan) and did not support the democratisation effort:

The move from communism to capitalism in Russia after 1991 was supposed to bring unprecedented prosperity. It did not. By the time of the rouble crisis of August 1998, output had fallen by almost half and poverty had increased from 2% of the population to over 40%. Russia's performance since then has been impressive, yet its gross domestic product remains almost 30% below what it was in 1990. At 4% growth per annum, it will take Russia's economy another decade to get back to where it was when communism collapsed.[31]

The analytic contrast is striking and illustrates the massive difference in appraising the role of the IMF. From the early 2000s, Russia benefited from a series of other plans, while IMF

---

[28] IMF, 'IMF Survey: Asia: Growth Remains Strong, Expected to Ease Only Modestly', IMF News (3 May 2016), available at www.imf.org/en/News/Articles/2015/09/28/04/53/socar050316b (accessed 21 December 2020).

[29] Jorge Martinez-Vazquez, Felix Rioja, Samuel Skogstad and Neven Valev, 'IMF Conditionality and Objections: The Russian Case', *American Journal of Economics and Sociology* (2001), 60, pp. 501–17.

[30] Michel Camdessus (Managing Director of the IMF), 'Russia and the IMF: Meeting the Challenges of an Emerging Market and Transition Economy', Address at the US–Russia Business Council (Washington, DC, 1 April 1998), available at www.imf.org/en/News/Articles/2015/09/28/04/53/sp040198 (accessed 21 December 2020).

[31] Joseph Stiglitz, 'The Ruin of Russia', *The Guardian* (9 April 2003), available at www.theguardian.com/world/2003/apr/09/russia.artsandhumanities (accessed 21 December 2020).

influence greatly exceeded its initial role, as it tried to shape democratic reform, with very mixed results. Yet some reforms, including the 2013–14 banking reforms and the recent tackling of inflation in coordination with the IMF, seem to have succeeded.[32]

15.3.1.4 The Argentine Crisis

In Argentina, history seems to repeat itself and the love/hate saga with the IMF is never-ending. By the end of 2018, Argentina had received the biggest loan package ever from the IMF: US$57.1 billion to be disbursed over the next three years. It was the biggest loan in history and not the first for Argentina. The new package came with stringent conditional-ities, including a commitment to a zero deficit for 2019. It aimed at tackling yet another currency crisis and double-digit inflation.[33] The package agreed on also planned for the following: an acceleration in the improvement of the fiscal position, a shift to monetary aggregates as the nominal anchor, a floating exchange rate and an increased level of benefits in the main social safety programmes. Argentina has repeatedly failed to meet the objectives set by the IMF and is facing a dramatic crisis, worsened by the Covid-19 pandemic.[34]

Argentina is the champion of IMF lending, as well IMF contestation. Since 2001, when the government declared default on its debt, the country has never stopped resorting to the Fund, while at the same hating it and drastically changing policy options from the election of one government to another. This instability has generated massive frustration, as well as numerous business conflicts, as in ISDS, where Argentina again tops the list of respondents, many of the disputes relating to policy changes in the context of IMF-advised privatisations and regulatory instability (see Chapter 14). It is difficult to conclude on the benefits expected or delivered by the IMF's various plans, but popular resentment against the organisation is very high, since it is perceived only to have imposed austerity plans, pushing more and more people into poverty.[35] Argentina, because of the lack of deep structural reforms, still faces one crisis after another. In May 2020, amid the Covid-19 pandemic, although not related to it, Argentina defaulted again.[36]

---

[32] For more detail, see the interview of the Russian Central Bank Governor, Elvira Nabiullina, 'Pursuing Stability', *Finance and Development* (2019), 56(1), available at www.imf.org/external/pubs/ft/fandd/2019/03/interview-with-russian-central-bank-governor-elvira-nabiullina.htm; as well as IMF, 'Russian Federation: Selected Issues', IMF Staff Country Reports (12 September 2018), available at www.imf.org/en/Publications/CR/Issues/2018/09/12/Russian-Federation-Selected-Issues-46227 (accessed 21 December 2020).

[33] IMF, 'IMF's Revised Stand-By Arrangement', Update on Argentina (updated on 26 October 2018), available at www.imf.org/en/Countries/ARG/argentina-update (accessed 21 December 2020); and generally on conditionalities, T. Stubbs, B. Reinsberg, A. Kentikelenis and L. King, 'How to Evaluate the Effects of IMF Conditionality', *Review of International Organizations* (2020), 15, pp. 29–73.

[34] See www.imf.org./en/Countries/ARG (accessed 21 December 2020).

[35] Ciara Nugent, 'Why Argentina's Talks with the IMF Are Enraging the Country', *Time* (11 May 2018), available at http://time.com/5272911/argentina-macri-imf-international-monetary-fund-economy/ (accessed 21 December 2020). See also IMF, 'Lessons from the Crisis in Argentina', Policy and Review Department (8 October 2003), available at www.imf.org/external/np/pdr/lessons/100803.pdf (accessed 21 December 2020).

[36] Michael Mussa, 'Argentina and the Fund: Anatomy of a Policy Failure', in Vines and Gilbert, *The IMF and its Critics*, pp. 316–62; and for more recent developments, Arturo C. Porzecanski, 'Sovereign Debt Restructuring after

15.3.2 Reforming the IMF?

From the above series of crises, it is clear, for a few decades, that the IMF is in great need of reform. In 2010, the IMF agreed a wide-ranging series of governance reform, to reflect, in particular, the importance of emerging market economies and to better support smaller and developing members. It consulted broadly, with leading economists and civil society organisations, and indeed reformed its governance to increase its legitimacy and efficacy. It has revised its quota policy and so given a greater say to emerging economies (China, in particular) and tried to better support the developing world; engaged in broader policy issues, from climate change to gender issues, and the Sustainable Development Goals (SDGs); paid more attention to the country's specificities in adjusting its lending policy and conditionalities, and so revamped its image in the direction of a more development-friendly organisation. Yet is it enough? And could something more be done? The very structure of the Fund as a quota-based organisation at the centre of which is the hyper-powerful US$, the global reserve currency, does not leave much margin for greater reform that would genuinely transform the organisation into an equality-based institution. In addition, the political economic orientation of the Fund in favour of trade liberalisation and market opening is also constraining, for it cannot fully take into consideration alternative paths for development and a human economy. It is interesting, yet also worrying, to see the Fund adopting the vocabulary and themes of UN agencies, from gender issues to SDGs. What, then, will be the specificity of the IMF? What, then, will differentiate the Fund from the World Bank? Is it part of its mandate to address gender equality? In short, is the system outdated and is it time to turn to another form of governance? As stressed in a recent report from the Council on Foreign Relations, however:

It would be utterly imprudent to shut down the IMF. It would be equally imprudent, however, to deny the need for reforming the Fund. The Fund must be empowered to deal more effectively with the functioning of the whole monetary system in a manner consonant with its stated purpose – promoting international monetary cooperation and providing a venue for consultation and cooperation among its major members. That process has now begun, although the outcome is uncertain.[37]

The IMF remains a key instrument in the management of global financial regulation and crisis prevention and resolution. But its existence and good functioning also depend on the true adherence of the most powerful countries, and the US in particular, to multilateralism.

Argentina', *Development* (2016), 59, pp. 100–6; Ilias Bantekas and Cephas Lumina (eds.), *Sovereign Debt and Human Rights* (Oxford University Press, 2018). In reaction to the 2020 Argentine debt crisis, a group of 138 economists from twenty countries, including Nobel laureates Joseph Stiglitz and Edmund Phelps, proposed alternative solutions: Joseph E. Stiglitz, Edmund S. Phelps and Carmen M. Reinhart, 'Restructuring Argentina's Private Debt Is Essential', *Project Syndicate* (6 May 2020), available at www.project-syndicate.org/commentary/argentina-sovereign-debt-restructuring-private-creditors-by-joseph-e-stiglitz-et-al-2020-05 (accessed 21 December 2020).

[37] Peter B. Kenen, *Reform of the International Monetary Fund*, CSR 29 (New York: Council on Foreign Relations, 2007), available at www.cfr.org/report/reform-international-monetary-fund (accessed 21 December 2020).

15.4 The European Monetary System

The IMF is not the sole regulator of international monetary activity. In order to balance US$ supremacy, Europe has attempted to create another monetary system, with its control mechanism, its ambitions and a number of as yet unresolved issues challenging its efficiency, if not its existence.

The eurozone is a geographic and economic region that consists of some of the European Union countries that have fully incorporated the euro as their national currency – today, there are nineteen countries: Austria, Belgium, Cyprus, Estonia, Finland, France, Germany, Greece, Ireland, Italy, Latvia, Lithuania, Luxembourg, Malta, the Netherlands, Portugal, Slovakia, Slovenia and Spain. The euro was first introduced in 1999 – as 'book' money. Around 340 million citizens live in the largest economic region of the world.

The history of the eurozone began in 1992, with the signing by the European Community of the Maastricht Treaty creating the European Union. The Maastricht Treaty promoted greater cooperation and the creation of truly common monetary and economic union, regulated by a banking system (the European Central Bank) and a common currency, the euro. Criteria were also defined for the euro to be used by the countries entering the system: limited public deficit and debt – two very controversial criteria; exchange rate stability; low inflation rates; and harmonisation of interest rates.

For some analysts, these stringent criteria did not suit all EU members and some were actually pushed into a period of massive budget cuts and, eventually, a crisis. The European debt crisis (or eurozone crisis) had begun by the end of 2009 and drastically affected a number of EU members: Greece, Portugal, Ireland, Spain and Cyprus in particular. They were unable to repay their debt and, as in the case of Greece, a combination of solutions had to be found involving the intervention of the European Central Bank, together with the IMF.

The eurozone system today seems to be in search of more credibility and long-term coherence. While the monetary policy is governed by the European Central Bank, together with each eurozone member's central bank, the economic policy, as well as the fiscal policies, remain national. The Covid-19 crisis has shown, once more, that a European consensus on financial policies was difficult to reach, if not impossible. The discussion on 'corona-bond' and how to put in place a solidarity package for the countries suffering from the crisis has highlighted European divisions.[38]

Box 15.5 Blockchain: a revolution for international finance and trade?

Cryptocurrencies, with Bitcoin, the digitalised decentralised currency at their head, have made the headlines since 2009. The American social media service Facebook has even proposed a controversial new digital currency, the 'Libra', with a launch planned for 2021.

---

[38] See www.ecb.europa.eu/home/search/coronavirus/html/index.en.html (accessed 21 December 2020).

Box 15.5 (cont.)

Blockchain is a decentralised, distributed record or ledger. It enables the storage of transactions in a nearly permanent and inalterable way using cryptographic techniques. It is not controlled by a single party, but by a network of peers. It is said to be more resilient to cyber-attacks than traditional databases. It can be public, private or managed by multiple partners, with or without permission to access.

The WTO itself has acknowledged its potential for trade, yet with a note of caution. Technology is not a solution to everything. Just as for 'smart contracts' or artificial intelligence, a legal framework needs to be put in place. While almost all WTO-related areas of trade could be positively impacted by blockchain and the efficiency it could bring – for instance, with the digitalisation of paperwork – a number of issues remain: scalability, security, interoperability (or the ability to communicate at the same technical and semantic level between different systems) and, naturally, the question of the legal status and framework for all these transactions. In 2017, UNCITRAL adopted a Model Law on Electronic Transferable Records. In 2020, the World Economic Forum Global Blockchain Council released the 'Presidio Principles', an aspirational document setting out foundational values for a decentralised future – in a word, a sort of code of conduct for blockchain. It is time to create an appropriate legal framework, with the GATS not entirely suited to address these new complex issues, as stressed in a recent WTO case. With Bitcoin reaching new heights, a number of countries are considering its ban, while others are investing in it.

On 28 December 2018, Venezuela requested consultations with the US concerning measures it imposed on goods and services, including the Venezuelan digital currency, the 'Petro'. According to Venezuela, these measures appeared to be inconsistent with the GATS, notably Articles II:1 (MFN) and XVII:1 (National Treatment). The main issue in demonstrating a violation is to rely on the GATS Schedule of Commitments, which does not yet include cryptocurrencies or anything really close to this new category. On 14 March 2019, the establishment of a WTO dispute settlement panel was requested.

Interesting developments should follow on both the dispute settlement and the regulatory fronts. In this regard, an integrated trade approach, blending trade and investment with international monetary law and finance, with the support of all related international organisations, seems very much needed.

To Go Further

Ganne, E., *Can Blockchain Revolutionize International Trade* (Geneva: World Trade Organization, 2018), available at www.wto.org/english/res_e/publications_e/blockchainrev18_e.htm (accessed 21 December 2020).

Patel, D. and Ganne, E., 'Blockchain and DLT in Trade: A Reality Check' (London: Trade Finance Global/World Trade Organization, 2019), available at www.wto.org/english/res_e/booksp_e/blockchainrev19_e.pdf (accessed 21 December 2020).

Box 15.5 (cont.)

Porges, A. and Enders, A., 'Data Moving Across Borders: The Future of Digital Trade Policy', E15 Expert Group on the Digital Economy, Think Piece (Geneva: International Centre for Trade and Sustainable Development and World Economic Forum, 2016), available at http://e15initiative.org/publications/data-moving-across-borders-the-future-of-digital-trade-policy/ (accessed 21 December 2020).

Razon, A. K., 'Liberalising Blockchain: An Application of the GATS Digital Trade Framework', *Melbourne Journal of International Law* (2019), 20(1), available at http://classic.austlii.edu.au/au/journals/MelbJIL/2019/6.html (accessed 21 December 2020).

UNCITRAL, Model Law on Electronic Transferable Records (adopted 2017), available at https://uncitral.un.org/en/texts/ecommerce/modellaw/electronic_transferable_records (accessed 21 December 2020).

World Economic Forum, Global Blockchain Council, 'Presidio Principles: Foundational Values for a Decentralized Future', available at www.weforum.org/communities/presidio-principles (accessed 21 December 2020).

WTO Dispute Settlement, DS574: *United States – Measures Relating to Trade in Goods and Services*, available at www.wto.org/english/tratop_e/dispu_e/cases_e/ds574_e.htm (accessed 21 December 2020).

15.5 When Public and Private International Law Meet: Private Activity Regulation

The regulation of private banking activity is not really in the realm of an essentially public international law-based textbook. However, as public and private law meet when a defragmented approach is adopted, this section aims at briefly introducing an interesting system of governance, the Basel Committee, which is at the crossroads between different legal and non-legal disciplines. Initially named the Committee on Banking Regulations and Supervisory Practices, it was established by the central bank governors of the Group of Ten countries at the end of 1974. The Committee, within the Bank for International Settlements in Basel, and was created to enhance financial stability. Its objective was to improve the quality of banking supervision globally, as well as regulatory cooperation. It met for the first time in 1975. It comprises now forty-five institutions from twenty-eight jurisdictions. It has established, on the basis of the Basel Accords I, II and III, a number of international standards for banking regulation. While the two first Basel Accords set the basis for international cooperation and regulation, Basel III responded to the 2007–09 financial crisis in issuing certain standards for liquidity risk measurement, monitoring and resilience. The standards were finalised in 2017.[39]

---

[39] Basel Committee on Banking Supervision, *Basel III: Finalising Post-Crisis Reforms* (Bank for International Settlements, December 2017), available at www.bis.org/bcbs/publ/d424.htm (accessed 21 December 2020); also Juan Ramirez, *Handbook of Basel III Capital: Enhancing Bank Capital in Practice* (Chichester: John Wiley, 2017).

Box 15.6 Bank for International Settlement

Created in The Hague on 20 January 1930, the Bank for International Settlement is the oldest financial institution. Its original members were Belgium, France, Germany, Italy, Japan, the UK and the Swiss Confederation. It comprises sixty central banks and monetary authorities today.

It was originally designed to administer Germany's First World War reparations payments. It was at the centre of controversies in the interwar period, for it is said to have directly cooperated with the Nazi regime and turned a blind eye on the gold it stole from the countries it occupied.

Today, its main activities include monetary and financial cooperation, known as the Basel process, and the fact of being a bank for central banks.

To Go Further

Bank for International Settlements, at www.bis.org (accessed 21 December 2020).
    'History: The BIS during the Second World War (1939–48)', available at www.bis.org/about/ history_2ww2.htm (accessed 21 December 2020).
Jones, C., 'BoE Helped Sell Looted Nazi Gold', *Financial Times* (30 July 2013), available at www.ft.com/content/43fa3cdc-f934-11e2-86e1-00144feabdc0 (accessed 21 December 2020).
Ziegler, J., *The Swiss, the Gold, and the Dead: How Swiss Bankers Helped Finance the Nazi War Machine* (New York: Penguin, 1999).

15.6 Conclusion

In a recent report, Professor Philip Alston, UN Special Rapporteur on extreme poverty and human rights, concluded that the IMF is the 'single most influential international actor, not only in relation to fiscal policy but also to social protection', yet he argues in favour of a profound reform of the system, which could help to tackle ever-increasing world inequalities. Growth is no longer sufficient to satisfy human development. As pointed out by US Treasury Secretary, Henry Morgenthau, in his inaugural speech to the Bretton Woods conference, 'Prosperity, like peace, is indivisible. We cannot afford to have it scattered here or there among the fortunate or enjoy it at the expense of others.'[40] And he argued further:

Poverty wherever it exists, is menacing to us all and undermines the well-being of each of us. It can no more be localized than war but spreads and saps the economic strength of all the more-favoured areas

---

[40] Department of State, 'Address by the Honorable Henry Morgenthau, Jr., at the Inaugural Plenary Session (July 1, 1944)', *United Nations Monetary and Financial Conference: Bretton Woods, Final act and related documents, New Hampshire, July 1 to July 22, 1944* (Washington, DC: Government Printing Office, 1944), 121, pp. 3–6, available at www.cvce.eu/content/publication/2003/12/12/34c4153e-6266-4e84-88d7-f655abf1395f/publishable_en.pdf (accessed 21 December 2020).

of the earth. We know now that the thread of economic life in every nation is inseparably woven into a fabric of world economy. Let any thread become frayed and the entire fabric is weakened. No nation, however great and strong, can remain immune.

Yet today, through fragmented disciplines and monolithic approaches to international law and economics, international organisations, and the IMF in particular, are not quite able to perform their initial role.

15.7 Summary

- International monetary law and finance involve trade and investment, as well as public and private actors.
- The Bretton Woods system created the two institutional pillars for finance and development: the IMF and the International Bank for Reconstruction and Development (now part of the World Bank).
- It also designed a financial system based on a (neo-)Gold Standard.
- The IMF was integrated into the (neo-)Gold Standard mechanism. It was the only authority to enable its members to change the par value of their currencies in case of 'fundamental disequilibrium'.
- This system ended in 1971, with the American decision to terminate the convertibility of the US$ to gold and was replaced by floating exchange rates.
- The IMF's structure consists of the Board of Governors, the Executive Board and a Managing Director.
- The IMF is a quota-based institution. These quotas determine IMF members' voting power, financial access and share in drawing rights allocations.
- The IMF's functions are surveillance, lending and capacity development.
- The IMF has played a significant role in major financial crisis management in Latin America, Asia and Europe.
- The Washington Consensus and the IMF system of 'conditionalities' have frequently been denounced as causing crises rather than bringing solutions to them.
- The eurozone provides another example of regulation.
- Private activity is also regulated on the basis of a mix between international public and private law.

15.8 Review Questions

1 What was the main objective of the Bretton Woods Conference?
2 What were Keynes' initial ideas about the restructuring of the post-Second World War financial system?
3 What is the Gold Standard? How long has it been in place? What replaced it?
4 What is the (neo-)Gold Standard?
5 When did the Bretton Woods system collapse, and for what reasons?

6 What are the main missions of the IMF?

7 How is it structured?

8 What forms does surveillance take?

9 What are quotas?

10 What are Special Drawing Rights?

11 What are the IMD conditionalities? Please give examples of recent conditionalities imposed by the IMF.

12 Is the IMF also invested in development and aid?

13 How has the IMF had an impact on regional crises?

14 Why has the IMF been scrutinised for its interventions in these crises?

15 What is the eurozone?

16 How is the eurozone governed?

17 Is the euro responsible for the euro debt crisis?

18 What are the Basel Accords for private banking?

19 How do the Basel Accords relate to the IMF mission?

20 What are blockchains and how can we approach them from an integrated trade perspective?

15.9 Exercises

(For background on the issue, please refer to previous Exercises in Chapters 13 and 14.)

Exercise 1

Hopeland investment policies have not resulted in the expected economic growth as they have not attracted enough FDI and fiscal revenues. In addition, Hopeland's generous social policies have forced the State to borrow on international markets. Private lenders have been rather keen to lend to Hopeland, in view of its expected large revenues from natural resources exploration and exploitation by domestic and foreign investors. However, with the recent droughts, which have affected the countries for the past two years, commodities earnings have drastically decreased, while the country has been unable to diversify its sources of revenue from wheat and soya beans culture in particular. Hopeland has not been able to meet its objectives. It has entered into a recession period for the past six months. It is now unable to pay the interest on its loans and is about to declare default.

Hopeland's government has always been reluctant to turn to international institutions for help, and the IMF in particular. It has very bitter memories of the 2001 intervention by the IMF, which was followed by a drastic austerity package, which Hopeland feels pushed even greater sections of the population into poverty. Hopeland's president has been elected on the promise of economic sovereignty and social justice. However, there is no other choice now than to turn to the IMF, albeit reluctantly.

LJCN, the reputed international law firm, which has advised Hopeland in the past, has been approached to liaise between the Ministries of Trade and Finance and the IMF. As a partner of the firm, in charge of the trade and development team, you are responsible for coordinating with the Fund to find the best possible rescue package for Hopeland. A US$10 billion loan agreement is negotiated to address macroeconomic vulnerabilities and promote inclusive growth and job creation. The significant drop in exchange reserves, as well as the large fiscal deficit and extremely high public debt, also have to be addressed. You need to come up with a plan that will quickly rescue Hopeland, without imposing too strict conditionalities.

Exercise 2

Two years after your first intervention, which indeed facilitated discussions between the IMF and Hopeland, the country is not in default anymore, but the economic situation is not good. More people seem to be living below the poverty line. Unemployment is very high among the country's young people, who represent 60 per cent of the population. Elections are coming and the party in power cannot afford to lose. There seems to be a number of systemic causes of these economic failures: outdated regulation of the banking system, unadjusted fiscal policies, poor efficiency of social spending, absence of transparency and corruption.

You are approached to work with the IMF on a second plan, which will involve longer-term capacity development. The recent crises in Russia, Egypt and Argentina are critically informing your work.

FURTHER READING

Alston, P. and Reisch, N. (eds.), *Tax, Inequality and Human Rights* (Oxford University Press, 2019).

Bantekas, I. and Lumina, C. (eds.), *Sovereign Debt and Human Rights* (Oxford University Press, 2018).

Carreau, D. and Juillard, P., *Droit international économique* (Paris: Dalloz, 2017).

Chaisse, J., *Legal Problems of Economic Globalisation: A Commentary on the Law and Practice* (Hong Kong: Wolters Kluwer, 2015).

Lastra, R. M., *International Financial and Monetary Law* (Oxford University Press, 2015).

Lim, C. and Mercurio, B. (eds.), *International Economic Law After the Global Crisis: A Tale of Fragmented Disciplines* (Cambridge University Press, 2015).

Lowenfeld, A. F., *International Economic Law* (Oxford University Press, 2008).

Roos, J. E., *Why Not Default? The Political Economy of Sovereign Debt* (Princeton University Press, 2019).

Sorel, J. M., 'Quelle normativité pour le droit des relations monétaires et financières internationales', *Collected Courses of the Hague Academy of International Law* (2019), 404, pp. 235–403.

Steil, B., *The Battle of Bretton Woods: John Maynard Keynes, Harry Dexter White, and the Making of a New World Order* (Princeton University Press, 2014).

Stiglitz, J. E., *Globalization and its Discontents* (London: Penguin, 2002).

Globalization and its Discontents Revisited: Anti-Globalization in the Era of Trump (London: Penguin, 2017).

Vines, D. and Gilbert, C. L. (eds.), *The IMF and its Critics: Reform of the Financial Architecture* (Cambridge University Press, 2004).

16 International Development and Aid

Table of Contents

Highlights

- While people and countries might be less poor today, inequalities are greater than twenty-five years ago.
- The issue of development is still very much relevant.
- But what is development? How is it defined and measured? Is there a universally accepted criterion?
- What challenges, but also what benefits, can the conceptual category of development bring in terms of special treatment and aid?
- Interdisciplinary in nature, international development and aid fit naturally in an ambitious international economic law approach.
- However, the concept of development remains one of the most controversial ideas in international economic and legal scholarship.
- Indeed, it assumes a departure from a pre-existing reality and a judgment on the same (undeveloped or underdeveloped), as well as the promise of progress towards something of a better nature.

- Development might not benefit all and could be imposed on countries by a few, hence reproducing forms of domination as in colonial times.
- The same critiques are formulated on the issue of foreign aid.
- From another perspective, one can approach development as a right.
- International development law is a field of international law that incorporates a variety of themes from the rule of law, to trade, finance and human rights.
- Critical approaches have questioned development models, as well as the role of law in development.
- There is a large variety of development and aid institutions and donors.
- Multilateral development banks are at the centre of the development edifice, with the World Bank Group playing a key role.
- The World Bank has been widely criticised for its involvement in controversial deals and support given to non-democratic regimes – not to mention its possible failure to really participate to development.
- Other development banks, either regional or specialised, are important actors too.
- The World Trade Organization offers a Special and Differential Treatment for developing countries, as well as special provisions for Least Developed Countries.
- A large number of multilateral organisations are also invested with a specific mandate to address development issues. Many of them belong to the United Nations family.
- Bilateral aid based on official development assistance represents the largest part of development funding.
- Of much less financial significance, yet interesting for their support to certain sectors or countries, are private charitable foundations.
- The global pandemic crisis has increased these inequalities to the extremes.

16.1   Introduction

Today, extreme poverty and extreme wealth coexist. According to Oxfam, twenty-six individuals possess the same wealth as 3.8 billion people representing 50 per cent of humanity.[1] While several developing countries are leading destinations for medical tourism, access to health remains a luxury for the vast majority of their nationals.[2] In Kenya, the growth of super-rich people is one of the fastest in the world, yet less than 0.1 per cent of the population (8,300 people) own more wealth than the bottom 99.9 per cent (more than

---

[1] Oxfam, 'Five Shocking Facts about Extreme Global Inequalities and How to Even it Up', available at www.oxfam .org/en/even-it/5-shocking-facts-about-extreme-global-inequality-and-how-even-it-davos; Oxfam, 'World's Billionaires Have More Wealth than 4.6 Billion People' (20 January 2020), available at www.oxfam.org/en/press-releases/worlds-billionaires-have-more-wealth-46-billion-people (both accessed 21 December 2020).

[2] Oxfam, 'India: Extreme Inequality in Numbers', available at www.oxfam.org/en/even-it/india-extreme-inequality-numbers (accessed 21 December 2020).

44 million people).[3] Despite being among the fastest-growing and largest economies in the world, which have lifted millions out of poverty in the past few decades of economic high growth, emerging economies like China, Brazil, South Africa and India also produce massive inequalities, to the detriment of vast sections of their populations.[4] The international institutions in charge of development and aid are coming to the same conclusions as civil society organisations and activists. The World Bank itself acknowledges that:

> without a significant reduction in inequality, especially in countries with high poverty and inequality, the world will not meet its goal to end extreme poverty by 2030. Inequality between all people in the world has declined since 1990, but within-country inequality is still higher today than 25 years ago, which means that an average person today is more likely to live in an economy with higher inequality compared to 25 years ago.[5]

Ten of the richest people in the world have literally exploded their wealth by more than £296 billion since the coronavirus pandemic began. The extra wealth accumulated by these ten men is more than the £284 billion the British government is estimated to have spent on tackling the pandemic and its impact on the UK's 66 million people (at time of writing). Yet, at the same time, global hunger is rising, as demonstrated by the UN World Food Programme, the recipient of the 2020 Nobel Peace Prize.[6]

The 2019 United Nations Development Programme (UNDP) *Human Development Report* focuses on inequalities, interrogating the ability of the world to meet the 2030 Agenda for Sustainable Development Goals, a set of seventeen interconnected targets, designed to 'end poverty, protect the planet and ensure that all people enjoy peace and prosperity'.[7]

Inequality and poverty are different, yet very much interrelated concepts and realities. It might well be that today's poverty level is lower than it was before, but does that mean that people live better? According to the World Bank, between 1993 and 2015, the percentage of people around the world who lived in extreme poverty fell from 33.5 per cent to 10 per cent, the lowest poverty rate in recorded history.[8] While for the World Bank, being extremely poor is living with less than US$1.90 a day, other research

---

[3] Oxfam, 'Kenya: Extreme Inequality in Numbers', available at www.oxfam.org/en/even-it/kenya-extreme-inequality-numbers (accessed 21 December 2020).

[4] See, for example, World Bank, Poverty & Equity Data Portal, available at http://povertydata.worldbank.org/poverty/home/ (accessed 21 December 2020).

[5] World Bank, 'Inequality and Shared Prosperity', available at www.worldbank.org/en/topic/isp/overview (accessed 21 December 2020).

[6] Forbes, The World's Real-Time Billionaires, data available at www.forbes.com/real-time-billionaires/#66fa10533d78; Rupert Neate, 'Ten Billionaires Reap $400bn Boost to Wealth during Pandemic', *The Observer*, available at www.theguardian.com/technology/2020/dec/19/ten-billionaires-reap-400bn-boost-to-wealth-during-pandemic; UN World Food Programme, available at www.wfp.org (all accessed 21 December 2020).

[7] UNDP, Sustainable Development Goals, available at www.undp.org/content/undp/en/home/sustainable-development-goals.html (accessed 21 December 2020).

[8] World Bank, 'Decline of Global Extreme Poverty Continues But Has Slowed', available at www.worldbank.org/en/news/press-release/2018/09/19/decline-of-global-extreme-poverty-continues-but-has-slowed-world-bank (accessed 21 December 2020).

organisations define poverty in less absolute terms.[9] For example, the Oxford Poverty and Human Development Initiative (OPHI) has developed an Index with the UNDP, which approaches poverty in a more multidimensional manner, taking into consideration not only the relative wealth of individuals, but also their ability to have access to food, education or health care.[10] Poverty does not mean the same in different national contexts, where the State may be more or less willing, or able, to support its population. It might be, as the World Bank demonstrates, that global poverty has declined in absolute terms in the past few years, but that inequalities are such that they limit States' progress towards inclusive and sustainable development.

So what is development? How is it defined and measured? How neutral is it? What is a developing country and what are the qualifications for this category? What challenges and benefits can this bring in terms of special treatment and aid?

This is another key area of international economic law, which often remains unfamiliar to academics and students alike. Interdisciplinary in nature, international development and aid is often taught in development economics, and for law students, in the context of a general course on international human rights, but rarely in a specialised international development law course. But development and aid fit naturally into an ambitious IEL textbook, for their main foundations and features have to do with the regulation of international economic relations and the global institutions designed for the same. Firmly grounded in general international law, our perspective encompasses a large variety of interrelated topics, which cannot be studied in the isolation of specialism.

We will therefore critically address development and aid as concepts, as well as development law as a field of law, to later delve into the study of the international institutions created to tackle these issues.

16.2 Development and Aid in Perspective

The concept of development remains one of the most controversial ideas in international economic and legal scholarship. Marked by the stigma of colonisation, development, like the idea of modernity, assumes a departure from a pre-existing reality (undeveloped or underdeveloped) and the promise of progress towards something better. Development rests on a judgement. On what ground is this judgement formulated? What are the values behind the concept of development? What is to be achieved by the process of development? Is development chosen or imposed? Does it benefit all or can be it bought up by a few? All these questions have informed heated debates, which have shaped not only intellectual

---

[9] World Bank, Understanding Poverty data, available at www.worldbank.org/en/understanding-poverty (accessed 21 December 2020).

[10] UNDP/OPHI, *How to Build a National Multidimensional Poverty Index (MPI): Using the MPI to Inform the SDGs* (New York: United Nations Development Programme, 2019), available at https://ophi.org.uk/wpcontent/uploads/How_to_Build_Handbook_2019_PDF.pdf (accessed 21 December).

discussions, but also the reality of development and aid policies, their practical implementations, their many failures as well as their successes. The sections below hence critically address development as a multifaceted idea and its translation into international law. They then approach the concept of foreign aid, to define its main traits and discuss some of the challenges it entails.

16.2.1 What Is Development?

Either purely based on economic growth indicators or on a more complex set of criteria, including access to public goods, literacy or even happiness, development is multifaceted and remains highly debated, if not controversial.

16.2.1.1 Fuelling Growth or Ending Poverty?

Development can equal economic growth. It is historically and intuitively associated with the idea of wealth. The richer the country, the more developed it could be. To gauge the wealth of nations, two systems are generally used, gross domestic product (GDP) or the gross national income (GNI), previously known as gross national product (GNP). Precision can then be added by adopting a per capita approach (divided by population). As an example, the World Bank regularly provides the GNI per capita in current US$.[11] In 2018, that of Afghanistan was of $550, compared to $3,920 for Algeria, $9,460 for China and $60,140 for Denmark.[12]

The two techniques are based on a few different criteria. GNI measures the country's income and includes all the wealth made by the country's residents and businesses, domestically and abroad. It also includes any product taxes not already counted, minus subsidies. GDP, on the other hand, measures the income of anyone domestically, in a given country (nationals and foreigners).

The OECD definitions of GDP and GNI provide an interesting critical approach in the form of a reflection on the inability of these indicators to take into consideration the well-being of populations. According to the OECD:

Gross domestic product (GDP) is the standard measure of the value added created through the production of goods and services in a country during a certain period. As such, it also measures the income earned from that production, or the total amount spent on final goods and services (less imports). While GDP is the single most important indicator to capture economic activity, it falls short of providing a suitable measure of people's material well-being for which alternative indicators may be more appropriate.[13]

---

[11] World Bank, 'GNI per Capita', available at https://data.worldbank.org/indicator/NY.GNP.PCAP.CD (accessed 21 December 2020).

[12] World Bank, 'GNI per Capita'.

[13] OECD, 'Gross Domestic Product', available at https://data.oecd.org/gdp/gross-domestic-product-gdp.htm (accessed 21 December 2020).

Gross national income (GNI) is defined as gross domestic product, plus net receipts from abroad of compensation of employees, property income and net taxes less subsidies on production. Compensation of employees receivable from abroad are those that are earned by residents who essentially live inside the economic territory but work abroad (this happens in border areas on a regular basis), or for people who live and work abroad for short periods (seasonal workers) and whose centre of economic interest remains in their home country. Property income receivable from/payable to abroad includes interest, dividends, and all (or part of) retained earnings of foreign enterprises owned fully (or in part) by resident enterprises (and vice versa).[14]

As alluded to above, GDP and GNI are standard indicators to measure development, but do not always prove useful to understanding its complexity, as explained in the following sections.

Box 16.1 What is the Third World?

Of less relevance today, the term Third World is still in use and has certainly been at the centre of development studies for decades. It was coined by the French demographer, anthropologist and historian, Alfred Sauvy, in an article published in the Magazine *L'Observateur*, on 14 August 1952. The 'Tiers Monde' referred, in an allusive manner, to the 'Tiers état' (Third Estate) – that is, all those who, at the time of the French Revolution, were not members of the two first estates, the nobility and the clergy. In the context of the cold war, it meant to describe those non-aligned with the Communist bloc or capitalist powers. It denounced, as in the French Revolution, the exploitation and despisal of the weakest.

The term has been used widely since that time, but has now been replaced by 'developing countries', 'least developed countries', 'emerging economies' or the 'Global South', depending on the context and issues at stake.

As we have started to see above, and as strange as it may seem, international organisations are not particularly clear on their definitions and measurement techniques of development. But the World Bank has made a clear effort at transparency.[15] It provides GNI data for all countries, removing the effect of exchange rates and presenting all results in US$, using the concept of 'purchasing power parity'. Purchasing power parity, however, is a limited instrument of measure, as it is based on products and services available in the US and is therefore sometimes of little or no use in the developing world. The approach per capita (divided by population) provides a closer look at the reality of a given country. China might now be rich, but it is also populated by 1.4 billion individuals. China's wealth then becomes quite relative when compared to that of the US, a country with 300 million

---

[14] OECD, 'Gross National Income', available at https://data.oecd.org/natincome/gross-national-income.htm (accessed 21 December 2020).

[15] World Bank, Data, Methodologies, available at https://datahelpdesk.worldbank.org/knowledgebase/articles/906531-methodologies (accessed 21 December 2020).

inhabitants. As a matter of fact, according to the World Bank, in 2018, China's GNI per capita was $9,460, compared to $63,080 for the US.[16]

As demonstrated by our introductory examples on India and Kenya, having great wealth in a country does not mean that poverty has been eradicated. Another way to approach development is to gauge the level of poverty and aim at its eradication. This is the objective of a series of international organisations with poverty at the centre of their agenda – the UNDP in particular. Here again, what is the meaning of poverty? The World Bank estimates than only 10 per cent of the world population lives on less than US$1.90 a day, down from nearly 36 per cent in 1990.[17] Does it mean that only 10 per cent of the population is poor or extremely poor? Of course not. Things are difficult to compare on the basis of a narrow figure. One cannot afford the same in all countries with US$1.90 a day. What about access to education, health care, sanitation, water or even energy? What about access to nutritious food, a decent living environment or remunerative labour? What about social, racial, ethnic or caste-based exclusion? What about rising poverty in the developed world? What to think of the American 'working poors', while the official poverty rate in the US in 2017 was 12.3 per cent?[18] Can one work full-time and still be poor?

Poverty entails much more than a lack of income. According to the UN, up to 42 per cent of the population in sub-Saharan Africa continues to live below the poverty line.[19] The UN came up with an ambitious agenda for development based on the SDGs and multidimensional measurements of poverty, as developed by the UNDP. The UNDP was established, in 1965, by the consolidation of the UN Expanded Programme of Technical Assistance and the UN Special Fund. Its aim is to support 'national processes to accelerate the progress of sustainable human development'.[20]

Poverty Facts and Figures
- 783 million people live below the international poverty line of US$1.90 a day.
- In 2016, almost 10 per cent of the world's workers and their families lived on less than US$1.90 per person per day.
- Most people living below the poverty line belong to two regions: Southern Asia and sub-Saharan Africa.
- High poverty rates are often found in small, fragile and conflict-affected countries.

[16] World Bank, 'GNI per Capita'.

[17] World Bank, Poverty, available at www.worldbank.org/en/topic/poverty (accessed 21 December 2020).

[18] The US Census Bureau released its annual report on poverty, stating that there are some 31–32 million poor Americans – a number greater than in 1965 – which, of course, needs to be put into perspective with population increase and a rise in general living standards; Income and Poverty in the United States: 2017, available at www .census.gov/data/tables/2018/demo/income-poverty/p60-263.html (accessed 21 December 2020).

[19] UN, Ending Poverty, available at www.un.org/en/sections/issues-depth/poverty/ (accessed 21 December 2020).

[20] See, for example, UNDP, 'Launch of the 2019 Human Development Report', with a clear focus on inequalities, taking stock of the work of Thomas Piketty and his team of the Paris School of Economics, available at www.undp .org/content/undp/en/home/news-centre/speeches/2019/launch-of-2019-human-development-report.html (accessed 21 December 2020).

- As of 2016, only 45 per cent of the world's population was effectively covered by at least one social protection cash benefit.[21]
- The Covid-19 pandemic has stressed these inequalities in terms of access to health, but also access to education and work, including in developed economies.

Box 16.2 Who qualifies as a developing country?

How does one qualify as a developing country? Is China still a developing country? What is a least developed country (LDC)?

As strange as it might seem, there are no harmonised criteria to define who is and who is not a developing country. Often, this status is a self-declaratory one.

The United Nations, in its *World Economic Situation and Prospects*, classifies countries into three broad categories: developed economies, economies in transition and developing economies. The categorisation intends to reflect basic economic conditions and is based on a country's level of development as measured by per capita GNI. Accordingly, countries have been grouped as high-income, upper-middle-income, lower-middle-income and low-income, as in the World Bank categorisation. The threshold levels of GNI per capita are indeed those established by the World Bank. Subgroups are also made by geography, as well as according to who is a 'fuel importer' or 'fuel exporter'. For the UN, an economy is classified as a fuel exporter if 'the share of fuel exports in its total merchandise exports is greater than 20 per cent and the level of fuel exports is at least 20 per cent higher than that of the country's fuel imports'. This criterion is drawn from the share of fuel exports in the total value of world merchandise trade. Fuels include coal, oil and natural gas. This measurement is slightly complex and does not necessarily clarify the categorisation.

The UN list of the least developed countries (LDCs) is decided upon by the United Nations Economic and Social Council and the General Assembly. It is drafted on the basis of recommendations made by the Committee for Development Policy. Here again, the main criterion is GNI. The UN *World Economic Situation and Prospects* also makes reference to the group of thirty-nine heavily indebted poor countries (HIPCs), which are considered by the World Bank and the IMF as part of their debt-relief initiative.

The World Bank has used an income classification system of high, upper-middle, lower-middle and low since 2016, based on GNI per capita in current US$. The classification is updated each year on 1 July. Two factors come into play: the GNI per capita, which can change with economic growth, inflation, exchange rates and population or the revisions to national accounts methods and data; and a classification threshold adjusted for inflation. Since the fiscal year 2019, the high-income threshold is

---

[21] UN, Poverty.

Box 16.2 (cont.)

also a factor for lending. Surcharges are applied for lending rates that have been categorised as high-income for two consecutive years. The IMF, in its *World Economic Outlook*, relies on GDP per capita and distinguishes two broad categories: *emerging market and developing economies*, and *advanced economies*. Naturally, the very notion of 'emerging' is debatable.

At the WTO, there are no definitions of 'developed' and 'developing' countries. Members of the organisation self-declare their status, which can then be challenged by other members. As we will see below, at the WTO, the status of developing country brings certain rights from longer transition periods to the benefit of the Generalised System of Preferences offered by developed countries. All these rights and benefits are not automatic and can be contested. The US has long contested China's status as a developing country, for example.

To Go Further

IMF, 'GDP per Capita, Current Prices', available at www.imf.org/external/datamapper/ NGDPDPC@WEO/OEMDC/ADVEC/WEOWORLD (accessed 21 December 2020).

UN, *World Economic Situation and Prospects* (New York: United Nations, 2019), available at www.un.org/development/desa/dpad/wp-content/uploads/sites/45/WESP2019_BOOK-web .pdf (accessed 21 December 2020).

World Bank, 'New Country Classifications by Income Level: 2019–2020, Data Blog (1 July 2019), available at https://blogs.worldbank.org/opendata/new-country-classifications-income-level-2019-2020 (accessed 21 December 2020).

WTO, Who Are the Developing Countries in the WTO?, available at www.wto.org/english/ tratop_e/devel_e/d1who_e.htm (accessed 21 December 2020).

16.2.1.2 Humane and Sustainable Development

The creation of the UNDP Human Development Index (HDI) was greatly influenced by the universally celebrated work of the Nobel Prize in Economic Sciences winner, Professor Amartya Sen, and his 2000 book, *Development as Freedom*.[22] It departs from economic growth and pure economic criteria based on GNI and puts the human being at its centre. Two countries with the same GNI per capita can end up with completely different HDIs. These differences notably relate to the role of the State and how it invests in education and

---

[22] Amartya Sen, *Development as Freedom* (New York: Anchor Books, 2000); Amartya Sen, *The Idea of Justice* (London: Penguin, 2010); Abhjit V. Banerjee and Esther Duflo, *Poor Economics: A Radical Rethinking of the Way to Fight Global Poverty* (New York: Public Affairs, 2012).

health, as well as in access to basic public goods. The HDI does not, however, reflect inequalities, which, as we have seen, are greater today than ever before.[23] The UNDP is now embarking on the production of a new generation of the *Human Development Report*, which aims to take inequalities more into account.

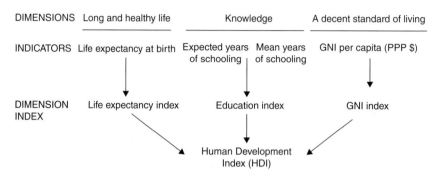

Figure 16.1 Human Development Index, 2018. Source: UNDP, Human Development Report 2018.

The UN SDGs also inform a just, inclusive and sustainable development. They were born at the UN Conference on Sustainable Development in Rio, in 2012. They are universal and measurable targets and replace the Millennium Development Goals. They were launched in 2000, to address 'the indignity of poverty', as per the UN words.[24] They are to be met in 2030, according to the *2030 Agenda for Sustainable Development*. They were eventually adopted in 2015, while, the same year, a series of related major agreements were finalised:

- Sendai Framework for Disaster Risk Reduction (March 2015);
- Addis Ababa Action Agenda on Financing for Development (July 2015);
- Transforming Our World: the 2030 Agenda for Sustainable Development (September 2015);
- Paris Agreement on Climate Change (December 2015).

Pure rhetoric or real commitment? The SDGs are referred to by all and in all circumstances, from higher education institutions to multinational companies, as being at the risk of diluting their substance. Is the intent genuine or are they used as communication tools? One can interrogate the instrumentalisation of these rather consensual objectives. Yet the reality they describe needs to be addressed by States and all stakeholders, public or private.

---

[23] UNDP, 'Human Development Index (HDI)', available at http://hdr.undp.org/en/content/human-development-index-hdi (accessed 21 December 2020).

[24] UNDP, Sustainable Development Goals, 'Background on the Goals', available at www.undp.org/content/undp/en/home/sustainable-development-goals/background.html (accessed 21 December 2020).

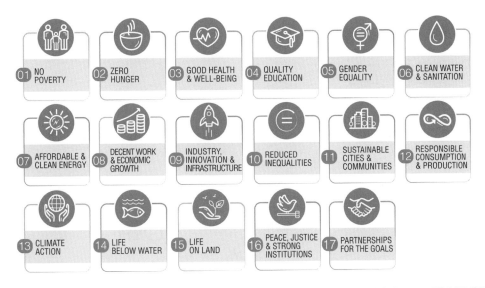

Figure 16.2 Sustainable Development Goals, 17 goals to transform our world. Source: UN SDGS.

Box 16.3 Development as happiness?

What if a more subjective criterion was adopted to gauge the development of a nation – that of happiness? Is it relevant or scientifically based?

In 2008, the Himalayan Kingdom of Bhutan enshrined the concept of gross national happiness (GNH) in its Constitution. The idea of gross national happiness was coined by His Majesty the Fourth King of Bhutan, Jigme Singye Wangchuck, in the 1970s, based on Buddhist principles of compassion, contentment and calmness. Thirty-three indicators were created to measure happiness in nine domains: psychological well-being, health, education, use of time, cultural diversity, good governance, community vitality, ecological diversity and resilience, and living standards.

Bhutan provides its citizens with free basic education and health care. More than 50 per cent of its land is designated for national parks, and more than 80 per cent is covered by natural forests. Bhutan is carbon-neutral and has a net zero-carbon footprint. Naturally, the rural and secluded kingdom of Bhutan still faces many challenges, including that of economic growth in attracting businesses and developing its domestic capacity. It has set up a GNH business certification, with the aim of developing a unique relationship with the private sector. On 19 July 2011, the UN General Assembly unanimously adopted a resolution, 'Happiness: towards a holistic approach to development', introduced by Bhutan with the support of sixty-eight member States, aimed at promoting sustainable happiness and well-being. Yet some have also criticised this approach as mere propaganda to distract international attention from human rights abuses.

Box 16.3 (cont.)

Figure 16.3 Gross
National Happiness

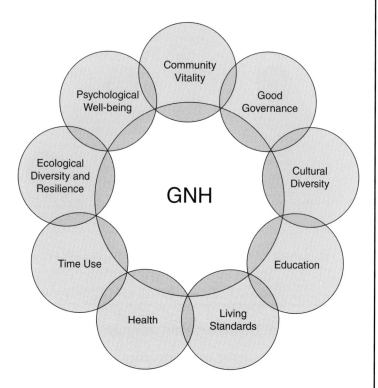

To Go Further

Case, J. H., 'The Law and Happiness in Bhutan: A New Law School in the Land of the Thunder Dragon', *Harvard Law Bulletin* (18 May 2017), available at https://today.law.harvard.edu/feature/law-happiness-bhutan/ (accessed 21 December 2020).

Centre for Bhutan Studies, 'Gross National Happiness Index Explained in Detail', available at www.grossnationalhappiness.com/docs/GNH/PDFs/Sabina_Alkire_method.pdf and https://sustainabledevelopment.un.org/partnership/?p=2212 (accessed 21 December 2020).

Centre for Bhutan Studies and GNH, available at www.grossnationalhappiness.com (accessed 21 December 2020).

Meier, B. M. and Chakrabarti, A., 'The Paradox of Happiness: Health and Human Rights in the Kingdom of Bhutan', *Health and Human Rights Journal* (2016), 18(1), available at www.hhrjournal.org/2016/04/the-paradox-of-happiness-health-and-human-rights-in-the-kingdom-of-bhutan/ (accessed 21 December 2020).

UN General Assembly, 'Happiness: Towards a Holistic Approach to Development', A/RES/65/309, available at https://digitallibrary.un.org/record/715187 (accessed 21 December 2020).

16.2.1.3   Just Development

Development could be based on the idea of justice, social justice naturally, but also the 'rule of law', and indeed the role of law and institutions. From this perspective, a series of human rights, first and foremost, should be guaranteed, from political and civil rights to economic, social and cultural rights. Just development entails the protection of private property and freedom of contract, the existence of an independent judiciary and the possibility for people to get redress. It stands firm against corruption. It supposes the existence of recourses against a possible arbitrary State and a political regime that allows all of the above to flourish – that is, a democracy. The role of law in development, as well as the political regimes on which development could be based, have been widely debated, along with the intervention of international organisations in the life of developing countries. A quick look at their programmes shows that all of them have 'rule of law'-related plans and ambitions. These often contradict more pragmatic actions, for example when lending to non-democratic oppressive regimes, which also aim at development, but one probably more centred on economic results.

16.2.1.4   Development as a Right

Another approach is to consider development as a right. The concept of the right to development has informed the discussions of the international community since the 1980s, and in particular since the adoption of UN General Assembly Resolution 41/128 on 4 December 1986.

Already present in the 1948 Universal Declaration of Human Rights, the idea of development was meant to include more than economic growth, but it materialised with the NIEO and decolonisation. It was indeed first recognised in 1981 in Article 22 of the African Charter on Human and Peoples' Rights and its Article 22(1), which provides that 'All peoples shall have the right to their economic, social and cultural development with due regard to their freedom and identity and in the equal enjoyment of the common heritage of mankind'.[25]

The right to development is now well-recognised by a series of declarations and programmes of actions for human rights and sustainable development, notably the Vienna Declaration and Programme of Action on Human Rights, the Rio Declaration on Environment and Development, and the Declaration on the Rights of Indigenous People. Some see the right to development as part of customary international law (see Introduction and Mini Chapter 1).

---

[25] African Charter on Human and Peoples' Rights, adopted in Nairobi, 27 June 1981, entered into force 21 October 1986.

General Assembly Resolution 41/128: The Right to Development (4 December 1986)

The General Assembly,

Bearing in mind the purposes and principles of the Charter of the United Nations relating to the achievement of international co-operation in solving international problems of an economic, social, cultural or humanitarian nature, and in promoting and encouraging respect for human rights and fundamental freedoms for all without distinction as to race, sex, language or religion,

Recognizing that development is a comprehensive economic, social, cultural and political process, which aims at the constant improvement of the well-being of the entire population and of all individuals on the basis of their active, free and meaningful participation in development and in the fair distribution of benefits resulting therefrom,

Considering that under the provisions of the Universal Declaration of Human Rights everyone is entitled to a social and international order in which the rights and freedoms set forth in that Declaration can be fully realized,

Recalling the provisions of the International Covenant on Economic, Social and Cultural Rights and of the International Covenant on Civil and Political Rights,

Recalling further the relevant agreements, conventions, resolutions, recommendations and other instruments of the United Nations and its specialized agencies concerning the integral development of the human being, economic and social progress and development of all peoples, including those instruments concerning decolonization, the prevention of discrimination, respect for and observance of human rights and fundamental freedoms, the maintenance of international peace and security and the further promotion of friendly relations and co-operation among States in accordance with the Charter,

Recalling the right of peoples to self-determination, by virtue of which they have the right freely to determine their political status and to pursue their economic, social and cultural development,

Recalling also the right of peoples to exercise, subject to the relevant provisions of both International Covenants on Human Rights, full and complete sovereignty over all their natural wealth and resources,

Mindful of the obligation of States under the Charter to promote universal respect for and observance of human rights and fundamental freedoms for all without distinction of any kind such as race, colour, sex, language, religion, political or other opinion, national or social origin, property, birth or other status,

Considering that the elimination of the massive and flagrant violations of the human rights of the peoples and individuals affected by situations such as those resulting from colonialism, neo-colonialism, apartheid, all forms of racism and racial

(cont.)

discrimination, foreign domination and occupation, aggression and threats against national sovereignty, national unity and territorial integrity and threats of war would contribute to the establishment of circumstances propitious to the development of a great part of mankind,

Concerned at the existence of serious obstacles to development, as well as to the complete fulfilment of human beings and of peoples, constituted, inter alia, by the denial of civil, political, economic, social and cultural rights, and considering that all human rights and fundamental freedoms are indivisible and interdependent and that, in order to promote development, equal attention and urgent consideration should be given to the implementation, promotion and protection of civil, political, economic, social and cultural rights and that, accordingly, the promotion of, respect for and enjoyment of certain human rights and fundamental freedoms cannot justify the denial of other human rights and fundamental freedoms,

Considering that international peace and security are essential elements for the realization of the right to development,

Reaffirming that there is a close relationship between disarmament and development and that progress in the field of disarmament would considerably promote progress in the field of development and that resources released through disarmament measures should be devoted to the economic and social development and well-being of all peoples and, in particular, those of the developing countries,

Recognizing that the human person is the central subject of the development process and that development policy should therefore make the human being the main participant and beneficiary of development,

Recognizing that the creation of conditions favourable to the development of peoples and individuals is the primary responsibility of their States,

Aware that efforts at the international level to promote and protect human rights should be accompanied by efforts to establish a new international economic order,

Confirming that the right to development is an inalienable human right and that equality of opportunity for development is a prerogative both of nations and of individuals who make up nations,

Proclaims the following Declaration on the Right to Development:

Article 1

1. The right to development is an inalienable human right by virtue of which every human person and all peoples are entitled to participate in, contribute to, and enjoy economic, social, cultural and political development, in which all human rights and fundamental freedoms can be fully realized.

(cont.)

2. The human right to development also implies the full realization of the right of peoples to self-determination, which includes, subject to the relevant provisions of both International Covenants on Human Rights, the exercise of their inalienable right to full sovereignty over all their natural wealth and resources.

Article 2

1. The human person is the central subject of development and should be the active participant and beneficiary of the right to development.
2. All human beings have a responsibility for development, individually and collectively, taking into account the need for full respect for their human rights and fundamental freedoms as well as their duties to the community, which alone can ensure the free and complete fulfilment of the human being, and they should therefore promote and protect an appropriate political, social and economic order for development.
3. States have the right and the duty to formulate appropriate national development policies that aim at the constant improvement of the well-being of the entire population and of all individuals, on the basis of their active, free and meaningful participation in development and in the fair distribution of the benefits resulting therefrom.

16.2.2 What Is Foreign Aid?

The concept of development aid or foreign aid goes back to the colonisation and in particular British policy. It is now referred to as 'development aid' or 'development cooperation', but also 'development assistance', 'technical assistance', 'international aid', 'overseas aid', 'official development assistance' or 'foreign aid'. It is as widely distributed as it is criticised for its many failures to provide effective relief to the poorest and really end poverty.[26] It is also greatly denounced for perpetuating what the British novelist and poet Rudyard Kipling had coined, in an infamous poem, as the 'white man's burden', when urging the US to take control of the Philippines for its betterment and, indeed, colonisation.[27] The expression now remains a euphemism of imperialism.

---

[26] William Easterly, *The White Man's Burden: Why the West's Efforts to Aid the Rest Have Done so Much Ill and so Little Good* (Oxford University Press, 2007).

[27] Text of the poem available at https://sourcebooks.fordham.edu/mod/kipling.asp (accessed 21 December 2020).

Box 16.4 China aid

How much is China spending on development and aid programmes, for whom and under what circumstances? As we have seen previously, China seems to adopt a quite different perspective to that of its Western counterparts, in terms of foreign investment and financial policy (see Chapter 12, Box 12.4 and Chapter 15, Box 15.1). Its loans are not based on IMF-type conditionalities, and its foreign aid (*duiwai yuanzhu*) policy distances itself significantly from the OECD official development assistance (ODA) criteria. It has been at the centre of intensive global scrutiny for its magnitude, but also for its absence of transparency.

Aid Policy

As for other major foreign policy programmes, Beijing Aid is officially based on a series of white papers reflecting the intentions of the government on a long-term basis. There are today two white papers on foreign aid (2011 and 2014). They form the official conceptual underpinning of China's aid policy. On this basis, one can identify three types of foreign aid: grants, interest-free loans and concessional loans. Generally, 'China prioritizes supporting other developing countries to develop agricultures, enhance education level, improve medical and health services and build public welfare facilities, and provide emergency humanitarian aid when they suffer severe disasters' (2014 White Paper).

Sectors and Actors

China's aid seems quite massive, although precise data are actually not available. According to non-official sources, and AidData in particular, between 2000 and 2014, the Chinese official financial contribution was US$354.3 billion, compared to US$394.6 billion for the US. However, most of the Chinese projects are not concessional and are of a more commercial nature. Energy generation and supply, but also transport and storage and industry, as well as mining and construction, make up most Chinese aid. To these sectors, one could naturally add all projects related to China's 'soft diplomacy' and expanding cultural influence, for example, with its vast Confucius Institutes Network. Close to 140 countries seem to have benefited from Chinese aid, with top recipients in developing Asia and Africa. The Chinese aid actors are very diverse: the Ministry of Foreign Affairs, the Ministry of Commerce, but also China EXIM Bank, the China Development Bank, the Asian Infrastructure Investment Bank and the BRICS Bank. China participates in multilateral programmes with the IMF, the World Bank and the UNDP. It acknowledges the 2030 agenda for sustainable development, but largely favours bilateral relations on a government-to-government basis.

Harmonisation

As a newcomer on the development and aid scene, China could well provide for harmonisation and a certain degree of transparency. The China International

Box 16.4 (cont.)

Development Cooperation Agency, created in 2018, which answers to the State Council, the highest executive body of China, is designed to improve domestic planning and coordination, as well as publishing aid-related data. Its precise mandate, however, seems still to be under development.

Challenges and Controversies

Transparency is certainly at the core of the numerous challenges faced by China's aid. In the recent context of the Belt and Road Initiative (BRI), which spans from Asia across Africa and Europe, with predicted total expenses for China of over US$1.2 trillion by 2027, as analysed by Morgan Stanley, a large number of countries, including recipient nations, are starting to question the realistic character of Chinese ambitions. More transparency and additional pragmatism on the ability of aided countries to refund their loans, and other forms of aid, seem very much needed.

To Go Further

AidData, available at www.aiddata.org/china-official-finance (accessed 21 December 2020).
Asian Infrastructure Investment Bank, available at www.aiib.org/en/index.html (accessed 21 December 2020).
China Development Bank, available at www.cdb.com.cn/English/ (accessed 21 December 2020).
China's Foreign Aid, White Papers, available at http://english.gov.cn/archive/white_paper/2014/08/23/content_281474982986592.htm (2014) and www.china.org.cn/government/whitepaper/node_7116362.htm (2011) (both accessed 21 December 2020).
China International Development Cooperation Agency, available at http://en.cidca.gov.cn (accessed 21 December 2020).
Confucius Institute, available at http://english.hanban.org (accessed 21 December 2020).
Export–Import Bank of China, available at http://english.eximbank.gov.cn (accessed 21 December 2020).
Grimm, S., Rank, R., McDonald, M. and Schickerling, E., 'Transparency of Chinese Aid: An Analysis of the Published Information on Chinese External Financial Flows' (Publish What You Fund/Centre for Chinese Studies, Stellenbosch University, 2011), available at www.die-gdi.de/en/others-publications/article/transparency-of-chinese-aid-an-analysis-of-the-published-information-on-chinese-external-financial-flows/ (accessed 21 December 2020).
New Development Bank, available at www.ndb.int (accessed 21 December 2020).

16.2.3 Critical and Conceptual Legal Approaches

Critical legal approaches are influenced by the 'law and development movement', which was born in the 1960s and 1970s and related to the thesis of a 'right to development', as discussed later by a number of developing countries (see above in this chapter, as well as the Introduction for a conceptual contextualisation). It also addressed the 'new law and development' of the years 2000–2010, in the context of a new NIEO.[28]

By the mid-1970s, the academics and practitioners David Trubek and Marc Galanter had published a now famous journal article, which concluded at the failure of the law and development movement, launched a decade before by the US Agency for International Development, the Ford Foundation and a number of other private institutions, in order to promote the reform of the legal and judicial systems of developing countries in Asia, Africa and Latin America. In all these projects, law was designed both as an instrument of economic development necessary for the proper functioning of the market, and as the guide of a political evolution towards a liberal democracy protected from political arbitrariness as itself subjected to law. Achieving this ambitious goal was deemed possible through training of legal professionals, judges and lawyers able to lead the whole society towards a different paradigm. The export of this 'legal liberalism', however, clashed with a principle of reality and was harshly criticised by its own promoters as an ethnocentric and naive model.

This heated debate on 'legal liberalism' lost its virulence from the second half of the 1970s. At the same time, another deep reflection, led by developing countries under UNCTAD, was to change the design of traditional international law by the proclamation of a 'right to development'. This claim in favour of greater equity comprised a right to trade ('trade not aid') and led to the adoption, by the UN General Assembly, of Resolutions 3201 and 3202 (S-VI), establishing an agenda for NIEO. This doctrinal creation also drew on Marxist theories on 'dependency', stressing that the end of decolonisation had not stopped the exploitation of the Third World by the capitalist West, helped by local elites. Twenty years later, the NIEO only appeared as a set of exceptions to the principles of liberalism. Developing States, subject to the conditionalities of the IMF and World Bank, received new technical assistance that they were constrained to seek in order to adapt their legal systems to new market imperatives.

Since the late 1990s, a small group of scholars have reinvestigated this issue. Their approach takes into account the legacy of the 1970s, while distancing from it. They generally associate the revival of the law and development movement with the promotion of good governance and the rule of law by major international donors and States, whether Western or not. A series of books reflecting on the evolution of the movement have been recently published (see the Further Reading section below).

More pragmatic, this perspective, often self-identifying as a third or fourth law and development movement, takes into account the evolution of the State and its relation to international law. But the authors remain marked by a relatively high uniformity of thought (American academic background and use of English language) and should be confronted

---

[28] For greater developments on this issue and the concept of emergence in IEL, see Leïla Choukroune, *Emerging Countries and International Trade and Investment Law* (Paris: Pedone, 2016). See also for a discussion on investments, notably, Sonia E. Rolland and David M. Trubek, *Emerging Powers in the International Economic Order* (Cambridge University Press, 2019).

with other and complementary standards applied to a different fieldwork. Moreover, these approaches are hardly based on concrete legal realities and, for instance, the international economic law practices of emerging powers such as China, Brazil or India. Other scholars who do not necessarily identify with the above movement have produced field-based analysis of great relevance, including, for example, the work of Marc Galanter or Upendra Baxi, to name just a few (see, generally, the Introduction for greater developments on conceptual approaches to IEL).

16.3   International Institutions for Development and Aid

16.3.1 World Bank Group: Five Members with a Broad Mandate

16.3.1.1   International Bank for Reconstruction and Development

The IBRD remains the world's largest development bank. It is a development cooperative bank, owned by its 189 members and working in 170 countries. Originating in the Bretton Woods system and founded in 1944, the IBRD, soon called the World Bank, later developed into a family of five interrelated institutions (the World Bank Group): the Bank itself, the International Development Association (IDA), the International Finance Corporation (IFC), the Multilateral Investment Guarantee Agency and the International Centre for the Settlement of Investment Disputes. They all embody the great variety of international economic law in action, while providing assistance to support economic growth, development, trade and investment. Originally, the Bank's loans helped to rebuild the countries devastated by the Second World War, but with the creation of the IFC, in 1956, the Group started to lend to the private sector, as well as to developing countries' newly independent institutions. With the launch of the IDA, in 1960, the Bank's focus was clearly directed towards the poorest. Today, the Bank's mandate is virtually limitless. It is precisely this omnipotence that is at the centre of a series of controversies, which have punctuated the Bank's history since the 1960s and its intervention in various developing countries.

The organisation of the Bank is officially based on an analogy to the functioning of a cooperative. The IBRD Articles of Agreement provides for the organisation of the Bank (Article V: Organization and Management).[29] Member countries act as shareholders and are represented by a Board of Governors (members' finance ministers, typically). They meet once a year at the IMF, with the World Bank and the IMF enjoying close links since their Bretton Woods creation. There are twenty-five Executive Directors (Board of Directors). Global power relations and imbalances are, unfortunately, reflected in these appointments, as the five largest shareholders appoint an Executive Director, while other members are represented by elected Executive Directors. The President of the World Bank is selected by the Board of Executive Directors, for a five-year renewable term. The support of the US has

---

[29] IBRD Articles of Agreement, available at www.worldbank.org/en/about/articles-of-agreement/ibrd-articles-of-agreement/article-V (accessed 21 December 2020).

proven key in this selection. Since its creation, the President of the World Bank has always been a US citizen proposed by the American government. Throughout the Bank's history (from 1944), the US has been the main shareholder and influencer. The headquarters of the Bank (like the IMF) is in Washington, DC, while the UN family is based in New York (and Geneva). This symbolism is more practically translated in the voting rights system, itself based on the financial strength of the Bank's members. Each member receives a voting power consisting of share votes (one vote for each share of the Bank's capital stock held by the member), as well as 'basic votes' (the sum of all basic votes needs to be equal to 5.55 per cent of the sum of basic votes and share votes for all members). In July 2019, the US held 16.57 per cent of the voting rights, against, for example, 3.80 per cent for the UK, 4.59 per cent for China and 0.02 per cent for Afghanistan.[30] While this allocation also reflects the financial commitment of the members of the Bank, it also gives the Washington Consensus critics more than enough to be getting on with (see Chapter 15). The Bank has shown itself willing, on numerous occasions, to support unstable regimes participating in Washington's geostrategic ambitions (Brazil, Nicaragua, Pinochet's Chile, Iraq), while at the same time refusing loans to countries perceived as too 'socialist' (France's immediate post-war government, Allende's Chile).[31]

Box 16.5 What is economic emergence?

The concept of economic emergence has gone through many incarnations since the 1990s. What was originally a rather abstract category, crafted to fill the vacant space between developed and developing countries, has eventually deeply impacted economic analysis and the work of international organisations.

In the early 1980s, in the framework of the IFC, a World Bank family member in charge of providing private support to developing countries, the economist Antoine van Agtmael coined the term 'emerging markets' in relation to the possible creation of a dedicated investment fund for promising Third World nations. The dynamic and evolving nature suggested by the idea of emergence immediately seduced the financial world – and the IFC, to begin with, which quickly saw the investment return potential in these new 'markets', as well as the efficient marketing theory behind the new label. As a matter of fact, while the database developed by the IFC was eventually sold to Standard & Poor's, a number of specialised investment funds were constituted, in the late 1980s, including by Antoine van Agtmael himself, who also created his own company. But the most successful initiative is certainly that of Morgan Stanley Capital International, launched in 1988 and now widely referred to all over the world. While economic development and GNI per capita matter to developed economies, what matters even

---

[30] IBRD, 'Subscriptions and Voting Power of Member Countries', available at http://pubdocs.worldbank.org/en/795101541106471736/IBRDCountryVotingTable.pdf (accessed 21 December 2020).

[31] Ha-Joon Chang (ed.), *Joseph Stiglitz and the World Bank: The Rebel Within* (London: Anthem Press, 2001).

Box 16.5 (cont.)

more to the 'emerging' are the number and size of companies of these countries, as well as the issue of liquidity and the accessibility (openness to foreign ownership, ease of capital inflow and outflow, efficiency and stability of the operational and institutional framework of a given market). An extremely important criterion is set here: that of the presence and progressive improvement of a sound regulatory framework for business, the building of which implies, if not complete adherence to, at least an acceptance of international norms. The BRICS illustrate this tendency. First coined in 2001 by Jim O'Neill, then economist at Goldman Sachs, the term BRIC (Brazil, Russia, India and China) was mentioned again in the 2003 Bank's second and more widely circulated report. So much so that the BRIC(S) (joined by South Africa in 2011) have regrouped. Since 2009, indeed, the BRICS have been holding annual summits during which they have sought to advance a common strategy, including the creation of their own institutions, as illustrated by the reflections initiated by India on the setting up of a 'New Development Bank' that would act as a counterweight to the World Bank and the IMF by responding more directly to their concerns in matters of development. Championing an economic globalisation model that has propelled China and India to the international front ranks, the BRICS seem to be seeking to ensure that 'their model', or more specifically, their choice of a heterodox approach to liberalisation of trade and investment, spreads to new spheres of influence in Asia, Africa and Latin America, expressing a 'go global' policy needed to consolidate their might. It would, of course, be illusory to think that the acronym, however apt, could erase the numerous political, economic and cultural disparities cutting across such a heterogeneous group of countries, which did not await – far from it – the twenty-first century to make a mark in the world. The economic difficulties faced by Russia, Brazil, South Africa or, to a lesser extent, India also interrogate the strength of a China-only-led grouping.

To Go Further

Choukroune, L., *Emerging Countries and International Trade and Investment Law* (Paris: Pedone, 2016).

International Finance Corporation, a member of the World Bank Group, is the largest global development institution focused on the private sector in emerging markets, available at www .ifc.org/wps/wcm/connect/corp_ext_content/ifc_external_corporate_site/home (accessed 21 December 2020).

Morgan Stanley Capital International, available at www.msci.com (accessed 21 December 2020).

O'Neill, J., 'Building Better Global Economic BRICs', Goldman Sachs, Global Economics Paper 66 (30 November 2001).

van Agtmael, A., *The Emerging Markets Century: How a New Breed of World-Class Companies is Overtaking the World* (London and New York: Free Press, 2007).

Wilson, D. and Purushothaman, R., 'Dreaming with BRICs: The Path to 2050', Goldman Sachs, Global Economics Paper 99 (1 October 2003).

16.3.1.2   International Development Association

The IDA is the World Bank's fund for the poorest.[32] It is one of the largest sources of aid in the world and provides for health, education, infrastructure, agriculture, and economic and institutional development generally. The IDA is responsible to its 173 shareholders. It is largely funded by its richest members, with additional funds from the World Bank and the IFC, as well as repayment from borrowers. The IDA gives loans ('credits') and grants on concessional terms (zero or very low interest rate), with a long repayment period of more than thirty years. As such, it complements the loans of the World Bank, while targeting its assistance to the poorest countries, including thirty-nine in Africa. Since 1960, the IDA has provided US$369 billion of support in 113 countries. The IDA evaluates the risk for developing country borrowers. Countries with a high risk of debt distress receive 100 per cent of their financial assistance in the form of grants, while those with a medium risk receive 50 per cent. Other countries receive credits (loans) on longer-term periods, up to thirty-eight years, and forty years for smaller States.

The IDA also provides debt relief through its HIPC programme, as well as the Multilateral Debt Relief Initiative (MDRI).[33] The HIPC Initiative began in 1996, launched by the World Bank, the IMF and a number of other multilateral, bilateral and commercial creditors. The HIPC and the MDRI, which was also related to the work of the IMF, have relieved thirty-six IDA countries, including thirty African nations, of US$99 billion debt. A country benefits from the programme on the basis of the following criteria:

- Facing an unsustainable debt situation after the full application of traditional debt relief mechanisms;
- Eligible for highly concessional assistance from the IDA and the IMF's Poverty Reduction and Growth Trust;
- Have a track record of reform monitored by the IMF and World Bank supported programmes;
- Develop a Poverty Reduction Strategy Paper that involves civil society participation.

Vast challenges remain to ensure that the debt of developing countries does not reach or remain at unsustainable levels. In this regard, the World Bank and the IMF have put in place rigorous mechanisms based on the lessons learnt in the 1980s and 1990s, with debt crises in Latin American and Asian countries (see Chapter 15).

16.3.1.3   International Finance Corporation

The IFC is the World Bank's arm for the private sector. It is based on the simple idea that the private sector also matters for development. It was established in 1956.[34] The IFC is

---

[32] International Development Association, 'What Is IDA?', available at http://ida.worldbank.org/about/what-is-ida (accessed 21 December 2020).

[33] World Bank, Heavily Indebted Poor Country (HIPC) Initiative, available at www.worldbank.org/en/topic/debt/brief/hipc (accessed 21 December 2020).

[34] IFC, *IFC, The First Six Decades: Leading the Way in Private Sector Development – A History*, 2nd ed. (Washington, DC: International Finance Corporation, 2016), available at www.ifc.org/wps/wcm/connect/5e70149f-6cad-407a-

owned by its 185 member countries and managed by a Board of Governors and a Board of Directors. It is the largest institution focusing on the private sector's contribution to development, with a presence in a hundred countries, 700 projects and a portfolio of US$1.3 billion. While part of the World Bank Group, the IFC has a separate identity from that of the World Bank and functions on the basis of its own Articles of Agreement.[35] The President of the World Bank Group, however, is also President of the IFC. It was first created to provide the private sector with loans to invest in the developing world. Its first ever loan consisted of US$2 million to Siemens' Brazilian associate to manufacture electrical equipment. In 1961, the IFC Charter was amended to allow equity investment. In 1976, it started its first commercial project with a loan to Kenya Commercial Bank, to enable it to lend to small local enterprises. In 1980, the IFC provided a loan to the Indian giant Tata and started looking at the 'emerging markets'. In the early 2000s, it was influential in the launch of the Equator Principles for responsible investment.[36] Since first being evaluated in 1989, the IFC has been rated triple-A every year by Standard and Poor's and Moody's, the financial market rating agencies. Indeed, since 2000, the IFC has been extremely active and has appeared to transform itself into an investment bank – a problematic turn for many of its detractors.

Box 16.6 The Indian fishermen US Supreme Court lawsuit against the IFC

In 2015, the Indian fishermen Budha Ismail Jam, Sidik Kasam Jam and Kashubhai Abhrambhai Manjalia, supported by the leading rights advocacy organisation Earth Right International, sued the World Bank Group's International Finance Corporation in US Federal Court in Washington, DC. They challenged the IFC's claim that it has 'absolute' immunity from lawsuit on the basis of its international organisation status. The original dispute, known as the *Jam Case*, relates to the IFC's contribution to finance the Indian multinational company Tata's Mundra Ultra Mega Power Plant coal-fired project in Gujarat. The plant is located near Tragadi village in Mandvi Taluka, and Navinal village in neighbouring Mundra Taluka in the state of Gujarat. It is the third-largest power plant in India. According to local communities, this massive project has been extremely harmful to their environment. About ten years ago, the IFC financed the construction of the coal-fired power plant in Gujarat Kutch District, providing US$450 million in loans to Coastal Gujarat Power Limited. It was not the only funder. The Asian Development Bank advanced a loan of US$450 million, the Export Credit Agency of Korea extended another US$800 million, and

---

944e-69d392079b47/IFC-History-Book-Second-Edition.pdf?MOD=AJPERES&CVID=lIwwdJi (accessed 21 December 2020).

[35] IFC Articles of Agreement, available at www.ifc.org/wps/wcm/connect/corp_ext_content/ifc_external_corporate_site/about+ifc_new/ifc+governance/articles/about+ifc+-+ifc+articles+of+agreement (accessed 21 December 2020).

[36] Equator Principles, available at https://equator-principles.com/about/ (accessed 21 December 2020).

Box 16.6 (cont.)

Coastal Gujarat Power Limited, the company to which the project was awarded, raised around Rs 1.5 billion from Indian banks. Under the terms of the IFC agreement, the project was required to comply with an environmental and social action plan. But it did not. The plant operates cooling technology that according to the plaintiffs requires much more water than the system it got environmental approval for. The water is eventually discharged into the sea and affects marine life. The fishermen first tried to seek redress at the IFC level, with the support of the Delhi-based NGO Centre for Financial Accountability, and through the organisation's mechanism for the resolution of disputes. It failed.

The legal issues pertaining to this case are fascinating, as they also relate to the question of immunity for international organisations:

1 The US law basis for immunity and whether it grants absolute immunity or not.
2 The interpretation of the IFC's Articles of Agreement, which could offer a waiver to immunity if a suit is not filed by its members.
3 The responsibility and liability of an international organisation for harm to the environment and human rights of the very communities it is supposed to help.

In a February 2019 decision, the US Supreme Court, with one judge abstaining, ruled that the IFC was entitled only to the same limited or 'restrictive' immunity that foreign governments currently enjoy. This opened quite a large avenue for the plaintiffs' subsequent procedures and possible redress.

To Go Further

Blokker, N. M. and Schrijver, N. J. (eds.), *Immunity of International Organizations*, Legal Aspects of International Organisations 55 (2015), available at https://brill.com/view/title/31796?lang=en (accessed 21 December 2020).

Centre for Financial Accountability, 'Tata Mundra: The Story of a Valiant Struggle' (11 April 2019), available at www.cenfa.org/projects-in-focus/tata-mundra-ultra-mega-project/tata-mundra-the-story-of-a-valiant-struggle/ (accessed 21 December 2020).

Earth Rights International, '*Budha Ismail Jam, et al*. v. *IFC*: An Indian Fishing Community Takes on the World Bank', available at https://earthrights.org/case/budha-ismail-jam-et-al-v-ifc/ (accessed 21 December 2020).

US Supreme Court Decision, *Jam et al.* v. *International Finance Corporation*, No. 17-1011, 27 February 2019, available at www.supremecourt.gov/opinions/18pdf/17-1011_new_d1o2.pdf (accessed 21 December 2020).

With rich nations and the US at its centre since its very inception, the IFC has naturally been widely criticised for fuelling a form of neocolonialism, based on the imperialism of Western multinational companies. Some of the most virulent criticism towards the IFC comes from the World Bank itself, for IFC operations often seem quite far away from the poor and their main concerns. While the IFC, as a money-maker, funds the IDA, this economic model can be problematic. The Institution has recently been marred by a number of financial scandals. From the financing of luxury resorts by the Shangri-La hotel group in the Maldives or Burma, to the support of a series of politically controversial deals led by developing world oligarchs, the IFC is at the centre of global controversy.[37] In an effort at transparency, the IFC has put in place a disclosure policy. A large part of its activities is now accessible online to all stakeholders.[38] However, the objective of the Institution is very much questioned. Is it to generate profit for the World Bank Group or to tackle development issues more directly?

16.3.1.4   Multilateral Investment Guarantee Agency and the ICSID

Like the IFC, the Multilateral Investment Guarantee Agency (MIGA) and the ICSID are at the crossroads between development assistance and international finance and investment.

The MIGA is a political risk insurer. The idea of covering the risk of investment in developing economies materialised, in 1985, at a key moment of the postcolonial liberalisation era, promoting foreign direct investment as a key driver for economic development. After a period of relative closure of their economies, developing countries were convinced by the donor agencies, in particular, that welcoming FDI was one of the best paths to take. Hence the surge, at the very same time, of investment treaties to promote and protect Western investments in the South (see Chapters 12 and 13). The Preamble of the 1988 MIGA Convention clearly defines the main objective of the Agency:[39]

> ### Convention Establishing the MIGA, 1988, Preamble
> *Considering* the need to strengthen international cooperation for economic development and to foster the contribution to such development of foreign investment in general and private foreign investment in particular;

---

[37] Claire Provost and Matt Kennard, 'The World Bank Is Supposed to Help the Poor: So Why Is it Bankrolling Oligarchs?', *Mother Jones* (January/February 2016), available at www.motherjones.com/politics/2016/03/world-bank-ifc-fund-luxury-hotels/; as well as the work of the Bretton Woods Project, which includes 7,000 NGOs and civil society members, available at www.brettonwoodsproject.org (both accessed 21 December 2020).

[38] IFC Project Information & Data Portal, available at https://disclosures.ifc.org/#/landing (accessed 21 December 2020).

[39] Convention Establishing the Multilateral Investment Guarantee Agency, available at www.miga.org/sites/default/files/archive/Documents/MIGA%20Convention%20(April%202018).pdf; Commentary on the Convention Establishing the Multilateral Investment Guarantee Agency, available at www.miga.org/sites/default/files/archive/Documents/commentary_convention_november_2010.pdf (both accessed 21 December 2020).

(cont.)

Recognizing that the flow of foreign investment to developing countries would be facilitated and further encouraged by alleviating concerns related to non-commercial risks;

Desiring to enhance the flow to developing countries of capital and technology for productive purposes under conditions consistent with their development needs, policies and objectives, on the basis of fair and stable standards for the treatment of foreign investment.

The MIGA was created as a legally and financially independent member of the World Bank family, to act as a complement to existing public and private investment insurers. It is now composed of 156 developing countries and 25 industrialised countries. It is managed by a Board of Directors representing the member countries' contribution. Its core mission is to provide political risk insurance to mitigate risk arising from complex political situations in developing countries and so support easier access to finance for the investor. It does not cover business risk. It is interesting, in this regard, to read the MIGA mandate in light of investment treaties, which also provide some protection, for example, with the controversial FPS standard. A less-known aspect of MIGA is that it also provides for alternative dispute settlement. In case of a conflict between the investor and the developing State, MIGA offers its 'good offices' to examine responsibilities and possible liabilities to help the parties reach an agreement.[40]

Faced with criticism denouncing its support for environmentally costly projects or a lack of interest in the realities of the poorest, the MIGA put forward a three-pillar strategy: (1) focus on the poorest through support for IDA country projects; (2) focus on fragile and conflict-affected States where private insurance firms refuse to operate; (3) commit to climate change mitigation and adaptation, with a target of 28 per cent of new issuance related to climate change mitigation or adaptation in 2020.[41]

In relation to investment again, the ICSID has been largely covered in Part II of this book. Let us recall that despite the recent waves of criticism and alternative proposals formulated by a variety of countries, it is still the main institutional body for the settlement of ISDS.

The five members of the World Bank Group have to be understood together. They complement each other in covering a large variety of development topics through different mechanisms using public and private resources.

---

[40] MIGA, Dispute Resolution, available at www.miga.org/dispute-resolution (accessed 21 December 2020).

[41] For updates, see IFC, COP 21, 'Private Sector: An Integral Part of Climate Action Post-Paris', available at www.ifc .org/wps/wcm/connect/news_ext_content/ifc_external_corporate_site/news+and+events/events/cop+21+landing +page (accessed 21 December 2020).

16.3.2 Other Multilateral Institutions for Development

The World Bank is not the only multilateral development institution. Since the 1950s, indeed, a significant number of regional or specialised banks have flourished. Like the World Bank, they provide financial support, accompanied by technical assistance, on the basis of various conditions for developing countries. The first to follow the path of the World Bank were the Inter-American Development Bank, created in 1959, the African Development Bank, which begun operations in 1964, and the Asian Development Bank, established in 1966. From the early decolonisation period, a number of other institutions also developed. They all have slightly different mandates and ways of functioning, but the objective is the same: to support development. The most prominent are: the European Investment Bank, the Islamic Development Bank, the European Bank for Reconstruction and Development, the Corporación Andina de Fomento – Banco de Desarrollo de América Latina, the Latin American Bank, the Caribbean Development Bank, the Central American Bank for Economic Integration, the East African Development Bank, the West African Development Bank (Banque Ouest Africaine de Développement), the Black Sea Trade and Development Bank, the Economic Cooperation Trade and Development Bank, the Eurasian Development Bank, the Arab Bank for Economic Development in Africa, and, more recently, the BRICS New Development Bank and the Asian Infrastructure Bank.

This rather complex panorama offers numerous possibilities to developing countries, but at the risk of unsustainable debt.

Box 16.7 More creditors, more debt?

With the recent creation of new development banks, as well as the growth of private funders, access to credit has never been easier for developing economies. This represents major risks and not all creditors have put in place surveillance and debt-relief mechanisms similar to those of the World Bank and the IMF.

The latest World Bank report on debt shows that the external debt stock of IDA-only countries totalled US$356 billion at end of 2017 – that is 11 per cent higher than the previous year. Over the past decade, the external debt stock of IDA-only countries has doubled. Borrowing from the private sector expands quickly. According to the Bank, external obligations to private creditors had risen to US$83 billion by the end of 2017 (26 per cent of long-term external debt). Twelve IDA countries accounted for 65 per cent of external debt stock at the end of 2017. Bangladesh was the largest borrower. Eleven low and middle-income countries, including Lebanon, Mongolia and Mozambique, have debt-to-GNI ratios of over 100 per cent. Not everybody can afford this debt ratio. While the IMF and the World Bank have long been criticised for their interventions, today's system is actually much more complex and requires even more scrutiny from the global community.

Box 16.7 (cont.)

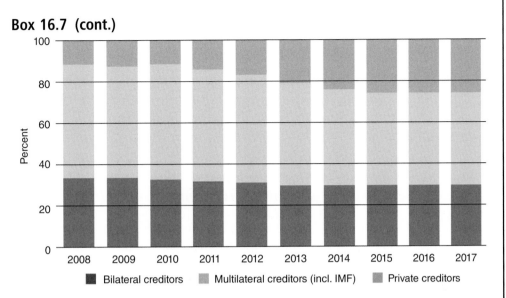

Figure 16.4 IDA-only borrowers' creditor composition of external debt stock, 2008–17. Source: World Bank Debtor Reporting System.

To Go Further

IBRD/World Bank, *International Debt Statistics 2019* (Washington, DC: World Bank, 2018), available at https://openknowledge.worldbank.org/bitstream/handle/10986/30851/IDS2019 .pdf?sequence=5&isAllowed=y (accessed 21 December 2020).
International Development Association, Debt, available at http://ida.worldbank.org/debt (accessed 21 December 2020).

16.3.2.1   World Trade Organization

The WTO Doha Development Agenda was designed to support developing countries.[42] It commenced, in 2001, at the Doha Ministerial Conference, under the mandate of then Director-General Mike Moore, with the idea of placing development at the centre of trade negotiations.[43]

---

[42] WTO, The Doha Round, available at www.wto.org/english/tratop_e/dda_e/dda_e.htm (accessed 21 December 2020).

[43] The issue of developing countries in the WTO has fascinated international legal scholarship, with a large production of books and papers, for example, Joel P. Trachtman and Chantal Thomas (ed.), *Developing Countries in the WTO Legal System* (New York: Oxford University Press, 2009); Gregory C. Shaffer and Ricardo Melendez Ortiz (eds.), *Dispute Settlement at the WTO: The Developing Country Experience* (Cambridge University Press, 2010); Donatella Alessandrini, *Developing Countries and the Multilateral Trade Regime: The Failure and Promise of the WTOs' Development Mission* (Oxford: Hart, 2010).

In the Hong Kong Ministerial Declaration of 2005, Members (re)emphasised the central importance of development to the Doha Round. The Aid for Trade initiative was also launched to help developing countries build their supply-side capacity to expand trade.[44] At the Bali Ministerial Conference in December 2013, a number of decisions were adopted under the developmental pillar to support least-developed countries' trade. Some, however, argue that these reforms are rather cosmetic, as the WTO failed developing countries, with the very basis of the advantages and benefits conferred to developing countries now questioned. In 2019, indeed, the US expressed its opposition to WTO developing country designation and the possible advantages it confers, arguing in a communication:[45]

An Undifferentiated WTO, Communication from the US

1.5. Despite the great development strides made in the years since the WTO's inception, the WTO remains stuck in a simplistic and clearly outdated construct of 'North–South' division, developed and developing countries. Each is a seemingly static set, regardless of economic, social, trade, and other indicators. This binary construct does not reflect the realities of 2019. Nor does it reflect how Members viewed development at the time the WTO was created. The preamble to the *Marrakesh Agreement Establishing the World Trade Organization* recognizes there are 'needs and concerns at different levels of economic development', implying there could be many levels of development.

   [...]

4.4. Self-declaration can lead to unpredictable and illogical results in the operation and implementation of existing WTO agreements. For example, Kazakhstan – ranked in UNDP's 'Very High Human Development' quartile and having made no previous claim to developing Member status – claimed such status for the first time for the purposes of implementing its obligations under the Trade Facilitation Agreement. Some of the wealthiest WTO Members – including Singapore; Hong Kong, China; Macao, China; Israel; the State of Kuwait; the Republic of Korea; United Arab Emirates; Brunei Darussalam; and Qatar – insist on being considered developing Members and can avail themselves of S&D provisions at their discretion – just like sub-Saharan Africa.

Unacceptable for some, and clearly targeted against China, the US document had the merit of pointing out the limits and incoherent nature of a self-declaration system in which

---

[44] WTO, Aid for Trade Global Review 2019: 'Supporting Economic Diversification and Empowerment', available at www.wto.org/english/tratop_e/devel_e/a4t_e/gr19_e/gr19programme_e.htm (accessed 21 December 2020).

[45] Communication from the US (Revision): 'An Undifferentiated WTO: Self-Declared Development Status Risks Institutional Irrelevance' (14 February 2019), WT/GC/W/757/Rev.1.

Singapore can potentially be treated on the same basis as Ethiopia.[46] Some differentiation and categorisation on the basis of UNDP or World Bank criteria could indeed be introduced, while taking into account the complexity of development.

That S&DT needs to be terminated is another question to which a group of quite heteroclite developing countries, comprising China, India, South Africa, Venezuela, Laos, Bolivia, Kenya, Cuba and Central African Republic, responded, starting with a quote from Thomas Jefferson: 'there is nothing more unequal than the equal treatment of unequal people', following up:[47]

Recent attempts by some Members to selectively employ certain economic and trade data to deny the persistence of the divide between developing and developed Members, and to demand the former to abide by absolute 'reciprocity' in the interest of 'fairness' are profoundly disingenuous. The world has indeed changed in many ways since the GATT and the establishment of the WTO, but in overall terms the development divide remains firmly entrenched. It is therefore of greater concern that some Members would attempt to ignore this reality in an effort to deprive developing Members of their right to develop.

In a rigorous demonstration, they also argued that the GATT system was originally created *by* and *for* the developed world, which made sure to control the rules and amend them to its own benefit. Rule makers de facto dominate international economic relations:

The claim by the United States that 'all rules apply to a few (developed countries)' totally ignores the 70 plus year history of GATT/WTO. First, 'Being carried along' due to capacity constraints is a factual description of the relationship between most developing Members and the multilateral trading system. A phenomenon of 'rules deficit' and 'development deficit' widely existed in the Uruguay Round as a result of the lack of capacity of developing Members and the dominant role developed Members played in those negotiations. Second, there were many instances wherein the developed Members secured exceptions and failed to adhere to even the fundamental principles of the multilateral trading system. Some of these exceptions were in place for decades, thereby undermining the rules and disciplines under the GATT/WTO. And during the Doha Round, many developed Members had secured country-specific carve-outs from rules that would have been generally applicable to them, for example country-specific carve-outs for some developed Members provided in the Draft Agriculture Modalities Text Rev.4, such as paragraphs 42 and Annex A of the Draft Modalities Text providing the United States an exception from the provision applicable for calculating product-specific limits on Blue Box, which gave the United States higher limits in product-specific support under Blue Box, particularly for corn, wheat, cotton and rice. In addition, exceptions for developed Members are also contained in the Nairobi Decision on Export Subsidies. While these were not labelled as S&DT

---

[46] On China's reaction, see Amanda Lee, 'China Hits Back at Donald Trump's "Absurd" Criticism of its WTO Developing Country Status', *South China Morning Post* (29 July 2019), available at www.scmp.com/economy/china-economy/article/3020474/china-hits-back-donald-trumps-absurd-criticism-its-wto (accessed 21 December 2020).

[47] Communication from China, India, South Africa, the Bolivarian Republic of Venezuela, Lao People's Democratic Republic, Plurinational State of Bolivia, Kenya and Cuba, 'The Continued Relevance of Special and Differential Treatment in Favour of Developing Members to Promote Development and Ensure Inclusiveness', WT/GC/W/765/Rev.1 (26 February 2019), available at https://docs.wto.org/dol2fe/Pages/FE_Search/FE_S_S009-DP.aspx?CatalogueIdList=251793 (accessed 21 December 2020).

provisions, it does not hide the reality that in effect these were S&DT provisions for some of the developed Members, which is usually referred to as 'reversed S&DT'. Such reserved S&DT has led to the long-lasting imbalances in the multilateral trading system as well as distortions in the international trade. It is, thus, inaccurate and disingenuous of the United States to assert that all rules have applied only to a few (developed countries).

While the world economy has progressed, the divide between the poorest and the richest is immense, as inequalities are growing. These have to be measured not only on the basis of GDP or GNI, but also on per capita data for countries with immense populations like China and India, as well as on concrete access to education, health care, culture, digital facilities, a clean and sustainable environment and so on.

More than two-thirds of WTO members are developing countries.[48] As demonstrated above, there are no formal criteria to justify a classification. The WTO developing country status is self-declaratory, but not automatic, in that it can, theoretically, be challenged, if not in a formal case, at least as a negotiation technique. In addition, the WTO offers a special regime for LDCs, the poorest members of the international community, on the basis of the UN classification. Among the forty-seven LDCs designated by the United Nations, thirty-six have become WTO Members, while nine LDCs are at different stages of negotiations to access the WTO.[49] The WTO Ministerial Conferences held in Bali in 2013 and in Nairobi in 2015 adopted several decisions in favour of LDCs, to assist their better integration into the multilateral trading system: duty-free and quota-free market access, preferential rules of origin and the LDC services waiver, for instance.

The WTO's approach to development is based on a series of principles and supported by a number of tools.

WTO Principles   The provisions contained in the WTO for developing countries are known under the term 'special and differential treatment' (S&DT). They consist of special rights allowing developed countries to treat developing countries more favourably than other WTO members. As such, they are a departure from key WTO principles, such as the MFN or NT, and the idea of reciprocity (see Chapter 1). According to the WTO, these S&DT provisions can be summarised under the following categories:[50]

1 Measures to increase trading opportunities
2 Provisions requiring all WTO members to safeguard the trade interests of developing countries

---

[48] WTO, Who Are the Developing Countries in the WTO?, available at www.wto.org/english/tratop_e/devel_e/d1who_e.htm (accessed 21 December 2020).

[49] WTO, Least-Developed Countries, available at www.wto.org/english/thewto_e/whatis_e/tif_e/org7_e.htm (accessed 21 December 2020).

[50] WTO, 'Special and Differential Treatment Provisions in WTO Agreements and Decisions: Note by the Secretariat', WT/COMTD/W/77, 25 October 2000, available at https://www.wto.org/english/tratop_e/devel_e/d2legl_e.htm (accessed 21 December 2020).

3 Capacity-building provisions (access to dispute settlement, technical standards)
4 LDCs-related special provisions
5 Waivers granted by the WTO General Council according to procedures set out in Article IX:3 of the WTO Agreement and the June 1999 General Council Decision on Waiver regarding Preferential Tariff Treatment for Least-Developed Countries (WT/L/304), allowing developing country members to provide preferential tariff treatment to products of least developed countries. The waiver was extended until 30 June 2019 in a decision (WT/L/759) adopted in 2009, as well as the WTO Ministerial Conference (WT/L/847) of December 2011 enabling developing and developed-country members to provide preferential treatment to services and service suppliers of LDCs, furthered in the Bali Ministerial Conference (WT/L/918).

Development provisions are present throughout the WTO Agreement: in the GATT, the GATS, the TRIPS, the Agreement on Agriculture, the SPS, the TBT and so on. Their wording, however, is vague, if not ambiguous, and developing countries are often not equipped to understand the potential usage and benefit. Their binding character is very much debated. For instance, the entire Part IV of the GATT includes provisions on the concept of non-reciprocal preferential treatment for developing countries, but developing countries claim that Part IV is of no practical value as it does not contain any obligations for developed countries.

The Committee on Trade and Development is mandated to identify which of those S&DT provisions are mandatory.

Examples of WTO S&DT Provisions as Provided for in Different Agreements

Chapeau of the Agreement Establishing the WTO

Recognizing further that there is need for positive efforts designed to ensure that developing countries, and especially the least developed among them, secure a share in the growth in international trade commensurate with the needs of their economic development.

GATT, Article XVIII: Governmental Assistance to Economic Development

1. The contracting parties recognize that the attainment of the objectives of this Agreement will be facilitated by the progressive development of their economies, particularly of those contracting parties the economies of which can only support low standards of living and are in the early stages of development.
2. The contracting parties recognize further that it may be necessary for those contracting parties, in order to implement programmes and policies of economic development designed to raise the general standard of living of their people, to take protective or other measures affecting imports, and that such measures are justified in so far as they

(cont.)

facilitate the attainment of the objectives of this Agreement. They agree, therefore, that those contracting parties should enjoy additional facilities to enable them (a) to maintain sufficient flexibility in their tariff structure to be able to grant the tariff protection required for the establishment of a particular industry and (b) to apply quantitative restrictions for balance of payments purposes in a manner which takes full account of the continued high level of demand for imports likely to be generated by their programmes of economic development.

3. The contracting parties recognize finally that, with those additional facilities which are provided for in Sections A and B of this Article, the provisions of this Agreement would normally be sufficient to enable contracting parties to meet the requirements of their economic development. They agree, however, that there may be circumstances where no measure consistent with those provisions is practicable to permit a contracting party in the process of economic development to grant the governmental assistance required to promote the establishment of particular industries with a view to raising the general standard of living of its people. Special procedures are laid down in Sections C and D of this Article to deal with those cases.

GATS, Article IV: Increasing Participation of Developing Countries

1. The increasing participation of developing country Members in world trade shall be facilitated through negotiated specific commitments, by different Members pursuant to Parts III and IV of this Agreement, relating to:
   (a) the strengthening of their domestic services capacity and its efficiency and competitiveness, inter alia through access to technology on a commercial basis;
   (b) the improvement of their access to distribution channels and information networks; and
   (c) the liberalization of market access in sectors and modes of supply of export interest to them.

2. Developed country Members, and to the extent possible other Members, shall establish contact points within two years from the date of entry into force of the WTO Agreement to facilitate the access of developing country Members' service suppliers to information, related to their respective markets, concerning:
   (a) commercial and technical aspects of the supply of services;
   (b) registration, recognition and obtaining of professional qualifications; and
   (c) the availability of services technology.

3. Special priority shall be given to the least-developed country Members in the implementation of paragraphs 1 and 2. Particular account shall be taken of the serious difficulty of the least-developed countries in accepting negotiated specific

(cont.)

commitments in view of their special economic situation and their development, trade and financial needs.

TRIPS, Article 66: Least-Developed Country Members

1. In view of the special needs and requirements of least-developed country Members, their economic, financial and administrative constraints, and their need for flexibility to create a viable technological base, such Members shall not be required to apply the provisions of this Agreement, other than Articles 3, 4 and 5, for a period of 10 years from the date of application as defined under paragraph 1 of Article 65. The Council for TRIPS shall, upon duly motivated request by a least-developed country Member, accord extensions of this period.
2. Developed country Members shall provide incentives to enterprises and institutions in their territories for the purpose of promoting and encouraging technology transfer to least-developed country Members in order to enable them to create a sound and viable technological base.

TRIPS, Article 67: Technical Cooperation

In order to facilitate the implementation of this Agreement, developed country Members shall provide, on request and on mutually agreed terms and conditions, technical and financial cooperation in favour of developing and least-developed country Members. Such cooperation shall include assistance in the preparation of laws and regulations on the protection and enforcement of intellectual property rights as well as on the prevention of their abuse and shall include support regarding the establishment or reinforcement of domestic offices and agencies relevant to these matters, including the training of personnel.

In direct relation to the S&DT is the *Enabling Clause*, officially called the Decision on Differential and More Favourable Treatment, Reciprocity and Fuller Participation of Developing Countries, adopted under the GATT in 1979. It allows S&DT and provides for the WTO legal basis for the GATT under which WTO developed country members offer non-reciprocal preferential treatment, on a unilateral basis (such as zero or low duties on imports, for example), to products originating in developing countries. In addition, the Global System of Trade Preferences (GSTP) allows developing countries to trade among themselves on preferable terms. Lastly, the Enabling Clause also provides the WTO with a basis for regional agreements between developing countries.

The WTO has put in place a series of tools to support the functioning of S&DT, which take the forms of committees: Committee on Trade and Development, Sub-Committee on Least Developed Countries, Working Group on Trade and Transfer of Technology,

Working Group on Trade, Debt and Finance. To this, three programmes can be added: the Aid for Trade programme, Trade-Related Technical Assistance and the Enhanced Integrated Framework (see, generally, Part II, and Chapter 2, in particular).

16.3.2.2 Other Multilateral Institutions

Without entering into the details of their functioning, one needs to mention the work of a series of other multilateral institutions for development. Some are part of the UN family while others are independent from it.

Part of the UN family, be they 'specialised agencies', 'funds' or 'special programmes' with different forms of legal status or funding, let us mention, notably, but not exclusively, the United Nations Development Programme, the United Nations Environment Programme, the United Nations Population Fund, the United Nations Human Settlements Programme or UN Habitat, the United Nations Children's Fund, the World Food Programme, the Food and Agriculture Organization, the International Fund for Agricultural Development, the International Labour Organization, the United Nations Educational, Scientific and Cultural Organization, the United Nations Industrial Development Organization, the World Health Organization, the Joint United Nations Programme on HIV/AIDS, the United Nations Conference on Trade and Development, and UN Women. Of particular relevance are the UNDP and UNCTAD, which cover numerous trade, investment and development issues in relation with WTO or World Bank initiatives, as well as regional organisations in charge of development policy.

With so many institutions, the question of *coordination* remains a massive issue. Numerous stakeholders are in charge of development-related programmes. Their policies are not necessarily coordinated and not always based on the same principles and objectives.

An interesting organisation for IEL specialists is the relatively unknown International Development Law Organization.[51] With an official mandate to create a 'culture of justice', it is devoted to promoting the rule of law. It is supported by governments, but also multilateral organisations, private foundations and the private sector. It was established as an intergovernmental organisation in 1988 and granted United Nations Observer status in 2001. It covers all areas of development, from trade to education, environment, health and women, with a particular emphasis on law, justice and the rule of law.

16.3.3 National Actors

National agencies also play a major part in international development policies and assistance. The list of actors is virtually unlimited. Let us mention a few: the United States Agency for International Development, the UK Department for International Development, l'Agence Française de Developpement, Japan International Cooperation Agency (JICA), China International Development Cooperation Agency, the Brazilian Cooperation Agency, and the India Development Partnership Administration.

---

[51] See www.idlo.int (accessed 21 December 2020).

A large number of these national actors, although not all of them, rely on the OECD ODA definition of development aid. Since 1969, ODA is defined by the OECD Development Assistance Committee as 'government aid that promotes and specifically targets the economic development and welfare of developing countries'. The Development Assistance Committee establishes a list of countries eligible to receive ODA, which is updated every three years and is based on per capita income.[52] In a number of countries, a given percentage of GDP (around 0.7 per cent, generally) is to be spent on development and aid, as per national policies, but also UN recommendations. At the second meeting of UNCTAD, held in New Delhi in 1968, its Secretary General, Raúl Prebisch, indeed proposed that a 'minimum figure of 0.75% of GNP could be established for net official aid'.[53] The Covid-19 pandemic has negatively impacted ODA budgets.

Box 16.8 What development aid policy post-Covid-19 crisis?

A health crisis, the Covid-19 pandemic revealed a much deeper human rights and human development crisis. All multilateral development and aid institutions put in place targeted responses to support the developing world in its capacity to manage the crisis and plan for the future. These include emergency financial assistance and debt relief to member countries, as proposed by the IMF, approved under the RCF, the RFI and the Catastrophe Containment and Relief Trust. The UNDP proposed an 'integrated response' to address a 'health, humanitarian and development crisis'.

The pandemic has drastically changed development and aid policies. A number of pressing questions have arisen:

- How to address a long-term crisis that differs from a disaster situation?
- How to coordinate multidonor initiatives?
- Are regional targeted responses preferable to multilateral initiatives?
- Are donors flexible enough to adapt to very fast-changing situations?
- What will be funded? Health only, to the detriment of other SDG priorities, such as education, gender equality or the environment?

To Go Further

Ugaz, P. and Sun, S., 'How Countries Can Leverage Trade Facilitation to Defeat the Covid-19 Pandemic' (UNCTAD, 22 April 2020), available at https://unctad.org/en/ PublicationsLibrary/dtlinf2020d2_en.pdf (accessed 21 December 2020).

World Bank, The World Bank Group's Response to the Covid-19 (Coronavirus) Pandemic, available at www.worldbank.org/en/who-we-are/news/coronavirus-covid19 (accessed 21 December 2020).

---

[52] OECD, 'What Is ODA?' (April 2020), available at www.oecd.org/dac/financing-sustainable-development/ development-finance-standards/What-is-ODA.pdf (accessed 21 December 2020).

[53] On the history of the 0.70 per cent ODA target, see OECD, Financing for Sustainable Development, available at www.oecd.org/dac/stats/ODA-history-of-the-0-7-target.pdf#page=2 (accessed 21 December 2020).

16.3.4 Private Actors

Lastly, it is important to acknowledge the significance of a large number of private actors in international development and aid. Private banks are playing a commercial role in lending to the developing world, as we have alluded to above. In addition, myriad NGOs and private foundations have blossomed. In 2018, the OECD released a report on private philanthropy's contribution to development, showing that these flows are relatively modest compared to ODA, but their contribution is substantial in certain sectors.[54] According to the OECD, private foundations provided US$23.9 billion for development during 2013–15 – that is, 5 per cent of the amount given through ODA. Most of these funds come from the US, in particular the Bill and Melinda Gates Foundation, which alone accounts for half of all philanthropic giving to developing countries. Other top countries for philanthropic funding for development are the UK (7 per cent), the Netherlands (5 per cent), Switzerland (2 per cent), Canada (2 per cent) and the United Arab Emirates (2 per cent). Of the total philanthropic giving during 2013–15, 81 per cent came from only twenty foundations. The private foundations direct their support mostly towards health-related issues. The poorest do not benefit so much from private foundations, as 67 per cent of philanthropic aid goes to middle-income countries, such as India (7 per cent of the total), Nigeria, Mexico, China and South Africa. A third of the country-allocable funding benefited the least-developed countries (28 per cent). Lastly, 97 per cent of philanthropic giving was implemented through NGOs or large foundations, such as Gavi, the Vaccine Alliance, the Rotary, and international organisations like the World Health Organization, PATH International and the United Nations Children's Fund.

Here again, the question of coordination and engagement with multilateral and national donors is key.

16.4 Conclusion

Development and foreign aid are complex and controversial concepts. They cover a vast landscape of notions, from pure economic growth to multidimensional components with access to public goods, education and health care, if not well-being and happiness. They are very much at the centre of IEL, with international organisations addressing issues of trade or finance, and indeed their related aspects in terms of human rights. Development is also a human right and is acknowledged as such by the United Nations.

There is a wide variety of development actors, at the centre of which remain States and governmental organisations. Their work, and that of the World Bank in particular, is under global scrutiny, for it has often failed people while contributing to economic development. A critical legal analysis helps us to better understand the complexity and challenges of development and aid.

---

[54] OECD, *Private Philanthropy for Development* (Paris: OECD Publishing, 2018), available at www.oecd.org/development/private-philanthropy-for-development-9789264085190-en.htm (accessed 21 December 2020).

16.5   Summary

- While the world is richer, development still matters.
- But development is also a controversial concept that needs to be analysed critically, and the same is true for foreign aid.
- The definition of development is complex. A wide variety of criteria must be taken into account, from pure economic data to a more qualitative analysis, as proposed by the UNDP HDI.
- Development can be very subjective and may rest on notions of happiness or well-being.
- The very category of a 'developing country' is not based on universally accepted criteria.
- The role of law in development needs to be addressed.
- There is a wide variety of development institutions, for instance, the World Bank, the Asian Development Bank, the European Bank of Reconstruction and Development and the New Development Bank.
- At the multilateral level, the World Bank Group plays a key role.
- Other development banks, either regional or specialised, are important actors too.
- With easy access to finance, developing countries face the challenge of unsustainable debt.
- The World Trade Organization offers S&DT for developing countries, as well as special provisions for LDCs.
- The UN family international organisations are key development actors.
- Bilateral aid on the basis of ODA also represents a very important part of development programmes.
- Of much less financial significance, yet still interesting, are private charitable foundations.
- The question of coordination of development and aid programmes has yet to be addressed.

16.6   Review Questions

1 How would you define the concept of development?
2 What are the indicators generally used to measure development?
3 Are these indicators questioned? Why? How can they be critically approached?
4 What is a developing country? Is there a universally accepted definition or categorisation of developing countries?
5 Why is the concept of development problematic?
6 What is the right to development?
7 What is the role of law in development? Has it been critically assessed?
8 What is foreign aid? Are there criteria to deliver it?
9 What is the role of the World Bank in promoting development?
10 Who are the main members of the World Bank Group and what are their functions?
11 What type of controversy surrounds the IFC?

12 Are there other development banks?

13 What advantages and benefits are conferred on developing countries by the WTO?

14 What are the categories of S&DT at the WTO?

15 Are there other multilateral agencies involved in development and aid?

16 What does the term ODA cover?

17 Are private actors playing a role in development and aid?

16.7 Exercise

(For background on the issue, please refer to previous Exercises in Chapters 12, 13 and 14.)

Hopeland is preparing its accession to the World Trade Organization. Its recent opening up to FDI, combined with the series of economic reforms put in place for the past ten years, has had a positive impact on its trade profile. However, Hopeland remains fragile compared to its main trade competitors and needs to grow domestic capacity. This process requires time and additional resources to address the complex issues faced by vital sectors of its economy. Farming and fishery are at the centre of the accession negotiation, for they are subsidised by the government and do not yet abide by a number of WTO SPS standards. In addition, its services sector is nascent and needs protection.

Accession negotiations are long and more difficult than expected. A number of developed trade partners are questioning the status of Hopeland and the advantages that this status could confer on the country in the WTO. Hopeland sees itself as an LDC and wishes to self-declare as such. Its arguments are also based on the World Bank and UN classifications, as well as comparisons with existing similar situations at the WTO. For its government, the best possible comparison would be with Cambodia and, to some extent, Nepal. Their Protocols of Accession to the WTO are of particular interest.

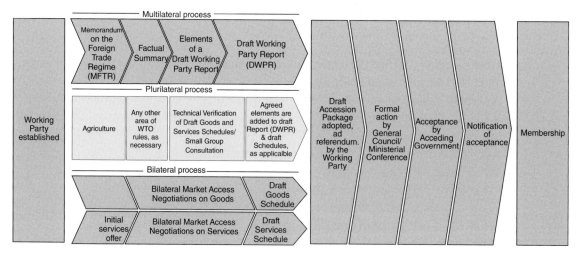

Figure 16.5 WTO accession process at a glance. Source: WTO.

When working for LJCN, the reputed international law firm, which had advised Hopeland at the time of its opening up to FDI, you gained considerable expertise of the WTO accession negotiation process. You were an adviser to the government of Cambodia and are now advising Bhutan in your own capacity. A few years ago, you set up your own firm, which also employs former staff of the Geneva-based Advisory Centre on WTO Law.

Now that the Working Party has been established, your task is to prepare a solid argumentation for each and every stage of the accession process (bilateral, multilateral and plurilateral). You expect discussions with the US to be difficult, on the basis of their 2019 General Council Communication on the self-declaration status for developing countries at the WTO. You know, as well, that other members might be more willing to accept your arguments. They challenged the American arguments in 2019 too.

To inform your reasoning, pay special attention to the following resources:

WTO, Accessions, Cambodia (key information on Cambodia's negotiations to join the WTO), available at www.wto.org/english/thewto_e/acc_e/a1_cambodge_e.htm (accessed 21 December 2020).

WTO, Accessions, Protocols of accession for new members since 1995, including commitments in goods and services, available at www.wto.org/english/thewto_e/acc_e/completeacc_e.htm#vnm (accessed 21 December 2020).

WTO, Member Information, Nepal and the WTO (key information on Nepal's participation in the WTO), available at www.wto.org/english/thewto_e/countries_e/nepal_e.htm (accessed 21 December 2020).

FURTHER READING

Alston, P. and Robinson, M. (eds.), *Human Rights and Development* (Oxford University Press, 2005).

Anghie, A., 'The Evolution of International Law: Colonial and Postcolonial Realities', *Third World Quarterly* (2006), 27, pp. 739–53.

Bunn, I. D., *The Right to Development and International Economic Law* (London: Hart, 2012).

Cassan, H., Mecure, P.-F., Bekhechi, M. A., *Droit international du développement* (Paris: Pedone, 2019).

Choukroune, L., *Emerging Countries and International Trade and Investment Law* (Paris: Pedone, 2016).

Chowdhury, S. R., de Waart, P. and Denters, E. (eds.), *The Right to Development in International Law* (Leiden: Martinus Nijhoff, 1992).

Faúndez, J. (ed.), *Law and Development* (London: Routledge, 2012).

Flory, M., *Droit international du développement* (Paris: Presses universitaires de France, 1977).

Kinley, D., *Civilizing Globalization* (Cambridge University Press, 2009).

Lee, Y. S., *Law and Development: Theory and Practice* (London: Routledge, 2019).

Sarkar, R., *International Development Law* (Oxford University Press, 2009).

Trebilcock, M. J. and Prado, M. M., *Law and Development* (Cheltenham: Edward Elgar, 2014).

Trubek, D. M., 'The Rule of Law in Development Assistance: Past, Present and Future', in D. M. Trubek and A. Santos (eds.), *The New Law and Economic Development: A Critical Appraisal* (Cambridge University Press, 2009), pp. 74–94.

Trubek, D. M. and Galanter, M., 'Scholars in Self-Estrangement: Some Reflections on the Crisis in Law and Development Studies in the United States', *Wisconsin Law Review* (1974), pp. 1062–101.

Vandenhole, W., 'Towards a Fourth Moment in Law and Development', *Law and Development Review* (2019), 12(2), pp. 265–83, available at https://doi.org/10.1515/ldr-2019-0013 (accessed 21 December 2020).

Part IV

International Economic Law at a Crossroads
Contemporary Illustrations of Multidisciplinary Approaches

Mini Chapter 1 International Economic Law and Human Rights

Are human rights taken into consideration in IEL? When analysing international trade treaties, investment agreements and international disputes, two simple answers rapidly come to mind: human rights are generally not addressed, and while some attempts have recently been made, these are rather timid, indirect and incoherent. Whether it is the unwillingness of treaty drafters to incorporate human rights provisions often perceived as detrimental to trade, or the reluctance of arbitrators to go beyond the letter of the law and interpret agreements in conjunction with general international norms and principles, the debate has occupied legal scholars for some time, but has not produced much change in legislation and jurisprudence. Interestingly, this apparent contradiction between international law branches could easily be resolved with a political and economic will to read the law from a holistic perspective, making use of its many flexibilities. Human rights are indeed at the core of international economic activity, even if not yet acknowledged as such by IEL.

A Negative Approach

A first general observation of the architecture of IEL shows that human rights, if ever taken into consideration, are approached negatively or by default. They are never put at the centre of the edifice, but voluntarily placed and maintained at the margin. They are exceptions to the main body of rules, for example, with the GATT 1994, Article XX, or investment treaties flexibilities and de facto exceptions or reservations.

In a WTO context, for example, these provisions are quite strangely referred to as 'non-trade concerns' (NTC) – as if, for example, the issue of labour in the global supply chain was not 'concerned' with trade and vice versa. The term itself is problematic. Why is the environment or gender equality a 'concern' and not simply a reality or, even better, an opportunity? Why are they not treated as rights, as in general international law? These 'concerns' appeared in relation to the interpretation of the WTO Agreement on Agriculture (AoA), which is said to be flexible enough to provide for the protection of food security, rural development, poverty alleviation and the environment.[1] In this context, the 'multifunctionality' of agriculture

---

[1] WTO, 'Non-trade' concerns: agriculture can serve many purposes, available at www.wto.org/english/tratop_e/agric_e/negs_bkgrnd17_agri_e.htm (accessed 21 December 2020).

already addressed by the OECD in its March 1998 communiqué was stressed by the WTO itself on the basis of the Agreement on Agriculture Preamble:

Noting that commitments under the reform programme should be made in an equitable way among all Members, having regard to non-trade concerns, including food security and the need to protect the environment; having regard to the agreement that special and differential treatment for developing countries is an integral element of the negotiations, and taking into account the possible negative effects of the implementation of the reform programme on least-developed and net food-importing developing countries.

The absence of a clear definition of what could be an NTC added to the confusion, along with developing countries' fear of seeing their trade policies impeded by externally imposed 'Western' values and standards. Developing and, to a lesser extent, emerging economies have traditionally associated their global attractiveness with a rather loose normative framework of protection for labour and the environment, hence creating a comparative advantage in trade. In addition, recent cases, such as the 'seal dispute' have reactivated the debate on the basis of the interpretation of the GATT 1994, Article XX (General Exceptions) and the protection of public morals (Article XX(a)), and indigenous communities' (Inuit) rights in particular (see Chapter 9). Yet no consensus could be achieved in treaty drafting or case law on the very coverage of NTC.

Keeping this in mind, one can also expand the same sort of non-definition to analyse the greater inclusion of non-investment concerns (NIC) in international investment treaties and today's megaregional deals, which encompass a broad vision of trade. The following elements could be considered as falling under the banner of NIC: the right to regulate – despite its many and problematic meanings – human rights, development, labour, CSR, the environment and anti-corruption. While certainly subjective, this list is based on today's most recurring treaty practices, responding, even timidly, to pressing 'societal' challenges that treaty drafters and adjudicators do not yet dare to formulate in a rights or, more precisely, human rights language. No matter their definition or the absence of the same, NTC/NIC are not generally accepted.

These views have only been reinforced by the technicalisation and strategic division of international law in many subdisciplines eventually read in isolation to meet short-term policy objectives. However, as analysed below, a number of human rights are key to IEL, even if not fully addressed by it.

Property: IEL Ambiguities Reflected

Since Article 17 of the 1789 French Declaration of the Rights of Man and Citizen, property has been a cornerstone in the liberal conception of international law and, by contrast, an obstacle to the socialist approach. The wording of the 1789 Declaration could easily be mistaken for twentieth-century investor-friendly BITs: 'Property being an inviolable and sacred right, no one may be deprived of it except when public necessity, as attested in law, manifestly requires it, and on condition of just compensation payable in advance'. IIL and dispute resolution can therefore be analysed as property-focused, with a vast majority of issues revolving around the concept of expropriation (see Chapters 11 and 12). International trade law, with the TRIPS Agreement also gives property a central space (see Chapter 7). But despite its general doctrinal importance, property remains ambiguously addressed by IEL, as it relies greatly on the protection of domestic law rather than on additional international obligations, as if IEL was only supporting domestic law's architecture with general international law mechanisms such as diplomatic protection. This ambiguity has much to do with the hesitation of general international law to treat property as a human right. Article 17 of the Universal Declaration of Human Rights offers rather limited coverage.

Universal Declaration of Human Rights, Article 17

(1) Everyone has the right to own property alone as well as in association with others.
(2) No one shall be arbitrarily deprived of his property.

But property was included in the Universal Declaration of Human Rights draft at a time when tensions between the Western and Eastern blocs were not yet at their peak. A few decades later, property could not be integrated into the 1966 International Covenant on Civil and Political Rights and the International Covenant on Economic Social and Cultural Rights, for the doctrinal divide between the liberals and the socialists was too deep. From a socialist angle, indeed, protecting property is equal to giving more to the haves, to the detriment of the have-nots. It is seen as a bourgeois right, a pillar of capitalism based on people's exploitation, something to overcome. One had to wait for more daring regional instruments, adopted in the wake of declining socialism, to acknowledge property as a human right, such as the 1986 African Charter on Human and Peoples' Rights (Article 14) or the 1978 American Convention on Human Rights (Article 21).

American Convention on Human Rights, Article 21: Right to Property

1. Everyone has the right to the use and enjoyment of his property. The law may subordinate such use and enjoyment to the interest of society.
2. No one shall be deprived of his property except upon payment of just compensation, for reasons of public utility or social interest, and in the cases and according to the forms established by law.
3. Usury and any other form of exploitation of man by man shall be prohibited by law.

In addition, international instruments on the right of indigenous peoples and the 2007 UN Declaration (UNGA Resolution 61/295) progressively linked land (property) rights and human rights to better protect marginalised indigenous populations.

General Assembly Resolution 61/295: UN Declaration on the Rights of Indigenous Peoples (13 September 2007)

Article 25

Indigenous peoples have the right to maintain and strengthen their distinctive spiritual relationship with their traditionally owned or otherwise occupied and used lands, territories, waters and coastal seas and other resources and to uphold their responsibilities to future generations in this regard.

Article 26

1. Indigenous peoples have the right to the lands, territories and resources which they have traditionally owned, occupied or otherwise used or acquired.
2. Indigenous peoples have the right to own, use, develop and control the lands, territories and resources that they possess by reason of traditional ownership or other traditional occupation or use, as well as those which they have otherwise acquired.
3. States shall give legal recognition and protection to these lands, territories and resources. Such recognition shall be conducted with due respect to the customs, traditions and land tenure systems of the indigenous peoples concerned.

From the angle of indigenous right protection, the right to property is not seen as a liability to social progress anymore, but rather as the key to independence. The rights of the powerless and marginalised can hence be fostered as included in an international law and international economic law architecture. The same objective to defragment international law fields is shared by the United Nations Guiding Principles on Business and Human Rights, endorsed by the Human Rights Council in June 2011, the implementation of which is supported by the UN Working Group on Business and Human Rights.[2] The 2014 Principles for Responsible Investment in Agriculture and Food Systems (RAI) echo the same ideas (see Chapter 11). However, ambiguities and contestations remain when addressing property right as illustrated by the controversies surrounding intellectual property and traditional knowledge (see Chapter 7).

---

[2] Office of the High Commissioner for Human Rights, *Guiding Principles on Business and Human Rights: Implementing the United Nations 'Protect, Respect and Remedy' Framework* (New York and Geneva: United Nations, 2011), available at www.ohchr.org/Documents/Publications/GuidingPrinciplesBusinessHR_EN.pdf (accessed 21 December 2020).

Rights and Rights Holders

Human rights are universal, indivisible, inalienable, interdependent and interrelated, as emphasised by the 1948 Universal Declaration and reiterated numerous times since its adoption, with the 1993 Vienna World Conference in particular.[3] One cannot choose one right and neglect another. Virtually all human rights interact with IEL. But a few have taken on greater importance in recent practice and debates, as demonstrated below.

The Right to Water and Sanitation

On 28 July 2010, with Resolution 64/292, the UN General Assembly recognised the human right to water and sanitation. It also acknowledged that clean drinking water and sanitation are essential to the realisation of all human rights, thus stressing the interrelatedness of all human rights. This was furthered, in November 2002, by General Comment No. 15 by the Committee on Economic, Social and Cultural Rights, on the right to water, defined as follows:[4]

> ## *OHCHR, General Comment No. 15: The Right to Water (Arts. 11 and 12 of the Covenant)*
>
> 2. The human right to water entitles everyone to sufficient, safe, acceptable, physically accessible and affordable water for personal and domestic uses. An adequate amount of safe water is necessary to prevent death from dehydration, to reduce the risk of water-related disease and to provide for consumption, cooking, personal and domestic hygienic requirements.
>   [...]
> 3. The right should also be seen in conjunction with other rights enshrined in the International Bill of Human Rights, foremost amongst them the right to life and human dignity.

Each and every term is important (sufficient, safe, acceptable, physically accessible and affordable). In interpreting the right to water in conjunction with other fundamental human rights, the Committee set the tone for the developments to come during the next decade, along with the progressive recognition by States, but also non-State actors, such as

---

[3] UN OHCHR, Vienna Declaration and Programme of Action (adopted by the World Conference on Human Rights in Vienna on 25 June 1993), available at www.ohchr.org/en/professionalinterest/pages/vienna.aspx (accessed 21 December 2020).

[4] *See* Resolution A/RES/64/292. United Nations General Assembly, July 2010 available at https://undocs.org/en/A/RES/64/292 and General Comment No. 15, at: *The Right to Water. UN Committee on Economic, Social and Cultural Rights, November 2002*, www.refworld.org/docid/4538838d11.html.

multinational corporations, of water (and then sanitation) as a human right. As a logical development, the UN stressed the presence of the State's obligation to realise people's access to safe drinking water and sanitation in a wide variety of international human rights treaties, such as the 1979 Convention on the Elimination of All Forms of Discrimination against Women, the 1985 International Labour Organization Convention No. 161 on Occupational Health Services, the 1989 Convention on the Rights of the Child and a vast number of regional human rights instruments, which sometimes contain direct human rights obligations related to access to safe drinking water and sanitation, such as the 1990 African Charter on the Rights and Welfare of the Child or the 2004 Arab Charter on Human Rights. Not to mention that a number of Constitutions (DRC, Ecuador, Kenya, South Africa, Uganda, Uruguay) explicitly refer to the right to water and sanitation, while others suggest a general obligation to be fulfilled by the State.[5]

When understood in an IEL context, the right to water refers to the quality of services provided by the State, which is responsible for the protection and implementation of human rights, as well as private companies, which should respect them.[6] Numerous investment law cases have dealt with the right to water. In this perspective, the following cases provide a useful insight into the use (or not) by the host State of the human right to water as a defence argument to justify contested measures, and also into some of the procedural developments alluded to above, with third-party intervention in the form of *amicus* brief submissions, as well as the reluctance (or not) of arbitrators to venture into the human rights arena while favouring other fields of law deemed more directly relevant (see Chapter 10): *Compañía de Aguas del Aconquija S.A. and Vivendi Universal S.A.* v. *Argentine Republic*;[7] *Suez, Sociedad General de Aguas de Barcelona S.A. and InterAguas Servicios Integrales del Agua S.A.* v. *Argentine Republic*;[8] *SAUR International S.A.* v. *Republic of Argentina*;[9] *Aguas del Tunari, S.A.* v. *Republic of Bolivia*;[10] and *Biwater Gauff* v. *Tanzania*.[11]

---

[5] See the studies produced by Office of the United Nations High Commissioner for Human Rights for easy access to constitutional and legislative developments, available at www2.ohchr.org/english/issues/water/contributions.htm (accessed 21 December 2020).

[6] Leïla Choukroune, 'Water and Sanitation Services in International Trade and Investment Law: For a Holistic Human Rights Based Approach', in Julien Chaisse (ed.), *The Regulation of the Global Water Services Market* (Cambridge University Press, 2016), pp. 196–219.

[7] *Compañía de Aguas del Aconquija S.A. and Vivendi Universal S.A.* v. *Argentine Republic*, ICSID Case No. ABR/97/3, available at www.italaw.com/cases/309 (accessed 21 December 2020).

[8] *Suez, Sociedad General de Aguas de Barcelona S.A. and InterAguas Servicios Integrales del Agua S.A.* v. *Argentine Republic*, ICSID Case No. ARB/03/17, available at www.italaw.com/cases/1048 (accessed 21 December 2020).

[9] *SAUR International S.A.* v. *Republic of Argentina*, ICSID Case No. ARB/04/4, available at www.italaw.com/cases/1456 (accessed 21 December 2020).

[10] *Aguas del Tunari, S.A.* v. *Republic of Bolivia*, ICSID Case No. ARB/02/3, available at www.italaw.com/cases/57 (accessed 21 December 2020).

[11] *Biwater Gauff (Tanzania) Ltd* v. *United Republic of Tanzania*, ICSID Case No. ARB/05/22, available at www.italaw.com/cases/157 (accessed 21 December 2020).

The Right to Food

The 'right to adequate food' is understood in relation with the possibility of living a life with dignity. It is realised when, as defined by the Committee on Economic Social and Cultural Rights, General Comment No. 12: 'every man, woman and child, alone or in community with others, has the physical and economic access at all times to adequate food or means for its procurement'.[12]

Malnutrition still affects 820 million people according to the Food and Agriculture Organisation.[13] While for decades the number of hungry people in the world has been declining, this is no longer true. From food insecurity to malnutrition, including obesity, challenges are immense and directly related to IEL, and the question of trade in agricultural products in particular (see Chapter 3).

The Right to Health

Another human right playing a central role in IEL, with related trade (TRIPS and access to medicine) and investment cases (*Phillip Morris*, for example), is the right to health. It has attained even greater visibility with the recent Covid-19 pandemic. The 1946 WHO envisaged already the 'highest attainable standard of health as a fundamental right of every human being'.[14] The right to health is naturally multifaceted and includes the concept of well-being. It is a legal obligation for States, to be realised progressively through the allocation of 'maximum available resources'. It includes freedoms (for example, sexual and reproductive rights, as well as the right to refuse treatment) and entitlements (access to health). It is also based, like other human rights, on core principles, such as accountability, equality and non-discrimination, and participation in particular. As defined in General Comment 14 of the Committee on Economic, Social and Cultural Rights, the right to health depends on certain conditions prevailing in a given State party: availability, accessibility, acceptability and quality.[15]

Gender

Also at the centre of today's IEL debates is the question of gender. IEL and international law are not gender-neutral. To correct inequalities of treatment and opportunities in trade and investment for women in particular, the WTO and a number of international

---

[12] CESCR General Comment No. 12: The Right to Adequate Food (Art. 11), available at www.refworld.org/docid/4538838c11.html (accessed 21 December 2020).

[13] FAO, The State of Food Security and Nutrition in the World, available at www.fao.org/state-of-food-security-nutrition/en/ (accessed 21 December 2020).

[14] WHO, Human rights and health, Key facts, available at www.who.int/news-room/fact-sheets/detail/human-rights-and-health (accessed 21 December 2020).

[15] CESCR General Comment No. 14: The Right to the Highest Attainable Standard of Health (Art. 12), available at www.refworld.org/pdfid/4538838d0.pdf (accessed 21 December 2020).

organisations like UNCTAD have engaged with the issue of gender. In December 2017, the Joint Declaration on Trade and Women's Economic Empowerment, adopted at the WTO Ministerial Conference in Buenos Aires, acknowledged 'the importance of incorporating a gender perspective into the promotion of inclusive economic growth, and the key role that gender-responsive policies can play in achieving sustainable socioeconomic development'. It was adopted in relation to the Goal 5 of the SDGs in the United Nations 2030 Agenda for Sustainable Development (Gender equality and women's empowerment). This Declaration echoes the International Covenant on Economic Social and Cultural Rights, Article 3, which provides for the right to equality between men and women in the enjoyment of all rights, and the Convention on the Elimination of All Forms of Discrimination against Women. Gender equality and neutrality in trade has now been integrated in a number of treaties. According to the WTO, in 2018, thirty-four agreements included provisions refer-ring to gender equality and women's participation.[16] Interestingly, Africa led the change, with Treaty of the Economic Community of West African States signed in 1993, which was the first RTA negotiated by developing countries with an article dedicated to 'Women and development'.

Development as a Right

As discussed in our Chapter 16, development has been considered a right. The concept of the right to development has indeed informed the discussions of the international community since the 1980s, and in particular since the adoption of the UN General Assembly Resolution 41/128 on 4 December 1986. Indeed, it was first recognised in 1981 in Article 22(1) of the African Charter on Human and Peoples' Rights, which provides that 'All peoples shall have the right to their economic, social and cultural development with due regard to their freedom and identity and in the equal enjoyment of the common heritage of mankind'.[17]

From a Negative Perspective to a Holistic Approach

Jus cogens, 'systemic integration' and references to Article 31(3)(c) of the VCLT are supposed to provide drafters and judges with solutions in favour of a pluralistic and integrative vision of international law and the integration of NTC in trade law.

Unfortunately, this is not enough. To address these pressing challenges, and indeed reconcile trade objectives with other imperatives of State policies, recent treaties have

---

[16] J.-A. Monteiro, 'Gender-Related Provisions in Regional Trade Agreements', Staff Working Paper ERSD-2018-15 (WTO, Economic Research and Statistics Division, 18 December 2018), available at www.wto.org/english/res_e/reser_e/ersd201815_e.pdf (accessed 21 December 2020).

[17] See www.achpr.org/legalinstruments/detail?id=49 (accessed 21 December 2020).

adopted a language of rights, if not yet binding norms. The trend started in the US and Canada in the late 1980s, for example, with the inclusion of labour issues in the US GSP and the adoption of the North American Agreement on Labour Cooperation, the side agreement to the 1994 NAFTA. Since around 2010, labour, gender, the environment, CSR and, to a lesser extent, human rights defined per se, are quite universally incorporated in the new generation of trade treaties, be it in their preambles or in more precise special provisions.[18] So much so that the EU, for instance, prides itself on the development of what it defines as a 'Human Rights Clause', which often covers democratic principles and the rule of law envisaged as a way to engage in a constructive dialogue with trade partners, but also to enable the taking of specific measures in response to serious treaty breaches – that is, the suspension of trade preferences.[19] This has yet to be seen. The integration of a 'Human Rights Clause' has as much to do with a response to European civil society's quest for State accountability as it has with a genuine defence of rights.[20]

Shifting the gaze would rather consist of adopting a human rights-based approach to IEL. In this regard, the UN Statement of Common Understanding on Human Rights-Based Approaches to Development Cooperation and Programming (the Common Understanding), adopted by the United Nations Development Group in 2003, provides an interesting first definition (having in mind that the objective of the UN was that of harmonisation between its many agencies).[21] The perspective is pragmatic, allowing simple

---

[18] For an interesting historical perspective on the incorporation of labour in trade treaties, see for example, F. Ebert and A. Posthuma, *Labour Provisions in Trade Arrangements: Current Trends and Perspectives* (Geneva: ILO, 2011), available at www.researchgate.net/publication/263734653_Labour_provisions_in_trade_arrangements_current_trends_and_perspectives; see also US Congressional Research Service, 'Labour Enforcement Issues in US FTAs', *In Focus* (updated 2 March 2020), available at https://fas.org/sgp/crs/row/IF10972.pdf (both accessed 21 December 2020).

[19] European Parliament Think Tank, 'Human Rights in EU Trade Agreements: The Human Rights Clause and its Application' (8 July 2019), available at www.europarl.europa.eu/thinktank/en/document.html?reference=EPRS_BRI(2019)637975 (accessed 21 December 2020).

[20] Leïla Choukroune, 'The Concern with Non-Concerns: For the End of Trade Dystopia', in M. K. Lewis, J. Nakagawa, R. J. Neuwirth et al. (eds.), *A Post-WTO International Legal Order: Utopian, Dystopian and Other Scenarios* (Cham, Switzerland: Springer, 2020), pp. 207–20.

[21] HRBA Portal, The Human Rights Based Approach to Development Cooperation: Towards a Common Understanding Among UN Agencies, available at https://hrbaportal.undg.org/the-human-rights-based-approach-to-development-cooperation-towards-a-common-understanding-among-un-agencies (accessed 21 December 2020). The Common Understanding is described as follows:

> All programmes of development co-operation, policies and technical assistance should further the realization of human rights as laid down in the Universal Declaration of Human Rights and other international human rights instruments.
>
> Human rights standards contained in, and principles derived from, the Universal Declaration of Human Rights and other international human rights instruments guide all development cooperation and programming in all sectors and in all phases of the programming process.
>
> Development cooperation contributes to the development of the capacities of 'duty-bearers' to meet their obligations and/or of 'rights-holders' to claim their rights.

integration of these human rights principles into the concrete work of UN agencies, based on fundamental concepts: universality and inalienability; indivisibility; interdependence and inter-relatedness; non-discrimination and equality; participation and inclusion; accountability and the rule of law. This human rights-based approach will not necessarily resolve difficult economic or social equations, for developing States in particular, but in expressly linking economic situations to rights, it provides a basic conceptual framework for negotiations with domestic and foreign private actors, enables the public to participate in decision-making and fosters State accountability. In doing so, it also departs from, as much as it renews the traditional international trade and investment approach often confined to risk prevention and remediation or exception justification.

Mini Chapter 2 New Architecture of Trade Agreements

At a time of 'mega-trade deals' negotiations, the architecture of trade agreements is evolving towards a much more complex structure. For well over the last decade, mega-regional trade agreements have been identified as an alternative to the Doha Development Round and overcoming the challenges of multilateral trade negotiations. The CETA, signed in 2016, and the CPTPP, concluded in 2018 by a group of Pacific Rim nations, are illustrations of this trend. Other examples include the African Continental Free Trade Area, which entered into force in May 2019, and the Regional Comprehensive Economic Partnership, signed by fifteen Asia-Pacific countries. In other words, 'mega-trade deals' exemplify the trend towards a new form of regionalism.

Regionalism is not a new phenomenon. It has been supported by the GATT and the WTO as a way to deepen multilateralism. The GATT Article XXIV, and the GATS Article V, along with the 2006 General Council Decision on the Transparency Mechanism for Regional Trade Agreements, facilitate the WTO Members' participation in RTAs. WTO members have to notify their participation in RTAs to the WTO. But their numbers have literally exploded since 2010. As of January 2020, 303 RTAs were in force.[1]

The multiplication and evolution of these deals becomes important, as they tend to address new concerns, in particular the impact of trade on human rights, labour standards and environmental regulations, among other issues. These mega-regional agreements go beyond the WTO and could complement the global trade system. Yet they also pose a number of challenges in terms of integration, regulatory harmonisation and dispute settlement. However, these agreements have used new templates, embraced new issues and developed innovative and pragmatic means of negotiation.

Trade agreements have traditionally displayed tariff reduction and tariff elimination goals, with occasional focus on regulating or disciplining non-tariff measures. The WTO Agreement was significantly novel, since it introduced new topics such as agriculture, trade in services and intellectual property rights, in addition to detailed agreements on various aspects of trade in goods. Nevertheless, a number of issues, such as investment, taxation (especially direct taxation), competition and currency practices were outside the scope of this multilateral framework.

---

[1] WTO, Regional trade agreements, available at www.wto.org/english/tratop_e/region_e/region_e.htm#facts (accessed 21 December 2020).

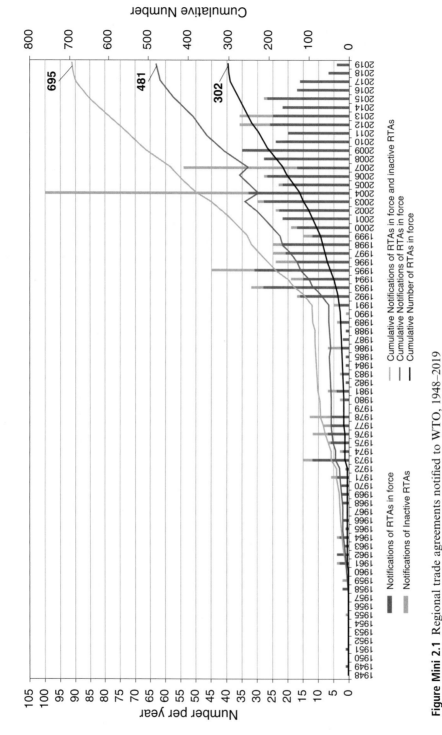

Figure Mini 2.1 Regional trade agreements notified to WTO, 1948–2019

Source: WTO Secretariat, RTA Section, September 2019. http://rtais.wto.org/UI/PublicMaintainRTAHome.aspx

Notifications of RTAs: goods, services and accessions to an RTA are counted separately. The cumulative lines show the number of RTAs/ notifications of RTAs that were in force for a given year. The notifications of RTAs in force are shown by year of entry into force, and the notifications of inactive RTAs are shown by inactive year.

In a way, the trendsetter for deeper liberalisation and market integration was not the WTO Agreement or its predecessor, the GATT 1947 (see Chapter 1), but European integration. The Coal and Steel Community was the first to be set up by virtue of the Treaty of Paris in 1951, followed by the Economic Community and an Atomic Energy Community (Treaties of Rome, 1957). After the creation of the European Economic Community, the first step was to foster economic cooperation between countries that traded with one another and were economically interdependent. Under the Single European Act (1986), the Communities finally dismantled all internal borders to establish a single market.[2] The Treaty on European Union, signed in Maastricht in 1992, created a European Union, combining a Community moving towards economic and monetary union with intergovernmental cooperation in certain areas. Following the entry into force of the Treaty of Lisbon on 1 December 2009, the European Union now has a legal personality and has acquired the competences previously conferred on the European Community. Community law has therefore become European Union law, which also includes all the provisions previously adopted under the Treaty on European Union, as applicable before the Treaty of Lisbon. Before the enactment of the Treaty of Lisbon in 2009, there were two treaties governing the EU – the Treaty establishing the European Community and the Treaty on European Union. The Treaty of Lisbon does not constitute a third treaty; rather, it amends both the existing Treaties.

At present, the EU is a single customs union, with a membership of twenty-seven countries (after Brexit) and a single trade policy and external tariff. The United Kingdom exiting the European Union highlighted the issues present in this form of integration, where it is difficult to balance the policy space of individual countries or members with the larger objectives of the integrated region. Brexit also poses questions about the political sustainability of deep integration agreements, which seek to liberalise, among other things, goods, services, capital and labour, in addition to harmonisation in regulatory approaches and monetary policy.

The other trendsetter was the NAFTA, concluded between the United States, Canada and Mexico that was concluded in 1992. The NAFTA provided an advanced template for trade negotiations. In fact, the NAFTA was the crucible for developing the 'new' trade policy agenda that the United States had been seeking to achieve in the multilateral arena. For example, the United States drove its intentions to include topics such as labour, the environment and innovative rules of origin under the NAFTA. In 2019, the upgraded version of the NAFTA, also known as the United States–Mexico–Canada Agreement, was finally negotiated and brought into force.[3] This agreement also comprehensively covers the issues of labour, environmental standards, intellectual property protections and digital trade.

---

[2] P. Craig and G. D. Búrca, *EU Law, Text, Cases and Materials*, 6th ed. (Oxford University Press, 2015), p. 6; P. Craig, 'The Evolution of the Single Market', in C. Barnard and J. Scott (eds.), *The Law of the Single European Market: Unpacking the Premises* (London: Bloomsbury, 2002), p. 2.

[3] Office of the US Trade Representative, Executive Office of the President, Agreement between the United States of America, the United Mexican States, and Canada 7/1/20 Text, available at https://ustr.gov/trade-agreements/free-trade-agreements/united-states-mexico-canada-agreement/agreement-between (accessed 21 December 2020).

The 1990s and the early 2000s also saw the emergence of regional arrangements in Africa, Latin America and Asia.[4] These are, mainly, the Common Market for Eastern and Southern Africa (COMESA), the East African Community (EAC), the South African Development Community (SADC), the Southern Common Market (MERCOSUR) and the ASEAN Free Trade Area (AFTA). These agreements were negotiated to suit the trade interests and economic development of these particular regions. These agreements pushed trade interests beyond reductions in tariffs and non-tariff barriers into deeper policy integration.

From the above it is evident that the newer trade agreements have witnessed a sea change in their architecture, scope and coverage. The changes include, for example, targeted preferential rules of origin of goods or a carefully calibrated definition of a 'juridical person', essentially in respect of services or investment, to ensure that the FTA benefits are limited only to the partner countries. In addition, the goods coverage of such agreements are subjected to certain exclusions or carve-outs. In relation to services, most FTAs use either a GATS-type positive list or, more increasingly, a negative list, and sometimes a hybrid of both the lists.

Plurilateral Approaches

The WTO Agreement was built on the concept of a 'single undertaking', which meant that nothing was agreed until everything was agreed. Article II.3 of the Marrakesh Agreement refers to a category of agreements included in Annex 4 to which not all WTO members may be parties. In other words, plurilateral agreements are binding only on those members that have accepted them. In other words, the conclusion of an Annex 4-type plurilateral agreement between or among certain members cannot alter or affect the obligations of other WTO members. At the same time, the benefits of such an agreement need not be applied to the entire membership.

There are only two such plurilateral agreements currently in force: the Agreement on Trade in Civil Aircraft and the Agreement on Government Procurement. However, plurilateral approaches have increasingly been suggested to overcome the stalemate commonly associated with multilateral approaches. At the 8th Ministerial Conference held in Geneva in 2011, the relevance of plurilaterals was also discussed in the context of the Doha Round negotiations. Several members, especially developing countries, opposed a formal endorsement of plurilateral approaches. One of the major achievements of the Uruguay Round was the adoption of the single undertaking approach, which rejected the GATT à la carte

---

[4] For a detailed discussion on agreements relating to Africa, see J. T. Gathii, 'Introduction', in *African Regional Trade Agreements as Legal Regimes* (Cambridge University Press, 2011); for Latin America's trade agreements, see B. Harper, 'Chart: Regional Trade Agreements in the Americas' (AS/COA, 17 October 2018), available at www.as-coa.org/articles/chart-regional-trade-agreements-americas (accessed 21 December 2020); for Asia's trade agreements, see M. Kawai and G. Wignaraja, *Asia's Free Trade Agreements: How Is Business Responding?* (Cheltenham: Edward Elgar, 2011).

approach, where contracting parties had the opportunity to choose trade agreements most beneficial to their interests. Most of the Tokyo Round (1974–79) Agreements, popularly known as 'Tokyo Codes' reflected this concept. The danger with this approach or concept is that trade agreements would fail to secure a meaningful balance between various interests among its signatories, and the weaker countries might be left with limited bargaining power or a limited role in rule-making.

The following section focuses on the negotiation approach adopted in such mega-trade agreements.

Exclusion List or Negative List

The purpose of FTAs or economic integration agreements is to eliminate or reduce tariffs or other restrictive regulations of commerce on most products. Also, these agreements provide different types of flexibilities to the parties for achieving deeper integration. In certain agreements, different tracks for product liberalisation are envisaged. Some of the commonly used tracks include normal track, sensitive track, highly sensitive track or the most sensitive track. The India–ASEAN FTA has provided for such multiple tracks of liberalisation for phasing out of tariffs. The most sensitive track is also referred to as the 'exclusion list', where a party may not undertake any tariff or other concessions. For example, under the India–ASEAN FTA, India did not offer tariff concessions on around 1,297 lines at the HS-8 digits level. However, the most sensitive or tariff exclusion lines were kept to a minimum in light of the overall trade liberalising objectives of these agreements. The RCEP also followed a similar approach for phasing out tariffs based on various tracks.

Positive List versus Negative List in Services

The agreements or chapters on trade in services comprise the text and the schedule of specific commitments. The text provides for the substantive obligations, while the schedule enumerates the sectors in which a party agrees to take commitments or the sectors/measures that are non-conforming with the obligations, stated in the agreement or chapter. There are two approaches for listing the commitments, namely the positive list and the negative list. Under the positive list, a party agrees to take commitments in the sectors or modes of trade in which a party has reasonable comfort in assuming trade obligations. It is also known as a 'bottom-up' approach. On the contrary, the negative list schedule contains all the measures that do not conform with the obligations under the main text of the agreement or chapter. In other words, the non-conforming measures pertaining to the specific service sectors need to be scheduled. There is a presumption that everything is liberalised unless specifically scheduled and excluded.

The positive list approach was followed under WTO members' Schedules of Specific Commitments under GATS, and subsequently adopted by a substantial number of WTO members (mainly developing and least developed countries) in their RTAs; the negative list emanates from the NAFTA-style approach. Under the NAFTA, the parties had to list only those sectors or subsectors that they wanted to limit or exclude by inscribing reservations for measures. Such exclusions were required if a party wanted to maintain a measure that might run counter to market access, the NT principle or any other trade obligations.

The negative list approach in services opens up all service sectors to obligations, for example, market access, national treatment, senior management and local presence, with the exception of enlisted non-conforming measures. There are two lists of non-conforming measures: (1) existing measures (usually under an Annex of non-conforming measures); and (2) future measures (usually under a different Annex of non-conforming measures). The measures under the first category are existing and non-conforming with the core obligations as on the date of the enforcement of the agreement. On the other hand, the measures under the second category are those measures in which a party reserves its policy space to enact restrictive regulations in the future. For instance, the US–Morocco FTA, which entered into force in 2006, has listed several non-conforming measures in the schedules. Non-conforming measures, which do not comply with the obligations of liberalisation, form the basis of future negotiations. Other elements that are inherent to the negative list approach are the concepts of 'standstill' and 'ratchet'.

Standstill Clause

A standstill clause is a mechanism through which the parties commit to keep the market at least as open as it was as at the time of the agreement. In other words, the parties agree not to take reservations for future measures. In practice, it means that, after the conclusion of a trade agreement, if a party decides to further open up its market and subsequently decides to fall back to a more trade restrictive framework, that framework should never fall below the level of openness committed to in the agreement.

Ratchet Clause

A ratchet clause is a mechanism through which the parties consent to a future unilateral decision to further open up their respective markets in one specific sector, where such opening would be 'locked in'. In other words, a party's trade commitments always need to reflect its existing level of openness.

An advantage of the ratchet clause is that trade commitments reflect the existing level of liberalisation. A ratchet clause also ensures that a free trade agreement is forward-looking. On the flip side, once a country has agreed to a ratchet clause, it would lose whatever policy flexibility it had in that sector. It could also discourage a country from undertaking unilateral or autonomous liberalisation.

Notwithstanding the above view, whenever parties have opened up a sector, be it through a positive or negative list, the parties retain their right to maintain or introduce non-discriminatory legislation. This is true even if the parties have agreed to include ratchet or standstill clauses. For example, regulatory requirements such as licensing or qualifications, or other prudential norms such as minimum capital requirements, or universal services obligations for public utility services such as telecom, postal or education, can still be maintained.

Hybrid List Approach

Countries often use hybrid approaches to inscribe commitments under the schedules. This includes the use of both positive and negative listing approaches for different sectors of service. It is understood that such a form of listing is less ambitious than the NAFTA-style approach of negative listing when scheduling services commitments. The FTAs signed by Singapore with the US[5] and Panama[6] have adopted a negative listing style, except for financial services, for which a positive list is adopted. The Trade in Services Agreement, negotiated by a few Members of the WTO, has also followed a hybrid approach.[7] This approach may also be seen in the RCEP agreement, where members have opted to use a mix of both positive and negative styles of listing for their services commitments. This approach allows the parties to incorporate the advantages of negative listing without compromising regulatory sovereignty.[8]

Certain trade agreements also include denial of benefits clauses in areas such as trade in services, investment or intellectual property rights. This clause allows parties under a trade agreement to deny the benefits of the agreement to a service supplier that is not owned or controlled by the nationals of the other party to such agreement. It can also be used in situations, for example, where an investor does not comply with the applicable laws and regulations of the domestic jurisdiction. In such cases, the benefits of the treaty can be denied to such an investor.

Side Letters

Side letters are bilateral instruments that enable two parties to a multi-party agreement to include special provisions relating to the relationship inter se without the need for other parties of the agreement to negotiate or agree to the contents of the side letter. The said two parties could mutually and bilaterally agree any departure (added obligation or reservation) from the standard obligation(s) of the agreement affecting the critical area. For example, in

---

[5] Singapore–USA FTA, entered into force 1 January 2004.

[6] Singapore–Panama FTA, entered into force 25 July 2006.

[7] European Commission, *Trade in Services Agreement (TiSA): Factsheet* (26 September 2016), available at https://trade.ec.europa.eu/doclib/docs/2016/september/tradoc_154971.doc.pdf (accessed 21 December 2020).

[8] Jane Kelsey, 'RCEP Services Chapter: Risks for Developing Countries' and LDCs' Policy Space and Regulatory Sovereignty' (4 August 2016), ch. 2, available at www.bilaterals.org/?rcep-services-chapter-risks-for&lang=fr (accessed 21 December 2020).

New Zealand's side letters with five CPTPP parties, these parties mutually agree not to initiate compulsory ISDS, as provided under Chapter 28 of the CPTPP. The remaining CPTPP parties can still invoke the ISDS provisions.[9]

Side letters are used in trade agreements in three main ways: (1) to provide additional clarification on how a particular provision of the agreement will apply to either of the parties to the FTA; (2) where either of the parties to the FTA wishes to make additional commitments that apply only to that country, as part of the overall agreement; and (3) where either of the parties to the FTA wishes to confirm to the other country how its current policies or systems operate.

In the context of the CPTPP, side letters have been exchanged on the date of signing of the CPTPP. Several side letters have been exchanged and accepted by all the parties to the CPTPP. Such side letters could be argued to qualify as an agreement relating to the treaty that was made between all the parties in connection with the conclusion of the treaty.[10] It is common practice to regard a treaty as concluded when it is signed.[11] As a result, these side letters could be used to interpret the commitments of a party to the FTA.

Side letters can also be regarded as a subsequent development of an FTA, if exchanged after the conclusion of the treaty.[12] According to Article 31(3)(a) of the VCLT, they may be considered as 'subsequent agreement' between the parties regarding the interpretation of the treaty or the application of its provisions. The agreement does not have to be part of the treaty, or be a treaty itself, but it must be a clear expression of the intention of the parties.[13] For instance, Article 2.4.4 of the CPTPP allows for agreement relating to bilateral modifications of a party's tariff concessions. Such agreements, concluded after the entry into force of the treaty, may be regarded as 'subsequent agreements' for the purposes of treaty interpretation.

Pursuant to Article 41 of the VCLT, two parties to a multilateral treaty may conclude an agreement to modify the treaty as between themselves alone if the modification in question is not prohibited by the treaty and does not affect the enjoyment by the other parties of their treaty rights or performance, or does not relate to a provision, derogation from which is incompatible with the effective implementation of the object and purpose of the treaty as a whole.[14] However, it is to be noted that the legal validity of side letters is yet to be tested. It is possible for an FTA party or non-FTA party to challenge side letters (providing differential tariff concessions) as inconsistent with the GATT MFN obligation. This would be because the GATT Article XXIV permits derogation from the WTO obligations only to the extent necessary for the formation of the FTA/RTA.[15]

---

[9] New Zealand has signed side letters with five members of the CPTPP – Brunei Darussalam, Malaysia, Peru, Vietnam and Australia – to exclude compulsory ISDS.

[10] VCLT 1969, Art. 31(2).   [11] R. Gardiner, *Treaty Interpretation* (Oxford University Press, 2015), p. 292.

[12] P. Xiong, *An International Law Perspective on the Protection of Human Rights in the TRIPS Agreement* (Leiden: Martinus Nijhoff, 2012), p. 324.

[13] A. Aust, *Modern Treaty Law and Practice* (Cambridge University Press, 2000), p. 189.   [14] VCLT 1969, Art. 41.

[15] Appellate Body Report, *Turkey – Textiles*, paras. 42–52.

Conclusion

Modern trade agreements are not purely trade liberalisation agreements. These agreements seek to achieve the goals of regulatory harmonisation and market integration. However, trade agreements also reflect the varying levels of diversity and the sensitivities of the domestic industry or the consumers. Accordingly, trade agreements often use tools such as positive listing, negative listing, denial of benefit clauses, product exclusions and carve-outs. These categories are purely illustrative. However, in order to make the trade agreements more meaningful and serve as instruments of liberalisation, concepts such as standstill and ratchet are also being used. Side letters have also recently been used in order to enable bilateral modifications or reservations to multi-party agreements.

The rapid conclusion of these mega trade agreements indicates that countries have the appetite to negotiate binding rules on new and expansive issues in the setting of a limited club agreement. These agreements can have adverse effects on economies that are not part of such groupings. Since these agreements tend to discriminate against non-parties and have a role in setting rules of global governance and standards, their potential impact needs to be studied more carefully. There is an apprehension that in the haste to conclude such agreements, countries might find their policy space restricted.

Mini Chapter 3   Digital Trade

Digital trade or, more generally, electronic commerce (e-commerce), is a twenty-first-century reality. Digital trade can be defined as the broad categories of 'economic activities which function by means of technology, especially electronic transactions made using the internet'.[1] A significant share of international trade, currently around 12–13 per cent, takes place through e-commerce.[2]

Digital trade is coming of age globally. The United States is the largest player in the e-commerce space, with the digital economy constituting more than one-third of its total GDP (roughly $6.5 trillion). The European Union, on the other hand, has, perhaps, the most robust regulatory regime, for example, with a comprehensive data protection law and an active antitrust regime.[3] China has recorded the highest growth in digitisation and has emerged as the largest exporter of electronically traded goods. Digital trade is also growing at a rapid pace in several industrialised as well as emerging economies, with the growth of internet penetration.

Regulating digital trade is a complex process. Digital trade involves the use of digital platforms and cross-border movement of data. It is, therefore, not surprising that some of the issues related to digital trade, such as cross-border movement of data, use and location of computing facilities and the protection of personal data, privacy and consumer protection, have acquired prominence. For instance, the EU's General Data Protection Regulation has raised many questions about the level of protection accorded to anonymised data.[4] Several countries have adopted domestic regulations that require data localisation or server localisation. Governments are also imposing measures that require the disclosure of trade secrets, including source codes and algorithms, or the use of specific encryption technologies as a condition for market access. While these restrictions address certain legitimate public policy concerns, these are often argued to create unnecessary barriers to trade and investment.

---

[1] UNCTAD, *Rising Product Digitalization and Losing Trade Competitiveness*, UNCTAD/GDS/ECIDC/2017/3 (2017), p. 7, available at https://unctad.org/en/PublicationsLibrary/gdsecidc2017d3_en.pdf (accessed 21 December 2020).

[2] J. Manyika, S. Lund, J. Bughin et al., *Digital Globalization: The New Era of Global Flows* (McKinsey Global Institute, March 2016).

[3] The EU enacted the General Data Protection Regulation (GDPR), which entered into force on 25 May 2018.

[4] H. Pearce and S. Stalla-Bourdillon, 'Rethinking the "Release and Forget" Ethos of the Freedom of Information Act 2000: Why Developments in the Field of Anonymisation Necessitate the Development of a New Approach to Disclosing Data', *European Journal of Law and Technology* (2019), 10(1), p. 2.

Digital Trade and the WTO

When the WTO was established in 1995, digital trade was in its nascent stage. Nevertheless, agreements such as the GATS and the TRIPS, being technology-neutral, had the potential to govern certain aspects of digital trade. However, unprecedented technological revolution in the following two decades warranted the need for an independent discipline governing digital trade. In 1998, during the Second WTO Ministerial Conference in Geneva, the members adopted a Declaration on Global Electronic Commerce.[5] In response to the Declaration, the WTO General Council introduced the Work Programme on Electronic Commerce, which established 'an exploratory process through which WTO Members examine questions about the application of WTO agreements to e-commerce'.[6]

According to the Declaration, the Work Programme assigned four WTO bodies, namely, the Council for Trade in Services, the Council for Trade in Goods, the TRIPS Council and the Committee for Trade and Development, responsibility for carrying out the Work Programme – that is, to examine issues related to e-commerce and report to the General Council.[7]

For the purpose of the Work Programme, the General Council defined e-commerce as 'the production, distribution, marketing, sale or delivery of goods and services by electronic means'. Three types of transactions are included in the scope of this limited definition of e-commerce:

Definition of E-commerce

(a) the provision of Internet access services themselves – meaning the provision of access to the Internet for businesses and consumers;
(b) the electronic delivery of services, meaning transactions in which services products are delivered to the customer in the form of digitized information flows;
(c) the use of the Internet as a channel for distribution services, by which goods and services are purchased over the net but delivered to the consumer subsequently in non-electronic form.[8]

The WTO definition of e-commerce includes goods and services that are produced, distributed, marketed, sold or delivered through the Internet. Subsequent discussions also touched on electronically transmitted goods that were previously delivered in tangible form, but could now be delivered in electronic form.

---

[5] WTO, Declaration on Global Electronic Commerce, Ministerial Conference, Second Session, WT/MIN(98)/DEC/2, adopted 20 May 1998.

[6] S. Wunsch-Vincent, 'WTO, E-commerce, and Information Technologies: From the Uruguay Round through the Doha Development Agenda – A Report for the UN ICT Task Force' (United Nations, 2008).

[7] Work Programme on Electronic Commerce, WT/L/274, adopted by the General Council on 25 September 1998.

[8] WTO Agreements and Electronic Commerce (Note by the Secretariat), WT/GC/W/90, 14 July 1998, paras. 1 and 2.

The Declaration also puts in place a moratorium during which members agreed to continue the practice of not imposing customs duties on electronic transmissions. This moratorium on customs duties on electronic transmissions has been extended through every Ministerial Decision so far, with the latest decision adopted at the 11th Ministerial Conference in Buenos Aires in 2017.[9]

Technological advancements have led to a debate on whether the commitments made under the WTO, especially under the services commitments during the Uruguay Round, continue to remain relevant. This is an important question, because global trade is moving in the direction of digital trade, with the Internet and technology at the centre of this shift. In spite of the perception that a member's schedule of commitments may cover e-commerce, there are several issues that arise, including classification issues. Classification of services is important for attaining harmonisation in services commitments. However, disruptive technologies are creating new service categories, or merging existing service categories. For example, services like cloud computing and video on demand may not fit within existing classifications.[10] A dispute filed by Venezuela against the United States raised the possibility of GATS covering even cryptocurrencies.[11]

Intellectual property rights also have considerable bearing on e-commerce, including the relationship with the TRIPS Agreement. Website and software features, such as source codes, object codes, data flow charts, algorithms and database contents, are capable of being protected as trade secrets. Since the TRIPS, like the GATS, is technologically neutral, there are specific gaps on how a member can regulate the IP aspects of electronic commerce. In addition, the fact that the WIPO Copyright Treaty and WIPO Performances and the Phonograms Treaty have not yet been integrated under TRIPS, contributes to the existing gaps in governance of e-commerce.

Negotiations on Disciplines of E-Commerce

Attempts to initiate negotiations on e-commerce have been made at the WTO since the beginning of the Doha Round. When the 11th Ministerial Conference was approaching, the United States tabled its proposal on e-commerce – a proposal that was modelled largely on the TPP text of July 2016.[12] At the 2017 Ministerial Conference in Buenos

---

[9] Work Programme on Electronic Commerce, Ministerial Decision of 13 December 2017, WT/MIN(17)/65. The most recent renewal of the moratorium was in 2019, where the General Council decided to extend it until the 12th Ministerial Conference scheduled for June 2020. See WTO, Work Programme on Electronic Commerce, General Council Decision, adopted 10 December 2019, WT/L/1079.

[10] Willemyns suggests that some of the new services, like cloud computing and video on demand, can be classified under existing services categories: Ines Willemyns, 'GATS Classification of Digital Services: Does "The Cloud" Have a Silver Lining?', *Journal of World Trade* (2019), 53(1), pp. 59–82.

[11] Request for the Establishment of a Panel by Venezuela, *United States – Measures Relating to Trade in Goods and Services*, WTO Doc. WT/DS574/2 (14 March 2019).

[12] WTO, Work Programme on Electronic Commerce, 'Non-Paper from the United States', JOB/GC/94 (July 2016).

Aires, there were three negotiating groups: (1) a group of members favouring launch of negotiations on a comprehensive agreement on e-commerce; (2) a group of members in favour of the status quo of continuing the moratorium but with no negotiations; and (3) a group of members in favour of creation of a working group, projecting a midway position between the first two groups.

While developed nations generally formed part of the first group, members such as India and South Africa tried to canvass attention towards their concerns, for example, about revenue loss due to the moratorium on customs duties on electronic transmission becoming permanent, a position proposed by the first group.[13]

Due to a lack of consensus, multilateral negotiations did not materialise, and the focus later shifted towards exploratory work on 'trade-related aspects of e-commerce' in a plurilateral setting after a joint statement by seventy-one countries.[14] Other countries, including China, agreed to join the statement in January 2019, at the World Economic Forum in Davos, to make it a group of seventy-six countries.[15] This resulted in a plurilateral discussion being initiated in March 2019.[16]

E-Commerce Moratorium

Discussions on the implications of the moratorium on e-commerce have focused on the long-term fiscal interests of member States, stated to be adversely affected on account of revenue loss.[17] It is noted that the moratorium leads to larger losses in revenue for developing countries than for developed ones.[18] This is exacerbated by the growth of 3D printing (or additive manufacturing), though still in its nascent stage. Additionally, it has been estimated that at the current growth rate, e-commerce, or digital trade, has the potential to replace 40 per cent of the present cross-border physical global trade. According to an UNCTAD study, cross-border bandwidth has grown by forty-five times since 2005 and is projected to grow nine times in the next five years.[19] This trend is likely to increase with the rise of 3D

---

[13] Communication from India and South Africa, WT/GC/W/747, 12 July 2018; S. Notani, A. Sathianathan and P. Jha, 'Multilateralism and E-Commerce: Assessing India's Position', *Global Trade and Customs Journal* (2019), 14(7/8), pp. 359–65.

[14] Joint statement on Electronic Commerce, WT/MIN(17)/60, 13 December 2017.

[15] Press release, '76 WTO Partners Launch Talks on E-Commerce' (25 January 2019), available at http://trade.ec.europa.eu/doclib/press/index.cfm?id=1974 (accessed 21 December 2020).

[16] D. James, 'Anti-Development Impacts of Tax-Related Provisions in Proposed Rules on Digital Trade in the WTO', *Development* (2019), 62(1), pp. 58–65.

[17] W. Cheng and B. Clara, 'Governing Digital Trade: A New Role for the WTO', German Development Institute Briefing Paper 6 (2019).

[18] Cheng and Clara, 'Governing Digital Trade'; R. Banga, 'Growing Trade in Electronic Transmissions: Implications for the South', UNCTAD Research Paper 29, (2019); James, 'Anti-Development Impacts of Tax-Related Provisions'.

[19] UNCTAD, *Rising Product Digitalization*.

printing. All these factors make the moratorium an important bone of contention during the discussions on e-commerce.[20]

If the members manage to discontinue the moratorium, the customs duties will have to be imposed based on the existing WTO framework, unless a new agreement for this purpose is negotiated. It is doubtful whether the GATT or the GATS would permit member States to impose the duties in a manner consistent with these agreements.[21]

Some of the other key issues include the application of the principles of non-discrimination to digital products,[22] and other barriers such as standards, privacy concerns, data localisation requirements and restrictions on cross-border flow of data.[23]

E-Commerce Chapter under FTAs

Regulatory cooperation is imperative in the field of digital trade. FTAs have played an important role in reconciling regulatory approaches of countries and will certainly play a much wider role in regulatory harmonisation.

The first FTA having substantial provisions and hard obligations on e-commerce was the Australia–Singapore FTA of 2013. Thereafter, other countries have concluded FTAs consisting of e-commerce chapters having substantive obligations.[24] The CETA, the TPP, or its newer version, the CPTPP, the USMCA, the United States–Japan Digital Trade Agreement[25] and the recent RCEP[26] cover some of the most extensive rules and obligations on digital trade.[27]

The CPTPP e-commerce chapter binds parties to grant non-discriminatory treatment to digital products originating from CPTPP parties,[28] makes the moratorium on customs duties

---

[20] WTO, 'Work Programme on Electronic Commerce: Trade Policy, the WTO, and the Digital Economy', Communication from Canada, Chile, Colombia, Côte d'Ivoire, the European Union, the Republic of Korea, Mexico, Paraguay and Singapore (Revision), JOB/GC/97/Rev.1 (22 July 2016); WTO, 'Work Programme on Electronic Commerce: Aiming at the 11th Ministerial Conference', Communication from the People's Republic of China and Pakistan (Revision), JOB/GC/110 (16 November 2016).

[21] S. T. Chandy, 'Customs Duties 2.0: Assessing the Legality of Imposing Customs Duties on Digital Products under the GATT and GATS', unpublished mimeo, March 2020 (on file with author).

[22] Non-Paper from the United States.

[23] WTO, Council for Trade in Services, The Work Programme on Electronic Commerce, Note by the Secretariat, S/C/W/68 (16 November 1998).

[24] J. P. Meltzer, 'A WTO Reform Agenda: Data Flows and International Regulatory Cooperation', *Global Economy and Development*, Working Paper 130 (2019); M. Wu, 'Digital Trade-Related Provisions in Regional Trade Agreements: Existing Models and Lessons for the Multilateral Trade System' (New York/Geneva: Inter-American Development Bank/ICTSD, 2017).

[25] Office of the US Trade Representative, US–Japan Digital Trade Agreement, available at ustr.gov/countries-regions/japan-korea-apec/japan/us-japan-trade-agreement-negotiations/us-japan-digital-trade-agreement-text (accessed 21 December 2020).

[26] Regional Comprehensive Economic Partnership, signed on 15 November 2020, available at https://rcepsec.org/legal-text (accessed 21 December 2020).

[27] Meltzer, 'A WTO Reform Agenda'.   [28] CPTPP, Art. 14.4.

permanent among the parties,[29] and prohibits localisation of computing facilities as a requirement for conducting business.[30] The CETA, similarly, makes the moratorium on customs duties permanent and preserves the rights of parties to adopt or maintain measures for the protection of personal information of users involved in e-commerce.[31] The CETA also requires taking into consideration international standards of data protection (set by relevant international organisations). The USMCA, among others, promotes the development of good regulatory practices related to e-commerce.[32]

Data Protection Provisions in FTAs

TPP, Article 14.8.2 (note 6)

For greater certainty, a Party may comply with the obligation in this paragraph by adopting or maintaining measures such as comprehensive privacy, personal information or personal data protection laws, sector-specific laws covering privacy, or laws that provide for the enforcement of voluntary undertakings by enterprises relating to privacy.

CETA, Article 16.4

Each Party should adopt or maintain laws, regulations or administrative measures for the protection of personal information of users engaged in electronic commerce and, when doing so, shall take into due consideration international standards of data protection of relevant international organizations of which both Parties are a member.

Recent trade agreements, such as the CPTPP, CETA, USMCA and the RCEP all contain extensive chapters on e-commerce, which cover a range of issues, although in varying detail, such as moratorium on customs duties, location of computing facilities, electronic authentication and electronic signatures, cross-border movement of data, source codes, cyber-security, consumer and privacy protection, online consumer protection, online data protection, paperless trading and cooperation on electronic commerce. The e-commerce chapters also include obligations such as the endeavour to take appropriate and necessary measures to regulate 'unsolicited commercial e-mails', and prohibition on requirements of the transfer of or access to source code. The scope of e-commerce obligations under FTAs continues to expand, with the e-commerce chapter under the USMCA having the widest scope so far.

---

[29] CPTPP, Art. 14.3.   [30] CPTPP, Art. 14.13.

[31] CETA, Art. 16.3; R. Wolfe, 'Learning about Digital Trade: Privacy and E-Commerce in CETA and TPP', *World Trade Review* (2019), 18(1), pp. 1–22.

[32] USMCA, Art. 28.2.

Conclusion

While cross-border digital trade has increased exponentially, WTO members have responded by adopting measures to mandate, regulate or restrict such flows. The 1998 WTO Work Programme on E-Commerce had the limited objective to explore trade-related issues of e-commerce and place a moratorium on the imposition of customs duties on electronically transmitted goods. However, the recent issues in e-commerce involve the treatment of data, restrictions on cross-border data, data privacy and protection issues. Countries are also becoming increasingly sensitive to negotiating internationally agreed norms on e-commerce. However, the divergent views on disciplining digital trade seem to have led countries to negotiate the rules at different forums. This has led to fragmentation of the rules. Nonetheless, considering the rapid growth in this sector, global cooperation in digital trade will be a matter of necessity, at least in the not-too-distant future.

Mini Chapter 4 Economic Sanctions

International economic law has become highly technical, but it also remains eminently political. Economic sanctions provide a very clear illustration of the political nature and practice of IEL. They are the expression of an 'economic control for political ends'.[1] Trade sanctions can be considered as a sort of subcategory of the broader term, 'economic sanctions', which include financial instruments in addition to commercial foreign policy tools. Although of prime importance in international affairs, economic sanctions tend to be marginalised in IEL scholarship. The recent US-led trade wars, Washington sanctions against Iran, the European Union restrictive measures vis à vis Russia, or WTO-supported US retaliatory actions in reaction to the European subsidies to the aeronautical giant firm Airbus are all showing the need to approach the issue of economic sanctions in an interdisciplinary fashion.[2] Sanctions are indeed at the crossroads between economic warfare and international regulation.

Sanctions in International Law

In 1935, the League of Nations' response to Italy's invasion of Abyssinia (now Ethiopia) triggered another international crisis. It questioned the very credibility of the international organisation. The League imposed limited sanctions against Italy and debated the possibility of an embargo on oil shipments. Italy ignored the sanctions, then quit the League, and managed to strike deals with Britain and France while keeping control of the annexed territory. This grave failure of multilateralism was later addressed by the United Nations Charter in its Chapter VII: Action with Respect to Threats to the Peace, Breaches of the Peace, and Acts of Aggression.

Economic sanctions can be imposed by an international organisation on the basis of a multilateral (UN) or regional treaty (EU, for example). They can also be taken unilaterally by an act of State. The latter sanctions are generally seen as contrary to international law

---

[1] As meaningfully summarised by Andreas F. Lowenfeld, who was probably the only scholar to approach this issue in great detail: Lowenfeld, *International Economic Law*, pp. 848–926.

[2] The US has imposed sanctions on Iran, under various legal grounds, since 1979 – that is, following the seizure of the US Embassy in Tehran: US Department of State, Economic Sanctions Policy and Implementation, Iran Sanctions, available at www.state.gov/iran-sanctions/ (accessed 21 December 2020). On 14 October 2019, the WTO authorised the US to retaliate in the case DS316, *European Communities and Certain Member States – Measures Affecting Trade in Large Civil Aircraft*. By this decision, the US was allowed to impose trade sanctions on up to $7.5 billion worth of EU goods, on the basis that European plane maker Airbus received illegal subsidies.

and highly debated. However, there is no universal definition of sanctions, nor any international body monitoring this practice.

An economic sanction can be defined as a measure of coercion of an economic nature, as opposed to diplomatic or military means, taken by States, either collectively or individually, in reaction to another State policy or practice, in order to produce a significant change of policy or practice. The legality, legitimacy and effectiveness of sanctions are often blurred and subject to multiple interpretations.

Collective Sanctions

The United Nations Security Council is at the centre of the collective sanctions edifice with its Chapter VII, and, specifically, Articles 39 and 41. There is a clear procedure to be followed: first, the determination of the 'existence of any threat to the peace, breach of the peace, or act of aggression' (Article 39), then the decision to resort to measures not involving the 'use of armed force' offered by Article 41. Sanctions are not listed, as such, but the allusion is clear.

UN Charter, Chapter VII: Action with Respect to Threats to the Peace, Breaches of the Peace, and Acts of Aggression

Article 39

The Security Council shall determine the existence of any threat to the peace, breach of the peace, or act of aggression and shall make recommendations, or decide what measures shall be taken in accordance with Articles 41 and 42, to maintain or restore international peace and security.

[...]

Article 41

The Security Council may decide what measures not involving the use of armed force are to be employed to give effect to its decisions, and it may call upon the Members of the United Nations to apply such measures. These may include complete or partial interruption of economic relations and of rail, sea, air, postal, telegraphic, radio, and other means of communication, and the severance of diplomatic relations.

Since 1966, the Security Council has established thirty regimes of sanctions in Southern Rhodesia, South Africa, the former Yugoslavia (two), Haiti, Iraq (two), Angola, Rwanda, Sierra Leone, Somalia and Eritrea, Eritrea and Ethiopia, Liberia (three), the Democratic Republic of Congo, Côte d'Ivoire, Sudan, Lebanon, the Democratic People's Republic of Korea, Iran, Libya (two), Guinea–Bissau, the Central African Republic, Yemen, South Sudan and Mali, as well as against the Islamic State of Iraq and the Levant (ISIL or Da'esh) and al-Qaida and the Taliban.[3] These sanctions have taken a wide variety of shapes, from trade measures to arms embargos, financial restrictions, travel bans or commodity access restrictions. The UN insists on the idea that these sanctions cannot operate 'in a vacuum', but should rather be seen as part of a larger apparatus to restore peace and security. They also argue, probably less convincingly, that: 'Contrary to the assumption that sanctions are punitive, many regimes are designed to support governments and regions working towards peaceful transition. The Libyan and Guinea–Bissau sanctions regimes all exemplify this approach.' As discussed below, the harmful effect of sanctions has long been demonstrated, while their efficacy remains to be proven. In 2020, fourteen UN supported programmes of sanctions were in place in the world. Each of them is administered by a sanction committee chaired by a non-permanent member of the Security Council. There are ten monitoring groups, teams and panels that support the work of eleven of the fourteen sanctions committees. Aware of the controversial nature of sanctions, the UN has put in place a system of monitoring with an ombudsperson and, since May 2015, the appointment by the Human Rights Council of a Special Rapporteur on the negative impact of the unilateral coercive measures.[4]

At the regional level, sanctions are, for example, one of EU's tools for the promotion of its Common and Foreign Security Policy, which consists of supporting 'peace, democracy and the respect for the rule of law, human rights and international law'.[5] The Council of the EU is in charge of sanctions-related decisions and all relevant legal acts are published in the Official Journal of the EU. These sanctions can target governments, but also private entities and individuals, such as terrorist groups or terrorists, and include embargos, trade restrictions, financial restrictions or restrictions on travel (visa or travel bans). More than thirty EU sanctions regimes are now in place.[6] Among these, are the 'Restrictive measures in view of Russia's actions destabilising the situation in Ukraine'.

Unilateral Sanctions

Unilateral sanctions are taken by a given State without a treaty basis. The US is championing this category, but other countries have had recourse to this mechanism. Here again, these economic sanctions can take a number of forms, from complete embargo – that is, the total interdiction to trade, travel, and conduct financial transactions – to more targeted measures, such as blocking or freezing financial assets, imposing restrictions on imports or exports on the basis of a licensing system, for example. The authority to take these measures is a matter of domestic law. However, the question of jurisdiction is particularly sensitive. Where and to whom could these sanctions be applied? If in the US, what about foreign companies operating

[3] UN Security Council, Sanctions, available at www.un.org/securitycouncil/sanctions/information (accessed 21 December 2020).

[4] OHCHR, Special Rapporteur on the negative impact of the unilateral coercive measures on the enjoyment of human rights, available at www.ohchr.org/EN/Issues/UCM/Pages/SRCoerciveMeasures.aspx (accessed 21 December 2020).

[5] European Commission, available at https://eeas.europa.eu/topics/common-foreign-security-policy-cfsp_en (accessed 21 December 2020).

[6] EU Sanctions Map, available at https://sanctionsmap.eu/#/main (accessed 21 December 2020).

on US territory or foreign assets? The issue of jurisdiction to impose and enforce sanctions remains very controversial. There is a clear extraterritorial element to the unilateral imposition of economic restrictive measures. In the language of the ILC, these unilateral sanctions are called 'countermeasures'. Chapter V, Article 22 of the Responsibility of States for Internationally Wrongful Acts provides a rather tortuous way to 'preclude': 'The wrongfulness of an act of a State not in conformity with an international obligation towards another State'.[7] The commentary goes on to explain further what is meant by 'countermeasures' and how these could be deemed legitimate in referring directly to the practice of sanctions:

> ### ILC, Articles on Responsibility of States for Internationally Wrongful Acts, with Commentaries (2001)
>
> In the literature concerning countermeasures, reference is sometimes made to the application of a 'sanction', or to a 'reaction' to a prior internationally wrongful act; historically the more usual terminology was that of 'legitimate reprisals' or, more generally, measures of 'self-protection' or 'self-help'. The term 'sanctions' has been used for measures taken in accordance with the constituent instrument of some international organization, in particular under Chapter VII of the Charter of the United Nations – despite the fact that the Charter uses the term 'measures', not 'sanctions'. The term 'reprisals' is now no longer widely used in the present context, because of its association with the law of belligerent reprisals involving the use of force. At least since the Air Service Agreement arbitration, the term 'countermeasures' has been preferred, and it has been adopted for the purposes of the present articles.

Close to the idea of self-defence, the measure at stake could be described as 'self-help' or 'self-protection'. The question of legality remains, even if analysed in reference to Part III, Chapter II (Countermeasures), which deals 'with the conditions for and limitations on the taking of countermeasures by an injured State'.

> ### Articles on the Responsibility of States for Internationally Wrongful Acts, Chapter V
>
> ### Article 22: Countermeasures in Respect of an Internationally Wrongful Act
>
> The wrongfulness of an act of a State not in conformity with an international obligation towards another State is precluded if and to the extent that the act constitutes a countermeasure taken against the latter State in accordance with chapter II of Part Three.

---

[7] UN, Articles on Responsibility of States for Internationally Wrongful Acts (2001), available at http://legal.un.org/avl/ha/rsiwa/rsiwa.html (accessed 21 December 2020); Articles on Responsibility of States for Internationally Wrongful Acts, with Commentaries.

Legality, Legitimacy and Effectiveness

Legality and Legitimacy

The *Nicaragua* case provides a clear illustration of the ambiguity and illegality of these measures. Economic sanctions were imposed by the United States to attain political goals in the comprehensive trade embargo levied against the government of Nicaragua in May 1985. The US was acting pursuant to the International Economic Emergency Powers Act of 1977 and the National Emergencies Act of 1976. A total embargo on all trade with Nicaragua was made, and service to the US by Nicaraguan airlines and flag vessels suspended. Nicaragua brought a complaint before the GATT Council. But the US argued that the measures had been taken in compliance with the GATT Article XXI for national security reasons. A panel was composed, but its ambiguous conclusions did not help Nicaragua. The embargo remained and only a change of power relations could ease the situation in 1990. This case remains a landmark in international law, with the ICJ judgment condemning the US for its military and paramilitary activities in Nicaragua and upholding Nicaragua's sovereignty.[8] Another example illustrating the extraterritorial effect of American sanctions is provided by the infamous Cuban Liberty and Democratic Solidarity (Libertad) Act of 1996 (see Chapter 9).

The US is not the only country to resort unilaterally to economic sanctions, as demonstrated by the example of the measures imposed by the UK on Bank Mellat in the context of the Iran crisis and the alleged links of the bank with Teheran's nuclear programme. In June 2019, an unprecedented $1.6 billion damages claim against the UK government by the Iranian Bank Mellat was successfully settled after a ten-year judicial battle. The claim was initiated by one of Iran's largest commercial banks against HM Treasury for the wrongful imposition of economic sanctions in 2009. In October 2009, indeed, HM Treasury made a direction under Schedule 7 to the Counter Terrorism Act 2008, requiring all persons operating in the UK financial sector not to undertake any business relationships or transactions with Bank Mellat and the Islamic Republic of Iran Shipping Lines ('2009 Order'). This sanction was subsequently followed by similar restrictive measures at the European level, as well as wide sectoral measures against almost the entire Iranian banking sector. After two unsuccessful attempts to challenge the restrictive measures imposed by the UK on its activities, Bank Mellat initiated a final appeal before the Supreme Court of England and Wales. In June 2013, the Supreme Court ruled in favour of the Bank and subsequently referred the matter back to the English Commercial Court for the assessment of losses suffered by the Bank as a result of the imposition of the 2009 Order. The damages claim initiated by Bank Mellat was the largest ever economic sanctions-related damages claim of its kind in the English Courts.[9]

---

[8] *Case Concerning Military and Paramilitary Activities in and against Nicaragua (Nicaragua* v. *United States of America), ICJ Reports 1986,* available at www.icj-cij.org/en/case/70 (accessed 21 December 2020).

[9] UK Supreme Court, *Bank Mellat* v. *Her Majesty's Treasury,* Judgment, 19 June 2013, [2013] UKSC 38 & [2013] UKSC 39, available at www.supremecourt.uk/cases/uksc-2011-0040.html; J. Croft, A. England and S. Provan, 'UK

Trade sanctions are an expression of discrimination. They contradict the idea of reciprocity and the basic principles of trade, the NT and MFN treatment. Yet the GATT Article XXI, as well as the GATS Article XIV*bis*, plan for security exceptions (see Chapter 9). These exceptions can de facto take the form of trade sanctions. They are legal if adopted according to the WTO rules and procedures, yet are they legitimate? What justifies their adoption? Are there possibly better alternatives? Are WTO-authorised retaliatory measures legitimising economic sanctions? These questions have been largely debated in international scholarship, along with the equally controversial issue of the effectiveness of economic sanctions.

GATT, Article XXI: Security Exceptions

Nothing in this Agreement shall be construed

(a) to require any contracting party to furnish any information the disclosure of which it considers contrary to its essential security interests; or

(b) to prevent any contracting party from taking any action which it considers necessary for the protection of its essential security interests
   (i) relating to fissionable materials or the materials from which they are derived;
   (ii) relating to the traffic in arms, ammunition and implements of war and to such traffic in other goods and materials as is carried on directly or indirectly for the purpose of supplying a military establishment;
   (iii) taken in time of war or other emergency in international relations; or

(c) to prevent any contracting party from taking any action in pursuance of its obligations under the United Nations Charter for the maintenance of international peace and security.

Effectiveness

While sanctions are still seen as a better alternative to the use of armed force, their effectiveness has never been proven. On the contrary, a vast body of international literature tends to demonstrate their lack of results to achieve the political objectives at stake, as well as their harmful effects on countries and populations. It has long been demonstrated that economic sanctions produce negative consequences on populations, such as a decline in economic growth, an increase in the poverty gap, income inequalities, widening the gap between rural and urban areas, negative effects on vulnerable populations and, in particular, women and minorities, reduce access to food, water and health, and, generally, participate in grave human rights violations.

Settles £1.3bn Lawsuit with Iran's Bank Mellat after Ten Years', *Financial Times* (18 June 2019), www.ft.com/content/58c4ae5c-91b0-11e9-b7ea-60e35ef678d2 (both accessed 21 December 2020).

On 26 September 2014, the Human Rights Council adopted Resolution 27/21[10] on the effect of coercive measures on human rights. Unilateral coercive measures are particularly targeted as contrary to international law, international humanitarian law, the UN Charter and the norms and principles governing peaceful relations between States.

HRC, Human Rights and Unilateral Coercive Measures

1. *Calls upon* all States to stop adopting, maintaining or implementing unilateral coercive measures not in accordance with international law, international humanitarian law, the Charter of the United Nations and the norms and principles governing peaceful relations among States, in particular those of a coercive nature with extraterritorial effects, which create obstacles to trade relations among States, thus impeding the full realization of the rights set forth in the Universal Declaration of Human Rights and other international human rights instruments, in particular the right of individuals and peoples to development;

2. *Strongly objects* to the extraterritorial nature of those measures which, in addition, threaten the sovereignty of States, and in this context calls upon all Member States neither to recognize these measures nor to apply them, and to take effective administrative or legislative measures, as appropriate, to counteract the extraterritorial application or effects of unilateral coercive measures;

3. *Condemns* the continued unilateral application and enforcement by certain powers of such measures as tools of political or economic pressure against any country, particularly against developing countries, with a view to preventing these countries from exercising their right to decide, of their own free will, their own political, economic and social systems;

4. *Expresses grave concern* that, in some countries, the situation of children and women is adversely affected by unilateral coercive measures not in accordance with international law and the Charter that create obstacles to trade relations among States, impede the full realization of social and economic development and hinder the well-being of the population in the affected countries, with particular consequences for women, children, including adolescents, the elderly and persons with disabilities;

5. *Reiterates* its call upon Member States that have initiated such measures to abide by the principles of international law, the Charter, the declarations of the United Nations and world conferences and relevant resolutions, and to commit themselves to their obligations and responsibilities arising from relevant provisions of the international law and human rights instruments to which they are parties by putting an immediate end to such measures;

---

[10] Human Rights Council, Human Rights and Unilateral Coercive Measures, 3 October 2014, A/HRC/RES/27/21, available at https://ap.ohchr.org/documents/dpage_e.aspx?si=A/HRC/RES/27/21 (accessed 21 December 2020).

(cont.)

6. *Reaffirms* in this context the right of all peoples to self-determination by virtue of which they freely determine their political status and freely pursue their own economic, social and cultural development;

7. *Also reaffirms* its opposition to any attempt aimed at the partial or total disruption of the national unity and territorial integrity of a State, which is incompatible with the Charter;

8. *Recalls* that, according to the Declaration on Principles of International Law concerning Friendly Relations and Cooperation among States in accordance with the Charter of the United Nations, and to the relevant principles and provisions contained in the Charter of Economic Rights and Duties of States, proclaimed by the General Assembly in its Resolution 3281 (XXIX) of 12 December 1974, in particular article 32 thereof, no State may use or encourage the use of economic, political or any other type of measure to coerce another State in order to obtain from it the subordination of the exercise of its sovereign rights and to secure from it advantages of any kind;

9. *Reaffirms* that essential goods, such as food and medicines, should not be used as tools for political coercion and that under no circumstances should people be deprived of their own means of subsistence and development;

10. *Underlines* the fact that unilateral coercive measures are one of the major obstacles to the implementation of the Declaration on the Right to Development, and in this regard calls upon all States to avoid the unilateral imposition of economic coercive measures and the extraterritorial application of domestic laws that run counter to the principles of free trade and hamper the development of developing countries;

11. *Rejects* all attempts to introduce unilateral coercive measures, as well as the increasing trend in this direction, including through the enactment of laws with extraterritorial application, which are not in conformity with international law.

In relation to this important resolution, the Human Rights Council has created the mandate of the Special Rapporteur on the negative impact of unilateral coercive measures on the enjoyment of human rights, as alluded to above. Mr Idriss Jazairy was appointed by the Human Rights Council, at its 28th session, as the first Special Rapporteur on the negative impact of the unilateral coercive measures on the enjoyment of human rights. He took office on 1 May 2015, and throughout his appointment he kept denouncing the imposition of unilateral sanctions and stressed the fact that unilaterally imposed sanctions against Cuba, Venezuela or Iran by the US violate human rights. In March 2020, Ms Alena Douhan took over the role.

Mini Chapter 5 International Taxation

Introduction

Does income have a naturally defined source? In relation to the taxation of income, there are two generally accepted principles: jurisdiction over the party earning the income (the country of residence of the taxpayer), and jurisdiction over the activity that produces the income (the country of source of the income). Under the residence principle, a country taxes the income of persons subject to its jurisdiction, irrespective of where those persons earn the income from. This type of taxation is often referred to as the worldwide system of taxation. Under the source principle, a country taxes income earned within its borders. This is known as the territorial system of taxation.

Why do countries follow different tax systems? Economic literature infers that if worldwide economic efficiency is the rationale of the tax policy, then source countries should forego taxes on foreign businesses operating within their jurisdiction. However, this is seldom followed in practice. Source countries generally require withholding of taxes whenever there is substantial business activity by foreign or domestic firms. And the resident country cannot prevent the source country from taxing that income. This could lead to double taxation, as the same income is taxed twice. This is an extremely competitive handicap for outbound investments.[1] In such circumstances, to mitigate the impact on the taxpayer, the resident country can either refrain from taxing the foreign source income or provide a tax credit for the foreign taxes paid. In the other scenario – that is, in the case of territorial tax systems – only the source country imposes the tax, with the resident country generally exempting the foreign source income from taxation. In other words, the differences between worldwide and territorial tax systems stems from the contrasting economic principles, namely, capital export neutrality (CEN) and capital import neutrality (CIN).[2] These two approaches have been sharply etched in tax policy literature for well over a century, since the enactment of the Revenue Act in the United States in 1913.[3] Importantly, CEN is neutral about a resident's choice between domestic and foreign investments, and also indifferent to which country collects the tax revenue. On the other hand, CIN subjects all business activity within a country's jurisdiction to the same overall taxation. CIN is agnostic to whether the economic activity is conducted by a foreigner or a resident. Generally

---

[1] See, generally, D. Shaviro, *Fixing US International Taxation* (Oxford University Press, 2014).

[2] M. J. Greaetz, 'Taxing International Income: Inadequate Principles, Outdated Concepts, and Unsatisfactory Policies' (David R. Tillinghast Lecture), *Tax Law Review* (2001), 54, pp. 261–336, at 270 and 271.

[3] Revenue Act of 1913, Public Law No. 63-16; see also Greaetz, 'Taxing International Income', p. 261.

speaking, capital-exporting countries preferred the CEN, whereas capital-importing coun-ties opted for CIN. However, these preferences are less important now, as most countries have significant inbound and outbound investments. In addition, most tax systems adopt a hybrid of CEN and CIN.

International taxation also came out with a concept of 'active income' and 'passive income'. Active income refers to the income derived from activities that the taxpayer had engaged in, for example, business income and wages. Passive income refers to the income from invest-ments not controlled by the taxpayer. Accordingly, active income is taxed primarily at the source, while passive income is mainly taxed at the residence.[4] Notwithstanding the above evolution, there is a clear absence of sourcing rules in international taxation. This absence has led to questions as to how countries can tax non-residents.

The two foregoing principles provide the basic framework for a contemporary inter-national tax regime and are reflected in international tax treaties. The simple question in this debate is this: who should get the 'first bite at the apple'? In recent times, several governments have tightened the rules on taxation, including the introduction of general anti-avoidance rules. Businesses, of course, were riled at this practice, and it is not surprising that various tax systems provided a patchwork solution to this problem.[5] The deferral rules, and even the creation of controlled foreign corporations (CFC), reflect an attempt to strike a balance between the urge of the State to tax on the one hand, and the need to mitigate the burden of taxation on businesses on the other.

Globalisation and the emergence of high-tech digital companies have also led to concerns that a substantial amount of global income is not taxed.[6] In a digital economy, services can be delivered from anywhere, while generating value and returns everywhere. Most of this income arises from rents and quasi-rents.[7] This is a separate issue from the problem of double taxation, which has been effectively addressed through a network of double taxation avoidance agreements (DTAAs). Under most tax treaties, business profits made by an enterprise resident in one contracting State are taxable exclusively by that State, unless the enterprise carries on business in the other State through a permanent establishment.[8] However, the emerging problem is that of 'double non-taxation' or 'stateless income'. Large multinational enterprises, epitomised by the expression GAFA (Google, Apple, Facebook, Amazon), enjoy substantial pre-tax profits and limited tax liability.[9] Most of these high-tech companies may not be present or locally resident in those locations from

---

[4] R. S. Avi-Yonah, *Advanced Introduction to International Tax Law*, 2nd ed. (Cheltenham: Edward Elgar, 2019), p. 13.

[5] J. Nedumpara, 'Corporate Tax Reforms in the United States: What Lesson Can Be Learned from the Past GATT/WTO Jurisprudence', *Indian Journal of International Law* (2012), 52(1), pp. 1–26, at 7.

[6] E. D. Kleinbard, 'The Lessons of Stateless Income', *Tax Law Review* (2011), 65, p. 99.

[7] J. Bankman, A. O. Sykes and M. Kane, 'Collecting the Rent: The Global Battle to Capture MNE Profits', *Tax Law Review* (2020), 72, pp. 197–233.

[8] OECD, *Tax Challenges Arising from Digitalisation – Interim Report 2018: Inclusive Framework on BEPS* (Paris: OECD/G20 Base Erosion and Profit Shifting Project, 2018), p. 168.

[9] S. Galloway, *The Four: The Hidden DNA of Apple, Amazon, Facebook, and Google* (New York: Random House, 2017).

which their income accrues. The larger question is whether the nations in which the MNEs operate but do not reside can be subject to location-specific taxation? Several countries have attempted to levy a digital service tax (DST) in respect of location-specific rents, an issue strongly contested by the multinational enterprises and their resident nations.[10] Hitherto US-based MNEs have been at the centre of this debate. The United States had initiated a Section 301 action against France in 2019, which proved extremely controversial. The French DST required companies to attribute revenues to France based on the proportion of users availing themselves of the service in France. Countries such as India have imposed an 'Equalisation Levy', based on the gross revenue from digital transactions, which seems consistent with the OECD's interim response plan.[11] Nonetheless, in June 2020, the United States initiated fresh Section 301 actions against several countries, including India, Indonesia, Turkey and several European countries, on their levy of DST.[12]

There are several other gaps in tax systems, a topic that cannot be examined within the confines of this mini chapter. However, this mini chapter does examine a key international development – the base erosion and profit shifting initiative (BEPS) at the OECD.

Base Erosion and Profit Shifting

Multinational enterprises and their international operations provide a readymade network of companies through which group funds can seamlessly flow. Within this framework, multinational enterprises often find it easy to exploit gaps and mismatches within tax systems, to avoid paying taxes. Base erosion is the result of financial measures and tax planning that an enterprise has undertaken to reduce a firm's taxable profits in a country. It is often achieved by structuring income to have more favourable tax treatment. This has the effect of reducing a company's tax liability below what it would otherwise have expected to pay.

As opposed to base erosion, profit shifting involves making payments to other group companies in order to move profits from high tax jurisdictions to low tax jurisdictions. The objective of profit shifting is to increase the overall profits available to group shareholders. Among transnational corporations, intra-group payments take the form of royalties, fees for technical services and interest payments, and these payments can be expensed. Such payments can be designed in such a manner to shift the profits to jurisdictions that have low tax rates. Another example is to use corporate structures with minimum capital structures for holding valuable IP rights, including royalties. The use of debt instruments is yet another contrivance to reduce corporate tax liability. Another concern is the excessive use of interest rate deductions.

---

[10] The EU has handled one part of this with new rules for VAT on digital services.

[11] OECD, *Addressing the Tax Challenges of the Digital Economy, Action 1: 2015 Final Report* (Paris: OECD/G20 Base Erosion and Shifting Project, 2015), ch. 7.

[12] Office of the US Trade Representative, 'USTR Initiates Section 301 Investigations on Digital Services Taxes' (2 June 2020), available at https://ustr.gov/about-us/policy-offices/press-office/press-releases/2020/june/ustr-initiates-section-301-investigations-digital-services-taxes (accessed 21 December 2020).

All economies are affected by such tax planning, although developing countries are comparatively more vulnerable to loss of revenue in view of their dependence on corporate income tax.[13] The OECD initiative on BEPS was begun in 2013 and was soon endorsed by the G20. The BEPS project is based on the OECD's fifteen-point Action Plan. Although it is not easy to harmonise taxation rules, it is possible to mitigate the negative effects through greater transparency and cooperation in tax matters. The OECD is coordinating this, and at the end of 2019 the BEPS Action Plan included 135 participating nations,[14] of which 92 countries are signatories to this multilateral instrument.[15]

Box Mini 5.1 Base erosion and profit shifting: OECD's fifteen-point Action Plan

1 *Addressing the challenges of the digital economy*: the objective of Action 1 is to examine the tax challenges arising from digitalisation and the manner in which the digital world actually functions.

2 *Neutralising the effects of hybrid mismatch arrangements*: Action 2 seeks to prevent tax exemption on payments that were tax-deductible for the payer; it seeks to deny deductions for interest or royalties paid to a related foreign person pursuant to a hybrid transaction or hybrid entity when the payments either are not includible or are deductible to the recipient in their home jurisdiction.

3 *Strengthening controlled foreign company (CFC) rules*: these rules impose a tax liability on parent companies for their subsidiaries' profits. According to the OECD, CFC rules have positive spillover effects in source countries because taxpayers have no (or much less of an) incentive to shift profits into a third, low-tax jurisdiction; Action 3 deals with strengthening CFC rules and provides recommendations for the design of those rules in the form of six building blocks, implying that jurisdictions are not obliged to implement the recommendations as minimum standards, but they may choose to do so.

4 *Limiting base erosion via interest deductions and other financial payments*: preferential tax regimes are under review, as they drive a race to the bottom. A core aim of this Action Plan is to reduce interest deducted for payments related to financing vehicles. The final report recommends a fixed ratio rule that would restrict an entity's net interest expense to a fixed percentage of its earnings before interest, taxes, depreciation and amortisation, along with a group ratio rule allowing an entity in a highly leveraged group to deduct net interest expenses in excess of the amount permitted under the fixed ratio rule.

---

[13] OECD, What is BEPS?, available at www.oecd.org/tax/beps/about/ (accessed 5 November 2020).

[14] OECD, Members of the OECD/G20 Inclusive Framework on BEPS (December 2019), available at www.oecd.org/tax/beps/inclusive-framework-on-beps-composition.pdf (accessed 5 November 2020).

[15] OECD, Signatories and Parties to the Multilateral Convention to Implement Tax Treaty Related Measures to Prevent Base Erosion and Profit Shifting (status as of 27 November 2020), available at www.oecd.org/tax/beps/beps-mli-signatories-and-parties.pdf (accessed 5 November 2020).

Box Mini 5.1 (cont.)

5 *Countering harmful tax practices more effectively, taking into account transparency and substance*: exchange of information on rulings relating to preferential regimes will be made compulsory, adapting current rules to work better in situations involving more than two countries. This is necessary to take into account the complexity of the global value chain. Currently, tax arrangements are only bilateral. The focus of this Action Plan is to align more closely apportionment of income with the economic activity that generates it, including checks on treaty abuse (a key source of BEPS concerns). This Action Plan takes note of the fact that concealment of information could give rise to BEPS.

6 *Preventing treaty abuse*: tax treaties will be updated to clarify that they are not intended to be used for 'double non-taxation'. DTAAs are intended to prevent double taxation, which hurts businesses, but the same instruments can also be used for double exemptions where possible. Some countries have implemented Action 6 recommendations in their tax treaties, while others have introduced anti-abuse rules in their domestic laws.

7 *Preventing the artificial avoidance of permanent establishment status*: Action 7 seeks to redefine permanent establishments to prevent undue avoidance of local taxes. Transfer pricing and arm's-length principles are related to this item to reduce shifting of income into low-tax systems.

8 *Transfer pricing of intangibles*: reducing the tax benefits of transferring intangibles within the same group. The OECD will define a broad but clear definition of intangibles, create well-defined valuation rules to apply to transfers of intangibles, find ways to price transfers of hard-to-value intangibles, and examine cost contribution arrangements.

9 *Transfer pricing of risks and capital*: preventing inappropriately large returns being enjoyed by a group entity simply for providing capital or assuming contractual risks. This Action Plan intends to ensure that the transfer pricing methods will allocate profits to the most important economic activities.

10 *Transfer pricing of other high-risk transactions*: intra-group transactions that would not ordinarily take place between third parties suggest that they may not be arm's-length transactions. Rules will be developed to clarify the application of transfer pricing methods like profit splits, in the face of global value chains, as well as to protect against management fees, head office expenses and other common base-eroding payments.

11 *Establishing methodologies to collect and analyse data on BEPS and the actions to address it*: data collection, data analysis and the selection of the appropriate metrics will be key to evaluating the scope of BEPS and the efficacy of counter-measures. Disclosure initiatives and co-operative compliance between taxpayers and tax authorities will increase transparency to drive this forward.

Box Mini 5.1 (cont.)

12 *Requiring taxpayers to disclose their aggressive tax planning arrangements*: this Action Plan focuses on requiring mandatory disclosure of international tax planning schemes that may fall under the scope of BEPS. The purpose of mandatory disclosure is to minimise the use of aggressive avoidance schemes by opening up the visibility of a taxpayer's global value chain.

13 *Re-examining transfer pricing documentation*: requiring multinationals to provide information of their transfer pricing arrangements to all relevant governments in a common template. The common template will help to ensure certainty and predictability for business, so that new rules do not introduce an undue additional reporting burden.

14 *Making dispute resolution systems more effective*: updating tax treaty dispute resolution mechanisms to use arbitration so that disputes can be resolved more efficiently and effectively through a 'mutual agreement procedure' (MAP).

15 *Developing a multilateral instrument*: the OECD proposes introducing a multilateral treaty that would amend consenting countries' bilateral tax arrangements in line with the OECD's recommendations.

There are major challenges in implementing tax rules in the digital economy. On 16 March 2018, the OECD released its Interim Report on Tax Challenges Arising from Digitalisation, in connection with Action 1 of its Action Plan on BEPS. The Interim Report outlines the BEPS Inclusive Framework's agreed direction of work on digitalisation and the international tax rules through 2020. The Interim Report does not make any specific recommendations to countries, as it is agreed that further work will need to be carried out to understand the various business models operated by enterprises offering digital goods and services, as well as digitalisation more broadly. However, despite the technical complexity and the diverse positions, the BEPS Inclusive Framework members agreed to undertake a coherent and concurrent review of the rules and achieve a consensus-based solution by 2020. The Interim Report was also presented to the G20 during their meeting in Buenos Aires, Argentina, on 19–20 March 2020.

International taxation is perhaps the only major area of IEL where multilateral instruments are absent. The signing of the new multilateral tax instrument (MLI) in November 2016, under the auspices of the OECD, is a major development. The MLI seeks to implement minimum standards to address treaty abuse and improve dispute resolution. This is a major initiative, although it falls way short of genuine multilateral cooperation.

Mini Chapter 6 The Blue Economy

Oceans cover three-quarters of the earth's surface; they contain 97 per cent of its water and 99 per cent of its living space by volume. As the single largest natural resource, oceans are the source of numerous benefits to humankind. They absorb 30 per cent of the carbon dioxide produced on the planet. They are the world's largest reserve of protein, with more than 2.6 billion people depending on oceans to find their primary source of protein. Marine fisheries, directly or indirectly, employ 200 million people. Oceans serve as a vital medium for international trade of goods, carrying about 80 per cent of world trade.[1] The period 2021–30 has been proclaimed by the United Nations as the 'Decade of Ocean Science for Sustainable Development'.[2]

It is in this general context that the concept of the 'blue economy' has emerged. It relates to the United Nations SDGs (see Chapter 16) and the SDG 14 in particular (Conserve and sustainably use the oceans, seas and marine resources).[3] According to the UNDP, the blue economy is based on 'an approach put forward by the international community to take into account the health of the oceans and seas as we strive to balance the three dimensions of sustainable development: economic, social and environmental'.[4] Of late, a large number of international organisations, as well as governments, businesses and civil society groups, have raised concerns about the need to safeguard marine wealth.

The World Bank defines the blue economy as the sustainable use of ocean resources for economic growth, improved livelihoods and jobs, while preserving the health of ocean ecosystems.[5] It has an impact on human activities such as fisheries, transport, renewable energy, waste management, climate change and tourism. In 2018, the Commonwealth nations adopted The Commonwealth Blue Charter, which affirmed a collective commitment to preserving and nurturing the world's oceans.[6]

---

[1] See https://unworldoceansday.org/event/world-oceans-day-2020-global-celebration-united-nations (accessed 21 December 2020).

[2] See www.oceandecade.org (accessed 21 December 2020).

[3] UN, Department of Economic and Social Affairs, Sustainable Development, Goal 14, available at https://sustainabledevelopment.un.org/sdg14 (accessed 21 December 2020).

[4] S. Chen, C. De Bruyne and M. Bollempalli, 'Blue Economy, Community Solutions' (New York: UNDP, 2018), available at www.undp.org/content/undp/en/home/librarypage/environment-energy/sgp/blue-economy–community-solutions.html (accessed 21 December 2020).

[5] World Bank, 'What Is the Blue Economy?' (6 June 2017), available at www.worldbank.org/en/news/infographic/2017/06/06/blue-economy (accessed 21 December 2020).

[6] The Commonwealth Blue Charter, available at https://bluecharter.thecommonwealth.org (accessed 21 December 2020).

Multidisciplinary by nature, the blue economy interacts with all areas of international law and international economic law. But what is the law of the blue economy?

The United Nations Convention on the Law of the Sea has served as an important instrument for the regulation of the blue economy. There are currently a number of key discussions under way on possible amendments of this regime, adopted in 1982, in Montego Bay, which will directly impact on developing economies. In the international trade law arena, the WTO has been at the forefront of debates on maritime wealth. The proactive – and still controversial – rulings by the Appellate Body in *US – Gasoline* and *US – Shrimp* changed how trade rules interact with environmental protection. Currently, and as discussed below, WTO

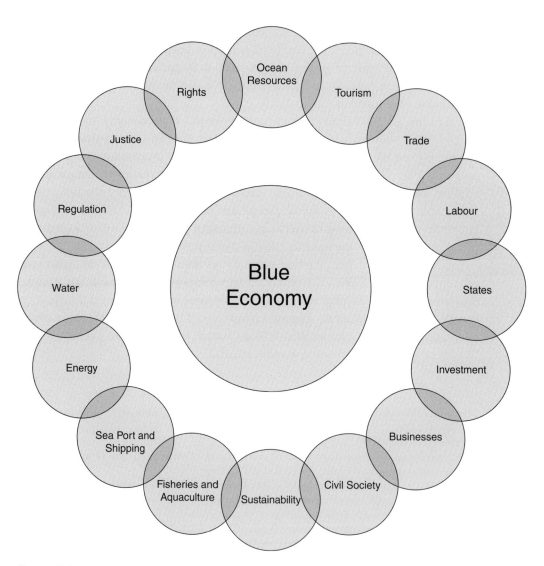

Figure Mini 6.1 Blue economy nexus

members are negotiating disciplines on fisheries subsidies to regulate illegal, unreported and unregulated fishing. Similarly, the interplay between the environment and international investment protection has gained importance.

At the crossroads between domestic and international norms, but also public and private law, the law of the blue economy presents numerous challenges in terms of harmonisation and implementation. For the purposes of this short chapter, we have chosen to focus on two aspects of this complex and interactive new field: a brief introduction to the UNCLOS regime and the key issue of fisheries and fisheries disciplines.

The UNCLOS

The oceans have long been ruled on the basis of the freedom of the sea doctrine. This principle was adopted in the seventeenth century to allow peaceful coexistence and commerce in limiting State sovereignty over the sea to a narrow belt along the coastline. Hugo Grotius, Dutch jurist and philosopher, and considered one of the fathers of international law, seems to have first pronounced the principle of freedom of the sea in his 1609 book *Mare Liberum*. He was, at the time, Counsel for the Dutch East India Company and a strong advocate of the freedom of the sea doctrine. His objective was to allow international trade and to fight against the doctrine of monopolies (*mare clausum* – closed sea) supported by Portuguese trade rivals.

With the advancement of technologies and the discovery of multiple marine resources, including oil and precious minerals, as well as onset of the Second World War, the freedom of the sea doctrine was progressively contested by a greater number of countries. In 1945, US President Harry S. Truman, under the pressure of oil producers, extended US jurisdiction over natural resources to the continental shelf. This was the first major challenge. It was soon followed by Argentina, which, in 1946, claimed its shelf and the epicontinental sea above it. With decolonisation and the emergence of new countries, the issue of freedom of the sea became truly contentious. Some countries, like Chile, Peru and Ecuador, extended their sovereignty over an area of 200 nautical miles, to control international foreign fishing and limit the exploitation of what they considered to be their resources. Large archipelagic nations like Indonesia or the Philippines also had claims over their waters, impacting their closest neighbours and maritime trade. In the late 1960s, the situation became untenable. It was time to codify international maritime relations. In a famous speech to the UN, on 1 November 1967, the Ambassador of Malta called for the establishment of an international regime.[7] A few years later, in 1973, a third Conference on the Law of the Sea was convened in New York. It ended, in 1982, with the adoption of the UNCLOS.[8] It came into force only on 16 November 1994, one year after its sixtieth ratification, with Guyana adhering to it.

---

[7] UNGA, 22nd Session, Official Records (1 November 1967), available at www.un.org/Depts/los/convention_agreements/texts/pardo_ga1967.pdf (accessed 21 December 2020).

[8] Oystein Jensen (ed.), *The Development of the Law of the Sea Convention* (Cheltenham: Edward Elgar, 2020).

This codification exercise was absolutely revolutionary and perceived as a victory for the developing world to be able to assert its claims and protect its resources. The UNCLOS is a complex instrument, which would deserve a detailed explanation, but its main provisions can be summarised as in Figure Mini 6.2.

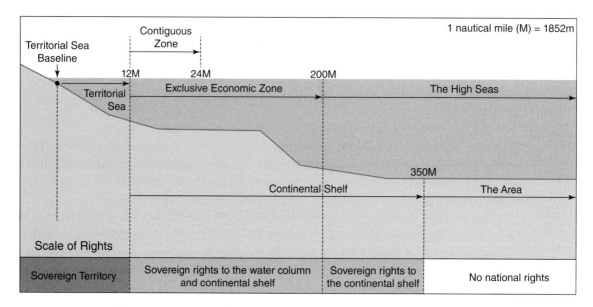

Figure Mini 6.2 Maritime territory delimitation. Source: Arctic Council, Arctic Marine Shipping Assessment 2009 Report.

The concept of 'freedom of the seas' can still be found in the UNCLOS under Article 87, which gives considerable freedom to States.[9]

UNCLOS, Article 87: Freedom of the High Seas

1. The high seas are open to all States, whether coastal or landlocked. Freedom of the high seas is exercised under the conditions laid down by this Convention and by other rules of international law. It comprises, inter alia, both for coastal and land-locked States:
   (a) freedom of navigation;
   (b) freedom of overflight;
   (c) freedom to lay submarine cables and pipelines, subject to Part VI;

---

[9] UNCLOS, available at www.un.org/depts/los/convention_agreements/texts/unclos/unclos_e.pdf (accessed 21 December 2020).

(cont.)

   (d) freedom to construct artificial islands and other installations permitted under international law, subject to Part VI;

   (e) freedom of fishing, subject to the conditions laid down in section 2;

   (f) freedom of scientific research, subject to Parts VI and XIII.

2. These freedoms shall be exercised by all States with due regard for the interests of other States in their exercise of the freedom of the high seas, and also with due regard for the rights under this Convention with respect to activities in the Area.

The most revolutionary feature of the UNCLOS is probably that of the exclusive economic zone (EEZ). It recognises the right of coastal States to jurisdiction over an area extending 200 nautical miles from their shores. As an example, about 87 per cent of all known and estimated hydrocarbon reserves fall under this area. This delimitation is also key in the fisheries regime.

The International Tribunal for the Law of the Sea (ITLOS) was established prior to the entry into force of the UNCLOS.[10] It is composed of twenty-one independent members, elected from among persons enjoying the highest reputation for fairness and integrity and of recognised competence in the field of the law of the sea. It has jurisdiction over any dispute concerning the interpretation or application of the UNCLOS, and over all matters specifically provided for in any other international agreement that confers jurisdiction on the ITLOS (Statute, Article 21). The UNCLOS gives the States parties a choice from among four procedures: the ITLOS, the ICJ, binding international arbitration procedures or special arbitration tribunals with expertise in specific types of disputes. An International Seabed Authority was also created on 16 November 1994.[11] Established under Part XI of the UNCLOS, it organises and controls activities in the seabed area, particularly with a view to administering its resources.

With new technological prospects, as well as climate change and environmental challenges, it is time to revisit the UNCLOS, but the treaty remains a fantastic instrument, too little studied by IEL specialists.

Fisheries Subsidies

Scientific studies have overwhelmingly indicated that several fish stocks are rapidly declining and that subsidies, both general and specific, provided by members are major contributors to illegal, unreported and unregulated (IUU) fishing, and overfishing and overcapacities.

---

[10] International Tribunal for the Law of the Sea, available at www.itlos.org (accessed 21 December 2020).

[11] International Seabed Authority, available at www.isa.org.jm (accessed 21 December 2020).

The United Nations General Assembly adopted the 2030 Agenda for Sustainable Development, which includes a standalone goal (SDG 14) for the ocean. Among the several targets contained therein, Target 14.6 particularly deals with control on fisheries subsidies.

SDG 14.6

By 2020, prohibit certain forms of fisheries subsidies which contribute to overcapacity and overfishing, and eliminate subsidies that contribute to IUU fishing, and refrain from introducing new such subsidies, recognizing that appropriate and effective special and differential treatment for developing and least developed countries should be an integral part of the WTO fisheries subsidies negotiation.

The discussion on fisheries subsidies was first taken up in the Doha Development Agenda of 2001, which led to a dedicated Negotiating Group on Rules to oversee disciplines on fisheries subsidies (as well as anti-dumping and RTAs, among other things).[12] The discussion was further expanded in the Hong Kong Ministerial Conference to include prohibition of subsidies that contribute to overcapacity and overfishing.[13] In December 2017, in Buenos Aires, the WTO Ministerial Conference agreed to constructively engage in negotiations with a view to reaching comprehensive and effective disciplines that prohibit subsidies that contribute to overfishing and overcapacity, and eliminate subsidies that contribute to IUU fishing.[14]

The period 2005–14 witnessed various fisheries negotiations. The discussions began because the Agreement on Agriculture excludes fisheries from its scope.[15] Furthermore, the SCM Agreement applies only to the fisheries subsidies that distort the market. In the words of members, '[SCM rules] do not adequately address other negative trade, environment and development impacts of fisheries subsidies, particularly the distinctive production distortions subsidies can cause in the fisheries sector'.[16]

Developed countries, including the United States, New Zealand and Australia, known in fisheries negotiation parlance as the 'Friends of Fish' advocated a top-down approach, where all the subsidies were prohibited except specific green box subsidies.[17] Developing countries such as China, Japan, India, South Korea and Taiwan defended such subsidies by favouring a bottom-up approach, where an ambitious list of prohibited subsidies was created. Their main defence was that there was no established link between the depletion

---

[12] L. Campling and E. Havice, 'Fisheries Subsidies, Development and the Global Trade Regime', *Trade and Environment Review 2016: Fish Trade*, UNCTAD/DITC/TED/2016/3 (UN, 2016), pp. 70–7.

[13] Ministerial Declaration, Doha Work Programme, Annex D, WT/MIN(05)/DEC (adopted 18 December 2005), para. 9.

[14] Fisheries Subsidies, Ministerial Decision of 13 December 2017, WT/MIN(17)/64.

[15] AoA, Annex 1, Entry (i), para. 1.

[16] The Doha Mandate to Address Fisheries Subsidies: Issues, Submission from Australia, Chile, Ecuador, Iceland, New Zealand, Peru, Philippines and the United States, TN/RL/W/3, 24 April 2002.

[17] K. Yoo, 'Fisheries Subsidies Negotiations in the WTO Framework: Trends and Prospects', *Hofstra Journal of International Business and Law* (2018), 18.

of fish stocks and the fisheries subsidies.[18] Developing countries such as Brazil, China, India and Indonesia pushed for special and differential treatment. The remaining small and vulnerable coastal economies, such as Barbados, Fiji and Papua New Guinea, argued that the fisheries sector that was a mainstay of their economies needed S&DT (see Chapter 16).

The negotiation for fisheries subsidies is particularly difficult when it comes to arriving at a consensus because of issues such as management, jurisdiction and dispute settlement. Some of these issues are discussed briefly below.

Fisheries Management

Under their sovereign rights, every member has the ability to exercise control over the natural resources lying in their national jurisdiction. The obligation of management or supervision becomes a concern, since the effect of subsidies in terms of IUU fishing, overfishing and overcapacity fishing has not yet been identified. A contentious issue is the determination of IUU fishing, overcapacity and overfishing. Members have a difference of opinion on whether the port State member or any other organisation should have the jurisdiction to determine the incidence of IUU fishing, overcapacity and overfishing. The disciplines for elimination of subsidies for IUU are to be based on the Food and Agriculture Organization's International Plan of Action, to deter, eliminate and prohibit IUU fishing adopted in 2001 (IPOA-IUU). Disciplines for prohibition of subsidies that contribute to overfishing and overcapacity are being developed either through a prohibition or capping of subsidies. Areas of EEZs of coastal States will also be covered by the national jurisdiction of the coastal member. However, there may be issues in cases of overlapping EEZs.

Regional fisheries management organisations/arrangements (RFMOs/As) are institutions charged with managing high seas fisheries under the UNCLOS and the United Nations Agreement relating to Straddling Fish Stocks and Highly Migratory Fish Stocks (UNFSA). They provide a forum where members agree on fisheries conservation and management measures. However, it would not be proper to assign RFMOs/As the task of managing fisheries under the current negotiations, unless they incorporate certain changes. RFMOs/As themselves suffer from numerous shortcomings. For instance, RFMOs/As need to be updated and reviewed. The last review under UNFSA took place in 2010. They are based on a consensus model and operate only between the members who are parties to it. They can only be as effective as the members agree for them to be.[19] In addition, the RFMOs/As mainly contemplate the management as to allocation of fishing rights rather than conservation.

---

[18] European Parliament, Directorate General for Internal Policies, Global Fisheries Subsidies, IP/B/PECH/IC/2013-146 (October 2013).

[19] K. M. Gjerde, D. Currie, K. Wowk and K. Sack, 'Ocean in Peril: Reforming the Management of Global Ocean Living Resources in Areas Beyond National Jurisdiction', *Marine Pollution Bulletin* (2013), 74, pp. 540–51.

Approaches to Prohibition of Fisheries Subsidies

Judging by the proposals submitted as of December 2020 in the Negotiating Group on Rules, three types of approaches have generally emerged – the 'listing', 'effect' and the 'hybrid' approaches.[20] Under the listing approach, a given list of subsidies is prohibited. Under the effect approach, it is proposed that all the subsidies that are effectively leading to IUU, overfishing or overcapacity be prohibited. The hybrid approach is a combination of the two.

The issue with the listing approach is that it provides a significant amount of room for countries in deciding what should be prohibited. The effect approach appears more rational. Members will retain the flexibility to determine the effect of subsidies. However, proving a causal relationship between the subsidy and overfishing and overcapacity will be a tedious task for members.[21]

Many members have started proposing various models for a capping approach in fisheries subsidies, similar to the approach in the AoA. A cap-based approach to address fisheries subsidies is premised on three elements: (1) the rights of members to marine fisheries resources depending on the length of the coastline and the size of the EEZ; (2) the livelihood and nutritional concerns relating to the marine fishers population; and (3) the need to calibrate the scope and nature of disciplines or commitments to the current level of subsidies maintained by WTO members. While framing a capping approach, members will have to consider numerous factors.

It has to be kept in mind that while a country may not have a significant share in world fisheries trade, its economy might be completely dependent on such trade. The United States and Australia have suggested an approach where members are divided into tiers on the basis of their share in the world fisheries trade.[22] Such an approach may suffer from various shortcomings, such as those listed above. China has also suggested certain elements and approaches for a cap-based approach. It has suggested that the capping and reduction of fisheries subsidies may be based on a percentage of the amount of the average base for capping provided by a member, or average landed value of the total wild marine capture, or on a per fisherman basis.[23] The provision for S&DT can be formulated or given effect in the capping approach, while listing the factors that will be taken into account for determining the cap.

The green box approach has to be used very carefully, and the drafting of a green box should only include subsidies aimed at biodiversity and conservation. A green box will push members to prove that their subsidies are not hurting the environment.[24]

---

[20] 'The WTO's Fisheries Subsidies Negotiations', South Centre's Trade for Development Programme in association with the African Trade Policy Centre, Analytical Note, SC/AN/TDP/2017/5 (Geneva, July 2017).

[21] G. Porter, 'Incorporating Impacts on Resources into Disciplines on Fisheries Subsidies: Issues and Options', Economics and Trade Branch Discussion Paper (Geneva: United Nations Environment Programme, 2004).

[22] Submission of Australia and the United States, 'A Cap-Based Approach to Addressing Certain Fisheries Subsidies', TN/RL/GEN/197 (22 March 2019).

[23] Communication from China, 'A Cap-Based Approach to Address Certain Fishing Subsidies that Contribute to Overcapacity and Overfishing', TN/RL/GEN/199 (3 June 2019).

[24] R. Parmentier, '*WTO Fisheries Negotiations: Failure Is Not an Option*', SDG Knowledge Hub (IISD, 25 June 2019), available at https://sdg.iisd.org/commentary/guest-articles/wto-fisheries-negotiations-failure-is-not-an-option/ (accessed 5 November 2020).

Transparency

Transparency in notifying subsidies has been a matter of perennial discontent at the WTO. The recent proposals by members in the Negotiating Group on Rules show that the transparency provision is not tied to any deterrent or legal implications, except for one proposal by the United States and Australia. They have suggested a tier-based capping model. Members from Tier 1 and Tier 2 will have to maintain up-to-date fisheries notifications in order to enjoy the benefit of their cap, and those from Tier 3 will have to provide notification in order to maintain their exemption status.[25]

A failure to notify a member's subsidies under Article 25 of the SCM Agreement does not entail any major consequences.[26] Consequently, the compliance rate with notifications has been characterised by the Chairman of SCM Committee as 'discouraging'.[27] The quality of notifications is another concern. The EU, in particular, has suggested certain reforms with respect to the transparency obligation and notification requirement in its concept note submitted to the WTO on 18 September 2018.[28]

Scope of Dispute Settlement

It has been put forth by the Philippines in one of its proposals that WTO dispute settlement should be limited only to the prohibition of subsidies resulting in IUU fishing, overfishing and overcapacity.[29] However, according to the Philippines, WTO Panels can look into complaints relating to IUU determination where the objections to the issue of territoriality are not frivolous. China has a very different view on this issue and is not in support of a review by a WTO Panel on territoriality. It must not determine territoriality, which is dealt with separately under the UNCLOS.

Similarly, the Canadian proposal states that members may identify the category of disputes that can be brought before the WTO DSB. Further, it is expected that some disputes may also involve a scientific determination that a WTO panel may not be best placed to assess or review. In such circumstances, members may agree on a separate and elaborate procedure for expert assistance to the panel.[30] The contours of the dispute

---

[25] Submission by Australia and United States (Revision), 'A Cap-Based Approach to Addressing Certain Fisheries Subsidies', TN/RL/GEN/197/Rev. 1. (6 May 2019).

[26] A. E. Appleton, 'Improving the Transparency of Fisheries Subsidies' (Geneva: ICTSD, December 2017).

[27] WTO, Concerns Grow about Slippage in Subsidy Notifications (25 April 2017).

[28] Concept Paper, 'WTO Modernisation: Introduction to Future EU Proposals', available at https://trade.ec.europa.eu/doclib/docs/2018/september/tradoc_157331.pdf (accessed 21 December 2020); WTO, 'Procedures to Enhance Transparency and Strengthen Notification Requirements under WTO Agreements' (Revision), Communication from Argentina, Australia, Canada, Costa Rica, the European Union, Japan, New Zealand, the Separate Customs Territory of Taiwan, Penghu, Kinmen and Matsu, and the United States, JOB/GC/204/Rev.1 (1 April 2019).

[29] WTO, Negotiating Group on Rules, Prohibition of Subsidies in Disputed Waters, Supplement by Philippines, TN/RL/GEN/196/Suppl.1 (December 2018).

[30] WTO, Negotiating Group on Rules, 'Dispute Settlement in a WTO Fisheries Subsidies Agreement: Discussion Paper', Communication from Canada, TN/RL/GEN/198 (10 May 2019).

settlement provision in a standalone agreement need to be framed in a manner that does not allow for forum shopping, and ensures that decisions made under the DSU do not contradict or undermine decisions made by fisheries management organisations.[31]

Members are involved in active discussions for achieving a framework on fisheries subsidies at the time of writing, in order to abide by the UNGA's timeline. The aim of the framework is the conservation of fish stocks while providing subsidies on fisheries. Territoriality and dispute settlement will be a challenge, considering the multiple set of rules present under the UNCLOS and other international agreements or conventions. The nature of prohibition and the manner in which such a prohibition is to be implemented is also contentious. Linked to the issue of prohibition is the provision of appropriate and effective S&DT for developing countries and LDCs. In a cap-based approach, the S&DT for developing countries and LDCs will have to be taken into account. The determination of IUUs, overfishing and overcapacity is another issue that cannot be tasked purely on national authorities or RFMOs/As, considering their limited powers and resources. Lastly, the transparency obligation under the negotiated framework will have to be made stringent by attaching some deterrent or legal implication to it. These issues continue to be discussed intensely by members at the WTO.

[31] Negotiating Group on Rules, 'Dispute Settlement in a WTO Fisheries Subsidies Agreement'.

Index